W9-BTH-301

Encyclopedia of Sociology

Editorial Board

Encyclopedia of Sociology

VOLUME 2

Edgar F. Borgatta
Editor-in-Chief
University of Washington, Seattle

Marie L. Borgatta
Managing Editor
University of Washington, Seattle

MACMILLAN PUBLISHING COMPANY
New York

MAXWELL MACMILLAN CANADA
Toronto

MAXWELL MACMILLAN INTERNATIONAL
New York · Oxford · Singapore · Sydney

Macmillan Publishing Company
866 Third Avenue, New York, NY 10022

Maxwell Macmillan Canada, Inc.
1200 Eglinton Avenue East, Suite 200
Don Mills, Ontario M3C 3N1

Printed in the United States of America

Library of Congress Catalog Card No.: 91-37827

printing number
3 4 5 6 7 8 9 10

Macmillan, Inc., is part of the Maxwell Communication Group of Companies.

Library of Congress Catalog in Publication Data
Encyclopedia of sociology / Edgar F. Borgatta, editor-in-chief, Marie L. Borgatta, managing editor.
p. cm.
Includes bibliographical references and index.
ISBN 0-02-897051-9 (set).—ISBN 0-02-897052-7 (v. 1) : $90.00
1. Sociology—Encyclopedias. I. Borgatta, Marie L.
HM17.E5 1991
301'.03—dc20 91-37827
CIP

EDITORIAL AND PRODUCTION STAFF

Philip Friedman, *Publisher*
Elly Dickason, *Editor in Chief*
Martha Goldstein, *Senior Project Editor*
Lynn Constantinou, *Production Manager*
Karin K. Vanderveer, *Assistant Editor*

The paper used in this publication meets the minimum requirements of American National Standard for Information Sciences—Permanence of Paper for Printed Library Materials. ANSI Z39.48–1984.

Encyclopedia of Sociology

ECOLOGY *See* Demography; Human Ecology and Environment.

ECONOMIC DETERMINISM Economic determinism refers to a kind of causality in which an economic variable *x* causes a condition of behavior *y*. This statement of direct causality contains very little actual economic determinism. But in stating that economic condition *x* is the most determining factor in causing behavior *y*, we have a model for economic determinism that is quite common in economics and sociology. This model appears in Weber's (1979) *Economy and Society;* in his discussion of domination he states:

> *Nor does domination utilize in every case economic power for its foundation and maintenance. But in the vast majority of cases, and indeed in the most important ones, this is just what happens in one way or another and often to such an extent that the mode of applying economic means for the purpose of maintaining domination, in turn exercises a determining influence on the structure of domination.* (p. 942)

The same model of economic determinism appears in Louis Althusser's (1970) *For Marx,* where the social formation has multiple determinants, but "the economy is determinant in the last instance" (p. 113). Neither model has the economic as a monocausal determinant of society, but economic categories, such as the economic market for Weber, clearly are part of a central structuring determination for society.

This model predates both Weber and Althusser and has its origins in eighteenth-century free market liberalism. In *The Federalist Papers,* James Madison assumes economic interests as the chief motivation of the people. In *The Wealth of Nations,* for Adam Smith it is "that in commercial society every man thus lives by exchanging, or becomes in some measure, a merchant "(1976, p. 26). For Smith people are buyers and sellers involved in production and consumption, and human behavior is an unending series of economic exchanges. Individuals pursue their own self-interest in rational ways, and their own self-interest consists of profit, which is regulated by competition in a predominantly self-regulating free market. In the pursuit of economic self-interest the individual promotes the social good, "led by an invisible hand to promote an end which was no part of his intention" (p. 477). In Smith's model an individual's pursuit of economic profit automatically structures the good for all of society.

Smith assumes an economic person who is always acting to optimize economic advantages. People here are determined by economic motives, that is, to increase profits and decrease losses. Modern neoclassical economists, such as Milton Friedman and Gary Becker, have continued the tradition of Adam Smith. For them the only limitation on the free market model is the amount of information to which a rational actor has access. Since information is not perfect, mistakes can occur. But in the pursuit of profit a rational actor learns even from mistakes; mistakes therefore increase the amount of information that a rational actor acquires, thus increasing the chances of making correct choices in the future. Thus, the free market not only structures human behavior but determines the inevitability that these actors, in rationally pursuing profit, will acquire the information needed to produce profits continuously for themselves and to mold—even if unintentionally—the social good.

The model of economic determinism offers sociology an easily quantifiable object, a phenomenon that can be subjected to scientific procedures—observed, measured, tested, and verified. As a positivist social science, sociology requires a transhistorical and universal phenomenon such as the physical sciences have, and economic determinism provides it in economic concepts such as the market, money, the circulation of capital, and so forth. It allows sociologists to speak the language of science and to reduce all social phenomena to mathematical formulas.

All positivist social sciences use mathematical representations of social reality to understand society, and economic determinism is but one attempt at creating a scientific sociology. Still, the model has offered sociology a formula that possesses broad powers for explaining social factors and avoids problems of indeterminate multiple causes. This is what science traditionally means by lawfulness. These lawlike social categories are representations of social reality and provide a framework in which the aggregate behavior of individuals can be structured in terms of economic interests. This behavior is patterned and can be studied and subjected to scientific procedures. Thus, the model of economic determinism informs sociological analysis and research.

Exchange theory provides an example of a positivist methodology that is based on the model of economic determinism. In exchange theory, economic exchange is the determinant principle of behavior. George C. Homans, the originator of this form of analysis, combines this economic model with a behaviorist psychology, but the economic is the determining structure. In *Social Behavior: Its Elementary Forms,* Homans states, "Human behavior as a function of its payoff: in amount and kind it depends on the amount and kind of reward and punishment it fetches" (1961, p. 13). Human relations have been reduced to the exchange and circulation of commodities. Homans assumes that a social actor is an economic person existing in a free market where individuals make rational choices to maximize profits and reduce costs. This is stated partly in the language of behavioral psychology, but the conditions of economic exchange are dominant. Thus, Homans sounds more like Adam Smith than like B. F. Skinner when he writes "we define psychic profits as rewards less costs, and we argue that no exchange continues unless both parties are making a profit" (1961, p. 61).

This model allows Homans to analyze individuals who live in a group, make numerous rational choices, and yet live a stable, patterned life. Individuals calculating their possibilities and making rational choices are led by something like Smith's "invisible hand" to maintain group life in "practical equilibrium."

Homans believed that his analysis was a value-neutral attempt to expand the scope of a scientifically valid sociology of human behavior. But, while exchanges are an important aspect of human interaction, the reduction of all human behavior to elementary exchanges is problematic. Homans has universalized the relations of individuals in the capitalist marketplace, relations that are historically specific and not the basis of a universal psychology of human behavior. Homans's exchange theory is a conservative sociological theory in which pecuniary relations structure human behavior.

Another form of sociological analysis that uses the model of economic determinism is Marxist sociology. In Weber's *The Protestant Ethic and the*

Spirit of Capitalism, Marx's analysis is called a "one-sided materialistic" interpretation (1958, p. 183). Marx provides evidence for Weber's contention when he argues that the economic base determines the ideological superstructure. In the preface to *A Contribution to the Critique of Political Economy,* Marx writes that "the totality of these relations of production constitutes the economic structure of society, the real foundation, on which arises a legal and political superstructure and to which correspond definite forms of social consciousness" (1970, p. 20). This famous passage, containing what is known as the base–superstructure model, became the hallmark statement for economic determinist Marxists from the Second International (Marxist Workers Congress) in 1889 to the present.

But Marx himself was not an economic determinist, even though many of his followers were. Marx theorized about a world in which human relations were subsumed under capitalist relations of production. His central concern was revolutionary change, which depended on the formation of a revolutionary class that could wage war against the dominant classes. But for Marx, class was determined not by economic conditions alone but by community and cultural conditions as well. Thus, he writes in *The Eighteenth Brumaire of Louis Bonaparte* on whether "small holding peasants" are or are not a class:

> *In so far as millions of families live under economic conditions of existence that separate their mode of life, their interests and their culture from those of other classes and put them in hostile opposition to the latter, they form a class. In so far as there is merely interconnection among these small holding peasants, and the identity of their interests begets no community, no national bond and no political organization among them, they do not form a class.* (Marx 1963, p. 124)

This is not "economics in the last instance" but a multivalent fitting together of a series of necessary conditions. Economic conditions are insufficient, and class formation and class struggle do not occur unless community occurs as well.

Later Marxists differ from Marx on a number of issues. First, many understand the base–superstructure model as a determinant condition of class. That is, class depends exclusively on the economic base for its formation. For Marx, however, it was an insufficient condition and a "moment" in his analysis of capitalism. Furthermore, economic determinist Marxists view class struggle as a secondary phenomenon, even though it is important. Finally, many Marxists have critiqued Marx's concept of class for its inability to predict revolutionary change with scientific accuracy. Erik Olin Wright, for instance, calls Marx's concept of class "vague" and "random"; it is much too relativistic for use as a neat, lawlike scientific formula. In his important book *Classes,* Wright preserves the Marxian tradition of the Second International and attempts to erect a positivist Marxist sociology whose propositions can be empirically verified. It is upon the base–superstructure model that Wright builds this science. As in exchange theory, Wright's model suggests that in capitalism rational actors make rational choices in pursuing their economic advantages. But Wright also attempts to build a scientific base for an analysis of class struggle, and in *Classes* he provides the causal link between capitalist exploitation and the actions of individuals in society. He does this by demonstrating that class structure is determined by property relations, a central determinant in modern society:

> *Class structure is of pervasive importance in contemporary social life. The control over society's productive assets determines the fundamental material interests of actors and heavily shapes the capacities of both individuals and collectivities to pursue their interests. The fact that a substantial portion of the population may be relatively comfortable materially does not negate the fact that their capacities and interests remain bound up with property relations and the associated processes of exploitation.* (Wright 1985, pp. 285-286)

Economic factors are crucial for understanding the social world. But society is not reducible to economic determinants; it is too complex to be reduced to a set of economic propositions, or any single determinant set of propositions, that imply unilinear causality. Still, economic determinism is seductive because it offers a theory that has broad explanatory powers, is easily quantifiable, and can be reduced to simple mathematical formulas. Thus, it is not surprising to see it continue and expand, seemingly unaware of its limitations. For instance, George Gilder writes in *Wealth and Poverty,* "The man's earnings, unlike the woman's, will determine not only his standard of living but also his possibilities for marriage and children—whether he can be a sexual man" (1981, p. 109). The reduction of sex and marriage to economic determinants is highly problematic, both as science and as common sense. Yet generalizations about social life wholly based on economic causes persist, under the names of both science and myth. One can restate Max Weber's warning against monocausal theories in the social sciences:

> *But it is, of course, not my aim to substitute for a one-sided materialistic an equally one-sided spiritualistic causal interpretation of culture and of history. Each is equally possible, but each if it does not serve as the preparation, but as the conclusion of an investigation accomplishes equally little in the interest of historical truth.* (1958, p. 183)

(SEE ALSO: *Capitalism; Economic Sociology; Marxist Sociology*)

REFERENCES

Aronowitz, Stanley 1988 *Science as Power: Discourse and Ideology in Modern Society.* Minneapolis: University of Minnesota Press.

Gilder, George 1982 *Wealth and Poverty.* New York: Bantam.

Homans, George C. 1961 *Social Behavior: Its Elementary Forms.* New York: Harcourt, Brace, and World.

Marx, Karl (1859) 1970 *A Contribution to the Critique of Political Economy.*

——— (1852) 1963 *The Eighteenth Brumaire of Louis Bonaparte.* New York: International.

Resnick, Stephen A., and Richard D. Wolff 1987 *Knowledge and Class: A Marxian Critique of Political Economy.* Chicago: University of Chicago Press.

Smith, Adam 1976 *An Inquiry into the Nature and Causes of the Wealth of Nations.* Chicago: University of Chicago Press.

Weber, Max (1947) 1979 *Economy and Society: An Outline of Interpretive Sociology.* Guenther Roth and Claus Wittich, eds. and trans. Berkeley: University of California Press.

——— (1904-1905) 1958 *The Protestant Ethic and the Spirit of Capitalism.* New York: Scribners.

Wright, Erik Olin 1985 *Classes.* London: Verso.

WILLIAM DIFAZIO

ECONOMIC DEVELOPMENT *See* Industrialization in Less-Developed Countries; Modernization Theory; Rural Sociology.

ECONOMIC INSTITUTIONS The analysis of economic institutions is central to the work of the classical figures of sociology—Marx, Weber, and Durkheim. These thinkers did not recognize a boundary line between sociological inquiry and economic inquiry; on the contrary, their efforts to make sense of the development of market capitalism led them to intensive analysis of market processes. Unfortunately, this thrust of sociological inquiry was largely abandoned by sociologists between World War I and the late 1960s. This was particularly true in the United States, where sociologists generally deferred to economists' claims of an exclusive mandate to study economic processes.

To be sure, there were a number of important intellectual figures during this period whose work integrated sociological and economic inquiry, but these individuals were rarely housed in sociology departments. Such economists as Thorstein Veblen, Joseph Schumpeter, and John Kenneth Galbraith have been retroactively recognized as sociologists. Similarly, the largely self-educated Hungarian scholar Karl Polanyi (1957, 1971) is now acknowledged to have made seminal contributions to the sociological analysis of economic institutions. Yet scholars working in the sociological mainstream either ignored economic topics or tended to incorporate the perspectives of neoclassical economics.

Since the late 1960s, however, the lines of inquiry pioneered by the classical writers have been revitalized. Sociologists working in a number of different intellectual traditions and on diverse empirical topics have developed sophisticated analyses of economic processes (Swedberg 1987). No longer content to defer to the expertise of professional economists, many of these writers have developed powerful critiques of the work of neoclassical economists (Zukin and DiMaggio 1990).

Although this body of work explores a range of different economic institutions, much of it can be understood through its analysis of the way that markets work. (Analyses of other economic institutions, such as the division of labor, money, and corporate organizations, are presented elsewhere in this volume.) In particular, an emergent economic sociological conception of market processes can usefully be contrasted with the conception of the market that is implicit in most economic writings.

THE ORGANIZATION OF MARKETS

Neoclassical economists tend to assume an ideal market situation that allows changes in prices to equilibrate supply and demand. In this ideal market situation, there are multiple buyers and sellers whose transactions are fundamentally impersonal; information on the product and the price are the only relevant variables shaping the action of market participants. Contemporary economists recognize that this ideal market situation requires a basic symmetry in the information available to buyers and sellers. When there are significant differences in information, it is likely that the resulting price will diverge from the price that would effectively equilibrate supply and demand. Nevertheless, contemporary microeconomics rests on the assumption that most markets approximate the ideal situation, including information symmetry (Thurow 1983)

The sociological view of markets is fundamentally different. It stresses the embeddedness of behavior within markets, the central role of imitation in structuring markets, and the importance of blocked exchanges. The concept of embeddedness challenges the idea that impersonality is an important feature of actual market situations. While the individual actor in economic theory is a rational actor who is able to disregard his or her social ties in the market situation, the sociological actor is seen as embedded in a network of social relations at the time that he or she engages in market transactions. This embeddedness means that a wide range of social ties exert continuing influence over how the actor will both make and respond to price signals (Polanyi 1957; Granovetter 1985).

The sociological view has two elements. First, the individual actor is decisively influenced by social ties. For example, a consumer might choose not to do business with retailers belonging to a stigmatized ethnic group, even when their prices are lower, because members of the consumer's ethnic group genuinely believe that the products of the other group will be inferior or that contact with the stigmatized group will jeopardize one's social position. The economists' argument that such an individual has a "taste for discrimination" does not adequately capture a reality in which discriminatory behavior often occurs with very little reflection because beliefs are deeply rooted. Second, the individual actor's dependence on social ties is necessary in order for him or her to accomplish a given economic goal. As Granovetter (1985, pp. 496–497) has pointed out, a purchasing officer at a corporation might well do business with a particular supplier regardless of price considerations because of long-standing ties to that individual. These ties provide assurance that the delivery will occur in a timely fashion and the merchandise will meet established quality standards. In other words, social bonds can provide protection against the uncertainties and risks that are always involved in transactions.

The standard economic view of markets tends to ignore these uncertainties; it is generally assumed that individuals will automatically obey the rules that make transactions possible. As Oliver Williamson (1975, p. 7) has noted, this represents a profound inconsistency in economic analysis. While individuals are assumed to be self-interested, they are also expected to avoid guile and deception. In the real world, however, every transaction involves the risk that one party is deliberately cheating the other, and the more "impersonal" the transaction—that is, the less one party knows about the other—the greater the risk becomes.

This is one of the reasons that actual markets tend to develop structures and rules designed to constrain and to embed individual behavior. Although commodity markets and stock markets most closely resemble the pure markets of economic theory, in which rapid price changes serve to balance supply and demand, these markets tend to evolve complex social structures. At one level, such markets appear to be completely impersonal, in that there is no contact between buyers and sellers. On another level, however, the actual transactions are handled by a community of brokers who are well known to each other and who are expected to follow a particular etiquette for managing transactions. This structure has evolved to provide protection against unknown brokers who might prove unreliable and to assure that known brokers will be discouraged from cheating their colleagues and clients (Adler and Adler 1984; Baker 1984a; Burk 1988).

The central point, however, is that the particular ways in which market behaviors are embedded have real and significant consequences. On the one hand, embeddedness allows market processes to go forward by diminishing the opportunities for guile and deceit. On the other hand, embeddedness assures that factors besides price will influence the behavior of market participants, so it can no longer be assumed that price will automatically equilibrate supply and demand.

One of the main implications of the concept of embeddedness is that actual markets will be characterized by imitative behavior. Economists assume that each economic actor will calculate his or her preference schedule independently of all other actors. In the sociological view, however, actors are continually making their choices in reference to the behavior of others. In deciding the price to be asked for a particular commodity, a market participant will set it in comparison with the prices of competitors (White 1981). This is one of the key reasons that in actual markets there is often less price competition than would be suggested either by economic theory or by considerable differences across firms in the costs of production.

This role of imitation plays a particularly important role in financial panics and bubbles. Panics occur when many holders of a particular kind of asset rush to convert their holdings to cash, leading to precipitous price declines. Bubbles occur when enthusiasm for a particular asset drives prices far higher than can be justified by expected returns (Kindleberger 1978). Economists have trouble explaining the behavior of individuals in most panics or bubbles because rational actors with complete information would not engage in such irrational behavior; they would understand that the underlying value of an asset is not likely to change so dramatically in a short period of time. However, actual individuals have limited information, and they cope with uncertainty by observing the behavior of their friends and neighbors. Such observation makes them quite susceptible to the collective enthusiasms of panics and bubbles.

The threat of panics is another reason that financial markets develop institutional structures to embed individual behavior. The New York Stock Exchange, for example, has an elaborate system of specialist firms who have the responsibility to smooth out the market for particular stocks. Such firms are expected to be purchasers of last resort in situations where there are too many sellers of a stock (Baker 1984b, pp. 111–112). The idea is that such action should help to reduce the likelihood of panic. While such an institutional arrangement diverges from the economists' conception of a self-regulating market, it makes sense in the context of imitative behavior.

Furthermore, in their emphasis on the virtues of markets, neoclassical economists often suggest a vision of society as a giant bazaar in which everything is for sale. Sociologists, in contrast, are more likely to recognize that the viability of markets depends upon a wide variety of restrictions that block certain types of exchanges. Blocked exchanges are transactions that are in violation of the law or of widely shared ethical standards (Walzer 1983). Instances of blocked exchange include prohibitions on the resale of stolen merchandise, laws that prevent government officials from selling their services to the highest bidder, and the criminalization of prostitution and the purchase of certain drugs.

More subtle blocked exchanges play an important role in structuring the economy. Lawyers are not allowed to switch sides in the middle of a civil suit in response to an offer of a higher fee by the other side. Accountants are not supposed to produce a more favorable audit in response to a higher fee (Block 1990, pp. 62–63). Loan officers at a bank are prohibited from approving loans in exchange for side payments from the applicant. The members of a corporate board of directors are supposed to place their fiduciary responsibility to the shareholders ahead of their self-interest in contemplating offers to buy out the firm. In a word, there is a complicated and sometimes shifting boundary between legitimate and illegitimate transactions in contemporary economies.

The importance of blocked exchanges sheds further doubt on arguments that markets can regulate themselves without governmental interference (Polanyi 1957). The construction of any particular market involves rules as to what kinds of exchange are open and what kinds are blocked, but the incentives to violate these rules are often quite substantial. At the same time, the incentives for market participants to police each other are often lacking. Hence, there is often no alternative to a governmental role in policing the boundary between legitimate and illegitimate exchanges. Moreover, debates about social policy are often framed in a language of individual rights that is profoundly insensitive to the importance and pervasiveness of blocked exchanges. For example, when a woman serving as a surrogate mother in exchange for a fee decides she wants to keep the baby, the issue is often debated in terms of contract law. The more fundamental issue, however, is whether the society believes that the rental of wombs is a legitimate or illegitimate transaction (Rothman 1989).

THE SCOPE OF MARKETS

A second important dimension of contemporary sociological work on economic institutions is a concern with the geographical scope of markets. Much of the sociological tradition has been oriented to the study of national societies or of subnational units. But an understanding of the scope of international markets calls that approach into question. Markets for raw materials, finished products, services, capital, and labor cross national boundaries and exert extraordinary influence over all aspects of social life (Swedberg 1987, pp. 91–104).

The most ambitious effort to date to chart the importance of these international markets has been the world system theory of Immanuel Wallerstein (1974a, 1974b, 1980, 1989). Instead of using national societies as the basic unit of analysis, Wallerstein has sought to shift sociological analysis to the level of the capitalist world system. For Wallerstein, this system is comprised of a world market and a competitive state system of divided sovereignties. Any analysis of patterns within a particular national society must begin by locating that society within the larger capitalist world system. A nation's location at the core, the periphery, or the semiperiphery of the capitalist world system can be expected to shape the nature of its economic and political institutions.

The existence of a single unified world market is central to Wallerstein's argument. Each nation that is part of the capitalist world system must struggle for relative advantage in that market, and this has implications for both social relations within nations and for the political–military relations among nations. Moreover, it is a central part of Wallerstein's project to detail the process by which various regions of the world have been incorporated into this unified world system. The capitalist world system began as a purely European phenomenon, but through colonization and the penetration of Western influence, this system became global. Regions that were once external to the system were progressively incorporated as peripheral areas that produced raw materials. Later-arriving nations such as the United States, Canada, and Japan moved to the semiperiphery and then to the core.

The contributions of Wallerstein and his followers have been extremely important in showing the systematic ways in which international markets shape developments within societies. The study of labor markets within the world system, for example, has been particularly fruitful in making sense of international migrations—the massive movements of people across national boundaries—that loom so large in understanding both core and peripheral societies (Portes and Walton 1981).

Wallerstein's work, however, is vulnerable to criticism because it sometimes implies that there is a single unified world market for commodities, for labor, and for capital that operates quite similarly to the markets of economic theory. Wallerstein devotes too little attention to analyzing the specific institutional structures of these various international markets that cut across geographical boundaries.

While it is true that virtually all nations in the modern world now attempt to increase their access to foreign exchange by selling a range of goods and services to other countries, it is important to realize that conceptualizing this process as a "world market" is only metaphoric. The metaphor captures the high level of interdependence that results from diverse nations' facing the same structural pressures to buy cheap and sell dear. However, there is no single world market; there are many different markets for particular commodities, and each of these particular markets has specific institutional structures. In some cases, there are international exchanges and networks of brokers who organize many of the transactions; in other cases, much of the activity occurs either within large transnational corporations or between such corporations and individual national markets.

The key point, however, is that the operation of such global markets is continually influenced and shaped by institutional arrangements within particular national societies. It makes a big difference, for example, whether the amount of oil produced in a given month by a major oil-producing country is the result of many local decisions by those who control the wells or of a decision by a government official. Similarly, the organization of the international market for apparel depends critically on the presence or absence of protectionist arrangements within the countries of the core.

Neoclassical economics sees these different possible boundaries between national markets and global markets as just so many different types of friction that interfere with one truly free world market. However, it is far more useful to see these national political measures as structuring the international market for particular commodities along particular lines. This is clearest, for example, in international markets for basic food products. All of the developed capitalist countries have agricultural policies that are designed to stabilize food prices and to provide some level of protection to farmers. These policies are devised and reshaped in response to what goes on abroad and, in turn, profoundly shape the nature of the international market for many foodstuffs (Hopkins and Puchala 1978).

However, if individual nations were completely free to shape these boundaries according to their own preferences, the idea of a "world market" would be a very poor metaphor. The price of any particular commodity would vary substantially depending upon which nation one was in. To minimize such a possibility, economically powerful nations have attempted to impose international regimes—sets of rules for managing the boundaries between national markets and international markets (Keohane and Nye 1977). For example, the nineteenth-century gold standard was a regime for regulating both trade relations and financial relations among nations. The idea of the gold standard was to reduce boundaries between national markets and the international market to an absolute minimum (Block 1977, pp. 4–7).

The contemporary world market has an elaborate institutional structure of international organizations, such as the International Monetary Fund and the General Agreement on Tariffs and

Trade, that attempt to enforce a common set of rules for managing international transactions. There are periods in which the rules are more or less strict in terms of the types of national policies that are prohibited, and there are periods in which international compliance with the rules is lower or higher.

The importance of these international rules and institutions in creating the structure of a world market has not been sufficiently emphasized in world system theory (Wood 1986, pp. 6–8). Moreover, this neglect is directly linked to the analysis of the relationship between capitalist and "socialist" states. Advocates of the world system perspective have insisted that the so-called socialist states—such as the Soviet Union and China—are still embedded in the capitalist world system (Wallerstein 1974b). The idea is that the continued need of "socialist" states for international trade subjects them to pressures to shape their domestic institutions in conformity with international market pressures. In the case of Eastern Europe, in particular, this argument makes it easier to understand how the growing participation of these countries in the capitalist world system through both trade and debt created pressures that led to the collapse of the state socialist regimes.

The important issue, however, is the degree to which different nations follow the rules governing international transactions. While it might make sense to say that both the Soviet Union in the 1930s and contemporary Switzerland are a part of the capitalist world system, the contrasts in the way these two countries manage the boundary between national markets and international markets is extremely significant. In fact, a good part of the underlying source of Cold War conflicts was the refusal of "socialist states" to conform to the regimes governing international transactions in trade and finance.

The point, quite simply, is that the world market, like any other market, has been structured in a particular way as a result of a series of political decisions (Block 1990, pp. 16–18). There is no single, objective world market that exists independent of and prior to political intervention. In fact, political understandings are necessary before international transactions can go forward in a predictable fashion. It follows that if the world market is socially constructed, it can be socially reconstructed. This means that when there are clashes between pressures of the world market and the pursuit of various goals within countries—whether they be development in the Third World, protection of the environment, or the improvement of social welfare—it is the task of the social analyst to remember that restructuring the world market is one possible choice.

(SEE ALSO: *Corporate Organizations; Economic Sociology; Money; Transnational Corporations*)

REFERENCES

Adler, Patricia, and Peter Adler (eds.) 1984 *The Social Dynamics of Financial Markets.* Greenwich, Conn.: JAI Press.

Baker, Wayne 1984a "The Social Structure of a National Securities Market." *American Journal of Sociology* 89:775–811.

——— 1984b "Floor Trading and Crowd Dynamics." In Patricia Adler and Peter Adler, eds., *The Social Dynamics of Financial Markets.* Greenwich, Conn.: JAI Press.

Block, Fred 1977 *The Origins of International Economic Disorder: A Study of United States International Monetary Policy from World War II to the Present.* Berkeley: University of California Press.

——— 1990 *Postindustrial Possibilities: A Critique of Economic Discourse.* Berkeley: University of California Press.

Burk, James 1988 *Values in the Marketplace: The American Stock Market Under Federal Securities Law.* New York: Walter de Gruyter.

Granovetter, Mark 1985 "Economic Action and Social Structure: The Problem of Embeddedness." *American Journal of Sociology* 91:481–510.

Hopkins, Raymond F., and Donald J. Puchala (eds.) 1978 *The Global Political Economy of Food.* Madison: University of Wisconsin Press.

Keohane, Robert, and Joseph Nye 1977 *Power and Interdependence: World Politics in Transition.* Boston: Little, Brown.

Kindleberger, Charles P. 1978 *Manias, Panics, and Crashes.* New York: Basic Books.

Polanyi, Karl (1944) 1957 *The Great Transformation.* Boston: Beacon Press.

——— 1971 *Primitive, Archaic and Modern Economies.* Boston: Beacon Press.

Portes, Alejandro, and John Walton 1981 *Labor, Class, and the International System.* New York: Academic Press.

Rothman, Barbara Katz 1989 *Recreating Motherhood: Ideology and Technology in a Patriarchal Society.* New York: Norton.

Swedberg, Richard 1987 "Economic Sociology: Past and Present." *Current Sociology* 35:1–221.

Thurow, Lester 1983 *Dangerous Currents: The State of Economics.* New York: Random House.

Wallerstein, Immanuel 1974a *The Modern World-System, I: Capitalist Agriculture and the Origins of the European World-Economy in the Sixteenth Century.* New York: Academic Press.

——— 1974b "The Rise and Future Demise of the Capitalist World-System: Concepts for Comparative Analysis." *Comparative Studies in Society and History* 16:387–415.

——— 1980 *The Modern World-System, II: Mercantilism and the Consolidation of the European World-Economy.* New York: Academic Press.

——— 1989 *The Modern World-System, III: The Second Era of Great Expansion of the Capitalist World-Economy, 1730–1840s.* New York: Academic Press.

Walzer, Michael 1983 *Spheres of Justice: A Defense of Pluralism and Equality.* New York: Basic Books.

White, Harrison 1981 "Where Do Markets Come from?" *American Journal of Sociology* 87:517–547.

Williamson, Oliver 1975 *Markets and Hierarchies: Analysis and Antitrust Implications.* New York: Free Press.

Wood, Robert 1986 *From Marshall Plan to Debt Crisis: Foreign Aid and Development Choices in the World Economy.* Berkeley: University of California Press.

Zukin, Sharon, and Paul DiMaggio 1990 *Structures of Capital: The Social Organization of the Economy.* New York: Cambridge University Press.

FRED BLOCK

ECONOMIC SOCIOLOGY Economic sociology constitutes its own distinct subfield in sociology and can be defined briefly as the sociological analysis of economic phenomena. Economic sociology has a rich intellectual tradition and traces its roots to the founders of sociology, especially to Max Weber. It should be noted that not only sociologists but also economists have made important contributions to economic sociology. This is particularly true for today's economic sociology, which is often referred to as "new economic sociology" and which is as much the result of works by economists (such as Gary Becker and Oliver Williamson) as by sociologists (such as Harrison White and Mark Granovetter).

To define economic sociology as the sociological analysis of economic phenomena may seem bland and even tautological. It is therefore important to stress that it entails a definite conception of what topics may be studied by sociologists; that it implies a certain division of labor between economists and sociologists; and that it also has direct consequences for how the relationship between economic theory and sociology is conceived. That this is the case comes out very clearly if we contrast this definition with two other ones that are commonly used: (1) that economic sociology deals primarily with a particular dimension of economic phenomena, namely their social dimension, and (2) that economic sociology is the study of social structures and organizations in the economy. That economic sociology deals with economic phenomena in general (the first definition) means that it addresses issues not only at the periphery of the economy (such as, say, the influence of religious values on the economy or of ethnicity on entrepreneurship) but also at its core (such as the way markets operate or investment decisions are made). Sociological theory here emerges as either an alternative to economic theory or as a direct challenge to it. To look at the social dimension of economic phenomena (the second definition) means, on the other hand, that sociologists look only at a limited number of economic issues, basically those left over once the economists have finished their analyses. Economists may, for example, decide with the help of standard economic theory what salaries and prices are like in a certain industry, while sociologists, by looking at a factory or a work group as a social system, may then add some additional information. Economic theory is not challenged by this type of economic sociology, since it deals only with those topics for which there is no economic theory. That economic sociology focuses on the social structures or on organizations in the economy (the third definition) means finally that also a purely economic analysis may be regarded as economic sociology as long as it deals with certain topics. Why a firm rather than the market is used for a specific type of transaction may, for example, be explained by the fact that transaction costs are higher in this specific case in the market. This type of economic sociology is close to economic theory and basically dispenses with traditional sociology (although not necessarily with rational choice sociology; see, e.g., Coleman 1990).

These three ways of looking at economic sociology all have their followers. The one that emphasizes that the sociological perspective in principle can be applied to *all* types of economic phenomena is, however, the one that has been used the most frequently throughout the history of economic sociology. That this is the case will become clear from the following brief overview of the field. That the two other definitions also have their adherents will become obvious as well.

Since the 1980s economic sociology has been going through something of a renaissance in the sociological profession, not only in the United States but also in other countries. Before the 1980s, however, three separate attempts had been made to create a vigorous economic sociology. Together these constitute the tradition of economic sociology. The first attempt was made in the early twentieth century by a group of German scholars of whom Max Weber is the most important. The second was made at the same time by Emile Durkheim and his followers in France. And the third attempt was made by some American sociologists, such as Talcott Parsons and Neil Smelser, in the 1950s. A few words shall be said about each of these attempts before we discuss the contemporary situation.

The most powerful attempt to create a solid economic sociology was made in Germany during the years 1890 to 1930 by a group of scholars who were all trained in economics. The three key figures were Max Weber, Werner Sombart, and Joseph Schumpeter. A major reason that economic sociology developed so forcefully in German-speaking academia is that this institution had a strong tradition of historical economics. There was also the fact that toward the end of the nineteenth century Gustav von Schmoller, the leader of the Historical School of Economics, got embroiled in a bitter academic fight with Carl Menger, one of the founders of marginal utility analysis. By the time Weber and Sombart became active, German economics had been polarized into two camps through the so-called battle of the methods or the *Methodenstreit,* one camp that was overly theoretical and one that was overly historical. The idea of "economic sociology" was conceived by both Sombart and Weber as an attempt to get out of this dead end and as a bridge between economic history and economic theory. Economic sociology should be analytical in nature but historically grounded. While Sombart, however, wanted economic sociology to replace economic theory totally, Weber thought differently. In his mind, a healthy science of economics (Weber used the term *Sozialoekonomie* or *social economics)* should be broad and draw simultaneously on economic theory, economic history, and economic sociology (Weber 1949). Schumpeter shared Weber's opinion, although economic theory would always rank higher in his mind than in Weber's. The idea of a broad-based social economics, however, never caught on.

Weber, Sombart, and Schumpeter all made a series of first-rate contributions to economic sociology. For one thing, all of them produced major studies of capitalism: Weber, *Economy and Society* (1978); Sombart, *Der moderne Kapitalismus* (1987); and Schumpeter, *Capitalism, Socialism, and Democracy* (1976). Weber emphasized that capitalism was becoming increasingly rationalized; Sombart was particularly interested in looking at the different historical stages of capitalism; and Schumpeter argued that modern capitalism was digging its own grave and was soon to be replaced by socialism. These visions of capitalism still dominate our thinking and are therefore of great interest. And so are many of these thinkers' shorter studies, such as Sombart's study of why there is no socialism in the United States, Weber's analysis of the relationship between Protestantism and the spirit of capitalism, and Schumpeter's two superb articles on imperialism and the tax state (Sombart 1976; Weber 1930; Schumpeter 1954; 1971).

A special mention must also be made of Georg Simmel's *The Philosophy of Money.* This work contains an ingenious analysis of money that ranges from philosophy to sociology. No general sociological theory of money is developed, but the author takes on a series of interesting topics, including credit, checks, and small change. Simmel should not only be credited with having made a serious attempt to develop a sociological approach to money; he was also the first to realize what an important role trust plays in economic life.

The only one to make a sustained effort to lay a theoretical foundation for economic sociology was, however, Max Weber. He did this in a chapter of *Economy and Society,* entitled "Sociological Categories of Economic Action." When Weber lectured on this chapter for his students, they found his analysis very abstract and dry. He therefore decided to give a lecture course in economic history to supplement his theoretical ideas. This course is today known as *General Economic History* (Weber 1981) and should be read together with *Economy and Society.* In *Economy and Society* Weber carefully constructs the various analytical categories that are needed in economic sociology. He starts with "the concept of economic action" and ends with macroeconomic phenomena such as "market economies and planned economies." He also defines and discusses such basic concepts as trade, money, and the market—all from a sociological perspective. At various points of his discussion Weber carefully underlines when economic theory and economic sociology differ. It is, for example, imperative for economic sociologists to use the concept of economic power in their analyses, while this plays no role in marginal utility theory. In economic theory it is assumed that consumers are price givers, but economic sociology assumes that they are price takers. In economic theory it is usually assumed that prices are simply the result of demand and supply, while in economic sociology it is necessary to look at the strength of the various social groups in order to understand the unfolding of the "price struggle." Finally, in economic sociology economic behavior must in principle be subjectively relevant to the actor in order to qualify as "economic action," something that is not the case in standard economic theory. To Weber, in other words, the concept of meaning is central to economic sociology: "all 'economic' processes and objects are characterized as such entirely by the *meaning* they have for human action" (Weber 1978, p. 64).

At about the same time that Weber, Sombart, and Schumpeter were active in Germany, a similar though independent effort to create an economic sociology was made in France. The key figures here are Emile Durkheim, Marcel Mauss, and François Simiand. All three felt that since economic theory is not a social theory (in the sense that it does not assign analytical priority to society as opposed to the individual), it should be replaced by a sociological approach to the economy or, more precisely, by economic sociology. In this they echoed Auguste Comte's critique in the early 1800s of the economic theorists for ignoring that the economy is part of society and that, as a consequence, there is no need for a separate economic theory (Swedberg 1987, pp. 14–17). The two most important studies in the French school of economic sociology are *The Division of Labor in Society* by Durkheim (1964) and *The Gift* by Marcel Mauss (1969; see also Simiand 1932). Mauss's work covers not only gift giving but also contains a series of brilliant remarks on credit, interest, and consumption. In *The Division of Labor in Society* Durkheim raises the question of how to bring about solidarity in industrial society. His answer, which is further elaborated in other works (see especially Durkheim 1962; 1983), is that no society in which the economic element predominates can survive. Economic life has to be restrained by a moral element; without a common morality, all persons would be at war with one another.

Both German and French economic sociology petered out in the 1930s. At around this time European sociology was exhausting itself, while U.S. sociology was in ascendency. Among the multiple subfields that now appeared, several are of interest to economic sociology, such as industrial sociology, sociology of professions, and stratification theory. None of these, however, dealt with core economic problems or with economic theory. Instead, there was a firm division of labor in U.S. social science around this time between economists, who studied economic topics only, and sociologists, who studied social topics only. In the 1950s, however, some sociologists decided to challenge this division of labor, and their efforts have become known as the economy and society approach. The reason for this is not only that two works with this title appeared (Moore 1955; Parsons and Smelser 1956) but that a conscious effort was made to bring two bodies of thought in the social sciences closer together at a time when most social scientists felt they should be kept separate (see also Polanyi et al. 1957). Talcott Parsons and Neil Smelser argued, for example, that the economy is part of society, or, in their terminology, "the economic sub-system" is part of "the social system." In this sense they assigned a certain priority to society and implicitly to sociology. On the other hand, they also felt that economic theory was essentially correct—even if it needed to be complemented by a sociological approach. This dual position also informs the first textbook as well as the first reader in economic sociology—both produced by Smelser (1963; 1965).

During the late 1960s and 1970s little of interest happened in economic sociology. Since the early 1980s, however, there has been a sharp increase of interest in this topic, and a new economic sociology has been born (see Friedland and Robertson 1990; Granovetter 1990; Zukin and DiMaggio 1990). Sociologists as well as economists have contributed to this development. Since the 1970s mainstream economists have become increasingly interested in the role of social structures and organizations in the economy. This has led to a movement usually referred to as new institutional economics. Sources of inspiration for this new institutionalism include transaction cost economics, agency-principal theory, and the theory of asymmetric information. Becker (1976) has convinced many economists that social phenomena can be analyzed with the help of the economist's tools; Arrow (1974) has taken on topics such as organizations and the role of norms in the economy; and Williamson (1975) has popularized the concept of transaction costs through his best-selling *Markets and Hierarchies* (see also Coase 1937 as well as Swedberg 1990). As a result of these and similar events, today's mainstream economists are interested not only in traditional issues relating to price formation but also in economic institutions. The last time that this happened in the United States was in the early twentieth century, when American institutionalism was born (see, e.g., Veblen 1899; Commons 1924; Gruchy 1947). There exists, however, an important difference between the old form of institutionalism and new institutional economics. While Thorstein Veblen and others tried to analyze economic institutions with the help of an approach that was very close to that of sociology, Becker and other rational choice theorists claim that the reasons that economic institutions emerged when they did and why they work the way they do are to be explained in terms of *efficiency* (defined as the maximization of utility). This is a thesis that has been severely criticized by some contemporary sociologists on the ground that it disregards the role of norms and values and what we know in general about economic organizations (e.g., Etzioni 1988).

New institutional economics has played an important role in provoking a response among sociologists and thereby awakening an interest in economic sociology. As a matter of fact, the article that signaled the birth of the new sociology of economic life (as today's economic sociology, as produced by sociologists, is sometimes called) was an article by Mark Granovetter, which contained a sharp critique of new institutional economics (Granovetter 1985). All economic action, Granovetter argued, is "embedded" in social networks, and this is something that is totally ignored by those economists who view economic institutions in terms of efficiency only. Granovetter's idea that networks are crucial to the functioning of the economy was to a large extent inspired by Harrison C. White, another key figure in today's economic sociology. White's most important contribution as of yet, however, has not been connected to this part of his work. His pioneering study of industrial production markets rests instead on the idea that buyers and sellers somehow succeed in creating a social structure—a market—by viewing each other in terms of social roles (White 1981).

White's idea that sociologists should try to analyze markets and not only marginal phenomena of economic life has increasingly become accepted by today's sociologists. Partly as a result of White's work and partly for other reasons, there has been a surge of sociological studies of markets in the 1980s. There exists today, for example, a fairly large sociological literature on labor markets and financial markets (e.g., Berg 1981; Baker 1984; Mintz and Schwartz 1985; Farkas and England 1988). The role of women in the economy —especially studies of segregated labor markets —has become another popular research topic (e.g., England et al. 1988). Today's economic sociologists have also displayed a great interest in various aspects of economic organization, from transfer pricing to the historical evolution of the American firm (e.g., Eccles 1985; Fliegstein 1990). Some of this has been in response to the works by Alfred Chandler and Oliver Williamson, but there also exists independent sources of inspiration in sociology to draw on—for example, in organizational sociology and industrial sociology (e.g., Gouldner 1954; Stinchcombe 1959; Hirsch 1972; Perrow 1986). Finally, a few sociologists have also tried to introduce a comparative approach and a cultural approach to the study of the economy. A fine example of comparative economic sociology can be found in a recent study of the organization of business in Taiwan, Japan, and South Korea (Hamilton and Biggart 1988; see also Stinchcombe 1983). That cultural factors play a distinct role in economic life has been most forcefully argued by Viviana Zelizer in her studies of life insurance and money (Zelizer 1983; 1989). In short, economic sociology has come alive again and seems headed for an interesting future.

(SEE ALSO: *Economic Determinism; Economic Institutions; Money; Transnational Corporations*)

REFERENCES

Arrow, Kenneth 1974 *The Limits of Organization.* New York: W. W. Norton.

Baker, Wayne E. 1984 "The Social Structure of a National Securities Market." *American Journal of Sociology* 89:775–811.

Becker, Gary 1976 *The Economic Approach to Human Behavior.* Chicago: University of Chicago Press.

Berg, Ivar, ed. 1981 *Sociological Approaches on Labor Markets.* New York: Academic Press.

Coase, Ronald H. 1937 "The Nature of the Firm." *Economica,* n.s. 4:385–405.

Coleman, James 1990 *Foundations of Social Theory.* Cambridge, Mass.: Harvard University Press.

Commons, John R. 1924 *The Legal Foundations of Capitalism.* New York: Macmillan.

Durkheim, Emile 1962 *Socialism.* New York: Collier Books.

——— 1964 *The Division of Labor in Society.* New York: Free Press.

——— 1983 *Professional Ethics and Civic Morals.* Westport, Conn.: Greenwood Press.

Eccles, Robert G. 1985 *The Transfer Pricing Problem: A Theory for Practice.* Lexington, Mass.: Lexington Books.

England, Paula, George Farkas, Barbara Kilbourne, and Thomas Dov 1988 "Explaining Occupational Sex Segregation and Wages: Findings from a Model with Fixed Effects." *American Sociological Review* 53:544–588.

Etzioni, Amitai 1988 *The Moral Dimension: Towards a New Economics.* New York: Free Press.

Farkas, George, and Paula England (eds.) 1988 *Industries, Firms, and Jobs: Sociological and Economic Approaches.* New York: Plenum.

Fliegstein, Neil 1990 *The Transformation of Corporate Control.* Cambridge, Mass.: Harvard University Press.

Friedland, Roger, and A. F. Robertson (eds.) 1990 *Beyond the Marketplace: Rethinking Economy and Society.* New York: Aldine.

Gouldner, Alvin 1954 *Patterns of Industrial Bureaucracy.* New York: Free Press.

Granovetter, Mark 1985 "Economic Action and Social Structure: A Theory of Embeddedness." *American Journal of Sociology* 91:481–510.

——— 1990 "The Old and the New Economic Sociology: A History and an Agenda." In Roger Friedland and A. F. Robertson, eds., *Beyond the Marketplace.* New York: Aldine.

Gruchy, Allan G. 1947 *Modern Economic Thought: The American Contribution.* New York: Prentice-Hall.

Hamilton, George G., and Nicole W. Biggart 1988 "Market, Culture, and Authority: A Comparative Analysis of Management and Organization in the Far East." *Supplement to the American Journal of Sociology* 94:S52–S94.

Hirsch, Paul 1972 "Processing Fads and Fashion: An Organization-Set Analysis of Cultural Industry Systems." *American Journal of Sociology* 77:639–659.

Mauss, Marcel 1969 *The Gift: Forms and Functions of Exchange in Archaic Societies.* London: Cohen and West, Ltd.

Mintz, Beth, and Michael Schwartz 1985 *The Power Structure of American Business.* Chicago: University of Chicago Press.

Moore, Wilbert E. 1955 *Economy and Society.* New York: Doubleday.

Parsons, Talcott, and Neil Smelser 1956 *Economy and Society: A Study in the Integration of Economic and Social Theory.* London: Routledge and Kegan Paul.

Perrow, Charles 1986 *Complex Organizations: A Critical Essay.* 3d ed. New York: Random House.

Polanyi, Karl, et al. (eds.) 1957 *Trade and Market in the Early Empires.* Glencoe, Ill.: Free Press.

Schumpeter, Joseph A. 1954 "The Crisis of the Tax State." *International Economic Papers* 4:5–38.

——— 1971 "The Sociology of Imperialisms." In Schumpeter, *Imperialism and Social Classes.* New York: Meridian Books.

——— 1976 *Capitalism, Socialism, and Democracy.* New York: Harper and Row.

Simiand, François 1932 *Le salaire, l'evolution sociale et la monnaie.* Paris: Alcan.

Simmel, Georg 1990 *The Philosophy of Money.* 2d enlarged ed. London: Routledge.

Smelser, Neil 1963 *The Sociology of Economic Life.* Englewood Cliffs, N.J.: Prentice-Hall.

——— (ed.) 1965 *Readings on Economic Sociology.* Englewood Cliffs, N.J.: Prentice-Hall.

Sombart, Werner 1976 *Why Is There No Socialism in the United States?* New York: Sharpe.

——— 1987 *Der moderne Kapitalismus.* Munich: Deutscher Taschebuch Verlag.

Stinchcombe, Arthur 1959 "Bureaucratic and Craft Administration of Production: A Comparative Study." *Administrative Science Quarterly* 4:168–187.

——— 1983 *Economic Sociology.* New York: Academic Press.

Swedberg, Richard 1987 "Economic Sociology: Past and Present." *Current Sociology* 35:1–221.

——— 1990 *Economics and Sociology—On Redefining Their Boundaries: Conversations with Economists and Sociologists.* Princeton: Princeton University Press.

Veblen, Thorstein 1899 *The Theory of the Leisure Class.* New York: Macmillan.

Weber, Max 1930 *The Protestant Ethic and the Spirit of Capitalism.* London: Allen and Unwin.

——— 1949 "'Objectivity' in Social Science and in Social Policy." In Weber, *The Methodology of the Social Sciences.* New York: Free Press.

——— 1978 *Economy and Society: An Outline of Interpretive Sociology.* Berkeley: University of California Press.

——— 1981 *General Economic History.* New York: Transaction Books.

White, Harrison C. 1981 "Where Do Markets Come From?" *American Journal of Sociology* 87:514–547.

Williamson, Oliver F. 1975 *Markets and Hierarchies: Analysis and Antitrust Implications.* New York: Free Press.

Zelizer, Viviana 1983 *Morals and Markets: The Development of Life Insurance in the United States.* New Brunswick, N.J.: Transaction Books.

——— 1989 "The Social Meaning of Money: 'Special Monies.'" *American Journal of Sociology* 95:342–377.

Zukin, Sharon, and Paul DiMaggio (eds.) 1990 *Structures of Capital: The Social Organization of the Economy.* Cambridge: Cambridge University Press.

RICHARD SWEDBERG

EDUCATIONAL ORGANIZATION Education and schooling are not synonymous. Education is the more encompassing concept, referring to the general process by which a social group—whether an entire society or just a family—transmits attitudes, beliefs, behaviors, and skills to its members. Within these broad boundaries, education greatly varies, with educational scholars typically distinguishing three general types: formal education, nonformal education, and informal education. These different kinds of education can be distinguished according to where they take place, the characteristics of teachers, the methods of instruction, and what is learned.

Informal education takes such forms as family child rearing, peer group socialization, and learning on one's own such skills as auto repair and guitar playing. It takes place in the context of everyday, intimate relationships, with teachers being family members or friends and learning occurring through observation and imitation ("hands on"). Formal education or schooling, meanwhile, takes place outside the family in institutions that specialize in education and that we call schools. Instruction is led by teachers who are not students' intimates, whose principal occupation is education, and who stress learning through verbal and written description and guided inquiry rather than through observation and imitation. Nonformal education, finally, includes on-the-job training, agricultural extension programs, and family planning outreach programs. It differs from informal education in that it takes place outside the family, but it also differs from formal education in that it does not take place in schools and its aims are more specific and short-term.

Virtually all societies utilize all three forms of education, but they differ in the relative predominance of these forms. In nonindustrialized societies, informal education dominates, with formal and nonformal education only marginally present. But in highly industrialized societies such as the United States, formal education rivals, if not exceeds, nonformal and informal education in its importance and its use of society's resources. Despite a common emphasis on formal education, the United States is quite different from other advanced industrial societies in how its school system is organized. Six divergences stand out (Dougherty and Hammack 1990, chap. 3).

First, the American school system is much larger. This is a product not just of the United States' large population but also of the fact that its schools enroll a far larger proportion of students, particularly among those above the age of compulsory school attendance. For example, in 1982, college students represented 5.3 percent of the entire U.S. population, while the comparable percentage was 2.3 in West Germany, 2.2 in France, 2.0 in Japan and the Soviet Union, and 1.6 in the United Kingdom.

Second, the American school system is far less centralized than the school systems of most advanced industrial societies (Hopper 1977). Most other industrial societies largely vest control of their school systems in a national ministry of education that finances the schools and sets basic rules for curriculum, admission, and graduation and for teacher education, hiring, and promotion. Such a pattern of strong national centralization, with minimal local voice, can be seen in Japan, France, Italy, and the Soviet Union (Ignas and Corsini 1981; King 1979). In the United States, meanwhile, the states have constitutional sovereignty over education and, furthermore, allow local districts great power over the day-to-day functioning of the schools (Campbell et al. 1985; Wirt and Kirst 1989). This decentralization of authority is enhanced by the fact that American schools receive most of their funds not from the national government but from state and local sources.

Because of its greater decentralization, the American school system is less homogeneous across different regions of the country than are the school systems in other advanced industrial societies. In comparison to French students living in different regions of their country, American students living in different states encounter greater differences in how much is spent on their education, how educated their teachers are, and what education they are provided.

A third distinctive feature of the American school system is that it is much less driven by examination requirements than are many other school systems. In good part because the American system is much less centralized, it does not have the system of nationwide exams that are present in most other advanced societies and that powerfully mold students' educational careers. In most other countries, exams taken before high school determine the kind of high school one can attend, and exams taken at the end of high school determine whether one can go on to higher education and what kind of college one can attend. As a result, exam taking assumes a critical and hellish importance in such countries as Japan, France, Germany, the Soviet Union, and England. In the United States, however, one can still get into college without doing well on the Scholastic

Aptitude Test (SAT) or American College Test (ACT) or even taking them at all. However, the American exemption from the "examination hell" may be disappearing as states and local school districts increasingly require students to pass a minimum competency test to receive a high school diploma or enter college.

While the American school system is less centralized and therefore less homogeneous across regions than the systems in most other industrial societies, it is also *more* homogeneous *within the same district.* This is the fourth major difference among industrial societies. The United States has long enrolled its students in "comprehensive" schools: that is, institutions that offer both academic and vocational subjects. Most other advanced industrial societies traditionally have had strongly differentiated secondary and postsecondary educational systems. Until recently, many students have enrolled in specialized high schools, whether vocational schools or elite academic high schools (the English grammar school, the French lycée, and the German gymnasium). In turn, higher education in most advanced societies has been strongly divided between academically oriented universities and less prestigious, vocationally oriented technical and teacher-training institutions. This curricular division has tended to coincide with social class divisions. The elite academic secondary schools and the universities have long drawn disproportionately from the upper class and upper middle class. Meanwhile, lower-middle-class and working-class students have gone to vocational schools and low-prestige comprehensive schools and, if they reached higher education, technical and teacher-training colleges. In the United States, meanwhile, students of all classes attend comprehensive schools and colleges because of the relatively small number of exclusively vocational or academic schools and colleges.

But if American schools in the same district evidence great homogeneity, this is purchased in good part through greater heterogeneity *within* those schools. This is the fifth difference between American schools and those of other countries. Unlike Japanese, French, and Soviet schools, American schools group students within schools according to apparent ability and interests—and, as a result, social class and ethnicity (Ignas and Corsini 1981; King 1979).

The sixth and final divergence is that U.S. schools typically take on far more tasks than is typical in other societies. Americans expect schools to address such problems as poor driving, drug abuse, sexual ignorance, and poor nutrition at home.

A closer examination of how U.S. schools are controlled is merited, for this is one of the more striking ways that they deviate from schools in other societies. In fact, the structure of control in U.S. schools produces recurrent political conflicts that tend to be unique to the United States.

A variety of entities sponsor education in the United States. The most prominent are governmental bodies. At the elementary and secondary school level, local school districts operate three-quarters of all schools. The nongovernmental patrons include religious bodies (above all the Catholic church) and independent nonprofit organizations. At the postsecondary level, governmental bodies sponsor 45 percent of all colleges and universities in the United States; these 1,500 public colleges account for three-quarters of all college enrollments. The biggest actors are state governments, followed by local governments and, far back in the distance, the federal government. The remaining 1,800 colleges are private, owned either by nonsectarian, nonprofit boards (25 percent), religious groups—especially the Protestant denominations (24 percent), or profit-making corporations (7 percent) (Dougherty and Hammack 1990, chap. 3).

Schools are controlled by four different mechanisms: bureaucracy, profession, politics, and markets. Schools are bureaucratic organizations because they serve explicit goals and are composed of a variety of people who do specialized work and whose efforts need to be coordinated. Formal rules specify which jobs are to be done within the organization, and there are explicit differences in the authority of members according to their places in the school's hierarchy (Bidwell 1965;

Corwin 1970). School boards, central school district officials, and state education authorities decide what the curriculum will include, what books to use, and what objectives they should strive to achieve. These goals and the means to achieve them descend to school-level principals and curriculum leaders and then to individual classroom teachers.

But schools are only partially bureaucratic organizations. Even as they aim to control teachers, they also have to give them considerable autonomy. Boards of education often have no clear consensus on what the goals of education should be or how to achieve them. The technology of teaching is relatively primitive, without "magic bullets" or drugs that can "heal" the patients or eradicate ignorance. Hence, school administrators often leave many decisions about the techniques and at times the very goals of education to teachers. Therefore, teachers often have great autonomy in the classroom. It is this autonomy that makes them professionals. But teaching is unlike other professions in that success is more problematic. Its technology is less certain in its result, in good part because it demands the active participation of the client. To be successful, teachers must successfully motivate students to value school achievement and to conform to the essential requirements of the classroom (Metz 1978; Meyer and Rowan 1978).

Schools are also governed by external political control. As noted earlier, the decentralized nature of the American school affords the opportunity for diverse groups to influence educational policy. One of these, of course, is voters. All adults can elect representatives to public school boards. In fact, citizens can even govern them directly, voting on school budgets, tax rates, and bond issues. In addition, organized interest groups—ranging from business to religious groups—influence school decisions through lobbying and their ability to shape the agenda for school policymaking (Campbell et al. 1985; Wirt and Kirst 1989).

Finally, schools are governed by market mechanisms. This is particularly obvious in the case of private schools, which do not have a guaranteed clientele and must recruit students every year. But public schools also face market forces because parents who are unhappy with their local schools may move to another neighborhood, leaving schools with fewer students and lower state aid. These market forces within public education have increased with recent efforts to increase parental choice within and even between districts: magnet schools, schools within schools, and voucher plans (Chubb and Moe 1990; Metz 1986; Spicer and Hill 1990).

The combination of bureaucratic, professional, political, and market controls makes schools unique organizations, with distinctive and recurrent tensions. A clash between bureaucracy and professionalism can be seen in the current conflict between those reformers calling for tighter administrative regulation of teachers' work and other reformers defending teachers' autonomy as professionals and intellectuals (Apple 1986; Aronowitz and Giroux 1985). In turn, those defending teachers' professional autonomy have also found themselves in conflict with groups calling for increased local community control. Schools are not only workplaces for teachers but also places where communities try to pass on their ways of life to their children. Professionalization threatens community control by shifting authority from lay people to educational experts, who do not necessarily have the promotion of local community values as their top priority. Our tradition of local control of public schools is inherently suspicious of educational decisions being made by officials who are not directly accountable to local citizens and taxpayers.

Another clash has come from the efforts of state bureaucratic authorities to eliminate local variation in school spending, curriculum, facilities, and outcomes. This effort has been actively resisted by local communities, teachers, and administrators. There have been great fights over school consolidation, school spending, and textbook content in recent decades (Peshkin 1978).

Finally, a clash between market and other forms of regulation is much in the news with the debate between those calling for greater parental choice (in order to increase competition between schools and thus force improvement) and those fearing that this will result in public schools becoming even more segregated by race and social class and less able to provide equal opportunity (Chubb and Moe 1990; Spicer and Hill 1990).

This concern about segregation is merited, given that American schools already differ greatly among themselves in student body composition: that is, in the social class, race, and ethnic distribution of their students (Dougherty and Hammack 1990, Chapter 3). Because of racial, ethnic, and economic segregation in residence patterns, as well as overt discrimination in drawing district boundaries, schools are often dominated by one social group and are thus segregated. From the Supreme Court's *Brown v. Board of Education of Topeka, Kansas* (1954) decision onward, civil rights rulings have altered this pattern somewhat. Yet the student composition of many schools still does not reflect the diversity of a community's population of young people.

In the case of higher education, one finds that as one moves from universities to four-year colleges to two-year colleges, the proportion of students who are male, white, upper class, or academically high performing drops. In addition, some colleges serve the needs of distinct populations of students: for example, the nearly 200 single-sex colleges and nearly 100 all-black colleges (U.S. National Center for Education Statistics 1985; Rudolph 1962; Solomon 1985).

Schools also differ among themselves in the programs they offer. While most elementary and secondary schools offer fairly similar programs, they often differ in how they package the common curriculum. High schools, especially, may emphasize a particular vocational connection to their curriculum—for example, by offering preparation for health or business careers.

Colleges also differ in their offerings. Universities offer doctoral and professional programs and produce a large number of graduates with doctorates or medical or dental degrees. "Comprehensive" institutions offer diverse undergraduate curricula and some graduate programs. "General baccalaureate" or "liberal arts" colleges emphasize undergraduate education and have very few, if any, graduate programs. "Specialized" colleges emphasize one field, such as engineering or the arts, offering either a baccalaureate or postbaccalaureate training. The nearly 1,300 "two-year colleges" specialize in subbaccalaureate degrees such as associate of arts and various kinds of vocational certificates in areas like dental assisting or auto repair (Brint and Karabel 1989; Cohen and Brawer 1989; Dougherty 1988). (The number of two-year institutions would be far greater if we were to include the many for-profit postsecondary schools, numbering 7,645 in 1986, that offer technical and vocational training.)

But if schools differ mightily between themselves, they are also as strongly or more strongly differentiated internally. Two students in the same school may experience educational environments as varied as those experienced by two students at different schools. One of the most important differentiations takes the form of "ability grouping" or tracking in elementary and secondary schooling. This pervasive practice involves breaking students up into different classes or groups within classes, ostensibly on the basis of academic aptitude, and teaching them different material or the same material but at different paces. This differentiation of students is said to be based mainly on test scores, but in actuality other factors also play an important role, such as students' interests, the number of students in the class, and the distribution of student ability. Hence, curriculum or instructional groups are often rather heterogeneous in test scores and only partially approach being ability groups. Many scholars argue that curriculum grouping plays a key role in producing class and race differences in educational attainment, because students differing in social class and race tend to be assigned to different tracks and because tracking has a significant impact on educational attainment, independent of the characteristics of students (Barr and Dreeben 1983; Dreeben and Gamoran 1986; Peterson, Wilkinson, and Hallinan 1984; and Rosenbaum 1980).

Elementary and secondary schools also engage in curriculum grouping in the form of special education, gifted education, and bilingual education. These programs have become targets of considerable criticism in recent years. The term *special education* applies to programs for those who have academic, physical, or emotional difficulties that require special educational provision. In recent years, however, many observers have argued that special education programs have become ghettos for nonwhite and working-class students, because they more often receive lower test scores than white or middle- and upper-class students. Gifted education, conversely, has become a reserve for white and, increasingly, Asian students. Gifted education has been developed ostensibly to meet the needs of students of such unusual ability that they require a specially enriched education. Many critics argue, however, that these programs have become devices for keeping white students in urban public schools by offering the prospect of largely white or Asian classmates. Bilingual education, finally, enrolls students whose native language is not English. These students are instructed in both English and their native language for the first few years so that they can keep pace academically with native students. In recent years, however, many have argued that these programs prevent assimilation into American culture (Dougherty and Hammack 1990, chap. 8).

Colleges and universities also engage in curriculum grouping in the form of different majors. These constitute different environments that result in different educational and occupational outcomes for students. However, this curricular differentiation has not been considered as problematic as elementary and secondary tracking, because it occurs at a higher level and involves greater student choice.

This article has traced a complex pattern of repeated differentiation in order to elucidate how education is organized. This complex structure produces certain recurrent tensions that repeatedly break into educational politics.

(SEE ALSO: *Socialization; Sociology of Education*)

REFERENCES

Apple, Michael 1986 *Teachers and Texts.* New York: Routledge, Chapman and Hall.

Aronowitz, Stanley, and Henry Giroux 1985 *Education under Siege.* South Hadley, Mass.: Bergin and Garvey.

Barr, Rebecca, and Robert Dreeben 1983 *How Schools Work.* Chicago: University of Chicago Press.

Bidwell, Charles 1965 "The School as a Formal Organization." In James G. March, ed., *Handbook of Organizations.* Chicago: Rand McNally.

Brint, Steven, and Jerome Karabel 1989 *The Diverted Dream.* New York: Oxford University Press.

Campbell, Roald F., Luvern L. Cunningham, Raphael O. Nystrand, and Michael D. Usdan 1985 *Organization and Control of American Schools,* 5th ed. Columbus, Ohio: Merrill.

Chubb, John E., and Terry Moe 1990 *Politics, Markets, and America's Schools.* Washington, D.C.: Brookings Institution.

Cohen, Arthur M., and Florence Brawer 1989 *The American Community College,* 2nd ed. San Francisco: Jossey-Bass.

Corwin, Ronald 1970 *Militant Professionalism: A Study of Organizational Conflict in High Schools.* New York: Appleton-Century-Crofts.

Dougherty, Kevin J. 1988 "The Politics of Community College Expansion." *American Journal of Education* 96:351–393.

———, and Floyd M. Hammack (eds.) 1990 *Education and Society.* San Diego: Harcourt Brace Jovanovich.

Dreeben, Robert, and Adam Gamoran 1986 "Race, Instruction, and Learning." *American Sociological Review* 51:660–669.

Hopper, Earl 1977 "A Typology for the Classification of Educational Systems." In Jerome Karabel and A. H. Halsey, eds., *Power and Ideology in Education.* New York: Oxford University Press.

Ignas, Edward, and Raymond Corsini (eds.) 1981 *Comparative Educational Systems.* Itasca, Ill.: F. E. Peacock.

King, Edmund 1979 *Other Schools and Ours,* 5th ed. New York: Oxford University Press.

Metz, Mary Haywood 1978 *Classrooms and Corridors.* Berkeley: University of California Press.

——— 1986 *Different by Design: Politics, Purpose, and Practice in Three Magnet Schools.* New York: Routledge, Chapman and Hall.

Meyer, John, and Brian Rowan 1978 "The Structure of Educational Organizations." In Marshall W. Meyer and Associates, *Environments and Organizations.* San Francisco: Jossey-Bass.

Peshkin, Alan 1978 *Growing Up American.* Chicago: University of Chicago Press.

Peterson, Penelope, Louise Cherry Wilkinson, and

Maureen Hallinan (eds.) 1984 *The Social Context of Instruction.* New York: Academic Press.

Rosenbaum, James 1980 "Social Implications of Educational Grouping." In David Berliner, ed., *Review of Research in Education.* Washington, D.C.: American Educational Research Association.

Rudolph, Frederick 1962 *The American College and University.* New York: Vintage.

Solomon, Barbara Miller 1985 *In the Company of Educated Women.* New Haven: Yale University Press.

Spicer, Michael W., and Edward W. Hill 1990 "Evaluating Parental Choice in Public Education." *American Journal of Education* 98:97–113.

U.S. National Center for Education Statistics 1985 *Traditionally Black Institutions of Higher Education: Their Development and Status, 1860–1982.* Washington, D.C.: U.S. National Center for Education Statistics.

Wirt, Frederick, and Michael Kirst 1989 *Schools in Conflict,* 2nd ed. San Francisco: McCutchan.

KEVIN DOUGHERTY
FLOYD M. HAMMACK

EDUCATION AND MOBILITY The role of education in relation to social mobility and reproduction has long been debated between those who emphasize its contribution to social mobility and those who focus on its contribution to social reproduction. In order to understand this debate, it is useful to review the key concepts and theoretical perspectives before considering the empirical evidence and then offering a resolution.

Social stratification refers to the class or status hierarchy in society and the inequality in social rewards between people who belong to different classes or have different status. *Class* is the term preferred by theorists who view the social order as consisting of distinctive economic groupings struggling to maximize their interests vis-a-vis each other, while *status* is preferred by theorists who perceive a continuing distribution of socioeconomic variation without clear-cut divisions and conflict. *Social mobility* is the movement from one class or status to another. The emphasis here, as with most studies of social mobility, is on *intergenerational mobility.* Intergenerational mobility refers to the change in class or status from parents to their adult children. An example of intergenerational mobility is when the daughter or the son of peasants becomes a doctor. In contrast, when the offspring of peasants ends up being a peasant, it is an example of *social reproduction.*

The social class or status positions that individuals occupy in society are usually attributed to both *ascriptive* and *achievement* processes. These are generally viewed as opposite or contradictory processes involving either ascribed characteristics based on biological factors and family of origin or achieved characteristics based on individual traits and behaviors. Stratification systems that emphasize ascriptive characteristics for class or status placement are defined as "closed" and lead to status inheritance or class reproduction. Those stratification systems that emphasize achieved characteristics are defined as "open" and are expected to lead to social mobility.

The opposing positions are formalized in the functionalist and conflict theories of social stratification. With respect to the role of education in producing social mobility, functionalists argue that different social roles require different skills and abilities and, if society is to function effectively, they must be filled by individuals possessing the appropriate skills and abilities (Davis and Moore 1945). The positions most valued by society are usually the most critical for societal functioning and the most demanding of individual skills and ability. In order to encourage individuals to invest the time and effort for training and to attract the best qualified individuals, these positions have to be accompanied by higher social and economic rewards. Education is widely viewed as both developing and reflecting individual skills and abilities and is therefore used as a means of social selection. Thus, education enhances social mobility by providing for social selection based on achieved rather than ascribed characteristics of individuals.

Conflict theorists start with the premise that society consists of different groups with conflicting interest, and they argue that stratification exists because groups that acquired power, wealth, and prestige want to maintain and enhance their position at the expense of less privileged groups. In respect to education, most conflict theorists agree that schools help to reproduce and legitimize the stratification system by portraying attainment as an achieved individual characteristic, while in fact they select and process individuals on the basis of ascriptive characteristics (Bowles and Gintis 1976; Willis 1977; Bourdieu 1977).

Empirical research on the role of education in the process of social mobility or reproduction has produced conflicting evidence. The argument of mobility through education as suggested by functional theories depends on the validity of two general conditions: (1) educational attainment must be used as a criterion of eventual social class or status position; and (2) the level of educational attainment of individuals must not be influenced by the level of their family's class or status. Boudon (1976) calls these two conditions necessary for social mobility "meritocracy" and "equality of educational opportunity" respectively. It is important to note that social mobility exists only if both conditions are met and that each of them alone is a necessary but insufficient condition for social mobility.

Many studies have tested empirically the meritocracy hypothesis, and almost all have found a significant relationship between educational and later socioeconomic attainments (Blau and Duncan 1967; Sewell, Haller, and Portes 1969; Duncan, Featherman, and Duncan 1972; Jencks et al. 1972). Indeed, most studies in the United States have found educational attainment to be among the most important determinants of occupational and status attainment, although the findings regarding its relationship with income are not as conclusive (Jencks et al. 1972). In short, the meritocracy condition is well supported by empirical evidence.

However, other studies of social mobility found that employing meritocracy in the allocation of occupational and social status has not resulted in substantial increases in social mobility (Boudon 1974; Collins 1979). Boudon, using data from Western industrialized countries, and Collins, analyzing data from the United States, found that the tremendous expansion of education in the last century left the opportunities for social mobility essentially unchanged. It did expand the educational attainment of many social groups, but, as the educational attainment of individuals from lower socioeconomic strata increased, individuals from higher strata acquired even more education, thus shifting the overall educational attainment of the population upward but keeping in tact the stratification of educational attainment (Boudon 1974; Collins 1979). Given that meritocracy in the allocation of social positions exists, these findings suggest the lack of equality of educational opportunity.

In relation to the latter, the functionalist position is that schools do provide equality of opportunity. For empirical support, they point to the numerous empirical studies suggesting that the process of educational attainment is an achievement process. The best-known model of educational and status attainment in the United States, known as the Wisconsin Model, describes the process as one whereby individual and background characteristics are translated into differential status attainment only after they have been transformed into individual performance and psychological variables (Sewell, Haller, and Portes 1969; Sewell, Haller, and Ohlendorf 1970). Although this model has been criticized for excluding social constraints and related structural variables (see Kerckoff 1976), its explanatory power remains strong, and it has withstood a number of replications (Alexander, Eckland, and Griffin 1978; Jencks, Crouse, and Mueser 1983). Indeed, most of the research on the social selection process that followed the Wisconsin Model has shown that schools select, process, and reward students based on individual traits and achievements such as aspirations and ability and that educational attainment in turn is the major determinant of occupational status attainment.

Conflict theorists and researchers, by contrast, have not been very successful in describing and explaining a social selection process that leads to social reproduction. The explanations and the evidence as to why individuals from higher social strata acquire consistently better education have not been able to dispute or account for the fact that the educational selection process is ostensibly an "achievement" process. In general, the argument from a conflict perspective is that structural limitations imposed on the schooling of some groups restrict their educational success, thus helping to reproduce the educational and social hierarchies.

Some structural limitations on both the quality and quantity of educational opportunity of children from low socioeconomic strata do indeed exist. Differential quality and quantity of schooling may have been especially influential in the past, but it still exists today. Some of the best schools at all educational levels in the United States are private, with high tuition, and obviously not all social groups have equal access to or success in these institutions. Also, fewer institutions, especially at the postprimary levels, are available in rural or low income areas. Nonetheless, the impact of variation in quality and quantity of schooling has been reduced over the years, and evidence does not indicate it as a major determinant of educational attainment. For example, the well-publicized report *Equality of Educational Opportunity* (Coleman et al. 1966) found that differences between public schools had no significant effect on student performance. In general, even though some relevant quality differences between schools may still exist today, this structural variable is a relatively weak factor in explaining differential educational attainment.

Other structural variables, such as curriculum tracking (Alexander, Cook, and McDill 1978), and differential treatment by teachers and counselors (Rist 1970; Karabel 1972) also have been found to exert significant influence on educational attainment. In addition, researchers have found that cultural differences linked to differential social origin are also responsible for the unequal educational attainment of students from different social groups (Bourdieu 1977; Bourdieu and Passeron 1977; DiMaggio 1982). Overall, however, structural limitations and cultural deficiencies account for only a small amount of attainment differences as compared to the individual achievement variables.

Summarizing the findings on equality of educational opportunity and meritocracy presents a paradoxical picture of social stratification and leaves the issue of social mobility through education largely unresolved: Status attainment research has shown that educational and status attainment is a meritocratic process based on individual achievement variables, but it has not explained the relatively low social mobility rates. Critical research, on the other hand, has shown reproduction of social status, but it has not been able to unseat the equality of opportunity thesis resting on the association of individual achievement with educational status attainment.

This apparent paradox may be due in part to the fact that research on educational and social stratification in the last few decades has been dominated by the ascription–achievement controversy without necessarily examining the relationship between this controversy and the broader mobility–reproduction debate. The underlying assumption of this focus seems to have been that achievement leads to mobility and ascription leads to reproduction. But however important achievement and ascription may be, they do not address the same issues as mobility and reproduction. A way out of this impasse may be to challenge the assumed correspondence between what we traditionally consider individual achievements on the one hand and social mobility on the other. There is no reason to assume that an empirical finding of schooling as an achievement process is necessarily incompatible with a theoretical argument of schooling as a process of reproduction. As long as individual qualities and achievements are determined by the social origin of the student, educational systems can promote not only social reproduction and individual achievement but social reproduction *through* achievement (Katsillis and Rubinson 1990).

One of the most consistent findings of the research on educational and status attainment is that the socioeconomic status of the family influences the whole educational process, including many, if not all, individual student achievements and abilities that lead to socioeconomic status attainment. Thus, once the assumption that achievement implies social status or class mobility is abandoned, there is no contradiction between the findings of status attainment research that indicate an achievement-oriented educational selection system and the findings of critical research that schools reproduce social status or class inequalities.

This, of course, poses some interesting questions, especially in relation to the meaning and the role of equality of educational opportunity as we understand it today: Does a process that transforms family status inequality into differential individual achievements or qualities and, subsequently, into unequal educational attainment constitute equality of educational opportunity? If it does not, what constitutes equality of educational opportunity, and how is it attained? We may have to rethink the whole process of equality of opportunity before we are able to provide satisfactory answers to the question of education and social mobility.

(SEE ALSO: *Equality of Opportunity; Social Mobility; Social Stratification; Sociology of Education; Status Attainment*)

REFERENCES

Alexander, K. L., M. A. Cook, and E. L. McDill 1978 "Curriculum Tracking and Educational Stratification: Some Further Evidence." *American Sociological Review* 43:47–66.

Alexander, K. L., B. K. Eckland, and L. J. Griffin 1978 "The Wisconsin Model of Socioeconomic Attainment: A Replication." *American Journal of Sociology* 81:324–342.

Blau, P. M., and O. D. Duncan 1967 *The American Occupational Structure.* New York: Wiley.

Bourdieu, P. 1977 "Cultural Reproduction and Social Reproduction." In J. Karabel and A. H. Halsey, eds., *Power and Ideology in Education.* New York: Oxford University Press.

———, and J. C. Passeron 1977 *Reproduction in Education, Society, and Culture.* Beverly Hills, Calif.: Sage Publications.

Bowles, S., and H. Gintis 1976 *Schooling in Capitalist America.* New York: Basic Books.

Coleman, J. S., E. Q. Campbell, C. J. Hobson, J. McPartland, A. M. Mood, F. D. Weinfall, and R. L. York 1966 *The Equality of Educational Opportunity.* Washington, D.C.: U.S. Department of Health, Education, and Welfare.

Davis, K., and W. Moore 1945 "Some Principles of Stratification." *American Sociological Review* 10:242–249.

DiMaggio, P. 1982 "Cultural Capital and School Success: The Impact of Status Culture Participation on the Grades of U.S. High School Students." *American Sociological Review* 47:189–201.

Duncan, O. D., D. L. Featherman, and B. Duncan 1972 *Socioeconomic Background and Achievement.* New York: Seminar Press.

Jencks, C., J. Crouse, and P. Mueser 1983 "The Wisconsin Model of Status Attainment: A National Replication with Improved Measures of Ability and Aspirations." *Sociology of Education* 56:3–19.

Jencks, C., M. Smith, H. Acland, J. M. Bane, D. Cohen, H. Gintis, B. Heyns, and S. Michelson 1972 *Inequality: A Reassessment of Family and Schooling in America.* New York: Basic Books.

Karabel, J. 1972 "Community Colleges and Social Stratification." *Harvard Educational Review* 42:521–562.

———, and A. H. Halsey (eds.) 1977 *Power and Ideology in Education.* New York: Oxford University Press.

Katsillis, J., and R. Rubinson 1990 "Cultural Capital, Student Achievement, and Educational Reproduction: The Case of Greece." *American Sociological Review* 55:270–279.

Kerckhoff, A. C. 1976 "The Status Attainment Process: Socialization or Allocation?" *Social Forces* 52:368–381.

Rist, R. C. 1970 "Student Social Class and Teacher Expectations: The Self-Fulfilling Prophecy in Ghetto Education." *Harvard Educational Review* 40:411–451.

Sewell, W. H., A. O. Haller, and G. W. Ohlendorf 1970 "The Educational and Early Occupational Status Attainment Process: Replications and Revisions." *American Sociological Review* 34:1,014–1,027.

Sewell, W. H., A. O. Haller, and A. Portes 1969 "The Educational and Early Occupational Status Attainment Process." *American Sociological Review* 34:82–92.

Willis, P. 1977 *Learning to Labor.* New York: Columbia University Press.

JOHN KATSILLIS
J. MICHAEL ARMER

ELITES *See* Intellectuals.

EMOTIONS *See* Affect-Control Theory.

ENDOGAMY/EXOGAMY *See* Incest; Kinship Systems and Family Types; Mate-Selection Theory.

ENVIRONMENT *See* Human Ecology and the Environment; Technological Risks and Society.

ENVIRONMENTAL IMPACT ASSESSMENT Environmental impact assessment has been defined in a variety of ways, but there is no single definition that is universally agreed upon. Still, one definition that is useful as a basis of discussion is offered by R. E. Munn. He describes environmental impact assessment (EIA) as "an activity designed to identify and predict the impact on the biogeophysical environment and on man's [sic] health and well-being of legislative proposals, policies, programmes, projects and operational procedures, and to interpret and communicate information about the impacts" (1979, p. 1).

The information about the potential environmental impacts of proposals, policies, programs, projects, and operational procedures is supposed to form the basis for logical and rational decisions (Clark 1983, pp. 4–5). The effectiveness of EIA in achieving this goal has been a question of serious and continuing debate (Wolf 1983, pp. 29–32).

Early attempts at EIA were project specific. The questions addressed in these early attempts were whether or not the project was technically feasible and whether or not the economic benefits outweighed the economic costs.

EIA has evolved so that other questions are now being addressed (Clark 1983, pp. 3–4). These include: (1) Is the project required, and, if so, when is it required? (2) How does this project compare with other alternatives? (3) What are the implications for levels of risk to public safety? and (4) To what extent should protection be provided for potentially endangered ecological systems, including human communities?

It could be argued that EIA was conceived and grew as a part of the environmental movement of the 1960s. Some authors suggest that the modern environmental movement began with public awareness of the effects of pesticides—awareness that was generated by the 1962 publication of Rachel Carson's book *Silent Spring* (Couch, Herity, and Munn 1983, p. 42; Wolf 1983, p. 22). Several environmental accidents had also occurred in the 1960s, and these accidents led to waning public confidence in scientific and technical opinion. Citizens' groups such as Friends of the Earth and Pollution Probe had formed and contributed to heightened public awareness. What came to be known as MEGA projects were being contemplated with greater frequency. These large-scale projects had the potential of serious environmental degradation (Couch, Herity, and Munn 1983, pp. 42–43). By 1970 the environmental movement had captured sufficient attention to inspire Earth Day, "an event which carried 'counterculture' hedonism of the Woodstock variety into the realm of social activism" (Wolf 1983, p. 22). In the United States the events of the 1960s and features of the social context combined in 1969 to produce the National Environmental Policy Act (NEPA), which requires environmental impact assessment for federal actions.

Events in themselves are rarely sufficient for the institutionalization of a new process such as EIA. Events must be interpreted in a social context, and there must be a social context for such an idea as EIA to be conceived and implemented. Wolf (1983, pp. 23–25) describes the features of this context in terms of pluralism, legalism, capitalism, pragmatism, and scientism. *Pluralism* in this context refers to the many different kinds of interest groups, societal actors, and governmental agencies that share concerns and responsibility for issues related to the environment. *Legalism* refers to the fact that in the United States the legal system is the ultimate arbiter of conflict. Legislation of environmental matters is, in direct proportion, accompanied by environmental litigation. *Capitalism* refers to the fact that the market is often relied upon to direct and inform environmental enforcement and regulation. *Pragmatism* refers to the political context in which environmental issues are debated and the essentially nonpolitical nature of concern with the environment. "There is no Ecology Party in the U.S. and environmental issues have never been seriously in dispute between the two major parties" (Wolf 1983, p. 25). The final term, *scientism,* refers to the attitude that environmental issues can be resolved by the application of science. According to Wolf, "the advancement of environmental science and of pollution control technology have made this position available; the inability to gain value consensus has made it acceptable" (1983, p. 25).

For the most part EIA has been project specific, that is, EIAs have been conducted for specific development projects. Attention is increasingly being given to the use of EIA in policy formulation at higher levels of policy. For example, a variety of projects might be affected by general policy, and an EIA might be conducted on the general policy. Higher levels of decision making are necessary in considering a series of projects that are potentially similar in environmental impacts and that would have cumulative environmental effects. It is more cost-effective to subsume specific projects under general policies that have considered environmental impacts in their formulation.

The EIA process usually results in a formal document called by various names, but usually it is called an "environmental impact statement" (EIS). The EIS is based upon, but is not identical to, the EIA. In the United States the content of the EIS for federal proposals is set by the Council on Environmental Quality (CEQ). The content is summarized in Table 1.

Operational procedures for EIA have been outlined by a number of authors. De Souza (1979, pp. 23–26) presents one of the more detailed summaries for the United States; Munn (1979, pp. 101–132) outlines these procedures for several countries; and Wathern (1988, p. 18) attempts to develop a generalized flowchart of the EIA system applicable to many countries.

TABLE 1
Content of an EIS for U.S. federal proposals as required by CEQ (1978)

Summary

Statement of purpose and need

Alternatives including proposed action

- Discussion of all options considered
- Discussion of 'no-action' option
- Identification of agency-preferred alternative
- Discussion of mitigation measures

Affected environment

- Baseline environmental description of area affected by each alternative

Environmental consequences

- Environmental impact of each alternative
- Unavoidable effects
- Relationship between local short-term use of environment and enhancement of long-term productivity
- Irreversible and irretrievable commitment of resources

List of preparers

SOURCE: Wathern 1988, p. 7.

Munn (1979, p. 125) outlines these procedures for the United States as follows:

1. The proponent agency develops a proposal for action. The agency must determine if the action will significantly affect the quality of the human environment. If so, it is responsible for preparation of the environmental impact statement.
2. If an environmental impact statement is required, the proponent may consult with the CEQ, the Environmental Protection Agency (EPA), and other federal agencies with special or unique expertise, state and local agencies in cases where projects might affect them, and the public in open hearings if needed to develop material for the draft environmental impact statement. The draft EIS is then filed with the EPA.
3. The draft must be reproduced and simultaneously circulated to the CEQ, the EPA, federal

expert agencies, state and local agencies, and the public for review and comment.

4. After this review process, a final environmental impact statement is filed by the proponent with the EPA and distributed to all of the above agencies and the public.
5. The final statement, which includes the comments of all of the reviewers, is submitted to the decision maker, who could be an agency head or secretary.
6. The decision maker reaches a decision. Where the proposed project requires legislation, the environmental impact statement will be submitted to Congress and the President for consideration in taking final action.
7. Initiation of the proposed action is begun only after all steps have been completed. In this connection, it is important to note that a citizen's suit may be brought to the courts.

"It would seem that EIA is a 'distinctively' American product" (Wolf 1983, p. 26), but EIA has now been adopted and adapted by many countries (Hill 1988, p. 197), regardless of their respective levels of industrialization, regardless of differences in economic systems, and in spite of diverse political systems. "Canada, Australia, the Netherlands and Japan, for example, adopted legislation in 1973, 1974, 1981 and 1984, respectively, while in July 1985 the European Community (EC), after nearly a decade of deliberation, finally adopted a directive making environmental assessments mandatory for certain categories of projects" (Wathern 1988, p. 3).

Third World countries have also adopted EIA processes or have developed projects that were accompanied by environmental impact assessments. In 1974, Colombia was the first Latin American country to use EIA. Thailand and the Philippines have formally adopted EIA procedures. Some African countries, including Rwanda, Botswana, and the Sudan, have sponsored projects that were accompanied by EIAs (Wathern 1988, p. 3).

The use of EIA is not restricted to capitalist or Third World countries. It is increasingly of interest in what were until recently the centrally planned economies of eastern Europe. Hungary and Poland are in the vanguard of these countries in promoting the use of EIA (Wathern 1988, p. 3). As of January 1988, the Soviet Union's State Committee established an EPA equivalent called *Goskompriroda,* the purpose of which is to protect nature. Within *Goskompriroda* there is interest in establishing a requirement for an environmental impact analysis for major projects within the Soviet Union (Cortese 1989, p. 1212). It is expected that the use of environmental impact assessments will spread even more widely as government agencies and people become more aware of effects of environmental degradation on humankind.

Countries that have adopted EIA have adapted it to fit their own individual circumstances. For example, following the establishment of NEPA in the United States, the Canadian Federal Department of the Environment was created in 1971. Canada began to explore the EIA process in 1972. These explorations led to the establishment of the Environmental Assessment and Review Process on December 20, 1973 (Couch, Herity, and Munn 1983, p. 43). The administrative, procedural, and jurisdictional structure of Canada's EIA process differs in major ways from that in the United States. For instance, in Canada the provinces have comparatively more responsibility and power over natural resources than have the states in the United States. This difference has led to more decentralized responsibility for EIA in Canada than in the United States, with the provinces having greater responsibility.

Further differences exist in the area of litigation. In the United States, the EIA process is perceived to be characterized by environmental litigation in the courts. In Canada a conscious attempt was made to minimize environmental litigation. In Canada greater emphasis is placed on an elaborate screening and public hearing process than on courts to resolve environmental disputes. In the United States litigation appears to be a first resort for environmental conflict resolution; in Canada litigation is a last resort.

International agencies are advocating EIA as part of their respective programs. These include the World Bank, Asian Development Bank, and United Nations agencies such as United Nations Environment Program (UNEP), the World Health Organization (WHO), and the United Nations Educational Scientific and Cultural Organization (UNESCO). Agencies promoting EIA also include regional economic groupings of nations such as the Economic Commission of Europe (ECE) and the Organization for Economic Cooperation and Development (OECD).

The interest of international agencies in EIA reflects a more profound recognition by these agencies that environmental issues and problems do not always respect national boundaries. Economic development is increasingly related to multinational economic relationships; environmental problems are related to economic development; therefore, environmental problems are multinaional. "Ecology and economy are becoming even more interwoven—locally, regionally, nationally, and globally—into a seamless net of causes and effects" (World Commission on Environment and Development 1987, p. 5).

Environmental problems are similar in many nations, and nations must share in environmental responsibility. As the Bruntland Commission puts it:

> *The onus lies with no one group of nations. Developing countries face the obvious life-threatening challenges of desertification, deforestation, and pollution, and endure most of the poverty associated with environmental degradation. The entire human family of nations would suffer from the disappearance of rain forests in the tropics, the loss of plant and animal species, and changes in rainfall patterns. Industrial nations face the life-threatening challenges of toxic chemicals, toxic wastes, and acidification. All nations may suffer from the releases by industrialized countries of carbon dioxide and of gases that react with the ozone layer, and from any future war fought with the nuclear arsenals controlled by those nations. All nations will have a role to play in changing trends, and in righting an international economic system that increases rather than decreases inequality, that increases rather than decreases numbers of poor and hungry.* (World Commission on Environment and Development 1987, p. 22)

A number of constraints to the adoption of EIA have been identified. These are most evident in developing countries and include: "a general lack of political will or awareness of the need; . . . insufficient public participation; lacking or inadequate legislative frameworks; lack of an institutional base; insufficient skilled manpower; lack of scientific data and information; and insufficient financial resources" (Kennedy 1988, p. 274).

It became evident very early in the evolution of EIA processes that the impacts of projects and policies ought to be assessed more extensively. It became necessary to extend the scope from the "biogeophysical" environment to include assessment of impacts on the social environment. Other questions needed to be addressed. For example, what are the social impacts of siting a surface coal mine and thermal power plant in an agricultural community? What are the impacts of such a development on farm operations, employment opportunities, internal migration, health, displacement of farmers from their land, and their relocation to other lands? What are the impacts on land values and on schools and other infrastructure needs? In short, there was a need for social impact assessment (SIA). SIA focuses on demographic, social, and economic aspects of development. Carley and Bustelo (1984, p. 5) suggest that SIAs focus on the following types of impacts:

1. Demographic impacts including labor force and population shift, employment multiplier effects, displacement and relocation problems, and changes in population make-up;
2. Socioeconomic impacts, especially changes in income and income multiplier effects, employment rates and patterns, and taxation and rates;
3. Institutional impacts including demands on local financial and administrative services, for example, in the fields of housing, water, sewers, schools, police, criminal justice, health and welfare, recreation, and others and especially changes in capital and operating budgets;
4. Psychological and community impacts, espe-

cially changes in intangible aspects of life, for example, social integration, community and friendship networks, sense of place, and community cohesion.

EIA and SIA evolved together, and initially they were not differentiated. SIA was a part of EIA. The two efforts are now more likely to be viewed as quite different activities. This difference is based on differences in subject matter and in the disciplines involved in that subject matter (Carley and Bustelo 1984, p. 4). EIA has come to concentrate on the biogeophysical environment and involves the natural sciences and associated methodologies, while SIA has come to supplement EIA by concentrating on the social environment and involving the social sciences and their associated methodologies. This bifurcation has led to problems of integrating information and conclusions in the planning and decision-making process. This bifurcation also highlights the multidisciplinary nature of the overall assessment process.

Because EIA and SIA evolved together, there are important similarities. For example, the steps in conducting these assessments are similar. First, a data base is established; then, the project is described, and sources of change to the environments are identified; last, forecasts of changes with and without the given project are made, as well as suggestions for mediating the negative changes (Carley and Bustelo 1984, p. 4).

The dimensions of impact in EIA and SIA are also similar (Carley and Bustelo 1984, pp. 5–6). First, impacts may be described as *direct* and *indirect.* Direct impacts are those that are immediate consequences of the proposed project or program. Indirect impacts are second-order effects of direct impacts. For example, a direct impact of a development in SIA might be inmigration of a work force; an indirect impact might be an increase in the school-age population. It is not so important to identify a hard and fast difference between direct and indirect impacts, but rather that a complex web of cause and effect can be set in motion by the intrusion of a project on a community.

Second, impacts may be described as *gross* and *net.* Gross impact is arrived at by comparing the present environment with a future environment that includes the proposed development. Net impact is arrived at by comparing the projected future environment including the proposed change with the projected future environment not including the proposed change. The study of gross impact may be appropriate for a small-scale development in a stable or static environment. The study of net impact is more appropriate in a changing environment with a large-scale intrusion over a longer time frame.

Third, impacts may be *concentrated* or *dispersed.* They may affect a particular social group or limited geographical area, or they may affect a generalized population or a widespread geographical area.

Fourth, impacts have a temporal dimension. Some impacts may be short in duration and others may continue indefinitely.

One of the continuing problems in integrating EIA and SIA is establishing relationships between biological, physical, and social impacts. For example in the operation of a surface coal mine, noise levels from drag lines and blasting are the same for both farmers and miners. It is a physical impact. But noise is socially defined. To the miner such noise is "good" noise; to the bucolic farmer such noise is socially defined as "bad" noise. Like noise, many physical phenomena have social definitions that cannot be discounted in assessing impact.

Interest in environmental impact assessment and its counterpart, social impact assessment, will expand as institutional interest in environmental preservation and conservation increases in response to public demand. It would be difficult to visualize society's return to a state of disregard for the natural and social environments of humankind. The involvement of applied social science in the provision of facts and analysis, and in consideration of policy options and possible consequences, is central to this development.

(SEE ALSO: *Human Ecology and the Environment; Technological Risks and Society*)

REFERENCES

Carley, M., and E. S. Bustelo 1984 *Social Impact Assessment and Monitoring: A Guide to the Literature. SIA Series no. VII.* Boulder, Colo.: Westview.

Carson, R. L. 1962 *Silent Spring.* Boston: Houghton Mifflin.

Clark, Brian D. 1983 "The Aims and Objectives of Environmental Impact Assessment." In PADC Environmental Impact Assessment and Planning Unit, eds., *Environmental Impact Assessment.* The Hague: Martinus Nijhoff.

Cortese, Anthony 1989 "Glasnost, Perestroika and the Environment." *Environmental Science and Technology* 23:1212–1213.

Couch, W. J., J. F. Herity, and R. E. Munn 1983 "Environmental Impact Assessment in Canada." In PADC Environmental Impact Assessment and Planning Unit, eds., *Environmental Impact Assessment.* The Hague: Martinus Nijhoff Publishers.

De Souza, Glenn R. 1979 *System Methods for Socioeconomic and Environmental Impact Analysis.* Toronto: Lexington Books, D. C. Heath.

Hill, Teresa 1988 "Our Common Future: Reshaping Canada's EIA Process." *Environmental Impact Assessment Review* 8:197–199.

Kennedy, W. V. 1988 "Environmental Impact Assessment and Bilateral Development Aid: An Overview." In Peter Wathern, ed., *Environmental Impact Assessment: Theory and Practice.* London: Unwin Hyman.

Munn, R. E. (ed.) 1979 *Environmental Impact Assessment: Principles and Procedures,* 2nd ed. SCOPE Reports. Chichester, England: John Wiley.

Wathern, P. 1988 "An Introductory Guide to EIA." In Peter Wathern, ed., *Environmental Impact Assessment: Theory and Practice.* London: Unwin Hyman.

Wolf, C. P. 1983 "The U.S. Model of Environmental Impact Assessment." In PADC Environmental Impact Assessment and Planning Unit, eds., *Environmental Impact Assessment.* The Hague: Martinus Nijhoff.

World Commission on Environment and Development 1987 *Our Common Future.* Oxford: Oxford University Press.

JOSEPH E. DISANTO

EPISTEMOLOGY The aim of epistemological inquiry is the justification of knowledge through the analysis of its origin, nature, and validity. In this sense, widely accepted in English-speaking cultures, epistemology is the general theory of knowledge. In continental Europe, however, its scope is restricted to scientific knowledge, and terms like *gnoseology* (*gnoséologie* in French, *gnoseologia* in Italian and Spanish) and *theory of knowledge* (*Erkenntnistheorie* in German) are usually preferred for the more general inquiry.

Epistemological themes and problems include the question of the possibility of valid knowledge, the analysis of the nature of such validity, the debate on the respective roles of reason and the senses in originating genuine knowledge, the investigation of the subject–object relationship, the analysis of different types of knowledge, the inquiry into the nature of truth, the assessment of the limits of meaningful knowledge, and the justification of methodological options and perspectives.

Epistemological awareness among sociologists is very recent, and epistemological themes and problems are either subsumed under the methodological quest or dealt with very unsystematically. Therefore, since methodological questions are usually resolved by technical procedures, epistemological validity is often reduced to technical validity. However, rational justification of technical validity requires the successful assessment of methodological validity, and this can be warranted only by a positive answer to the epistemological question it presupposes: "Is it possible to acquire knowledge of human social reality by means of empirical data?" The corresponding methodological question is, instead, "Given that it is possible to acquire knowledge of human social reality by means of empirical data, how is it possible?" Although their answers are related, the two questions are obviously of different natures. Those sociologists who do not perceive or who deny the difference between the two questions maintain that a positive answer to the methodological question also resolves the epistemological problem. The rationale is that showing how it is possible demonstrates that it is possible. But this rationale rests on the assumption that the "how" is indeed adequate to acquire valid knowledge of human social reality. This assumption is generally upheld by those sociologists who maintain that their discipline is a natural science that uses the scientific method, while those sociologists who do not share this view would reject it.

The acceptance or rejection of the scientific method as the legitimate general procedure for collecting data and making inferences in the realm of human social life represents of course an epistemological choice, and it opens a cleavage between scholars of different sociological traditions. In fact, sociology as a discipline originated as the positivistic science of human society and aligned itself against the metaphysical and philosophical speculations about social life. From Comte to Quetelet, from Spencer to Mill, the idea of a positivistic social science implied the straight application of the scientific method used in physics to the analysis of human society and the extensive use of quantification (Lazarsfeld 1961). The first serious challenge to this epistemological view of sociology came from Wilhelm Dilthey, the major representative of the nineteenth-century German Historical School. Against Mill's proposal of introducing the methods of physics into the "moral sciences" ([1834] 1947, Part 6), Dilthey argued that human sciences—or "spiritual sciences" (*Geisteswissenschaften*), since this term was used in translating Mill's "moral sciences" into German in 1863—were of a radically different type from the natural sciences and that they could not share the same method ([1883] 1966). The human sciences were sociohistorical, and their objects were states of mind, or spiritual experiences, which could be apprehended only by means of an "empathic understanding" (*Verstehen*). This understanding is not mediated by sense perceptions and produces a direct and intuitive knowledge-by-acquaintance. Without this particular understanding, external observation would miss its aims because, as human beings, we do not understand others through external experiences but by means of psychic and subjective life experiences (*Erlebnisse*). We could explain the external courses of actions, but if we do not understand them they will remain meaningless. In this way, a major, long-lasting distinction was posited, that is that the aim of the natural sciences is to explain (*erklären*) by means of external sense data, while the scope of the human sciences is to understand (*verstehen*) through an intrapsychic experience. Later, Wilhelm Windelband and Heinrich Rickert, both members of the German Historical School, insisted on stressing the difference between the natural and the social sciences. Windelband ([1894] 1914) argued that only the former could aim at establishing general laws, while the latter, being historical, had to interpret and understand the individual character of the historical event. Therefore, natural sciences were "nomothetic" (from the Greek term for laws, *nomos*), and the sociohistorical sciences were "idiographic" (from *idios*, peculiar). Moreover, this individuality preserved and investigated by the social scientist had to be isolated by an interpretive grasp of the values that gave significance to the sociohistorical event. Rickert further developed the notion of the necessity of referring to values as a foundation for sociohistorical knowledge ([1896] 1913): It was only through this reference to values that sociohistorical events could be understood and generalized beyond the particular case.

The German Historical School had a profound influence on Max Weber, and, although he was critical of its idealistic orientation, he accepted the school's main epistemological tenets and argued for their importance for the sociohistorical sciences. In his methodological essays ([1904–17] 1949) Weber undertakes an inquiry into the nature and validity of methods used in the social sciences and presents a general epistemological framework for his "interpretive sociology" (*verstehende Soziologie*). He argued in particular for the necessity, in investigating social actions, (1) of resorting to an "interpretive understanding"; (2) of preserving the cultural and social uniqueness of the historical event, using the ideal-type methodology; and (3) while avoiding "value judgements," of establishing "value relevances" (*Wertbeziehungen*) of the subject matter as criteria for its cultural importance and scientific pertinence. These three points constitute Weber's elaboration of the epistemological choices of the German Historical School, to which he remained faithful. In his last years, however, he accepted sociology as a generalized and nomothetic science and argued for the complementarity of interpretive understanding and causal explanation; that is, a researcher's personal understanding should be balanced by empirical and statistically established regularities of scientific explanation (Weber [1913] 1968).

The epistemological legacy of the German Historical School has strongly influenced contemporary interpretive sociology (through Weber and Simmel) and the phenomenological tradition in sociology (through Schutz). Its impact has been widespread, however, and it is manifest in the antipositivistic methodological choices of many sociologists as different as Sorokin (1959) and C. Wright Mills (1959). Some sociologists, like the Frankfurt School (Adorno 1976; Habermas 1976), advocate the necessity of the dialectical method in sociology. Their epistemological choices are derived partly from Weber and partly from Marx, particularly for what concerns the use of dialectics in social analysis. Dialectical epistemology implies (1) the holistic approach, that is, the necessity of considering the totality in order to understand the parts; (2) the denial of the separation of sociological theory and history; and (3) a demystifying attitude in undertaking critical analysis of society.

Altogether, interpretive, phenomenological, and dialectical sociologies answer negatively the epistemological question about the possibility of acquiring knowledge of human social reality by means of empirical data alone. They reject the methodological unity of the natural and social sciences and do not accept the straight application of scientific method to sociological analysis. Most of their studies are speculative and nonempirically oriented. Those few who do undertake empirical research resort to methodologies that result from the researcher's epistemological choices. These methodological perspectives tend to reject technical terminologies and quantification, to privilege common-sense conceptualization and language, and to take the point of view of the social actor instead of the researcher and the scientific community. Qualitative methodologies of this kind are also favored by other sociologies—such as symbolic interactionism, ethnomethodology, and sociologies of daily life of different varieties—that have not been directly influenced by the idealistic and antipositivistic attitudes of the German Historical School. Although seldom explicitly stated, their epistemological foundations, which tacitly direct their choice of methods and tools of social research, are consonant with those of interpretive, phenomenological, and dialectical sociologies.

The large majority of sociologists, however, think that knowledge of human affairs can be attained by empirical means and accept scientific method as the appropriate and valid method of the social sciences. Traditionally, this epistemological choice was based on positivistic foundations. Yet in this century the term *positivist* has been abused, and very few epistemologists would care to be known as such (Popper 1976). Classical positivism was radically sensist: Knowledge originated only with experiences through the senses. Concepts that did not have a direct tie with empirical experiences were considered meaningless. Observability and verifiability were generally understood in terms of sense experiences. At the beginning of the century, a neopositivistic movement with emphasis on logical analysis of language discarded the sensist views and renewed empiricism on new bases. Logical neopositivism still maintained that only empirically verifiable knowledge was meaningful, that science was a cumulative process based on induction, that the method of physics was the method of all sciences including social sciences, and that the discovery of natural and general laws was the fundamental aim of any science. But it discarded direct observation as the only means of hypothesis testing, and it considered verification as "testability in principle." It also accepted theoretical constructs without direct empirical referents as meaningful. In order, however, to avoid the connotations of classical positivism, many members preferred the term *logical empiricism* to *logical neopositivism.* Moreover, since the 1960s the movement, under criticism from many sources, has dissolved in a plurality of approaches. Currently, scientific epistemology is quite diversified, and rationales for using scientific method in the social sciences come from a wide range of perspectives. Among sociologists, the most influential contributions are those of Nagel (1961), who delves into the methodological problems of the social sciences in the tradition of logical empiricism, of Popper (1972), who has developed a "critical rationalism," which raises new issues with respect to traditional scientific epistemolgies, and of Campbell (1988), who advocates realism and objectivity in all sciences in the framework of a natural selection paradigm.

The characteristic aspects of scientific methods have been subjected to rigorous analysis and widespread criticism, and several traditional features have been reconsidered. Since all efforts to justify induction have failed, the logic of scientific method is more and more considered to be hypothetic-deductive. The notion of scientific experiences is not confined anymore to direct observation nor to controlled experimental conditions. Moreover, all scientific experience seems theory-laden. In particular, verification always depends on observational theories that are often derived from the same substantial theory from which hypotheses under test have been deducted, making their test logically inconclusive. The notion of verification itself is being dropped in favor of that of falsification, in the sense that a hypothesis can be definitely considered false if it fails an adequate test, while if it is congruent with data this does not necessarily mean it is true. Yet three types of falsification have been identified—the naive, the dogmatic, and the methodological—and only the last one seems epistemologically sound (Lakatos 1970). Currently, epistemological analyses of scientific method agree only on considering it as a method of critical discussion of alternative views, but there is a wide range of disagreement about the way the method has to be understood and applied. For example, Feyerabend (1970; 1975) speaks of the incommensurability of scientific theories and of scientific methodology as "an ornament."

The "methodological anarchism" of Feyerabend represents an extreme and paradoxical view. In fact, the scientific method remains the only rational procedure for deciding and agreeing upon which theory is more adequate to describe and explain a state of affairs in the natural as well as in the social worlds. Of course, rationality depends upon common premises and procedures. The advantage of accepting them is of great import because it is through them that intersubjectivity is achieved. Scientific objectivity resides neither in the object of knowledge, as classical positivism maintained, nor in the subject, as idealists tend to believe, but in the intersubjectivity that results when researchers adopt the same procedures and accept the premises on which they are based. It is the reproducibility of methods, techniques, and tools of scientific research that secures the replicability of results. And their reproducibility is due largely to their being public procedures—easily scrutinized and reapplied. The results of research in the natural sciences may be more objective than those in the social sciences, but this is due to the standardization and publicity of procedures in the natural sciences. There is no ground for supposing that natural scientists possess a special objective attitude, while social scientists possess a value-oriented attitude. The problem is that many research procedures in the social sciences are not reproducible because they often reflect a private state of mind communicated through linguistic expressions full of connotative meanings often not shared by all in the research community. The advantages of quantitative over qualitative techniques of data collection and analysis are, more than precision and rigor, standardization and reproducibility.

It is difficult, however, to justify quantification for all types of sociological data. Many sociologists believe that not all aspects of social phemomena could be subject to the rules of quantification. And some of them think that quantitative and qualitative methods and techniques are complementary. Yet such an integrated and pluralistic methodology needs to be justified by an explicit epistemology, and at present such an epistemology is lacking. There are, nonetheless, some indications that the old cleavages between naturalistic and interpretive sociologies may slowly fade away. Behavioral sociologists no longer consider empathic understanding (*Verstehen*) with contempt, confining it solely to the context of discovery, as was the case a few decades ago (Abel 1953). They are progressing toward an empirical epistemology that takes into account subjective experiences, intentions, feelings, and other states of mind by means of a private knowledge based on an intuitive kind of understanding (Baldwin and Baldwin 1978). On the other side, only philosophers like Winch (1958) would insist on excluding from sociological research any type of causal–analytical explanation. In fact, many qualitative sociologists do not consider the current massive flow of quantitative research useless or meaningless. Quantitative sociologists, for their part, often find qualitative research helpful and enlightening. Therefore, the time seems ripe for a new epistemological foundation for an emerging pluralistic sociological methodology.

(SEE ALSO: *Metatheory; Scientific Explanations; Validity*)

REFERENCES

Abel, Theodore (1948) 1953 "The Operation Called *Verstehen.*" In H. Feigl and M. Brodbeck, eds., *Readings in the Philosophy of Science.* New York: Appleton-Century-Crofts.

Adorno, Theodor W. (1957) 1976 "Sociology and Empirical Research." In G. Adey and D. Frisby, eds. and trans., *The Positivist Dispute in German Sociology.* London: Heinemann.

Baldwin, John B., and Janice I. Baldwin 1978 "Behaviorism on *Verstehen* and *Erklären.*" *American Sociological Review* 43:335–347.

Campbell, Donald T. (1974) 1988 "Evolutionary Epistemology." In E. Samuel Overman, ed., *Methodology and Epistemology for Social Science.* Chicago: University of Chicago Press.

Dilthey, Wilhelm (1883) 1966 *Einleitung in die Geisteswissenschaften.* Vol. 1 of *Gesammelte Schriften.* Stuttgart: Teubner.

Feyerabend, Paul K. 1970 "Consolations for the Specialist." In I. Lakatos and A. Musgrave, eds., *Criticism and Growth of Knowledge.* Cambridge: Cambridge University Press.

——— 1975 *Against Method: Outline of an Anarchist Theory of Knowledge.* London: NBL.

Habermas, Jürgen. (1963) 1976 "The Analytical Theory of Science and Dialectics." In G. Adey and D. Frisby, eds., and trans., *The Positivist Dispute in German Sociology.* London: Heinemann.

Lakatos, Imre 1970 "Falsification and Methodology of Scientific Research Programmes." In I. Lakatos and A. Musgrave, eds., *Criticism and Growth of Knowledge.* Cambridge: Cambridge University Press.

Lazarsfeld, Paul F. 1961 "Notes on the History of Quantification in Sociology." In H. Woolf, ed., *Quantification.* New York: Bobbs-Merrill.

Mill, John S. (1834) 1947 *A System of Logic.* New York: Longmans.

Mills, C. Wright 1959 *The Sociological Imagination.* New York: Oxford University Press.

Nagel, Ernest 1961 *The Structure of Science: Problems in the Logic of Scientific Explanation.* New York: Harcourt, Brace and World.

Popper, Karl R. 1972 *Objective Knowledge: An Evolutionary Approach.* Oxford: Clarendon Press.

——— (1970) 1976 "Reason or Revolution?" In G. Adey and D. Frisby, eds. and trans., *The Positivist Dispute in German Sociology.* London: Heinemann.

Rickert, Heinrich (1896) 1913 *Die Grenzen der naturwissenschaftlichen Begriffsbildung.* Tübingen: Mohr.

Sorokin, Pitirim A. 1959 *Fads and Foibles in Modern Sociology and Related Sciences.* New York: Henry Regnery.

Weber, Max (1904–17) 1949 *The Methodology of the Social Sciences.* E. A. Shils and H. A. Finch, trans. and eds., New York: Free Press.

——— (1913) 1968 "Uber einege Kategorien der verstehenden Soziologie." In *Gesammelte Aufsätze zur Wissenschaftslehre.* Tübingen: Mohr.

Winch, Peter 1958 *The Idea of a Social Science.* London: Routledge and Kegan.

Windelband, Wilhelm (1894) 1914 "Geschichte und Naturwissenschaft." In Wilhelm Windelband, *Präludien.* Tübingen: Mohr.

PAULO AMMASSARI

EQUALITY OF OPPORTUNITY

Equality of opportunity refers to the fairness of processes through which individuals with different backgrounds or from different social groups reach particular outcomes, such as educational or occupational goals. Sociologists have developed several alternative approaches to defining and assessing equality of opportunity in each outcome domain, including residual differences after relevant qualifications are taken into account, process differences in the variables linking individual attributes to outcomes, and structural differences in the barriers encountered in preparing for, learning about, or obtaining particular educational or occupational achievements. Each approach has advantages and disadvantages for particular scientific, policy, and practical purposes.

RESIDUAL DIFFERENCES IN EQUALITY OF OPPORTUNITY

Equality of opportunity is usually judged with reference to major social groupings, such as race, sex, or socioeconomic status. The issue is whether individuals from major population subgroups have the same chances to achieve educational or occupational success, assuming that they possess the same distributions of personal attributes to qualify for success. Because any initial average outcome gaps between subgroups can be due to unequal possession of relevant qualifications, as well as to unfair access to the opportunities that link qualifications to achievements, it is necessary to take into account differences in personal qualifications before deciding that unequal opportunities exist.

Researchers have frequently tested for inequalities of opportunity by estimating the residual gap between the educational or occupational success of selected race, sex, or social class groups after individual differences in relevant credentials or competencies and educational or labor market locations have been statistically controlled for. The usual methodology is to estimate a prediction equation or to use other methods of standardization for selected individual resource variables that permit a researcher to compare the actual group difference in an educational or occupational outcome with the residual gap that would be expected if one group's productivity resources were replaced by the average resources of the other group (Farley and Allen 1987, chap. 11). For example, the actual average difference in annual earnings of African-American and white workers in the North would be compared against the residual earnings gap when one assumes that African-American workers' resources (such as education and labor market experience) deliver the same rate of return in earnings as that experienced by white workers. Some problems are inherent in this approach, including the risk of overestimating the residual gap if some important qualification variables are omitted or poorly measured, and the chance of underestimating the residual gap when some groups are deprived of relevant qualifications due to earlier unequal opportunities not reflected in the estimation methodology. Nevertheless, several important residual race, sex, or social class gaps have been identified for various important educational and occupational outcomes. However, these gaps are often associated with some subgroups but not others, and some gaps have been changing more rapidly than others in recent years.

Numerous national and regional studies have been conducted since the 1960s to estimate the inequality of job opportunities, including research that examines residual subgroup differences in unemployment rates, occupational distributions, and dollar returns from holding a job. Studies of race, sex, and social class residual gaps in earnings and income of employed workers have been particularly noteworthy, with more than twenty-five major national studies having been published since 1965 (Farley and Allen 1987).

The research on earnings gaps that estimates the "cost of being black" due to inequality of job opportunities has contrasted the experiences of male and female workers and reported the continuing but declining significance of race. After taking into account differences in educational attainment, age or years of potential labor market experience, hours of work, and regional location, large residual gaps in earnings are found between male African-American and white workers, with African-Americans earning 10 to 20 percent less than comparable whites in various regions and at various educational levels. Women continue to earn much less than men of the same race with similar educational credentials, but the residual race gap for women is no longer the same as reported for men. In 1960, African-American women earned less than white women at all educational levels except college graduate, but this gap had been eliminated or reversed by 1980, when college-educated African-American women actually reported greater earnings, largely because of greater hours of employment. The residual race gap in earnings for employed workers also appeared to grow somewhat smaller for men between 1960 and the 1980s, but still remains between 10 and 15 percent at all educational levels.

At the same time, evidence is mounting that race gaps in rates of unemployment are significant and have been growing worse since the 1960s for African-American men in most age and education categories; they are especially severe for unmarried young African-American men in the North who have limited educational attainments (Jaynes and Williams 1989, ch. 6; Farley and Allen 1987, chaps. 8–11).

Inequalities of educational opportunity have been examined by estimating residual race, sex, or social class gaps in outcomes net of initial resources, especially for college enrollment and completion rates. Among the earliest evidence of a social class gap in college attendance net of academic ability is data from the 1960s showing that even after controlling on standardized test performance, students from lower categories of socioeconomic status are much less likely to enter college within five years of high school graduation. The talent loss due to unequal social class background was estimated to be 50 percent of top-ability students who do not enter college from the lowest socioeconomic quartile, compared with a loss of only 5 percent of high-ability students from the highest socioeconomic quartile (U.S. Department of Health, Education and Welfare 1969). The importance of social class factors for educational equity was reinforced by extensive research on Wisconsin high school students that included measures of race as well as student achievement on standardized tests. Social class disparities in educational attainment net of academic ability were again in evidence, as it was reported that top-ability students were only half as likely to attend college or to graduate from college if they came from the lowest quarter, rather than the highest quarter, in socioeconomic status (Sewell and Hauser 1980). These studies also estimated that observed African-American–white differences in years of educational attainment can largely be accounted for by social class differences between the racial groups.

Other race differences in educational outcomes are not so well explained by socioeconomic status alone, including differences in students' achievement test performance and choice of major fields of study, whereas race contrasts in labor market discrimination, residential segregation, and the quality of schooling available to African-Americans are often weakly related to social class differences but strongly related to student motivation and performance in school (Jaynes and Williams 1989).

PROCESS DIFFERENCES IN OPPORTUNITIES

Another approach to assessing equality of opportunity is to compare the attainment processes that link personal resources or investments to educational or occupational achievements for different social groups. Opportunities can be defined as unequal when the major avenues to advancement used by one group are not as effective for another. Researchers have frequently reported attainment process differences in the degree to which various population subgroups have been able to capitalize on advantages of family background or have experienced a high rate of return on investments in building relevant competencies or credentials. Some of this work has been criticized for possible shortcomings of methodology and interpretation.

Studies of social group differences in an attainment process are important because they help to estimate the long-run prospects for closing existing achievement gaps (Featherman and Hauser 1978, chap. 6). The prospects are positive if each subgroup has access to an attainment process that will translate improvements of personal and family resources into achievement outcomes, especially when programs and policies are available for investments in upgrading resources of groups that at present are weak. But if some groups are lagging in relevant skills and credentials, and are exposed only to attainment processes that provide poor returns in comparison with other groups, then the prospects are dim for closing existing gaps.

Studies of general social mobility processes have identified the special problems of African-American males in translating any advantages from the family of origin into attainments in their own adult lives. For the white male population in this country, clear intergenerational processes have been evidenced in which sons can build upon a middle- or upper-class family background, as shown by the strong relationship between father's and son's occupational status for whites over many recent decades. In contrast, through the 1960s, African-American males have not been as able to capitalize on any family advantages in building their occupational careers, as shown by the weak relationship for intergenerational mobility and the frequency with which substantial proportions of African-American males from nonmanual or white-collar households are downwardly mobile and unable to benefit from their family advantages. There is some indication that since the 1970s race differences for males in the opportunities to benefit from any inheritance of family social class advantages have closed (Featherman and Hauser 1978; Farley and Allen 1987).

Race differences in the processes of school effects on achievement hawe been reported in two national studies by the sociologist James S. Coleman and his research coworkers. In a 1966 national study of public schools, differences in school resources and learning environments were found to have larger average effects on African-American students' achievement than on white students' achievement (Coleman et al. 1966). The result was interpreted as a differential sensitivity of disadvantaged students to school improvements, because these students from poor families relied more on good schools for their development of academic skills. A similar race difference in educational processes was found in the 1980s with national data from public and private high schools (Coleman and Hoffer 1987). African-Americans, Latinos, and students from low socioeconomic backgrounds were found to do better in Catholic schools than in public high schools, in terms of both higher test scores and lower dropout rates. It was argued that these students especially benefited from the greater academic demands that can be enforced by the sense of community established by Catholic schools, which compensates for family disadvantages of many of these students. Again, minority and disadvantaged students were found to be more responsive to changes in school environments that have effects on high school students' achievement and completion rates. Other researchers have questioned the recent results on the grounds that key student/family self-selection variables were not controlled in the analyses of public–Catholic school differences and that the sizes of the race interaction effects were not impressive by conventional statistical standards (Alexander and Pallas 1985; McPartland and McDill 1982).

Research has indicated that race inequalities are currently much less evident in educational attainment processes than in occupational attainment processes. Analyses using appropriate statistical tests of the processes that yield important educational achievements—such as additional years of schooling and scholastic outcomes including grades and test scores—have found great similarities between African-Americans and whites (Gottfredson 1981; Wolfle 1985; Pallas 1987). Thus, not only have African-American–white differences in the frequency of high school graduation and college education been diminishing, the processes that link social background and school input variations to educational achievements have become very similar for African-Americans and whites. At the same time, race gaps in school test scores have been closing more slowly, and serious disparities persist in the level of financing and concentration of single-race and disadvantaged student bodies in schools attended by racial minorities, even though education attainment processes would translate improvements of such inputs into attainments for African-Americans (Jaynes and Williams 1989).

However, major race and sex differences continue in the occupational domain regarding both the processes of attainment and the gaps in achievement. Labor market disparities by race and sex are much more apparent than differences in educational opportunities, but the disparities are exhibited in complex patterns or processes according to individuals' social class position, labor market location, career stage, and other factors (Jaynes and Williams 1989; Featherman and Hauser 1978; Farley and Allen 1987; Wilson 1987). The chances are equally good for African-Americans and whites of each sex who are highly educated to gain entry to good jobs, but advancement opportunities to higher positions at later career stages are more likely to be missed by African-Americans. At the same time, African-American male workers with less advanced credentials are much more likely to have periods of unemployment or reduced hours, and to be paid less when employed, than white males with equivalent years of schooling. The greatest race discrepancies are observed for poorly educated young African-American males, who are much more likely than comparable whites to be unemployed, to have dropped out of the labor force, or to report no annual earnings. William J. Wilson has developed a theory of the "declining significance of race" that considers the growing social class gaps within the African-American population in occupational success, as well as the special difficulties faced by poorly educated African-American males in urban racial ghettos, whom he views as "the truly disadvantaged" (Wilson 1987).

STRUCTURAL BARRIERS TO EDUCATIONAL OPPORTUNITIES

While careful studies of residual differences and attainment process differences can document the existence of unequal opportunities, other research is required on specific interactions and practices in schools or labor markets to understand the actual barriers that unfairly inhibit individuals because of their sex, race, or social class position. For education, research on differential access to specific components of schooling, studies of tracking and grouping policies in elementary and secondary schools, and examinations of financial aid practices in higher education have identified some specific structural barriers in educational opportunities.

A landmark study was conducted in response to a congressional request under the 1964 Civil Rights Act and published in 1966 with the title *Equality of Educational Opportunity* (EEO). Also known as the "Coleman Report," after the sociologist James S. Coleman, who directed the research, EEO was both influential and controversial for the way it examined educational opportunities and for its major findings (Coleman et al. 1966). Based on a large national survey of students and schools at both elementary and secondary levels, EEO collected the most comprehensive data available at that time on equity issues in education. It was not satisfied to compare only the average school input resources experienced by different race and ethnic groups—such as textbooks, libraries and laboratories, per-pupil expenditures, teacher qualifications, or class size. EEO also considered race and ethnic differences on student outcomes as measured by standardized tests in major subjects, and asked how different school components contributed to student learning, in order to weigh inequalities of school inputs by their importance for student outcomes. The simultaneous examination of school inputs, student outcomes, and their relationships to one another had not been attempted before in assessing equity issues, and the published results have been a continuing source of reanalysis and reinterpretation.

EEO did find large differences in test scores between white and most racial and ethnic minority groups that existed from the time students began school and were not reduced, on the average, as students moved from grade 1 to grade 12. These differences in student outcomes could not be explained by variations in the school input factors measured by the EEO surveys, because within each region no great disparities of school inputs appeared for different racial and ethnic groups, and these factors did not relate strongly to student outcomes in any case after family background and social class factors were statistically controlled. In fact, when school factors were combined into three clusters for analysis—(a) instructional materials and resources, (b) teacher and staff characteristics, and (c) student body composition —the most important component in accounting for variations in student test scores net of family background was the attributes of fellow students. Thus, the large observed group differences in student outcomes were not found to be accounted for by existing variations in conventional school and teacher components, although attending a school with fellow students who were college bound did seem to make a positive contribution to the learning environment.

Subsequent investigations have confirmed the general picture drawn by EEO of an educational system that does little to reduce the large racial and ethnic differences in academic test scores with which students begin elementary grades (Mosteller and Moynihan 1972; Jencks et al. 1972). But specific limitations of EEO data prevented researchers from identifying factors within schools and classrooms that have potential for improving educational opportunities, and other conditions that have likely consequences on equality of opportunities have changed since the 1960s.

EEO data did not measure within-school differences in educational resources and learning environments, and consequently was unable to analyze major barriers to equal opportunities from specific internal school practices, such as tracking and ability grouping. Other research has shown that when students are tracked into separate programs or separate courses according to their earlier test scores or grades, those in the lower-level groups are likely to encounter serious barriers to their educational growth and progress. Lower tracks and lower-level courses have been shown to offer weaker educational resources, such as fewer expert teachers and poorer educational climates with lower academic expectations, that can lead to lower average student achievement test scores and decreased probabilities of completing high school and continuing education in college (Oakes 1985; Gamoran 1986; Hallinan 1988). Tracking is now seen as a major barrier to equal educational opportunities because tracking and ability grouping are very common practices in American schools, and minorities and socioeconomically disadvantaged students are much more likely to be assigned to the lower-level programs and courses within their schools (Bowles and Gintis 1976; Oakes 1985; Braddock 1990).

Moreover, the educational resources available at the school level are thought to be more unequal for minorities and disadvantaged students at the present time than they were found to be in the 1966 EEO assessments (Smith and O'Day 1991). Since the 1960s, demographic trends have created greater concentrations of poverty in large urban schools, and changes in funding support for public education in central city districts have reduced those districts' relative ability to purchase adequate classroom supplies and materials, and to recruit and retain highly qualified teachers. Consequently, school-level barriers to equal educational opportunities have worsened since the 1960s, because the changing urban demographics and negative fiscal trends have dramatically altered the student body composition and the quality of the teaching staff that the EEO study found to be the most important factors of a good school.

Barriers have been identified in college educational opportunities, which also may have gotten worse, especially for African-American males, in recent years. Minorities have long been underrepresented as students at four-year colleges, in scientific major fields, and in obtaining advanced degrees (ISEP 1976; Thomas 1986; Trent and Braddock 1987). Some of these gaps had been closing through the 1970s, but since that time, uniform progress is no longer evident and some actual downturns in minority enrollments and attainments have been recorded (Jaynes and Williams 1989). African-American and Latino students often encounter special problems in pursuing college programs because of insufficient social and academic support on campus or of inadequate prior educational experiences (Green 1989). Recent reversals in minority enrollments have been explained by increasing tensions related to race and ethnicity on some college campuses and to changes from grants to loans in many financial assistance programs which poor students are less likely to receive or use (Blackwell 1990).

STRUCTURAL BARRIERS TO OCCUPATIONAL OPPORTUNITIES

To help account for residual sex or race gaps in job success and in the career attainment process, research has identified specific structural barriers to sex equality and to racial equality in occupational opportunities.

Studies of the large average earnings differences between men and women workers show that very large gaps remain after statistically controlling on individual differences in input variables such as education and experience, but these gaps are substantially reduced by adding measures of each person's occupation or occupational group. This result indicates that sex gaps in earnings have much of their source in the extreme job segregation by sex in the American labor market—many occupations are primarily filled by women or primarily filled by men—and the wage levels are much lower for "female" occupations (Treiman and Hartmann 1981). Since fully two-thirds of men and women would have to change jobs to achieve similar representation of each sex across occupations, full enforcement of antidiscrimination laws against unequal pay for men and women in the same occupation can achieve only modest improvements in wage differentials by sex. Other suggested approaches to reducing sex segregation of jobs and associated wage gaps—such as enriching the socialization experiences toward a wider range of career exposures for children and youth of both sexes, or incorporating policies of "comparable worth" that establish wage rates by job features, irrespective of sex or race of incumbents (Hartmann 1985; Marini 1989)—have not yet made large inroads.

To specify how occupational opportunities continue to be unequal for racial or ethnic minorities, research has identified structural barriers at each stage of the occupational career process. Barriers can appear at the job candidate stage, when employers are recruiting the pool of candidates for job openings; at the job entry stage, when an individual is actually selected to fill a vacancy; and at the job promotion stage, when transfers are made within a firm to fill spots at higher levels (Braddock and McPartland 1987; Feagin and Feagin 1978; Marini 1989).

At the job candidate stage, qualified minorities of either sex may fail to learn about many desirable job openings because they are excluded from useful social networks that provide others with information about and contacts for particular employment opportunities. Employers find job candidates more frequently from walk-ins and friends of current employees (the result of informal social networks) than any other recruitment means for lower- and middle-level jobs. The social contacts used by many minorities are racially segregated networks that on the average are not as well tied to good job information as the social networks available to whites. This barrier to equal opportunities at the job candidate stage is partially kept in place by the continued racial segregation of the schools and neighborhoods that create many social networks, and by the underrepresentation of minorities in the upper levels of firms, where informal information for friends and relatives about job openings is often best acquired (Rossi, Berk, and Eidson 1974; Crain 1970).

At the job entry stage, otherwise qualified minorities are often not selected because of barriers of statistical discrimination and information bias. Employers who do not wish to invest much to obtain extensive information about job applicants will often use a group identifier, such as sex or race, in hiring decisions when they believe that traits on which subgroups may differ statistically predict job performance. For example, such "statistical discrimination" can occur when an employer selects a white over a minority applicant for a job requiring good academic skills, based on a belief in average racial group differences on academic test scores rather than on actual individual candidates' differences in academic skills shown on tests administered or obtained by the employer during the screening process (Thurow 1975; Bielby and Baron 1986; Braddock et al. 1986).

Even when qualification data from individuals are relied upon in hiring decisions, other barriers to equal opportunities occur due to "information bias" of data on minority candidates. References and recommendations from school or employment officials for African-American applicants may be viewed as less credible by white employers who are less familiar with an African-American school, a member of the African-American clergy, or an African-American firm, or who may be more wary of information provided by minority sponsors due to stigmas or stereotypes attached to these sources. Similarly, minority job applicants who grow up in communities that have high youth unemployment rates will be less able to satisfy prospective employers' interests in previous employment experiences and references (Braddock and McPartland 1987).

At the job promotion stage, minorities may face unfair barriers due to internal recruitment methods or because they are poorly positioned within internal labor markets. However, findings from a national study indicate the potential benefits to minorities of seeking internal promotions: The average pay differential between African-American and white workers is less for jobs filled from inside a firm than for jobs filled from outside for individuals of the same sex and education level, suggesting that unfair selection is reduced when employers process information on applicants' actual job performance within their firm. On the other hand, the same study showed that unless an internal vacancy is widely advertised within a firm, whites are more likely to be sought out for available promotions (Braddock and McPartland 1987). Moreover, research has shown that minorities are less likely to have entered a firm on a career ladder that ordinarily leads to promotion opportunities, so they may never be eligible to compete for advancement through an internal labor market (Rosenfield 1980).

POLICIES AND PRACTICES

Governments and courts have established policies and practices in recent decades that are intended to eliminate race and sex discrimination and to ensure equality of opportunity. These range from the 1954 Supreme Court decision against segregated schools to the civil rights legislation of the 1960s and the executive orders to establish affirmative action guidelines in employment (Jaynes and Williams 1989; Burstein 1985).

Although it is difficult to distinguish the effects of one governmental action from those of another in improving the life chances of women and minorities, clear advances have been made that can be attributed to the combined impacts of various public policies for equal rights. For example, from 1970 to 1990 the race gaps in academic test scores of schoolchildren decreased between 25 and 50 percent for different age groups (Smith and O'Day 1991). Reductions in the race gaps in terms of years of school completed have been dramatic, especially among female students. Greater equity is also evident in some labor market behaviors, including the distribution of occupations by race within sex groups. On the other hand, racial improvements are not so evident in employment rates and income levels of adult males, and extensive racial segregation of housing and schooling remains a dominant feature of American life (Jaynes and Williams 1989). Still, progress in equal opportunities for sex and race groups clearly has been coincident with the major thrusts of legislation and court decisions to foster civil rights.

Controversy continues to accompany further efforts to sustain current policies and to institute new practices for equal opportunities. The differences are most evident on whether outcome-based policies are required to overcome systemic barriers—for instance, affirmative action programs that use guidelines and timetables—or whether efforts should concentrate only on intentional discrimination or on specific aspects of the processes that inhibit equal rights (Levinger 1987).

(SEE ALSO: *Affirmative Action; Discrimination; Education and Mobility; Ethnicity; Equity Theory; Social Mobility; Race*)

REFERENCES

Alexander, Karl A., and Aaron M. Pallas 1985 "School Sector and Cognitive Performance." *Sociology of Education* 58:115–127.

Bean, Frank D., and Marta Tienda 1987 *The Hispanic*

Population of the United States. New York: Russell Sage Foundation.

Bielby, William T., and James N. Baron 1986 "Men and Women at Work: Sex Segregation and Statistical Discrimination." *American Journal of Sociology* 91:759–799.

Blackwell, James E. 1990 "Current Issues Affecting Blacks and Hispanics in the Educational Pipeline." In Gail E. Thomas, ed., *U.S. Race Relations in the 1980s and 1990s.* New York: Hemisphere.

Blau, Peter M., and Otis D. Duncan 1967 *The American Occupational Structure.* New York: Wiley.

Bowles, Samuel, and Herbert Gintis 1976 *Schooling in Capitalist America.* New York: Basic Books.

Braddock, Jomills H., II 1990 *Tracking: Implications for Student Race-Ethnic Subgroups.* Report No. 2. Center for Research on Effective Schooling for Disadvantaged Students, The Johns Hopkins University, Baltimore, Md.

———, and James M. McPartland 1987 "How Minorities Continue to Be Excluded from Equal Employment Opportunities: Research on Labor Market and Institutional Barriers." *Journal of Social Issues* 43 (1):5–39.

———, et al. 1986 "Applicant Race and Job Placement Decisions: A National Survey Experiment." *International Journal of Sociology and Social Policy* 6:3–24.

Burstein, Paul 1985 *Discrimination, Jobs and Politics: The Struggle for Equal Employment Opportunity in the United States Since the New Deal.* Chicago: University of Chicago Press.

Coleman, James S. 1968 "The Concept of Equality of Educational Opportunity." *Harvard Educational Review* 38:7–22.

———, and Thomas Hoffer 1987 *Public and Private High Schools.* New York: Basic Books.

———et al. 1966 *Equality of Educational Opportunity.* Washington, D.C.: U.S. Government Printing Office.

Crain, Robert L. 1970 "School Integration and Occupational Achievement of Negroes." *American Journal of Sociology* 75:593–606.

Duncan, Otis D. 1969 "Inheritance of Poverty or Inheritance of Race?" In Daniel P. Moynihan, ed., *Understanding Poverty.* New York: Basic Books.

Farley, Reynolds, and Walter R. Allen 1987 *The Color Line and the Quality of Life in America.* New York: Russell Sage Foundation.

Feagin, J. R., and C. B. Feagin 1978 *Discrimination American Style: Institutional Racism and Sexism.* Englewood Cliffs, N.J.: Prentice-Hall.

Featherman, David L., and Robert M. Hauser 1978 *Opportunity and Change.* New York: Academic Press.

Gamoran, Adam 1986 "Instructional and Institutional Effects of Ability Grouping." *Sociology of Education* 59:185–198.

Gottfredson, Denise C. 1981 "Black–White Differences in the Educational Attainment Process: What Have We Learned?" *American Sociological Review* 46:542–557.

Granovetter, Mark S. 1974 *Getting a Job: A Study of Contacts and Careers.* Cambridge, Mass.: Harvard University Press.

Green, Madeleine F. 1989 *Minorities on Campus: A Handbook for Enhancing Diversity.* Washington, D.C.: American Council on Education.

Hallinan, Maureen T. 1988 "Equality of Educational Opportunity." *Annual Review of Sociology* 14:249–268.

Hartmann, Heidi I. (ed.) 1985 *Comparable Worth: New Directions for Research.* Washington, D.C.: National Academy Press.

Institute for the Study of Educational Policy. 1976 *Equal Educational Opportunity for Blacks in U.S. Higher Education: An Assessment.* Washington, D.C.: Howard University Press.

Jaynes, Gerald David, and Robin M. Williams, Jr. (eds.) 1989 *A Common Destiny: Blacks and American Society.* Washington, D.C.: National Academy Press.

Jencks, Christopher, et al. 1972 *Inequality: A Reassessment of the Effect of Family and Schooling in America.* New York: Basic Books.

———1979 *Who Gets Ahead? The Determinants of Economic Success in America.* New York: Basic Books.

Levinger, George (ed.) 1987 "Black Employment Opportunities: Macro and Micro Perspectives." *Journal of Social Issues* 43:1–156.

Marini, Margaret Mooney 1989 "Sex Differences in Earnings in the United States." *Annual Review of Sociology* 15:343–380.

McPartland, James M., and Edward L. McDill 1982 "Control and Differentiation in the Structure of American Education." *Sociology of Education* 55:65–76.

Mosteller, Frederick, and Daniel P. Moynihan (eds.) 1972 *On Equality of Educational Opportunity.* New York: Random House.

Oakes, Jeannie 1985 *Keeping Track.* New Haven, Conn.: Yale University Press.

Pallas, Aaron M. 1987 "Black-White Differences in Adolescent Educational Outcomes." Paper prepared for Committee on the Status of Black Americans. Washington, D.C.: National Research Council.

Reskin, Barbara F. (ed.) 1984 *Sex Segregation in the Workplace.* Washington, D.C.: National Academy Press.

Rosenbaum, James E., Takehiko Kariya, Rick Settersten, and Tony Marier 1990 "Market and Network Theories of the Transition from High School to Work: Their Application to Industrialized Societies." *Annual Review of Sociology* 16:263–299.

Rosenfield, Rachel A. 1980 "Race and Sex Differences in Career Dynamics." *American Sociological Review* 45:583–609.

Rossi, Peter H., Richard A. Berk, and Betty K. Eidson 1974 *The Roots of Urban Discontent: Public Policy, Municipal Institutions and the Ghetto.* New York: Wiley.

Sewell, William H., and Robert M. Hauser 1980 "The Wisconsin Longitudinal Study of Social and Psychological Factors in Aspirations and Achievements." In Alan C. Kerckhoff, ed., *Research in Sociology of Education and Socialization,* Vol. I. Greenwich, Conn.: JAI Press.

Smith, Marshall S., and Jennifer O'Day 1991 "Educational Equality: 1966 and Now." In Deborah Verstegen, ed., *Spheres of Justice in American Schools.* New York: Harper Business.

Thomas, Gail E. 1986 *The Access and Success of Blacks and Hispanics in U.S. Graduate and Professional Education.* Working Paper, Office of Scientific and Engineering Personnel, National Research Council. Washington, D.C.: National Academy Press.

Thurow, Lester 1975 *Generating Inequality.* New York: Basic Books.

Treiman, Donald J., and Heidi I. Hartmann (eds.) 1981 *Women, Work and Wages: Equal Pay for Jobs of Equal Value.* Washington, D.C.: National Academy Press.

Treiman, Donald J., Heidi I. Hartmann, and Patricia A. Roos, 1984 "Assessing Pay Discrimination Using National Data." In Helen Remick, ed., *Comparable Worth and Wage Discrimination.* Philadelphia: Temple University Press.

Trent, William T., and Jomills Henry Braddock II 1987 "Trends in Black Enrollment and Degree Attainment." In John B. Williams, ed., *Title VI Regulation of Higher Education: Problems and Progress.* New York: Teachers College Press.

U.S. Department of Health, Education and Welfare 1969 *Toward a Social Report.* Washington, D.C.: U.S. Government Printing Office.

Wilson, William Julius 1980 *The Declining Significance of Race: Blacks and Changing American Institutions,* 2nd ed. Chicago: University of Chicago Press.

———1987 *The Truly Disadvantaged: The Inner City, the Underclass and Public Policy.* Chicago: University of Chicago Press.

Wolfle, Lee M. 1985 "Postsecondary Educational Attainment Among Whites and Blacks." *American Educational Research Journal* 22:501–525.

JOMILLS HENRY BRADDOCK II
JAMES M. MCPARTLAND

EQUILIBRIUM THEORY *See* Social Dynamics.

EQUITY THEORY The concept of fairness or justice is basic to social life. It is a "central moral standard" in human affairs and is concerned with the necessity of "assuring that each person receives what she or he is due" (Cohen 1986; p. 1). Debate surrounds the question of what each is due and the principles and procedures to be used to make this determination. One of the fundamental problems in applying the moral standard of justice is that there is often little consensus about the principles to be used to evaluate the fairness or justice of matters arising in social life. It is clear that a range of competing principles—equality, equality of opportunity, equity, rights or entitlement, and need—are all prevalent in most realms of social existence. As will be clear throughout this presentation, the principle of equity is one of many standards used to evaluate fairness or justice in social life. And, while the essay focuses primarily on "justice," the heading "equity theory" is used because of the way in which these issues are often phrased within sociology. These various principles compete for recognition and application in human affairs. Indeed, as will be evident in the following review of research on this topic, there is less than complete consensus among philosophers, social and behavioral scientists, and others regarding the principles of justice that should be employed in the understanding of human behavior.

The question of justice, or fairness, comes up in virtually all aspects of social life. It arises both in interpersonal interaction and exchange, or what will here be referred to as microsocial settings for interaction, and in the relationship of the individual to the larger social collective, or what we will call macrosocial settings or situations. Thus, people's perceptions of justice, that is, their sentiments about the fairness of social exchange, social relationships, the treatment of themselves and others by the social group or by society as a whole, represent a ubiquitous aspect of social life. It is important to recognize that questions of justice and its evaluation are posed with respect to both microsocial and macrosocial matters.

Justice issues pervade many aspects of social relationships, particularly when inequality of outcomes exists. Spheres where justice issues are especially important concern (a) aspects of social life where issues of dependence/independence arise from interdependence, and from matters of the extent of power and influence held by actors and other parties to the relationship; (b) material outcomes of existence, where the well-being of parties to the relationship is at issue; and (c) the realm of status, respect, and the sense of worth given and received in social interaction. These spheres concern the political, economic, and social realms of existence, respectively.

Although issues of justice frequently arise in the presence of inequality, as noted above, it is often the case that equality of outcomes also raises questions of justice. In his *Nichomachean Ethics,* Aristotle (1953) put it in these terms: "For if the persons are not equal, they will not have equal shares; it is when equals possess or are allotted unequal shares, or persons not equal, equal shares that quarrels and complaints arise." Thus, equality of outcomes may in certain circumstances be perceived as unjust, even as inequality of results may be seen as perfectly just. The distinction between equality and justice is, thus, extremely important in understanding these phenomena. And it is important to realize that a person's beliefs about the sources of inequality importantly affect evaluations of justice (see Kluegel and Smith 1981, 1986; Robinson and Bell 1978).

As noted above, justice sentiments occur with respect to what each person receives relative to what he or she is expected to receive, wherein expectations may be governed by the application of some principle of justice, and expectations are formed not only by recipients but by others as well, including both others who are involved in the relationship and other observers. Justice sentiments, thus, derive from comparisons of what is received with what one believes should be received, that is, a comparison of the real with the ideal. The evaluation of the difference between these two entities or quantities engages human faculties of perception, cognition, and emotion. And, if we know little else about justice evaluation, we know it is subjective. As noted by Walster and her colleagues (Walster et al. 1973), "justice is in the eye of the beholder." Of course, these facts complicate even further the application of justice principles, because, even setting aside the problem of which principle of justice to invoke in a given situation, actors may not agree on what is real, that is, what exists. But, to paraphrase a theme in interactionist sociology (from W. I. Thomas), *what is real in the perceptions of humans is real in its consequences.* Thus, if individuals perceive the social mechanisms for allocating scarce social rewards as just, then the resulting distribution of outcomes will also be perceived as just.

Because questions of justice in society are so pervasive, most social science disciplines lay some claim to understanding the ways in which human society deals with them. Thus, the literature on justice is massive. Extensive scholarship on justice exists in philosophy (see Buchanan and Mathieu 1986), anthropology (see Nader and Sursock 1986), economics (Boulding 1981; Solo and Anderson 1981; Worland 1986), psychology (see Deutsch 1975, 1986; Folger 1984; Furby 1986; Greenberg and Cohen 1982; Mikula 1980; Messick and Cook 1983), political science (Barry 1981; DiQuattro 1986; Hochschild 1981; Rae 1981), and sociology (Alwin 1987; Markovsky 1985; Rytina 1986; Jasso 1980). Justice is a prominent theme in many traditions within sociology, but the issues of justice have been studied primarily by those working within the tradition of social psychology; thus the present discussion reflects that emphasis.

PHILOSOPHICAL ROOTS

The historical roots of Western conceptions of justice lie in classical philosophy, the Judeo-Christian religious traditions, and the theoretical underpinnings of economic and political arrangements. Aristotle's *Nichomachean Ethics* (Book V) provides the classical formulation of the problem of justice. His formulation sought to clarify principles of distributive and retributive justice and to formulate the rules for the regulation of social exchange. The Aristotelian logic of justice in market relationships involving social exchange stressed the proportionality of expected rewards given considerations of merit, and that just contracts and purchases comply with the going rate of exchange (Cohen and Greenberg 1982, p. 4). Worland suggests that there is a crucial dilemma revealed in Aristotle's work:

> *It becomes clear that the reference to* two *different kinds of justice and* two *different rules or proportions poses a crucial dilemma. If commodities sell at their fair price—or at a price that reflects the "fair" rate of exchange—then how can society guarantee that exchange at such prices will also provide society's participants with an income proportionate to their relative "merit" or standing in the community? How is the rule requiring distribution of common goods in proportion to "merit" to be reconciled with the rule requiring "reciprocal proportionate equality" in the contractual, private exchange of commodities?* (1986, p. 48)

Eighteenth- and nineteenth-century philosophers and social theorists addressed this dilemma, resolving it in a number of competing ways. Karl Marx's labor theory of value (Buchanan and Mathieu 1986, p. 12) suggested that the need for principles of justice was evidence that social institutions should be restructured, abolishing the market system and private goods. Although the notion of communal ownership of the means of production can be traced in history at least to Plato, this has not been viewed as the most adequate solution to Aristotle's dilemma. Indeed, the recent unpopularity of communism as a political and economic system, as implemented in the twentieth-century, perhaps provides some evidence of this. The existence of a market for social exchange seems to represent an important component in understanding the fairness of social exchange (Lane 1986, p. 384). This point is recognized within recent traditions of social psychological thinking (see Thibaut and Kelley 1959).

Adam Smith, the philosophical father of modern capitalism, on the other hand, posed the Aristotelian dilemma somewhat differently. He observed that the modern economic system had become specialized in the sense that the production, distribution, and exchange of social goods had evolved to a stage where economic activity was highly differentiated as an institution (Worland 1986, p. 50). Smith believed it was an empirical question of scientific merit to determine the "natural" rules by which markets developed and the moral issues of justice were resolved. What is just, then, was clearly a question of what individual actors considered just, not only at the subjective level but also at the macrosocial level. The operation of the principles of supply and demand to set a going rate was seen to provide the answer to the moral question of justice. And, thus, Smith gave an early example of a principle later articulated in the social psychological literature—the principle that "what is" determines "what ought to be" (see Homans 1974, p. 250; Heider 1958, p. 235). This, however, falls short of resolving the Aristotelian dilemma.

As Worland (1986, p. 57) suggests, Marx's theory of surplus value, in which he identified the real sources of profit and nonwage income as exploitation of working people by the capitalist class, did much to clarify what can now be seen as a condemnation of capitalist economies in Aristotelian terms. The twentieth-century response to Marx's critique of capitalism in economics is known as marginal utility theory, which handles issues of injustice in terms of market imperfections and the existence of monopolistic forms of capitalism in contrast with real free enterprise. The neoclassical response is, according to Worland (1986, p. 81) able only to isolate and clarify "the rules that a market society needs in order to comply with the Aristotelian moral imperative." It does not answer the deeper question of moral psychology, concerning "whether such a society would be able to achieve the social consensus necessary for the practical implementation of the rules."

The perspective offered by neoclassical economics on moral issues of justice is often seen as more of a justification for social inequalities than as a "natural law" of justice. It reminds the observer of Cohen and Greenberg's (1982) suggestion that each social and economic system evolves its own unique concept of justice. For neoclassical economics the idea that there may be merit tied to nonproductive activities or considerations is a foreign one. By contrast, contemporary political philosophers have attempted to address the broader question of merit. Rawls (1971), on the other hand, evaluates the Aristotelian imperative from a nonmaterial, nonutilitarian, rational Kantian perspective. Rawls's principles of justice are as follows (quoted from Buchanan and Mathieu 1986, p. 27):

1. The principle of greatest equal liberty: Each person is to have an equal right to the most extensive system of equal basic liberties compatible with a similar system of liberty for all.
2. The principle of equality of fair opportunity: Offices and positions are to be open to all under conditions of equality of fair opportunity—persons with similar abilities and skills are to have equal access to offices and positions.
3. The difference principle: Social and economic institutions are to be arranged so as to benefit maximally the worst off.

According to Rawls, these principles are ordered in terms of their primacy, that is, if the principles conflict, the first listed takes precedence. These principles, obviously, refer not only to social contracts and exchanges but also to the basic structure of society, including economic, political, legal, and social institutions. In most societies that includes charters and constitutions, the means of production, competitive markets, the family, the legal system of laws and procedures, and so forth. The basic structure of society is said to specify how and by what principles society is to distribute primary goods, such things as basic liberties, powers, authority, opportunities, income, and wealth. The principle of greatest equal liberty specifies Rawls's theory of how basic liberties are distributed. The principle of equality of fair opportunities regulates the distribution of life chances or prospects in the domains of power and authority. And the difference principle governs the distribution of income and wealth (see Buchanan and Mathieu 1986, p. 28).

It is beyond the scope of this essay to review Rawls's theory in full, or to summarize the critical comment that followed, except to note that his theory is utopian in the sense that it describes an ideal society run on the basis of just principles. He does not spell out how one moves from states of injustice (such as those found in present society) to the ideal situation. Still, no single book has generated more discussion and critique than Rawls's *A Theory of Justice.* A prominent contemporary critique is Nozick's (1974) entitlement theory, which departs radically from Rawls and which stresses a libertarian view that a person is entitled to the ownership of a social good if it was acquired through just principles. And Walzer (1983) argues that it is not possible to write a general theory of justice in the abstract without any attempt to assay the "substantive ways of life" of different cultures. To Walzer *justice* is a relative term, and no abstract theory of the ideal society can really work because *justice* does not exist in an abstract theoretical sense, but only in terms of social meanings ordained by a particular way of life.

SCARCITY, GOODS, AND SATISFACTION

The social goods, or primary goods, that are of concern in questions of distributive justice include a wide array of things, including basic freedoms, political enfranchisement, power, authority, status, income and wealth, education and employment opportunities, housing, health care, and the like. In most discussions it is assumed that such things are scarce, although in some cases this is clearly not so—for example, there should be an unlimited supply of basic freedoms in a well-ordered society. But even if social goods are not scarce, they have inherent satisfaction value—they are things that bring both extrinsic and intrinsic satisfaction to the individual.

The relation between justice issues and human satisfaction can be summarized in the following propositions (Alwin 1989):

1. Generally, when people get what they want, they are more satisfied. However, people differ in their preferences and therefore want different things. Differential preferences, or values, may need to be taken into account in assessing satisfaction.
2. What persons want is determined, in part, by individual and social definitions of what is deserved. The concept of what is deserved may be defined in terms of any possible principle of justice—need, contributions, equality, entitlement, equality of opportunity.
3. What is deserved, from individual and/or social perspectives, is a function of (a) existential expectations, (b) justice principles or standards, and (c) referential comparisons, that is, what other persons or categories of persons receive. In this case existential expectations are simply *what is* and *what has been.* Justice principles represent abstract utopian principles or absolutes that govern the distribution of social goods—need, equality, opportunity, and so on. Comparison with others is basic to social life. Similar social categories often are a basis for invidious comparisons.
4. Fairness or justice evaluation is characterized by a comparison of actual rewards against fair or just rewards. Actual rewards are simply the quantity of social goods an individual receives. These may be thought of as resources and/or rewards. Just or fair rewards represent those levels of rewards an individual expects, needs, deserves, or otherwise believes are just. Justice is subjective, that is, the outcome of justice evaluation is relevant to the individual but nonetheless has implications for collective outcomes.
5. Satisfaction with social goods, such as material rewards, or any component of overall satisfaction, is dependent upon the comparison of actual rewards with just rewards.

EQUITY THEORY

Responding to what they saw as the need for a general theory of social behavior, Walster and her colleagues (see Walster, Walster, and Berscheid 1978; Walster, Berscheid, and Walster 1973; Berkowitz and Walster 1976) formulated equity theory to integrate the insights from a variety of social psychological theories, including reinforcement theory, cognitive consistency theory, psychoanalytic theory, and exchange theory (Walster et al. 1978, p. 2). Building upon the work of Homans, Lerner, and others, equity theory, as given by Walster et al. (1978, p. 6), contains four basic propositions:

Proposition I: Individuals will try to maximize their outcomes.

Proposition IIA: Groups can maximize collective reward by evolving accepted systems for equitably apportioning resources among members. Thus, groups will evolve such systems of equity, and will attempt to induce members to accept and adhere to these systems.

Proposition IIB: Groups will generally reward members who treat others equitably, and generally punish members who treat others inequitably.

Proposition III: When individuals find themselves participating in inequitable relationships, they will become distressed. The more inequitable the relationship, the more distress individuals will feel.

Proposition IV: Individuals who discover they are in an inequitable relationship will attempt to eliminate their distress by restoring equity. The greater the inequity that exists, the more distress they will feel and the harder they will try to restore equity.

While it is clear that self-interest is a strong motive for behavior in many types of situations, and it may be a safe assumption to make in competitive situations, there are clearly other motivations for behavior. This can be seen as one of the unnecessarily restrictive assumptions of equity theory—the prevalence of altruism, cooperation, and other forms of pro-social behavior strongly question this basic assumption. There is plenty of evidence that competitive behavior in mixed-motive games like the Prisoner's Dilemma can evolve into stable cooperation under certain conditions, such as the anticipation of future interaction (Axelrod 1984). And in relationships where intimacy and identification are present, the importance of self-interest as a motive for behavior is considerably lessened (Austin 1977). As noted earlier, Rawls's (1971) theory of justice, for example, suggests that one principle which underlies the moral judgments made in human society is the principle that social and economic arrangements are made to maximally benefit those who are less advantaged with respect to desirable social goods. Thus, one can see that equity theory as stated by Walster et al. (1978) probably overstates the need to specify a type of utilitarian-based logic for defining justice.

To define justice, equity theory distinguishes inputs and outcomes, both of which are expressed in the same units, say dollars, or points, or some conceivable unit in which both can be expressed. Then, assuming that inputs are positive (for simplicity), the equity principle states that under conditions of justice there is an equality of relative gains. For two actors (persons, groups, nations, etc.) engaged in social exchange, equity is said to exist when the ratio of profits (outcomes minus inputs) to inputs is the same for both actors involved in the exchange.

The experimental literature in social psychology indicates that when persons perceive "inequitable" inequalities, they frequently experience cognitive tensions and a drive to reduce those tensions either by changing their judgments about relative investments and contributions or by changing their values regarding the importance of reward-relevant criteria. Research also shows that when experimental subjects in task-oriented settings have well-defined expectations linked to objective indicators of contributions and investments, they find reward inequalities more acceptable (Brickman 1977; Cook 1975).

FROM EQUITY TO DISTRIBUTIVE JUSTICE

In the early 1970s Deutsch (1975) began to question the proportionality principle implicit in so much of the theorizing on equity theory. He, among others, began arguing that equity is only one of several principles used to evaluate the justice of outcomes in social life. Principles of justice are used as a basis for "judging individual persons and in judging the basic structure of societies" (Cohen 1986; p. 1). There are at least five competing principles—equality, equality of opportunity, equity, rights or entitlement, and need—that are applied in most realms of social existence. While these principles may more or less exhaust the possible criteria for evaluating justice, it is perhaps true that the equity principle has been seen as most relevant in many cases. For example, in the work of George Homans (1974) the proportionality principle is given a prominent place in the discussion of distributive justice, and it is clearly present in many discussions of equity theory (see Adams 1965; Berkowitz and Walster 1976).

However, with time, theoretical work and empirical research have begun to cast the problem of equity into a broader framework of distributive justice, wherein justice may be evaluated by one of many different principles. Contemporary interest in the study of distributive justice can be traced to the early articulation of relative deprivation theory, particularly the work of Stouffer, Merton, and Homans (see Williams 1975). Within the past several decades, issues of distributive justice have received attention primarily in the work of social psychologists studying the psychological and behavioral consequences of patterns of social reward distributions in small group settings (see reviews by Adams 1965; Berkowitz and Walster 1976; Crosby 1976; Cohen and Greenberg 1982), and more recently by sociologists studying principles of justice evaluation (Jasso and Rossi 1977; Jasso 1978, 1980; Alves and Rossi 1978). Much current research on distributive justice traces its theoretical roots to Homans's (1974, p. 249) discussion of the "rule of distributive justice," which hypothesizes that unless persons' perceived inputs (contributions, investments, resources) are equal, some inequality of outcomes or rewards will be expected, and that, generally, rewards are expected to be allocated in proportion to inputs (see also Heider 1958, p. 288).

There are also some parallels between issues of distributive justice and issues of status congruence or status inconsistency, since models dealing with either topic share a cognitive balance framework. In a general sense, the consistency expectations that emerge because of the correlation of statuses are similar to the expectation states of theories of distributive justice. The latter are unique, however, in their theoretical distinctions among statuses, particularly between inputs and rewards.

Justice Evaluation and Social Comparison. Current theories of distributive justice implicitly or explicitly specify the reference standards that persons use in the evaluation of the fairness of social rewards. The following discussion summarizes the author's theory of justice evaluation and social comparison (Alwin 1987). Most theories assume that in evaluating the fairness of a particular reward allocation, persons compare themselves with others (see Berger et al. 1972; Pettigrew 1967; Williams 1975; Gartrell 1982). For example, Homans's "rule of distributive justice" is often given as follows (e.g., Walster et al. 1976):

$$\text{Justice} = \left[\frac{\text{P's Reward}}{\text{P's Inputs}}\right] - \left[\frac{\text{O's Reward}}{\text{O's Inputs}}\right] = 0 \qquad (1)$$

Here P and O are two persons in a local exchange, where P is assumed to evaluate his/her comparison ratio of rewards to inputs against that of another individual, O. If P perceives O's comparison ratio to equal his/her own, then he/she will perceive a state of fairness or justice. If not, some degree of injustice is presumed to exist, in which case P will perceive that he/she is either underrewarded or overrewarded relative to O.

The term *inputs* is used in equation 1 to represent the general reward-relevant characteristics of individuals that are involved in making assessments of the fairness of rewards. These may be contributions, investments, resources, or global status characteristics (see Cook 1975; Cook and Yamagishi 1983). This formulation ignores the concept of costs and their effects on rewards and inputs. In other words, inputs and rewards are thought of as positive quantities. For a somewhat different formulation involving negative inputs and rewards, see Walster et al. (1976).

Several investigators (e.g., Blau 1971; Berger et al. 1972; Jasso 1978) have pointed out that in objectively viewing this identity (equation 1), it is impossible to determine which parties are over- or underrewarded when perfect justice does not prevail. From this point of view, formulations of justice evaluation as local comparisons cannot cope with the possibility that, from the perspective of a more general referential standard, both P and O may be unjustly rewarded, even though their comparison ratios may be equal. This view in no way intends to deny that persons in fact make local comparisons of such ratios. The point is simply that when persons make local comparisons, referential standards existing outside the local situation are typically invoked to evaluate fairness.

Berger et al. (1972, p. 122) criticize the above formulation, arguing that distributive justice issues arise only in the presence of a "stable frame of reference," and that justice evaluations are inherently made on the basis of reference to "generalized individuals" rather than to specific others. Using this observation as a basis for reconceptualizing the classical exchange-based conception of justice, Berger et al. (1972) formulate a "theory of status value" that formalizes the process by which persons evaluate the fairness of rewards. They formulate the process in terms of referential standards—frames of reference that contain existing information regarding the characteristics and rewards of generalized others. According to this theory, through social exchange persons develop normative expectations about the reward levels typically associated with general classes of individuals, and when persons perceive their reward-relevant characteristics to be similar to a particular general class of individuals, they come to expect their reward levels also to be similar. The referential structure, as formalized by Berger et al., consists of information about the relation between levels of characteristics possessed by general classes of persons and the associated levels of social reward. As a consequence of these beliefs about "what is," normative expectations are formed about reward levels that persons can legitimately claim (1972, p. 139). This conclusion is consistent with Homans's (1974, p. 250) and Heider's (1958, p. 235) observation that the "ought" is determined in the long run by the "is," and with recent sociological theorizing which argues that social inequalities are often themselves the major basis for their own legitimization (Sennett and Cobb 1972; Della Fave 1980; Stolte 1983).

The Berger et al. (1972) status-value formulation is limited in its consideration of the process by which a person selects a referential comparison standard. Referential comparisons may be based upon relatively small groups of persons, such as one's coworkers, or quite large classes of persons, such as occupational categories. This may appear to be a flaw in the status-value theory, since such a wide range of comparison points is available. However, this may actually be viewed as an asset rather than a flaw, in that it allows flexibility in specifying the role of various types of referential standards in justice evaluation processes.

Referential Comparisons. While near consensus exists in the social psychological literature that persons use referential comparisons to evaluate how satisfactory their income is, Gartrell (1982) observes that little is known about the origin and visibility of comparative frames of reference. In his own research, for example, he finds that information on wage rates is often invisible, and such information for persons in other jobs frequently originates from concrete, personal referents rather than from knowledge of rates for broad social categories. Moreover, the awareness of wage comparisons frequently appears to relate to somewhat idiosyncratic factors, such as informal social contacts (see also Walster et al. 1976). This is consistent with other studies of relative deprivation and status comparison, wherein persons are found to rely heavily on information from their own social circles (see Runciman 1966; Rainwater 1974; Coleman and Rainwater 1978). Thus, it may be more difficult to specify the origin or basis of a person's referential comparison with any objective accuracy. Some experimental research (Major and Forcey 1985) suggests that subjects are most interested in same-sex and same-job wage comparisons.

Moreover, the individual's subjective judgment regarding the "fairness" of a given reward outcome may be the more relevant concept. Jasso's (1978, 1980) theory of distributive justice introduces the term "just reward" to refer to the reward level individuals expect on the basis of referential comparisons conceived in general terms. She formulates the status-value model of justice evaluation as follows (1978, p. 1402):

$$\text{Justice} = \text{P's Actual Reward} - \text{P's Just Reward} = 0 \qquad (2)$$

That is, for a person to determine the fairness of his/her reward, the actual level of reward is simply compared against the reward expected on the basis of existential (or other) criteria. This formulation is more general than that given by Berger et al. (1972), because it permits a wide range of reference group comparisons and because both existential and nonexistential criteria may be used in the calculus for the "just reward" (see Jasso 1978, 1980). As Blau (1971, pp. 58–59) points out in his criticism of Homans (1974), "not all existing practices reflect justice; some are unjust by prevailing moral standards, and the fact that they are expected to continue to exist does not make them just." There are obviously both existential and nonexistential standards of justice.

This "comparison difference" formulation of distributive justice makes the nature of over- or underreward clear, unlike the formulation phrased by most equity theorists (e.g., Walster et al. 1976). Moreover, in contrast with the classical formulation given in equation 1, both quantities in the equation are expressed in the same units, that is, units of reward. Further, it satisfies the notion that the individual's subjective judgment regarding the expected or "deserved" reward may be the most relevant concept. And finally, the distinction between kinds and degrees of injustice can be measured on a scale that has zero as its origin, where "perfect justice" occurs. Southwood (1978, p. 1157) has proposed a model very similar to Jasso's model involving what he calls "subtractive interaction," intended to estimate the effects of departures of actual reward from expected (or just) reward. This model simply involves estimating the effects of the quantity $x_1 - x_2$, where x_1 represents actual reward and x_2 the expected reward.

Reformulating the Justice Evaluation Model. Using Jasso's concept of the just reward, it is possible to reformulate the classical exchange-based conception of justice evaluation in a way that permits the measurement of the direction and magnitude of departures from justice. First, it is necessary to recast the rule of distributive justice given in the expression in equation 1 as an equivalence of the ratio of P's and O's rewards to the ratio of their inputs (see Patchen 1961; Adams 1965; Homans 1974, 1976), as follows:

$$\text{Justice} = \left[\frac{\text{P's Reward}}{\text{O's Reward}}\right] - \left[\frac{\text{P's Inputs}}{\text{O's Inputs}}\right] = 0 \qquad (3)$$

Here the comparison ratios are made up differently. They now involve terms in common units, reward units on the one hand and units of input on the other. The present formulation of the classical model has two nice properties: it is intuitively simpler to have the numerator and denominator of such ratios in the same units, *and* this formulation fits with the psychological mechanisms often assumed in justice evaluation—that persons expect their inputs (contributions, investments, resources, or general status characteristics) to be in a constant proportion to the rewards they associate with some standard of comparison.

If the Berger et al. (1972) theory of status value is correct in stating that a person (*P*) uses referential structures specifying levels of reward-relevant characteristics that are similar, indeed equivalent, to his/her own (see also Pettigrew 1967; Williams 1975), then it is possible to equate P's and O's inputs on the right-hand side of equation 3, setting the second term on the right of the equation to unity, as follows:

$$\text{Justice} = \left(\frac{\text{P's Reward}}{\text{O's Reward}}\right) - 1 = 0 \qquad (4)$$

And if then we generalize the concept of "O's Reward" to be the same as Jasso's "just reward," the justice evaluation process devolves to a comparison of P's actual and expected (or just) rewards:

$$\text{Justice} = \left(\frac{\text{P's Actual Reward}}{\text{P's Expected Reward}}\right) - 1 = 0 \qquad (5)$$

An examination of this expression indicates that the classical formulation restated in this way permits the distinction between kinds and degrees of injustice measured on a scale that has zero as its origin, where perfect justice prevails. These units may conveniently be thought of as justice units, because when the comparison exceeds zero, overreward occurs, and when it is less than zero, *P* is said to be underrewarded.

Jasso argues, however, that the simple ratio of actual to just rewards does not capture the justice evaluation phenomenon precisely. It does not account for the fact that positive departures from justice (overreward) are not equivalent to negative departures (underreward), and "this appears to violate the human experience that deficiency is felt to be more unjust than a comparable excess" (Jasso 1978, 1403). In other words, the injustice created by an actual reward above the just reward k is not equivalent to the injustice created by an underreward of the same magnitude. Jasso (1978, p. 1415) resolves the problem by proposing the natural logarithm of the comparison ratio [Actual Reward/Just Reward]. Such a formulation assumes that an overreward of k times is equal in magnitude of injustice to an underreward of $1/k$ times.

Note the convergence of the reformulation of the classical model given here with that proposed by Jasso (1978), which she derived empirically from the analysis of vignette data. The natural logarithm of equation 5, derived from classical exchange and status-value theories, equals the formulation for justice evaluation proposed by Jasso. I have thus derived theoretically a principle of justice evaluation that is equivalent to Jasso's (1978, 1980) empirically derived "Universal Law of Justice Evaluation." This formulation can be used as a basis for defining departures from justice. Alwin (1987) empirically examine Jasso's hypothesis that the effects of underreward are more potent than the effects of overreward, using measures of satisfaction with material well-being as the theoretically relevant criterion variable. While support was found for the importance of the sense of injustice for the prediction of material satisfaction, the hypothesis that the extent of satisfaction depends upon measured departures from justice was not supported (Alwin 1987).

DISTRIBUTIVE VS. PROCEDURAL JUSTICE

Distributive justice issues arise in the consideration of two sets of questions: Who gets what, and how? Who should get what, and how? Some have suggested that the distinction between the concepts *procedural justice* and *distributive justice* is critical to a complete understanding of the ways in which humans evaluate justice (see Cohen 1981; Thibaut and Walker 1975; Tyler 1984, 1986). *Procedural justice* refers to the mechanisms or decision rules by which reward allocations of social goods are made, while *distributive justice* is concerned with the resulting allocation. These are two aspects of the same process and are clearly related, but conceptually they purport to refer to two distinct features of justice. Typically, distributive justice issues are thought of in terms of the comparison of rewards received by a person or a group with some standard of fairness or deservedness, whereas procedural justice issues refer to the "mechanics" of the system that regulates the process of distribution.

It may be useful to distinguish three components of the distributive justice process: (1) the principles for the allocation of goods, (2) the system that governs the application of these allocative principles, and (3) the resulting distribution. While separable in this sense, these are *all* components of what is best thought of in terms of distributive justice, which is the overriding concept. This view agrees with that of Deutsch (1986, p. 35), who states that "procedural justice is a key aspect of distributive justice" and not something that is necessarily separate or separable. Procedural justice matters come to the forefront, suggests Deutsch, and arouse complaints of injustice more often than do the principles of justice, primarily because justice principles are often taken for granted, whereas procedural matters are not.

From this formulation we can see that these three components—principles, procedures, and distributive outcomes—are likely to be confounded and confused in social life. If there is consensus on evaluative principles, and a clear set of procedures can be said to exist to implement those values—and, thus, allocate rewards within a social group or in society—then distributive justice will exist. In such a situation the evaluation of justice is unproblematic. If, on the other hand, there is lack of consensus on the allocative principles to be used, or even if there is consensus but procedures are seen as ineffective or corrupted, then distributive justice will be called into question. In such situations the evaluation of distributive justice focuses on the evaluative principles that should be used, or on the application of the principle, or both. It may be the case, then, that the principles of allocation and the procedural aspects of allocation are intrinsically inseparable, and it may not be clear whether unjust outcomes result from the "wrong" principle being used or from the misapplication of the "right" principle.

In sum, while it seems useful to distinguish "procedural" justice from other components of the distributive process, it is not at all clear that "procedural" and "distributive" justice are really different forms of justice. Rather, they are different aspects of the same process. From the above point of view, distributive justice issues arise when persons perceive the allocative mechanisms to be unjust, or when they perceive imperfections in the application of just mechanisms to real life. It can be seen, then, that overall evaluations of justice, either at the microsocial or the macrosocial level may be influenced by perceptions of the fairness of either procedural or distributive justice issues. However, it ultimately becomes an empirical issue whether, and under what set of conditions, distributive versus procedural injustice is perceived by the actors involved.

(SEE ALSO: *Decision-Making Theory and Research; Social Psychology; Utopian Analysis and Design*)

REFERENCES

Adams, J. Stacy 1965 "Inequity in Social Exchange." In L. Berkowitz, ed., *Advances in Experimental Social Psychology,* vol. 9. New York: Academic Press.

Alves, Wayne M., and Peter H. Rossi 1978 "Who Should Get What? Fairness Judgments of the Distribution of Earnings." *American Journal of Sociology* 84:541–564.

Alwin, Duane F. 1987 "Distributive Justice and Satisfaction with Material Well-Being." *American Sociological Review* 52:83–95.

——— 1989 "Distributive Justice in the United States: Expectations, Fulfillment and Morale." International Conference on Perceptions of Justice, Dubrovnik, Yugoslavia.

Anderson, Norman H., and Arthur J. Farkas 1975 "Integration Theory Applied to Models of Inequity." *Personality and Social Psychology Bulletin* 1:588–591.

Aristotle 1953 *Nichomachean Ethics,* J. A. K. Thompson, trans. London: George Allen and Unwin.

Austin, William 1977 "Equity Theory and Social Comparison Processes." In J.M. Suls and R.L. Miller, eds., *Social Comparison Processes: Theoretical and Empirical Perspectives.* Washington, D.C.: Hemisphere Publishing.

Axelrod, Robert 1984 *The Evolution of Cooperation.* New York: Basic Books.

Barry, Brian 1981 "Social Science and Distributive Justice." In Robert A. Solo and Charles W. Anderson, eds., *Value Judgment and Income Distribution.* New York: Praeger.

Berger, Joseph, Maurice Zelditch, Bo Anderson, and Bernard P. Cohen 1972 "Structural Aspects of Distributive Justice: A Status-Value Formulation." In J. Berger, M. Zelditch, and B. Anderson, eds., *Sociological Theories in Progress,* vol. 2. Boston: Houghton-Miffin.

Berkowitz, Leonard, and Elaine Walster, eds. 1976 *Equity Theory: Toward a General Theory of Social Interaction. Advances in Experimental Social Psychology,* vol. 9. New York: Academic Press.

Blau, Peter M. 1971 "Justice in Social Exchange." In H. Turk and R. L. Simpson, eds., *Institutions and Social Exchange: The Sociologies of Talcott Parsons and George C. Homans.* New York: Bobbs-Merrill.

Boulding, Kenneth E. 1981 "Allocation and Distribution: The Quarrelsome Twins." In R. A. Solo and C. W. Anderson, eds., *Value Judgment and Income Distribution.* New York: Praeger.

Brickman, Philip 1977 "Preferences of Inequality." *Sociometry* 40:303–310.

Buchanan, Allen, and Deborah Mathieu 1986 "Philosophy and Justice." In R. L. Cohen, ed., *Justice: Views from the Social Sciences.* New York: Plenum.

Cohen, Ronald L. 1981 "Procedural Justice and Participation." *Human Relations* 38:643–663.

——— 1986 *Justice: Views from the Social Sciences.* New York: Plenum.

———, and Jerald Greenberg 1982 "The Justice Concept in Social Psychology." In J. Greenberg and R. L. Cohen, eds., *Equity and Justice in Social Behavior.* New York: Academic Press.

Coleman, Richard P., and Lee Rainwater 1978 *Social Standing in America.* New York: Basic Books.

Cook, Karen S. 1975 "Expectations, Evaluations and Equity." *American Sociological Review* 40:372–388.

———, and Toshio Yamagishi 1983 "Social Determinants of Equity Judgments: The Problem of Multidimensional Input." In D.M. Messick and K. A. Cook, eds., *Equity Theory: Psychological and Sociological Perspectives.* New York: Praeger.

Crosby, Faye 1976 "A Model of Egoistical Relative Deprivation." *Psychological Review* 83:85–113.

Davis, James A. 1959. "A formal interpretation of the theory of relative deprivation." *Sociometry* 22:280–296.

Della Fave, L. Richard 1980 "The Meek Shall Not Inherit the Earth: Self-Evaluation and the Legitimacy of Social Stratification." *American Sociological Review* 45:955–971.

Deutsch, Morton 1975 "Equity, Equality and Need: What Determines Which Value Will Be Used as the Basis of Distributive Justice." *Journal of Social Issues* 31:137–149.

——— 1986 *Distributive Justice: A Social Psychological Perspective.* New Haven, Conn.: Yale University Press.

DiQuattro, Arthur 1986 "Political Studies and Justice."

In R. L. Cohen, ed., *Justice: Views from the Social Sciences.* New York: Plenum.

Farkas, Arthur J., and Norman H. Anderson 1979 "Multidimensional Input in Equity Theory." *Journal of Personality and Social Psychology* 37:879–896.

Folger, Robert 1984 *The Sense of Injustice: Social Psychological Perspectives.* New York: Plenum.

Furby, Lita 1986 "Psychology and Justice." In R. L. Cohen, ed., *Justice: Views from the Social Sciences.* New York: Plenum.

Gartrell, C. David 1982 "On the Visibility of Wage Referents." *Canadian Journal of Sociology* 7:117–143.

——— 1985 "Relational and Distributional Models of Collective Justice Sentiments." *Social Forces* 64:64–83.

Greenberg, Jerald, and Ronald L. Cohen 1982 *Equity and Justice in Social Behavior.* New York: Academic Press.

Heider, Fritz 1958 *The Psychology of Interpersonal Relations.* New York: Wiley.

Hochschild, Jennifer L. 1981 *What's Fair? American Beliefs about Distributive Justice.* Cambridge, Mass.: Harvard University Press.

Homans, George C. (1961) 1974 *Social Behavior: Its Elementary Forms.* New York: Harcourt Brace Jovanovich.

——— 1976. "Commentary." In L. Berkowitz and E. Walster, eds., *Equity Theory: Toward a General Theory of Social Interaction.* New York: Academic Press.

Jasso, Guillermina 1978 "On the Justice of Earnings: A New Specification of the Justice Evaluation Function." *American Journal of Sociology* 83:1398–1419.

——— 1980 "A New Theory of Distributive Justice." *American Sociological Review* 45:3–32.

——— 1981 "Some Consequences of the Sense of Distributive Justice: Small Group Applications." In D. M. Messick and K. A. Cook, eds., *Theories of Equity: Psychological and Sociological Perspectives.* New York: Praeger.

———, and Peter H. Rossi 1977 "Distributive Justice and Earned Income." *American Sociological Review* 42:639–651.

Kluegel, James R., and Eliot R. Smith 1981 "Beliefs about Stratification." *Annual Review of Sociology* 7:29–56.

——— 1986 *Beliefs About Inequality: Americans' Views of What Is and What Ought to Be.* New York: Aldine De Gruyter.

Lane, Robert 1986 "Market Justice, Political Justice." *American Political Science Review* 80:383–402.

Major, Brenda, and Blythe Forcey 1985 "Social Comparisons and Pay Evaluations: Preferences for Same-Sex and Same-Job Wage Comparisons." *Journal of Experimental Social Psychology* 21:393–405.

Markovsky, Barry 1985 "Toward a Multilevel Distributive Justice Theory." *American Sociological Review* 50:822–839.

Merton, Robert K. 1949 *Social Theory and Social Structure.* New York: Free Press.

———, and Alice S. Kitt 1950 "Contributions to the Theory of Reference Group Behavior." In R. K. Merton and P. F. Lazarsfeld, eds., *Continuities in Social Research: Studies in the Scope and Method of the American Soldier.* New York: Free Press.

Messick, David M., and Karen A. Cook 1983 *Equity Theory: Psychological and Sociological Perspectives.* New York: Praeger.

Mikula, Gerald 1980 *Justice and Social Interaction: Experimental and Theoretical Contributions from Psychological Research.* New York: Springer-Verlag.

Nader, Laura, and Andrée Sursock 1986 "Anthropology and Justice." In R. L. Cohen, ed., *Justice: Views from the Social Sciences.* New York: Plenum.

Nozick, Robert 1974 *Anarchy, State, and Utopia.* New York: Basic Books.

Patchen, Martin 1961. *The Choices of Wage Comparisons.* Englewood Cliffs, N.J.: Prentice-Hall.

Pettigrew, Thomas F. 1967 "Social Evaluation Theory: Convergences and Applications." In D. Levine, ed., *Nebraska Symposium on Motivation.* Lincold: University of Nebraska Press.

Rae, Douglas 1981 *Equalities.* Cambridge, Mass.: Harvard University Press.

Rainwater, Lee 1974 *What Money Buys.* New York: Basic Books.

Rawls, John 1971 *A Theory of Justice.* Cambridge, Mass.: Harvard University Press.

Robinson, Robert V., and Wendell Bell 1978 "Equality, Success and Social Justice in England and the United States." *American Sociological Review* 43: 125–143.

Runciman, W. 1966 *Relative Deprivation and Social Justice.* Berkeley: University of California Press.

Rytina, Steve 1986 "Sociology and Justice." In R. L. Cohen, ed., *Justice: Views from the Social Sciences.* New York: Plenum.

Sennett, Richard, and Jonathan Cobb 1972 *The Hidden Injuries of Class.* New York: Vintage Books.

Solo, Robert A., and Charles W. Anderson 1981 *Value Judgment and Income Distribution.* New York: Praeger.

Soltan, Karol 1986 "Public Policy and Justice." In R. L.

Cohen, ed., *Justice: Views from the Social Sciences.* New York: Plenum.

Southwood, Kenneth E. 1978 "Substantive Theory and Statistical Interaction: Five Models." *American Journal of Sociology* 83:1154–1203.

Stolte, John F. 1983 "The Legitimation of Structural Inequality." *American Sociological Review* 48:331–342.

Stouffer, Samuel, et al. 1949 *The American Soldier: Adjustment During Army Life.* Princeton, N.J.: Princeton University Press.

Thibaut, John W., and Harold H. Kelley 1959 *The Social Psychology of Groups.* New York: Wiley.

Thibaut, John W., et al. 1975 *Procedural Justice: A Psychological Analysis.* Hillsdale, N.J. L. Erlbaum.

Tyler, Tom R. 1984 "Justice in the Political Arena." In R. Folger, ed., *The Sense of Injustice: Social Psychological Perspectives.* New York: Plenum Press.

——— 1986 "The Psychology of Leadership Evaluation." In Hans W. Bierhoff, Ronald L. Cohen, and Jerald Greenberg, eds., *Justice in Social Relations.* New York: Plenum Press.

Thurow, Lester C. 1981 "The Illusion of Economic Necessity." In R. A. Solo and C. W. Anderson, eds., *Value Judgment and Income Distribution.* New York: Praeger.

Walster, Elaine, Ellen Berscheid, and G. William Walster 1973 "New Directions in Equity Research." *Journal of Personality and Social Psychology* 25:151–176.

———, G. William Walster, and Ellen Berscheid 1978 *Equity: Theory and Research.* Boston: Allyn and Bacon.

Walzer, Michael 1983 *Spheres of Justice: A Defense of Pluralism and Equality.* New York: Basic Books.

Williams, Robin M., Jr. 1975 "Relative Deprivation." In L. A. Coser, ed., *The Idea of Social Structure: Papers in Honor of Robert K. Merton.* New York: Harcourt Brace Jovanovich.

Worland, Stephen T. 1986. "Economics and Justice." In R. L. Cohen, ed., *Justice: Views from the Social Sciences.* New York: Plenum.

DUANE F. ALWIN

ETHNICITY Ethnicity is a salient feature of numerous societies throughout the world. Few societies are ethnically homogeneous, even when they proclaim themselves to be. Consequently, ethnicity has been a preoccupation of sociologists since the early days of the discipline (although more so in the United States than elsewhere).

Yet there is not complete agreement on how the subject should be defined. In the past, it was common to highlight cultural difference as an essential feature of ethnic distinctiveness (see van den Berghe 1967). Recently, this has been deemphasized on the grounds that cultural differences may vary from one setting to another and from one historical period to another. Following an approach attributed to Barth (1969), recent definitions have therefore focused on the existence of a recognized social boundary. Perhaps the most useful definition is still the classic one of Max Weber ([1922] 1968, p. 389): An ethnic group is one whose members "entertain a subjective belief in their common descent because of similarities of physical type or of customs or both, or because of memories of colonization and migration." Weber adds insightfully, "it does not matter whether or not an objective blood relationship exists."

Despite definitional disagreements, a number of characteristics are generally recognized as hallmarks of ethnicity; not all of them will be present in every case, but many will be. They include features shared by group members, such as the same or similar geographic origin, language, religion, foods, traditions, folklore, music, and residential patterns. Also typical are: special political concerns, particularly with regard to a homeland; institutions (e.g., social clubs) to serve the group; and a consciousness of kind or a sense of distinctiveness from others (for the full listing, see Thernstrom, Orlov, and Handlin 1980, p. vi).

There is further disagreement over whether race should be viewed as a form of ethnicity. In this context, "race" should not be understood as a bundle of genetically determined traits that generate of themselves social differences—a view that has been repudiated by the vast majority of social scientists—but as a kind of social classification used by members of a society. Some scholars distinguish between ethnicity and race. For example, van den Berghe (1967) defines race as a social classification based on putative physical traits, and ethnicity as a classification based on cultural ones. But more commonly, race is seen as a variant of ethnicity: A racial group is, then, an ethnic group whose members are believed, by others if not also by themselves, to be physiologically distinctive. This is the approach adopted in this article.

Sociologists recognize that the imprint of history on the contemporary ethnic relations of any society is deep, and this gives rise to another distinction that is potentially central to any discussion of ethnicity. It pertains to the mode of entry of a group into a society and has been formulated by Lieberson (1961) in terms of the situation that obtains just after contact between an indigenous group and one migrating into an area. One possibility is that the migrant group dominates, typically through conquest (often aided by the introduction of new diseases). This is exemplified in the contacts between indigenes and European settlers in Australia and the United States. The other is that the indigenous group dominates, as occurred during the century of mass immigration (1830–1930) into the United States. The crux of the matter here is whether a group is incorporated into a society through force or through more or less voluntary migration. Lieberson argues that a group's mode of entry is fateful for its trajectory of development in a society, and this is amply borne out in the literature on ethnicity.

Stated in very broad terms, three approaches dominate the sociological study of ethnicity (see Sakong 1990). One, the *assimilation* perspective, focuses on social processes and outcomes that tend to dissolve ethnic distinctions, leading to the assimilation of one ethnic group by another or by the larger society. The second approach could be labeled as *stratification.* As the name implies, it is concerned with the origins and consequences of inequalities of various kinds among ethnic groups. The third approach focuses on *ethnic group resources.* Its domain encompasses such processes as mobilization and solidarity, by which the members of ethnic groups attempt to use their ethnicity to compete successfully with others.

No one of these three approaches could be described as preeminent, and each is a major presence in contemporary research on ethnicity. Other approaches are possible but are not as theoretically and empirically developed as these three. One other possibility seeks a basis for ethnicity in sociobiology, viewing ethnicity as a form of genetic nepotism, a generalization of the presumably universal tendency among animals to favor kin. Van den Berghe (1981) has been an exponent of such an approach, but as yet no body of evidence has been developed to distinguish it from more sociological approaches; other sociologists have not followed his lead. Ethnicity has also been viewed as "primordial," deriving from deeply seated human impulses and needs that are not eradicated by modernization (Isaacs 1975). But this viewpoint has not led to sociologically interesting research, and it has lacked exponents in recent decades. The newest attempt stems from "rational choice theory" (Banton 1983; Hechter 1987) and seeks to explain ethnic phenomena in terms of the efforts of individuals to maximize their advantages (or, in technical language, utilities). The use of rational choice theory is still too novel to draw up a meaningful balance sheet.

The assimilation approach has deep roots in classical social theory as well as in American sociology, where it is often traced to Robert E. Park's 1926 formulation of a race relations cycle of "contacts, competition, accommodation, and eventual assimilation" (Park 1950; p. 150) The canonical statement of the assimilation approach is by Gordon (1964). Although Gordon was addressing the role of ethnicity in the United States, his formulation is so general that it can be readily applied to other societies. At the heart of his contribution is the recognition that assimilation is a multidimensional concept. He distinguished, in fact, among seven types of assimilation, but the critical distinction lies between two: *acculturation* and *structural* (or social) *assimilation.* Acculturation means the adaptation by an ethnic group of the cultural patterns of the surrounding society (recognizing that these patterns may themselves be changed by the group's presence). Such acculturation encompasses not only external cultural traits, such as dress and language, but also internal ones, such as beliefs and values. Gordon (1964; p. 77) theorized that acculturation is typically the first of the types of assimilation to occur and that the stage of "'acculturation only' may continue indefinitely''—hence the importance of the second assimilation type, structural assimilation. Structural assimilation is defined by Gordon to mean the entry of an ethnic group's members into close, or primary, relationships with members of the dominant group (or, at least, with ethnic outsiders). The cardinal hypothesis in Gordon's scheme is that structural assimilation is the key that unlocks all other types: "Once structural assimilation has occurred . . . all of the other types of assimilation will naturally follow" (Gordon 1964, p. 81). Once structural assimilation occurs, the way is open to widespread intermarriage, an abating of prejudice and discrimination, and the full participation of ethnic-group members in the life of a society.

Gordon discussed certain models or theories of the assimilation process (they might also be described as ideologies because of their value-laden character). Although these were again developed for the U.S. context, Gordon's discussion is so lucid that the models have passed into more general application. One is labeled "Anglo-conformity" by Gordon, and it describes an assimilation that is limited to acculturation to the behavior and values of the core ethnic group, taken in the American context to be Protestants with ancestry from the British Isles. A second model is that of the "melting pot." It envisions an assimilation process that operates on cultural and structural planes. One outcome is a culture that contains contributions from numerous ethnic groups and is adopted by their members. A parallel outcome on a structural plane is a pattern of widespread marriage across ethnic lines, in which the members of all ethnic groups participate, leading ultimately to population made up of individuals of quite intermixed ancestry. The melting pot idea corresponds with some popular notions about U.S. society, but so does the last model explicated by Gordon—namely, "cultural pluralism." Cultural pluralism corresponds with a situation in which ethnic groups remain socially differentiated, often with their own institutions and high rates of ingroup marriage, and retain some culturally distinctive features. It is, in fact, an apt description of many societies throughout the world.

Urban ecology, dating back to the origins of the Chicago School of American sociology, is quite compatible with the assimilation approach. The core tenets of this tradition, as updated in the model of *spatial assimilation* (Massey 1985), are that residential mobility follows from the acculturation and socioeconomic mobility of ethnic-group members and that residential mobility is an intermediate step on the way to more complete (i.e., structural) assimilation. The model envisions an early stage of residential segregation, as the members of ethnic groups—typically, immigrants and their children—are concentrated in urban enclaves, which frequently result from the displacement of other groups. But as the members of an ethnic group acculturate and establish themselves in the labor markets of the host society, they attempt to leave behind less successful coethnics and to convert socioeconomic and assimilation progress into residential gain by "purchasing" residence in places with greater advantages and amenities. This process implies, on the one hand, a tendency toward dispersion of an ethnic group, opening the way for increased contact with members of ethnic majority, and, on the other hand, greater resemblance in terms of residential characteristics between successful ethnic-group members and their peers from the majority. This model has been applied to immigrant groups in six different societies by Massey (1985).

The assimilation perspective has been successfully applied to American ethnic groups derived from European immigration (although the ultimate assimilation of these groups is still debated). In a review of the evidence, Hirschman (1983) documents the abating of ethnic differences in the white population in terms of socioeconomic achievement, residential location, and intermarriage. To cite some representative research findings, Lieberson and Waters (1988, chap. 5), comparing the occupations of European-ancestry men in 1900 and 1980, find a marked decline in occupational concentrations, although these still show traces of the patterns of the past. These authors and Alba (1990) also demonstrate the great extent to which interethnic marriage now takes place within the white population: Three of every four marriages in this group involve some degree of ethnic boundary crossing.

Much of the evidence on assimilation and ethnic change is derived from cross-sectional studies rather than those over time; the latter are difficult to conduct because of the limited availability of comparable data from different time points. Cross-sectional analyses involve some dissection of an ethnic group into parts expected to display a trajectory of change. One basis for such a dissection is generational groups. *Generation* here refers to distance in descent from the point of entry into a society. (By convention, generations are numbered with immigrants as the "first," so that their children are the "second," their grandchildren are the "third," etc.) Generally speaking, later generations are expected to be more assimilated than earlier ones. Another basis for dissection is *birth cohorts,* defined as groups born during the same period. Cohort differences can provide insight into historical changes in a group's position. Both kinds of differences have been used to study ethnic changes in the United States (for an application of the generational method, see Neidert and Farley 1985; for the cohort method, see Alba 1988).

The second major approach to the study of ethnicity and race, labeled above as "stratification," is considerably less unified than the assimilation approach, encompassing quite diverse theoretical underpinnings and research findings. Yet there are some common threads throughout. One is an assumption that ethnic groups generally are hierarchically ordered: There is typically a dominant or *superordinate* group, which is often described as the *majority* group (even though in some societies, such as South Africa, it may be a numerical minority of the population). There are also *subordinate* groups, often called *minorities* (although they may be numerical majorities). Second, these groups are assumed to be in conflict over scarce resources, which may relate to power, favorable occupational position, educational opportunity, and so forth. In this conflict, the dominant group employs a variety of strategies to defend or enhance its position, while minority groups seek to challenge it. Often, the focus of the stratification approach is on the mechanisms that help preserve ethnic inequalities, although there has also been some attention to the means that enable minorities successfully to challenge entrenched inequality.

One tradition in ethnic stratification research has looked to mechanisms of inequality that are rooted in ideologies, in belief systems that are then manifested in the outlooks and behavior of individuals. This is, in fact, a common meaning for the word *racism.* A long-standing research concern has been with *prejudice,* which is generally defined as a fixed set of opinions and attitudes, usually unfavorable, about the members of a group (Allport 1954). Prejudice is frequently an outgrowth of *ethnocentrism,* the tendency to value positively one's own group and denigrate others. It can lead to *discrimination,* which is a behavior: the denial of equal treatment to a group's members, exemplified by the refusal to sell homes in certain neighborhoods to minority group members. The investigation of prejudice was one of the early testing grounds for survey research. In the United States, this research uncovered a dimension of *social distance,* expressing the specific gradations of social intimacy the majority is willing to tolerate with the members of various ethnic groups (Bogardus 1928). Recent research has revealed a paradoxical set of changes: on the one hand, a secular decline in prejudiced attitudes and beliefs, most notably those held by whites toward blacks; on the other, little increase in support for government policies that implement principles of racial equality (Schuman, Steeh, and Bobo 1985).

However persuasive as explanatory factors prejudice and discrimination may appear to the lay person, sociologists have in recent decades more and more neglected them in favor of *institutional* or *structural* mechanisms of inequality. One reason for this shift has been skepticism that prejudice and discrimination by themselves are adequate to account for the depth and durability of racial and ethnic cleavages in industrial societies, especially since these factors have seemed to decline in tandem with rising educational levels.

(However, the emphasis on structural mechanisms can itself be faulted for neglecting the ideological component in racism.)

One expression of the focus on structural factors has been the notion of *institutional racism* (Blauner 1972). According to this notion, inequality among racial and ethnic groups depends not so much on individual acts of discrimination as it does on the workings of such institutions as the schools and the police, which process and sort individuals according to their racial and ethnic origins and ultimately impose very different outcomes on them. An assumption of this approach is that this sort of discrimination can occur on a wide scale without equally widespread prejudice. Indeed, it may even be possible without any discriminatory intent on the part of individuals in authority. An example would be educational tracking systems that sort students according to racial background based on culturally and socially biased cues that are presumed by teachers and administrators to be related to intellectual ability. Studies deriving from the notion of institutional racism have in fact provided some compelling analyses of the perpetuation of inequalities (on education, see Persell 1977), although they also can easily descend into controversy, as when any unequal outcome is declared to indicate the operation of racism.

A major theme in the stratification approach is the often complicated relationship or interaction between ethnicity and social class. In treating this theme, one viewpoint is that ethnicity is, to some degree at least, a manifestation of deeply rooted class dynamics. This has led to analyses that emphasize the economic and material foundations of what appear superficially to be cultural and ethnic distinctions. Analyses of this type have sometimes been inspired by Marxism, but they are hardly limited to Marxists. For example, Herbert Gans ([1962] 1982), in an influential analysis of second-generation Italians in a Boston neighborhood, argued that many of their distinctive traits could be understood as a function of their working-class position, which was not greatly changed from the situation of their southern Italian ancestors. In a related vein, Steinberg (1981) argues that cultural explanations of ethnic inequalities, which impute "undesirable" characteristics to some groups and "desirable" ones to others, are often rationalizations of economic privilege.

It is sometimes argued that inequalities that once rested on an ethnic basis now rest primarily on one of class. An important, if controversial, instance is Wilson's (1978, 1987) claim of a "declining significance of race" for American blacks. One part of Wilson's argument focuses on an increasing socioeconomic split within the black population. This is held to result from the increasing opportunities available to young, well-educated African-Americans since the 1960s. However, while improvements have been registered for a minority of the group, the lot of the black poor has not improved—it has even worsened. Wilson describes their situation as one of an *underclass,* which he defines in terms of isolation from the mainstream economy and society. His explanations for the emergence of the underclass are structural, not individualistic, and include: the spatial concentration of the black poor in rundown urban neighborhoods, which have been stripped of their institutional fabric and middle class residents; and the exodus of suitable job opportunities from central cities to suburbs and Sunbelt areas. This interpretation gives insight into the emergence of deviant characteristics in these ghettoes, such as high rates of out-of-wedlock births.

An economic approach has also been used to explain ethnic conflict, which is seen as an outgrowth of the conflicting material interests of different ethnic groups. An exemplar is provided by the theory of the ethnically *split labor market* (Bonacich 1972). Such a labor market develops when two ethnically different groups of workers compete (or could compete) for the same jobs *at different costs to employers.* It is typical in such situations for the higher priced group of workers to have the same ethnic origins as employers and therefore for the lower priced group to be ethnically different from both. Nevertheless, it is in the interest of employers to substitute lower priced workers for higher priced ones wherever possible, despite the ethnic ties they share with the latter. Intense ethnic conflict can therefore develop between the two groups of workers, as the higher priced group seeks to eliminate the threat to its interests. Two strategies may be employed: exclusion of the lower priced group (for example, through legal restrictions on the immigration of its members); or creation of a caste system (i.e., the limitation of the lower priced group to a separate sphere of undesirable jobs). Split labor market theory has been applied to black–white relations in South Africa and the United States.

Yet, even in terms of a strictly economic approach, the precise genesis of the conflict between different ethnic groups of workers is open to question, and the theory of *segmented labor markets* gives another picture (Piore 1979). This theory divides the economies and labor markets of advanced capitalist societies into a primary sector, which combines relatively secure, well-paid jobs with decent working conditions and the opportunity for advancement, and a secondary sector, made up of insecure, dead-end jobs at low wages. Regardless of their class position, workers from the dominant group prefer to avoid jobs in the secondary sector and usually can manage to do so. Even unemployment may not be sufficient to force them into the secondary sector because the benefits and resources available to most members of the dominant group, such as relatively generous unemployment compensation and seniority rights, enable them to wait out periodic unemployment. Hence, there is a need for another supply of workers, typically drawn from minorities and immigrants, who have no alternative but to accept employment in the secondary sector. Immigrants, in fact, are often willing to take these jobs because, as sojourners, the social stigma attached to the work is less meaningful for them than for the native born. In contrast to the theory of the split labor market, which takes the existence of an ethnic difference among workers as a given, segmented labor market theory explains why ethnic differences, especially between natives and immigrants, are so prevalent and persistent in the industrial societies of the West.

An economic explanation of ethnic differences is sometimes placed in a context of worldwide colonialism and capitalist exploitation (Rex 1981). Indeed, ethnic inequalities *within* a society are sometimes seen as the consequence of international relations between colonizers and the colonized. The notion that subordinate groups form economically exploited *internal colonies* in Western societies is an important expression of this (Blauner 1972). This notion is compatible with a hypothesis of a *cultural division of labor,* according to which positions in the socioeconomic order are assigned on the basis of cultural markers and hence ethnic origin (Hechter 1975).

The stratification approach need not focus exclusively on socioeconomic differences. Some scholars, in fact, prefer to see inequalities of power as more fundamental (Horowitz 1985; Stone 1985). This is a very general perspective on ethnic stratification and is quite compatible with such fundamental notions as dominant and subordinate groups. According to it, social class relations are but one instance, no matter how important, of the institutionalized inequalities between ethnic groups. Equally important, ethnic dominance cannot be reduced to, or explained solely in terms of, social class mechanisms. (An implication is that class analysis of ethnic relations can be reductionist, an attempt to explain away ethnicity's causal independence.) Thus, the antagonism and sectarian violence between Catholics and Protestants in Northern Ireland is not comprehensible solely in the terms of a social class analysis, even though aggregate class differences between the groups exist as a result of centuries-long Protestant domination. This domination, the legacy of colonial treatment of Ireland by the British, is manifest in a number of areas—in separate residential neighborhoods and schools, in social relations between members of the two groups, and in the political system. In short, domination encompasses much more than social class privilege and gives even working-class members of the Protestant group a sense of status and superiority.

Distinguishing empirically between ethnic stratification based on power and that rooted in economic structure has proven difficult. In one attempt, Blalock (1967) has formulated a *power threat hypothesis,* to be contrasted with one derived from economic competition between groups. These two hypotheses can be tested in the relationship between discrimination and the size of a minority group. In particular, threats to the power of the dominant group are expected to result in discrimination that rises sharply with increases in the size of a minority; the same is not true for economic competition. So far, this test has been applied mainly to the American South.

Theories concerning power differentials among ethnic groups border on the final major approach to the study of ethnicity, with its focus on ethnic group resources (a term borrowed for this context from Light and Bonacich 1988 and Sakong 1990). This approach, like the stratification approach, takes its point of departure from the inequalities among groups. However, its vision is less one of the domination of some groups over others than it is of a more balanced competition, which is affected by characteristics of the groups, such as their numbers, their solidarity, and their ability to form separate ethnic subeconomies. Such characteristics can give the group and its members relative advantages or disadvantages in this competition. Insofar as advantages are conferred, there may be incentives for individuals to maintain their attachments to a group rather than to assimilate. In a sense, theories of ethnic group resources can be seen as counterarguments to assimilation theories.

This is certainly clear in Glazer and Moynihan's (1970) politically based explanation for the continuing importance of ethnicity in the United States. These authors acknowledge that immigrant cultures fade quickly under the impact of the assimilation process; assimilation is accomplished to this degree. However, ethnicity comes to coincide with differences in American circumstances, such as residential and occupational concentrations, which are similarly affected by government policies and actions. Hence, ethnicity takes on importance in the political sphere: Ethnic groups become "interest groups," reflecting the interests of many similarly situated individuals. This role breathes new life into what might otherwise languish as an Old World social form. Glazer and Moynihan give many examples of the working of such interest groups in New York City.

Others have argued that ethnicity has become "politicized" in many contemporary societies, including many industrialized ones, and this leads to an unanticipated ethnic "resurgence." Bell (1975) states one basis for this point of view, claiming that politics is increasingly replacing the market as the chief instrument of distribution and that politics recognizes only group claims, thus enhancing ethnicity's political import. Horowitz (1985), on the other hand, sees the ethnic political conflict characterizing many third world nations as originating in part in colonial policies and then intensified by the anxieties of groups over their status in the post-colonial order. On a different note, Nielsen (1985) contends that ethnicity offers a wider basis for political recruitment than the chief alternative, social class.

Students of ethnic politicization have focused especially on the phenomenon of ethnic mobilization, which is epitomized in separatist movements in modern states as in Brittany, Eritrea, and Quebec (Olzak 1983). Mobilization can be regarded as one manifestation of ethnic solidarity, a core concept in the literature on ethnicity. *Solidary* ethnic groups can be defined as self-conscious communities whose members interact with each other to achieve common purposes, and *mobilization* occurs when members take some collective action to advance these purposes. Recent research on ethnic movements appears to demonstrate that they are not generally interpretable in modern polities as the vestiges of traditional loyalties that have yet to be submerged by the modernization processes attendant upon development; rather, such movements can be outcomes of these processes and thus increase as economic development proceeds. The specific causes of this linkage are disputed, however (Olzak 1983).

Culture is another domain in which the search for group resources has been carried out. The group resources approach is compatible with the cultural pluralist description of society, described earlier. More commonly in the past than today, the relative success of ethnic groups has been explained in terms of cultural traits. Quite often, the advantages these give have been analyzed in social psychological terms. A well-known attempt along these lines was that of Rosen (1959), who matched American ethnic groups against the profile of the "achievement syndrome," a configuration of values that is presumed to predispose individuals to success. Included are an orientation to the future rather than the past and a downplaying of fatalism. In Rosen's analysis, the presence or absence of these traits in the culture of a group was explained according to the group's history and experience and frequently in terms of the culture of the society from which it came.

This sort of analysis, presuming stable cultural traits and rooting socioeconomic success in social-psychological prerequisites, has fallen into disfavor of late. In fact, it is often seen as more popular myth than social science (Steinberg 1981). Cultural explanations, however, are not limited to the social-psychological realm. As one example, Light (1972) has devised an intriguing partial explanation for the entrepreneurial proclivities of different groups—in terms of the extent to which their cultures sponsor mechanisms that generate capital for the start-up of small businesses. Light argues that the business success of some Asian groups can be understood in part as an outcome of the rotating credit association, a traditional social form imported from their home societies. Nevertheless, sociologists recently have stressed the malleability of culture and have tended to view it more as an adaptation to, and hence outcome of, socioeconomic position than as a cause of it. Consequently, cultural interpretations currently play only a minor role in the study of ethnicity. This may be a neglect engendered by cyclical intellectual fashion. In the future, they may loom larger.

A final theory that fits under the group resources umbrella focuses on the ability of some ethnic groups to form separate economic sectors, which can shelter ethnic entrepreneurs and workers from the disadvantages they would face in the mainstream economy. In the guise of *ethnic enclave* theory, this set of ideas recently has been highly developed by Portes and various colleagues (e.g., Portes and Bach 1985), although its intellectual ancestry is considerably older. Examining the trajectories of recent, non-European immigrant groups in the United States, Portes and his coauthors argue that the mode of economic incorporation is fateful for the group. The members of immigrant groups that lack an independent economic base have little alternative but to offer their labor power in the mainstream economy, where they typically find themselves disadvantaged by language, by foreign educational backgrounds, and by their ethnic ancestry itself. The story can be quite different for the members of groups that are able to establish their own niches, or ethnic enclaves, in the economy. (Portes and Bach 1985 cite Cubans as a case in point.) These groups, which typically contain a high-status stratum composed of individuals with professional occupations, capital, or both, are able to establish networks of businesses in specific industrial sectors. The success of these businesses is predicated upon ethnic loyalty to some degree. Where suppliers and purchasers of materials for production (in, say, the garment industry) share the same ethnic background, an advantage based on ethnicity is created, for suppliers have a guaranteed outlet for their product and purchasers a guaranteed source, and perhaps credit, to satisfy their production needs. Where workers and bosses share the same ethnicity, a further advantage may exist. Workers may be willing to work longer hours or for lower wages, thus enhancing the profitability of a business, because they are able to work in a culturally familiar environment (usually speaking their mother tongue, for example). Workers may also have the opportunity to learn about running a business, and some eventually graduate to become entrepreneurs themselves.

Once established, an enclave economy offers an alternative to assimilation into the mainstream economy. This is evident in two ways. First, participants in the enclave economy receive income returns on their education and other human capital equivalent to those obtained by participants in the mainstream economy. There is, then, no economic loss associated with the enclave. Second, because ethnic solidarity is the linchpin of the enclave, the formation of an enclave economy in turn fosters the perpetuation of solidarity and its cultural and social underpinnings. Thus, an enclave economy creates countercurrents to the general tide of assimilation.

Despite its attractiveness on theoretical grounds, the implications of the enclave economy are disputed. One criticism is that such an economy offers few benefits for workers; the economic gains accrue to ethnic entrepreneurs (Sanders and Nee 1987). Another is that the success of the enclave depends on very low-cost *female* labor and thus on gender exploitation (Zhou and Logan 1989). If true, both criticisms suggest that the enclave as a positive alternative to the mainstream, and thus the incentives to resist assimilation, may be overstated. What is clear is that more research is needed to clarify both the conditions under which an enclave economy will prosper and its ramifications for an ethnic group.

The literature on ethnicity remains unsettled in its theoretical core. The persistence—perhaps even the resurgence—of ethnic difference and conflict in societies throughout the world has attracted much attention from sociologists and other social scientists. But the paradoxes associated with ethnicity, evidenced in the United States by the assimilation of some groups and the continued separateness and even subordination of others, have yet to be resolved. They remain fruitful for sociology, nevertheless: The study of ethnicity has produced some of the discipline's most striking findings and, no doubt, will continue to do so.

(SEE ALSO: *Culture; Discrimination; Nationalism; Social Mobility; Social Stratification*)

REFERENCES

Alba, Richard 1988 "Cohorts and the Dynamics of Ethnic Change." In Matilda White Riley, Bettina Huber, and Beth Hess, eds., *Social Structures and Human Lives.* Newbury Park, Calif.: Sage.

——— 1990 *Ethnic Identity: The Transformation of White America.* New Haven, Conn.: Yale University Press.

Allport, Gordon 1954 *The Nature of Prejudice.* New York: Addison-Wesley.

Banton, Michael 1983 *Racial and Ethnic Competition.* Cambridge: Cambridge University Press.

Barth, Frederik 1969 "Introduction." In Frederik Barth, ed., *Ethnic Groups and Boundaries.* Boston: Little, Brown.

Bell, Daniel 1975 "Ethnicity and Social Change." In Nathan Glazer and Daniel P. Moynihan, eds. *Ethnicity: Theory and Experience.* Cambridge, Mass.: Harvard University Press.

Blalock, Hubert 1967 *Toward a Theory of Minority-Group Relations.* New York: Capricorn.

Blauner, Robert 1972 *Racial Oppression in America.* New York: Harper and Row.

Bogardus, Emory 1928 *Immigration and Race Attitudes.* Boston: D. C. Heath.

Bonacich, Edna 1972. "A Theory of Ethnic Antagonism: The Split Labor Market." *American Sociological Review* 37:547–559.

Gans, Herbert (1962) 1982 *The Urban Villagers: Group and Class in the Life of Italian Americans.* New York: Free Press.

Glazer, Nathan, and Daniel Patrick Moynihan 1970 *Beyond the Melting Pot: The Negroes, Puerto Ricans, Jews, Italians, and Irish of New York City,* 2nd ed. Cambridge, Mass.: MIT Press.

Gordon, Milton 1964 *Assimilation in American Life.* New York: Oxford University Press.

Hechter, Michael 1975 *Internal Colonialism: The Celtic Fringe and British National Development.* Berkeley: University of California Press.

——— 1987 *Principles of Group Solidarity.* Berkeley: University of California Press.

Hirschman, Charles 1983 "America's Melting Pot Reconsidered." *Annual Review of Sociology* 9:397–423.

Horowitz, Donald 1985 *Ethnic Groups in Conflict.* Berkeley: University of California Press.

Isaacs, Harold 1975 "Basic Group Identity: The Idols of the Tribe." In Nathan Glazer and Daniel P. Moynihan, eds., *Ethnicity: Theory and Experience.* Cambridge, Mass.: Harvard University Press.

Lieberson, Stanley 1961 "A Societal Theory of Race and Ethnic Relations." *American Sociological Review* 26:902–910.

———, and Mary Waters 1988 *From Many Strands: Ethnic and Racial Groups in Contemporary America.* New York: Russell Sage Foundation.

Light, Ivan 1972 *Ethnic Enterprise in America: Business and Welfare Among Chinese, Japanese, and Blacks.* Berkeley: University of California Press.

———, and Edna Bonacich 1988 *Immigrant Entrepreneurs: Koreans in Los Angeles, 1965–1982.* Berkeley: University of California Press.

Massey, Douglas 1985 "Ethnic Residential Segregation: A Theoretical Synthesis and Empirical Review." *Sociology and Social Research* 69:315–350.

Neidert, Lisa, and Reynolds Farley 1985 "Assimilation in the United States: An Analysis of Ethnic and Generation Differences in Status and Achievement." *American Sociological Review* 50:840–850.

Nielsen, François 1985 "Toward a Theory of Ethnic Solidarity in Modern Societies." *American Sociological Review* 50:133–149.

Olzak, Susan 1983 "Contemporary Ethnic Mobilization." *Annual Review of Sociology* 9:355–374.

Park, Robert E. 1950 *Race and Culture.* New York: Free Press.

Persell, Caroline 1977 *Education and Inequality: The Roots of Stratification in America's Schools.* New York: Free Press.

Piore, Michael 1979 *Birds of Passage: Migrant Labor and Industrial Societies.* New York: Cambridge University Press.

Portes, Alejandro, and Robert Bach 1985 *Latin Journey: Cuban and Mexican Immigrants in the United States.* Berkeley: University of California Press.

Rex, John 1981 "A Working Paradigm for Race Relations Research." *Ethnic and Racial Studies* 4:1–25.

Rosen, Bernard 1959 "Race, Ethnicity, and the Achievement Syndrome." *American Sociological Review* 24:47–60.

Sakong, MyungDuk 1990 "Rethinking the Impact of the Enclave: A Comparative Analysis of Korean Americans' Economic and Residential Adaptation." Ph.D. diss., State University of New York, Albany.

Sanders, Jimy, and Victor Nee 1987 "Limits of Ethnic Solidarity in the Enclave Economy." *American Sociological Review* 52:745–767.

Schuman, Howard, Charlotte Steeh, and Lawrence Bobo 1985 *Racial Attitudes in America: Trends and Interpretations.* Cambridge, Mass.: Harvard University Press.

Steinberg, Stephen 1981 *The Ethnic Myth: Race, Ethnicity, and Class in America.* New York: Atheneum.

Stone, John 1985 *Racial Conflict in Contemporary Society.* London: Fontana Press/Collins.

Thernstrom, Stephan, Ann Orlov, and Oscar Handlin 1980 *Harvard Encyclopedia of American Ethnic Groups.* Cambridge, Mass.: Harvard University Press.

van den Berghe, Pierre 1967 *Race and Racism: A Comparative Perspective.* New York: Wiley.

——— 1981 *The Ethnic Phenomenon.* New York: Elsevier.

Weber, Max [1922] 1968 *Economy and Society.* New York: Bedminster Press.

Wilson, William J. 1978 *The Declining Significance of Race: Blacks and Changing American Institutions.* Chicago: University of Chicago Press.

——— 1987 *The Truly Disadvantaged: The Inner City, the Underclass, and Public Policy.* Chicago: University of Chicago Press.

Zhou, Min, and John Logan 1989 "Returns on Human Capital in Ethnic Enclaves: New York City's Chinatown." *American Sociological Review* 54:809–820.

RICHARD D. ALBA

ETHICS IN SOCIAL RESEARCH The immediacy of subject matter in social science underscores the importance of ethical issues in research by social scientists. This is particularly true in sociology. A rather small percentage of sociologists use historical documents or cultural products as data. The majority rely upon interviews with actively cooperating subjects, records relating to persons still living or recently alive, unobtrusive observation of live actors, or participant studies within interacting groups. Sociological research typically focuses on relatively large study populations and poses questions relevant to many dimensions of individual and social life. Both the process and application of sociological inquiry may conceivably affect large numbers of subjects in an adverse manner. Thus, the question of "right" and "wrong" in research has been a continual (though not always powerful or explicit) concern within the profession.

Ethics may be conceptualized as a special case of norms governing individual or social action. In any individual act or interpersonal exchange, ethics connotes principles of obligation to serve values over and above benefits to the people who are directly involved. Examination of ethical standards in any collectivity provides insights into its fundamental values; identification of ethical issues provides clues to its basic conflicts. This is as true of sociology as a profession as it is of other social systems.

The most abstract and general statements about ethics in sociological literature reflect broad agreement about the values that social inquiry should serve. Bellah (1981) writes that ethics constitutes an important though typically implicit topic in the thinking of sociology's founders (such as Durkheim and Weber) and leading contemporary practitioners (such as Shils and Janowitz). Even while consciously striving to distinguish their emerging discipline as a science free of values and moralizing, the early sociologists appeared to have a distinct ethical focus. The discipline's founders implied and sometimes stated that sociology necessarily involved ethical ends, such as identification of emerging social consensus or the development of guidelines for assessing social good. Modern sociologists have emphasized improvement of society's understanding of itself as the discipline's principal ethical end, as opposed to determining a specific direction or developing technology for social change. In the broadest sense, contemporary sociologists seem to consider the raising of consciousness as quintessentially ethical activity and social engineering by private or parochial interests as ethically most objectionable. In the phraseology of Edward Shils, this means contributing to "the self-understanding of society rather than its manipulated improvement" (Shils 1980, p. 76).

The American Sociological Association (ASA) *Code of Ethics* (American Sociological Association 1989) addresses more specific, concrete, and immediate matters. Research constitutes the largest area of interest in the code, concentrating on three areas: (1) full disclosure of motivations for and background of research; (2) avoidance of material harm to research subjects, with special emphasis on issues of confidentiality; and (3) qualifications to the technical expertise of sociology.

The first area appears concerned primarily with a fear among sociologists that agencies of social control (such as military or criminal justice units) may seek intelligence under the guise of social research. Thus, the code advises sociologists not to "misuse their positions as professional social scientists for fraudulent purposes or as a pretext for gathering intelligence for any organization or government." The mandate for disclosure has implications for relations not only between professionals and research subjects but among professionals. Another provision of the code reads, "Sociologists must report fully all sources of financial support in their publications and must note any special relation to any sponsor."

The second area of concern in the code places special emphasis on assurance of confidentiality to research subjects. It stresses the need for extraordinary caution in making and adhering to commitments. As if to recognize the absence of legal protection for confidentiality in the research relationship and to mandate its protection nevertheless, the code states: "Sociologists should not make any guarantees to respondents, individuals, groups, or organizations—unless there is full intention and ability to honor such commitments. All such guarantees, once made, must be honored" (p. 2).

As a subject of professional ethics, the third area is extraordinary. Provisions mandating disclosure of purpose and assurance of confidentiality might appear in the code of ethics of any profession dealing regularly with human clients or subjects. But it is surprising to find, as a provision in the ASA *Code of Ethics,* the mandate that sociologists explicitly state the shortcomings of methodologies and the openness of findings to varying interpretation. The following illustrate provisions of this nature:

> *Since individual sociologists vary in their research modes, skills, and experience, sociologists should always set forth* ex ante *the limits of their knowledge and the disciplinary and personal limitations that condition the validity of findings.*
>
> *To the best of their ability, sociologists should . . . disclose details of their theories, methods and research designs that might bear upon interpretation of research findings.*
>
> *Sociologists should take particular care to state*

all significant qualifications on the findings and interpretations of their research. (p. 2)

Themes in the *Code of Ethics* dealing with disclosure and confidentiality reflect widely shared values and beliefs in the profession. Sociology stands out among the learned professions as critical of the authority of established institutions such as governments and large business firms. But propositions about the limitations of theories and methodologies and the openness of findings to varying interpretation suggest conflict. In the late twentieth century, sociological methodologies encompassed both highly sophisticated mathematical modeling of quantitative data and observation and theory building based entirely on qualitative techniques. Acknowledgment of the legitimacy of these differences as an *ethical* principle reflects a strenuous attempt by sociology as a social system to accommodate subgroups whose basic approaches to the discipline are inconsistent with each other in important respects.

A review of historical developments, events, and controversies of special importance to sociologists in the decades preceding the 1989 *Code of Ethics* promotes a further appreciation of the concerns it embodies. Perhaps the most far-reaching development in this era was the introduction of government funding into new areas of the sociological enterprise. Like many areas of science, government funding provided opportunities to expand the scope and sophistication of research. But it created new ethical dilemmas and accentuated old ones.

Increased government funding created interrelated problems of independence for the sociological researcher and anonymity for the research subject. A report by Trend (1980) on work done under contract with the U.S. Department of Housing and Urban Development (HUD) illustrates one aspect of this problem. Possessing a legal right to audit HUD's operations, the General Accounting Office (GAO) could have examined raw data complete with individual identifiers despite written assurances of confidentiality to the subjects by the research team. Sensitivity on the part of the GAO and creativity by the sociologists averted an involuntary though real ethical transgression in this instance. But the case illustrates both the importance of honoring commitments to subjects and the possibility that ethical responsibilities may clash with legal obligations.

Paradoxically, legal provisions designed explicitly to protect human subjects have fostered controversy among scientists. Regulations developed by the U.S. Department of Health and Human Services (DHHS) in the 1970s and 1980s required that universities, laboratories, and other organizations requesting funds establish institutional review boards (IRBs) for protection of human subjects. Some would argue that deliberations of these boards take place in the absence of appropriate standards or methods of analysis. Ordinarily, moreover, sociological research poses risks that are less calculable and considerably less substantive than traditional scientific fields. In the words of one commentator, the requirement by IRBs that researchers predict adverse consequences of proposed studies encourages sociologists to engage in exercises of "futility, creativity, or mendacity" (Wax and Cassell 1981, p. 226).

The Vietnam era saw increasing suspicion among sociologists that government might use their expertise to manipulate populations both at home and abroad. A sentinel event during this period was controversy over a U.S. Army–funded research effort known as Project Camelot. One commentator describes the objective of Project Camelot as a study of "the conditions that might lead to armed insurrections in a variety of developing countries so as to enable United States authorities to help friendly governments eliminate the causes of such insurrections or to deal with them should they occur" (Davison 1967, p. 397). Critical scrutiny by scholars, diplomats, and congressional committees led to cancellation of the project. But provisions in the *Code of Ethics* on disclosure and possible impacts of research clearly reflect its influence.

Perhaps because ethics involves issues that are fundamentally ambiguous, sociologists who share basic values may draw different conclusions when faced with specific questions. Basic values themselves—for example, the right to inquiry versus the right to privacy—may contradict each other. As an ethical principle, utilitarianism provides a convenient decision rule. The dominant morality among modern cosmopolitans, utilitarianism applies the principle of the greatest net gain to society in deciding questions of research ethics. This perspective places emphasis on degrees of risk or magnitude of harm that might result from a given research effort. Under this perspective, even Project Camelot may have deserved more favorable reception.

Davison (1967) suggests that completion of the project would probably not have caused appreciable harm. He comments:

> *If past experience is any guide, it would have contributed to our knowledge about developing societies, it would have enriched the literature, but its effects on this country's international relations would probably have been tangential and indirect.* (p. 399)

As an ethical principle, however, utilitarianism presents conceptual and practical problems. Bok (1978) points out the difficulty in estimating risks of harm (as well as benefits) from any research activity—areas of particular uncertainty in the social sciences. More traditional ethical principles contradict utilitarianism; ethical arguments that are *deontological* in nature (Frankena 1973, p. 15) assess acts on the basis of abstract acceptability (such as their consistency with religious beliefs) rather than on their material consequences. The ASA *Code of Ethics* seems to include both utilitarian and deontological principles. A utilitarian-seeming passage in the code's preamble states that sociological practice, teaching, and scholarship should "maximize the beneficial effects that sociology may bring to humankind and minimize the harm that might be a consequence of sociological work." Other statements are considerably less relativistic. A provision of the code, for example, reads: "Sociologists should not mislead respondents involved in a research project as to the purpose for which the research is being conducted."

Resolution of these and other ethical issues may determine the scope and significance of sociological research. Even studies that have no adverse personal consequences for individual subjects may have undesirable social impacts. Opinion polling, the sociological research technique most familiar to the public, may have consequences of this nature. The asking of survey questions falls squarely in the realm of legitimate social research and under the protection of the right of free speech. But interviewers typically do not disclose the sponsorship and purpose of a public opinion survey to the respondent in much detail. Unknown to the respondent, the poll in which he or she participates may partially supplant traditional political processes, as both candidates and office-holders evaluate policy alternative through immediate public responses to hypothetical options. Seen in its worst light, polling may serve as a technique of social control. As Sievers comments,

> *Information gained from survey research can easily be translated into manipulative techniques designed to gain public acceptance for whatever is purveyed, whether products, television programs, or political candidates.* (Sievers 1983, p. 331)

Even a purely academic piece of research under truly neutral sponsorship may be abused by interested parties with access only to published findings.

Studies by sociologists with exemplary motives have initiated major ethical controversies. Among the best known is Laud Humphreys's study of impersonal sex in public places (1975). Humphreys gained access to the secret world of male homosexuals seeking contacts in public restrooms by volunteering his services as a lookout. Despite its obvious deception, Humphreys's work received the support of several homophile organizations (Warwick 1973, p. 57), in part because it illustrated the prevalence of sexual preferences once widely considered abnormal. In his study of mental institutions, Rosenhan (1973) placed normal (i.e., nonpsychotic) observers in the wards without the knowledge or consent of most staff. His study generated highly useful information on the imperfections of care in these institutions, but the deception and manipulation of his subjects (hospital staff) is undeniable.

It may be argued that the most potentially consequential research in sociology is also the most ethically risky. The utilitarian approach to ethical decisions appears to be a necessary condition for important research in this field. Because they cannot fully anticipate the consequences of their activities, sociological researchers may never be able to avoid problems of ethical uncertainty.

(SEE ALSO: *Medical Sociology; Professions*)

REFERENCES

American Sociological Association 1989 *Code of Ethics.* Washington, D.C.: American Sociological Association.

Bellah, R. N. 1983 "The Ethical Aims of Sociological Inquiry." In N. Haan, R. N. Bellah, P. Rabinow, and E. M. Sullivan, eds., *Social Science as Moral Inquiry.* New York: Columbia University Press.

Bok, S. 1978 "Freedom and Risk." *Daedalus* 107 (Spring): 115–127.

Davison, W. P. 1967 "Foreign Policy." In P. F. Lazarsfeld, W. H. Sewell, and H. L. Wilensky, eds., *The Uses of Sociology.* New York: Basic Books.

Frankena, W. K. 1973 *Ethics.* Englewood Cliffs, N.J.: Prentice-Hall.

Humphreys, L. 1975 *Tearoom Trade: Impersonal Sex in Public Places.* Chicago: Aldine.

Rosenhan, D. L. 1973 "On Being Sane in Insane Places." *Science* 179 (January 1973): 250–258.

Shils, E. 1980 *The Calling of Sociology: Essays on the Pursuit of Learning.* Chicago: University of Chicago Press.

Sievers, B. 1983 "Believing in Social Science: The Ethics and Epistemology of Public Opinion Research." In N. Haan, R. N. Bella, P. Rabinow, and W. M. Sullivan, eds., *Social Science as Moral Inquiry.* New York: Columbia University Press.

Trend, M. G. 1980 "Applied Social Research and the Government: Notes on the Limits of Confidentiality." *Social Problems* 27:343–349.

Warwick, D. P. 1973 "*Tearoom Trade:* Ends and Means in Social Research." *The Hastings Center Studies* 1:27–38.

Wax, M. L., and J. Cassell 1981 "From Regulation to Reflection: Ethics in Social Research." *The American Sociologist* 16:224–229.

HOWARD P. GREENWALD

ETHNOCENTRISM *See* Ethnicity; Nationalism.

ETHNOMETHODOLOGY Ethnomethodology is a field of sociology that studies the common-sense resources, procedures, and practices through which the members of a culture produce and recognize mutually intelligible objects, events, and courses of action. The field emerged in the late 1960s in reaction to a range of sociological perspectives, most prominently structural functionalism, which treated conduct as causally determined by social structural factors. In contrast, ethnomethodology stressed that social actions and social organization are produced by knowledgeable agents who guide their actions by the use of situated common-sense reasoning. Rather than treating the achievement of social organization as a given from which the analysis of social structure could proceed, ethnomethodological research was directed at the hidden social processes underlying that achievement. The resulting research focus on the properties of common-sense knowledge and reasoning represents one strand of what has been termed the *cognitive revolution* in the social sciences. As a sociological perspective, however, ethnomethodology deals with the socially shared and publicly accountable nature of common-sense reasoning rather than with psychological aspects of cognitive processes. Its primary research stance has been descriptive and naturalistic rather than explanatory or experimental.

BACKGROUND AND DEVELOPMENT

The basic outlook of ethnomethodology was developed by Harold Garfinkel (1967a) during a twenty-year period spanning graduate research at Harvard, under the supervision of Talcott Parsons, and an extensive number of empirical investigations at the University of California at Los Angeles. Garfinkel's starting point was the vestigial treatment in the sociological analyses of the

1950s of how actors employ knowledge to understand and act in ordinary social contexts (Heritage 1984). With respect to the prevailing treatment of internalized norms as motivational "drivers" of behavior, Garfinkel noted that goal achievement requires actions based on knowledge of real circumstances and that where coordinated action is necessary knowledge must be socially shared. What is the character of this knowledge? How is it implemented and updated? By what means are shared and dynamically changing knowledge and understandings concerning actions and events sustained? Merely to raise these questions was to point to fundamental deficiencies in extant theories of action.

In developing answers to these questions, Garfinkel drew on the theoretical writings of the phenomenological sociologist Alfred Schutz (Schutz 1962–1966). Schutz observed that each actor approaches the social world with a "stock of knowledge at hand" made up of common-sense constructs and categories that are primarily social in origin. The actor's grasp of the real world is achieved through the use of these constructs which, Schutz stressed, are employed presuppositionally, dynamically, and in a taken-for-granted fashion. Schutz also observed that these constructs are held in typified form, that they are approximate and revisable, that actions are guided by a patchwork of "recipe knowledge," and that intersubjective understanding between actors who employ these constructs is a constructive achievement that is sustained on a moment-to-moment basis. Ethnomethodology took shape from Garfinkel's efforts to develop these theoretical observations into a program of empirical research.

A major component of these efforts took the form of the famous "breaching experiments" which were inspired by the earlier "incongruity experiments" pioneered by Asch and Bruner. The breaching experiments employed a variety of techniques to engineer drastic departures from ordinary expectations and understandings about social behavior. By "making trouble" in ordinary social situations, Garfinkel was able to demonstrate the centrality of taken-for-granted background understandings and contextual knowledge in persons' shared recognition of social events and in their management of coordinated social action. He concluded that understanding actions and events involves a circular process of reasoning in which part and whole, foreground and background, are dynamically adjusted to one another. Following Mannheim (1952), he termed this process *the documentary method of interpretation.* In this process, basic presuppositions and inferential procedures are employed to assemble linkages between an action or an event and aspects of its real-worldly and normative context. The character of the action is thus grasped as a "gestalt contexture" (Gurwitsch 1966) that is inferentially and procedurally created through the interlacing of action and context. Here, temporal aspects of actions and events assume a central significance (Garfinkel 1967a, pp. 38–42), not least because background and context have to be construed as dynamic in character. Within this analysis, presuppositions, tacit background knowledge, and contextual detail are the inescapable resources through which a grasp of events is achieved.

Garfinkel also showed (1967a, pp. 1–7, 18–24) that the description or coding of actions and events is an inherently approximate affair. The particulars of objects and events do not have a "one-to-one" fit with their less-specific representations in descriptions or codings. The fitting process therefore inevitably involves a range of approximating activities that Garfinkel terms *ad hoc practices* (Garfinkel 1967a, pp. 21–24). This finding is, of course, the inverse of his well-known observation that descriptions, actions, and so on have *indexical* properties: their sense is elaborated and particularized by their contextual location. An important consequence of these observations is that shared understandings cannot be engendered by a "common culture" through a simple matching of shared words or concepts, but rather can only be achieved constructively in a dynamic social process (Garfinkel 1967a, pp. 24–31). Similar conclusions apply to the social functioning of rules and norms.

In summary, Garfinkel's research indicates that every aspect of shared understandings of the social world depends on a multiplicity of tacit *methods of reasoning*. These methods are procedural in character, they are socially shared, and they are ceaselessly used during every waking moment to recognize ordinary social objects and events. A shared social world, with its immense variegation of social objects and events, is jointly constructed and recognized through, and consequently ultimately rests on, a shared base of procedures of practical reasoning that operationalize and particularize a body of inexact knowledge.

In addition to functioning as a base for understanding actions, these procedures also function as a resource for the production of actions. Actors tacitly draw on them so as to produce actions that will be *accountable*—that is, recognizable, describable—in context. Hence, shared methods of reasoning are publicly available on the surface of social life because the results of their application are inscribed in social action and interaction. As Garfinkel (1967a, p. 1) put it, "The activities whereby members produce and manage the settings of organized everyday affairs are identical with members' procedures for making these settings 'account-able'."

While the results of Garfinkel's experiments showed that the application of joint methods of reasoning is central to the production and understanding of social action, they also showed that the application of these methods is strongly "trusted" (Garfinkel 1963; 1967a, pp. 76–103). This "trust" has a normative background and is insisted on through a powerful moral rhetoric. Those whose actions could not be interpreted by means of this reasoning were met with anger and demands that they explain themselves. Garfinkel's experiments thus showed the underlying *morality* of practical reasoning and that the procedural basis of action and understanding is a part—perhaps the deepest part—of the moral order. Such a finding is consistent with the view that this procedural base is foundational to organized social life and that departures from it represent a primordial threat to the possibility of sociality itself.

CONTEMPORARY RESEARCH INITIATIVES

Garfinkel's writings have stimulated a wide range of commentary, theoretical reaction, and empirical initiatives. In what follows, only the latter will be described. Empirical research in ethnomethodology will be discussed under three headings: social structures as normal environments, the creation and maintenance of social institutions and social worlds, and studies of work.

SOCIAL STRUCTURES AS NORMAL ENVIRONMENTS

In his theoretical writings, Schutz (1962) argued that human consciousness is inherently typifying and that language is the central medium for the transmission of socially standardized typifications. In a number of his empirical studies, Garfinkel developed this idea in relation to social process, noting the ways in which common-sense reasoning is used—often within a moral idiom—to typify and normalize persons and events. A number of influential ethnomethodological studies have taken up this theme and focused on the ways in which participants may be actively or tacitly engaged in creating or reproducing a texture of normality in their everyday affairs.

Much of this work was concentrated in the fields of deviance and bureaucratic record keeping. This emphasis was far from accidental. In both fields, the participants are concerned with the administration of socially consequential categories and in both—with their indigenous preoccupation with classification and definition—normalizing processes are close to the surface of organizational life and are readily accessible to analysis. Pioneering studies in this area included Sudnow's (1965) analysis of "normal crimes" in which he showed that California lawyers employed models of "typical" offenders and offenses in plea-bargaining procedures that departed substantially from the provisions of the California criminal code. Zimmerman's (1969) work on record keeping in a public welfare agency showed that bureaucratic records utilized typifications of clients that could only be interpreted by reference to detailed background knowledge of the organization's procedures (see also Garfinkel 1967a, pp. 186–207). Wieder's (1974) work on a halfway house for paroled narcotics offenders showed that a "convict code" profoundly shaped how staff and inmates perceived events inside the institution—with disastrous consequences for its success.

Related works on deviance—by Cicourel (1968) on the policing of juveniles and by Atkinson (1978) on suicide—crystallized points of friction between ethnomethodology and more traditional approaches to the study of deviant behavior. Both studies examined the social processes underlying the classification of deviants. Each of them detailed a complex of common-sense considerations that enter into the determination of the nature of a deviant act and (in the case of juvenile offenders) the treatment of its perpetrator.

Cicourel's study showed that police treatment of juveniles was informed by a lay theory that posited a connection between juvenile offenses and the home background of the offender. Offenses by juveniles from "broken homes" were treated more seriously than offenses by those from other social backgrounds. In consequence, offenses by juveniles from broken homes were more likely to be officially reported, were more commonly the object of court proceedings, and had a greater tendency to result in custodial sentences. Police records, Cicourel showed, embodied a related process of idealization and typification in which case records, as they were developed through the system, became increasingly concise, selective, and consistent with the assumptions, objectives, and dispositions of the legal agencies. At the core of Cicourel's argument was the claim that the processing of juvenile offenders exhibits a circular process. Basic assumptions about the causal factors associated with juvenile crime were being used to normalize offenders and were built into the differential treatment of juveniles. From this point, these assumptions became built into police records and statistics and, finally, into social scientific treatments of the statistics which "recovered" the initial assumptions as valid explanations of juvenile crime.

Similar conclusions were reached by Atkinson (1978) in relation to the treatment of suicide. Drawing on the work of Douglas (1967), Atkinson argued that police conceptions of "typical suicides" profoundly influenced how particular cases of sudden death were investigated and treated. These conceptions not only influenced individual verdicts but, through the accumulation of verdicts, the official statistics of suicide. Atkinson concluded that sociological studies of suicide based on official statistics are unavoidably engaged in decoding the common-sense typifications of suicide that were constitutive in the recognition of, and verdicts on, individual cases and that accumulate in the statistical record.

In sum, ethnomethodological studies of typification in relation to deviance and organizational records have had both "constructive" and "deconstructive" moments. New and important social processes that inform the categorial activities of public agencies of various kinds have been uncovered. At the same time, these discoveries have challenged traditional sociological treatments of official statistics. The "deconstructive" conclusion that official statistics of social phenomena may be largely artifactual and, in many cases, can tell us only about the kinds of assumptions and practices that animate the relevant officials has provoked debates in the discipline that are unresolved to date.

THE CREATION AND MAINTENANCE OF SOCIAL INSTITUTIONS AND SOCIAL WORLDS

An important aspect of ethnomethodological theorizing is the notion that social institutions are sustained as real entities through vocabularies of accounts (or accounting frameworks) through which the events of the social world are recognized and acted on. Although this idea can be traced back to C. Wright Mills (1940), it found vivid expression in Garfinkel's (1967a, pp. 116–185) analysis of a transsexual individual; he used this as an occasion to investigate the nature of gender as (1) the achievement of a particular individual that (2) was made possible by the person's grasp of, and subscription to, appropriately "gendered" practices and accounting frameworks that are generally hidden or taken for granted by normally sexed people.

A number of subsequent studies have developed this preoccupation with the role of accounting frameworks, which are employed in the taken-for-granted production and reproduction of social institutions and social realities. An early and influential work was Wieder's (1974) study, mentioned before, of the role of the "convict code" in a halfway house for paroled narcotics offenders. Wieder showed the ways in which the code—which prescribed a range of activities hostile to staff members—functioned both as a fundamental way of seeing "what was going on" in the halfway house and as a resource that could be invoked in accounting for noncompliant conduct in interaction with staff members. Of particular interest is Wieder's finding that the "code" functioned in these ways among both offenders and staff despite their distinctive and conflicting perspectives on the activities of the halfway house. In transcending the formal power structure of the institution, the code was the predominant medium through which events were defined and acted on by all participants and, for this reason, served as a source of power and control for the offenders.

At a still more general level, Pollner (1974; 1987) has explored the ways in which a version of reality is socially sustained within a collectivity. Our sense of reality, he argues, is a social institution that is sustained by particular socially organized practices that he labels "mundane reason." Within this framework of practices, we start from the presumption that real-world objects and events are intersubjectively available as determinate, noncontradictory, and self-identical. That this presumption is actively sustained, he shows, emerges in environments—ranging from those of everyday events to more specialized contexts such as the law courts, mental hospitals, and research science—where witnesses disagree in their depiction of objects and events. In such contexts, Pollner observes, a range of procedures are invoked that discount one version of events and privilege the other. The invocation of such procedures sustains (by restoring or repairing) persons' belief in a single noncontradictory reality. "Explaining away" a witness's testimony—by, for example, arguing that he couldn't have seen what he saw, was not competent to do so, or was lying or even insane—functions in the way described by Evans-Pritchard (1937) as the "secondary elaboration of belief." Such "secondary elaborations," Pollner observes, are inevitably used in defense of the factual status of all versions of the world. They are the universal repair kit of the real. Pollner's work has stimulated a range of empirical studies in a variety of settings varying from mental hospitals (Coulter 1975) to a research community of biochemists (Gilbert and Mulkay 1984) and has strongly influenced the recent "discourse analysis" movement in social psychology.

STUDIES OF WORK

In recent years, Garfinkel and a number of collaborators have initiated a new program of ethnomethodological research known as "studies of work." This research represents an extension of earlier work into the practical task-oriented activities of jurors (Garfinkel 1967a, pp. 104–115) or coroners (Garfinkel 1967b), but in the more recent studies there is a deepening preoccupation with the technical competencies that manifest themselves in complex work domains.

The focus of the "studies of work" program is what Garfinkel has termed the *quiddities* or *just whatness* of occupational activities. Its challenge is to extend the descriptive power of social science to depict the embodied courses of practical reasoning and action that are involved in the technically competent performance of work tasks that range from playing jazz (Sudnow 1978) to proving a mathematical theorem (Livingston 1986) or laboratory work in brain science (Lynch 1985). Practitioners' descriptions of these activities characteristically omit the detailed texture of shoptalk and workbench practice that comprise recognizably competent work and inform the production of results (Lynch, Livingston, and Garfinkel 1983). Yet it is these taken-for-granted "backstage" details that practitioners attend to in assessing the competence, efficacy, and achievements of their peers. Thus, sociologically analyzable courses of action and reasoning can inform decisions about whether an astronomical observation (Garfinkel, Lynch, and Livingston 1981) or a neurological specimen (Lynch 1985) is evidence or artifact. The "studies of work" program undertakes the description and analysis of these practices. These studies, which echo Husserl's (1970) concern with the embeddedness of scientific findings in the practices of the mundane world (or *lebenswelt*), show the extent to which the objects of scientific inquiry are found and secured as demonstrable facts in and through embodied courses of inquiry.

CONCLUSION

Since its emergence in the 1960s, ethnomethodology has developed as a complex set of research initiatives that have raised topic areas, problems, and issues for analysis where none were previously seen to exist or perceived as relevant. A number of these initiatives have had a pronounced "deconstructive" dimension that has sometimes appeared iconoclastic or even nihilistic (Pollner 1991). Yet in its oscillation between constructive and deconstructive tendencies, ethnomethodology has been a significant site of theoretical and empirical innovation within sociology. It is exerting a continuing impact on the sensibility of the discipline. Finally, it has also had a wide-ranging influence on a spectrum of adjacent disciplines—such as linguistics (Levinson 1983) and artificial intelligence (Suchman 1987)—that are concerned with communication, action, and practical reasoning.

(SEE ALSO: *Case Studies; Conversion Analysis; Field Research Methods; Sociolinguistics*)

REFERENCES

Atkinson, J. M. 1978 *Discovering Suicide: Studies in the Social Organization of Sudden Death.* London: Macmillan.

Cicourel, A. V. 1968 *The Social Organization of Juvenile Justice.* New York: Wiley.

Coulter, J. 1975 "Perceptual Accounts and Interpretive Asymmetries." *Sociology* 9:385–396.

Douglas, J. 1967 *The Social Meanings of Suicide.* Princeton, N.J.: Princeton University Press.

Evans-Pritchard, E. E. 1937 *Witchcraft, Oracles and Magic among the Azande.* Oxford: Oxford University Press.

Garfinkel, H. 1963 "A Conception of, and Experiments with, 'Trust' as a Condition of Stable Concerted Actions." In O. J. Harvey, ed., *Motivation and Social Interaction.* New York: Ronald Press.

——— 1967a *Studies in Ethnomethodology.* Englewood Cliffs, N.J.: Prentice-Hall.

——— 1967b "Practical Sociological Reasoning: Some Features of the Work of the Los Angeles Suicide Prevention Center." In E. S. Schneidman, ed., *Essays in Self-Destruction.* New York: International Science Press.

Garfinkel, H., M. Lynch, and E. Livingston 1981 "The Work of a Discovering Science Construed with Materials from the Optically Discovered Pulsar." *Philosophy of the Social Sciences* 11:131–158.

Gilbert, G. N., and M. Mulkay 1984 *Opening Pandora's Box: A Sociological Analysis of Scientists' Discourse.* Cambridge: Cambridge University Press.

Gurwitsch, A. 1966 *Studies in Phenomenology and Psychology.* Evanston, Ill.: Northwestern University Press.

Heritage, J. 1984 *Garfinkel and Ethnomethodology.* Cambridge, England: Polity Press.

Husserl, E. 1970 *The Crisis of European Sciences and Transcendental Phenomenology: An Introduction to Phenomenological Philosophy.* Evanston, Ill.: Northwestern University Press.

Levinson, S. C. 1983 *Pragmatics.* Cambridge: Cambridge University Press.

Livingston, E. 1986 *Ethnomethodological Foundations of Mathematics.* London: Routledge.

Lynch, M. 1985 *Art and Artifact in Laboratory Science.* London: Routledge.

Lynch, M., E. Livingston, and H. Garfinkel 1983 "Temporal Order in Laboratory Work." In K. Knorr-Cetina and M. Mulkay, eds., *Science Observed.* London: Sage.

Mannheim, K. 1952 "On the Interpretation of *Weltanschauung.*" In Mannheim, *Essays on the Sociology of Knowledge,* trans. and ed. P. Kecskemeti. London: Routledge and Kegan Paul.

Mills, C. W. 1940 "Situated Actions and Vocabulaties of Motive." *American Sociological Review* 5:904–913.

Pollner, M. 1974 "Mundane Reasoning." *Philosophy of the Social Sciences* 4:35–54.

——— 1987 *Mundane Reason: Reality in Everyday and*

Sociological Discourse. Cambridge: Cambridge University Press.

——— 1991 "Left of Ethnomethodology." *American Sociological Review* 56.

Schutz, A. 1962 "Commonsense and Scientific Interpretation of Human Action." In A. Schutz, *Collected Papers.* Vol. 1, *The Problem of Social Reality,* ed. M. Natanson. The Hague: Martinus Nijhoff.

——— 1962–1966. *Collected Papers,* 3 vols. The Hague: Martinus Nijhoff.

Suchman, L. 1987 *Plans and Situated Action.* Cambridge: Cambridge University Press.

Sudnow, D. 1965 "Normal Crimes." *Social Problems* 12:255–276.

——— 1978 *Ways of the Hand.* Cambridge, Mass.: Harvard University Press.

Wieder, D. L. 1974 *Language and Social Reality.* The Hague: Mouton.

Zimmerman, D. 1969 "Record Keeping and the Intake Process in a Public Welfare Agency." In S. Wheeler, ed., *On Record: Files and Dossiers in American Life.* Beverly Hills, Calif.: Sage.

JOHN HERITAGE

EVALUATION RESEARCH Sociologists do not have a monopoly on the field of evaluation. Rather, it includes a broad range of applied research activities undertaken by persons trained in all of the social science disciplines and in various professional schools including education, management, public health, public administration, social welfare, and urban planning. Its place in sociology rests on the relatively large cadre of persons with training in the discipline who are engaged in evaluation activities, on the dependence of evaluators on more-or-less commonplace sociological research method, and on the inclusion of sociological and sociopsychological variables as independent, control, or outcome measures in most evaluations.

SCOPE OF THE FIELD

A simple definition that most persons in the field would embrace is that *evaluation research is the systematic application of social research procedures to assess the conceptualization, design, implementation, impact, and benefit-to-cost ratios of social intervention programs* (Rossi and Freeman 1989). Some, of course, would regard this definition as too broad, others as too narrow. It might be regarded as overly extensive, for example, by those who view *implementation research* as a separate field or a planning activity and not part of evaluation research (Schneider 1982). It would be considered overly constrained by persons who object to including the word *social* before *intervention programs,* since the same procedures are used to evaluate economic intervention programs as ones undertaken in business and industry to maximize productivity and to market various products. But the definition proposed more or less captures the work undertaken by the majority of sociologists who identify themselves as *evaluation researchers* or *evaluators* (the terms have lost whatever separate meanings they had and are now pretty much used interchangeably).

VERY BRIEF HISTORY OF EVALUATION RESEARCH

Although it is possible to trace the development of evaluation research back several centuries, it is essentially a modern invention (Freeman 1977). In part, the growth of evaluation research is a product of the changes in values that pretty much began after World War I and that gradually shifted primary responsibility for community members' welfare from family members, individual citizens, and local charities to government bureaucracies, foundations, and large-scale voluntary organizations. A strong case could be made that the burgeoning of social programs, particularly since World War II—in education, income security and job training, medical and mental-health care, public safety and criminal justice, social services, and housing and urban development, to name some of the most important areas—underlies the rapid development of the evaluation field (Cronbach and associates 1980).

But it is also true that the evaluation research field was spawned at the same time that sociology and the other social sciences were making a place for themselves in colleges and universities as legitimate intellectual endeavors, when methods of social research—particularly sample surveys, field experiments, and regression analyses—were rapidly developing and being taught in graduate departments, and when support for social research investigations began to be forthcoming from government and national foundations. Public health and industrial productivity experiments during the 1930s and employment programs of the federal government to mitigate somewhat the Great Depression, as well as the scarcity of jobs in academia, stimulated social researchers to go into applied work.

Then came World War II, and applied social research flourished including evaluations of morale building, health enhancement, work productivity, and propaganda programs (Williams 1989). But the boom period in evaluation activities arrived after World War II. In a comparatively short number of years, programs to assist foreign nations, particularly the developing ones, were widely implemented, and initiatives designed to reduce poverty, decrease crime, improve public and higher education, and prevent and manage disease became the commitment of the federal government and many state and local public agencies (Levine, Solomon, and Hellstern 1981). These efforts could hardly be designed, implemented, and managed, let alone evaluated in any sense of the term, solely by the political appointees who formerly occupied most of the positions in the executive branches of the federal, state, and local governments. Thus, all levels of government, as well as foundations and voluntary groups, turned to persons trained in the social science and professional schools with curricula rooted in these disciplines to get the work done.

CURRENT STATUS OF THE FIELD

Evaluation research is no longer the growth industry it was in the 1960s and 1970s (Haveman 1987). Rather, it is an accepted component of social program development and implementation and is undertaken as part of both established and innovative human service activities. Sponsors and staffs of programs, with varying degrees of enthusiasm, look to evaluations to implement and judge the performance and utility of social programs, and the various stakeholders in these programs have become increasingly sophisticated about using evaluations in their advocate and protagonist roles. Moreover, while earlier evaluations were viewed mainly as a tool of "the left," that is no longer the case. While the programs advocated differ today from those of the Great Society days, and the substantive research questions are different, resource constraints continue, and, if anything, there is increased scrutiny of both the conduct and results of programs. Consequently, whether conservatives or liberals are in political control, evaluation activities continue to receive a fair degree of support (Freeman 1983).

Historically, and to this day, there has been a fundamental and unresolved issue that confronts all evaluators, particularly those trained in sociology and kindred disciplines. On the one hand, there continue to be advocates of "scientific evaluations," associated perhaps most often with the name of Donald Campbell (1969), who sought to promote an "experimenting society." On the other, there are the "realists," who argue that research and evaluation are qualitatively different. Perhaps the most important figure on this side of the debate is Lee Cronbach (Cronbach and associates 1980).

The former prefer theory-grounded work and press for randomized experiments, although they are inclined to accept quasi-experiments in which experimental and comparison groups are adjusted or matched and time-series analyses when true experiments are not possible (Cook and Campbell 1979). The latter see themselves much more as social-change agents themselves or contractors working for such persons and groups and are inclined to use a "good enough" and not the "gold" standard in undertaking evaluation activities and judging the products of others (Cronbach 1982). In the training of social science students, scientific evaluations are usually emphasized. In fact, however, most evaluations conducted for policy and management purposes are hardly perfect studies at best, but then again neither are most so-called basic research studies.

There is another critical difference between evaluation research and most other sociological investigations including most of applied sociology. It is the pervasiveness of politics in evaluation activities (Chelimsky 1987). Evaluators are unavoidably engaged in a political process, except when simply "crunching numbers" for others to use. Thus, it is essential that they be astute about the parameters and features of the "policy space" in which they work. In brief, the evaluation researcher must have not only substantive knowledge of the etiology and amelioration of social problem areas and an extensive repertoire of research methods but also a temperament to cope with, and a sensitivity to successfully negotiate, the political areas in which he or she must become involved.

WORK OF EVALUATORS

Evaluators are involved in four sets of tasks, as discussed next.

Diagnosing Human and Social Problems That Require Communal Action. Sociologists in general, not just those engaged in program evaluation, expend considerable effort in identifying social problems, in estimating their incidence and prevalence, and in forecasting their growth trajectories (Berk and Rossi 1976). Obviously these activities are essential for program development, implementation, and assessment of impact. However, the evaluator needs to undertake these tasks so that the program staff can identify the target population of the intervention, estimate its size and characteristics, and plan the resources required in the future to extend the program if it proves efficacious and cost beneficial. For example, in order for a program to reduce alcohol addiction to be well planned and carried out, it is necessary to define the problem so that the alcohol-dependent person can be distinguished from the recreational drinker. Also, it is necessary to know the number of alcoholics currently in the population and the number of new cases that will arise during, say, the next five years and to specify indicators that allow the identification of the population at risk.

Planning, Refining, and Revising Intervention Programs. This set of tasks includes specifying intervention programs' objectives in measurable terms, developing an intervention model or *causal theory* that can guide the development of the actual intervention, defining the elements of the program, designing and testing the delivery system for providing the services to the targets, and assuring that the intervention is evaluable in terms of impact and possibly the ratio of benefits to costs (Wholey 1979). Take this simple example: Staff of a program to reduce crime by assigning automobiles to police for their personal use might regard a reduction in reports of crime, either to the police or on victimization surveys, as the measurable objective of the program; have as the intervention model the idea that visibility of police riding in their cars acts as a deterrent to crime; define the targets as the one-quarter of the census tracts with the highest crime rates in or near which sufficient police resided; and value being able to undertake the intervention in a random subset of these tracts.

Monitoring Program Implementation. There are two major monitoring tasks. The first is to measure by observation, treatment records, surveys, or other means whether or not the program is delivered as specified in its design. The second is to estimate the extent to which the appropriate targets are being served (Raizen and Rossi 1981). In this respect, the concern is with *undercoverage,* that is, the extent to which appropriate targets are served, and *overcoverage,* the extent to which inappropriate targets are served. For example, a program to increase the educational skills of children whose reading and mathematics performance is marginal by providing one hour of instruction to each of them should be monitored to make certain that each child receives one hour of appropriate instruction (and is not, for example, playing games on the computer). Moreover, it is necessary to be sure that marginal-scoring children have not been overlooked in selecting targets and that children at the top of the class have been enrolled.

Assessing Program Efficacy and Efficiency. These two activities are the glamorous aspects of evaluation research. Program impact, or efficacy, studies focus on whether or not a program makes a difference, compared with either one or more competing programs or no program at all. Efficiency analyses refer to contrasting the costs of programs with their outcomes (Rossi and Freeman 1989). Cost-benefit analyses express both inputs and outputs in monetary terms, and they have the advantage of being able to compare programs in different areas because a common unit is used, for example dollars. Cost-effectiveness analyses use monetary units in expressing program inputs but substantive measures in expressing outcomes, such as number of arrests and mortality rates. They are preferred whenever it is problematic to convert outcome measures into dollars.

A wide range of procedures is used to measure efficacy. The underlying framework for most procedures to measure program impact is the randomized experiment, in which two or more groups are contrasted in terms of outcome, at least one of which is subject to an intervention, or treatment, program (Riecken and Boruch 1974). While such true experiments are more common than many social researchers imagine, even many programs that are potentially amenable to such designs cannot be so evaluated. Sometimes the administrative problems of assigning targets interfere, other times stakeholders raise issues about denying services, and in many instances targets either do not cooperate from the outset or depart from their assigned groups in systematically different ways during the conduct of the evaluation.

Consequently, many evaluations that began as randomized experiments end up as *quasi-experiments;* others are designed as quasi-experiments from the outset because of the difficulties of randomization (Cook and Campbell 1979). Commonly now, quasi-experiments adjust differences between experimental and comparison groups by multivariate statistical procedures. Earlier matching procedures, which were used more than currently, were those in which targets in treatment and nontreatment groups were paired.

For example, the impact of a videotape to train physicians in taking a sexual history, in order to identify persons at high risk of acquiring AIDS, might be studied by a randomized experiment. The experimental group would receive the tape on taking a sexual history, and the comparison group would receive a tape containing a "week in review in medicine" program. But if, say, one-third of the experimental and two-fifths of the comparison group either did not want to view the tape or mislaid it, a quasi-experimental analysis would be undertaken. Without an analysis that sought to adjust for the presumed selection biases, given the differential viewing rates, it would be difficult to argue that the two groups were similar in relevant characteristics that might impinge on the outcome measures (Lewis et al. 1986).

A variety of other procedures are also employed, including *time-series analyses,* in which changes in experimental and, ideally, comparison groups are tracked over a sufficient time with enough observation points so that, with adjustments for group differences, fairly firm estimates of impact can be made. Generally, efforts to assess impact by means of time series evaluations involve economists, for few other social researchers are familiar with this family of analytical methods (McCleary and Hay 1980). A typical study would be one designed to obtain information on the number of murders and serious woundings of persons that occurred month by month for, say, five years prior to the introduction of a stiff gun registration law and for three years after it was in place. One would expect that, taking seasonal variations and population changes into account, it should be possible to arrive at a reasonable conclusion about the law's impact.

In addition, there are "softer" approaches employed such as measuring within-treatment group changes before and after a program is implemented and having observers with varying degrees of expertise report on results and estimate what they think might have occurred if there had been no program. At the extreme, in this respect, are evaluators who promote *qualitative evaluations* that range from field research efforts to phenomenological and ethnomethodological inquiries. In general, however, highly quantitative studies that use an experimental framework are the most highly regarded for obtaining firm estimates of program impact.

UTILIZATION OF EVALUATIONS

Evaluators tend to be preoccupied, some say overly so, with the utilization of their work. An important distinction made in this respect is immediate, direct use of findings, compared with "conceptual," later utilization (Leviton and Hughes 1981). As evaluators have gained more experience in relating to policymakers and program staffs, it has become clear that decisions are rarely made on a zero-sum basis and that the decision-making process is a complex one in which there is a large number of inputs that vie for attention. Most of the recent efforts to understand and gauge the utility of evaluations provide evidence of both the direct and the conceptual utility of many evaluations. Indeed, the demonstrated utility of evaluations accounts for the support they receive from the public and private sectors (Leviton and Boruch 1983).

(SEE ALSO: *Applied Sociology; Quasi-Experimental Research Designs; Scientific Method*)

REFERENCES

Berk, Richard A., and Peter H. Rossi 1976 "Doing Good or Worse: Evaluation Research Politically Re-Examined." *Social Problems* 23:337–349.

Campbell, Donald T. 1969 "Reforms as Experiments." *American Psychologist* 24:409–429.

Chelimsky, E. 1987 "The Politics of Program Evaluation." *Society* 25(1):24–32.

Cook, T. D., and D. T. Campbell 1979 *Quasi-Experimentation Design and Analysis Issues for Field Settings.* Skokie, Ill.: Rand McNally.

Cronbach, L. J. 1982 *Designing Evaluations of Educational and Social Programs.* San Francisco: Jossey-Bass.

———, and associates 1980 *Toward Reform of Program Evaluation.* San Francisco: Jossey-Bass.

Freeman, Howard E. 1977 "The Present Status of Evaluation Research." In M. A. Guttentag and S. Saar, eds., *Evaluation Studies Review Annual,* Vol. 2, pp. 17–51. Beverly Hills, Calif.: Sage.

Freeman, Howard E. 1983 "A Federal Evaluation Agenda for the 1980s: Some Speculations and Suggestions." *Educational Evaluation and Policy Analysis* 5:185–194.

Haveman, Robert H. 1987 "Policy Analysis and Evaluation Research after Twenty Years." *Policy Studies Journal* 16:191–218.

Levine, R. A., M. A. Solomon, and G. M. Hellstern, eds. 1981 *Evaluation Research and Practice: Comparative and International Perspectives.* Beverly Hills, Calif.: Sage.

Leviton, L. C., and R. F. Boruch 1983 "Contributions of Evaluations to Educational Programs." *Evaluation Review* 7:563–599.

Leviton, L. C., and E. F. X. Hughes 1981 "Research on the Utilization of Evaluations: A Review and Synthesis." *Evaluation Review* 5:525–548.

Lewis, C. E., et al. 1987 "AIDS-Related Competence of California's Primary Care Physicians." *American Journal of Public Health* 77:795–799.

McCleary, R., and R. Hay, Jr. 1980 *Applied Time Series Analysis for the Social Sciences.* Beverly Hills, Calif.: Sage.

Raizen, S. A., and P. H. Rossi 1981 *Program Evaluation in Education: When? How? To What Ends?* Washington, D.C.: National Academy Press.

Riecken, H. W., and R. F. Boruch, eds. 1974 *Social Experimentation: A Method for Planning and Evaluating Social Intervention.* New York: Academic Press.

Rossi, Peter H., and Howard E. Freeman 1989 *Evaluation: A Systematic Approach,* 4th ed. Newbury Park, Calif.: Sage.

Schneider, A. L. 1982 "Studying Policy Implementation." *Evaluation Review* 6:715–730.

Wholey, J. S. 1979. *Evaluation: Promise and Performance.* Washington, D.C.: Urban Institute.

Williams, Robin M. 1989 "The American Soldier: An Assessment, Several Wars Later." *Public Opinion Quarterly* 53:155–174.

HOWARD E. FREEMAN

EVENT HISTORY ANALYSIS Event history analysis is a collection of statistical methods for the analysis of longitudinal data on the occurrence and timing of events. These methods have become quite popular in sociology during the last decade, with applications to such diverse events as divorces (Bennett, Blanc, and Bloom 1988), births (Kallan and Udry 1986), deaths (Moore and Hayward 1990), job changes (Carroll and Mayer 1986), organizational foundings (Halliday, Powell, and Granfors 1987), migrations (Baydar, White, Simkins, and Babakol 1990), and friendship choices (Hallinan and Williams 1987). Although event history methods have been developed and utilized by statistical practitioners in a variety of discplines, the term *event history analysis* is used primarily in sociology and closely allied disciplines. Elsewhere the methodology is known as survival analysis (biomedicine), failure-time analysis (engineering), or duration analysis (economics). Introductory treatments for social scientists can be found in Teachman (1983), Allison (1984), Tuma and Hannan (1984), Kiefer (1988), and Blossfeld, Hamerle, and Mayer (1989). For a biostatistical point of view, see Lawless (1982) or Cox and Oakes (1984).

EVENT HISTORY DATA

The first requirement for an event history analysis is event history data. An event history is simply a longitudinal record of when events occurred for an individual or a sample of individuals. For example, an event history might be constructed by asking a sample of people to report the dates of any past changes in marital status. If the objective is a causal analysis, the event history should also include information on explanatory variables. Some of these, like sex, will be constant over time, while others, like income, will vary. If the timing of each event is known with considerable precision (as in the case of exact dates of marriages), the data are called continuous-time data. Frequently, however, events are known only to have occurred within some relatively large interval of time, for example, the year of a marriage. These are referred to as discrete-time data or grouped data.

Event history data are often contrasted with panel data, in which the individual's status is known only at a set of fixed points in time (although panel data collected at frequent intervals can often be treated as discrete-time event history data). Event history data have two relative advantages, both of which are a consequence of the more complete and detailed information. The first advantage is an increase in statistical precision. The second advantage is an enhanced capacity to disentangle causal orderings. While this capacity is by no means unequivocal, the combination of event history data and event history analysis is perhaps the best available nonexperimental methodology for studying causal relationships.

PROBLEMS WITH CONVENTIONAL METHODS

Despite the enormous potential of event history data, they typically possess two characteristics that make conventional statistical methods highly unsuitable. Censoring is the most common problem. Suppose, for example, that the aim is to study the causes of divorce. The sample might consist of a number of married couples who are followed for the first ten years of marriage. For the couples who get divorced, the timing of the divorce is the principal variable of interest. But many of the couples will not get divorced during this interval, and these cases are called censored. The problem is to combine the data on timing with the data on occurrence and nonoccurrence in a statistically consistent fashion. Ad hoc methods like excluding the censored cases or assigning the maximum length of time observed can lead to large biases or loss of precision.

The second problem is time-varying explanatory variables (also known as time-dependent covariates). Suppose, in the divorce example, that the aim is to test the hypothesis that as the number of children increases, the likelihood of divorce goes down. If there were no censored cases, one might be tempted to regress the length of the marriage on the number of children at the end of the marriage. But longer marriages are likely to have produced more children simply because more time is available to have them. A correct test of the causal hypothesis requires an entirely different method.

One method for dealing with the censoring problem has been around since the seventeenth century and is still widely used: the life table. The life table is one example of a variety of methods that are concerned primarily with estimating the distribution of event times without regard for the effects of explanatory variables. For a comprehensive survey of such methods, see Elandt-Johnson and Johnson (1980). On the other hand, most recent interest in event history methods in sociology has centered on regression methods, in which the aim is to estimate a model predicting the occurrence of events based on a set of explanatory variables. The remainder of this article will focus on regression methods.

ACCELERATED FAILURE TIME MODELS

Suppose that the events are first marriages, and the sample consists of women who are interviewed at age twenty-five. From each woman ($i = 1, \ldots n$), we learn her age in days at the time of the marriage, denoted by T_i. For women who still were not married at age twenty-five (the censored cases), T_i^* is their age in days at the time of the interview. We also have data on a set of explanatory variables $x_{i1}, \ldots, x_{ik}$. For the moment, let us assume that none of these variables changes over time.

One class of models that is appropriate for data like these is the accelerated failure time (AFT) model. The general formulation is shown in equation 1.

$$\log T_i = \beta_0 + \beta_1 x_{i1} + \ldots + \beta_k x_{ik} + \epsilon_i \qquad (1)$$

The purpose in taking the logarithm on the left-hand side is to ensure that T_i is always greater than 0. Specific submodels are obtained by choosing particular distributions for the random disturbance ϵ_i. The most common distributions are normal, extreme-value, logistic, and log-gamma. These imply that T_i has distributions that are, respectively, lognormal, Weibull, log-logistic, and gamma, which are the names usually given to these models. The disturbance ϵ_i is assumed to be independent of the x's and to have constant variance.

If there are no censored data, these models can be estimated easily by ordinary least squares regression of log T on the x's. The resulting estimators are unbiased and efficient. But the presence of censored data requires something different. The standard approach is maximum likelihood, which combines the censored and uncensored data in an optimal fashion. Maximum likelihood estimation for these models is now widely available in several statistical packages.

PROPORTIONAL HAZARDS MODELS

A second class of regression models for continuous-time data is the proportional hazards (PH) model. To explain this model, it is first necessary to define the hazard function, denoted by $h(t)$, which is the fundamental dependent variable. Let $P(t, t+s)$ be the conditional probability that an event occurs in the time interval $(t, t+s)$, given that it has not already occurred prior to t. To get the hazard function, we divide this probability by the length of the interval s and take the limit as s goes to 0 (equation 2).

$$h(t) = \lim_{s \to 0} \frac{P(t, t+s)}{s} \qquad (2)$$

Other common symbols for the hazard function are $r(t)$ and $\lambda(t)$. The hazard may be regarded as the instantaneous likelihood that an event will occur at exactly time t. It is not a probability, however, since it may be greater than 1.0 (although never less than zero). If $h(t)$ has a constant value c, it can be interpreted as the expected number of events in a one-unit interval of time. Alternatively, $1/c$ is the expected length of time until the next event. Like a probability (from which it is derived), the hazard is never directly observed. Nevertheless, it governs both the occurrence and timing of events, and models formulated in terms of the hazard may be estimated from observed data.

The general proportional hazards model is given in equation 3,

$$\log h_i(t) = \alpha(t) + \beta_1 x_{i1} + \ldots + \beta_k x_{ik} \quad (3)$$

where $\alpha(t)$ may be any function of time. It is called the proportional hazards model because the ratio of the hazards for any two individuals is a constant over time. Notice that, unlike the AFT model, there is no disturbance term in this equation. That does not mean that the model is deterministic, however, because there is random variation in the relationship between $h(t)$ and the observed occurrence and timing of events.

Different versions of the PH model are obtained by choosing specific forms for $\alpha(t)$. For example, the Gompertz model sets $\alpha(t) = \alpha_0 + \alpha_1 t$, which says that the hazard is an increasing (or decreasing) function of time. Similarly, the Weibull model has $\alpha(t) = \alpha_0 + \alpha_1 \log t$. (The Weibull model is the only model that is a member of both the AFT class and the PH class.) The exponential model—a special case of both the Weibull and the Gompertz—sets $\alpha(t) = \alpha$, a constant over time. For any specific member of the PH class, maximum likelihood is the standard approach to estimation.

In a path-breaking paper, the British statistician David Cox (1972) showed how the PH model could be estimated without choosing a specific functional form for $\alpha(t)$, using a method known as partial likelihood. This method is very much like maximum likelihood, except that only a part of the likelihood function is maximized. The partial likelihood method has since become extremely popular because, although some precision is sacrificed, the resulting estimates are much more robust. Computer programs that implement this method are now widely available.

The partial likelihood method also allows one easily to introduce time-varying explanatory variables. For example, suppose that the hazard for first marriage is thought to depend both on race (x_1) and income (x_2). A suitable PH model might be the model shown in equation 4,

$$\log h(t) = \alpha(t) + \beta_1 x_1 + \beta_2 x_2(t) \quad (4)$$

which says that the hazard at time t depends on income at time t, on race, and on time itself. If longitudinal data on income are available, models like this can be estimated in a straightforward fashion with the partial likelihood method.

MULTIPLE KINDS OF EVENTS

To this point, it has been assumed that all events are to be treated alike. In many applications, however, there is a compelling need to distinguish among two or more types of events. For example, if the events of interest are job terminations, one might expect that explanatory variables would have vastly different effects on voluntary and involuntary terminations. The statistical analysis should take this into account.

All of the methods already discussed can be easily applied to multiple kinds of events. In doing an analysis for one kind of event, one simply treats other kinds of events as though the individual were censored at the time when the event occurred, a method known as "competing risks." Thus, no additional methodology is required to handle this situation.

An alternative approach is to estimate a single event history model for the timing of events without distinguishing different event types. Then, after eliminating all the censored cases, one estimates a logit regression model for the determinants of the type of event. This method of analysis is most appropriate when the different kinds of events are functionally alternative ways of achieving a single objective.

REPEATED EVENTS

The discussion so far has presumed that each individual experiences no more than one event. Obviously, however, such events as child births, job changes, arrests, and car purchases can occur multiple times over the life of an individual. The methods already described have been applied routinely to cases of repeated events, taking either of two alternative approaches. One approach is to do a separate analysis for each successive event.

For example, one event history model is estimated for the birth of the first child, a second model is estimated for the birth of the second child, and so on. The alternative approach is to break each individual's event history into a set of intervals between events, treat each of these intervals as a distinct observation, and then pool all the intervals into a single analysis.

Neither of these alternatives is entirely satisfactory. The sequential analysis is rather tedious, wastes information if the process is invariant across the sequence, and is prone to selection biases for later events in the sequence. The pooled analysis, on the other hand, presumes that the process really is invariant across the sequence and that the multiple intervals for a single individual are independent, both questionable assumptions. Several new methods have been proposed for the analysis of repeated events (Yamaguchi 1986), but these are either impractical, very limited in scope, or not yet embodied in software. The most promising innovation is the recently developed marginal likelihood method of Wei, Lin, and Weissfeld (1989), but currently available software for this method leaves much to be desired.

DISCRETE-TIME METHODS

When event times are measured coarsely, the continuous-time methods already discussed may yield somewhat biased estimates. In such cases, methods specifically designed for discrete-time data are more appropriate (Allison 1982). Moreover, such methods are easily employed and are particularly attractive for handling large numbers of time-varying explanatory variables.

Suppose that the time scale is divided into a set of equal intervals, indexed by $t = 1, 2, 3, \ldots$. The discrete-time analog of the hazard function, denoted by P_t, is the conditional probability that an event occurs in interval t, given that it has not occurred prior to t. A popular model for expressing the dependence of P_t on explanatory variables is the logit model (equation 5),

$$\log\left[\frac{P_{it}}{1-P_{it}}\right] = \alpha_t + \beta_1 x_{it1} + \ldots + \beta_k x_{itk} \qquad (5)$$

in which the subscript on α_t indicates that the intercept may differ for each interval of time. Similarly, the explanatory variables may take on different values at each interval of time. This model can be estimated by the method of maximum likelihood, using the following computational strategy:

1. Break each individual's event history into a set of discrete time units (e.g., person-years).
2. Create a dependent variable that has a value of 1 for time units in which events occurred, otherwise 0. Explanatory variables are assigned whatever values they had at the beginning of the time unit.
3. Pool all of these time units, and estimate a logistic (logit) regression model using a standard maximum likelihood logit program.

Other models and computational methods are also available for the discrete-time case. These methods can be easily extended to allow for multiple kinds of events and repeated events.

(SEE ALSO: *Comparative Historical Analysis; Longitudinal Research*)

REFERENCES

Allison, Paul D. 1982 "Discrete Time Methods for the Analysis of Event Histories." In Samuel Leinhardt, ed., *Sociological Methodology 1982*. San Francisco: Jossey-Bass.

——— 1984 *Event History Analysis*. Beverly Hills, Calif.: Sage.

Baydar, Nazli, Michael J. White, Charles Simkins, and Ozer Babakol 1990 "Effects of Agricultural Development Policies on Migration in Peninsular Malaysia." *Demography* 27:97-109.

Bennett, Neil G., Ann Klimas Blanc, and David E. Bloom 1988 "Commitment and the Modern Union: Assessing the Link between Premarital Cohabitation and Subsequent Marital Stability." *American Sociological Review* 53:127–138.

Blossfeld, Hans-Peter, Alfred Hamerle, and Karl Ulrich Mayer 1989 *Event History Analysis*. Hillsdale, N.J.: Erlbaum.

Carroll, Glenn R., and Karl Ulrich Mayer 1986 "Job-shift Patterns in the Federal Republic of Germany: The Effects of Social Class, Industrial Sector, and Organizational Size." *American Sociological Review* 51:323–341.

Cox, David R. 1972 "Regression Models and Life Tables." *Journal of the Royal Statistical Society,* series B, 34:187–202.

———, and D. Oakes 1984 *Analysis of Survival Data.* London: Chapman and Hall.

Elandt-Johnson, R. C., and N. L. Johnson 1980 *Survival Models and Data Analysis.* New York: Wiley.

Halliday, Terence C., Michael J. Powell, and Mark W. Granfors 1987 "Minimalist Organizations: Vital Events in State Bar Associations, 1870–1930." *American Sociological Review* 52:456–471.

Hallinan, Maureen, and Richard A. Williams 1987 "The Stability of Students' Interracial Friendships." *American Sociological Review* 52:653–664.

Kallan, Jeffrey, and J. R. Udry 1986 "The Determinants of Effective Fecundability Based on the First Birth Interval." *Demography* 23:53–66.

Kiefer, Nicholas M. 1988 "Economic Duration Data and Hazard Functions." *Journal of Economic Literature* 26:646–679.

Lawless, J. F. 1982 *Statistical Models and Methods for Lifetime Data.* New York: Wiley.

McLanahan, Sara S. 1988 "Family Structure and Dependency: Early Transitions to Female Household Headship." *Demography* 25:1–16.

Moore, David E., and Mark D. Hayward 1990 "Occupational Careers and Mortality of Elderly Men." *Demography* 27:31–53.

Teachman, Jay D. 1983 "Analyzing Social Processes: Life Tables and Proportional Hazards Models." *Social Science Research* 12:263–301.

Tuma, Nancy Brandon, and Michael T. Hannan 1984 *Social Dynamics: Models and Methods.* Orlando, Fla.: Academic Press.

Wei, L. J., D.Y. Lin, and L. Weissfeld 1989 "Regression Analysis of Multivariate Incomplete Failure Time Data by Modeling Marginal Distributions." *Journal of the American Statistical Association* 84:1065–1073.

Yamaguchi, Kazuo 1986 "Alternative Approaches to Unobserved Heterogeneity in the Analysis of Repeated Events." In Nancy Brandon Tuma, ed., *Sociological Methodology 1986.* Washington, D.C.: American Sociological Association.

PAUL D. ALLISON

EVOLUTION: BIOLOGICAL, SOCIAL, CULTURAL The diverse forms of life on earth have apparently emerged from a common source through a process of evolution that has the following characteristics:

1. The course of evolution does not always proceed along a straight path, for example, from simple to complex forms. Instead, it can meander like a stream, directed largely by environmental circumstances, and occasionally it appears to reverse direction in certain respects. Our own distant ancestors, for instance, became adapted to life in the trees, but our more recent ancestors readapted to living on the ground. When the course of evolution does reverse direction, it generally does so with respect to comparatively few features only; a complex evolutionary development never comes close to being totally reversed. Thus, we humans retain various characteristics evolved earlier in connection with life in the trees: stereoscopic vision, visual acuity, reduced sense of smell, hands adapted for grasping, and so forth.

2. Different groups of organisms sometimes evolve in similar directions in certain respects when exposed to similar environmental conditions. Thus, whales—descendants of mammals that lived on land—acquired fishlike shapes when they adapted to life in the water.

3. However, parallelism in evolutionary development generally remains limited: Different evolutionary lines do not come close to "merging." Whales, even though living in the ocean and acquiring fishlike shapes, retain basic anatomical and physiological features of mammals, quite different from those of fish.

The life-cycle of an individual human involves fixed stages (infancy, childhood, adolescence, adulthood, old age) that represent an unfolding of innate potentialities, that millions of people pass through, and that culminate in inevitable death. The evolution of a new biological species, by contrast, is a unique historical development involving movement in directions shaped primarily in response to environmental pressures, without any inevitable "death" or other predetermined end.

A "Lamarckian" evolutionary process (named, somewhat inappropriately, after Jean Baptiste Lamarck, 1744–1829) would involve inheritance of acquired characteristics. Thus, if evolution followed the Lamarckian pattern, giraffes might have acquired their long necks because in each generation necks were stretched (perhaps to obtain food high up in trees or to detect approaching enemies) and because the effect of each generation's stretching tended to be inherited by the generation that followed. However, Lamarckian ideas were found to be invalid long ago.

An alternative approach developed by Charles Darwin (1859) and others does not assume that acquired characteristics (such as effects of neck-stretching) are inherited. Rather, it assumes (1) random or randomlike variation among the offspring in each generation (with some giraffes happening by chance to have longer necks than others); (2) natural selection, involving tendencies for certain variants (longer-necked giraffes) to survive and reproduce more than others; and (3) preservation through inheritance of the effects of natural selection (longer-necked giraffes tending to have similarly long-necked offspring, although—as suggested above—there would still be some random variation among these offspring with respect to neck length).

Darwinian ideas challenged traditional Christian religious beliefs by suggesting (1) that humans are descended from more primitive creatures and, ultimately, from elementary life forms; (2) that our evolution was basically an unplanned outcome of diverse environmental pressures rather than something planned in advance; and (3) that the earth is old enough for evolutionary processes to have had time to produce the variety and complexity of life forms that we actually find. Although still resisted today by many on religious grounds, Darwinian theory ultimately came to be generally accepted by biologists, with important modifications and certain disagreements about details, and in combination with new knowledge in other areas of biology and other scientific disciplines that was not available to Darwin (see Gould 1982; Mayr 1982, pp. 299–627; and Stebbins and Ayala 1985).

In the late nineteenth and early twentieth centuries, evolutionary concepts and associated slogans such as "survival of the fittest" came to provide a rationale for a "social Darwinist" social policy. Various business, political, ideological, and military leaders in several countries, along with some scholars in several disciplines (including the sociologists Herbert Spencer and William Graham Sumner), emphasized the importance of the struggle for survival in maintaining a hardy population and a vigorous society and opposed social welfare measures that they thought would encourage "unfit" people to reproduce. Supporters of this approach differed among themselves in several ways: Some emphasized individual struggle, others group (e.g., racial or national) struggle; some emphasized nonviolent means (e.g., economic competition); and others emphasized armed conflict (see Hofstadter 1955).

The emergence of evolutionary theory in biology was also accompanied by the emergence of theories about human societal change that came to be called "evolutionary," although this label may be misleading. The idea that human society evolves from simple beginnings through comparatively fixed stages came to be commonly accepted in the nineteenth century, although different theorists had different conceptions of what these stages were. Examples include analyses of transitions from theological to metaphysical and then "positivistic" thought styles (Comte 1875); from savagery to barbarism and finally to civilization (Morgan 1877); from tribalism to slavery, feudalism, capitalism, and then communism (Marx and Engels 1947, first published 1846); and from simple to compounded, doubly compounded, and then triply compounded societies (Spencer 1967, first published 1885-1886).

When societies, cultures, or civilizations are said to pass from childhood to adulthood and then to old age, or are said to grow and then decline, there is an analogy not with the evolution of a species but rather with the human life-cycle, as illustrated in the works of Oswald Spengler and Arnold J. Toynbee. Nineteenth-century "social-evolutionary" theories departed from the life-cycle model in that they did not involve the idea of decline or old age followed by death as the end point of a cycle. Quite the opposite: The trends they described tended to culminate in triumphant achievements: "positivism" (Comte), "civilization" (Morgan), "communism" (Marx and Engels), and societies "compounded" many times (Spencer). In this one respect, but only in this respect, these theories resembled the bioevolutionary model: Biological species do not have to become extinct—even though many of them actually do—in the same sense in which individuals have to die. However, these theories nevertheless reflect a life-cycle model insofar as they involve one society after another following essentially the same pattern of development, just as one infant after another follows the same general route to adulthood. And, they do not appear to involve, in any major way, the evolutionary mechanisms of random variation and selection. In fact, they are primarily theories of progress, not of evolution in any sense that biologists would recognize, regardless of the "evolutionary" label commonly attached to them (Nisbet 1969).

The social-evolutionary idea fell into disfavor around the turn of the century but was revived several decades later, for example, with Talcott Parsons's analysis of primitive, intermediate, and modern societies (1977), and Lenski and Lenski's (1982) analysis of transitions from hunting-and-gathering to horticultural, agrarian, and industrial societies. Although based on more accurate and more extensive facts than were available in the nineteenth century, the newer social-evolutionary schemes are nevertheless fundamentally similar to their nineteenth-century predecessors in that they present various societies as passing through specific stages in a predominantly unidirectional pattern—which, as noted above, represents a sharp divergence from the bioevolutionary model. This is not necessarily a defect: The development of new types of society simply may not be a process to which concepts of a bioevolutionary sort are fully applicable.

Such concepts are more readily applicable to the development of culture, especially in the areas of science (Hull 1988) and technology (Basalla 1988) in which the cumulative character of culture is most strongly manifested. Competing scientific hypotheses are the "randomlike variations" in science as an evolutionary process; research results that evaluate such hypotheses select some of them for survival and others for extinction; and the knowledge that constitutes the outcome of this process in any given generation of scientists is "inherited" by subsequent generations through textbooks, teaching, and research publications. In technological evolution, positive selection (i.e., acceptance) of variations (innovations) depends not only on research results (i.e., on how well they "work") but also on costs, competitive pressures, compatibility with prevailing culture, and other factors.

The bioevolutionary model is not useful when applied to social or cultural changes that are cyclical, easily reversed, or primarily planned, innately determined, or repetitive. It may be usefully applied when a complex transformation that would be hard to repeat or reverse occurs gradually without being planned, through environmentally determined selections from among divergent alternative directions of change (see Campbell 1965; Richter 1982, pp. 19–34).

(SEE ALSO: *Culture*)

REFERENCES

Basalla, George 1988 *The Evolution of Technology.* New York: Cambridge University Press.

Campbell, Donald T. 1965 "Variation and Selective Retention in Socio-Cultural Evolution." In Herbert R. Barringer, George I. Blanksten, and Raymond W. Mack, eds., *Social Change in Developing Areas.* Cambridge, Mass.: Schenkman.

Comte, Auguste 1875 *The Positive Philosophy,* 2nd ed. Harriet Martineau, trans. and cond. London: Trubner.

Darwin, Charles 1859 *On the Origin of Species.* London: Murray.

Gould, Stephen Jay 1982 "Darwinism and the Expansion of Evolutionary Theory." *Science* 216:380–387.

Hofstadter, Richard 1955 *Social Darwinism in American Thought.* Boston: Beacon Press.

Hull, David L. 1988 *Science as a Process.* Chicago: University of Chicago Press.

Lenski, Gerhard, and Jean Lenski 1982 *Human Societies: An Introduction to Macrosociology.* New York: McGraw-Hill.

Marx, Karl, and Friedrich Engels 1947 *The German Ideology.* New York: International Publishers.

Mayr, Ernst 1982 *The Growth of Biological Thought.* Cambridge, Mass.: Harvard University Press, Belknap Press.

Morgan, Lewis H. 1877 *Ancient Society.* Chicago: Charles H. Kerr.

Nisbet, Robert A. 1969 *Social Change and History.* London: Oxford University Press.

Parsons, Talcott 1977 *The Evolution of Societies,* ed. Jackson Toby. Englewood Cliffs, N.J.: Prentice-Hall.

Richter, Maurice N., Jr. 1982 *Technology and Social Complexity.* Albany: State University of New York Press.

Spencer, Herbert 1967 *The Evolution of Society,* ed. Robert L. Carneiro. Chicago: University of Chicago Press. Excerpted from *Principles of Sociology,* vols. 1 and 2, rev. ed. London: Williams and Margate, 1885–1886.

Stebbins, G. Ledyard, and Francisco J. Ayala 1985 "The Evolution of Darwinism." *Scientific American* 253: 72–82.

MAURICE N. RICHTER, JR.

EXCHANGE THEORY One of the major theoretical perspectives in sociology is exchange theory, which views social behavior primarily in terms of the pursuit of rewards and the avoidance of punishment (and other forms of cost). In exchange theory the basic unit of analysis is the relationship between actors. Individuals engage in interaction in order to meet their needs. Social relations and the social structures generated by the ties that bind people into different forms of association are viewed as the central objects of sociological inquiry by exchange theorists. Major topics of study within this tradition of research include the nature and effects of the interconnections among actors and the distribution of power within exchange structures. Power and status relations among actors in different types of social structures are defined as key forces determining the nature of structural change over time. The major exchange theorists all treat power, structural sources of power, and the dynamics of power use as primary in their theoretical formulations.

Exchange theory derives from several distinct lines of theoretical work in the social sciences: social behaviorism, utilitarianism, and functionalism (Turner 1986). Major proponents of the exchange perspective within sociology include Homans (1958, 1974), Blau (1964, 1987) and Emerson (1962, 1972a, 1972b). Within psychology the work of Thibaut and Kelley (1959; Kelley and Thibaut 1978) bears a strong resemblance to exchange theory, because of its emphasis upon the interdependence of actors and the social implications of different forms of interdependence. Anthropologists like Malinowski (1922), Mauss ([1925] 1950), Schneider (1974) and Lévi-Strauss (1949) have all contributed in different ways to the emergence of this theoretical perspective (see Ekeh 1974). In addition, the basic foundation of microeconomics has much in common with some variants of exchange theory (Heath 1976). This affinity is clearest in Blau's (1964) book, *Exchange and Power in Social Life,* and in subsequent theoretical developments (e.g., Cook and Emerson 1978; Coleman 1972, 1990). The breadth of the intellectual heritage of exchange theory accounts, in part, for its continued significance in the social sciences.

George Homans's seminal essay "Social Behavior as Exchange," published in the *American Journal of Sociology* in 1958, clarified the nature of this particular theoretical orientation and introduced it into mainstream sociology. Further elaboration of the perspective was published in the volume *Social Behavior: Its Elementary Forms* (1974; first published in 1961). An important distinguishing feature of Homans's work was its reliance on the language and propositions of behavioral psychology. The use of operant psychology as the behavioral basis of the theory created much of the early controversy surrounding the utility of this perspective for sociologists. In particular, the corresponding claim made by Homans that laws of social behavior could be "reduced to" the basic underlying principles of psychological behaviorism generated much debate (e.g., Deutsch 1964). According to Homans, "the general propositions we shall use in explanation are psychological in two senses: they refer to the actions of individuals and they have . . . been formulated and tested by psychologists" (1974, p. 12). However, Homans explicitly took as the major theoretical task the explanation of social phenomena. It is this emphasis upon social behavior and the social structures generated and altered by human social interaction that has sustained the influence of exchange theory in sociology. In this regard, Homans viewed the line drawn between psychology and sociology as fundamentally arbitrary.

The initial theoretical formulation developed by Homans in 1961 and revised in 1974 included five main propositions. All have to do with the fact that behavior is a function of its payoffs, the consequent rewards and punishments. The first proposition is the "success proposition," which states that the more frequently an activity is rewarded, the greater the likelihood of its performance. Behavior that generates positive consequences for the individual is likely to be repeated. The second proposition, the "stimulus proposition," stipulates that similar environmental or situational circumstances will stimulate behavior that has been rewarded in such circumstances in the past. This allows for the generalization of behavioral responses to "new" situations. The third, the "value proposition," specifies that the more valuable the result of an action is to the actor, the more likely that action is to be performed. This proposition is qualified by the fourth proposition, the "deprivation–satiation" proposition, which introduces the general idea of diminishing marginal utility. According to this proposition, the more often a person has recently received a particular reward for an action, the less valuable is an additional unit of that reward. Thus, some rewards become less effective over time in eliciting specific actions, though this is less true for generalized rewards, like money and affection, or anything for which satiation is less likely to occur except at extreme levels. The fifth theoretical proposition in Homans's basic framework specifies the conditions under which people react emotionally to different reward situations. It has two parts. People who do not receive what they anticipate are expected to become angry and behave aggressively, based on the original Miller and Dollard (1941) "frustration–aggression" hypothesis (see Homans 1974, p. 37). People who receive more than they expect, or do not receive anticipated punishments, will be happy and will behave approvingly. This system of propositions forms the original core set of ideas of what has come to be called, in many variants, social exchange theory.

Homans uses this set of theoretical ideas to explain phenomena like the exercise of power and authority, cooperation, conformity and competition, structures of sentiment and interaction, status and influence, satisfaction and productivity, leadership, distributive justice, and the emergence of stratification. He addressed these social phenomena primarily in terms of the nature of the interpersonal relations involved. Furthermore, he emphasized "elementary" forms of behavior, or what he referred to as the "subinstitutional" level of analysis. "We gain our fullest understanding of the elementary features of social behavior by observing the interactions between members of small, informal groups," argued Homans (1974, p. 356). By studying such forms of behavior he hoped to illuminate the elementary, informal, subinstitutional bases of more complex forms of social behavior, often more formal and institutionalized. What he bequeathed to modern day sociology, besides his particular form of theorizing, was his emphasis upon the microfoundations of social structures and social change.

Whereas Homans focused on elementary forms of behavior and the subinstitutional level of analysis, Blau (1964, 1986) moved beyond the micro level to the institutional level, dealing with authority and power, conflict, and change in the context of institutionalized systems of exchange. In disagreement with Homans's reductionistic strategy, Blau (1986, p. ix) claims that his own "theory is rooted in the peculiarly social nature of exchange, which implies that it cannot be reduced to or derived from psychological principles that govern the motives of individuals, as Homans aims to do." In distinct contrast to Homans's reductionism Blau assumed that social structures had "emergent" properties that could not be explained by characteristics or processes involving only the subunits. Thus, Blau parted company from Homans in two major ways. First, his framework was not based on principles of behavioral psychology; instead he introduced some microeconomic reasoning into the analysis of distinctly social exchange. Second, he explicitly introduced the notion of emergent processes into his theoretical treatise, not only rejecting reductionism but also expanding the theory to extend far beyond its original subinstitutional base.

Blau (1964) developed a general framework for analyzing macrostructures and processes based on an extension of his micro-level theory of social exchange processes. Drawing upon Simmel's understanding of social life he explains the general structure of social associations rooted in psychological processes like attraction, approval, reciprocation, and rational conduct. Group formation, cohesion, and social integration as well as processes of opposition, conflict, and dissolution are explained in terms of social exchange processes. These forms of social association generated by exchange processes come to constitute over time very complex social structures (and substructures). These more complex social structures are then examined by Blau as they are created and changed by power processes and the dynamics of legitimation and political opposition. Common values mediate and make possible indirect exchanges and thus the coordination of action in large collectivities. According to Blau, they also legitimate the social order. Throughout this major work he contrasts and compares social exchange processes in simple structures with those in more complex social structures and institutions. The major social forces he analyzes include differentiation, integration, organization, and opposition, which sets up the dialectic necessary for the explanation of structural change.

The strategy of building a theory of macrostructure and processes upon an explicitly micro-level theory was a major distinguishing feature of Blau's (1964) original work and is currently the focus of a major stream of theoretical work in sociology on the "micro–macro link." Ironically, Blau (1986) himself challenged the utility of this approach in his recent writings (see also Blau 1987), fueling the debate further. In his introduction to the second printing of his book on exchange and power, he argues that microsociological and macrosociological theories "require different approaches and conceptual schemes though their distinct perspectives enrich each other" (1986, p. xv). This theoretical debate will not be over soon since it is at the heart of the nature of sociological analysis and relates to broad issues of the primacy of particular units and levels of analysis as well as to complex metatheoretical and methodological issues.

Blau (1964) and Emerson (1962, 1972a, 1972b) made power the central focus of analysis. Blau treated power, authority, opposition, and legitimation as key topics in his discussion of macrostructures and the dynamics of structural change. Emerson's (1962) theory of power–dependence relations was partially incorporated into Blau's (1964) treatment of power imbalance and the conditions of social independence. For Emerson (1962) these strategies were power-balancing mechanisms. The central proposition in Emerson's classic essay was that power, defined in relational terms, was a function of the dependence of one actor upon another. In a two-party exchange relation, the power of one party (A) over another party (B) is a function of the dependence of B upon A. Dependence is a function of the value one actor places upon the resources (or valued behavior) mediated by the other and the availability of those resources from alternate sources. The greater the availability of these resources from other actors (i.e., alternative sources) the lower one actor's dependence upon another. This relational conception of power became the basis for most of the subsequent work on exchange and power in the 1970s and 1980s.

Emerson (1972a, 1972b) expanded his treatment of power and dependence to form a more extensive exchange theory of social relations. In many ways his work was a composite of the approaches of Homans (1961) and Blau (1964). In the original formulation Emerson (1972a) adopted the language and principles of behavioral psychology to form a theory of social relations. However, he moved quickly beyond behavioral principles to the formation of more complex propositions regarding the emergence of various kinds of social structures. Here the theory picks up the Simmelian focus of Blau's work as well as the concern with emergent properties and complex social structures. Emerson (1972b), like Blau (1964, 1986), viewed the major task of exchange theory as the creation of a framework in which the primary dependent variable was social structure and structural change. The major task was eminently sociological, not psychological, even though all three theorists explicitly incorporated into their thinking notions about the psychology of actors. Recent versions of Emerson's and Cook's work (e.g., Cook and Emerson 1978) adopt a more cognitive perspective on the actors involved in social exchange. Molm's (e.g., 1981, 1987) work extends the original behavioral underpinnings of the theory.

Exchange theory, though originally dyadic in focus, has been extended in recent theoretical and empirical work to apply to the analysis of exchange networks. Both Homans and Blau recognized the ubiquity of social networks and different forms of social association, but Emerson (1972b) made networks and corporate groups a central focus of his theoretical formulation. The definition of exchange relations as "connected" in various ways to form network structures was the key to this development in the theory. Power-balancing mechanisms were postulated to explain some of the ways in which structures change either to maintain and preserve existing structural arrangements and distributions of power or to alter them. For example, coalition formation is presented as one mechanism by which power-disadvantaged actors in less powerful network positions can gain power through the collective advantage gained in cooperative action. Division of labor, or specialization within the network, can also result in changes in the distribution of power in a network through modifications in the distribution of resources and the nature of the structural arrangements. Various theorists have continued this line of work, specifying the principles that predict the distribution of power in different exchange structures (e.g., Cook et al. 1983; Markovsky, Willer, and Patton 1988; and Bonacich 1987).

Additional developments in the theory include the formulation of explicit propositions concerning the use of power in different types of exchange network structures. Cook and Emerson (1978) and Molm (e.g., 1981) contrast rates of power use in power-balanced and power-imbalanced networks and specify some of the determinants of the use of structural power. These include factors like concern over the fairness of the distribution of outcomes, commitments between actors, the formation of coalitions, particular strategies of action, and whether or not the power is reward power or punishment power (see Molm 1989). Future developments will focus even more attention on the structural determinants of power and methodologies for specifying the distribution of power in complex network structures. Interest in this topic is, in part, driven by the potential for synthesizing exchange-theoretic conceptions of power with network models of social structure (see Cook 1987). Another arena of current theoretical and empirical work is the specification of dynamic models of power use and structural change. These efforts will be significant if exchange theory is to fulfill its promise of providing one approach to the problem of linking micro-level theories of action and interaction with macro-level explanations of structure and processes of social change. This is an agenda that was set by Homans, Blau, and Emerson, among others, and it remains an important theoretical agenda for sociologists in the 1990s.

(SEE ALSO: *Interpersonal Power; Social Psychology*)

REFERENCES

Blau, P. M. 1964 *Exchange and Power in Social Life.* New York: Wiley.

——— 1986 *Exchange and Power in Social Life,* rev. ed. New Brunswick, N.J.: Transaction Books.

——— 1987 "Microprocess and Macrostructure." In

K. S. Cook, ed. *Social Exchange Theory.* Newbury Park, Calif.: Sage.

Bonacich, P. 1987 "Power and Centrality: A Family of Measures." *American Journal of Sociology* 92:1,170–1,182.

Coleman, J. S. 1972 "Systems of Social Exchange." *Journal of Mathematical Sociology* 2:145–163.

——— 1990 *The Foundations of Social Theory.* Cambridge, Mass.: Harvard University Press.

Cook, K. S. (ed.) 1987 *Social Exchange Theory.* Newbury Park, Calif.: Sage.

———, and R. M. Emerson 1978 "Power, Equity, and Commitment in Exchange Networks." *American Sociological Review* 43:721–739.

———, et al. 1983 "The Distribution of Power in Exchange Networks: Theory and Experimental Results." *American Journal of Sociology* 89:275–305.

Deutsch, M. 1964 "Homans in the Skinner Box." *Sociological Inquiry* 34:156–165.

Ekeh, P. P. 1974 *Social Exchange Theory: The Two Traditions.* Cambridge, Mass.: Harvard University Press.

Emerson, R. M. 1962. "Power–Dependence Relations." *American Sociological Review* 27:31–40.

——— 1972a "Exchange Theory, Part I: A Psychological Basis for Social Exchange." In J. Berger, M. Zelditch, and B. Anderson, eds., *Sociological Theories in Progress,* vol. 2. Boston: Houghton Mifflin.

——— 1972b "Exchange Theory, Part II: Exchange Relations and Networks." In J. Berger, M. Zelditch, and B. Anderson, eds. *Sociological Theories in Progress,* vol. 2. Boston: Houghton Mifflin.

Heath, A. 1976 *Rational Choice and Social Exchange: A Critique of Exchange Theory.* Cambridge: Cambridge University Press.

Homans, G. C. 1958 "Social Behavior as Exchange." *American Journal of Sociology* 62:597–606.

——— 1974 *Social Behavior: Its Elementary Forms,* 2nd ed. New York: Harcourt, Brace and World.

Kelley, H. H., and J. Thibaut 1978 *Interpersonal Relations: A Theory of Interdependence.* New York: Wiley.

Lévi-Strauss, C. 1949 *Les structures élémentaires de la parenté.* Paris: Presses universitaires de France. Published in English as *The Elementary Structures of Kinship.* Boston: Beacon Press. 1969.

Malinowski, B. 1922 *Argonauts of the Western Pacific.* London: Routledge and Kegan Paul.

Markovsky, B., D. Willer, and T. Patton 1988 "Power Relations in Exchange Networks." *American Sociological Review* 53:220–236.

Mauss, M. (1925) 1950 *Essai sur le don in sociologie et anthropologie.* Paris: Presses universitaires de France. Published in English as *The Gift.* New York: Free Press. 1954.

Miller, N. E., and J. Dollard 1941 *Social Learning and Imitation.* New Haven: Yale University Press.

Molm, L. D. 1981 "The Conversion of Power Imbalance to Power Use." *Social Psychology Quarterly* 44:151–163.

——— 1987 "Power–Dependence Theory: Power Processes and Negative Outcomes." In E. J. Lawler and B. Markovsky, eds., *Advances in Group Processes,* vol. 4. Greenwich, Conn.: JAI Press.

——— 1989. "Punishment Power: A Balancing Process in Power–Dependence Relations." *American Journal of Sociology* 94:1,392–1,418.

Schneider, H. K. 1974 *Economic Man: The Anthropology of Economics.* New York: Free Press.

Thibaut, J., and H. H. Kelley 1959 *The Social Psychology of Groups.* New York: Wiley.

Turner, J. H. 1986 *The Structure of Sociological Theory,* 4th ed. Chicago: Dorsey Press.

KAREN S. COOK

EXPECTATION STATES THEORY Expectation states theory is an ongoing research program investigating various aspects of group interaction. The focus is on small, task-oriented groups; the central interest is in the processes through which group members assign levels of task competence to each other, and in the consequences this assignment has for their interaction. Originating as a single theory developed by Joseph Berger (1958), expectation states theory has grown to include various branches sharing a core of basic concepts and propositions, as well as a set of substantive, methodological, and metatheoretical assumptions. Thus the program in fact contains not one theory but several. (Unless otherwise specified, the expression "expectation states theory" refers here to the entire program rather than to any particular theory within it.) Expectation states theory has received strong support from extensive empirical research.

Two key concepts in the program are "status characteristic" and "performance expectation." A status characteristic is any valued attribute implying task competence. Such characteristics are viewed as having at least two levels (e.g., being high or low in mechanical ability, being male or female), one carrying a more positive evaluation than the other. They are also defined as varying from specific to diffuse, depending on the range of their perceived applicability. For instance, mechanical ability is usually considered to be relatively specific, or associated with well-defined performance expectations. Sex, on the other hand, tends to be treated as diffuse, or to carry both limited and general performance expectations. The "diffuseness" refers to the fact that since there is no explicitly set limit to the expectations, the characteristic is viewed as relevant to a large, indeterminate number of different tasks. Other attributes commonly treated as diffuse status characteristics are ethnicity, race, social class, level of education, organizational rank, age, and physical attractiveness.

Performance expectations link status characteristics to observable behavior. Thus, levels of these characteristics are associated with degrees of competence and corresponding expectations that, in turn, determine what is known as "the power and prestige order of the group." This consists of a set of interrelated behaviors: the unequal distribution in the offer and acceptance of opportunities to perform, the type of evaluations received for each unit of performance, and the rates of influence exerted among group members. Performance expectations are distinguished from evaluations of units of performance: While the latter are evaluations of a single act, the former refer to the level of competence that a person is predicted to exhibit over a number of such performances. Once established, expectations tend to be stable, since the behaviors that make up the power and prestige order of a group operate in a way that reinforces the status quo.

Research in expectation states theory follows a situational approach. Propositions are formulated from the point of view of a person (also referred to as "self" or "focal actor") who performs a given task with a partner ("other"). Performance expectations are therefore relative to a specific pair of actors, and an individual is not seen as holding high (or low or medium) expectations for self but, rather, an "expectation state" that is defined in terms of self *and* other. In other words, the focal actor is said to hold expectations for self that are higher than, lower than, or equal to, the expectations he or she holds for the partner. Such expectations are also seen as relative to a particular situation. It follows, then, that with a different partner or in the context of a different task, for example, a person's expectation state could vary. It should also be noted that an expectation state is a theoretical construct, not an observable phenomenon. In particular, although expectations are seen as reflecting a person's beliefs about the distribution of task competence in the group, they are *not* assumed to be self's conscious calculations of either advantage or disadvantage in this respect. Rather, what is proposed are models to be used to predict the focal actor's behavior, and this person is to be seen only *as if* he or she performed the operations specified in the models.

Propositions in expectation states theory also have been formulated within well-defined scope conditions, or statements specifying the limits within which the propositions apply. Since scope conditions are part of the theory, they are expressed in abstract terms, as are the key concepts "status characteristic" and "performance expectation." Two important scope conditions are that the focal actor is assumed to be task-oriented (motivated to do the task well) and collectively oriented (prepared to accept the partner's ideas if they are thought to contribute to the task solution). In other words, the latter scope condition specifies that solving the task has to be more important to this actor than any other considerations, such as having his or her individual contributions accepted, or being liked by the partner.

The situational approach and the use of scope conditions are part of an overall analytical strategy whereby the initial focus is on the simplest contexts, which are studied with the aid of minimum assumptions. Complexities are added gradually as knowledge accumulates. More recent expectation states research has, for example, extended the investigation from dyads to larger groups. Similarly, the scope conditions of task orientation and collective orientation could be relaxed in the future, in order to study the extent to which status still affects expectations when such circumstances are changed.

The core of the theory investigates the performance expectations an individual forms about self and other in settings where the two are engaged in the joint solution of a task. As indicated previously, the focal actor is assumed to be both task-oriented and collectively oriented. It is also assumed that competence at the task is valued and thus constitutes a status characteristic for him or her. Basically, the assignment of levels of this characteristic and corresponding performance expectations may occur in one of two ways: directly, from actual evaluations of task performance, or indirectly, on the basis of other status characteristics of the performers that the person perceives to be relevant to the task. For simplicity, let us first consider situations where expectations are formed exclusively in one fashion or the other. The two ways comprise the major branches of expectation states theory, the former focusing on the effects of performance evaluations and the latter on the effects of other status information. These branches are described below. (Because of space limitations, the emphasis in this article is on the basic ideas. Thus, for the most part, specific references are given only for selected work in the earlier development of the program. It should be mentioned, however, that expectation states theory has been a collaborative effort from its beginnings, and that a considerable number of researchers have worked in it. For references to their individual contributions at the various stages of the program, see the works mentioned at the end of this article.)

Initial work in the first branch of the theory investigated the formation of performance expectations in situations where two actors begin their interaction as status equals (they have no information from either inside or outside the group that would enable them to assign different levels of task competence to each other). In this case, the assignment of levels of competence that eventually occurs is the result of a generalization from evaluations of units of performance. These evaluations may be made by the performers themselves as they resolve disagreements between each other regarding the correct solution to the task (Berger and Conner 1969; Berger and Snell 1961), or by a "source" or third party with the right to evaluate the performers (Webster 1969; Webster and Sobieszek 1974). Moreover, the evaluations may or may not be made through the use of objective criteria. Various other topics have been investigated within this branch. These include the effects on expectations of the type of evaluations received (positive or negative), the consistency of these evaluations (across performances or across sources), and the attributes that confer evaluative competence on a source (such as level of task competence or vicarious exposure to the task). More recent work has dealt with the effects of applying either strict or lenient standards for competence (and for lack of competence) to the processing of evaluations. The study of second-order expectations (those based on self's perceptions of the expectations held by the partner) also has received attention in this program, and is of direct relevance to this branch.

The second branch of the theory is primarily concerned with situations where the actors differ in status. It is in this branch, which has come to be known as "status characteristics theory," that a large proportion of expectation states research has been conducted. This work started with the investigation of situations in which the two actors are differentiated with respect to a single diffuse status characteristic (Berger, Cohen, and Zelditch 1966, 1972; Moore 1968). Furthermore, this difference constitutes the only information that the person has about self and other, and he or she treats the attribute as a diffuse status characteristic (that is, attaches different evaluations to its various levels and holds different performance expectations, specific as well as general, for each).

The basic proposition in this branch states that unless the focal actor believes the characteristic to be irrelevant to the task at hand, he or she will use the status difference between self and other to organize their interaction. In other words, performance expectations for the task at hand will be the result of importing information from outside the group. This process is known as "status generalization.'' Let us consider sex as an example (with "male" carrying a more positive evaluation than "female") and assume that the focal actor is a man and that his partner is a woman. The theory predicts different expectations, depending on what the individual believes the sex linkage of the task to be. If it is perceived as masculine, self will use this information to infer that he is the better of the two. If he has no information about its sex linkage (perceives the task as neither associated with nor dissociated from sex differences), the burden-of-proof principle will apply: Those of lower status will be considered to have inferior task competence, unless they demonstrate the opposite. Accordingly, the man will still expect to be more competent than his female partner at the task. On the other hand, the theory predicts that he will *not* form expectations of his own superiority if the task has been explicitly dissociated from sex. Finally, if the valued task is perceived to be one at which women excel, the male actor will consider himself inferior to his female partner.

It is important to emphasize that the above predictions assume that sex is a diffuse status characteristic for the focal actor (and that in the example "male" carries a higher value than "female"). If sex is not such a characteristic, the propositions do not apply. Because of the inclusion of this scope condition, the theory is sensitive to cultural, historical, and individual differences. Thus, it incorporates the fact that although sex is such a characteristic in most societies, it is more so in some than in others. The extent to which this is the case also may vary within a given society and from one historical period to another. Furthermore, the theory reflects the fact that even in strongly sexist societies there are likely to be individuals who are less sexist than the majority, and perhaps some who are not sexist at all. (This may be due, for example, to variations in socialization practices within a given culture, and/or to their various degrees of success.) Note that the theory assumes that women, *as well as* men, may treat sex as a diffuse status characteristic and devalue women's performances.

Let us, then, analyze the earlier example from the point of view of the female actor, and assume that she considers sex to be a diffuse status characteristic to the same degree that her male partner does. She will then form expectations that are exactly complementary to those of her partner. Thus, if she either views the task as masculine or relates it to sex differences through a burden-of-proof process, she will consider herself the less competent of the two performers. (She will not form such expectations if the task has been dissociated from sex, and will believe herself to be the better performer if the task has been defined as feminine.) However, as with most status systems, those persons who benefit from the existing order should be expected to be more supportive of it than those who do not, socialization practices notwithstanding. Thus it could be that men tend to meet this scope condition more than women do. This is not an issue about the theory itself, but an empirical matter regarding the concrete instances to which it applies. Also, while the preceding discussion has been limited to sex for the sake of providing an example, the comments are meant to apply to any diffuse status characteristic. In general, the strength of the link between status and expectations is a function of the extent to which the attribute is a status characteristic for the focal actor.

Performance expectations formed through status generalization may of course be affected by other factors. Accordingly, the basic ideas of the initial formulation of status characteristics theory have been expanded and elaborated in several directions. In particular, these include the study of situations where actors possess more than one status characteristic. These may be either specific or diffuse, or consistent or inconsistent with each other in terms of their implied levels of competence. Furthermore, as a set, they may either equate or differentiate the performers to various degrees (Berger, Fisek, Norman, and Zelditch 1977). This extended formulation specifies the conditions under which the available status items will become salient (or "activated"), as well as the rules by which they will be processed. It is proposed that all (and only) activated items will be used and that they will be combined according to the following principles: Inconsistent information will have more impact than consistent information, and each additional item of consistent information will have less weight than it would by itself. Furthermore, this version includes referent actors (nonparticipating actors who serve as objects of comparison for the performers) and their role in the formation of expectations.

The two main branches of the program have not developed independently of each other. In fact, the branches touch and intertwine at various points, as expectations are formed on the basis of *both* performance evaluation and status information. For example, the extent to which the focal actor accepts the evaluations from a source is often affected by the diffuse status characteristics of everyone involved. Of particular interest is the resilience of status-based expectations when these are contradicted by actual performance evaluations. This resistance shows itself in, for example, the higher level of performance that lower-status actors have to achieve in order to escape the effects of status generalization. The issue is of course a special case of the extension of status characteristics theory to more than one attribute. A recent proposal in this area links the resilience to the use of double (or multiple) standards for competence and incompetence that protect higher-status actors and penalize lower-status ones.

Other expectation states research, also of relevance to both branches, has included a rich variety of topics. For example, theoretical and empirical work has investigated the relationship between performance expectations and reward expectations, the status value view of distributive justice, the transfer of expectations across actors and situations, and the legitimation of status positions. The latter work examines how and why individuals come to view the status hierarchies in which they are involved as right and proper. Also of special interest is the analysis of the way task settings generate emotional reactions and how these, in turn, affect performance expectations. Other important areas have been the role that status cues (such as accent, dress, demeanor), personality characteristics (such as friendly, rigid, outgoing), and moral characteristics (such as honest, fair, selfish) play in the assignment of task competence.

No review of the expectation states program would be complete without a discussion of three features that, together with those mentioned earlier, serve to characterize it. First, a sizable portion of the research has used a standardized experimental situation involving two subjects (Webster and Sobieszek 1974, Appendices 1 and 2). The utilization of an experimental approach clearly is well suited to the program's analytical strategy of investigating the effects of a few variables at a time, and the standardized setting has contributed to cumulativeness in the research findings by allowing comparability across studies. In this setting, the task consists of a series of trials, each involving a binary choice regarding perceptual stimuli, and the subjects are allowed to interact only indirectly with each other. The situation consists of two phases. In the first phase, performance expectations are formed on the basis of information controlled by the experimenter. These may include evaluations of each person's task performance, cues regarding the participants' other status characteristics, or a combination of the two. In the second phase, each trial consists of an individual initial choice, the experimentally controlled communication of the partner's choice, and a final individual choice. In most trials, that communication indicates that the partner disagrees with the subject. The dependent variable of central interest is the amount of influence (one of the components of the power and prestige order of the group) that a partner exerts on the performer in the resolution of those disagreements. (Additional bases of empirical support for the theory include direct evidence from studies conducted in classrooms and other research settings—such as those mentioned below—as well as indirect evidence from work originating in various other theoretical traditions. For a review of the different types of support for the theory, see Berger, Wagner, and Zelditch 1989.)

Second, the program has been characterized by an effort to state propositions as part of deductive systems. These systems have been formalized to various extents, and different techniques (such as stochastic models, a Bayesian approach, graph theory, fuzzy set theory) have been used. The most comprehensive of these formulations is the graph theoretic model of the extended version of status characteristics theory (Berger, Fisek, Norman, and Zelditch 1977). Third, from its beginnings the program has shown a definite interest in application and intervention research, designed to understand and alleviate concrete social problems. A large portion of this work has included the development of techniques to reduce the effects of status generalization, particularly those based on ethnicity and race, in classroom settings (Cohen 1972; Entwisle and Webster 1972). It is important to note that this research has progressed in close association with theoretical work; thus applications and interventions have both stimulated and benefited from the development of abstract formulations.

Expectation states theory continues to develop in several directions. For example, the refinement, expansion, and integration of various aspects of the program are currently under way. There are also some exciting new areas of research, such as the study of the relationship between status and affect (emotions and sentiments) in the assignment of task competence. Furthermore, the notion of an "expectation state" has been generalized from its original reference to status-based processes, to those concerning affect and control. Finally, the research methodology has been extended to include other settings and tasks, including face-to-face contexts, interactions where selected aspects of formal organizations have been re-created, computerized tasks, and larger groups. For reviews and assessments of the expectation states program at various stages, see Berger (1988); Berger, Rosenholtz, and Zelditch (1980); Berger, Wagner, and Zelditch (1985, 1989); Meeker (1981); Webster and Foschi (1988a). For edited collections of work on various topics, see Berger, Conner, and Fisek (1974); Berger and Zelditch (1985); Webster and Foschi (1988b). For three examples of the more recent research, see Ridgeway (1989); Ridgeway and Johnson (1990); Wagner, Ford, and Ford (1986). For discussions of the program's methodological and metatheoretical assumptions, see Berger, Zelditch, and Anderson (1972); Cohen (1989, esp. chap. 6); Zelditch (1969).

(SEE ALSO: *Interpersonal Power; Social Psychology*)

REFERENCES

Berger, Joseph 1958 "Relations Between Performance, Rewards, and Action-Opportunities in Small Groups." Ph.D. diss., Harvard University.

——— 1988 "Directions in Expectation States Research." In Murray Webster, Jr., and Martha Foschi, eds., *Status Generalization: New Theory and Research.* Stanford, Calif.: Stanford University Press.

———, Bernard P. Cohen, and Morris Zelditch, Jr. 1966 "Status Characteristics and Expectation States." In Joseph Berger, Morris Zelditch, Jr., and Bo Anderson, eds., *Sociological Theories in Progress,* vol. 1. Boston: Houghton Mifflin.

——— 1972 "Status Characteristics and Social Interaction." *American Sociological Review* 37:241–255.

Berger, Joseph, and Thomas L. Conner 1969 "Performance Expectations and Behavior in Small Groups." *Acta Sociologica* 12:186–198.

Berger, Joseph, Thomas L. Conner, and M. Hamit Fisek (eds.) 1974 *Expectation States Theory: A Theoretical Research Program.* Cambridge, Mass.: Winthrop.

Berger, Joseph, M. Hamit Fisek, Robert Z. Norman, and Morris Zelditch, Jr. 1977 *Status Characteristics and Social Interaction: An Expectation-States Approach.* New York: Elsevier.

Berger, Joseph, Susan J. Rosenholtz, and Morris Zelditch, Jr. 1980 "Status Organizing Processes." In Alex Inkeles, Neil J. Smelser, and Ralph H. Turner, eds., *Annual Review of Sociology,* vol. 6. Palo Alto, Calif.: Annual Reviews.

Berger, Joseph, and J. Laurie Snell 1961 "A Stochastic Theory for Self–Other Expectations." Technical Report no. 1. Stanford, Calif.: Laboratory for Social Research, Stanford University.

Berger, Joseph, David G. Wagner, and Morris Zelditch, Jr. 1985 "Expectation States Theory: Review and Assessment." In Joseph Berger and Morris Zelditch, Jr., eds., *Status, Rewards and Influence: How Expectations Organize Behavior.* San Francisco: Jossey-Bass.

——— 1989 "Theory Growth, Social Processes, and

Metatheory." In Jonathan H. Turner, ed., *Theory Building in Sociology: Assessing Theoretical Cumulation.* Newbury Park, Calif.: Sage.

Berger, Joseph, and Morris Zelditch, Jr. (eds.) 1985 *Status, Rewards and Influence: How Expectations Organize Behavior.* San Francisco: Jossey-Bass.

Berger, Joseph, Morris Zelditch, Jr., and Bo Anderson 1972 "Introduction." In Joseph Berger, Morris Zelditch, Jr., and Bo Anderson, eds., *Sociological Theories in Progress,* vol. 2. Boston: Houghton Mifflin.

Cohen, Bernard P. 1989 *Developing Sociological Knowledge: Theory and Method,* 2nd ed. Chicago: Nelson-Hall.

Cohen, Elizabeth G. 1972 "Interracial Interaction Disability." *Human Relations* 37:648–655.

Entwisle, Doris R., and M. Webster, Jr. 1972 "Raising Children's Performance Expectations: A Classroom Demonstration." *Social Science Research* 1:147–158.

Meeker, Barbara F. 1981 "Expectation States and Interpersonal Behavior." In Morris Rosenberg and Ralph H. Turner, eds., *Social Psychology: Sociological Perspectives.* New York: Basic Books.

Moore, James C., Jr. 1968 "Status and Influence in Small Group Interactions." *Sociometry* 31:47–63.

Ridgeway, Cecilia L. 1989 "Understanding Legitimation in Informal Status Orders." In Joseph Berger, Morris Zelditch, Jr., and Bo Anderson, eds., *Sociological Theories in Progress: New Formulations.* Newbury Park, Calif.: Sage.

———, and Cathryn Johnson 1990 "What Is the Relationship Between Socioemotional Behavior and Status in Task Groups?" *American Journal of Sociology* 95:1189–1212.

Wagner, David G., Rebecca S. Ford, and Thomas W. Ford 1986 "Can Gender Inequalities Be Reduced?" *American Sociological Review* 51:47–61.

Webster, Murray, Jr. 1969. "Source of Evaluations and Expectations for Performance." *Sociometry* 32:243–258.

———, and Martha Foschi 1988a "Overview of Status Generalization." In Murray Webster, Jr., and Martha Foschi, eds., *Status Generalization: New Theory and Research.* Stanford, Calif.: Stanford University Press.

——— (eds.) 1988b *Status Generalization: New Theory and Research.* Stanford, Calif.: Stanford University Press.

Webster, Murray, Jr., and Barbara Sobieszek 1974 *Sources of Self-Evaluation: A Formal Theory of Significant Others and Social Influence.* New York: Wiley.

Zelditch, Morris, Jr. 1969 "Can You Really Study an Army in the Laboratory?" In Amitai Etzioni, ed., *A Sociological Reader on Complex Organizations,* 2nd ed. New York: Holt, Rinehart and Winston.

MARTHA FOSCHI

EXPERIMENTS Sociologists usually reserve the term *experiment* for studies in which the researcher *manipulates* one or more key independent variables; that is, for studies in which the experimenter *controls* the decision as to which subjects are exposed to what level of the independent variable. Although experiments comprise a minority of sociological research studies, they are still quite common. Laboratory versions are traditional in much of sociological social psychology (recent examples are Molm 1990; Bonacich 1990). Field experiments are prominent in program evaluations, particularly in applied areas such as education (e.g., Slavin and Karweit 1985), criminal justice (e.g., Rossi, Berk, and Lenihan 1980; see also Zeisel 1982), and even large-scale social policy efforts such as studies of a proposed guaranteed minimum income (Hannon, Tuma, and Groenveld 1977). Questionnaire experiments (e.g., Schuman and Presser 1981) test various methodological questions, while "vignette" experiments (e.g., Rossi and Nock 1982) have become popular approaches to the study of attitudes.

The primary attraction of the experimental method is undoubtedly that it is more persuasive than other methods in its fit with *causal* arguments (Kish 1987). Campbell and Stanley, whose 1963 book is the most influential discussion of experiments for contemporary sociologists, call this "internal validity" (for other historically important discussions of experiments, see especially Fisher 1935 and Cochran and Cox 1957). To them, "true" experiments are studies in which subjects are *randomly* allocated into "experimental" and "control" groups. The former receive a "treatment," such as an educational program, while the latter do not. Randomization allows the researcher to *assume* the similarity of groups at the beginning of the treatment, *with known statistical chances of error,* and to avoid a variety of "threats" to the validity of the conclusion that the treatment "caused" any found differences between the groups in post-treatment behavior or other outcome. In contrast, "quasi-experiments" (most other forms of research), which do not use randomization, require a variety of additional, often heroic, assumptions in order to make causal inferences.

A MODEL

Consider an experiment to test the proposition that increasing the sensitivity to Hispanic cultures of non-Hispanic second-grade teachers will improve the performance of Hispanic children in their classes, particularly students with poor English-language skills. Teachers are randomly assigned to attend one of three seminars on Hispanic cultures, which vary in intensity (experimental treatments), or a seminar on Asian cultures (control). Following the approach of Alwin and Tessler (1974), Figure 1 presents a model of this experiment. Our proposition is tested by estimating the relationship between two "unobservable" variables—student performance in second grade (*Y*) and the sensitivity of their teachers (*X*). The variables are "unobservable" in the sense that we cannot unambiguously and directly measure the rather complex concepts we have. For example, true "student performance" probably includes

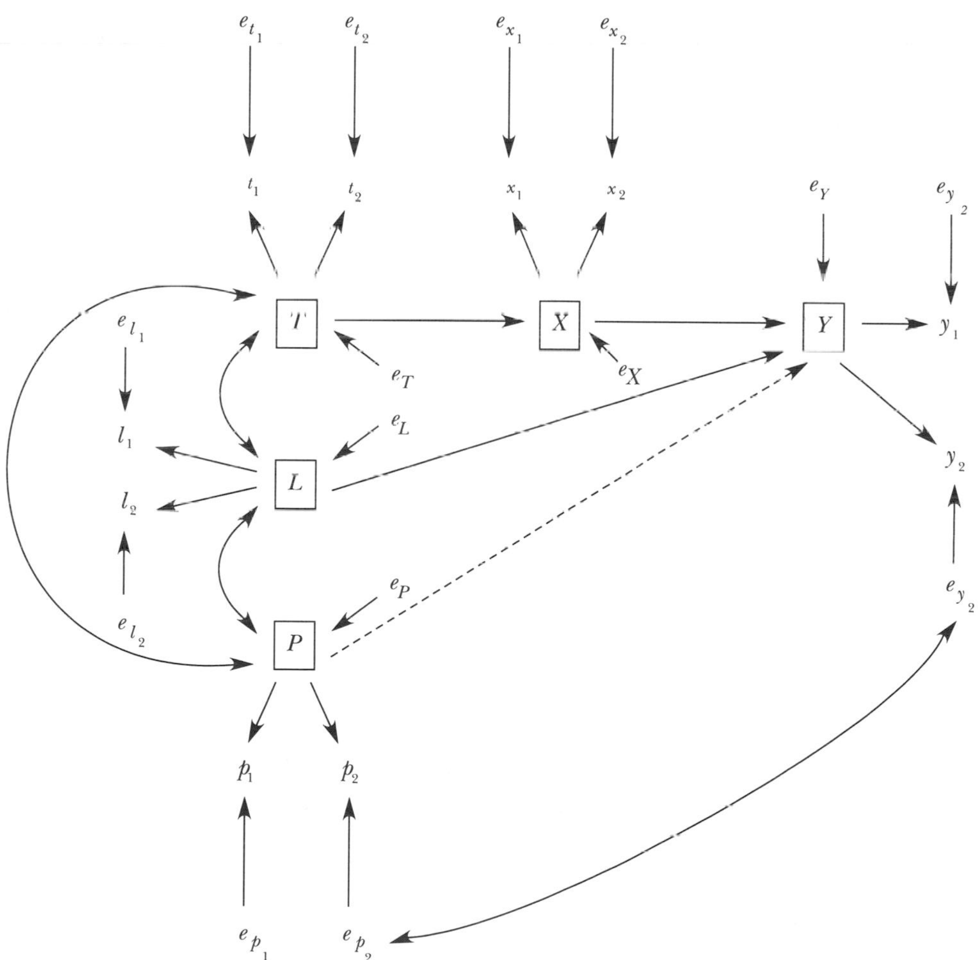

Figure 1
Model based on Alwin and Tessler

facility with mathematics, language acquisition, and many other components, each of which we can measure only imperfectly. The model also contains two other variables that may be unobservable—the "Hispanic intensity" of the course (*T*) and the English-language skill of the student (*L*)—and should include a fifth unobservable (as indicated by the broken line), which is the student's performance in first grade (*P*). Including *P* allows us to test for the effect of taking the seminar on *change* in student performance.

As is conventional in such models, each unobservable variable is measured by indicators (x_1, x_2, t_1, etc.) and is affected by a stochastic term representing our inability to measure the concept perfectly with our indicators (e_x, e_t, etc.) as well. It is obvious that student performance (*Y* and *P*) would be best measured by a series of indicators such as teachers' ratings, grades in various topics, and performances on standardized tests. Since similar or identical measures of *Y* and *P* might be used, errors could be correlated, as shown by the curved line between e_{y2} and e_{p2}.

Alwin and Tessler (1974) call x_1 and x_2 "manipulation checks." Hispanic culture seminars (*T*) may or may not change a given teacher's sensitivity toward Hispanic students (*X*). It is even possible that Asian culture seminars make teachers more sensitive to all minorities, including Hispanics. In other words, we cannot *assume* that *T* successfully manipulated *X*. There may actually be no differences in sensitivity (*X*) between experimentals and controls. We will have to check, which means that we will have to measure *X*.

What experimenters rarely realize is that they should often also measure *T*. If the treatment is complicated, assigning a subject to be treated does not guarantee that he or she receives the treatment that is intended. The instructor in one of the culture seminars might do a poor job of presenting the materials. A teacher might be ill and miss one of the sessions. Most experimenters assume that the relationship between *T* and *X* is 1.0, but that is not necessarily the case. To estimate the actual effect of *T* on *X*, various "treatment checks" (t_1, t_2) would be required.

MULTIPLE COMPARISONS

Note that a sophisticated experimental design may often require many levels of the "treatment" and even of the "control." Or there may be no "control" at all, just comparison among different treatments. If *X* is conceptualized as a continuous variable, such as the intensity of the seminar (where *T* may be number of sessions), there is no reason to have only three levels of *T*. Instead, we might randomly assign each member of the treatment group to a different number of sessions, from one to a whole semester (if the seminar was being offered at the university anyway). This is particularly important in something like a guaranteed income experiment, where a wide range of levels of guaranteed income is possible. We might even wish to have every family receive a different level of income support, so as to represent the possible range well and help us choose the best level of support for an actual program.

Furthermore, note that in our example the control group is *not* comprised of teachers who get no seminars at all. This is to avoid what has been commonly termed the "Hawthorne effect," in which experimental subjects respond to the attention they get by being sent to a seminar, rather than to the content (Hispanic culture) of the seminar itself. Designs that do not attend to the effects of just being treated are always subject to errors of interpretation. Of course, an even more sophisticated design might include a second control group of teachers who were not even informed that others were attending seminars (and perhaps other control groups at various levels of "intensity" of the Asian culture seminar, as well). The "no seminar" group would provide data that allow us to estimate the size of the difference in class performance between students whose teachers had attended sensitivity seminars and students in a school system with no sensitivity program at all.

BLOCKING

In most studies, a number of variables other than *X* may seem to the researcher to be probable causes of *Y*. These are not manipulated, either because such manipulation is impossible or because it is otherwise undesirable. For instance, facility with the English language (L) would probably affect the performance of most second-grade students in the United States. The experimenter cannot manipulate this characteristic of the subjects. Because of randomization we *expect* T, and hence X, to be uncorrelated with L (see Figure 1), and with all other variables. However, sampling variation means that we might be unlucky, so that T and L are empirically correlated among the students we are actually studying. Under these conditions our estimate of the relationship between X and Y may be unbiased, but it is also less efficient than when L is controlled, because we add sampling error to other sources of error.

We can increase the efficiency of the estimate by using L as a "blocking variable," perhaps by using their ranks on L to create matched pairs of students. We then randomly assign one of the two highest-rated students to the experimental group, and the other to the controls, one of the next two highest to the experimental, and so forth, until the lowest L pair is assigned. We thus guarantee a correlation of 0 between T and L. In our analysis, we can statistically estimate the effects of blocked variables such as L on Y, and reduce the variance that we attribute to "error."

COST

Efficiency is particularly important because experiments are often very expensive. When "real life" manipulates the independent variables (e.g., making one person male and the other female, one born to rich parents and another to poor), the researcher does not have to pay for the "treatment." But experiments usually require the researcher to get the subject to do something—which can often be done only through pay—and then to do something to the subject, which also usually costs money. In our example, the teachers will have to be paid for their time going to the seminars, and so will the instructors of those seminars. These costs generally mean that experimenters strongly need to keep the number of subjects they study small, which threatens the internal (and external; see below) validity of the research.

GENERALIZATION

The most frequent criticism of experiments, however, is that their results are often difficult to generalize, a problem Campbell and Stanley (1963) call "*external* invalidity." Because treatments tend to require special arrangements, the sample studied is usually restricted to some relatively "special" group, which is therefore unrepresentative (Kish 1987) of the population to whom we might like the results to apply. For example, getting students from more than one or two school systems to participate in our study is hard to imagine. Certainly a random sample from all the Hispanic students in the whole country is impossible. Yet the school system to which we have access, and within which we do the study, might be very atypical. For instance, it may be a suburb whose Hispanic community is comparatively well-off. A strong relationship between X and Y might exist in a poorer community, but our study might estimate the relationship as 0. It *is* possible to do representative samples in experiments (see Marwell and Ames 1979), especially those involving such things as question wording (e.g., Schuman and Presser 1981). However, such opportunities are rare.

Experiments also usually prescribe strong "control" over various extraneous conditions. To assure that they all get the identical treatment, the teachers might be brought to a tightly run seminar at the university. However, if the program were actually implemented as a regular policy by a number of school systems, many of the seminars would be taught at the schools, at various times, by various leaders, and so on. Can one generalize from the experiment to everyday practice? As Kish (1987) points out, experiments are often necessarily weak on the *reality* of the conditions they impose on subjects.

Campbell and Stanley (1963) spend much of their time discussing the possibility that the very process of measuring the variables of interest may make the experiment unrepresentative of other situations. For example, if we measure performance in both the second (*Y*) and first (*P*) grades with the same standardized test, some students might have had their learning during the second grade affected by taking the test in the first grade. They might have become sensitized to the material asked in the early test, and "learned" it more than would students in the "real world" who had not been tested. Again, the issue is whether what appears to be the effects of *X* on *Y* might not be the effects of some interaction between *X* and *P*, and therefore not generalizable to the usual situation in the school. This is one reason Campbell and Stanley recommend using "post-test only" designs (i.e., without *P*) where feasible, relying on randomization to make groups equivalent.

In fact, interactions with nonmanipulated independent variables are a particular problem for experiments. If the program works only for Hispanic students with very poor English-language skills, and we did not measure this variable, we may not uncover this fact when we test the *X–Y* relationship for the whole sample (Smith 1990).

CONCLUSIONS

Although recognizing the advantages of experimental studies for making causal inferences, sociologists have tended to associate experiments with laboratory-based studies, and to denigrate the possibility of generalizing from their results. A broader view of experiments sees them as serving a variety of purposes in a variety of settings, while retaining the association with causal models that makes them attractive.

One of the less recognized of these advantages is that experiments tend to force the researcher to clarify the causal model underlying her or his argument, since such theoretical clarity is necessary for the development of an effective design.

(SEE ALSO: *Analysis of Variance and Covariance; Quasi-Experimental Research Designs*)

REFERENCES

Alwin, Duane F., and Richard C. Tessler 1974 "Causal Models, Unobservable Variables, and Experimental Data." *American Journal of Sociology* 80:58–86.

Bonacich, Philip 1990 "Communication Dilemmas in Social Networks: An Experimental Study." *American Sociological Review* 55:427–447.

Campbell, Donald T., and Julian C. Stanley 1963 *Experimental and Quasi-Experimental Designs for Research.* Chicago: Rand McNally.

Cochran, W. G., and G. Cox 1957 *Experimental Designs.* New York: Wiley.

Fisher, R. A. 1935 *The Design of Experiments.* London: Oliver and Boyd.

Hannan, Michael, Nancy Brandon Tuma, and Lyle Groenveld 1977 "Income and Marital Events." *American Journal of Sociology* 82:1,186–1,211.

Kish, Leslie 1987 *Statistical Design for Research.* New York: Wiley.

Marwell, Gerald, and Ruth Ames 1979 "Experiments on the Provision of Public Goods. I: Resources, Interest, Group Size and the Free Rider Problem." *American Journal of Sociology* 84:1,335–1,360.

Molm, Linda 1990 "Structure, Action and Outcomes: The Dynamics of Power in Social Exchange." *American Sociological Review* 55:427–447.

Rossi, Peter H., and Steven L. Nock 1982 *Measuring Social Judgments: The Factorial Survey Approach.* Beverly Hills, Calif.: Sage.

———, Richard A. Berk, and Kenneth J. Lenihan 1980 *Money, Work, and Crime: Experimental Evidence.* New York: Academic.

Schuman, Howard, and Stanley Presser 1981 *Questions and Answers in Attitude Surveys: Experiments on Question Form, Wording, and Context.* Orlando, Fla.: Academic.

Slavin, Robert E., and Nancy C. Karweit 1985 "Effects of Whole Class, Ability Grouped and Individual Instruction on Mathematics Achievement." *American Educational Review Journal* 22:351–367.

Smith, Herbert L. 1990 "Specification Problems in Experimental and Nonexperimental Social Research." *Sociological Methodology* 20:59–92.

Zeisel, Hans 1982 "Disagreement over the Evaluation of a Controlled Experiment." *American Journal of Sociology* 88:378–389.

GERALD MARWELL

F

FACTOR ANALYSIS Factor analysis is a mathematical and statistical technique for analyzing differences among units of analysis and the structure of relationships among variables assessing those units. The units of analysis may be persons, groups, organizations, ecological units, or any other justifiable basis of aggregation. The chief purpose of the method is the attainment of scientific parsimony, which is achieved by positing a set of latent common factors that underlie the data. The factor model was developed by Charles Spearman (1904a; 1927) to be used to describe economically the correlations among mental test scores observed for persons. Spearman's famous bi-factor model of intelligence held that measures of mental abilities had two major sources: a factor common to all measures of ability, which he called the *g*-factor (factor of general ability), and a specific component of variation (an *s*-factor) unique to the test. For example, a test of numerical ability may be affected in part by a general factor of intelligence as well as a factor specific to numerical aptitude. This model, although never the predominant psychological theory of mental tests, has persisted in the culture in the sense that people often believe there is a general factor of intelligence underlying performance across different domains (see Gould 1981 for a critique of this view).

Although Spearman's work did not go very far beyond such a simple model, his approach to model construction and theory testing using tetrad differences has provided the basis for much further work (see, e.g., Glymour et al. 1987). Many contemporaries of Spearman—Cyril Burt, Karl Pearson, Godfrey Thomson, J. C. Maxwell Garnett, and others—working in the fields of human abilities and statistics also contributed to the development of factor analysis. Several worked to modify Spearman's bi-factor model to include multiple factors of intelligence. But the most radical departure from the *g*-factor view of human intelligence came with Thurstone's (1938) publication of *Primary Mental Abilities,* in which he demonstrated empirically through the application of *multiple factor analysis* that several factors were necessary to explain correlations among measures of human abilities. While Thurstone (1947) is usually credited with the popularization of this more general technique, the concept of multiple factor analysis first arose in the work of Garnett (1919–1920; see Harman 1976).

Multiple factor analysis proved to be a major advance over the Spearman model, which was later to be seen as a special case (the one-factor case). Multiple factor analysis permitted a general solution to the possibility of positing multiple factors (k) in a set of variables (p). Within this framework, two competing research strategies emerged, each resting on distinct principles. One was based on Pearson's principle of *principal axes,* which was later developed by Hotelling (1933) as the method of *principal components.* This approach emphasized the objective of "extracting" a maximum of variance from the set of p variables so that the k factors explained as much of the variance in the variables as they could. This tradition still exists in approaches to factor analysis that rely on principal components analysis, and, although many researchers use the technique, they are likely to be unaware of the objectives underlying the approach.

In contrast to the strategy of maximizing the variance explained in the variables, the other basic strategy—more squarely in the tradition of Spearman—emphasized the objective of reproducing the observed correlations among the variables. These two objectives—one emphasizing the extraction of maximum variance in the variables and the other emphasizing the fit to the correlations among the variables—eventually became the object of serious debate. However, with time has emerged a consensus that the "debate" between these approaches rested on a misconception. The method of principal axes, which is the basis of principal components analysis—involving the analysis of a correlation matrix with unities in the diagonal—is now better understood as a computational method and not a model, as the factor analysis approach is now considered (see Maxwell 1977).

The early developments in the field of factor analysis and related techniques were carried out primarily by psychometricians. These early developments were followed by many important contributions to estimation, computation, and model construction during the post–World War II period. Some of the most important contributions to the method during the 1950s were made by a sociologist, Louis Guttman. Guttman made important contributions to the resolution of the issue of deciding upon the best number of latent factors (Guttman 1954), the problem of "factor indeterminacy" (Guttman 1955), and the problem of estimating communalities (Guttman 1956), among many others. Guttman (1960) also invented yet a third model, called *image analysis,* which has a certain elegance but is rarely used (see Harris 1964; Kaiser 1963).

Research workers in many fields made contributions to the problem of deciding how best to represent a particular factor model in a theoretical/geometrical space, via the transformation or rotation of factors. Methods of rotation included the quartimax (Neuhaus and Wrigley 1954), varimax (Kaiser 1958), and oblimax (Harman 1976), among others. Several contributions were made during the early development of factor analysis with respect to the most useful strategies for estimating factor scores (see reviews by Harris 1967 and McDonald and Burr 1967) and for dealing with the problem of assessing factorial invariance (e.g., Meredith 1964a; 1964b; Mulaik 1972). Within recent years—from the mid-1960s —the new developments in the field of factor analysis have focused on the development of maximum-likelihood estimation techniques (Lawley and Maxwell 1971; Jöreskog 1967; Jöreskog and Lawley 1968), alternative distribution-free techniques (Bentler and Weeks 1980; Bentler 1983; 1989; Browne 1974; 1984; Browne and Shapiro 1988), the development of confirmatory factor analysis, which permits the setting of specific model constraints on the data to be analyzed (Bentler 1989; Jöreskog 1966; 1967; 1970; 1971a; 1973; Jöreskog and Sörbom 1986), and the development of factor analysis strategies for categoric variables (Christofferson 1975; Jöreskog and Sörbom 1988; Muthén 1983; 1988).

Factor analysis is used extensively by sociologists as a research tool. It is used in at least four related ways. First, it is frequently used as a data reduction or item analysis technique in index construction. Second, it is used as an exploratory device for examining the dimensional structure of content within a well-specified domain. Third, it is used as a confirmatory, hypothesis-testing tool aimed at testing prior hypotheses about the dimensional structure of a set of variables. And fourth, it is used to conceptualize the relationships of multiple indicators of latent variables in a causal modeling framework in which a factor model is assumed for the relationships between latent variables and their indicators. After a brief introduction to each of these four ways in which factor analytic tools are used in sociological research, this discussion covers the basic factor model and issues that arise in its application, either in the *exploratory* or *confirmatory* frameworks of analysis.

DATA REDUCTION APPROACHES

When a researcher wishes to build a composite score from a set of empirical variables, factor analysis and related techniques are often useful. Indeed, it is perhaps in this area of "index construction" that factor analysis is most often used by sociologists. There are various related data reduction approaches that fall under the heading of "dimensional analysis" or "cluster analysis," but the basic goal of all these techniques is to perform some decomposition of the data into sets of variables, each of which is relatively independent and homogeneous in content. When factor analysis is used in this way the researcher is essentially interested in determining the sets of linear dependence among a set of variables that are intended to measure the same general domain of content. The factor analysis of such variables may proceed in a number of different ways, but the basic goal is to determine the number of clusters of homogeneous content and the extent of relationship among various clusters or factors. Relationships among factors may be conceptualized either in terms of uncorrelated (or orthogonal) sets of factors or in terms of correlated (or oblique) factors. Such analyses are often supplemented with information on how to build "factor scores", with item-analysis information, such as item-to-total score correlations, and with information estimating the "internal consistency" or "reliability" of such composite scores (see Greene and Carmines 1980; Maxwell 1971).

When using factor analysis and related techniques as a basis for index construction, one of two situations is typically the case. Either the investigator has some a priori basis for expecting that items in a set have a common factor (or common factors) underlying them, and therefore the investigator has certain well-founded expectations that the items can be combined into a scale, *or* the investigator has no a priori set of hypotheses for what clusters will be found and is willing to let the inherent properties of the data themselves determine the set of clusters. In either case the use of factor analysis as a data reduction tool is aimed at the development and construction of a set of "scores," based on factor analysis, that can then be introduced as variables in research.

EXPLORATORY FACTOR ANALYSIS

As noted above, in situations where the researcher has no a priori expectations of the number of factors or the nature of the pattern of loadings of variables on factors, we normally refer to applications of factor analysis as exploratory. In the case of exploratory factor analysis the goal is to find a set of k latent dimensions that will best reproduce the correlations among the set of p observed variables. It is usually desirable that k be considerably less than p and as small as possible. In exploratory factor analysis one typically does not have a clear idea of the number of factors but instead begins with uncertainty about what the data will reveal. The most common practice is to find k orthogonal (uncorrelated) dimensions that will best reproduce the correlations among the variables, but there is nothing intrinsic to the factor analytic model that restricts the conceptual domain to several orthogonal dimensions.

CONFIRMATORY FACTOR ANALYSIS

Confirmatory factor analysis, in contrast, refers to situations in which the investigator wishes to test some hypotheses regarding the structure of relationships in the presence of a strong set of assumptions about the number of factors, the values of the factor pattern coefficients, the presence or absence of correlations of factors, or other aspects of the model. In confirmatory factor analysis it is essential that one begin with a theory that contains enough detailed specification regarding constraints that should be imposed on the data in order to provide such a test, whereas in exploratory factor analysis there is no requirement that one specify the number of factors and expected relationships to be predicted in the data. Confirmatory approaches are thus more theory-driven, whereas exploratory approaches are more data-driven (see Alwin 1990). However, much of the so-called confirmatory factor analysis that is carried out in modern social and behavioral science is in fact exploratory, and much current research would be more realistically appraised if such confusion did not exist. Often, there is considerable tinkering with "confirmatory" models in order to improve their fit to the data, either by removing variables or by loosening up (or "freeing") certain parameters. It is also often the case that the "confirmatory" factor analyses are actually preceded by an exploratory analysis, and then a confirmatory model based on these results is fit to the same data. Although very common, this approach "capitalizes" on chance and gives an illusory sense that one has confirmed (or verified) a particular model. Placed in the proper perspective, there is nothing in principal wrong with the approach, as long as the "test" of the model is cross-validated in other data.

FACTOR ANALYSIS AND MULTIPLE INDICATOR CAUSAL MODELS

In the 1960s and 1970s, with the introduction of causal modeling strategies in social science (see Blalock 1964; Duncan 1966; 1975; Heise 1968), a fundamental shift occurred in the nature and uses of the common factor models by sociologists. Methods and the logic of causal modeling with nonexperimental statistical designs had been around for a long time. Due largely to the influence of Lazarsfeld (1968), causal inference strategies had been prevalent especially among analysts of sample survey data since the 1940s, but the research strategies were based on tabular presentation of data and the calculation of percentage differences. In the early 1960s there was a general infusion of techniques of causal modeling in sociology and other social science disciplines. Path analysis, principal of these newly adopted techniques, of course, was invented before 1920 by the great geneticist Sewall Wright, but his contributions were not appreciated by social and behavioral scientists, including the psychometricians responsible for the development of factor analysis. Wright (1921) developed path models as *deductive* systems for deriving correlations of genetic traits among relatives of stated degree. He also used the method inductively to model complex economic and social processes using correlational data (Wright 1925).

Psychometricians, like Spearman, had been dealing with models that could be thought of as "causal models," which could be understood in Wright's path analysis framework—common factors were viewed as the causes underlying the observed variables—but Spearman and others who developed common factor models were unfamiliar with Wright's work. None of the early psychometricians apparently recognized the possibility of causal relationships among the latent variables of their models, or for that matter among their indicators. However, with the publication of work by Jöreskog (1970) and others working in the "new" field of *structural equation models* (see Hauser and Goldberger 1971; Goldberger 1971; 1972; Goldberger and Duncan 1973), the convergence and integration of linear models in the path analysis tradition and those in the factor analysis tradition provided a basic "breakthrough" in one of the major analytic paradigms most prevalent in sociology. These developments were assisted by the interests of sociologists in conceptualizing measurement errors within a causal analysis framework. A number of researchers began to incorporate conceptions of measurement error into their causal analyses (Alwin 1973a; 1974; Blalock 1965; 1969; 1970; Costner 1969; Duncan 1972; Heise 1969; Siegel and Hodge 1968), ushering in a new approach that essentially combined factor models and path models.

At about this same time, Karl Jöreskog and his colleagues were developing efficient procedures for estimating the parameters of such models—called LISREL models, named after Jöreskog and his colleagues' computer program, LISREL—and this provided a major impetus for the widespread use of confirmatory approaches to the estimation of structural equation models. Jöreskog's early contributions to maximum-likelihood factor analysis (1967) became readily applied by even the most novice of researchers. Unfortunately, the widespread availability of these techniques to researchers who do not understand them has led to serious risks of abuse. This can be true of any technique, including the techniques of exploratory factor analysis. In any event, the proper use and interpretation of the results of LISREL-type model estimation is a significant challenge to the present generation of data analysts.

THE COMMON FACTOR MODEL

The formal mathematical properties of the common factor model are well known and can be found in many of the accompanying references. It is useful for purposes of exposition briefly to review its salient features. Although the model can be most compactly represented using vector and matrix notation, it is normally best to begin with a scalar representation for the data, such as in equation 1

$$\begin{aligned} z_1 &= a_{11} f_1 + a_{12} f_2 + \ldots + a_{1k} f_k + u_1 \\ z_2 &= a_{21} f_1 + a_{22} f_2 + \ldots + a_{2k} f_k + u_2 \\ &\ldots \\ z_p &= a_{p1} f_1 + a_{p2} f_2 + \ldots + a_{pk} f_k + u_p \end{aligned} \quad (1)$$

Here the z variables are empirical quantities observed in a sample of units of observation (e.g., persons, groups, ecological units), and for present purposes the variables are standardized to have a mean of zero and standard deviation of unity. This scaling is not a requirement of the model. In fact, in confirmatory factor models, it is often desirable to leave the variables in their original metric, especially when comparing the properties of these models across populations or subpopulations (see Alwin 1988b).

According to the common factor model, each observed z variable is, then, a linear function of a set of k latent or unobserved variables and a residual variable, u_i (also unobserved), which contains variation specific to that particular variable and random measurement error. The a coefficients in equation 1 are "factor loadings." They reflect the linkage between the "observed" variables and the "unobserved" factors. In the case of uncorrelated factors these loadings equal the correlations of the variables with the factors. The loadings thus provide a basis for interpreting the factors in the model; factors obtain their meaning from the variables to which they are linked and vice versa. Thus, in many investigations the primary objective is to estimate the magnitudes of these factor loadings in order to obtain a meaningful understanding of the nature of the data.

The k latent variables are called *common* factors because they represent common sources of variation in the observed variables. As such, these common factors are thought to be responsible for covariation among the variables. The unique parts of the variables, by contrast, contribute to lack of covariation among the variables. Covariation among the variables is greater when they measure the same factors, whereas covariation is less when the unique parts of the variables dominate. Indeed, this is the essence of the model—variables correlate because they measure the same things. This was the basis of Spearman's original reasoning about the correlations among tests of mental ability. Those tests correlated *because* they measured the same general factor. In the general case those variables that correlate do so because of their multiple sources of common variation.

Common variation in the aggregate is referred to as *communality*. More precisely, a variable's communality is the proportion of its total variation that is due to its common sources of variation. The communality of variable i is denoted h_i^2. A variable's *uniqueness*, denoted u_i^2, is the complement of the communality; that is, $u_i^2 = 1.0 - h_i^2$. The uniqueness is thought of as being composed of two independent parts, one representing *specific* variation and one representing *random measurement error* variation; that is, $u_i^2 = s_i^2 + e_i^2$. (This notation follows traditional psychometric factor analysis notation. Each of these quantities is a variance, and, thus, in the covariance modeling or structural equation modeling tradition these quantities would be represented as variances, such that $\sigma_{u_i}^2 = \sigma_{s_i}^2 + \sigma_{e_i}^2$ [see below].) Specific variance is *reliable* variance, and thus the reliability of variable i can be expressed as $r_i^2 = h_i^2 + s_i^2$. Unfortunately, because of the presence of specific variance in most variables, it is virtually impossible to use the traditional form of the common factor model as a basis for reliability estimation (see Alwin 1989; Alwin and Jackson 1979). The problem is that the common factor model typically does not permit the partitioning of u_i^2 into its components, s_i^2 and e_i^2. In the absence of specific variance, classicial reliability models may be viewed as a special case of the common factor model, but in general it is risky to assume that $e_i^2 = u_i^2$. Alwin and Jackson (1979) discuss this issue in detail. Some attempts have been made to augment the traditional latent "trait" model inherent in the common factor model by adding "method" factors based on the *multitrait-multimethod* design of measurement within the framework of confirmatory factor models (see Alwin 1974; Alwin and Jackson 1979; Werts and Linn 1970). This provides a partitioning of the specific variance due to method, but it does not provide a general solution to the problem of handling specific variance.

Returning to the above example (in equation 1), in Spearman's case (the one factor case) each variable contains a common factor and a specific factor, as shown in equation 2.

$$\begin{aligned} z_1 &= a_{11} f_1 + s_1 \\ z_2 &= a_{21} f_2 \text{ n } s_2 \\ &\ldots \\ z_p &= a_{p1} f_1 + s_p \end{aligned} \tag{2}$$

In this case $h_i^2 = a_i^2$ and $u_i^2 = s_i^2$. Spearman's (1927) theory in essence assumes perfect measurement, not unlike most sociological theories. However, unlike researchers of today, Spearman was very concerned about measurement errors, and he went to great lengths to correct his observed correlations for imperfections due to random errors of measurement (Spearman 1904b). Thus, when applied to such corrected correlational data, these assumptions may not be inappropriate.

As can be seen from the equations for Spearman's model (equation 2), the correlations among variables z_i and z_j, $r_{ij} = E\,[z_i\, z_j]$ (the expected value of the cross-products of the z scores for the two variables) may be written as $r_{ij} = a_i\, a_j$. For example, if $p = 3$, the correlations among the variables can be written as $r_{12} = a_1a_2$, $r_{13} = a_1a_3$, and $r_{23} = a_2a_3$. In vector notation (introduced in greater detail below), the common parts of the correlations among the variables of the model are composed of the matrix product AA'. In the case where $p = 3$, the matrix A is written as in equation 3,

$$\begin{bmatrix} a_1 \\ a_2 \\ a_3 \end{bmatrix} \tag{3}$$

and the product AA' is written as in equation 4.

$$\begin{bmatrix} a_1a_1 & a_1a_2 & a_1a_3 \\ a_2a_1 & a_2a_2 & a_2a_3 \\ a_3a_1 & a_3a_2 & a_3a_3 \end{bmatrix} \tag{4}$$

The variances of the variables are also affected by the common factors, but, as indicated in the foregoing, there is a residual portion of variance containing specific and unreliable variance. In Spearman's model the variance of variables i is as shown in equation 5.

$$\begin{aligned} \sigma_{z_i}^2 &= 1.0 = a_i^2 + \sigma_{u_i}^2 \\ &= a_i^2 + \sigma_{s_i}^2 + \sigma_{e_i}^2 \end{aligned} \tag{5}$$

Then it can be seen that the correlation matrix is equal to $R = AA' + U^2$, where the matrix U^2 for the $p = 3$ case is written in matrix form as in equation 6.

$$\begin{bmatrix} \sigma_{u_1}^2 & 0 & 0 \\ 0 & \sigma_{z_2}^2 & 0 \\ 0 & 0 & \sigma_{u_3}^2 \end{bmatrix} \tag{6}$$

These results have general applicability, as will be seen below.

ESTIMATION AND TESTING OF THE FACTOR MODEL

Before proceeding to the more general uses of the model, it is important to review the logic behind Spearman's approach. In the general Spearman case, the correlation of two variables is equal to the product of their loadings on the general factor; that is, $r_{ij} = a_i a_j$. Recall that under this model the a coefficients represent the correlations of the variables with the factor. Spearman reasoned therefore that if the model were true (that is, if a single unobserved common factor could account for the correlations among the observed variables), then certain things had to hold in the empirical data.

Spearman reasoned that, if the single factor model holds, the partial correlation between any two variables, holding constant the underlying common factor, $r_{ij.f}$, should be zero. This stems from the fact that the numerator of this partial correlation, $r_{ij} - r_{if}\, r_{jf}$, is zero, because *under the model* $r_{ij} - a_i a_j = a_i a_j - a_i a_j = 0$. Of course, it is not possible to calculate such a partial correlation from the data because the factor score, f, does not exist except in the theory. Spearman, however, recognized a specific pattern to the components of the correlations *under the model*. He noted that, if the single factor model held for $p = 4$, the intercorrelations of the variables had to satisfy two independent conditions, referred to by Spearman (1927) as *vanishing tetrads*, shown in equation 7.

$$\begin{aligned} r_{12}\, r_{34} - r_{14}\, r_{23} &= 0 \\ r_{13}\, r_{24} - r_{14}\, r_{23} &= 0 \end{aligned} \tag{7}$$

Note that the case of $p = 3$ is a trivial case, since a one factor model can always be used to describe the intercorrelations among three variables. For $p = 5$ there are $[p(p - 1)\,(p - 2)\,(p - 3)]/8$ different tetrads (see Harman 1976), which equals fifteen. Not all of the possible tetrad differences formed from these fifteen are independent, and for one factor to explain the correlations, there are $p\,(p - 3)/2$ independent tetrad differences. Thus, in the case of five variables there are five tetrad differences that must vanish, and for six there are nine, and so forth.

Although in recent years there has been a revival of interest in Spearman's vanishing tetrads for sets of four variables (Glymour et al. 1987), at the time he developed this logic there was little that could be done computationally with very large problems. Thurstone (1947) developed the *centroid* method as an approximation to the principal axes approach involved in Spearman's early work, which was in common use during the 1940s and 1950s, but with the development of the high-speed computer, principal axes methods became (and remain) quite common in many applications of the model.

In exploratory factor analysis, where the number of factors of the model is not known beforehand, estimation is carried out by way of an eigen-value/eigen-vector decomposition of some matrix, either R or some estimate of $R - U^2$. There is a wide variety of types of factor analyses that can be done—principal component factor analysis (which analyzes the p first nonzero components of R), communality-based factor analysis (which analyzes R with a communality estimate in the diagonal), alpha factor analysis, canonical factor analysis, or image analysis (see Harris 1963; 1964). Few developments have been made in these approaches since the 1960s, although there continues to be considerable debate about the desirable properties of these various approaches (e.g., see Widaman 1991).

Perhaps the most important developments affecting exploratory factor analysis since the 1960s has been the development of maximum-likelihood factor analysis. Maximum-likelihood estimation, however, requires the prior estimate of the number of factors. These methods are most often discussed in connection with confirmatory factor analysis, although the approach to exploratory factor analysis discussed by Lawley and Maxwell (1971) illustrates how a form of traditional exploratory factor analysis can be done by setting minimal constraints on the model and testing successive hypotheses about the number of factors. A discussion of these models occurs in a subsequent section on confirmatory factor analysis. Before this, a more formal presentation of the factor model in matrix form is given, along with a discussion of several of the long-standing problems that dominate the literature on factor analysis, specifically the problem of estimating communality, the problem of estimating factor scores, and the problem of determining factorial invariance.

THE FACTOR MODEL IN MATRIX NOTATION

We can generalize the model given above for the case of multiple factors, k, in matrix notation. And again, the factor model can be easily represented in terms of the data matrix at hand. (The model can also be written compactly in vector notation for populations of interest. This is the approach taken in the subsequent discussion of confirmatory factor analysis.) The data matrix in this case can be represented as a p by n array of variable scores. Let Z' symbolize this p by n data matrix. Using this notation, write the common factor model for a set of p variables as $Z' = AF' + UW'$ where Z' is as defined above, A is a p by k *factor pattern matrix* (in the case of uncorrelated factors A is called the *factor structure matrix), F'* is a k by n matrix of hypothetical factor scores, U is a p by p diagonal matrix of unique-score standard deviations (defined such that the element u_i is the square root of the unique variances, $\sigma^2_{u_i}$) and W' is a p by n matrix of hypothetical unique scores. Note that the factors (both common and unique) are never observed—they exist purely at the hypothetical level. Note also that because we have standardized the variables (the *z*s) to be centered about the mean and to have standard deviations of unity, the factor scores in this model are theoretically standardized in the same fashion. In other words, $E(F'F) = I_k$, and the variances of the unique scores are equal to $E(W'W) = U^2$, assumed to be a diagonal matrix.

Traditionally, the factor model assumed that the factors of this model were uncorrelated, that the unique parts of the data (the W) are uncorrelated with the common parts (the F), and that the unique variation in variable i is uncorrelated with the unique variation in variable j, for all i and j. In matrix notation, the factor model assumes that $E(F'F) = I_k$, $E(W'W) = U^2$, and $E(F'W) = E(W'F) = 0$. In other words, the factors of the model are uncorrelated with one another and have variances of unity. Also, the common factors and unique factors are uncorrelated, and the unique factors are uncorrelated among themselves.

This type of notation helps clarify the fact that factor analysis is in effect interested in the "reduced" data matrix, $Z' - UW'$, rather than Z'. Consequently, the factor model is concerned with the decomposition of the matrix $R - U^2$ (the correlation matrix with communalities in the diagonal) rather than R (the correlation matrix with unities in the diagonal), since in equation 8 we demonstrate the following:

$$
\begin{aligned}
R &= E(Z'Z) = E(AF' + UW')\,(AF' + UW')' \\
&= AA' + U^2 \qquad (8) \\
\text{and } R - U^2 &= AA'.
\end{aligned}
$$

This demonstrates an often misunderstood fact—namely, that factor analysis focuses on the reduced-correlation matrix, $R - U^2$, rather than on the correlation matrix (with 1s in the diagonal). As will be clarified below, this is the fact that differentiates factor analysis from principal components analysis—the latter operates on the correlation matrix. In factor analysis, then, one must begin with some estimate of $I - U^2$ or H^2, the matrix of communalities, and then work on the decomposition of $R - U^2$. This poses a dilemma, since neither the common nor unique factors are observed, and it is therefore not possible to know U^2 and H^2 beforehand. The objective is to come up with an estimate of H^2 that retains a positive semidefinite property to $R - U^2$. At the same time, H^2 is one aspect of what one wants to discover from the analysis, and yet in order to estimate the model one must know this matrix beforehand. The solution to this problem is to begin with an "estimate" of the communalities of the variables, and then through an iterative procedure new estimates are obtained and the solution is reached through convergence to some criterion of fit.

COMMUNALITY ESTIMATION AND THE NUMBER OF FACTORS

Determining the number of factors in exploratory factor analysis is one of the fundamental problems involved in arriving at a solution to the parameters of the factor model. The problem essentially involves determining the rank, *k,* of the matrix $R - U^2$, where these matrices are as defined above. Technically, we want to find a matrix U^2 that will retain the property of positive semidefiniteness in $R - U^2$ with the smallest possible rank (Guttman 1954). The rank of this matrix in this case is the minimum number of factors necessary to reproduce the off-diagonal elements of *R*. Thus, the problem of determining *k* is closely related to the communality estimation problem, that is, determining an estimate for the diagonal of $R - U^2$, that is, H^2.

Guttman (1954) outlined the problem of deciding on the number of factors and compared three principles for estimating *k* via solutions to the communality estimation problem. He described a "weak lower bound" on the number of factors, k_1, as the nonnegative roots (eigen values) of the matrix $R - I$. This is equivalent to the number of roots of *R* greater or equal to unity, since *R* and $R - I$ differ only by *I,* and their roots differ therefore only by unity. Guttman shows that k_1 is a lower bound to *k,* that is, $k \geq k_1$. A second principle, one that also implies another approach to estimating communality, is based on the matrix $R - D$, where *D* is a diagonal matrix whose elements, $1 - r_j^2$ ($j = 1, p$), are the result of unity minus the square of the largest correlation of variable *j* with any of the $p - 1$ other variables. Guttman shows that k_2 is also a lower bound to *k,* such that $k \geq k_2$. A third and perhaps the most common approach to estimating communalities is based on the idea that the squared multiple correlation for each variable predicted on the basis of all the other variables in the model is the upper limit on what the factors of the model might reasonably explain. If we define the matrix $R - C^2$, where C^2 is a diagonal matrix whose elements C_j^2 $(1, p)$ are equal to $1 - r_j^2$, where r_j^2 is the squared multiple correlation of variable *j* with the remaining $p - 1$ variables. Guttman shows that k_3 is also a lower bound to *k.* This third lower bound is often referred to as Guttman's *strong* lower bound since he showed the following relationships among the lower bounds: $k \geq k_3 \geq k_2 \geq k_1$. In practice, k_1 may be adequate but it could be wrong, and, if wrong, it is likely to be too small. The use of k_1 is probably questionable in the general case. The use of k_2 is obsolete and not practicable. It estimates communality in the way of the Thurstone centroid method, which is only a rough approximation to a least-squares approach. Perhaps the best solution is the choice of k_3. It is less likely to overlook common factors, as k_1 might, since $1 - s_j^2$ is a lower bound to h_j^2. It should be pointed out that the lower bounds k_1 and k_3 are what distinguish the two main approaches to factor analysis, namely an incomplete principal components decomposition (referred to as principal components factor analysis) and the principal factor method of analysis.

FACTOR ANALYSIS VERSUS PRINCIPAL COMPONENTS ANALYSIS

It was mentioned above that it is not understood well enough that factor analysis is concerned mainly with the matrix $R - U^2$ rather than with *R*. This is in fact one of the things that distinguishes factor analysis from principal components analysis. However, the differences between the two are more fundamental. Factor analysis is based on a *model,* a particular theoretical view (hypothesis, if you like) about the covariance (or correlational) structure of the variables. This model states (as given above) that the correlation matrix for a set of variables can be partitioned into two parts—one representing the common parts of the data and one representing uniqueness—that is, $R = A'A + U^2$. The factor model states, first, that the off-diagonal elements of $A'A$ equal the off-diagonal elements of *R* and, second, that the elements of U^2 (a diagonal matrix) when added to the diagonal elements of $A'A$ give the diagonal elements of *R*. Thus, the factor model posits a set of *k* hypothetical variables ($k << p$) that can account for the interrelationships (or correlations) of the variables but not for their total variances.

In contrast to this, principal components is not a model in the same sense—it is best viewed as a method. It is one method for obtaining an initial approximation to the common factor model (see Guttman's weak lower bound, discussed above), but it is extremely important to distinguish such an "incomplete" principal components solution (one associated with the roots of R that are equal to or greater than unity) from the full-rank principal components decomposition of R (see Maxwell 1977).

Any square symmetric nonsingular matrix, for example, $R = R'$, can be written in the form $R = QD^2Q'$, where D^2 is a diagonal matrix of order p containing eigen values ordered according to decreasing magnitude, and Q is a matrix of unit-length eigen vectors (as columns) associated with the eigen values. Q is an orthonormal matrix, $Q'Q = I = QQ'$. This model is referred to as the principal components decomposition of R. Typically, one either analyzes a correlation matrix with 1s in the diagonal, or a covariance matrix with variances in the diagonal, in the application of this decomposition. In this model the correlation matrix, R, is formed by a centered or deviation-score data matrix scaled so that the variables have variances of unity. Let Z' be the $p \times n$ data matrix, as above. Note that the expected value of $Z'Z = QD^2Q'$, since $Z' = QDY'$.

If the correlation matrix is of full rank, then there will be p columns in Q. This means that in this case the principal components model involves a transformation of p variables into a set of p orthogonal components. When the correlation matrix is singular, meaning that the rank of the matrix is less than p, the principal components decomposition is said to be incomplete, but from the point of view of factor analysis this is often irrelevant since it is the matrix $R - U^2$ that is of interest to the factor analyst.

If P is an $r \times p$ components matrix ($P = QD$), and $r = p$, then it is well known that $Y' = (P'P)^{-1}P'Z' = P^{-1} Z'$, where Y' is a set of r component scores, P is as defined above, and Z' is a $p \times n$ data matrix involving p variables and n units of observation (e.g., persons, cities, social organizations). In other words, component scores (in contrast to factor scores) are directly calculable.

THE ROTATION PROBLEM—CORRELATED VERSUS UNCORRELATED FACTORS

Principal components are by definition *uncorrelated* with one another. The basic objective of the method is to obtain a set of p orthogonal (uncorrelated) new variables via a linear transformation of the p original variables. Factors are different. Factors may be uncorrelated, and in classical exploratory factor analysis one always begins with a set of uncorrelated factors, but in general this is not a requirement. Indeed, in exploratory factor analysis the factors one obtains are uncorrelated because of the nature of the methods used, but normally one performs a transformation or rotation of these factors to achieve a more pleasing representation for interpretation purposes.

Two types of rotations are available—those that preserve the uncorrelated nature of the factors, such as the varimax and quartimax rotations (see Kaiser 1958; Neuhaus and Wrigley 1954), and those that allow the factors to be correlated. The latter are called "oblique" rotations because they move the factors out of the orthogonal reference into a vector space that reduces the geometric angles between them. Using either of these approaches, the basic goal of rotation is to achieve what Thurstone called *simple structure,* the principle that variables should simultaneously load highly on one factor and low on all other factors. These rotational approaches are relatively straightforward and discussed in all of the textbook descriptions of factor analysis.

FACTORIAL INVARIANCE

Following Thurstone's (1938; 1947) discussions of factor analysis, students of the method have frequently been concerned with the problem of the correspondence between factors identified in separate studies or in subgroups of the same study. Using Thurstone's terminology, a concern with the correspondence of factors refers to the *invariance* of factors. The concern with factorial invariance has generated an array of methods for comparing factors (see Mulaik 1972). The most common approach to the problem involves the computation of an index of *factor similarity* for corresponding factors given estimates of a factor model using the same variables in two or more samples. The details of various strategies for estimating factor similarity will not be covered here, as descriptions can be found in a variety of factor analysis textbooks.

These approaches were developed primarily for results obtained from exploratory factor analysis, and it can be argued that the issues of factorial invariance can be more fruitfully addressed using the methods of confirmatory factor analysis (see Jöreskog 1971b; Lawley and Maxwell 1971). The technical aspects of these methods will not be reviewed here, as they have been exposited elsewhere (see Alwin and Jackson 1979, 1981). Suffice it to say that issues of factorial invariance can be phrased, not only with respect to the correspondence of the factor pattern coefficients (the A matrix) across populations, but also with respect to other parameters of the model as well, particularly the matrix of factor interrelationships (correlations and covariances) and the matrix of disturbance covariances.

It is perhaps useful in this context to raise a more general question regarding the nature of factorial invariance that is sought in the analysis of the factorial content of measures. In general there is no consensus regarding whether stronger or weaker forms of invariance are necessary for comparisons across populations or subpopulations. Horn, McArdle, and Mason (1983), for example, suggest that rather than the "equivalence" of factor structures across populations, weaker "configurational" forms of invariance are "more interesting" and "more accurate representations of the true complexity of nature." By contrast, Schaie and Hertzog (1985, pp. 83–85) argue that the condition of factorial invariance, that is, "the equivalence of unstandardized factor loadings across multiple groups," is critical to the analysis of differences among groups and developmental changes within groups.

Clearly, these represent extremes along a continuum of what is meant by the question of factorial invariance. On the one hand, for strict comparison of content across groups, it is necessary to have the same units of measurement, that is, invariance of metric. This requires the same variables measured across populations, and some would also argue that such invariance of metric requires that the relationships of the variables and the factors be equivalent across populations (see Jöreskog 1971a). On the other hand, if the same pattern of loadings seems to exist, it may be an example of misplaced precision to require equivalence in the strictest sense. Of course, the resolution of these issues has implications for other uses to which factor analysis is typically put, especially the construction of factor scores and the use of causal modeling strategies to compare substantive processes across groups.

THE PROBLEM OF FACTOR SCORE ESTIMATION

Researchers using the common factor model as a data reduction tool typically engage in the estimation of such models in order to obtain scores based on the factors of the model, which can then be used to represent those factors in further research. As will be shown here, *factor scores* can never be computed directly (as in the case of *component scores*). Factor scores are always estimated, and, due to the nature of the factor model, "estimated factor scores" never correlate perfectly with the underlying factors of the model. An important alternative to factor scores is what have come to be called "factor-based" scores, which are scores derived from the results of the factor analysis, using unit versus zero weightings for the variables instead of the factor score weights derived from one or another method of estimating factor scores. Factor-based scores, which are frequently more easy to justify and much more practical, typically correlate so highly with factor score estimates as to make one skeptical of the need for factor score estimates at all (see, e.g., Alwin 1973b).

However, it is important that factor analysts understand the nature of the factor score estimation problem, regardless of whether factor score estimates become any more appealing than the simpler and more stable factor-based scores. The factor score estimation problem can best be seen in terms of an interest in solving for the matrix F' in the above matrix representation of the common factor model, $Z' = AF' + UW'$. This can be done analytically, but, as will be seen, it is not possible to do so empirically because of the nature of the model. To solve for F' in this model we arrive at the following representation (without going through all of the necessary steps): $F' = (A'A)^{-1} A' [Z' - UW']$. The calculations implied by this expression cannot actually be carried out because one never knows W'. This is known as the "factor measurement problem," which results in the fact that factor scores cannot be computed directly and must therefore be estimated.

The question, then, becomes whether it is possible to estimate factor scores in a manner that is useful, given what is known—Z, A, and U^2. Several approaches have been set forth for estimating the factors, all of which involve some transformation of the data matrix Z' into a set of k scores that vary in their properties (see Harris 1967; McDonald and Burr 1967). Most of these methods bear some resemblance to the analytic solution for F' above, but there are some technical differences. One of the most commonly misunderstood facts involved in the estimation of factor scores is that the factor pattern coefficient matrix, A, *cannot* be applied directly to the estimation of factors; that is, F' cannot be estimated by $A'Z'$. This, of course, should be clear from the above representation, but it is often used, probably due to ignorance of the more "correct" factor score estimation strategies.

There are four recognized strategies for estimating scores representing the common factors of the model, given Z, A, and U^2 (Alwin 1973b). All of these approaches are typically discussed for a model such as that discussed above, namely a set of uncorrelated factors scaled to have 0 means and standard deviations of 1. It is not the purpose of the present discussion to evaluate the properties of these various approaches to factor score estimation, but a brief summary can perhaps provide a guide to the technical literature on this topic. It is important to emphasize that *none* of these approaches produces factor score "estimates" that are perfectly correlated with the underlying factors of the model. Some of these approaches produce *univocal* score estimates, meaning that each factor score correlates *only* with the factors they are intended to measure and not with factors they are not intended to measure. Only one of the approaches produces a set of factor score estimates that reflect the property of uncorrelated factors with unit standard deviations. But it is difficult in practice to evaluate the desirability of any of the properties of factor score estimates.

METHODS OF CONFIRMATORY FACTOR ANALYSIS

Confirmatory factor analysis, unlike the methods of exploratory factor analysis, begins with prior knowledge regarding the number of factors and something about the nature of their relationships to the observed variables. In the absence of such knowledge, confirmatory factor analysis is not appropriate. In the typical situation of confirmatory factor analysis, then, the investigator begins with some specific theoretical hypotheses involving a model that can be tested against the data. Naturally, there is an extremely large number of such possible models, so it should be obvious that the techniques cannot easily be used to "search" for the best possible set of restrictions involving k factors (but see Glymour et al. 1987).

The bulk of this review has been devoted to the use of exploratory techniques of factor analysis. This imbalance is perhaps justified, given what is known within sociology about the common factors in our data. Exploratory factor analysis techniques are likely to be much more useful, especially at a stage where less knowledge has been developed. And within a field like sociology, where there is a broad variety of competing concepts and paradigms, exploration of data may often be the most salutary strategy. There are, however, clear-cut instances where the use of confirmatory factor analysis techniques is in order, and the remainder of this discussion focuses on these situations.

Consider the following model for a set of p variables: $y = v + \Lambda \eta + \epsilon$, where v is a vector of location parameters or constants representing the origins of measurement of the p observed variables, η is a vector of k latent variables or factors, and ϵ is a vector of random disturbances for the p observed variables. The covariance properties associated with η and ϵ are basically the same as those discussed in the section on exploratory factor analysis for F and W, except that in general these are not required to be uncorrelated within the common factor set. And, of course, there is no restriction on the metric of the variables; that is, the p variables and k factors are not necessarily standardized to have 0 means and standard deviations of unity. The coefficient matrix, Λ, is a matrix of regression coefficients relating the p observed variables to the k latent factors. In the case of a single population, one can easily consider the p variables centered (which would remove the vector of location constants) and scaled to have unit variance, but in the situation where one wants to compare populations neither of these constraints is probably desirable.

The use of these models requires the distinction between constrained and unconstrained parameters. Typically, one refers to parameters of the model as *fixed* if they are constrained to have a particular value, such as a factor loading of 0 or, in the case of the variance of a latent factor, a variance of unity. By contrast, the unknown parameters of the model, for example the λs, are referred to as *free* parameters, which means that they are estimated in the model under the constraints specified for *fixed* parameters. Thus, one speaks of fixed or constrained parameters on the one hand and free or estimable parameters on the other. The major breakthrough in the use of this type of model was the development of computer programs that allow one to fix certain parameters of the model to known quantities while estimating the free parameters under these constraints. The general approach also allows one to specify causal connections among the latent factors of the model, and it allows one to specify correlations among the errors in the variables and the errors in the equations connecting the latent factors.

Consider the factor model for the situation where there are $p = 4$ variables and $k = 2$ factors, with the pattern of factor pattern coefficients shown in equation 9, where the first two variables are believed to measure η_1 and the third and fourth variables are said to measure η_2. This is the kind of situation described by Costner (1969), who developed an approach to confirmatory factor analysis using Spearman's tetrad differences. Of course, there are more efficient estimation strategies than those proposed by Costner. In any event, the point of this example is that the investigator begins, not only with a specific number of factors in mind, but also with a specific set of assumptions about the pattern of loadings.

$$\Lambda = \begin{bmatrix} \lambda_{11} & 0.0 \\ \lambda_{21} & 0.0 \\ 0.0 & \lambda_{32} \\ 0.0 & \lambda_{42} \end{bmatrix} \tag{9}$$

In the general case the covariances and correlations of the common factors of the model, $E(\eta'\eta)$, can be symbolized by Ψ (sometimes this matrix is denoted as Φ, but there are many ways in which to symbolize these quantities), and the covariances of the disturbances (or errors) on the variables can be symbolized by Θ_ϵ. Neither of these two matrices, Ψ and Θ_ϵ, is required by the model to be diagonal, although in the simplest form of the confirmatory model, Θ_ϵ is often assumed to represent a set of uncorrelated disturbances. In more complicated forms of the model, within constraints placed by the identification problem, both of these matrices can be nondiagonal. In either case, the model here is written with the assumption that the investigator has prior theoretical knowledge regarding the number of sources of common variation and that the η vector exhausts those sources.

Any application of this model requires that it be *identified,* which essentially means that there must be enough independent information within the covariance and correlation structure being analyzed sufficient to solve for the unknown parameters of the model. In general, there need to be k^2 constraints on a particular common factor model, that is, in the parameters in Λ and Ψ. Other constraints, of course, are possible. Space does not permit the discussion of these matters, but a detailed treatment of these issues can be found elsewhere (see Alwin and Jackson 1979; Alwin 1988a).

In contrast to methods of exploratory factor analysis and available computer programs for getting results, programs for confirmatory factor analysis are somewhat less accessible, and the sophistication required for using them can be quite high. There are now three generally available computer programs that are capable of handling this type of confirmatory factor models: LISREL (Jöreskog and Sörbom 1986), EQS (Bentler 1989), and LISCOMP (Muthén 1988). These programs are all quite flexible in terms of the kinds of models they estimate, but each has a number of unique advantages. The program manuals for these routines are self-explanatory, and there is little advantage to reviewing their capabilities in the present context. However, there are several special cases of the confirmatory factor analysis model that can be briefly reviewed.

The True-Score Models. It can be shown that a well-known class of measurement models that form the basis for *classical test theory* (Lord and Novick 1968) can be specified as a special case of confirmatory factor analysis (see Jöreskog 1971a; Alwin and Jackson 1979). In brief, by placing particular constraints on the Λ and Θ_ϵ matrices of the model, one can estimate the parameters of models that assume the measures are *parallel, tau-equivalent,* or *congeneric.* Of course, as indicated earlier, in order to use the common factor model in such a fashion, one must be reasonably sure that there is little or no specific variance in the measures. Otherwise, one runs the risk of confusing reliable specific variance with measurement error variance.

Multitrait-Multimethod Models. In addition to the application of confirmatory factor analysis to the estimation of classical true-score models, several attempts have been made to augment the traditional latent "trait" model, inherent in the classical model, by the addition of "method" factors based on the *multitrait-multimethod* design of measurement within the framework of confirmatory factor models (see Alwin 1974; Alwin and Jackson 1979; Werts and Linn 1970). This provides a partitioning of the specific variance due to method, but it does not provide a general solution to the problem of handling specific variance. While these models can be very useful for partitioning item-level variance into components due to trait, method, and error, they place relatively high demands on the measurement design. And while the required designs are relatively rare in practice, these models help sensitize the researcher to problems of correlated method error (see, e.g., Costner 1969).

Multiple-Indicator, Multiple-Cause Models. One of the simplest forms of causal models involving latent common factor models is one in which a single latent endogenous variable having several indicators is determined by several perfectly measured exogenous variables. Jöreskog (1974) and Jöreskog and Goldberger (1975) refer to this as a *multiple-indicator, multiple-cause* (MIMC) model. This kind of model has certain similarities to the canonical correlation problem (see Hauser and Goldberger 1971).

Analysis of Change—Simplex Models. One type of model that can be viewed as a confirmatory factor model, and is useful in analyzing change with respect to the latent common factors over time, falls under the rubric of *simplex* models (Jöreskog 1974). Such models are characterized by a series of measures of the same variables separated in time, positing a Markovian (lag-1) process to describe change and stability in the underlying latent variable. This model can be used in situations where there is a single variable measured over time (see Heise 1969) or in situations where there are multiple measures of the latent variable at each time (see Wheaton, et al. 1977).

Causal Modeling of Factors. If one obtains multiple measures of factors, for which common factor models are believed to hold, and the factors can be specified to be causally related, then it is possible to use confirmatory techniques to estimate the causal influences of factors on one another. Of course, one must be able to justify these models strongly in terms of theoretical considerations, and there must be considerable prior knowledge (as in the use of confirmatory factor analysis) that justifies the specification of such measurement models. The logic involved in dealing with the linkage between observed and unobserved variables is essentially that involved in confirmatory factor analysis, while the logic applied in dealing with the causal linkages among factors is that involved in path analysis and structural equation modeling. The main point is that the parameters of models that essentially contain two parts—a measurement part specifying a model linking observed and latent variables and a structural model linking the latent variables—can be estimated within the framework of LISREL-type models. The measurement part can typically be viewed within the framework of confirmatory factor analysis.

CONCLUSION

The fact that sociologists studying individual differences among persons, social groups, ecological units, and other units of analysis often utilize concepts that involve latent variables, often depicted at a relatively high level of abstraction, reinforces the importance of factor analysis as a method that can assist in the construction of sociological theory. Research by sociologists, as indicated at the outset, relies on factor analysis typically in one of four ways: (1) data reduction for index construction; (2) exploratory factor analysis; (3) confirmatory factor analysis; and (4) multiple-indicator causal models. This review has given primary emphasis to the first two of these basic objectives of the factor model, both because these are areas where one sees more routine use of factor analysis and because the cumulation of knowledge requires in its initial phases an emphasis on exploration, description, and classification. Verification is also an important goal of sociology, and in many contexts the knowledge base is such that the confirmatory factor models have also proven to be useful.

This review has been designed to provide an overview of the major issues involved in the use of factor analysis as a research tool, including both exploratory and confirmatory techniques. Regardless of one's background before entering the field of factor analysis, there are several areas covered above wherein one can find suggestions of further reference material. There are several textbook discussions of factor analysis that will aid those who require further introduction to these issues. Among these, the texts by Gorsuch (1984), Harman (1976), Mulaik (1972), McDonald (1985), and Lawley and Maxwell (1971) are especially valuable.

(SEE ALSO: *Causal Inference Models; Measurement; Measurement Instruments; Multiple Indicator Models; Validity*).

REFERENCES

Alwin, D. F. 1973a "Making Inferences from Attitude–Behavior Correlations." *Sociometry* 36:253–278.

———1973b "The Use of Factor Analysis in the Construction of Linear Composites in Social Research." *Sociological Methods and Research* 2:191–214.

———1974 "Approaches to the Interpretation of Relationships in the Multitrait-Multimethod Matrix." In H. L. Costner, ed., *Sociological Methodology 1973–74.* San Francisco: Jossey-Bass.

———1988a "Structural Equation Models in Research on Human Development and Aging." In K. Warner Schaie, Richard T. Campbell, William Meredith, and Samuel C. Rawlings, eds., *Methodological Issues in Aging Research.* New York: Springer.

———1988b "Measurement and the Interpretation of Coefficients in Structural Equation Models." In J. S. Long, ed., *Common Problems/Proper Solutions: Avoiding Error in Quantitative Research.* Beverly Hills, Calif.: Sage.

———1989 "Problems in the Estimation and Interpretation of the Reliability of Survey Data." *Quality and Quantity* 23:277–331.

———1990 "From Causal Theory to Causal Modeling:

Conceptualization and Measurement in Social Science." In J. J. Hox and J. De-Jong-Gierveld, eds., *Operationalization and Research Strategy*. Amsterdam: Swets and Zeitlinger.

Alwin, D. F. and D. J. Jackson 1979 "Measurement Models for Response Errors in Surveys: Issues and Applications." In K. F. Schuessler, ed., *Sociological Methodology 1980*. San Francisco: Jossey-Bass.

———1981 "Applications of Simultaneous Factor Analysis to Issues of Factorial Invariance." In D. J. Jackson and E. F. Borgatta, eds., *Factor Analysis and Measurement in Sociological Research*. Beverly Hills, Calif.: Sage.

———1982 "Adult Values for Children: An Application of Factor Analysis to Ranked Preference Data." In R. M. Hauser et al. eds., *Social Structure and Behavior*. New York: Academic Press.

Bentler, P. M. 1983 "Some Contributions to Efficient Statistics for Structural Models: Specification and Estimation of Moment Structures." *Psychometrika* 48:493–517.

———1989 *EQS Structural Equations Program Manual, Version 3.0*. Los Angeles: BMDP Statistical Software.

Bentler, P. M. and D. G. Weeks 1980 "Linear structural equations with latent variables." *Psychometrika* 45:289–308.

Blalock, H. M., Jr. 1964 *Causal Inferences in Nonexperimental Research*. Chapel Hill: University of North Carolina Press.

———1965 "Some Implications of Random Measurement Error for Causal Inferences." *American Journal of Sociology* 71:37–47.

———1969 "Multiple Indicators and the Causal Approach to Measurement Error." *American Journal of Sociology* 75:264–272.

———1970 "Estimating Measurement Error Using Multiple Indicators and Several Points in Time." *American Sociological Review* 35:101–111.

Browne, M. W. 1974 "Generalized Least Squares Estimators in the Analysis of Covariance Structures." *South African Statistical Journal* 8:1–24.

———1984 "Asymptotically Distribution-Free Methods for the Analysis of Covariance Structures." *British Journal of Mathematical and Statistical Psychology* 37:62–83.

Browne, M. W. and A. Shapiro 1988 "Robustness of Normal Theory Methods in the Analysis of Linear Latent Variate Models." *British Journal of Mathematical and Statistical Psychology* 41:193–208.

Christofferson, A. 1975 "Factor Analysis of Dichotomized Variables." *Psychometrika* 40:5–32.

Costner, H. L. 1969 "Theory, Deduction, and Rules of Correspondence." *American Journal of Sociology* 75:245–263.

Duncan, O. D. 1966 "Path Analysis: Sociological Examples." *American Journal of Sociology* 72:1–16.

———1972 "Unmeasured Variables in Linear Models for Panel Analysis." In H. L. Costner, ed., *Sociological Methodology 1972*. San Francisco: Jossey-Bass.

———1975 *Introduction to Structural Equation Models*. New York: Academic Press.

Garnett, J. C. M. 1919–20 "On Certain Independent Factors in Mental Measurement." *Proceedings of the Royal Society of London*. A. 96:91–111.

Glymour, C., R. Scheines, P. Spirtes, and K. Kelly 1987 *Discovering Causal Structure: Artificial Intelligence, Philosophy of Science, and Statistical Modeling*. New York: Academic Press.

Goldberger, A. S. 1971 "Econometrics and Psychometrics: A Survey of Communalities." *Psychometrika* 36:83–107.

———1972 "Structural Equation Models in the Social Sciences." *Econometrika* 40:979–999.

———, and O.D. Duncan 1973 *Structural Equation Models in the Social Sciences*. New York: Seminar Press.

Gorsuch, R. L. 1984 *Factor Analysis*. 2d ed. Hillsdale, N.J.: Lawrence Erlbaum.

Gould, S. J. 1981 *The Mismeasure of Man*. New York: Norton.

Greene, V. L. and E. G. Carmines 1979 "Assessing the Reliability of Linear Composites." In K. F. Schuessler, ed., *Sociological Methodology 1980*. San Francisco: Jossey-Bass.

Guttman, L. 1954 "Some Necessary Conditions for Common Factor Analysis." *Psychometrika* 19:149–161.

———1955 "The Determinacy of Factor Score Matrices with Implications for Five Other Basic Problems of Common-Factor Theory." *British Journal of Statistical Psychology* 8:65–81.

———1956 "'Best Possible' Systematic Estimates of Communalities." *Psychometrika* 21:273–285.

———1960 "The Matrices of Linear Least-Squares Image Analysis." *British Journal of Statistical Psychology* 13:109–118.

Harman, H. H. 1976 *Modern Factor Analysis*. Chicago: University of Chicago Press.

Harris, C. W. 1963 "Canonical Factor Models for the Description of Change." In C. W. Harris, ed., *Problems in Measuring Change*. Madison: University of Wisconsin Press.

———1964 "Some Recent Developments in Factor Analysis." *Educational and Psychological Measurement* 24:193–206.

———1967 "On Factors and Factor Scores." *Psychometrika* 32:363–379.

Hauser, R. M. 1972 "Disaggregating a Social Psychological Model of Educational Attainment." *Social Science Research* 1:159–188.

Hauser, R. M. and A. S. Goldberger 1971 "The Treatment of Unobservable Variables in Path Analysis." In H. L. Costner, ed., *Sociological Methodology 1971.* San Francisco: Jossey-Bass.

Heise, D. R. 1968 "Problems in Path Analysis and Causal Inference." In E. F. Borgatta, ed., *Sociological Methodology 1969.* San Francisco: Jossey-Bass.

———1969 "Separating, Reliability and Stability in Test–Retest Correlation." *American Sociological Review* 34:93–101.

———1972 "Employing Nominal Variables, Induced Variables, and Block Variables in Path Analysis." *Sociological Methods and Research* 1:147–174.

Heise, D. R., and G. W. Bohrnstedt 1970 "The Validity, Invalidity, and Reliability of a Composite Score." In E. F. Borgatta and G. W. Bohrnstedt, eds., *Sociological Methodology 1970.* San Francisco: Jossey-Bass.

Horn, J. L., J. J. McArdle, and R. Mason 1983 "When Is Invariance Not Invariant?: A Practical Scientist's Look at the Ethereal Concept of Factor Invariance." *The Southern Psychologist* 1:179–188.

Hotelling, H. 1933 "Analysis of a Complex of Statistical Variables into Principal Components." *Journal of Educational Psychology* 24:417–441, 498–520.

Jöreskog, K. G. 1966 "Testing a Simple Structure Hypothesis in Factor Analysis." *Psychometrika* 31: 165–178.

———1967 "Some Contributions to Maximum-Likelihood Factor Analysis." *Psychometrika* 32:443–482.

———1970 "A General Method for Analysis of Covariance Structures." *Biometrika* 56:239–251.

———1971a "Simultaneous Factor Analysis in Several Populations." *Psychometrika* 36:409–426.

———1971b "Statistical Analysis of Sets of Congeneric Tests." *Psychometrika* 36:109–133.

———1973 "A General Method for Estimating a Linear Structural Equation System." In A. S. Goldberger and O. D. Duncan, eds., *Structural Equation Models in the Social Sciences.* New York: Seminar Press.

———1974 "Analyzing Psychological Data by Structural Analysis of Covariance Matrices." In D. H. Kranz, et al. eds., *Measurement, Psychophysics, and Neural Information Processing.* San Francisco: Freeman.

Jöreskog, K. G. and A. S. Goldberger 1975 "Estimation of a Model with Multiple Indicators and Multiple Causes of a Single Latent Variable." *Journal of the American Statistical Association* 70:631–639.

Jöreskog, K. G. and D. N. Lawley 1968 "New Methods in Maximum-Likelihood Factor Analysis." *British Journal of Mathematical and Statistical Psychology* 21:85–96.

Jöreskog, K. G. and D. Sörbom 1986 *LISREL: Analysis of Linear Structural Relationships by the Method of Maximum-Likelihood.* User's Guide, Version 6. Chicago: Scientific Software.

———1988 *PRELIS: A Program for Multivariate Data Screening and Data Summarization (A Preprocessor for LISREL).* Version 1.8, 2d ed. Chicago: Scientific Software.

Kaiser, H. F. 1958 "The Varimax Criterion for Analytic Rotation in Factor Analysis." *Psychometrika* 23:187–200.

———1963 "Image Analysis." In C. W. Harris, ed., *Problems in Measuring Change.* Madison: University of Wisconsin Press.

Lawley, D. N. and A. E. Maxwell 1971 *Factor Analysis as a Statistical Method.* London: Butterworths.

Lazarsfeld, P. F. 1968 "The Analysis of Attribute Data." In D. L. Sills, ed., *International Encyclopedia of the Social Sciences,* vol. 15. New York: Macmillan and Free Press.

Lord, F. M. and M. L. Novick 1968 *Statistical Theories of Mental Test Scores.* Reading, Mass.: Addison-Wesley.

McDonald, R. P. 1985 *Factor Analysis and Related Methods.* Hillsdale, N.J.: Lawrence Erlbaum.

McDonald, R. P. and E. J. Burr 1967 "A Comparison of Four Methods of Constructing Factor Scores." *Psychometrika* 32:381–401.

Maxwell, A. E. 1971 "Estimating True Scores and Their Reliabilities in the Case of Composite Psychological Tests." *British Journal of Mathematical and Statistical Psychology* 24:195–204.

———1977 *Multivariate Analysis in Behavioral Research.* London: Chapman and Hall.

Meredith, W. 1964a "Notes on Factorial Invariance." *Psychometrika* 29:177–185.

———1964b "Rotation to Achieve Factorial Invariance." *Psychometrika* 29:187–206.

Mulaik, S. A. 1972 *The Foundations of Factor Analysis.* New York: McGraw-Hill.

———1975 "Confirmatory Factor Analysis." In D. J. Amick and H. J. Walberg, eds., *Introductory Multivar-*

iate Analysis for Educational, Psychological, and Social Research. Berkeley: McCutchan Publishing Corp.

Muthén, B. 1978 "Contributions to Factor Analysis of Dichotomous Variables." *Psychometrika* 43:551–560.

———1983 "Latent Variable Structural Equation Modeling with Categorical Data." *Journal of Econometrics* 22:43–65.

———1988 *LISCOMP—Analysis of Linear Structural Equations with a Comprehensive Measurement Model: A Program for Advanced Research.* Version 1.1. Chicago: Scientific Software.

Neuhaus, J. O., and C. Wrigley 1954 "The Quartimax Method: An Analytical Approach to Orthogonal Simple Structure." *British Journal of Statistical Psychology* 7:81–91.

Schaie, K. W. and C. Hertzog 1985 "Measurement in the Psychology of Adulthood and Aging." In J. E. Birren and K. W. Schaie, eds., *Handbook of the Psychology of Aging.* New York: Van Nostrand.

Siegel, P. M. and R. W. Hodge 1968 "A Causal Approach to Measurement Error." In H. M. Blalock, Jr., and A. B. Blalock, eds., *Methodology in Social Research.* New York: McGraw-Hill.

Spearman, C. 1904a "'General Intelligence,' Objectively Determined and Measured." *American Journal of Psychology* 15:201–293.

———1904b "The Proof and Measurement of Association between Two Things." *American Journal of Psychology* 15:88–103.

———1927 *The Abilities of Man.* New York: Macmillan.

Thurstone, L. L. 1931 "Multiple Factor Analysis." *Psychological Review* 38:406–427.

———1938 *Primary Mental Abilities.* Psychometric Monographs, no. 1. Chicago: University of Chicago Press.

———1947 *Multiple Factor Analysis.* Chicago: University of Chicago Press.

Werts, C. E. and R. L. Linn 1970 "Path Analysis: Psychological Examples." *Psychological Bulletin* 74:194–212.

Wheaton, B., et al. 1977 "Assessing Reliability and Stability in Panel Models." In D. R. Heise, ed., *Sociological Methodology 1977.* San Francisco: Jossey-Bass.

Widaman, K. 1991 "Common Factor Analysis vs. Component Analysis: Differential Bias in Representing Model Parameters." Department of Psychology, University of California, Riverside. Typescript.

Wiley, D. E. and J. A. Wiley 1970 "The Estimation of Measurement Error in Panel Data." *American Sociological Review* 35:112–117.

Wright, S. 1921 "Systems of Mating." *Genetics* 6:111–178.

———1925 *Corn and Hog Correlations.* U.S. Dept. of Agriculture, Bulletin no. 1300L1-60. Washington, D.C.: U.S. Government Printing Office.

DUANE F. ALWIN

FAMILY AND HOUSEHOLD STRUCTURE The family system of the United States is often characterized as consisting of nuclear family households (Lee 1982). In fact, there has never been a point in American history where extended family households predominated, either normatively or statistically (Seward 1978). Today only 3.7 percent of all families in the United States are "related subfamilies"—a married couple or single parent with children living with a related householder (U.S. Bureau of the Census 1989a, Table 58).

This does not mean that all remaining households contain the stereotypical nuclear family of two parents and dependent children, however. There is great diversity among American households, and this diversity is increasing. Table 1 presents data on the composition of American households and families from 1960 to 1988. Even over this relatively brief period, substantial changes are apparent. The average size of both households and families has decreased dramatically. Fewer households contained families and married couples in 1988 than in 1960, while the proportion of nonfamily households has nearly doubled, as has the proportion of single-person households. Female householders have increased as a proportion of both all households and all families.

There are many factors responsible for these changes. To understand them, changes in marriage rates and age at marriage, divorce and remarriage rates, rates of nonmarital cohabitation, the departure of children from their parents' homes, and the predilection of unmarried persons to live alone will be briefly examined. Each of these factors has affected household structure.

TABLE 1
Changes in U.S. Households and Families, 1960–1988

	1960	*1970*	*1980*	*1988*
Number of households (in 1000s)	52,799	63,401	80,776	91,061
Average size	3.33	3.14	2.76	2.64
Family households (%)	85.0	81.2	73.7	71.5
Married-couple households (%)	74.3	70.5	60.8	56.9
Female householder (%)	8.4	8.7	10.8	11.6
Nonfamily households (%)	15.0	18.8	26.3	28.5
Single-person households (%)	13.1	17.1	22.7	24.0
Number of families (in 1000s)	45,111	51,586	54,550	65,113
Average size	3.67	3.58	3.29	3.17
Married couple families (%)	87.2	86.8	82.5	79.5
Female householder (%)	10.0	10.8	16.0	16.3

SOURCE: U.S. Bureau of the Census (1989a, Table 58, p. 45).

Marriage rates have declined considerably since 1960 (Table 2). This is not apparent from the "crude" rate (the rate per 1,000 population) because this rate does not take the marital status or age distributions of the population into account. The crude marriage rate was artificially low in 1960 because, as a result of the postwar baby boom, a large proportion of the population consisted of children too young to marry. The rates per 1,000 unmarried women (for both ages fifteen and over and ages fifteen to forty-four) show the frequency of occurrence of marriage for persons exposed to the risk of marriage, and here there is clear evidence of decline. Some of this, however, is attributable to increases in the median age at first marriage, which declined throughout the twentieth century until about 1960 but has been increasing rapidly since 1970. As age at marriage increases, more and more people remain temporarily unmarried each year, thus driving the marriage rate down.

These changes do not mean that marriage is becoming a minority pattern, however. Norton and Moorman (1987) estimate that the propor-

TABLE 2
Changes in U.S. Marriage and Divorce, 1960–1987

	1960	*1970*	*1980*	*1987*
Marriages:				
Rate per 1,000 population	8.5	10.6	10.6	9.9
Rate per 1,000 unmarried women 15+	73.5	76.5	61.4	55.7
Rate per 1,000 unmarried women 15–44	148.0	140.2	102.6	92.4
Median age at first marriage: Males	22.8	23.2	24.7	25.9[a]
Females	20.3	20.8	22.0	23.6[a]
Divorces:				
Rate per 1,000 population	2.2	3.5	5.2	4.8
Rate per 1,000 married women 15+	9.2	14.9	22.6	20.8

[a] Rate for 1988

SOURCES: Marriage rates: National Center for Health Statistics (1990b, Table 1). Age at Marriage: U.S. Bureau of the Census (1989b, Table A-2). Divorce rates: National Center for Health Statistics (1990c, Table 1).

tion of all women who marry at some point in their lives will decrease from its historic level of about 95 percent to approximately 90 percent among women born after 1950. However, those who do marry will marry somewhat later in their lives, leaving a larger pool of young adults who are unmarried at any single point in time.

The rising divorce rate has also contributed greatly to the declining proportion of married-couple households and the increases in female householders and single-person households. The crude divorce rate rose from 2.2 in 1960 to 5.2 in 1980 (reaching peaks of 5.3 in both 1979 and 1981) but has declined modestly in the 1980s. The most recent estimates (National Center for Health Statistics 1990a) indicate a rate of 4.7 per 1,000 population in 1989. Martin and Bumpass (1989), however, point out that this decline is somewhat illusory because the large baby boom cohorts are aging out of the most divorce-prone years. The rate of divorce per 1,000 married women fifteen and over increased from 9.2 in 1960 to 22.6 in 1980, then declined marginally to 20.8 in 1987 (National Center for Health Statistics 1990b). However, estimates of the proportion of all first marriages among today's young adult cohorts that will ultimately end in divorce or separation range from 55 percent (Norton and Moorman 1987) to 64 percent (Martin and Bumpass 1989). Divorce rates are slightly higher for second and higher-order marriages.

Schoen, Woodrow, and Baj (1985) estimate that over 80 percent of divorced men and over 75 percent of divorced women ultimately remarry. Rates of remarriage after divorce have been decreasing since the late 1960s, however (Norton and Moorman 1987). Annual remarriage rates were 204.5 per 1,000 divorced men and 123.3 per 1,000 divorced women in 1970; by 1987 they had declined to 115.7 for men and 80.7 for women (National Center for Health Statistics 1990c).

Decreasing marriage and remarriage rates and increasing divorce rates have combined to produce increases in single-person and single-parent households. This trend is mitigated somewhat by the increasing prevalence of nonmarital heterosexual cohabitation, however. Most such unions (those without children) appear as nonfamily households in Table 1. Bumpass and Sweet (1989) report that, according to estimates from a 1987 national survey, about 4 percent of persons ages nineteen and over are currently cohabiting. In itself this does not seem like an extremely large proportion, although it is a substantial increase from even 1970. However, this estimate pertains to a single point in time. Bumpass and Sweet report that, of those married for the first time between 1980 and 1984, 44 percent cohabited prior to marriage; rates are even higher for those who remarried. For the entire sample, 45 percent had cohabited at some point by their early thirties. Bumpass and Sweet also show that the declining marriage rate among young adults is largely, although not entirely, offset by the increasing rate of cohabitation. Further, about 60 percent of all cohabitations eventuate in marriage. Although cohabiting unions are less stable than marriages, and marriages begun by cohabitation are somewhat more likely to eventuate in divorce, ignoring cohabitation results in substantial underestimates of the prevalence of heterosexual unions in the United States.

In spite of this trend, changes in marriage and divorce behavior have had substantial effects on household and family structure in the United States since 1960. Fewer people are marrying, those who marry are doing so at later ages, more married people are divorcing, and fewer divorced people are remarrying. Largely for these reasons, the rate of growth in the number of households has substantially exceeded the rate of growth in the number of families. Referring again to Table 1, it is apparent that from 1960 to 1988 the number of households increased by over 72 percent, while the increase in number of families was under 45 percent. Over the same time period, the total population of the United States increased by approximately 35 percent (U.S. Bureau of the Census 1989a, Table 2).

A major cause of the decline in household size shown in Table 1 is decreased fertility. The fertility rate (number of births per 1,000 women ages fifteen to forty-four) in the United States was 118.0 in 1960 and had decreased to 65.7 by 1987

(National Center for Health Statistics 1989); clearly the trend toward smaller households and families is reflective to some extent of decreases in the number of children per family.

However, household and family size also depend on the extent to which adults live together or separately. Note that the proportional decline in household size shown in Table 1 is much greater than the proportional decline in family size. Santi (1987) has shown that the increased tendency of adults to live in separate households (single-person and single-parent households) was an even more important cause of declining household size in the early 1980s than was decreased fertility.

For these reasons, the American population is now distributed in more households, particularly more single-person households, than ever before. Single-person households consist of three types of persons: the never-married, who are primarily young adults; the divorced and separated who are without coresident children and who are primarily young and middle-aged; and the widowed who live alone and who are primarily elderly. Each of these types has increased but for somewhat different reasons; each type therefore must be examined separately.

As noted previously, average ages at marriage have risen markedly since 1970, and the proportion of adults below age thirty-five who have never married has increased (Norton and Moorman 1987). This has been accompanied by a long-term decrease (since World War II) in the average age of leaving the parental home (Goldscheider and LeBourdais 1986). Prior to 1970, most of this decline was driven by decreasing ages at marriage, but since then it has reflected an increasing gap between leaving the family of orientation and beginning the family of procreation (Goldscheider and DaVanzo 1989). Goldscheider and LeBourdais (1986) showed that, of all unmarried males between the ages of eighteen and twenty-four, only 1 percent headed their own households in 1940 and 1950; this figure increased to 3.3 percent in 1960 and 13.3 percent in 1980.

There is, however, some evidence that the age at leaving home may have increased somewhat in the 1980s and that some young adults who do leave home may, for a variety of reasons, temporarily return (Glick and Lin 1986). From 1980 to 1988, the proportion of persons ages eighteen to twenty-four living with their parent(s) increased from 48.4 percent to 54.4 percent (U.S. Bureau of the Census 1989b); the percentage of family householders and nonfamily householders in this age category correspondingly decreased.

The increase in divorce and decrease in remarriage have contributed to the rise in single-person households as formerly married persons establish their own residences and, increasingly, maintain them for longer periods of time. They have also contributed to the rise in family households that do not contain married couples. As shown in Table 1, families headed by females (without husband present) increased from 10 percent of all families in 1960 to 16.3 percent in 1988. Families headed by males (without wife present) also increased, from 2.8 percent of all families in 1960 to 4.2 percent in 1988. Among families with children under eighteen, 19.7 percent were headed by women without husbands, and 3.3 percent by men without wives, in 1988 (U.S. Bureau of the Census 1989c, Table 1).

As a consequence of these changes plus the rise in nonmarital childbearing (Wojtkiewicz, McLanahan, and Garfinkel 1990), the proportion of children under eighteen living with both parents has decreased from 87.7 percent in 1960 to 72.7 percent in 1988 (U.S. Bureau of the Census 1989b, Table A-4). In addition, there is a large race difference in the living arrangements of children. Only 38.6 percent of black children lived with two parents in 1988, compared to 78.9 percent of white children. Over one-half (51.1 percent) of all black children lived with their mothers only.

These factors primarily influence the household and family structures of young and middle-aged persons. At the other end of the life cycle, the living arrangements of older persons have also changed considerably in recent history, but here a somewhat longer perspective is necessary to observe these changes. Smith (1979), in an analysis of census data from 1900, estimated that over 60 percent of all elderly persons (sixty-five and over) with surviving children lived with a child. By 1962 this proportion had decreased to 17 percent, and there was essentially no change in this figure by 1984 (18 percent; Crimmins and Ingegneri 1988). Coward, Cutler, and Schmidt (1989) estimated from 1980 census data that just under 20 percent of all elderly Americans lived in two- or three-generation families, but about 5 percent of these persons (1 percent of the total) were living with their own parent(s). Today, then, just under one-fifth of all older persons with children live with a child, which is a substantial decrease from the three-fifths who did so at the beginning of the century. Virtually all of this change, however, occurred prior to 1960.

Two sets of factors appear to be primarily responsible for this change. First, the family life cycle was quite different in 1900 from today. People married a bit later (and markedly later than in the 1960s and early 1970s), had more children, and had children later in life. Consequently, a significant proportion of people in their sixties had unmarried children who simply had not yet left the parental home. Smith (1979) showed that about one-half of the older persons in 1900 who lived with a child lived with an unmarried child.

Second, economic factors played a major role. Social Security did not exist until 1940. In 1900, 85 percent of all men between the ages of sixty-five and sixty-nine were in the labor force, as were 49 percent of all men eighty-five and over. However, this option was much less available to women; the comparable proportions were 12 percent and 6 percent (Smith 1979). Many older persons, particularly women, had no means of support other than their children. Rates of coresidence of aging parents with their adult children have decreased as the prosperity of the elderly has increased; more can now afford to live independently.

Today, about 15 percent of elderly men and 40 percent of elderly women live alone (Coward, Cutler, and Schmidt 1989). Over one-half (51.5 percent) of all women seventy-five years of age and older live alone (Soldo and Agree 1988); the figure among comparable men is only 21.8 percent. The reason for this difference is, of course, the difference in marital status between men and women. Among men seventy-five and over, nearly two-thirds are married and less than one-quarter are widowed; among women these figures are almost exactly reversed (Soldo and Agree 1988). The proportion of all elderly persons living alone increases from 22 percent among those sixty-five to sixty-nine to over 41 percent among those eighty-five to eighty-nine, then drops to 33 percent for those ninety and over (Coward, Cutler, and Schmidt 1989). Older persons who have lost their spouses through death are clearly exhibiting a tendency to live alone as long as possible, which for many of them extends into the latest years of life.

Older persons now constitute over 12 percent of the total population of the United States, compared to about 4 percent in 1900. With so many of them maintaining their own residences, either with their spouses or alone following widowhood, their contribution to the proliferation of small and single-person households is substantial.

If so many older persons lived with their children in 1900, why did the United States have so few extended families? There were three primary reasons. First, because of more limited life expectancies, older people constituted a much smaller proportion of the population, as noted above. Second, also as noted, many older persons lived with an unmarried child; unless other relatives are present, this arrangement constitutes a nuclear family household regardless of the age of the parent or child. Third, while these cohorts of older persons typically had many children, they almost invariably lived with only one (Smith 1979); their remaining children lived in nuclear families. But it is nonetheless very significant that, in comparison to the beginning of the century, older persons today are much less likely to live with children and much more likely to live alone.

To this point, factors that have contributed to long-term decreases in household and family size and the proliferation of small and single-person households have been elucidated. There is evidence of changes in these directions in all age segments of the population. These trends do not mean, however, that more complex family households are not part of the American experience.

As was noted at the outset, the United States has never been characterized by either a normative or a statistical predominance of extended family households; the model family in our culture is nuclear. But extended family households do occur. At any single point in time, they constitute no more than 7 percent of all households (Angel and Tienda 1982; Beck and Beck 1989). However, a dynamic perspective presents a somewhat different picture.

Beck and Beck (1989) analyzed the household structures of a large sample of middle-aged women who were followed from 1969 to 1984. The presence of non-nuclear kin in their households was noted for specific years and was also calculated for the entire fifteen-year period. In 1984, when these women were between the ages of forty-seven and sixty-one, only 8 percent of white married women and 20 percent of white unmarried women (ages forty-seven to sixty-one at that time) lived in households containing their parents, grandchildren, or other non-nuclear kin. The proportions were higher for comparable black women: 27 percent of the married and 34 percent of the unmarried. However, over the fifteen years covered by the survey, about one-third of all white women and fully two-thirds of the black women lived in a household containing extended kin at some point. These are actually underestimates since the survey was not done every year and some short-term episodes of extended family living were undoubtedly missed.

One reason that rates of extended family households are higher among blacks than among whites is that blacks are more likely to be unmarried, and unmarried persons are more likely to live with non-nuclear kin. However, even within marital status categories, blacks are more likely than are whites to live with parents, grandchildren, or other relatives. This is partly a response to the more limited economic resources of blacks (Angel and Tienda 1982); extended family households allow pooling of resources. Beck and Beck (1989, p. 165) conclude that "when a crisis or situation of perceived need occurs, the modified-extended family often responds by becoming an 'intermittent-extended family'; that is, an extended family household is formed temporarily to help one or more family members through a crisis or period of need."

The evidence examined in this article highlights the dynamic nature of household and family arrangements. It is clearly overly simplistic to characterize the family system of the United States as nuclear and leave it at that. More and more Americans are living in single-person households, before, between, and after marriages. More are living in single-parent households. Collectively, Americans are spending smaller proportions of their lives in families of any description than they did in the past (Watkins, Menken, and Bongaarts 1987). However, they are more likely than ever before to live in nonmarital heterosexual unions, and many of them live in households that contain non-nuclear kin at some point in their lives.

The growth of small and single-person households is in many ways indicative of the fact that more Americans can now afford to remain unmarried, leave unhappy marriages, and maintain their own residences in later life. The proliferation of households represents the proliferation of choices. It suggests not that the fabric of our social structure is irreparably torn but rather that the social structure is different from what it was.

(SEE ALSO: *American Families; Family Law; Family Roles*)

REFERENCES

Angel, Ronald, and Marta Tienda 1982 "Determinants of Extended Household Structure: Cultural Pattern or Economic Need?" *American Journal of Sociology* 87:1,360–1,383.

Beck, Rubye W., and Scott H. Beck 1989 "The Incidence of Extended Households among Middle-Aged Black and White Women: Estimates from a Fifteen-Year Panel Study." *Journal of Family Issues* 10:147–168.

Bumpass, Larry L., and James A. Sweet 1989 "National Estimates of Cohabitation." *Demography* 26:615–625.

Coward, Raymond T., Stephen Cutler, and Frederick Schmidt 1989 "Differences in the Household Composition of Elders by Age, Gender, and Area of Residence." *Gerontologist* 29:814–821.

Crimmins, Eileen M., and Dominique G. Ingegneri 1988 "Changes in Family Structure and Family Interaction among Older Americans: 1962–1984." Paper presented at the annual meetings of the National Council on Family Relations, Philadelphia, Pa., Nov. 12–16.

Glick, Paul C., and Sung-Ling Lin 1986 "More Young Adults Are Living with Their Parents: Who Are They?" *Journal of Marriage and the Family* 48:107–112.

Goldscheider, Frances K., and Julie DaVanzo 1989 "Pathways to Independent Living in Early Adulthood: Marriage, Semiautonomy, and Premarital Residential Independence." *Demography* 26:597–614.

Goldscheider, Frances K., and Celine LeBourdais 1986 "The Falling Age at Leaving Home, 1920–1979." *Sociology and Social Research* 70:99–102.

Lee, Gary R. 1982 *Family Structure and Interaction: A Comparative Analysis,* 2nd ed. Minneapolis: University of Minnesota Press.

Martin, Teresa Castro, and Larry L. Bumpass 1989 "Recent Trends in Marital Disruption." *Demography* 26:37–51.

National Center for Health Statistics 1989 "Advance Report of Final Natality Statistics, 1987." *Monthly Vital Statistics Report.* Series 38, no. 3. Hyattsville, Md.: U.S. Public Health Service.

———1990a "Births, Marriages, Divorces, and Deaths for 1989." *Monthly Vital Statistics Report.* Series 38, no. 12. Hyattsville, Md.: U.S. Public Health Service.

———1990b "Advance Report of Final Divorce Statistics, 1987." *Monthly Vital Statistics Report.* Series 38, no. 12, supp. 2. Hyattsville, Md.: U.S. Public Health Service.

———1990c "Advance Report of Final Marriage Statistics, 1987." *Monthly Vital Statistics Report.* Series 38, no. 12, supp. Hyattsville, Md.: U.S. Public Health Service.

Norton, Arthur J., and Jeanne E. Moorman 1987 "Current Trends in Marriage and Divorce among American Women." *Journal of Marriage and the Family* 49:3–14.

Santi, Lawrence L. 1987 "Change in the Structure and Size of American Households: 1970 to 1985." *Journal of Marriage and the Family* 49:833–837.

Schoen, Robert, Karen Woodrow, and John Baj 1985 "Marriage and Divorce in Twentieth-Century American Cohorts." *Demography* 22:101–114.

Seward, Rudy R. 1978 *The American Family: A Demographic History.* Beverly Hills, Calif.: Sage Publications.

Smith, Daniel 1979 "Life Course, Norms, and the Family System of Older Americans in 1900." *Journal of Family History* 4:285–298.

Soldo, Beth J., and Emily M. Agree 1988 "America's Elderly." *Population Bulletin.* Series 43, no. 3. Washington, D.C.: Population Reference Bureau.

U.S. Bureau of the Census 1989a *Statistical Abstract of the United States, 1989.* Washington, D.C.: U.S. Government Printing Office.

———1989b "Marital Status and Living Arrangements: March 1988." *Current Population Reports.* Series P-20, no. 433. Washington, D.C.: U.S. Government Printing Office.

———1989c "Household and Family Characteristics: March 1988." *Current Population Reports.* Series P-20, no. 437. Washington, D.C.: U.S. Government Printing Office.

Watkins, Susan Cotts, Jane A. Menken, and John Bongaarts 1987 "Demographic Foundations of Family Change." *American Sociological Review* 52:346–358.

Wojtkiewicz, Roger A., Sara S. McLanahan, and Irwin Garfinkel 1990 "The Growth of Families Headed by Women: 1950–1980." *Demography* 27:19–30.

GARY R. LEE

FAMILY AND POPULATION POLICY IN LESS DEVELOPED COUNTRIES

The term *family policy* is defined variously, with little consensus about its precise referent other than involving the government's orientation or actions toward "the family" (itself an ill-defined term). For example, in a review of usages, Kamerman and Kahn (1978, pp. 3–8) suggest that "family policy" is used in three distinct ways. In the first usage, the term refers to a field of planning or activity in which certain objectives for the family are defined, and programs or regulations intended to achieve these objectives are created. In the second usage, goals for the family are used as a rationale or rationalization for other, possibly less legitimate, objectives—for example, as a way of increasing or reducing the supply of female workers to the labor market. In the third usage, objectives for the family are used as a criterion by which to evaluate all social policy choices—that is, a government's family policy becomes a yardstick against which military, land use, housing, educational, welfare, and other social policies are measured. There do not appear to be societies where this last usage holds true, but some social policy specialists advocate that it be established, for example, by requiring "family impact statements" whenever social programs are proposed (Kamerman and Kahn 1978, p. 2).

Kamerman and Kahn suggest that family policy ultimately refers to "everything that government does to and for the family" (1978, p. 3) or, more specifically, to "deliberate actions taken [by government] toward the family, such as day care, child welfare, family counseling, family planning, income maintenance, some tax benefits, and some housing policies" (p. 3). They make a distinction between *explicit* family policy, that is, "programs and policies which deliberately do things to and for the family" (p. 3), in some cases guided by specific and explicit overarching goals for the family and in other cases without such goals, and *implicit* family policy, consisting of governmental "actions and policies not specifically or primarily addressed to the family, but which have indirect consequences" (p. 3). An example of the latter is policy to improve literacy by creating a mass public educational system, a development that has been argued to bring about such changes as reductions in average family size (Caldwell 1980) and improvement in the status of women (Mason 1984).

In other usages, "policy" refers to a set of goals for the family and is distinguished from the laws, regulations, and programs that are used to implement the policy or that are evaluated in terms of it. This last usage is less confusing than the usages in which goals and actions are lumped together, so long as it is recognized that implicit family policies can be inferred only by analyzing governmental actions. In these terms, then, *a family policy is a set of explicit or implicit governmental goals for various aspects of family composition or functioning,* goals that are implemented or inferable through the government's regulatory, distributive, or redistributive actions. Common arenas of government action through which explicit family policies are implemented (or implicit policies are inferred) include (1) the enactment or enforcement of family-related laws; (2) the creation of taxation policies affecting family composition or functioning; and (3) the implementation or encouragement of social service programs that influence the family.

Often all three mechanisms will be used to achieve the same goal. For example, a division of labor between spouses in which the wife specializes in domestic chores and child care while the husband provides the household's income may be reinforced through family law (such as making a woman's failure to provide domestic services or a man's failure to provide income, but not the reverse, grounds for divorce; Weitzman 1981, pp. 1–134); through taxation policy (for instance, not taxing a wife's earnings if they are small, as is done in Japan); and through the provision of particular social services (such as public assistance payments for women with dependent children and no husband, but not for men with dependent children and no wife).

Population policies are distinct from family policy because they are oriented toward achieving particular demographic goals rather than particular goals for the family per se. Especially common in today's less developed countries are policies designed to reduce the population growth rate by reducing the birth rate (United Nations 1990), and policies that seek to change the geographic distribution of the population by encouraging or discouraging migration into and out of particular areas of a country (United Nations 1981). Because these demographic outcomes arise from the accumulated decisions of individual family units, however, many population policies are also family policies, at least implicitly. For example, policies designed to reduce the average number of children that couples bear not only may affect family size (itself important as an aspect of the family) but also may reduce the older generation's authority over offspring or increase the wife's autonomy from the control of her husband or mother-in-law. Confusion between population and family policies often arises because the chief population policy in less-developed countries since the 1960s has been to encourage "family planning," a term referring to actions that limit or space births. This phrase dominates public discourse; the phrase *family policy* is rarely heard. The focus of this essay is family policy. Population policies are touched on here insofar as they involve goals for the family.

In every known society, the family/kinship system is a critical social institution, not least because it regulates resource use and allocation, and ensures the continuity of society by rearing the new generation. The composition and functioning of families are governed by moral precepts and social norms. While not all of these regulate behavior strictly (as do, for example, incest taboos), they are strongly felt by most of the population. For this reason, the conduct of family life (for example, the distribution of property among children, or the distribution of rights to children's loyalty and labor among adult family members) is rarely a matter of moral or emotional neutrality, both at the mass level and in government. In this sense, every known society has an "unconscious" family policy consisting of its values and norms about the formation of family units and the conduct of family life.

The universality of strong moral codes concerning the family does not, however, result in the universal existence of explicit government family policies. Among less developed countries today there is great variation in the extent to which explicit family policies can be found (United Nations 1987). Almost all countries have laws intended to regulate important aspects of family life, such as marriage, divorce, and inheritance; but while some have explicit goals for the family —as implied, for example, by the statement in the Philippines' constitution that "the State shall strengthen the family as a basic social institution" (Romero 1983, p. 413)—others have no such goals and no explicit policies beyond of those embodied in the law (United Nations 1987).

One reason for this variation among countries is that explicit policies are often enacted in order to bring about change in the family, a goal that not all governments share. The desire to change traditional family morality has often motivated the enactment of laws on marriage, divorce, dowry, women's family rights, and other aspects of family behavior. For example, in the decade after independence, the government of India sought to change a number of traditional aspects of the Hindu family system by enacting legislation that outlawed polygyny, made remarriage legally possible for Hindu women, gave married daughters a right to their father's estate, and proscribed dowry (Sethi and Sibia 1987). The desire to reduce population growth by regulating age at marriage and, hence, marital childbearing underlies family legislation in some countries—for example, China during the 1970s, when the later–longer–fewer policy was introduced (the three words refer to marriage, interbirth intervals, and children, respectively; Greenhalgh 1990).

Variation among countries in family policy occurs not only because of variation in government attitudes toward family change but also because of variation in internal conflicts over the family. Even where government statements suggest consensus on family issues, considerable discord often exists within the population. For example, the above statement from the Philippines' constitution of 1986 reflects not consensus but conflict between Roman Catholic conservative groups and more liberal elements of Filipino society (Philippine Population Journal 1986). While most governments favor social change, not all sectors of society share that view or agree about the desirable direction of change. Conflict about social change in general, and about the family in particular, is often found between social classes, between groups with varying degrees of exposure to Western or other "outside" cultures, and especially among the ethnic and religious groups that were artifically aggregated into nation-states during the colonial or postcolonial period in many regions of the world.

Whether less developed countries adopt explicit family policies may also reflect the strength of the state and the extent of its struggle to wrest control from local organizations (Migdal 1988). Especially where large kinship groups, such as clans or lineages, have formed the traditional basis of social control, the creation of the modern state may be perceived by leaders to require the curtailment of the power of family groups and, hence, a change in the way that families are formed and function. The state's attempt to gain control through family change may be exacerbated by ethnic heterogeneity in family systems within the society (see Shah 1989 on India). The ongoing contest between traditional and "modern" elements, and between societies and states, can be observed in many settings, though with important variations. In much of Africa, states are attempting to meld diverse tribal systems of custom and law. Church influence (as in the Philippines), the adoption of Western values, and the general extent of centralized planning in the government are other factors that may motivate the creation of an explicit family policy and that help to explain variation among countries in the existence of such policy.

In addition to variation among countries in their adoption of explicit family policies is variation in the content of family policy, both explicit and implicit. For example, some countries have explicit goals to "strengthen" the family, while in others, the goal has clearly been to weaken it (as in China in the two decades following the establishment of the People's Republic [Greenhalgh 1990] or Iran prior to the 1979 revolution). Despite this variation across countries in the content of family policy, however, certain concerns about family-related issues are shared by a number of today's less-developed countries' governments. Demographic problems that many of these countries face are one source of shared concern. Paramount among these is rapid population growth, a concern that has motivated a variety of family-oriented laws and programs, including raising the minimum legal age for marriage in order to reduce the reproductive span during which women are exposed to regular sexual activity (Piepmeier and Hellyer 1977), providing family planning services to married couples, and, in countries such as Singapore and China, offering incentives and disincentives for childbearing that involve the provision or withholding of housing, paid maternity leave, and medical or educational services (Quah 1990; Greenhalgh 1990).

Another demographic problem faced by many less developed countries that influences family policy is the lengthening of adolescence and the attendant development of an independent youth culture caused by declining ages at puberty and rising ages at marriage (United Nations 1989). A number of less developed countries' governments, especially in Asia, have established sex education or "family life education" policies and programs oriented toward the adolescent population, in part in response to the growing youth culture and extension of adolescence, and in part as a way of maintaining government family planning programs in the face of increasingly low levels of marital fertility (Xenos 1990). States have increasingly differentiated youth from adults in their constitutions (Boli-Bennett and Meyer 1978), and youth policies are an increasingly important element of family policy (see Central Committee on Youth 1988; Paxman 1984).

Still another emerging demographic problem that is influencing family policy in many less-developed countries is the proportionate growth of the aged population that invariably occurs when birth rates fall. How a growing population of the aged is to be cared for, and whether the family or the state should provide this care, are topics receiving increasing attention in the less-developed countries that have experienced a decline in the birth rate. In some countries, policies are being considered to keep this burden within families rather than making it a government responsibility (Martin 1988).

In addition to common areas of concern caused by demographic trends are areas of concern that reflect the global movement toward equal rights for oppressed groups (including those based on gender and age) and fundamentalist countermovements, especially those associated with Islam. Many less developed countries' governments have moved to grant women equal (or more equal) rights with men, a change that invariably has affected family policy. In many countries, legislation outlawing bigamy or polygyny, the dowry, exclusive property inheritance by males, the prohibition of remarriage for women, men's exclusive right to initiate divorce, and the control of married women's property and earnings by husbands or fathers has been enacted. The passage of such laws has by no means guaranteed their enforcement or the population's compliance with them (see Sethi and Sibia 1987 for evidence of this in India), and in some countries, in response to fundamentalist movements, a trend toward reducing women's family rights can be found (as in Iran and Pakistan). But the point is that many governments have been motivated to alter the legal arrangements surrounding family relationships by the desire to change women's rights vis-à-vis men.

Rising divorce rates and the accompanying perception of family "breakdown" is another concern affecting family policy in less developed countries. Although divorce rates have fallen in some countries where they were traditionally high (such as Malaysia and Indonesia), other countries that historically had little divorce have seen an increase. As in the West, this has often led to concern about the breakdown of traditional family arrangements, especially those involving the care of children. Traditional and contemporary patterns vary widely across world regions, with high rates of out-of-wedlock childbearing and child rearing having existed in some areas for a century or more (such as the Caribbean); nor are responses to this problem uniform. Nevertheless, if divorce rates continue to rise, it seems likely that less developed countries' governments will enact new legislation and programs touching on this problem.

In discussing family policy it is important to recognize that the object of this policy—the family—is a diverse entity, both within and between countries. The bounded, economically independent conjugal unit consisting of husband, wife, and dependent children that is often thought of as constituting "the" family in the West is not recognized as a meaningful unit in some traditional cultures, especially in sub-Saharan Africa. In that part of the world, the lineage, the mother–child unit, or the sibling group often is the important unit within which the economic, social, political, and child-rearing work of the family takes place (Goody 1972). Family systems vary enormously within the Third World—for example, the ideal of the patrilineal, patrilocal "grand family" found in China and India is largely absent in Southeast Asia, where a far more "conjugalized" system tends to dominate (Xenos 1988)—and family policy often varies according to the nature of the ideal family system. For example, in Japan, where the ideal of a patrilateral stem family in which the eldest son remains in the parental home has dominated for a century or more (Ueno 1987), it is not surprising that the government continues to emphasize the family as the most desirable source of care for the aged.

Recognition of important variation in what constitutes "the" family raises an important issue: the strain in many countries between an imported, Westernized vision of the family that is supported by the government, and the traditional family forms supported at the grass roots. In many less developed countries, the government vision of the family may result from the colonial experience (although in some instances, such as India, the colonial power has been more laissez faire about native family forms than the postindependence government), or it may reflect the exposure of the urban elite to Western society, or the perceived consonance between a more Westernized family system and other governmental goals, such as economic development or undermining the power of large kin groups. Where political struggle focuses on family policy, the underlying issue that is often at stake involves alternative definitions of the family. The proponents of these alternative definitions often are distinguished by elite versus mass background, as well as by membership in different elites.

Social policy in developing countries has been much influenced by emerging global viewpoints and by the sanction given to them by international organizations. For example, various arms of the United Nations offer explicit recommendations on a range of policies, including those on education, family health, women's labor force participation, and the family (United Nations 1987). Moreover, such recommendations are closely tied to the system of international aid. An important outcome has been the development of consistent systems for collecting social data and monitoring social change. There is a remarkable homogeneity across less developed countries in the types of data available to inform national debate on family and other social policies that has resulted from the effort of international agencies to ensure uniform social statistics.

(SEE ALSO: *Demographic Transition; Family Planning; Population*)

REFERENCES

Boli-Bennett, John, and John W. Meyer 1978 "The Ideology of Childhood and the State: Rules Distinguishing Children in National Constitutions, 1870–1970." *American Sociological Review* 43:797–812.

Caldwell, John C. 1980 "Mass Education as a Determinant of the Timing of Fertility Decline." *Population and Development Review* 6 (June):225–255.

Central Committee on Youth 1988 *Report on Youth Policy.* Hong Kong: Central Committee on Youth.

Goody, Jack 1972 "The Evolution of the Family." In P. Laslett and R. Wall, eds., *Household and Family in Past Time.* Cambridge: Cambridge University Press.

Greenhalgh, Susan 1990 *State–Society Links: Political Dimensions of Population Policies and Programs, with Special Reference to China.* Research Division Working Papers, no. 18. New York: Population Council.

Kamerman, Sheila B., and Alfred J. Kahn, (eds.) 1978 *Family Policy: Government and Families in Fourteen Countries.* New York: Columbia University Press.

Martin, Linda G. 1988 "The Aging of Asia." *Journal of Gerontology* 43, no. 4:S99–S113.

Mason, Karen Oppenheim 1984 *The Status of Women: A Review of Its Relationships to Fertility and Mortality.* New York: Rockefeller Foundation.

Midgal, Joel S. 1988 *Strong Societies and Weak States: State–Society Relations and State Capabilities in the Third World.* Princeton, N.J.: Princeton University Press.

Paxman, John M. 1984 *Law, Policy and Adolescent Fertility: An International Overview.* London: International Planned Parenthood Federation.

Philippine Population Journal 1986 "Proceedings of the Constitutional Commission on the Family, 1986 (Part 1)." *Philippine Population Journal,* 2, nos. 1–4: 135–156.

Piepmeier, Katherine B., and Elizabeth Hellyer 1977 "Minimum Age at Marriage: 20 Years of Legal Reform." *People* 4, no. 3 [data chart].

Quah, Stella R. 1990 "The Social Significance of Marriage and Parenthood in Singapore: Policy and Trends." In S. R. Quah, ed., *The Family as an Asset: An International Perspective on Marriage, Parenthood and Social Policy.* Singapore: Times Academic Press.

Romero, Flerida Ruth P. 1983 "New Policy Directions in Philippine Family Law." *Philippine Journal of Public Administration* 27 (October):412–417.

Sethi, Raj Mohini, and Kiran Sibia 1987 "Women and Hindu Personal Laws: A Socio-Legal Analysis." *Journal of Sociological Studies* 6 (January):101–113.

Shah, A. M. 1989 "Parameters of Family Policy in India." *Economic and Political Weekly,* March 11, pp. 513–516.

Ueno, Chizuko 1987 "The Position of Japanese Women Reconsidered." *Current Anthropology* 28 (August–October):S75–S84.

United Nations 1981 *Population Distribution Policies in Development Planning.* New York: United Nations, Department of International Economic and Social Affairs.

———1987 *The Family.* No. 3: *National Family Policies: Their Relationship to the Role of the Family in the Development Process.* New York: United Nations, Department of International Economic and Social Affairs.

———1989 *Adolescent Reproductive Behaviour: Evidence from Developing Countries,* vol. II. New York: United Nations, Department of International Economic and Social Affairs.

———1990 *World Population Trends and Policies: 1989 Monitoring Report.* New York: United Nations, Department of International Economic and Social Affairs.

Weitzman, Lenore J. 1981 *The Marriage Contract: Spouses, Lovers, and the Law.* New York: Free Press.

Xenos, Peter 1988 "Family Theory and the Southeast Asian Family." Paper prepared for the IUSSP/NIRA Seminar on Theories of Family Change, Tokyo, November 29–December 2, 1988.

———1990 "Youth, Sexuality and Public Policy in Asia: A Research Perspective." In S. R. Quah, ed., *The Family as an Asset: An International Perspective on Marriage, Parenthood and Social Policy.* Singapore: Times Academic Press.

KAREN OPPENHEIM MASON
PETER XENOS

FAMILY LAW Family law is that body of law having to do with creating, ordering, and dissolving marital and family groups. Although the exact scope of family law is given differently by different authors, at its core family law is concerned with such issues and events as marriage, separation, divorce, alimony, custody, child support, and adoption, as well as the more arcane topics of annulment, paternity, legitimacy, artificial insemination, and surrogate parenting.

This entry on family law in the United States should be read with two important caveats in mind. First, it is somewhat misleading to write of "United States" family law. Because the power to regulate domestic life is not one of the powers delegated to the federal government by the Constitution, in the United States most family law has been "a virtually exclusive province of the states" (*Sosna v. Iowa*, 419 U.S. 393 [1975]). Despite considerable variation in state law, however, certain general trends can be identified. Moreover, researchers have identified similar trends in a number of European countries (Glendon 1989).

Second, many kinds of law that affect the family cannot be discussed here. These include laws that are not ordinarily listed under the rubric of "family law" but that have significant effects on family life in this country. These range from the laws of inheritance to zoning regulations and regulations about social welfare programs. While the impact on the family of a diversity of laws seems to become increasingly significant, this is not a uniquely modern phenomenon. For example, 200 years ago poor laws affected family life in ways that anticipated the impact of modern welfare laws (tenBroek 1964).

As was typical of much of early law in this country, most American family law was received from English law; but family law was atypical in that much of it was not derived from secular or "temporal" English law. In England, from the late twelfth century (Pollock and Maitland 1898, Vol. 2, p. 367) until the passage of the Matrimonial Causes Act of 1857, issues pertaining to marriage and divorce were governed by canon law, and most family matters were thus subject to the jurisdiction of ecclesiastical courts. While the American colonies had no ecclesiastical courts, English canonical rules concerning family relations were incorporated—either by statute or by common law tradition—into the laws of the colonies and, later, the states (Clark 1980).

Notwithstanding its religious heritage, family law in this country was completely secular. Although marriages were frequently performed by members of the clergy, the authority to solemnize marriages was vested in them by the state, not the church. In legal theory, at the basis of the family was a marriage that was a civil contract and not a religious sacrament.

This contractual view of marriage had some interesting consequences. For example, it led to official recognition of informal as well as formal marriage. This informal union, the so-called common law marriage, was effected by the simple express agreement of a man and a woman to be married, followed by their cohabitation. (Contrary to popular myth, common law marriages did not require a specific number of years to go into effect.) While today they are recognized only in fourteen states, until the twentieth century common law marriages were as valid as formal marriages in nearly every state (Wardle, Blakesley, and Parker 1988, § 3:17). Recognition of common law marriage meant that settlers on the geographic fringes of society, without access to officials, could enjoy the same protection of their property rights and their children's legitimacy as was afforded in formal marriages. In 1833, Chief Justice Gibson of Pennsylvania ruled that rigid marriage laws were "ill adapted to the habits and customs of society as it now exists." Not recognizing common law marriage, or so Gibson suggested, would "bastardize the vast majority of children which have been born within the state for half a century" (*Rodenbaugh v. Sanks*, 2 Watts 9).

After the Civil War, there was a movement to strengthen state regulation of marriage. Most states already required marriage licenses, but in antebellum America, courts had treated these licenses as a means "to register, not to restrict marriage" (Grossberg 1985, p. 78). By the end of the nineteenth century, however, marriage licenses had clearly become a means of social control. Because the process of acquiring a marriage license brought the couple under scrutiny of some official, licensing requirements helped states prevent marriages of people who were too young or too closely related, either by blood (consanguinity) or marriage (affinity). Official scrutiny of those seeking to wed also helped to enforce laws against bigamy and polygamy.

But legislators, encouraged by eugenicists who believed that crime, mental illness, and other social ills could be traced to hereditary biological factors, also enacted laws enumerating other kinds of forbidden marriages. For example, marriage was prohibited to those not mentally capable of contracting owing to conditions variously labeled as insanity, lunacy, idiocy, feeblemindedness, imbecility, or unsound mind (Clark 1968, pp. 95–96). Marriage was also prohibited to those physically incapable of performing the "marriage essentials." Generally, this latter criterion involved only the capacity to have "normal" or "successful" sexual intercourse, not necessarily the ability to procreate. As one author explained it, "Copula, not fruitfulness, is the test" (Tiffany 1921, p. 29).

Eugenics also justified, scientifically, laws that prohibited people with certain diseases (e.g., epilepsy, tuberculosis, and venereal disease) and statuses (e.g., habitual criminal, rapist) from marrying. In most cases, such obstacles could be overcome only if the person consented to sterilization. Many believed such statutes were necessary to "prevent the demise of civilized society" (Linn and Bowers 1978, p. 629). Even some of the most respected legal thinkers joined the eugenicists. Justice Oliver Wendell Holmes of the United States Supreme Court, for example, wrote that it would be "better for all the world, if instead of waiting to execute degenerate offspring for crimes, or to let them starve for their imbecility, society can prevent those who are manifestly unfit from continuing their kind" (*Buck v. Bell*, 274 U.S. 200 [1927]).

The most notorious marriage impediment was race. By 1930, thirty states had enacted statutes prohibiting interracial marriages (Clark 1968, p. 91). For the most part, these antimiscegenation laws forbade marriages between whites and blacks, but in several cases, the prohibition was extended to, for example, white and Malays, whites and Mongolians, whites and Native Americans, and blacks and Native Americans (Kennedy 1959, pp. 59–69).

Divorce was even more strictly regulated than marriage. However, the absence of ecclesiastical restrictions made divorces much easier to obtain in the United States than in England. This was especially true in the northern states. A few states even allowed divorce simply where the cause seemed "just and reasonable." Connecticut, for example, permitted divorce for conduct that "permanently destroys the happiness of the petitioner and defeats the purpose of the marriage relation" (Clark 1968, p. 283). During the latter part of the nineteenth century such generous statutes were repealed, and divorce was allowed only in response to specific types of fault—usually adultery, desertion, cruelty, or long-term imprisonment.

Despite stringent regulation of entrance to and exit from marriage, husbands and wives in intact marriages were generally protected from legal scrutiny. Indeed, traditionally, the principle of nonintervention was so strong that neither husbands nor wives could invoke the law to resolve marital disputes even when they wished to. In one case, for example, the wife of a well-to-do but stingy husband asked the Nebraska courts to require him to pay for indoor plumbing and to provide a reasonable allowance to her. The court agreed that, given his "wealth and circumstances," the husband's attitude "leaves little to be said in his behalf." But, said the court, "the living standards of a family are a matter of concern to the household and not for the courts to determine" (*McGuire v. McGuire*, 157 Neb. 226, 59 N.W.2d 336 [1953]). Similarly, the courts preferred a hands-off approach to parent–child relationships. As the United States Supreme Court ruled in 1944, "the custody, care, and nurture of the child reside first in the parents, whose primary function and freedom include preparation for obligations the state can neither supply nor hinder. . . . It is in recognition of this that [earlier] decisions have respected the private realm of family life which the state cannot enter" (*Prince v. Massachusetts*, 321 U.S. 158 [1944]).

The extent of the courts' reluctance to intervene in family matters or, as it was sometimes put, to "disrupt family harmony," was shown in the rule that spouses could not sue one another for personal torts or injuries. If, for example, a husband assaulted or battered his wife, she was enjoined from taking legal action against him in civil court (Keeton, Dobbs, and Owen 1984, pp. 901–902). In theory, the husband could be prosecuted in criminal court, but police and criminal courts too were reluctant to interfere in domestic matters (Pleck 1987, p. 187).

The practice of nonintervention was carried a step further at the turn of the century when the courts invented the doctrine of "parental immunity." Owing to reasons of "sound public policy, designed to subserve the repose of families and the best interests of society" (*Hewellette v. George*, 68 Miss. 703, 9 So. 885 [1891]), an unemancipated minor was barred from suing his or her parents for negligent or intentional wrongdoing.

Owing to the state's reluctance to intervene, the family has had a great deal of autonomy in this country, even to the extent that some have referred to the family as a "minisovereignty" (O'Donnell and Jones 1982, p. 7). In recent times, this autonomy has been justified on the basis of privacy rights. Speaking of the married couple's right to make decisions about the use of contraception, the United States Supreme Court said in 1965, for example, "we deal with a right of privacy older than the Bill of Rights" (*Griswold v. Connecticut*, 381 U.S. 479 [1965]).

But things began to change in the late twentieth century. First, beginning in the 1960s, strict regulation of entrance to and exit from marriage began to unravel. In the 1967 case of *Loving v. Virginia*, the United States Supreme Court ruled unconstitutional all antimiscegenation laws, saying that the states had no right to "prevent marriages between persons solely on the basis of racial classification." "Marriage," said the Court, "is one of the 'basic civil rights of man,' fundamental to our very existence and survival" (388 U.S. 1; quoting *Skinner v. Oklahoma*, 316 U.S. 535 [1942]). Since *Loving*, many other marriage restrictions have been repealed or eased. Age requirements in many states have been lowered; the mental ability needed to contract marriage has been ruled to be less than that required for other sorts of contracts; and the necessary mental competency is presumed to be present unless there is "clear and definite" proof to the contrary. Moreover, "there is a trend in modern times to abolish affinity restrictions" (Wardle, Blakesley, and Parker 1988, § 2:09); only one state (Missouri) still prohibits epileptics to marry (Wardle, Blakesley, and Parker 1988, § 2:47) and in many states, even prison inmates are deemed to have a right to marry (*In re Carrafa*, 77 Cal. App.3d 788 [1978]).

These changes reflect the courts' willingness to protect the rights of individuals to make their own choices about marriage and related matters. The decision to marry, according to the Supreme Court, is among "the personal decisions protected by the right to privacy" (*Zablocki v. Redhail*, 434 U.S. 374 [1978]).

Presumably, much the same can be said about the decision to divorce; recent changes in divorce laws have, if anything, been even more dramatic than changes in marriage laws. Implicitly accepting the principle that there is a right to divorce, the Supreme Court ruled in 1971 that welfare recipients could not be denied access to divorce courts because they could not afford to pay court costs and fees (*Boddie v. Connecticut*, 101 U.S. 371 [1971]). By the mid-1980s, every state had either replaced fault-based divorce laws with no-fault laws, or added no-fault grounds to existing laws (Freed and Walker 1986, p. 444). No longer, then, must there be a "guilty" and an "innocent" party in a divorce. Instead, one spouse simply needs to assert that the couple is no longer getting along or has been living apart for a certain amount of time.

While regulations governing entrance to and exit from marriage and family life have decreased, there has been a corresponding increase in regulations affecting relations in ongoing families. Spousal immunity has been abolished in most states. Moreover, in many states the law recognizes the crime of "marital rape." Similarly, children now have more rights that can be asserted against their parents. For example, minors have the right to obtain information about and to use birth control without a parent's consent (*Carey v. Population Services International*, 431 U.S. 678 [1977]); to receive psychiatric care (*In re Alyne E.*, 113 Misc. 2d 307, 448 N.Y.S.2d 984 [1982]); and perhaps even to separate from their parents should the parents and children prove "incompatible" (*In re Snyder*, 85 Wash. 2d 182. 532 P.2d 278 [1975]). At base, says the Supreme Court, children "are 'persons' under the Constitution" and have rights that should be protected by the state (*Tinker v. Des Moines Independent School District*, 393 U.S. 503 [1969]).

Both the easing of marriage and divorce restrictions and the loss of family autonomy can be traced to the growth of individual rights that began in the 1960s. The idea of family autonomy and privacy and, hence, the policy of nonintervention were traditionally based on "paternal" authority; the authority of the family patriarch. This pattern can be traced back to the Roman idea of *patria potestas*—or the right of the father to exert absolute control over his family, including the power of life or death.

Family autonomy and privacy that is based on paternal power is viable only when other members of the family are unable to invoke the power of the state against the father. It was for this reason, then, that traditionally the woman's power to invoke the law was suspended from the moment of her marriage (Blackstone [1769] 1979, Vol. 1, p. 430). Children, likewise, had no legal standing until they reached the age of majority.

Things are much different today: While children still have many "legal disabilities," they can no longer be regarded as chattel. Women have achieved at least technical legal equality (though whether this has served to their advantage in divorce law is still subject to debate—compare Weitzman 1985 and Jacob 1988). Although the courts still speak of "family privacy," it is becoming clear that such privacy is based on family members' individual rights and exists only as long as family members are not in serious conflict about how they wish to assert those rights.

Some mourn the loss of near total family autonomy; the family, they say, has lost its integrity (Peirce 1988). There is no doubt that the notion of family autonomy or privacy served an important value: It has been "a convenient way for dealing with a problem . . . [that is] especially acute in the United States—that of devising family law which is suited to the needs and desires of persons with different ethnic and religious backgrounds, different social status, and different standards of living" (Glendon 1989, p. 95). In many instances, however, nonintervention created private Hobbesian jungles in which the strong ruled and the weak could not call upon the law for help.

(SEE ALSO: *Family and Household Structure*)

REFERENCES

Blackstone, William (1769) 1979 *Commentaries on the Laws of England*, 4 vols. Chicago: University of Chicago Press.

Clark, Homer H., Jr. 1968 *Law of Domestic Relations*. St. Paul, Minn.: West.

——— 1980 *Cases and Problems on Domestic Relations*. 3rd ed. St. Paul, Minn.: West.

Freed, Doris J., and Timothy B. Walker 1986 "Family Law in the Fifty States: An Overview." *Family Law Quarterly* 20:439–587.

Glendon, Mary A. 1989 *The Transformation of Family Law, State, Law, and Family in the United States and Western Europe*. Chicago: University of Chicago Press.

Grossberg, Michael 1985 *Governing the Hearth: Law and Family in Nineteenth-Century America*. Chapel Hill: University of North Carolina Press.

Jacob, Herbert 1988 *Silent Revolution*. Chicago: University of Chicago Press.

Keeton, W. Page, Dan B. Dobbs, Robert E. Keeton, and David G. Owen 1984 *Prosser and Keeton on the Law of Torts*. 5th ed. St. Paul, Minn.: West.

Kennedy, Stetson 1959 *The Jim Crow Guide to the USA*. London: Lawrence and Wishart.

Linn, Brian J., and Lesly A. Bowers 1978. "The Historical Fallacies behind Legal Prohibitions of Marriages Involving Mentally Retarded Persons: The Eternal Child Grows Up." *Gonzaga Law Review* 13:625–690.

Long, Joseph R. 1905 *A Treatise on the Law of Domestic Relations.* St. Paul, Minn.: Keefe-Davidson.

O'Donnell, William J., and David A. Jones 1982 *The Law of Marriage and Marital Alternatives.* Lexington, Mass.: D. C. Heath.

Pleck, Elizabeth 1987 *Domestic Violence: The Making of American Social Policy against Family Violence from Colonial Times to the Present.* New York: Oxford University Press.

Peirce, Dorothy S. 1988 "*BRI v. Leonard*: The Role of the Courts in Preserving Family Integrity." *New England Law Review* 23:185–219.

Pollock, Frederick, and Frederic W. Maitland 1898 *The History of English Law before the Time of Edward I,* 2 vols. Cambridge: Cambridge University Press.

tenBroek, Jacobus 1964 *Family Law and the Poor.* Westport, Conn.: Greenwood.

Tiffany, Walter C. 1921 *Handbook on the Law of Personal and Domestic Relations.* 3rd ed. St. Paul, Minn.: West.

Wardle, Lynn D., Christopher L. Blakesley, and Jacqueline Y. Parker 1988 *Contemporary Family Law: Principles, Policy, and Practice.* 4 vols. Deerfield, Ill.: Callaghan.

Weitzman, Lenore 1985 *The Divorce Revolution.* New York: Free Press.

LISA J. MCINTYRE

FAMILY PLANNING Most people want to have children at some time in their lives. Americans generally want two children, and, on average, women have 1.8 births over their lifetime. In order to limit lifetime births to such a small number, family planning or fertility control is a necessity; couples must either abstain from intercourse, have high levels of contraceptive use, or resort to abortion. Indeed, sexually active women from ages fifteen to forty-four would average eighteen births if they used no contraception and no induced abortion. This chapter summarizes information regarding sexual activity, the timing of desired pregnancies and births, infertility, the risk of unintended pregnancy, contraceptive use, and levels of pregnancy, birth, and abortion in the United States.

COMPARISON WITH OTHER WESTERN, INDUSTRIALIZED COUNTRIES

We are similar to women and men in most other developed countries in both the desire for small families and the achievement of low birth or fertility rates, but we have a relatively high pregnancy rate and high abortion rate. American women average 2.6 pregnancies (not including those that end in miscarriage) and have 0.8 abortions. Table 1 gives data for the nine Western, developed countries that have complete and recent data on pregnancy and the planning status of pregnancies, summarized into estimates of the average number of pregnancies, births, and abortions a woman in each of the countries would have over her reproductive life (i.e., between the ages of fifteen and forty-four). Although there is variation between countries, the range of difference in pregnancy rates in developed countries is quite small. Total pregnancy rates differ by less than one per woman, and the total fertility rates differ by only 0.4 births per woman across the nine countries. Compared with the other countries, however, the United States falls at the high end of each measure. France and Denmark also have relatively high rates; the lowest pregnancy, birth, and abortion rates are in the Netherlands.

The greatest difference between the United States and other countries is in the rate of unplanned pregnancies. Slightly more than one-half of all pregnancies in the United States are unintended, for a total unplanned pregnancy rate of 1.3 per woman. This is similar to the rate in France but substantially higher than other countries, especially Canada, the Netherlands, Sweden, and Great Britain, where the average unplanned pregnancy rate is 0.8 per woman or less. Relative rankings of the nine countries in Table 1 by the level of contraceptive use shows that the three countries with high use of methods considered the most effective—sterilization, oral contraceptives, and the intrauterine contraceptive device (IUD)—have the lowest levels of unplanned pregnancy. Denmark, France, and the United States, which

TABLE 1
Total Pregnancy Rates,* by Planning Status and by Outcome, and Relative Level of Contraceptive Use Among Women Ages Fifteen to Forty-four, in Selected Countries, 1977–1985

		Planning status		Outcome		Contraceptive	
Country	*Total pregnancy rate*	*Total planned pregnancy rate*	*Total unplanned pregnancy rate*	*Total fertility rate*	*Total abortion rate*	*Any method*	*Effective method*
Belgium	2.00	1.17	0.83	1.71	0.29	H	M
Canada	2.03	1.24	0.79	1.67	0.36	H	H
Denmark	2.50	1.32	1.18	1.75	0.75	M	M
Finland	2.09	1.03	1.06	1.63	0.46	H	M
France	2.53	1.18	1.35	1.87	0.66	H	M
Netherlands	1.65	1.37	0.28	1.47	0.18	H	H
Sweden	2.19	1.39	0.80	1.62	0.57	M	M
Great Britain	1.98	1.35	0.63	1.68	0.30	H	H
United States	2.56	1.25	1.31	1.80	0.76	L	M

* Pregnancies ending in miscarriage are not included.
NOTE: L-low; M-moderate; H-high.
SOURCE: Jones et al. 1989. Tables 2.1, 2.2, 2.5, and Appendix B.

have the highest levels of unplanned pregnancy and abortion, all fall in the moderate level of effective contraceptive use rankings.

EXPOSURE TO RISK OF PREGNANCY

Most Americans begin to have intercourse during their late adolescence and continue to be sexually active throughout their reproductive lives. In 1988, one-half of all men in the United States had had intercourse by age 16.5, and, by age 17.4, one-half of all women had had sex. Table 2 shows information for women by age groups. The proportion who never had intercourse decreases quickly from 47 percent of teens ages fifteen to nineteen to 1 to 2 percent of all women ages thirty to forty-four. About 7 percent of women in each group have had intercourse but are not currently in a relationship (i.e., they have not had sex within the last three months). Some 6 percent of women ages fifteen to forty-four are infertile or noncontraceptively sterile because of illness, surgery (that was not for contraceptive purposes), menopause, or some other reason. The proportion that is infertile increases steadily with age, from 1 to 2 percent of women under age thirty to about 20 percent of those ages forty to forty-four. Many of these women want to have a child or another child, especially those in their mid-twenties to early thirties. The proportion of women who are pregnant, postpartum, or trying to become pregnant (and not known to be infertile) is highest among women ages twenty to thirty-four.

Women who are at risk for an unintended pregnancy account for two-thirds of all women ages fifteen to forty-four at any point in time. Women at risk are those who are currently in a sexual relationship, are fertile, and wish to avoid becoming pregnant. The proportion at risk of unintended pregnancy increases from 41 percent of teenagers to 72 to 75 percent of all women ages twenty-five to forty-four. Women who are currently married or cohabiting are most likely to be at

TABLE 2
Percentage Distribution of Women Ages Fifteen to Forty-four According to Exposure to the Risk of Unintended Pregnancy, by Age, 1988

Risk Status	*Total*	*15–19*	*20–24*	*25–29*	*30–34*	*35–39*	*40–44*
Total	100.0	100.0	100.0	100.0	100.0	100.0	100.0
Not at risk	33.1	59.3	32.8	27.9	26.6	25.2	28.5
Noncontraceptively sterilized	6.1	0.5*	1.2*	1.7	5.6	11.7	18.2
Pregnant/Postpartum/ Trying	8.6	4.3	11.1	14.4	12.3	4.9	1.9
Infrequent intercourse	6.9	7.7	6.9	6.6	6.7	6.5	7.3
Never had intercourse	11.5	46.8	13.6	5.2	2.0	2.1	1.1*
At risk	67.0	40.8	67.1	72.1	73.4	74.8	71.5

*Denotes percentages with relative standard errors of 30 percent or more.
SOURCE: J. D. Forrest and S. Singh 1990 "Sexual and Reproductive Behavior of American Women, 1982–1988: Findings from the National Survey of Family Growth." *Family Planning Perspectives* 22:5.

risk for unintended pregnancy—79 percent of them are at risk, compared with 63 percent of formerly married women and 49 percent of never-married women not currently in union. The most common reason some married and cohabiting women are not at risk of unintended pregnancy is that they are pregnant, postpartum, or trying to become pregnant. Among women who never have been married, no intercourse or infrequent intercourse are the most common reasons. Among never-married women who have had intercourse, the proportion at risk of unintended pregnancy is almost as high as among women currently in union—74 percent.

CONTRACEPTIVE USE

Women and men in the United States have a variety of contraceptive methods available to them, although fewer than couples in some other countries. Surgical contraceptive sterilization is available for both women and men. Physician visits and prescriptions are required for oral contraceptives, the IUD, the diaphragm, contraceptive implants, and the contraceptive cap. Other methods —condoms and spermicidal foam, cream, jelly, and film—can be purchased over the counter in pharmacies or other stores. Instruction in periodic abstinence is available from physicians and other family planning providers as well as through classes where only that method is taught.

Nine in ten women ages fifteen to forty-four in 1988 who were classified as being at risk of unintended pregnancy were using a contraceptive method, as shown in Table 3. Thirty-five percent relied on contraceptive sterilization of themselves or their partner, 55 percent used reversible methods, and 10 percent were currently using no contraceptive, even though they were at risk of unintended pregnancy.

Patterns of use differ by age. Younger women at risk of unintended pregnancy are most likely to be using no method of contraception. Twenty-one percent use no method, compared to 6 to 8 percent of women at risk ages thirty to forty-four. The proportion using reversible methods declines with age. Oral contraceptives are the most commonly used method among women ages fifteen to twenty-nine. About one in five women—and 28 percent of teens—at risk of unintended pregnancy rely on the condom, diaphragm, or a spermicidal method for contraception, methods that reduce

TABLE 3
Percentage Distribution of Women at Risk of Unintended Pregnancy According to Contraceptive Method Used, by Age, 1988

Contraceptive method	*Total*	*15–19*	*20–24*	*25–29*	*30–34*	*35–39*	*40–44*
Total	100.0	100.0	100.0	100.0	100.0	100.0	100.0
Sterilization	35.3	1.4*	5.7	20.6	43.1	60.5	67.6
Female	24.8	1.2*	4.1	15.2	30.1	42.1	47.1
Male	10.5	0.2*	1.6*	5.4	13.0	18.4	20.5
Reversible methods	54.8	77.5	82.0	69.0	49.5	33.3	24.6
Pill	27.7	46.3	59.8	39.8	19.9	4.9	2.9
Condom	13.1	25.8	12.7	13.9	11.1	11.1	9.7
Diaphragm	5.2	0.8*	3.2	5.0	8.2	7.2	3.6
Spermicides	2.7	1.3*	1.5*	3.4	3.0	4.2	1.5*
Periodic abstinence	2.1	0.7*	1.5*	2.2	2.5	2.8	2.0*
IUD	1.8	0.0	0.3*	1.2*	2.7	2.5	3.4
Other+	2.2	2.6*	3.0	3.5	2.1	0.6*	1.5*
No Method	9.9	21.2	12.3	10.5	7.3	6.2	7.7

+ Includes withdrawal, douche, and other unspecified methods.
* Denotes percentages with relative standard errors of 30 percent or more.
SOURCE: Tabulation from the 1988 National Survey of Family Growth.

the risk of both pregnancy and sexually transmitted disease. As women become older and complete their families, male and female contraceptive sterilization become increasingly common, rising steeply from 6 percent of women at risk ages twenty to twenty-four to 21 percent of women in their late twenties and to over 60 percent of those ages thirty-five to forty-four. Among women in their twenties, female sterilization is about three times more common than vasectomy. The margin narrows among older women to slightly more than two times more common.

The proportion of women at risk of unintended pregnancy who use no contraceptive method is highest among never-married women who are not in a cohabiting union, 20 percent as compared to 6 percent of those who are currently married or in a cohabiting union, and 12 percent of formerly married women. Sterilization is the most frequently used method among women who are currently married or cohabiting (44 percent) as well as formerly married women who are not currently in a union (49 percent). The pill is the most commonly used method among never-married women (47 percent). One in five women at risk who are not currently in a union use methods that also help protect against sexually transmitted disease—11 percent of the formerly married and 23 percent of never-married women.

Poorer women (those with family incomes less than 200 percent of the federal poverty level) at risk of unintended pregnancy are almost twice as likely to be using no contraceptive method as higher income women, 15 versus 8 percent. At each age, they are less likely to rely on reversible methods and more likely to rely on sterilization than higher income women. Eleven percent of poor women at risk ages twenty to twenty-four and 33 percent of those ages twenty-five to twenty-nine use sterilization as their method, compared with 2 and 15 percent of higher income women in these age groups. Poor women relying on sterilization are much more likely than higher income women to have been sterilized themselves rather than have a partner who has a vasectomy. Female sterilization accounts for 85 percent of all contraceptive sterilization among poor women, compared with 63 percent among those with higher incomes.

CONTRACEPTIVE SERVICE PROVISION

About 45,000 general and family practitioners in the United States (84 percent of those providing office-based patient care) and essentially all 23,000 obstetrician-gynecologists provide reversible contraceptive services. Obstetrician-gynecologists serve more than two-thirds of all women visiting private physicians for reversible contraception. Services are also provided at 5,100 family planning clinic sites. Prescriptive and nonprescriptive supplies can be obtained from the more than 58,000 pharmacies in the country.

Women strongly prefer private physicians for family planning care because they are seen as providing more personal and higher quality care. Sixty-nine percent of women making a medical visit for reversible contraceptives go to a private physician, and the others obtain services from family planning clinics. Family planning clinics were set up, most with federal funding, to provide care to those who could not afford services from private physicians or who cannot use private physicians for other reasons. In the mid-1980s, for example, an initial contraceptive visit with a general or family practitioner cost about $39, while a visit to an obstetrician-gynecologist cost $66; an annual supply of oral contraceptives cost $169. Fewer than one in five health insurance participants are covered for routine family planning visits, and contraceptive supplies are often also considered to be preventive care and not covered. Only one-half of the physicians providing reversible contraceptive care will accept Medicaid, the federal and state program paying for medical care for very poor people, and no more than 15 percent will provide services at reduced fees for women who cannot afford their charge. In addition, only 65 percent of the physicians will provide contraception to unemancipated minors without parental consent.

In almost all family planning clinics, on the other hand, minors are offered confidential services, Medicaid is accepted, and the cost of services depends on a patient's income. Family planning clinics are run by public health departments (serving 40 percent of all clients), Planned Parenthood agencies (28 percent), hospitals (11 percent), and other organizations such as neighborhood health centers, women's health centers, and other community-based groups (21 percent). They tend to be situated in lower income areas of communities and often operate only a few times a week in a medical facility used for other services as well. Poor women are more likely than others to depend on clinics for care. Fifty-seven percent of women under the federal poverty level who make a medical visit for reversible contraception go to a family planning clinic; another 14 percent go to private physicians who are paid through Medicaid. Lower income women who go to clinics instead of private physicians do so primarily because they cannot afford private physicians' fees or because the clinic will accept Medicaid. One-half of all teens who make a medical visit go to clinics. Adolescents who go to clinics do so because of the free or low-cost services and because they are afraid a private physician will tell their parents about their contraceptive use. In addition, some women, especially teenagers who have never been to a physician on their own, go to clinics because they do not know a private physician who would serve them. Clinic patients usually shift to private physicians when their incomes rise and as they become older or when they become pregnant and must look elsewhere for obstetric care.

About 80 percent of female sterilizations are done by obstetrician-gynecologists. Almost all (94 percent) obstetrician-gynecologists and 18 percent of the general and family practitioners in office-based private practice perform female sterilizations. About one-half of all vasectomies are done by urologists, 89 percent of whom (6,000) perform the operation. In addition, one-half of the general surgeons (12,000) and 26 percent of general and family practitioners (14,000) do vasectomies. About one-fifth of family planning agencies offer female or male sterilization services, but they are not offered at all clinic sites in an agency, and patients are often referred for the surgery to a private physician who is paid under contract from the agency. Eighty-three percent of private physicians performing tubal sterilizations and 95 percent of vasectomy providers place some conditions on whom they will serve. The most common are spousal consent (50 and 79 percent of providers, respectively), minimum age (47 and 40 percent), and waiting periods (39 and 44 percent). Where there is an age limit, the average minimum age for tubal ligation is set at twenty-three years and, for vasectomy, at twenty-five years. Thirty percent of providers require that the woman or man have at least one child. Only 22 percent of private physicians performing tubal ligations and 51 percent of those doing vasectomies will accept Medicaid; 4 and 12 percent, respectively, will reduce their fees for women and men who cannot afford them.

Most tubal ligations are done in a hospital; 52 percent are performed on an inpatient basis, 41 percent take place in hospitals on an outpatient basis, and most of the others occur in ambulatory nonhospital clinics. Most vasectomies occur in physicians' offices (64 percent); 23 percent are performed on an outpatient basis in a hospital facility, and only 8 percent are done on an inpatient basis. In 1983, the most recent year for which data are available, physician and hospital charges for an inpatient or outpatient tubal ligation averaged $1,300, and the fee for an office vasectomy was $240.

ATTITUDES ABOUT CONTRACEPTIVE METHODS

Women are most likely to have favorable attitudes about oral contraceptives (77 percent of women ages fifteen to forty-four), the condom (61 percent), vasectomy (61 percent), and female sterilization (57 percent). Fewer than one-third have favorable opinions of other available methods. Among those currently using a method, at least eight in ten have a favorable opinion of the one they are using. Almost nine in ten women relying on sterilization have a favorable opinion of it, but one-quarter say they would like more children, and one in ten would like it reversed. It is not clear to what extent this reflects actual dissatisfaction with sterilization or with their being in a situation in which they feel they cannot have more children.

The reason most often given by those at risk of unintended pregnancy for not using a contraceptive method or for using the condom, diaphragm, or spermicides is concern about side effects and health risks. The condom and spermicidal methods are being used increasingly for protection against sexually transmitted disease as well as for pregnancy protection. Thirteen percent of all women ages fifteen to forty-four in 1988 who had ever had intercourse were using condoms (12 percent) or spermicides (1 percent) to prevent STDs. About one-third were seeking to prevent both pregnancy and STDs; the others were using these methods only to prevent STDs. Women using oral contraceptives, the IUD, and sterilization do so primarily because of concerns about the effectiveness of other methods and because other methods interfere with intercourse and can be inconvenient to use.

Fears of health risks from contraceptives, especially oral contraceptives, are common in the United States, even though this method is most favorably rated. Three-quarters of adult women and two-thirds of men think using the pill represents substantial risks, primarily from cancer and from blood clots. Extensive medical studies show that, except for women with risky behavior such as heavy smoking or with preexisting health conditions, using oral contraceptives or any other method is safer than using no contraceptive at all if women are at risk of unintended pregnancy. Some of the health risk comes from use of the method itself and some from pregnancies that occur to contraceptive users. If those pregnancies end in abortion rather than in birth, the health risks are substantially lowered.

CONTRACEPTIVE EFFECTIVENESS

Pregnancies occur to couples using contraceptive methods for two reasons—because of the inadequacy of the method itself or because it was not used correctly or consistently. It is not possible to measure the theoretical success or failure (the method effectiveness) of a contraceptive independent from what happens when it is actually used. Studies instead measure the use effectiveness, which relates to the experience of an actual group of users. Failure rates differ by method, with some consistently showing higher effectiveness than others; rates also differ by sociodemographic subgroup within study populations. Clinical studies of specially selected and followed patients tend to show lower failure rates than when methods are used by the general population.

Table 4 shows estimates of what the method failure rates of the most commonly used reversible contraceptive methods might be, along with the rates actually observed across age, race, and marital status subgroups of women in the United States. In each case, the observed rates are substantially higher than the estimated method failure rates, and, for most methods, the difference between the lowest and highest subgroup rates is quite wide. The lowest failure rates are achieved with oral contraceptives, while spermicidal methods have the highest failure rates. In general, women who are young, unmarried, poor, and nonwhite have higher failure rates. The differences in failure rates between methods and between subgroups are much greater than what any difference in method effectiveness or in the biology of women would cause and are assumed primarily to reflect differences in the correctness and consistency of method use.

UNINTENDED PREGNANCY AND ABORTION

Of the 110 pregnancies each year per 1,000 women ages fifteen to forty-four in the United States, 48 are intended; of these, 40 end in births and 8 end in miscarriage. The peak ages of intended pregnancy in the United States are the twenties, when about 8 percent of all sexually active women have planned pregnancies each year.

Over one-half of all pregnancies in the United States are unintended, that is, they occur to women who want to have a baby later but not now (generally called "mistimed") or to women who did not want to have any children in the future (called "unwanted"). An estimated 56 percent of all pregnancies are unintended, and 6 percent of women ages fifteen to forty-four have an unintended pregnancy each year. Of the 110 total pregnancies per 1,000 women ages fifteen to forty-four, 27 are unintended pregnancies that end in birth, 27 end in abortion, and 8 are unintended pregnancies that end in miscarriage. Forty percent of all births are unintended, 28 percent are mistimed, and 12 percent were reported by the mother as having been unwanted.

The proportion of pregnancies that are unintended is highest among adolescents—81 per-

TABLE 4
Estimated Percentage of Women Who Experience a Contraceptive Failure During the First Twelve Months of Use Given Perfect Use, and Observed Failure Rates by Method Across Age, Race, and Marital Status Groups

		Observed rates		
Method	*Perfect Use*	*All Users*	*Lowest*	*Highest*
Oral contraceptives*	0.1–0.5	6.2	1.9	18.1
Condom	2.0	14.2	3.3	36.3
Diaphragm	3.0	15.6	10.3	57.0
Periodic Abstinence*	2.0–10.0	16.2	6.2	34.1
Spermicide*	3.0–8.0	26.3	9.1	38.7

*Rate varies by type of method or formulation used.
SOURCE: E. F. Jones and J. D. Forrest 1989 "Contraceptive Failure in the United States: Revised Estimates from the 1982 National Survey of Family Growth." *Family Planning Perspectives* 21:3, 103.

cent. Among every 1,000 women ages fifteen to nineteen, 127 become pregnant each year, 102 of them unintentionally. Almost as many unintended pregnancies among adolescent women end in birth (forty-three per 1,000) as end in abortion (forty-six per 1,000), and thirteen per 1,000 end in miscarriage. Because only slightly more than one-half of all women ages fifteen to nineteen have had intercourse, rates among all teenagers understate the frequency of pregnancy. Among those who have ever had intercourse, 24 percent become pregnant each year; 20 percent of those who have had sex have an unintended pregnancy annually.

The proportion of pregnancies that are unintended varies widely by age. It decreases from eight in ten of the pregnancies to adolescents to four in ten among women ages thirty to thirty-four and then rises again to almost eight in ten among women ages forty to forty-four. The proportion of unintended pregnancies that end in abortion varies little by age up to age thirty-five, from 47 to 51 percent. More unintended pregnancies to older women, however, end in abortion—55 percent of those to women ages thirty-five to thirty-nine and 50 percent of unintended pregnancies to women ages forty to forty-four.

One-quarter of all pregnancies in the United States end in induced abortion. Because of the high level of unintended pregnancy in the United States, each year almost 3 percent of all women ages fifteen to forty-four have an abortion. At current levels of abortion, it is estimated that almost one-half of all women will have at least one abortion in their lifetime and that many will have more than one.

Approximately 2,600 facilities provide abortion services in the United States. Hospitals represent 40 percent of all abortion providers, even though only about one in five short-term general hospitals provides abortion services. Four percent of abortion service facilities are private physician offices serving fewer than 400 women a year for abortion. Hospitals and private physician facilities serve relatively small numbers of women and account for only 10 and 4 percent of all patients, respectively. Nonhospital clinics serve 86 percent of women having abortions. Almost all abortions are provided as ambulatory procedures, even if done in a hospital. Abortion services in the United States are heavily concentrated in larger metropolitan areas of the country. In 1988, 90 percent of all providers, which performed 98 percent of all abortions, were located in metropolitan areas. Thirty-one percent of women of reproductive age live in counties where there are no abortion providers, and 42 percent live where there are no providers serving at least 400 abortion patients per year. Facilities set limits on the maximum gestation at which they will provide abortion services; 57 percent perform them only at twelve or fewer weeks since the last menstrual period, and 76 percent only do so at sixteen weeks or less. Some states require that unemancipated minors notify or obtain consent from a parent or parents before they may have an abortion or that they obtain a court ruling that they are sufficiently mature to make the decision themselves or that having an abortion is better for them than giving birth. In addition, some facilities, especially hospitals, require parental consent or notification for abortion services provided to young adolescents. Funding for abortion for women covered by Medicaid is restricted to abortions for the purpose of preserving a woman's health or to abortions to women in the few states that provide state funds for abortion services.

Because of the uneven distribution of abortion services around the country, about 40 percent of women who have abortions obtain them from providers in another county or state. There are no data on what proportion of women giving birth wanted to have an abortion and would have done so if services were more accessible. One-half of all abortions are performed within eight weeks of the woman's last menstrual period, and 91 percent are performed within twelve weeks. Four percent occur at sixteen or more weeks since the last menstrual period and 1 percent at twenty-one weeks or more. About one-quarter of those having abortions at sixteen or more weeks said the chief reason for not having had the abortion earlier was difficulty making arrangements, especially obtaining money for the abortion quickly enough. As of mid-1985, the average cost for a nonhospital abortion at ten weeks' gestation with local anesthesia was $238. Abortions performed later in gestation or using general anesthesia are more expensive, and the cost of hospital abortions, even those done on an outpatient basis, are more than double the average nonhospital cost.

LINKS BETWEEN CONTRACEPTIVE USE AND UNINTENDED PREGNANCY

Women who are using no contraceptive method account for about 10 percent of women at risk of unintended pregnancy, but, because they are more likely to become pregnant than those using a method, they account for the majority of unplanned pregnancies, an estimated 57 percent. Significant reductions in unintended pregnancy and abortion could occur with decreased levels of sexual activity, with increased contraceptive use, with more effective use of existing methods, and with the development and marketing of additional methods. It has been estimated that eliminating nonuse could result in a 57 percent reduction in the level of unintended pregnancy and a 48 percent reduction in abortion.

SEE ALSO: *Birth and Death Rates; Fertility Determinants; Family Size*)

REFERENCES

Forrest, Jacqueline Darroch, Rachel Benson Gold, and Asta-Maria Kenney 1989 *The Need, Availability, and Financing of Reproductive Health Services.* New York: Alan Guttmacher Institute.

Harlap, Susan, Kathryn L. Kost, and Jacqueline Darroch Forrest 1991 *Preventing Pregnancy, Protecting Health: A New Look at Birth Control Choices in the United States.* New York: Alan Guttmacher Institute.

Henshaw, Stanley, and Jennifer Van Vort (eds.) 1991 *Abortion Services in the United States, Each State and Metropolitan Area, 1987–1988.* New York: Alan Guttmacher Institute.

Jones, Elise F., Jacqueline Darroch Forrest, Stanley K. Henshaw, Jane Silverman, and Aida Torres 1989 *Pregnancy, Contraception, and Family Planning Services in Industrialized Countries.* New Haven, Conn.: Yale University Press.

Mastroianni, Luigi, Jr., Peter J. Donaldson, and Thomas T. Kane (eds.) 1990 *Developing New Contraceptives: Obstacles and Opportunities.* Washington, D.C.: National Academy Press.

Pratt, William F., William D. Mosher, Christine A. Bachrach, and Marjorie C. Horn 1984 "Understanding U.S. Fertility: Findings from the National Survey of Family Growth, Cycle III." *Population Bulletin* 39.

JACQUELINE DARROCH FORREST

FAMILY POLICY IN WESTERN SOCIETIES The dramatic growth in the industrial capacities and economic power of the United States and the countries of Western Europe since World War II has demonstrably improved the per capita income and quality of life of the average citizen in these countries. Based on such indicators as available health services, declining death rates, unemployment protection, and retirement benefits, it is reasonable to infer that, more than at any other time in human history, the majority of the people in these countries are assured that they can obtain the basic elements necessary for their survival and the survival of their families. Moreover, their quality of life, as measured by education, availability and quality of housing, ownership of automobiles and other durable goods, and available leisure time, suggests a life-style heretofore reserved for only the rich.

It is ironic that this unparalleled affluence has been accompanied by fundamental changes in family structure and family relationships—changes that challenge our basic conceptions of how families are organized and function. Over the last thirty years virtually all of the highly industrialized countries have evidenced accelerating increases in divorce rates, decreasing family size, increases in pregnancies among unmarried women, and an increase in childless marriages. Unlike the third world countries where population is growing at a rapid rate, birthrates in Western countries are below the level of population replacement (see Van de Kaa 1987 for Western Europe; Sweet and Bumpass 1987 for the United States).

There is general agreement among students of

the family that these changes are due, at least in part, to the expanding number of married women in the labor force. In 1920, about 9 percent of the families in the United States consisted of wives who were employed outside the home (Hayghe 1990, p. 14); by 1987 the number of dual-earner families outnumbered families in which the husband was the only breadwinner by two to one (Baca Zinn and Eitzen 1990, p. 180). This situation does not change appreciably when children enter the family. Labor participation for married women with children under the age of six increased from 18.6 percent of all married women in 1960 to 53.4 percent in 1985. For married women with children between the ages of six and seventeen the rate increased from 39 percent in 1960 to 68 percent in 1985. Similar data exist for countries in Western Europe. Haavio-Mannila and Kauppinen (1990) note that full-time homemaking has almost disappeared in the Nordic Countries. These changes have had a direct impact on the division of labor in the family and an indirect effect on marital role relationships.

Closely linked to women's growing labor market activity is the fact that they are making better use of the educational opportunities available to them. There is evidence that educational achievement is converging for males and females in most of the Western world (Haavio-Mannila 1988).

As both educational and occupational career opportunities increase for women, there is a tendency to delay marriage. In the United States, the median age for marriage among women was higher in 1985 than it had been at any point since 1890 (Lindsey 1990). Moreover, with growing educational equality and an increased ability to compete effectively for jobs in markets that value the skills obtained through education, the time such women spend raising children becomes more costly, both economically and psychologically (Sweet and Bumpass 1987, p. 398). The result is fewer children per family and an increase in surrogate parenting for families with children.

These changes have altered the ways in which marital and parental roles are conducted within families. Sweet and Bumpass (1987), describing the situation for U.S. families, claim that although husbands have made only a modest contribution to sharing household duties, they can no longer claim the role of "breadwinner." The conception of the prototypical family as consisting of a legally married husband and wife living together for a lifetime, raising children in a household managed by the wife and mother and financially supported by the husband and father, is anachronistic. Indeed, such family structures are now in the minority in the United States and other Western countries (see Gerson 1985, p. 237, for the United States; and Poponoe 1988, pp. 167–182, for Sweden).

Many scholars regard this decline in traditional family structures with considerable alarm. The decline is associated with values that emphasize individualistic and self-oriented goals over family well-being and, by extension, concern for others in the community. We are no longer "our brother's keeper," and the result, it is argued, is social isolation, growing levels of interpersonal distrust, and individuals engaged in an endless and empty search for gratification (see, for example, Bellah et al. 1985).

Other scholars, though not sanguine about the human problems created by these changes, tend to consider them as an inevitable consequence of increased individual opportunity and freedom. Such freedom can only occur when the developed societies establish equality between the sexes and underwrite the financial and social risks of illness, job loss, and aging. To the extent that greater individual autonomy and freedom of opportunity are gained at the cost of stable family relations, that cost should be borne (Myrdal 1967). Most important, those who look positively upon these changes point with approval to the changing role of women. The increased participation of women in the labor force in all industrialized countries has increased women's freedom to choose their own life-styles, both in the worlds of work and in the family (Kamerman and Kahn 1978). If changes in family structure contribute to greater equality and greater opportunities for women to achieve their full potential, then, it is argued, society as a whole benefits (see Poponoe 1988, pp. 143–155, for a review of these arguments).

Interestingly, people on both sides of the debate tend to define themselves as profamily. Virtually everyone seems to acknowledge the social importance of the family in caring for and socializing children. There is also a recognition of the importance of the family as a sanctuary that provides its members with protection, affection, and succor in what is often a hostile and, generally, impersonal environment. For the most part advocates of both perspectives accept as problematic the fact that, increasingly, families fail to carry out these functions. The high divorce rate, single-parent households, teenage pregnancy, and wife and child abuse are disturbing components in modern family life, and there is general agreement that something should be done about them. There is a consensus in all of the advanced industrialized countries that the family is a proper concern of public policy.

There are, however, fundamental differences in the conceptions of what that policy should be, what institutions or groups should be responsible for implementing the policy, and what types of families or individuals should be the targets of such policy.

Some want to reverse the trends of the last three decades by shoring up the traditional family. They advocate reinforcing the importance of legal marriages, making divorce more difficult, emphasizing parental responsibility for the care and protection of their children, and, more generally, strengthening the family by protecting it from government intrusions. Governments, from this perspective, should be restrained from taking over responsibilities that "rightfully" belong to the family. Only limited indirect support in the form of tax relief or tax credits to assist families to care for its dependent members and to make home ownership easier are considered appropriate forms of government involvement (Carlson 1988, pp. 273–279). Advocates for restricting government involvement maintain that families, if left alone, would function quite well. Thus Berger and Berger (1983) join a chorus of critics who attribute the concern about public assistance for families to the advocacy of self-interested groups like family social workers, psychologists, and so forth who define situations in such a way that their services are deemed important.

Some critics of government involvement in family life argue for the privatization of most social services geared toward helping families. The essential claim is that privately organized and funded services to families would be more efficient and would protect the sacred right of the family to make choices for itself (Brodkin and Young 1989).

At the other extreme there are those who believe that the appropriate role of government is to assist the family in fostering free choice and maximizing individual potential for each family member. They maintain that, in democratic societies, government should mediate between various interest groups, each seeking its own advantages. Only the government, responsible to the electorate, is in a position to protect the public interest. Far from weakening the family, the government, it is argued, is the only institution in a position to use its resources to support and strengthen families and their members. This is especially true for families with children living under current conditions of rapid social change. Thus, it is argued that "social and demographic changes have combined to diminish the likelihood that families can assure their children's healthy growth and development without help from outside the family" (Schorr, Miller, and Fine 1986).

Some have maintained that the question of government intervention is a moot point; governments as political entities serve the purposes of their most influential constituencies. For example, they point to the tendency of the U.S. government to assist businesses in the form of tax incentives, the building of highways in the 1950s to benefit the automobile industry, and the readiness to come to the aid of the Chrysler Corporation and various banks during times of crisis. In brief, for many observers, the notion of "minimalist government," the ideal advocated in the rhetoric of the Reagan administration in the 1980s, is not a reality in any modern country (Kahn and Kamerman 1975). The real question is not whether government should come to the aid of its citizens, but which citizens will be the beneficiary of such aid.

William J. Wilson's (1987) answer to the question is that government services should be as universal as possible. Rather than limiting services to crises and emergencies or providing aid just to the disadvantaged, public services should be expanded to cover all citizens. Wilson maintains that only when public programs serve all segments of a society will it be possible to prevent system breakdowns and integrate all elements as productive members of the society.

The disagreements about what is appropriate family policy are so basic that it is hard to identify "objective" investigations or investigators. Policy implies advocacy and advocacy implies bias. As a consequence debates circle around such fundamentals as what is meant by the phrase *family policy;* indeed, there is disagreement on what is meant by *family.* Consider the following three definitions: (1) "The family is a society limited in members but nonetheless a true society, anterior to every state or nation, with rights and duties of its own, wholly independent of the commonwealth" (Pope Leo XIII quoted in Strong and DeVault 1989, p. 6); (2) "The family consists of two or more persons living together and related by blood, marriage or adoption" (U.S. Bureau of the Census 1988); and (3) "One or more adults related by blood, marriage, or affiliation who cooperate economically, share a common dwelling place, and *may* rear children" (Strong and DeVault 1989, p. 6; emphasis in original). Note that definition (1) places the family as independent and free from the state. By implication, what goes on in the family is none of the government's business. Definition (2) restricts the family to shared residence and formal kin ties determined by blood or legal marriage, whereas definition (3), by introducing the vague term *affiliation,* is intended to include under the family label such "family" forms as "cohabiting families . . . and gay and lesbian families" (Strong and DeVault 1989, p. 6). Still other definitions point to the fact that families need not always reside in the same household to maintain familial bonds and obligations, while others define family in terms of the social functions it serves.

Those who define the family as the Census Bureau does are more likely to advocate policies that support only households whose members are linked through legally defined ties of kinship. Those who adhere to definition (3), on the other hand, are more likely to advocate government recognition of and assistance to different kinds of heterosexual and homosexual unions formed only by the consent of the participants without any state recognition or sanction. Adherents of definitions (1) or (2) are more likely to maintain that governmental aid to some of the groups that fit definition (3) is not aid to families but a major contribution toward the declining significance of the family in modern life (Poponoe 1988).

Despite these disagreements concerning an adequate definition, some shared understanding of what is meant by "family" is necessary to provide a referent for the discussion that follows. The working definition provided below is designed to incorporate essential elements that make up most definitions. It is, however, not likely to satisfy staunch advocates of any particular policy orientation. The family is defined here as *any group of individuals who are bound together by publicly acknowledged and socially sanctioned kinship ties.* The key to this definition is in the concept of *kinship.* Kinship is a special type of social relationship determined by ancestry, marriage, and adoption. Within every society certain kin have designated duties toward and responsibilities for other members of the kin group. These responsibilities are obligatory; the only way an individual can free him- or herself from such obligations is by ceasing to be kin, a difficult, if not impossible, task. These obligations tend to be lifelong. For key kin the obligations can pertain to virtually all physical and emotional needs of family members. For example, in modern industrial societies parents are expected not only to care for their children's physical needs but to provide them with love and affection and to prepare them to function effectively in the real world. Failure to do so can result in severe sanctions against the parent. Thus all Western industrialized countries have laws designed to require that parents provide financial support and care for their children, even if the husband and wife are separated. Each country also has laws designed to punish parents for physically abusing and emotionally neglecting their minor children. Similar obligations accrue as a consequence of marriage. Formal marriages are legal entities sanctioned by the state (and often the church), and violations of the marital agreement are monitored and adjudicated by reference to secular laws, sacred laws, or both.

Whereas the care, nurturance, and socialization of children continue to be the responsibility of parents, the care of aging parents by adult children is becoming less common. Social security and retirement pensions, national health programs, and public support for housing for the elderly have been introduced in all highly industrialized countries. As these programs increase, family obligations decline.

This tendency toward declining family responsibility for its members extends beyond care for the elderly. Over the years, as modes of production have changed, the family has gradually relinquished responsibility for providing either employment or occupational training for its members. It is also no longer directly responsible for formal and religious education, and, more recently, responsibility for child care has tended to be relegated to nonfamily institutions. As the family gives up these functions to the workplace, schools, and churches, its relative power and influence on the economic and political life of the society diminishes. The issue thus becomes whether public policy, established and administered by agents of the governmental or economic segments of society, should be used to assist this weakened institution. More specifically, the question arises whether public services in the form of health care, housing, unemployment insurance, support for education, maternity benefits, support for child care, and so forth help to strengthen the family in its remaining responsibility for the care, nurturance, and socialization of its members or further weaken it by making family members dependent on nonfamily sources for benefits and social support. This is the key question surrounding the debate over what is a proper family policy in the Western world.

The term *policy,* like *family,* is burdened with multiple meanings and definitions. It has been variously described as the means for focusing on fundamental problems of individuals in relation to societies (Lasswell 1968), a set of decisions designed to support an agreed-upon course of action (Zimmerman 1988), or as "governmental goals" (Dumon and Aldous 1979). Thus the different definitions have covered the gamut, from means to process to goals. Kahn's (1969, p. 131) conception of policy incorporates these elements within a context that gives it specific meaning. He refers to policy as "the general guide to action, the cluster of overall decisions relevant to the achievement of the goal, the guiding principles, the standing plan." Thus, a definition that seems to have some consensual meaning would hold that policy is a commitment to action that utilizes a consciously designated strategy designed to attain specified goals.

Although some writers insist that the term *policy* is applicable only to governmental action, the more general view is that any actor, whether an individual or a large collectivity, can make and implement policy (Zimmerman 1988). What is important, and the source of considerable debate, is the fit between the policy goals and the actor's ability to implement those goals. For example, individual families of moderate means are not likely, by themselves, to be able to implement a policy for attaining high-standard, low-cost day care for their children; conversely, neither national governments nor national corporations are likely to be able effectively to develop policies for resolving neighborhood conflicts between ethnic groups. The difficulty is not only in matching appropriate levels of scale (i.e., community problems are best solved by community organizations), it also lies in the actor's ability to bring the right resources to bear on a given problem. This requires access to relevant information, the ability to influence the parties involved, the ability to recruit appropriate personnel, and control over the appropriate resources.

The debate about family policy generally focuses on three primary issues: goals, the strategies designed to attain those goals, and the appropriate agencies for implementing these strategies. The sharpest differences concerning these issues are apparent at the national level.

These differences between policy goals, strategies, and designated agents are most evident when we compare the approach to family policy in the United States with the industrialized nations of Western Europe. As noted earlier, the United States shares many of the same family problems with these countries. The solutions offered in the form of public policy, however, differ considerably. The United States, often referred to as the "reluctant welfare state," has tended to be less forthcoming than the Europeans in providing funds or services for its families or individuals. Moreover, there has been a strong inclination to have agencies other than government administer and implement social programs. America's revolutionary history has left its citizens with a pervasive distrust of government; rather than viewing government as a source of aid and assistance to its people, it is often considered a threat capable of usurping individual freedom and autonomy (Schorr 1979). When the family is considered, this fear of government is enhanced by the tradition in Anglo-Saxon jurisprudence of noninterference in family life (Glendon 1989).

Differences in approach to family policy in the United States and Western Europe are also affected by the different cultural, racial, and ethnic composition of the various countries. For example, despite the recent immigration of foreign workers in European countries like West Germany, Switzerland, and Sweden, no European country approximates the United States in its ethnic and racial heterogeneity. Whereas minorities make up between 6 and 7 percent of the population of countries like West Germany and Sweden, the nonwhite and Hispanic minorities in the United States represent 20 percent of the population (Statistisches Jahrbuch für die Bundesrepublik Deutschland 1989; Statistical Abstract of Sweden 1990; U.S. Bureau of the Census 1987).

Also important are the differences between the countries in the extent to which governments are centralized and can make policy at the national level. With the exception of Switzerland, the Western European countries tend to be more centralized. This makes it possible to have a meaningful national debate about the pros and cons of a national family policy. Such a debate in the United States is less conclusive, principally because decision-making power on such an issue is distributed among federal, state, and local governments (Dumon and Aldous 1979).

These factors tend to contribute to one incontrovertible fact: The United States has less legislation directly concerned with assisting families and provides less financial support designated to aid families than any other advanced Western industrial society (Kahn and Kamerman 1983; Kamerman and Kahn 1981, p. 239).

Americans have been more reluctant than Europeans to pass legislation that can be interpreted as violating the sanctity and the privacy of the family. Legislators in most European countries seem willing to write laws designed to protect the child's safety, health, and psychological well-being without great concern that such legislation might interfere with family perogatives (Glendon 1989, p. 100). Although the reluctance of the U.S. courts to venture into the family domain is gradually changing (the courts have found it necessary to protect wives against violence and children against abuse and neglect), they have moved much more slowly and reluctantly in this area than their counterparts in the Scandinavian countries, France, the Netherlands, and West Germany. It would be unheard of, for example, for the courts or legislatures in the United States to follow the Swedish example and forbid parents to spank their children.

Although divorce is a common condition in all of the Western developed countries, the United States and England have been unwilling to interfere in the financial arrangements accompanying the divorce on behalf of the children involved. This is not the case in the Nordic countries or in continental Europe where, according to Glendon (1989, pp. 236–237), there is "genuine judicial supervision of the spouses' financial arrangements for children: mechanisms to ensure that child support is fixed at realistic and fair levels; highly efficient collection systems; 'maintenance advance systems' in which the state not only collects unpaid child support, but partially absorbs the risk of non-payment of advancing support up to a fixed amount in cases of default."

With the possible exception of social security benefits for the elderly, the available data indicate that the United States is not as generous as most of the European countries with regard to funding programs designed to assist families (Kahn and Kamerman 1983). This is most apparent when we consider families with children. The United States has tended to limit its assistance to such programs as Aid to Dependent Children, which is geared toward providing financial aid to single-parent families who are living below the poverty line. Some additional assistance is provided to poor families through food stamps (unique to the United States) and, in the short run, unemployment insurance. Financial assistance to all families with children generally takes the form of a standard income tax deduction of $2,000 for each dependent child. For families whose income is below $10,000 an earned income credit is provided.

Most of the countries of Western Europe, on the other hand, provide direct cash payments to families for each child. These payments are tax free and serve as family income supplements. The per child payments tend to increase with increased family size. Funds are also provided to assist families during the childbearing phase in the form of direct grants to cover income loss and pre- and postnatal medical care (Kamerman and Kahn 1981).

The Nordic states and Western continental Europe also provide direct housing assistance for both rental and home ownership payments. Housing allowances generally decrease as income rises, thus providing an income leveling mechanism in these countries (Herrstrom 1986). Unlike the U.S. policy of tax deductions for interest paid on mortgages, which benefit better-off families, the European housing allowances tend to favor the lower-income families (Kahn and Kamerman 1983; Herrstrom 1986).

In addition to these direct income transfer programs, many of the countries in Western Europe provide a variety of benefits designed to assist families with the child rearing problems associated with both parents working outside the home. Sweden, for example, provides a guaranteed pregnancy leave as well as a nine-month parental leave at 90 percent of salary (Poponoe 1988, p. 203). Efforts are underway in Finland to extend this type of parental leave to three years. Sweden has committed itself to providing publicly supported preschool child care services for every child needing such services by 1991 (Poponoe 1988, p. 204). In the Nordic countries parents during the first three years of a child's life can choose to obtain state support for one parent to remain home with the child or to use the funds for day care services. By comparison, in the United States in 1990 President Bush vetoed a bill designed to allow mothers six months maternal leave without pay but with guaranteed job protection.

Regardless of the merits of the American and European approaches to family policy, one significant current fact differentiates family conditions in the United States from those in the developed countries of continental Europe: In the United States one-fifth of children live under conditions of poverty (Phillips 1990, pp. 204–206). This high level of poverty in the midst of affluence has produced a growing sense of despair and hopelessness concerning the life chances of these children. Miller (1990) summarizes the available data as follows: "Many studies have documented the much poorer health status of poor and minority children, the greater rates of child abuse, the higher incidence of injuries and death attributable to violence and crime, high rates of illiteracy, teenage pregnancy, educational failure and school dropouts." He goes on to note that the communities in which these children live are more dangerous, the schools are less adequate, and rates of drug abuse are higher than in the general population. A sizable proportion of these children, but by no means all, are black, Hispanic, or Native American. The majority live in female-headed, single-parent families, a phenomenon increasingly referred to as the "feminization of poverty" in the United States.

Thus, the essential issue concerning family policy for Americans is inextricably linked with the questions of poverty and what to do about it. The fact that this situation does not exist in the other advanced countries of Europe (with the possible exception of the United Kingdom) raises the inevitable question whether the family policies of these "welfare states" have anything to offer Americans in their search for solutions to the problem of family poverty.

It will come as no surprise that expert opinion on this issue is greatly divided. Differences exist even among those who usually share the same ideological perspective. Some who are concerned with providing greater equality in our society advocate programs such as those in Western Europe. Wilson (1987, p. 149) refers to such programs as "universal programs of reform," that is, programs that provide services for all citizens rather than earmarking aid for just minorities or the poor. The advantages of such programs are that since all citizens benefit, there is no stigma attached to being a recipient and no resentment among nonrecipients that taxes are being spent to benefit others.

This position is not universally shared even among those committed to equalitarian solutions. Some feel strongly that massive resources must be put into play to assist just those families under the greatest risk of being trapped in an abyss of poverty and hopelessness (Schorr 1988).

Predictably, those more concerned with issues of freedom than equality have argued that the problem of poverty in the United States is not the result of inadequate public services but rather is a consequence of such services. According to Carlson (1988, p. 273), the "matriarchal welfare state . . . has produced family disruptive results" and the "poverty crisis, the ageism crisis, the teen pregnancy crisis, the overpopulation crisis, the juvenile delinquency crisis, the eugenics crisis, the child abuse crisis, the youth suicide crisis" have all contributed to expanding the power of the state at the expense of the family. Charles Murray (1984) compiled an impressive amount of data that purports to illustrate that public services designed to reduce poverty in the United States were ineffectual. Murray's data have been challenged by a number of investigators, and the ensuing debate reaffirms the difficulty in interpreting data relevant to this issue in ways that are free of bias. The difficulty is that socioeconomic conditions change so rapidly that it is not likely that any single factor can or should be justified as constituting the cause for poverty.

Whatever the causes, poverty is a reality in the United States, and increasingly, the discrepancies in the distribution of wealth within this country demand the attention of policy makers (Phillips 1990). It also seems apparent that, given the ubiquity of the family in social life, any policy regarding poverty must also be a policy pertaining to families. Whether that policy will be concerned with all families or just the poor remains to be seen; whether it is a national policy or policies instigated and implemented at the state levels, and whether its funding is in the form of direct grants or tax benefits and incentives, is also hard to predict. It is likely, however, given American traditions and the deep differences that exist within the country about family policy, that the eventual solutions and compromises reached will be different from those that have evolved in Europe. Nevertheless, in this world of instant communication and visibility, the state of the family in Europe and the resources available to European families must have an impact on the policy decisions made in the United States.

(SEE ALSO: *Alternative Life-Styles; American Families; Family Law; Family Planning; Family Size; Fertility Determinants; Marriage and Divorce Rates*)

REFERENCES

Baca Zinn, Maxine, and D. Stanley Eitzen 1990 *Diversity in Families,* 2nd ed. New York: HarperCollins.

Bellah, Robert N., Richard Madsen, William M. Sullivan, Ann Swidler, and Steven M. Tipton 1985 *Habits of the Heart: Individualism and Commitment in American Life.* Berkeley: University of California Press.

Berger, Brigitte, and Peter L. Berger 1983 *The War over the Family: Capturing the Middle Ground.* Garden City, N.Y.: Anchor Press.

Brodkin, Evelyn Z., and Dennis Young 1989 "Making Sense of Privatization: What Can We Learn from Economic and Political Analysis?" In Sheila B. Kamerman and Alfred J. Kahn, eds., *Privatization and the Welfare State.* Princeton, N.J.: Princeton University Press.

Carlson, Allan C. 1988 *Family Questions: Reflections on the American Social Crisis.* New Brunswick, N.J.: Transaction Books.

Dumon, Wilfried, and Joan Aldous 1979 "European and United States Political Contexts for Family Policy Research." In Gerald W. McDonald and F. Ivan Nye, eds., *Family Policy.* Minneapolis: National Council on Family Relations.

Gerson, Kathleen 1985 *Hard Choices: How Women Decide about Work, Career, and Motherhood.* Berkeley: University of California Press.

Glendon, Mary Ann 1989 *The Transformation of Family Law: State, Law, and Family in the United States and Western Europe.* Chicago: University of Chicago Press.

Haavio-Mannila, Elina 1988 "Converging Tendencies in Gender Roles." Paper presented at symposium, Can America Continue to Learn from Sweden and Finland? University of Delaware, Newark, Del. Oct. 19–21.

———, and Kaisa Kauppinen 1990 "Women's Lives and Women's Work in the Nordic Countries." In Hilda Kehore and Janet Giele, *Women's Lives and Women's Work in Modernizing and Industrial Countries.* Boulder, Colo.: Westview Press.

Hayghe, Howard V. 1990 "Family Members in the Work Force." *Monthly Labor Review* 113 (3):14–19.

Herrstrom, Staffan 1986 "Swedish Family Policy." *Current Sweden* 348 (September).

Kahn, Alfred J. 1969 *Theory and Practice in Social Planning.* New York: Russell Sage Foundation.

Kahn, Alfred J., and Sheila B. Kamerman 1975 *Not for the Poor Alone: European Social Services.* Philadelphia: Temple University Press.

———1983 *Income Transfers for Families with Children.* Philadelphia: Temple University Press.

Kamerman, Sheila B., and Alfred J. Kahn 1978 *Family Policy: Government and Families in Fourteen Countries.* New York: Columbia University Press.

———1981 *Child Care, Family Benefits, and Working Parents: A Comparative Study.* New York: Columbia University Press.

———1989 *Privatization and the Welfare State.* Princeton, N.J.: Princeton University Press.

Laswell, Harold 1968 "The Policy Orientation." In Daniel Lerner and Harold Lasswell, eds., *Policy Sciences.* Stanford, Calif.: Stanford University Press.

Lindsey, Linda L. 1990 *Gender Roles: A Sociological Perspective.* Englewood Cliffs, N.J.: Prentice-Hall.

Miller, Gary J. 1990 "A Contextual Approach to Child Development." Working Paper No. 9. Minneapolis: The City Inc. Photocopy.

Myrdal, Alva 1967 "Forward." In Edmund Dahlstrom, ed., *The Changing Roles of Men and Women.* London: Gerald Duckworth.

Murray, Charles 1984 *Losing Ground: American Social Policy, 1950–1980.* New York: Basic Books.

Phillips, Kevin 1990 *The Politics of Rich and Poor: Wealth and the American Electorate in the Reagan Aftermath.* New York: Random House.

Poponoe, David 1988 *Disturbing the Nest.* New York: Aldine De Gruyter.

Schorr, Alvin L. 1979 "Views of Family Policy." In Gerald McDonald and F. Ivan Nye, eds., *Family Policy.* Minneapolis: National Council on Family Relations.

Schorr, Lisbeth B. 1988 *Within Our Reach.* New York: Anchor Books.

———, C. Arden Miller, and Amy Fine 1986 "The Social Policy Context for Families Today." In Michael W. Yogman and T. Berry Brazelton, eds., *In Support of Families.* Cambridge, Mass.: Harvard University Press.

Statistical Abstract of Sweden 1990. Stockholm: Statistiska Centralbyran.

Statistisches Jahrbuch für die Bundesrepublik Deutschland 1989. Bonn: W. Kohlhammer.

Strong, Bryan, and Christine De Vault 1989 *The Marriage and Family Experience.* St. Paul: West Publishing Co.

Sweet, James A., and L. L. Bumpass 1987 *American Families and Households.* New York: Russell Sage Foundation.

United States Bureau of the Census 1988 *Statistical Abstracts of the United States.* Washington, D.C. U.S. Government Printing Office.

Van de Kaa, Kirk J. 1987 "Europe's Second Demographic Transition." *Population Bulletin* 42:1–57.

Wilson, William Julius 1987 *The Truly Disadvantaged: The Inner City, the Underclass, and Public Policy.* Chicago: University of Chicago Press.

Zimmerman, Shirley, L. 1979. "Policy, Social Policy, and Family Policy: Concepts, Concerns, and Analytic Tools." In Gerald W. McDonald and F. Ivan Nye, eds., *Family Policy*. Minneapolis: National Council on Family Relations.

———1988 *Understanding Family Policy*. Newbury Park, Calif.: Sage Publications.

IRVING TALLMAN
GINNA M. BABCOCK

FAMILY ROLES For a family to survive and function well, an optimal division of labor among adult family members is necessary. This labor includes not only such tangible work as housework, child care, and making a living, but also such intangibles as making decisions for the family and helping to maintain the happiness and psychological well-being of its members. How these tasks are divided among family members is, to a great extent, prescribed by the social norms of the society in which the family resides. These patterns of the division of labor are called *family roles*. Thus, family roles may be defined as "prescriptions for interpersonal behavior associated with one's position in the family" (Heiss 1976, p. 3). Put another way, family roles are socially constructed "beliefs or expectations that [family members] ought or ought not to behave in certain ways" (Burr, Leigh, Day, and Constantine 1979, p. 54).

Attempts to describe observed differences between the family roles of husbands and wives led to the concept of "instrumental" and "expressive" roles. Earlier research on small groups had shown that when a group was given a task to solve, two leaders tended to emerge (Bales 1958). The first leader was the one who talked most during the discussion, expressed many opinions, and gave out information. This person might have contributed a great deal to solving the task, but she or he usually was not the one most liked by other group members. The other leader was the one who showed solidarity and agreement more than did the others and tried to release tension among group members. This second leader was most liked by the others. These two leaders were called the "instrumental leader" and the "expressive leader," respectively. Because this instrumental–expressive differentiation occurs in most task-solving groups, particularly after the group has worked together for some time, it was assumed that this role differentiation was universal to all small groups, including the family. Because a husband "must provide for his family" and is "responsible for the support of his wife and children" (Zelditch 1955, p. 339), the instrumental role was attributed to the husband and the expressive one to the wife.

As dual-income couples have become the majority in the United States and other industrialized countries, the instrumental–expressive role differentiation of husbands and wives has lost some, but not all, of its validity. Child care, which requires affectionate and emotional interactions with children, is still assumed more by the wife than by the husband. Major financial decisions, such as whether or where to move or whether to buy a house, are still made by the husband in many families. This differentiation, however, may not be solely the result of husband–wife role differentiations but rather the result of more specific attributes of each spouse in realms outside family, such as employment status, income, and occupation.

The provider–homemaker dichotomy is another way of explaining the difference in family roles. Goods and services necessary to family life are produced or obtained through the enactment of the "provider" role, while the same goods and services are maintained or converted for family use by someone acting as the "homemaker." Thus, these two roles complement each other (Slocum and Nye 1976). Until recently, family labor was divided into these two roles in middle class American families: market labor by the husband as provider and household labor by the wife as homemaker. This provider–homemaker role differentiation, however, is far from universal. This pattern became typical only after the family's place of production and place of consumption became separated: The home became the site of family consumption, and the farm, factory, or office became the place of production. Furthermore, in traditional agricultural families, this provider–homemaker role differentiation was never as well established as one might think. In most farming families, husbands and wives worked very much together in the field, particularly during the harvest.

In contemporary American society, the distinction between these two roles has become less clear because more than half of all married women now are gainfully employed. In a family of an early industrialized society, the husband exchanged his earned money and social status for different but complementary resources—time, energy, and skill at household work—provided by the wife. In many contemporary families, however, the resources exchanged between husband and wife are the same: Monetary resources and household work are provided by both spouses. Recent research has found that the husband's share of the household work increases when his wife is gainfully employed, when she has a large income, or both (Kamo 1988). In other words, the husband's contribution in household labor (traditionally part of the homemaker role) is associated with his wife's contribution in market labor (traditionally part of the provider role). Nevertheless, it also has been found that the husband's contribution to the household work is not nearly as large as the wife's, even when they have provided roughly the same income (Kamo 1988). This suggests that the differentiation of provider–homemaker roles is not a simple function of both spouses' work status. It has been argued that husbands do not assume the homemaking role to the extent that wives assume the provider role. Alternatively, some scholars argue that, even though both spouses are gainfully employed, the wife may not be assuming the duty of providing for the family and that the husband may not be relinquishing his provider-role responsibilities (Perry-Jenkins 1988). The spouses' expectations of the roles and behaviors associated with each gender then become crucial in explaining the role differentiation in contemporary societies.

The importance of the spouses' gender-role attitudes to their household division of labor has been widely demonstrated (Coverman 1985; Bird, Bird, and Scruggs 1984). Those who believe in traditional gender-role differentiation share household work accordingly, regardless of how much income each generates or whether or not both are employed. Nevertheless, the relationship between one's attitude toward provider–homemaker roles and one's enactment of those roles is not perfect. Specifically, although both husbands and wives say they support sharing the provider and homemaker roles equally, their actual behavior indicates otherwise.

In some societies, individual behaviors are strictly prescribed by traditions and rules, and so are family roles. In many early industrialized societies, for example, there were inviolable rules about the roles individuals played within the family. In nineteenth-century rural France, family roles were rigid, and sanctions for deviating from them were harsh. A husband had to maintain authority at home, and if his wife battered him in a fight, he was ridiculed in a community ceremony, called "charivari," by being mounted backward on top of a donkey, with the donkey's tail in his hands (Segalen 1983). The same punishment was used for an adulterous couple, indicating the seriousness with which violation of certain family roles was regarded. Also ridiculed were "feminized" husbands who stayed home cooking meals, which was considered to be strictly the wife's role.

Comparative and historical analyses of family roles suggest that rigid family roles may be accounted for by the strength of social norms based on tradition and culture and by the social structure of a given society. Where sanctions for deviating from family roles are weak, such as in contemporary America, family behaviors become more spontaneous and innovative. In other words, although family roles used to be universally determined in traditional societies, in contemporary society family roles are more flexible and determined by specific family situations. The behavior expected of certain family members is determined more by such specific attributes as personality, individual preference, work status, and income rather than by the universal status of being a husband or a wife.

The family roles of a given society are closely

related to that society's more general gender roles, which include behaviors expected in other areas such as education, politics, and community involvement. Likewise, an individual's attitude toward family roles is closely related to his or her gender-role attitude. Family roles, therefore, are a link between the behavior of family members and their status in the larger society. The latter includes whether they are employed, in what type of work, how much they earn, and what roles they play in their community. When several groups are compared, either cross-culturally or within a society, the general status of men and women in the society will have a direct relationship to what is expected of a husband or a wife. Through careful examination of family roles and behaviors—even those as basic as the domestic division of labor—we may reach a better understanding of the human behaviors in the family, in the work place, and in the community.

(SEE ALSO: *Alternative Life-Styles; American Families*)

REFERENCES

Bales, Robert F. 1958 "Task Roles and Social Roles in Problem-Solving Groups." In E. E. Maccoby, T. M. Newcomb, and E. L. Hartley, eds., *Readings in Social Psychology,* 3rd ed. New York: Holt.

Bird, Gloria W., Gerald A. Bird, and Marguerite Scruggs 1984 "Determinants of Family Task Sharing: A Study of Husbands and Wives." *Journal of Marriage and the Family* 46:345–355.

Burr, Wesley R., Geoffrey K. Leigh, Randall D. Day, and John Constantine 1979 "Symbolic Interaction and the Family." In W. Burr, R. Hill, F. I. Nye, and I. Reiss, eds., *Contemporary Theories about the Family.* New York: Free Press.

Coverman, Shelley 1985 "Explaining Husband's Participation in Domestic Labor." *Sociological Quarterly* 26:81–97.

Heiss, Jerold 1976 "An Introduction to the Elements of Role Theory." In J. Heiss, ed., *Family Roles and Interaction: An Anthology.* Chicago: Rand McNally.

Kamo, Yoshinori 1988 "Determinants of Household Labor: Resources, Power, and Ideology." *Journal of Family Issues* 9:177–200.

Perry-Jenkins, Maureen 1988 "Future Directions for Research on Dual-Earner Families: A Young Professional's Perspective." *Family Relations* 37:226–228.

Segalen, Martine 1983 *Love and Power in the Peasant Family: Rural France in the Nineteenth Century,* trans. Sarah Matthews. Chicago: University of Chicago Press.

Slocum, Walter L., and F. Ivan Nye 1976 "Provider and Housekeeper Roles." In F. Ivan Nye, ed., *Role Structure and Analysis of the Family.* Beverly Hills, Calif.: Sage Publications.

Zelditch, Morris, Jr. 1955 "Role Differentiation in the Nuclear Family: A Comparative Study." In Talcott Parsons and Robert F. Bales, eds., *Family, Socialization, and Interaction Process.* New York: Free Press.

YOSHINORI KAMO

FAMILY SIZE Family size may be considered from two perspectives. At the individual (micro) level, it defines one aspect of an individual's family background or environment. As such, it represents a potential influence on the development and accomplishments of family members. At the societal (macro) level, family size is an indicator of societal structure that may vary over time, with concomitant implications for individual development and social relations in different cohorts. In this essay, consideration is given to both aspects of family size, as it is reflected in sociological theory and research.

While the term *family size* is sometimes used to represent the total number of individuals comprising a family unit, Treas (1981) argues convincingly for decomposing the concept into two components: numbers of children and numbers of adults in the household. This distinction is important, as observed patterns of change in overall family size may be attributable to one component or the other, as may effects of overall family size. In the present discussion, family size is defined in terms of the number of children in the household.

A further distinction is made between family size in the parental and filial households, sometimes referred to as the family of origin (or orientation) and the family of procreation. Some use the term *sibship size* to refer to the number of children in an individual's parental family (Blake

1989; Ryder 1986). However, the two are not directly comparable: mean family size takes into account those families which have no children, while mean sibship size is necessarily restricted to families with children.

Family size can also be differentiated from fertility, which reflects the aggregate numbers of births relative to the numbers of women in the population, without regard for the distribution of those births across family units. Fertility and family size are both important characteristics of cohorts; however, for assessing relationships at the individual level, family size or sibship size is the more meaningful construct (Ryder 1986).

The subsequent sections address the following aspects of family size: demographic trends in family size, antecedents and correlates of family size, and implications of sibship size and family size for child and adult members of the family.

DEMOGRAPHIC TRENDS

The twentieth century has witnessed substantial change in both fertility and family size (as indicated by the number of children in the household), with the overall trend being toward smaller families. Such trends can be examined through comparisons of fertility rates and mean family size, and also through investigation of parity distributions—that is, the numbers of families with zero, one, two (and so on) children.

Drawing on fertility tables compiled by the National Center for Health Statistics, Ryder (1986) presents time-series data for successive cohorts of women in the United States born between 1867 and 1955 (and who would thus be bearing children between approximately 1885 and 1975) that show the following general trends in fertility and family size:

1. Total fertility declined by 52 percent in the period being considered, from 4.00 for women born in 1867–1870 to 1.92 for women born in 1951–1955. A similar rate of decline occurred in marital fertility.
2. This decline was punctuated by a temporary upsurge in fertility for women born in 1916–1940, who were bearing children during the two decades following World War II (the "babyboom" years).
3. Variation in fertility rates increased for cohorts through 1910, and since then has consistently decreased, suggesting that in recent years there have been fewer women bearing no children or large numbers of children and an increasing concentration of families of moderate size.
4. Family size (the mean number of children in the family) decreased by 61 percent, from a high of 7.3 for women born in 1867–1870 to 2.8 for women born in 1951–1955.

It thus appears that during the period under consideration, mean family size decreased at an even faster rate than fertility. Further, the increased fertility during the "babyboom" years appears to have been offset by reduced variation in fertility for those cohorts of women, with the result that mean family size held relatively constant during that period, then continued its pattern of decline.

Treas (1981) examined changes in family size between 1955 and 1978 for whites and for nonwhites, using data from the March Current Population Surveys. Throughout the period, nonwhites consistently had larger families than did whites: In 1955 the mean number of children was 1.26 in white families and 1.80 in nonwhite families; in 1978 the corresponding figures were 1.04 and 1.56. During this period Treas found similar patterns of increases in family size through the 1960s, followed by decreasing family size in the 1970s, for both groups. However, the shifts were considerably more pronounced among nonwhite families.

Data obtained from the U.S. census on the distribution of family sizes (parity distributions) provide further insight on the trend toward smaller families. During the years between 1970 and 1988 the proportion of families with no children under eighteen increased substantially, from 44 percent to 51 percent, while the proportion of families with one child or two children increased only slightly (from 18 percent to 21 percent, and from 17 percent to 18 percent, respectively). However, the proportion of families with three or more children decreased markedly, from 20 percent to 10 percent during this period. Among black and Hispanic families, the increase in families with no children was not as pronounced as among white families, but the increases in families with one or two children were greater, as were the decreases in families with three or more children (U.S. Bureau of the Census 1990, p. 51).

Further insight into the decline in family size is provided by investigations of parity progression, or the probability of having (or intending to have) an additional child at each parity level. Decomposing his time-series data into parity progressions, Ryder (1986) reports that the "babyboom" was the result of an increase in progression from parities one and two, but that progression from parities three and higher have shown consistent declines. Similarly, data on intended parities show that the proportions intending progression from parity one have increased over time, while the intended progression ratios for parity three and higher have declined.

Other data on ideal, or normative, family sizes support this pattern of increasing concentration of smaller families. West and Morgan (1987) cite historical data showing that fertility norms have fluctuated in parallel with fertility rates and family sizes: During the 1930s and early 1940s two- and three-child families were preferred. During the post-World War II era three- and four-child families became the ideal, but in the late 1960s preferences reverted to the two- or three-child family. They further report that, among a sample of contemporary adults, a significant majority (64.8 percent) view the two-child family as ideal; that belief was surprisingly consistent across various subgroups defined by current family size, marital status, race, and religion.

At the same time that families have tended to become smaller on average, there has been increased variability in the timing of childbearing. One trend that has been widely noted has been the increase in childbearing among teenagers, particularly among lower SES, nonwhite, and less academically able youth (Card and Wise 1978). At the same time, there has been an increase in the proportion of women who delay childbearing until their early and mid thirties or who remain childless (Bloom and Trussell 1984). As will be discussed below, the timing of the first birth has implications for the eventual family size, and thus for the development and accomplishment of family members.

In sum, in the United States there appears to have been a strong shift toward smaller families, with the ideal being a two- or three-child family. A similar trend toward smaller families is found in other developed countries, while in developing countries families are more likely to be larger (Lopreato and Yu 1988). One exception to this generalization concerns countries, such as the Peoples' Republic of China, that are trying to implement a policy of restricting families to one child. However, while the policy appears to have led to lower mean family sizes, numerous families have continued to have two or more children, and a preferred family size of two continues to be the mode (Whyte and Gu 1987).

ANTECEDENTS AND CORRELATES OF FAMILY SIZE

Determinants of family size have been investigated at both the societal and the individual level. At the societal level, researchers have sought to account for differences in fertility and family size over time or between societies. Easterlin (1980) advanced a theory to account for changes in fertility and family size over time, as a function of individuals' economic resources and aspirations. He attributes the "babyboom" surge in fertility and family size to the generation of young men following World War II who experienced high wages, as a result of the expanding economy, and had relatively low material aspirations, as a result of being raised during the Depression. Conversely, the "babyboom" generation confronted increased competition for jobs, which, combined with higher aspirations, led to the "babybust" of the 1970s and 1980s. One implication of Easterlin's theory is that smaller birth cohorts are likely to experience more favorable labor markets, resulting in higher fertility.

A variation of this theory is presented by

Devaney (1983), who argues that the decline in fertility observed during the 1960s and 1970s can be attributed to increases in female wages and female employment, which in turn served to depress fertility, rather than to conscious decisions to limit fertility in the face of disadvantageous economic conditions. Her analyses, based on national fertility data and data on female labor force participation rates and male and female earnings, suggest that (1) female labor force participation and fertility are highly and negatively correlated, and (2) that female wage rates are the dominant factor in explaining recent variations in fertility and female employment. While this model differs from Easterlin's in terms of the process by which economic factors are thought to influence fertility, they are similar in viewing fertility as a response to economic market conditions.

Studies of developing countries have focused on several sociocultural as well as socioeconomic factors associated with fertility and family size: modernization (Levy 1985), contraceptive use and family planning programs (Koenig, Phillips, Simmons, and Khan 1987), and cultural attitudes and values, such as the perceived old-age security value of children (Rani 1986) or the view of children as risk insurance (Robinson 1986).

At the individual level, researchers have examined the extent to which fertility and family size may vary depending on individuals' family backgrounds, social and psychological characteristics, or economic status. Inverse relationships between social class and family size have been documented in a number of data sets: Individuals from larger families tend to have less-well-educated fathers who have lower-status occupations. Also, farm background is associated with larger family sizes (Blake 1989).

Parents' sibship size (the number of siblings that each parent had) is a second major determinant of family size: Women and men from larger families are more likely to have larger families (Ben-Porath 1975; Thornton 1980). This gives rise to an apparent paradox: While there is an overall trend toward small families, a high proportion of children come from larger families (Blake 1989). This paradox arises from the distinction noted above between cohort fertility rates, which are based on all women or all families, and children's sibship sizes, which are necessarily limited to women or families who have had children.

Retherford and Sewell (1988) investigated the relationship between intelligence and family size in their analysis of data from the Wisconsin Longitudinal Study of the High School Class of 1957, finding that the overall relationship between IQ and family size was negative for both sexes. However, the relationship proved to be much stronger for females, who showed consistent declines in family size as IQ increased. Among men the relationship was less consistent. Retherford and Sewell also reviewed the results of other, earlier studies, noting that the negative relationship between IQ and family size appears to have become more pronounced in the post-"babyboom" cohorts.

Additional factors associated with family size pertain primarily to family and achievement-related characteristics of the mother: More education, later age at marriage, longer interval between marriage and the birth of the first child, and employment status are all associated with smaller families—that is, fewer children (Wagner, Schubert, and Schubert 1985). Family configuration has also been found to be associated with increased family size, with the probability of having an additional child being higher in families with all children of the same sex (Gualtieri and Hicks 1986). Also, only children are disproportionately likely to come from broken families (Blake 1989).

The interaction between wives' employment and childbearing has been a topic of much study, as women have increasingly entered or remained in the work force, but the results obtained are inconsistent. Waite and Stolzenberg (1976) found a significant negative relationship between wife's work and family size. However, based on analyses of longitudinal data that allowed for the study of recursive processes as well as inclusion of several additional measures, Bagozzi and Van Loo (1988) found no causal relationships between wife's employment and family size, and suggested that both labor force participation and family size are codetermined by the wife's achievement motivation, sex role norms, and perceived value of children.

Oropesa (1985) used data from the NORC General Social Surveys to test the hypotheses represented in Easterlin's model at the micro level, using relative affluence as the predictor and expected family size as the outcome of interest. He found that relative affluence is more likely to be associated with expected births for women than for men, and that the effects are stronger with regard to expected births in the short term than with total expected family size.

The research cited above focuses on static determinants of childbearing and family size. However, some investigators have examined fertility and childbearing decisions as a dynamic process, influenced by life situation and life events, that may change over time, as well as by relatively fixed individual characteristics. One line of investigation has focused on timing of first birth as a determinant of eventual family size. Card and Wise (1978) and Hofferth and Moore (1979) demonstrated that early first births are associated with larger families; Bloom and Trussell (1984) similarly demonstrated that delayed childbearing is associated with smaller average family sizes, as well as with childlessness.

A second line of research has investigated the relationships between parity level and fertility decisions. Udry (1983) examined the relative influence of initial fertility plans and intervening life events (such as births during the interval, change in household income, change in education, female work status, change in marital satisfaction) on couple's fertility decisions at different parity levels. He found that including intervening events in the analyses improved the prediction of both fertility plans and, especially, actual fertility behavior, providing support for a sequential model of fertility decision making. White and Kim (1987) investigated whether the determinants of fertility choices vary by parity, and found a nonlinear relationship between fertility determinants and childbearing, especially with regard to factors related to women's roles. Both sex-role traditionalism and achievement in nonfamily roles were associated with a higher probability of having a child at parity zero or one, but a lower probability of having a child among women at higher parities. These findings are somewhat contrary to those based on cross-sectional analyses of family size, suggesting the importance of taking parity level into account in such investigations.

IMPLICATIONS OF FAMILY SIZE

The effects of sibship/family size and family composition on children and on adults has long been a topic of popular interest, and in recent years has become the focus of a considerable body of sociological and psychological inquiry. In particular, attention has been directed to effects of sibship size on children's cognitive development, physical and social-psychological development, educational attainment, and socioeconomic attainment and mobility. Consideration is also given to effects of family size on parents and on family well-being.

Cognitive Development. Interest in the relationship between sibship size and intelligence dates back to Anne Anastasi's (1956) review, which found an inverse relationship between the two. Subsequent empirical studies, in the United States as well as in Europe, using various measures of ability and controlling for family background characteristics, have confirmed this finding (Belmont and Marolla 1973; Breland 1974; Claudy, Gross, and Strause 1974). Blake (1989) provides a comprehensive review of this literature, including a discussion of limitations and weaknesses in the prior studies.

Only children present a special case. Numerous studies have reported that only children do not perform as well on intelligence measures as do children from two-child families. Indeed, in the Belmont and Marolla study (1973), only children were found to be lower in intelligence than firstborns in families up to size four, and lower than second-borns in families up to size three. Claudy et al. (1974) obtained similar results after controlling for differences in SES. However, when differences in family composition were taken into account by restricting the sample to only children in two-parent families, the differences between only children and firstborn children in larger families became nonsignificant (Claudy, Farrell, and Dayton 1979).

In an effort to account for the observed relationships between sibship size and intellectual ability, Zajonc (1976) introduced the "confluence model," which postulates that the intellectual environment in the home, defined by the combined intellectual levels of the parents and children, accounts for the observed relationships. According to his theory, the intellectual level is at its peak in families with two adults and no children; as the number of children in the home increases, the intellectual environment afforded to any individual child is effectively diluted. There are two implications of the "confluence model": Children from smaller families should show higher intelligence, and children born earlier in families should show higher intelligence. While the former hypothesis has been supported by a number of empirical studies, the latter did not account for the findings pertaining to only children. In response, Zajonc expanded the confluence model, postulating that younger siblings provide an opportunity for teaching, thus enriching the intellectual experience of older children; the lower intellectual performance of only children is attributed to the fact that they cannot avail themselves of this opportunity. While the confluence model has generated considerable discussion and debate, particularly regarding possible interactions between family size and birth order, and with family SES (see, for example, Steelman 1985; Zajonc 1986), a systematic test of the model remains to be conducted.

Blake (1989) identifies two limitations in the previous work: lack of differentiation of various kinds of intellectual ability (such as verbal and nonverbal) and potential interactions with SES. She finds that the inverse relationship between sibship size and intelligence holds for measures of verbal skill, but not for measures of nonverbal ability, and that the verbal ability deficits observed among children in large families are not limited to those from more disadvantaged backgrounds.

Physical and Social-Psychological Development. Compared with other outcome measures, relatively little attention has been given to the study of sibship size effects on children's physical and social-psychological development. Mednick, Birgitte, Baker, and Hocevar (1985) and Wagner et al. (1985) provide brief reviews of this literature. Family size has been found to be inversely related to children's height and weight; it is also positively correlated with morbidity and mortality. With regard to social-psychological development, children from larger families have been found to have poorer self-concepts, value conformity, and self-control rather than independence and self-expression, and to show a greater tendency toward antisocial behavior. They are also less likely to be interested in white-collar occupations.

Blake (1989) investigated the relationship between sibship size and educational expectations, using data from three different cohorts of youth, and found that young people from smaller families, as well as from higher-status families, tend to have higher educational goals. These effects, however, are mediated through ability and grades, and through parents' expectations.

Educational Attainment. Blake's (1989) book, *Family Size and Achievement,* provides the most comprehensive assessment to date of this area. Two sets of questions are addressed: First, does sibship size affect educational expectations and attainment, and if so, where in the educational process? Second, what is the relative importance of sibship size, relative to other measures of family background?

With regard to the first question, sibship size does appear to have a substantial effect on educational attainment. Individuals from small families had approximately two additional years of schooling, relative to their peers from larger families—net of differences attributable to parental characteristics. The greatest impact on education occurred at the high school level, with individuals from larger families more likely to drop out of high school.

With regard to the second question, relative to other background variables in the analysis, sibship size was consistently second in importance for years of schooling, behind father's education. However, the negative effects of large families were somewhat mitigated by high parental SES and by membership in certain religious or ethnic groups. Similarly, the effects of parental SES were somewhat mitigated for youth in small families.

Some have argued that sibship size is simply a proxy for otherwise unmeasured characteristics of parents' family background, and does not exert any independent effect on education in its own right. To address this concern, Blake (1989) examined the extent to which children from different-sized families have different home environments that might, in turn, influence educational attainment. In particular, attention was given to characteristics of the home setting (such as time spent reading newspapers, reading books, watching television) and to parental behaviors directed toward the child (such as encouragement, correction, goal setting). Children from smaller families were more likely to spend time in intellectual and cultural pursuits, to spend time playing alone, to have been read to as children, and to have had music or dance lessons. However, no significant differences were found in parental values for their children or in parenting style after parents' education and SES were taken into account. Thus, while there appear to be differences in the home environments afforded to children in smaller versus larger families, these differences do not appear to be attributable to differences in parental values or parenting style.

Socioeconomic Attainment and Mobility. A long tradition of research has addressed the question of how family background conditions or constrains individuals' socioeconomic attainment and social mobility. While primary consideration has been given to the impact of family social resources (father's education and occupation) on children's attainment, sibship size also was found to be related to occupational attainment (Blau and Duncan 1967). Among both women and men, those from larger families were more likely to have lower-status jobs and lower earnings, even after adjusting for differences in fathers' SES and educational attainment, both of which are correlated with family size. Among women, the effect of sibship size on earnings was stronger than the effect of father's occupation (Featherman and Hauser 1976). Using path analysis to model both indirect and direct relationships, however, Duncan, Featherman, and Duncan (1972) found that the negative effect of sibship size on men's occupational status could be accounted for primarily by the effect of sibship size on educational attainment. This finding lends some support to arguments that larger families result in a dilution of family economic resources, thus constraining the opportunities available to children.

Parents' Economic Well-Being. Duncan et al. (1972) examined the impact of family size (as contrasted with sibship size) as a contingency in men's socioeconomic attainment, finding a slight and negative effect on occupational status but a positive effect on earnings, net of other background variables. Studies that included women found evidence of reciprocal relationships between family size and labor force participation, which in turn affected women's career attainment (Waite and Stolzenberg, 1976). However, as noted previously, Bagozzi and Van Loo (1988) suggested that women's work and family size are not causally related but are mutually dependent on other, achievement-related characteristics of the wife.

Relationships have been reported between the timing of childbearing and subsequent economic well-being. Card and Wise (1978) found that teenage parents of both sexes tended to have less education, lower job prestige, and lower earnings, relative to later childbearers, net of differences in background characteristics. Investigating this relationship in greater depth, Hofferth and Moore (1979) found that the effects of early childbearing on women's subsequent earnings were primarily attributable to the larger family sizes of these women, and the consequent implications for (less) work experience. However, they also found that early childbearing was less of a handicap for black women, due to weaker relationships between early childbearing and subsequent education and employment. Hofferth (1984) found that among women aged sixty or over, the number of children per se was not related to measures of economic well-being, but that the timing of childbearing was: Those who delayed the first birth until after age thirty had higher family incomes and higher standards of living than did women whose first child was born before age thirty. This relationship was most pronounced among delayed childbearers who had small families, suggesting an interaction between timing of childbearing and family size.

Massagli (1987) has argued for a life cycle model of the process of stratification that incorporates information on family size in both the parental and the filial generations. He hypothesizes that sibship size does not affect socioeconomic attainment directly but, rather, is related to the timing of early life cycle transitions and to marital fertility; the observed negative effects of sibship size on attainment are attributed to the product of the relationship with life cycle transitions and marital fertility and the negative effect of marital fertility on attainment.

Parental Attitudes and Well-Being. Wagner et al. (1985) review a number of studies of effects of family size on parental attitudes and parental health. They find that parental attitudes and treatment of children vary with family size: Larger families are more family centered, with a greater role played by fathers; at the same time, parents in larger families tend to be more authoritarian, and more inclined to treat all children alike. Parents in larger families have also been found to have poorer marital relations. Finally, men and women who have many children are at greater risk of hypertension and other physical ailments.

In sum, sibship size and family size both appear to exert significant influence on the children and on the parents. Sibship size is closely related to family socioeconomic background, however, which is also a major influence on children's development and attainment. As a result, care must be taken to differentiate between effects of sibship size per se and effects of socioeconomic background. Similarly, family size among adults (the number of children they have) is highly correlated with socioeconomic status, intelligence, and other characteristics; again, it is important to consider the effects of family size net of these other factors. In many instances, the effects of sibship size and family size appear to be indirect. For example, sibship size is highly correlated with educational attainment, and thus with subsequent occupational attainment. Similarly, among adults, family size is correlated with employment, and thus with socioeconomic attainment. Finally, family size is often closely related to other characteristics of the family: Among children, it may be related to birth order, and among parents, it may be related to the timing of childbearing. Understanding these indirect as well as direct relationships yields a better understanding of the ways in which, and the extent to which, sibship size and family size may affect the lives of children and adults.

(SEE ALSO: *Family Planning; Family Policy in Western Societies; Fertility Determinants*)

REFERENCES

Anastasi, A. 1956 "Intelligence and Family Size." *Psychological Bulletin* 53:187–209.

Bagozzi, Richard P., and M. Frances Van Loo 1988 "An Investigation of the Relationship Between Work and Family Size Decisions over Time." *Multivariate Behavioral Research* 23:3–34.

Belmont, L., and F. A. Marolla 1973 "Birth Order, Family Size, and Intelligence." *Science* 182:1096–1101.

Ben-Porath, Y. 1975 "First-Generation Effects on Second-Generation Fertility." *Demography* 12:397–405.

Blake, Judith 1986 "Number of Siblings, Family Background, and the Process of Educational Attainment." *Social Biology* 33:5–21.

——— 1989 *Family Size and Achievement.* Berkeley: University of California Press.

Blau, Peter M., and Otis D. Duncan 1967 *The American Occupational Structure.* New York: Free Press.

Bloom, David E., and James Trussell 1984 "What Are the Determinants of Delayed Childbearing and Permanent Childlessness in the United States?" *Demography* 21:591–611.

Breland, H. M. 1974 "Birth Order, Family Configuration, and Verbal Achievement." *Child Development* 45:1011–1019.

Card, Josefina J., and Lauress L. Wise 1978 "Teenage Mothers and Teenage Fathers: The Impact of Early Childbearing on the Parents' Personal and Professional Lives." *Family Planning Perspectives* 10:199–205.

Claudy, John G., William S. Farrell, Jr., and Charles W. Dayton 1979 "The Consequences of Being an Only Child: An Analysis of Project TALENT Data." Final report. Palo Alto, Calif.: American Institutes for Research.

Claudy, John G., David E. Gross, and Rebecca D. Strause 1974 "Two Population Studies: I. Family Size, Birth Order, and Characteristics of Young Adults, and II. A Study of Married Couples in Knox County, Tennessee." Final report. Palo Alto, Calif.: American Institutes for Research.

Devaney, Barbara 1983 "An Analysis of Variations in U.S. Fertility and Female Labor Force Participation Trends." *Demography* 20:147–161.

Duncan, Otis D., David L. Featherman, and Beverly Duncan 1972 *Socioeconomic Background and Achievement.* New York: Seminar Press.

Easterlin, Richard A. 1980 *Birth and Fortune.* New York: Basic Books.

Featherman, David L., and Robert M. Hauser 1976 "Sexual Inequalities and Socioeconomic Achievement." *American Sociological Review* 41:462–483.

Gualtieri, C. Thomas, and Robert E. Hicks 1986 "Family Configuration and Family Size." *Social Biology* 33:146–147.

Hofferth, Sandra L. 1984 "Long-Term Economic Consequences for Women of Delayed Childbearing and Reduced Family Size." *Demography* 21:141–155.

———, and Kristin A. Moore 1979 "Early Childbearing and Later Economic Well Being." American Sociological Review 44:784–815.

Koenig, Michael A., James F. Phillips, Ruth S. Simmons, and Mehrab A. Khan 1987 "Trends in Family Size Preferences and Contraceptive Use in Matlab, Bangladesh." *Studies in Family Planning* 18:117–127.

Levy, Victor 1985 "Cropping Pattern, Mechanization, Child Labor, and Fertility Behavior in a Farming Economy: Rural Egypt." *Economic Development and Cultural Change* 33:777–791.

Lopreato, Joseph, and Mai-yu Yu 1988 "Human Fertility and Fitness Optimization." *Ethology and Sociobiology* 9:269–289.

Massagli, Michael P. 1987 "Effects of Family Size on the Process of Stratification: A Structural Equation Model for White Couples in the U.S. in 1962 and 1973." In *Research in Social Stratification and Mobility,* vol. 6, Robert V. Robinson, ed. Greenwich, Conn.: JAI Press.

Mednick, Birgitte R., Robert L. Baker, and Dennis Hocevar 1985 "Family Size and Birth Order Correlates of Intellectual, Psychosocial, and Physical Growth." *Merrill-Palmer Quarterly* 31:67–84.

Oropesa, R. S. 1985 "Subject Relative Affluence and Expected Family Size." *Sociology and Social Research* 69:501–515.

Rani, Usha D. 1986 "Old Age Security Value of Children and Fertility in Relation to Social Policy." Paper presented at the annual meeting of the International Sociological Association.

Retherford, Robert D., and William H. Sewell 1988 "Intelligence and Family Size Reconsidered." *Social Biology* 35:1–40.

Robinson, W. C. 1986 "High Fertility as Risk-Insurance." *Population Studies* 40:289–298.

Ryder, Norman B. 1986 "Observations on the History of Cohort Fertility in the United States." *Population and Development Review* 12:617–643.

Steelman, Lala C. 1985 "A Tale of Two Variables: A Review of the Intellectual Consequences of Sibship Size and Birth Order." *Review of Educational Research* 55:353–386.

Thornton, A. 1980 "The Influence of First Generation Fertility and Economic Status on Second Generation Fertility." *Population and Environment* 3:51–72.

Treas, Judith 1981 "Postwar Trends in Family Size." *Demography* 18:321–334.

Udry, J. Richard 1983 "Do Couples Make Fertility Plans One Birth at a Time?" *Demography* 20:117–128.

U.S. Bureau of the Census 1990 *Statistical Abstract of the United States: 1990.* Washington, D.C.: U.S. Government Printing Office.

Wagner, Mazie E., Herman J. P. Schubert, and Daniel S. P. Schubert 1985 "Family Size Effects: A Review." *Journal of Genetic Psychology* 146:65–78.

Waite, Linda J., and Ross M. Stolzenberg 1976 "Intended Childbearing and Labor Force Participation of Young Women: Insights from Nonrecursive Models." *American Sociological Review,* 41:235–252.

West, Kirsten K., and Leslie A. Morgan 1987 "Public Perceptions of the Ideal Number of Children for Contemporary Families." *Population and Environment* 9:160–171.

White, Lynn K., and Hyunju Kim 1987 "The Family-

Building Process: Childbearing Choices by Parity." *Journal of Marriage and the Family* 49:271–279.

Whyte, Martin K., and S. Z. Gu 1987 "Popular Response to China's Fertility Transition." *Population and Development Review* 13:471–494.

Zajonc, Robert B. 1976 "Family Configuration and Intelligence." *Science* 192:227–236.

———1986 "Family Factors and Intellectual Test Performance: A Reply to Steelman." *Review of Educational Research* 56:365–371.

LAURI STEEL

FAMILY VIOLENCE Physical violence of all types, from slaps to murder, probably occurs more frequently in the family than in any other setting or group except the armed services in time of war or riot. This article summarizes the incidence rates and examines reasons for the high rates, with emphasis on the characteristics of the family as a social institution and on social inequality.

Physical violence is defined as an act carried out with the intention or perceived intention of causing physical pain or injury to another person (Gelles and Straus 1979). For certain purposes, the term *assault* is preferable because much intrafamily violence is a statutory crime. However, not all violence is criminal. Hitting a misbehaving child is legal and expected in all but a few countries. Hitting an "errant wife" was legal under the common law in the United States until the 1870s (Calvert 1974).

Child abuse was not regarded as a widespread social problem by sociologists, family therapists, or the public until the 1960s (Nelson 1984; Pfohl 1977), and wife beating not until the 1970s. The subsequent emergence of public concern and research on these and other aspects of family violence reflects major social changes, including the following:

1. The social activism of the 1960s, which sought to aid oppressed groups of all types, was extended to this aspect of the oppression of children and women.
2. The rising homicide and assault rate, violent political and social protest and assassinations, terrorist activity, and the Vietnam war sensitized people to violence.
3. Disenchantment with the family in the 1960s and early 1970s facilitated perceiving negative features of family life, including violence.
4. The growth of paid employment by married women provided the economic means for them no longer to tolerate the abuse that had long been the lot of women.
5. The reemerged women's movement made battering a central issue in the mid 1970s and gave it wide publicity.
6. The creation by the women's movement of a new social institution—shelters for battered women—did more than provide material assistance. Shelters were ideologically important because they concretized and publicized a phenomenon that had previously been ignored.
7. Changes in theoretical perspectives in sociology put the consensus model of society under attack by conflict theory. The inevitability of conflict in all human groups, including the family, was recognized, along with the possibility of violent conflict.

PREVALENCE OF FAMILY VIOLENCE

Homicide. In the United States, about one-quarter of all murders involve family members (Straus 1986). In other industrialized countries the percentage is much higher, for example, 48 percent in Canada and 67 percent in Denmark (Straus 1987). These high percentages occur because Canada and Denmark have *low* homicide rates. The few family homicides that occur are a large proportion of the low overall rate. This suggests that when homicide has been almost eliminated in a society such as Denmark, the family is the setting in which it is most likely to persist.

Official Statistics on Child Abuse and Spouse Abuse. National statistics on child abuse cases reported to welfare authorities in the United States have been published since 1976. In that year 669,000 cases were reported, of which about one-quarter (167,000) were physical abuse (American Association for the Protection of Children 1986). These statistics vastly underestimate the actual extent of child abuse. Many times more children are severely beaten each year but do not come to public attention. Officially reported cases grew by about 10 percent per year during the period 1976–1985, for a total increase of about 300 percent. However, rather than an increase, historical and survey evidence suggests that the true incidence of child physical abuse has been slowly decreasing since the late seventeenth century (Radbill 1987; Straus and Gelles 1986). The growth in officially known cases from 1976 to 1985 did not occur because more children were assaulted but because the child abuse education campaigns and the social changes listed earlier led the public and professionals to report cases that in previous times would have been ignored.

There are no official statistics for the United States on violence between spouses because the Uniform Crime Reporting System used by almost all police departments does not classify assaults on the basis of relationship between victim and offender. Even if such data were gathered, only a small fraction of the cases would be included because most do not come to the attention of the police (Kaufman Kantor and Straus 1990). A similar problem makes the U.S. National Crime Survey (Gaquin 1977–1978; U.S. Department of Justice 1980) vastly underestimate the incidence of wife beating. The public tends to consider assault by a spouse as a "family problem" rather than a "crime" and rarely informs the survey interviewer of such events.

The National Family Violence Surveys. National surveys of U.S. families were conducted in 1975 and 1985 to secure a better estimate of the incidence and prevalence of family violence. These surveys were made possible by the development of the "Conflict Tactics Scales" to measure family violence (Straus 1979, 1990). The following rates are based on the 6,002 families in the 1985 study (Straus and Gelles 1986, 1990). The resulting annual incidence rates are many times greater than rates based on cases known to child welfare professionals, the police, shelters, or the National Crime Survey, but are still believed to be lower-bound estimates.

Sixteen percent of the couples surveyed reported one or more incidents involving physical violence during 1985. Attacks by husbands on wives that were serious enough to warrant the term "wife beating" (because they involved punching, biting, kicking, choking, etc.) were reported for 3.2 percent of wives, resulting in a lower-bound estimate of 1.7 million beaten women in 1985. The 1975 and 1985 National Family Violence Surveys, and all other studies of marital violence that do not use samples selected from the clientele of shelters and similar agencies, find that women assault their husbands at about the same rate as men assault their wives (Straus 1990); however, men are injured at only one-seventh the rate of injury to women (Stets and Straus 1990; Straus 1990).

The most violent role within the family is that of parent, because almost all parents use physical punishment. Over one-fifth of the parents of infants in the 1985 National Family Violence Survey reported hitting their child that year. Over 90 percent of parents of three-year-old children used physical punishment. The figure decreased steadily from age five on, but one-third of parents of children fifteen to seventeen years old reported hitting the child that year.

Child abuse is more difficult to operationalize than *physical punishment* because the line differentiating *abuse* from *physical punishment* is to a considerable extent a matter of social norms. Two different rates, based on different normative assumptions, were therefore computed from the National Family Violence Survey data. The first rate indicates the percentage of children who were kicked, bitten, punched, beaten, scalded, or attacked with a knife or gun. This resulted in a child abuse rate of 2.4 percent, and a lower-bound estimate of 1.5 million U.S. children abused in 1985. Hitting children with an object such as a stick or a belt was not included in the first rate because the courts and much of the general public continue to uphold its legality. However, the proportion of the public who accept such acts as legitimate physical punishment seems to be decreasing. Consequently, a second rate, which classifies hitting a child with an object as abusive, was computed. This resulted in a rate of 11 percent and an estimate of more than 6.9 million U.S. children physically abused in 1985. The first of these two estimates is about six times greater than the number of cases reported to protective service agencies in 1985, and the second of the estimates is twenty-seven times greater.

Intrafamily relationships between children are extremely violent. But, like violence of parents, it is not perceived as such because there is an implicit normative tolerance. Almost all young children hit a sibling, and more than 20 percent hit a parent. Even in their late teens (age fifteen to seventeen) the rate of violence between siblings is enormous: More than two-thirds of that age group hit a sibling during the year of the survey.

Comparison of the two National Family Violence Surveys found a substantial reduction in the rates of child abuse and wife beating (Straus and Gelles 1986), reflecting a centuries-long trend. Nevertheless, the rates just reported show that American society still has a long way to go before a typical citizen is as safe in his or her own home as on the streets or in the workplace.

EXPLANATIONS OF FAMILY VIOLENCE

High Level of Family Conflict. A characteristic of the family that helps accounts for the high rate of violence is its inherently high level of conflict. One reason for high conflict is that, as in other primary groups, family members are concerned with "the whole person." Consequently, there are more issues over which conflict can occur than in nonprimary relationships. Moreover, when conflict does occur, the deep commitment makes arguments emotionally charged. A disagreement about music with colleagues at work is unlikely to have the same emotional intensity as when children favor rock and parents favor Bach. The likelihood of conflicts is further multiplied because families usually consist of both males and females and parents and children, thus juxtaposing differences in the orientations and interests of different genders and generations. The family is the prime locus of the "battle of the sexes" and the "generation gap."

Norms Tolerating or Requiring Violence. Although conflict is endemic in families, it is not the only group or institution with a high level of conflict. Conflict is also high in academic departments and congressional committees, yet physical violence is practically nonexistent in those groups. Additional factors are needed to explain why violence is so much more frequent in the family than in other groups. One of these is the existence of cultural norms that tolerate or require violence. The clearest example is the right and obligation of parents to use physical force to train, protect, and control a child. Eighty-four percent of Americans believe "It is sometimes necessary to discipline a child with a good hard spanking" (Lehman 1989). These norms contrast with those prevailing within other institutions. Even prison authorities are no longer permitted to use corporal punishment.

Similar norms apply to husband–wife relations. However, they are implicit and taken for granted, and therefore largely unrecognized. Just as parenthood gives the right to hit, so the marriage license is also a hitting license (Greenblat 1983; Straus 1976). As with other licenses, rules govern its use. Slapping a spouse, for example, is tolerable if the spouse is perceived to be engaged in a serious wrong and "won't listen to reason." Many of the men and women interviewed by Gelles (1974, p. 58) expressed this normative principle with such phrases as "I asked for it" or "She needed to be brought to her senses."

The common law right of a husband to "physically chastise an errant wife" was recognized by U.S. courts until the late nineteenth century (Calvert 1974). Informally, it lived on in the behavior of the public, the police, and the courts, and continues to do so. Under pressure from the women's movement, this is changing, but slowly. There have been major reforms in police and court procedures (Lerman 1981; Sherman and

Cohn 1989), but the public and many police officers continue to believe that "it's their own business" if spouses are violent to each other, provided the blow is not severe enough to cause an injury that requires medical treatment, whereas they would not tolerate a similar pattern of assault in an office, factory, or church. Only a very small percent of men in the 1985 National Family Violence Survey believed that a legal sanction would be likely if they assaulted their wife (Carmody and Williams 1987). Of the more than six hundred women in this survey who were assaulted by their husbands, the police were involved in only 6.7% of the incidents and an arrest was made in only five cases (Kaufman Kantor and Straus 1990). The probability of legal sanction for assaulting a wife is even less than the .008 indicated by those five cases, because two-thirds of the six hundred women were assaulted more than once during the year of the survey.

Family Socialization in Violence. In a certain sense it begs the question to attribute the high rate of family violence to norms that tolerate, permit, or require violence because it does not explain why the norms for families are different from those for other social groups or institutions. There are a number of reasons, but one of the most fundamental is that the family is the setting in which physical violence is first experienced, and in which the normative legitimacy of violence is learned. Learning about violence begins with physical punishment, which, as noted above, is experienced by over 90 percent of American children. Physical punishment is used to teach that certain types of behavior are not condoned, but simultaneously, social learning processes teach the legitimacy of and behavioral script for violence.

The first step in the process is the association of love with violence. Since physical punishment begins in infancy, parents are the first, and usually the only, ones to hit an infant. From the earliest level of psychosocial development, children learn that those to whom they are most closely bonded are also those who hit. Second, since physical punishment is used to train the child in morally correct behavior or to teach about danger to be avoided, it establishes the normative legitimacy of hitting other family members. Third, physical punishment teaches the cultural script for use of violence. For example, parents often refrain from hitting until their anger or frustration reaches a certain point. The child therefore learns that anger and frustration justify the use of physical force.

As a result of these social learning processes, use of violence becomes internalized and generalized to other social relationships, especially such intimate relationships as husband and wife and parent and child. Both National Family Violence Surveys found that the more physical punishment experienced as a child, the higher the probability of hitting a spouse (Straus 1983; 1991; Straus, Gelles, and Steinmetz 1980). Many children do not even need to extrapolate from physical punishment of children to other relationships because they directly observe role models of physical violence between their parents.

Gender Inequality. Despite egalitarian rhetoric and the trend toward a more egalitarian family structure, male dominance in the family and in other spheres remains an important cause of family violence (Straus 1976). Most Americans continue to think of the husband as the "head of the family," and many believe that status gives him the right to have the final say. This sets the stage for violence because force is ultimately necessary to back up the right to have the final say (Goode 1971).

Numerous structural patterns sustain the system of male dominance: The income of women employed full-time is about a third lower than the income of men, and money is a source of power. Men tend to marry women who are younger, shorter, and less well educated; and age, physical size, and education form a basis for exercising power. Thus, the typical marriage begins with an advantage to the man. If the initial advantage changes or is challenged, many men feel morally justified in using their greater size and strength to maintain the right to have the final say, which they perceive to have been agreed on at the time of the marriage (LaRossa 1980). As a result, male-dominant marriages have been found to have the highest rate of wife beating (Coleman and Straus 1986; Straus, Gelles, and Steinmetz 1980), and societies in which male-dominant marriages prevail have higher rates of marital violence than more egalitarian societies (Levinson 1989; Straus 1977).

The privileged economic position of men also helps to explain why beaten wives so often stay with an assaulting husband (Kalmuss and Straus 1983). As recently as the 1980 U.S. census, about half of all married women with children had no earned income of their own. The other half earned only about half of the male wage. When marriages end, children stay with the mother in about 90 percent of the cases. Child support payments are typically inadequate and typically not made after a year or two. No-fault divorce has worked to the economic disadvantage of women (Weitzman 1986). Consequently, many women stay in violent marriages because the alternative is bringing up their children in poverty.

Other Factors. Many other factors contribute to the high rate of intrafamily violence in the United States, even though they do not explain why the family is, on the average, more violent than other groups. Space permits only some of these to be identified briefly.

The empirical evidence shows that the greater the number of stressful events experienced by a family, the higher the rate of marital violence and child abuse (Makepeace 1983; Straus 1980; Straus and Kaufman Kantor 1987). In addition to specific stressful events that impinge on families, chronic stresses, such as marital conflict and poverty, are also strongly associated with child abuse and spouse abuse.

Almost all studies that have investigated this issue find a strong association between drinking and family violence (Coleman and Straus 1983; Kaufman Kantor and Straus 1987). However, even though heavy drinkers have two to three times the violence rate of abstainers, most heavy drinkers do *not* engage in spouse abuse or child abuse (Kaufman Kantor and Straus 1987).

The higher the level of nonfamily violence in a society, the higher the rate of child abuse and spouse abuse (Levinson 1989; Straus 1977). The nonfamily violence can be in the form of violent crime or socially legitimate violence such as warfare. The carryover of violent behavior from one sphere of life to another may be strongest when the societal violence is "legitimate violence" rather than "criminal violence," because most individual acts of violence are carried out to correct some perceived wrong. Archer and Gartner (1984) and Huggins and Straus (1980) found that war is associated with an increase in interpersonal violence. Straus constructed an index to measure differences between the states of the United States in the extent to which violence was used or supported for socially legitimate purposes such as corporal punishment in the schools, or expenditure per capita on the National Guard (Baron and Straus 1989). The higher the score of a state on this Legitimate Violence Index, the higher the rate of *criminal* violence such as homicide (Baron and Straus 1988) and rape (Baron and Straus 1989).

Family violence occurs at all social levels, but it is more prevalent at the lowest socioeconomic level and among disadvantaged minorities. Socioeconomic group differences in physical punishment of children or slapping of spouses are relatively small, but the more severe the violence, the greater the socioeconomic difference. Thus, punching, biting, choking, attacking with weapons, and killing of family members occur much more often among the most disadvantaged sectors of society (Straus, Gelles, and Steinmetz 1980; Bachman, Linsky, and Straus 1988).

The Overall Pattern. No single factor, such as male dominance or growing up in a violent family, has been shown to account for more than a small percentage of the incidence of child abuse or spouse abuse. However, a study of the potential effect of twenty-five such "risk factors" found that in families where only one or two of the factors existed, there were no incidents of wife beating during the year studied. On the other hand, wife beating occurred in 70 percent of the families with twelve or more of the twenty-five factors (Straus, Gelles, and Steinmetz 1980, p. 203). Similar results were found for child abuse. Thus, the key to unraveling the paradox of family violence appears to lie in understanding the interplay of numerous causal factors.

THE FUTURE

During the period 1965 to 1985, the age-old phenomena of child abuse and wife beating underwent an evolution from "private trouble" to "social problem"—and in the case of wife beating, to a statutory crime. Every state in the United States now employs large numbers of "child protective service" workers, and there are national and local voluntary groups devoted to prevention and treatment of child abuse. There are about a thousand shelters for battered women, whereas none existed in 1973. There are growing numbers of counseling programs for batterers and of family dispute mediation programs. Criminal prosecution of violent husbands, although still the exception, is increasing.

Child protective services, shelters for battered women, and treatment programs for wife beaters are essential services. However, the root causes of child abuse and spouse abuse lie in the characteristics of the family and of other social institutions. Consequently, social services for abused children, shelters, counseling, and prosecution are unlikely to have a major or lasting effect unless there are also changes in those institutional characteristics. The changes must address the pervasive inequality between men and women within the family and in society at large; the high incidence of normatively legitimate violence, ranging from the almost universal practice of physical punishment to capital punishment, and bombing countries engaged in "state terrorism"; social norms tolerating violence between spouses; and the stress and frustration experienced by the millions living in poverty and under racial oppression.

(SEE ALSO: *Incest; Sexual Violence and Abuse*)

REFERENCES

American Association for the Protection of Children 1986 *Highlights of Official Child Neglect and Abuse Reporting 1984.* Denver: The Association.

Archer, Dane, and Rosemary Gartner 1984 *Violence and Crime in Cross-National Perspective.* New Haven, Conn.: Yale University Press.

Bachman, Ronet, Arnold S. Linsky, and Murray A. Straus 1988 "Homicide of Family Members, Acquaintances, and Strangers, and State-to-State Differences in Social Stress, Social Control and Social Norms." Paper presented at the meeting of the American Sociological Association; Atlanta. Durham: Family Research Laboratory, University of New Hampshire.

Baron, Larry, and Murray A. Straus 1988 "Cultural and Economic Sources of Homicide in the United States." *The Sociological Quarterly* 29:371–390.

——— 1989 *Four Theories of Rape in American Society: A State Level Analysis.* New Haven, Conn.: Yale University Press.

Calvert, Robert 1974 "Criminal and Civil Liability in Husband–Wife Assaults." In Suzanne K. Steinmetz and Murray A. Straus, eds., *Violence in the Family.* New York: Harper and Row.

Carmody, Diane C., and Kirk R. Williams 1987 "Wife Assault and Perceptions of Sanctions." *Violence and Victims* 2:25–38.

Coleman, Diane H., and Murray A. Straus 1983 "Alcohol Abuse and Family Violence." In E. Gottheil, K. A. Druley, T. E. Skolada, and H. M. Waxman, eds., *Alcohol, Drug Abuse and Aggression.* Springfield, Ill.: C. C. Thomas.

——— 1986 "Marital Power, Conflict, and Violence in a Nationally Representative Sample of American Couples." *Violence and Victims* 1:141–157.

Gaquin, Deirdre A. 1977–1978 "Spouse Abuse: Data from the National Crime Survey." *Victimology* 2:632–643.

Gelles, Richard J. 1974 *The Violent Home: A Study of Physical Aggression Between Husbands and Wives.* Beverly Hills, Calif.: Sage.

Gelles, Richard J., and Murray A. Straus 1979 "Determinants of Violence in the Family: Toward a Theoretical Integration." In W. R. Burr, R. Hill, F. I. Nye, and I. L. Reiss, eds., *Contemporary Theories About the Family.* New York: Free Press.

Goode, William J. 1974 "Force and Violence in the Family." In Suzanne K. Steinmetz and Murray A. Straus, eds., *Violence in the Family.* New York: Harper and Row.

Greenblat, Cathy S. 1983 "A Hit Is a Hit Is a Hit . . . or Is It? Approval and Tolerance of the Use of Physical Force by Spouses." In David Finkelhor, Richard J. Gelles, Gerald T. Hotaling, and Murray A. Straus, eds., *The Dark Side of Families.* Beverly Hills, Calif.: Sage.

Huggins, Martha D., and Murray A. Straus 1980 "Violence and the Social Structure as Reflected in Children's Books From 1850 to 1970." In Murray A. Straus and Gerald T. Hotaling, eds., *The Social Causes of Husband–Wife Violence.* Minneapolis: University of Minnesota Press.

Kalmuss, Debra S., and Murray A. Straus 1983 "Feminist, Political, and Economic Determinants of Wife Abuse Services in American States." In David Finkelhor, Richard J. Gelles, Gerald T. Hotaling, and Murray A. Straus, eds., *Issues and The Dark Side of Families.* Beverly Hills, Calif.: Sage.

Kaufman Kantor, Glenda, and Murray A. Straus 1987 "The 'Drunken Bum' Theory of Wife Beating." *Social Problems* 34:213–230.

———1990 "Response of Victims and the Police to Assaults on Wives." In Murray A. Straus and Richard J. Gelles, eds., *Physical Violence in American Families: Risk Factors and Adaptations to Violence in 8,145 Families.* New Brunswick, N.J.: Transaction Books.

LaRossa, Ralph E. 1980 "And We Haven't Had Any Problem Since: Conjugal Violence and the Politics of Marriage." In Murray A. Straus and Gerald T. Hotaling, eds., *The Social Causes of Husband–Wife Violence.* Minneapolis: University of Minnesota.

Lehman, Betsy A. 1989 "Spanking Teaches the Wrong Lesson." *Boston Globe,* March 13, p. 27.

Lerman, Lisa 1981 *Prosecution of Spouse Abuse: Innovations in Criminal Justice Response.* Washington, D.C.: Center for Women Policy Studies.

Levinson, David 1989 *Family Violence in Cross-Cultural Perspective.* Newbury Park, Calif.: Sage.

Makepeace, James M. 1983 "Life Events Stress and Courtship Violence." *Family Relations* 32:101–109.

Nelson, Barbara J. 1984 *Making an Issue of Child Abuse: Political Agenda Setting for Social Problems.* Chicago: University of Chicago Press.

Pfohl, Stephen J. 1977 "The Discovery of Child Abuse." *Social Problems* 24 (February):310–323.

Radbill, Samuel X. 1987 "A History of Child Abuse and Infanticide." In Ray E. Helfer and C. Henry Kempe, eds., *The Battered Child,* 4th ed. Chicago: University of Chicago Press.

Sherman, Lawrence W., and Ellen G. Cohn 1989 "The Impact of Research on Legal Policy: The Minneapolis Domestic Violence Experiment." *Law and Society Review* 23, no. 1:117–144.

Stets, Jan E., and Murray A. Straus 1990 "Gender Differences in Reporting Marital Violence and Its Medical and Psychological Consequences." In Murray A. Straus and Richard J. Gelles, eds., *Physical Violence in American Families: Risk Factors and Adaptations to Violence in 8,145 Families.* New Brunswick, N.J.: Transaction Books.

Straus, Murray A. 1976 "Sexual Inequality, Cultural Norms, and Wife-Beating." In E. C. Viano, ed., *Victims and Society.* Washington, D. C.: Visage Press. Also in *Victimology* 1 (Spring 1976):54–76; and in J. R. Chapman and M. Gates, eds., *Women into Wives: The Legal and Economic Impact of Marriage.* Sage Yearbook in Women Policy Studies, Vol 2. Beverly Hills, Calif.: Sage, 1977.

———1977 "Societal Morphogenesis and Intrafamily Violence in Cross-Cultural Perspective." *Annals of the New York Academy of Sciences* 285:719–730.

———1979 "Measuring Intrafamily Conflict and Violence: The Conflict Tactics (CT) Scale." *Journal of Marriage and the Family 41:*75–88.

———1980 "Social Stress and Marital Violence in a National Sample of American Families." In F. Wright, C. Bahn, and R. Rieber, eds., *Forensic Psychology and Psychiatry.* New York: New York Academy of Sciences. *Annals of the New York Academy of Sciences,* 347.

———1983 "Ordinary Violence Versus Child Abuse and Wife Beating: What Do They Have in Common?" In David Finkelhor, Gerald T. Hotaling, Richard J. Gelles, and Murray A. Straus, eds., The Dark Side of Families: *Issues and Controversies in the Study of Family Violence.* Beverly Hills, Calif.: Sage.

———1986 "Domestic Violence and Homicide Antecedents." *Bulletin of the New York Academy of Medicine* 62, no. 5:446–465.

———1987 "Primary Group Characteristics and Intra-family Homicide." Paper presented at the Third National Conference for Family Violence Researchers, Family Research Laboratory, University of New Hampshire, Durham.

———1989 "Assaults by Wives on Husbands: Implications for Primary Prevention of Marital Violence" Paper presented at 1989 meeting of the American Society of Criminology, Reno, Nev. Durham: Family Research Laboratory, University of New Hampshire.

———1990 "The Conflict Tactics Scale and Its Critics: An Evaluation and New Data on Validity and Reliability." In Murray A. Straus and Richard J. Gelles, eds., *Physical Violence in American Families: Risk Factors and Adaptations to Violence in 8,145 Families.* New Brunswick, N.J.: Transaction Books.

———1991 "Discipline and Deviance: Physical Punishment of Children and Violence and Other Crime in Adulthood." *Social Problems* 38, no. 2.

Straus, Murray A., and Richard J. Gelles 1986 "Societal Change and Change in Family Violence from 1975 to 1985 as Revealed by Two National Surveys." *Journal of Marriage and the Family* 48:465–479.

———, eds. 1990 *Physical Violence in American Families: Risk Factors and Adaptations to Violence in 8,145 Families.* New Brunswick, N.J.: Transaction Books.

Straus, Murray A., Richard J. Gelles, and Suzanne K. Steinmetz 1980 *Behind Closed Doors: Violence in the American Family.* New York: Doubleday/Anchor.

Straus, Murray A., and Glenda Kaufman Kantor 1987 "Stress and Physical Child Abuse." In Ray E. Helfer and C. Henry Kempe, Eds., *The Battered Child,* 4th ed. Chicago: University of Chicago Press.

U.S. Department of Justice 1980 *Intimate Victims: A Study of Violence Among Friends and Relatives. A National Crime Survey Report.* Washington, D.C.: Bureau of Justice Statistics.

Weitzman, Lenore J. 1986 *The Divorce Revolution.* New York: Free Press.

MURRAY A. STRAUS

FEMININITY/MASCULINITY Femininity and masculinity (*gender*), in a social or psychological sense, are distinguished from male and female (*sex*), in a biological sense (Lindsey 1990). The focus of this article is on the former. Conceptions of the nature of femininity and masculinity are varied and have changed over the past several decades (Maccoby 1987). In discussing the nature of femininity/masculinity, researchers have referred variously to gender-related dispositions, traits, and temperaments, to gender roles, and to gender identities. Often they use these terms almost interchangeably. There is a general belief that biological sex, gender roles, and masculine and feminine psychological characteristics and gender identities are all tightly interrelated (Spence and Helmreich 1978). Whether or not this interrelationship is true, however, it is necessary to keep the concepts distinct and not confuse them. What is true with respect to one (for example, gender identities) may not be true with respect to another (for example, gender roles).

Gender identity refers to the way in which people view themselves along feminine/masculine lines. There are two parts to this. The first is basic gender identification or the cognitive knowledge that one is male or female. By the age of two, most children have established their basic gender identification (Money and Ehrhardt 1972). The second is gender-role identity or the nature of the view of the self as a male or female in society (Kagan 1964). For example, a person may know himself to be a male (basic gender identification) but view himself as somewhat feminine (gender-role identity). Gender-role identity, in this sense, develops more slowly over time as the result of socialization (Kagan 1964; Smith and Lloyd 1978).

Gender role refers to the ways in which males and females behave (or are expected to behave) in society. In the United States, for example, males traditionally are expected to behave in a logical, competitive, and ambitious way, while females traditionally are expected to behave in a gentle, sensitive, and warm manner (Broverman et al. 1972).

Gender-related personality traits and temperaments refer to the underlying dispositions and emotional characteristics distinguishing males from females. Temperament and personality dispositions are thought by some researchers to underlie the observable differences between the behavior of men and women. Early research addressed issues of sex differences in temperament with a concern that such differences may be innate (cf. Mead 1935). While the issue of innate differences is not dead (Money 1987), most current research and thinking about issues of femininity/masculinity in the social and behavioral sciences bypass questions of innate sex differences in temperaments and traits. Instead, such research examines how men and women are socialized to be different (learned gender-related traits).

INNATE TEMPERAMENT

Gender-role differentiation is fairly universal across societies. Men and women are assigned different behaviors, tasks, rights, obligations, privileges, and resources. In Western culture (stereotypically), men are aggressive, competitive, and instrumentally oriented, while women are passive, cooperative, and expressive. Early thinking often assumed that this division was based on underlying innate differences in traits, characteristics, and temperaments of males and females. Measures of femininity/masculinity might be used to diagnose problems of basic gender identification.

Margaret Mead addressed the issue of sex differences in temperament in her 1935 study *Sex and Temperament in Three Primitive Societies.* This study concludes that there are no necessary differences in traits and temperaments between the sexes. Observed differences in temperament between men and women are not a function of their biological differences. Rather, they result from differences in socialization and the cultural expectations held for each sex.

Mead came to this conclusion because the three societies she studied showed patterns of temperament that varied greatly from our own. Among the Arapesh, both males and females display what we would consider a "feminine" temperament (passive, cooperative, and expressive). Among the Mundugamor, both males and females display what we would consider a "masculine" temperament (active, competitive, and instrumental). Finally, among the Tchambuli men and women display temperaments that are different from each other but opposite to our own pattern. In that society, men are emotional and expressive, while women are active and instrumental.

Mead's study caused people to rethink the nature of femininity/masculinity. Different gender-related traits, temperaments, roles, and identities could no longer be tied inextricably to biological sex. Since Mead's study, the nature–nurture issue has been examined extensively and with much controversy, but no firm conclusions are yet clear (Maccoby and Jacklin 1974). While there may be small sex differences in temperament at birth (and the evidence on this is not consistent), there is far more variability within each sex group (Spence and Helmreich 1978). Further, the pressures of socialization and learning far outweigh the impact of possible innate sex differences in temperament.

BEHAVIORS, PERSONALITY TRAITS, AND ROLES

The high degree of variability in temperament within each sex group, and the strong trends toward behaviorism in the 1950s and 1960s, led many researchers to examine observable, behavioral differences between men and women and to pay less attention to questions of innate temperament. Two approaches to the study of such behavioral differences developed during this time, each based within an academic discipline. On the one hand, psychologists understood the differences in behavior between men and women to be the result of differences in conditioning and socialization. They believed personality traits developed from socialization and then instigated behavior. Sociologists, on the other hand, viewed behavior less as the result of individual motivation and instigation and more as the result of society organizing and shaping individuals into various roles. For them the question was how society formed and organized masculine and feminine gender roles. However, since both roles and personality traits are inferences made from observed behavior, researchers tend often to be confused about what is being studied (Locksley and Colten 1979).

On the sociological side, Parsons and Bales (1955), in a merger of grand social theorizing and careful observation of moment-to-moment behaviors of individuals interacting in groups, proposed a model of leadership-role differentiation. The idea was that in any group, including the family, there were two basic issues with which a group needs to deal. One concerns satisfying the group's need to perform instrumental tasks and attain its goals. The other centers on the need of the group to maintain the emotional and expressive bonds among its members. Parsons and Bales suggested that the pursuit of the group's instrumental tasks and goals by some individuals often disrupts the social bonds. This makes it very difficult for these same individuals to pursue the emotional and expressive needs of the group. As a result, other individuals play the expressive role, which results in a division of labor. One person becomes the instrumental, task-oriented leader, and another becomes the social-emotional, expressive leader in a group (Bales and Slater 1955).

The parallel between these instrumental and expressive leadership roles and the masculine and feminine gender roles in American society was not unnoticed. The gender-role division was said to grow out of the functioning of the nuclear family (cf. Parsons 1955; Zelditch 1955). Gender roles, within the functionalist framework of Parsons and Bales, are the result of inevitable social forces at play in groups, organizations, and societies (Bales and Slater 1955), not differences in the personality traits of males and females. The ideologically conservative justification of the status quo (male dominance) implied by this functionalist theory has been noted (Lindsey 1990). However, there is nothing in the theory that forces a sex link to the instrumental and expressive dimensions. The question of what makes instrumental activity be male sex-linked and expressive activity be female sex-linked has never been answered fully. By focusing on behaviors, however, one is not tied inevitably to that sex link.

On the psychological side, Bakan (1966), again noting the wide variability of "masculine" and "feminine" tendencies in all people, suggested that persons have both male (agency) and female (communion) tendencies or traits. He further suggested that culture and socialization mold the particular combination of these personality traits in individuals. Based on this reasoning, both Bem (1974) and Spence, Helmreich, and Stapp (1974) developed scales to measure separately these masculine and feminine personality traits in both males and females. In each case, the characteristics or behaviors that are included in the scales are those that are positively valued for either sex but are more "appropriate" for either males (M scales) or females (F scales). "Appropriate," of course, is judged relative to the norms and standards of the culture.

For the Bem scale, descriptions for the masculine scale include, for example, "acts as leader," "makes decisions easily," and "willing to take risks." Descriptions for the feminine scale include "affectionate," "gentle," and "sensitive to the needs of others." For the Spence, Helmreich, Stapp scales, masculinity was measured with bipolar items like "very independent" (vs. "not at all independent") and "can make decisions easily" (vs. "has difficulty making decisions"). Femininity was measured with items such as "very emotional" (vs. "not at all emotional") and "very helpful to others" (vs. "not at all helpful to others"). In addition to the masculinity and femininity scales, Spence, Helmreich, and Stapp developed a third scale, which they labeled MF. This scale had bipolar items that were "appropriate" for males on one end of the continuum, and "appropriate" for females on the other end of the continuum. For example, "very submissive" (vs. "very dominant") and "feelings not easily hurt" (vs. "feelings easily hurt") are typical items.

With separate measures of masculinity and femininity, it is possible to ask about the relationship between them. When this relationship was examined, it was found that the two scales were not strongly negatively related, as would be expected if a masculine gender role were the opposite of a feminine gender role. Instead, the two ratings were relatively uncorrelated (Bem 1974; Spence and Helmreich 1978). People had all combinations of scores in relatively equal proportions. People who combined high scores on masculinity with high scores on femininity were said to be *androgynous* with respect to their gender roles (Bem 1977; Spence and Helmreich 1978). The other classifications were *masculine* (high M and low F scores), *feminine* (high F and low M scores), and *undifferentiated* (low M and low F scores) gender roles. Those classified as masculine or feminine are either sex typed (gender appropriate) or cross sex typed (gender inappropriate).

These measures of masculinity, femininity, and androgyny were usually interpreted in terms of individual personality characteristics and orientations rather than as gender-role performances, though this was not uniformly true. Additionally, the measures were often vaguely thought of as measures of gender self-concept (since they were obtained by respondents providing self-descriptions using the scales). The language of many research reports is confusing on this conceptual issue (Locksley and Colten 1979).

Once these M and F scales were developed to measure masculinity and femininity, a great deal of research ensued. Studies found that sex-typed individuals were more likely to choose behaviors that are consistent with their own gender than androgynous or cross sex-typed individuals (Bem and Lenney 1976; Helmreich, Spence, and Holahan 1979). They also avoided gender-inappropriate activities (Bem, Martyna, and Watson 1976). On the other hand, several studies have found that androgynous people who combine masculine and feminine characteristics are more adaptable, flexible, and mentally healthy (Bem 1975; Helmreich, Spence, and Holahan 1979). They also have higher self-esteem (Spence and Helmreich 1978), although this finding is somewhat problematic since the measures of masculinity and femininity contain traits that are desirable for anyone in our society. (Bem 1974; Spence and Helmreich 1978).

GENDER-ROLE IDENTITIES AND SELF-CONCEPTS

Masculinity and femininity, considered as desirable personality characteristics for men and women, respectively, are labels provided by the researcher. Masculinity and femininity may also be considered as part of the self-descriptions or self-concepts that men and women apply to themselves and, as such, are also a source of motivation for action (Foote 1951; Burke 1980). In this latter sense, it is possible to speak of gender-role identities.

Gender-role identities are the self-meanings of masculinity or femininity one has as a male or female member of society and are inherently derived from and tied to social structure. Masculinity and femininity, considered as personality traits as in the last section, are individual attributes that are neither a source of motivation nor necessarily tied to social structure. The self-meaning of one's gender-role identity helps to form the self-concept, which is understood as the hierarchical organization of a set of role identities ordered by centrality or salience (McCall and Simmons 1978, Stryker 1968). Role identities are the meanings of the self-in-role as an object to the self (Burke and Tully 1977). In this sense, gender identities would consist of the self-relevant meanings of being a male or a female in society. These self-meanings are formed in social situations and are based on a role's similarities and differences with counterroles (Lindesmith and Strauss 1956; Turner 1968). Because there are only two gender roles, the meanings of masculine and feminine in this context necessarily contrast. For gender identities, masculinity and femininity would be based on the similarities and differences between the male role and the female role in society. To be a male (masculine) is not to be a female (feminine) and vice versa (Storms 1979).

Starting from an interactionist theoretical position, Burke and Tully (1977) used the semantic differential (Osgood, Succi, and Tannenbaum 1957) to develop procedures for measuring self-meanings based on (1) differences between either actual or stereotypical meanings of target roles and counterroles, and (2) views of the self in relation to these differences. Using this procedure, they then examined the gender-related self-meanings (gender identities) of a large sample of middle school girls and boys. The items that defined gender for these children included, for example, "soft" (vs. "hard"), "weak" (vs. "strong"), and "emotional" (vs. "not emotional"). The gender-identity scores for both boys and girls were approximately normally distributed along the masculine–feminine dimension. About 18 percent of the sample consisted of individuals who had a gender identity that was closer to the modal identity of the opposite sex.

Burke and Tully (1977) found that the children with cross-sex identities (boys who thought of themselves in ways similar to the way most girls thought of themselves, and vice versa) were more likely than children with gender-appropriate identities (1) to have engaged in gender-inappropriate behavior; (2) to have been warned about engaging in gender-inappropriate behavior; and (3) to have been called names like "tomboy," "sissy;" or "homo." Finally, they found that boys and girls with cross-sex gender identities were more likely to have low self-esteem.

In other studies using the Burke-Tully measure, gender identity was found to be related to a variety of behaviors from performance in school to abuse in dating relationships. Among middle school children, boys and girls with a more feminine gender identity had higher marks than those with a more masculine gender identity. This was true independent of the child's sex, race, grade, subject area, or sex of teacher (Burke 1989). Among college students, males and females with a more feminine gender identity were more likely to inflict and to sustain both physical and sexual abuse in dating relationships (Burke, Stets, and Pirog-Good 1988). In each case, the behaviors were consistent with the relationship orientation and emotional expressiveness of the cultural definitions of gender-role performance.

Because masculinity and femininity using the Burke-Tully measure are on opposite sides of a single scale, and one's gender identity is the location of the self somewhere along this dimension, it is conceptually impossible to be both masculine and feminine in one's gender identity. Androgyny, thus, cannot be a combination of masculinity and femininity as in the Spence, Helmreich, and Stapp measure or in the Bem measure. Instead, androgyny is defined by Burke (1980) as the range or span of the gender scale across which an individual is comfortable interacting in situations. The link between this definition of androgyny and notions of flexibility, openness, and so forth is quite clear. Additionally, such a conception prevents contamination of the concept of androgyny with self-esteem or social desirability, from which the Bem scale suffers.

BASIC ISSUES AND OPEN QUESTIONS

The biggest issue that has plagued social scientists in defining the concepts of masculinity, femininity, and androgyny has been the variety of conceptions and confusions that exist in the literature. Future research and discussion must be more careful to distinguish between masculine and feminine as applied to gender identities, gender roles, personality traits resulting from socialization practices, and genetic dispositions. Had such clarity of reference been maintained in the past, the debate between the bipolar and the dualistic conceptions of masculinity and femininity, for example, would likely not have arisen. When we distinguish between identities (bipolar distinctions between two groups) and roles (a dualistic mix of instrumental and expressive behaviors), it is clear that there is no debate. Each view is appropriate in the correct context (Spence and Helmreich 1978).

Another issue is the nature–nurture question. This is basically a false distinction, and researchers today are less prone to waste time with it. There is no way that nature and nurture can be separated one from the other. Genetic, biological differences play themselves out in a social world; social factors work with the genetic and biological beings that we are. On the other hand, the issue captures people's imagination as they ask questions like that raised by Margaret Mead (1949, p. 13) "In educating women like men, have we done something disastrous to both men and women alike, or have we only taken one further step in the recurrent task of building more and better on our original human nature?" The answer, of course, depends upon values, not upon science.

Finally, as was pointed out, the different bases of masculinity and femininity (genes, traits, roles, and identities), while not the same, are all interrelated. There is clearly some general phenomenon underlying all of this, and it needs to be understood. A first attempt at such an understanding lies in the concept of gender schema. A schema is a cognitive structure that organizes and guides an individual's perception. Bem (1981) introduced the idea or theory of a gender schema that sorts persons, attributes, and behaviors into masculine and feminine categories. She suggests that gender schema are supplied by culture as fundamental ways of dealing with information. Sex typing derives, in part, from gender-schematic processing of information on the basis of sex-linked associations derived from our culture. While it is clear that gender identities are built upon the gender schema supplied by society, it is less clear how that same gender schema colors all perceptions of social and physical reality, politicizing and polarizing the world into masculine and feminine. How and why this is the case needs to be understood.

(SEE ALSO: *Gender; Role Models; Sex Differences*)

REFERENCES

Bakan, David 1966 *The Duality of Human Existence.* Chicago: Rand McNally.

Bales, Robert F., and Philip E. Slater 1955 "Role Differentiation in Small Decision-Making Groups." In Talcott Parsons and Robert F. Bales, eds., *Family, Socialization and Interaction Process.* New York: Free Press.

Bem, Sandra L. 1974 "The Measurement of Psychological Androgyny." *Journal of Consulting and Clinical Psychology* 42:155–162.

———1975 "Sex-Role Adaptability: One Consequence of Psychological Androgyny." *Journal of Personality and Social Psychology* 31:634–643.

———1977 "On the Utility of Alternate Procedures for Assessing Psychological Androgyny." *Journal of Consulting and Clinical Psychology* 45:196–205.

———1981 "Gender Schema Theory: A Cognitive Account of Sex Typing." *Psychological Review* 88:354–364.

———, and E. Lenney 1976 "Sex Typing and the Avoidance of Cross-Sex Behavior." *Journal of Personality and Social Psychology* 33:48–54.

———, W. Martyna, and C. Watson 1976 "Sex Typing and Androgyny: Further Exploration of the Expressive Domain." *Journal of Personality and Social Psychology* 34:1016–1023.

Broverman, I. K., et al. 1972 "Sex-Role Stereotypes: A Current Appraisal." *Journal of Social Issues* 28:59–78.

Burke, Peter J. 1980 "The Self: Measurement Implications from a Symbolic Interactionist Perspective." *Social Psychology Quarterly* 43:18–29.

———1989 "Gender Identity, Sex and School Performance." *Social Psychology Quarterly* 52:159–169.

———, Jan E. Stets, and Maureen Pirog-Good 1988 "Gender Identity, Self-Esteem, and Physical and Sexual Abuse in Dating Relationships." *Social Psychology Quarterly* 51:272–285.

———, and Judy Tully 1977 "The Measurement of Role/Identity." *Social Forces* 55:880–897.

Foote, Nelson N. 1951 "Identification as the Basis for a Theory of Motivation." *American Sociological Review* 26:14–21.

Helmreich, Robert L., Janet T. Spence, and Carole K. Holahan 1979 "Psychological Androgyny and Sex-role Flexibility: A Test of Two Hypotheses." *Journal of Personality and Social Psychology* 37:1631–1644.

Hull, Jay G., and Alan S. Levy 1979 "The Organizational Functions of Self: An Alternative to the Duval and Wicklund Model of Self-Awareness." *Journal of Personality and Social Psychology* 37:756–768.

Kagan, Jerome 1964 "Acquisition and Significance of Sex Typing and Sex Role Identity." In Martin L. Hoffman and Lois W. Hoffman, eds., *Review of Child Development Research,* vol. 1. New York: Russell Sage Foundation.

Lindesmith, Alfred R., and Anselm L. Strauss 1956 *Social Psychology.* New York: Holt, Rinehart and Winston.

Lindsey, Linda L. 1990 *Gender Roles: A Sociological Perspective.* Englewood Cliffs, N.J.: Prentice-Hall.

Locksley, Anne, and Mary Ellen Colten 1979 "Psychological Androgyny: A Case of Mistaken Identity?" *Journal of Personality and Social Psychology* 37:1017–1031.

McCall, George J., and J. L. Simmons 1978 *Identities and Interactions,* rev. ed. New York: Free Press.

Maccoby, Eleanor E. 1987 "The Varied Meanings of 'Masculine' and 'Feminine'." In June M. Reinisch, Leonard A. Rosenblum, and Stephanie A. Saunders, eds., *Masculinity/Femininity: Basic Perspectives.* New York: Oxford University Press.

Maccoby, Eleanor E., and Carol N. Jacklin 1974 *The Psychology of Sex Differences.* Stanford, Calif.: Stanford University Press.

Mead, Margaret 1935 *Sex and Temperament in Three Primitive Societies.* New York: Dell Publishing.

———1949 *Male and Female: A Study of the Sexes in a Changing World.* New York: Dell Publishing.

Money, John 1987 "Propaedeutics of Diecious G-I/R: Theoretical Foundations for Understanding Dimorphic Gender-Identity/Role." In June M. Reinisch, Leonard A. Rosenblum, and Stephanie A. Saunders, eds., *Masculinity/Femininity: Basic Perspectives.* New York: Oxford University Press.

Money, John, and A. E. Ehrhardt 1972 *Man and Woman, Boy and Girl.* Baltimore: Johns Hopkins University Press.

Osgood, Charles E., George J. Succi, and Percy H. Tannenbaum 1957 *The Measurement of Meaning.* Urbana: University of Illinois Press.

Parsons, Talcott 1955 "Family Structure and the Socialization of the Child." In Talcott Parsons and Robert F. Bales, eds., *Family, Socialization and Interaction Process.* New York: Free Press.

———, and Robert F. Bales 1955 *Family, Socialization and Interaction Process.* New York: Free Press.

Smith, Caroline, and Barbara Lloyd 1978 "Maternal Behavior and Perceived Sex of Infant: Revisited." *Child Development* 49:1263–1265.

Spence, Janet T., and Robert L. Helmreich 1978 *Masculinity and Femininity: Their Psychological Dimensions, Correlates, and Antecedents.* Austin: University of Texas Press.

Spence, Janet T., Robert L. Helmreich, and J. Stapp 1974 "The Personal Attributes Questionnaire: A Measure of Sex-Role Stereotypes and Masculinity–Femininity." *JSAS Catalogue of Selected Documents in Psychology* 4:127.

Storms, Michael D. 1979 "Sex Role Identity and Its Relationships to Sex Role Attitudes and Sex Role Stereotypes." *Journal of Personality and Social Psychology* 37:1779–1789.

Stryker, Sheldon 1968 "Identity Salience and Role Performance." *Journal of Marriage and the Family* 4:558–564.

Turner, Ralph 1968 "The Self Conception in Social Interaction." In C. Gorden and K. J. Gergen, eds., *The Self in Social Interaction.* New York: Wiley.

Zelditch, Morris, Jr. 1955 "Role Differentiation in the Nuclear Family: A Comparative Study." In Talcott Parsons and Robert F. Bales, eds., *Family, Socialization and Interaction Process.* New York: Free Press.

PETER J. BURKE

FEMINIST THEORY The term *feminist theory* is an invention of the academic branch of the mid- and late twentieth-century feminist movement. It refers to generating systematic ideas that define women's place in society and culture, including the depiction of women large questions, indeed. The task of feminist theorists is necessarily monumental. It requires the wisdom, courage, and perseverance that Penelope displayed as she wove and unwove her tapestry to trick the suitors who sought to appropriate her kingdom and so steal her child's birthright.

For many reasons the task of feminist theorists is difficult. First, it is interdisciplinary. Literary critics, art historians, musicologists, historians, and philosophers—to name some specialists associated with the humanities—have all offered powerful and sometimes conflicting ideas about women in society and culture. So have sociologists, anthropologists, economists, psychologists, and psychoanalysts. Although the biological and physical sciences do not usually make fruitful contributions to contemporary debates about social and cultural issues, feminist scientists have posed questions that challenge the presuppositions of their own fields. They too have augmented the scope of feminist theory. Indeed, specialists in so many disciplines have offered apt ideas that no one essay or writer can even pretend to outline the scope of contemporary feminist theory. This presentation will concentrate on ideas developed in the social sciences.

Second, because feminist theory has its basis in the current women's movement, it is necessarily infused with the political concerns of the contemporary era. (Any system of arranging facts, including the writing of history, is necessarily influenced by the dominant concerns and ideologies of its times.) The most important of these is the relationship among race (ethnicity), gender, and class, both cross-culturally and historically. For even as Americans and Europeans have sought to confront institutionalized racism and sexism, as well as the unequal distribution of income and wealth in their own nations, women in developing nations have posed issues regarding the application of generalizations based on those experiences to their own situations. So, too, historical research has raised the challenge of process—namely the problem that any particular historical outcome is not predetermined, so that the development of relationships among gender, class, and race (or ethnicity) may vary greatly. Such variations make the act of generalizing hazardous, if not foolhardy.

Third, feminist theory has not merely existed in

a socio-political context but has been informed by it. This means that many theorists realize that their ideas have been influenced by their own material conditions and cultures. Thus, they have had to confront epistemological issues, including the meaning of objectivity and the way male dominance has shaped notions important to all branches of human inquiry. Put somewhat differently, theorists have broached two issues: (1) the inextricable association between ideas and methods of inquiry and (2) how both dominant ideas and methods have been influenced by the male hegemony over academic and scientific discourse. As is true in most contemporary fields of study, each of these issues is controversial.

Given these challenges, one might well wonder why anyone would try to generate feminist theory. But feminist academics felt that they could make a significant contribution by using their training first to document and later to analyze women's place in society. When the feminists of academe began to debate their understandings of women's place in society and culture, no sure path seemed available. With the exception of Simone de Beauvoir's *The Second Sex* (1952), men had penned the two canonized (nineteenth-century) texts most familiar to these academics, namely John Stuart Mill's *The Subjection of Women* and Frederich Engels's *The Origins of Private Property, the Family, and the State.* Although Western women had debated their own situation since at least 1400, when, as Joan Kelly (1982) notes, Christine de Pisan "sparked . . . the four-century-long debate . . . known as the *querelle des femmes,*" twentieth-century academics were largely ignorant of that polemical tradition. Instead, they had been schooled in the thought of great men—whose writings were included in the first anthologies of feminist thought, such as Miriam Schneir's *Feminism: The Essential Historical Writings* (1972) and Alice Rossi's *The Feminist Papers* (1973). Such anthologies also introduced American academics to great women outside their own fields.

Nonhistorians learned of the generative ideas of participants in the Seneca Falls convention of 1848, as well as about Susan B. Anthony, Emma Goldman, and the British activist Emily Pankhurst; noneconomists met Charlotte Perkins Gilman; nonliterary critics met Virginia Woolf. Although feminist intellectuals might find strength in the knowledge that other women had provided trail markers to guide their way, antifeminists were not convinced that gender inequality still existed.

Thus, the first task confronting feminist theory was to document both past and present inequalities. Many of the early writings addressing this project discussed women as either "other" or "victim." These characterizations ran through writings that might be classed as either liberal (the belief that women have the same capabilities as men and should receive equal treatment); socialist Marxist (variations of the notion that capitalism created or augmented gender inequality); or radical feminist (versions of the idea that women were inextricably different from men and at least equal, and possibly superior, to them).

WOMAN AS OTHER AND AS VICTIM

To some extent the notions of "other" and "victim" are implicit in any mid-twentieth-century demonstration of inequality. Those who are maltreated for unacceptable reasons appear to be victims, as implicit in the late 1960s' and early 1970s' political slogan "Don't blame the victim." They seem to be "others" because of the historic and cross-cultural tendency of dominant groups to justify discriminatory actions by arguing that members of subdominant groups are "alien," not fully human, or simply "not like us." (In the American case, blacks were deemed "not fully human" when procedures for counting the male population were defined in the early years of the Republic.) This dichotomy between "subject" and "object," "self" and "other," has also been crucial to modern European thought, including the philosophic basis for de Beauvoir's *The Second Sex,* which was Jean-Paul Sartre's concept of existentialism. Such notions seemed to provide a conceptual framework with which to document *sexism,* a term introduced by those members of the American women's movement who had participated in the civil-rights movement and who wished for a term that reverberated with connotations of despicable conduct implicit in the more familiar term *racism.* That is, academic feminists could view themselves as demonstrating how specific practices or institutions viewed women as "others," maltreated them, and so transformed them into "victims" not responsible for their "despised" status. Once those processes were identified, feminist activists could seek to reform or to revolutionize the relevant institutions.

Social scientists provided confirmation of victimization by gathering data comparing women and men. Men were more likely to dominate professions (even such "female work" as grade school teaching and librarianship, in which men were likely to be principals and department heads), earn more money, receive higher education, be awarded scholarships and fellowships, earn advanced degrees, hold positions of political leadership, be granted credit cards, be treated as legally responsible for their actions, and be permitted to make decisions about their own bodies. (Both theorists and activists hotly discussed the "body issues" such as abortion, incest, rape, and sexual harassment and wife-battering.) Psychologists and psychiatrists pointed out that their colleagues had equated mental health with supposedly male characteristics. Humanists demonstrated that in art, music, and literature, men had inscribed themselves in the "cultural canon." Not only did the canon identify men's accomplishments as the "most important" Western works, but the so-called Western cultural tradition also represented history, literature, art, and philosophy from a male point of view. Sometimes these great works dwelled on the dichotomy between the concepts of madonna and whore; sometimes on the secular objectification of women's sexuality (as seen in renditions of the female nude). Whether religious or secular, both the cultural canon and academic knowledge were discovered to ignore or belittle women in various ways, as well as to devalue their contributions to civic and cultural life throughout the centuries.

Feminists confronted the dilemma of what to do about this devaluation. Liberal feminists seemed to echo one theme implicit in de Beauvoir's *The Second Sex* and Mill's *The Subjection of Women:* Become more like men—that is, remove the barriers preventing women from having the same opportunities as men, and, in the future, women will accomplish as much as men. Because, as some psychologists argued, there is no innate difference between women and men, equal treatment and equal opportunity will result in equal accomplishment.

The solution offered by Marxist- and socialist-feminists was not all that different from the ideas of liberals. They, too, believed that the eradication of obstacles would liberate women. But Marxist- and socialist-feminists were haunted by the "problem of the hyphen." That is, for them, the barriers confronting women were not simply posed by what all feminists termed "patriarchy" (shorthand for "male dominance"). Rather, as they saw it, patriarchy was itself inextricably related to capitalism. So, disentangling that relationship was a complex task. If capitalism had been a primary cause of women's inferior position, then women should have found greater equality in noncapitalist nations. In actuality, women had *not* prospered under the brands of communism found in the Soviet Union, Eastern Europe, or China. In those nations, too, women were clustered in jobs that paid less than those filled by men of equivalent education.

As feminists learned, communist lands had treated women favorably while still in their revolutionary stages. For example, in the Soviet Union of the 1920s, "changes in property relationships and inheritance laws weakened the family as an economic unit and reduced the dominance of the male household head, while new family codes undermined the legal and religious basis of marriage and removed restriction on divorce" (Lapidus 1978, p. 60). By undercutting the power of both the church and the traditional family, these measures strengthened the state. Once the communist party had institutionalized its power and declining birth rates challenged economic growth, however, it redefined the family as "the bulwark of the social system, a microcosm of the new socialist society . . . [supposed] to serve above all as a model of social order" (Lapidus 1978, p. 112).

Divorce became difficult; motherhood was defined as a contradiction, simultaneously a joy and the "supreme obligation of Soviet women." As in capitalist countries, the Soviet Union then began to glorify women's role in the family, (what feminist theory identified as the private sphere).

The discrepancy that arose between communist practice and socialist theory created a theoretical dilemma. One might insist that the so-called communist countries had radically departed from the theoretical ideal, and so the impact of socialism on women's lives had yet to receive a valid test. One might point to the relatively enlightened laws of the Scandinavian societies, where social policies assisted women who tried to combine work and family life. But even in these nations, women assumed more of the responsibility for children than did men. Although Scandinavian laws enabled father or mother to take parental leave after the birth or adoption of a child, few men exercised that legal right. Thus, another option seemed necessary: One might seek to reconceptualize the link between private property and patriarchy.

Anthropologists and historians were among the first feminists to attempt that (re)vision. Three of their solutions were particularly influential. First, drawing on de Beauvoir, some anthropologists (and at least one sociologist) returned to the idea of woman as other (see Rosaldo and Lamphere 1974). They suggested that extant societies embodied an analogy: Woman is to nature as man is to culture. That is, traditional and industrialized societies assumed that woman is closer to nature than man is. Men had supposedly thrust themselves upon nature and transformed it.

Second, some theorists incorporated Marxist notions by pointing out that men had defined women as private property. Rubin (1975) offered the most influential argument about what she termed "the sex/gender system." Assuming that women and men are more like than unlike one another, she asked how societies create "difference" or transform sex into gender. Answering her question, she retained her anthropologist's conviction that kinship relations are at the basis of society while she drew on her own "freely interpretive" readings of Claude Lévi-Strauss and Sigmund Freud. In essence, Rubin argued, men exchange women to create and to cement their own social relationships. This exchange "does imply a distinction between gift and giver. If women are the gifts, then men are the exchange partners. And it is the partners, not the presents, upon whom reciprocal exchange confers its quasi-mystical powers of social linkage. The relations of such a system are such that women are in no position to realize the benefits of their own circulation. As long as the relations specify that men exchange women, it is the men who are the beneficiaries of the product of such exchanges—social organization" (Rubin 1975, p. 174).

Prohibitions on incest keep this exchange system going because they intend to ensure the availability of women to be exchanged. Yet the women must be willing to be "gifts"; that is, they must have internalized the appropriate societal norms. Supposedly, what Freud describes as the Oedipal complex provides that internalization. According to Rubin, the Oedipal complex is a record of "how [contemporary] phallic culture domesticates women" (1975, p. 198). Furthermore, psychoanalytic findings about women's inferiority to men is a palimpsest "of the effects in women of their domestication" (p. 198). Thus, any society based on the exchange of women has molded the inequalities of the sex/gender system into its very essence. According to Rubin, this generalization is as applicable to today's industrialized societies as to nonindustrial societies. What feminists term *patriarchy* is actually the operation of the sex/gender system. By implication, to achieve equality, feminists had to challenge the sex/gender system.

Third, some historians and anthropologists responded to the conflation of capitalism and patriarchy by seeking nonindustrial models where women held power. Mainly they sought examples of women as a force in the public sphere. Eleanor Leacock wrote about one classic case, the Iroquois. In the Iroquois Confederation, women elected the (male) chiefs and were also empowered to remove them from office. In medieval society,

Joan Kelly maintained, (aristocratic) women had power over the education of their daughters. During the Renaissance, men absconded with that power, devalued the knowledge women had shared, deprived women of the right to educate one another, and also denied women equal access to the then newly discovered "classics." Kelly concluded her article by suggesting that the Renaissance had a different meaning for women and men; and so, by challenging historians' periodization, another conclusion was also possible. One might infer that during the Renaissance, men transformed women into victims.

By viewing women as either other or victim, all these theorists were implicitly accepting the male assumption that the public sphere is more important than the private. Even the search for examples of women who had once collectively held significant political power can be viewed as an affirmation of the dominant (male) view that the public sphere is more important than the private (home). However, the third approach—the search for examples of institutionalized female power—also foreshadowed a new phase of feminist theory: "The (re)vision of public and private spheres." As introduced by the poet Adrienne Rich, the term *(re)vision* is a deliberate pun referring to both a reconsideration of past ideas and a new vision of women's role in society.

THE (RE)VISION OF PUBLIC AND PRIVATE SPHERES

In the late 1970s, the feminist movement was maturing; many middle- and upper-class women (including nonfeminists) began to flock to the male-dominated professional schools from which they had once been excluded. Feminists in several fields began to reassess the value of activity in the private sphere—the world of the home in which most women were ensconced. Could the private sphere serve as a launchpad for social change? Had it ever done so? Are these spheres indeed separate, or does the persistence of this dichotomy conflate the errors of nineteenth-century thought? (A reconsideration of the relationship between the public and private spheres is implicit in the titles of such books as *Beyond Separate Spheres* and *Private Woman, Public Stage.* In sociology, Marxist and Sociolist feminists use different language to discuss women's and men's spheres.)

Nineteenth-century social theories had implied that the private sphere was of equal importance to the public world of work. Although the early nineteenth-century "cult of domesticity" banished women to the home where they were to serve as models of religiosity and virtue, they were also enshrined as "mothers of civilization"—a role that might imply power. But from the vantage of the late twentieth century, the role of "mother of civilization" did not seem so vital. If the private sphere was so important, why was the role of "parent of civilization" not available to men, who historically seemed almost to have monopolized positions of power? If the roles of women and men (wives and husbands) were of equal importance, as Talcott Parsons had implied, why were American women more likely than men to complain of the sorts of physical and mental ailments associated with an inferior social position?

Yet, in the late 1970s, historians, anthropologists, and some sociologists began to find positive aspects of women's role in the private sphere. According to historians, women had used their roles to initiate social reforms. They had been especially active in trying to ameliorate some of the social problems resulting from the transformation of an agricultural society into an industrial one. For example, through voluntary associations, middle- and upper-class women in New York tried to decrease the destructive impact of poverty on the poor, especially on poor women. In Oneida County, they sought to reform the behaviors of the many single men who had moved to the city from the farms, lived in boarding houses, and sometimes disrupted the civil order. That the activities of the volunteers resulted in the enshrinement of women in the home once their activities had been successful is a historical irony (Ryan 1981). But that outcome is irrelevant to the main theoretical point offered by feminist theorists: Activity that nineteenth-century women had viewed as an extension of their roles in the private sphere had indeed influenced the public sphere. Put somewhat differently, the domestic and public spheres are not necessarily dichotomous.

Yet problems remain. First, variations suggest that generalization is premature. Second, rejection of the dichotomy between domestic and public spheres challenges the residues of nineteenth-century thought remaining in twentieth-century theories but does not necessarily lead to new theoretical formulation. Indeed, neither historical nor anthropological discoveries of variations on the common pattern—male dominance—*necessarily* facilitate theorizing. Rather, they might and did lead some feminists to search for the origins of male dominance (as in the article by Gayle Rubin) and to champion causal explanations.

Yet the (re)vision of public and private spheres did enable some feminist theorists to ask new questions. The anthropologist M. Z. Rosaldo (1980) explains:

> *Sexual asymmetry can be discovered in all human social groups, just as can kinship systems, marriages, and mothers. But asking "Why?" or "How did it begin?" appears inevitably to turn our thoughts from an account of the significance of gender for the organization of all human institutional forms (and reciprocally, of the significance of all social facts to gender) toward dichotomous assumptions that link the roles of men and women to the different things that they, as individuals, are apt to do.*

Rosaldo (1980) continues:

> *What traditional social scientists have failed to grasp is not that sexual asymmetries exist but that they are as fully social as the hunter's or the capitalist's role, and that they figure in the very facts, like racism or social class, that social science claims to understand. A crucial task for feminist scholars emerges, then, not as the relatively limited one of documenting pervasive sexism as a social fact—or showing how we can now hope to change or have in the past been able to survive it. Instead, it seems that we are challenged to provide new ways of linking the particulars of women's lives, activities, and goals to inequalities wherever they exist.*

To advance beyond naivete, feminist theories must grasp *how* meanings of gender are constructed, not why they exist.

Sociologist Nancy Chodorow provided one such demonstration in her now classic but still controversial *The Reproduction of Mothering.* Using psychoanalytic object-relations theory and some elements of Marxist thought, she argued that in contemporary capitalist societies the roles of women and men within the family (re)produce the roles women and men are expected to fill in Western societies. Because women are responsible for the care of small children, young girls and boys initially identify with their mothers. Girls are encouraged to continue this relational identification with their mothers; boys are not. For girls, the omnipresence of women in early childhood leads to a problem of boundaries—of knowing where their mothers end and they begin. As adults, this lack of boundaries may be advantageous: Out of their ability to see the world as others do, they may have a richer emotional life than men and also be more emphathic than they are. For boys, the omnipresence of women means that men learn the meaning of masculinity through the eventual demand that they separate from their mothers and identify with a role (male gender). Theirs is a positional identification. Ultimately, Chodorow argues, these scenarios play themselves out so that women and men try to reproduce the sorts of modern families in which they were reared. Additionally, Chodorow (1978) claims,

> *An increasingly father-absent, mother-involved family produces in men a personality that both corresponds to masculinity and male dominance as these are currently constituted in the sex-gender system, and fits appropriately with participation in capitalist relations of production. Men continue to enforce the sexual division of spheres as a defense against powerlessness in the [capitalist] labor market. Male denial of dependence and of attachment to women helps to guarantee both masculinity and performance in the world of work.*

She continues,

> *The relative unavailability of the father and the overavailability of the mother create negative defini-*

tions of masculinity and men's fear and resentment of women, as well as the lack of inner autonomy in men that enables, depending on the particular family constellation and class origin, either rule-following or the easy internalization of the values of the organization.

Chodorow's theory is controversial. Some liberals object to the inference that women are more emphathetic than men. They claim that psychological studies show that women and men have the same innate emotional capabilities. Nevertheless, radical feminists—people who believe that male dominance is the primary cause of women's subjugation—sometimes celebrate women's alleged superiority to men.

Others challenge Chodorow's theory by questioning whether any theory about the modern American family can possibly be applied to other historical epochs or cultures. Yet this objection misses the point in two ways. First, Chodorow discusses a specific time and place—contemporary America. Her contrast between how women and men learn their (relational or positional) roles should be even more important today than it was in 1978 when *The Reproduction of Mothering* was first published. Since 1978 the percentage of female-headed households has increased. Concomitantly, more young boys have even less contact with men; they must form the positional identifications that, Chodorow claims, prepare them to uphold the orientations to work and family required to maintain postindustrial capitalism. Second, Chodorow anticipated Rosaldo's call to understand how gender is socially constructed to articulate with other roles. She did not ask the origin of all sex/gender systems.

Chodorow's argument is important in a third way: she transforms "normal" understandings of men's and women's roles. She turns one current interpretation of Freud's thought, object relations theory, on its head. Woman-centered (written from the perspective of a feminist) yet comparative (examining both women and men), Chodorow's book anticipated the challenge that feminist scholarship currently offers other theoretical projects.

CHALLENGING CONVENTIONAL INTERPRETATIONS

The theme of difference is key to Carol Gilligan's *In a Different Voice* (1981). Extending and (re)vising Lawrence Kohlberg's work on the development of moral judgments among men, Gilligan argues that Kohlberg's scale of moral maturity slights women. Kohlberg argues that the highest stages of maturity involve the application of "rules to universal principles of justice" (Gilligan 1981, p. 18). In Kohlberg's model, women seem stuck at an intermediate stage because of their lack of opportunity to enter the public sphere and so to master and to apply those universal principles. Gilligan contends that Kohlberg has erred in his assessment of women (and other subordinated groups). In the case of women, he has not understood how their concepts of morality are based on their socialization. On the basis of her empirical studies and Chodorow's argument, Gilligan concludes that women do not make inferior moral judgments but different ones. They employ a relational ethic that stresses interpersonal caring, including a responsibility for self and others.

Gilligan's theory is as controversial as Chodorow's—perhaps even more so. Radical feminists cite this theory to argue again that women are morally superior to men. Some liberal feminists, who are interested in pushing for women's entry to upper levels of corporate management, use Gilligan's theory to claim that women are better equipped than men to develop innovative management styles that bind teams to the corporation. Other liberals (e.g., Epstein 1989) insist that there are no *innate* psychological distinctions between women and men.

However, both Chodorow and Gilligan raise an additional issue, potentially more controversial than the debates about "innate" gender differences. They try at one and the same time to follow the practices of their respective discipline and to view social life from a woman's perspective. Since science, social science, and the literary canon are based on male perspectives (as is true of Kohlberg's studies), how are we to forge an epistemology (and hence a methodology) that can simultaneously claim veracity and be true to women's experience of the social world? Can any theory that is either androcentric (man-centered) or gynocentric (woman-centered) be valid?

FEMINIST THEORY AND THE PROBLEM OF KNOWLEDGE

Some scientists or social scientists might believe that the question of validity applies only to explicitly interpretive work. After all, many decades have passed since Heisenberg enunciated his famous principle that the technologies (and by extension the theories and methods) used to view a phenomenon necessarily influence what is viewed. Supposedly, scientists and social scientists have been taking this principle into account as they explain how their generalizations apply "all other things being equal." But feminist theorists, like postmodern theorists, have challenged the very basis of the deductive methods at the heart of contemporary science and social science. They "question the very foundation of post-Enlightenment science and social science: the "objectivist illusion" (Keller 1982) that observation can be separated from explanation, the knower from the known, theory from practice, the public from the private, culture from nature, and other dualism that undergird systems of social stratification" (Hess 1990, p. 77). The feminist challenge differs from other deliberations about epistemology because, as Hess observes, it is "more political."

The work of scientist Evelyn Fox Keller is exemplary of this controversy. Keller has written rather abstract philosophic essays on such issues as Plato's epistemology and Bacon's notions of mastery and obedience to argue that modern science is infused with "male" notions. Rather than attempt to present these complex arguments briefly, let us concentrate on a more concrete work, Keller's biography of biologist Barbara McClintock, *A Feeling for the Organism* (1982).

In this biography, Keller claims that McClintock accomplished her Nobel prize-winning research on the transposition of genes in part because McClintock's research style radically departed from the dominant male model, molecular genetics. According to Keller, the dominant model presumed a hierarchical structure of genetic organization that resembles organizational charts of corporate structure and assumes a unidirectional flow of information. That assumption permitted the quick payoffs in research on the structure of specific bacteria that facilitates significant scientific findings (and so careers). The hierarchical model, though, is also supposedly a "male" model.

McClintock, however, believed in a more complex and less hierarchical "old-fashioned" model: "To McClintock, as to many other biologists, mechanism and structure have never been adequate answers to the question 'How do genes work?' To her an adequate understanding would, by definition, have to include an account about how they function in relation to the rest of the cell, and, of course, to the organism as a whole" (Keller 1985, p. 168). In this view, even a genome is an organism, and it, too, must be considered in relation to its environment.

Keller does not claim that McClintock's model was female: McClintock was trained by men. Keller does argue that many biologists have missed the essence of McClintock's vision. Keller includes among them biologists who are trying to incorporate McClintock's work on transposition into the hierarchical model. And, Keller believes,

> *The matter of gender never does drop away. . . . The radical core of McClintock's stance can be located right here. Because she is not a man, in a world of men, her commitment to a gender-free science has been binding; because concepts of gender have deeply influenced the basic categories of science, that commitment has been transformative. In short, the relevance of McClintock's gender in this story is to be found not in its role in her personal socialization but precisely in the role of gender in the construction of science.* (Keller 1982, p. 174)

For, Keller explains, contemporary science names the object of its inquiry (nature) "as female and the parallel naming of subject (mind) as male" (p. 174). Thus, women scientists are faced with a necessary contradiction between the roles in the world and their role as scientist. Even as the social structure of science tends to place women on the periphery of the invisible colleges that constitute the scientific world, that contradiction may limit the creative scientific imagination of both women and men.

However, as Keller readily admits, not all men believe in the hierarchical model. Nor, to paraphrase Keller, have they all "embraced" the notion of science as a female to be put on the rack and tortured to reveal her secrets. But Keller insists, both the naming of subject and object and the hierarchical model are androcentric and limit the possibilities of scientific inquiry.

Keller's work has been challenged on a number of grounds. Stephen Jay Gould has launched the most telling attack. His field, paleontology, is also dominated by men but rejects the hierarchical "male" model. Unlike nineteenth-century evolutionary thought, contemporary theories do not view human beings as the proud culmination of the past. Other life forms have been more successful. Furthermore, to reconstruct the past, paleontologists must grasp "wholes." Cynthia Fuchs Epstein adds that one cannot even argue that, as social scientists, women have been more empathic or observant than men. Epstein's counterexample is Erving Goffman, whose ability to "see" is almost legendary among sociologists.

For the purposes of this article, it is irrelevant whether Keller, Gould, or Epstein is correct. What matters is that developments in feminist theory have led feminists to participate in the postmodern debate about the nature of knowledge. During the late 1980s, this debate has been at the center of controversies in the social sciences and the humanities. It will probably remain important for some years to come. The debate infuses interpretations of literary works, reconstructions of the past, and understandings of social scientific models. It seems to transcend schools of thought. Marxists are divided about postmodernism as are liberals and, within the feminist community, radicals. Feminist theory has followed the course of all contemporary theories because feminists too are members of the societies about which they write and which they are trying to change.

Throughout this essay, terms such as *liberal, Marxist* or *socialist,* and *radical* feminists have been intended to distinguish different political orientations and experiences that shaped each group of feminists, as so well documented in histories and sociologies of the mid-twentieth-century feminist movement. In 1990, these very different groups of feminists are self-consciously aware; that is, many understand that even as feminism has sought social change, it too has shaped and been shaped by its environment. For instance, Stacey (1990) argues that in the late 1960s and early 1970s, as feminism stressed female participation in the public sphere and denigrated motherhood, it contributed to rising divorce rates and devaluation of feminine tasks. Such a self-conscious awareness that theories have social consequences is part of the promise of feminist theory. For self-reflective theories that question their own philosophic and practical consequences may ultimately lead to new questions and new knowledge.

(SEE ALSO: *Comparable Worth; Gender; Social Movements*)

REFERENCES

Chodorow, Nancy 1978 *The Reproduction of Mothering.* Berkeley: University of California Press.

de Beauvoir, Simone 1952 *The Second Sex.* New York: Alfred A. Knopf.

Gilligan, Carol 1981 *In a Different Voice.* Cambridge, Mass.: Harvard University Press.

Hess, Beth 1990 "Beyond Dichotomies: Drawing Distinctions and Embracing Differences." *Sociological Forum* 5:75–94.

Keller, Evelyn Fox 1982 *A Feeling for the Organism.* New York: W. H. Freeman.

——— 1985 *Reflections on Gender and Science.* New Haven: Yale University Press.

Kelly, Joan 1982 "Early Feminist Theory and the *Querelle des femmes,* 1400–1789." *Signs* 8:4–28.

Lapidus, Gail 1978 *Women in Soviet Society.* Berkeley: University of California Press.

Rosaldo, M. Z. 1980. "The Uses and Abuses of Anthropology." *Signs* 5:389–417.

———, and Louise Lamphere (eds.) 1974 *Women, Culture, and Society.* Stanford, Calif.: Stanford University Press.

Rossi, Alice S. (ed.) 1973 *The Feminist Papers*. New York: Columbia University Press.

Rubin, Gayle 1975 "The Traffic in Women: Notes on the Political Economy of Sex." In Rayna Rapp Reiter, ed., *Toward an Anthropology of Women*. New York: Monthly Review Press.

Ryan, Mary P. 1981 *Cradle of the Middle Class*. New York: Cambridge University Press.

Schneir, Miriam (ed.) 1972 *Feminism: The Essential Historical Writings*. New York: Random House.

Stacey, Judith 1990 *Brave New Families*. Berkeley: University of California Press.

GAYE TUCHMAN

FERTILITY DETERMINANTS Fertility refers to the actual childbearing performance of individuals, couples, groups, or populations. A common measure of fertility is the *crude birthrate*, in which the numerator is the number of live births in a given population in the course of a year, and the denominator is the total population in that year. Other measures of fertility limit the births and the population to specific groups. For example, demographers sometimes calculate marital fertility rates (with births to married women in the numerator, and the total number of married women in the population in the denominator) or out-of-wedlock fertility rates (with births to unmarried women in the numerator, and the total number of unmarried women in the denominator). Since the ability to conceive and bear a child varies by age, demographers also calculate age-specific birthrates. Summing the age-specific fertility rates between ages fifteen and fifty provides a convenient measure of the average number of children a woman would have over her reproductive years; this is called the *total fertility rate*.

Currently, crude birthrates vary from around 45–50 births/1,000 population/year in many African countries, where there is little use of contraception, to about 10–15 births/1,000 population/year in Western Europe. The total fertility rate (TFR) is 6 to 7 in nations where there is little use of contraception but around 2 in countries where most couples use effective means of contraception. Note that the total fertility rate is an average; thus, a population with an average TFR of 7 might include some women with well over fifteen children as well as some women with none.

FERTILITY DETERMINANTS IN PRETRANSITION SOCIETIES

The fertility transition is defined not in terms of a change in level (from high to low) but rather in terms of reproductive practices. Pretransition societies are those in which *married* couples do not effectively stop childbearing once they reach the number of children they desire; correspondingly, the onset of the fertility transition is marked by the adoption of practices to effectively stop childbearing before the couple's physiological capacity to reproduce is exhausted. Specifically, in pretransition societies, behavior is not parity-specific that is, it does not depend on the number of children the couple has already borne (Henry 1961). Nonetheless, in pretransition societies, fertility varies across individuals, couples and groups: observed total fertility rates for a population are as high as 12 (the Hutterites) and as low as 4 to 5 (the Kung hunters and gatherers). Important advances in understanding the sources of this variation followed a distinction between the "proximate" determinants of fertility and the "true" determinants of fertility, a distinction that owed much to an earlier systematic classification of influences on fertility made by Kingsley Davis and Judith Blake (1956) and is embodied in the currently dominant research paradigm of Richard Easterlin and Eileen Crimmins (1985; see also Bulatao and Lee 1983). The proximate determinants are *direct* determinants of fertility, the combination of biological and behavioral characteristics through which the "true" determinants—the social, economic, psychological, and environmental factors—affect fertility (Bongaarts 1978). Evaluating the relative influence of the various proximate determinants has been particularly important in understanding variations in fertility in pretransition societies. To account for the modern decline of fertility, as well as to understand fertility differentials in modern societies, more emphasis has been placed on the "true" determinants of fertility.

Demographers typically group the proximate determinants into two categories, those that determine the length of the woman's reproductive span and those that determine the length of the birth interval, or the period of time between one child and the next (Bongaarts 1978). The reproductive span begins with the onset of the ability to conceive and bear a live child (menarche), although when most sexual unions occur within marriage the age of marriage is a better marker of the beginning of the reproductive span. The reproductive span ends with menopause. Whether the birth interval is long or short is determined by: (1) the duration of postpartum infecundability (a period following a birth when women do not ovulate); (2) the level of fecundability (the monthly probability of conceiving among women who menstruate regularly but do not practice contraception); (3) the use of contraception; (4) the risk of spontaneous intrauterine mortality; and (5) induced abortion.

Let us consider first variations in fertility in societies—some historical, some in the contemporary developing world—where there is little contraception or induced abortion. Evidence for past societies comes primarily from the investigation by historical demographers of genealogies and of parish registers in which priests recorded baptisms, burials, and marriages, and then from censuses and from the registration of vital events required by the state (births and marriages, as well as deaths). Two exemplary studies for the pretransition period are those of John Knodel (1988) for Germany, and of E. A. Wrigley and Roger Schofield (1981) for England. Evidence for contemporary developing societies comes largely from surveys, although census information is increasingly available and reliable. The World Fertility Survey, which covered forty-two countries and is therefore the largest social survey ever undertaken, has been especially important (Cleland and Hobcraft 1985). While it is reasonable to be suspicious of the recording of fertility both in historical societies and developing ones, demographers have developed methods of adjusting the estimates, for instance, for the underregistration of births.

In accounting for differences in fertility across and within these societies, marriage patterns are of consequence, since in most societies childbearing occurs primarily within marriage. Hence, the age at which women marry, as well as the likelihood that their marriages will be disrupted by divorce or the death of their spouse, is important in determining the length of the reproductive span. The age at which the reproductive span normally ends varies with the individual, but it varies little across societies, and is thus not a significant determinant of aggregate fertility differences. Disease, however, may be associated with earlier sterility.

There is a striking difference between the marriage patterns of Western Europe and countries of European settlement such as the United States, Australia, and New Zealand, and societies in other parts of the world, particularly Asia and Africa. The distinctiveness of the Western European marriage pattern was first noticed by John Hajnal (1965), and it appears to have characterized Western Europe since at least the fourteenth century. In societies west of a line drawn between Leningrad and Trieste, typically several years intervened between menarche and marriage; in Western Europe the average age at which women married was twenty-three or older. In addition, 10 percent or more of women remained lifelong spinsters. The average age of female marriage in nineteenth-century America was somewhat younger; although some women did marry in their teens, the average was usually above twenty (Wells 1982). In Asia and Africa, in contrast, menarche and marriage were closely associated: as soon as a woman was able to bear a child she married (in some groups, marriage even preceded menarche), and virtually all women married. Obviously, the reproductive span in Western Europe was on average much shorter than that in Asian and African societies.

Recent research suggests that the differences in marriage patterns between Western Europe and other parts of the world were associated primarily with different norms or customs about the family, and especially about residence after marriage. In Western Europe, couples set up their own households after marriage; in Asia and Africa, in contrast, the ideal was usually that sons would bring their wives into their parents' household, while daughters would go to live in the parental households of their husbands (Laslett 1972). Since the ability to support one's own household is associated with age, it is not surprising that the age of marriage was later in Western Europe than elsewhere.

Within marriage, the major determinant of variations in fertility across groups in populations in which little or no contraception is practiced is known to be the duration of breastfeeding (Bongaarts and Menken 1983; Casterline et al. 1984). Nursing inhibits the return of ovulation, and although some individuals ovulate while they are still nursing, on average the period of postpartum amenorrhea is longer when breastfeeding is extended than when it is brief (Lesthaeghe and Page 1980). In addition, in some societies it is thought that sexual intercourse spoils the milk of a nursing mother; thus, there are taboos on intercourse during the period of breastfeeding.

Once the child is weaned and ovulation resumes, the woman is considered to be "fecundable" (at risk of pregnancy) until conception occurs again. In modern societies, the major proximate determinant of the length of the fecundable period is the use of contraception. In pretransition societies with little or no use of contraception, differences in the length of the fecundable period are due primarily to differences in the frequency of intercourse. More frequent intercourse increases the probability that it occurs during the fertile period of the woman's monthly cycle. Evidence about the frequency of intercourse in pretransition societies comes almost totally from surveys in developing countries. Differences among groups in intercourse frequency are relatively small, and they do not account for much of the observed variation in fertility. Intrauterine mortality (e.g., spontaneous miscarriage) does not seem to be an important determinant of differences in levels of fertility. Whereas it was thought that differences in nutrition might account for variations in postpartum amenorrhea, in the length of the fecundable period, or in intrauterine mortality, this does not seem to be the case (Menken, Trussell, and Watkins 1981).

In pretransition societies, the two most important of the proximate determinants of the overall level of fertility are marriage patterns and breastfeeding patterns. Although differences in these two proximate determinants account for much of the observed differences in levels of fertility across groups, it is unlikely that their variation reflects variation in ideal family size, either for the individual or the couple. Whether marriage was early or late, or whether breastfeeding was short or long, seems largely the outcome of other social concerns, such as establishing an independent household at marriage or the compatibility of women's work with nursing. Therefore, although these proximate determinants had the effect of limiting fertility, it is unlikely that they were usually intended to have that effect. Moreover, it is probable that the timing of marriage and the duration of breastfeeding were determined by community norms or social structures, rather than individual preferences: communities seem to have differed more in these respects than did individuals within these communities.

THE FERTILITY TRANSITION AND AFTER

Now let us turn to the fertility transition. The fertility transition represents a striking decline in fertility, as well as a revolution in reproductive practices. In pretransition societies, most women bear children from the time they marry until they reach menopause (or death or divorce intervene); in posttransition societies, most women (or couples) limit severely the number of children they bear. The deliberate and effective control of fertility within marriage is thus an innovation. Differences in the timing of the onset of the fertility transition, as well as differences in the pace and pervasiveness of the spread of this innovative behavior within populations, account for fertility differentials during the transition.

The earliest sustained fertility transitions at the national level occurred in France, where fertility decline began around the time of the French Revolution, and in the United States, where fertility control was evident in a number of New England communities by the end of the first quarter of the nineteenth century, and widespread among women who married on the eve of the Civil War. Indeed, urban white women who married around the time of the Civil War bore, on average, between two and three children, very "modern" levels of fertility (David and Sanderson 1987). The fertility decline occurred later in the U.S. South and among blacks.

Other fertility transitions spread throughout Europe between 1870 and 1930 (Coale and Watkins 1986), with very similar timing in Australia. These changes began in the core countries of northwest Europe and occurred later in the periphery of central Europe and the Mediterranean countries, with Ireland and Albania following even later. Aristocracies, Jews, and urban populations were early forerunners of the fertility transition (Livi-Bacci 1986).

In non-Western countries, time series of fertility measures are rare. Most analysts agree, however, that there was little evidence of a decline in marital fertility anywhere in the developing world before 1960, except for Argentina, Uruguay, and Chile (largely populated by settlers from Western Europe). Fertility decline was evident in a few city-states (Hong Kong, Singapore) and island populations (Mauritius, Fiji) in the mid-1960s, shortly thereafter in many countries with Chinese-origin populations, and then in many parts of Latin America. Some of the declines have been very rapid indeed, and fertility is now as low or nearly as low in some Asian countries as it is in the United States and in European countries. The TFR in Japan and South Korea is 1.6, in Taiwan 1.8, and in China 2.3, compared to 1.3 in Italy, 1.8 in France, the United Kingdom, and Hungary, and 2.0 in the United States (Population Reference Bureau 1990). A sustained decline in marital fertility has not yet begun in parts of North Africa and the Middle East, in Pakistan and Bangladesh, and in sub-Saharan Africa. Even in these parts of the world, however, there is evidence of incipient marital fertility decline among the more educated groups in the larger urban areas.

Although rises in female marriage age have contributed to the decline in fertility, this decline is largely due to the adoption of new behavior in marriage. In Europe, this was initially the use of abortion, withdrawal, and/or abstinence by married couples to stop childbearing, and only later the use of modern contraceptives to space children as well as to limit their number. In the Third World, fertility decline was closely associated with the use of modern contraceptives. The course of fertility decline in countries where fertility is now low suggests that once the process of the fertility transition has started, fertility levels decline monotonically until very low levels are reached. Moreover, there is no turning back: the new reproductive behavior is not abandoned. The rise in fertility in most developed countries after World War II (the babyboom) is an apparent exception to this generalization, but closer inspection shows that it was largely a shift in the timing of childbearing rather than the number of children women bore over their lifetime (Ryder 1980).

Why did fertility decline? Why did couples start to deliberately limit the number of children they bore? What are the "true" determinants of fertility? While a comprehensive theory of fertility would account for both the shift from high to low fertility and variations in fertility at each stage of the fertility transition, most of the attempts to understand the social, economic, and cultural influences on fertility have focused on attempts to understand the onset of the fertility transition. Almost anything that distinguishes traditional from modern societies has been considered relevant to the explanation of the fertility decline (Cleland 1985). The most influential explanation, called the theory of the demographic transition, is based on the assumption that the means of fertility control used in the early stages of the fertility transition were always known. Hence, the decline was attributed to changes in the motivations of individuals or couples, changes thought to be related to "modernization," especially increasing literacy, urbanization, the shift to paid, nonagricultural labor, and declines in infant and child mortality. Classic statements of demographic transition theory (e.g., Thompson 1929; Davis 1963; Notestein 1953; Freedman 1961–1962) emphasized changes in these macro-level conditions. Neoclassical economic theory, and in particular the New Home Economics associated with Gary Becker (1960), provides a translation from macro-level structural changes to the micro-level calculus of parents (for a more thorough review, see Jones 1982).

Empirical evidence on the fertility decline in Western Europe as well as developing countries supports some of the expectations of these theories, but others are called into question. In general, the urban dweller, the literate, and those in nonagricultural occupations were the leaders in the transition to low fertility. Almost all studies of fertility during the period of transition show that some part of the differentials can be accounted for by the increased proportion of the population in these categories (Watkins 1986). On the other hand, these studies have contradicted some of the expectations, and thus raised a number of questions. Fertility declines have occurred in largely rural or relatively poor populations (France in the eighteenth century, Sri Lanka recently); conversely, fertility declines began rather later in some countries than might have been expected (fertility did not decline in England until the last quarter of the nineteenth century). There is no threshold either of development or of mortality decline that invariably stimulated marital fertility change. Indeed, the transition has occurred at lower levels of development in the Third World (Knodel and van de Walle 1986; World Bank 1984). And although generally the more economically advanced segments of the population adopted the new reproductive behavior earliest, others—for example, rural, illiterate farmers—followed quickly. This suggests that the diffusion of information about techniques, or perhaps the legitimacy of their use—from one segment of the population to another—may have been as important as changes in the material circumstances of couples that would motivate them to desire fewer children (Watkins 1987). Both in Europe and in developing countries, cultural factors such as language, ethnicity, or region appear to be major independent determinants of the onset of the decline (Cleland 1985).

Currently, interesting research focuses on several alternative interpretations to classical demographic transition theory. A major alternative perspective emphasizes ideational change. The shift to small families has been part and parcel of a shift in ideational systems toward individualism. These doctrines offered justification for challenge to traditional authorities and practices, including those that concerned reproduction (Lesthaeghe 1983). In a similar vein, John Caldwell argues that much of the fertility decline in developing countries can be explained in terms of the introduction of images of the egalitarian Western family into the more patriarchal family systems of the developing world. It was not so much that the relative balance of costs and benefits of children changed, but that the moral economy shifted: it came to be seen as inappropriate to derive economic benefit from one's children (Caldwell 1982).

There has also been considerable interest in institutional determinants of fertility change. These are typically social institutions (e.g., systems of landholding) but occasionally emergent properties of the collective behavior of individuals (Smith 1989). Therefore, in understanding the frequent association between education and fertility decline, it may be more relevant to ask what proportion of the community has attended school than to ask whether a particular individual has. Similarly, both class relations (Cain 1981) and gender relations (Mason 1986) are aspects of the community rather than the individual, and both are likely to be associated with fertility change.

Much attention has been devoted to evaluating the role of family planning programs in the fertility decline in the Third World, where it seems that the methods used initially in the West were either not known or considered too costly in personal terms (Knodel, Napaporn, and Pramualratana 1984). It is likely that family planning programs speed rather than initiate the decline. Most analyses have shown family planning programs to have an effect that is independent of the socioeconomic setting, although dollar for dollar, family planning programs are more effective in countries or areas that have experienced development (Lapham and Mauldin 1985; Population Information Program 1985). The effect of family planning programs is generally less than that of the socioeconomic setting, but it is significant. In some cases, family planning programs seemed not only to reduce the disparity between desired and achieved family size, but also to affect desired family size itself (Westoff 1978). Where a powerful state has energetically pushed family planning programs (e.g., China) adoption of contraception has been particularly rapid.

Distinguishing between (1) the socioeconomic progress of individuals and households; (2) ideational change; and (3) institutional change is difficult, for they do not operate independently of one another. Economic advance stimulates and supports expanded government programs. Government programs change the social and economic conditions facing individuals and can accelerate the adoption of new ideas or, as in the case of Iran, attempt to insulate the population from outside influences. It does seem likely, however, that further advances in understanding the fertility transition will require integrating macro-level characteristics of communities with micro-level behavior.

In modern, low-fertility societies there is less variation in fertility than there was either in pretransition societies or during the transition (Watkins 1991). Most couples desire only a few children (rarely more than two), and most use effective means to achieve their desires. Accordingly, analysts have concentrated on the determinants of fertility in specific subgroups of the population, such as teenagers or ethnic or racial minorities. In doing so they have drawn on much the same combination of socioeconomic characteristics, institutional factors, and ideational change. For example, the higher fertility of teenagers is usually explained in terms both of their differing socioeconomic characteristics and of their lesser access to effective contraception, as well as to an unwillingness to use it.

What will happen to fertility in the future? Few expect fertility to rise. Some temporal fluctuations are expected, but these are likely to be related more to shifts in the timing of childbearing than changes in number. When childbearing is postponed, *period* measures of fertility (e.g., those calculated for a single year) will decline, even though *cohort* measures (those that measure the lifetime reproduction of a group of women, such as those born or married in the same year) may stay the same. The most comprehensive explanation for temporal fluctuations proposes that the size of a cohort is related to its fertility (Easterlin 1980). Larger cohorts (e.g., those born in the United States at the end of World War II) competed with each other for jobs, thus bidding down labor force rewards and causing them to delay marriage and childbearing until they could afford what they felt was an appropriate household in which to begin marriage. Smaller cohorts, in contrast, are advantaged on the job market, and hence marry earlier.

Some, however, predict further declines in fertility. These predictions are based on a combination of proximate and true determinants. Since the 1960s, marriage age has risen sharply in most of the developed countries, as have divorce rates; if these trends continue—and as long as most children continue to be born within marriage—lower fertility will follow. There has also been some increase in the proportion who are unable to bear children, in part because some couples postpone marriage and childbearing so long that they are unable to have the children they want, and in part because it is likely that involuntary sterility associated with sexually transmitted diseases may have increased at least slightly (Menken 1985).

But the major predictions of lower fertility in the future emphasize the characteristics of modern societies that make childbearing less rewarding compared to the other opportunities available to women, and the continued inroads into the family that individualism is making (Preston 1986; Keyfitz 1986). A striking feature of recent decades has been the degree to which the trends—in marriage, in divorce, in cohabitation, in fertility—are virtually synchronous across most social groups within the same country, as well as across most developed countries. This suggests that the determinants of fertility in the future as well as the past need to be sought not only at the level of individuals, but at the macro-level. The greater integration of modern nations, and trends toward a global society, would seem to be evident in fertility as well as in other aspects of social life.

(SEE ALSO: *Demographic Transition; Family and Population Policy in Less Developed Countries; Family Planning; Family Policy in Western Society; Family Size*)

REFERENCES

Becker, Gary S. 1960 "An Economic Analysis of Fertility." In *Demographic and Economic Change in Developed Countries,* Universities-National Bureau Conference Series, no. 11. Princeton, N.J.: Princeton University Press.

Bongaarts, John 1978 "A Framework for Analyzing the Proximate Determinants of Fertility." *Population and Development Review* 4:105–132.

———, and Jane Menken 1983 "The Supply of Children: A Critical Essay." In Rodolfo A. Bulatao and Ronald D. Lee, eds., *Determinants of Fertility in Developing Countries.* New York: Academic Press.

Bulatao, Rodolfo A., and Ronald D. Lee, eds. 1983 *Determinants of Fertility in Developing Countries.* New York: Academic Press.

Cain, Meade 1981 "Risk and Insurance: Perspectives on Fertility and Agrarian Change in India and Bangladesh." *Population and Development Review* 7:435–474.

Caldwell, John C. 1982 *Theory of Fertility Decline.* New York: Academic Press.

Casterline, John, et al. 1984 "The Proximate Determinants of Fertility." In *WFS Comparative Studies.* Voorburg, Netherlands: International Statistical Institute.

Cleland, John 1985 "Marital Fertility Decline in Developing Countries: Theories and the Evidence." In John Cleland and John Hobcraft, eds., *Reproductive Change in Developing Countries.* London: Oxford University Press.

———, and John Hobcraft (eds.) 1985 *Reproductive Change in Developing Countries.* London: Oxford University Press.

———, and Chris Wilson 1987 "Demand Theories of the Fertility Decline: An Iconoclastic View." *Population Studies* 41:5–30.

Coale, Ansley J., and Susan C. Watkins, eds. 1986 *The Decline of Fertility in Europe.* Princeton, N.J.: Princeton University Press.

David, Paul A., and Warren C. Sanderson 1987 "The Emergence of a Two-Child Norm among American Birth-Controllers." *Population and Development Review* 13:1–41.

Davis, Kingsley 1963 "The Theory of Change and Response in Modern Demographic History." *Population Index* 29:345–366.

———, and Judith Blake 1956 "Social Structure and Fertility: An Analytic Framework." *Economic Development and Cultural Change* 4:211–235.

Easterlin, Richard A. 1980 *Birth and Fortune: The Impact of Numbers on Personal Welfare.* New York: Basic Books.

———, and Eileen Crimmins 1985 *The Fertility Revolution: A Supply-Demand Analysis.* Chicago: University of Chicago Press.

Freedman, Ronald 1961–1962 "The Sociology of Human Fertility." *Current Sociology* 10/11:35–119.

Hajnal, John 1965 "European Marriage Patterns in Perspective." In D. V. Glass and D. E. C. Eversley, eds., *Population in History.* London: Edward Arnold.

Henry, Louis 1961 "Some Data on Natural Fertility." *Eugenics Quarterly.* 8:81–91.

Jones, Gavin W. 1982 "Fertility Determinants: Sociological and Economic Theories." In J. A. Ross, ed., *International Encyclopedia of Population.* New York: Free Press.

Keyfitz, Nathan 1986 "The Family That Does Not Reproduce Itself." *Population and Development Review* 12 (suppl.):139–154.

Knodel, John 1988 *Demographic Behavior in the Past.* Cambridge: Cambridge University Press.

———, and Etienne van de Walle 1986 "Lessons from the Past: Policy Implications of Historical Fertility Studies." In Ansley J. Coale and Susan C. Watkins, eds., *The Decline of Fertility in Europe.* Princeton, N.J.: Princeton University Press.

———, Havanon Napaporn, and Anthony Pramualratana 1984 "Fertility Transition in Thailand: A Qualitative Analysis." *Population and Development Review* 10 2:297–328.

Lapham, R. J., and W. P. Mauldin 1985 "Contraceptive Prevalence: The Influence of Organized Family Planning Programs." *Studies in Family Planning* 16:117–137.

Laslett, Peter 1972 "Introduction: The History of the Family." In Peter Laslett and Richard Wall, eds., *Household and Family in Past Time.* Cambridge: Cambridge University Press.

Lesthaeghe, Ron 1983 "A Century of Demographic and Cultural Change in Western Europe." *Population and Development Review* 9:411–435.

———, and Hilary J. Page 1980 "The Postpartum Nonsusceptible Period: Development and Application of Model Schedules." *Population Studies* 34: 143–170.

Livi-Bacci, Massimo 1986 "Social Group Forerunners of Fertility Control in Europe." In Ansley J. Coale and Susan C. Watkins, eds., *The Decline of Fertility in Europe.* Princeton, N.J.: Princeton University Press.

Mason, Karen O. 1986 "The Status of Women: Conceptual and Methodological Issues in Demographic Studies." *Sociological Forum* 1:284–300.

Menken, Jane 1985. "Age and Fertility: How Late Can You Wait?" *Demography* 22(4):469–483.

———, James Trussell, and Susan Cotts Watkins 1981 "The Nutrition-Fertility Link: An Examination of the Evidence." *Journal of Interdisciplinary History* 11:425–444.

Notestein, Frank 1953 "Economic Problems of Population Change." *Proceedings of the Eight International Conference of Agricultural Economists.* London: Oxford University Press.

Population Information Program 1985 *The Impact of Family Planning Programs on Fertility,* Series J, No. 29. Baltimore, Md.: Johns Hopkins University.

Population Reference Bureau 1990 *World Population Data Sheet.* Washington, D.C.: Population Reference Bureau, Inc.

Preston, Samuel H. 1986 "Changing Values and Falling Birth Rates." *Population and Development Review* 12 (Suppl.):176–195.

Ryder, Norman B. 1980 "Components of Temporal Variations in American Fertility." In R. W. Hiorns, ed., *Demographic Patterns in Developed Societies.* London: Taylor and Francis.

Smith, Herbert L. 1989 "Integrating Theory and Research on the Determinants of Fertility." *Demography* 26:171–184.

Thompson, Warren S. 1929 "Population." *American Journal of Sociology* 34:959–975.

Watkins, Susan Cotts 1986 "Conclusions." In Ansley J. Coale and Susan C. Watkins, eds., *The Decline of Fertility in Europe.* Princeton, N.J.: Princeton University Press.

——— 1987 "The Fertility Transition: Europe and the Third World Compared." *Sociological Forum* 2 (4):645–673.

Watkins, Susan Cotts 1991 *From Provinces into Nations: The Demographic Integration of Western Europe.* Princeton, N.J.: Princeton University Press.

Wells, Robert V. 1982 *Revolutions in American Lives.* Westport, Conn.: Greenwood Press.

Westoff, Charles 1978 "The Unmet Need for Birth Control in Five Asian Countries." *International Family Planning Perspectives and Digest* 4:9–17.

World Bank 1984 *World Development Report 1984.* New York: Oxford University Press.

Wrigley, E. A., and Roger S. Schofield 1981 *The Population History of England, 1541–1871.* Cambridge: Harvard University Press.

SUSAN COTTS WATKINS

FIELD RESEARCH METHODS Field research examines people acting and interacting in the context of their everyday lives. Fieldworkers enter social worlds to learn firsthand about how people live, how they talk and behave, and the ways in which circumstances affect their conduct. Contemporary field research has come to connote something more than simply naturalistic inquiry, however. It is also a range of methods for describing and understanding social organization. Immersion—even participation—in others' social worlds is recommended both to provide immediate, direct access to those worlds and to avail field-workers of the subjective meanings and concerns of the persons they study.

Field research is sometimes distinguished from other research methods by the place and manner of data collection; any and all research conducted "in the field" may be called field research. The important feature is that data are collected *in situ,* and field researchers avoid as much as possible any artificial alterations of the settings studied. Field research also may be distinguished by its approach to understanding social phenomena. It is a distinctive "way of knowing" that results from deep involvement in, or intimate familiarity with, the settings, activities, and persons studied. In this regard it is not geographic proximity to subjects that distinguishes the approach as much as field-workers' ability to grasp the native social and cognitive processes, practices, and meanings that constitute the social worlds under consideration. The concept of "field" itself is currently a matter of theoretical debate and critique (Clifford and Marcus 1986; Emerson 1983; Gubrium and Silverman 1989).

HISTORICAL DEVELOPMENT OF FIELD RESEARCH

Entering subjects' natural habitats to collect data systematically has its origins in early twentieth-century anthropology. Prior to this, anthropological analysis depended on the unsystematic reports of explorers, traders, and military or missionary expeditions for details of indigenous life and culture. To study western Pacific people, however, anthropologist Bronislaw Malinowski lived among his subjects and recognized that the means of understanding people and cultures "consist[s] in cutting oneself off from the company of other white men, and remaining in as close contact with the natives as possible, which really can only be achieved by camping out right in their villages" (1961, p. 6). Malinowski inspired generations of cultural anthropologists to adopt and refine field research techniques.

Sociological fieldwork developed in the same period, but sprang from social reform movements. Researchers sought descriptions of the real-life conditions of disadvantaged urban populations to ameliorate the impoverished circumstances of the city. This reforming impulse and direct observational methods were hallmarks of the University of Chicago school of sociology, which dominated the discipline in its formative years. Robert Park, for example, was concerned with the diverse moral regions and social worlds that composed urban life, and urged sociological field researchers to

> *go and sit in the lounges of the luxury hotels and on the doorsteps of the flophouses; sit on the Gold Coast settees and on the slum shakedowns; sit in Orchestra Hall and in the Star and Garter Burlesk. In short, gentlemen, go get the seat of your pants dirty in real research* (McKinney 1966, p. 71).

Park and others recommended both the social survey—extensive and in-depth interviews with knowledgeable subjects—and the observational methods of anthropologists as models for field research. Chicago sociologists also developed the intensive case study and life history method as a way of thoroughly documenting the subjective experiences of daily life. This approach relies on data collected through interviews, autobiographies assembled by informants, letters, diaries, journalistic stories, and official records and documents from courts, social service agencies, and the police, among many others. The researcher's goal is to assemble as many documents as possible to reveal social life through individual experience.

As field research came to dominate anthropological research and establish itself as a viable sociological method, field-workers developed increasing sensitivity to field processes and relations in their own right. Participant observation came to be known as the primary method of gaining access to subjects' meanings and orientations, and its ascendance was accompanied by concern for how this involvement affected research findings. Early field-workers—often immersed in their social reform activities—typically faced the problem of sufficiently distancing and detaching themselves from their subjects or phenomena to analyze them objectively. As sociological interest spread to groups and settings associated with diverse political interests, the processes of gaining access, establishing trust and rapport, and sustaining personal relations across racial, ethnic, and class boundaries began to compete with objectivity as central methodological concerns. Thus was formed the perennial tension for field researchers between developing intimacy and sympathetic understanding, on the one hand, and maintaining analytic objectivity, on the other.

The Chicago school of field research was closely associated with the development of symbolic interactionism (Blumer 1969). This focused research on social processes—which all but required naturalistic observation—and increased field-workers' sensitivity to their own interactions and roles in sociological analyses. The idea that sociological observation could proceed in the fashion of observation in the natural sciences was increasingly questioned. Field researchers could not expect simply to document preexisting, objective meanings, because meaning was understood to emerge from, and change with, social interaction.

People interpret the world they inhabit, and these interpretations motivate and shape their actions and experiences. To understand the social world, then, researchers must discern the meanings that actions, events, and circumstances have for those being studied. To grasp and appreciate subjects' meanings, researchers are compelled to comprehend and describe the subjective experience of their subjects and to interpret the world as it appears to those subjects. Thus, sociological understandings are "second order" constructions (Schutz 1962). Appreciation of the need for *verstehen,* or interpretive understanding, has become a major justification for observational field research at a time when the discipline of sociology has become progressively committed to quantification. Field research is the vehicle for understanding subjects' holistic, subjective experiences —their lives, thoughts, motivations, and actions as they apprehend them. Done systematically, field research aspires to rigorous knowledge grounded in "the perspectives of the actors themselves and upon the categories of distinctions which the actors recognize and respond to" (Wax 1967, p. 329).

THE OBJECTIVES OF FIELD RESEARCH

While the ultimate aim of field research is to develop theoretical statements about social life, its more immediate goal is to provide empirically derived descriptions. As field research has increasingly rejected the possibility of doing literal description—as if actions had fixed and invariant meanings—field-workers have abandoned the notion that observation is a mechanical process of merely recording what is there "for all to see." Where to look, what to look at, and how to report what is seen have become major theoretical as well as technical issues. Observation and description are admittedly guided by the field-worker's conceptual assumptions, formulations, and theories, acknowledging that description is inevitably selective, partial, and perspectival. The distinction between method and theory—between observation and analysis—is thus blurred.

In this context, description is a theoretically informed "re-presentation" of acts or events that vary according to observers' theoretical assumptions. There are alternate approaches to developing and using these preinterpreted versions of indigenous scenes and actions. Clifford Geertz (1973), for one, argues that field research should provide "thick description" of social and cultural circumstances and activities, advocating a documentation of the intimate details of the actions, events, and settings that are consequential and important to those experiencing them. Connections between actions and events must be explicitly specified to reflect local participants' awareness and understanding. Geertz emphasizes an "experience near" appreciation of social contexts, to provide understandings that approximate those of actual participants. The approach rejects a priori attempts to standardize data collection procedures, including instruments based on predetermined classifications or categories. From this standpoint, the goal of fieldwork is not to count and correlate the presence of precategorized conditions or variables, but to describe locally meaningful complexes of activities. Geertz suggests that "thick," "experience near" descriptions may then be connected to more theoretical statements regarding the general contours of social life.

Field research informed by ethnomethodological theory (Garfinkel 1967; Heritage 1984) is most concerned with the ways in which members of particular groups *use* common sense or folk knowledge to provide their everyday lives and activities with a sense of order. Members' articulation of meanings and descriptions of their social worlds are important from this perspective because they are seen as constitutive of those worlds. Rather than treat members' descriptions as reports about their worlds, the ethnomethodologically informed field researcher examines how descriptions are used to manage and sustain the sensible, organized character of the circumstances in which (and about which) descriptions are offered. Since descriptions are produced for practical purposes, close attention is paid to what is thereby *accomplished* through socially situated descriptions and accounts. Ethnomethodological field research aims to identify and document these reality-producing, -managing, and -sustaining procedures.

DOING FIELD RESEARCH

While there are as many ways of doing field research as there are field-workers and theories of the field, most naturalistic, observational research projects deal with a similar set of issues concerning what to study, how to study it, and how to formulate research findings. Field researchers begin with a general notion of the problems or issues that interest them, and have some sense for the settings that will be relevant for examining these problems or issues. Some formulate tentative hypotheses about the social relations they intend to study. While research questions are rarely preformulated in great detail, they suggest research sites that might provide insights into the issues of concern. Alternatively, researchers may find particular settings or situations especially interesting and study the dynamics of those settings more completely and systematically. Research questions and theoretical issues emerge as the setting is explored. In either case, a field setting must be designated, and access to the setting obtained.

A number of concerns arise in gaining entry into a research setting. Most obviously, permission may sometimes be required, especially in institutional settings. Researchers must also consider subjects' informed consent to participate in the study. And this, of course, relates to the decision about whether to enter the field openly as researchers, or to conduct research covertly without revealing the actual purpose of being in the setting. Some researchers study settings of which they are already integral parts, or undergo extensive training and socialization to become members of settings to be studied. Others enter settings without revealing their identity or purpose, secretly to observe activities without subjects' knowledge, let alone consent. The ethics of covert research are continually debated among field researchers (Denzin 1989; Silverman 1985).

Concerns about access to research settings also relate to the issue of "reactive" effects—that is, how a researcher changes the circumstances studied by his or her presence. Covert entry is generally believed to be less reactive, but there may be good reason for entering a setting as a known researcher. Researchers may have access to persons and places in a setting that may be denied regular participants. Additionally, indigenous informants may be more willing to reveal their lives to researchers than to other indigenous persons, who may be perceived as having particular interests in the setting.

Once field researchers enter a setting, myriad factors must be considered in collecting data. Researchers must decide on the roles they will occupy in the setting—complete observer, observer as participant, participant as observer, or complete participant, among others. To ascertain the meaning of the things they are told and shown, observers must take into account the identities attributed to them within the settings they study. They must develop relationships with persons in those settings, and sustain the rapport necessary to cultivate reliable informants. Field researchers must familiarize themselves with the circumstances and social dynamics of the setting so they can recognize indigenous members' meanings—how the meanings are developed, and their impact on actions and interpretations. This involves carefully watching, listening, and recording the details of everyday activity in the setting under study—that is, translating their observations into systematically organized data.

Recording and organizing field notes is perhaps the most arduous and time-consuming aspect of a field study. Field-workers record direct observations of activities, events, conversations, and settings. They talk with and question participants in the settings, conduct formal and informal interviews, and inspect formal organizational documents and informal records (e.g., diaries and letters). Audio and video recordings of naturally occurring interactions and interview conversations are increasingly employed. The actual methods vary according to the special needs, theoretical orientations, objectives, and practices of individual field-workers.

Producing analytic descriptions of field settings —*ethnographies*—is the culmination of field research. Here, too, are many approaches to analyzing field data, involving diverse analytic strategies, techniques, and objectives. Most hold in common the desire to produce theoretical generalizations or propositions grounded in the settings or conduct studied. Perhaps the best-known system for generating theory from field research is the "grounded theory" approach (Glaser and Strauss 1967). This approach involves systematic theorizing about social processes and rests on the assertion that the discovery and elaboration of theory are distinct from theory verification. It suggests that the value of field research lies in its ability to reveal concepts and discover theoretical generalizations. In the grounded theory approach, data collection and analysis proceed simultaneously. Grounded theorists shape their data collection from their analytic interpretations and discoveries; they check and elaborate emerging ideas by collecting further data relevant to those ideas. Data are used to suggest conceptual categories, and then more data are collected by theoretical sampling—selection of cases to examine aspects of the emerging theory specifically. New observations are made to pursue analytically relevant concerns and to elaborate or modify the original, tentative theoretical propositions. The researcher continually checks emerging categories against data from the field to develop a set of conceptual abstractions that explain what is going on in the setting under study. Tentative theoretical formulations may subsequently be verified or rejected using formal hypothesis-testing procedures.

The method called "analytic induction" (Robinson 1951) denies the distinction between generating and verifying theory. Its intent is to develop propositions that apply to all cases of the problem under analysis. In this approach, researchers begin with a rough formulation of the phenomenon of interest and formulate tentative hypotheses. They then examine a limited number of cases to see if the hypothesis is adequate for explaining those cases. If it is not, either the hypothesis is reformulated or the phenomenon is redefined so the cases are accounted for. The procedure continues to more cases, with the researcher recasting the theoretical formulations in light of each negative case encountered. Practical certainty is achieved when a small number of cases can be adequately explained, but the discovery of negative cases requires constant reformulation. Field researchers are obligated to search for negative cases to test the adequacy of their theorizing. The procedure continues until all cases can be accounted for.

Numerous other analytic strategies are applied in field research. Erving Goffman's dramaturgic approach (1959) focuses on persons' staged interaction, metaphorically framing analysis in the language of the theater. Interactions are construed as performances, and field data are used to document the presentation of self, facework, role-taking, and other interaction rituals that sustain social encounters. In a related fashion, interactional strategy analysis (Lofland 1976) attempts to specify the social tactics used by actors to manage roles and relationships.

These data analysis strategies are more or less grounded in symbolic-interactionist theory. Their objectives are to describe and explain the structures and meanings of social worlds. Ethnomethodologically informed analyses of field data take a different approach. Their concern is for the interactional practices through which the observable, reportable features of everyday life are locally accomplished and managed. Analyses focus on the fine details of interaction—everyday discourse and conversation in particular. The aim is to describe the interactional methods by which persons situationally create, sustain, and manage the appearances of a meaningful social world while they maintain the sense that this world exists apart from their mundane, constitutive activities. In contrast to symbolic-interactionist strategies, ethnomethodologists emphasize the constitution of everyday life, not its social distribution or performances. Ethnomethodological field research thus focuses on the ways in which people use commonsense constructs and categories to produce and manage social realities.

Some approaches to field research have attempted to combine concerns for social structure with interests in the activities that create and sustain the sense of social structure. "Constitutive ethnography" (Mehan 1979) aims to show how the social facts of the world emerge from interactual "structuring" work to become external and constraining features of social worlds. "Practical ethnography" (Gubrium 1988) treats the production of meaning as a practical matter located within concrete, everyday settings. Analysis of field data from this perspective focuses on how "practitioners of everyday life" manage and apply generally recognized categories, ideas, and accounts to sort, design, and execute their everyday activities meaningfully. The approach thus links ethnomethodology's emphasis on the social accomplishment of social reality with more traditional concerns with social structure.

(SEE ALSO: *Case Studies; Ethnomethodology*)

REFERENCES

Blumer, Herbert 1969 *Symbolic Interactionism.* Englewood Cliffs, N.J.: Prentice-Hall.

Clifford, James, and George E. Marcus (eds.) 1986 *Writing Culture: The Poetics and Politics of Ethnography.* Berkeley: University of California Press.

Denzin, Norman K. 1989 *The Research Act,* 3rd ed. Englewood Cliffs, N.J.: Prentice-Hall.

Emerson, Robert M. (ed.) 1983 *Contemporary Field Research.* Boston: Little, Brown.

Garfinkel, Harold 1967 *Studies in Ethnomethodology.* Englewood Cliffs, N.J.: Prentice-Hall.

Geertz, Clifford 1973 *The Interpretation of Cultures.* New York: Basic Books.

Glaser, Barney G., and Anselm L. Strauss 1967 *The Discovery of Grounded Theory.* Chicago: Aldine.

Goffman, Erving 1959 *The Presentation of Self in Everyday Life.* Garden City, N.Y.: Doubleday.

Gubrium, Jaber F. 1988 *Analyzing Field Reality.* Newbury Park, Calif.: Sage Publications.

———, and David Silverman (eds.) 1989 *The Politics of Field Research.* London: Sage Publications.

Heritage, John C. 1984 *Garfinkel and Ethnomethodology.* Cambridge, U.K.: Polity Press.

Lofland, John 1976 *Doing Social Life.* New York: John Wiley.

Malinowski, Bronislaw 1961 *Argonauts of the Western Pacific.* New York: E. P. Dutton.

McKinney, John C. 1966 *Constructive Typology and Social Theory.* New York: Appleton-Century-Crofts.

Mehan, Hugh 1979 *Learning Lessons.* Cambridge, Mass.: Harvard University Press.

Pollner, Melvin 1987 *Mundane Reason.* Cambridge: Cambridge University Press.

Robinson, W. S. 1951 "The Logical Structure of Analytic Induction." *American Sociological Review* 16:812–818.

Schutz, Alfred 1962 *The Problem of Social Reality.* The Hague: Martinus Nijhoff.

Silverman, David 1985 *Qualitative Methodology and Sociology.* Brookfield, Vt.: Gower.

Wax, Murray L. 1967 "On Misunderstanding *Verstehen.*" *Sociology and Social Research* 51:323–333.

JAMES A. HOLSTEIN
JABER F. GUBRIUM

FIELD THEORY It was perhaps only the youthful optimism of a new science that allowed Kurt Lewin and his colleagues to believe that they had within their grasp the key elements of a "field theory of the social sciences." Social psychology made great strides in the 1930s and 1940s. Lewin and Lippitt (1938) seemed to have demonstrated in the laboratory the inherent superiority of democracy over autocracy. Lewin (1948) provided a theoretical framework for resolving social conflicts, and after his death his colleagues quickly shaped his legacy into a social scientific field theory (Lewin 1951). How could they resist? The physicists had just announced developments that shook the foundations of Newtonian physics. It was expected that Einstein, safely ensconced in the Institute for Advanced Study, would any day announce the "unified field theory" that would once again make the physical world an orderly place. Could they ask less of the social sciences?

By 1968 one of Lewin's former students, Morton Deutsch, would declare field theory—and all other grand theories of social psychology—moribund. A few years later, Nicholas Mullins (1973) would eulogize the entire field of small group research as "the light that failed," a victim of the untimely death of its only real intellectual leader, Kurt Lewin. Mullin's borrowing of the Kipling title is compelling not only because it suggests that small group research promised much and failed to deliver but because it suggests that field theory extended its reach beyond its grasp. In recent years there has been a revival of interest in field theory, though, for better or worse, much of the youthful optimism has faded.

LEWIN AND THE ORIGINS OF FIELD THEORY

Lewin's (1935) *A Dynamic Theory of Personality* called for a shift in psychology from the Aristotelian to the Galilean mode of thought. Epitomized by the now-classic formulation "behavior is a function of personality and environment," or $B = f(PE)$, the new perspective placed social psychology squarely at the intersection of psychology and sociology. It required abandoning the hope that social behavior could be explained by reference to personality variables and sought explanations in the dynamic relationships among actors and situations. In this book, Lewin defined the building blocks of the field theory that was to come: force (a vector directed at a point of application), valence (the push or pull of the force), and conflict (the opposition of roughly equivalent forces). At this point he clearly had in mind a metric space of social life, the concepts of vector and direction having limited meaning in topological (or nonmetric) space.

The young field of topological mathematics freed Lewin from the necessity of defining a metric space of social life. In *Principles of Topological Psychology,* he defined the new nonmetric space: "By this term is meant that we are dealing with mathematical relationships which can be characterized without measurement. No distances are defined in topological space" (Lewin 1936, p. 53). The concept was a failure; his presentation to the mathematicians at MIT made it clear that he had overreached. He had ventured into the murky mathematical realm of topology when, in fact, he always intended to return to metric space. Two additional difficulties also appear in this volume. First, Lewin insisted that the new topological psychology deal with the entire life–space of the individual. Much as Simmel (1955) conceived of the individual as lying at the intersection of various "social circles," Lewin saw the individual life–space as made up of the totality of available social relations. For practical purposes, this made the full specification of a single life–space almost impossibly complex. If one then tried to understand even a small group of actors by merging life–spaces, the problem became overwhelming. Second, Lewin seemed often to think of life–space in terms of physical space. Thus, locomotion almost literally meant moving from one physical location to another. This confusion of metaphor with reality prevented Lewin from proposing a consistent conceptual space of the sort suggested by Borgatta (1963), Bales (1985), and others.

A collection of Lewin's (1948) more applied American papers, *Resolving Social Conflicts,* appeared the year after he died. Figure 1 illustrates the way Lewin translated concrete conflicts into abstract life–space capsules. This particular example illustrates the concept of "range of free movement" as "a topological region encircled by other regions that are inaccessible" (Lewin 1948, p. 5). In the same volume, Lewin defined two useful characteristics of the boundaries between sectors of the life–space: sharpness (the clarity of boundaries) and rigidity (the ease with which boundaries shift).

Field Theory in Social Science, a collection of Lewin's more theoretical writings, appeared in 1951. In these papers, Lewin introduced the most crucial concepts. Conflict is defined as "the overlapping of two force fields," force as "the tendency toward locomotion," and position as "a spatial relation of regions" (1951, pp. 39–40). The example of a conflict between husband and wife, as reproduced in Figure 1, illustrates Lewin's concepts of "subjective" and "objective" social fields. The subjectively defined life–spaces of two people differ, and so a single interpersonal act may have very different meanings for the two actors. Repeated reality testing is necessary to bring the individuals to a consensually defined "objective" social life–space.

Lewin never really succeeded in developing a predictive theory of group dynamics: "The clarification of the problem of past and future has been much delayed by the fact that the psychological field which exists at a given time contains also the views of that individual about his future and past" (Lewin 1951, p. 53). The field is still struggling with this problem, lacking an adequate theory even of state-to-state transition.

In the years following Lewin's death, the focus shifted from the theoretical to the applied. Much of the work done at the University of Michigan's Research Center for Group Dynamics and at National Training Laboratory's facilities in Bethel, Maine, has been only very loosely tied to the concepts of field theory. While Lewin is often credited with founding the field of organization development (Weisbord 1987), his careful work on the nature of the social field is often ignored in favor of his deceptively simple comments such as "There's nothing so practical as a good theory." While Lewin believed that he could not be sure

FIGURE 1
A Conflict between Husband and Wife, Represented in Life–space Diagrams and Narrative Form.

In the life-space of the husband the region "friendship of husband with third person" does not overlap with the "marriage region"; it definitely overlaps in the life-space of the wife.

M, marriage region
Bu, business life of husband
Cl, club life of husband
hl, home life
ch, life with children
se, sexual relation between husband and wife
so, social life of husband and wife
fr, friendship of husband with third person

The intimate relationship of one partner to a third person not only makes the second partner "lose" the first one, but the second partner will have, in addition, the feeling that something of his own intimate life is thrown open to a third person . . . The life space of the husband might be represented through Figure 1a. His friendship to the third person (fr) might have grown out of his business relations. It may have become a rather important region for him personally, while still retaining its place in the business region, or at least clearly outside his marriage (M) life . . . The same situation may appear in an entirely different light to the wife. In her life space (Fig. 1b), the whole life of the husband is embraced in the marriage relationship and particularly any kind of friendly or intimate relation profoundly affects the marriage region.

Reproduced from: Lewin, K. (1948). *Resolving Social Conflicts.* New York: Harper, pp. 99–100.

that he had fully understood a social situation unless he could change it, he never assumed that the ability to bring about change implied understanding. Only in the past several years has attention returned to the difficult legacy of an incomplete field theory.

RECENT DEVELOPMENTS AND PROSPECTS FOR THE FUTURE

Current research on field theory has come from three directions. First, members of the recently founded Society for the Advancement of Field Theory have concentrated on a variety of practical applications while calling for a renewed focus on theory building. In addition, writers in the field of organization development have continued to build, both implicitly and explicitly, on Lewinian constructs. Finally, the group process school, which had developed independent of Lewinian thought, has recently begun to integrate field theory with process-based models of social space.

The Society for the Advancement of Field Theory was founded at a Temple University conference in 1984. Stivers and Wheelan (1986) have since published the proceedings of the conference as *The Lewin Legacy.* Papers from the two subsequent biennial meetings of the society have also been circulated.

The book of proceedings from the 1984 conference includes historical essays and applications of field theory to therapy, education, organizational development, and community psychology. A brief set of papers at the end calls for a revitalization of Lewinian thought, particularly within the tradition of action research. It is clear, however, that the authors are responding more to Lewin's research philosophy than to the theoretical constructs of his field theory.

The papers from the 1986 and 1988 field theory conferences continue to focus on application but with more explicit reference to theory. A paper titled "The Two Field Theories" addresses the issue of whether field theory is a "real theory" or simply an "approach." It distinguishes between the theory as described above and the approach or "meta-theory" that has served as the guide for the generations of scholars that followed Lewin. Pointing out that much of social psychology has drifted away from the consideration of social life–space toward the understanding of internal cognitive processes, the author calls for a revitalization of the Galilean mode of thought. Building on this suggestion, another paper calls for a new model of social psychology that takes into account time, place, and context. The remainder of the volume is once again directed toward the solution of practical problems. The authors deal with families, psychiatry, human development, education, conflict, organizations, and cross-cultural concerns. Virtually all of this work seems to draw on Lewin's "approach" or "meta-theory" rather than his "specific field theory."

Weisbord (1987) has made explicit the debt that organization development owes to field theory. Citing Marrow's (1969) excellent biography of Lewin, Weisbord draws parallels between the lives of Frederick Taylor and Kurt Lewin. Lewin's "Humanization of the Taylor System" can be thought of as a blueprint for achieving the central goal of organizational development: increasing organizational effectiveness through the application of social science knowledge. The origins of participatory management, teambuilding, feedback, process consultation, and third party intervention lie in both the theoretical and empirical work of Lewin and his colleagues.

The group process school, with its origins in Parsonian functionalism, has recently moved toward integration with the group dynamics school. Bales (1985), tracing the origins of field theory to Dewey's (1896) "reflex arc," suggested that his new three-dimensional conceptual space of social interaction made possible a new field theory. He argued for the universality of the dimensions but stopped short of offering the integration: "The new field theory in social psychology is the needed framework, I believe, for the long-desired integration of social psychology. But to explore that thesis is a major undertaking, and here we must be content with a tentative case for the major dimensions of the framework" (Bales 1985, p. 17).

Polley (1989) validated an updated set of di-

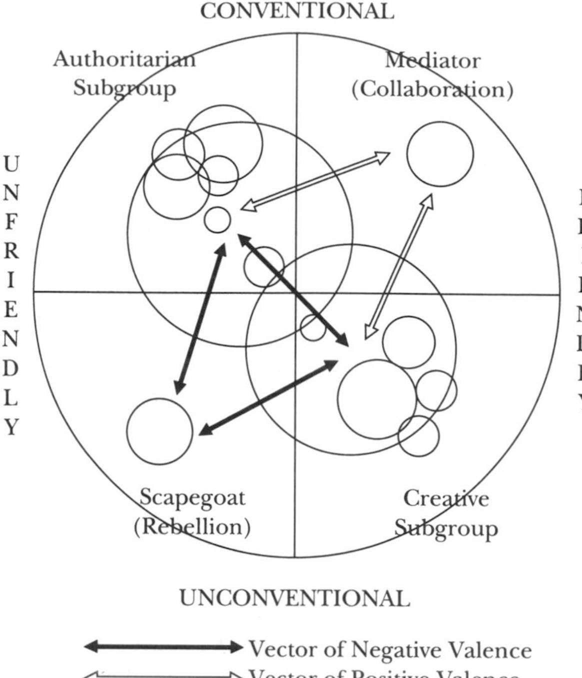

FIGURE 2
A Three-Dimensional Field Diagram, Showing Two Subgroups, a Mediator, and a Scapegoat.

mensions and offered a series of explicit operational definitions for the basic concepts of Lewinian field theory. Figure 2 presents a "field diagram" that illustrates some of the basic principles. Two dimensions of interpersonal behavior (Friendly–Unfriendly and Conventional–Unconventional) define the plane of the field diagram, and the third (Dominant–Submissive) is represented by circle size. Larger circles represent more dominant members, while smaller circles represent less dominant members. Members close together in the plane of the field diagram are drawn closer by vectors of positive valence, while distinct subgroups repel one another via vectors of negative valence. Members positioned at right angles to the central conflict between two subgroups tend to serve as mediators if they lie toward the "friendly" side of the space and as scapegoats if they lie toward the "unfriendly" side of the space. Both have the potential to draw opposing subgroups together, reducing the severity of the conflict.

While field theory has suffered from neglect in the past, there seems to be resurgence of interest. The atheoretical approach to organizational development and action research seems to have run its course, and basic field theoretic constructs are beginning to reemerge.

(SEE ALSO: *Social Psychology*)

REFERENCES

Bales, Robert F. 1985 "The New Field Theory in Social Psychology." *International Journal of Small Group Research* 1:1–18.

Borgatta, Edgar 1963 "A New Systematic Interaction Observation System." *Journal of Psychological Studies* 14:24–44.

Deutsch, Morton 1968 "Field Theory in Social Psychology." In G. Lindzey and E. Aronson, eds., *The Handbook of Social Psychology.* Reading, Mass.: Addison-Wesley.

Dewey, John 1896 "The Reflex Arc Concept in Social Psychology." *Psychological Review* 3:357–370.

Lewin, Kurt 1920 "Die Sozialisierung des Taylorsystems." *Praktischer Sozialismus* 4:5–36.

———1935 *A Dynamic Theory of Personality.* New York: McGraw-Hill.

———1936 *Principles of Topological Psychology.* New York: McGraw-Hill.

———1948 *Resolving Social Conflicts.* New York: Harper.

———1951 *Field Theory in Social Science.* New York: Harper.

Lewin, Kurt, and Ronald Lippitt 1938 "An Experimental Approach to the Study of Autocracy and Democracy: A Preliminary Note." *Sociometry* 1:292–300.

Marrow, Alfred 1969 *The Practical Theorist.* New York: Basic Books.

Mullins, Nicholas C. 1973 *Theories and Theory Groups in Contemporary American Sociology.* New York: Harper and Row.

Polley, Richard B. 1989 "Operationalizing Lewinian Field Theory." In E. Lawler and B. Markovsky, eds., *Advances in Group Process: Theory and Method.* Greenwich, Conn.: JAI Press.

Simmel, Georg 1955 *Conflict and the Web of Group Affiliation,* trans. K. H. Wolf and R. Bendix. New York: Free Press.

Stivers, Eugene, and Susan Wheelan 1986 *The Lewin Legacy.* Berlin: Springer-Verlag.

Weisbord, Marvin R. 1987 *Productive Workplaces.* San Francisco: Jossey-Bass.

RICHARD BRIAN POLLEY

FILIAL RESPONSIBILITY The term *filial responsibility* denotes the "responsibility for parents exercised by children. The term emphasizes duty rather than satisfaction and is usually connected with protection, care, or financial support" (Schorr 1980, p. 1). Although there is popular belief that the obligation of children to care for their parents has origins in antiquity which are based on widely held moral beliefs, both historical and sociological evidence suggests that neither element of this belief is true (Finch 1989; Schorr 1980).

HISTORICAL PATTERNS OF SUPPORT

One source of the persistent belief in both the historical existence of filial responsibility and its moral derivation stems from an equally persistent belief that there was a time in the past when "the family" had a stronger sense of responsibility toward looking after its aging members (Finch 1989). However, a consistent literature on the history of families and demographic trends has emerged that refutes this belief (Laslett 1972). Central to this literature is an understanding of the effects of the demographic transition, medical advances, and changes in social and health practices that have resulted in a significant increase in the numbers of persons living into old age. Together these factors have resulted in dramatic changes in the population structure of modern societies wherein the aging segments account for a significantly higher proportion of the population than ever before. Put simply, until recent history only an extremely small segment of the population survived into an extended and dependent old age (Anderson 1980; Johansson 1977).

Furthermore, as a result of the nature of the preindustrial economy, those persons who did survive into old age were not dependent upon the goodwill or a sense of obligation on the part of their children to assure their financial support. In preindustrial economies both land and businesses that served as the family's source of sustenance were owned by the older generation and passed down to the younger generation only after the older's death. Hence, it was not the older generation who was dependent upon the younger generation; rather, it was the younger generation who was dependent upon the older generation for housing and income. What care may have been provided to parents was therefore not necessarily based on a sense of moral obligation but stemmed from economic necessity (Demos 1978; Schorr 1980).

As long as this economic basis for support existed, there was no need for filial responsibility laws (Schorr 1980; Finch 1989). Only with the introduction of an industrial economy that provided a means for children to leave the parental home and obtain an income was there a need for the community to regulate filial responsibility. Finch (1989, p. 84) notes:

> *Much of the historical evidence . . . suggests that under the harsh conditions of poverty which prevailed for most people in the early industrial period, family relationships necessarily were highly instrumental, with support being offered only if there was . . . hope of mutual benefit precisely because*

anything else would have been an unaffordable luxury.

The shift to an industrial economy changed the financial base of the family and introduced the possibility of children's independent access to financial resources. This shift effectively emphasized the possibility of elders becoming destitute (Bulcroft et al. 1989).

LEGAL MANDATES

Crowther (1982) argues that the legal mandate for filial responsibility which began with the Elizabethan poor laws originated in the need to keep down public expenditure. The poor laws established for the first time in history that the community would help an indigent parent only after the means of his or her child or children had been exhausted (Schorr 1980). The poor laws were not simply laws about poverty; they were laws to govern the lower class in order to keep down public expenditure. This motivation continues to underlie current laws and practices concerning the care of the elderly in both England and the United States, even when legal support for family responsibilities has been presented as a moral matter (Abel 1987; Finch 1989). Despite the moral rhetoric in which filial responsibility laws are often couched, these laws, which currently exist in some form in thirty states, emerged not as a result of moral values but in response to a threat of a growing financial burden that dependent elders posed to an industrial society (Bulcroft et al. 1989).

Perhaps this absence of a moral basis for filial responsibility laws accounts for the inconsistency among states in the statement of filial responsibility and its capricious enforcement (Bulcroft et al. 1989). Filial responsibility laws are variously located in domestic statutes, poor laws, penal codes, and human resource laws. Among the state laws there are variations in the specificity as to which members of the family are responsible and the conditions under which they are responsible. A consistent order does exist, however, that places responsibility first on spouses, second on parents, and third on children. For the most part filial responsibility as incorporated in laws is limited to financial support; and, for the most part, these laws have gone unenforced. Clearly such laws do not account for the prevalence of children as caregivers either in historical or in modern times.

ATTITUDES TOWARD FILIAL RESPONSIBILITIES

Just as the discrepancy between the existence of filial responsibility laws and the lack of their enforcement suggests an equivocal attitude toward children's responsibilities, so results of surveys of attitudes about filial responsibility have been inconsistent. Surveys generally yield respectable percentages of responses favoring filial responsibility as long as the question is limited to ethical and general terms (Schorr 1980). However, when the question is reframed to introduce an individual's own responsibility or to force a choice between the child and other sources of support, a majority of aged persons opposed filial responsibility (Schorr 1980; Sussman 1976). Generally there has been a movement toward acceptance of the government or insurance programs as the source for financial support of the elderly. This trend is witnessed by the introduction of Social Security and Supplemental Security Income. Similarly, adult children and their parents express a preference for independent living arrangements for the two generations.

Current practices of filial responsibility correspond to these expressed preferences. For most families, the flow of financial support between generations is primarily from the older generation to the younger generation and the two generations reside in separate housing units (Sussman 1976; Mindel and Wright 1982). Furthermore, when parents and adult children live together, it is usually as a result of the needs of the younger generation or the mutual benefits for both generations. The situation of a parent moving into the home of an adult child is relatively rare and is usually associated with a need for personal care rather than for housing.

PERSONAL CARE

The most significant change in family roles and filial responsibility practices in recent history has been the assumption by large numbers of adult children of responsibility for the welfare and direct care of their parents. Although the motives that prompt adult children to care for their frail parents are not well understood, the predominance of adult children among informal caregivers is undisputed when all types and levels of assistance are considered (Stone 1987). The prevalence of children as sources of emotional support, assistance with transportation and banking matters, and help with household chores and activities of daily living has been widely documented (Brody 1985; Shanas 1979b).

There is, however, a significant difference between sons and daughters in their caregiving activities and experience. Almost uniformly studies have shown that greater numbers of daughters than of sons assist their parents with a wide range of tasks, and that daughters' predominance is especially strong with respect to direct personal assistance to their impaired parents (Horowitz 1985b; Stone et al. 1987). Daughters are more likely to provide assistance to their parents, and there is a substantial difference in the way in which sons and daughters engage in and are affected by the caregiving role. As a rule, daughters are more likely than sons to help elders with household chores, especially food preparation and laundry, as well as with personal care tasks that require "hands-on" care and daily assistance (Horowitz 1985a; Montgomery and Kamo 1989). In contrast, sons are more likely to perform home repair and maintenance tasks (Coward 1987; Stoller 1990). Indicative of the different types of tasks that sons and daughters tend to assume, daughters spend more hours each week in parent care (Montgomery and Kamo, 1989).

CAREGIVING ROLES

The difference in the types of tasks that sons and daughters perform is related to the types of caregiving roles that the two sexes tend to assume. Daughters are not only more likely to engage in caregiving tasks but also are more likely to assume the role of primary caregiver (Abel 1987; Montgomery and Kamo 1989; Stoller 1990). As such, they are more likely to provide "routine" care over longer periods of time (Matthews and Rosner 1988; Montgomery and Kamo 1989; Stoller 1990). Sons, in contrast, assume supportive roles that require commitments over shorter periods of time and tend to be peripheral helpers within a caregiving network rather than the central actors.

Numerous explanations have been advanced to account for the observed divergence of caregiving behaviors between sons and daughters. Most of these explanations center on differences in male and female roles and differences in power within the family and within society in general (see Finley 1989). However, there is little evidence to support any of the hypothesized explanations, and none of them account for the persistence of parent care activities.

AFFECTION AND OBLIGATION

The relatively recent emergence of the parent care role as it exists in the United States today is most often attributed to the unprecedented size of the elderly population, especially that segment requiring assistance with household and personal tasks (Stone et al. 1987). Yet the physically determined needs of parents for assistance do not fully account for the now widely documented willingness of adult children to assume caregiving roles to meet these needs (Brody 1985; Stone 1987). The persistence of these parent care activities, despite the absence of legal or economic imperatives, has often led researchers and policymakers to focus on affection as the primary source for these filial responsibility practices (Jarrett 1985). Numerous studies have noted the relationship between affection and the felt obligation to provide for parent care (Horowitz 1985b), as well as the importance of attitudes of obligation as correlates of contact with and assistance to parents (Walker et al. 1990).

However, there is a growing literature that

questions the importance of "affection" as the primary force underlying filial responsibility and/or the performance of caregiving tasks (Jarrett 1985). Repeatedly it has been shown that there can be emotional closeness between parent and child without contact or aid being given (Shanas 1979a; Walker et al. 1989). At the same time, it has been demonstrated that children who do not feel great affection for their parents are still able and willing to provide needed assistance (Walker et al. 1989, 1990). Furthermore, there is growing evidence that caregiving is governed by a plurality of motives that encompass both affection and obligation (Walker et al. 1989, 1990). For many children, affection may influence the way in which responsibilities are experienced, but these children frequently provide care simply because parents need it (Leigh 1982) or because children perceive few alternatives (Brody 1985; Birkel and Jones 1989).

SOCIAL POLICY AS A SOURCE

It has been suggested that the lack of alternatives for parent care is due to existing social policy that incorporates assumptions about filial responsibility although it does not necessarily explicitly legislate this responsibility (Abel 1987; Finch 1989; Montgomery and Borgatta 1987). Specifically, as implemented and practiced, policies and programs concerned with services for the elderly in both England and the United States reflect the belief that there is a latent willingness, presumably based upon a residual sense of responsibility that can be activated. This assumption is reinforced in reality by rationing the use of scarce public services and concentrating them upon people who have no relatives providing informal care. It is also evidenced in debates among policymakers and policy analysts regarding the appropriate role of the family in the care of the elderly (Maroney 1980; Callahan et al. 1980).

Taken together, the evidence regarding filial responsibility suggests trends in laws and practice that reflect a decline in expectation for financial support of the elderly while at the same time there is a continued and growing expectation for children, especially daughters, to support parents in more direct ways (Finch 1989). Also, there is an indication that filial responsibility, as practiced in terms of both financial and direct care, stems largely from necessity and is created by social policies and practices that tend to invoke a questionable or mythical moral basis for such responsibility.

(SEE ALSO: *In-Law Relationships; Intergenerational Relations; Intergenerational Resource Transfers*)

REFERENCES

Abel, E. K. 1987 *Love Is Not Enough.* Washington, D.C.: American Public Health Association.

Anderson, M. 1980 *Approaches to the History of the Western Family 1500–1914.* London: Macmillan.

Birkel, R., and C. J. Jones 1989 "A Comparison of the Caregiving Network of Dependent Elderly Individuals Who Are Lucid and Those Who Are Demented." *The Gerontologist* 29, no. 114–119.

Brody, E. M. 1985 "Parent Care as a Normative Family Stress." *The Gerontologist* 25, no. 1:19–29.

Bulcroft, K., J. Van Leynseele, and E. F. Borgatta 1989 "Filial Responsibility Laws." *Research on Aging* 11, no. 3:374–393.

Callahan, J. J., Jr., L. D. Diamond, J. Z. Giele, and R. Morris 1980 "Responsibility of the Family for Their Severely Disabled Elders." *Health Care Financing Review,* 1 (Winter):29–48.

Coward, R. T. 1987 "Factors Associated with the Configuration of the Helping Networks of Noninstitutionalized Elders." *Journal of Gerontological Social Work* 10:113–132.

Crowther, M. A. 1982 "Family Responsibility and State Responsibility in Britain Before the Welfare State." *Historical Journal* 25, no. 1:131–145.

Demos, J. 1978 "Old Age in Early New England." In J. Demos and S. Boocock, eds., *Turning Points.* Chicago: University of Chicago Press.

Finch, J. 1989 *Family Obligations and Social Change.* Cambridge: Polity Press and Basil Blackwell.

Finley, N. J. 1989 "Theories of Family Labor as Applied to Gender Differences in Caregiving for Elderly Parents." *Journal of Marriage and the Family* 51, no. 1:79–86.

Gilligan, C. 1982 *In a Different Voice.* Cambridge, Mass.: Harvard University Press.

Horowitz, A. 1985a "Family Caregiving to the Frail Elderly." *Annual Review of Gerontology and Geriatrics* 6:194–246.

——— 1985b "Sons and Daughters as Caregivers to Older Parents: Differences in Role Performance and Consequences." *The Gerontologist* 25, no. 6:612–617.

Jarrett, W. H. 1985 "Caregiving Within Kinship Systems: Is Affection Really Necessary?" *The Gerontologist* 25, no. 1:5–10.

Johansson, S. R. 1977 "Sex and Death in Victorian England: An Examination of Age- and Sex-Specific Death Rates 1840–1910." In M. Vicinus, ed., *A Widening Sphere: Changing Roles of Victorian Women.* London: Methuen.

Laslett, P. 1972 "Introduction: The History of the Family." In P. Laslett and R. Wall, eds., *Household and Family in the Past Time.* Cambridge: Cambridge University Press.

Leigh, G. K. 1982 "Kinship Interaction over the Family Life Span." *Journal of Marriage and the Family* 44, no. 1:197–208.

Maroney, R. M. 1980 *Families, Social Services and Social Policy: The Issue of Shared Responsibility.* Washington, D.C.: Department of Health and Human Services, U.S. Government Printing Office.

Matthews, S. H., and T. T. Rosner 1988 "Shared Filial Responsibility: The Family as the Primary Caregiver." *Journal of Marriage and the Family* 50:185–195.

Mindel, C. H., and R. Wright, Jr. 1982 "Satisfaction in Multigenerational Households." *Journal of Gerontology* 37, no. 4:483–489.

Montgomery, R. J. V., and Edgar F. Borgatta 1987 "Aging Policy and Societal Values." In Borgatta and Montgomery, eds., *Critical Issues in Aging Policy: Linking Research and Values.* Newbury Park, Calif.: Sage.

Montgomery, R. J. V., and Y. Kamo 1989 "Parent Care by Sons and Daughters." In J. A. Mancini, ed., *Aging Parents and Adult Children.* Lexington, Mass.: Lexington Books/D. C. Heath.

Schorr, A. L. 1980 *Thy Father and Thy Mother . . . A Second Look at Filial Responsibility and Family Policy.* Social Security Administration Publication No. 13–11953. Washington, D.C.: U.S. Government Printing Office.

Shanas, E. 1979 "The Family as a Social Support System in Old Age." *The Gerontologist* 19, no. 2:169–174.

Stoller, E. P. 1990 "Males as Helpers: The Role of Sons, Relatives, and Friends." *The Gerontologist* 30, no. 2:228–235.

Stone, R. 1987 *Exploding the Myths: Caregiving in America.* Select Committee on Aging, House of Representatives, Publication No. 99–611. Washington, D.C.: U.S. Government Printing Office.

———, G. Cafferata, and J. Sangl 1987 "Caregivers of the Frail Elderly: A National Profile." *The Gerontologist* 27:616–626.

Sussman, M. 1976 "The Family Life of Old People." In R. H. Binstock and E. Shanas, eds., *Handbook of Aging and the Social Sciences.* New York: Van Nostrand Reinhold.

Walker, A. J., C. C. Pratt, H. Y. Shin, and L. L. Jones 1989 "Why Daughters Care: Perspectives of Mothers and Daughters in a Caregiving Situation." In J. A. Mancini, ed., *Aging Parents and Adult Children.* Lexington, Mass.: Lexington Books/D. C. Heath.

———, 1990 "Motives for Parental Caregiving and Relationship Quality." *Family Relations* 39, no. 1: 51–56.

RHONDA J. V. MONTGOMERY

FRENCH SOCIOLOGY In France, just as elsewhere, all classical domains of sociology can be found, but French sociology differs in the high priority it places on seeking to reveal, through a scientific approach, the general functioning of society. In a phrase, French sociology aims to produce a theory of society. This quest for theory, shared for example with Parsons, can be partly explained by a direct descendence from Durkheim, but it is also due to the very recent professionalization of sociology in France, dating back no further than 1960. Current French sociological theoreticians have a philosophical background and have not quite forgotten their original discipline.

There are three French theoreticians whose work well describes this type of French sociology: Raymond Boudon, Pierre Bourdieu, and Alain Touraine. However, their work cannot be comprehensively presented here since they have evolved and focused on many sociological domains. What follows is a representative, albeit incomplete, idea of their mode of thought.

RAYMOND BOUDON: METHODOLOGICAL INDIVIDUALISM

Boudon's individualism, borrowed from the field of economics, is fundamentally methodological, with its roots in the theory of rational behavior. His fundamental guiding idea is that if a person does something, he or she has good reason to do so. If an observer believes that a person does something because it is a custom or a habit, or because the person is not aware of his own hidden interests, then, Boudon believes, there is a high risk of ethnocentricity, that is, the observer's own set of rationalities is, in the end, substituted for that of the subject, or, in a far too facile way, the observer is masking his or her own intellectual laziness.

Boudon has on different occasions (1984; 1986) used the following example. In the view of some observers, a society like India's is easily characterized by general social principles that take into consideration the fixity of various behaviors. Some see India as the model of hierarchical society, and this alone could sufficiently explain its resistance to change. But this is a generalization soon proven inadequate when the consequences of concrete attempts to modernize established practices are examined.

If we look closely at the effects of introducing irrigation in southern Indian villages, we notice that they are ambiguous. Some cultural characteristics are reinforced, while others are altered, and such effects can be seen as the result of rational behavior.

An example of a modified traditional characteristic is son–father dependence, which has been weakened to a certain extent. This situation is explained by the fact that sugar cane produced on irrigated land is purchased by the administration, which has implemented a quota system in order to prevent overproduction. The adaptation of a family's rational behavior to this situation is a reversal of old practices. Traditionally, fathers delayed ceding their land to descendants in order that the land could remain viable for the longest possible time. Given the new scenario, it is more reasonable to cede land to sons as soon as possible so as to increase the production quota permitted by the administration. It is obvious that this new procedure is not without its own effects on the relationship between children and their parents and in fact puts distance between them, which is contrary to tradition.

Conversely, the material impossibility of dividing up the land into too many parcels means that some sons have to be sent to work in the towns, from which they send home modest but non-negligible income. Given that this source of revenue is directly proportional to the number of children per family, the strategy of an extended family is reinforced by technological change. Thus, to suggest that the permanence of extended families is due to the weight of tradition reveals ignorance of the real situation.

This is a typical example of Boudon's reasoning. His examples are always selected on the basis of the same two criteria: their explanatory coherence and their polemic nature. The author wants to show that other French theoreticians, in particular Bourdieu and Touraine, favor theories that presume what he calls a "hypersocialized" conception of human beings, in which the individual is the pure expression of the sociocultural environment (criticism aimed at Bourdieu), or in which the individual is subjected to the decisive impact of social movements essential to the dynamics of society (aimed at Touraine).

PIERRE BOURDIEU: THE RULES OF THE GAME REVEALED

Whether or not one is of the same mind as Pierre Bourdieu, he has had an incontestable impact in France and elsewhere. The best proof of this has been his election, as a sociologist, to the most prestigious French academic institution, the Collège de France.

The social impact of Bourdieu's theories can easily be explained by the fact that in the opinion of many, in particular teachers, he revealed that social openness was only appearance and that the rules of the social game were understood and used correctly only by the privileged few who had established these rules, even if they did not realize it themselves. He thus liberated many people who believed barriers to their own social advancement were due to their personal lack of skill or talent and who, thanks to Bourdieu, discovered that what they really lacked was inside information and social contacts.

Bourdieu's first book (coauthored by Jean-Claude Passeron), which had a considerable social impact, focused on students (1964). In this work, he shows that most students come from the upper classes and that teaching, especially that of the arts, is based on the culture of the privileged classes, which constitutes the natural environment for these students from birth. What is taught, therefore, is not *savoir-faire,* but *savoir-vivre.* A student from a poor social background is not born into this upbringing, and such a student's apprenticeship is a struggle since it is informal, unspoken, and undeclared. Officially, if people do not succeed, it is because they are not "gifted," while in reality these gifts are only a reflection of a privileged social background where much is inherent knowledge.

The subjects of this book, the "inheritors," have more or less become part and parcel of normal academic baggage, and many people are in fact unaware that the term *cultural heritage,* which is today taken for granted, was originally coined in this work (and in that of Basil Berstein).

In Bourdieu's view, the sociologist's role must be that defined by Durkheim: Given that every society has a preconceived and inaccurate idea of its own functioning (Durkheimian pre-notion), scientific work consists of inducing a break of critical force. In the case of students: "The unmasking of cultural privilege destroys the justificatory ideology which enables the privileged classes, the main users of the educational system, to see their success as the confirmation of natural, personal gifts. Since the ideology of the gift is based essentially on blindness to social inequalities in schooling and culture, mere description of the relationship between academic success and social origin has a critical force."

Through this revelation, a scientific as well as a political work is created. In demonstrating that what seems "natural" in society is in fact the fruit of a socially created phenomenon, we increase our knowledge of society and simultaneously enable those who were excluded from the game to participate by discovering the real rules.

Since the mid-1960s, Bourdieu's theory, via the publication of many books and a review called *Les actes de la recherche en sciences sociales,* has developed in two areas. First, in the case of previously explored territory, a fair part of the social universe has been the subject of research and theory: forms of social classification (social classes, age classes, and sex classification, for example), artists, the Catholic church, doctors, lawyers, academics, athletes, the use of speech, and so forth. Second, in relation to the elaboration of theoretical instruments, Bourdieu believes the task is particularly difficult since any social group resists revealing its true internal functioning. Before this information can be disclosed, a solid basis of rigorous technical competence must be acquired to ensure scientific validity. Following are the concepts Bourdieu has elaborated over time.

Habitus. The medieval concept of *habitus* is reused to demonstrate the paradox by which, without explicit knowledge of the real rules of society, some actors are apt to play an efficient role while others are not. In fact, the capable ones have, since birth, received essential practical training that enables them to find the right response in different situations. Taking again the founding example of the "inheritors," the coherence between university teaching and the habitus of the privileged classes permits members of the latter to integrate philosophy or the arts with their prior cultural inheritance, derived from attending all kinds of artistic presentations and regular discussions on art or politics.

In a wider sense, habitus describes an individual's socially acquired capacity that endows him or her with the potential automatically to make the right move at the right time. In other words, it is as if an immediate and appropriate response to a given situation was natural. Bourdieu often uses the idea of a game because it clearly shows that, although practical acts can be the fruit of a long apprenticeship, this does not prevent them from being, at the right moment in time, an "instinctive" response. Such social training, which a group passes on to its members, once acquired in the form of a habitus, seems quite natural and enables the right choices to be made in all circumstances. The "right choices" are those, of course, that conform to the group's culture (its ethos).

Cultural and Symbolic Capital. The "inheritors" receive "cultural capital" from their families, that is, knowledge and information that become virtually natural to them and whose absence during studies can be a handicap to those who do not come from privileged backgrounds. This is the same as the habitus referred to above, but cultural capital may also be legitimized, or made official, with an academic diploma.

Bourdieu speaks of noneconomic capital in an attempt to point out that actors, active in different social domains, are led to mobilize different types of resources, including their economic capital, but also other qualities that seem to enjoy an equivalent status, thus also warranting the label *capital.* For example, Bourdieu noted in his ethnological research in Kabylie (Algeria) that a marriage evokes economic considerations as well as those of honor, reputation, and prestige, which he refers to as "symbolic capital." In our societies, economic, cultural, and symbolic capital can be grouped together under the same concept of capital in that, on the one hand, they are the object of an investment, but, on the other hand, they are also the object of profitability. Moreover, in some cases, they can be exchanged or used as equivalencies. High academic capital can have financial worth, given that a diploma can help a person earn higher wages, while high economic capital can also be a source of prestige.

Investments vary according to the different domains in which they are active. Bourdieu calls these domains *fields.*

Fields. Social actors belong to several areas of society, and their strategies in a given field are related to the balance of power that regulates and, at the same time, defines the field. Bourdieu has studied several of these fields, first and foremost, education, then art, then various others such as cultural production, power, economics, universities, literature, religion, and science. In each of these cases, by disassembling the balance of power regulating a specific field, Bourdieu puts a stop to the fake transparence that gives the impression of "natural" social divisions. For example, in the scientific field, membership in a group imposes a specific paradigmatic vision of reality, but the symbolic capital available to members of the group means a different rationality could be made available. On first appraisal, this may seem paradoxical, as "rationality" should be accepted of itself and should not have to be "imposed."

The complex relationships described above (habitus, cultural and symbolic capital, and fields) permit, in a given area, to destroy natural truths, and to substitute them with a more rigorous description which will show the effects of domination and classification, as well as of taste, attitude, and behavior. This analysis makes it possible to study strategies, oppositions, and conflicts within a stable society (synchrony). Touraine, however, is more concerned with what brings about in-depth changes in society (diachrony).

ALAIN TOURAINE: SOCIAL MOVEMENTS

For many years, Touraine developed theories of social structure (1965; 1969; 1973; 1974), but in his more recent work (1984) some earlier theoretical elements have lost their importance, and the accent is on social movements.

Of these three theoreticians, Touraine seems to be the closest to political and social action, given his numerous public appearances and more fundamentally the relationship between his theory and his analysis of the social role attributed to sociological analysis. In his view, the state of our societies is not characterized principally by being postmodern but by being postindustrial. While the ideology of the Enlightenment and its faith in rationality has been shaken by the bloody developments of our century (thus robbing modernity of its role as an ideal), technical rationality still has an effect on society. In the past, it enabled society to produce (the industrial society). Today it helps society control its social reproduction by an ever-growing command, not only over material aspects, but also over social organizational aspects themselves.

This new power gives human beings the ability to affect the course of history, and Touraine calls this effect *historicity*. But the control of this power is obviously in the hands of the ruling classes, who easily manage to have their interests—their cultural models—identified as those of society as a whole.

If the fruit of modernity is having abolished all the metasocial guarantors of society (divinity, providence, or tradition), the control of society's investments for its own future, of its choices made by those who govern it, can be contested only by social groups capable of proposing alternative possibilities for development. Touraine and the researchers who work with him have devoted most of their work to the study of these social movements. This work has led them to develop research methods, similar to participant observation, that have been applied to a certain number of concrete cases: the workers' movement, the antinuclear movement, the French regional Occitan movement, and the Polish Solidarity movement. Through his work, Touraine has attempted to participate actively in the struggle against technical, bureaucratic ideology, which contributes to the establishment of absolute power.

Even if these three most important theoreticians of contemporary French sociology do not agree with each other, similarities between them emerge when they are placed in comparative perspective. Boudon and Bourdieu both react against earlier Marxist social or structural-functional theories. This leads them both to take into account the social individual, including the individual's interests and strategies, and to demonstrate concretely how the interaction between the individual and society occurs. They differ in that Boudon considers the higher level to be a result of an aggregation of individual acts, while Bourdieu's individual incorporates attitudes that are inevitable due to his situation in a given field. Since the actor is also a feature of Touraine's research (1984), we can see that this emphasis on the social individual plays a dominant role in French sociology today, a product indeed of individualist and neoliberal trends.

It would be dangerous, however, to use this association between these theoreticians and their era to criticize them. If in a given age the accent is placed on an aspect that clearly corresponds to a social demand, there remains the overall theoretical contribution, which remains a vast edifice. It would be illusory to judge these contributions on the basis of the few elements proposed here.

REFERENCES

Ansart, Pierre 1990 *Les sociologies contemporaines.* Paris: Le Seuil.

Boudon, Raymond 1973 *L'inégalité des chances.* Paris: Armand Colin.

——— 1977 *Effet pervers et ordre social.* Paris: Presses Universitaires de France.

——— 1979 *La logique du social.* Paris: Hachette.

——— 1984 *La place du désordre.* Paris: Presses Universitaires de France.

——— 1986 "Individualisme et holisme dans les sciences sociales." In Pierre Birnbaum and Jean Leca, *Sur l'individualisme.* Paris: Presses de la Fondation nationale des sciences politiques.

Bourdieu, Pierre 1979 *La distinction, critique sociale du jugement.* Paris: Editions de Minuit.

——— 1980 *Le sens pratique.* Paris: Editions de Minuit.

——— 1980 *Questions de sociologie.* Paris: Editions de Minuit.

——— 1982 *Ce que parler veut dire.* Paris: Fayard.

——— 1984 *Homo academicus.* Paris: Editions de Minuit.

——— 1987 *Choses dites.* Paris: Editions de Minuit.

——— 1989 *La noblesse d'état.* Paris: Editions de Minuit.

———, Jean-Claude Chamboredon, and Jean-Claude Passeron 1968 *Le métier de sociologue.* Paris: Mouton-Bordas.

———, and Jean-Claude Passeron 1964 *Les héritiers.* Paris: Editions de Minuit. Translated by Richard Nice, under the title *The Inheritors.* Chicago: University of Chicago Press, 1979.

Durand, Jean-Pierre, and Robert Weil 1989 *Sociologie contemporaine.* Paris: Vigot.

Touraine, Alain 1965 *La sociologie de l'action.* Paris: Le Seuil.

——— 1969 *La société post-industrielle.* Paris: Denoël.

——— 1973 *Production de la société.* Paris: Le Seuil.

——— 1974 *Pour la sociologie.* Paris: Le Seuil.

——— 1984 *Le retour de l'acteur.* Paris: Fayard.

———, F. Dubet, M. Wieviorka, and J. Strzelecki 1982 *Solidarité.* Paris: Le Seuil.

———, Z. Hegedus, F. Dubet, and M. Wieviorka 1980 *La prophétie antinucléaire.* Paris: Le Seuil.

———, M. Wieviorka, and F. Dubet 1984 *Le mouvement ouvrier.* Paris: Fayard.

PHILIPPE CIBOIS
KARL M. VAN METER
LISE MOUNIER
MARIE-ANGE SCHILTZ

Groupe Méthodologie Sociologique, Paris

FUNCTIONALISM Functional theorizing in sociology emerged in the nineteenth century as the result of an analogy: Society is like a biological organism, and, hence, its parts can be analyzed in terms of their functions for maintaining the "body social." Analogies of this kind had a long tradition —beginning as early as the Greeks, moving through early Christianity and the limited scholarship of the Middle Ages, to the organismic imagery of Hobbes and Rousseau—but it was Auguste Comte (1830–1842, 1851–1854) who explicitly welded organismic analogies to sociology. According to Comte, there is a "true correspondence between Statical Analysis of the Social Organism in Sociology, and that of the Individual Organism in Biology" (1851–1854, p. 239). Moreover, Comte went so far as to "decompose structure anatomically into *elements, tissues,* and *organs*" (1851–1854, p. 240) and to "treat the Social Organism as definitely composed of the Families which are the true elements or cells, next the Classes or Castes which are its proper tissues, and lastly, of the cities and Communes which are its real organs" (pp. 211–212). Yet, since these analogies were not systematically pursued by Comte, his main contribution was to give sociology its name and to reintroduce organismic reasoning into the new science of society.

It was Herbert Spencer who used the organismic analogy to create an explicit form of functional analysis. Drawing upon materials from his monumental *The Principles of Biology* (1864–1867), Spencer's *The Principles of Sociology* (1874–1896) is filled with analogies between organisms and society as well as between ecological processes (variation, competition, and selection) and societal evolution (which he saw as driven by war). Spencer did not see society as an actual organism; rather, he conceptualized "super-organic systems" (organization of organisms) as revealing certain similarities in their "principles of arrangement" to biological organisms (1874–1896, part 2, pp. 451–462). In so doing, he introduced the notion of "functional requisites" or "needs," thereby creating functionalism. For Spencer, there were three basic requisites of superorganic systems: (1) the need to secure and circulate resources, (2) the need to produce usable substances, and (3) the need to regulate, control, and administer system activities (1874–1896, part 2, p. 477). Thus, any pattern of social organization reveals these three classes of functional requisites, and the goal of sociological analysis is to see how these needs are met in empirical social systems.

Later functionalists produced somewhat different lists of requisites. Emile Durkheim argued that sociological explanations "must seek separately the efficient cause (of a phenomenon)—and the function it fulfills" (1895, p. 96), but, in contrast to Spencer, he posited only one functional requisite: the need for social integration. For Durkheim, then, sociological analysis would involve assessment of the causes of phenomena and their consequences or functions for meeting the needs of social structures for integration.

Were it not for the activities of theoretically oriented anthropologists, functionalism probably would have died with Durkheim, especially since Spencer's star had faded by World War I (Turner and Turner 1990). As the traditional societies studied by early anthropologists were generally without a written history, anthropologists were confronted with the problem of explaining the existence of activities and structures in these societies. The explanatory problem became particularly acute in the post-World War I period with the demise of evolutionism and diffusionism as deciphering tools (Turner and Maryanski 1979). Functional analysis provided a novel alternative: Analyze structures such as kinship or activities such as rituals in terms of their functions for maintaining the society. It was A. R. Radcliffe-Brown (1914, 1935, 1952) who sustained the Durkheimian tradition by emphasizing the importance of integrative needs and then analyzing how structures—most notably kinship systems—operate to meet such integrative requisites. In contrast, Bronislaw Malinowski (1913, 1944) extended functional analysis in a more Spencerian direction, emphasizing that there are distinct system levels (biological, social, and cultural), each of which reveals its own distinctive requisites. Extending Spencer and anticipating Talcott Parsons, Malinowski (1944) posited four basic requisites at the social system level: (1) production and distribution; (2) social control and regulation; (3) education and socialization; and (4) organization and integration.

Thus, functionalism was carried to the midpoint of the twentieth century by anthropological work. Yet, during the 1930s, a group of Harvard sociologists—led by a graduate student, Robert Merton (1949)—began thinking about functional analysis, especially as it had been carried forth by Radcliffe-Brown and Malinowski (Turner and Maryanski 1979). As a result, many of Merton's fellow students became the leading figures in the revival of functionalism in sociology. This revival began with Kingsley Davis's and Wilbert Moore's classic article on "Some Principles of Stratification" (1945), followed by Davis's basic text, *Human Societies* (1948), and a variety of articles and books by others listing the "functional requisites" of societies (e.g., Levy 1952). But it was Talcott Parsons, a young Harvard instructor during Merton's tenure as a graduate student, who was to become the arch-functionalist of modern times (Parsons 1951; Parsons, Bales, and Shils 1953). For Parsons, the social universe was conceptualized in terms of four distinct types and levels of "action systems" (culture, social, personality, and organismic/behavioral), with each system having to meet the same four functional needs: (1) adaptation (securing and distributing environmental resources); (2) goal attainment (mobilizing resources to goals or ends); (3) integration (coordinating system parts); and (4) latency (managing tensions within parts and generating new parts). The operation and interchanges of structures and processes within and between system levels were then analyzed with respect to these basic requisites.

As functional theorizing became dominant in American theory in the 1950s and 1960s, criticism escalated. Opposition came from several different quarters and took a number of distinctive lines of attack. From interactionist theorizing came criticism about functionalism's failure to conceptualize adequately the nature of actors and the process of interaction (Blumer 1969); from Marxist-inspired theory, which was just emerging from the academic closets in the post-McCarthy era, came attacks on the conservative and static nature of analysis that emphasized the functions of phenomena for maintaining the status quo (e.g., Dahrendorf 1958; Coser 1956; Mills 1959); from theory construction advocates came questions about the utility of excessively classificatory or typological theories that pigeonholed phenomena in terms of their functions (e.g., Merton 1957, pp. 44–61); and from philosophers and logicians came questions about tautology and illegitimate teleology in explanations that saw phenomena as meeting needs and needs as generating phenomena (e.g., Dore 1961). The result was the decline of functional theorizing in the early 1970s.

In the 1980s, however, functional theorizing was revived under what is sometimes termed "neofunctionalism" (Alexander 1985; Alexander and Colomy 1985). Neofunctionalism is a label for diverse kinds of activity, however. Some who labor under the neofunctionalist umbrella are unrepentant functionalists, usually of Parsonian persuasion, who analyze phenomena in terms of specific functional requisites (e.g., Münch 1982); others downplay functional requisites and examine a variety of phenomena, although the agenda is often the same as early functional theory, revolving around conceptualizations of social differentiation, integration, and social evolution (e.g., Luhmann 1982); and still others stress cultural processes and the functions of ritual, ideology, and values for integrating social structures (e.g., Wuthnow 1987). In most cases, the functionalism—that is, concern with how phenomena meet or fail to meet system needs—is deemphasized, often making neofunctionalism somewhat nonfunctional (Turner and Maryanski 1988).

Functional theorizing has not only generated critics, who then used their criticism to launch or sustain alternative perspectives; it has also served as a source of inspiration for approaches that have lost much of their functional character. These perspectives are all derived from Durkheim's more muted functionalism and can be grouped under the label "structuralist" theorizing.

In Durkheim's (1893, 1895) earlier work, he implicitly borrowed Comte's distinction between statics and dynamics, although Durkheim conceptualized social statics in Montesquieu terms as social "morphology." Static or morphological analysis was seen to involve an assessment of the "nature," "number," "interrelations," and "arrangement" of parts in a systemic whole (Durkheim 1895, p. 85). For Durkheim, sociological explanation still sought to discover "cause" and "function," but the basic structural units of sociological analysis—that is, the "things" that are caused and functioning—are to be classified by "the nature and number of the component elements and their mode of combination" (Durkheim 1895, p. 81). British structuralism, as it evolved into modern day social network analysis, was to stay very close to this materialist conceptualization of structure, whereas French structuralism, as it developed into a broad intellectual movement, was to turn Durkheim on his head and posit a more mentalistic view of structure (although key scholars like Lévi-Strauss emphasized a universal material base, lodged in the biochemistry of the human brain).

French structuralism stood Durkheim on his head through Claude Lévi-Strauss's (1945a, [1949] 1969, 1963) adoption of ideas in less sociologically prominent works by Durkheim and his nephew, Marcel Mauss. In Durkheim's "Incest: The Nature and Origin of the Taboo" (1898) as well as his and Mauss's *Primitive Classification* (1903), emphasis shifts to the origins and functions of rules of exogamy for human classification systems and modes of symbolic thought. For Durkheim and Mauss, the way that humans cognitively perceive and classify this world reflects the morphological or material structure of society (nature, number, arrangement, and combination of parts). In developing this argument, which Durkheim repeats in less extreme form in *Elementary Forms of the Religious Life* (1912), Durkheim and Mauss posit all the basic elements of Lévi-Strauss's (1963) structuralism. First, although societies differ in their evolutionary development, they are all fundamentally similar because they are based upon the same "underlying principles" (Durkheim and Mauss [1903] 1963, p. 74), and these principles provide individuals with a basis for classifying and constructing their universe. Second, "mythology" is a universal method of classification. Third, such classification systems represent "relations of things" to each other and "are thus intended, above all, to connect ideas, to unify knowledge" (p. 81). Fourth, classification systems are, in essence, created by oppositions in the material social world—sacred–profane, pure–impure, friends–enemies, favorable–unfavorable.

This last idea, which Lévi-Strauss was to conceptualize as "binary oppositions," is carried further by Mauss (in collaboration with Henri Beuchat) in *Seasonal Variations of the Eskimo: A Study in Social Morphology* ([1904–1905] 1979) where the sharp dualisms of Eskimo life are outlined, as these are created by the seasonal nature of Eskimo activities. Later, in *The Gift* ([1925] 1941), Mauss reasserts Durkheim's earlier conclusion that activity, such as the famous Kwakiutl potlatch, is a surface exchange reflecting a "deeper" and "more complex" underlying structure in which gifts symbolize and assure the continuation of social relations among diverse groups.

Lévi-Strauss regarded *The Gift* as the inauguration of a new era in the social sciences and saw Mauss as a new Moses "conducting his people all the way to a promised land whose splendour he would never behold" (Lévi-Strauss [1950] 1987, pp. 41–45). Following directly in Mauss's footsteps, Lévi-Strauss ennobled the concept of exchange as a "total social phenomena" by arguing in his first major work, "The Elementary Structures of Kinship," that a "principle of reciprocity" is the most general and universal property of society, with the exchange of women as the most fundamental expression of this principle (Lévi-Strauss [1949] 1969, pp. 60–62).

Yet, it is doubtful that these ideas alone would produce structuralism. Two other scholars are critical to Lévi-Strauss's transmutation of Durkheim and Mauss. One is Robert Hertz, a young member of Durkheim's "Année School." Before his death in World War I, Hertz produced a number of essays, the two best known being published in *Death and the Right Hand* ([1909] 1960). In this work, Hertz continues the Durkheim/Mauss theme of the duality in the structure of society and documents how this is reflected in ideas about society (myths, classifications, and other "representations"), but the imagery is much more like modern structuralism in that the goal of inquiry is (1) to show the meaning of observed facts in their interrelations, and (2) to uncover the underlying structural principles beneath the surface of such observed phenomena.

The final and perhaps most critical influence on Lévi-Strauss's reversal of Durkheim is the Swiss linguist Ferdinand de Saussure ([1915] 1966), whose lectures, posthumously published under the title *Course in General Linguistics,* serve as the pioneering and authoritative work for modern-day structural linguistics. De Saussure appears to have influenced Lévi-Strauss indirectly through Nikolai Trubetzkoi ([1949] 1964; 1968) and Roman Jakobson (1962; 1971), but they simply extend Saussure's key insight that language is a system whose units—whether sounds or morphemes—are only points in an overall structure. Moreover, while speech (*parole*) can be directly observed, it reflects an underlying system or language structure (*langue*), and, thus, it is critical to use *parole* to discover the *langue.*

In Lévi-Strauss's hands, this combined legacy was to produce French structuralism. At times, Lévi-Strauss is critical of Durkheim, but he concludes in the end that Durkheim's work "is an inspiration" (Lévi-Strauss 1945b, p. 522) and that "the entire purpose of the French school lies in an attempt to break up the categories of the layman, and to group the data into a deeper, sounder classification" (Lévi-Strauss 1945b, pp. 524–525). In early work such as *The Elementary Structures of Kinship* (Lévi-Strauss [1949] 1969), there is a clear debt to Durkheim and Mauss as Lévi-Strauss seeks to uncover the underlying principles (such as "reciprocity") of bridal exchanges, but soon he turns to the methods of structural linguistics and sees surface social structures (Durkheim's "morphology") as reflecting a more fundamental reality, lodged in the human unconscious and biochemistry of the human brain and involving "rules and principles" to organize "binary oppositions" that are used to create empirically observable patterns of social reality (Lévi-Strauss 1953). But these empirical patterns (e.g., myths, beliefs, kinship structures) are not the "really real" structure; they are like *parole* is to *langue,* a reflection of a deeper structural reality of which existing phenomena are only the surface realizations.

This mode of thought has stimulated a widespread structuralist movement in such fields as linguistics, anthropology, and literary analysis, but within sociology its impact has been diverse, stimulating concern with textual analysis of works (Barthes 1972; Lamont and Wuthnow 1990), with assertions that "society is text" (e.g., Brown 1987), with processes of "structuring" and "structuration" out of elementary rules and codes (Giddens 1984), with various brands of neofunctionalism and cultural analysis (Wuthnow 1987), and with a new relativism that is used to attack the scientific pretensions of sociology (Lemert 1990).

In contrast, British structuralism sustains the materialist and scientific emphasis of the early Durkheim. The key figure is A. R. Radcliffe-Brown, who, in his early research on the Andaman Islanders, employed Durkheimian analysis, especially the emphasis on structure and the functions of rituals that sustain the integration of such structure (Radcliffe-Brown [1914] 1922). While still a graduate student under the guidance of his mentors, A. C. Haddon and W. H. R. Rivers, the young Radcliffe-Brown became an advocate of the Durkheimian school. During his tenure among the Andamanese Islanders, he rejected the historical approach and took up the French functional method. As he comments:

> *Every custom and belief of a primitive society plays some determinate part in the social life of the community, just as every organ of a living body plays some part in the general life of the organism. . . . The life of a society is not less real, or less subject to natural laws, than the life of an organism* ([1914] 1922, pp. 229–230).

In later works, as these grew out of his analysis of kinship structures (Radcliffe-Brown 1924), he increasingly became concerned with theoretical questions, leading him to create structural functionalism with more emphasis on the nature of structure. For example, he argued that "the concept of function . . . involves the notion of a structure consisting of a set of relations among unit entities, the continuity of the structure being maintained by a life-process made up of the *activities* of the constituent units" (1935, p. 396). Indeed, Radcliffe-Brown was so perplexed by Lévi-Strauss's transformation of Durkheim's functionalism that he wrote to Lévi-Strauss, asserting "for you, social structure has nothing to do with reality but with models that are built up, I regard the social structure as a reality" (Murdock 1953, p. 109).

Following Radcliffe-Brown, S. F. Nadel (1957) retained both Durkheim's (1895) emphasis on "nature, number, and arrangement of parts" and Radcliffe-Brown's view of structure as a social reality made up of "sets of relations amongst unit entities," but at the same time he sought to give more precision to the concepts of entities, units, and relations while integrating them with role theory. In so doing, he initiated the British tradition (e.g., Mitchell 1974) in what we would now term "network analysis." This early tradition was paralleled in the United States by Jacob Moreno's (1953) sociometry, by early studies of communication processes (e.g., Leavitt 1951), and by the use of graph theory to represent social structure (e.g., Cartwright and Harary 1956). Today, the American and British traditions are merged; and while the American branch never drew much inspiration from Durkheimian functionalism, the major inspiration for the British side has been the Durkheimian view of morphology as it was initially preserved in anthropology by Radcliffe-Brown.

In sum, then, functionalism and structuralism are more connected, intellectually and historically, than is commonly recognized. For during the rise of functionalism, and then during its domination in the 1950s and early 1960s, as well as its critical flogging in the late 1960s and 1970s and resurrection as neofunctionalism in the 1980s, two offspring of functionalism were produced, each growing in influence and, in the long run, each likely to be more influential than functionalism ever was.

(SEE ALSO: *Scientific Explanation; Social Stratification*)

REFERENCES

Alexander, Jeffrey C. (ed.) 1985 *Neofunctionalism.* Beverly Hills, Calif.: Sage.

———, and Paul Colomy 1985 "Toward Neofunctionalism." *Sociological Theory* 3:11–32.

Barthes, Roland 1972 *Mythologies.* New York: Hill and Wang.

Blumer, Herbert 1969 *Symbolic Interaction: Perspective and Method.* Englewood Cliffs, N.J.: Prentice-Hall.

Brown, Richard 1987 *Society as Text: Essays on Rhetoric, Reason, and Reality.* Chicago: University of Chicago Press.

Cartwright, Dorin, and Frank Harary 1956 "Structural Balance: A Generalization of Heider's Theory." *Psychological Review* 63:277–293.

Comte, Auguste 1830–1842 *Cours de Philosophie Positive,* 5 vols., Paris: Bachelier.

——— 1851–1854 *Système de Politique: ou, Traité de Sociologie, Instituant la Religion de L'Humanité.* Paris: L. Mathias.

Coser, Lewis A. 1956 *The Functions of Social Conflict.* London: Free Press.

Dahrendorf, Ralf 1958 "Out of Utopia: Toward a Reorientation of Sociological Analysis." *American Journal of Sociology* 74 (September):115–127.

Davis, Kingsley 1948 *Human Societies.* New York: Macmillan.

———, and Wilbert Moore 1945 "Some Principles of Stratification." *American Sociological Review* 4: 431–442.

Dore, Phillip Ronald 1961 "Function and Cause." *American Sociological Review* 26:843–853.

Durkheim, Emile 1893 *The Division of Labor in Society.* New York: Free Press.

——— 1895 *The Rules of the Sociological Method.* New York: Free Press.

——— 1898 "Incest: The Nature and Origin of the Taboo." *Année Sociologique* 1:1–70.

——— 1912 *Elementary Forms of the Religious Life.* New York: Macmillan.

———, and Marcell Mauss. (1903) 1963 *Primitive Classification.* London: Cohen and West.

Giddens, Anthony 1984 *The Constitution of Society: Outline of the Theory of Structuration.* Berkeley: University of California Press.

Hertz, Robert (1909) 1960 *Death and the Right Hand.* London: Cohen and West.

Jakobson, Roman 1962 *Selected Writings I: Phonological Studies.* The Hague: Mouton.

——— 1971 *Selected Writings II: Word and Language.* The Hague: Mouton.

Lamont, Michèle, and Robert Wuthnow 1990 "Betwixt and Between: Recent Cultural Sociology in Europe and the United States." In G. Ritzer, ed., *Frontiers of Social Theory.* New York: Columbia University Press.

Leavitt, Harold J. 1951 "Some Effects of Certain Communication Patterns on Group Performance." *Journal of Abnormal and Social Psychology* 36:38–50.

Lemert, Charles C. 1990 "The Uses of French Structuralisms in Sociology." In G. Ritzer, ed., *Frontiers of Social Theory.* New York: Columbia University Press.

Lesser, Alexander 1935 "Functionalism in Social Anthropology." *American Anthropologist* 37:386–393.

Lévi-Strauss, Claude 1945a "The Analysis of Structure in Linguistics and in Anthropology." *Word* 1:1–21.

——— 1945b "French Sociology." In Georges Gurvitch and Wilbert E. Moore, eds., *Twentieth Century Sociology.* New York: Philosophical Library.

——— (1949) 1969 *The Elementary Structures of Kinship.* Boston: Beacon Press.

——— (1950) 1987 *Introduction to the Work of Marcel Mauss.* London: Routledge and Kegan Paul.

——— 1953 "Social Structure." In A. Kroeber, ed., *Anthropology Today.* Chicago: University of Chicago Press.

——— 1963 *Structural Anthropology.* New York: Basic Books.

Levy, Marion J. 1952 *The Structure of Society.* New Haven, Conn.: Yale University Press.

Luhmann, Niklas 1982 *The Differentiation of Society.* New York: Columbia University Press.

Malinowski, Bronislaw 1913 *The Family Among the Australian Aborigines.* New York: Schocken.

——— 1944 *A Scientific Theory of Culture.* Chapel Hill: University of North Carolina Press.

Mauss, Marcel (1904–1905) 1979 *Seasonal Variations of the Eskimo: A Study in Social Morphology.* London: Routledge and Kegan Paul.

——— (1925) 1941 *The Gift, Forms and Functions of Exchange in Archaic Societies.* New York: Free Press.

Merton, Robert K. 1949 "Manifest and Latent Functions." In *Social Theory and Social Structure.* New York: Free Press.

——— 1957 *Social Theory and Social Structure.* Rev. ed. New York: Free Press.

Mills, C. Wright 1959 *The Sociological Imagination.* New York: Oxford University Press.

Mitchell, Clyde 1974 "Social Networks." *Annual Review of Anthropology* 3:279–299.

Moreno, Jacob 1953 *Who Shall Survive?,* rev. ed. New York: Beacon House.

Münch, Richard 1982 *Theory of Action: Reconstructing the Contributions of Talcott Parsons, Emile Durkheim, and Max Weber,* 2 vols. Frankfurt: Suhrkamp.

Murdock, George P. 1953 "Social Structure." In Sol Tax, Loren Eiseley, Irving Rouse, and Carl Voegelin, eds., *An Appraisal of Anthropology Today.* Chicago: University of Chicago Press.

Nadel, S. F. 1957 *The Theory of Social Structure.* New York: Free Press.

Parsons, Talcott 1951 *The Social System.* New York: Free Press.

———, Robert F. Bales, and Edward Shils 1953 *Working Papers in the Theory of Action.* New York: Free Press.

Radcliffe-Brown, A. R. (1914) 1922 *The Andaman Islanders.* Cambridge: Cambridge University Press.

——— 1924 "The Mother's Brother in South Africa." *South African Journal of Science* 21:42–63.

——— 1935 "On the Concept of Function in Social Science" (reply to Lesser 1935). *American Anthropologist* 37:394–402.

——— 1952 *Structure and Function in Primitive Society.* London: Cohen and West.

Saussure, Ferdinand de (1915) 1966 *Course in General Linguistics.* New York: McGraw-Hill.

Spencer, Herbert 1864–1867. *The Principles of Biology,* 3 vols. New York: D. Appleton.

——— 1874–1896 *The Principles of Sociology,* 3 vols. New York: D. Appleton.

Trubetzkoi, Nikolai (1949) 1964. *Principes de Phonologie.* Paris: Klincksieck.

——— 1968 *Introduction to the Principles of Phonological Description.* The Hague: Martinus Nijhoff.

Turner, Jonathan H., and Alexandra Maryanski 1979 *Functionalism.* Menlo Park, Calif.: Benjamin-Cummings.

——— 1988 "Is Neofunctionalism Really Functional?" *Sociological Theory* 6 (1):110–121.

Turner, Stephan Park, and Jonathan H. Turner 1990 *The Impossible Science: An Institutional Analysis of Sociology.* Newbury Park, Calif.: Sage.

Wuthnow, Robert 1987 *Meaning and Moral Order: Explorations in Cultural Analysis.* Berkeley: University of California Press.

ALEXANDRA MARYANSKI
JONATHAN H. TURNER

G

GAME THEORY AND STRATEGIC INTERACTION A *game* is a situation that involves two or more persons (decision makers called *players*), where (1) each player has at least two behavioral options; (2) each player strives to achieve the greatest payoff (reward) possible; and (3) the payoff obtained by a player depends not only on the option that he chooses but also on the options chosen by the other players. Players in a game typically have opposing interests, at least to some degree. Due to this opposition of interests, players' interaction in games is usually proactive and strategic.

The *theory of games* is a branch of applied mathematics that treats rigorously the topic of optimal behavior in two-person and *n*-person games. Its origins go back at least to 1710, when the German mathematician-philosopher Leibniz foresaw the need for a theory of games of strategy. Soon afterward, James Waldegrave (in Montmort 1713) formulated the concept of maximin, a decision criterion that is central to game theory. In his book *Mathematical Psychics,* Edgeworth (1881) made explicit the similarity between economic processes and games of strategy. Later, theorists such as Zermelo (1913) stated specialized propositions for certain games (e.g., chess). Not until the work of Borel ([1921] 1953) and von Neumann (1928), however, did a true theory of games emerge. The *Theory of Games and Economic Behavior,* a landmark of the modern era by von Neumann and Morgenstern (1944), extended game theory to problems involving more than two players. Luce and Raiffa (1957) published the first widely regarded textbook in game theory. For more details regarding the early history of game theory, see Rives (1975).

Game theory has continued to develop in recent years. Many readable introductions to the modern mathematical theory are available. Among these are Jones (1980), Owen (1982), Szep and Forgo (1985), and Friedman (1986).

Beyond its status as a branch of applied mathematics, game theory serves social scientists as a tool for studying situations and institutions that involve multiple decision makers. Some of these investigations are empirical, while others are primarily analytic in character. The dependent variables of central concern in games include allocation of payoffs (i.e., who receives what rewards or bears what costs) and formation of coalitions (i.e., which alliances among players occur in a game). Other concerns include whether outcomes of a game are stable or enforceable, whether outcomes are collectively efficient, and whether outcomes are fair in some sense.

GAME-THEORETIC CONCEPTS

Mathematical game theory provides three main tools that assist in the analysis of multiperson decision problems. These include a descriptive framework, a typology of games, and a variety of solution concepts.

Descriptive Framework. At base, a description of any game requires a list of all players, the strategies available to each player, the logically possible outcomes in the game, and the payoff of each outcome to each player. In some instances, a game's description will also include a specification of the dynamic sequence of play and of the information sets available to players. Payoffs in a game are expressed in terms of *utility;* this provides a standard means of comparing otherwise diverse outcomes.

An analyst can model or represent a game in various forms. *Extensive form* depicts in tree format all possible strategies of players. It is especially useful for modeling games in which play occurs in stages or over time. *Strategic form* (also called normal form or a "payoff matrix") shows payoffs to players as a function of all strategy combinations. *Characteristic function form* lists the minimum payoffs to all coalitions in a game. Whereas extensive and normal forms pertain to virtually all types of games, characteristic function form pertains only to cooperative games (i.e., games that permit coalitions).

Typology of Games. The second tool from game theory is a general typology of games. This provides a means of codifying or classifying games vis-a-vis one another. For instance, games can be *two-person* or *n-person* (more than two players). Further, games can be classified as either *constant-sum* or *nonconstant-sum.* In constant-sum games, the payoffs to players always add to some constant value. Players in these games have diametrically opposing interests, and the interaction in these games is very adversarial. In nonconstant-sum games, the payoffs to players do not add to a constant value, and players do not have diametrically opposing interests. Interaction in games of this type is not strictly adversarial, for it will involve mixed motives.

Another important distinction is that between *cooperative games* and *noncooperative games.* Cooperative games permit players to communicate before reaching decisions, and they include some mechanism that enables players to make binding agreements regarding strategies. Noncooperative games do not permit players to communicate or to form binding agreements. Stated another way, cooperative games permit players to form coalitions while noncooperative games do not.

Among cooperative games, some are *sidepayment games* while others are *nonsidepayment games.* Sidepayment games permit players to transfer payoffs (utility) within coalitions; nonsidepayment games do not. Cooperative sidepayment games can be either *simple games* or *nonsimple games.* Simple games are those whose characteristic function assumes only two values. Nonsimple games are those whose characteristic functions have more than two values. Analysts use simple games primarily to model social processes with binary outcomes (e.g., win–lose, succeed–fail, etc.).

Solution Concepts. The third set of tools provided by game theory is a variety of solution concepts. A *solution concept* is a theory of equilibrium that predicts (behaviorally) or prescribes (normatively) the payoffs to players in games. In other words, a solution concept predicts how a game will turn out when played. For this reason, solution concepts are of special interest to social and behavioral scientists. They are perhaps the most important contribution of game theory.

Game theorists have developed numerous solution concepts. These differ both in underlying conception and in the predictions they make. For noncooperative games, the most prominent solutions include the Nash equilibrium (Nash 1951), the strong equilibrium (Aumann 1959), and the perfect equilibrium (Selten 1975). Important extensions appear in van Damme (1987). Other recent approaches are those of Harsanyi and Selten (1988) and Fraser and Hipel (1984).

For cooperative games, prominent solutions include the imputation set, the core (Gillies 1959; Aumann 1961), the Shapley value (Shapley 1953), and the nucleolus (Schmeidler 1969). Other solutions include the disruption nucleolus (Gately

1974; Littlechild and Vaidya 1976), the disruption value (Charnes, Rousseau, and Seiford 1978), the p-center solution (Spinetto 1974), and the aspiration solution (Bennett 1983). Some solutions make payoff predictions contingent upon coalitions that form. This class includes the $M_1(i)$ bargaining set (Aumann and Maschler 1964; Aumann and Dreze 1974), the competitive bargaining set (Horowitz 1973), the kernel (Davis and Maschler 1965), and the alpha-power set (Rapoport and Kahan 1982). Beyond these, a variety of specialized solutions exist for certain subtypes of games.

LABORATORY EXPERIMENTAL STUDIES OF GAMES

Laboratory experimentation on two-person and *n*-person games commenced in the early 1950s (e.g., Flood 1952), and it continues to the present. Some gaming studies are primarily descriptive in nature, while others investigate the predictive accuracy of various solution concepts.

Experiments of Two-Person Games. Investigators have conducted literally thousands of laboratory experiments on two-person games. Most of these treat only noncooperative games, although some do treat cooperative games in various forms. Some studies investigate constant-sum games, while others treat nonconstant-sum games (primarily such archetypal games as the prisoner's dilemma, chicken, battle of the sexes, etc.).

The major dependent variables in the two-person studies are the strategies used by players (particularly the frequency of cooperative choices) and the payoffs received by players. Independent variables include the type of game, strategy of the confederate, information set available, interpersonal attitudes of players, sex of players, motivational orientation of players, magnitude and form of payoffs, and so on (Vinacke 1969).

Some of this work seeks to comprehend how differences in game matrices affect play (Rapoport, Guyer, and Gordon 1976; Harris 1972). Another portion describes how players' strategies vary as a function of the confederate's strategy (i.e., partner's history of play over time). A useful review of empirical studies of confederate's strategies appears in Oskamp (1971), and a discussion of metastrategies appears in Howard (1971). Another portion of this work investigates the extent to which predictions from the minimax theorem approximate observed payoffs in constant-sum games. Colman (1982, chapter 5) reviews these findings. Still other work covers cooperative bargaining models (Roth 1979). General reviews of experimental research on two-person games appear in Guyer and Perkel (1972), Pruitt and Kimmel (1977), and Colman (1982).

Experiments of *n*-Person Noncooperative Games. There are several lines of experimentation on *n*-person noncooperative games. One line investigates multiperson compound games derived from 2 × 2 matrices (e.g., *n*-person chicken, *n*-person battle of the sexes, etc.). Most important of these is the *n*-person dilemma (NPD) game (Hamburger 1973; Schelling 1973). In the NPD, individually rational strategies produce outcomes that are not collectively rational. The NPD serves an abstract model of many phenomena including conservation of scarce natural resources, voluntary wage restraint, and the "tragedy of the commons" (Hardin 1968). There are many experimental studies of the NPD. Reviews of some research on NPDs appear in Dawes (1980) and Messick and Brewer (1983).

A related line of research is that by experimental economists on markets and auctions (Smith 1982). This work investigates market structures (such as competitive exchange, oligopoly, and auction bidding) in laboratory settings (Friedman and Hoggatt 1980; Plott and Sunder 1982). Most of these structures can be viewed as noncooperative games. Plott (1982) provides a useful review of studies investigating equilibrium solutions of markets—the competitive equilibrium, the Cournot model, and the monopoly (joint maximization) model.

There is an increasingly large experimental literature on auctions, some of which is game-theoretic in character (e.g., Vickrey and Nash solutions). These studies investigate the effects on bidding behavior of such variables as risk aversion, differential information, and asymmetric beliefs.

They also investigate different institutional forms such as English auctions, Dutch auctions, double auctions, and sealed bid-offer auctions (e.g., Smith et al. 1982; Cox, Smith, and Walker 1984). Reviews of the large theoretical literature on auctions appear in Engelbrecht-Wiggans (1980) and McAfee and McMillan (1987).

Experiments of *n*-Person Weighted Majority Games. Weighted majority games are an important subclass of cooperative, sidepayment, simple games. They serve as models of legislative or voting systems. Theorists have developed many special solution concepts for these games. The major early theories applicable to weighted majority games were the minimum resource theory (Gamson 1961) and the minimum power theory (Shapley and Shubik 1954). More recent theories for weighted majority games include the weighted probability model (Komorita 1974), the bargaining theory (Komorita and Chertkoff 1973) and the equal excess model (Komorita 1979). The bargaining theory posits that players in a coalition will divide payoffs in a manner midway between equality and proportionality to resources (votes) contributed. The equal excess model is similar but uses the equal excess norm in place of proportionality.

Numerous experiments on coalition bargaining in weighted majority games have tested these theories (e.g., Michener, Fleishman, and Vaske 1976; Komorita and Tumonis 1980; Miller 1980). Results of these studies generally support the bargaining theory and the equal excess model over the others, although all have deficiencies. Reviews of the many experiments in this line appear in Komorita and Kravitz (1983) and Komorita (1984).

Experiments of Other *n*-Person Cooperative Games. Beyond weighted majority games, investigators have studied a wide variety of *n*-person cooperative games in other forms. The primary objective of the work is to discover which game-theoretic solution concepts predict most accurately the outcomes of these games.

Numerous studies have investigated cooperative sidepayment games in characteristic function form (e.g., Rapoport and Kahan 1984; Murnighan and Roth 1980; Michener et al. 1986). Other studies have investigated similar games in strategic form (Michener, Yuen, and Sakurai 1981). This work shows that in games with empty core, solution concepts such as the nucleolus and the kernel predict well. In games with nonempty core, however, the Shapley value is relatively more accurate. Reviews of this body of research appear in Murnighan (1978), Michener and Potter (1981), and Kahan and Rapoport (1984).

Other studies have investigated cooperative nonsidepayment games. Some of this research pertains to bargaining models in sequential games of status (Laing and Morrison 1974; Friend, Laing, and Morrison 1977). Other research tests various solution concepts (core, lambda transfer value) in nonsidepayment games in strategic form (McKelvey and Ordeshook 1982; Michener et al. 1985).

Another line of experimentation on cooperative nonsidepayment games is that conducted by political scientists interested in committee games or spatial voting games. These are *n*-person voting games in which policies are represented as positions in multidimensional space. For the most part, this research attempts to test predictions from alternative solution concepts (Ordeshook and Winer 1980; Ferejohn, Fiorina, and Packel 1980). Some of this work has led to new theories, such as the competitive solution (McKelvey, Ordeshook, and Winer 1978), or to new developments regarding established ones, such as methods for computing the Copeland winner (Grofman et al. 1987).

INSTITUTIONAL ANALYSIS VIA GAME THEORY

Economists and political scientists have long used game theory in the analysis of social institutions. In work of this type, an analyst specifies an institution (such as a Cournot oligopoly or an approval voting system) in hypothetical or ideal-typical terms and then applies game-theoretic solution concepts. Work of this type yields insight regarding which payoffs will result at equilibrium. Through this approach, an analyst can compare alternative institutional forms with respect to stability, efficiency, and fairness. Broad discussions and reviews of this literature appear in Schotter (1981), Shubik (1982, 1984), and Schotter and Schwodiauer (1980).

Economic Institutions. Von Neumann and Morgenstern (1944) were among the first to explore the role of n-person game theory in economic analysis. Since that time, economists have analyzed a variety of institutions in game-theoretic terms. One of these institutions is *oligopoly*. Markets in which there are only a few sellers (oligopoly), two sellers (duopoly, a type of oligopoly), one buyer and one seller (bilateral monopoly), and so on, lend themselves readily to game-theoretic analysis because the payoffs to each player depend on the strategies of the other players.

Economists have modeled oligopolies both as noncooperative games and as cooperative games. Several analyses of oligopolies as noncooperative games show that the standard Chamberlin price-setting strategy is equivalent to a Nash equilibrium in pure strategies (Shubik 1959a; Telser 1972). Beyond that, various analyses have treated oligopoly as a noncooperative multistage game. These analyses have produced generalizations concerning the effects of adjustment speed, of demand and cost functions, and of incomplete information regarding demand on the dynamic stability of the traditional Cournot solution and other equilibria (Friedman 1977; Gates, Rickard, and Wilson 1977; Radner 1980).

Analyses of collusion among oligopolists usually view this as a cooperative game. These treatments analyze outcomes via such solution concepts as the core or the bargaining set (Kaneko 1978). Detailed reviews and discussion of game-theoretic models of oligopoly appear in Shubik (1984) and Friedman (1983).

A second topic of interest to game-theoretic economists is general equilibrium in a *multilateral exchange economy*. An early paper (Arrow and Debreu 1954) modeled a general competitive exchange economy (involving production, exchange, and consumption) as a noncooperative game and then showed that a generalized Nash equilibrium existed for the model. Other theorists have modeled a multilateral exchange economy as a cooperative n-person game. Shubik (1959b) showed that core of such a game is identical to Edgeworth's traditional contract curve. More generally, Debreu and Scarf (1963) showed that the core converges to the Walrasian competitive equilibrium.

By representing an economy as an n-person cooperative game, analysts can investigate general equilibrium even in markets that do not fulfill neoclassical regularity assumptions such as convexity of preferences, divisibility of commodities, and absence of externalities (Shapley and Shubik 1966; Rosenthal 1971; Telser 1972). Beyond that, some economists model general equilibrium in game-theoretic terms because they can introduce and analyze a variety of alternative institutional arrangements. This includes, for instance, models with or without trade, with or without production, with various types of money, and with various types of financial institutions such as common stock, central banks, and bankruptcy rules (Shapley and Shubik 1977; Dubey and Shubik 1977). Depending on the models used, such cooperative solutions as the core, Shapley value, and nucleolus play an important role in these analyses, as does the Nash noncooperative solution.

A third concern of game-theoretically oriented economists is the analysis of *public goods and services* (i.e., bridges, roads, dams, harbors, libraries, police services, public health services, and the like). Of special relevance is the pricing and cross-subsidization of public utilities; a central issue is how different classes of customers should divide the costs of providing public utilities.

Theorists can model such problems by letting the cost function of a public utility determine the characteristic function of a (cooperative) "cost-sharing game." Games of this type are amenable to analysis via such solution concepts as the Shapley value (Loehman and Whinston 1974), the nucleolus (Littlechild and Vaidya 1976; Nakayama and Suzuki 1977), and the core (Faulhaber 1975;

Littlechild and Thompson 1977), each of which represents alternative cost-sharing criteria. Other work has used game-theoretic concepts to model bargaining with respect to provision of public goods (Schofield 1984a).

Political Institutions. Like economists, political scientists have analyzed a variety of institutions in game-theoretic terms. One broad line of work—termed the study of *social choice*—investigates various methods for aggregating individual preferences into collective decisions. Of special concern is the stability of outcomes produced by alternative voting systems (Nurmi 1987; Ordeshook 1986). Analysts have studied many different voting systems (e.g., majority voting, plurality voting, weighted voting, approval voting, and so on).

Strikingly, this work has demonstrated that in majority voting systems where voters choose among more than two alternatives, the conditions for equilibria (i.e., the conditions that assure a decisive winner) are so restrictive as to render equilibria virtually nonexistent (Fishburn 1973; McKelvey 1976; Riker 1982).

Topics in voting include the detailed analysis of cyclic majority phenomenon (generalized Condorcet paradox situations), the analysis of equilibria in novel voting systems such as weighted voting (Banzhaf 1965) and approval voting (Brams and Fishburn 1983), and the development of predictive solution concepts for voting systems that possess no stable equilibrium (Ferejohn and Grether 1982).

A second line of work by game theorists concerns the strategic manipulation of political institutions to gain favorable outcomes. One topic here is the consequences of manipulative *agenda control* in committees (Plott and Levine 1978). Another topic is the effects of *strategic voting*—that is, voting in which players strive to manipulate the decision by voting for candidates or motions other than their real preferences (Farquharson 1969; Bjurulf and Niemi 1981; Niemi and Frank 1982). Analyses by Gibbard (1973) and Satterthwaite (1975) showed that no voting procedure can be completely strategy-proof (in the sense of offering voters no incentive to vote strategically) without violating some more fundamental condition of democratic acceptability. In particular, any voting mechanism that is strategy-proof is also necessarily dictatorial. An important issue here is how to design voting systems with at least some desirable properties that encourage sincere revelation of preferences (i.e., use of maximax strategies). An integrative discussion of the theory of voting appears in Moulin (1983).

A third broad line of work concerns the *indexing of players' power* in political systems (Owen 1982, chap. 10). Frequently this entails assessing differences in a priori voting strength of members of committees or legislatures. For example, a classic study applied the Shapley–Shubik index of power to the U.S. legislative system and assessed the relative power of the president, senators, and representatives (Shapley and Shubik 1954). Other measures of power include the Banzhaf–Coleman index (Banzhaf 1965; Dubey and Shapley 1979) and Straffin's probabilistic indices (Straffin 1978).

A fourth interest of game-theoretically oriented political scientists is *cabinet coalition formation,* especially in European governments. This topic is of interest because political fragmentation can produce instability of cabinet coalitions, which in turn can lead to collapse of entire governments. Work on this problem ties in with that on spatial voting games and weighted majority games, discussed above. Some cabinet coalition models stress policy (or ideological) alignment among members, while other models stress the transfer of value (payoffs) among members. Important theoretical models include Riker (1962), DeSwaan (1973), Winer (1979), and Grofman (1982). For European data, the most successful model of coalition formation is one predicting coalitions that are both minimal winning and minimal connected winning (Schofield 1984b).

Other Analyses. Analysts have also used game theory to study a diversity of other phenomena. Investigators have scrutinized faith versus rationality in the biblical stories—an interesting topic because God usually has more information than the other players (Brams 1980), the resolution of international conflicts such as various

World War II battles, the Suez Crisis, and the Cuban Missile Crisis (Fraser and Hipel 1984), the structure of dramaturgical plays (Howard 1971), the optimal allocation of resources during political campaigns (Young 1978; Lake 1979), the conflictive behavior of various animal species such as fiddler crabs (Maynard Smith 1974; Hyatt, Smith, and Raghaven 1979), the optimal use of deception (Brams 1977; Axelrod 1979), and the strategic character of U.S. presidential primary campaigns (Aldrich 1979).

EMPIRICAL APPLICATIONS OF GAME THEORY IN NATURAL SETTINGS

Game-theoretic models require a large amount of initial information. That is, any empiricist attempting to model a specific real-world situation as an *n*-person game must obtain data about players, strategies, information sets, payoffs, and institutional norms to construct a complete model. This task is usually difficult and occasionally impossible (as, for example, in situations where the players have so much at stake that they are unwilling to reveal their preferences and strategies to anyone). This constraint has hampered the widespread application of game-theoretic constructs to specific empirical situations (Bennett and Huxham 1982; Colman 1982, chap. 13).

Nevertheless, one can point to several studies that successfully model specific, real-world situations (not just hypothetical situations or institutional forms) as games. Many of the game-theoretic studies by political scientists of cabinet coalition formation, cited above, are empirical in nature, and some utilize historical data regarding European governments (e.g., Schofield 1984b). Beyond this, economists and others have conducted empirical game-theoretic research about the pricing of public goods. Included here, for instance, are studies of river pollution caused by three cities (Loehman, Pingry, and Whinston 1974), water resource management (Heaney 1979), allocation of costs in managing a medical library (Bres et al. 1979), allocation of aircraft landing fees among different sizes of aircraft (Littlechild and Thompson 1977), determination of user fees in a telephone system (Billera, Heath, and Raanan 1978), and analysis of regional cooperation regarding investment in electric power (Gately 1974). Roth (1984) has studied the organization and operation of the labor market for medical interns from the standpoint of the matching problem.

DYNAMIC GAMES

Some have criticized game theory as providing only static models of social phenomena. Perhaps this criticism was once justified, for traditional game theory treated equilibrium primarily as single-period. During the last two decades, however, theorists increasingly have modeled games as occurring over time. There is today a growing literature on such topics as dynamic games, supergames, and evolutionary games. Readable introductions to dynamic games appear in Thomas (1984), Friedman (1986), and Owen (1982).

Dynamic (or differential) games are games played over time in which at least one player can use a strategy that depends on previous actions. The classic works include Isaacs (1965) and Friedman (1971). Other important works include Leitmann (1974), Hajek (1975), and Basar and Olsder (1982).

A *supergame* is a sequence of (ordinary) games played by a fixed set of players. A *repeated game* is a supergame in which the same game is played at each stage in the sequence. Certain repeated games are of interest because they allow collectively rational outcomes to result from noncooperative equilibrium strategies. Axelrod (1984) discusses the evolution of cooperation in repeated games. Aumann (1981) provides a survey of repeated games.

Finally, biologists have recently used game-theoretic concepts to study *evolutionary games,* that is, dynamic models that explain why certain inherited traits (i.e., behavioral patterns) arise in an animal population and remain stable over time. In games of this type, strategy selection derives from behavioral phenotypes rather than from rational thought processes. Theorists have advanced various concepts of stability for evolutionary games (Maynard Smith 1982; Bomze and Potscher 1989).

(SEE ALSO: *Decision-making Theory and Research; Experiments; Social Psychology*)

REFERENCES

Aldrich, J. H. 1979. "A Model of the U.S. Presidential Primary Campaign." In S. J. Brams, A. Schotter, and G. Schwodiauer, eds., *Applied Game Theory.* Wurzburg: Physica-Verlag.

Arrow, K. J., and G. Debreu 1954 "Existence of an Equilibrium for a Competitive Economy." *Econometrica* 22:265–290.

Aumann, R. J. 1959 "Acceptable Points in General Cooperative *n*-Person Games." In A. W. Tucker and R. D. Luce, eds., *Contributions to the Theory of Games,* vol. 4. Annals of Mathematics Studies, no 40. Princeton, N.J.: Princeton University Press.

———1961 "The Core of a Cooperative Game without Sidepayments." *Transactions of the American Mathematical Society* 98:539–552.

———1981 "Survey of Repeated Games." In R. J. Aumann et al., *Essays in Game Theory.* Mannheim: Bibliographisches Institut.

Aumann, R. J., and J. H. Dreze 1974 "Cooperative Games with Coalition Structures." *International Journal of Game Theory* 3:217–237.

Aumann, R. J., and M. Maschler 1964 "The Bargaining Set for Cooperative Games." In M. Dresher, L. S. Shapley, and A. W. Tucker, eds., *Advances in Game Theory.* Annals of Mathematics Studies, no. 52. Princeton, N. J.: Princeton University Press.

Axelrod, R. 1979 "Coping with Deception." In S. J. Brams, A. Schotter, and G. Schwodiauer, eds., *Applied Game Theory.* Wurzburg: Physica-Verlag.

———1984 *The Evolution of Cooperation.* New York: Basic Books.

Banzhaf, J. F., III 1965 "Weighted Voting Doesn't Work: A Mathematical Analysis." *Rutgers Law Review* 19:317–343.

Basar, T., and G. J. Olsder 1982 *Dynamic Non-Cooperative Game Theory.* New York: Academic Press.

Bennett, E. 1983 "The Aspiration Approach to Predicting Coalition Formation and Payoff Distribution in Sidepayment Games." *International Journal of Game Theory* 12:1–28.

Bennett, P. G., and C. S. Huxham 1982 "Hypergames and What They Do." *Journal of the Operational Research Society* 33:41–50.

Billera, L. J., D. C. Heath, and J. Raanan 1978 "Internal Telephone Billing Rates: A Novel Application of Non-Atomic Game Theory." *Operations Research* 26:956–965.

Bjurulf, B. H., and R. G. Niemi 1981 "Order-of-Voting Effects." In M. J. Holler, ed., *Power, Voting, and Voting Power.* Wurzburg: Physica-Verlag.

Bomze, I. M., and B. M. Potscher 1989 *Game Theoretic Foundations of Evolutionary Stability.* Berlin: Springer-Verlag.

Borel, E. (1921–1927) 1953 " 'The Theory of Play and Integral Equations with Skew Symmetric Kernels,' 'On Games that Involve Chance and the Skill of the Players,' and 'On Systems of Linear Forms of Skew Symmetric Determinant and the General Theory of Play.' " *Econometrica* 21:97–117.

Brams, S. J. 1977 "Deception in 2 × 2 Games." *Journal of Peace Science* 2:171–203.

———1980 *Biblical Games: A Strategic Analysis of Stories in the Old Testament.* Cambridge, Mass.: MIT Press.

———, and P. C. Fishburn 1983 *Approval Voting.* Cambridge, Mass.: Birkhauser.

Bres, E., A. Charnes, D. Cole Eckels, S. Hitt, R. Lyders, J. Rousseau, K. Russell, and M. Schoeman 1979 "Costs and Their Assessment to Users of a Medical Library: A Game-Theoretic Method for Allocating Joint Fixed Costs." In S. J. Brams, A. Schotter, and G. Schwodiauer, eds., *Applied Game Theory.* Wurzburg: Physica-Verlag.

Charnes, A., J. Rousseau, and L. Seiford 1978 "Complements, Mollifiers, and the Propensity to Disrupt." *International Journal of Game Theory* 7:37–50.

Colman, A. M. 1982 *Game Theory and Experimental Games.* Oxford: Pergamon Press.

Cox, J. C., V. L. Smith, and J. M. Walker 1984 "Theory and Behavior of Multiple Unit Discriminative Auctions." *Journal of Finance* 39:983–1010.

Davis, M., and M. Maschler 1965 "The Kernel of a Cooperative Game." *Naval Research Logistics Quarterly* 12:223–259.

Dawes, R. M. 1980 "Social Dilemmas." *Annual Review of Psychology* 31:169–193.

Debreu, G., and H. E. Scarf 1963 "A Limit Theorem on the Core of an Economy." *International Economic Review* 4:235–246.

DeSwaan, A. 1973 *Coalition Theories and Cabinet Formation.* San Francisco: Jossey-Bass.

Dubey, P., and L. S. Shapley 1979 "Mathematical

Properties of the Banzhaf Power Index." *Mathematics of Operations Research* 4:99–130.

Dubey, P., and M. Shubik 1977 "Trade and Prices in a Closed Economy with Exogenous Uncertainty, Different Levels of Information, Money and Compound Future Markets." *Econometrica* 45:1657–1680.

Edgeworth, F. Y. 1881 *Mathematical Psychics.* London: Kegan Paul.

Engelbrecht-Wiggans, R. 1980 "Auctions and Bidding Models: A Survey." *Management Science* 26:119–142.

Farquharson, R. 1969 *Theory of Voting.* New Haven, Conn.: Yale University Press.

Faulhaber, G. R. 1975 "Cross-Subsidization: Pricing in Public Enterprises." *American Economic Review* 65:966–977.

Ferejohn, J. A., M. P. Fiorina, and E. W. Packel 1980 "Nonequilibrium Solutions for Legislative Systems." *Behavioral Science* 25:140–148.

Ferejohn, J. A., and D. M. Grether 1982 "On the Properties of Stable Decision Procedures." In P. C. Ordeshook and K. A. Shepsle, eds., *Political Equilibrium.* Boston: Kluwer-Nijhoff Publishing.

Fishburn, P. C. 1973 *The Theory of Social Choice.* Princeton, N.J.: Princeton University Press.

Flood, M. M. 1952 "Some Experimental Games." Research Memorandum RM-789. Santa Monica, Calif.: The Rand Corporation.

Fraser, N. M., and K. W. Hipel 1984 *Conflict Analysis: Models and Resolutions.* New York: Elsevier.

Friedman, A. 1971 *Differential Games.* New York: Wiley.

Friedman, J. W. 1977 *Oligopoly and the Theory of Games.* Amsterdam: North-Holland.

——— 1983 *Oligopoly Theory.* New York: Cambridge University Press.

——— 1986 *Game Theory with Applications to Economics.* New York: Oxford University Press.

———, and A. C. Hoggatt 1980 "An Experiment in Noncooperative Oligopoly." *Research in Experimental Economics.* Vol. 1, supplement 1. Greenwich, Conn.: JAI Press.

Friend, K. E., J. D. Laing, and R. J. Morrison 1977 "Game-Theoretic Analyses of Coalition Behavior." *Theory and Decision* 8:127–157.

Gamson, W. A. 1961 "A Theory of Coalition Formation." *American Sociological Review* 26:373–382.

Gately, D. 1974 "Sharing the Gains from Regional Cooperation: A Game Theoretic Application to Planning Investment in Electric Power." *International Economic Review* 15:195–208.

Gates, D. J., J. A. Rickard, and D. J. Wilson 1977 "A Convergent Adjustment Process for Firms in Competition." *Econometrica* 45:1349–1363.

Gibbard, A. 1973 "Manipulation of Voting Schemes: A General Result." *Econometrica* 41:587–601.

Gillies, D. B. 1959 "Solutions to General Non-Zero-Sum Games." *Annals of Mathematics Studies* 40:47–85.

Grofman, B. 1982 "A Dynamic Model of Protocoalition Formation in Ideological N-Space." *Behavioral Science* 27:77–90.

———, G. Owen, N. Noviello, and A. Glazer 1987 "Stability and Centrality in Legislative Choice in the Spatial Context." *American Political Science Review* 81:539–552.

Guyer, M., and Perkel, B. 1972 "Experimental Games: A Bibliography (1945–1971)." Communication no. 293. Ann Arbor: Mental Health Research Institute, University of Michigan.

Hajek, O. 1975 *Pursuit Games.* New York: Academic Press.

Hamburger, H. 1973 "*N*-Person Prisoner's Dilemma." *Journal of Mathematical Sociology* 3:27–48.

Hardin, G. 1968 "The Tragedy of the Commons." *Science* 162:1243–1248.

Harris, R. J. 1972 "An Interval-Scale Classification System for All 2 × 2 Games." *Behavioral Science* 17:371–383.

Harsanyi, J. C., and R. Selten 1988 *A General Theory of Equilibrium Selection in Games.* Cambridge, Mass.: MIT Press.

Heaney, J. P. 1979 "Efficiency/Equity Analysis of Environmental Problems—A Game Theoretic Perspective." In S. J. Brams, A. Schotter, and G. Schwodiauer, eds., *Applied Game Theory.* Wurzburg: Physica-Verlag.

Horowitz, A. D. 1973 "The Competitive Bargaining Set for Cooperative *n*-Person Games." *Journal of Mathematical Psychology* 10:265–289. (Erratum: 1974, 11:161.)

Howard, N. 1971 *Paradoxes of Rationality: Theory of Metagames and Political Behavior.* Cambridge, Mass.: MIT Press.

Hyatt, G. W., S. D. Smith, and T. E. S. Raghaven 1979 "Game Theory Models of Intermale Combat in Fiddler Crabs (Genus UCA)." In S. J. Brams, A. Schotter, and G. Schwodiauer, eds., *Applied Game Theory.* Wurzburg: Physica-Verlag.

Isaacs, R. 1965 *Differential Games.* New York: Wiley.

Jones, A. J. 1980 *Game Theory: Mathematical Models of Conflict.* Chichester, U.K.: Ellis Horwood.

Kahan, J. P., and Amnon Rapoport 1984 *Theories of Coalition Formation.* Hillsdale, N.J.: Erlbaum.

Kaneko, M. 1978 "Price Oligopoly as a Cooperative Game." *International Journal of Game Theory* 7:137–150.

Komorita, S. S. 1974 "A Weighted Probability Model of Coalition Formation." *Psychological Review* 81:242–256.

———1979 "An Equal Excess Model of Coalition Formation." *Behavioral Science* 24:369–381.

———1984. "Coalition Bargaining." In L. Berkowitz, ed., *Advances in Experimental Social Psychology.* Vol. 18. New York: Academic Press.

Komorita, S. S., and J. M. Chertkoff 1973 "A Bargaining Theory of Coalition Formation." *Psychological Review* 80:149–162.

Komorita, S. S., and D. A. Kravitz 1983 "Coalition Formation: A Social Psychological Approach." In P. B. Paulus, ed., *Basic Group Processes.* New York: Springer-Verlag.

Komorita, S. S., and T. M. Tumonis 1980 "Extensions and Tests of Some Descriptive Theories of Coalition Formation." *Journal of Personality and Social Psychology* 39:256–268.

Laing, J. D., and R. J. Morrison 1974 "Sequential Games of Status." *Behavioral Science* 19:177–196.

Lake, M. 1979 "A New Campaign Resource Allocation Model." In S. J. Brams, A. Schotter, and G. Schwodiauer, eds., *Applied Game Theory.* Wurzburg: Physica-Verlag.

Leitmann, G. 1974 *Cooperative and Non-Cooperative Many Player Differential Games.* New York: Springer-Verlag.

Littlechild, S. C., and G. E. Thompson 1977 "Aircraft Landing Fees: A Game Theory Approach." *Bell Journal of Economics* 8:186–207.

Littlechild, S. C., and K. G. Vaidya 1976 "The Propensity to Disrupt and the Disruption Nucleolus of a Characteristic Function Game." *International Journal of Game Theory* 5:151–161.

Loehman, E., E. D. Pingry, and A. Whinston 1974 "Cost Allocation for a Regional Pollution Treatment System." In J. R. Conner and E. Loehman, eds., *Economics and Decision Making for Environmental Quality.* Gainesville: University Presses of Florida.

Loehman, E., and A. Whinston 1974 "An Axiomatic Approach to Cost Allocations for Public Investments." *Public Finance Quarterly* 2:236–251.

Luce, R. D., and H. Raiffa 1957 *Games and Decisions: Introduction and Critical Survey.* New York: Wiley.

Maynard Smith, J. 1974 "The Theory of Games and the Evolution of Animal Conflicts." *Journal of Theoretical Biology* 47:209–221.

———1982 *Evolution and the Theory of Games.* Cambridge: Cambridge University Press.

McAfee, R. P., and J. McMillan 1987 "Auctions and Bidding." *Journal of Economic Literature* 25:699–738.

McKelvey, R. D. 1976 "Intransitivities in Multidimensional Voting Models and Some Implications for Agenda Control." *Journal of Economic Theory* 12: 472–482.

McKelvey, R. D., and P. C. Ordeshook 1982 "An Experimental Test of Solution Theories for Cooperative Games in Normal Form." In P. C. Ordeshook and K. A. Shepsle, eds., *Political Equilibrium.* Boston: Kluwer-Nijhoff Publishing.

McKelvey, R. D., P. C. Ordeshook, and M. D. Winer 1978 "The Competitive Solution for *n*-Person Games without Transferable Utility, with an Application to Committee Games." *American Political Science Review* 72:599–615.

Messick, D. M., and M. D. Brewer 1983 "Solving Social Dilemmas: A Review." In L. Wheeler and P. Shaver, eds., *Review of Personality and Social Psychology.* Vol. 4. Beverly Hills, Calif.: Sage.

Michener, H. A., D. C. Dettman, J. M. Ekman, and Y. C. Choi 1985 "A Comparison of the Alpha- and Beta-Characteristic Functions in Cooperative Non-Sidepayment *n*-Person Games." *Journal of Mathematical Sociology* 11:307–330.

Michener, H. A., J. A. Fleishman, and J. J. Vaske 1976 "A Test of the Bargaining Theory of Coalition Formation in Four-Person Groups." *Journal of Personality and Social Psychology* 34:1,114–1,126.

Michener, H. A., G. B. Macheel, C. G. Depies, and C. A. Bowen 1986 "Mollifier Representation in Non-Constant-Sum Games: An Experimental Test." *Journal of Conflict Resolution* 30:361–382.

Michener, H. A., and K. Potter 1981 "Generalizability of Tests in *n*-Person Sidepayment Games." *Journal of Conflict Resolution* 25:733–749.

Michener, H. A., K. Yuen, and M. M. Sakurai 1981 "On the Comparative Accuracy of Lexicographical Solutions in Cooperative Games." *International Journal of Game Theory* 10:75–89.

Miller, C. E. 1980 "A Test of Four Theories of Coalition Formation: Effects of Payoffs and Resources." *Journal of Personality and Social Psychology* 38:153–164.

Montmort, P. R. de 1713 *Essay d'analyse sur les jeux de hazard.* 2d ed. Paris: Quillau.

Moulin, H. 1983 *The Strategy of Social Choice.* Amsterdam: North-Holland Publishing Co.

Murnighan, J. K. 1978 "Models of Coalition Behavior: Game Theoretic, Social Psychological, and Political Perspectives." *Psychological Bulletin* 85:1,130–1,153.

———, and A. E. Roth 1980 "Effects of Group Size and Communication Availability on Coalition Bargaining in a Veto Game." *Journal of Personality and Social Psychology* 39:92–103.

Nakayama, M., and M. Suzuki 1977 "The Cost Assignment of Cooperative Water Resource Development: A Game Theoretical Approach." In R. Henn and O. Moeschlin, eds., *Mathematical Economics and Game Theory.* Berlin: Springer-Verlag.

Nash, J. F., Jr. 1951 "Non-Cooperative Games." *Annals of Mathematics* 54:286–295.

Niemi, R. G., and A. Q. Frank 1982 "Sophisticated Voting under the Plurality Procedure." In P. C. Ordeshook and K. A. Shepsle, eds., *Political Equilibrium.* Boston: Kluwer-Nijhoff Publishing.

Nurmi, H. 1987 *Comparing Voting Systems.* Dordrecht: D. Reidel Publishing Co.

Ordeshook, P. C. 1986 *Game Theory and Political Theory.* Cambridge: Cambridge University Press.

———, and M. Winer 1980 "Coalitions and Spatial Policy Outcomes in Parliamentary Systems: Some Experimental Results." *American Journal of Political Science* 24:730–752.

Oskamp, S. 1971 "Effects of Programmed Strategies on Cooperation in the Prisoner's Dilemma and Other Mixed Motive Games." *Journal of Conflict Resolution* 15:225–259.

Owen, G. 1982 *Game Theory.* 2d ed. New York: Academic Press.

Plott, C. R. 1982 "Industrial Organization Theory and Experimental Economics." *Journal of Economic Literature* 20:1,485–1,527.

———, and M. E. Levine 1978 "A Model of Agenda Influence on Committee Decisions." *American Economic Review* 68:146–160.

———, and S. Sunder 1982 "Efficiency of Experimental Securities Markets with Insider Information." *Journal of Political Economy* 90:663–698.

Pruitt, D. G., and M. J. Kimmel 1977 "Twenty Years of Experimental Gaming: Critique, Synthesis, and Suggestions for the Future." *Annual Review of Psychology* 28:363–392.

Radner, R. 1980 "Collusive Behavior in Noncooperative Epsilon-Equilibria of Oligopolies with Long but Finite Lives." *Journal of Economic Theory* 22:136–154.

Rapoport, Amnon, and J. P. Kahan 1982 "The Power of a Coalition and Payoff Disbursement in Three-Person Negotiable Conflicts." *Journal of Mathematical Sociology* 8:193–224.

———1984 "Coalition Formation in a Five-Person Market Game." *Management Science* 30:326–343.

Rapoport, Amnon, M. Guyer, and D. G. Gordon 1976 *The 2 × 2 Game.* Ann Arbor: University of Michigan Press.

Riker, W. H. 1962 *The Theory of Political Coalitions.* New Haven: Yale University Press.

———1982 "Implication from the Disequilibrium of Majority Rule for the Study of Institutions." In P. C. Ordeshook and K. A. Shepsle, eds., *Political Equilibrium.* Boston: Kluwer-Nijhoff Publishing.

Rives, N. W., Jr. 1975 "On the History of the Mathematical Theory of Games." *History of Political Economy* 7:549–565.

Rosenthal, R. W. 1971 "External Economies and Cores." *Journal of Economic Theory* 3:182–188.

Roth, A. E. 1979 *Axiomatic Models of Bargaining.* Berlin: Springer-Verlag.

———1984 "The Evolution of the Labor Market for Medical Interns and Residents: A Case Study in Game Theory." *Journal of Political Economy* 92:991–1,016.

Satterthwaite, M. A. 1975 "Strategy-Proofness and Arrow's Conditions: Existence and Correspondence Theorems for Voting Procedures and Social Welfare Functions." *Journal of Economic Theory* 10:187–217.

Schelling, T. C. 1973 "Hockey Helmets, Concealed Weapons, and Daylight Saving: A Study of Binary Choices with Externalities." *Journal of Conflict Resolution* 17:381–428.

Schmeidler, D. 1969 "The Nucleolus of a Characteristic Function Game." *SIAM Journal of Applied Mathematics* 17:1,163–1,170.

Schofield, N. 1984a "Bargaining over Public Goods." In M. J. Holler, ed., *Coalitions and Collective Action.* Wurzburg: Physica-Verlag.

———1984b "Political Fragmentation and the Stability of Coalition Governments in Western Europe." In M. J. Holler, ed., *Coalitions and Collective Action.* Wurzburg: Physica-Verlag.

Schotter, A. 1981 *The Economic Theory of Social Institutions.* New York: Cambridge University Press.

———, and G. Schwodiauer 1980 "Economics and the Theory of Games: A Survey." *Journal of Economic Literature* 18:479–527.

Selten, R. 1975 "Reexamination of the Perfectness Concept for Equilibrium Points in Extensive

Games." *International Journal of Game Theory* 4:25–55.

Shapley, L. S. 1953 "A Value for *n*-Person Games." In H. W. Kuhn and A. W. Tucker, eds., *Contributions to the Theory of Games.* Annals of Mathematics Studies, no. 28. Princeton: Princeton University Press.

Shapley, L. S., and M. Shubik 1954 "A Method of Evaluating the Distribution of Power in a Committee System." *American Political Science Review* 48:787–792.

———1966 "Quasi-Cores in a Monetary Economy with Nonconvex Preferences." *Econometrica* 34:805–827.

———1977 "Trade Using One Commodity as a Means of Payment." *Journal of Political Economy* 85:937–968.

Shubik, M. 1959a *Strategy and Market Structure.* New York: Wiley.

———1959b "Edgeworth Market Games." In A. W. Tucker and R. D. Luce, eds., *Contributions to the Theory of Games.* Annals of Mathematics Studies, no. 40. Princeton: Princeton University Press.

———1982 *Game Theory in the Social Sciences.* Cambridge, Mass.: MIT Press.

———1984 *A Game-Theoretic Approach to Political Economy.* Cambridge, Mass.: MIT Press.

Smith, V. L. 1982 "Microeconomic Systems as an Experimental Science." *American Economic Review* 72:923–955.

———, A. W. Williams, W. K. Bratton, and M. G. Vannoni 1982 "Competitive Market Institutions: Double Auctions vs. Sealed Bid-Offer Auctions." *American Economic Review* 72:58–77.

Spinetto, R. 1974 "The Geometry of Solution Concepts for *n*-Person Cooperative Games." *Management Science* 20:1,292–1,299.

Straffin, P. D., Jr. 1978 "Probability Models for Power Indices." In P. C. Ordeshook, ed., *Game Theory and Political Science.* New York: New York University Press.

Szep, J., and F. Forgo 1985 *Introduction to the Theory of Games.* Dordrecht: D. Reidel Publishing Co.

Telser, L. 1972 *Competition, Collusion, and Game Theory.* Chicago: Aldine-Atherton.

Thomas, L. C. 1984 *Games, Theory and Applications.* Chichester, U.K.: Halsted Press.

van Damme, E. 1987 *Stability and Perfection of Nash Equilibria.* Berlin: Springer-Verlag.

Vinacke, W. E. 1969 "Variables in Experimental Games: Toward a Field Theory." *Psychological Bulletin* 71:293–318.

von Neumann, J. 1928 "Zur Theorie der Gesellschaftsspiele." *Mathematische Annalen* 100:295–320.

———, and O. Morgenstern 1944 *Theory of Games and Economic Behavior.* Princeton: Princeton University Press.

Winer, M. 1979 "Cabinet Coalition Formation: A Game-Theoretic Analysis." In S. J. Brams, A. Schotter, and G. Schwodiauer, eds., *Applied Game Theory.* Wurzburg: Physica-Verlag.

Young, H. P. 1978 "The Allocation of Funds in Lobbying and Campaigning." *Behavioral Science* 23:21–31.

Zermelo, E. 1913 "Uber eine Anwendung der Mengenlehre auf die Theorie des Schachspiels." In E. W. Hobson and A. E. H. Love, eds., *Proceedings of the Fifth International Congress of Mathematicians.* Vol. 2. Cambridge: Cambridge University Press.

H. ANDREW MICHENER

GENDER

GENDER Despite the enormous weight of scientific evidence that differences between women and men are deceptive (Epstein 1988), societies continue to create and maintain these differences (Hess 1990). In an effort to analyze the processes of differentiation, as well as to trace their effects and perhaps derive some policies with which to modify them, sociologists have been wrestling with the conceptualization of gender (Lorber and Farrell 1991).

Gender is the organized pattern of social relations between women and men, not only in face-to-face interaction and within the family but also in the major institutions of society, such as social class, the hierarchies of large-scale organizations, and the occupational structure (Acker 1988, 1990; Reskin 1988). In order to sustain these patterns, women and men need to be demonstrably different—they have to be perceived as clearly separable.

The social reproduction of gender in individuals sustains the gendered societal structure; as individuals act out the expectations of their gender status in face-to-face interaction, they are constructing gender and, at the same time, gendered systems of dominance and power (West and Zimmerman 1987). In most societies, women and men are not only perceived as different but are also differently evaluated, and these supposed differences in characteristics and capabilities justify the power differences between them. As Joan Wallach Scott (1988) says, "Gender is a constitutive element of social relationships based on perceived differences between the sexes, and gender is a primary way of signifying relationships of power" (p. 42).

Gender is so pervasive that, in our society, we assume it is bred into our genes. Given our naturalistic orientation, it is hard to believe that gender is constantly created and recreated out of human interaction, out of social life, and at the same time is the texture and order of that social life. Gender signs and signals are so ubiquitous that we usually fail to notice them. If we meet someone whose gender signals are ambiguous, however, and we cannot tell whether the person is a woman or a man, we are uncomfortable until we have successfully placed that person in some gender category (Devor 1990). In our society, the category can be transvestite (someone who dresses in sex-inappropriate clothing) or transsexual (someone who has had a sex-change operation); these categories confine the ambiguity without disturbing the gender dichotomy. There could be no cross-dressing if there were no distinction between what women and men should wear, and so, underneath the inappropriate clothing, the transvestite is still, we believe, a woman or a man. Actually, the transvestite is a biological female masquerading as a man or a biological male masquerading as a woman. A female-to-male or male-to-female transsexual has traversed the boundaries of gender but has ended up securely in a conventional category, the status of man or woman.

In most instances, a glance places a person in a gender category; the interaction can then proceed along lines established for people of the same or different gender, depending on the context and on other status markers, such as age, race, education, occupational position, religion. Deeply embedded in these established, taken-for-granted rules of everyday interaction are signifiers of power. In "doing gender," as West and Zimmerman (1987) point out, "men are also doing dominance and women are doing deference" (p. 146).

In all societies, the belief that women and men are inherently different provides the moral justification for allocating certain kinds of work to women and to men, and for relegating the rearing of children to women. Religion, language, education, and culture (both popular and high) teach and reinforce the society's values for women and men. The result is a gendered moral order. The acceptance of the legitimacy of this moral order by those who have lesser access to the rewards of the society (property, power, and prestige) makes the dominant moral order hegemonic.

Most analyses of gender and authority try to separate gender effects from standards of competence, demonstrated leadership, or value to the group. Legitimacy—the right to compete for or be appointed to positions of power and prestige—may be used as an intervening variable to see if the same standards apply to women and men (Ridgeway 1988). Only when women and men have the same right to compete are the same standards applied to both, evenhandedly. But where does legitimacy—the sense of the right to a position of authority—come from? Situational theorists argue that it comes from what people in face-to-face interaction bring to the encounter and also, if the dyad or group meets regularly, from the norms and expectations they build up (Stewart 1988; Wagner 1988). Under certain conditions, the group experience can counteract the effect of stereotyped expectations of women and men and even carry over into different groups (Pugh and Wahrman 1983). Given enough such counteractions, new expectations of the leadership potential of women may attain legitimacy.

However, it is difficult to separate gender, competence, leadership, power, and legitimacy. Whether the candidate for leadership is a woman or a man influences the assessment of that person's competence, potential for leadership, and right to a high-status position of power. Gender is not *added* to task-oriented and expressive behaviors; they are *defined by* gender, as in "men are rational; women are emotional" (Hochschild 1983). More research is needed on the conservatism and malleability of gendered status expectations in face-to-face encounters.

Similarly, social institutions and their established positions are so gendered (doctors and nurses, teachers and supervisors, priests and nuns) that when gender boundaries are broken, the prevailing gender dichotomy remains (references to a president, police officer, fire fighter, Supreme Court Justice need to be qualified when the incumbent is a woman; nurse, kindergarten teacher, social worker, secretary need a qualifier when referring to a man). Work and family, the main institutions of most societies, are almost completely gendered. With little rationale or uniformity from society to society, occupations, professions, and jobs within occupations and professions are divided into women's work and men's work (Roos 1985). In the family, all the main kin statuses are gendered, as signified by their names (mother, father, daughter, son, sister, brother, aunt, uncle), although lesser relationships may not be (cousin, stepchild). Here, too, gender is built into the structure of the institution and also played out in its practices, particularly the division of household labor (Berk 1985). Research examining the processes that build gender into paid work and work for the family would be more useful at this point than further studies of what kinds of jobs women and men are tracked into and what kinds of household labor each does.

Finally, gender is not just one among many elements in the stratification systems of complex societies; wherever there is unequal distribution of society's rewards, the lesser distribution of property, power, and prestige to women is considered perfectly equable. Within classes and within racial ethnic groups, whether the group's share of valued resources is larger or smaller, if there are any valued resources at all to be distributed, men monopolize them (Almquist 1987). Gender equality exists under conditions of scarce resources and no permanent property or privileges, as in gathering-hunting societies and in slums, barrios, and ghettos. In the worst human conditions—slavery, concentration camps—women suffer more than men do because they are subject to sexual exploitation and violence from the men in power.

In complex societies, the dominant social group or groups use agencies of social control (government, law, education, medicine, the military, religion) to reinforce the moral order and repress or minimize the effects of resistance and rebellion against the gendered social order. Women's responsibility for reproduction and child rearing justifies men's control over their sexuality in societies in which descent comes through the male line; in matrilineal societies, women have greater sexual freedom. The use of violence (rape and battering) against women is considered an illegitimate means of social control in societies ruled by law; nonetheless, violence against women is a prevalent form of gendered social control that is ambiguously sanctioned (Connell 1987; MacKinnon 1989). In all societies, women are encouraged or coerced into having children or not having them, depending on the needs of the group for current or future workers, and also for future mothers and future soldiers. To the extent that women are coerced into having or not having children by state policy, that policy becomes an additional form of gendered social control (Jenson 1986).

In sum, gender patterns face-to-face interaction; structures work, family, and other social institutions; determines the distribution of scarce and valued resources as well as life chances; and provides the moral legitimacy that keeps most women and men from questioning, challenging, and, to a great extent, even thinking about why these things are the way they are.

DOING RESEARCH ON GENDER

There have been many studies comparing women and men, but few analyzing gender itself. First, the concept is usually sex, not gender—that is, an assumed biological "fact" and not a social construction. Also, there is almost no recognition that both sex, as a social category, and gender, as a social construction, are problematic. That there are two sexes or two genders is taken as a given (Kessler and McKenna 1978); furthermore, it is assumed that any interviewer can recognize which of the two the respondent is. If a respondent claims to be a woman, it is assumed that a "normal, natural woman" is meant, but the person could instead be a permanent transvestite or a transsexual or someone in transition. It is also assumed that no one ever lies about it.

So sex and gender are twofold variables in most research—and assumed to be the cause, a prior condition, and not an effect. Another assumption is that men and women are so different they can be put into discrete categories. The researcher then usually goes on to see what difference sex, or gender, makes to the variation in the topic under study (attitudes, or voting behavior, or capacity for various kinds of work, for nurturance, etc.). If differences are found, they are taken to be the result of whatever is different about those in the category, males and females, or men or women, which is a tautology, since the researcher had to start out with the assumption of difference in order to put women and men in different categories in the first place. If differences are not found, it is concluded that sex or gender is not salient to this particular variable, without really disturbing the overall belief that women and men are, basically, different.

Another way of studying gender is to take the point of view of the subject. For the most part, in sociology today, such research is done by women about women (Smith 1987), although there have also been fine studies of men's lives (Brod 1987; Kimmel and Messner 1989). Taking the standpoint of the subject allows for insightful understanding of the perspectives of others, and others' experiences and the meanings of those experiences produce rich and complex data. The problem is that women and men vary by race and ethnicity, social class, language, culture, religion, and politics, by where they were born and where they live at the time of the research, and by sexual practices. So who can take whose standpoint, and what group of women or men can be taken as representative of "woman" or "man"?

In either quantitative or qualitative research, it might be useful to consider the components of gender when designing the research. Gender is not a unitary essence but has many components (cf. West and Zimmerman 1987) that link up as follows:

Sex—actual combination of genes and genitalia; prenatal, adolescent, and adult hormonal input; and procreative capacity (*assumed* to be congruous with one another and with sex category assignment);

Sex category—assignment at birth based on appearance of genitalia;

Sex-gender identity—sense of gendered self as a member of a sex category, sense of female or male body, socially contextualized;

Gender as process—learning, being taught, picking up cues, enacting behavior already learned to be gender-appropriate (or inappropriate if rebelling, testing), "doing gender" as a member of a sex category; and

Gender as status and structure—the individual's gender status as part of the society's structure of prescribed gender relations, especially patterns of dominance and subordination, and the gendered division of labor in the home and at paid work.

In any research on gender, the design should specify which components are being examined and should be careful to confine comparisons to the same component. That is, if women's and men's statuses are the subject of study, their sex category should not be the basis for comparison, since a transsexual has a woman's gender status but was not assigned to the sex category female at birth. The cause or the effect of gender status, therefore, cannot be reduced to biological sex.

If gender as process is the research question, it would be useful to compare the socialization of those who were assigned the sex category female, were brought up as girls, and took on the adult status of woman, with those who took on the adult status of man (for example, passed for men so they could work as men or had sex-change surgery). Similarly, one could compare subjects who were assigned the category male, were brought up as boys, and took on the adult status of man, with those who took on the adult status of woman (permanent transvestites and transsexuals). Then all of these groups could be compared with one another. In this design, there are *four to six* genders, not two.

Research on the intersection of gender status and gendered social institutions has compared women who have gender-inappropriate careers with men in the same occupation to see whether the processes that led to their occupational choices and to their achievements are similar or different (Epstein 1981; Kanter 1977; Lorber 1984). What is needed is more research that compares men in gender-inappropriate family roles with women, such as Beer's study of "househusbands" (1982) and Risman's study of single fathers (1987).

THE INTERSECTION OF GENDER, RACE, AND SOCIAL CLASS

Gender has a material base in the production of food and the reproduction of children. Gender patterns and orders economic production and social reproduction, creating cooperation, reciprocal exchange, and competition for scarce resources, bonds of trust and loyalty, and also conflict. For individuals, gender, race, and social class greatly affect opportunities for a good education, well-paying jobs, and positions of authority. For the society as a whole, gender, race or ethnicity, and social class are the main building blocks of the stratification system that structures the distribution of power, prestige, and property.

The outcome of these patterns is often inferior status for all women (Chafetz 1984) and oppression for the women of the most disadvantaged races and classes, particularly in developing countries (Benéria and Stimpson 1987; Brydon and Chant 1989; Leacock and Safa 1986; Mies, Bennholdt-Thomsen, and von Werlhof 1988; Nash and Fernández-Kelly 1983). In the United States, black working-class women are subject to discrimination by white men and white women and may also suffer from sexist attitudes of black men (Hooks 1984). Similar patterns occur among Asian Americans (Chow 1987) and Hispanic Americans (Garcia 1989). Much more work is needed at this point on the intersection of gender, race, and class, particularly in family structure (Zinn 1990), and further work needs to be done on the articulation of work for the family and work for pay along the lines of Hartsock's *Money, Sex, and Power* (1983) and Sokoloff's *Between Money and Love* (1980).

Although there are many past and present instances of subversion and rebellion on the part of women and men of all groups to the strictures of gender, race, and class, societies and communities that have tried to become egalitarian have never seriously restructured the gendered division of work or family roles (Agassi 1989; Chafetz and Dworkin 1986). Nor have they tried to structure a society where women and men, defined as different, are equal (Lapidus 1978; Stacey 1983). To do so would entail scrupulously monitoring women's and men's rights, responsibilities, and rewards to make sure neither group becomes dominant (Chafetz 1990).

The question of social orders without gender, or with significantly different gender patterns, has been explored in science fiction (LeGuin 1969; Piercy 1976), but has not been extensively discussed in social theory (Lorber 1986). While such "thought experiments" might be seen as fanciful, they would challenge the underlying assumption of most current sociological theory and research that gender and sex are interchangeable and that these variables are dichotomies.

(SEE ALSO: *Comparable Worth; Feminist Theory; Role Models; Sex Differences; Socialization*)

REFERENCES

Acker, Joan 1988 "Class, Gender, and the Relations of Distribution." *Signs* 13:473–497.

———1990 "Hierarchies, Jobs, and Bodies: A Theory of Gendered Organizations." *Gender & Society* 4: 139–158.

Agassi, Judith Buber 1989 "Theories of Gender Equality: Lessons from the Kibbutz." *Gender & Society* 3:160–186.

Almquist, Elizabeth M. 1987 "Labor Market Gendered Inequality in Minority Groups." *Gender & Society* 1:400–414.

Beer, William R. 1982 *Househusbands.* New York: Praeger.

Benéria, Lourdes R., and Catherine R. Stimpson, eds. 1987 *Women, Households, and the Economy.* New Brunswick, N.J.: Rutgers University Press.

Berk, Sarah Fenstermaker 1985 *The Gender Factory.* New York: Plenum.

Brod, Harry (ed.) 1987 *The Making of Masculinities.* Boston: Allen and Unwin.

Brydon, Lynne, and Sylvia Chant 1989 *Women in the Third World.* New Brunswick, N.J.: Rutgers University Press.

Chafetz, Janet Saltzman 1984 *Sex and Advantage.* Totowa, N.J.: Rowman & Allenheld.

———1990 *Gender Equity.* Newbury Park, Calif.: Sage.

———, and Anthony Gary Dworkin 1986 *Female Revolt.* Totowa, N.J.: Rowman & Allenheld.

Chow, Esther Ngan-Ling 1987 "The Development of Feminist Consciousness among Asian American Women." *Gender & Society* 1:284–299.

Connell, Robert W. 1987 *Gender and Power.* Stanford, Calif.: Stanford University Press.

Devor, Holly 1990 *Gender Blending.* Bloomington: Indiana University Press.

Epstein, Cynthia Fuchs 1981 *Women in Law.* New York: Basic Books.

———1988 *Deceptive Distinctions: Sex, Gender and the Social Order.* New Haven, Conn.: Yale University Press.

Garcia, Alma M. 1989 "Chicana Feminist Discourse: 1970–1980." *Gender & Society* 3:217–238.

Hartsock, Nancy C. M. 1983 *Money, Sex, and Power: Toward a Feminist Historical Materialism.* New York: Longman.

Hess, Beth B. 1990 "Beyond Dichotomy: Drawing Distinctions and Embracing Differences." *Sociological Forum* 5:75–93.

Hochschild, Arlie Russell 1983 *The Managed Heart.* Berkeley: University of California Press.

Hooks, Bell 1984 *Feminist Theory: From Margin to Center.* Boston: South End Press.

Jenson, Jane 1986 "Gender and Reproduction: or, Babies and the State." *Studies in Political Economy* 20:9–46.

Kanter, Rosabeth Moss 1977 *Men and Women of the Corporation.* New York: Basic Books.

Kessler, Suzanne J., and Wendy McKenna 1978 *Gender: An Ethnomethodological Approach.* Chicago: University of Chicago Press.

Kimmel, Michael S., and Michael M. Messner (eds.) 1989 *Men's Lives.* New York: Macmillan.

Lapidus, Gail Warshofsky 1978 *Women in Soviet Society.* Berkeley: University of California Press.

Leacock, Eleanor, and Helen I. Safa 1986 *Women's Work: Development and the Division of Labor by Gender.* South Hadley, Mass.: Bergin and Garvey.

LeGuin, Ursula K. 1969 *The Left Hand of Darkness.* New York: Ace.

Lorber, Judith 1984 *Women Physicians: Careers, Status, and Power.* New York and London: Tavistock.

———1986 "Dismantling Noah's Ark." *Sex Roles* 14:567–580.

———, and Susan A. Farrell (eds.) 1991 *The Social Construction of Gender.* Newbury Park, Calif.: Sage.

MacKinnon, Catharine A. 1989 *Toward a Feminist Theory of the State.* Cambridge, Mass.: Harvard University Press.

Mies, Maria, Veronika Bennholdt-Thomsen, and Claudia von Werlhof 1988 *Women: The Last Colony.* London: Zed Books.

Nash, June, and Patricia Fernández-Kelly (eds.) 1983 *Women, Men, and the International Division of Labor.* Albany: State University of New York Press.

Piercy, Marge 1976 *Woman on the Edge of Time.* New York: Fawcett Crest.

Pugh, M. D., and Ralph Wahrman 1983 "Neutralizing Sexism in Mixed-Sex Groups: Do Women Have to Be Better Than Men?" *American Journal of Sociology* 88:746–762.

Reskin, Barbara 1988 "Bringing the Men Back In: Sex Differentiation and the Devaluation of Women's Work." *Gender & Society* 2:58–81.

Ridgeway, Cecilia L. 1988 "Gender Differences in Task Groups: A Status and Legitimacy Account." In Murray Webster, Jr., and Martha Foschi, eds., *Status Generalization: New Theory and Research.* Stanford, Calif.: Stanford University Press.

Risman, Barbara J. 1987 "Intimate Relationships from a Microstructural Perspective: Men Who Mother." *Gender & Society* 1:6–32.

Roos, Patricia A. 1985 *Gender and Work: A Comparative Analysis of Industrial Societies.* Albany: State University of New York Press.

Scott, Joan Wallach 1988 *Gender and the Politics of History.* New York: Columbia University Press.

Smith, Dorothy E. 1987 *The Everyday World as Problematic.* Toronto: University of Toronto Press.

Sokoloff, Natalie J. 1980 *Between Money and Love.* New York: Praeger.

Stacey, Judith 1983 *Patriarchy and Socialist Revolution in China.* Berkeley: California University Press.

Stewart, Penni 1988 "Women and Men in Groups: A Status Characteristics Approach to Interaction." In Murray Webster, Jr., and Martha Foschi, eds., *Status Generalization: New Theory and Research.* Stanford, Calif.: Stanford University Press.

Wagner, David G. 1988 "Gender Inequalities in Groups: A Situational Approach." In Murray Webster, Jr., and Martha Foschi, eds., *Status Generalization: New Theory and Research.* Stanford, Calif.: Stanford University Press.

West, Candace, and Don Zimmerman 1987 "Doing Gender." *Gender & Society* 1:125–151.

Zinn, Maxine Baca 1990 "Family, Feminism, and Race in America." *Gender & Society* 4:68–82.

JUDITH LORBER

GENERAL LINEAR MODEL

GENERAL LINEAR MODEL The *general linear model* refers to the application of the linear regression equation to solve analysis problems that initially do not meet the assumptions of linear regression analysis. Specifically, there are three situations in which the assumptions of linear regression are violated but regression techniques can still be used: (1) the use of nominal-level measures (such as race, religion, marital status) as independent variables—a violation of the assumption that all variables are measured at the interval or ratio level; (2) the existence of interaction effects between independent variables—a violation of the assumption of additivity of effects; and (3) the existence of a curvilinear effect of the independent variable on the dependent variable—a violation of the assumption of linearity. The linear regression equation can be applied in all of these situations provided certain procedures and operations are carried out on the variables. These situations and their solutions within the linear regression model will be described in greater detail below.

REGRESSION WITH DUMMY VARIABLES

In situations where the dependent variable is measured at the interval level of measurement (ordered values at fixed intervals) but one or more independent variables are measured at the nominal level (no order implied between values), analysis of variance/covariance procedures is usually more appropriate than linear regression. Linear regression analysis can be used in these circumstances, however, as long as the nominal-level variables are first "dummy coded." The results will be consistent with those obtained from an analysis of variance/covariance, but can also be interpreted within a regression framework.

Dummy coding is a procedure in which a separate dichotomous variable is created for each category of the nominal-level variable. For example, in a study of the effects of racial experience, the variable for race can have several values that imply no order nor degree. Some of the categories might be white, black, Hispanic, Indian, Asian, and Other. Since these categories imply no order nor degree, the variable for race cannot be used in a linear regression analysis.

The alternative is to create five dummy variables—one for each race category except one. Each of these variables measures whether the respondent is the particular race. For example, the first variable might be for the category "white," where a value of zero is assigned if the person is any race but white, and a value of one is assigned if the person is white. Similarly, separate variables would be created to identify membership in the black, Hispanic, Indian, and Asian groups. A dummy variable is not created for the "Other" category because its values are completely determined by values on the other dummy variables (for instance, all persons with the racial category "Other" will have a score of zero on all of the dummy variables). This determination is illustrated below.

	VALUES ON DUMMY VARIABLES				
RESPONDENT'S RACE	D1	D2	D3	D4	D5
White	1	0	0	0	0
Black	0	1	0	0	0
Hispanic	0	0	1	0	0
Indian	0	0	0	1	0
Asian	0	0	0	0	1
Other	0	0	0	0	0

Since there are only two categories or values for each variable, the variables can be said to have interval-level characteristics and can be entered into a single regression equation such as the following:

$$Y = a + b_1D1 + b_2D2 + b_3D3 + b_4D4 + b_5D5,$$

where Y is the score on the dependent variable; a is the constant or Y-intercept; b_1, b_2, b_3, b_4, and b_5 are the regression coefficients representing the effects of each category of race on the dependent variable; and D_1, D_2, D_3, D_4, and D_5 are dummy variables representing separate categories of race. If a person is black, then his/her predicted Y score would be equal to $a + b_2$, since $D2$ would have a value of 1 ($b_2D2 = b_2 * 1 = b_2$) and $D1$, $D3$, $D4$, and $D5$ would all be 0 (for instance, $b_1D1 = b_1 * 0 = 0$). The effect of race would then be the addition of each of the dummy variable effects. Other dummy or interval-level variables could then be included in the analysis and their efforts could be interpreted as "controlling for" the effects of race.

Estimating Analysis-of-Variance Models. The use of dummy variables in regression makes it possible to estimate analysis-of-variance models as well. In the example above, the value of a is equal to the mean score on the dependent variable for those who had a score of "Other" on the race variable (the omitted category). The mean scores for the other racial groups can then be calculated by adding the appropriate b value (regression coefficient) to the a value. For example, the mean for the Hispanic group would be $a + b_3$. In addition, the squared multiple correlation coefficient (R^2) is equivalent to the measure of association used in analysis of variance (ETA-squared), and the F test for statistical significance is equivalent to the one computed using conventional analysis-of-variance procedures. For a more detailed discussion of these similarities, as well as more elaborate dummy coding procedures, see Kerlinger and Pedhazur (1973) and Nie et al. (1975).

Regression with Interaction Effects. An interaction is said to exist when the effect of one variable on some outcome varies depending on the effect of some third variable. For example, Bulcroft (1991) found that, for early adolescent boys, physical development had no overall effect on conflict with parents. However, when level of parental independence giving was taken into consideration, he found that some types of physical development heightened conflict with parents when independence was not given and reduced conflict when independence was given. Such interaction effects are not detectable in normal linear regression, since the assumption is that each independent variable has an "additive" effect on the dependent variable. The general linear model can be used, however, to detect and estimate interaction effects if certain operations are first performed on the data.

To assess interaction effects, special "interaction terms" need to be computed and then entered into the regression equation. These terms are simply the product of the two variables thought to be interacting in their effects on the dependent variable. In the interest of finding the simplest model (one without interaction terms), the conventional approach is to enter each independent variable first (the "main effects") and then to enter the interaction term in a second step. If the interaction explains significant variance in the dependent variable over and above that explained by the separate variables, then an interaction is said to exist and the main effects are not normally interpreted.

The actual interpretation of interaction effects is complicated by the coding used for the separate variables comprising the interaction term. Basically, the interaction term can be conceptualized as a transformation of one's score on one of the interacting variables "weighted" by one's score on the other interacting variable. For example, in the study mentioned above, respondents' scores on the physical change variable were enhanced when they also scored high on parental independence giving. As a result, those adolescents whose parents granted little independence had the lowest scores on the interaction term regardless of how much change they experienced, whereas those adolescents whose parents gave a great deal of independence had scores on the interaction term that varied from low to very high, depending on how much physical change they experienced. When a significant *negative* coefficient was found for the interaction term after controlling for the main effects of physical change and independence, this indicated that physical change *under conditions of high independence* tended to reduce levels of conflict with parents.

In addition to interpretation problems, the use of interaction terms in regression poses technical problems stemming from the fact that the two variables comprising the interaction terms are not usually orthogonal. As a result, unambiguous statements about the "relative" contributions of main effects and interactions to the explanation of variance in the dependent variable are difficult to make, and problems with multicollinearity may arise. Therefore, standardized regression coefficients are invalid for interaction terms and it is generally advisable to assess multicollinearity prior to interpreting any regression involving interaction terms. For a more detailed discussion of interaction terms, see Allison (1977).

REGRESSION WITH CURVILINEAR EFFECTS

The final situation where the assumptions of regression are violated but regression techniques can still be used to analyze the data involves a nonlinear relationship between the dependent and independent variables. An example of a nonlinear relationship would be the effects of age on marital satisfaction among the elderly. According to Gilford (1984), among persons fifty-five or older, increasing age initially results in an increase in positive social interactions; after age sixty-nine, however, the effect of increasing age on positive social interaction is negative. As a result, the highest level of positive social interaction is found among couples between the ages of sixty-three and sixty-nine, with lower levels among younger and older age groups. If these data were analyzed using standard linear regression techniques, the results would suggest that the two variables were not linearly related. The general linear model can still be used, however, as long as the variables in the equation are first transformed.

There are two options available for transforming variables for use in regression when a curvilinear relationship exists: (1) taking the log of the dependent variable and then using the transformed variable in a standard regression, and (2) taking successive powers of the independent variable and entering them stepwise into a standard regression equation (polynomial regression).

If the precise form of the distribution can be predicted from a theory, this form can sometimes be represented by taking the log of the dependent variable. The resulting values would then appear to be linearly related to the independent variables, although the results would be interpreted as nonlinear (specifically, resembling a log scale). This procedure is also used when the dependent variable has a strong negative or positive skew and a linear effect is predicted.

If the precise form of the nonlinear relationship is not known a priori, polynomial regression is the preferred method for assessing the relationship. In polynomial regression, the independent variable is first entered into the regression equation, followed by the square of the independent variable, the cube, and so on. Increasing powers of the independent variable are entered until they no longer add significantly to the variance explained. If the first polynomial term entered is not significant, then a linear relationship is assumed and accepted as the simplest explanation of variance in the dependent variable. If the square of the independent variable is significant, then a single curve in the bivariate distribution is indicated. If the cube of the independent variable is also significant, then the bivariate distribution has two curves. Each additional power of the independent variable represents an additional curve in the distribution. In all of the above cases, however, the actual form of the relationship can be seen only by graphing the bivariate distribution.

CONCLUSION

General linear model refers to the use of the linear regression equation to estimate the relationship between two or more variables when the assumptions of linear regression are violated. The three most common violations involve the use of nominal-level independent variables, the presence of interaction effects, and the possibility of curvilinearity. In all three cases, linear regression techniques can still be used as long as simple transformations are performed on the variables involved.

(SEE ALSO: *Analysis of Variance and Covariance; Correlation and Regression Analysis*)

REFERENCES

Allison, Paul 1977 "Testing for Interaction in Multiple Regression." *American Journal of Sociology* 83(1): 144–153.

Bulcroft, Richard A. 1991 "The Value of Physical Change in Adolescence: Consequences for the Parent–Adolescent Exchange Relationship." *Journal of Youth and Adolescence* 20(1):86–104.

Gilford, Rosalie 1984 "Contrasts in Marital Satisfaction Throughout Old Age: An Exchange Theory Analysis." *Journal of Gerontology* 39(3):325–333.

Kerlinger, Fred N., and Elazar J. Pedhazur 1973 *Multiple Regression in Behavioral Research.* New York: Holt, Rinehart and Winston.

Nie, Norman H., et al. 1975 *SPSS: Statistical Package for the Social Sciences,* 2nd ed. New York: McGraw-Hill.

RICHARD A. BULCROFT

GENOCIDE

GENOCIDE The adoption in December 1948 of the United Nations Convention for the Prevention and Punishment of the Crime of Genocide held out promise of revolutionary change in the internal relations of groups within member states and in the international relations of the states themselves. But in fact the United Nations convention has contributed little to the eradication of genocide, described in the convention as an odious scourge that has inflicted great losses on humanity throughout all periods of history.

Indeed, the recognition of genocide as a crime under international law is a recent development. In antiquity the annihilation of peoples was common enough, whether as punishment for resistance, as incidental to conquest, or as a means of spreading terror. The deity or deities might be participants, thereby sanctifying the destruction. In Europe, during the Middle Ages and later, religious conflict or challenge often resulted in the eradication of dissident sects, and pogroms were associated with periods of religious effervescence, such as the Crusades and Easter, or disaster such as famine or the Black Death.

The current rejection of genocide is a product of the Enlightenment, the influence of the natural law of human rights, the acceptance of humanitarian intervention in the internal affairs of states for the protection of persecuted minorities, the humanitarian conventions regulating warfare, and above all the revulsion against the systematic annihilation of victim peoples by Nazi Germany.

DEFINITION

The free creation of definitions greatly impedes the comparative study of genocide. Yet a curious anomaly is that, notwithstanding this diversity, scholars working on genocide as a general phenomenon agree appreciably on their selection of case studies.

The definitions derive from the perspectives of different disciplines and under the influence of varied ideological commitments, theoretical or ethnocentric. If the emphasis is on the broad category of massacres, then an arbitrary element may enter into the selection of types of massacres deemed to constitute genocide. The scope of genocide may be extended to the one-sided mass murder of any group or fantasized social category. Or the definition may be based on the recognition of the central role of the state in most genocides, which are then viewed as state crimes, with special concern for the types of states that have engaged in genocide. Ethnocentric perspectives are associated, for example, with an excluding emphasis on the genocide perpetrated against one's own group, as in the Holocaust of Jews, and a diminished significance attached to the genocides perpetrated against other groups.

The United Nations convention defines genocide as follows:

> *any of the following acts committed with intent to destroy, in whole or in part, a national, ethnical, racial or religious group, as such:*
>
> *(a) killing members of the group;*
> *(b) causing serious bodily or mental harm to members of the group;*

(c) *deliberately inflicting on the group conditions of life calculated to bring about its physical destruction in whole or in part;*
(d) *imposing measures intended to prevent births within the group;*
(e) *forcibly transferring children of the group to another group.*

This definition has the advantage of being the internationally accepted legal definition, incorporated in a convention that provides some mechanisms for punishment and prevention. It represents, moreover, a crystallization of the varied national and historical experiences and cultural perspectives of the participants in the debates on the convention, and it has now been ratified by over 100 states, though with reservations by a number of signatories.

As is to be expected in a definition arrived at on the basis of consensus and compromise, there are many defects in the final text. The phrase "in whole or in part" is imprecise, and "in part" will be interpreted here to signify an appreciable part of the victimized group. "As such," which qualifies the intent to destroy, replaces an original formulation specifying motive but gives rise to varied interpretations. The present discussion does not view motivation as a legal requisite for commission of the crime, however significant in other respects. The phrase "as such" is here interpreted to signify that the criterion for selection of the victims is membership of the targeted group. And finally, the acts specified as constituting the crime are of very different orders, but they are drawn together as expressions of the intent to destroy.

Selecting from the United Nations convention, the definition of genocide may be summarized as the deliberate destruction of a racial, ethnic, national, or religious group, in whole or appreciable part, by killing members of the group or imposing conditions inimical to survival. This links genocide to central concerns in the social sciences—namely the relations between racial, ethnic, national, and religious groups, illuminating these relations by examining them in the extremes of annihilatory violence and directing attention to the processes of polarization.

TYPOLOGIES

Genocide is not a uniform phenomenon, save at a high level of abstraction, and its manifestations are quite varied. Typologies may be derived inter alia from motivations, objectives, or, if the emphasis is on genocide as a crime committed by states, the nature of the state.

A primary distinction must be drawn between "domestic" genocides, based on internal divisions within a society, and genocide in the course of international war, though bearing in mind that wars may be the occasion for domestic genocides, as in the Turkish genocide of Armenians in World War I and the Nazi Holocaust of Jews, Gypsies, and other groups in World War II. Moreover, the global competition between the superpowers, the so-called cold war, has been waged appreciably by intervention of the superpowers or their surrogates in the domestic conflicts of other states, thereby raising the level of annihilatory violence. The following typology of domestic genocides is based on a classification of the victims in their varied societal contexts. The first two categories may be viewed as perpetually at risk.

Small indigenous groups, often hunters and gatherers, are particularly vulnerable if they inhabit areas with exploitable resources. These are the so-called victims of progress, threatened by settlers, multinational corporations, or governmental agencies.

The second groups are often described as "middleman minorities," engaged in trade or other desirable occupations and usually of a culture and religion different from the dominant groups. Assaults on these groups are relatively unpredictable because the groups are in effect hostages to the fortunes of the host society.

The major sources of domestic genocides are the struggles by racial, ethnic, or religious groups for power, greater autonomy, secession, or more equal participation and freedom from discrimination.

Domestic genocides are phenomena of plural societies. These societies comprise different racial, ethnic, national, or religious groups within a single polity but maintain well-defined divisions between the constituent units; these divisions result from the superimposition of differences—for example, in culture, occupations, political rights, and spatial distribution of the constituent units. By reason of this superimposition, conflicts readily move from one social sector to another, thereby reverberating throughout the society and sometimes escalating to indiscriminate massacre and a point of no return. The processes of polarization in these societies are well known and readily predictable, having been studied in many societies: Algeria, Burundi, German South-West Africa (the Hereros), northern Nigeria, Rwanda, the Sudan, the Ukraine (the "Man-Made Famine of 1932–33"), and Zanzibar.

Many genocides have been committed in the creation of plural societies by colonization and later struggles for decolonization.

THEORIES

Apart from theories of the plural society, which are illuminating for the analysis of domestic genocides, there are more general theories, derived from conceptions of human nature and the social conditions predisposing groups to genocide.

Two antithetical views of the biological nature of human beings or of their personality structure, as molded by the advance of civilization, have been influential in the analysis of genocide. The first, as, for example, in the works of Lorenz (1977) and Koestler (1978), emphasizes human destructiveness in human nature. Since this is presumably a constant, and since many societies have lived for long periods of time in peaceful relations with other societies and with their own inhabitants, it is clear that, even accepting the premise, analysis must be directed to the preconditions that precipitate genocide, such as the responses to the crises of traumatic events.

By contrast, a widely accepted theory postulates dehumanization of the victims, as in the animal or evolutionary analogies of colonization, or the demonization of Jews, as a necessary condition for genocide. This presupposes powerful inhibitions in human society against the mass murder of one's own kind, but it is hardly consistent with the evidence of the vast destruction of human lives in the two world wars of the twentieth century, contemporary genocides, the institutionalization of torture in many societies as a routine instrument of government, and the frequent reports of the joyous abandon of perpetrators in the annihilation of their victims.

An alternate thesis, the brutalization of the perpetrators, with its consequent detachment from empathy with the victims is certainly a major predisposing condition. In societies with highly developed technologics and bureaucracies, this brutalized detachment is promoted by distancing individuals from the killing fields, facilitating the participation of genteel strata.

Contemporary developments as manifested in the Nazi genocide and in nuclearism encourage the development of a new genocidal class, the "killing professionals," analyzed by Lifton and Markusen (1990). However, direct participation in the killing fields is by no means excluded, many Nazi doctors having applied their medical skills, with greater facility and assurance of success, to the annihilation of their helpless victims.

Functional theories, frustration and aggression, Malthusian restraints on population growth, and the expendability of redundant populations are all invoked in theories explaining genocide. The complexity of genocide, and its varied manifestations, certainly call for eclectic interdisciplinary approaches, with particular attention to predisposing conditions and processes.

Ideologies, in a broad societal context of other predisposing conditions, are often a significant element in genocide, contributing to motivation or serving as justification. Differences in religion are a common element in genocide, even when the conflicts do not relate to issues of doctrine or ritual and sectarian challenge. Some sacred texts can readily be interpreted as legitimizing and, indeed, sanctifying genocide, these warrants for genocide entering as predisposing conditions. Secular ideologies, with comparable Manichean perspectives, often serve the same function.

NUCLEARISM AND THE THREAT OF OMNICIDE

At the level of process, movement along the continuum of destruction facilitates genocide in the domestic conflicts between racial, ethnic, and religious groups. The same process has also been significant in the threat to the survival of our species by nuclearism.

The habituation to mass killings in the world wars of the twentieth century, the progressive abolition of the distinction between civilians and combatants in the bombing of London, Coventry, Liverpool, and Rotterdam, and more particularly in the pattern bombings of Dresden and Hamburg and the fire bombing of Tokyo, heralded the advent of nuclearism. The atomic holocausts of Hiroshima and Nagasaki represent the most significant movement on the continuum of destruction toward total war and the rejection of humanitarian rules of war, preparing the way for the proliferation of increasingly sophisticated and annihilatory nuclear weapons. Nuclear bombs, warheads, and missiles are weapons of indiscriminate effect—genocidal weapons par excellence.

Nuclearism has produced an ultimate absurdity, analyzed by Lifton and Markusen (1990), which greatly magnifies the nuclear threat. Incredibly, we rely for protection on the proliferation of the very weapons that threaten our survival, enhancing their lethal power by the continuous invention of technological improvements, and we seek prevention in deterrence, which to be realistic implies a readiness to engage in nuclear war.

The movement toward nuclearism appears to have a momentum of its own, propelled by the involvement of leading scientists seeking to control the elemental forces of nature, and the competitive interests of giant bureaucracies and great industrial empires. Perhaps the reconciliation in the early 1990s between the superpowers holds promise for the future. This reconciliation has initiated a reversal of the superpowers' race to deploy more powerful weapons. But in the meantime, nuclear technology has proliferated beyond the superpowers' borders, and this still poses a threat to the survival of our species.

Lifton and Markusen seek a long-term solution in the development of "species consciousness," defined as "an expansion of collective awareness, an altered sense of self that embraces our reality as members of a single species" (1990, p. 255). It is the theoretical antithesis of the genocidal mentality activating genocide and nuclearism.

PREVENTION

Meanwhile, domestic genocides continue, seemingly unabated. Development projects still routinely threaten the survival of small indigenous groups. Conflicts between racial, ethnic, and religious groups take their deadly toll of lives. Starvation, a traditional weapon in forcing submission, is deployed, as in the Sudan, Somalia, and Eritrea, even when relief aid is immediately available. And there are grounds for anticipating a mounting wave of genocide as a result of the increasing pressure of population on resources, the ready availability of more lethal weapons in a vigorous national and international arms trade, and the seeming condonation implicit in the failure of preventive measures.

The United Nations convention relied appreciably on punishment as a deterrent. But to be effective, provision should have been made for universal jurisdiction, as in the crimes of piracy or the forging of currency. Instead, jurisdiction is vested in a competent tribunal of the state in which the act was committed or in an international penal tribunal whose jurisdiction has been accepted. Because no such tribunal has been established, or seems likely to be established, and because domestic genocides are generally committed by or with the complicity of governments, there is an implicit absurdity in vesting jurisdiction in the offending governments. It is only when the government has been overthrown that punitive action might be instituted, and even then the former leaders are likely to find sanctuary in other countries.

This same characteristic of genocide as primarily a government crime inhibits preventive action in the United Nations. Contracting parties to the convention may bring complaints of genocide to the International Court of Justice, but no such complaint has ever been filed, and a well-prepared initiative charging genocide by the Khmer Rouge in Cambodia foundered because no state was willing to sponsor the action. And in deliberations within the United Nations, regional and ideological alliances and calculations of national self-interest protect offending states.

Nevertheless, preventive action can be effective in the early stages of genocidal conflict, when the many infringements of human rights provide opportunities for applying restraint and alerting international opinion. And other intergovernmental forums, such as the European Assembly and Parliament, provide more favorable milieus for preventive action.

States, and particularly wealthy donor states, can apply diplomatic, trade, and other sanctions. But much of the initiative has come from the many nongovernmental organizations that have proliferated in recent years to compensate for the inadequacies of intergovernmental institutions. Their continued active involvement remains an indispensable prerequisite for effective preventive action.

(SEE ALSO: *International Law; Race; War*)

REFERENCES

Becker, Elizabeth 1986 *When the War Was Over: The Voices of Cambodia's Revolution and Its People.* New York: Simon and Schuster.

Chaliand, Gerard, and Yves Ternon 1983 *The Armenians: From Genocide to Resistance.* London: Zed Press.

Chalk, Frank, and Kurt Jonassohn 1990 *The History and Sociology of Genocide.* New Haven, Conn.: Yale University Press.

Charney, Israel 1984 *Toward the Understanding and Prevention of Genocide.* Boulder, Colo.: Westview Press.

Charney, Israel (ed.) 1988 *Genocide: A Critical Bibliographic Review.* New York: Facts on File.

Dadrian, Vahakn N. 1989 "Genocide as a Problem of National and International Law: The World War I Armenian Case and Its Contemporary Legal Ramifications." *Yale Journal of International Law* 14:221–334.

Davis, Shelton H. 1977 *Victims of the Miracle: Development and the Indians of Brazil.* Cambridge: Cambridge University Press.

Drechsler, Horst 1980 *"Let Us Die Fighting": The Struggle of the Herero and the Nama against German Imperialism.* London: Zed Press.

Fein, Helen 1979 *Accounting for Genocide: National Responses and Jewish Victimization during the Holocaust.* New York: Free Press.

Grosser, Alfred 1989 *Le Crime et la mémoire.* Paris: Flammarion.

Hirsch, Herbert, and Roger Smith 1990 "The Language of Extermination." In Israel Charney, ed., *Genocide: A Critical Bibliographic Review.* New York: Facts on File.

Hovannisian, Richard G. (ed.) 1986 *The Armenian Genocide in Perspective.* New Brunswick, N.J.: Transaction Books.

Koestler, Arthur 1978 *Janus: A Summing Up.* London: Hutchinson.

Kuper, Leo 1981 *Genocide: Its Political Use in the Twentieth Century.* New Haven, Conn.: Yale University Press.

——— 1985 *The Prevention of Genocide.* New Haven, Conn.: Yale University Press.

Lemarchand, René, and David Martin 1974 *Selective Genocide in Burundi.* Report No. 20. London: Minority Rights Group.

Lemkin, Raphael 1944 *Axis Rule in Occupied Europe.* Washington, D.C.: Carnegie Endowment.

Lifton, Robert J. 1986 *The Nazi Doctors: Medical Killing and the Psychology of Genocide.* New York: Basic Books.

———, and Erik Markusen 1990 *The Genocidal Mentality: Nazi Holocaust and Nuclear Threat.* New York: Basic Books.

Lorenz, Konrad 1977. *On Aggression.* New York: Harcourt, Brace, and World.

Melson, Robert 1982 "A Theoretical Inquiry into the Armenian Massacres of 1894–1895." *Comparative Studies in Society and History* 2:481–509.

Staub, Ervin 1989 *The Roots of Evil: The Origins of Genocide and Other Group Violence.* Cambridge: Cambridge University Press.

Walliman, Isidor, and Michael N. Dobkowski (eds.) 1987 *Genocide and the Modern Age: Etiology and Case Studies of Mass Death.* New York: Greenwood Press.

LEO KUPER

GERMAN SOCIOLOGY "German Sociology" has two specific traits: It is part of the general humanities tradition of German culture —that is, it has a philosophical orientation—and it emphasizes epistemological reflection, favoring the understanding of human action through *verstehen* (intuitive oneness with the explanandum). This is the way in which Raymond Aron (1935) characterized sociology in Germany, studying it at the time of the Nazi regime, when it was mainly a memory and not a living field of knowledge or profession.

Since then a large number of books and essays in the United States have treated sociology as practiced in Germany, at least some of which broaden the image (Nisbet 1966; Fletcher 1971; Oberschall 1965, 1972; Schad 1972; Freund 1978). The dominant meaning of the intellectual commodity called German sociology—as continued in the works of Salomon (1945), Barnes (1938), Coser (1977), Zeitlin (1981), and especially Meja, Misgeld, and Stehr (1987)—is that of grand theory with a teleological meaning. This "German Sociology" is only a small part of sociology in Germany, but it is the aspect to which the intellectual community at large reacts; and it is reinforced by selectivity in translation and citation. For the social sciences in the United States, those parts of sociology in other countries which are least like American sociology are searched out as welcome completions.

THE CLASSICAL PERIOD

By the turn of the twentieth century, sociology had become an exciting intellectual concern in the United States, France, England, and Germany. Since an educated person at that time was expected to know English, German, and French, there was intensive direct interaction. Of special importance were the exchanges among Albert Schäffle (1884), Ferdinand Tönnies (1887), Emile Durkheim (e.g., 1887), and Georg Simmel (1890). Durkheim first made a name for himself in France by reviewing German social science literature by authors such as Wilhelm Wundt and, especially, Ferdinand Tönnies, and was therefore attacked as a Germanophile. Tönnies's distinction *Gemeinschaft* (community) and *Gesellschaft* (society) influenced Durkheim's dichotomy mechanical and organic solidarity, and Tönnies in turn commented on Durkheim's notion of the division of labor as the central element in social evolution (Gephardt 1982). Initially the builders of large "systems," such as Ludwig Gumplowitz (1883), Gustav Ratzenhofer (1893), and Theodore Abel (1929), dominated German sociological literature.

In a review of the period up to 1914, Leopold von Wiese (1959) lists Ferdinand Tönnies, Max Weber, and Werner Sombart as the most important sociologists; the list should also include Alfred Vierkandt, Franz Oppenheimer, Alfred Weber, Roberto Michels, and Hermann Kantorowicz (Käsler 1984). This inner circle of sociologists of the "classical period" is still influential today.

In the closing days of the German empire, sociology was established in an elitist academy with Tönnies as president, Sombart as vice president, and von Wiese as the eminence gris. Simmel and Weber were considered to be the leading scholars within this academy, even though both had become merely observers. In 1912, after numerous editions, Tönnies's *Gemeinschaft und Gesellschaft,* first published in 1887, at last achieved wide recognition among the educated public, paralleling the impact of Edward A. Ross's *Social Control* in the United States.

THE WEIMAR PERIOD

Upon the reestablishment of sociology in 1919, von Wiese was able to retain bureaucratic control over the policy of the academy and largely over its conventions. Not until the end of the 1920s was the first chair of sociology instituted in Frankfurt. However, during the fourteen years of the Weimar Republic, forty professorships were created that combined sociology with another discipline, such as economics, philosophy, or law. Eight periodicals had *Sociology* in their titles, and another eight regularly published sociological contributions. Von Wiese was instrumental in founding the first permanent research institute at the University of Cologne, Forschungsinstitut für Sozial- und Verwaltungswissenschaften, in 1919 (Alemann 1978), followed in 1923 by the Institut für Sozialforschung in Frankfurt (Jay 1973). In the early 1930s nearly all universities in Germany regularly offered courses in sociology, and by the mid-1920s the Deutsche Gesellschaft für Soziologie had begun to question the wisdom of opposing a degree curriculum in the universities.

The 1920s were a time of abrasive partisanship in German intellectual life. René König groups the various positions along a dividing line between left and right Hegelians, the Kantian tradition having paled in the humanities (König 1987). Left Hegelian translates into Marxism, but that itself was very heterogeneous. When Eisenstadt and Curelaru (1976, p. 122) and Zeitlin (1981, p. v) maintain that "a critical reexamination of Marxism" is a main focus of German sociology, this is an error; Marxists and non-Marxists mostly tended to ignore each other, although not in the 1920s.

"In the 1920s there was no dominant figure in sociology, which evolved in a number of milieus with little common direction. Even within its local centers in the Weimar Republic there was practically no paradigmatic unity" (Lepsius 1987, p. 40). These local centers were Frankfurt, Cologne, Berlin, and (later) Leipzig. In this characterization of the Weimar turmoil, there are two omissions: Max Weber's influence is not mentioned, and the Frankfurt School is bypassed. In both cases it is done for the same reason: at that time they were not very important for sociology. Shortly after accepting a professorship in Munich, Weber died in 1920. Some of his most important works on religion had appeared during the war, and his magnum opus, *Wirtschaft und Gesellschaft* (Economy and Society) was published posthumously by his wife Marianne Weber. Other works by Weber were not readily available until after about 1925.

The Institut für Sozialforschung in Frankfurt did not see itself as an institute for sociologists. Felix J. Weill, who obtained the funds for the institute from his grain merchant father, would have preferred to call it Institute for Marxism, but it was then judged prudent to choose the neutral title Social Research. All of the members shared an aesthetic disgust with bourgeois society, though they themselves were from well-off-to-very-rich families, and they wanted to convert fellow intellectuals to this view. The most important effect of the institute until the 1940s, however, was to give younger social scientists a chance to develop their talents: Max Horkheimer, Karl August Wittfogel, Franz Borkenau, Leo Löwenthal, Herbert Marcuse, and Theodor Adorno. "Although without much impact in Weimar, and with even less during the period of exile that followed, the Frankfurt School was to become a major force in the revitalization of Western European Marxism in the postwar years" (Jay 1973, p. 4).

AN END TO SOCIOLOGY

It is easier to name sociologists who did not emigrate as the Nazi regime came to power than to list the émigrés. Of all the sociologists with a reputation, only the social philosopher Hans Freyer welcomed the new regime. Werner Sombart, who during his lifetime took just about every political stance available, was in an anticapitalist-anti-Semitic phase around 1933. It must have protected him when, in 1938, he ridiculed racism and the glorification of the people. Franz Oppenheimer and Eric Vögelin were eventually forced to emigrate, even though they tried to remain. Othmar Spann lost his professorship in 1938 and was imprisoned. Ferdinand Tönnies, whose show of opposition bordered on the suicidal, was ostracized. Alfred Weber was dismissed. Alfred Vierkandt had to cease lecturing. Alfred von Martin resigned. The Deutsche Gesellschaft für Soziologie was suspended in 1934 by von Wiese in order to avoid a takeover. Von Wiese stopped publishing the *Kölner Zeitschrift* in the same year, and from then on, lectured only on the history of economic thought. René König, a young candidate for a professorial career who had to emigrate in 1935, attributes to the Nazis a complete stoppage of sociology worthy of its name (König 1978, p. 14).

A SECOND BEGINNING

Sociology after 1945 could not have been a continuation of a tradition; and even if it had been possible, it would not have been a discipline in which basic issues had been settled. This is especially true for the issue of professionalization, which translates into the question "What public are the sociologists addressing?"

Emigrants returning to Germany (René König, Max Horkheimer, Theodor W. Adorno, Siegfried Landshut, Helmut Plessner, Arnold Bergsträsser, Emmerich K. Francis, and, much later, Norbert Elias) often had been influenced by developments in America. American sociology was most influential, since books from the United States often were the only ones available. The "Young Turks" of sociology born between 1926 and 1930—Karl Martin Bolte, Rainer M. Lepsius, Burkhart Lutz, Renate Mayntz, Erwin K. Scheuch, and Friedrich Tenbruck—studied the subject in American universities.

Three of the five research centers of the period of reconstruction were financed by foreign sources: the Sozialforschungsstelle Dortmund with funds from the Rockefeller Foundation; the UNESCO Institute for Social Research in Cologne, through the initiative of Alva Myrdal; and the Institut für Sozialwissenschaftliche Forschung in Darmstadt, with American government money. The trade unions established sociology as a "democratic discipline" in Hamburg at the Akademie für Gemeinschaft. Von Wiese reopened the institute in Cologne that later was integrated into the university. With generous financing from American sources, such as the government-sponsored Voice of America, the Institut für Sozialforschung in Frankfurt resumed operations. And in Göttingen, Hans Paul Bahrdt took up the tradition of industrial sociology of the late Weimar times and founded the Soziologisches Forschungsinstitut, Göttingen—the SOFI Institut. Thus, from the resumption of sociology in Germany, there was an infrastructure for empirical social research well connected to the international community. With the exception of von Wiese's institute, however, it later proved to be impossible to integrate these institutes for empirical research into the universities, and therefore the UNESCO Institute, the Sozialforschungsstelle Dortmund, and the Darmstadt group ceased to exist.

Empirical social research at that time was largely understood to be an import from the United States. At the UNESCO Institute in Cologne and in Darmstadt, important community studies inspired by American studies of the 1930s and 1940s were carried out. The reports by Renate Mayntz and Erich Reigrotzki are still very much worth reading. Parallel to this, survey research was developed as a commercial service; here, too, the American standards of the time were immediately imported. Of great influence were the survey units that the American and British governments had begun as their troops moved into Germany. It was in these survey units that the core personnel of the later German institutes learned their techniques (Scheuch 1990b).

The 1950s were characterized by a coexistence of professors who had learned sociology largely on their own before 1945 and a larger number of sociologists born between 1926 and 1930 who were virtually identical in skill and outlook with their American contemporaries. For this generation Weimar sociology was forgotten, and the classics were read with an American selectivity and perspective.

By the end of the 1950s sociology—in terms of chairs, curricula, students, and volume of empirical research—had surpassed the level of 1933. Much against the wishes of von Wiese and Horkheimer, the German Sociological Association had been transformed from an elitist academy into a professional association with increasingly important sections or research committees in which the Young Turks were able to attract followers. The sections for industrial sociology (for the more theoretically minded) and for methodology (for the mainly empirically oriented) offered an alternative to the plenary meetings that were still dominated by professors who were the last academic mandarins of German tradition. In research nearly everyone who later influenced the discipline worked on social stratification, which as a central topic succeeded the community studies of the first half of the 1950s. Among the Young Turks and their following a structural functional approach was the common paradigm, and Talcott Parsons was held to be the great theorist of the time.

Sociology was a deeply divided discipline. One dividing line pitted those who had emigrated against sociologists who had supported the Nazi regime. Hans Freyer, Arnold Gehlen, and Helmut Schelsky were accused of collaborating with the regime; Gunter Ipsen did more than that; and Karl-Heinz Pfeffer and Karl Valentin Müller were justly denounced as racists. In 1960 the German Sociological Association nearly split along the dividing line between collaborators with the Nazi regime and the majority led by former immigrants.

However, it was not possible simply to dismiss Gehlen and Schelsky as former Nazi sympathizers. While they had been exactly that, they now did important scholarly work. Gehlen developed an anthropology that included perhaps the best approach to the analysis of social institutions, and Schelsky had initiated many important studies on youth, the family, and social stratification. The two men published a textbook in sociology that saw four editions within three years (Gehlen and Schelsky 1955).

The second dividing line ran between the Frankfurt Institute and all others. Horkheimer, Adorno, and Pollack had been successful in the United States, the home of modern sociology. By now their Marxism had toned down to a variant of left Hegelianism that they christened "critical theory." Initially a political camouflage, it now characterized the retained commitment to cultural criticism of bourgeois society. The combination of Marxism with cultural criticism proved to be a winning message with the cultural establishment.

The opposition to Schelsky/Gehlen and Adorno/Horkheimer crystallized around René König, whom von Wiese had invited to Cologne. Originally a pure humanist—he wrote what is considered the standard monograph on Niccolo Machiavelli (1941)—in exile he had identified with the post-Durkheim school in France. Upon returning to Germany in 1950, he recognized the need to familiarize the young generation of sociologists and sociology students with mainstream American sociology. Although himself not a quantitatively minded scholar, he encouraged quantitative social research as an antidote to the temptations of speculative grand theory. Knowing his personal preference for cultural anthropology and French culture, it is ironic that he was the key figure in thoroughly Americanizing the larger part of an academic generation in sociology.

König's *Soziologie heute* (Sociology Today, 1949), a sociological rendering of existentialist philosophy, was the first postwar best-seller in sociology. The dictionary of sociology that he edited (1958) brought together most of the Young Turks and became the largest selling sociology book ever in Germany, with more than twenty editions and almost half a million copies. Most important for the profession, however, was the two-volume handbook of empirical social research (1962) that he edited, conceived along the lines of Gardner-Lindzey's *Handbook of Social Psychology* (König 1962). The handbook is still a standard for empirical sociology and has gone through several editions. All of these works were translated into English, French, Spanish, and Italian, and some into Japanese as well.

The different positions in the first phase of sociology after 1945 were sorted into three "schools" that were to constitute sociology in Germany: the Frankfurt School, the Cologne School, and the Schelsky school. Within the discipline the Cologne school set standards for curricula and research, the *Kölner Zeitschrift* being stronger than the Dortmund-based *Soziale Welt.* The readers of these two largest social science journals do not overlap much. *Kölner Zeitschrift* is the journal for the discipline, while *Soziale Welt* is for practitioners of social science in bureaucracies and the helping professions. Thus, the publics of the three "schools" were different and have remained so: the Frankfurt school for the cultural intelligentsia; the Cologne school for social scientists; the Schelsky school for practical applications in welfare and bureaucracy. It was largely the pressure from the respective audiences more than the preferences of the professors that for a long time caused sociology in Germany to be divided into these three camps.

THE TIME OF EXPANSION

The second most formative decade was the 1960s. It marked a return to important subjects of the classics and to some authors of that time. The Americanization of the discipline had peaked.

After the vituperous quarrels in the Deutsche Gesellschaft in the 1950s it was agreed to meet in closed session at Tübingen in 1961, to discuss basis issues in a purely scholarly atmosphere. Unexpectedly this led to a controversy between two radically different views of social science, the chief protagonists of which were Theodor W. Adorno and Karl Popper (Adorno 1962), between science as a vehicle for emancipation and a scientific view of science. Popper's work is in the philosophy of science rather conventional sociology. For Adorno empiricism means supremacy of instrumental reasoning, which subjugates reason to the rule of facts; empiricism is tantamount to "treating facts as fetishes" (Adorno 1969, p. 14). This dispute was continued by two nonsociologists —the economist Hans Albert and the philosopher Jürgen Habermas—as the "positivism controversy," Habermas representing the Frankfurt school of critical theory and Albert the Cologne school of neopositivism (Adorno 1975). This was a revival of the methodological controversies in the Verein für Socialpolitik in the decade prior to 1914.

The controversy between Habermas und Albert occurred during the 1964 sociology convention that was dedicated to the rediscovery of Max Weber. The topic that sent shock waves throughout the cultural establishment (Stammer 1965) was the revival of the debate on value judgments as part of science. The "radical" sociologists who began to appear at this time took as their central argument the charge that positivism was blind to the forces its research served.

The repercussions were much larger: the arguments of critical theory against positivism became a credo among the cultural intelligentsia. It is important for an understanding of sociology in Germany that this old controversy did not spring from developments within the discipline; rather, it became an unavoidable topic because the intellectual environment forced it onto sociology.

Meanwhile, a seeming alternative to the Cologne and Frankfurt Schools, though closely related to the latter in its concerns, became the major intellectual success: Ralf Dahrendorf with his *Gesellschaft und Demokratie in Deutschland* (1965). How was the Nazi regime possible? Could it reappear in a different guise? This topic keeps emerging in Germany as a central focus in intellectual attempts at self-analysis. In the 1980s the intellectual public expected answers from a controversy among historians; in the 1960s the expectations were focused on sociology and Dahrendorf.

Dahrendorf, trained as a philosopher, is a self-taught sociologist. By temperament he is a moralist, as is evident in his dissertation exploring the idea of justice in Marx's thought (1954). He was subsequently among the Young Turks who concentrated on industrial sociology, and published an immensely successful book on the subject (Dahrendorf 1956) that overshadowed a more original monograph by Heinrich Popitz, Hans Paul Bahrdt, Ernst-August Jüres and Hanno Kesting (1957) that is yet to be recognized internationally as a classic. Among younger sociologists Dahrendorf became a central focus of controversy as a result of his long essay on role theory, in which he characterizes modern society as a cage of obligations that prevent individuality from asserting itself (Dahrendorf 1959b). While the profession largely rejected this notion as a misperception of role theory and economics, the book *Homo Sociologicus* remained for decades the most popular sociological treatise among students (Dahrendorf, 1959b). An essay on chances for complete social equality was Dahrendorf's contribution to the topic of social stratification (Dahrendorf 1961), then dominant among the Young Turks. A much more important publication for an understanding of his concerns is his treatment of the United States as the one case where presumably there was an attempt to construct a society in the spirit of the French Enlightment (Dahrendorf 1963). Characteristically, Dahrendorf takes as his point of departure a source of general intellectual importance, in this case Alexis de Tocqueville's report on the United States in the 1830s.

As Adorno had introduced the concerns of the cultural public into the profession, so Dahrendorf did the same for the intelligentsia concerned with public affairs. In the English-speaking world he is often included in sociological curricula as a conflict theoretician, but there is no conflict theory in his writings, except for an attempt at a taxonomy of conflicts. The label *conflict theoretician* was affixed because of his criticism of Talcott Parsons, whose structural functionalism he accused of glorifying social harmony. Dahrendorf's central theme is to explore the chances for the values of British liberalism to become the guiding principle in society. In practical life this orientation met with mixed success.

In the 1970s Dahrendorf returned to England to become the first foreign president of the London School of Economics. He later became a professor at Oxford and remains a respected commentator on public affairs with a continuing interest in sociology as an intellectual endeavor. Although frequently in error in his statements that have empirical content, he is invariably sensitive in choosing topics that relate the discipline to an intellectual public.

The mood of the times was moving away from the liberal creed of Dahrendorf. The controversies in the United States, stimulated by the Vietnam intervention, were taken up by politicized students in Germany. Marxism was believed to provide answers that the liberal promise of the postwar Western world apparently could not. The varieties of Marxism were studied with religious fervor.

At the 1968 convention of the German Sociological Association demands for an alternative to mainstream sociology, especially the "Cologne Americanism," exploded. Adorno had chosen as the congress's theme, "Late Capitalism or Industrial Society"—alternative ways of conceptualizing the same reality. The term "late capitalism" was favored by Neo-marxists as implying that the demise of bourgeois society was imminent. It also implied that the notion of a basic sameness of all industrial societies—that the United States and the Soviet Union were structurally related as industrial socieites—was wrong. The Neo-Marxist conceptualization "late capitalism" and, by contrast, critical theory implied that the social orders of the Soviet Union and the United States were dedicated to a different telos, and that this difference was what mattered most (Adorno 1969).

With the May 1968 uprising in Paris, the student movement in Germany turned into a crusade for leftism as the mandatory creed on campus, and specifically for sociologists. For a moment the adherents of the Frankfurt school could see the student movement as the realization of their hopes. Max Horkheimer had always rejected any methodological constraints on philosophizing, and on any scholarship. Methodology would restrict science to the factual, while for Horkheimer, Adorno, and Bloch the prime goal of scholarship was creative utopianism. According to Horkheimer, it was now up to science to provide the answers given earlier by religion (Horkheimer 1968). The student movement, however, accused the Frankfurt school of running away from reality, and critical theory of having only negative messages and no direction for positive action. Adorno had always maintained this view (Adorno 1969). Deposing a ruling class would not change the basic character of relations that were permeated with instrumental reasoning; there was no longer a revolutionary subject to realize the cause of emancipation. After some very ugly clashes, Adorno died in 1969. Dahrendorf turned against the student movement, as did such well-known sociologists as Helmut Schelsky and Helmut Schoeck. Erwin Scheuch's *Anabaptists of the "Affluent Society"* (1968) became a best-seller. Even Habermas, irritated by the uncompromising nature of the New Left, severed his connection by diagnosing its "left fascism" (Habermas 1969).

In the turbulent years that followed 1968, sociologists were more concerned with reacting to the New Left than with developments of their own. Sociology had been utterly surprised by a student movement that it neither predicted nor understood. Rainer Lepsius contrasts this situation with the immediate success of empirical sociology in analyzing the right-wing protest NPD party (National-Demokratische Partei Deutschlands) of the late 1960s (Lepsius 1976, p. 7).

The public, however, identified sociology with the New Left. An explosion of leftist literature, using sociological terminology, buried the output of sociologists. The public image of sociology became one of a haven for radicals opposed to bourgeois society. For about ten years after 1968, sociology became the quarry for cultural discourse. Academic fields that were based on shared beliefs in civil society and cultural values—such as pedagogy, art appreciation, literary criticism, and political education—had their criteria damaged, even destroyed. Sociology was used to provide an alternative rationale: service to the cause of emancipation from bourgeois society. Tenbruck (1984) has charged that sociology had "colonized" the humanities, and even life in general. It actually was the other way round: as the humanities lost their belief in civil society, they raided sociology for arguments in the name of society. Professional sociology completely lost control over the use of its vocabulary—with disastrous results for the self-selection of students of sociology and the standing of the field in the world of scholarship.

The student protest movement, and various alternative cultures loosely associated with it, became a regular part of public life in Germany, as it had in the United States. It became fashionable to call a great number of protest forms *sociology* while denouncing the profession carrying out "normal science" (Kuhn 1970) as "bourgeois" sociology. Sociologists were asked to react to fashionable topics of the day, such as permissive education, Third World dependency, mind-expanding drugs, feminism, gay power, autonomous living. Many of the newly appointed professors went along, contributing to the erroneous public impression that sociology was spearheading the cultural revolution in the name of anticapitalism. The opposite was true: sociologists often caved in to demands from the protest movements.

Even in a less turbulent intellectual environment, the period between 1968 and 1973 would have been most unsettling, because it was a period of unique expansion. By the mid-1960s social democratic state governments had been convinced by proponents of the Frankfurt school that sociology should be included in the curricula of secondary education. The profession was divided on this, and as late as 1959 Dahrendorf counseled against the inclusion of sociology in degree curricula even at universities. With the youth, however, sociology was a huge success; many teachers were needed, and that meant many more professors. In 1968 there were 55 tenured positions as professor of sociology in the Federal Republic of Germany; in 1973 there were 190 (Lamnek 1991). From that year, the rate of expansion levelled, and by 1980 there were 252 "chairs" (Sahner 1982, p. 79).

Lepsius modified this feeling of an avalanche of sociology overwhelming academe (Lepsius 1976, p. 12). At the beginning of the 1970s, sociology had 1.3 percent of all the positions in university budgets, no larger a share than ten years earlier; 1.2 percent of the students took a major in sociology, also the percentage before the expansion; public money for sociological research had always hovered around 1 to 2 percent of all grants. The universities had expanded with explosive rapidity, and in this general explosion sociology merely kept its former share.

As a discipline, sociology, however, was among those least prepared to keep its place during an expansion that within a few years quadrupled the number of students in the Federal Republic. Consequently a great many sociologists were appointed to tenured positions who in other times would not have been. In this process the discipline lost cohesion and common scholarly standards.

THE CONSOLIDATION

After 1968 the Deutsche Gesellschaft für Soziologie was taken over by the Young Turks; from their ranks Dahrendorf, Scheuch, and Lepsius were successively president. The leadership of the association was tired of conventions serving as forums for all kinds of protests, thus further damaging the reputation of the field. Consequently, biannual sociological conventions were suspended until 1974, when a meeting was held in Kassel. While the field had a Babel of views, there was now agreement to coexist.

At the Kassel convention of 1974, a custom was started called *Theorievergleich* (comparison of theory). This is in reality a juxtaposition of sociological "denominations," not a weighing of alternative theoretical propositions (Lepsius 1976, sec. II). At that time four such denominations were defined: (a) behaviorism, the chief proponent of which in Germany was Karl-Dieter Opp; (b) action theory as represented by Hans-Joachim Hummel; (c) functionalism and systems theory, with Niklas Luhman as its prominent representative; and (d) historical materialism, which translates into Marxism. Somewhat later, parts of behaviorism and action theory amalgamated to become rational choice; two German-speaking Dutch sociologists, Reinhard Wippler and Siegwart Lindenberg, are its best-known proponents. Phenomenological sociology has been successful especially among young sociologists, with Jürgen Helle as the chief representative.

The lines between these denominations keep shifting as new variants emerge. In general, though, this approach to theory—to choose a topic such as evolution and then listen to what each denomination has to say about it—appears to have spent itself.

Concern with theory in Germany again means reacting to theory builders, a most dissimilar pair of whom dominated the scene in the 1970s and early 1980s: Jürgen Habermas and Niklas Luhmann. Luhmann is a self-taught sociologist who studied law and became a career administrator. His first specialty was the sociology of organization, which showed a strong influence of Chester I. Barnard. Subsequently Luhmann analyzed phenomena of the *Lebenswelt* (the key term of phenomenology for the world of immediate, unreflected experience—in contrast to the world that science portrayed) at that time influenced by the phenomenologist Edmund Husserl, as in Luhmann's monograph on trust as the basis for social cohesion. Luhmann later met Talcott Parsons, whose work he understood from the perspective of a systems theorist. From then on, he focused on pure theory, going so far as to reject the application of theoretical statements to the empirical world, declaring empirical evidence to be irrelevant for his theoretizing (Luhmann 1987). Since Luhmann writes prolifically in English, his views should be well known outside Germany.

It will be helpful to note his shift in emphasis over the years. The central notion was first functional differentiation as the guiding principle in evolution. This results in an increasing competence of the system if the functionally differentiated areas are allowed to develop their area-specific rationality (*Eigenlogik*). The economy is seen as a prime example of an *Eigendynamik,* provided it is not shackled by attempts at political or ethical guidance. Differentiated systems, according to Luhman, need constant feedback to permit a creative reaction. Luhman conceptualizes these feedbacks as *selbstreferenzielle Prozesse* (self-referential processes). More recently he has become interested in chaos theory and has given self-organization—which he calls *Autopoiesis*—a central place in explaining system functioning. It appears that the interest in Luhman has increased as his writings have become more abstract and his terms more outlandish—something he does self-consciously, since he can be a lucid writer.

This is less true for Jürgen Habermas, a philosopher who is self-taught in sociology. He calls his approach *critical sociology,* a choice that expresses his initial indebtedness to left Hegelianism of the Frankfurt school. While he has included Marxist terminology in his writings, he is probably best understood as a sociological disciple of the idealistic philosopher Fichte. In this perspective society is a problem for man's true calling: emancipation. He understands emancipation in the spirit of the French Enlightenment. The characteristic element of Habermas's "critical sociology" is *doppelte Reflexivität* (double feedback): the sociologist reflects on the context of discovery, and again on the context of utilization of his findings. With this attitude Habermas approaches the problematic relationship between theory and praxis (a Hegelian variant of practice) at a time when human existence is determined by a technological *Eigendynamik*. Habermas's writings, available in translation, are internationally known. Viewed over a period of around thirty years, it seems that he is sliding into a position of Great Cultural Theory, of the kind like Pitirim Sorokin's. And in becoming a synthesizer, he becomes more empirically minded, as Luhman ascends into the more abstract.

SOCIOLOGY AS "NORMAL SCIENCE"

While practically all German universities offer degrees in sociology up to the doctoral level, there are some centers in terms of number of students, research facilities, and number of teaching personnel. In terms of faculty size, these centers are Bielefeld, Berlin, and Frankfurt, Munich, Cologne, and Mannheim. If one includes among the criteria the number of degrees granted, then Bochum, Hamburg, and Göttingen must be added as centers.

There is now a very developed infrastructure for empirical research. In addition to many public service research institutes both inside and outside universities, there are some 165 commercial institutes for market and social research, the largest employing 600 academics and having a business volume of 90 million dollars. There is an academic network of three service institutions with a yearly volume of ten million dollars from the budgets of state and federal governments: the Informationszentrum, in Bonn, providing on-line information on research projects and literature abstracts; ZUMA, Zentrum für Umfragen, Methoden und Analysen, in Mannheim, doing some of the work of NORC, National Opinion Research Center, Chicago, and helping anyone in need of methodological support; and the Zentralarchiv in Cologne, which provides data for secondary analysis, as the Roper Center in the United States does. All three together form GESIS, Gesellschaft sozialwissenscaftliche Infrastruktureinrichtungen, Bonn, a package that can be used by the mostly small research institutes of German universities. There are also larger institutes, the biggest in terms of number of academics employed being the Deutsche Jugendinstitut (German Youth Institute) and the largest in terms of finance (eleven million dollars) being the Wissenschaftszentrum Berlin (Social Science Center in Berlin). All have regular budgets from tax money.

There is a yearly survey on work in progress, and between 1978 and 1988, 29,000 research projects were reported. The Zentralarchivs keeps a count on quantitative research, and limiting its attention only to such work where data are in machine readable format, the yearly academic production in quantitative research is around 900 projects. The preferred method is the personal interview, which during the years had a share of 50 percent for all projects where quantitative data were collected. The doorstep interview is being replaced by the telephone interview, although to a lesser extent than in the United States.

Among the more than 1,000 members of the German Sociological Association the attention given to applied fields is dominant. A content analysis of journal articles shows that only 15.4 percent of all published manuscripts—the rejection rate is around 80 percent of all articles submitted—deal with theory. The most important applied fields are (in order of frequency) industrial sociology, social psychology, methods of quantitative research, sociology of politics, and sociology of the family. All these have shares in publications above five percent. Twenty other fields of sociology contribute alltogether 50 percent to journal publications (Sahner 1982).

Heinz Sahner's (1991) content analysis of the theoretical paradigms used in journal articles between 1970 and 1987 found the expected correlation with the intellectual climate. Marxism declined rapidly from the late 1970s, and it never dominated in German professional journals. Structural functional sociology is still the single most important theoretical paradigm, with phenomenological approaches gaining steadily. Even more so than earlier, sociology in Germany is now a multiparadigm field, including as a prominent part, "German Sociology."

REFERENCES

Abel, Theodore 1929 *Systematic Sociology in Germany.* PhD diss. Columbia University, New York.

Adorno, Theodor W. 1962 "Zur Logik der Sozialwissenschaften." In *Kölner Zeitschrift für Soziologie und Sozialpsychologie* 14:249–263.

———1975 *Der Positivismusstreit in der deutschen Soziologie,* 4th ed. Neuwied: Luchterband.

———, ed. 1969 *Spätkapitalismus oder Industriegesellschaft. Verhandlungen des 16. Deutschen Soziologentages.* Stuttgart: Entce.

Alemann, Heine von 1978 "Geschichte und Arbeitsweise des Forschungsinstituts für Sozialwissenschaften in Köln." In Erwin K. Scheuch and Heine von Alemann, eds., *Das Forschungsinstitut.* Erlangen: Universität, Institut für Gesellschaft und Wissenschaft.

Aron, Raymond 1935 *La sociologie allemande contemporaine.* Paris: pr. univer. de France. Translated into English as *German Sociology.* New York, 1964.

Barnes, Harry E., and Howard Becker 1938 *Social Thought from Love to Science,* vol. 2. New York: D. C. Heath.

Coser, Lewis A. 1977 *Masters of Sociological Thought,* 2nd ed. New York: Harcourt Brace Jovanovich.

Dahrendorf, Ralf 1954 *Marx in Perspektive.* Hannover: Dietz.

———1956 *Industrie- und Betriebssoziologie.* Berlin: De Gruyter.

———1959a "Betrachtungen zu einigen Aspekten der gegenwärtigen deutschen Soziologie." *Kölner Zeitschrift für Soziologie und Sozialpsychologie* 11:132–153.

———1959b *Homo sociologicus.* Opladen: Westdeutscher Verlag.

———1961 *Über den Ursprung der Ungleichheit unter den Menschen.* Tübingen: Mohr.

———1963 *Die angewandte Aufklärung.* Munich: Piper.

———1965 *Gesellschaft und Demokratie in Deutschland.* Munich: Piper.

Durkheim, Emile 1887 "La philosophie dans les universités allemandes." In *Revue internationale de l'ensieignement,* Bd. 13.

Eisenstadt, Shmuel Noah, and Miriam Curelaru 1976 *The Form of Sociology.* New York: Wiley.

Fletcher, Ronald 1971 *The Making of Sociology,* 2 vols. London: Nelson.

Freund, Julien 1978 "German Sociology in the Time of Max Weber." In Tom Bottomore and Robert Nisbet, eds., *A History of Sociological Analysis.* New York: Basic Books.

Gehlen, Arnold, and Helmut Schelsky 1955 *Sociologie: Ein Lehr- und Handbuch.* Düsseldorf Köln: Diederich Verlag.

Gephardt, Werner 1982 "Soziologie im Aufbruch." *Kölner Zeitschrift für Soziologie und Sozialpsychologie* 34:1–24.

Gumplowitcz, Ludwig 1883 *Der Rassenkampf: Sociologische Untersuchungen.* Innsbruck: Wagner.

Habermas, Jürgen 1969 *Protestbewegung und Hochschulreform.* Frankfurt a.M.: Suhrkamp.

Horkheimer, Max 1968 *Kritische Theorie.* In Alfred Schmidt, ed., *Eine Dokumentation.* Frankfurt: S. Fischer. a.M.

Jay, Martin 1973 *The Dialectical Imagination.* London: Heinemann.

Käsler, Dirk 1984 *Die frühe deutsche Soziologie 1909–1934.* Opladen: Westdeutscher Verlag.

———1985 *Soziologische Abenteuer.* Opladen: Westdeutscher Verlag.

König, René 1941 *Niccolo Machiavelli: Zur Krisenanalyse einer Zeitenwende.* Erlenbach-Zürich: Rentsch.

——— 1949 *Soziologie heute.* Zùrich: Regio-Verlag.

——— 1958 *Sociologie.* Frankfurt: Fischer.

1062 *Handbuch der empirischen Socialforschung.* Stuttgart: Enke.

——— 1987 *Soziologie in Deutschland.* Munich: Hauser-Verlag, pp. 230–257.

——— (ed.) 1978 *Soziologie,* 11th ed. Frankfurt: Fischer.

Kuhn, Thomas Samuel 1970 *The Structure of Scientific Revolutions.* Chicago: Univ. of Chicago Press.

Lamnek, Siegfried 1991 "Gesellschaftliche Interessen und Geschichte der Ausbildung." In Harald Kerber, and Arnold Schmieder, eds., *Soziologie Theorien, Arbeitsfelder, Ausbildung: Ein Grundkurs.* Reinbek and Hamburg: Rowolt.

Lepenies, Wolfgang (ed.) 1981 *Gëschichte der Soziologie,* 4 vols. Frankfurt: Suhrkamp.

Lepsius, Mario Rainer (ed.) *Zwischenbilanz der Soziologie.* Stuttgart: Enke. 1976

———1987 "Sociology in the Interwar Period." In Volker Meja, Dieter Misgeld, and Nico Stehr, eds., *Modern German Sociology.* New York: Publisher.

Luhmann, Niklas 1987 "Soziologische Aufklärung." In vol. 4, *Beiträge zur funktionalen Differenzierung der Gesellschaft.* Opladen: Westdeutscher Verlag.

Meja, Volker, Dieter Misgeld, and Nico Stehr (eds.)

1987 *Modern German Sociology.* New York: Publisher.

Nisbet, Robert A. 1966 *The Sociological Tradition.* London: Heinemann.

Oberschall, Anthony 1965 *Empirical Social Research in Germany, 1848–1914.* Paris: Mouton.

——— 1972 *The Establishment of Empirical Sociology.* New York: Harper and Row.

Popitz, Heinrich, et al. 1957 *Das Gesellschaftsbild des Arbeiters.* Tübingen: Mohr.

Ratzenhofer, Gustav 1893 *Wesen und Zweck der Politik.* Leipzig: F. A. Brockhaus.

Sahner, Heinz 1982 *Theorie und Forschung.* Opladen: Westdeutscher Verlag.

——— 1991 "Paradigms Gained—Paradigms Lost: Die Entwicklung der Nachkriegssoziologie im Spiegel der Fachzeitschriften." In *Soziale Welt,* Index for vols. 1–40.

Salomon, Albert 1945 "German Sociology." In Georges Gurvitch and Wilbert E. Moore, eds., *Twentieth Century Sociology.* New York: Basie Books.

Schad, Susanna Petra 1972 *Empirical Social Research in Weimar Germany.* Paris: Mouton.

Schäffle, Albert 1885 *Gesammelte Aufsätze.* Tubingen: J. C. B. Mohr.

Scheuch, Erwin K. 1968 *Anabaptists of the "Affluent Society."*

——— 1990a "Von der deutschen Soziologie zur Soziologie in Deutschland." *Österreichische Zeitschrift für Soziologie* 15:30–50.

———1990b "Von der Pioniertät zur Institution." In Dieter Franke and Joachim Scharioth, eds., *40 Jahre Markt- und Sozialforschung in der Bundesrepublik Deutschland.* Munich: Oldenbourg Verlag.

Simmel, Georg 1890 *Über Soziale Differenzierung: Soziologie und psychologie Untersuchungen.* Leipzig: Duncker & Humblod.

Stammer, Otto (ed.) 1965 *Max Weber und die Soziologie heute: Verhandlungen des 15. Deutschen Sociologentages.* Tübingen: Mohr.

Tenbruck, Friedrich H. 1984 *Die unbewaltigten Sozialwissenschaften oder die Abschaffung des Menschen.* Graz: Styria.

Tönnies, Ferdinand (1887) 1912 *Gemeinschaft und Gesellschaft.* 2nd ed. Berlin: Carl Curtius.

Vanberg, Viktor 1975 *Die Zwei Sozialogien: Individualismus und Kollektivismus in der Sozialtheorie.*

Vierkandt, Alfred 1931 *Handwörterbuch der Soziologie.* Stuttgart: Entze.

Wiese: Leopold von 1926 *Soziologie: Geschichte und Hauptprobleme.* Berlin: de Gruyter.

———1959a "Die Deutsche Gesellschaft für Soziologie." *Kölner Zeitschrift für Soziologie und Sozialpsychologie* 11:11–20.

———1959b "Deutsche Gesellschaft für Soziologie." In *Handwörterbuch für Sozialwissenschaften,* vol. 2. Stuttgart: Fischer.

Zeitlin, Irving M. 1981 *Ideology and the Development of Sociological Theory,* 2nd ed. Englewood Cliffs, N.J.: Prentice-Hall.

ERWIN K. SCHEUCH

GERONTOLOGY *See* Social Gerontology.

GLOBAL SYSTEMS ANALYSIS Since the 1960s mounting empirical pressure has forced sociology to abandon the assumption that national societies could be understood without looking beyond their borders. The nation-state remains a crucial unit of analysis, but it must be analyzed as operating within the context of a larger global social system. Global flows of culture, technology, people, goods, and capital transform national societies.

The value of international trade has grown more rapidly than the value of goods and services produced and sold within national boundaries. Manufacturing means assembly of components from around the globe. Electronic youth culture in the United States revolves around Japanese cartoon characters while a generation of Third World television viewers take their cultural cues from North American TV serials. Capital markets operate around the globe and around the clock as trading moves from Tokyo to London to New York over the course of each day. Sociologists cannot yet claim to understand the working of this global system, but a number of fruitful avenues of analysis have emerged.

The approaches favored by sociologists have differed from the study of "international relations," as it has been traditionally defined. International relations has traditionally seen the global system as structured primarily by interactions in which nations were unitary actors (see Waltz 1979). The international relations perspective has also focused more on "West–West" interactions (those among advanced industrial countries) or

"East–West" interactions, in which "national security" was the principal issue at stake. The global system is presumed to be structured largely by the distribution of national power among the advanced nations. Hegemonic, bipolar, and multipolar power distributions are argued to have quite different implications for conflict and cooperation in the global political economy (Keohane 1984). Sociologists, on the other hand, have been very interested in how the global system is structured by flows of resources, people, ideas, and attitudes across geographic boundaries, flows that often occur without, or even in spite of, national actors. Relations between the rich countries of the "north" and the poor countries of the "south" have played a more prominent role in stimulating sociological approaches.

Investigating the prevalence of that complex of ideas and attitudes associated with "modernity" provided an initial impetus to taking a global look at the diffusion of culture and social structures. In a classic study, Inkeles and Smith (1974) analyzed the attitudes of citizens in six Third World countries spread around the globe. Modern attitudes were found in social contexts more characteristic of advanced industrial countries. The more time respondents spent living in cities or working in factories the more their attitudes resembled those associated with the culture of advanced industrial countries. These findings suggested a global system structured largely by processes of diffusion. The implicit model was one of gradual convergence around a similar set of "modern" values and attitudes. The spread of modern social institutions helps inculcate modern values and attitudes; the values and attitudes in turn reinforce the institutions.

The work of John Meyer and his associates shows how ideas and institutions originating in the advanced industrial countries become embodied in a global culture which in turn shapes local institutions in all countries. Boli-Bennett (1979), for example, examines the way in which national constitutions reflect global legal norms rather than local conditions. Ramirez and Boli (1982) look at the ways in which schools take on similar shapes around the global as conceptions of what constitutes an effective educational institution come to be shared with surprising speed across geographic boundaries. The global diffusion of institutional patterns is facilitated by the existence of formal organizations that span international boundaries, but informal flows of ideas, people, and goods are also important.

Approaches that focus less on cultural attributes and more on political economy tend to emphasize divergent trends in different geographical regions rather than convergence. Deriving their initial inspiration from economists like Raul Prebisch (1962) and Paul Baran (1957), sociologists who analyzed the global system from a "dependency" perspective emphasized the extent to which Third World political economies evolve differently because they confront a world dominated by already industrialized countries. Rather than seeing the global system as consisting simply of a set of nations which can be ranked along various continuums according to individual characteristics such as size and wealth, the dependency approach viewed the global system as consisting of a "core" of advanced industrial countries connected both economically and politically to a larger "periphery" of poor nations. The structure of the global system was conceptualized primarily in terms of trade and capital flows reinforced by political domination. The principal concern was with the consequences of these ties for social, political, and economic change in the countries of the periphery.

Cardoso and Faletto's *Dependency and Development in Latin America* ([1969]1979) is still the best exemplar of this tradition. Their analysis shows that the way in which economic elites are connected to the global economy shapes not only their strategies of investment but also their willingness to make political alliances with other groups and classes. For example, Latin American countries whose primary ties to the core were formed by mineral exports under the control of foreign capital experienced a different political history than countries that relied on agricultural exports controlled by local elites.

The expectations of the dependency approach with regard to changes in the structure of the global system over time stand in sharp contrast not only to those of modernization theory but also to those of traditional Marxist approaches. The basic Marxist presumption, like that of modernization theory, is that the global system is dominated by processes of diffusion. In the words of the *Communist Manifesto* the expansive character of capitalist production "draws all, even the most barbarian, nations into civilization." Contemporary advocates of the traditional Marxist position continue to argue that it is only by the expansion of economic ties to core countries, principally in the form of importing more foreign capital, that poor nations are likely to be able to reduce the gap that separates them from rich nations (see Warren 1980). The dependency perspective, on the other hand, emphasizes the ways in which economic elites and their allies in the periphery have an interest in preventing the full diffusion of economic capacities from core to periphery. For example, those who have an interest in the system of trading agrarian exports for core country manufactures may consider nascent local industrialists competitors for both labor and political power.

Empirical work generated by the dependency perspective suggested that the consequences of core-periphery capital flows, rather than being the most important stimulus to the growth of the periphery as Marxists like Bill Warren suggested, might in fact create obstacles to growth. Cross-national quantitative analyses discovered that the buildup of stocks of foreign capital had negative, rather than the expected positive consequences for growth (Chase-Dunn 1975; Bornschier, Chase-Dunn, and Rubinson 1978). While the findings of these studies are still contested by economists (e.g., Singh 1988), they clearly demonstrate that the results of transnational capital flows are not those predicted by a simple diffusionist model.

One of the criticisms that can be leveled against the dependency approach is that it has focused too much on capital and not enough on labor. Whereas dependency theorists have been concerned with the consequences of transnational capital flows for labor in both periphery and core (e.g., Frobel, Heinrich, and Kreye 1981), the tradition contains no series of cross-national quantitative analyses of either wage levels or the structure of international labor flows studies comparable to the literature on international capital flows. With some notable exceptions (e.g., Portes and Walton 1981), the global structure of labor flows and their consequences is understudied.

The logic of the dependency approach does not imply a global system in which the structure of relations among nations is frozen. To the contrary, analysts of "dependent development" (Cardoso 1974; Evans 1979) argue that intensification of ties with core countries is a dynamic element in reshaping the political economies of Third World countries. Dependent development shares with classic Marxist approaches the assumption that capital flows between core and periphery can play a significant role in generating industrialization in the Third World. It emphasizes, however, that both the economic character of this industrialization and its social and political concomitants are likely to be different from the experience of core countries.

Again, quantitative cross-national studies played a valuable role in specifying the consequences of industrializing in an already industrialized world. Chase-Dunn (1975) found that a greater role for foreign capital was associated with high levels of inequality, and his findings were confirmed by a variety of subsequent studies (e.g., Rubinson 1976; Evans and Timberlake 1980). These studies also confirm the political consequences of global economic ties. Rubinson (1979) and Delacroix and Ragin (1981) show that peripheral status in terms of trade relations is associated with weak state apparatuses. Bornschier and Ballmer-Cao (1979) argue on the basis of cross-national data that core-peripheral capital flows strengthen the political position of traditional power-holders at the expense of labor and middle-class groups.

Although most of the emphasis in the dependency tradition has been on looking at the consequences of position in the global system for local political and economic development, it is important to underline that strong interactive assumptions are built into the approach as well. In

Zeitlin's (1984) work on Chile, for instance, he argues that the outcome of the political struggles among economic elites in the nineteenth century were determinative of Chile's retaining its role as an exporter of raw materials rather than moving in the direction of trying to transform its mineral resources into more processed exports. Likewise, Taiwan and Korea are used as examples of the way in which internal dynamics may allow construction of more effective state apparatuses that in turn enable a country to improve its position in the global system (Evans 1987).

Despite the fruitfulness of the dependency approach in stimulating work on the domestic consequences of international variables, the approach's contribution to our understanding of the international system has been limited by the fact that it does not focus directly on the structure of the global system itself. The "world-system" approach, launched by Wallerstein (1974) and others (see Chase-Dunn 1989) at the beginning of the 1970s, took the overall structure of the system as its starting point.

Wallerstein's contribution lay not only in directing attention to analysis of the global system itself but also in setting the contemporary capitalist world-system in the context of previous systems spanning more than one society. Some of the most interesting work stimulated by world-system thinking has involved analysis of systems that antedated the emergence of the contemporary one (e.g., Abu-Lughod 1989). Wallerstein argues that systems prior to the current one were primarily of two types. "Mini-systems" extended across boundaries defined by unified political control and ethnic solidarity but did not come close to being global in scope. "World empires" joined various ethnic and social groups in a single division of labor by extending political control over a broader geographic area. Only the contemporary capitalist world-system, however, unites such a broad geographic region (essentially the entire globe) in a single division of labor without unified political control of corresponding scope.

Wallerstein's world system is, like that envisioned by the dependency approach, definitely hierarchical. More important, the hierarchical structure of the system is postulated as essential for its survival. The geographic expansion of northwestern Europe's economic and political influence beginning at the end of the 'long' fourteenth century was, in Wallerstein's view, essential to the transformation of productive organization in that region. Subsequent interchange among regions with different modes of extraction has been central to sustaining the process of accumulation in the system as a whole. Wallerstein envisions at least three structural positions within the system. Defined in terms of the nature of their exchange relations with other regions, they are: the "core," which exports goods produced by processes more intensive in their use of capital and new technology; the periphery, which relies on the production of labor- and resource-intensive goods; and the semiperiphery, which "trades both ways."

Quantitative cross-national analysis provides support for the idea that countries can be categorized according to their interactions with other nations, and that countries in the same position experience shared benefits (or costs). Snyder and Kick (1979), analyzing data on trade networks and military interventions using "block-modeling" techniques (see White, Boorman, and Brieger 1976), found a block of nations whose characteristics corresponded roughly to those of the "core," several blocks that corresponded to the periphery, and a set of nations with the intermediary properties attributed to the semiperiphery. David Smith and Douglas White (forthcoming) used a similar methodology but improved on the work of Snyder and Kick by examining longitudinal changes in the structure of the system. They were able to demonstrate changes in the structure of relations within and between blocks of nations and chart the mobility of individual nations within the system.

The primary criticism of the world-system perspective is that its focus on global analysis may lead to neglect of the role of domestic dynamics in determining the position of individual nations within the system and, by extension, shaping the structure of the system itself. Few would quarrel with the proposition that prospects of individual countries are conditioned by their position in the global system and by the swings in economic growth that characterize the system as a whole. A given nation may indeed find itself experiencing hardship or economic decline, not because of contradictions that have developed in its domestic economy, but because of the reverberation of changes occurring elsewhere in the world system. The question is whether the kind of interactive logic discussed earlier in relation to the dependency approach is sufficiently built into the world-system perspective.

The issue of domestic dynamics is especially important in relation to explanations of the mobility of individual nations from one position to another. Such mobility obviously takes place. Spain and Portugal, which once formed the core, later moved to the semiperiphery, where they are joined by Taiwan and Korea, which have moved up from the periphery. While such mobility depends in part on changes in the system as a whole, it also depends on the outcome of domestic political struggles. Zeitlin's analysis of Chile, as discussed earlier, shows how the outcome of domestic political contest can perpetuate peripheral status. Brenner's (1976, 1977) interpretation of England's rise to the core provides another example of the domestic roots of systemic mobility. In Brenner's view, the differences between the agrarian strategies of England on the one hand and Spain and Portugal on the other were not simply the result of trade possibilities generated by changes at the level of the world system. They depended crucially on interactions between peasant communities and agrarian elites at the local level, which were in turn rooted in long-standing historical characteristics of the peasant communities themselves.

Assessing the role of domestic dynamics in shaping changes in the global system requires an integration of analysis at the international level with comparative work on domestic social structures. Such integration is clearly already under way. Over the course of the 1970s and 1980s, a growing body of work emerged that took the influence of the global system seriously in its analysis of change at the domestic level but used analysis of domestic political struggles and their economic consequences to explain changing ties with the global system (see Evans and Stephens 1988). These attempts to integrate international and comparative analysis are not unique to sociology. A parallel trend can be observed in political science as well (see Gourevitch 1986; Putnam 1988).

A second interesting trend in current sociological work on the global system is the increasing concern of sociologists with the politics of international relations among states. The third volume of Wallerstein's epic analysis of the modern world-system (1989) makes it clear that the world-system perspective, often accused of being excessively "economistic," is now focusing much more on the logic of interstate politics. At the same time, other major sociological figures have turned their attention to the political and military aspects of the international system (e.g., Giddens 1985; Mann 1988; Tilly 1989). Given the possibilities for interplay between the structure of the global system as it has been portrayed by the dependency and world-systems perspectives and existing models of the interstate system such as those proposed by "hegemonic stability theory" (see Snidal 1985), this convergence between sociology and political science should be quite fruitful. A similar interplay between the more economically oriented aspects of sociological approaches to the global system and the theorizing on trade, capital flows, and international labor migration produced by the discipline of economics could be just as interesting. Unfortunately, with the exception of some recent thinking on "strategic trade theory" (see, e.g., Krugman 1987), such interplay does not seem to be in the offing.

Overall, our understanding of the global system must still be considered a project "under construction" rather than a finished set of tools easily applied to specific problems. Some things are clear nonetheless. We know that trajectories of change in national societies cannot be analyzed without reference to the global system in which they are embedded any more than the analysis of change in individual communities can be attempted without awareness of the national society in which they are embedded. We also know that the character of relations between an individual state and the larger system is shaped, not just by the evolution of the global system, but also by political struggles at the local level. We know that diffusion of ideas and norms throughout the global system has a powerful influence on how social institutions are structured in individual nations, but we also know that this diffusion takes place within a system that has a very hierarchical structure. We know that the nations located at the bottom of this structure are disadvantaged economically as well as politically, but we also know that mobility is possible. We know that the contemporary global system is an invention of the last half-dozen centuries; predicting how long it will endure is another question.

(SEE ALSO: *Industrialization in Less Developed Countries; Modernization Theory*)

REFERENCES

Abu-Lughod, Janet 1989 *Before European Hegemony.* New York: Oxford University Press.

Baran, Paul 1957 *The Political Economy of Growth.* New York: Monthly Review Press.

Boli-Bennett, John 1979 "The Ideology of Expanding State Authority in National Constitutions, 1870–1970." In J. Meyer and M. Hannan, eds., *National Development and the World System.* Chicago: University of Chicago Press.

Bornschier, Volker, and T.-H. Ballmer-Cao 1979 "Income Inequality: A Cross-National Study of the Relationships between MNC-Penetration, Dimensions of Power-Structure and Income Distribution." *American Sociological Review* 44:487–506.

Bornschier, Volker, Christopher Chase-Dunn, and Richard Rubinson 1978 "Cross-National Evidence of the Effects of Foreign Investment and Aid on Economic Growth and Inequality: A Survey of Findings and a Re-analysis." *American Journal of Sociology* 84:651–683.

Brenner, Robert 1976 "Agrarian Class Structure and Economic Development in Pre-industrial Europe." *Past and Present* 70:30–75.

———1977 "The Origins of Capitalist Development: A Critique of Neo-Smithian Marxism." *New Left Review* 104:24–92.

Cardoso, F. H. 1974 "As Tradições de Desenvolvimento-associado." *Estudos Cebrap* 8:41–75.

———, and E. Faletto (1969) 1979 *Dependency and Development in Latin America.* Berkeley: University of California Press.

Chase-Dunn, Christopher 1975 "The Effect of International Dependence on Development and Inequality: A Cross-National Study." *American Sociological Review* 40:720–738.

———1989 *Global Formation: Structures of the World Economy.* New York: Blackwell.

Delacroix, Jacque, and Charles Ragin 1981 "Structural Blockage: A Cross-National Study of Economic Dependence, State Efficacy and Underdevelopment." *American Journal of Sociology* 86:1311–1347.

Evans, Peter B. 1987 "Class, State, and Dependence in East Asia: Some Lessons for Latin Americanists." In F. Deyo, ed., *The Political Economy of the New Asian Industrialism.* Ithaca, N.Y.: Cornell University Press.

———1979 *Dependent Development: The Alliance of Multinational State and Local Capital in Brazil.* Princeton, N.J. Princeton University Press.

———, and John Stephens 1988 "Development and the World Economy." In Neil Smelser, ed., *Handbook of Sociology.* Beverly Hills, Calif.: Sage.

———, and Michael Timberlake 1980 "Dependence, Inequality and the Growth of the Tertiary: A Comparative Analysis of Less Developed Countries." *American Sociological Review* 45:531–553.

Frobel, Folker, Jurgen Heinrich, and Otto Kreye 1981 *The New International Division of Labor: Structural Unemployment in Industrialized Countries and Industrialization in Developing Countries.* Cambridge: Cambridge University Press.

Giddens, Anthony 1985 *The Nation-State and Violence.* Berkeley: University of California Press.

Gourevitch, Peter 1986 *The Politics of Hard Times.* Ithaca, N.Y.: Cornell University Press.

Inkeles, Alex, and David Smith 1974 *Becoming Modern: Individual Change in Six Developing Countries.* Cambridge, Mass.: Harvard University Press.

Keohane, Robert 1984 *After Hegemony: Cooperation and Discord in the World Political Economy.* Princeton, N.J.: Princeton University Press.

Krugman, Paul 1987 "Strategic Sectors and International Competition." In Robert Stern, ed., *U.S. Trade Policies in a Changing World Economy.* Cambridge, Mass.: MIT Press.

Mann, Michael 1988 *States, War and Capitalism.* Oxford: Blackwell.

Portes, Alejandro, and John Walton 1981 *Labor, Class*

and the International System. New York: Academic Press.

Prebisch, Raul 1962 "The Economic Development of Latin America and Its Principal Problems." *Economic Bulletin for Latin America* 7 (February):1–22.

Putnam, Robert 1988 "Diplomacy and Domestic Politics: The Logic of Two-level Games." *International Organization* 42 (Summer):427–460.

Ramirez, F., and J. Boli 1982 "Global Patterns of Educational Institutionalization." In P. Albach et al., eds. *Comparative Education.* New York: Macmillian.

Rubinson, Richard 1976 "The World Economy and the Distribution of Income Within States." *American Sociological Review* 41:638–659.

Singh, Ram D. 1988 "The Multinationals' Economic Penetration, Growth, Industrial Output, and Domestic Savings in Developing Countries: Another Look." *Journal of Developmental Studies* 25:55–82.

Smith David A., and Douglas R. White (Forthcoming) "Structure and Dynamics of the Global Economy: Network Analysis of International Trade, 1965–1980." *Social Forces.*

Snidal, Duncan 1985 "The Limits of Hegemonic Stability Theory." *International Organizaiton* 39 (4):580–614.

Snyder, David and Edward Kick, 1979. "Structural Position in the World System and Economic Growth, 1955–1970: A Multiple Network Approach," *American Journal of Sociology* 84:1096–1126.

Tilly, Charles 1989 "Coercion, Capital and European States, AD 990–1990," unpublished.

Wallerstein, Immanuel 1974 *The Modern World-System I: Capitalist Agriculture and the Origins of the European World-Economy in the Sixteenth Century.* New York: Academic Press.

———1989 *The Modern World-System III: The Second Era of Great Expansion of the Capitalist World Economy, 1730's–1840's.* New York: Academic Press.

Waltz, Kenneth 1979 *Theory of International Relations.* Reading, Mass.: Addison-Wesley.

Warren, Bill 1980 *Imperialism: Pioneer of Capitalism.* London: New Left Books.

White, Harrison, Scot Boorman, and Ronald Brieger 1976 "Social Structure from Multiple Networks: I. Block Models of Roles and Position." *American Journal of Sociology* 81:730–780.

Zeitlin, Maurice 1984 *The Civil Wars in Chile (Or the Bourgeois Revolutions That Never Were).* Princeton, N.J.: Princeton University Press.

PETER B. EVANS

GOVERNMENT REGULATION Government regulation is part of a larger area of study encompassing state policymaking and administration. Along with political scientists, economists, legal scholars, and historians, sociologists studying regulation contribute to an interdisciplinary growth industry. There is no uniformly agreed-upon concept of regulation that separates it from other kinds of government activity. Mitnick (1980, pp. 3–19) offers a good overview of concepts of regulation. Narrow definitions typically focus on government action affecting private business by policing market entry and exit, rate or price, and profit structures and competitive environment. Some narrow definitions confine regulatory activity to that undertaken by administrative agencies. Law enforcement by courts is excluded, no matter what its object. On the other hand, the broadest definitions conceptualize regulation as government action affecting private businesses or private citizens. "Regulation" thus becomes virtually coterminous with all government policymaking and administration, whether by legislatures, administrative agencies, or courts.

Sabatier (1975) has offered a useful definition of regulation in between these two extremes. The definition is based on the goals and content of government policy, not on the means of enforcement, and it highlights the distinction between government policing of behavior and government allocation of goods and services. Distributive (e.g., defense contracts) and redistributive (e.g., the income tax, social welfare legislation) policies allocate goods and services. Government policing is self-regulatory if it polices behavior to the benefit of the group whose behavior is policed; it is regulatory if it "seek[s] to change the behavior of some actors in order to benefit others" (Sabatier 1975, p. 307). Antipollution, antidiscrimination, consumer protection, occupational safety and health, and antitrust are examples of regulatory policies. Sociologists often distinguish between economic and social regulation. Whereas economic regulation controls market activities—for example, entry and exit or price controls—social regulation controls aspects of production—for example, occupational safety and health standards and pollution control (e.g., Szasz 1986). The term *social regulation* also is used to signal regulation that directly affects people rather, or more than, markets (Mitnick 1980, p. 15).

Regulation is dynamic. It is an "an ongoing process or relation" (Mitnick 1980, p. 6) between regulator and regulated parties. Because of the nature of the legal system in the United States, regulation tends to involve the issuance and application of legal rules (Sabatier 1975, p. 307). For example, Congress has legislated federal statutes to promote competitive markets, to prevent race and gender discrimination in employment, and to increase workplace safety. These laws have been interpreted and enforced by the appropriate federal administrative agencies and by the federal courts. Federal regulatory agencies include the Interstate Commerce Commission (ICC), Federal Trade Commission (FTC), Federal Communications Commission (FCC), Securities and Exchange Commission (SEC), Equal Employment Opportunity Commission (EEOC), National Labor Relations Board (NLRB), Environmental Protection Agency (EPA), Food and Drug Administration (FDA), and Occupational Safety and Health Administration (OSHA). (See Wilson 1980b; Derthick and Quirk 1985 for case studies of many of these agencies.)

Consistent with the U.S. emphasis on legal rules as mechanisms to constrain or implement regulation, institutional forms used to reach regulatory goals are varied. Breyer (1982) provides an overview of the ideal-typical workings of various regulatory forms, including cost-of-service ratemaking (e.g., public utility regulation), standard setting (e.g., administrative rule making and enforcement by the EPA and OSHA), and individualized screening (e.g., the FDA regulations pursuant to which direct food additives can be marketed). Mitnick (1980) also provides an overview of regulatory forms and contrasts regulation by directive (e.g., administrative and adjudicative rule making) with regulation by incentive (e.g., tax incentives, effluent charges, and subsidies).

THEORIES OF REGULATION

There are various general theoretical approaches to regulation. Most are concerned with regulatory origins or processes, but often they also address questions of impact, at least implicitly. Mitnick (1980) and Moe (1987) provide detailed exposition and evaluation of theories of regulation. All are theories of "interest." Marver Bernstein's classic life-cycle theory (see Mitnick 1980, pp. 45–50) argues that regulatory agencies designed in the public interest become captured by the powerful private interests they are designed to regulate. The diffuse majority favoring regulation loses interest once the initial statute is legislated, leaving the agency with few political resources to confront strong, well-organized regulatory parties with a large stake in agency outcomes.

Arguing that regulatory agencies are not simply captured by private interests but are designed from the beginning to do their bidding, Stigler (1971) and others have developed the economic theory of regulation. This theory assumes that all actors behave rationally in their self-interest and so try to use government to achieve their own ends. But economic interest does not necessarily result in effective mobilization of resources. Because "there is a mobilization bias in favor of small groups, particularly those having one or more members with sizeable individual stakes in political outcomes" (Moe 1987, pp. 274–75), concentrated business interests have great advantages over diffuse groups in mobilizing for regulatory legislation. When costs of regulation fall upon a concentrated group (e.g., a particular industry such as railroads or airlines) and benefits on a diffuse one (e.g., consumers) "capture" will result. Similarly, when benefits fall upon a concentrated group and costs on a diffuse one, regulation will be designed to benefit regulated parties.

The economic theory of regulation does not always predict capture. Generally, regulatory policies result from a chain of control running from economic groups to politicians to bureaucrats and reflect the underlying balance of power among economic groups, whatever that balance may be. Considering different distributions of regulatory costs relative to regulatory benefits, Wilson (1980a, pp. 364–72) sketches four different political scenarios for the origins of regulation. Exemplified by the origin and operation of the Civil Aeronautics Board, "client politics" is consistent with Stigler's prediction that regulation reflects the regulated industry's desires. Client politics results when costs are widely distributed and benefits are concentrated. When both costs and benefits are narrowly concentrated, both sides have strong incentives to organize and exert influence, so "interest group politics" results. Wilson views passage of the Commerce Act in 1886 as a product of conflict over rate regulation, in which interest group participants included railroads, farmers, and shippers. When both costs and benefits are widely distributed, interest groups have little incentive to form around regulatory issues because none can expect to capture most of the benefits or to avoid most of the costs. "Majoritarian politics," in which the mobilization of popular opinion is likely to play an important role, governs passage of such legislation. "Entrepreneurial politics" characterize the dynamics of mobilization around policies that offer widely distributed benefits but narrowly concentrated costs. Here, although policy opponents benefit from the mobilization bias of small numbers and have strong incentives to organize, a "policy entrepreneur" can "mobilize latent public sentiment . . . [and] put the opponents" on the defensive (Wilson 1980a, p. 370). For Wilson, antipollution laws enforced by the EPA exemplify entrepreneurial politics. Although the traditional economic theory of regulation predicts ultimate capture of agencies created by entrepreneurial politics, Sabatier (1975) argues that such agencies can avoid capture by concentrated business interests if they actively develop a supportive constituency able to monitor regulatory policy effectively.

Economic theories of regulation have much to say about the political dynamics of social groups seeking and resisting regulation, but they do not attend to political and regulatory institutions. In contrast, the positive theory of institutions "traces the congressional and bureaucratic linkages by which interests are translated into public policy" (Moe 1987, p. 279). It argues that political institutions and rules of the game matter. Although political actors try to create rules that lead to outcomes they favor, institutionalized rules may well be out of sync with underlying economic interests. Whether congressional regulatory policies reflect any given economic interest depends on the distribution of that interest across congressional districts, the location of Congress members who support that interest on particular committees with particular prerogatives and jurisdictions, and the rules of the congressional game.

The positive theory of institutions ordinarily begins with and focuses on the self-interest of actors in Congress and the regulatory agencies rather than of actors outside these political and regulatory institutions. It argues that legislative choice of regulatory forms as well as of regulatory content can be modeled as a function of the costs and benefits to legislators of selecting particular regulatory strategies (see, e.g., Fiorina 1982). These costs and benefits are a function of the distribution of economic interests across districts and the political-institutional rules of the game. In general, electoral incentives prevent members of Congress from placing high priority on controlling administrative agencies. The principal–agent models of control employed by the positive theory of institutions "suggest . . . that even when legislators do have incentives to control agencies toward specific ends, they are likely to meet with some measure of failure, owing to . . . conflicts of interest, information asymmetries, and opportunities for bureaucratic 'shirking'" (Moe 1987, p. 281). Game-theoretic models of regulatory enforcement developed in this theory indicate ample opportunity for the capture of regulators by regulated parties (Ayres and Braithwaite 1989). However, where some forms of capture are economically undesirable, others are economically (Pareto) efficient.

Other theoretical perspectives used by sociologists to study regulation include various forms of neo-Marxist political economy or class theory (see Levine 1988; Yeager 1990) and the political-institutional view developed by Theda Skocpol and others (Weir, Orloff, and Skocpol 1988). Where the former parallels the economic theory of regulation in focusing on the organization and mobilization of nongovernmental actors—specifically classes and segments of classes—in support of their interests, the latter parallels the positive theory of institutions in stressing the import of political structures and rules of the game. But in contrast to economic and positive theories, which largely model comparative statics (Moe 1987), class and political-institutional theories focus on historical dynamics.

Political institutionalists stress, for example, the importance of feedback from prior to current regulatory policies and of political learning by government actors. Class theorists stress how regulatory enforcement and cycles of regulation and deregulation evolve over time in response both to the structural constraints of a capitalist economy and to active struggles over regulation by classes and class segments. For example, Yeager (1990) argues that because government depends on tax revenues from the private accumulation of capital, it tends to resolve conflict conservatively over such negative consequences of production as air and water pollution, so as not to threaten economic growth. Many aspects of regulatory processes make it likely that laws passed against powerful economic actors will be limited in impact or will have unintended effects that exacerbate the problems that initially caused regulation.

The effectiveness of regulatory statutes may be limited by implementation decisions relying on cost–benefit considerations because ordinarily costs are more easily determined than benefits and because cost–benefit analyses assert the primacy of private production. Moreover, government relies upon signals from private business to gauge when regulation is preventing adequate economic growth. Limited effectiveness of regulation also results from enforcement procedures tilted in favor of regulated parties that have the technical and financial resources needed to negotiate with agency officials. Corporate organizational forms encourage regulatory leniency and negotiations regarding compliance; corporate officials are seldom prosecuted for criminal violations because the corporate form makes it difficult to locate individual culpability. Because courts emphasize proper legal reasoning when reviewing agency decisions, regulatory agencies may focus on procedure rather than substance. This too tilts enforcement toward the interests of regulated parties. Finally, because no unit of government has complete control over any given policy from legislation through funding and implementation, parties bearing the cost of regulation need thwart regulation at only one point in the process, while supporters of regulation must promote it effectively at all points. In implementation, advocates of tough enforcement are likely to lose to more resource-rich segments of business seeking to limit regulation (Yeager 1990).

Notwithstanding forces that load regulatory processes in favor of the regulated business community and particularly the larger, more powerful corporations at the expense of smaller firms, consumers, environmentalists, and labor, class theorists also see limits on regulatory leniency and on the success of deregulatory movements by business. For example, Yeager (1990) argues that antipollution enforcement biased toward large corporations dominating the U.S. economy will reproduce both the dominance of this business segment and large-scale pollution. Economic growth facilitated by lenient enforcement is accompanied by technological development that fosters both higher pollution risks and greater capacity to detect pollution. Regulatory ineffectiveness may lead to a loss of legitimacy for government as the public responds to higher risk and to perceived governmental failure by pressuring for additional antipollution efforts.

Finally, although the concept of interest is central to theories of regulation, sociologists studying regulation are sensitive to the causal role of norms and ideas as well as of economic and political interests. Ayres and Braithwaite (1989) have approached the problem of regulatory capture with a synthesis of economic interest and socialization mechanisms. Seeking a social framework to facilitate economically efficient forms of capture while deterring inefficient capture, they point to benefits obtainable if all participants in regulatory processes that empower public interest groups adhere to a culture of regulatory reasonableness. For example, social and self-disapproval sanctions in a regulatory ethic that is firm but reasonable will inhibit regulators from capitulation to law evasion by industry and from punitive enforcement when industry is complying with regulatory law. Yeager (1990) views limits on regulatory law as a function of prevailing systems of cultural belief as well as of class and group relations. Notions of regulatory responsiveness and reasonableness are negotiated in enforcement interactions between regulators and regulated parties within an overall cultural framework that attributes moral ambivalence rather than unqualified harm to regulated conduct. This facilitates adoption of a technical orientation to solving "noncompliance" problems rather than of a more punitive approach. Because the regulation of business has to be constantly justified within U.S. culture, administering regulation itself becomes morally ambivalent. This also contributes to less aggressive enforcement.

EMPIRICAL STUDIES OF REGULATION

Empirical research on regulation includes studies of regulatory origins (e.g., Sanders 1981; 1986; Steinberg 1982), processes (e.g., Moe 1987; Yeager 1990), and impact (e.g., Beller 1982; Mendeloff 1979). There also are studies of deregulation (e.g., Derthick and Quirk 1985; Szasz 1986). Studies of processes look at the evolution of regulatory forms (e.g., Stryker 1989; 1990) as well as of the substance of regulatory rules (Melnick 1983; McCammon 1990). Researchers employ a variety of methodologies, from quantitative assessment of causes and consequences of regulation (e.g., Steinberg 1982; Mendeloff 1979) or models of regulatory processes (e.g., Yeager 1990) to qualitative, historical, and comparative accounts of regulatory evolution (e.g., Sanders 1981; Stryker 1990; Moe 1987). It is difficult to generalize about findings from empirical studies of regulation. It is clear, however, that (1) no general theory or perspective on regulation enjoys unqualified support when stacked up against the variety and complexity of actual regulatory experiences; and (2) all theories have something to offer the empirical analyst.

First, economic interests and resources are major, but they are not the sole, determining factor of the dynamics of political struggles over regulatory origins and administration (Sanders 1986; Stryker 1989; 1990; Yeager 1990; Szasz 1986; Moe 1987). Political structures and rules of the game matter because they are the mechanisms through which economic and social actors must translate their interests into regulatory policy (Moe 1987). But for legislative, administrative, and judicial participants in policy processes, these institutional mechanisms also create independent interests in, and resources for, regulatory policymaking. Sanders (1981) shows that the regulation of natural gas has been a function of four sets of regionally based economic interests, including gas producer regions of the United States and gas deficit consumer regions, as well as of electoral rules and structures. Regulatory outcomes have resulted from a dynamic relationship among political actors who reflect the changing market positions of their constituents. "The potential for sectional conflict is exacerbated by the territorial basis of elections, the weakness of the party system, and a federal structure that not only encloses different political cultures and legal systems, but also supports fifty sets of elected officials sensitive to encroachments on their respective turfs" (Sanders 1981, p. 196). Current regulatory structures and policies do have feedback effects constraining and providing opportunities for subsequent regulatory policies as well as for subsequent action by parties with interests at stake in regulation (see, e.g., Sanders 1981; Steinberg 1982; Stryker 1990).

Second, the legal structures and culture through which most regulation is administered in the United States significantly shape regulatory processes and outcomes. For example, Melnick (1983) shows how the narrow, highly structured, reactive, and adversarial legal processes through which antipollution enforcement takes place in the United States have led to court decisions that simultaneously extend the scope of EPA programs and lessen agency resources for achieving antipollution goals. Appellate judges tend to promote stringent antipollution standards because they are removed from local concerns and are likely to be inspired by broad public goals. In a different institutional location, trial judges observe the impact on local businesses and citizens of imposing strict regulation. Their flexibility in response to the perceived harm of strict regulation generates an equity-balancing enforcement that counteracts what is accomplished in standard setting.

Third, regulatory implementation is influenced by internal agency politics as well as by the agency's external environment. For example, Stryker (1989; 1990) has shown how, in conjunction with class and political-institutional factors, intra-NLRB conflict between agency economists and lawyers over the proper administrative use of social science caused Congress to abolish the NLRB's economic research unit. Katzmann (1980) has indicated how internal jockeying by economists within the FTC changed enforcement priorities and outcomes through the 1970s.

Fourth, regulation often has unintended effects. Yeager (1990) shows how EPA sanctioning decisions and processes, while rational in the face of economic, political, and legal constraints on the agency, reproduce private sector inequality by favoring large corporations that have financial and technical resources. Large companies have greater access to agency proceedings than do small companies. Agency proceedings often change antipollution requirements in favor of regulated firms so that ultimately large corporations have fewer pollution violations. In decisions to apply the harshest sanctions—criminal and civil prosecutions—the EPA may well avoid tangling with the most resource-rich firms, for fear of losing in court. Melnick (1983, p. 354) indicates a similar dynamic. Ostensibly neutral procedures, then, create inequitable law application and also may help reproduce the problems that led to the initial antipollution legislation.

Fifth, although capture of administrative agencies by regulated parties can and does occur (see Sabatier 1975; Sanders 1981), it need not. Enactment of regulatory legislation also can lead to cycles of aggressive enforcement alternating with periods of capture or, similarly, to enforcement that oscillates between or among the interests at stake in regulation or between periods of regulation and deregulation. For example, over time, FTC enforcement has alternated between favoring big or small business and core or peripheral economic regions of the country (Stryker 1990). Sanders' (1981) study of natural gas regulation shows that initial federal legislation mixed the goals of consumer protection and of industry promotion. Federal Power Commission interaction with its environment did not result in stable capture by gas producers but rather in oscillation between "capture" by gas consumers and capture by gas producers. Clearly, consumers, labor, and other subordinate groups can and have benefited from regulation (see, e.g., Steinberg 1982; Sanders 1981; Stryker 1989). But the political economy of capitalism also sets structural and cultural limits to these benefits (Szasz 1986; McCammon 1990; Yeager 1990).

A major challenge to theories and empirical research in the future is to model the historical dynamics of various types of regulation. Ideally, the juxtaposition of abstract theory and concrete, historical research can lead to integrated theories of regulatory origins, processes, and impact. Such theories must be sensitive to economic and organizational interests and resources, to political structures and rules, and to regulatory cultures. They also must be sensitive to periods or cycles in which different economic or institutional arrangements, incentives, and constraints operate and to feedback effects from past to future regulatory policies and processes.

(SEE ALSO: *Bureaucracy; Organizational Structure; Public Policy Analysis*)

REFERENCES

Ayres, Ian, and John Braithwaite 1989 "Tripartism, Empowerment, and Game-Theoretic Notions of Regulatory Capture." American Bar Foundation Working Paper 8902. Chicago: American Bar Foundation.

Beller, Andrea H. 1982 "Occupational Segregation by Sex: Determinants and Changes." *Journal of Human Resources* 17:371–392.

Breyer, Stephen 1982 *Regulation and Its Reform.* Cambridge, Mass.: Harvard University Press.

Derthick, Martha, and Paul Quirk 1985 *The Politics of Deregulation.* Washington D.C.: Brookings Institution.

Fiorina, Morris P. 1982 "Legislative Choice of Regulatory Forms: Legal Process or Administrative Process?" *Public Choice* 39:33–66.

Katzmann, Robert A. 1980 *Regulatory Bureaucracy: The Federal Trade Commission and Antitrust Policy.* Cambridge, Mass.: MIT Press.

Levine, Rhonda 1988 *Class Struggle and the New Deal: Industrial Labor, Industrial Capital, and the State.* Lawrence: University of Kansas Press.

McCammon, Holly J. 1990 "Legal Limits on Labor Militancy: U.S. Labor Law and the Right to Strike since the New Deal." *Social Problems* 37:206–229.

Melnick, R. Shep 1983 *Regulation and the Courts: The Case of the Clean Air Act.* Washington D.C.: Brookings Institution.

Mendeloff, John 1979 *Regulating Safety: An Economic and Political Analysis of Occupational Safety and Health Policy.* Cambridge, Mass.: MIT Press.

Mitnick, Barry M. 1980 *The Political Economy of Regulation: Creating, Designing, and Removing Regulatory Forms.* New York: Columbia University Press.

Moe, Terry 1987 "Interests, Institutions, and Positive Theory: The Politics of the NLRB." *Studies in American Political Development* 2:236–299.

Sabatier, Paul 1975 "Social Movements and Regulatory Agencies: Toward a More Adequate—and Less Pessimistic—Theory of 'Clientele Capture'." *Policy Sciences* 6:301–342.

Sanders, M. Elizabeth 1981 *The Regulation of Natural Gas: Policy and Politics, 1938–78.* Philadelphia: Temple University Press.

———1986 "Industrial Concentration, Sectional Competition, and Antitrust Politics in America, 1880–1980." *Studies in American Political Development* 1:142–214.

Steinberg, Ronnie 1982 *Wages and Hours: Labor and Reform in Twentieth-Century America.* New Brunswick, N.J.: Rutgers University Press.

Stigler, George 1971 "The Theory of Economic Regulation." *Bell Journal of Economic and Management Science* 2:3–21.

Stryker, Robin 1989 "Limits on Technocratization of the Law: The Elimination of the National Labor Relations Board's Division of Economic Research." *American Sociological Review* 54:341–358.

———1990 "A Tale of Two Agencies: Class, Political-Institutional, and Organizational Factors Affecting State Reliance on Social Science." *Politics and Society* 18:101–141.

Szasz, Andrew 1986 "The Reversal of Federal Policy Toward Worker Safety and Health." *Science and Society* 50:25–51.

Weir, Margaret, Ann Shola Orloff, and Theda Skocpol 1988 "Understanding American Social Politics." In M. Weir, A. Orloff, and T. Skocpol, eds., *The Politics of Social Policy in the United States.* Princeton, N.J.: Princeton University Press.

Wilson, James Q. 1980a "The Politics of Regulation." In J. Q. Wilson, ed., *The Politics of Regulation.* New York: Basic Books.

———, ed. 1980b *The Politics of Regulation.* New York: Basic Books.

Yeager, Peter 1990 *The Limits of Law: The Public Regulation of Private Pollution.* Cambridge: Cambridge University Press.

ROBIN STRYKER

GROUP COHESIVENESS *See* Small Groups.

GROUP PROBLEM SOLVING From the early 1900s social psychologists have been interested in the effect of the presence of other persons on an individual's behavior in problem solving and in other forms of activity. By the 1920s experiments were performed to observe problem solving in groups (Hare 1976, pp. 384–395). The comparison of the individual problem solver with a group has continued through the present day since there are economic and social costs in maintaining a group to solve problems. Thus, the question remains, for what types of problems are individuals best able to find a solution and for what types is it best to have a group? In answer to this question, a summary of research comparing individuals and groups will be presented first, followed by a comparison of different types of groups (Hare 1976, chaps 14, 15; Hare et al. 1991, chaps 8, 11, 12).

INDIVIDUAL VERSUS GROUP

For many group tasks an individual is first required to reach an individual decision or perform some individual activity before sharing or combining the individual product with that of other group members to form a group decision or a group product. Thus, the first phase of a group task is often carried out by individuals in a group situation. Any effect of the presence of other persons on an individual's activity becomes important at this time. A person performing an individual task in the presence of others may do less well, as well, or better than when performing alone. Zajonc (1965) hypothesized that, when subjects are aroused by the presence of others, well-learned or easy (hence dominant) responses would be enhanced by the presence of others, while performance on novel, poorly learned, or complex tasks would deteriorate because the dominant response would be to make errors. Arousal may be increased because of a drive based on survival, or knowledge that others may reward or punish behavior, or because the others distract the subject's attention and it becomes necessary to deal with both the task and the distraction. The performance of an individual in the presence of others is lower if the others interfere with the activity in some way and higher if the others provide high-performance role models.

For research comparing the productivity of an individual with that of a group, the task has to be one that is capable of being performed by an individual. There would be no contest if the task required a set of actions, to be performed simultaneously, that would be impossible for an individual. Thus, we should not be surprised to find that, for these types of problem-solving situations, an individual can be just as effective as a group.

When individuals are compared with groups on the same task, groups are generally found to be better than the average individual but seldom better than the best (Hill 1982). The productivity of the group tends to be less than that of the same number of individuals if no division of labor is required, if there are problems of control, or if the group develops a norm against high productivity. In terms of the number of individual hours required for a task, an individual is usually more productive than a group. When groups appear to be better than individuals, part of the group effect is simply having a larger number of persons to remember facts, identify objects, or produce ideas, especially for tasks requiring low levels of creativity. The average of a number of judgments is usually more accurate than that of a single individual. In addition, the result of a group decision by majority opinion may be more accurate than that of the average of the same number of individuals because the majority decision will not include deviant opinions that would be included in the average.

The fact that groups do better than individuals on difficult and complex tasks, requiring high levels of creativity, may result from having at least one skilled problem solver in the group (Laughlin and Futoran 1985). This is especially true for puzzles for which the correct answer is obvious once one person discovers it. Thus, "truth" wins the decision. Groups may do less well if the type of feedback they are given makes it difficult to locate their errors.

Individuals' productivity in groups may be lower if they engage in "social loafing" and put in less effort than they would in doing the same task on their own (Latané, Williams, and Harkins 1979). This is more likely to happen if there is shared responsibility for the outcome, if the individuals believe their efforts are dispensable or cannot be identified, or if their motivation is low. These effects are more likely to result with tasks requiring low levels of creativity.

The group process called "brainstorming" was developed as a method of enhancing creativity in a group by having individuals generate ideas without criticism from other group members. However, as with other tasks, sets of individuals working alone produce more ideas than the same number of persons working in a group (Street 1974). Part of the problem in groups is a "production block" that results when group members use valuable time as they take turns talking (Diehl and Stroebe 1987). For both individuals and groups it is easier to produce ideas if there is no limit on their practical usefulness.

Several systems have been suggested to take advantage of the problem-solving abilities of a number of individuals without having them participate in a group discussion. In these "nominal" groups individual judgments are combined by some system of averaging (Rohrbaugh 1981).

Some research continues to explore the possibility that individuals will make more "risky" decisions when they participate in group discussion. However, the body of research indicates that the factors that influence "choice" in a group are the same as those that influence any other type of behavior, namely attributes of the situation, the group, and the individual (Isenberg 1986). Individual choice shift as a result of group discussion is influenced by social comparison and persuasive argumentation. The process of social comparison appears to involve an exaggerated perception of the group norm on the part of individual members or a shift to a position more extreme than the group norms (overconformity). Group members are also found to be sensitive to the number of arguments in a particular direction as well as to the novelty and persuasiveness of the arguments. Some norms and arguments may be sex- or personality-linked and thus only have an effect in particular contexts or with particular tasks.

GROUP VERSUS GROUP

Productive groups have a commitment to a clear goal and a combination of personalities, skills, structure, role assignment, morale, and problem-solving experience that is appropriate for the task (McGrath 1984). Although competition between members may result in higher total output, it may also result in lower member satisfaction. However, if the group members are interdependent, and some cooperation is necessary, then competition will lower efficiency (Rosenbaum et al. 1980).

Groups composed of individuals whose personality traits enable them to take initiative, act independently, and act compatibly with other members will be more productive. When possible, group members will develop a group structure that is compatible with their personalities. For example, members who value authority will create a bureaucratic structure, and those who value intimate relations will create a collaborative structure (Friedlander and Green 1977). When a structure is imposed on a group, productivity will be higher when the structure fits the personality characteristics.

High cohesiveness, measured by members' desire to belong to the group, is associated with high productivity. In sports groups, group success leads to a further increase in cohesiveness.

For a discussion task, a five-member group is optimal (Bales 1954; Yetton and Bottger 1983). In general, groups will be less efficient if they have either fewer or more members than those actually required for the task.

Productivity is increased if group members have appropriate information, adequate time for task completion, and a communication network that allows for maximum communication. It usually helps to have a leader designated to coordinate group activity, unless group members are accustomed to sharing the coordination functions. Training for the group task, feedback about the performance, or previous experience with the same task results in improved performance.

A variety of decision-making rules have been suggested for increasing group efficiency. All have the effect of leading members to a more systematic consideration of the facts and members' abilities. For example, Janis (1982) has labeled as "group think" defective policy planning by political decision-making groups. This phenomenon can be avoided if measures are taken to ensure that all negative information is thoroughly considered and group members are given a second chance to express doubts. As a safeguard, more than one set of members and experts may be asked to reach a decision, and the results could be compared.

A decision-making rule that calls for a majority agreement and one that requires unanimity (all members have, or at least agree to, the same opinion) usually result in the same decision. However, a decision made by consensus (members unite in their support of a decision after considering the needs and interests of the individual members) has been viewed as superior to majority rule in terms of decision quality, valuing of all members, and conflict resolution, although a decision may take longer to reach (Hare 1982, pp. 146–154).

Research on the decisions of juries has been conducted using simulations (Tindale and Davis 1985). In much of the research no actual interaction between the "jurors" occurs. Typically a court case is compiled with variations in the sex or apparent guilt of the accused. Subjects are then asked to give their verdicts. Aside from the facts that the decision is about another human being, leading to more sympathy for the defendant of one's own sex, and a greater certainty of guilt and willingness to convict if the subject has had actual jury experience, the results of simulated jury deliberations are similar to those of other task groups. It is easier for a jury to reach a decision under a majority decision rule than one requiring a unanimous decision, although under the majority rule there may be a dissatisfied minority. After deliberation, individuals' opinions may become polarized. The initial distribution of opinions among the members of a jury is a good predictor of the final outcome.

As noted in the comparison of individual and group decisions, when the cost of bringing group members together is high, a decision method that combines individual opinions statistically may produce satisfactory solutions. Even without a conscious decision rule, when the answer to a problem is immediately evident, once it has been proposed by one member, the answer will be accepted by the group (the case where "truth wins"). In laboratory groups, when no decision rule is specified, members seem to use an "equiprobability" scheme in which each strategy advocated by a member has an equal probability of being selected (Davis, Hornik, and Hornseth 1970). Group members also try to be fair, allowing most members to reach their own level of aspiration. Resulting decisions are often the median of the individual opinions.

Group success tends to be attributed to the skill and effort of the members. Opposing teams or other external features are likely to be blamed for failure.

For additional reviews of the literature on group problem solving, see Brandstätter, Davis, and Stocker-Kreichgauer (1982); Davis and Stasson (1988); Kaplan (1989); McGrath (1984); McGrath and Kravitz (1982); and Silver, Cohen, and Rainwater (1988).

(SEE ALSO: *Decision-Making Research and Analysis; Small Groups; Social Psychology*)

REFERENCES

Bales, Robert F. 1954 "In Conference." *Harvard Business Review* 32:44–50.

Brandstätter, Hermann, James H. Davis, and Gisela Stocker-Kreichgauer, eds. 1982 *Group Decision Making.* London: Academic Press.

Davis, James H., John Hornik, and John P. Hornseth 1970 "Group Decision Schemes and Strategy Preferences in a Sequential Response Task." *Journal of Personality and Social Psychology* 15:397–408.

Davis, James H., and Mark F. Stasson 1988 "Small Group Performance: Present Research Trends." *Advances in Group Processes* 5:245–277.

Diehl, Michael, and Wolfgang Stroebe 1987 "Productivity Loss in Brainstorming Groups: Toward the Solution of a Riddle." *Journal of Personality and Social Psychology* 53:497–509.

Friedlander, Frank, and P. Toni Green 1977 "Life Styles and Conflict Coping Structures." *Group and Organization Studies* 2:101–112.

Hare, A. Paul 1976 *Handbook of Small Group Research.* New York: Free Press.

——— 1982 *Creativity in Small Groups.* Beverly Hills, Calif.: Sage.

———, Herbert H. Blumberg, Martin F. Davies, and M. Valerie Kent 1991 *Small Group Research: A Handbook.* Norwood, N.J.: Ablex Publishing Co.

Hill, Gayle W. 1982 "Group Versus Individual Performance: Are $N + 1$ Heads Better Than One?" *Psychological Bulletin* 91:517–539.

Isenberg, Daniel J. 1986 "Group Polarization: A Critical Review and Meta-Analysis." *Journal of Personality and Social Psychology* 50:1,141–1,151.

Janis, Irving L. 1982 *Groupthink: Psychological Studies of Policy Decisions and Fiascos.* Boston: Houghton Mifflin.

Kaplan, Martin F. 1989 "Task, Situational, and Personal Determinants of Influence Process in Group Decision Making." *Advances in Group Processes* 6:87–105.

Latané, Bibb, Kipling Williams, and Stephen Harkins

1979 "Social Loafing." *Psychology Today* October, pp. 104–110.

Laughlin, Patrick R., and Gail C. Futoran 1985 "Collective Induction: Social Combination and Sequential Transition." *Journal of Personality and Social Psychology* 48:608–613.

McGrath, Joseph E. 1984 *Groups: Interaction and Performance.* Englewood Cliffs, N.J.: Prentice-Hall.

———, and David A. Kravitz 1982 "Group Research." *Annual Review of Psychology* 33:195–230.

Rohrbaugh, John 1981 "Improving the Quality of Group Judgment: Social Judgment Analysis and the Nominal Group Technique." *Organizational Behavior and Human Performance* 28:272–288.

Rosenbaum, Milton E., Danny L. Moore, John L. Cotton, Michael S. Cook, Rex A. Hieser, M. Nicki Shovar, and Morris J. Gray 1980 "Group Productivity and Process: Pure and Mixed Reward Structures and Task Interdependence." *Journal of Personality and Social Psychology* 39:626–642.

Silver, Steven D., Bernard P. Cohen, and Julie Rainwater 1988 "Group Structure and Information Exchange in Innovative Problem Solving." *Advances in Group Processes* 5:169–194.

Street, Warren R. 1974 "Brainstorming by Individuals, Coacting and Interacting Groups." *Journal of Applied Psychology* 59:433–436.

Tindale, R. Scott, and James H. Davis 1985 "Individual and Group Reward Allocation Decisions in Two Situational Contexts: Effects of Relative Need and Performance." *Journal of Personality and Social Psychology* 48:1148–1161.

Yetton, Philip, and Preston Bottger 1983 "The Relationships Among Group Size, Member Ability, Social Decision Schemes, and Performance." *Organizational Behavior and Human Performance* 32:145–159.

Zajonc, Robert B. 1965 "Social Facilitation." *Science* 149:269–274.

A. PAUL HARE

GROUP SIZE EFFECTS Group size has been a variable of interest to sociologists and social psychologists since the earliest experimental work with groups. From the turn of the century, research has been directed toward the effects of the presence of other persons on individual performance and on the characteristics of social interaction and problem solving in different sized groups (Hare 1976, pp. 214–231; Hare et al. 1991).

Although the size of the natural group varies with the age and other social characteristics of the members, casual work or play groups most often have only two or three members (Bakeman and Beck 1974), while the modal size of an adolescent gang is about ten members.

As each additional member joins a group, the number of potential relationships between individuals and subgroups increases rapidly, thus placing more demands on the leader in coordinating group activity. With an increase in group size, the time available to each member for communication decreases, the gap between the top participater and other group members grows proportionately greater, and an increased proportion of the members feel threatened and inhibited (Bales et al. 1951).

The larger group has some advantages because, with the addition of new members, the resources of the group are increased so that a variety of problems may be solved more efficiently. However, after some point, depending upon the task, the addition of new members brings diminishing returns (cf. Smith and Murdoch 1970). Although the group may take less time to complete the task, it is less efficient as measured by how much time each person spends, and the range of available ideas is increased at the expense of greater difficulty in reaching agreement in the absence of any clear-cut criteria for judgment. For types of problems for which the group is given credit for solving the problem if at least one member can find the answer, the advantage of a large group is simply that a larger sample of potential problem solvers is provided.

Of special interest in the United States has been the comparison of six-person and twelve-person juries, because state legislatures have shown an interest in reducing jury size. In one study, jury size had no effect on conviction when apparent guilt of the defendant was low. But when apparent guilt was high the six-person juries were more likely to convict (Valenti and Downing 1975), perhaps because the probability of a dissenter being present was reduced.

In a decision-making process, the quality of interaction among group members changes as group size increases: Groups use more mechanical methods of introducing information, are less sensitive in the exploration of different points of view, and make more direct attempts to reach a solution, whether or not all members agree. Individuals with initially different opinions are more likely to conform to the majority in larger groups, although the effect of size is nonlinear. The extent of "social impact" and minority influence are important variables. Group size has most effect on an individual's conformity if the other group members are perceived as having their own separate opinions rather than being part of a single group (Wilder 1977).

The number of members in a group compared to the number needed for the task has been referred to as "manning." Tasks may be "undermanned" or "overmanned." Having more members than necessary is found to produce weaker and more variable feelings of involvement (Wicker et al. 1976). In a situation where there are less than the required number of persons, members work harder. Overmanned groups are more likely to reject a deviant member. In a simple task that requires a low level of creativity (rope pulling, for example), individual performance declines significantly with the addition of one or two coworkers (Ingham et al. 1974). For simple tasks or tasks in which the individual's contribution is not clearly recognized, members are inclined to decrease their effort and engage in "social loafing" as more members are added to a group (Latané, Williams, and Harkins 1979).

The interaction pattern in a group of two has unique characteristics that suggest a delicate balance of power in making decisions. Over time, one member of the pair becomes more active. Research on intimate relations is similar to early research on the dyad and on friendship (Kelley et al. 1983; Levinger 1980). Relations between intimate pairs include intimate disclosure, knowing each other's personal feelings, joint development of pair norms, and mutual responsibility for one another's outcomes, with strong mutual attraction. Relationships are generally closer if the persons have similar social characteristics and compatible personality traits.

In groups of more than two, there are differences between those with even and those with odd numbers of members. Possibly as a result of the fact that a group often splits into two opposing subgroups of equal size, there is more disagreement and antagonism in even-sized groups. In laboratory groups of three, two members characteristically form a coalition, leaving one member isolated; however, the same tendency is not observed in family groups of mother, father, and son. When coalitions do form between members of unequal power, a pair will join forces to maximize their reward and minimize the temptation to form a different coalition (cf. Knowles 1978; Stokols 1976).

The optimum size for a small discussion group appears to be five members because members are generally less satisfied with smaller or larger groups (Bales 1954). In smaller groups, members may be forced to be too prominent, and in larger groups they may not have enough opportunities to speak, and more control may be required. In a group of five, strict deadlocks can be avoided and members can shift roles swiftly. To select the appropriate-sized group for a given problem, Thelen (1949) has suggested the "principle of least group size." The group should be just large enough to include individuals with all the relevant backgrounds and skills for the problem's solution. For example, in the use of "Synectics," a form of creative problem-solving developed primarily for business applications, Gordon (1961, pp. 72–73) finds that five persons representing a cross-section of a business firm are enough to provide all the necessary skills and points of view.

If the number of persons is too large for the space it is given to occupy, members are more likely to feel crowded, even when everyone can be seen. Under crowded conditions persons react more negatively to each other. However, in contrast to men, women tend to find smaller rooms more comfortable and intimate. When possible, people will avoid crowded situations.

Research on helping behavior provides additional evidence concerning the influence of different-sized sets of persons or groups (Latané and Nida 1981). Although many studies of helping behavior involve field experiments in which an accomplice drops things in public or appears to need assistance in some other way, the basic design is similar to the early experiments recording the influence of the presence of an audience or a group on individual behavior. In this case, the focus is not on problem solving but on a manifestation of positive behavior, namely helping. The larger the number of observers who are not helping someone in need, the less likely a subject is to help, especially if the costs of helping are high and help is not important. As with other tasks, the kind of group involved and its relationship to the subject makes a difference in the likelihood of helping. The number of bystanders present is frequently found to be inversely related to the intervention (if the persons are unacquainted) because the onlooker may feel less responsible. However, if the bystanders are part of a cohesive group, there may be an increase in the salience of the norm of social responsibility.

The contrasts between small groups and larger groups are similar to those between groups led by democratic leaders and those led by authoritarian leaders, groups with decentralized communication networks and those with centralized communication networks, and groups whose members are cooperating and those whose members are competing. For large groups, authoritarian leadership, centralized communication networks, and groups whose members are competing, one finds an increase in productivity coupled with low satisfaction for the average member. Thus, the effects of increasing the size of a group may well be countered by the influence of some other variable such as leadership, communication network, or the requirements of the task.

(SEE ALSO: *Small Groups; Social Psychology*)

REFERENCES

Bakeman, Roger, and Stephen Beck 1974 "The Size of Informal Groups in Public." *Environment and Behavior* 6:378–390.

Bales, Robert F. 1954 "In Conference." *Harvard Business Review* 32:44–50.

———, Fred L. Strodtbeck, Theodore M. Mills, and Mary E. Roseborough 1951 "Channels of Communication in Small Groups." *American Sociological Review* 16:461–468.

Gordon, William J. 1961 *Synectics: The Development of Creativity*. New York: Collier Books.

Hare, A. Paul 1976 *Handbook of Small Group Research*. New York: Free Press.

———, Paul, Herbert H. Blumberg, Martin F. Davies, and M. Valerie Kent 1991 *Small Group Research: A Handbook*. Norwood, N.J.: Ablex Publishing Co.

Ingham, Alan G., George Levinger, James Graves, and Vaughn Peckham 1974 "The Ringelmann Effect: Studies of Group Size and Group Performance." *Journal of Experimental Social Psychology* 10:371–384.

Kelley, Harold H., Ellen Berscheid, Andrew Christensen, John H. Harvey, Ted L. Huston, George Levinger, Evie McClintock, Letitia Anne Peplau, and Ronald R. Peterson 1983 *Close Relationships*. New York: Freeman.

Knowles, Eric S. 1978 "The Gravity of Crowding: Application of Social Physics to the Effects of Others." In A. Baum and Y. Epstein, eds., *Human Response to Crowding*. Hillsdale, N.J.: Erlbaum.

Latané, Bibb, and Steve Nida 1981 "Ten Years of Research on Group Size and Helping." *Psychological Bulletin* 89:308–324.

Latané, Bibb, Kipling Williams, and Stephen Harkins 1979 "Social Loafing." *Psychology Today* October, pp. 104–110.

Levinger, George 1980 "Toward the Analysis of Close Relationships." *Journal of Experimental Social Psychology* 16:510–544.

Smith, Gene F., and Peter Murdoch 1970 "Performance of Informed versus Noninformed Triads and Quartets in the 'Minimal Social Situation'." *Journal of Personality and Social Psychology* 15:391–396.

Stokols, Daniel 1976 "The Experience of Crowding in Primary and Secondary Environments." *Environment and Behavior* 8:49–86.

Thelen, Herbert A. 1949 "Group Dynamics in Instruction: Principle of Least Group Size." *School Review* 57:139–148.

Valenti, Angelo C., and Leslie L. Downing 1975 "Differential Effects of Jury Size on Verdicts Following Deliberation as a Function of the Apparent Guilt of a

Defendant." *Journal of Personality and Social Psychology* 32:655–663.

Wicker, Allan W., Sandra L. Kirmeyer, Lois Hanson, and Dean Alexander 1976 "Effects of Manning Levels on Subjective Experience, Performance, and Verbal Interaction in Groups." *Organizational Behavior and Human Performance* 17:251–274.

Wilder, Davis A. 1977 "Perception of Groups, Size of Opposition, and Social Influence." *Journal of Experimental Social Psychology* 13:253–268.

A. PAUL HARE

H

HAWTHORNE EFFECT The *Hawthorne effect* refers to confounding influences on research outcomes caused by subjects' reactions to being studied. The popular belief is that subjects react to some aspect of experimental participation by increasing their effort. Based on evidence of increased worker output caused by this type of "reactivity," the initial Hawthorne study findings gave rise to the field of organizational psychology and prompted researchers in many fields of sociology, psychology, and education to further examine and control for the potential interactions among research methods, outcomes, and subjects' reactivity to being studied. Although the causal process that produced the Hawthorne results was not clear from the original studies, several rudimentary social-psychological explanations have since been postulated.

The Hawthorne effect gets its name from a series of experimental field studies conducted between 1924 and 1932 at the Hawthorne Works of the Western Electric Company (Roethlisberger and Dickson 1939; Mayo 1933). The studies were designed to examine the effects of different working conditions, such as changes in rest cycles and illumination, on work productivity, for example, rates of assembling relays, inspecting parts, and winding coils. The surprising outcome from several (not all) of these studies was that each change in a working condition, even seemingly adverse changes such as decreasing normal work-space illumination by 50 to 70 percent, resulted in increased work productivity. Furthermore, at the conclusion of the first "Relay Assembly Test Room Study," during which productivity increased in response to changes in weekly and daily work schedules, lengths of rest periods, and amount of lunch provided by the company, production rates remained at an increased level even after workers were returned to prestudy work conditions.

What is it about being studied that subjects react to? Although the Hawthorne investigations show evidence of behavioral changes due, in some way, to the process of being studied, the specific causal elements of the Hawthorne effect are not well understood. The ambiguity is due to: (1) misinterpretation and exaggeration of the Hawthorne findings by subsequent writers and researchers; (2) inconsistent results from attempts to replicate Hawthorne effects and isolate the social-psychological mediating factors; and (3) problems in the original Hawthorne studies such as poor control group designs and simultaneous influences of many uncontrolled experimental conditions. The last problem has been used to suggest that a clear analysis of the Hawthorne effect may not be possible from the original studies (Carey 1967). Nevertheless, subsequent research has advanced several explanations and corresponding control procedures.

To examine explanations and supporting evidence for Hawthorne effects, Adair and his colleagues (Adair 1984; Adair, Sharpe, and Huynh 1989) reviewed eighty-six educational studies that explicitly controlled for Hawthorne effects. The three most common explanations of the Hawthorne effect were: (1) subjects respond to the *special attention,* by researchers and/or supervisors, accorded them as study participants; (2) mere *awareness* of participating in a study affects subject's performance; and (3) subjects react to *novelty* created by some aspect of study procedures. Control procedures employed in these studies generally corresponded to one or more of these explanations. For example, to match treatment and control group subjects on experimental "awareness," subjects in a Hawthorne control group would be told explicitly that they were participating in an experiment. Although results of the research review supported none of the three explanations (Adair, Sharpe, and Huynh 1989), the potential problem presented by subject reactivity and need for appropriate control procedures is not diminished. Instead, the review findings underscore the need for exploring more systematically the specific causes of outcomes like those evidenced in the original Hawthorne studies so that an articulated model of processes involved in subject reactivity can be developed and used to improve research designs and procedures.

To articulate the processes underlying the Hawthorne effect, it will be necessary to better understand the subject's experience of study procedures, expectations about the goals of the researcher and hypotheses under investigation, and how these relate to the subject's own goals and motivations. This perspective is not new. Since the 1950s, Martin T. Orne and others have proposed that subject reactivity can be understood as a response to the "demand characteristics" of a study:

> *[Demand characteristics] include the scuttlebutt about the experiment, its setting, implicit and explicit instructions, the person of the experimenter, subtle cues provided by him, and, of particular importance, the experimental procedure itself. All of these cues are interpreted in the light of the subject's past learning and experience. Although the explicit instructions are important, it appears that subtler cues from which the subject can draw covert or even unconscious inference may be still more powerful* (Orne 1969, p. 146).

Because the goals, procedures, and moment-to-moment subject–researcher interactions are rarely similar in any two studies, demand characteristics and, consequently, the expression of subject reactivity, may vary tremendously across studies. It may therefore be unrealistic to expect that a single social-psychological model underlies subject reactivity or can explain the Hawthorne study results. Instead, if research progresses in this area it is likely that several different forms of Hawthorne effects and the processes that determine them will evolve.

(SEE ALSO: *Industrial Sociology; Quasi-Experimental Research Designs*)

REFERENCES

Adair, J. G. 1984 "The Hawthorne Effect: A Reconsideration of the Methodological Artifact." *Journal of Applied Psychology* 69:334–345.

———, D. Sharpe, and C. L. Huynh 1989 "Hawthorne Control Procedures in Educational Experiments: A Reconsideration of Their Use and Effectiveness." *Review of Educational Research* 59:215–228.

Carey, A. 1967 "The Hawthorne Studies: A Radical Criticism." *American Sociological Review* 32:403–416.

Mayo, E. 1933 *The Human Problems of an Industrial Civilization.* New York: Macmillan.

Orne, M. T. 1969 "Demand Characteristics and the Concept of Quasi-Controls." In R. Rosenthal and R. L. Rosnow, eds., *Artifact in Behavioral Research.* New York: Academic.

Roethlisberger, F. J., and W. J. Dickson, 1939 *Management and the Worker.* New York: Wiley.

ERIC LANG

HEALTH AND ILLNESS BEHAVIOR

Health behavior usually refers to preventive orientations and the positive steps people take to enhance their physical well-being and vitality. Traditionally, work in health behavior has focused on the use of preventive services such as immunizations, medical checkups, hypertensive screening, and prophylactic dentistry (Becker 1974). It also includes research on such behaviors as cigarette smoking, substance abuse, nutritional practices, and exercise.

The conventional approach to health behavior has been limited, focusing on the origins of particular behaviors damaging to health and strategies to modify them. The most widely used general model—the health belief model—conceptualizes preventive health action within a psychological cost-benefit analysis (Rosenstock 1974). Behavior change is seen as following motives that are salient and perceived as yielding valuable benefits in situations where people have conflicting motives. An important component of the model involves cues to action, since an activating stimulus often appears to be necessary in the initiation of a new behavioral sequence. Over the years, this model has been expanded (Becker and Maiman 1983), but it serves more as an organizing framework for study of preventive health behavior than as a successful predictive model. Most studies applying the model achieve only modest success in prediction.

Efforts to develop a general theory are limited by the fact that behavior conducive to health derives from diverse and sometimes conflicting motives. The correlations among varying positive health practices tend to be modest, although there are clusters of behaviors (such as smoking, marijuana use, and alcohol consumption) that are somewhat more highly intercorrelated (Mechanic 1979; Langlie 1977). Nevertheless, there is no simple identifiable positive health orientation that can serve as a basis for promoting risk aversion and health maintenance.

The lack of such a general orientation results because most behaviors with important implications for health arise from motives not related to health and are significantly programmed into the daily patterns and institutional life of communities and families (Mechanic 1990). Health-protective behaviors that are consequences of accepted, everyday, conventional activities require neither conscious motivation nor special efforts to be sustained. The favorable health experience of Mormons, for example, is a product of their belief systems and patterns of activity reinforced by the way of life of this cultural community (Mechanic 1990).

One implication is that promoting health is more a matter of changing culture and social structure than of modifying personal motives or intentions. Patterns of behavior that depend on sustained conscious motivation are less stable than those that are a natural consequence of the accepted norms and understandings within a community. Expectations not only affect the prevalence of varying behaviors but also establish constraints on the acquired behaviors of children and adolescents. Changes in the last decade in the social constraints on smoking, and the growing unacceptability of smoking in varying social contexts, may have more significance than any program to change personal behavior.

Although there is no evidence for a unitary health orientation, some social factors, particularly socioeconomic status (SES), predict good outcomes across a wide range of health indicators (Bunker, Gomby, and Kehrer 1989). Persons of higher SES have less morbidity and lower mortality, are less likely to smoke and abuse drugs, more readily seek and use preventive health opportunities, and are more interested in health and acquire more information about it. Across nations, education is the most powerful predictor of health outcomes, particularly maternal education—a factor crucial for the reduction of infant mortality and maintenance of child health (Caldwell 1986). The precise ways in which SES affects these outcomes are not understood, although there are many plausible hypotheses. Beyond the income advantages and related opportunities that education commonly brings, schooling also enhances knowledge, self-concept, sense of control, personal autonomy, and social participation. Education is also the single best predictor of "psychological modernity,'' an orientation conducive to family planning, health, and social involvement (Inkeles 1983; Inkeles and Smith 1974).

A variety of behaviors noxious to health (smoking, drug use, and drinking) develop or increase during adolescence and young adulthood. However, young people who have a good relationship with their parents and who are attuned to parent-oriented values as measured by school performance, attending religious services, and having meals with parents do relatively well across a variety of health measures (Hansell and Mechanic 1990). In contrast, high engagement with peer-oriented social activities is associated with increases in behavior associated with health risk.

Individuals' appraisals of their health depend as much on their global sense of well-being as they do on specific patterns of illness (Mechanic 1978). Studies of perceptions of health show that they are independently influenced both by the prevalence of symptoms and illness conditions and by the person's psychological well-being (Tessler and Mechanic 1978). Individuals tend to assess their health holistically in terms of vitality and capacity to perform their social activities and roles. Psychological distress often diminishes vitality and functioning as much as serious medical conditions. The RAND Medical Outcomes Study found that depressive symptoms were more disabling than many chronic physical conditions that physicians view as extremely serious (Wells et al. 1989). Several longitudinal studies of the elderly have found that subjective self-assessments of health predict future mortality after taking account of known risk factors and socio-demographic measures. Such self-assessments prospectively predict longevity better than physician assessment (Kaplan and Camacho 1983; Mossey and Shapiro 1982).

An important issue is how sense of well-being becomes incorporated into people's judgments of their physical health. One approach is to study health appraisals among children and adolescents who have little serious illness. A recent prospective study found that adolescents who were more competent and more engaged in age-related activities as measured by school performance and participation in sports and other exercise rated their health more highly (Mechanic and Hansell 1987). Adolescents' health assessments are shaped by their overall sense of functioning, and they do not seem to differentiate among physical and psychological aspects of well-being in making general assessments of how they feel. These findings may help explain the common inclination of adults to express general malaise and psychosocial problems through physical complaints.

The study of illness behavior, in contrast to health behavior, is concerned with the way people monitor their bodies, define and interpret bodily indications, make decisions about needed treatment, and use informal and formal sources of care (Mechanic 1986). Illness behavior begins prior to the use of services and shapes decisions about whether to seek care and what pathways to follow.

A wide range of factors affects the appraisal of symptoms and response to perceived illness (McHugh and Vallis 1986). Sickness is an accepted role in society, bringing sympathetic attention and legitimate release from expected performance (Parsons 1951). Determinations of illness may involve intense negotiations about individuals' claims that, when legitimized, may justify failure to meet expectations or allow escape from onerous obligations (Mechanic 1978). In some situations the sick role becomes a point of tension and conflict between the claimant, who seeks legitimation of sickness with its special privileges, and other interested parties including families, employers, and welfare administrators, who may seek to limit release from social obligations or diminish special privileges granted to the sick and disabled (Field 1957). Most illness situations are neither problematic nor sources of conflict, but the contested cases make evident the social assumptions and expectations around which illness is organized.

Like other behavior, illness behavior is learned through socialization in families and peer groups and through exposure to the mass media and education. There is great diversity of attitudes, beliefs, knowledge, and behavior all of which affect the definitions of problematic symptoms, the meanings and causal attributions that explain them, socially anticipated responses, and the definition of appropriate remedies and sources of care. Motivation and learning affect the initial recognition of symptoms, reactions to pain, the extent of stoicism and hypochondriasis, the readiness to seek release from work, school, and other obligations and to seek help (Mechanic 1978).

Processes of symptom appraisal are influenced by the manner in which symptoms occur and their characteristics, by knowledge, and by past experiences with illness (Mechanic 1972; Leventhal 1986). Some symptoms are so painful and incapacitating that they inevitably lead to intervention without significant inquiry. Others are so familiar and generally understood as self-limited that they also are dealt with routinely. Many symptoms, however, are neither familiar nor easily understood, resulting in a process of interpretation within the context of personality, situational cues and stressors, and environmental influences. Only a small proportion of symptoms leads to formal consultation or care. The vast majority are denied, normalized, or evaluated as having little significance.

In situations where there are no obvious explanations for the occurrence of symptoms, individuals seek meanings for changes in their feeling states. The common-sense theories they apply may either be idiosyncratic or drawn from socially prevalent conventional explanations such as stress, lack of sleep, overwork, and overeating. These lay explanations are influential on subsequent behavior such as care-seeking and use of medication (Kleinman 1980; Leventhal, Meyer, and Nerenz 1980; Leventhal, Prohaska, and Hirschman 1985). For example, it is commonly believed that stress increases blood pressure and that relaxation reduces it. Most individuals, however, cannot assess whether their blood pressure is high or low on the basis of available cues, yet many believe they can. Persons with hypertension, an asymptomatic condition, commonly use self-assessments of their stress levels or relaxation as an indicator of their blood pressure levels and adjust their medication accordingly, despite medical advice to the contrary (Leventhal, Prohaska, and Hirschman 1985). Similarly, many patients with limited understanding of the biological processes through which drugs such as antibiotics or antidepressants act increase or decrease medication in relation to changes in how they feel and environmental cues.

In short, illness appraisal is a two-step process (Mechanic 1972). In the initial step, persons monitor their bodies to assess the location, duration, intensity, and persistence of discomfort. In the second stage, which may occur almost concurrently, they seek explanations for perceived changes. If an obvious explanation is not available, or is disconfirmed by further checking, individuals look to their environment for new cues and explanations. These interpretations, in light of knowledge and other beliefs, may then play a role in the formal initiation of care.

Persons seeking medical care commonly express their distress and lowered sense of well-being through many diffuse physical complaints such as fatigue, insomnia, and aches and pains in different bodily systems, a process referred to as somatization (Kleinman 1986). Although much of the existing literature focuses on somatization as a problematic process, it is by far the predominant pattern for expressing distress. Until the last forty or fifty years it was uncommon to conceptualize distress in psychological terms, and even now such expressions are used primarily among well-educated populations receptive to psychological interpretations. General distress has both physical and psychological concomitants; the language that people use to characterize distress depends on the cultural context, the perceived appropriateness of psychological complaints, and the stigma attached to emotional disorder.

There is controversy as to whether psychological idioms are inaccessible to many people due to cultural factors or limited schooling, or whether somatization represents a choice among alternative idioms because such presentations are seen as more consistent with the medical care context. Rates of reported depression in Chinese cultures, for example, are extremely low, although "neurasthenia" is a common diagnosis in Chinese medical care settings (Kleinman 1986). Psychiatrists in China routinely view neurasthenia as a "disorder of brain function involving asthenia of cerebral cortical activity," but alternatively the symptoms reported are strikingly similar to the physical manifestations of depressive disorders more commonly seen in Western countries. It remains unclear whether these diagnoses characterize the same underlying disorders that are expressed differently in varying cultural groups or whether they are fundamentally different. This debate shares common features with the discussion of gender differences in the prevalence of psychiatric disorder. While depression is seen more commonly among women, men have higher rates of antisocial behavior and substance abuse. Researchers differ on whether these are fundamentally different disorders or alternative manifestations of common underlying difficulties. The debate is difficult to resolve because it reflects two fundamentally different models of the nature of illness itself. Within one perspective depression reflects a discrete underlying disorder, while in the other it is simply one alternative adaptive pattern (Mechanic 1989).

The social complexity of the relationships between illness and illness behavior are illustrated by a prospective study of Chinese patients diagnosed as neurasthenic who also met the criteria for a diagnosis of major depression consistent with American diagnostic standards. Kleinman (1986) treated these patients with antidepressant drugs but found on follow-up that while a majority showed significant improvements in clinical psychiatric symptoms, they continued to be impaired, to function badly, and to seek help for their condition. They also remained skeptical of the drug treatment they received. Kleinman links these responses to the patients' needs for the medical legitimation of their "illness" to explain past failures and to justify continuing difficulties in meeting social expectations.

Certification of illness becomes a public issue when physicians have moral and legal authority to define illness and disability and to sanction the sick role. Such influence is found in certifying justified absenteeism for employers, in litigation, and in decisions on eligibility in insurance and disability entitlement programs. Efforts are often made to maintain the illusion that these are objective decisions based solely on medical expertise and clinical experience, but judgments often depend on who the physician represents. The state or other formal organizations may thus attempt to control physicians by limiting their discretion, as happened in the Soviet Union when physicians were viewed as allowing people excuses to escape work too easily (Field 1957), or by taking physicians acting as patients' agents out of the decision-making loop as in the American disability determination system. The need for bureaucratic control tends to be refocused on the new alternative decision-makers as evidenced by the continuing efforts of the Social Security Administration to constrain the decisions of state agencies and administrative law judges (Osterweis, Kleinman, and Mechanic 1987). In short, the definition of illness and disability is the "rope" in a tug of war in which competing parties seek determinations in their own interest.

The study of illness behavior has many applications in research, clinical care, public health, and social policy (Mechanic 1986). Such patterns of behavior substantially affect pathways into care and selectively shape the samples studied in clinical contexts. Failure to understand these selection effects and how they operate lead to erroneous conclusions about the nature of basic disease processes. A common error is to attribute to the etiology of the illness influences triggering use of services, a problem that plagues much research on stress and illness. At the clinical level, awareness of how people construe illness, present symptoms, and respond to care can improve understanding and communication and help health professionals to guide more effectively the treatment regimen. Much of illness behavior, as illustrated, is an alternative to other types of coping and environmental mastery. Increasing evidence suggests that a personal sense of control (Rodin 1986) and self-esteem (Mechanic 1980) contribute to physical vitality and satisfaction and promote health. These areas of concern are important for the public health agenda.

Health and illness behavior studies make clear that the forces affecting health and treatment outcomes transcend medical care and the transactions that take place between doctor and patient. In recent decades there have been increasing tendencies toward the medicalization of social problems and a failure to address the complicated longitudinal needs of patients with serious chronic illness and disabilities. Moreover, the problems of managing the frailties of old age, characterized by a combination of medical, instrumental, and psychosocial needs, increasingly challenge the operating assumptions of treatment focused on narrow definitions of disease and care. Studies of illness behavior teach the importance of moving beyond initial complaints and narrow definitions of problems and examining the broad context of individuals' lives and the factors that affect social function and quality of life. They point to the diverse adaptations among persons with comparable physical debility and potential. They reinforce the need to take account of the environmental and social context of people's lives, their potential assets, and their disease. A medical care system, responsive to these broad concerns, would be better prepared for the impending health care challenges of the 1990s.

(SEE ALSO: *Health Promotion; Health Status Measurement; Medical Sociology; Mental Health; Mental Illness and Mental Disorders)*

REFERENCES

Becker, Marshall (ed.) 1974 *The Health Belief Model and Personal Health Behavior.* Thorofare, N.J.: Slack.

———, and Lois Maiman 1983 "Models of Health-Related Behavior." In D. Mechanic, ed., *Handbook of Health, Health Care and the Health Professions.* New York: Free Press.

Bunker, John, Deanna Gomby, and Barbara Kehrer, eds. 1989 *Pathways to Health: The Role of Social Factors.* Menlo Park, Calif.: Kaiser Family Foundation.

Caldwell, John 1986 "Routes to Low Mortality in Poor Countries." *Population and Development Review* 12:171–220.

Field, Mark G. 1957 *Doctor and Patient in Soviet Russia.* Cambridge, Mass.: Harvard University Press.

Hansell, Stephen, and David Mechanic 1990 "Parent and Peer Effects on Adolescent Health Behavior." In Klaus Hurrelman and Friedrich Losel, eds., *Health Hazards in Adolescence.* New York: De Gruyter.

Inkeles, Alex 1983 *Exploring Individual Modernity.* New York: Columbia University Press.

———, and D. H. Smith 1974 *Becoming Modern: Individual Change in Six Developing Countries.* Cambridge, Mass.: Harvard University Press.

Kaplan, George, and Terry Camacho 1983 "Perceived Health and Mortality: A Nine-Year Follow-Up of the Human Population Laboratory Cohort." *American Journal of Epidemiology* 117:292–304.

Kleinman, Arthur 1980 *Patients and Healers in the Context of Culture.* Berkeley: University of California Press.

———1986 *Social Origins of Distress and Disease: Depression, Neurasthenia, and Pain in Modern China.* New Haven: Yale University Press.

Langlie, Jean 1977 "Social Networks, Health Beliefs, and Preventive Health Behavior." *Journal of Health and Social Behavior* 18:244–260.

Leventhal, Howard 1986 "Symptom Reporting: A Focus on Process." In Sean McHugh and T. Michael Vallis, eds., *Illness Behavior: A Multidisciplinary Model.* New York: Plenum.

———, Daniel Meyer, and David Nerenz 1980 "The Common-Sense Representation of Illness Danger." In Stanley Rachman, ed., *Contributions to Medical Psychology.* New York: Pergamon.

———, Thomas Prohaska, and Robert Hirschman 1985 "Preventive Health Behavior across the Life Span." In James Rosen and Laura Solomon, eds., *Prevention in Health Psychology.* Hanover: University Press of New England.

McHugh, Sean, and T. Michael Vallis (eds.) 1986 *Illness Behavior: A Multidisciplinary Model.* New York: Plenum.

Mechanic, David 1972 "Social Psychologic Factors Affecting the Presentation of Bodily Complaints." *The New England Journal of Medicine* 286:1132–1139.

———1978 *Medical Sociology.* 2nd ed. New York: Free Press.

———1979 "The Stability of Health and Illness Behavior: Results from a Sixteen-Year Follow-Up." *American Journal of Public Health* 69:1142–1145.

———1980 "Education, Parental Interest, and Health Perceptions and Behavior." *Inquiry* 17:331–338.

———1985 "Health and Illness Behavior." In J. M. Last and Maxcy-Rosenau, eds., *Preventive Medicine and Public Health.* 12th ed. New York: Appleton-Century Crofts.

———1986 "Illness Behavior: An Overview." In S.

McHugh and T. M. Vallis, eds., *Illness Behavior: A Multidisciplinary Model.* New York: Plenum.

———1989 *Mental Health and Social Policy.* 3rd ed. Englewood Cliffs, N.J.: Prentice-Hall.

———1990 "Promoting Health." *Society* 27(2):16–22.

Mechanic, David, and Stephen Hansell 1987 "Adolescent Competence, Psychological Well-Being and Self-Assessed Physical Health." *Journal of Health and Social Behavior* 28:364–374.

Mossey, Jane, and Evelyn Shapiro 1982 "Self-Rated Health: A Predictor of Mortality among the Elderly." *American Journal of Public Health* 72:800–808.

Osterweis, Marian, Arthur Kleinman, and David Mechanic (eds.) 1987 *Pain and Disability: Clinical, Behavioral and Public Policy Perspectives.* Washington, D.C.: National Academy Press.

Parsons, Talcott 1951 *The Social System.* New York: Free Press.

Rodin, Judith 1986 "Aging and Health: Effects of the Sense of Control." *Science* 233:1,271–1,276.

Rosenstock, Irwin 1974 "The Health Belief Model and Preventive Health Behavior." In Marshall Becker, ed., *The Health Belief Model and Personal Health Behavior.* Thorofare, N.J.: Slack.

Tessler, Richard, and David Mechanic 1978 "Psychological Distress and Perceived Health Status." *Journal of Health and Social Behavior* 19:254–262.

Wells, Kenneth, Anita Stewart, Ron D. Hays, Audrey Burnam, William Rogers, Marcia Daniels, Sandra Berry, Sheldon Greenfield, and John Ware 1989 "The Functioning and Well-Being of Depressed Patients: Results from the Medical Outcomes Study." *Journal of the American Medical Association* 262:914–919.

DAVID MECHANIC

HEALTH AND THE LIFE COURSE

Health and *the life course* are two broad concepts of interest to sociologists. Each of these concepts must be nominally defined.

CONCEPTIONS OF HEALTH

Health can be conceptualized in three major ways: the medical model (or physical definition); the functional model (or social definition); and the psychological model (or the subjective evaluation of health; Liang 1986). In the medical model, health is defined as the absence of disease. The presence of any disease condition is determined by reports from the patient, observations by health practitioners, or medical tests. The social definition of health is derived from Parsons's (1951) work and refers to an individual's ability to perform roles, that is, to function socially. Illness or impairment is a function of reduced capacity to perform expected roles, commonly measured in terms of activities of daily living (ADLs—eating, dressing, bathing, walking, grooming, etc.). The psychological model, or the subjective evaluation of health, is often based on the response to a single question asking one to rate one's health on a scale from poor to excellent. The definition of health used by the World Health Organization since 1946 reflects this multidimensional perspective: "a state of complete physical, mental, and social well-being and not merely the absence of disease or infirmity."

It has been suggested (e.g., Schroots 1988) that a distinction be made between *disease* and *illness.* It is argued that disease refers to an objective diagnosis of a disorder, while illness refers to the presence of a disease plus the individual's perception of and response to the disease. Thus, one may have a disease, but as long as one does not acknowledge it and behave accordingly (e.g., take medicine), one will perceive oneself as healthy (Birren and Zarit 1985).

A distinction should also be made between *acute* and *chronic* conditions. These two types of health conditions are differentially related to older and younger age groups (discussed more below). That is, there is a morbidity shift from acute to chronic diseases as an individual ages. In addition, Western societies experienced a dramatic shift from infectious diseases (a form of acute condition) to chronic, degenerative diseases in the late nineteenth century and the first half of the twentieth century.

CONCEPTIONS OF THE LIFE COURSE

The life course is a progression through time (Clausen 1986), in particular, social time. Social time is a set of norms governing life transitions for particular social groups. These transitions may vary from one group to another (e.g., working class versus middle class) and from one historical period to another. The life course approach focuses on "age related transitions that are *socially created, socially recognized,* and *shared*" (Hagestad and Neugarten 1985, p. 35). Historical time plays a key role in life course analysis because of the emphasis on social time and social transitions (Elder 1977; Hareven 1978). Changes that take place in society lead to a restructuring of individual life courses. Thus, life courses will vary from one cohort (generation) to the next.

The life course perspective should be differentiated from the lifespan perspective or other developmental models of psychology. In these latter approaches the focus is on the individual, especially on personality, cognition, and other intrapsychic phenomena (George 1982). In these developmental approaches, change results from within the individual, and this change is universal —it is a function of human nature. Typically, developmental changes are linked to chronological age, with little or no reference to the social context or the sociohistorical or individual-historical context. The life course perspective, in contrast, focuses on transitions when the "social persona" (Hagestad and Neugarten 1985, p. 35) undergoes change.

CONCEPTIONS OF AGING

In order to understand health and the life course it is also important to understand the aging process. Aging is best understood in a life course perspective. Persons do not suddenly become old at age sixty or sixty-five or at retirement. Aging is the result of a lifetime of social, behavioral, and biological processes interacting with one another. While genetics may play a part in predisposing individuals to certain diseases or impairments, length and quality of life have been found to be highly dependent on behaviors, life-styles, and health-related attitudes (e.g., Haug and Ory 1987).

A distinction is often made between primary and secondary aging (see Schroots 1988). Primary aging, or normal aging, refers to the steady declines in functioning in the absence of disease or despite good health. Secondary aging, or pathological aging, refers to the declines that are due to illnesses associated with age but not to aging itself. This suggests that secondary aging can be reversed, at least in principle (Kohn 1985).

VARIATIONS IN HEALTH AND LIFE EXPECTANCY

The largest cause of death in America for people under age forty-five is accidents and adverse effects (National Center for Health Statistics 1989). For people five to fourteen years of age and twenty-five to forty-four years of age, malignant neoplasms (tumors) rank second as a cause of death. For persons fifteen to twenty-four years of age, homicide, followed closely by suicide, are the next leading causes of death.

For adults ages sixty-five and over the causes of death are quite different. Cardiovascular disease, malignant neoplasms, cerebrovascular disease, and influenza and pneumonia are the most common causes of death (Schroots 1988; White et al. 1986). Older persons, too, are more likely to suffer from chronic, and often limiting, conditions. Most common among these are arthritis, hypertension, hearing impairments, heart conditions, chronic sinusitis, visual impairments, and orthopedic impairments (e.g., back). Interestingly, these same conditions are among the most commonly mentioned by persons ages forty-five to sixty-four, though their prevalence is generally considerably less than that of persons sixty-five and older.

At the turn of the century, life expectancy for a person sixty-five years of age was almost twelve years. By 1978, life expectancy for a sixty-five-year-old was fourteen years for males and eighteen years for females. Many of the improvements in life expectancy came about before large-scale immunization programs. These programs largely affected the health of those born during the 1940s and 1950s. These programs have, however, reduced infant mortality and reduced the likelihood of certain debilitating diseases (e.g., polio).

The chance of surviving to old age with few functional disabilities is strongly related to socioeconomic position, educational level, and race (Berkman 1988). People in lower classes and with less education have higher mortality risk and have higher incidence and prevalence of diseases and injuries. They have more hospitalizations, disability days, and functional limitations.

Life expectancy also varies by social class. At age twenty-five life expectancy, for those with four or fewer years of education, is forty-four years for men and almost forty-seven years for women. For men and women with some college education, life expectancy is forty-seven years and fifty-six years respectively. After age sixty-five, however, this relationship becomes less clear-cut, suggesting that for older cohorts a different set of factors is involved.

ISSUES AND IMPLICATIONS

Differences in health conditions by age raise at least two issues regarding the analysis and understanding of health. First, it has been suggested that in trying to understand health and health behavior of the elderly, especially as our models become more complex, the *individual* is the critical unit of analysis (Wolinsky and Arnold 1988). That is, we must focus on individual differentiation over the life course. Aging is a highly individual process, resulting from large inter- and intraindividual differences in health and functioning.

The second issue concerns the extent to which many processes thought to be life course processes may in fact be cohort differences (see Dannefer 1988). An assumption is often made that the heterogeneity within older cohorts is an intracohort, life course process: Age peers become increasingly dissimilar as they grow older. This conclusion is, however, often based on cross-sectional data and may lead to a life course fallacy. Age differences may reduce to cohort differences. If each succeeding cohort becomes more homogeneous, older cohorts will display greater heterogeneity compared to younger cohorts. Evidence suggests that for several cohort characteristics this may be the case. For example, there has been increasing standardization of years of education, age of labor-force entry and exit, age at first marriage, number of children, and so on. Thus, younger age groups would exhibit less diversity than older cohorts.

Not all health deterioration is a normal process of aging. Some of it appears to be the result of an accumulation of life experiences and behaviors. Many of the experiences and behaviors are different for older and younger cohorts, suggesting that an understanding of factors affecting health for older cohorts may not hold for younger cohorts as they age.

Two possible scenarios exist. One is that older people in the future will experience less morbidity than today's elderly, even though later life will be longer. That is, they will be older longer, sick for a very short period of time, and then die. An alternative situation is one in which elderly live longer and are sick or impaired for many of those years. That is, they will be sick for an extensive period of their later life. Given the fact that more people are living longer, the general expectation is that the demand for health care by elderly will be greater in the future. The extent of the demand will depend, in part, on which of these two scenarios is closer to the truth. The conservative approach, and the one generally adopted, is that estimates of tomorrow's needs for care are based on data from today's elderly. However, a life course perspective might yield quite a different picture because the life experiences, behaviors, and health attitudes of today's elderly may be quite different from those of younger cohorts, tomorrow's elderly.

(SEE ALSO: *Health and Illness Behavior; Life Course; Life Expectancy; Social Gerontology*)

REFERENCES

Berkman, Lisa F. 1988 "The Changing and Heterogeneous Nature of Aging and Longevity: A Social and Biomedical Perspective." In G. L. Maddox and M. P. Lawton, eds., *Varieties of Aging*. Vol. 8 of *Annual*

Review of Gerontology and Geriatrics. New York: Springer.

Birren, James E., and Judy M. Zarit 1985 "Concepts of Health, Behavior, and Aging." In J. E. Birren and J. Livingston, eds., *Cognition, Stress and Aging*. Englewood Cliffs, N.J.: Prentice-Hall.

Clausen, John A. 1986 *The Life Course: A Sociological Perspective*. Englewood Cliffs, N.J.: Prentice-Hall.

Dannefer, Dale 1988 "Differential Gerontology and the Stratified Life Course: Conceptual and Methodological Issues." In G. L. Maddox and M. P. Lawton, eds., *Varieties of Aging*. Vol. 8 of *Annual Review of Gerontology and Geriatrics*. New York: Springer.

Elder, Glen H., Jr. 1977 "Family History and the Life Course." *Journal of Family History* 2:279–304.

George, Linda K. 1982 "Models of Transitions in Middle and Later Life." *Annals of the Academy of Political and Social Science* 464:22–37.

Hagestad, Gunhild O., and Bernice L. Neugarten 1985 "Age and the Life Course." In R. H. Binstock and E. Shanas, eds., *Handbook of Aging and the Social Sciences*. New York: Van Nostrand Reinhold Company.

Hareven, T. K. 1978 *Transitions: The Family and the Life Course in Historical Perspective*. New York: Academic Press.

Haug, Marie R., and Marcia G. Ory 1987 "Issues in Elderly Patient–Provider Interactions." *Research on Aging* 9:3–44.

Kohn, R. R. 1985 "Aging and Age-Related Diseases: Normal Processes." In H. A. Johnson, ed., *Relations between Normal Aging and Disease*. New York: Raven Press.

Liang, Jersey 1986 "Self-Reported Physical Health among Aged Adults." *Journal of Gerontology* 41:248–260.

National Center for Health Statistics 1989 "Advance Report of Final Mortality Statistics, 1987." *Monthly Vital Statistics Report*. Vol. 38 No. 5, Supp. Hyattsville, Md.: Public Health Service.

Parsons, Talcott 1951 *The Social System*. New York: Free Press.

Schroots, Johannes J. F. 1988 "Current Perspectives on Aging, Health, and Behavior." In J. J. F. Schroots, J. E. Birren, and A. Svanborg, eds., *Health and Aging: Perspectives and Prospects*. New York: Springer.

White, Lon R., William S. Cartwright, Jean Cornoni-Huntley, and Dwight B. Brock 1986. "Geriatric Epidemiology." In C. Eisdorfer, ed., *Annual Review of Gerontology and Geriatrics,* Vol. 6. New York: Springer.

Wolinsky, Fredric D., and Connie Lea Arnold 1988 "A Different Perspective on Health and Health Services Utilization." In G. L. Maddox and M. P. Lawton, eds., *Varieties of Aging*. Vol. 8 of *Annual Review of Gerontology and Geriatrics*. New York: Springer.

DONALD E. STULL

HEALTH-CARE FINANCING The most important feature of health care in the United States is its high growth rates, especially during the 1970s and 1980s. The average annual growth rate in health expenditures has been 14.8 percent for the period 1980 to 1988, while the consumer price index has averaged 4.6 percent annually during that same period (Consumer Price Index 1989). In 1990, the United States is expected to spend $661 billion on health care, which represents a 10.4 percent increase over the previous year (U.S. Department of Commerce, International Trade Administration 1990). The annual growth rate for health expenditures is expected to continue to increase at 10 to 14 percent from 1990 to 1995, well above the general level of inflation (U.S. Department of Commerce, International Trade Administration 1990). Total health expenditures are expected to represent 11.5 percent of the gross national product in 1990 (U.S. Department of Commerce, International Trade Administration 1990). This has increased since 1970, when health expenditures were 7.3 percent of the GNP, and from 1980, when expenditures were 9.1 percent (U.S. Department of Commerce, International Trade Administration 1990). The United States spends more on health than any other country, both in absolute dollars and relative to gross national product (Schieber and Poullier 1989).

In spite of a number of public-policy changes during this time, the projections are for continued high growth rates in costs during the 1990s. This has a tremendous impact on the public, who must pay for such care either directly, to health-care providers or in the form of health-insurance premiums or public taxes, or indirectly in the form of tax exemptions to businesses that provide health insurance.

SOURCES OF FUNDS

Most of the funds for health care in the United States come from private programs (58 percent in 1988), while the remainder (42 percent) come from public programs (U.S. Office of National Cost Estimates 1990). This represents a growing trend to pay for health care through public sources, having increased since 1965, when government programs were 25 percent of the total health expenditures (Levit, Freeland, and Waldo 1989; Letsch, Levit, and Waldo 1988).

In examining the original sources of funds for health care, in 1987 the funds came directly from out-of-pocket expenditures by individuals (25 percent); from individual purchase of private insurance, Medicare taxes and premiums, or philanthropy (17 percent); from private businesses (28 percent); and only 30 percent from government expenditures supported by tax dollars (Levit, Freeland, and Waldo 1989). In contrast, in 1965 the amount paid by government from taxes was 26 percent; the amount paid by individual purchase of insurance and premiums on philanthropy was 9 percent and by private business was 17 percent, while the proportion of direct out-of-pocket expenditures from individuals was 48 percent (Levit, Freeland, and Waldo 1989).

The two major U.S. public programs that pay for health care are Medicare and Medicaid. In 1988, Medicare paid for 18.8 percent, Medicaid for 10.9 percent, and other government programs for 10.9 percent of personal health-care expenditures (U.S. Office of National Cost Estimates 1990). Medicare is a federal insurance program, initiated in 1965 under the Social Security Act, with a mandatory hospital program (which provides hospital, home health, and hospice care) and an optional supplementary medical insurance program (which provides physician, outpatient, and other services). Medicare is financed by payroll taxes levied on employers and employees for the hospital insurance program and by premiums and general revenue for the medical insurance program. It provided protection for 33 million aged and disabled workers and their dependents and spent $90 billion on 25 million users in 1988 (U.S. Office of National Cost Estimates 1990).

Medicaid, also initiated in 1965 under the Social Security Act, is a federally supported and state administered program for low income individuals and families. The program provided a wide range of services for the 23 million recipients in 1988, of whom 30 percent were aged, blind, and disabled and 70 percent were women and children eligible for the Aid to Families with Dependent Children program. While the number of Medicaid recipients has remained stable since 1974, the program expenditures increased from $10.6 billion that year to $52 billion in 1988 (U.S. Office of National Cost Estimates 1990). Other public programs offering health services are sponsored by the Department of Defense, the Department of Veterans Affairs, the Indian Health Service, and the Alcohol, Drug Abuse, and Mental Health Administration.

TYPES OF EXPENDITURES

Of the total estimated $661 billion spent on health-care services in 1990, 89 percent are for personal care, 4 percent for program administration, 3 percent for government public health administration, and 4 percent for research and the construction of medical facilities. The greatest proportion of personal health-service expenditure is for hospital care (43 percent in 1990) and physician services (23 percent; U.S. Department of Commerce, International Trade Administration 1990). Nursing homes account for 9 percent of expenditures, drugs for 8 percent, dental care for 6 percent, other professional services for 6 percent, and the remainder for other health services and supplies (U.S. Department of Commerce, International Trade Administration 1990). Since 1965, expenditures for hospital, nursing home, and other professional services have grown somewhat as a proportion of the total, those for drugs and dental services have declined, and those for physician services have remained steady in relationship to other service expenditures (U.S. Office of National Cost Estimate 1990).

FACTORS AFFECTING COST INCREASES

The causes of high growth rates in health care have been examined by health economists. In 1988, general price inflation contributed 43 percent of the total growth, medical price inflation (increases in the costs of labor and technology and increases in the use of services) contributed 24 percent, and population growth contributed 10 percent (U.S. Office of National Cost Estimates 1990). The remaining 23 percent was caused by price inflation by health providers and can be considered the "greed factor." It is the latter that is a great concern to public-policy makers.

One factor encouraging high costs is the large growth in the supply of physicians. The number of nonfederal physicians increased from 124 per 100,000 population in 1965 to 189 in 1987 (American Medical Association forthcoming). Physicians create the demand for their own services and are responsible for most decisions regarding the use of health-care services and consequently for generating health expenditures. Fuchs (1978) found that a 10 percent increase in the surgeon-to-population ratio results in a 3 percent increase in per capita utilization. Feldstein (1988) suggests that physicians set their own prices to meet a targeted or desired income level and that each physician may generate $200,000 to $300,000 in other medical expenses annually. Others suggest there are too many specialists who tend to order expensive services and too few general practitioners.

Another factor in health-care costs is the number of employees in the health field. The number of health workers has increased from 7.6 percent of all employed civilians in the United States in 1988 (an increase from 5.5 percent in 1970; U.S. Department of Health and Human Services 1990). The number of nurses employed in hospitals has increased from 56 nurses per 100 adjusted average daily census (AADC) in 1975 to 72 per 100 in 1980 and 98 per 100 in 1987 (a 75 percent increase; American Hospital Association 1989). The total number of hospital personnel per patient has also increased by 35 percent during the same period (American Hospital Association 1989). The increase in ratios of personnel to patients and in their educational and training levels contribute to increases in the cost of care.

Health insurance is also a key component of the health industry. There are over 1,000 for-profit commercial health insurers and eighty-five Blue Cross and Blue Shield plans operating in a competitive environment (Feldstein 1988, p. 161). The administrative costs and profits for these companies range from about 35 percent of total premium dollars for individual policies to 7 to 14 percent of total premium dollars for group plans and vary by type of plan (Feldstein 1988, p. 161).

The rapid increases in health-care costs, particularly for private health insurance, has stimulated the growth in managed health care, including health maintenance organizations (HMOs) and preferred provider organizations (PPOs). HMOs provide basic health-care services to those who voluntarily enroll, and they charge a fixed monthly premium regardless of how often an individual uses the services; HMOs do not charge on a fee-for-service basis. PPOs are modified HMOs that offer limited numbers of providers who are reimbursed at negotiated rates or discount fees. In 1988, the number of HMOs increased to 607 and of PPOs to 620 (U.S. Department of Commerce, International Trade Administration 1990). The number enrolled in such systems has increased from 3 percent in the 1970s to 25 percent of the total U.S. population in 1988 (U.S. Department of Commerce, International Trade Administration 1990). HMOs and PPOs have been able to control costs primarily by reducing hospital admission rates (Feldstein 1988, p. 331).

POLICY REFORMS

During the last decade, public policymakers have introduced payment reforms for public programs in an effort to control health expenditures. In 1983 Medicare introduced for hospital payments a prospective payment system (PPS) by diagnosis. At that time, Blue Cross, private insurers, and other third party payers also changed to prospective payment systems. There was an immediate reduction in the national average length of hospital stay (from 10.1 days in 1982 to 8.8 days for those over age 65; U.S. Office of National Cost Estimates 1990; Guterman et al. 1988). The number of admissions dropped from thirty-eight million in 1982 to 33.5 million in 1988, the total inpatient days declined, and hospital occupancy rates dropped from 75 percent in 1982 to 65 percent in 1988 (U.S. Office of National Cost Estimates; Guterman et al. 1988). Hospital revenues declined, and the hospital expenditure growth rates declined from 14 percent in 1981–1982 to 9 percent in 1987–1988 (U.S. Office of National Cost Estimates 1990).

After the changes in payment systems for inpatient hospital services, growth rates for hospital outpatient services more than doubled (U.S. Office of National Cost Estimates 1990). Physician expenditures also increased from 10 percent in 1981–1982 to 13 percent in 1987–1988 (U.S. Office of National Cost Estimates 1990). Thus, in an effort to control costs, Congress adopted in 1989 a new payment system for physicians under Medicare (U.S. Congress, House 1989). Although these policy changes have had some impact in reducing expenditures, government regulation of only its share of overall spending can only have a limited impact in reducing the nation's spending on health care.

THE UNINSURED AND THEIR HEALTH

An estimated thirty-seven million individuals in the United States have no private health care insurance and no Medicare, Medicaid, or other form of public coverage (Short, Monheit, and Beauregard 1989). This number represents 15.5 percent of the population. Another large portion of the population is underinsured. The number of uninsured has increased since the 1980s, as there were cutbacks in public-health expenditures during the Reagan administration and as the unemployment rate increased with the downturns in the U.S. economy (Palmer and Sawhill 1982).

Of those who are uninsured, 75 percent are employed or the dependents of employees in businesses that do not offer health benefits. Most uninsured who are employed (57 percent) earn minimum wages, and many are employed by small firms, self-employed, or are unskilled, part-time, or temporary workers (U.S. Department of Commerce, International Trade Administration 1990). Others are uninsured because they are unemployed or unable to purchase insurance because of preexisting medical conditions.

The United States and South Africa are the only two existing industrialized countries without national health insurance. The lack of access to financial coverage by either public or private insurance limits access to needed health-care services and has been demonstrated to have negative consequences for those who are poor. In 1986, the United States was nineteenth in its overall life expectancy rates for men and twenty-second in its infant mortality rates (having moved from nineteenth for infant mortality in 1981; U.S. Department of Health and Human Services 1990). A number of studies have examined health status, service utilization, and access to services for the poor and minorities. The poor and minorities have less financial and organizational access to services, lower utilization rates for all types of services, less preventive care, and poor health status in terms of morbidity and mortality compared to other social groups (Dutton 1989; Schlesinger 1987).

While the United States has the highest per capita spending on health and the highest proportion of its GNP spent on health care, its health outcomes are poor because so many individuals are excluded from the health-care system. A number of proposals have been developed to address the problem of the uninsured. These proposals range from small incremental expansion of the Medicaid program for the poor, to mandating that employers offer private insurance to employees, to a comprehensive national health insurance program that would be similar to the one in Canada. Canada's plan is a mandatory program financed with tax dollars, is comprehensive in its coverage, and uses private sector providers to provide services (Himmelstein and Woolhandler 1989).

FINANCING LONG-TERM CARE

Another major problem with the current financing of health care in the United States is the lack of financial coverage for long-term care insurance. Long-term care includes nursing home care, home health care, and other services for those with disabilities and chronic illnesses. Although 95 percent of hospital services and 81 percent of physician services in the United States are covered by private or public coverage, only 52 percent of nursing home services are covered by public or private insurance. The remaining 48 percent ($26 billion in 1990) for nursing home care must be paid for directly out-of-pocket by individuals or their families (U.S. Department of Commerce, International Trade Administration 1990). Most of the public expenditures for nursing home services (48 percent of the total) are paid by Medicaid, while Medicare, other public programs, and private insurance cover only 4 percent (U.S. Congressional Budget Office 1987). Home care and other long-term care services also are poorly covered by Medicare or private insurance.

Thus, individuals with large long-term care expenses frequently spend down their personal funds. The average $29,000 in costs for nursing home care in 1987 is beyond the level that many individuals can afford (Rivlin and Wiener 1988). Eventually, they may become impoverished and then eligible for Medicaid coverage for these services. This financial burden, which falls primarily on the aged and disabled, has become of increasing concern to public policy makers who have been examining various public and private financing options for long-term care (Harrington 1990).

SUMMARY

The United States has developed a unique health program that is primarily privately financed and operated. While government programs are increasingly used to supplement the existing system primarily for the poor and the aged and disabled, these public programs generally have financed the existing private sector service delivery without making reforms in service delivery. The limited financing for only the most needy, low income individuals and Medicare beneficiaries has created a growing number of individuals and families without financial access to health-care services.

Government has made only limited attempts to regulate the rapidly increasing costs of health care, yet the United States has the most expensive health-care system in the world, while it offers only limited financial coverage for the population. As costs continue to rise, politicians, reluctant to use regulatory powers, are concerned that the United States cannot afford to adopt a more universal health-care plan for its population. Although there is a growing public demand for national health insurance in the United States, the reluctance of policymakers to intervene in the private financing and delivery of health care leads the country toward fiscal crisis and unsatisfactory health outcomes.

(SEE ALSO: *Health Policy Analysis; Health Services Utilization; Long-Term Care*)

REFERENCES

American Hospital Association 1989 *Hospital Statistics.* Chicago: American Hospital Association.

American Medical Association (Forthcoming) *Physician Characteristics and Distribution in the U.S., 1988 Edition.* Chicago: American Medical Association.

Consumer Price Index 1989 *Statistical Abstract of the United States: 1988.* Washington, D.C.: U.S. Government Printing Office.

Dutton, Diana B. 1989 "Social Class, Health, and Illness." In P. Brown, ed., *Perspectives in Medical Sociology.* Belmont, Calif.: Wadsworth.

Feldstein, Paul J. 1988 *Health Care Economics.* New York: Wiley.

Fuchs, Victor R. 1978 "The Supply of Surgeons and the Demand for Operations." *Journal of Human Resources* 13 (suppl.):35–38.

Guterman, Stuart, Paul W. Eggers, Gerald Riley, Timothy F. Greene, and Sherry A. Terrell 1988 "The First

Three Years of Medicare Prospective Payment: An Overview." *Health Care Financing Review* 9 (no. 1): 67–77.

Harrington, Charlene 1990 "The Organization and Financing of Long-Term Care." In L. H. Aiken and C. M. Fagin, eds., *Nursing and Health Policy: Issues of the 1990s.* Philadelphia: J. B. Lippincott.

Himmelstein, David U., and Steffie Woolhandler 1989 "A National Health Program for the United States." *New England Journal of Medicine* 320 (no. 2):102–105.

Letsch, Suzanne W., Katharine R. Levit, and Daniel R. Waldo 1988 "National Health Expenditures, 1987." *Health Care Financing Review* 10 (no. 2):109–129.

Levit, Katharine R., Mark S. Freeland, and Daniel R. Waldo 1989 "Health Spending and Ability to Pay: Business, Individuals, and Government." *Health Care Financing Review* 10 (no. 3):1–11.

Palmer, John L., and Isabel V. Sawhill, eds. 1982 *The Reagan Experiment.* Washington, D.C.: Urban Institute Press.

Rivlin, Alice M., and Joshua M. Wiener 1988 *Caring for the Disabled Elderly: Who Will Pay?* Washington, D.C.: Brookings Institution.

Schieber, George J., and Jean-Pierre Poullier 1989 "Overview of International Comparisons of Health Care Expenditures." *Health Care Financing Review.* Annual Supplement, 1–7.

Schlesinger, Mark 1987 "Paying the Price: Medical Care, Minorities, and the Newly Competitive Health Care System." *The Milbank Quarterly* 65:270–291.

Short, Pamela Farley, Alan C. Monheit, and Karen Beauregard 1989 *A Profile of Uninsured Americans,* National Medical Expenditure Survey. Research Findings 1. Washington, D.C.: National Center for Health Services Research and Health Care Technology Assessment, Department of Health and Human Services.

U.S. Congress, House 1989 *Omnibus Budget Reconciliation Act.* 101st Cong., 1st sess. H.R. 3299.

U.S. Congressional Budget Office 1987 State of Nancy Gordon, Assistant Director for Human Resources and Community Department, CBO, before the Health Task Force Committee on the Budget, U.S. House of Representatives. Washington, D.C.

U.S. Department of Commerce, International Trade Administration 1990. *Health and Medical Services: U.S. Industrial Outlook 1990.* Washington, D.C.: U.S. Department of Commerce.

U.S. Department of Health and Human Services 1990 *Health United States, 1989.* DHHS 90–1,232. Hyattsville, Md.: U.S. Department of Health and Human Services.

———U.S. Office of National Cost Estimates 1990 "National Health Expenditures, 1988." *Health Care Financing Review* 11(4):1–41.

CHARLENE HARRINGTON

HEALTH POLICY ANALYSIS Health policy analysis is of increasing interest to sociologists in the areas of medical sociology and health services research. Health policy analysis draws on multidisciplinary perspectives, using virtually all the social science disciplines from anthropology and economics to political science and sociology, as well as the applied disciplines of public health, public administration, and public policy.

The various disciplines, substantive specializations, and methodologies represented in such work have contributed an array of perspectives to the definition of health policy analysis, how it is conducted, and how professional training is organized and implemented. There is a lack of consensus, and no reigning paradigms, on the approach to health policy analysis in schools of public policy, public health, public administration, and social work and in sociology and other social science disciplines. As the number of programs offering general policy or specific health policy specializations has increased, the academic respectability of this type of work has grown. One indicator of advances in the field of policy studies is the publication of the *Policy Studies Review Annual,* which commenced in 1977 (Nagel 1977) and continues to describe the field with an editorial advisory board of distinguished university professors from a broad spectrum of social science disciplines.

Health services research contributes two types of knowledge: engineering and enlightenment (Weiss 1977). In the engineering model, which provides visibly and immediately useful knowledge for practical problem solving, researchers assume the values inherent in existing policy as givens when they address specific questions and evaluate alternative technical solutions to achieve policy goals. In the enlightenment model, research based on variant theoretical premises provides the essential (and often irreverent) critical investigation of the conceptualization and empirical generalizations in a field or problem area. Rather than dealing with how things work in the technical or engineering sense, research that provides enlightenment knowledge contributes to the root understanding of a problem, clarifying and opening the way for advances in the basic knowledge base—often with the effect of promoting what Thomas Kuhn (1970) calls "paradigm shift," or transformation in the basic way of looking at a problem.

Based on research, health policy analysis necessarily concerns itself with timeliness, pragmatism, and specificity in an effort to improve health and health care delivery. Research and analysis are utilized to further the formulation of social policy by (1) illuminating aspects of human organization and human behavior that are relevant to health policy planning, (2) identifying the social and health problems that require formulation or changes of health policy, and (3) providing data that monitor the effects and outcomes of health policy decisions and the relative impact of programmatic alternatives.

The products of health policy analysis range from journalistic and descriptive treatises to sophisticated quantitative explanatory analyses and projections. Many of the most influential health policy analyses appear first as fugitive documents directed to internal governmental audiences, addressing particularistic needs and interests of government agencies and actors, and are based on reports designed with an evaluative purpose. Policy analysis is primarily funded and supported by government, with a lesser role played by private foundations. The other leading sources of policy analysis are scholars in twenty to thirty university-based health policy and health services research centers and institutes and the myriad and growing number of private sector "think tanks" such as the Brookings Institution, the Urban Institute, RAND, the National Bureau of Economic Research, Project Hope, and the American Enterprise Institute.

Major federal agencies that both contribute to and conduct health policy analysis include the National Center for Health Statistics (NCHS); the Health Care Financing Administration (HCFA); the Agency for Health Care Policy and Research (AHCPR); the Alcohol, Drug Abuse, and Mental Health Administration (ADMHA); the Social Security Administration; the National Institute on Aging (NIA); and the Office of the Assistant Secretary for Planning and Evaluation. The primary professional association promoting the advancement of knowledge relevant to health policy analysis is the Association for Health Services Research and the Foundation for Health Services Research, with an annual meeting drawing more than one thousand researchers from all social science and health professional fields.

Several journals are sources for the latest developments in health policy analysis: *Health Affairs, Health Care Financing Review, Health Services Research, Journal of Health and Social Behavior, Journal of the American Medical Association, Milbank Quarterly, New England Journal of Medicine,* and *Journal of Health Politics, Policy and Law.*

Sociology has a long and venerable tradition of reformism and interest in the pursuit of scientific knowledge toward the solution of applied problems. Robert Lynd's *Knowledge for What?* (1986) called sociologists to the task, and a long line of American sociologists have worked within the applied tradition. Particular examples are from the Chicago School (Park 1952; Bulmer 1984; Deegan 1988; Deegan and Burger 1981) and Columbia University, where Paul Lazarsfeld and his colleagues were mobilized to advance the field of applied research by the events of World War II. These efforts were quickly followed by serious reflective work on the uses of sociology (Lazarsfeld, Sewell, and Wilensky 1967) and applied sociology (Gouldner and Miller 1965), and a burgeoning of various sociological subfields devoted to such topics as social problems and medical sociology. These forerunners of present-day work in policy analysis laid the foundation for what has become an increasingly credible scientific enterprise: the study of health policy.

Howard Freeman's 1978 observation on the nature of health policy analysis as a scientific enterprise remains applicable: that policy studies are rather specialized and "content-limited," demonstrating few attempts to develop overriding conclusions about the policy process; hence, "there is practically no effort at 'grand theory' and little at 'middle-range theory' either" (Freeman 1978, p. 11). Nevertheless, the extremely narrow, highly specialized studies are not policy studies if they have no use beyond the most limited and specialized areas of concern. "Policy studies . . . need to be broad in implications, insightful to those beyond the narrow band of experts in a particular field, and intermeshed with work in related areas" (Freeman 1978, p. 12). The stimulation of and funding for policy analyses are driven largely by the immediacy of existing (rather than emerging) problems that catch the attention of policymakers. Therefore, there is tension between the need to conduct carefully controlled definitive studies and the need to enlarge the focus of such research to contribute broader application and significance.

The growth and fortunes of health policy research and analysis were dramatically shaped by the social-problem definitions of health care from the 1960s to the 1980s (Rist 1985) and these, in turn, have been shaped by the political and economic exigencies of these periods. Health care was defined in the 1960s by the crisis of access, in the 1970s by the crisis of fragmentation and lack of comprehensive planning, and in the 1980s by the crisis of cost and the resurgence of market forces in health care. Beginning with the passage of Medicare and Medicaid in 1965, increased political attention has been accorded health care delivery. Federal research funding, although limited, has assured the slow but gradual accumulation of health services research knowledge, the mother's milk of health policy analysis. The cost of medical care continues to rise at two or three times the rate of inflation; the costs to business, government, and individuals skyrocket; more and more Americans are uninsured each year; the annual expenditure on the medical–industrial complex climbs above $600 billion; and the population is aging. In the wake of these dramatic developments, the health care system and the policies creating it have been increasingly exposed to criticism and investigation. The key health policy issues for the 1990s are the cost, quality, and outcomes of care; the organization, financing, and delivery of acute and long-term care services; and the access to care.

(SEE ALSO: *Health-Care Financing; Health Promotion; Health Services Utilization; Medical-Industrial Complex; Medical Sociology*)

REFERENCES

Bulmer, Martin 1984 *The Chicago School of Sociology: Institutionalization, Diversity and the Rise of Sociological Research.* Chicago, Ill.: University of Chicago Press.

Deegan, Mary Jo 1988 *Jane Addams and the Men of the Chicago School, 1892–1918.* New Brunswick, N.J.: Transaction Books.

———, and John S. Burger 1981 "W. I. Thomas and Social Reform: His Work and Writings." *Journal of the History of Behavioral Sciences* 17:114–125.

Freeman, Howard E. (ed.) 1978 *Policy Studies Review Annual,* vol. 2. Beverly Hills, Calif.: Sage.

Gouldner, Alvin W., and S. M. Miller (eds.) 1965 *Applied Sociology: Opportunities and Problems.* New York: Free Press.

Kuhn, Thomas 1970. *Structure of Scientific Revolutions,* 2nd ed. Chicago, Ill.: University of Chicago Press.

Lazarsfeld, Paul F., William H. Sewell, and Howard L. Wilensky 1967 *The Uses of Sociology.* New York: Basic Books.

Lynd, Robert S. 1986 *Knowledge for What? The Place of Social Science in American Culture.* Middletown, Conn.: Wesleyan University Press.

Nagel, Stuart S. (ed.) 1977 *Policy Studies Review Annual,* vol. 1. Beverly Hills, Calif.: Sage.

Park, Robert Ezra 1952 *Human Communities.* Glencoe, Ill.: Free Press.

Rist, Ray C. 1985 "Introduction." In Ray C. Rist, ed., *Policy Studies Review Annual,* vol. 7, pp. 1–3. New Brunswick, N.J.: Transaction Books.

Weiss, Carol H. 1978 "Research for Policy's Sake: The Enlightenment Function of Social Research." In Howard Freeman, ed., *Policy Studies Review Annual,* vol. 2, pp. 67–81. Beverly Hills, Calif.: Sage.

CARROLL L. ESTES

HEALTH PROMOTION Health promotion and disease prevention are vital activities that help a society maintain a well-functioning, long-lived population. This statement may appear obvious, but an examination of health-relevant knowledge, attitudes, or behaviors shows that health promotion and disease prevention play only small roles in the U.S. health care system. The basic principles of health promotion receive little attention in medical textbooks or in the journals that physicians regularly read. Furthermore, little funding has been forthcoming for these activities.

The U.S. health care system revolves around treatment and attempts to cure existing health problems. A vast biomedical, surgical, pharmaceutical, mechanical, and human technology has emerged. This technological armamentarium is primarily devoted to medical treatment of injury and disease, and physicians frequently use this technology when taking heroic measures to save lives. Unfortunately, most of the rescued individuals have not experienced wellness programs nor other organized health promotion efforts that might have prevented their health problems from developing or from reaching the stage where massive intervention was required.

The field of health promotion may become increasingly important as society acknowledges the rapidly rising cost of maintaining our medical technology. Many influential people are concerned about the economic burden and are beginning to call for health promotion programs in worksites and elsewhere. It is noteworthy that the "ounce of prevention" philosophy is increasingly espoused. There is greater willingness to accept the notion that health promotion activities are worthwhile.

THE GOALS OF HEALTH PROMOTION

The federal government has spearheaded efforts to focus the nation's attention on health promotion as a meaningful medical goal. The U.S. Public Health Service (1989) believes that the health and well-being of the U.S. population can be significantly improved by the year 2000 by engaging in specific health promotion activities. This body has defined five national health promotion goals for the new century. These are:

1. Reducing infant mortality to no more than seven deaths per 1,000 live births (the present rate is ten per 1,000).
2. Increasing life expectancy at birth to at least seventy-eight years (currently seventy-five).
3. Reducing the proportion of people disabled by chronic conditions to no more than 6 percent of the population (current chronic disease disability rates are 9 percent).
4. Increasing years of healthy life (quality-adjusted life years) to at least sixty-five (estimated to be sixty years in 1987).
5. Decreasing the disparity in life expectancy between white and minority populations to no more than four years (in 1990 there was a six-year gap).

To achieve these goals the U.S. Public Health Service targeted seven areas: nutrition; physical activity and fitness; tobacco use; alcohol and drug use; sexual behavior; violent/abusive behavior; and vitality and independence of older people. Education and interventions in these areas can significantly reduce the illness burden and greatly enhance the health of the public.

It is noteworthy that the U.S. Public Health Service has singled out violent and abusive behavior. Social scientists have long regarded violence as a social problem. Yet, in a broader context, violence-induced problems not only threaten human life, dignity, and the social order but pose serious strain to our health care resources. Victims of violent and abusive behavior crowd hospital emergency rooms. Many require lifelong treatment for injuries they have sustained.

HEALTH PROMOTION ACTIVITIES

Health promotion activities incorporate health education, health screening, an active surveillance system for present and potential health problems, preventive services, and medical care for serious and minor health problems. Some health promotion activities are directed at the physical environment (e.g., pollution control), others are focused on the social environment (e.g., stress-reduction clinics), still others relate to human biology or human behavior (e.g., immunization and anti-smoking campaigns). It is believed that health promotion is best accomplished by a lifetime health monitoring program.

Most experts conclude that health promotion activities involve the primary, secondary, and tertiary prevention of disease. These terms are used in relationship to the stage of illness. *Primary prevention* applies to the period prior to the onset of a disease. Thus, health promotion is directed toward those persons without disease manifestations and includes activities that will help individuals to maintain a healthy, well-functioning body. In contrast, *secondary* and *tertiary prevention* occur after a disease has been detected. These health promotion efforts are directed at individuals who are already afflicted with a condition, and they consist of interventions that can slow the progress of disease. Thus, secondary and tertiary prevention actually fall under the sphere of medical treatment for disease.

Primary prevention is defined as actions that avert the occurrence of disease, injury, or defects. The aim of primary prevention is to maintain health by eliminating the factors that cause disease or can cause a departure from health. Hence, a disease or illness never manifests itself because the individual has either avoided exposure or has engaged in activities that retard the onset of a condition. An example is a society's efforts to prevent polio by immunization. Another example is increased regulation of smoking in public places; doing so can help prevent major lung and heart diseases.

Activities under the rubric of primary prevention include educational efforts addressed toward the reduction of chronic disease. Five chronic illnesses account for most of the deaths, hospital care, and disability of the U.S. population. These illnesses are: arthritis, hypertension, heart disease, bronchitis, and diabetes. They are so prevalent that the National Center for Health Statistics found that in 1984, 124 of every 1,000 Americans were hypertensive and 133 suffered from arthritis (National Center for Health Statistics 1986). The problem increases in magnitude as persons age. There is a significant increase in chronic disease after the sixth decade, and arthritis, hypertension, and heart disease rates are at least ten times as high for persons over sixty-five as for their counterparts who are less than forty-five years old.

If the progress of chronic disease is traced, it becomes obvious that chronic conditions are readily amenable to preventive action. Fries and Crapo (1986) illustrated the typical decline from specific chronic diseases over a fifty-year period. The conditions they traced all had behavioral etiologies associated with lifestyle, habits, and health-risk behaviors. The problems actually began when individuals were in their twenties, as optimal physiological response was altered. By the time people were in their forties there were subclinical manifestations of the disease, and by age fifty the threshold stage had been reached. As people reached their sixties the severe phase of chronic disease was reached, and in the seventies there was endstage disease that could cause death.

The development of heart disease provides a good example of this process. While most individuals do not develop major heart conditions before age sixty-five, after this time the disease is very prevalent (there are over four million heart patients aged sixty-five or older). For most of these individuals the disease process began decades before. At age twenty, elevated cholesterol readings might have been detected; small plaques may have been discernible on an arteriogram at age thirty and would have been much more visible at age forty. If the patient reported leg pain when exercising as he or she reached their fifties, physicians may have detected the threshold phase of the disease. This may have progressed to angina pectoris around age sixty. Finally, as the person reached his or her seventies, a heart attack would be the likely outcome.

Primary prevention of heart disease and most other chronic conditions begins with risk-factor reduction. Health promotion efforts that involve eliminating or reducing cardiac risk behaviors can lessen the likelihood of heart disease. The major cardiovascular risk factors are cigarette smoking, high blood pressure (hypertension), obesity, physical deconditioning, high lipid count (dyslipidemia), heredity, and impaired glucose tolerance. Most of these also constitute risk for cerebrovascular and diabetic disease. Yet all of the above, with the exception of the hereditary factor, are modifiable (Kannel et al. 1987; Herd et al. 1987). Persons who change their behaviors with regard to even one of these significantly decrease their risk of developing heart disease. They are also much less likely to die from a heart condition. Typical risk-reduction instruction for heart disease emphasizes no smoking, weight control, dietary change, exercising, and regular blood pressure and urine tests.

Secondary prevention contrasts with primary prevention because it involves control of a condition observed by medical practitioners. The aims of secondary prevention are to ensure early detection of conditions, followed by prompt treatment. Efforts toward halting, slowing, or possibly reversing the progression of a condition are given major attention.

One important tool for persons involved in secondary prevention is health screening. Procedures to screen individuals include blood pressure tests, chest X-rays, Pap smears, glaucoma, hearing, and similar tests, as well as thorough investigations of urine and blood. Electrocardiograms, breast examinations, and dental examinations are often included in screening efforts. These secondary prevention efforts can be widespread, involving community agencies and the public health sector; they can be limited to the workplace; or they can be restricted to physicians and allied health professionals using their clinical practice sites.

These procedures are immensely valuable. They are considered to be the best means for postponing disability and preventing chronic conditions from progressing to dangerous clinical thresholds. For example, urine testing that detects diabetes early in the course of the disease can prevent the development of impaired circulation; this testing can, in turn, prevent amputation of limbs. These procedures can also enhance the quality of life of the ailing person. Blindness and deterioration of vision can be prevented if diabetes is treated promptly with dietary modification, medication regimes, or both so the individual can retain sight indefinitely. Not only can secondary prevention efforts forestall further development of the disease and improve life quality, but they can prevent premature death.

Unfortunately, secondary prevention procedures are used less than is optimal or even desirable. In a recent survey of physicians, office practices regarding early cancer detection were investigated. Data showed that internists offered their patients the most opportunity for standard cancer detection tests (Pap tests, chest X-rays, mammograms, stool blood determinations, and prostate, breast, digital rectal, and proctoscopic examinations), but that fewer than half of all physicians surveyed indicated they would schedule proctoscopic exams and chest X-rays for asymptomatic patients with no personal history of cancer (American Cancer Society 1990).

Tertiary prevention refers to medical interventions that prevent disability associated with bodily deterioration from a well-established disease. The aim of tertiary intervention is to provide good health care to an individual. This is likely to halt the downward trajectory of a serious illness while reducing the likelihood of preventable complications. Thus, effective medical treatment of disease and injury represent tertiary prevention efforts.

In the United States, tertiary prevention practices illustrate our most successful health promotion efforts. They reflect the vast technological armamentarium available to our health care system. Breakthrough medical interventions have resulted. Unfortunately, this type of prevention is responsible for much of the accelerating cost of health care.

Cardiovascular disease is again the example of the use of tertiary prevention practices. In the 1980s, mortality from heart conditions declined steadily (National Center for Health Statistics 1986). While some have argued that this resulted from better dietary practices (primary prevention) and hypertension screening (secondary prevention), many experts believe that tertiary prevention efforts are responsible. They cite medical advances including the following: (1) the introduction of new categories of heart drugs that prevent cardiac deterioration and, in some instances, actually dissolve the blood clot associated with a heart attack; (2) the massive use of surgical interventions such as coronary artery bypass graft surgery, which replaces diseased arteries to the heart so that blood flow is increased; (3) semisurgical procedures such as coronary angioplasty, involving temporary insertion of a "balloon" device to remove arterial blockages; and (4) newer medical management strategies used in the hospital setting. In addition, the practice of heart transplantation is used increasingly. These practices have given many thousands of persons the chance to enjoy life with less pain and fewer limitations and to survive longer. Yet, as has been found for all tertiary prevention practices, there is only so much that can be accomplished because the person's body has been ridden with heart and circulatory disease for many years and has typically suffered anatomical and physiological decline. Furthermore, when the cost of providing these interventions is calculated (the *New York Times* of April 29, 1990, cited the average cost of a heart transplant to be $162,000), it is clear that tertiary prevention is not the best societal focus.

HEALTH PROMOTION BARRIERS

Some health promotion activities are popular and widely used while others are not. Most people agree that health promotion is a worthwhile goal, but not all concur with the U.S. Public Health Service that it should be a societal priority. Especially as defined in the five goals for the nation presented earlier, there is little consensus on whether these defined areas should be emphasized. There is even less consensus on what specific activities should receive greater support, on where the responsibility lies for health promotion, or on how to pay for these efforts.

Health promotion activities do not typically include all seven areas denoted by the U.S. Public Health Service. For example, nutrition, physical activity and fitness, tobacco use, alcohol and drug use, sexual behavior, violent/abusive behavior, and vitality and independence of older people do not receive equal attention. There are educational programs to impart the dangers of smoking to the public, yet efforts to prevent sexually transmitted disease were rarely noticed until the AIDS epidemic, and few pregnant women besides those receiving regular prenatal care are instructed about alcohol and drug use during pregnancy. Even in the area of nutrition, many of the health education efforts have been fad-related. As calcium or fat ingestion practices become popular, materials are circulated that provide information about their proper use. However, many people have not been exposed to the health risks of poor and unbalanced diets. Similarly, the risks associated with poor or inappropriate exercise are not well understood. Exercise is often neglected in educational efforts or may be misrepresented. A large proportion of health education material advises the public to "get more exercise." However, the American Heart Association guidelines on exercise for a "healthy heart" (National Heart, Lung, and Blood Institute 1988) are not known to most people. They have not been exposed to material about specifically beneficial types of exercise (aerobic), nor do they have adequate information about the frequency or duration of exercise.

The responsibility for health promotion has been alternatively assigned to public agencies, the health care system, health professionals, and individuals. Each, in turn, has been considered to be the major player.

Many people believe that the individual has sole responsibility for his or her health status. If someone is to remain healthy, or even to avoid death from a condition, it is that person who must act in a health-promoting manner. The failure of individuals to exert control over their health behaviors is often cited as a major contributor to our disease rates. A recent article (Rastam, Luepker, and Pirie 1988) showed that only 57 percent of persons identified as having elevated cholesterol levels during public screening programs actually visited a physician after being notified. This type of report is often used to promulgate the notion that people do not care enough about their health to take appropriate action.

Physicians are often held responsible for health

promotion. According to this view, the physician must take the initiative, advise patients of their personal risk, and propose means of risk reduction. Data are cited that indicate few patients (especially the aged) are given adequate information by their doctor.

The health care system and public agencies are often considered responsible. According to this view, the Surgeon General of the United States, the U.S. Public Health Service, the National Institutes of Health, and other governmental agencies bear the responsibility for a healthy public. It is considered to be the job of these agencies to provide health information and health screening to the public at large. Furthermore, the government is expected to fund preventive services so that all persons can have financial access to this care.

Clearly, the patient, his or her physician, the health care system, and the public sector all have roles to play. Health promotion must represent a combined effort. Schools, workplaces, and local agencies must impart information about health maintenance and health risks; health providers must advise at-risk people that they are likely candidates for a particular disease; private and public health facilities must be available to screen and provide treatment; there must be a means for payment for the health care or advice received; individuals must comply with the advice and health-promoting behaviors that have been proposed.

CONCLUSIONS

Health promotion is an often-used term. The principle appeals to most people, but it is not a widely supported activity. Our society has traditionally focused on providing a wide range of medical treatment services rather than on educational and applied efforts to prevent the development of deteriorating diseases and injuries. Furthermore, there is little consensus about what should constitute a health promotion program or what primary, secondary, or tertiary activities this type of program requires to reach health-promotion and disease-prevention goals. Yet without a widespread program, little control can be exerted over the human, social, and financial cost of illness. For this or any society to maintain the health and vitality of its citizens; for reduction of the illness burden to both the population and society; for greater longevity, health promotion must be a societal priority.

(SEE ALSO: *Health and Illness Behavior; Health Policy Analysis; Health Services Utilization; Medical Sociology*)

REFERENCES

American Cancer Society 1990 "1989 Survey of Physicians' Attitudes and Practices in Early Cancer Detection." *Ca-A Cancer Journal for Clinicians* 40:77–101.

Fries, James F., and Lawrence M. Crapo 1986 "The Elimination of Premature Disease." In Ken Dychtwald, ed., *Wellness and Health Promotion for the Elderly.* Rockville, Md.: Aspen.

Herd, J. Alan, Alastair J. J. Wood, James Blumenthal, James E. Daugherty, and Raymond Harris 1987 "Medical Therapy in the Elderly." *Journal of the American College of Cardiology* 10:29–34.

Kannel, William B., Joseph T. Doyle, Roy J. Shephard, Jeremiah Stamler, and Pantel S. Vokonas 1987 "Prevention of Cardiovascular Disease in the Elderly." *Journal of the American College of Cardiology* 10A:25–28.

National Center for Health Statistics 1986 "Current Estimates from the National Health Interview Survey, United States, 1984." *Vital and Health Statistics.* Series 10, No. 156. DHHS Pub. No. (PHS) 86-1584. Public Health Service. Washington, D.C.: U.S. Government Printing Office.

National Heart, Lung, and Blood Institute 1988 *Blood Pressure Month Information Kit.* Washington, D.C.: NHLBI Information Center.

Rastam, Lennart, Russell V. Luepker, and Phyllis L. Pirie 1988 "Effect of Screening and Referral on Follow-up and Treatment of High Blood Cholesterol Levels." *American Journal of Preventive Medicine* 4:244–248.

U.S. Public Health Service 1989 *Promoting Health/ Preventing Disease: Year 2000 Objectives for the Nation.* Draft for Public Review and Comment. Washington, D.C.: U.S. Department of Health and Human Services.

ROSALIE F. YOUNG

HEALTH SERVICES UTILIZATION

The study of the use of health services is at the center of the field of medical sociology. In part, this is because, either directly or indirectly, all facets of medical care have to take into account the quantity and types of services that community members utilize (Freeman et al. 1987). In part, it is related to the intellectual attraction of the area for persons of different conceptual and methodological leanings. To estimate and explain the use of health services, it is necessary to draw upon the full range of available micro- and macrosociological knowledge and to use the entire spectrum of research methodologies (Freeman and Levine 1989).

A MICROPERSPECTIVE

Health and illness remain social concepts even in today's medical care world, where the extensive training given to physicians and other providers and the widespread use of high technology have increased the validity and reliability of diagnoses (Parsons 1951). Persons with the same biomedical conditions and manifesting the same symptoms differ considerably in their self-evaluations of health status, in their willingness to comply with suggested regimens to prevent more serious conditions and to improve their health status, and in their competence to deal with providers and health care organizations.

Likewise, individual medical providers vary greatly in their identification of persons as sick or well, in the treatments they prescribe, and in the ways they relate to patients. Because of these well-documented findings, there has been extensive sociopsychological research on the provision and utilization of health services (Andersen, Kravits, and Anderson 1976).

Perhaps the most researched area, in which considerable work goes on now, is how to encourage persons to participate in preventive programs (Becker and Rosenstock 1989). While perhaps not health services in the strict sense, current efforts to modify diet and increase exercise are seen as means to reduce illness and disease. But it goes beyond that, ranging from following generally regarded frequencies of visits to providers, depending upon health status, age, sex, and other characteristics, to practicing safe sex in the face of the AIDS epidemic and the number of seropositive persons in the community. Thus, there is extensive interest in a "health belief model" and in "social power" strategies for modifying health care behavior (Becker and Joseph 1988).

Of course, microdimensions are not independent of macro ones. This is illustrated by the well-known concept of the *sick role* discussed by Parsons (1951) several decades ago. He observed that the sick role was a means for persons to minimize their participation in instrumental roles normatively expected of them. Similarly, public health efforts to minimize the AIDS epidemic depend upon developing efficacious programs for reducing unsafe sex and eliminating needle sharing.

A MACROPERSPECTIVE

Understanding the utilization of health services, however, requires bringing in social structural and organizational dimensions as well. Although a persistent area of sociological study, interest in the relations between structural and organizational arrangements for care and the quantity, types, and quality of health care utilized has increased markedly in recent years because of the spiraling costs of health services for everyone (Shortell and Kaluzny 1987).

Health insurance now represents a major economic burden for even reasonably well-to-do families and their employers, and public medical care costs are a significant tax burden for community members. As a consequence, new forms of medical care organizations have emerged, and they have been the focus of intensive study (Freeman et al. 1990).

A frequently encountered type is the *staff model* health maintenance organization (HMO), where primary-care physicians may practice on a salary and the focus is on prevention and early detection, in order to minimize expensive inpatient and high-tech services. They operate on a capitation basis, with employers or individuals paying a fee to cover all or almost all of their health care costs (Luft 1983).

Unfortunately, not all such HMOs have prospered, because of the failure to manage them properly, the extensiveness of the services provided, or the selection of such settings by persons requiring extensive care. Other common options are *preferred provider organizations* (PPOs), in which groups of primary-care physicians, who may be salaried or may work for fees, provide routine care but refer out patients for specialty services. Some of these PPOs permit patients to choose their own specialists, although they are usually required to pay part of the medical care costs if they do so. There are a number of variant models of *managed care,* as well as physicians who arrange with insurance carriers to provide care under a variety of different fiscal arrangements. Each innovation in the way health care is delivered affects the utilization of services, creating literally endless opportunities for research. So, too, does the emergence of new disorders and the redefinition of the social dimensions of others. AIDS and the HIV virus are a clear example of the former; the medical ramifications of domestic violence and the abuse of family members by each other, of the latter.

But there are other reasons for organizational change in medicine. For example, organizational arrangements are a major factor in the training of health providers and, thus, in the types of patients who utilize their services (Ludmerer 1985). Fledgling providers select and are selected differently, depending upon organizational features of settings; receive quite different substantive educations once there; and have their career trajectories determined to a large degree by the sites in which they have been trained. The patients of a doctor with an MD from Harvard, a residency at Johns Hopkins, and a practice that is teaching-hospital based receive markedly different care than the patients of a doctor who went to a foreign medical school, interned at a community hospital for one year, and maintains a solo practice in a small-sized community.

At the same time, there are some research concerns that have persisted since sociologists began to study medical care and the utilization of services. Since their beginnings, hospitals have been class structured, ranging from "charity hospitals" for the impoverished to "doctors' hospitals" for the rich. Utilization of health services still varies, depending upon access to hospitals and health care providers (Iglehart 1985). Access to care today continues to differ, depending upon the social characteristics of patients. Health insurance coverage, furthermore, is a major determinant of the type, quantity, and quality of care that a patient receives.

Moreover, the organizational arrangements under which medical care is provided are major determinants of the extent and nature of health services that community members receive. This is the case for both ambulatory and hospital care, whether one takes a national perspective and pursues research opportunities in a single nation or an international one and undertakes comparative investigations.

Ambulatory Care. At one time the image of the solo practitioner traveling to the patient's bedside and diagnosing and treating with the few instruments and medicines contained in his black bag was rooted in fact. Most doctors were generalists and had limited technical training. There was only a small number of specialists to call upon for consultation, and few tests were available to help confirm diagnoses. Further, there were marked variations in the quantity and quality of care received by different income groups. For the most part, costs of doctors' visits and prescriptions were borne by individual patients, and differences in access to care were much greater than now (Mechanic and Aiken 1989).

Today, of course, ambulatory care is delivered primarily by providers who undergo extensive training, have a broad array of technology to employ in making diagnoses, and frequently refer patients to superspecialists for both diagnostic procedures and treatment (Aiken and Freeman 1980). Indeed, current concern centers on the problems of too many physicians being trained in many specialties, excess use of technology, and overtreatment of patients. In part, present concerns are stimulated by the intense interest in cost containment; in part, by skepticism that high-tech "modern medicine" necessarily benefits patients from either a medical care or psychological standpoint.

The differentials in care related to socioeconomic characteristics may have narrowed, but there are still major barriers to care faced by many of the poor in the United States, in some of the other industrialized countries, and in all of the less-developed ones. For example, it is advisable that adult women have regular breast examinations including mammograms. Most middle-income women with health insurance in the United States have no economic barriers to receiving what is now a well-established preventive procedure, one that results in early detection of cancer and reduced mortality. At the same time, Medicaid, the federal–state program that provides health care for many poor women, in many states does not include mandatory payment for mammograms or many other preventive services. Moreover, emergency rooms staffed primarily by students and physicians-in-training become the site of care for many of the poor, particularly the uninsured. In contrast, the insured, economically fortunate, community members are treated by highly trained and experienced primary-care physicians who often refer patients to their superspecialist colleagues for consultations and nonroutine treatment.

Variations in ambulatory care have received extensive sociological study. It is a much more complicated area for research than it may seem at first glance. A major reason is the difficulty of differentiating and measuring *need* and *demand.* Ideally, the former concept would be reserved for the care required from a medical perspective; and the latter, for what the patient wishes to receive.

But, as noted in the discussion of the microdimension, need generally has its social components as well as biomedical ones and patients are rarely autonomous in their search for health care. For example, on the one hand, a somewhat compulsive person with hypertension can be taught to take her or his blood pressure weekly and, if compliant about taking the medication, need see her or his physician every six months (although she may demand to do so much more often). On the other, a person unwilling to regularly take her or his blood pressure and medicine may need to see a provider monthly, although such patients only demand care when they manifest disabling symptoms.

The concept of access is used to differentiate the use of health services over time and, more important, between groups such as the insured and the uninsured, Anglos and Hispanics and Afro-Americans, and rural and urban dwellers. These community and national studies are posited on the position that, given equity in access, if anything, there should be higher use of services among economically and socially disfranchised groups. This view is held because of the association identified early in the history of social medicine between poor health and disadvantageous quality of life. Thus, the health care utilization of the advantaged groups is used as the "gold standard." While it is difficult to develop ways of measuring need, particularly on large samples and without extensive medical examinations, there are continuing efforts to develop proxies for it that are useful in epidemiological research and surveys on use of health services (McKinlay, McKinlay, and Beaglehole 1989). In part this is because of the intrinsic interest in social structural differences in access; in part, because advocates of disadvantaged groups legally and politically bring pressure to remedy the lack of services of these groups, compared with the more economically fortunate and better insured in the population.

Institutional Care. Ambulatory care is simple to study and understand, compared with the institutional care of patients. The settings providing inpatient care range from small homelike places providing convalescent care to huge, bureaucratic organizations with thousands of patients and employees, complex vertical and horizontal structures, and all of the organizational features of large conglomerates (American Hospital Association 1986). Indeed, some are just that, for national profit and nonprofit multihospital corporations are publicly held and truly "big business."

In all medical institutions, however, the services

available and received by patients are determined only in part by the resolution of need and demand differences and the likelihood that they will benefit the recipients. Other determinants include the costs of care; the probability of reimbursement; the risks of malpractice and other legal actions; the extent to which the mission of the institution is patient care, compared with teaching students and young doctors and doing research; and the likelihood that the actions taken will enhance the power and standing of individual providers and the institution as a whole.

All of the determinants just mentioned, individually and collectively, have been the subject of sociological studies using every conceptual framework imaginable and just about all research methodologies. Because of the variations in types of health services provided and the differences in settings, sociologists often specialize in subareas, for example, in the study of the use of services and the impact of the organizations on them among persons with psychiatric illnesses, acute and chronic physical health conditions, and so on.

Moreover, the research undertaken is often not purely sociological. To research problems of institutional care (and only to a slightly lesser extent, ambulatory care) in these times one needs to consider the economics of medical care and a host of management and human resource problems. In fact, some researchers become so multidisciplinarily oriented that they lose their identity as sociologists and become health services researchers (Freeman 1988). But they, as well as their peers who maintain their disciplinary identity, are assured of continued opportunities for research, for the gaps and differentials in use of health services undoubtedly will continue to confront persons in all communities and every nation.

(SEE ALSO: *Health-Care Financing; Health Policy Analysis; Medical Sociology*)

REFERENCES

Aiken, Linda H., and Howard E. Freeman 1980 "Medical Sociology and Science and Technology in Medicine." In P. T. Durbin, ed., *A Guide to the Culture of Science, Technology and Medicine.* New York: Free Press.

American Hospital Association 1986 *Hospital Statistics 1986.* Chicago: American Hospital Association.

Andersen, R., J. Kravits, and O. W. Anderson 1976 *Two Decades of Health Services: Social Survey Trends in Use and Expenditure.* Cambridge, Mass.: Ballinger.

Becker, M. H., and J. G. Joseph 1988 "AIDS and Behavioral Change to Reduce Risk: A Review." *American Journal of Public Health* 78:394–410.

Becker, Marshall H., and Irwin M. Rosenstock 1989 "Health Promotion, Disease Prevention, and Program Retention." In H. E. Freeman and S. Levine, eds., *Handbook of Medical Sociology,* 4th ed. Englewood Cliffs, N.J.: Prentice-Hall.

Freeman, Howard E. 1988 "Medical Sociology." In E. Borgatta and K. Cook, eds., *The Future of Sociology.* Beverly Hills, Calif.: Sage.

Freeman, Howard E., Linda H. Aiken, Robert J. Blendon, and Christopher R. Corey 1990 "Uninsured Working-Age Adults: Characteristics and Consequences." *Health Services Research* 24(6):811–823.

Freeman, Howard E., Robert J. Blendon, Linda H. Aiken, Seymour Sudman, Connie F. Mullinix, and Christopher R. Corey 1987 "Americans Report on Their Access to Health Care." *Health Affairs* 6(1):6–18.

Freeman, Howard E., and Sol Levine 1989 *Handbook of Medical Sociology,* 4th ed. Englewood Cliffs, N.J.: Prentice-Hall.

Iglehart, J. W. 1985 "Medical Care of the Poor: A Growing Problem." *New England Journal of Medicine* 313:59–63.

Ludmerer, Kenneth 1985 *Learning to Heal: The Development of American Medical Education.* New York: Basic Books.

Luft, Harold S. 1983 "Health Maintenance Organizations." In D. Mechanic, ed., *Handbook of Health, Health Care and the Health Professions.* New York: Free Press.

McKinlay, John B., Sonja M. McKinlay, and Robert Beaglehole 1989 "Trends in Death and Disease and the Contribution of Medical Measures." In H. E. Freeman and S. Levine, eds., *Handbook of Medical Sociology,* 4th ed. Englewood Cliffs, N.J.: Prentice-Hall.

Mechanic, David, and Linda H. Aiken 1989 "Access to Health Care and Use of Medical Care Services." In H. E. Freeman and S. Levine, eds., *Handbook of Medical Sociology,* 4th ed. Englewood Cliffs, N.J.: Prentice-Hall.

Parsons, Talcott 1951 "Illness and the Role of the Physician: A Sociological Perspective." *American Journal of Orthopsychiatry* 21:452–460.

Shortell, Stephen M., and Arnold D. Kaluzny 1987 "Organization Theory and Health Care Management." In S. M. Shortell and A. D. Kaluzny, eds., *Health Care Management.* New York: John Wiley.

HOWARD E. FREEMAN

HEALTH STATUS MEASUREMENT

Healers throughout the world use indicators to assess the state of their patients' health. In some traditional settings it may consist of peering into the patient's eyes or feeling the pulse, or, in more contemporary settings, using the stethoscope, the percussion hammer, and the penlight. In the United States and in some other advanced industrialized countries, the patient who appears for an annual examination may expect to have blood pressure measured, blood and urine analyzed, or, depending on age, gender, and history, to be the recipient of several other procedures as well. In many cases, the validity and reliability of these procedures are problematic. It is well known, for instance, that different blood pressure readings of the same patient may be obtained in successive measures at brief intervals in the course of an hour, and when taken by different people, for example, the physician, the nurse, or the secretary.

In recent years clinicians and investigators have gone beyond obtaining physiological measures of the patient's condition and have tried to document the patient's functional performance or quality of life (Elinson and Siegmann 1979; Donald et al. 1978). In this context we do not refer to quality of life features, such as level of crime, satisfaction with government, or standard of living, that may emanate from basic social conditions (Campbell, Converse, and Rodgers 1976). Instead, we refer to features that are health-related and that may be influenced by health interventions. One of the main reasons for this new emphasis in health is that there has been a dramatic increase in the prevalence of chronic diseases throughout this century. Arthritis, hypertension, heart disease, diabetes, mental illness, various forms of cancer, and other chronic diseases are not very amenable to cure. The crucial questions in treating chronic diseases are how to control the disease as much as possible, how to enhance the patient's quality of life, and how to foster the patient's ability to function with family members and friends, at work, and in the community.

In addition, the rising costs in the health sector have become a widespread concern in the population. Policymakers are viewing the burgeoning of new, costly, and sophisticated medical technologies with increasing skepticism. In question is whether the new technologies can not only extend life but also improve the quality of the life that is extended. Finally, some major social and cultural developments have been reflected in growing criticism of the biomedical approach to patient care. Women, minorities, and holistic health advocates have urged that health care become more humanized and that more attention be paid to the patient's social functioning and well-being (Croog and Levine 1989).

Early functional classification scales included several indexes specifically designed for cardiac and arthritic patients; they provided clinicians with measures of the capacities of the more severely disabled patients. Other scales such as the Katz Index of Daily Living and the Barthel Index tapped such self-care functions as bathing, dressing, and toileting (Kazis 1991). Although these scales represented improved methods of measuring health status, most of them were narrow in focus and in need of more rigorous testing. These initial tests, however, constituted important innovations in going beyond physiological measurements and in focusing on aspects of the patient's functional performance and quality of life.

One major problem in quality of life studies is that there has been a lack of agreement about the meaning of quality of life or the components that are encompassed by the concept. In some studies quality of life measures have been appended or added as an afterthought (Bergner 1989). A more explicit operational definition of the concept is needed. Nevertheless, the concept has served as a general rubric to guide the work of a good number of investigators. In addition, investigators appear to agree about some of the main components to be included in generic measures of quality of life: performance of social roles, physiological and emotional state, cognitive or intellectual functioning, and the patient's sense of well-being or general satisfaction.

A number of new instruments effectively measure different dimensions of physical and mental health and social and physical functioning. These tests meet the basic standards of psychometric tests (Kazis 1991), including validity (the test measuring what it is supposed to measure), reliability (consistency in test results), and sensitivity (the ability of the test to detect significant small changes of improvement or worsening).

Another issue in ascertaining the quality of life of patients is whether to rely on measures that are generic (used for a wide variety of diseases or conditions) or disease-specific (designed especially for a specific condition or disease). Some of the better-known measurement instruments designed for generic purposes are the Sickness Impact Profile (SIP), the Duke-UNC Health Profile, the RAND Health Insurance Experiment (HIE) measures, the Index of Well-Being, the McMaster Health Index Questionnaire, the SF-36 (a short form that emerged from the Medical Outcomes Study), and the Nottingham Health Profile. Illustrative of the disease-specific measures are the Karnofsky Performance Status Measures (cancer), the New York Heart Association Functional Classification, and the Arthritis Impact Measurement Scales (Kazis 1991; Patrick and Deyo 1989). A number of tests are being modified and refined.

Generic measures as well as disease-specific measures have their respective merits (Patrick 1990). A judicious combination of the two types of measures is often warranted, depending on the purpose of the study. One factor in favor of using at least some disease-specific items is that some features of a patient's quality of life are attributable to the specific medications prescribed. Thus, some widely used antihypertensive medications may occasionally cause fatigue, nightmares, loss of mental acuity, dry mouth, itching, and sexual impotence. These specific aspects of quality of life might not be identified if disease-specific measures were not used.

Another major methodological issue in assessing quality of life is whether this can be provided by a single summary assessment score for each patient. There are clear advantages in having a single summary score for descriptive and analytical purposes. However, a summary score may be overly simplistic for assessing a complex phenomenon for which there is no known underlying dimension. A possible solution to this problem is to have a profile format that includes summary ratings for each major component of quality of life, such as the patient's cognitive functioning, job performance, and anxiety state. Changes in each of the patient's life areas, as well as total configurations, can be charted and analyzed (Croog and Levine 1989; Ware 1984).

It is one task to develop tests or scales that may be used in studying different population groups. It is another task to develop instruments that can chart an individual patient's progress over time. Researchers hope that health status assessments may serve the needs of both clinicians working with patients and of research investigators conducting health surveys or clinical trials. The purpose for which the instrument is used would determine what instruments are appropriate and how they are employed. Some investigators are making progress in developing some short-form measures that can be used with patients as well as with general populations (Stewart, Hays, and Ware 1988). Clinicians need relatively brief instruments that can be completed easily by patients, scored quickly and conveniently, and incorporated into daily clinical practice. It is also necessary to produce questions that can elicit valid data when administered to persons of different socioeconomic and cultural backgrounds.

It is not easy to incorporate health status assessments into routine clinical practice. This entails more than introducing a simple new diagnostic procedure. The physician who has been accustomed to relying on clinical judgment and to working mainly with physiological measures must acquire both new habits and a significantly new orientation. Patients, too, may require reorientation, though there is good evidence that they have often been frustrated in their eagerness to discuss their quality of life with their physicians. Patients, therefore, are expected to welcome the physician's greater interest in their functional performance. Although physicians have been gathering information on the functional performance of their patients for years, they have not done so reliably and systematically. The new health outcome measurements are intended to provide physicians with firm and standardized benchmarks with which they can chart their patients' progress. A crucial question is the degree to which this new information will change the clinical behavior of the physician. The ultimate question, of course, is the degree to which the use of health outcome measurements will improve the patient's functional performance and well-being.

(SEE ALSO: *Health and Illness Behavior; Medical Sociology; Quality of Life)*

REFERENCES

Bergner, M. 1989 "Quality of Life, Health Status, and Clinical Research." *Medical Care* (Suppl.) 27:148–151.

Campbell, A., P. E. Converse, and W. L. Rodgers 1976 *The Quality of American Life.* New York: Russell Sage Foundation.

Croog, S. H., and S. Levine 1989 "Quality of Life and Health Care Interventions." In H. E. Freeman and S. Levine, eds., *Handbook of Medical Sociology.* Englewood Cliffs, N.J.: Prentice-Hall.

Donald, C. A., J. E. Ware, R. H. Brook, and A. Davies-Avery 1978 *Conceptualization and Measurement of Health for Adults in the Health Insurance Study,* vol. 4, *Social Health.* Santa Monica, Calif.: RAND Corporation.

Elinson, J., and A. E. Siegmann 1979 *Socio-medical Health Indicators.* Bloomingdale, N.Y.: Baywood Publishing.

Kazis, L. E. 1991 "Health Outcome Assessments in Medicine: History, Applications, and New Directions." *Advances in Internal Medicine* 36:109–130.

Patrick, D. L. 1990 "Assessing Health Related Quality of Life Outcomes." In K. A. Haithoff and K. N. Lohr, eds., *Effectiveness and Outcomes in Health Care.* Washington, D.C.: National Academy Press.

———, and R. A. Deyo 1989 "Generic and Disease-Specific Measures in Assessing Health Status and Quality of Life." *Medical Care* 27:217–232.

Stewart, A. L., R. D. Hays, and J. E. Ware 1988 "The MOS Short-form General Health Survey: Reliability and Validity in a Patient Population." *Medical Care* 26:724–735.

Ware, J. E. 1984 "Methodological Considerations in the Selection of Health Status Assessment Procedures." In N. K. Wenger, M. E. Mattson, C. D. Furberg, and J. Elinson, eds., *Assessment of Quality of Life in Clinical Trials of Cardiovascular Therapies.* New York: Le Jacq.

SOL LEVINE

HETEROSEXUAL BEHAVIOR PATTERNS Social science researchers have learned a great deal about human sexual behavior since Alfred Kinsey and his colleagues conducted their pioneering studies on male and female sexuality in the late 1940s and early 1950s (Kinsey et al. 1953; Kinsey, Pomeroy, and Martin 1948). However, much of what has been learned has focused on sexuality issues within a "social problems" context. Relatively little attention has been devoted to studying the expression of sexuality in noncontroversial, everyday life circumstances. Moreover, research typically has been conducted in a manner consistent with popular culture's image that individuals' sexuality reflects their innate biological and psychological traits (see Stein 1989 for a review of the major theoretical models guiding sex research, and for contemporary sociological theoretical statements on sexuality see Reiss 1986; Simon and Gagnon 1986).

The politics of sex research has clearly thwarted researchers' efforts to overcome the sharpest criticism of Kinsey's earlier work—biased sampling (see Callero and Howard 1989). Even the contemporary political climate, at least in the final decision-making stages, has impeded the scientific objective of developing a reliable, systematic understanding of individuals' sexual attitudes and behaviors. For example, during 1989 the U.S. House Appropriations Committee deleted 11 million from the 1990 fiscal appropriations bill for the Departments of Labor, Health and Human Services, Education and Related Agencies which had been targeted for a national survey of 20,000 Americans' sexual attitudes and behaviors. Similarly, Britain's former Prime Minister Margaret Thatcher canceled in the same year Britain's largest national sex survey, $1.2 million and 20,000 respondents, before it was fielded.

Thus, nationally representative data on sexuality issues remain quite limited and are restricted typically to descriptive questions about age at first intercourse and frequency of sexual relations. Consequently, our knowledge about the more diverse and dynamic aspects of sexual experience is based on research with varying degrees of generalizability and scientific rigor. In general, sex researchers are probably challenged more by issues related to response bias, sample representativeness, measurement, and ethics than most social scientists because of the sensitive nature of sexuality. With these methodological issues in mind (see Bentler and Abramson 1980; Jayne 1986; Kelley 1986), and given this chapter's space limitations, this review assesses the available research on *heterosexual behavior* within the United States (individual chapters in this volume address homosexuality and lesbianism). The brevity of this chapter precludes reviewing the plethora of literature on individuals' subjective perceptions about sexuality. Although this discussion is not meant to be exhaustive, it does take into account four basic and interrelated features of sexuality: (1) its varied meaning throughout the life course; (2) the consensual and coercive contexts within which sex occurs; (3) the gendered aspects of its expression; and (4) the relationship between the HIV epidemic and sexual behavior. Finally, while this chapter reviews primarily social scientific literature, a number of authors have published books in the popular press—some of which have received considerable attention by the lay population—based on empirical findings often derived from self-selected samples of persons who returned magazine surveys (see Kelley 1990 for a review of these works).

CHILDHOOD SEXUAL BEHAVIOR

Anthropological research has shown quite clearly that, while individuals in Western cultures tend to view children as asexual, children are viewed as being capable of sexual activity within many nonindustrialized, non-Western countries (Ford and Beach 1951). Parents in these non-Western countries may sometimes tolerate and even encourage their children to pursue heterosexual behaviors (including intercourse), homosexual behaviors (e.g., fellatio), or both. In some societies mothers actually masturbate their children in order to soothe them. Given the Western view of children, it should not be surprising that little social science research has been conducted on childhood sexuality in the United States. Available research does indicate that boys are much more likely to masturbate and to do so at younger ages than are girls. For example, Hunt (1974) found that 63 percent of boys and 33 percent of girls in his nonrepresentative urban sample could recall having an orgasm while masturbating before the age of thirteen. Boys also appear to participate throughout childhood in both heterosexual and homosexual play activities that have sexual overtones (e.g., "doctor and nurse"). These activities typically include some element of exhibition, exploration, and experimentation.

Thorne and Lurias' (1986) participant observation study of nine- to eleven-year-old boys and girls within a school context provides fresh insights into studying childhood sexuality. Although this study does not address sexual behavior as defined in conventional "adult" terms, it is nevertheless an important contribution because it clarifies how children structure their social worlds in response to gender and sexuality issues. In the process, these authors assess the ways in which children structure their behavior by drawing upon and employing sexual meanings in their gender-differentiated environments. It seems reasonable to argue that these processes are likely to influence children's sexual behaviors later on in life as well.

ADOLESCENT AND YOUNG ADULT SEXUAL BEHAVIOR

In contrast to the small amount of research on childhood sexuality, an expansive body of literature on adolescent sexual behavior has emerged during the past two decades (see Hofferth 1987; Marsiglio 1988; Walsh 1989). Much of this research has used one of several national data sets to document and examine rates and trends for age at first intercourse, with particular attention given to racial patterns. Overall, the bulk of the evidence suggests that there was a sizable increase in the rate of sexual activity among teenage females during the 1970s, although this increase appears to have leveled off during the 1980s. Rates among black and white females converged during this period. Sexual activity rates among comparably aged males have also increased and have always been higher than those for females. While the rates for females and males converged during this period, some evidence suggests that this trend may have peaked.

One study that employed data from three separate national surveys compared the retrospective reports of females living in metropolitan areas at age fourteen who had been born between 1959 and 1963 and found that between 10.2 and 19 percent of whites had become sexually active before the age of sixteen and between 54.2 and 56.9 percent had had intercourse before their nineteenth birthday (Kahn, Kalsbeek, and Hofferth 1988). Meanwhile, the comparable range of percentages for black females was 18 to 42.3 and 73.4 to 85.5. Another study compared two separate national samples of metropolitan males born between 1959 and 1963 with those born between 1969 and 1973 and found that the more recent cohort was significantly more likely to initiate sex at younger ages (Sonenstein, Pleck, and Ku 1989). Whereas 55.7 and 77.5 percent of seventeen- and nineteen-year-old males from the older cohort were sexually active, 71.9 and 87.8 percent of the seventeen- and nineteen-year-olds in the more recent cohort of teenage males had already had intercourse.

Attempts to explain why youth initiate sex have focused primarily on the direct and indirect influence of sociodemographic, social psychological, and biological factors. In her review of research on sexual initiation, Hofferth (1987) posits a model that assesses the impact of both biological and psychosocial factors. Most of the research designs are not ideal for concluding a causal relationship between beliefs, attitudes, or values and sexual behavior because these variables tend to be measured simultaneously. Despite this methodological shortcoming, Hofferth identifies a number of factors that appear to be related positively (in a multivariate context) to the probability of individuals initiating intercourse at a young age: being black, living in a poverty area, having weak religious beliefs, attending a segregated school (for blacks), attending an integrated school (for whites), lower parental education, having a mother who was sexually active at a young age, living in a single parent household, having more siblings, and having a low level of academic achievement.

In addition to these social variables, Udry (1988) and his associates have employed biosocial models to conduct a series of novel studies of the sexual behavior of school-age youth in a southern public school setting. This research provides preliminary evidence that adolescents' sexuality (both attitudes and behavior) is related to hormonal factors and that models that posit an interaction between hormones and social variables may explain sexual behavior more fully than sociological models alone. While some sociologists have criticized this research because of the importance it places on the biological substratum, others have advocated the merits of developing biosocial models that take into account the complex interrelationship between the pubertal process, sexual identity development, sexual behavior, and societal norms.

While most research has focused on sexual intercourse, a number of studies of adolescent and college populations have examined issues related to other types of sex acts and the sequencing of petting behaviors. Researchers have shown, for example, that the prevalence of oral sex has grown tremendously during this century. Kinsey's data revealed that very few college women born between 1910 and 1935 performed fellatio (11 percent) or received cunnilingus (12 percent). More recent studies in California and North Carolina suggest that between one-third and one-half of adolescents fifteen to eighteen have engaged in oral sex (Hass 1979; Newcomer and Udry 1985), while nonrepresentative studies of college students in the United States and Canada indicate that between 32 and 86 percent of females have administered oral sex and between 44 and 68 percent say they have received it (Herold and Way 1983; Young 1980). Furthermore, Kinsey's data suggested that oral sex was primarily experienced only among those who also had experienced coitus (only 5 percent of male and female virgins reported performing it), but more recent research indicates that a sizable minority of youth are experiencing oral sex while they are still technically "virgins."

One recent fourteen-year study of three cohorts of women at the same Northeastern private university concluded that college women had not changed their sexual practices in terms of the frequency with which they engaged in fellatio, cunnilingus, and anal intercourse (Debuono et al. 1990). However, female students in 1989 were at least twice as likely to report using condoms "always or almost always" than their counterparts were in 1986. Another survey of college students at Rhode Island University in 1986 (Carroll 1988) found that 40 percent reported that their concern over AIDS had altered their sexual behavior. Among those sexually active, 54 percent had changed their behavior with 30 percent reporting that they exercised greater discretion when selecting partners—although this did *not* mean that they were more likely to enter an exclusive relationship, nor did it mean that they reduced coital frequency. Fifteen percent of the nonactive students said they had not engaged in sexual intercourse because of their concerns about AIDS.

Although researchers have used college populations to examine different aspects of young adults' sexual behavior, relatively little research has considered the sexual behavior of young and middle-aged heterosexual single adults, especially those not enrolled in college. One recent exception to this pattern that also dealt with the issue of HIV infection is the controversial epidemiological study by Masters, Kolodny, and Johnson (1988), which received extensive media coverage. Their study was based on a nonrandomly selected sample of 800 sexually active, self-identified heterosexuals, twenty-one to forty years of age, who had not had a blood transfusion or injected illegal drugs since 1977. Respondents were enrolled from one of four cities (Atlanta, Los Angeles, New York, and St. Louis), with half (200 men and 200 women) reporting that they had had at least six sexual partners during each of the preceding five years and the other half reporting that they were in a monogamous relationship for at least five years. The authors' major conclusion was that public health officials had grossly underestimated the incidence and spread of HIV. The authors contended that in the heterosexual population this rate would continue to climb because the most sexually active persons were insensitive to the possibility of HIV infection; none of the men and only 3 percent of the women reported using condoms regularly during the preceding year.

SEXUALLY COERCIVE BEHAVIOR

Although most sexual interaction involves consenting partners, some does not. In response to the feminist movement, scholars increasingly have focused on the power dimension of sexuality by documenting and explaining the various forms of coercive sexuality (i.e., sexual relations that occur because of the threat or actual use of physical force or other controlling behaviors) and other exploitative forms of sexuality (for a macrosociological perspective on rape, see Baron and Straus 1987). The scientific rigor of research in this area has improved over the years, but questions concerning the validity of data persist, given the moral and criminal nature of these issues.

It is exceedingly difficult to estimate the prevalence of the various forms of coercive sexuality because the Uniform Crime Reports are widely believed to underreport the true rate of sex crimes, and anonymous, self-report surveys vary widely in their sampling techniques and findings. Nevertheless, Grauerholz and Solomon's (1989) succinct review of research in this area suggests that a large proportion of the U.S. population has or will experience coercive sexual relations at one time or another, either as a victim, a perpetrator, or both. Researchers' estimates of the pervasiveness of incest may vary the most. Whereas some researchers have observed that about 1 percent of U.S. females have been incest victims (Kempe and Kempe 1984), others have reported much higher figures. For example, Russell (1984) found that 16 percent of her large household sample of women eighteen years of age and older in San Francisco had experienced incest before age eighteen, and 20 percent of Finkelhor's (1979) predominantly white, middle class, New England college student sample who were raised primarily in nonmetropolitan areas reported having been an incest victim. While females are more likely to be the victims of coercive and exploitative sexuality, studies also indicate that many young boys are victimized in this manner (Finkelhor 1979; Moore, Nord, and Peterson 1989).

Mary Koss and her colleagues (Koss et al. 1985; Koss et al. 1988), using a recent national survey of college students, found that 38 percent of female college students reported sexual victimization that met the legal criterion for rape or attempted rape, and 7.7 percent of males actually admitted they had either raped or attempted to rape at least one woman since their fourteenth birthday, a finding supported by other studies (Mosher and Anderson 1986; Rapaport and Burkhart 1984). Using data from the 1987 wave of the National Survey of Children, Moore, Nord, and Peterson (1989) also found that about 7 percent of U.S. adults aged eighteen to twenty-two (females being more likely than males) confirmed that they had had sex against their will or had been raped at least on one occasion. Other researchers have reported that between 10 and 12 percent of women report having been raped by dates and between 8 and 14 percent of wives report that their husbands have sexually assaulted or raped them (Finkelhor and Yllo 1985; Russell and Howell 1982).

Having documented that coercive sexuality is quite prevalent, the question remains: Why do many men, and some women, coerce others to have sex with them? Some theorists argue that males are more likely to engage in various forms of coercive sexuality if they have strong ties to a peer group that supports sexually aggressive behavior. Compared to their less stereotypically masculine counterparts, men studied in the research noted above who possess strong "macho" personality characteristics and hold rigid, conservative views of sex-role stereotypes are more likely to report that they have used physical force and threats to have sex and that they would probably use physical force to obtain sex if they could be assured that they would not be prosecuted. Other theorists have argued that a small percentage of women may even facilitate different forms of coercive sexuality by playing sexually receptive or seductive roles. Not surprisingly, it is common for rapists to believe, or at least report, that their victims were willing participants who actually enjoyed themselves while being raped—even though these perceptions are clearly *inconsistent* with rape victims' own accounts (Scully and Marolla 1984).

While the several forms of coercive sexuality share a number of common themes, such as the objectification of women, individual factors and circumstances may be more or less significant in accounting for why particular types of coercive sexuality occur. One of the important factors that seems to distinguish the typical stranger or the acquaintance rapist from the "average" date rapist is the former's greater tendency to have been sexually or physically abused by his parents or others. Date rape incidences tend to involve partners who knew one another and had established at least a modicum of interpersonal trust by making a commitment to spend some time together. The dynamic nature of interaction episodes that typify date rapes, and the fact that at least one of the persons often has been influenced by drugs, alcohol, or both, can obscure participants' intentions and behavior. Furthermore, the more that individuals' sexual scripting is influenced by traditional gender-role socialization, the more likely coercive sexuality will occur because of sexual miscommunication and males' reliance on coping strategies that emphasize dominance and aggression. Many males assume that women will tend to offer token resistance to their sexual advances in order to create an impression that they are not sexually "promiscuous" (Check and Malamuth 1983). Indeed, one study of 610 female undergraduates revealed that almost 40 percent had engaged in this type of token resistance at least once (Muehlenhard and Hoolabaugh 1988). While these patterns should not be used to justify date rape in any way, it should come as no surprise that some males grossly distort the consensual petting that generally precedes date rape as a woman's way of acknowledging her willingness to engage in more intimate forms of sexual interaction—even if this means that in some cases males will be required to pursue it forcefully. Finally, while there are many factors related to fathers' incestuous behavior, one of the more frequently noted arguments underscores the common pattern whereby a father pursues sexual and emotional intimacy with his female children (usually a series of episodes over time with the eldest female child) in order to compensate for his unfulfilling relationship with the adult female, who generally has withdrawn from her roles as mother and wife (partner).

Pornography represents the final factor we discuss that may be related to coercive sexuality. Edward Donnenstein and N. Malamuth have conducted an ambitious series of social psychological experimental studies to examine the relationship between viewing pornographic materials (especially versions that depict male aggression toward women) and various forms of coercive sexuality. Donnenstein and Linz (1986, p. 212) conclude their review of the research that addresses the question of whether pornography influences men's attitudes and behaviors toward women by arguing that "there is no evidence for any 'harm'-related effects from sexually explicit materials. But research may support potential harmful effects from aggressive materials. Aggressive images are the issue, not sexual images."

From a feminist perspective, instances of coercive sexuality all involve a critical power or control dimension; however, the issue of sexual discretion and availability must also be discussed in relation to many instances of coercive sexuality, especially date and marital rape. By definition, men can only engage in coercive sexuality with women if women do not want to have sex in a given instance. Unfortunately, data are not available that would enable a reliable analysis of historical trends to determine the ways and extent to which the change in norms regarding the sexual double standard, which was brought about by the women's movement, have altered rates (either increased or decreased) for different forms of coercive sexuality.

PROSTITUTION

Contemporary sociological research on prostitution has typically involved small-scale, convenience samples. Unfortunately, Kinsey's nonrepresentative data, which are more than forty years old, are probably the best available data on clients of prostitutes. Gagnon (1977) suggested that the six most common reasons men visit prostitutes include: (1) sex without negotiation; (2) involvement without commitment; (3) sex for eroticism and variety; (4) a form of socializing; (5) sex away from home; and (6) sex for those who fear rejection most.

Many commentators have indicated that rates of prostitution, a form of commercialized sex that had in the past provided men with sexual opportunities in a less sexually open society, have decreased drastically since World War II. Kinsey reported that prior to the war between 60 and 70 percent of adult men had visited a prostitute and about 15 to 20 percent used them regularly. Some sociologists believed that prostitution served a useful societal function in that it provided men with a convenient sexual outlet, which in turn minimized the numbers of sexual transgressions against "respectable" women. One reason males may be using prostitutes less often during recent decades is that they can obtain sex more easily now and women appear to be more inclined to engage in sexual activities (e.g., oral-genital sex) that they previously had found less appealing. In addition, anecdotal and journalistic accounts suggest that some men today are avoiding prostitutes because they fear they would be exposed to the AIDS (HIV) virus.

ELDERLY SEXUAL BEHAVIOR

Although the proportion of the U.S. population over fifty continues to grow, research addressing the relationship between aging and sexuality, and in particular the sexual behavior of the elderly population (sixty-five and older), is still quite limited due to its frequent use of small, nonrepresentative samples, its cross-sectional research designs, and its narrow, youth-oriented definitions of sexuality as coitus. Consequently, generalizations are difficult to make, and most of the research on elderly persons' sexual behavior deals with the physiological and psychological aspects of this phenomenon. Several reviews of sexuality among the elderly currently exist (Ludeman 1981; Riportella-Muller 1989; Starr 1985).

Two of the more frequently cited studies of aging and sexuality issues include the Starr-Weiner Report (1981) and the second Duke Longitudinal Study (George and Weiler 1981), neither of which were based on random sampling techniques. The former included 800 sociodemographically diverse participants in senior centers, while the latter included a panel design of men and women health-insurance program participants, who were forty-six to seventy-one years of age at the first observation period in 1969 and were followed for six years (n = 348 for those enrolled in all four data collection points). Seventy-five percent of the respondents in the first study reported that sex felt as good or better than when they were younger. Results from an analysis restricted to the 278 *married* respondents who had been retained throughout the Duke study revealed that patterns of sexual interest and activity remained fairly stable over time, men reported higher levels of sexual interest and activity than their female age peers, and younger cohorts of respondents reported higher levels of sexual interest and activity.

Compared to earlier studies (e.g., the Kinsey reports), the Starr-Weiner and Duke studies as well as more recent ones have found higher levels of sexual activity among older persons. Accordingly, Riporetella-Muller (1989, p. 214) concluded that "for those elderly who remain sexually active and have a regular partner, the rate of decline is not as great as formerly believed." However, many older persons do not remain sexually active. Indeed, George and Weiler (1981) found, using data from the second Duke study, that of those who were at least fifty-six years of age at the first observation date, 21 percent of men and 39 percent of women reported six years later that they had either abstained from sexual relations throughout the study or were currently inactive.

In a recent study using data from a nationally representative household sample, Marsiglio and Donnelly (forthcoming) found that about 53 percent of all married persons sixty years of age and older reported having coitus within the past month with 65 percent of those sixty to sixty-five years old being sexually active compared to 44 percent of those sixty-six or older. Among those who had been coitally active during the past month, the overall mean frequency for coitus was 4.3 times. In a multivariate context, persons were most likely to have had coitus during the past month if they were younger, married to a spouse who self-reported his or her health status as favorable, and had a higher sense of self-worth and competency. Surprisingly, when an interaction term was used to compare husbands and wives, no significant differences were observed in the way their partner's health status was related to their coital behavior, although other research has found that both husbands and wives report that males' attitudes or physical condition tends to be the principal reason why they have curtailed or ceased to have sexual relations. Meanwhile, other research indicates that being widowed is the most frequently cited reason for not being sexually active among older women overall. While data on persons who are institutionalized are scarce, it appears as though their sexual activity levels are rather low.

Being without a spouse does not necessarily mean that older persons will be sexually inactive. Brecher (1984) reported, for example, that among unmarried persons sixty years of age and older, about 75 percent of men and 50 percent of women were sexually active. These findings are reinforced by Starr and Weiner's (1981) finding that 70 percent of their respondents over sixty were sexually active, although only 47 percent were married. Finally, masturbation is another option used by some elderly to express their sexuality, presumably in a nonsocial setting. A few studies have found that about one-third of women and slightly less than one-half of men over seventy report masturbating.

CONCLUSION

This brief review has documented the extensive efforts of social scientists during recent decades to enhance our understanding of human sexual behavior. Indeed, our knowledge of sexual behavior has increased dramatically since the days of Kinsey's early studies. This review also serves as a reminder, however, that our knowledge about human sexual behavior, in some areas more so than others, remains quite limited. Moreover, our knowledge is a function of both moral and political decisions. Just as social scientists can largely be held accountable for any shortcomings associated with the prevailing theoretical approaches to sexuality issues, the larger society and its institutionalized mechanisms for providing research support, are responsible in various ways for impeding the research community's efforts to understand sexual behavior. Because sexual activity tends to be a highly private social experience, social scientists' incremental advances in documenting and explaining it are linked inevitably to the lay population's commitment to this type of research endeavor.

(SEE ALSO: *Courtship; Sexual Behavior and Marriage; Sexual Orientation; Sexual Violence and Abuse*)

REFERENCES

Baron, Larry, and Murray A. Straus 1987 "Four Theories of Rape: A Macrosociological Analysis." *Social Problems* 34:467–489.

Bentler, P. M., and P. R. Abramson 1980 "Methodological Issues in Sex Research: An Overview." In R. Green and J. Weiner, eds., *Methodological Issues in Sex Research.* Rockville, Md.: National Institute of Mental Health, U.S. Department of Health and Human Services.

Brecher, Edward 1984 *Love, Sex, and Aging: A Consumer Union Report.* Mount Vernon, N.Y.: Consumers Union.

Callero, Peter L., and Judith A. Howard 1989 "Biases of the Scientific Discourse on Human Sexuality: Toward a Sociology of Sexuality." In Kathleen McKinney and Susan Sprecher, eds., *Human Sexuality: The Societal and Interpersonal Context.* Norwood, N.J.: Ablex.

Carrol, Leo 1988 "Concern with AIDS and the Sexual Behavior of College Students." *Journal of Marriage and the Family* 50:405–411.

Check, J. V. P., and N. M. Malamuth 1983 "Sex Role Stereotyping and Reactions to Depictions of Stranger vs. Acquaintance Rape." *Journal of Personality and Social Psychology* 45:344–356.

Debuono, Barbara A., Stephen H. Zinner, Maxim Daamen, and William M. McCormack 1990 *The New England Journal of Medicine* 322:821–825.

Donnenstein, E., and D. Linz 1986 "Mass Media Sexual Violence and Male Viewers." *American Behavioral Scientist* 29:601–618.

Finkelhor, D. 1979 *Sexually Victimized Children.* New York: Free Press.

———, and K. Yllo 1985 *License to Rape.* New York: Holt, Rinehart and Winston.

Ford, Clellan, and F. Beach 1951 *Patterns of Sexual Behavior.* New York: Harper.

Gagnon, John 1977 *Human Sexualities.* Glenview, Ill.: Scott, Foresman.

George, L. K., and S. J. Weiler 1981 "Sexuality in Middle and Late Life." *Archives of General Psychiatry* 38:919–923.

Grauerholz, Elizabeth, and Jennifer Crew Solomon 1989 "Sexual Coercion: Power and Violence." In Kathleen McKinney and Susan Sprecher, eds., *Human Sexuality: The Societal and Interpersonal Context.* Norwood, N.J.: Ablex.

Hass, W. 1979 *Teenage Sexuality.* New York: Macmillan.

Herold, W., and L. Way 1983 "Oral-Genital Sexual Behavior in a Sample of University Females." *The Journal of Sex Research* 19:327–338.

Hofferth, Sandra L. 1987 "Factors Affecting Initiation of Sexual Intercourse." In Sandra L. Hofferth and Cheryl D. Hayes, eds., *Risking the Future: Adolescent Sexuality, Pregnancy, and Childbearing.* Washington, D.C.: National Academy Press.

Hunt, M. 1974 *Sexual Behavior in the 1970s.* Chicago: Playboy Press.

Jayne, C. E. 1986 "Methodology on Sex Research in 1986: An Editor's Commentary." *The Journal of Sex Research* 22:1–5.

Kahn, Joan R., William D. Kalsbeek, and Sandra L. Hofferth 1988 "National Estimates of Teenage Sexual Activity: Evaluating the Comparability of Three National Surveys." *Demography* 25:189–204.

Kelley, Gary F. 1990 *Sexuality Today: The Human Perspective.* Guilford, Conn.: Dushkin Publishing.

Kelley, K. 1986 "Integrating Sex Research." In D. Bryne and K. Kelley, eds., *Alternative Approaches to the Study of Sexual Behavior.* Hillsdale, N.J.: Erlbaum.

Kempe, R. S., and H. Kempe 1984 *The Common Secret: Sexual Abuse of Children and Adolescents.* New York: Freeman and Co.

Kinsey, Alfred, C., Wardell Pomeroy, and Clyde Martin 1948 *Sexual Behavior in the Human Male.* Philadelphia: Saunders.

Kinsey, Alfred, C., Wardell Pomeroy, Clyde Martin, and Paul Gebhard 1953 *Sexual Behavior in the Human Female.* Philadelphia: Saunders.

Koss, Mary, Thomas E. Dinero, Cynthia A. Seibel, and Susan L. Cox 1988 "Stranger and Acquaintance Rape: Are There Differences in the Victim's Experience?" *Psychology of Women Quarterly* 12:1–23.

Koss, Mary, Kenneth E. Leonard, Dana A. Beezley, and Cheryl J. Oros 1985 "Nonstranger Sexual Aggression: A Discriminant Analysis of the Psychological Characteristics of Undetected Offenders." *Sex Roles* 12:981–992.

Ludeman, Kate 1981 "The Sexuality of the Older Person: Review of the Literature." *Gerontologist* 21:203–208.

Marsiglio, William 1988 "Adolescent Male Sexuality and Heterosexual Masculinity: A Conceptual Model and Review." *Journal of Adolescent Research* 3:285–303.

———, and Denise Donnelly forthcoming "Sexual Intercourse in Later Life: A National Study of Married Persons." *Journal of Gerontology.*

Masters, William H., V. E. Johnson, and R. C. Kolodny 1988 *Crisis: Heterosexual Behavior in the Age of AIDS.* New York: Grove Press.

Moore, Kristin Anderson, Christine Winquist Nord, and James L. Peterson 1989 "Nonvoluntary Sexual Activity among Adolescents." *Family Planning Perspectives* 21:110–114.

Mosher, D. L., and R. D. Anderson 1986 "Macho Personality, Sexual Aggression, and Reactions to Guided Imagery of Realistic Rape." *Journal of Research in Personality* 20:77–94.

Muehlenhard, C. L., and L. C. Hollabaugh 1988 "Do Women Sometimes Say No When They Mean Yes: The Prevalence and Correlates of Women's Token Resistance to Sex." *Journal of Personality and Social Psychology* 54:872–879.

Newcomer, S., and J. Udry 1985 "Oral Sex in an Adolescent Population." *Archives of Sexual Behavior* 14:41–46.

Rapaport, K., and B. R. Burkhart 1984 "Personality and Attitudinal Correlates of Sexual Coercive College Males." *Journal of Abnormal Personality* 93:216–221.

Reiss, Ira L. 1986 *Journey into Sexuality: An Exploratory Voyage.* Englewood Cliffs, N.J.: Prentice-Hall.

Riportella-Muller, Roberta 1989 "Sexuality in the Elderly: A Review." In Kathleen McKinney and Susan Sprecher, eds., *Human Sexuality: The Societal and Interpersonal Context.* Norwood, N.J.: Ablex.

Russell, D. E. 1984 *Sexual Exploitation.* Beverly Hills, Calif.: Sage.

Russell, D. E. H., and N. Howell 1982 *Rape in Marriage.* New York: Macmillan.

Scully, D., and J. Marolla 1984 "Convicted Rapists' Vocabulary of Motive: Excuses and Justifications." *Social Problems* 31:530–544.

Simon, William, and John H. Gagnon 1986 "Sexual Scripts: Permanence and Change." *Archives of Sexual Behavior* 15:97–120.

Sonenstein, Freya, Joseph Pleck, and Leighton C. Ku 1989 "Sexual Activity, Condom Use and AIDS Awareness Among Adolescent Males." *Family Planning Perspectives* 21:152–158.

Starr, Bernard D. 1985 "Sexuality and Aging." *Annual Review of Gerontology and Geriatrics* 5:97–126.

———, and Marcella B. Weiner 1981 *The Starr-Weiner Report on Sex and Sexuality in the Mature Years.* Briarcliff Manor, N.Y.: Stein & Day.

Stein, Arlene 1989 "Three Models of Sexuality: Drives,

Identities, and Practices." *Sociological Theory* 7:1–13.

Thorne, Barrie, and Zella Luria 1986 "Sexuality and Gender in Children's Daily Worlds." *Social Problems* 33:176–190.

Udry, J. Richard 1988 "Biological Predispositions and Social Control in Adolescent Sexual Behavior." *American Sociological Review* 53:709–722.

Walsh, Robert H. 1989 "Premarital Sex among Teenagers and Young Adults." In Kathleen McKinney and Susan Sprecher, eds., *Human Sexuality: The Societal and Interpersonal Context.* Norwood, N.J.: Ablex.

Young, M. 1980 "Attitudes and Behaviors of College Students Relative to Oral-Genital Sexuality." *Archives of Sexual Behavior* 9:61–67.

WILLIAM MARSIGLIO
JOHN H. SCANZONI

HISPANIC-AMERICAN STUDIES Despite their common linguistic heritage, Hispanic-Americans are a heterogeneous and rapidly growing population that includes no less than twenty-three distinct national identities and combines recent immigrants with groups whose ancestors predated the formation of the United States as we know it today. In 1989 the U.S. Census Bureau estimated the Hispanic population at 20.1 million, with nearly two-thirds (63 percent) of Mexican origin, while 12 percent traced their origins to Puerto Rico, 5 percent to Cuba, and 13 percent to other Central and South American nations. An additional 8 percent of Hispanics were of unspecified national origin, which includes mixed Spanish-speaking nationalities, Spaniards, and "Hispanos," the descendants of the original Spanish settlers in what came to be known as Colorado and New Mexico.

The two largest groups also have the oldest established communities in the United States, but the Cuban presence is clearly evident in southern Florida and selected neighborhoods of various northeastern and midwestern cities. Furthermore, the late 1970s and 1980s witnessed the proliferation of Central and South American ethnic neighborhoods in various cities across the United States but especially the major cities of southern California, Texas, New York, Florida, and Illinois. Although small Cuban and Puerto Rican communities can be traced back to the turn of the century and before, these settlements were tiny and geographically contained compared to the Mexican presence in the Southwest.

Social science interest in Hispanic-Americans has increased greatly since 1960, and the scope of topics investigated has expanded accordingly. Whereas studies conducted during the 1960s and through the mid-1970s tended to focus on one highly localized population, the 1980s witnessed a proliferation of designs that compared group experiences. This shift in the research agenda brought into focus the theme of diversity and inequality among national origin groups. Beyond cultural, generational, and socioeconomic heterogeneity as a defining feature of Hispanic-Americans, two additional themes stand out in recent writings about this population. One concerns the rate of growth and persisting residential concentration, and the second, which is related to the first, concerns their long-term prospects for social integration. As one of the most rapidly growing minority populations in the United States, the growing Hispanic presence has raised fears about the potential "Latinization" or "Hispanicization" of the United States. Such nativist sentiments are particularly evident in areas where Hispanics are highly concentrated.

Larger numbers are not likely to be the most decisive force shaping the Hispanic imprint on the U.S. ethnic landscape, for size does not automatically confer power. As numbers increase, politics also become increasingly important in determining the social and economic destiny of Hispanic origin groups. To evaluate the likely imprint of Hispanics in the United States, the following article summarizes several themes that have unfolded in the sociological literature on Hispanic-Americans. These include: the changing social and demographic composition of the population; the origin of current ethnic labels; the roots of diversification; and the political implications of recent social and economic trends. A concluding section summarizes key lessons from existing studies and identifies areas for further investigation.

RECENT DEMOGRAPHIC AND SOCIOECONOMIC TRENDS

Until World War II, virtually all people currently classified as Hispanics were of Mexican origin, but after the war this picture changed radically with the advent of heavy migration from Puerto Rico to the Northeast and the arrival of thousands of Cubans in south Florida and the Northeast following the 1959 Cuban Revolution. Although immigration has figured prominently in the growth of the Hispanic population since 1941, its influence on demographic growth has been especially pronounced since 1965. In 1960 the Hispanic population was just under seven million; but by 1980 the population had doubled, and it had tripled by 1990! The significance of this growth—phenomenal by any standard—is accentuated when evaluated against evidence that the growth rate of the non-Hispanic white population has slowed. Hence, by 1989 approximately 8 percent of the U.S. population was Hispanic, compared with 4 percent in 1960.

Consistent with the theme of increasing differentiation along national-origin lines, growth rates differed among the major nationality groups. Owing to continued high fertility and heavy immigration during the 1980s, the Mexican share of the total rose from 60 to 63 percent, while the Puerto Rican share declined from 14 to 12 percent. This decline resulted from lower fertility and the absence of a strong net inmigration flow from the island. Furthermore, as immigration from Central and South America continued, these groups increased their shares of the Hispanic population from 7 to 12 percent. This increase in population shares was also accompanied by changes in the country-of-origin composition. By 1980 over one in three Hispanics from Central America and the Caribbean traced their origins to the Dominican Republic, compared to less than one in five two decades earlier. When military and political events in Central America escalated during the 1980s, the presence of immigrants from El Salvador, Guatemala, and Nicaragua also began to rise. However, the future prospects of these flows remain highly uncertain.

The visibility of distinct Hispanic communities is heightened by persisting regional concentration along national origin lines. Two states—California and Texas—housed half of all Hispanics in 1989, with Mexicans and Central Americans disproportionately concentrated in these states. Despite some tendency toward residential dispersion, Puerto Ricans remain concentrated in the Northeast—predominantly in the large cities of New York and New Jersey—while Cubans have become bimodally distributed in south Florida and large northeastern cities (Bean and Tienda 1987). Residential segregation compounds geographic concentration further by spatially isolating some Hispanics—particularly those of low socioeconomic status and recent immigrant groups—from non-Hispanic whites. This segregation reinforces the cultural distinctiveness of Hispanics in regions where visible communities have been established.

A social and economic profile of the Hispanic population since 1960 provides signals of optimism and pessimism about the long-term economic prospects of distinct nationality groups. Trends in educational attainment are quite revealing in themselves and in terms of their implications for labor-market prospects. On the one hand, from 1960 to 1988 Hispanics witnessed an unmistakable improvement in their educational achievement. On the other hand, high school noncompletion rates remain disturbingly high for Mexicans and Puerto Ricans—the two groups with the longest history in the United States. That Cubans outperform these two groups undermines simplistic explanations that immigration and language are the reasons for the continued educational underachievement of Mexicans and Puerto Ricans.

These educational disadvantages carry into the labor market. Since 1960 the labor-force standing of Puerto Rican men and women has deteriorated, while Cubans have become virtually indistinguishable from non-Hispanic whites in terms of participation rates, unemployment rates, and occupational profiles. Mexicans stand somewhere between these extremes, with greater success than Puerto Ricans in securing employment. However, Mexicans are more highly represented among the working poor than are whites. Puerto Rican men witnessed unusually high rates of labor-force withdrawal during the 1970s, and their labor-force behavior has converged with that of economically disadvantaged blacks (Tienda 1989). Numerous explanations have been provided for the deteriorating labor-market position of Puerto Ricans, including the unusually sharp decline of manufacturing jobs in the Northeast; the decline of union jobs in which Puerto Ricans traditionally concentrated; increased labor-market competition with Colombian and Dominican immigrants; and the placement of Puerto Rican workers at the bottom of a labor queue. However, empirical tests of these working hypotheses—all of which have merit—have not been forthcoming.

Less debatable than the causes of weakened labor-market position are its economic consequences. During the 1970s median family incomes of blacks and whites respectively increased 8 and 6 percent in real terms, compared with increases of 18 and 20 percent enjoyed by Mexicans and Cubans. However, during this same decade, family incomes of Puerto Ricans and Central and South Americans weathered real declines of about 4 to 6 percent (Tienda and Jensen 1988). For the latter, this decline can be traced to changes in the class composition of recent immigrants coupled with deleterious effects of the recession of the early 1980s. Again, the reasons for the decline in Puerto Rican incomes are more perplexing and in any event must be associated with the weakened labor-market standing of this group. It is also unclear why the deleterious effects of recessions take their heaviest toll on minority groups, but this phenomenon is consistent with the premises of queuing theory, which claims that groups at the bottom of a status hierarchy will benefit most from economic expansion and lose most from economic contraction (Lieberson 1980). The merits of this perspective have yet to be explored systematically with Hispanic groups.

ETHNIC LABELS AMIDST DIVERSITY

Ethnic labels are partly imposed by the host society and partly taken by immigrant groups who wish to preserve their national identity. The labels *Spanish Origin* and *Hispanic* originally were coined as terms of convenience for official reporting purposes. Essentially these labels serve as an umbrella to identify persons of Latin American origin who reside in the United States. Before the mid-1960s, Hispanics were unfamiliar to most observers outside the Southwest, where persons of Mexican ancestry were well represented, and the Northeast, where Puerto Rican communities began to flourish after World War II. Therefore, until 1960 the "Spanish-surname" concept was adequate for identifying persons of Mexican origin residing in the Southwest, and "Puerto Rican stock" was used to identify persons who resided in the Northeast (predominantly New York) and who were born in or whose parents were born in Puerto Rico. However, with increasing intermarriage and residential dispersion, these concepts became progressively less useful to identify persons from Mexico and Puerto Rico. Furthermore, the influx of immigrants from Central and South America and the Spanish-speaking Caribbean into areas traditionally inhabited by Mexicans and Puerto Ricans required labels that could better represent the growing diversity along national origin lines.

In recognition of the growing residential and marital heterogeneity of the Spanish-speaking population, in 1970 the U.S. Census Bureau adopted the "Spanish Origin concept," which was based on self-identification and could be administered to the U.S. population on a national level (Bean and Tienda 1987). And in 1980 the term *Hispanic* accompanied *Spanish Origin* on the census schedule to identify persons from Latin America. However, through the 1980s the term *Latino* came into popular use as an alternative to *Hispanic.* As a symbol of self-determination and self-definition, it is the label preferred by many ethnic scholars—second, of course, to specific national identities. The label *Hispanic* was used in the 1990 census to identify persons from Latin America (except Brazil) and Spain, or whose ancestors were traced to these countries, but whether the label *Latino* will appear in the census of 2000 remains to be seen.

Despite their popular use and administrative legitimacy, generic terms such as *Latino* or *Hispanic* are less precise ethnic labels than Puerto Rican, Venezuelan, Cuban, or Mexican. In fact, the considerable socioeconomic and generational diversity of Hispanic-Americans undermines the value of a common ethnic label—except for administrative efficiency. The diverse immigration histories and settlement patterns of Mexicans, Puerto Ricans, Cubans, and persons from Central and South America manifest themselves in distinct subpopulations with clearly discernible social and economic profiles and with apparently unequal opportunities to succeed. Not surprisingly, diversity along national origin lines became a major intellectual theme in the scholarly writings about Hispanics during the mid- to late 1980s.

THE ROOTS OF DIVERSITY

The cultural and socioeconomic heterogeneity of Hispanic-Americans can be traced to the diverse modes of incorporation into the United States. Nelson and Tienda (1985) proposed a framework for conceptualizing the emergence, consolidation, and persistence of distinct Hispanic ethnicities. They identified three domains of immigrant incorporation that are pertinent for understanding socioeconomic stratification of Hispanics: (1) the mode of entry, namely whether groups were colonized or migrated voluntarily; (2) the mode of integration, that is, the climate of reception at the time of mass entrance to the host society; and (3) the reaffirmation of national origin. The latter emphasizes the distinction between the cultural or symbolic content of Hispanic origin and the economic consequences of ethnicity that result in the formation of minority groups. This distinction between the economic and the cultural underpinnings of Hispanic national origins is pertinent for theorizing about the long-term integration prospects of Hispanics.

Along these three domains of ethnic incorporation, the major national origin groups exhibit considerable diversity. For example, the origin of the Mexican and Puerto Rican communities can be traced to annexation, although the timing and particulars of both cases were quite distinct. The annexation of Mexican territory resulted from a political settlement subsequent to military struggle and was followed by massive and voluntary wage-labor migration throughout the twentieth century, but particularly after 1960. The Puerto Rican annexation will remain an incomplete process until statehood or independence is achieved, but, like the Mexican experience, it was characterized by a massive wage-labor flow well after Puerto Rico was officially made a Commonwealth of the United States.

These distinct modes of incorporation are sharpened by the Cuban experience, whose socioeconomic success is as striking as the socioeconomic failure of Puerto Ricans. The Cuban community was established by political events that eventuated in the creation of a wave of political refugees who were themselves differentiated by social classes. The so-called golden exile cohort, which virtually gutted the Cuban middle class, was followed by the exodus of skilled and semiskilled workers who made up the vast majority of Cuban emigres. Although the distinction between political and economic migrants is murky, unlike wage-labor migrants, political refugees commanded immediate acceptance from the host society, however symbolic in character. Hence, the Cuban experience also stands in sharp contrast to that of recent political refugees from Central America (Guatemala and El Salvador, primarily) whose refugee story is one of clandestine entry and extended legal and political struggles for recognition. These groups have yet to be officially recognized as political refugees.

Immigration from Central and South America has continued to diversify not only the country-of-origin composition of the Hispanic population but also the socioeconomic position of the various groups. However, the future role of immigration in stratifying the Hispanic population is highly uncertain, as these depend both on changes in U.S. foreign policy toward Central and South America and on revisions in immigration policy concerning the disposition of undocumented aliens and quotas on future admissions. Nonetheless, a comparison of wage-labor migration histories of Hispanics clearly illustrates how diverse modes of entry and integration fueled the diversification of Hispanic-Americans.

Ethnic reaffirmation and consolidation can best be understood as immigrant minority communities define themselves vis-a-vis the host society. For groups who were relatively successful in adapting to the host society, such as Cubans, national heritage acquired a highly symbolic character, used for economic relationships when expedient and downplayed otherwise. Alternatively, for immigrants destined to become minorities, class position and national origin become inextricably linked when social opportunities are limited or blocked altogether, as seems to have occurred for Mexicans and especially Puerto Ricans, or when illegal status forces many underground, as occurred among large segments of the Dominican, Colombian, and Mexican labor pools. Thus, the distinction between symbolic ethnicity and minority status revolves around the degree of choice groups have in controlling their socioeconomic destiny (Gans 1979; Vincent 1974). This distinction is pertinent for understanding the increasing socioeconomic and demographic heterogeneity among Hispanic-Americans.

INTEGRATION PROSPECTS

The changing demography of Hispanics has direct implications for the integration of Hispanic immigrant minority groups. First, the rapid growth and residential concentration of the groups raise questions about the prospects for assimilation of Hispanics. Second, the rising salience of immigration as a component of demographic growth serves to revitalize Hispanic cultures even as earlier arrivals are culturally assimilated, while also reactivating nativist sentiments when economic opportunities shrink and Hispanic immigrants are seen to be in competition for jobs.

Puerto Ricans are U.S. citizens by definition and enjoy most of the privileges that citizenship confers, while Mexicans who enter legally must wait at least five years to apply for citizenship. Those who enter illegally continue to have an uncertain status in the United States. That Puerto Ricans have been less successful economically than Mexicans places in question the significance of citizenship as a requisite for socioeconomic integration. The newest wage-labor migrants—Colombians, Dominicans, and some Central Americans—seem to be faring better than Puerto Ricans, posing yet another challenge to conventional understandings about immigrant assimilation processes, but it is too early to determine their placement in the ethnic queue because the process of assignment appears to be quite fluid. Furthermore, the growing number of illegals among these groups could undermine their political leverage over the short to medium term.

Although it is difficult to predict the long-term integration prospects of any group, the diversity of the Hispanic experience complicates this task further because of the uncertain future of immigration and the state of the economy and because the political participation of Hispanics traditionally has been low. While the spatial concentration of Hispanics allows native languages to flourish and under some circumstances promotes ethnic enterprises, some observers interpret the rise and proliferation of ethnic neighborhoods as evidence of limited integration prospects, irrespective of whether the segregation is voluntary or involuntary. An alternative interpretation of rising residential segregation among Hispanics is that of ethnic resilience. This perspective maintains that in the face of interethnic tension and economic adversity, individuals rely on their ethnic compatriots for social supports and hence promote solidarity along ethnic lines. One implication of this view is that ethnic resilience is the *consequence* rather than the *cause* of unequal integration prospects, and their tendency to elaborate ethnic ties reflects their tentative acceptance by the dominant society. As such, ethnic traits become enduring rather than transitional features of Hispanic neighborhoods (Portes and Bach 1980).

A similar debate over the integration prospects of Hispanics clouds the issue of Spanish retention, which is politically significant because it provides a ready target for policies designed to assimilate linguistically diverse populations and because Spanish retention is a ready scapegoat for the poor educational achievement of Mexicans and Puerto Ricans. While there exists considerable controversy about the socioeconomic consequences of bilingualism, the preponderance of research shows that Spanish retention and bilingualism per se are not the sources of Hispanic underachievement. Rather, the failure to acquire proficiency in English is the source of underachievement. In support of the distinction between bilingualism and lack of proficiency in English, there is some evidence that bilingualism may be an asset, albeit only among the middle classes who are able to convert this skill to social and financial resources (Lopez 1976; Tienda 1982). The failure of many Hispanics to achieve proficiency in English certainly limits their economic opportunities, but it is facile to equate lack of proficiency in English with bilingualism, which does not preclude proficiency in English.

Finally, the socioeconomic prospects of the Hispanic population depend on whether and how groups from specific localities or national origin groups mobilize themselves to serve ethnic interests. The record on Hispanic political participation shows great room for improvement. While Hispanics compose 8 percent of the total population, they hold less than 2 percent of elected offices and hold less than 2 percent of the seats available in Congress (*Southwest Voter Research Notes* 1989). Obviously, Hispanics do not represent a unified political force nationally, and the fragility of their coalitions could easily be undermined by the trend toward greater socioeconomic inequality. Furthermore, greater numbers are insufficient to guarantee increased representation, particularly for a population with a large number of persons under voting age, coupled with low rates of naturalization and, among eligible voters, a dismal record at the polls. That voter turnout also varies by national origin will further divide the fragile Hispanic political alliances, such as the Hispanic Caucus, by splitting the Hispanic vote along class and party lines.

SUMMARY

Several lessons can be culled from the scholarly literature and public discourse over the social and economic future of Hispanic-Americans. One is that generic labels, like *Hispanic* and *Latino,* are not useful for portraying the heterogeneous socioeconomic integration experiences of the Hispanic national origin groups. A second major lesson is that the evolving differentials in economic standing of Hispanic national origin groups are rooted in the distinct *modes of incorporation* of each group, which in turn have profound implications for integration prospects. A third major lesson, which is related to the second, is that the socioeconomic imprint of Hispanic-Americans will be as varied as the population itself. Changes in immigrant composition and residential segregation will play decisive parts in determining how Hispanics shape the ethnic landscape of the United States into the twenty-first century.

The nagging question is: Why does there persist a close association between Hispanic national origin and low social standing? On this matter there is much debate, but both sides accord great emphasis to the role of immigration in deciding the socioeconomic destiny of Hispanic-Americans. One interpretation—the replenishment argument—emphasizes how immigration continues to diversify the composition of the population by introducing new arrivals on the lower steps of a social escalator, while earlier arrivals experience gradual improvements in their economic and social statuses. Consistent with the predictions of classical assimilation theory, this view implies that observed differences in socioeconomic standing among Hispanics will disappear with time, irrespective of country of origin or period of arrival. Lending support to this prediction is a growing body of evidence showing that later arrivals fare better in the U.S. labor market and social institutions than do earlier arrivals.

Despite some compelling aspects of the replenishment argument, it falls short of accounting for the limited social mobility of Mexicans and Puerto Ricans, the two groups with the longest exposure to U.S. institutions and traditions. These experiences challenge the replenishment argument and place greater emphasis on the complex set of circumstances that define distinct modes of incorporation for the major national origin groups and entry cohorts. The structural interpretation emphasizes the role of unique historical circumstances under which each national origin group established its presence in the United States and acknowledges that social opportunities depend greatly on the state of the economy and public receptiveness toward new arrivals.

Unfortunately, it is too early to evaluate the relative merits of the two hypotheses, especially in the absence of longitudinal data required to trace socioeconomic trajectories of successive generations. That the future of immigration (its volume, source countries, and composition) is highly indeterminate further aggravates the difficulties of assessing these hypotheses. Of course, the greatest uncertainty about immigration concerns the flow of illegal migrants—both in terms of its volume and source countries. Finally, the socioeconomic fate of Hispanic-Americans as a whole and as separate national origin groups will depend also on the extent to which Hispanic elected and appointed officials use ethnicity as a criterion for defining their political agendas. The 1990s will be pivotal in resolving these uncertainties.

(SEE ALSO: *Discrimination; Ethnicity*)

REFERENCES

Bean, Frank D., and Marta Tienda 1987 *The Hispanic Population of the United States.* New York: Russell Sage Foundation.

Gans, Herbert J. 1979 "Symbolic Ethnicity: The Future of Ethnic Groups and Cultures in America." *Ethnic and Racial Studies* 2:1–19.

Lieberson, Stanley 1980 *A Piece of the Pie.* Berkeley: University of California Press.

Lopez, David E. 1976 "The Social Consequences of Home/School Bilingualism." *Social Problems* 24: 234–246.

Nelson, Candace, and Marta Tienda 1985 "The Structuring of Hispanic Ethnicity: Historical and Contemporary Perspectives." *Ethnic and Racial Studies* 8: 49–74.

Portes, Alejandro, and Robert L. Bach 1980 *Latin Journey.* Berkeley: University of California Press.

Southwest Voter Research Notes 1989 Vol. 3, No. 2. October.

Tienda, Marta 1982 "Sex, Ethnicity, and Chicano Status Attainment." *International Migration Review* 16:435–472.

——— 1989 "Puerto Ricans and the Underclass Debate." *Annals of the American Academy of Political and Social Sciences* 501:105–119.

———, and Leif I. Jensen 1988 "Poverty and Minorities: A Quarter-Century Profile of Color and Socioeconomic Disadvantage." In Gary D. Sandefur and Marta Tienda, eds., *Divided Opportunities.* New York: Plenum Press.

Vincent, Joan 1974 "The Structuring of Ethnicity." *Human Organization* 33:375–379.

MARTA TIENDA

HISTORICAL ANALYSIS *See* Comparative-Historical Analysis; Event-History Analysis; Historical Sociology.

HISTORICAL SOCIOLOGY Used as a category to identify social scientific research that constructs or illustrates theory by careful attention to culturally, geographically, and temporally located facts, historical sociology (or from the historian's vantage point, sociological history) exists as a self-conscious research orientation within both of its parent disciplines. Popular assertions in the 1950s and 1960s that history involved the study of particular facts while sociology involved the formulation of general hypotheses (see Lipset 1968, pp. 22–23; cf. Mills 1959, pp. 143–164) had turned around by the early 1980s, at which time Abrams claimed that "sociological explanation is necessarily historical" (Abrams 1982, p. 2; see Burke 1980, p. 28).

Abrams's claim is true for much of sociological theorizing, and sociologists realize that seminal research in their discipline has been informed by careful attention to historical information. Nonetheless, fundamental differences exist between history and sociology regarding the choice of research strategies and methodologies. Historical research emphasizes the sociocultural context of events and actors within the broad range of human culture, and when examining events that occurred in early periods of the human record it borrows from archeology and cultural anthropology, two companion disciplines. Historians, therefore, who examine premodern material often borrow anthropological rather than sociological insights to elucidate areas where the historical record is weak, under the assumption that preindustrialized societies share basic similarities that sociological theory rarely addresses (Thomas 1963; 1971; cf. Thompson 1972). Historians are likely to choose research topics that are culturally and temporally delimited and that emerge "from the logic of events of a given place and period" (Smelser 1968, p. 35; see Bonnell 1980, p. 159). They tend to supplement secondary sources with primary texts or archival data (see Tilly 1981, p. 12).

In contrast, sociological research stresses theory construction and development, and its heavy emphasis on quantification limits most of its research to issues that affect societies after they begin to modernize or industrialize (and hence develop accurate record keeping that researchers can translate into data [see Burke 1980, p. 22]). Many of their methodological techniques—including surveys, interviews, qualitative fieldwork, questionnaires, various statistical procedures, and social-psychological experimentation—have little if any applicability to historians (Wilson 1971, p. 106). Given their orientation toward theory, sociologists are likely to choose research topics that are "rooted in and generated by some conceptual apparatus" (Smelser 1968, p. 35; Bonnell 1980, p. 159). Their data sources infrequently involve archival searches (see Schwartz 1987, p. 12) or heavy dependence on primary texts. Sociologists seem more willing than historians both to "undertake comparative analysis across national and temporal boundaries" and to present generalizations that relate to either a number of cases or universal phenomena (as opposed to a single case [Bonnell 1980, p. 159]). Reflecting these basic differences, social history, which developed out of the historical discipline, concentrates on speaking about lived experiences, while traditional historical sociologists concentrate on analyzing structural transformations (Skocpol 1987, p. 28).

Although some historical sociological studies attempt either to refine concepts or rigorously to test existing theoretical explanations, more often they attempt "to develop new theories capable of providing more convincing and comprehensive explanations for historical patterns and structures" (Bonnell 1980, p. 161). When testing existing theories, historical sociologists argue deductively (by attempting to locate evidence that supports or refutes theoretical propositions), case-comparatively (by juxtaposing examples from equivalent units), or case-illustratively (by comparing cases to a single theory or concept [Bonnell 1980, pp. 162–167]). Both case comparisons and case illustrations can show either that cases share a common set of "hypothesized causal factors" that adequately explain similar historical outcomes or that they contain crucial differences that lead to divergent historical results (Skocpol 1984, pp. 378–379).

Sociology's founding figures—Marx and Engels, Weber, Tocqueville, and, to a limited degree, Durkheim—utilized history in the formulation of concepts and research agendas that still influence the discipline. In various works Marx and Engels demonstrated adroit sociohistorical skills, particularly in *The Eighteenth Brumaire of Louis Bonaparte* (Marx [1885] 1963) and *The Peasant War in Germany* (Engels 1870). In these studies they moved deftly among analyses of "short-term, day-to-day phenomena" of socio-political life, the underlying structure of that life, and "the level of the social structure as a whole" (Abrams 1982, p. 59) to provide powerful examples of historically grounded materialist analysis (see Abrams 1982, p. 63; Sztompka 1986, p. 325).

Weber, who was steeped in ancient and medieval history of both the East and West, believed that through the use of heuristically useful ideal types, researchers could "understand on the one hand the relationships and cultural significance of individual events in their contemporary manifestations and on the other the causes of their being historically *so* and not *otherwise*" (Weber 1949, p. 72). However much contemporary researchers have faulted his *Protestant Ethic and the Spirit of Capitalism* (1930) for misunderstanding Puritan religious traditions (MacKinnon 1988a, 1988b; Kent 1990) and interpreting them through preexisting philosophical categories (Kent 1983, 1985), it remains the quintessential example of his historically informed sociological studies (see Marshall 1982).

Variously assessed as a historian and a political scientist, Tocqueville also contributed to historical sociology with books that examined two processes —democratization (in the United States) and political centralization (in France)—that remain standard topics of historical sociological research (Tocqueville [1835] 1969, [1858] 1955; see Sztompka 1986, p. 325; Poggi 1972). Similar praise, however, for historical sensitivity has not always gone to a fellow Frenchmen of a later era, Emile Durkheim, whose concepts were scornfully called by one historical sociologist an "early form of ahistoricism" (Sztompka 1986, p. 324). Bellah, nevertheless, asserted that "history was always of central importance in Durkheim's sociological work" (Bellah 1959, p. 153), and even argued that "at several points Durkheim went so far as to question whether or not sociology and history could in fact be considered two separate disciplines" (Bellah 1959, p. 154). Abrams's compromise interpretation may be most accurate; he acknowledges that Durkheim identified the broad process of the Western transition to industrialization, even though his "extremely general framework" demands specific historical elaboration (Abrams 1982, p. 32).

Despite the prominence of history within major studies by sociology's founding figures, subsequent sociologists produced few historically informed works until the late 1950s (cf. Merton 1938). Also during this period (in 1958) the historian Sylvia Thrupp founded the journal *Comparative Studies in Society and History*, and since then other journals have followed that are sympathetic to historical sociology (including *Journal of Family History, Journal of Interdisciplinary History, Journal of Social History, Labor History, Social History, Social Science History, Journal of Historical Sociology*, and *Past and Present* [Bart and Frankel 1986, pp. 114–116]). The output of interdisciplinary books continued growing throughout the 1960s, and by the 1970s "the sociological study of history achieved full status within the discipline" (Bonnell 1980, p. 157; see p. 156).

Four research areas that currently produce the most respected historical sociology studies include capitalist expansion, "the growth of national states and systems of states," collective action (Tilly 1981, p. 44), and the sociology of religious development.

Studies of capitalist expansion examine such topics as the emergence and consequences of the Industrial Revolution, the rise of the working class, population growth, and the developmental operations of the modern world system. Exemplary studies include Smelser's *Social Change in the Industrial Revolution* (1959) and Wallerstein's *The Modern World System* (1974). Basing his middle-range model upon Parsons's general theory of action, Smelser deduced a supposedly universal sequence through which all changes move that involve structural differentiation in industrializing societies (see Bonnell 1980, p. 162; Skocpol 1984, p. 363). He illustrated the applicability of his framework by drawing examples from the economic changes within the British cotton industry during the nineteenth century, followed by additional examples of changes to the lives and activities of workers in that industry. These historical facts, however, were secondary to the model itself.

Wallerstein borrowed from Marxism and functionalism to devise a "world system" theory of the global economy that purports to be universal in its interpretive and explanatory power. He argued that after the late fifteenth and early sixteenth centuries, a "world economy" developed in which economically advantaged and politically strong areas called "core states" dominated other, economically nondiversified and politically weak "peripheral areas." Through "semi-peripheral areas" that serve as "middle trading groups in an empire," resources flow out of the peripheral areas and into the core states for capitalist development, consumption, and often export back to their areas of origin (Wallerstein 1974, pp. 348–350). Within this model Wallerstein mustered a phalanx of historical facts in order to demonstrate the emergence of the world economy above the limited events in various nation-states, and in doing so he "has promoted serious historical work within sociology" (Tilly 1981, p. 42).

E. P. Thompson's exemplary study (1963) took the sociological concept of "class" and presented its historical unfolding in England between 1780 and passage of the parliamentary Reform Bill in 1832 (Thompson 1963, p. 11). He argued that "the finest-meshed sociological net cannot give us a pure specimen of class. . . . The relationship [of class] must always be embodied in real people and in a real context" (p. 9). By the end of the era that he examined, "a more clearly-defined class consciousness, in the customary Marxist sense, was maturing, in which working people were aware of continuing both old and new battles on their own" (p. 712). His study stands among the finest examples of historically careful development of a sociological concept.

In contrast to the economic focus of issues involving capitalist expansion, studies of the growth of national states and systems of states examine political topics such as state bureaucratization, the democratization of politics, revolutions, and the interaction of nations in the international arena. Three heralded historical sociology studies in this genre are Eisenstadt (1963), Moore (1966), and Skocpol (1979). Eisenstadt studied twenty-two preindustrial states that had centralized, impersonal, bureaucratic empires through which political power operated. After a tightly woven and systematic analysis of comparative social, political, and bureaucratic patterns, he concluded that "in any of the historical bureaucratic societies, their continued prominence was dependent upon the nature of the political process that developed in the society: first, on the policies of the rulers; second, on the orientations, goals, and political activities of the principal strata; and third, on the interrelations between these two" (Eisenstadt 1963, p. 362).

Moore's case studies of revolutions in England, France, the United States, China, Japan, and India sought "to understand the role of the landed upper classes and peasants in the bourgeois revolutions leading to capitalist democracy, the abortive bourgeois revolutions leading to fascism, and the peasant revolutions leading to communism" (Moore 1966, p. xvii). His own sympathies, however, lay in the development of political and social systems that fostered freedom, and he realized the importance of "a violent past" in the development of English, French, and American democracies (pp. 39, 108, 153). He concluded "that an independent nobility is an essential ingredient in the growth of democracy" (p. 417) yet realized that a nobility's efforts to free itself from royal controls "is highly unfavorable to the Western version of democracy," unless these efforts occur in the context of a bourgeois revolution (p. 418).

Skocpol scrutinized the "causes and processes" of social revolutions in France, Russia, and China "from a nonvoluntarist, structural perspective, attending to international and world-historical, as well as intranational, structures and processes." While doing so she moved "states—understood as potentially autonomous organizations located at the interface of class structures and international situations—to the very center of attention" (Skocpol, 1979, p. 33). She concluded that "revolutionary political crises, culminating in administrative and military breakdowns, emerged because the imperial states became caught in cross-pressures between intensified military competition or intrusions from abroad and constraints imposed on monarchical responses by the existing agrarian class structures and political institutions" (p. 285).

Virtually unnoticed by theorists of historical sociology is the growing number of studies that apply sociological categories and concepts to the emergence and development of historically significant religious traditions (see Swatos 1977). By doing so, these scholars have surpassed the traditional sociological and historical colleagues who limit their efforts primarily to political and structural issues, especially ones arising during the late eighteenth to twentieth centuries. Swanson (1960), for example, coded material on fifty hunting and gathering societies in an effort to connect religion and magic to social structure and subsequently analyzed relationships between constitutional structures and religious beliefs around the period of the Protestant Reformation (Swanson 1967). The emergence and early development of major religious traditions has received considerable sociological attention—for example, analyses of early Christianity as a social movement (Blasi 1988) and a millenarian movement (Gager 1975; see Meeks 1983, pp. 173–180; Lang 1989, p. 339). Concepts from sociological studies of modern sectarianism have informed historical studies of Mahayana Buddhism (Kent 1982) and Valentinian Gnosticism (Green 1982). Weberian examinations continue to influence historically grounded studies of numerous world religions including ancient Judaism (Zeitlin 1984), Islam (Turner 1974) and additional religious traditions from around the world (see Swatos 1990).

The historically grounded research in the sociology of religion, along with the works of Eisenstadt and others, suggests that future historical sociological studies will continue pushing beyond the confines of modern, macrosociological topics and into a wide range of premodern historical areas. Likewise, historical issues likely will become more consciously developed in microsociological studies (see Abrams 1982, pp. 227–266), and there will appear more sociologically informed historical examinations of cultural development (still exemplified by Elias 1978). Nonetheless, considerable macrosociological research still needs to be performed on historical issues affecting preindustrializing and third world countries as well as on recent international realignments between forms of capitalism and communism.

(SEE ALSO: *Comparative-Historical Analysis; Event History Analysis*)

REFERENCES

Abrams, Philip 1982 *Historical Sociology.* Shepton Mallet, England: Open House.

Bart, Pauline, and Linda Frankel 1986 *The Student Sociologist's Handbook,* 4th ed. New York: Random House.

Bellah, Robert N. 1959 "Durkheim and History." *American Sociological Review* 24:447–461. Reprinted in Robert A. Nisbet, ed., *Émile Durkheim,* Englewood Cliffs, N.J.: Prentice-Hall, 1965.

Bendix, Reinhard 1956 *Work and Authority in Industry: Ideologies of Management in the Course of Industrialization.* New York: Wiley.

Blasi, Anthony J. 1988 *Early Christianity as a Social Movement.* New York: Peter Lang.

Bonnell, Victoria E. 1980 "The Uses of Theory, Concepts, and Comparison in Historical Sociology." *Comparative Studies in Society and History* 22:156–173.

Burke, Peter 1980 *Sociology and History.* London: George Allen and Unwin.

Eisenstadt, S. N. 1963 *The Political Systems of Empires.* New York: The Free Press.

Elias, Norbert 1978 *The Civilizing Process.* Vol. 1, *The History of Manners.* Edmund Jephcott, trans. New York: Urizen Books.

Engels, Frederick [1870] 1926 *The Peasant War in Germany.* 2nd ed. Moissaye J. Olgin, trans. New York: International Publishers.

Gager, John G. 1975 *Kingdom and Community: The Social World of Early Christianity.* Englewood Cliffs, N.J.: Prentice Hall.

Green, Henry A. 1982 "Ritual in Valentinian Gnosticism: A Sociological Interpretation." *Journal of Religious History* 12:109–124.

Kent, Stephen A. 1982 "A Sectarian Interpretation of the Rise of Mahayana." *Religion* 12:311–332.

——— 1983 "Weber, Goethe, and the Nietzschean Allusion." *Sociological Analysis* 44:297–319.

——— 1985 "Weber, Goethe, and William Penn." *Sociological Analysis* 46:315–320.

——— 1990 "The Quaker Ethic and the Fixed Price Policy: Max Weber and Beyond." In William H.

Swatos, ed., *Time, Place, and Circumstance: Neo-Weberian Studies in Comparative Religious History.* Westport, Conn.: Greenwood Press.

Lang, Graeme 1989 "Oppression and Revolt in Ancient Palestine: The Evidence in Jewish Literature from the Prophets to Josephus." *Sociological Analysis* 49:325–342.

Lipset, Seymour Martin 1950 *Agrarian Socialism: The Cooperative Commonwealth Federation in Saskatchewan.* Berkeley: University of California Press.

———1968 "History and Sociology: Some methodological considerations." In Seymour Martin Lipset and Richard Hofstadter, eds. *Sociology and History: Methods.* New York: Basic Books.

MacKinnon, Malcolm H. 1988a "Calvinism and the Infallible Assurance of Grace: The Weber Thesis Reconsidered." *British Journal of Sociology* 39:143–177.

———1988b "Weber's Exploration of Calvinism." *British Journal of Sociology* 39:178–210.

Marshall, Gordon 1982 *In Search of the Spirit of Capitalism: An Essay on Max Weber's Protestant Ethic Thesis.* New York: Columbia University Press.

Marx, Karl (1885) 1963 *The Eighteenth Brumaire of Louis Bonaparte.* 3rd ed. New York: International Publishers.

Meeks, Wayne A. 1983 *The First Urban Christians: The Social World of the Apostle Paul.* New Haven: Yale University Press.

Merton, Robert 1938 "Science, Technology, and Society in Seventeenth-Century England." *Osiris* 4:360–632. Reprinted with a new preface, New York: Harper Torchbooks, 1970.

Mills, C. Wright 1959 *The Sociological Imagination.* New York: Oxford University Press.

Moore, Barrington, Jr. 1967 *Social Origins of Dictatorship and Democracy.* Boston: Beacon Press.

Poggi, Gianfranco 1972 *Images of Society: Essays on the Sociological Theories of Tocqueville, Marx, and Durkheim.* Stanford, Calif.: Stanford University Press.

Schwartz, Mildred A. 1987 "Historical Sociology in the History of American Sociology." *Social Science History* 11:1–16.

Skocpol, Theda 1979 *States and Social Revolutions.* London: Cambridge University Press.

———1984 "Emerging Agendas and Recurrent Strategies in Historical Sociology." In Theda Skocpol, ed., *Vision and Method in Historical Sociology.* Cambridge: Cambridge University Press.

———1987 "Social History and Historical Sociology: Contrasts and Complementarities." *Social Science History* 11:17–30.

Smelser, Neil, J. 1959 *Social Change in the Industrial Revolution: An Application to of Theory to the British Cotton Industry.* Chicago: University of Chicago Press.

———1968 *Essays in Sociological Explanation.* Englewood Cliffs, N.J.: Prentice-Hall.

Swanson, Guy 1960 *The Birth of the Gods: The Origin of Primitive Beliefs.* Ann Arbor: University of Michigan Press.

———1967 *Religion and Regime: A Sociological Account of the Reformation.* Ann Arbor: University of Michigan Press.

Swatos, William H., Jr. 1977 "The Comparative Method and the Special Vocation of the Sociology of Religion." *Sociological Analysis* 38:106–114.

———. ed. 1990. *Time, Place, and Circumstance: Neo-Weberian Studies in Comparative Religious History.* Westport, Conn.: Greenwood Press.

Sztompka, Piotr 1986 "The Renaissance of Historical Orientation in Sociology." *International Sociology* 1:321–337.

Thomas, Keith 1963 "History and Anthropology." *Past and Present* 24:3–24.

———1971 *Religion and the Decline of Magic.* New York: Scribner's.

Thompson, E. P. 1972 "Anthropology and the Discipline of Historical Context." *Midland History* 1:41–55.

Tilly, Charles 1981 *As Sociology Meets History.* New York: Academic Press.

Tocqueville, Alexis de (1835) 1969 *Democracy in America,* 2 vols. George Lawrence, trans. London: Collins.

———(1858) 1955 *The Old Regime and the French Revolution* 4th ed. Stuart Gilbert, trans. Garden City, N. Y.: Doubleday.

Turner, Bryan S. 1974 *Weber and Islam: A Critical Study.* London: Routledge and Kegan Paul.

Wallerstein, Immanuel 1974 *The Modern World System.* New York: Academic Press.

Weber, Max 1930 *The Protestant Ethic and the Spirit of Capitalism.* Talcott Parsons, trans. and ed. New York: Scribners.

———1949 *The Methodology of the Social Sciences.* E. Shils and F. Finch, trans. and ed. New York: Free Press.

Wilson, B. R. 1971 "Sociological Methods in the Study of History." *Transactions of the Royal Historical Society* (5th ser.) 21:101–118.

Zeitlin, Irving 1984 *Ancient Judaism: Biblical Criticism from Max Weber to the Present.* New York: Polity Press.

STEPHEN A. KENT

HOMELESSNESS *Literal* homelessness—lacking permanent housing of one's own—is a condition that has been present throughout human history. It has always been dangerous as well, given the necessity of shelter for survival. Nevertheless, the routine occurrence of homelessness in the past probably prevented the problem from generating any extraordinary degree of collective concern. Members of premodern societies often experienced losses or disruptions of residence as a result of food scarcity, natural disaster, epidemic disease, warfare, and other environmental and self-inflicted circumstances. Such forces contributed to the likelihood, if not the expectation, that most people would be homeless at some point in the life cycle.

Ironically, now that homelessness is relatively rare in Western societies, it has achieved a special notoriety. When shelter security becomes the norm, the significance of housing evolves beyond the purely functional. Homes, like jobs, constitute master statuses, anchoring their occupants in the stratification system. Hence, being without a home portends a more general and threatening *disaffiliation,* defined as "a detachment from society characterized by the absence or attenuation of the affiliative bonds that link settled persons to a network of interconnected social structures" (Caplow, Bahr, and Sternberg 1968, p. 494). This is the broadest meaning associated with the concept of homelessness, at the opposite end of the continuum from its literal definition.

Homelessness, broadly construed, began to assume major proportions as a social problem in the United States near the end of the nineteenth century. Over the several preceding decades, urban homeless populations had emerged in response to a series of events at the national level, including Civil War displacement; the arrival of impoverished European immigrants; seasonal employment patterns in agriculture, construction, and the extractive industries; and severe economic setbacks in the early 1870s and 1890s (Hoch 1987; Rooney 1970). As a temporary remedy, downtown warehouses and old hotels were converted into inexpensive, dormitory-style lodging facilities. The proximity of the lodging facilities to one another, along with the distinctive mix of service and recreational establishments growing up around them, served to concentrate the homeless physically in areas that came to be known as *skid rows* (supposedly named for a "skid road" in Seattle used to slide logs downhill).

The manpower needs created by World War I drained skid row districts of their inhabitants, but a pool of footloose veterans replenished them at war's end. An even greater surge in homelessness—one extending well beyond the boundaries of skid row—was soon sparked by the Great Depression. The widespread hardship of the period forced previously domiciled individuals into a migrant life-style, and shantytowns (dubbed "Hoovervilles") sprang up in urban and rural settings alike. These new manifestations of homelessness in turn stimulated the first generation of sustained research on the subject among sociologists. Anderson (1940), Sutherland and Locke (1936), and other scholars conducted studies of different segments of the homeless population as part of the Depression-era relief effort.

A second generation of research started in the 1950s. Large-scale single-city surveys—many of which were funded by urban renewal agencies—informed the debate over what to do about skid row areas (Bahr and Caplow 1974; Bogue 1963). Demographic data obtained during the surveys showed homeless respondents to be predominantly male, white, single, older, and of local origins. The surveys also lent credibility to the popular image of the homeless as deviant "outsiders." Depending upon the city under examination, between one-fourth and one-half reportedly were problem drinkers, a higher percentage had spent time in jail or prison, most were unable or unwilling to hold down steady employment, many suffered from poor health, and few were enmeshed in supportive social networks. This negative image based on the survey findings was countered by a parallel body of ethnographic evidence. Field observers like Wallace (1965) portrayed the homeless of skid row in subcultural terms, as a cohesive group with their own language, norms, and status hierarchy. Participation in the subculture was believed to help members cope with a problem more serious than their presumed deviance: extreme poverty.

In the 1970s, almost a century after skid row first appeared as a recognizable entity in the American city, its demise seemed imminent. Urban renewal and redevelopment projects had eliminated much of the infrastructure of skid row while a slackening demand for short-term unskilled labor was eroding one of the few legitimate economic roles the area could claim to play. Consequently, several investigators predicted skid row's disappearance and, by implication, the decline of the U.S. homeless population (Bahr 1967; Lee 1980). Yet within a decade of such forecasts, homelessness had resurfaced as an important national issue. During the 1980s media coverage of the so-called *new homeless* increased dramatically, and federal legislation (most notably the McKinney Act) was formulated to address their plight. The amount of social scientific inquiry rose as well. Indeed, over the past eight years the outpouring of scholarly monographs on the topic may have surpassed that of any prior generation of research.

Despite this renewed interest, what is known about contemporary homelessness remains limited, for several reasons. Unlike most groups surveyed by sociologists, the homeless are not easily reached at residential addresses or telephone numbers. The demolition of skid row districts in general and of single-room-occupancy (SRO) hotels in particular has intensified the difficulties involved in finding homeless people, pushing a higher percentage of them onto the streets and into more dispersed locations. Those referred to as the *doubled up,* who stay on an irregular basis with settled relatives or friends, are virtually inaccessible to investigators. Even among the homeless who can be found, participation rates fall far short of perfect. Some individuals have always been too suspicious and others too incoherent to take part in an interview, and their numbers may be increasing.

Finally, the political context surrounding the latest wave of research magnifies the significance of each methodological obstacle just identified. Because the homelessness issue has been transformed into a referendum on the ability of the state to meet its citizens' needs, liberals and conservatives both use the slightest technical shortcoming as ammunition with which to attack any study unfavorable to their own position. Thus, apparently straightforward "facts" about homelessness—and there are few of these to begin with—become matters open to debate.

Data on the size of the national homeless population illustrate the uncertain nature of the existing knowledge base. According to an early assertion by advocates, the number of homeless in the United States as of 1982 stood at 2.2 million, or approximately 1 percent of the total population of the country (Hombs and Snyder 1982). However, only two years later the U.S. Department of Housing and Urban Development (1984) compiled a series of point estimates, extrapolated from street counts and surveys of informants and shelter operators, that yielded a "most reliable" range of 250,000 to 350,000. More recently, an Urban Institute study has arrived at a figure—500,000 to 600,000 homeless nationwide on a single day—that falls between the advocate and HUD extremes (Burt and Cohen 1989). Whatever its true size, the homeless population is thought to have grown rapidly over the past decade, by as much as 25 percent annually in some places. That growth rate could be inflated, though, given the relative stability documented in one of the few large cities (Nashville, Tennessee) for which longitudinal observations are available (Lee 1989).

While definitional differences underlie much of the disagreement over the magnitude of the homeless population, generalizations about its composition have been complicated by (1) the selective emphasis of many inquiries on atypical "slices" of the whole (homeless veterans, the mentally ill, etc.), and (2) real variation in the characteristics of the homeless across communities. Contrary to media reports and popular perceptions that suffer from such distorting influences, the modal homeless individual is still an unattached white male with local roots, similar in fundamental ways to his skid row counterpart of two decades ago. Yet there clearly have been striking compositional shifts during the intervening period. Blacks and other minorities, rarely found on skid row, are now overrepresented among the homeless, and women, children, young adults, and high school graduates constitute larger segments of the population both absolutely and proportionally than they once did (Momeni 1989; Rossi 1989; Wright 1989). Family groupings, usually headed by the mother alone, have become more common as well. Taking these elements of demographic continuity and change together, perhaps the safest conclusion to be drawn is that a trend toward greater diversity distinguishes the new homelessness from the old.

The same conclusion applies fairly well with respect to deviant characteristics. Alcoholism, which previously constituted the most noticeable form of deviance among the homeless, is now rivaled by other kinds of substance abuse, and mental illness has surpassed physical illness as an object of public concern. Beyond a rough consensus regarding the greater variety of such problems in the current homeless population, little of a definitive nature is known about them. For example, a recent review of nine studies cited mental illness prevalence rates that run from a low of one-tenth to a high of one-half of all homeless (U.S. General Accounting Office 1988), and occasional reports suggest that as many as 90 percent are at least mildly clinically impaired. This wide range leaves room for opposing arguments: on the one hand, that pervasive mental illness is the principal cause of contemporary homelessness (Bassuk 1984; Eagle and Caton 1990); on the other, that its presumed causal role represents a stereotypic "myth" created by the visibility of a small minority of disturbed folk (Snow, Baker, and Anderson 1986).

Even if the extent of mental illness has been exaggerated, there can be no doubt that the general well-being of the homeless remains low. This is hardly surprising in light of the stresses that accompany life on the street. The absence of shelter exposes homeless persons to the weather, criminal victimization, and other threatening conditions. They have trouble fulfilling basic needs that most Americans take for granted, such as finding work, obtaining nutritionally adequate meals, getting around town, washing clothes, storing belongings, and locating toilet and bathing facilities. Fortunately, the percentage of the homeless who have to confront these difficulties over an extended period appears to be smaller today than in the past. Results from several local surveys suggest that the median episode of homelessness lasts between six months and one year (Rossi 1989, pp. 94–95; U.S. Department of Housing and Urban Development 1984). Some people, of course, still experience the longer-duration bouts common in the skid row era; as many as 10 percent may be homeless for five continuous years or more.

Whether temporarily or chronically homeless, few choose to be in that state. But if choice can be ruled out, what forces do account for the new homelessness? Among the numerous answers elicited by this question so far, two general classes are discernible. *Structural* explanations treat homelessness as a consequence of societal trends, including changes in the economy (a decline in limited-skill jobs, deindustrialization), mental health policy (deinstitutionalization), and welfare provision (shrinkage of the social service "safety net"). Arguably, the availability of affordable housing has received the most attention of any structural factor. The thrust of the housing thesis is that government action, a supply-demand "squeeze," inner-city revitalization, and related events have not only priced many low-income households out of rental status but have also eliminated a key fallback option historically open to them: SRO units in downtown residential hotels (Hoch and Slayton 1989; Ringheim 1990; Wright and Lam 1987). With the depletion of the SRO stock, displacement from other sectors of the housing market may lead directly to a homeless outcome.

In contrast to the structural approach, *individ-*

ualistic explanations posit traits or attributes internal to the person as the main causes of homelessness. Older thinking about the inherent immorality and wanderlust of skid row denizens has given way to revisionist claims that the primary antecedents are deficits in talent or motivation (Main 1983; McMurry 1988) or the debilitating effects of mental illness. Interestingly, many scholars who subscribe to some version of the individualistic view have had to invoke associated structural trends—deinstitutionalization in the case of mental illness, for example—in order to explain the size and compositional changes that have occurred in the homeless population in recent years.

The tendency to draw on both individualistic and structural perspectives has grown more pronounced with the realization that a theory of homelessness, like that of any social phenomenon, can never be fully satisfying when cast in exclusively micro- or macro-level terms. To date, the work of Rossi (1989) offers the most compelling cross-level synthesis. He contends that structural changes have put everyone in extreme poverty at higher risk of becoming homeless, especially those poor people who exhibit an "accumulation of disabilities," such as drug abuse, bad health, unemployment, and a criminal record. Being "disabled" forces one to rely on a network of friends and family for support, often over prolonged periods. If the strain placed on this support network is too great and it collapses, homelessness is the likely result.

Though Rossi's central idea—that structural factors and individual problems combine to make certain segments of the poor more vulnerable to homelessness than others—seems reasonable to social scientists, it could prove less acceptable to members of the general public. In fact, based on previous research into public beliefs about the causes of poverty (Kluegel and Smith 1986), most Americans might be expected to hold the homeless responsible for their lot. However, the small amount of evidence that bears directly on this expectation contradicts rather than confirms it. Findings from a local survey, supplemented with data from a national opinion poll, indicate that (1) more people blame homelessness on structural variables and bad luck than on individualistic causes, and (2) many hold a mixture of structural and individualistic beliefs, consistent with the complex roots of the condition (Lee, Jones, and Lewis 1990).

The relative frequency of the two types of beliefs is a matter of substantial political significance, since the study just cited shows that each type implies a distinctive set of policy attitudes. As a rule, members of the public who believe in structural causes consider homelessness a very important problem, feel that the response to it has been inadequate, and endorse a variety of ameliorative proposals, including a tax increase and government-subsidized housing. This policy orientation stands at odds with that for individualistic believers, who tend to devalue homelessness as an issue and favor restrictive measures (vagrancy enforcement, access limitation, etc.) over service provision. Regardless of which orientation ultimately registers the greatest impact on policymaking, the sharp contrast between them says much about how homelessness has managed to stay near the top of the U.S. domestic social agenda for the past decade.

The United Nations' designation of 1987 as the "Year of Shelter for the Homeless" attests that homelessness has been an international concern as well. The situation is particularly acute in the developing countries of the Third World, where rapid population growth outstrips the expansion of the housing stock by a wide margin (Burns and Grebler 1977). Compounding the growth-housing mismatch are prevailing patterns of spatial redistribution: rural-to-urban migration streams have created huge pools of homeless people in tenements, in squatter communities, and on the streets of many large cities. Besides such demographic trends, periodic events of the kind that once created literal homelessness in premodern societies—drought, food shortages, war, and the like—still contribute to the problem today outside the West. Sadly, the prospects for effective intervention must be judged slim in the face of the financial debts, service demands, and other burdens under which Third World governments operate. Possibly because these burdens are so overwhelming, homelessness—while important—has yet to achieve dominant-issue standing. As one informed observer put the matter, "neither the resources to address the plight of the homeless nor the degree of aroused public sympathy present in the United States are in evidence in the developing world" (Knight 1987, p. 268). However, that is the sector of the world in which a vast majority of all homeless persons will continue to live for the foreseeable future.

(SEE ALSO: *Income Distribution in the United States; Poverty)*

REFERENCES

Anderson, Nels 1940 *Men on the Move.* Chicago: University of Chicago Press.

Bahr, Howard M. 1967 "The Gradual Disappearance of Skid Row." *Social Problems* 15:41–45.

———, and Theodore Caplow 1974 *Old Men Drunk and Sober.* New York: New York University Press.

Bassuk, Ellen L. 1984 "The Homelessness Problem." *Scientific American* 251:40–45.

Bogue, Donald J. 1963 *Skid Row in American Cities.* Chicago: Community and Family Study Center, University of Chicago.

Burns, Leland S., and Leo Grebler 1977 *The Housing of Nations.* London: Macmillan.

Burt, Martha R., and Barbara E. Cohen 1989 *America's Homeless: Numbers, Characteristics, and the Programs That Serve Them.* Washington, D.C.: Urban Institute.

Caplow, Theodore, Howard M. Bahr, and David Sternberg 1968 "Homelessness." In David L. Sills, ed., *International Encyclopedia of the Social Sciences,* Vol. 6. New York: Macmillan.

Eagle, Paula F., and Carol L. M. Caton 1990 "Homelessness and Mental Illness." In Carol L. M. Caton, ed., *Homeless in America.* New York: Oxford University Press.

Hoch, Charles 1987 "A Brief History of the Homeless Problem in the United States." In Richard D. Bingham, Roy E. Green, and Sammis B. White, eds., *The Homeless in Contemporary Society.* Newbury Park, Calif.: Sage.

Hoch, Charles, and Robert A. Slayton 1989 *New Homeless and Old: Community and the Skid Row Hotel.* Philadelphia: Temple University Press.

Hombs, Mary E., and Mitch Snyder 1982 *Homelessness in America: A Forced March to Nowhere.* Washington, D.C.: Community for Creative Non-Violence.

Kluegel, James R., and Eliot R. Smith 1986 *Beliefs About Inequality: Americans' Views of What Is and What Ought to Be.* New York: Aldine de Gruyter.

Knight, Rudolph H. 1987 "Homelessness: An American Problem?" In Richard D. Bingham, Roy E. Green, and Sammis B. White, eds., *The Homeless in Contemporary Society.* Newbury Park, Calif.: Sage.

Lee, Barrett A. 1980 "The Disappearance of Skid Row: Some Ecological Evidence." *Urban Affairs Quarterly* 16:81–107.

———1989 "Stability and Change in an Urban Homeless Population." *Demography* 26:323–334.

———, Sue Hinze Jones, and David W. Lewis 1990 "Public Beliefs About the Causes of Homelessness." *Social Forces* 69:253–265.

Main, Thomas J. 1983 "The Homeless of New York." *Public Interest* 72:3–28.

McMurry, Dan 1988 "Hard Living on Easy Street." *Chronicles* 12 (8):15–19.

Momeni, Jamshid A. (ed.) 1989 *Homelessness in the United States, Volume I: State Surveys.* New York: Greenwood.

Ringheim, Karin 1990 *At Risk of Homelessness: The Roles of Income and Rent.* New York: Praeger.

Rooney, James F. 1970 "Societal Forces and the Unattached Male: An Historical Review." In Howard M. Bahr, ed., *Disaffiliated Man: Essays and Bibliography on Skid Row, Vagrancy, and Outsiders.* Toronto: University of Toronto Press.

Rossi, Peter H. 1989 *Down and Out in America: The Origins of Homelessness.* Chicago: University of Chicago Press.

Snow, David A., Susan G. Baker, and Leon Anderson 1986 "The Myth of Pervasive Mental Illness among the Homeless." *Social Problems* 33:407–423.

Sutherland, Edwin H., and Harvey J. Locke 1936 *Twenty Thousand Homeless Men.* Chicago: J. B. Lippincott.

U.S. Department of Housing and Urban Development 1984 *A Report to the Secretary on the Homeless and Emergency Shelters.* Washington, D.C.: Office of Policy Development and Research, U.S. Department of Housing and Urban Development.

U.S. General Accounting Office 1988 *Homeless Mentally Ill: Problems and Options in Estimating Numbers and*

Trends. Washington, D.C.: Program Evaluation and Methodology Division, U.S. General Accounting Office.

Wallace, Samuel E. 1965 *Skid Row as a Way of Life.* Totowa, N.J.: Bedminster.

Wright, James D. 1989 *Address Unknown: The Homeless in America.* New York: Aldine de Gruyter.

———, and Julie A. Lam 1987 "Homelessness and the Low Income Housing Supply." *Social Policy* 17:48–53.

BARRETT A. LEE

HOMICIDE. *See* Violent Crime.

HOMOSEXUALITY. *See* Sexual Orientation; Sexually Transmitted Diseases.

HUMAN ECOLOGY AND THE ENVIRONMENT The term *ecology* comes from the Greek word *oikos* (house) and, significantly, has the same Greek root as the word *economics,* from *oikonomos* (household manager). Ernst Haeckel, the German biologist who coined the word *ecology* in 1868, viewed ecology as a body of knowledge concerning the economy of nature, highlighting its roots in economics and evolutionary theory. He defined ecology as the study of all those complex interrelations referred to by Darwin as the conditions of the struggle for existence.

Ecologists like to look at the environment as an ecosystem of interlocking relationships and exchanges that constitute the web of life. Populations of organisms occupying the same environment (habitat) are said to constitute a community. Together, the communities and their abiotic environments constitute an ecosystem. The various ecosystems taken together constitute the ecosphere, the largest ecological unit. Living organisms exist in the much narrower range of the biosphere, which is said to extend a few hundred feet above the land or under the sea. On its fragile film of air, water, and soil, all life is said to depend. For the sociologist, the most important ecological concepts are diversity and dominance, competition and cooperation, succession and adaptation, evolution and expansion, and carrying capacity and the balance of nature. Over the years, three distinct approaches have come to characterize the field of human ecology.

CONVENTIONAL HUMAN ECOLOGY

The Chicago sociologists Louis Wirth, Robert Ezra Park, Ernest W. Burgess, and Roderick McKenzie are recognized as the founders of the human ecological approach in sociology. In the early decades of the twentieth century, American cities were passing through a period of great turbulence due to the effects of rapid industrialization and urbanization. The urban world, with its fierce competition for territory and survival, appeared to mirror the very life-world studied by the plant ecologists. In their search for the principles of order, the human ecologists started looking at the process of city development in terms of the process of "succession," which involved an orderly sequence of invasions and displacements leading to a climax or equilibrium state. In their hands, human ecology became synonymous with the ecology of space. Park and Burgess identified the "natural areas" of land use, which come into existence without a preconceived design. Quite influential and popular for a while was the "Burgess Hypothesis" regarding the spatial order of the city as a series of concentric zones emanating from the central business district. However, Hawley (1984) has pointed out that with urban characteristics now diffused throughout society, one in effect deals with a system of cities in which the urban hierarchy is cast in terms of functional rather than spatial relations.

Park (1936) identified the problematics of human ecology as the investigation of the processes by which biotic balance and social equilibrium are maintained by the interaction of the three factors constituting what he termed the "social complex" (population, technological culture [artifact], and nonmaterial culture [custom and belief]) with the fourth, natural resources of the habitat. Essentially the same factors reappear as the four POET variables (population, organization, environment, and technology) in Otis Dudley Duncan's Ecological Complex, indicating its point of contact with the early human ecology (Duncan 1964). In any case, it was McKenzie who, by shifting attention from spatial relations to the analysis of sustenance relations, provided the thread of continuity between the two approaches. His student Amos Hawley, who has been the "exemplar" of conventional human ecology since the 1940s, defines it as the attempt to deal holistically with the phenomenon of organization.

Hawley (1986) views the ecosystem as the adaptive mechanism that emerges out of the interaction of population, organization, and the environment. Organization is the adaptive form that enables a population to act as a unit. The process of system adaptation involves members in relations of interdependence to secure sustenance from the environment. Growth is the development of the system's inner potential to the maximum size and complexity afforded by the existing technology for transportation and communication. Evolution is the creation of higher potential for resumption of system development through the incorporation of new information that enhances the capacity for the movement of people, materials, and messages. In this manner, the system moves from simple to more complex forms.

Through the use of the ecological concept of "expansion," Hawley (1979) has applied his framework to account for the growth phases that intervene between stages of development. The evolution of a system takes place when its scale and complexity do not go hand in hand. Thus, an imbalance between population and the carrying capacity of the environment may create external pressures for branching off into colonies and establishing niches in a new environment. However, when complexity and scale do advance together, the normal condition for growth or expansion arises from the colonization process itself. Hawley identifies the technology of movement as the most critical variable. It determines accessibility and, therefore, governs the spread of settlements, changes in hierarchy and division of labor, and the creation of interaction networks among the settlements. According to Hawley, the process can work on any scale and is limited only by the level of technological development of communication and transportation.

Hawley (1979) points out that while expansionism in the past relied on political domination, its modern variant aims at structural convergence along economic and cultural axes to obviate the need for direct rule by the center. In this way, free trade and "resocialization" of cultures and whole populations into standardized organizational forms and procedures create a far more efficient and cost-effective global reach. At the same time, as polities try to bring larger portions of system territories under their jurisdictions, the management of scale becomes highly problematical. Lacking a single supranational polity, the international pecking order is then subject to increasing instability, challenge, and change.

The system tends to return to scale as the costs of administration mount. This results in decentralization and some local autonomy. But improvements in technology of movement start the growth process all over again. The picture thus is that of a global system thoroughly interlinked by transportation and communication networks. Hawley (1979, p. 29) believes that the growth of social systems has now reached a point at which the evolutionary model has lost its usefulness in explaining cumulative change. However, since a single world order has only a small tolerance for errors, this situation harbors the grave danger that a fatal error may destroy the whole system.

The real irony of this relentless global expansion elaborated by Hawley lies, however, in the coexistence of extreme opulence and affluence of the few with stark poverty and misery of the majority at home and abroad. The large metropolitan centers provide a very poor quality of life. The very scale of urban decay underscores the huge problems facing the city—congestion, polluted air, untreated sewage, high crime rates, dilapidated housing, domestic violence, and broken lives. One therefore needs to ask: What prospect does this scale and level of complexity hold for the future?

Industrial and industrializing nations are now beset with more or less the same devastating problems of air, land, and water pollution and environmental destruction. Large numbers of lakes and rivers that were not naturally eutrophic have now become so as a result of pollution and chemical runoffs. In the United States, Love Canal and Times Beach, Missouri, made headlines in the 1980s as much as Chernobyl did in 1986 in the Soviet Union. Sulfur dioxide emissions from industrial and power plants cause acid rain that inflicts irreparable damage on buildings, monuments, marine life, trees, and plants. Over sixty thousand synthetic chemicals are now on the market, of which a sizable number contaminate the environment and pose health hazards. Over half a million tons of toxic wastes are produced each year in the United States, where the five-year cost of cleaning the nuclear waste, which remains dangerously radioactive for thousands of years, may well exceed thirty billion dollars. The soil and the lake water and groundwater near nuclear power and weapons plants are heavily contaminated with such toxins as mercury, arsenic, and many types of solvents, and with deadly radioactive materials such as plutonium, tritium, and strontium-90. The contamination is so bad in eight states that huge tracts of land are said to be totally unfit for human habitation and pose serious health hazards for the surrounding communities.

The environmental destruction is far more serious and widespread in Eastern Europe and the Soviet Union. These countries are the site of some of the world's worst pollution. Lakes and rivers are dead or dying. Water is so contaminated in some areas that it is undrinkable. Chemical runoff and sewage and wastewater dumping have created serious groundwater contamination. Lignite (brown coal), the major source of energy for industry and homes in some of these nations, is responsible for heavy concentration of sulfur dioxide and dust in the air that has caused serious respiratory problems and additional health damage. The haze-covered cities are an environmental disaster. According to Worldwatch estimates, the Soviet Union alone accounts for a fifth each of global carbon dioxide and sulfur dioxide emissions—the former are implicated in global warming; the latter are the principal ingredient of acid rain. As a result, environment and politics are becoming an explosive mix and the source of action and instability in the region (French 1990, p. 9). Zhores Medvedev believes the Soviet Union is losing its forests at the same rate as rain forests are being destroyed in Brazil. Between 1960 and 1989, it lost more land through land and environmental degradation than the combined total cultivable area in Belgium and Ireland. Besides the effects of Chernobyl and other major nuclear disasters, it lost more agricultural land and pastureland to radioactive contamination than the total cultivated acreage in Switzerland (Medvedev 1990, p. 28). Experts fear that from twenty-five thousand to seventy-five thousand persons in Russia and Europe may die prematurely from cancer and other effects of the radiation fallout from Chernobyl, history's worst nuclear disaster. A quarter to a third of the forests in eastern Europe show signs of dying from air pollution. These environmental problems are thus not only transboundary, they also cut across ideological labels. Between them, the United States and the Soviet Union produce more than 40 percent of the carbon dioxide emissions every year.

In non-Western nations, a million people suffer acute poisoning and twenty thousand persons die every year from pesticides. Pesticides are a major source of environmental and health problems in the United States as well. But the United States alone exports over half a billion pounds of pesticides that are restricted or banned for domestic use. The ecology, natural environment, and resources of these non-Western nations are being destroyed and contaminated at a frightening rate. Irreversible damage is being done by large-scale destruction of rain forests and the intensive use of marginal lands and by the imbalances that result from population pressures and the practices of multinational firms and national elites. Desertification now threatens a third of the earth's land surface. Poverty, hunger, starvation, famine, and death are endemic throughout much of the world.

ENVIRONMENTAL SOCIOLOGY AND THE NEW HUMAN ECOLOGY

The mounting public concern during the 1970s about fuel shortages, oil spills, nuclear power-plant accidents, acid rain, dying lakes, urban smog, famine and death in the Sahel, rain forest destruction, and the like made social scientists realize that overexploitation of the ecosystem may destroy the very basis of our planetary survival. Many environmentalists blamed the dominant social paradigm of industrial societies for the destruction of the fragile balance among the components of the ecological complex.

The antiecological worldview of the dominant social paradigm, which was shaped by the experience of a seemingly limitless frontier and of extraordinary abundance, is said to be a major reason for the neglect of the physical environment by American sociologists. Another reason is related to the Durkheimian emphasis on explaining social facts by other social facts. Together with the general aversion of sociologists to any form of determinism, these reasons ruled out the due consideration of environmental factors even by human ecologists (Freudenberg and Gramling 1989). William Catton and Riley Dunlap (1978) point out that the exaggerated emphasis by conventional human ecologists on culture, science, and technology as "exceptional" human achievements has led to the illusion that humans are "exempt" from bioecological constraints to which all species are subject. This awareness has led Catton and Dunlap to develop the fields of new human ecology (Buttel 1987) and "environmental sociology" to deal with the reciprocal interaction between human activities and the physical environment. They believe that the POET model, broadened to include the role of human agency and culture, provides a useful analytical framework for grounding environmental sociology in the ecological perspective. In addition, they have identified the important subfield of the sociology of environmental issues, which is concerned with the study of the environmental movement, wildland recreation, and resource management problems and the like, but mainly within the sociological tradition.

In a comprehensive review of the new field, Buttel (1987) has made two essential points. He argues that both the cleavage between the conventional and the new human ecology, and the conflict-versus-consensus cleavage of mainline sociology, continue to be important. Buttel would also like to shift the focus of environmental sociology from the imbalance of population and resources, emphasized by Catton, to the reality of the unequal distribution of these resources. Allan Schnaiberg's idea of the "treadmill of production" (1980), which emerges from a dialectical relationship between economic growth and ecological structures, points to the need for focusing on production institutions as the primary determinants of economic expansion and for incorporating a conflict dimension in environmental analysis. Buttel's own work in environmental sociology draws upon the "political economy tradition" of the neo-Marxists and the neo-Weberians. Catton's major contributions, on the other hand, are in the neo-Malthusian tradition.

Thus, while the problem of order created by the harsh realities of industrial life and expansionism defined the central problematics of sociology and conventional human ecology, the problem of survival now defines the central problematics of environmental sociology and the new human ecology: to the earlier question of how social order is possible is now added the more urgent concern with survival itself.

THE POLITICAL ECONOMY APPROACH

A "new urban sociology" conflict paradigm in the political economy tradition has been put forward by M. Gottdiener and Joe Feagin (1988) as an alternative to the conventional and the new human ecology paradigms. Societies, in their view, are neither mere population aggregates nor unified biotic communities, but are specified by their mode of production. Crisis tendencies and profit generation constitute the core of societal development, which is dominated by the capital accumulation process. Thus, to take one example, conventional human ecologists like to regard central-city restructuring as a consequence of adaptation to increasing population size and the growing complexity of social organization. They then relate these changes to the size of the metropolitan hinterland. The new urban paradigm, on the other hand, emphasizes the impact of a global economy, the multinational corporations, the shift to functional specialization in world-system financial and administrative activities, the constant subsidization by the state, the efforts of pro-growth coalitions, and changes in labor force requirements leading to some renovation and central city gentrification. The following are some of the basic questions that the new urban sociology paradigm seeks to answer: What is the character of power and inequality? How do they relate to "ecological" patterns? How do production and reproduction processes of capital accumulation, as well as the processes of crisis adjustment, manifest themselves in sociospatial organization?

RELATION BETWEEN POPULATION AND THE ENVIRONMENT

For human ecology, the most salient aspect of the population–environment relationship is the way it affects human survival and the quality of human life. Under the impact of the interlocking crisis of overpopulation, resource depletion, and environmental degradation, issues of sustainability and survival have come to occupy center stage. Corresponding to the main approaches in human ecology, three broad positions may be identified for discussion: the pro-growth (expansionist), the neo-Malthusian, and the political economy perspectives. The discussion of these positions is followed by a consideration of the Brundtland Report, issued by the World Commission on Environment and Development, and of the traditional-Gandhian view of the ecological crisis. Extended treatment of the issues involved may be found in Catton (1980), Schnaiberg (1980), Humphrey and Buttel (1982), Redclift (1987), Mellos (1988), and de la Court (1990).

The Pro-Growth (Expansionist) Perspective. In expansionist thinking, scale, complexity, and acceleration—that is, the constant broadening of the limits of the maximum permitted by prevailing circumstances—mark the human–environment encounter. The basic conviction is that man through his unaided reason can comprehend and control the processes of the world. This is the meaning of Hawley's apparently guarded conviction that evolution as a mode of change has disappeared from human social systems (1979, p. 29)—that is, that by grasping the very mainspring of evolution, man has already seized "the tiller of the world," in the words of Teilhard de Chardin. In responding to the concern of the neo-Malthusians about population outrunning resources, Hawley (1986, pp. 110–112), points to the inherently expansive nature of populations, technology, and organization, which through resource substitutions, intensive use and exploitation of land and resources, and the exploration and discovery of new frontiers and new resources, can allay concerns regarding environmental finitude. In his view, the problem of food and resource shortages is really rooted in poverty rather than in resource scarcity. In short, Hawley believes that industrial systems have no known upper limits on either the number of specializations or the size of the populations that can be supported. Similar pro-growth sentiments are expressed by other expansionist thinkers.

While Colin Clark directly links population numbers to power, Herman Kahn (1974) views population increase as a necessary stimulus to economic growth and believes the earth can easily support fifteen billion people at twenty thousand dollars per capita for a millennium. In fact, he believes that the wider the gap between the rich and the poor, the more the riches will percolate downward. In any case, he is unconvinced that the rich would agree to part with their income to ensure a more equitable distribution of wealth. Roger Revelle (1974) believes the earth can actually support nearly thirty times the present population in terms of food supplies, and that it would take almost 150 years to hit that mark. While economic development is necessary to provide people with the basis to control their fertility, Revelle is certain the world would drown in its own filth if most of the people in the world were to live at Western standards. Finally, the postindustrial sociologist Daniel Bell (1977) is convinced that economic growth is necessary to reduce the gap between the rich and the poor nations. He has little doubt that the "super-productivity society," with less than 4 percent of its labor force devoted to agriculture, could feed the whole population of the United States, and most of the world as well. In his opinion, pollution exists because the market principle has never been applied to the use of collective goods. Actually, Bell suggests that the government itself could utilize the market to demand a public accounting from all parties on issues of public interest, levy effluent charges for pollutants, and bring effective compliance through the price mechanism.

However, while corporations have shown greater sensitivity and self-regulation, there is evidence that the attempts to enforce the "polluter pays" principle are likely to be resisted or the costs passed on to the public. The negative impact of governmental policies that alleviate energy and resource scarcities is more likely to be felt at the lower socioeconomic levels (Morrison 1978). Dunlap (1979) presents evidence to show that the effects of pollution and the costs of cleaning the environment are borne disproportionately by the poor and may actually serve to reinforce class inequalities.

The Neo-Malthusian Perspective. The neo-Malthusian perspective is based on the well-known Malthusian law of a geometric increase in population far outstripping the arithmetic increase in food supplies in the absence of constraints. The disparity between the two growth rates poses a perpetual threat to the human prospect and serves as a natural brake on unlimited population increase by triggering war, widespread famine, disease, and death. In place of these harsh "positive checks," Malthus (1766–1834) wished to substitute the "preventive check" of "moral restraint," not the artificial methods of birth control and abortion. The crucial linking concept between population and environment is the biological concept of "carrying capacity." The carrying capacity for humans is the maximum population that can be supported indefinitely by a particular environment under exploitation by specified technology and organization (Catton 1978, p. 231). With each technological breakthrough, humans have so far been able to raise their carrying capacity through extending their territorial and environmental reach, which now goes to the ends of the globe. A more or less stable population of five hundred million in 1650 jumped to a billion in 1850. In 1930, it was two billion; and in 1975, four billion. Now humans number 5.2 billion, with prospects of the earth's population doubling about once every thirty years. Three-fourths of the earth's inhabitants live in non-Western nations. The 1990 U.S. population of 250 million is expected to jump to 300 million in 30 years.

Compounding the environmental effects of the poverty-stricken and "food hungry" populations of the world are the impacts of massive consumption and pollution of the "energy hungry" nations (Miller 1972, p. 117). The latter rise sharply with even a slight growth in population of Western nations, where one-quarter of the world's population is responsible for over 85 percent of world wide consumption of natural resources and the environmental sinks. Within the United States a bare 6 percent of the world's population consumes over half of the world's nonrenewable resources and over a third of all the raw materials produced. Miller (1972, p. 122) believes that the real threat to our life-support system, therefore, comes not from the poor but from the affluent megaconsumers and megapolluters who occupy more space, consume more of natural resources, disturb the ecology more, and directly and indirectly pollute the land, air, and water with ever-increasing amounts of thermal, chemical, and radioactive wastes. While the Club of Rome (Meadows et al. 1972) and the other neo-Malthusians give a grace period of thirty or so years, Catton believes we have already overshot the maximum carrying capacity, and are now on a catastrophic downward crash course. In any case, he is convinced that our best bet would be to act *as if* a crash were imminent and to take advance measures to minimize its impact.

However, these premises of Malthusian theory have not stood the test of time. The social and economic forces unleashed by the Industrial Revolution not only telescoped the doubling of human population within a shorter time span, they also brought about ever-rising material standards of living due to astronomical increases in the scale and speed of agricultural and industrial production in the advanced nations. Worldwide, the annual rate of population growth fell to 1.8 percent in 1990, and is expected to stabilize around 1.5 percent by the year 2000. Annual food production in the developing countries is increasing by 4.4 percent, over twice the rate of population growth. What has caused the huge increase in numbers in poor nations is the fact that while the birthrate has declined, the death rate has gone down as well. In Western nations, on the other hand, fertility rates registered a dramatic decline between the two world wars, boomed thereafter to everybody's disbelief, and have again hit such low levels that population replacement has become a major concern for many industrial nations. The Western nations are thus said to have completed a "demographic transition." In the initial stage, population is kept stable as high birthrates are balanced by high death rates due to the operation of the Malthusian positive checks. In the second stage, population increases rapidly as death rates decline but birthrates soar due to an increase in food supply and improved health care. In the third stage, birthrates decline more rapidly than death rates due to the use of family planning and birth control measures. Finally, low birthrates and low death rates lead to a stabilization of the population at a lower level. A decline in fertility rates to a level below replacement (1.3 per woman) in industrialized countries such as Germany and Denmark is said to constitute the current "second demographic transition." France and the Soviet Union have officially encouraged childbearing to counter falling birthrates. Thus, in the present era, the challenges and opportunities opened up by declining fertility rates and record food surpluses have totally eclipsed the Malthusian specter for the rich nations while again casting its shadow on the poor. In any case, population is but one factor, albeit a most significant one, in the complex interaction between social structure and the environment.

To revert to the neo-Malthusian argument: The tragedy of numbers is compounded by the "free rider," who derives personal benefits from the collective efforts of others, and the more serious "tragedy of the commons" (Hardin 1966), where each herdsman will add cattle without limit, ignoring the costs imposed on the others and must, therefore, degrade the land held in common. Hardin believes that the administrative system, supported by a common standard of judgment and having access to "mutual coercion mutually agreed upon," can avoid the collective tragedy. However, unless the users jointly own the commons and exercise joint control over the resources and their use, Hardin's cure may place them at the mercy of the custodians, leaving them worse off individually and collectively. The threat of imminent ethnocide facing the remaining native populations is a case in point.

On the other hand, the "development" of poor nations has created a new set of claimants for the resources needed to maintain the high material standard of living of affluent nations. As the poor nations begin to assert control over their own resources, try to set terms of their exchange, or resist outside pressures to transform them into "environmental preserves" or the "global commons," the prospects of conflict, particularly over critical mineral and energy resources, are greatly magnified. Amartya Sen (1981) has looked at the famine situation as essentially a "crisis of entitlement," not so much because there is lack of food but because the many are denied any claims to it because of their lowly position in society. In the West, the entitlement revolution has entailed huge welfare expenditures, which could be financed either by economic growth or by direct redistribution of income (Bell 1977, p. 20). For Bell and the neo-Malthusians, the latter is out of the question. There is thus a natural progression from Hardin's "commons" view to his "lifeboat ethics." While he admits it is possible to significantly increase food supply to match the demand, he is convinced that every Indian life saved would only diminish the quality of life of those aboard the "lifeboat" and of their descendants. The situation, he feels, demands a world authority to take control of reproduction and resource use. In a piece published in 1969 in the *Stanford Alumni Almanac*, and appropriately titled "The Immorality of Being Softhearted," Hardin is quite clear that food would be the worst thing to send to the poor. Nothing short of the final solution will do. "Atomic bombs would be kinder. For a few moments the misery would be acute, but it would soon come to an end for most of the people, leaving a very few survivors to suffer thereafter." These solutions, which bring about decimation of entire populations, have been called ecofascist. Such sentiments are by no means uncommon among the neo-Malthusians.

The "tragedy of the commons" is really the tragedy of individualism from which all constraints of private and common morality have been removed. However, others have been quick to point to the equal or far greater extent of environment pollution and ecological destruction in socialist countries as one more evidence of the inevitable convergence of capitalism and socialism! Many environmental problems are clearly transideological and transnational. Acid rain, oil spills, destruction of the ozone layer, threat of global warming—all call for common responsibility and joint regulation. Ironically, it appears that the expressed concern about the destruction of the global commons through overpopulation or industrial pollution is seldom matched by a parallel commitment by powerful nations to preserve or clean up the environment or provide support for international population control efforts. Instead, one witnesses a mad scramble to divide up the remaining oceanic and other planetary resources without regard to equity, ecology, or environment. As a result, the air and the oceans, as well as the forests and lands of other nations, are being overexploited or used as garbage and toxic dumps with impunity.

Of no small consequence globally is the environmental impact of waste, widespread corruption at all levels, hoarding and price-fixing, and poor storage, distribution, and transportation networks. B. B. Vohra, a top Indian government official, has pointed out how "formidable mafias based on a triangular alliance between the corrupt bureaucrat, the corrupt politician and the corrupt businessman emerged in all [Indian] States and became a most powerful threat to the conservation of the country's tree cover" (1985, p. 50). When one adds to this list the role of political and economic elites and multinational corporations, and of huge debts, huge dams, and huge arms stockpiles, it becomes clear that povery, hunger, malnutrition, and starvation may have far more to do with political, cultural, and socioeconomic components of food shortages than with sheer numbers alone. This is not to underestimate the immensity of the population problem or to minimize the difficulty of its solution.

The Political Economy Perspective. Barry Commoner (1974) faults socialist as much as capitalist economic theories for neglecting the biosphere as a major factor of production, but regards both poverty and growth of population as outcomes of colonial exploitation. The world, he believes, has enough food and resources to support nearly twice its present population. The problem, in his view, is a result of gross distributive imbalances between the rich and the poor, and requires a massive redistribution of wealth and resources to abolish poverty and raise standards of living in order to wipe out the root cause of overpopulation. The alternative to this humane solution is the unsavory one of genocide or natural destruction.

A study of environmental destruction in southern Honduras by Susan Stonich (1989) illustrates the power of a perspective that combines the concerns of political economy, ecology, and demography. Her conclusion is that environmental degradation arises from fundamental social structure and is intricately connected to problems of land tenure, unemployment, poverty, and demography. She identifies political and economic factors and export-promotion policies of international lending institutions and aid agencies as the key elements of a development policy for the whole of

Central America that is likely to lead to destruction of the remaining tropical forests, worsen poverty and malnutrition, and increase inequality and conflicts within and between nations. Government policies encourage commercial agriculture for earning foreign exchange in the face of mounting external debt, which rose by 170 percent in just seven years to cover three-fourths of the 1986 gross national product. The expansion of export-oriented agriculture and the integration of resource-poor rural households into the capitalist sector, often by ruthless and violent means, concentrates highest population densities in the most marginal highland areas and encourages intensive land-use and adaptive strategies that accelerate ecological decline. Between 1952 and 1974, as a result of changes in land-use patterns, forest land declined by over two-fifths and the area in fallow by three-fifths. In the same period, food crop production was reduced drastically while the pasture area rose by more than half regionally and by over 150 percent in the highlands, where the number of cattle rose by about 70 percent. By 1974, a third of all rural families were landless; two-fifths were below the subsistence level in 1979.

The result has been the evolution of a class of rich peasants raising export-oriented cattle and cash crops, a class of land-poor and landless peasants and wage laborers, and a class of middlemen operatives who serve as transportation links in an expanding regional and national network. The whole socioeconomic structure has a most deleterious effect on the regional ecology and environment. These patterns are being repeated all over Africa and Asia. Even the "green revolution" provides only a temporary respite. Its recurrent and increasing high capital requirements for seed, fertilizer, insecticide, water, land, and machinery wipe out the small farmers and landless laborers. It destroys peasant agriculture, exposes the monocultures to destruction by disease and pests, magnifies inequality, and sows the seeds of social instability and rural strife. To those who subscribe to the political economy perspective, the biological explanation thus appears to be too simplistic. It overlooks the social context of development and land distribution within which worldwide destruction of traditional agriculture and the rain forests is now occurring.

In sum, these considerations bring out the fact that debates surrounding resource distributions and the control of population and consumption patterns are neither entirely scientific nor purely ecologically inspired. As Barry Commoner (1974) points out, they are political value positions. Will the changes come voluntarily, or will they involve totalitarian nightmares? "Sustainable development" and "traditional ecology" hold out two contrasting possibilities for the future.

THE BRUNDTLAND REPORT

At the heart of the 1987 Brundtland Report of the World Commission on Environment and Development is the idea of "sustainable development" that has become the rallying point for diverse agendas linking poverty, underdevelopment, and overpopulation to environmental degradation and "environmental security." The report defines sustainable development as "development which meets the needs of the present without compromising the ability of future generations to meet their own needs." Its popularity lies in its ability to accommodate the opposing idea of limits to growth within the context of economic expansion, but with a new twist. As pointed out by Gro Brundtland (1989), the "central pivot" of the notion of sustainable development remains "progress, growth, the generation of wealth, and the use of resources." The imposition of limits on consumption is then justified in order to protect the resource base of the environment both locally and globally. At the same time, continuous economic growth is held essential to meeting the needs of the world's neediest. In fact, the Brundtland Report indicates that "a five- to tenfold increase in world industrial output can be anticipated by the time world population stabilizes sometime in the next century."

Sustainable development is also seen as a strategy to enhance global security by reducing the threat posed by conflict and violence in an inequitable and resource-hungry world. To this end, it promotes a commitment to multilateralism, with a call for strong international institutions to ward off the new threats to security and for the collective management of global interdependence (Brundtland 1989, p. 14). As a result, the interests of economic growth and the environment are seen as mutually reinforcing rather than contradictory (Arnold 1989, p. 22). The Brundtland Report (1987) duly notes that ecology and economy "are becoming ever more interwoven—locally, regionally, nationally, and globally—into a seamless net of causes and effects." The 1990 Worldwatch Institute Report predicts that the world will have a sustainable society by the year 2030 (Brown et al. 1990, p. 175). Meanwhile, the challenge, as Arnold states, is to ensure that the sustainability vision "is not trivialized or, worse, used as one more way to legitimize the exploitation of the weak and vulnerable in the name of global interest and solidarity."

To its credit, the Brundtland Report singled out some forms of economic growth that destroy resources and the environment. The present one-trillion-dollar expenditure on armaments, for example, constitutes "more than the total income of the poorest half of humanity." According to the 1990 United Nations estimates, military expenditures in developing countries, which account for 75 percent of the arms trade, have multiplied by seven times since 1965 to almost two hundred billion dollars, compared with a doubling by the industrialized countries. In addition, burgeoning debt, adverse trade policies, and internal instability constitute the overwhelming obstacles to sustained development. With Africa's total debt approaching two hundred billion dollars (half of its overall gross national product and three to four times its annual income from exports), average debt repayments amount to more than half the export income. The debt burden forces the African nations to concentrate on monocrop export agriculture to the detriment of food crop production, and pushes hungry and landless farmers and nomads to marginal lands that they overgraze and overexploit in order to survive. However, with respect to fixing the responsibility for deforestation, the Brundtland Report appears to be of two minds (de la Court 1990). In asserting that to "most farmers, especially the poor ones, wood is a 'free good' until the last available tree is cut down," the report partly sides with the "tragedy of the commons" argument, accusing the poor farmers of being "both victims and agents of destruction." On the other hand, it also points to a different cause: "The fuelwood crisis and deforestation—although related—are not the same problems. Wood fuels destined for urban and industrial consumers do tend to come from the forests. But only a small proportion of that used by the rural poor comes from forests. Even in these cases, villagers rarely chop down trees; most collect dead branches or cut them from trees." (quoted in de la Court 1990, p. 68).

In any case, the Brundtland Report is now the focal point for global environmental efforts, even though in the United States it remains what the environmental activist Bettie Eisendrath has called "America's best-kept secret." It will undoubtedly play a crucial role in the United Nations conference on the global environment to be held in Brazil in 1992.

TRADITIONAL ECOLOGY AND THE ENVIRONMENT

Patterns of human social organization and technology use reflect the vision a people have of themselves and of their place in the universe. According to Karl Polanyi (1974), the question of how to organize human life in a machine society confronts us with a new urgency: "Behind the fading fabric of competitive capitalism there looms the portent of an industrial civilization with its paralyzing division of labor, standardization of life, supremacy of mechanism over organism, and organization over spontaneity. Science itself is haunted by insanity. This is the abiding concern" (p. 213–214). Bell (1976) has made the critical point that while the dominant nineteenth-century view of society as an interrelated web, a structured whole unified by some inner principle, still rules Marxist and functionalist thought, it is no longer applicable. On the contrary, society today is composed of three distinct realms—the technoeconomic structure, the polity, and the culture—each obedient to a different axial (governing) principle, having different rhythms of change, and each following different norms that legitimate different and even contradictory types of behavior. The discordances between these realms are responsible for various contradictions within society. Bell has proposed the creation of a "public household" to overcome the disjunctions between the family, the economy, and the state through the use of modified market mechanisms to further social goals. At the same time, he is convinced that the crisis is a spiritual one of belief and meaning. "But today what is there left in the past to destroy, and who has the hope for a future to come? . . . What holds one to reality, if one's secular system of meanings proves to be an illusion?" he asks (1976, p. 29). His answer is the return in Western society of some conception of religion to restore the continuity of generations and provide a ground for humility and care for others. The task is truly formidable, for as he admits, "such a continuity cannot be manufactured, nor a cultural revolution engineered" (1976, p. 30).

It is doubtful that the problems of order created by the "normal" but dangerous disrelation between the life-sustaining (ecology–economy) and order-maintaining (sociopolitical) systems of contemporary society can be corrected by the creation of a miracle hybrid "public household," protected and nurtured by the polity and the household to serve the interests of the technoeconomic structure, and by the side-door entry of the "religious" to provide for the integrative and "higher"-order needs of a socially disjointed and spiritually vacuous society. Even the frantic use of a "holistic" ecological approach is bound to fail if its actual goal is somehow to dominate or hold on desperately to a sundered reality in which everything is so hopelessly *dis*related to everything else. The high-powered technoeconomic structure, driven by the insatiable demand for energy, resources, and markets, is inherently antiecological. Its immensity of scale and utilitarian thrust not only destroy traditional socioeconomic structures but also set in motion irreversible and ecologically damaging global processes whose attempted solutions greatly magnify the problems. Marston Bates states that humans now truly constitute a new geological force. While the West is involved in a massive effort to take over the life-support systems of the earth, it is clear that a dependent part cannot grow infinitely at the expense of the others, or usurp the whole for its own purposes within conditions of environmental finitude.

A. K. Saran (1978) does not doubt in the least that the ecological crisis is a self-inflicted one, because an entropic environmental system and an infinitely expanding economy and technology are mutually incompatible. Furthermore, he points out that in the modern, historicist, horizontal framework of thought governed by a demiurgic anthropology, there can only be a technological solution to the problem of order in the sociopolitical realm. Ideally, it would require the destruction of this cosmos and the reconstruction of a new heaven, a new earth, "for if it were of a lesser order, a fundamental alteration of the nature of earth and sky could release forces and generate possibilities that must necessarily prove beyond the powers of the supposed masters of the earth to control. . . . For not having the power to reverse processes once started, [they] become their victims at the next stage" (Saran 1978, pp. 25, 31).

Saran's main argument is that since the modern system excludes a truly vertical dimension, it has absolutely no authoritative foundation. It does not provide a coherent worldview or the proper regulative principle to satisfy the needs of the different orders in a unitive way. Where centricity and true hierarchy have been rejected, a piecemeal approach will be relied on in the interest of the strong to deal with the consequences of a discordant and disharmonious order. In addition to generating tremendous violence, universal disorder, and planetary destruction in the desperate attempt to hold the parts together under its hegemony, such an approach is bound to fail. Since the symbolic is not an integral part of the modern literal consciousness, the attempt to appropriate Mother Earth or other symbols, such as that by the proponents of Gaia, may be ideologically seductive but is both scientifically irrelevant and spiritually vacuous. Since evolution has been the master concept to organize and rearrange the world in human terms, the ontology of modern science is necessarily anthropocentric. Saran's conclusion, therefore, is that there can be no ecological science unless it is grounded in traditional cosmology.

In a study of the Tukano Indians of the northwest Amazon, G. Reichel-Dolmatoff shows how aboriginal cosmologies, myths, and rituals

> *. . . represent in all respects a set of ecological principles . . . that formulate a system of social and economic rules that have a highly adaptive value in the continuous endeavor to maintain a viable equilibrium between the resources of the environment and the demands of society.* (1977, p. 5)
>
> *The cosmological myths which express the Tukano world-view do not describe Man's Place in Nature in terms of dominion, or mastery over a subordinate environment, nor do they in any way express the notion of what some of us might call a sense of "harmony with nature". Nature, in their view, is not a physical entity apart from man and, therefore, he cannot confront it or oppose it or harmonize with it as a separate entity. Occasionally man can unbalance it by his personal malfunctioning as a component, but he never stands apart from it. Man is taken to be a part of a set of supra-individual systems which—be they biological or cultural—transcend our individual lives and within which survival and maintenance of a certain quality of life are possible only if all other life forms too are allowed to evolve according to their specific needs, as stated in cosmological myths and traditions.* (1977, p. 11)
>
> *. . . This cosmological model . . . constitutes a religious proposition which is ultimately connected with the social and economic organization of the group. In this way, the general balance of energy flow becomes a religious objective in which native ecological concepts play a dominant organizational role. To understand the structure and functioning of the ecosystem becomes therefore a vital task to the Tukano.* (1977, p. 6)

However, modernity in its essence has been totally destructive of the traditional vision of human nature, our proper place in the "web of life," and our conception of the ultimate good. Polanyi points out how with the modern separation of "economy" as the realm of hunger and gain, our

> *animal dependence upon food has been bared and the naked fear of starvation permitted to run loose. Our humiliating enslavement to the "material", which all human culture is designed to mitigate, was deliberately made more rigorous. This is the root of the "sickness" of an acquisitive society that Tawney warned of. . . . [T]he task of adapting life in such surroundings to the requirements of human existence must be resolved if man is to continue on earth.* (1974, p. 219)

The post-World War II creation of the global economy through the idea of "development" is the other half of the story. As pointed out by Wolfgang Sachs, and in line with Hawley's observation, the concept of development provided the United States with the vision of a new global order in which the former colonies were held together not through political domination but through economic interdependence. But

> *[t]o define the economic exploitation of the land and its treasures as "development" was a heritage of the productivist arrogance of the 19th century. Through the trick of a biological metaphor, a simple economic activity turns into a natural and evolutionary process. [Soon] traditions, hierarchies, mental habits—the whole texture of societies—were all dissolved in the planner's mechanistic models . . . patterned on the American way of life.* (Sachs 1990, p. 42)

However, even after nearly two decades of development work, the results were far from heartening. Instead of declining, inequality, poverty, unemployment, hunger, and squalor actually increased manyfold in all "developing" countries.

To summarize: While the expansionist vision ties ecology, economy, and polity together, and the neo-Malthusians add biology to the list, it is in "sustainable development" that all these orders are firmly knit together—but at a price. The paradoxical nature of the term *sustainable development* arises from the fact that it attempts to combine the contradictory notions of limits to growth and active growth promotion. However, if the key to maintaining ecological integrity is economic self-sufficiency and production for use, then the problem today is surely one of the inhuman scale of enterprise based on the "techniques of degradation" (Marcel 1962, p. 70), which serve nothing higher than human self-interest, and of the concept of man as an economically rather than a spiritually determined nature (Coomaraswamy 1946, p. 2).

Roy Rappaport (1976) has documented how the Maring of New Guinea support as many as two hundred people per square mile by cultivating nearly forty-five acres of cleared forest at a time, without damaging the environment. But then they look at the world through very different eyes!

THE ENVIRONMENTAL MOVEMENT

Sociologists have paid significant attention to the study of the nature and dynamics of the environmental movement, which by the early 1980s involved over 3,000 organizations in the United States alone, though only about 250 operated on the national or multistate level (Humphrey and Buttel 1982).

The overriding emphasis of the environmental movement has been reformist. Concern with conservation and efficiency in resource and energy use, rather than with reallocating the production surplus among social classes, has dominated its agenda. Thus, the radical challenge to the dominant high-technology "treadmill of production," and the "softening" of the resource perspective of environmentalism by the emergence of equity concerns surrounding the new "appropriate technology" and "deep ecology" movements (Morrison 1980), have remained largely rhetorical, even as the focus on efficient resource use in production has made common cause between their membership and elite interests. Schnaiberg (1983), however, sees no upswelling of such redistributive politics in the near future.

One of the major research contributions has been the finding that public concern with the environment follows the same issue-attention cycle that is characteristic of most social movements. Thus, a review of current research by Dunlap (1986) revealed that public concern with environmental quality, which rose sharply in the latter half of the 1960s but peaked by 1970, declined throughout the 1970s, then rose again in force in the 1980s. As a result of the second Earth Day (1990), and the intense national and global publicity and debate on environmental issues, such as global warming and the unprecedented "environmental terrorism" in the Gulf region, public concern is at an all-time high in this United Nations "Decade of the Environment."

Environmental sociologists have explored the charge of "elitism" leveled against the environmental movement. A review by Morrison and Dunlap (1986) points out that the class composition of the environmentalists is similar to that of participants in other mass movements, that their ideological commitments range from the cause of the privileged to the problems of the poor, and that reforms do appear to have had a somewhat disproportionate negative impact at the lower end of the socioeconomic scale. Research in this and other areas is summarized in Buttel (1987).

Overall, while the environmental movement has had a significant worldwide impact on the way people and politicians look at the environment and its problems, this change has not yet been translated into comprehensive and effective policies to promote and protect environmental interests. Internationally, the United Nations' 1972 Stockholm Conference marks a watershed in the history of global action to protect the environment. It led to the formation of the United Nations Environment Programme and to various important declarations, protocols, and treaties on deforestation, desertification, management of oceanic and other common resources, transboundary pollution, global climatic change, international legal and regulatory mechanisms to ensure compliance, and the like (Leonard 1990). A concise and comprehensive history of the birth and growth, and the philosophy, of the global environmental movement is given in Sinh (1985). Sinh also has outlined the agenda to harness the tremendous potential power of people's elected representatives in the service of the environment. The 1992 global conference on the environment to be held in Brazil will review two decades of progress since Stockholm, and is likely to bring the deeply divergent views of the North and the South on the environment into sharper focus.

A PROACTIVE ENVIRONMENTAL SOCIOLOGY

The newly emerging concern with human ecology and the environment has moved into the mainstream of public life as a major national and international concern. This provides important opportunities for environmental sociologists to contribute to the understanding and solution of these problems. Constance Holden (1989) has highlighted the report of the National Academy of Sciences that outlines an agenda for both micro and macro social scientific studies of "anthropogenic" stresses on the resources and the environment in the north circumpolar region, which has general application. The fragile arctic region has a great wealth of natural resources. It comprises one-tenth of the global area and has eight million people, of whom a quarter are natives. The report placed major emphasis on interdisciplinary studies, particularly those linking the social and physical sciences and basic and applied research. It emphasized the need for drawing on native knowledge and put urgent priority on issues such as cultural survival and the allocation of scarce resources. It also asked the social scientists to come up with models generalizable to other areas.

An interesting insight concerns how each of the several identities of the Arctic (e.g., as homeland for the natives, as a "colony" exploited for its natural resources, and as the last wilderness) results in a distinctive approach to the human–environment relationships. "These approaches have come increasingly into conflict as subsistence hunters and commercial interests vie for limited stocks of fish and game; communities are shaken by boom and bust cycles in scrambles for mineral resources; and rapid modernization has inflicted trauma on native cultures" (Holden 1989, p. 83). The committee identified three areas of interest to the social scientist. In the area of human–environment relationships, there is need for studies on conflict resolution to strike a balance between commercial needs and the interests of subsistence hunters, sportsmen, and conservation. The second area pertains to community viability, for which a systematic approach is needed to help develop physical and social services infrastructure to meet the special climatic needs of the region. A final area pertains to the study of the impact of rapid social change (single-industry cash economy, the snowmobile revolution), which is exacting a heavy price from the local inhabitants in terms of higher rates of alcoholism, suicide, stress, loneliness, accidents, and violence.

The commitment to protect growth or a certain way of life has led conventional human ecologists and the neo-Malthusians to disregard the minimum well-being or sheer survival of the rest of humankind. In fact, Hawley (1986, p. 127) admits that while "competition," resulting from demand exceeding the carrying capacity, may account for the exclusion of some contestants from access to their share of a limited resource, it does not shed "any light on what happens to the excluded members of a population after their exclusion." This serious neglect of the concern for the underdog and the undermined is matched by the self-admitted tendency of the human ecologists "not [to] confront policy matters directly" (Hawley 1986, p. 127).

Edgar Borgatta (1989) has sought to develop an important field called "proactive sociology," with a view to closing the wide gap between sociological theory and practice and to save sociology from sheer irrelevance. Sociological approaches, even when application-oriented, have been largely timid, inactive, or merely reactive. Rather than waiting to study only the aftereffects of "all in the path"—the Three Mile Island radiation leak or the *Exxon Valdez* oil spill—or stepping in at the end of the "issue-attention" cycle, when the problem is historically interesting but socially irrelevant, a proactive sociology will concern itself with the dynamics out of which problems arise, anticipating potential problem areas and their alternative solutions as the means to translate desired values into effective policy. This will involve identifying possible futures and the consequences of action or inaction for their attainment, a policy dimension ignored by sociologists, despite their belief that this may make all the difference in a fast-changing and turbulent world in which the ability to handle and manage change requires the ability to anticipate change and to adapt social structures to changing requirements. To this end, the sociologist needs to ask if what he or she is doing will make an impact and be useful to society. The fundamental assumption here is that if we know something about the impact of social structure on behavior, we should be able to propose models for changes in social structures that will effectively implement values which have priority status in society (Borgatta 1989, p. 15). Sociologists are then obligated to "address societal values more directly by providing alternate models of potential changes and exploring the consequences these changes may produce if identified values are implemented" (Borgatta and Hatch 1984, p. 354).

Following this lead, a "proactive environmental sociology" would broaden the scope of the "sociology of environmental issues" by focusing specifically on the changes that are required to effectively implement stated values (equity, social justice, "future generations," conservation, sharing the global commons, clean and healthy environment, changes in life-styles and consumption patterns, and the like), and by exploring the possible consequences of these changes. Thus, David Mahar, an adviser to the World Bank, has argued that blaming peasant colonists for deforestation is "tantamount to blaming the victim" for "misguided public policies" that promote road building, official colonization of the forest, and extensive livestock development, and that "purposely or inadvertently encourage rapid depletion of the forest." This definition of the situation led Mahar to propose an "alternative development model" that would put government action on hold so that, based on land-use surveys, "(l)ands found to have limited agricultural potential—virtually whole of *terra firme* [sic] of Amazonia—would be held in perpetuity as forest reserves. . . ." These and other unconventional conclusions are stated by Mahar as his own and carry the disclaimer that they do not necessarily represent the views and policies of the World Bank itself (cited in Hildyard 1989).

This example also brings out Borgatta's point that a proactive stance may involve the espousing of unpopular positions. It may lead a proactive environmental sociologist to examine the role of established institutions and values (crass individualism and the impact of "anthropocentric," "cowboy," "superpower," and "sustained development" approaches to the use of finite resources and a fragile environment, corporate nonaccountability and the global impact of multinationals, the state, and the like) in order to facilitate the creation of environmentally sustainable social structures that implement stated values. On this basis, a systematic concern with the application of knowledge would lead to a "proactive environmental sociology" that would prompt the sociologist to formulate alternative policies with respect to the set of environmental values or goals that are to be implemented (cf. Borgatta and Cook 1984, p. 17). This will also ensure that the applied aspects of "environmental sociology" will flourish within the discipline and not become detached from sociology, as has been the fate of industrial sociology and many other areas in the past (Borgatta 1989).

OVERVIEW

Environmental sociologists have complained of the lack of a unifying focus within the field, and have noted its specialized, fragmented, and dualistic tendencies, which hinder concept and theory development (Buttel 1987, p. 466). This should be a cause for serious concern insofar as the new human ecology is supposed to provide a holistic, integrated understanding of human–environment interactions. In addition to the problems surrounding functionalist as well as Marxist categories and assumptions is the difficulty of adapting bioecological concepts to the human context. Notions such as ecosystem, niche, succession, climax communities, balance of nature, even evolution, have no clear social referents and pose formidable problems of inappropriate or illegitimate transferral of concepts. Thus, while one finds constant reference to urban or social "ecosystems" in the literature, the wide-ranging, even global, energy-exchange patterns make the boundaries so diffuse that it becomes impossible to locate an urban *ecosystem* in time and space, at least in biological terms (Young 1983, p. 195). Or, if humans are defined as niche dwellers, the term *niche,* "if adopted directly from biology would produce only one worldwide niche for the entire global species, a result that would render the concept useless. How can the species problem be overcome in adapting such a concept to human ecology?" (Young 1983, p. 795).

Terms such as *the environment* are not easy to define or conceptualize; nor are ecological chain reactions, multiple causal paths, and feedback mechanisms in complex ecosystems easy to delineate. In recognition of the substantial difference between human and bioecological orders, some human ecologists, such as Hawley, have moved away from bioecological models. Thus, Hawley is highly critical of the neo-Malthusian application of the "carrying capacity" notion, on the ground that "while the argument may be suitable for plants and animals, its transfer to the human species is highly questionable" (1986, p. 53). While still shying away from assigning a critical role to human agency, or even a policymaking role to the human ecologist, Hawley has nonetheless broadened the scope of his theory by incorporating culture and norms as ecosystem variables. Rappaport has raised more basic objections: To treat the components of the environment as if they were mere resources is to view them exclusively in economic terms and invite "the use and abuse of biological systems of all classes and the neglect of moral and aesthetic considerations in general. Whatever may be meant by the phrase 'quality of life,' exploitation does not enhance it" (1978, pp. 266–267).

Human ecologists, in general, have not dealt adequately with such concerns nor with the problems of power, domination, and the role of the state and of "values" in human–environmental relationships. At a minimum, one needs to know the role of the state in the regulation, maintenance, expansion, suppression, and "resocialization" of peoples and societies. If ecosystems are constituted of interdependent parts, one needs to know the nature of the reciprocal relationships among the parts and among the parts and the ecosystem. Rappaport (1978) has drawn attention to the maladaptive tendency of subsystems to become increasingly powerful and to dominate and use the larger system for their own benefit, to the detriment of the general interest and the adaptive flexibility of the system. He mentions the dominating positions occupied by huge corporations and the "military industrial complex" as examples. More broadly, Rappaport ties pollution, "resource" depletion, and the diminution of the quality of life and the destruction of its meanings to the scale of modern societies and the voracious appetites of their industrial metabolisms. Thus, while he does not deny that population increase may have a negative impact on the quality of life, he has little doubt that the real cause of ecosystem destruction and the deterioration of the quality of life is to be found in the way societies are organized, not in their population trends. If that is so, what alternative do humans have?

Within the human ecological perspectives, environmental problems are seen as arising either from the unplanned nature of growth and expansionism, and its attendant externalities and "commons" tragedies, and growth and market restrictions (the pro-growth, expansionist perspective), or as a result of the excess of population over the carrying capacity of the environment (the neo-Malthusian perspective). To restore ecological balance and environmental health, human ecologists place their faith in value consensus, rational planning, systems theory, computer models, economic growth, trickle-downs, market mechanisms, technological fixes (the pro-growth perspective) or in limits to growth, sustainable development, sticks and carrots, benign neglect, the triage, die-offs, outright compulsion, even genocide (the neo-Malthusian perspective). Within the political economy perspective, on the other hand, the emphasis is on internal contradictions, uneven development, center–periphery relations, capitalist exploitation, the role of multinationals and the state, trade imbalances, and the treadmill of production. To ensure environmental protection, distribution, social justice, and equality, the proposals from a political economy standpoint range from social revolution, conflict, and confrontation to social welfarism and mixed economies.

The political economy perspective is critical of the basic assumption of the Chicago ecologists that changes in population, organization, and the technologies of movement explain expansionary movements and territorial arrangements. By allowing planners to alter spatial forms to dissipate class conflict and social unrest, Smith (1979, p. 255) believes, the perspective becomes a powerful depoliticizing weapon in their hands. He favors "client-centered" planning, which does not assume that "physical structure determines social structure," but holds that both are shaped by the economic and political structures of society which provide selective access to opportunities, and further discriminatory patterns of land use and investment. Smith, therefore, offers "conflictual planning" on behalf of the poor and the powerless, to call attention to the hidden social costs of development and to increase the political costs of pursuing repressive policies disguised as rationally planned allocational, locational, and investment choices. This approach poses three basic questions: "Whose values, interests, and social actions will determine the purpose, pace, and direction of historical change? Can the costs and benefits of historical change be distributed fairly? Can the changes that do occur further the cause of social justice?" (Smith 1979, p. 288).

Schnaiberg (1980) has identified three responses to the contradiction between production expansion and ecological limits: (1) the expansionist, which will be temporary, increasingly unequal, environmentally stressful, and authoritarian; (2) the business-as-usual, which will be unstable, socially regressive, unequal, and of limited environmental value; (3) the ecological, involving appropriate technology, reduced consumption, and reduced inequality, which will be the most durable but also the most socially disruptive and the least desirable. William Ophuls (1977) has called for a rejection of Alexander Hamilton's ruling vision of power in order to realize the Jeffersonian vision of republican simplicity. Schnaiberg's own preference, short of a social revolution, is for a mixed social democratic system like Sweden's, with some production expansion and improved welfare distribution under close state supervision.

However, this solution does not quite address the critical concerns of the environment or the needs of three-fourths of humanity. It presents to the world the antiecological model of the "treadmill of production" under a more benign form. The common problem, as Hilary French (1990) points out in a Worldwatch paper on environmental reconstruction in socialist nations, is that of finding the proper balance between sufficiency and excess, which he says will be as difficult for the socialist countries as it has been for the West. He is afraid that under the impact of powerful forces, the socialist countries may end up repeating some of the West's errors. In this context, he points out how Czechoslovakia's president, Vaclav Havel, has identified "the omnipresent dictatorship of consumption, production, advertising, commerce, and consumer culture" as the common enemy. Nancy Anderson, the well-known New England environmental educator and activist, blames uncontrolled greed for the frightening global environmental degradation and for overpowering our sense of responsibility to future generations.

Gandhi, aware both of the fatal attraction and the destructive potential of wanton materialism, saw it as constituting the gravest threat to human freedom, survival, and environmental security. He therefore opted for a simple, nonexploitative, and ecologically sustainable social order. Such a decentralized social order, based on truth and nonviolence, is to be governed by the metaphysically determined optimum levels of wants, technology, and resource use fitted to the requirements of the human scale. In the interim, he demanded that the rich become trustees of the poor in order to serve justice, to mitigate the negative impacts of the differentials of wealth and power, and to avoid class conflicts. His radical vision of a normal social order, nowhere realized as yet, provides a useful yardstick for measuring how ecologically sound and environmentally sustainable a society is in its actual operation (Saran 1977; see also Bharadwaj 1984). Noting that the world has enough for everyone's needs but not for everyone's greed, Gandhi was convinced that such a social order would come about

> *only if the means of production of the elementary necessaries of life remain in the control of the masses. These should be freely available to all as God's air and water are or ought to be; they should not be made a vehicle of traffic for the exploitation of others. Their monopolization by any country, nation or group of persons would be unjust. The neglect of this simple principle is the cause of the destitution that we witness today not only in this unhappy land but in other parts of the world too.* (quoted in Sinha 1976, p. 81)

From this point of view, while there is little disagreement that overpopulation aggravates environmental and other problems, the attempts to eradicate the root causes of social instability, inequality, and poverty are bound to be far more effective in the long run than the impressive but partially effective approaches to population control. Brian Tokar (1988) has pointed out that, historically, rapid increases in population occur when people become dislocated from their traditional land base and become less secure about their personal and family survival. On the other hand, populations become stable when the future is secure, the infant mortality rate is low, social choices for women are expanding, and parents are not worried about who will support them in their old age.

How to effect the radical changes required to restore the proper ecological balance and preserve the biocultural integrity and diversity of the global "household," but "without the most fantastic 'bust' of all time" (Ehrlich 1968, p. 169), is the formidable challenge and the urgent task facing humankind. This will involve a redirection of the vast, creative human energies away from a self-defeating and ecodestructive expansionist and wasteful orientation, and their rechanneling into the life-giving and life-promoting forms of human action and human social organization.

(SEE ALSO: *Demographic Transition; Population; Technological Risks and Society*)

REFERENCES

Arnold, Steven H. 1989 "Sustainable Development: A Solution to the Development Puzzle." *Development, Journal of SID* 2/3:21–24.

Bell, Daniel 1976 *The Cultural Contradictions of Capitalism.* New York: Basic Books.

——— 1977 "Are There 'Social Limits' to Growth?" In Kenneth D. Wilson, ed., *Prospects for Growth: Changing Expectations for the Future.* New York: Praeger.

Bharadwaj, L. K. 1984 "The Contribution of Gandhian Thinking to the Understanding of the World Crisis." *Revue internationale de sociologie* 20:65–99.

Borgatta, Edgar F. 1989 "Towards a Proactive Sociology." Paper presented at the 29th International Congress of the International Institute of Sociology, Rome.

———, and Karen S. Cook 1988 "Sociology and Its Future." In Edgar F. Borgatta and Karen S. Cook, eds., *The Future of Sociology.* Newbury Park, Calif.: Sage.

———, and Laurie Russell Hatch 1988 "Social Stratification." In Edgar F. Borgatta and Karen S. Cook, eds., *The Future of Sociology.* Newbury Park, Calif.: Sage.

Brown, Lester R., Christopher Flavin, and Sandra Postel 1990 "Picturing a Sustainable Society." In Lester R. Brown and associates, *State of the World 1990: A Worldwatch Institute Report on Progress Toward a Sustainable Society.* New York: W. W. Norton.

Brundtland, Gro Harlem 1989 "Sustainable Development: An Overview." *Development, Journal of SID* 2/3:13–14.

Buttel, Frederick H. 1987 "New Directions in Environmental Sociology." *Annual Review of Sociology* 13:465–488.

Catton, William R., Jr. 1978 "Carrying Capacity, Overshoot, and the Quality of Life." In J. Milton Yinger and Stephen J. Cutler, eds., *Major Social Issues: A Multidisciplinary View.* New York: Free Press.

——— 1980 *Overshoot.* Urbana: University of Illinois Press.

———, Jr., and Riley E. Dunlap 1978 "Environmental

Sociology: A New Paradigm." *American Sociologist* 13:41–49.

Commoner, Barry 1974 "Interview on Growth." In Willem L. Oltmans, ed., *On Growth: The Crisis of Exploding Population and Resource Depletion.* New York: Capricorn Books.

Coomaraswamy, A. K. 1946 *The Religious Basis of the Forms of Indian Society.* New York: Orientalia.

de la Court, Thijs 1990 *Beyond Brundtland: Green Developments in the 1990s.* New York: New Horizon Press.

Duncan, Otis Dudley 1964 "Social Organization and the Ecosystem." In Robert E. L. Faris, ed., *Handbook of Modern Sociology.* Chicago: Rand McNally.

Dunlap, Riley E. 1979 "Environmental Sociology." *Annual Review of Sociology* 5:243–273.

———1986 "Two Decades of Public Concern for Environmental Quality: Up, Down and Up Again." Paper presented at the Annual Meetings of the American Sociological Association, New York.

Ehrlich, Paul R. 1968 *The Population Bomb.* New York: Ballantine Books.

French, Hilary F. 1990 *Green Revolutions: Environmental Reconstruction in Eastern Europe and the Soviet Union.* Worldwatch Paper 99:1–62. Washington, D.C.: Worldwatch Institute.

Freudenberg, William R., and Robert Gramling 1989 "The Emergence of Environmental Sociology: Contributions of Riley E. Dunlap and William R. Catton, Jr." *Sociological Inquiry* 59:439–452.

Gottdiener, M., and Joe R. Feagin 1988 "The Paradigm Shift in Urban Sociology." *Urban Affairs Quarterly* 24:163–187.

Hardin, Garrett 1968 "The Tragedy of the Commons." *Science* 162:1243–1248.

Hawley, Amos H. 1979 "Cumulative Change in Theory and in History." In Amos H. Hawley, ed., *Societal Growth: Processes and Implications.* New York: Free Press.

———1984 "Sociological Human Ecology: Past, Present, and Future." In Michael Micklin and Harvey M. Choldin, eds., *Sociological Human Ecology: Contemporary Issues and Applications.* Boulder, Colo.: Westview.

———1986 *Human Ecology: A Theoretical Essay.* Chicago: University of Chicago Press.

Hildyard, Nicholas B. 1989 "Adios Amazonia? A Report from Altimira Gathering." *The Ecologist* 19:53–67.

Holden, Constance 1989 "Environment, Culture, and Change in the Arctic." *Science* 243:883.

Humphrey, Craig R., and Frederick H. Buttel 1982 *Environment, Energy, and Society.* Belmont, Calif.: Wadsworth.

Kahn, Herman 1974 "Interview on Growth." In Willem L. Oltmans, ed., *On Growth: The Crisis of Exploding Population and Resource Depletion.* New York: Capricorn Books.

Leonard, Pamela 1990 *Effective Global Environmental Protection: World Federalist Proposals to Strengthen the Role of the United Nations.* Washington, D.C.: World Federalist Association. (In collaboration with Walter Hoffman.)

Meadows, Donella, Dennis Meadows, Jorgen Randers, and William Behrens 1972 *The Limits to Growth: A Report for the Club of Rome's Project on the Predicament of Mankind.* New York: Universe Books.

Medvedev, Zhores A. 1990 "The Environmental Destruction of the Soviet Union." *The Ecologist* 20: 27–29.

Mellos, Koula 1988 *Perspectives on Ecology: A Critical Essay.* New York: St. Martin's.

Micklin, Michael, and Harvey M. Choldin (eds.) 1984 *Sociological Human Ecology: Contemporary Issues and Applications.* Boulder, Colo.: Westview.

Miller, G. Tyler, Jr. 1972 *Replenish the Earth: A Primer in Human Ecology.* Belmont, Calif.: Wadsworth.

Morrison, Denton E. 1976 "Growth, Environment, Equity and Scarcity." *Social Science Quarterly* 57: 292–306.

———1978 "Equity Impacts of Some Major Energy Alternatives." In Seymour Warkov, ed., *Energy Policy in the United States: Social and Behavioral Dimensions.* New York: Praeger.

———1980 "The Soft, Cutting Edge of Environmentalism: Why and How the Appropriate Technology Notion Is Changing the Movement." *Natural Resources Journal* 20:275–298.

———, and Riley E. Dunlap 1986 "Environmentalism and Elitism: A Conceptual and Empirical Analysis." *Environmental Management* 10:581–589.

Ophuls, William 1977 "Buddhist Politics: In Politics as in Economics, 'Small Is Beautiful.'" *The Ecologist* 7:82–87.

Park, Robert E. 1936 "Human Ecology." *American Journal of Sociology* 42:1–15.

Polanyi, Karl 1974 "Our Obsolete Market Mentality." *The Ecologist* 4:213–220. Reprint of 1947 article.

Rappaport, Roy A. 1976 "Forests and Man." *The Ecologist* 6:240–246.

———1978 "Biology, Meaning, and the Quality of Life." In J. Milton Yinger and Stephen J. Cutler, eds., *Major Social Issues: A Multidisciplinary View.* New York: Free Press.

Redclift, Michael 1987 *Sustainable Development: Exploring the Contradiction.* New York: Methuen.

Reichel-Dolmatoff, G. 1977 "Cosmology as Ecological Analysis: A View from the Rain Forest." *The Ecologist* 7:4–11.

Revelle, Roger 1974 "Interview on Growth." In Willem L. Oltmans, ed., *On Growth: The Crisis of Exploding Population and Resource Depletion.* New York: Capricorn Books.

Sachs, Wolfgang 1990 "On the Archeology of the Development Idea." *The Ecologist* 20:42–43.

Saran, A. K. 1977 *Gandhi and the Concept of Politics: Toward a Normal Civilization.* New Delhi: Nehru Memorial Museum and Library.

———1978 "The Traditional Vision of Man." UNESCO Seminar, Hyderabad, India. Mimeo.

Schnaiberg, Allan 1980 *The Environment: From Surplus to Scarcity.* New York: Oxford University Press.

———1983 "Redistributive Goals Versus Distributive Politics: Social Equity Limits in Environmental and Appropriate Technology Movements." *Sociological Inquiry* 53:200–219.

Sen, Amartya K. 1981 *Poverty and Famines: An Essay on Entitlement and Deprivation.* Oxford: Clarendon Press.

Sinh, Digvijay 1985 *The Eco-Vote: Peoples' Representatives and Global Environment.* New Delhi: Prentice-Hall of India.

Sinha, Radha 1976 *Food and Poverty: The Political Economy of Confrontation.* London: Croom Helm Ltd.

Smith, Michael P. 1979 *The City and Social Theory.* New York: St. Martin's.

Stonich, Susan C. 1989 "The Dynamics of Social Processes and Environmental Destruction: A Central American Case Study." *Population and Development Review* 15:269–296.

Tokar, Brian 1988 "Social Ecology, Deep Ecology and the Future of Green Political Thought." *The Ecologist* 18:132–141.

Vohra, B. B. 1985 "Why India's Forests Have Been Cut Down." *The Ecologist* 15:50–51.

World Commission on Environment and Development 1987 *Our Common Future.* New York: Oxford University Press (The Brundtland Report).

Young, Gerald (ed.) 1983 *Origins of Human Ecology.* Stroudsburg, Pa.: Hutchinson Ross.

LAKSHMI K. BHARADWAJ

HUMANISM *See* Religious Orientation.

HUMAN NATURE Debates over the nature of human nature have characterized social theory since it emerged in the Renaissance. As Thomas Sowell has argued, these debates generally take two forms: the optimistic and the pessimistic (Sowell 1987). The former position, associated with Rousseau and anarchists such as William Goodwin, holds that humans are essentially good, but they are turned bad by the institutions of their society. The latter position is rooted in the assumption that humans are fundamentally egoistic and selfish, thereby requiring either a strong state to regulate them or, in a less pessimistic account, an institution like the market to guide their affairs toward an optimal result.

For sociologists, neither position became the dominant way of thinking about human nature; instead, the plasticity of human experience was emphasized. Durkheim (1973) wrote the most important defense of a pluralistic approach to the subject, one that remains unsurpassed to this day in its clarity of presentation. Human nature was dualistic, he argued, speaking to the needs of both body and soul, the sacred and the profane, the emotional and the cognitive, and other such dualities. We are, in short, what we make ourselves. This version of a flexible approach to human nature would come to characterize contemporary theorists such as Parsons, who spoke of "much discussed 'plasticity' of the human organism, its capacity to learn any one of a large number of alternative patterns of behavior instead of being bound by its generic constitution to a very limited range of alternatives" (1951, p. 32).

In current sociological debates, the plasticity of human nature is emphasized by the general term *social construction.* If one argues that we ought to speak of gender roles rather than sex roles—the former is recognized to be the product of how people arrange their cultural rules, whereas the latter is understood to be fixed biologically—one is making a case for plasticity (Epstein 1988). Indeed, given the importance of feminism in contemporary theory, which tends to argue that "nothing about the body, including women's reproductive organs, determines univocally how social divisions will be shaped" (Scott 1988, p. 2), the strength of a plasticity approach to human nature is probably stronger than ever before.

Current research in many areas of sociology is premised on a social construction approach. Work stimulated by ethnomethodology is one clear case. In contrast to a Chomskian understanding of language as originating in rules hard-wired in the brain, the tradition of conversation analysis examines how human beings in real conservation twist and shape their utterances to account for context and nuance (Schegloff and Sacks 1979; Scheff 1986). Moreover, since the language we use is a reflection of the way we think, it is possible to argue that the mind itself is socially constructed, that the a priori nature of the way we think is relatively minimal (Coulter 1979). Accounts of sociological practice based on the assumption of plasticity do not end there. It has been argued that homosexuality is not driven by biological destiny but is a socially constructed phenomenon (Greenberg 1988). Morality, as well, can be understood as socially constructed (Wolfe 1989). Underlying a wide variety of approaches to sociology—from symbolic interactionism to social problems—is an underlying premise that human nature is not driven by any one thing.

The only dissent from a general consensus over human nature's plasticity is rational choice theory. At least among economists who believe that economic methodologies can be used to study social institutions such as the family, there is a belief that "human behavior is not compartmentalized, sometimes based on maximizing, sometimes not, sometimes motivated by stable preferences, sometimes by volatile ones, sometimes resulting in an optimal accumulation, sometimes not" (Becker 1976, p. 14). Yet there are many versions of rational choice theory; at least one of them, that associated with Jon Elster, is committed to methodological individualism, but is also willing to concede the existence of a "multiple self" (Elster 1986). It is far more common in contemporary sociology to speak of egoism and altruism as existing in some kind of unstable combination rather than giving the priority totally to one or the other (Etzioni 1988).

Arguments about human nature, in turn, are related to the philosophical anthropology that shaped so much social theory. It has been a consistent theme of the sociological enterprise to argue that humans are different from other species. From the emphasis on *homo faber* in Marx and Engels through Weber's notions about the advantages of culture to Mead's account of why dogs and other animals are incapable of exchanging significant symbols, humans have been understood to possess unique characteristics that determine the organization of their society. Twentieth-century theorists such as Arnold Gehlen or Helmuth Plessner carried forward this tradition and are increasingly translated and read (for an overview, see Honneth and Joas 1988). Even Niklas Luhmann, whose work is heavily influenced by biology and cybernetics, can still claim that "the decisive advantage of human interaction over animal interaction stems from this elemental achievement of language" (1982, p. 72).

The most important shift in philosophical anthropology in recent years is a shift from an essentially materialist understanding of human capacities to an essentially mental one. Powers of interpretation and narrative, it has been argued, constitute the essential features of the human self (Taylor 1989). Just as an argument about the plasticity of human nature enables sociology to avoid reduction into psychological categories, an emphasis on the interpretive powers of humans prevents a reduction of sociology to sociobiology and other basically algorithmic ways of thinking about evolution.

As with the issue of plasticity, not all sociologists agree either that there are specific human characteristics or that, if there are, they ought to be understood as primarily mental and interpretive. Sociobiologists argue that not only are humans driven by their genetic structure more than they would like to believe, but other animals also possess cultural skills. There is therefore no fundamental difference between human and nonhuman species, merely points along a continuum (Lumsden and Wilson 1981). Both sociologists and anthropologists, consequently, have argued for the use of sociobiological approaches in the social sciences (Lopreato 1984; Wozniak 1984; Rindos 1986), although there are also critics who question such an enterprise (Blute 1987).

Another challenge to the anthropocentric view that social scientists have taken toward humans has arisen with cognitive science and artificial intelligence. Whereas classical sociological theory compared humans to other animal species, we can now compare them to machines. Computers, after all, process information just as human brains do, use language to communicate, reason, and can, especially in new approaches to artificial intelligence called connectionist, learn from their mistakes. There are, consequently, some efforts to apply artificial intelligence to sociology as there are efforts to use the insights of sociobiology (Gilbert and Heath 1986), although here, again, there are strong critical voices (Wolgar 1985; Wolfe 1991). In the more recent work of Luhmann, as well as in the writings of some other theorists, emphasis is placed on information science, systems theory, even thermodynamics, all of which are approaches based on a denial that human systems require special ways of understanding that are different from other systems (Luhmann 1989; Beniger 1986; Bailey 1990).

In spite of efforts to develop sociological theory on the basis of algorithmic self-reproducing systems, it is unlikely that assumptions about the unique, interpretative, meaning-producing capacities of humans will be seriously challenged. It is the capacity to recognize the contexts in which messages are transmitted and thereby to interpret those messages that make human mental capacities distinct from any organism, whether natural or artificial, that is preprogrammed to follow explicit instructions. One reason humans are able to recognize contexts is precisely the plasticity of their mental capacities. The plastic theory of human nature, in short, overlaps with an emphasis on philosophical anthropology to produce an understanding of human behavior that does not so much follow already-existing rules so much as it alters and bends rules as it goes along.

Both understandings of human nature and accounts of specifically human capacities will be relevant to future efforts in sociological theory to reconcile micro and macro approaches. Although there has been a good deal of effort to establish a micro–macro link (Alexander et al. 1987), the more interesting question may turn out not to be not whether it can be done but whether (and how) it ought to be done. Systems theory and the information sciences provide a relatively easy way to make a link between parts and wholes: each part is understood to have as little autonomy as possible so that the system as a whole can function autonomously with respect to other systems. The micro, like a bit of information in a computer program, would be structured to be as dumb as possible so that the macro system itself can be intelligent. Nonhuman enterprises—computers on the one hand and the structure of DNA in other animal species on the other—show that there is a major bridge between the macro and the micro. But the cost of constructing that bridge is the denial of the autonomy of the parts, a high cost for humans to pay.

But conceptions of human beings as preprogrammed rule followers are not the only way to conceptualize micro sociological processes. The traditions of ethnomethodology and symbolic interactionism, which are more compatible with notions emphasizing the plasticity of human nature, imagine the human parts of any social system as engaged in a constant process of renegotiating the rules that govern the system. When the micro is understood as plastic, the macro can be understood as capable of existing even in imperfect, entropy-producing states of disorder. Indeed, for human systems, as opposed to those of machines and other species, disorder is the norm, integration the exception. If there is going to be a micro–macro link in sociology, it may well come about not by denying human plasticity and uniqueness, but rather by accounting for the particular and special property humans possess of having no fixed nature but a repertoire of social practices that in turn make human society different from any other kind of system.

(SEE ALSO: *Evolution: Biological, Social, Cultural; Intelligence; Sex Differences*)

REFERENCES

Alexander, Jeffrey C., Bernhard Giesen, Richard Münch, and Neil J. Smelser 1987 *The Macro-Micro Link.* Berkeley: University of California Press.

Bailey, Kenneth D. 1990 *Social Entropy Theory.* Albany: State University of New York Press.

Becker, Gary 1976 *The Economic Approach to Human Behavior.* Chicago: University of Chicago Press.

Beniger, James R. 1986 *The Control Revolution: Technological and Economic Origins of the Information Society.* Cambridge, Mass.: Harvard University Press.

Blute, Marion 1987 "Biologists on Sociocultural Evolution: A Critical Analysis." *Sociological Theory* 5:185–193.

Coulter, Jeff 1979 *The Social Construction of Mind.* London: Macmillan.

Durkheim, Emile 1973 "The Dualism of Human Nature and Its Social Conditions." In Robert N. Bellah, ed., *Emile Durkheim on Morality and Society: Selected Writings.* Chicago: University of Chicago Press.

Elster, Jon (ed.) 1986 *The Multiple Self.* Cambridge: Cambridge University Press.

Epstein, Cynthia 1988 *Deceptive Distinctions: Sex, Gender, and the Social Order.* New Haven, Conn.: Yale University Press.

Etzioni, Amitai 1988 *The Moral Dimension.* New York: Free Press.

Gilbert, C. Nigel, and Christian Heath (eds.) *Social Action and Artificial Intelligence: Surrey Conferences on Sociological Theory and Method 3.* Aldershot, England: Gower.

Greenberg, David 1988 *The Construction of Homosexuality.* Chicago: University of Chicago Press.

Honneth, Axel, and Hans Joas 1988 *Social Action and Human Nature.* Cambridge: Cambridge University Press.

Lopreato, Joseph 1984 *Human Nature and Biocultural Evolution.* Boston: Allen and Unwin.

Luhmann, Niklas 1982 *The Differentiation of Society,* trans. Stephen Holmes and Charles Larmore. New York: Columbia University Press.

——— 1989 *Ecological Communication,* trans. John Bednarz. Chicago: University of Chicago Press.

Lumsden, Charles J., and Edward O. Wilson 1981 *Genes, Mind, and Culture: The Coevolutionary Process.* Cambridge, Mass.: Harvard University Press.

Parsons, Talcott 1951 *The Social System.* New York: Free Press.

Rindos, David 1986 "The Evolution of the Capacity for Culture: Sociobiology, Structuralism, and Cultural Selectiveness." *Current Anthropology* 27:315–332.

Scheff, Thomas J. 1986 "Micro-Linguistics and Social Structure: A Theory of Social Action." *Sociological Theory* 4:71–83.

Schegloff, Emmanuel, and Harvey Sacks 1979 "Opening Up Closings." In Ray Turner, ed., *Ethnomethodology: Selected Readings.* Baltimore: Penguin.

Scott, Joan Wallach 1988 *Gender and the Politics of History.* New York: Columbia University Press.

Sowell, Thomas 1987 *A Conflict of Visions.* New York: William Morrow.

Taylor, Charles 1989 *Sources of the Self: The Making of the Modern Identity.* Cambridge, Mass.: Harvard University Press.

Wolfe, Alan 1989 *Whose Keeper?: Social Science and Moral Obligation.* Berkeley: University of California Press.

——— 1991 "Mind, Self, Society, and Computer: Artificial Intelligence and the Sociology of Mind." *American Journal of Sociology* 96:1073–1096.

Woolger, Steve 1985 "Why Not a Sociology of Machines?: The Case of Sociology and Artificial Intelligence." *Sociology* 19:557–572.

Wozniak, Paul R. 1984 "Making Sociobiological Sense out of Sociology." *Sociological Quarterly* 25:191–204.

ALAN WOLFE

HUMAN RIGHTS *See* Apartheid; Political Crime; Protest Movements; Segregation and Desegregation.

HYPOTHESIS TESTING *See* Scientific Explanation; Statistical Inference.

I

IDENTITY THEORY Identity theory, in the present context, has its referent in a specific and delimited literature that seeks to develop and empirically examine a theoretical explanation, derived from what has been called a structural symbolic-interactionist perspective (Stryker 1980), of role choice behavior. It is only one of a large number of formulations—social scientific, therapeutic, humanistic—in which the concept of identity plays a central role, formulations having their roots in a variety of disciplines ranging from theology through psychoanalysis to psychology, social psychology, and sociology. Further mention of these diverse formulations will be forgone in order to focus on identity theory as specified above; those who desire leads into the literature of sociology and social psychology to which identity theory most closely relates will find them in Weigert (1983); Weigert, Teitge, and Teitge (1986); Reynolds (1990); Hewitt (1989); McCall and Simmons (1978); and Stryker (1980).

The prototypical question addressed by identity theory, phrased illustratively, is, Why is it that one person, given a free weekend afternoon, chooses to take his or her children to the zoo while another person opts to spend that time on the golf course with friends? The language of this prototypical question implies a scope limitation of the theory that is important to recognize at the outset of the discussion. The theory is intended to apply to situations where alternative courses of action are reasonably, and reasonably equivalently, open to the actor. A defining assumption of the symbolic-interactionist theoretical framework is that human beings are actors, not merely reactors. Identity theory shares this assumption, which recognizes the possibility of choice as a ubiquitous feature of human existence. At the same time, however, identity theory recognizes the sociological truth that social structure and social interaction are equally ubiquitous in constraining—not in a strict sense "determining"—human action. That constraint is variable. It may be true in an abstract and philosophical sense that people are "free" to act in any way they choose in any situation in which they may find themselves, including choosing to endure great punishment or even death rather than to behave in ways demanded by others; but surely it is entirely reasonable to presume that jailed prisoners have no viable options with respect to many—likely most—facets of life and in any event have fewer viable options than persons who are not jailed. Identity theory has more to say on the latter persons than on the former, and more to say on the perhaps few aspects of life about which the former do have reasonable choice than on those many aspects of prisoner life where options, as a practical matter, do not exist.

As a derivative of a symbolic-interactionist theoretical framework, identity theory shares a number of the assumptions or premises of interactionist thought in general. One, that human beings are actors as well as reactors, has already been suggested. A second is that human action and interaction are critically shaped by definitions or interpretations of the situations of action and interaction, which definitions and interpretations are based on shared meanings developed in the course of interaction with others. A third premise is that the meanings which persons attribute to themselves, their self-conceptions, are especially critical to the process producing their action and interaction. And a fourth premise is that self-conceptions, like other meanings, are shaped in the course of interaction with others and are, at least in the initial instance and at least largely, the outcomes of others' responses to the person.

The fourth premise has sometimes been phrased as, Self reflects society. Taken in conjunction with the third premise, it gives rise to the basic theoretical proposition or formula of symbolic interactionism: Society shapes self, which shapes social behavior. That formula, it must be noted, admits of and, indeed, insists upon the possibility of reciprocity among its components—social behavior impacts self and society, and self can impact society. Identity theory builds upon refinements of the traditional symbolic-interactionist framework and specifications of its basic formula.

The refinements essentially have to do with three facets of the traditional symbolic-interactionist framework as it evolved from Mead (1934), Cooley (1902), Blumer (1969), and others: the conceptualization of society, the conceptualization of self, and the relative weight to be accorded social structure versus interpretive processes in accounts of human behavior. The traditional framework tends to a view of "society" as unitary, as a relatively undifferentiated and unorganized phenomenon with few, if any, internal barriers to the evolution of universally shared meanings. It also tends to a view of "society" as an unstable and ephemeral reflection, even reification, of relatively transient, ever-shifting patterns of interaction. On this view of society, social structures, as these are typically conceived of by sociologists, have little place in accounts of persons' behaviors; these accounts tend to be innocent of a coherent sense of extant social constraints on those behaviors, and there are few means of linking the dynamics of social interaction in reasonably precise ways to the broader social settings that serve as context for persons' action and interaction.

Further, and enlarging this theme of an inadequate conceptualization and consequent neglect of social structure, this view of society tends to dissolve social structure in the universal solvent of subjective definitions or interpretations, thus missing the obdurate reality of social forms whose impact on behavior is undeniable. To say this does not deny the import for social life of the definitional and interpretative processes central to interactionist thinking and explanation. It is, however, to say that seeing these processes as in large degree unanchored and without bounds, as open to any possibility whatsoever without recognizing that some are much more probable than others, results in visualizing social life as less a product of external constraints and more a product of persons' phenomenology than is likely warranted. Finally, on the premise that self reflects society, this view of society leads directly to a view of self as unitary, as equivalently internally undifferentiated, unorganized, unstable, and ephemeral.

Contemporary sociology's image of society is considerably different from that contained in traditional symbolic interactionism, and it is the contemporary sociological conceptualization of society that is incorporated into the structural symbolic-interactionist frame from which identity theory derives. This contemporary conceptualization emphasizes the durability of the patterned interactions and relationships that are at the heart of sociology's sense of social structure. It emphasizes social structure's resistance to change and its tendency to reproduce itself. The contemporary image differs as well by visualizing societies as highly differentiated yet organized systems of interactions and relationships; as complex mosaics of groups, communities, organizations, institutions; and as encompassing a wide variety of crosscutting lines of social demarcation based upon social class, age, gender, ethnicity, religion, and more. This vast diversity of parts is seen as organized in multiple and overlapping ways—interactionally, functionally, and hierarchically. At the same time, the diverse parts of society are taken to be sometimes highly interdependent and sometimes relatively independent of one another, sometimes implicated in close and cooperative interaction and sometimes conflicting.

The symbolic-interactionist premise that self reflects society now requires a very different conceptualization of self, one that mirrors the altered conception of society. Self must be seen as multifaceted, as comprised of a variety of parts that are sometimes interdependent and sometimes independent of other parts, sometimes mutually reinforcing and sometimes conflicting, and that are organized in multiple ways. It requires a sense of self in keeping with James's (1890) view that persons have as many selves as there are other persons who react to them, or at least as many as there are groups of others who do so.

Equally important, viewing both society and self as complex and multifaceted as well as organized opens the way to escaping the overly general, almost banal, and essentially untestable qualities of the basic symbolic-interactionist formula by permitting theorization of the relations between particular parts of society and particular parts of self, and by permitting reasonable operationalizations of those parts.

In identity theory, this theorization proceeds by specifying the terms of the basic symbolic-interactionist formula, doing so by focusing on particulars hypothesized as especially likely to be important in impacting role choice. That is, first of all, the general category of social behavior is specified by taking role choice—opting to pursue action meeting the expectations contained in one role rather than another—as the object of explanation. Role choice is hypothesized to be a consequence of identity salience, a specification of the general category of self; and identity salience is hypothesized to be a consequence of commitment, a specification of society. Identity theory's fundamental proposition, then, is, Commitment impacts identity salience impacts role choice.

The concept of identity salience develops from the multifaceted view of self articulated above. Self is conceptualized as comprised of a set of discrete identities, or internalized role designations, with persons potentially having as many identities as there are organized systems of role relationships in which they participate. Identities require both that persons be placed as social objects by having others assign a positional designation to them and that the persons accept that designation (Stone 1962; Stryker 1968). By this usage, identities are self-cognitions tied to roles and, through roles, to positions in organized social relationships; one may speak of the identities of mother, husband, child, doctor, salesman, employee, senator, candidate, priest, tennis player, churchgoer, and so on.

But self is not only multifaceted; it is also postulated to be organized. Identity theory takes hierarchy as a principal mode of organization of identities; in particular, it assumes that identities will vary in their salience, and that self is a structure of identities organized in a salience hierarchy. Identity salience is defined as the probability that a given identity will be invoked, or called into play, in a variety of situations; alternatively, it can be defined as the differential probability, across persons, that a given identity will be invoked in a given situation. Identity theory's fundamental proposition hypothesizes that choice between or among behaviors expressive of particular roles will reflect the relative location in the identity salience hierarchy of the identities associated with those roles.

The concept of commitment has its basic referent in the networks of social relationships in which persons participate. Associated with the "complex mosaic of differentiated parts" image of society is the recognition that persons conduct their lives not in the context of society as a whole but, rather, in the many contexts of relatively small and specialized social networks, networks made up of persons to whom they relate by virtue of occupancy of particular social positions and the playing of the associated roles. To say that persons are committed to some social network is to say that their relationships to the other members of that network depend on their playing particular roles and having particular identities: To the degree that one's relationships to specific others depend on being a particular kind of person, one is committed to being that kind of person. Thus, commitment is measured by the costs of giving up meaningful relations to others should an alternative course of action be pursued. Commitment, so defined and measured, is hypothesized by identity theory to be the source of the salience attached to given identities (Stryker 1968, 1980, 1987a).

Two analytically distinct and possibly independent dimensions or forms of commitment have been discerned: interactional and affective (Stryker 1968; Serpe 1987). The former has its referent in the number of relationships entered by virtue of having a given identity and by the ties across various networks of relationships (for instance, one may relate as husband not only to one's spouse, her friends, and her relatives but also to members of a couple's bridge club and other such groups). The latter has its referent in the depth of emotional attachment to particular sets of others.

Reciprocity among the three terms of the identity theory formula is again recognized; but the dominant thrust of the process is hypothesized to be as stated by the proposition, on the grounds that identity, as a strictly cognitive phenomenon, can change more readily than can commitment, whose conceptual core is interaction rather than cognition.

The empirical evidence brought to bear on the hypotheses contained in the fundamental identity theory formula has been supportive. Stryker and Serpe (1982) demonstrate that both time spent acting out a religious role and preferred distribution of time to that role are tied to the salience of the identity associated with the role; they demonstrate as well that the salience of the religious identity is tied to commitment (in this case, the measure of commitment combines interactional and affective commitment) to others known through religious activities. Burke and various associates (Burke and Tully 1977; Burke and Reitzes 1981; Burke and Hoelter 1988) show the link between identity and gender, academic attainment and aspirations, and occupational aspirations, finding evidence that the linkage reflects the commonality of meaning of identity and behavior. Serpe and Stryker (1987), using data on student-related identities obtained at three points in time from students entering a residential college, provide evidence that the salience of these identities is reasonably stable over time; that in a situation in which earlier commitments have been attenuated by a move to a residential university, high identity salience leads to efforts to reconstruct social relationships that permit playing the role associated with the salient identity, efforts taking the form of joining appropriate organizations; and that when such efforts are not successful, the level of salience of the identity subsequently drops and self-structure is altered. Callero (1985), Callero, Howard, and Piliavin (1987), and Charng, Piliavin, and Callero (1988) show that commitment and identity salience add appreciably to the ability to account for the behavior of repeated blood donors. Serpe (1987) shows that over time there is indeed a reciprocal relationship between commitment to various student role relationships and the salience of identities associated with those roles, and that the identity theory hypothesis arguing the greater impact over time of commitment on salience than vice versa is correct.

The success of identity theory attested to in this brief review of empirical evidence notwithstanding, however, there is reason to believe that the theory requires development and extension beyond the basic proposition which has been the major focus of attention to this point. Indeed, such work has begun; and it has a variety of thrusts. How to incorporate varying degrees of situational constraint into the theory—the impact that variations in "choice" have on the ways in which the relationships among commitment, identity salience, and role performances play themselves out—is one such thrust (Serpe 1987). Another seeks to explore mechanisms underlying the linkages among commitment and identity salience, and identity salience and behavior; to this end, current work (especially by Burke and Reitzes 1981, 1990) exploits the basic symbolic-interactionist idea that it is commonality of meaning which makes social life possible. Some attention has been given to extending the applicability and predictive power of identity theory by incorporating into it other than strictly role-based identities; in particular, the concern has been with what have been termed "master statuses" (such as age, gender, and class) and personal traits (such as aggressiveness and honesty), and the suggestion is that master statuses and traits may affect identity processes by modifying the meaning of the roles from which identities derive (Stryker 1987a).

An effort is being made to correct the almost totally cognitive focus of identity theory (as well as its parent and grandparent interactionist frameworks) by recognizing the importance of affect and emotion to the processes with which the theory is concerned. The earliest statement of the theory (Stryker 1968) posited a cathectic modality of self that parallels the cognitive modality from which the emphasis on identity flows; however, subsequent work on the theory has not pursued that idea. More recently Stryker (1987b) has attempted to integrate emotion into the theory by arguing, with Hochschild (1979), that emotional expressions carry important messages from self and, beyond Hochschild, that the experiences of emotions are messages to self informing those who experience those emotions of the strength of commitments and the salience of identities.

Finally—and here work has barely begun—it is time to make good on the promise to provide more adequate conceptualization of the linkages between identity theory processes and the wider social structures within which these processes are embedded. From the point of view of a structural symbolic interactionism, structures of class, ethnicity, age, gender, and so on operate as social boundaries making it more or less probable that particular persons will form interactional networks; in this way, such social structures enter identity theory directly through their impact on commitments. However, the relation of such structures to identity processes clearly goes beyond this direct impact; they affect not only the probabilities of interaction but also the content (meanings) of the roles entailed in interaction and, thus, the meanings of identities, the symbolic and material resources available to those who enter interaction with others, and the objectives or ends to which interactions are oriented. Explication of these impacts, both direct and indirect, of social structure on the processes that relate commitment, identity salience, and role performance remains to be accomplished.

(SEE ALSO: *Self-Concept; Social Psychology; Symbolic Interaction Theory*)

REFERENCES

Blumer, Herbert 1969 *Symbolic Interactionism: Perspective and Method.* Englewood Cliffs, N.J.: Prentice-Hall.

Burke, Peter J., and Jon W. Hoelter 1988 "Identity and Sex–Race Differences in Educational and Occupational Aspirations Formation." *Social Science Research* 17:29–47.

Burke, Peter J., and Donald C. Reitzes 1981 "The Link Between Identity and Role Performance." *Social Psychology Quarterly* 44:83–92.

——— 1990 "An Identity Theory Approach to Commitment." Unpublished manuscript.

Burke, Peter J., and Judy Tully 1977 "The Measurement of Role/Identity." *Social Forces* 55:880–897.

Callero, Peter L. 1985 "Role–Identity Salience." *Social Psychology Quarterly* 48:203–215.

———, Judith A. Howard, and Jane A. Piliavin 1987 "Helping Behavior as Role Behavior: Disclosing Social Structure and History in the Analysis of Pro-social Action." *Social Psychology Quarterly* 50:247–256.

Charng, Hong-Wen, June Allyn Piliavin, and Peter L. Callero 1988 "Role-Identity and Reasoned Action in the Prediction of Repeated Behavior." *Social Psychology Quarterly* 51:303–317.

Cooley, Charles H. 1902 *Human Nature and Social Order.* New York: Scribners.

Hewitt, John P. 1989 *Dilemmas of the American Self.* Philadelphia: Temple University Press.

Hochschild, Arlie R. 1979 "Emotion Work, Feeling Rules, and Social Structure." *American Journal of Sociology* 85:551–575.

James, William 1890 *Principles of Psychology.* New York: Holt.

McCall, George, and J. S. Simmons 1978 *Identities and Interaction,* rev. ed. New York: Free Press.

Mead, George H. 1934 *Mind, Self and Society.* Chicago: University of Chicago Press.

Reynolds, Larry T. 1990 *Interactionism: Exposition and Critique,* 2nd ed. Dix Hills, N.Y.: General Hall.

Serpe, Richard T. 1987 "Stability and Change in Self: A Structural Symbolic Interactionist Explanation." *Social Psychology Quarterly* 50:44–55.

———, and Sheldon Stryker 1987 "The Construction of Self and the Reconstruction of Social Relationships." In Edward J. Lawler and Barry Markovsky, eds., *Advances in Group Processes,* vol. 4. Greenwich, Conn.: JAI Press.

Stone, Gregory P. 1962 "Appearance and the Self." In Arnold M. Rose, ed., *Human Behavior and the Social Process.* Boston: Houghton Mifflin.

Stryker, Sheldon 1968 "Identity Salience and Role Performance." *Journal of Marriage and the Family* 30:558–564.

———1980 *Symbolic Interactionism: A Social Structural Version.* Menlo Park, Calif.: Benjamin/Cummings.

———1987a "Identity Theory: Developments and Extensions." In Krysia Yardley and Terry Honess, eds., *Self and Society: Psychosocial Perspectives.* New York: Wiley.

———1987b "The Interplay of Affect and Identity: Exploring the Relationships of Social Structure, Social Interaction, Self and Emotion." Paper presented at a meeting of the American Sociological Association, Chicago.

———, and Richard T. Serpe 1982 "Commitment, Identity Salience, and Role Behavior: Theory and Research Example." In William Ickes and Eric S. Knowles, eds., *Personality, Roles, and Social Behavior.* New York: Springer-Verlag.

Weigert, Andrew J. 1983 "Identity: Its Emergence Within Sociological Psychology." *Symbolic Interaction* 6:183–206.

———, J. Smith Teitge, and Dennis W. Teitge 1986 *Society and Identity: Toward a Sociological Psychology.* Cambridge: Cambridge University Press.

SHELDON STRYKER

ILLEGAL ALIENS/UNDOCUMENTED IMMIGRANTS *See* International Migration.

ILLEGITIMACY Until the 1960s, it was widely assumed that marriage was a universal or nearly universal institution for licensing parenthood. Marriage assigned paternity rights to fathers (and their families) and guaranteed social recognition and economic support to mothers and their offspring. According to Malinowski (1930), who first articulated "the principle of legitimacy," and to Davis (1939, 1949), who extended Malinowski's theory into sociology, marriage provides the added benefit to children of connecting them to a wider network of adults who have a stake in their long-term development.

This functional explanation for the universality of marriage as a mechanism for legitimating parenthood became a source of intense debate in anthropology and sociology during the 1960s. Evidence accumulated from cross-cultural investigations showed considerable variation in marriage forms and differing levels of commitment to the norm of legitimacy (Bell and Vogel 1968; Blake 1961; Goode 1961; Coser 1964). More recently, historical evidence indicates that the institution of marriage was not firmly in place in parts of Western Europe until the end of the Middle Ages (Laslett 1972; Gillis 1985).

The accumulation of contradictory data led Goode (1960, 1971) to modify Malinowski's theory to take account of high rates of informal unions and nonmarital childbearing in many New World nations and among dispossessed cultural minorities. Goode (1971) argued that the norm of legitimacy was likely to be enforced only when fathers possessed wealth and property or when their potential economic investment in child rearing was high. Therefore, he predicted that when "giving a name" to children offers few material, social, or cultural benefits, the norms upholding marriage will become attenuated.

So vast have been the changes in the perceived benefits of marriage since the 1960s in the United

States and most Western nations that even Goode's modification of Malinowski's theory of legitimacy now seems to be in doubt (Davis 1985; Popenoe 1988; Cherlin and Furstenberg 1988). Indeed, the term *illegitimacy* has fallen into disfavor precisely *because* it implies inferior status to children born out of wedlock. The nuclear unit (biological parents and their offspring)—once regarded as the cornerstone of our kinship system—remains the modal family form, but it no longer represents the exclusive cultural ideal, as was the case in the mid-1960s. The incentives for marriage in the event of premarital pregnancy have declined, and the sanctions against remaining single have diminished (Cherlin 1988; Bane and Jargowsky 1988; Thornton 1989).

TRENDS IN NONMARITAL CHILDBEARING

Premarital pregnancy has never been rare in the United States or in most Western European nations (Vinovskis 1988; Smith 1978; Goode 1961). Apparently the tolerance for pregnancy before marriage has varied over time and varies geographically at any given time. Throughout the first half of the twentieth century, premarital pregnancy almost always led to hasty marriages rather than out-of-wedlock births—even for very young women (Vincent 1961; O'Connell and Moore 1981). Rates of nonmarital childbearing were actually higher in the middle of the nineteenth century in England, Wales, and probably the United States (Clague and Ventura 1968) than a century later. In 1940, illegitimacy was uncommon in the United States, at least among whites. Nonmarital births were estimated at about 3.6 per 1,000 unmarried white women, while the comparable rate for nonwhites was 35.6. For all age groups, and among whites and nonwhites alike, a spectacular rise occurred over the next two decades (Clague and Ventura 1968; Cutright 1972).

In the 1960s and 1970s, nonmarital childbearing rates continued to increase for younger women, albeit at a slower pace, while for women in their late twenties and thirties rates temporarily declined. Then, in the late 1970s, nonmarital childbearing rose again for all age groups and among both whites and African-Americans. Current levels in the United States are unprecedented. Moreover, since rates of marriage and marital childbearing have fallen precipitously since the 1960s, the ratio of total births to single women has shot up (National Center for Health Statistics 1990, Tables 1-31–1-33). More than a quarter of all births (25.7 percent) in 1988 occurred out of wedlock, more than five times the proportion in 1955 (4.5 percent) and nearly twice that in 1975 (14.3 percent). The declining connection between marriage and parenthood is evident among all age groups but is especially pronounced among women in their teens and early twenties. Nearly two-thirds of births to teens and close to one-third of all births to women ages twenty to twenty-four occurred out of wedlock. Virtually all younger blacks who had children in 1988 (over 90 percent) were unmarried, while half of white teens and a quarter of women twenty to twenty-four were single.

Nonmarital childbearing was initially defined as a problem among teenagers and black women (Furstenberg 1991). But these recent trends strongly suggest that the disintegration of the norm of legitimacy has spread to all segments of the population. First the link between marriage and sexual initiation dissolved, and now the link between marriage and parenthood has become weak. Whether this trend is temporary or a more permanent feature of the Western family system is not known. But public opinion data suggest that a high proportion of the population finds single parenthood acceptable. A Roper study (Virginia Slims American Women's Opinion Poll 1985) revealed that 49 percent of women agreed that "There was no reason why single women should not have children and raise them if they want to."

Citing similar attitudinal evidence from the National Survey of Families and Households in 1987–1988, Bumpass (1990) concludes that there has been an "erosion of norms" proscribing nonmarital childbearing. He concludes that this behavior is not so much motivated by the desire to have children out of wedlock as it is by the reduced commitment to marriage and the limited sanctions forbidding nonmarital childbearing. Bumpass argues that much of the nonmarital childbearing is unplanned and ill-timed.

THE CONSEQUENCES OF NONMARITAL CHILDBEARING

Although extensive research exists on the economic, social, and psychological sequelae of single parenthood for adults and children, relatively little of this research distinguishes between the consequences of marital disruption and nonmarriage (Garfinkel and McLanahan 1986; Furstenberg 1989; Furstenberg and Cherlin 1991). A substantial literature exists on the consequences of nonmarital childbearing, but it is almost entirely restricted to teenage childbearers (Hofferth and Hayes 1987; Chilman 1983; Moore, Simms, and Betsey 1986; Miller and Moore 1990). It is difficult, then, to sort out the separate effects of premature parenthood, marital disruption, and out-of-wedlock childbearing on parents and their offspring.

Nonmarital childbearing most certainly places mothers and their children at risk of long-term economic disadvantage (McLanahan and Booth 1989). Out-of-wedlock childbearing increases the odds of going on welfare and of long-term welfare dependency (Duncan and Hoffman 1990). The link between nonmarital childbearing and poverty can probably be traced to two separate sources. The first is "selective recruitment," that is, women who bear children out of wedlock have poor economic prospects before they become pregnant, and their willingness to bear a child out of wedlock may also reflect the bleak future prospects of many unmarried pregnant women, especially younger women (Hayes 1987; Hogan and Kitagawa 1985; Geronimus 1987; Furstenberg 1990). But it is also likely that out-of-wedlock childbearing—particularly when it occurs early in life—directly contributes to economic vulnerability because it reduces educational attainment and limits a young woman's prospects of entering a stable union (Hofferth and Hayes 1987; Trussell 1988; Furstenberg 1991).

If nonmarital childbearing increases the risk of lengthy periods of poverty for women and their children, it is also likely that it restricts the opportunities for intra- and intergenerational mobility of families formed as single-parent units. Growing up in poverty restricts access to health, high-quality schools, and community resources that may promote success in later life (Ellwood 1988; Wilson 1987). Apart from the risks associated with poverty, some studies have shown that growing up in a single-parent family may put children at greater risk because they receive less parental supervision and support (McLanahan and Booth 1989; Dornbush 1989). As yet, however, researchers have not carefully distinguished between the separate sources of disadvantage that may be tied to nonmarital childbearing: economic disadvantage (that could restrict social opportunities or increase social isolation) and psychological disadvantage (that could foster poor parenting practices or limit family support).

Even though nonmarital childbearing may put children at risk of long-term disadvantage, it is also possible that over time the advantages conferred by marriage may be decreasing in those segments of the population that experience extremely high rates of marital disruption (Bumpass 1990). Moreover, the social and legal stigmata once associated with nonmarital childbearing have all but disappeared in the United States and many other Western nations (Glendon 1989). Over time, then, the hazards associated with nonmarital childbearing (compared with ill-timed marital childbearing) for women and their children could be declining (Dechter and Furstenberg 1990).

NONMARITAL CHILDBEARING AND PUBLIC POLICY

Growing rates of nonmarital childbearing in the United States and many Western nations suggest the possibility that the pattern of childbearing before marriage or between marriages may be spreading upward into the middle class. In Scandinavia, where marriage has declined most dramatically, it is difficult to discern whether formal matrimony is being replaced by a de facto system of informal marriage (Hoem and Hoem 1988). If this were to happen, the impact on the kinship system or the circumstances of children might not be as dramatic as some have speculated. But if the institution of marriage is in serious decline, then we may be in the midst of a major transformation in the Western family.

The weakening of marriage has created confusion and dispute over parenting rights and responsibilities. A growing body of evidence indicates that most nonresidential biological fathers, especially those who never marry, typically become disengaged from their children (Furstenberg and Nord 1985; Setzer, Schaeffer, and Charng 1989; Teachman 1990). Most are unwilling or unable to pay regular child support, and relatively few have constant relationships with their children. Instead, the costs of child rearing have been largely assumed by mothers and their families, aided by public assistance. A minority of fathers do manage to fulfill economic and social obligations, and some argue that many others would do so if they had the means and social support for continuing a relationship with their children (Smollar and Ooms 1987). Some researchers observe that the role of biological fathers is often assumed by surrogates, who may come to assume some or most paternal responsibilities (Mott 1990). In short, it is possible that social parenthood is becoming more important than biological parenthood.

Nevertheless, the uncertain relationship between biological fathers and their children has created a demand for public policies to shore up the family system. Widespread disagreement exists over specific policies for readdressing current problems. Advocates who accept the current reality of high levels of nonmarriage and marital instability propose more generous economic allowances and extensive social support to women and their children to offset the limited economic role of men in disadvantaged families (Ellwood 1988). Critics of this approach contend that such policies may further erode the marriage system (Vinovskis and Chase-Lansdale 1988). Yet few realistic measures have been advanced for strengthening the institution of marriage (Furstenberg and Cherlin 1991).

One policy—enforcement of child support—has attracted broad public support. A series of legislative initiatives culminating in the Family Support Act of 1988 has increased the role of federal and state governments in collecting child support from absent parents (typically fathers) and standardizing levels of child support. Some states, notably Wisconsin and New York, have designed but not yet implemented measures for creating a child support assurance system that will guarantee payments to single mothers and their children. It is too early to tell whether these sweeping measures will succeed in strengthening the economic contributions of fathers who live apart from their children. And, if it does, will greater economic support by absent parents reinforce social and psychological bonds to their children (Furstenberg 1989; Garfinkel and McLanahan 1991).

As for the future of marriage, few, if any, sociologists and demographers are predicting a return to the status quo or a restoration of the norm of legitimacy. Short of a strong ideological swing favoring marriage and condemning nonmarital sexual activity and childbearing, it is difficult to foresee a sharp reversal in present trends (Blankenhorn, Bayme, and Elshtain 1990). Predicting the future, however, has never been a strong point of demographic and sociological research.

(SEE ALSO: *Deviance; Law and Society; Legitimacy*)

REFERENCES

Bane, M. J., and P. A. Jargowsky 1988 "The Links Between Government Policy and Family Structure: What Matters and What Doesn't." In A. Cherlin, ed., *The Changing American Family and Public Policy.* Washington, D.C.: Urban Institute Press.

Bell, N. W., and E. F. Vogel (eds.) 1968 *A Modern Introduction to the Family.* New York: Free Press.

Blake, J. 1961 *Family Structure in Jamaica.* New York: Free Press.

Blankenhorn, D., S. Bayme, and J. B. Elshtain 1990 *Rebuilding the Nest.* Milwaukee, Wisc.: Family Service America.

Bumpass, L. 1990 "What's Happening to the Family?

Interactions Between Demographic and Institutional Change." *Demography* 27:483–498.

Cherlin, A. 1988 "The Weakening Link Between Marriage and the Care of Children." *Family Planning Perspectives* 20:302–306.

———, and F. F. Furstenberg, Jr. 1988 "The Changing European Family: Lessons for the American Reader." *Journal of Family Issues* 9:291–297.

Chilman, C. S. 1983 *Adolescent Sexuality in a Changing American Society: Social and Psychological Perspectives for the Human Services Professions.* New York: Wiley.

Clague, A. J., and S. J. Ventura 1968 *Trends in Illegitimacy: United States 1940–1965.* Vital and Health Statistics, Public Health Service Publication no. 1000, ser. 21, no. 15. Washington, D.C.: U.S. Government Printing Office.

Coser, R. L. (ed.) 1964 *The Family: Its Structures and Functions.* New York: St. Martin's Press.

Cutright, P. 1972 "Illegitimacy in the United States, 1920–1968." In C. Westoff and R. Parks, eds., *Demographic and Social Aspects of Population Growth.* Washington, D.C.: U.S. Government Printing Office.

Davis, K. 1939 "Illegitimacy and the Social Structure." *American Journal of Sociology* 45:215–233.

———1949 *Human Society.* New York: Macmillan.

———1985 *Contemporary Marriage: Comparative Perspectives on a Changing Institution.* New York: Russell Sage Foundation.

Dechter, A., and F. F. Furstenberg, Jr. 1990 "The Changing Consequences of Adolescent Childbearing: A Comparison of Fertility and Marriage Patterns Across Cohorts." Paper presented at the annual meetings of the American Sociological Association, Washington, D.C., August.

Dornbush, S. M. 1989 "The Sociology of Adolescence." *Annual Review of Sociology* 15:233–259.

Duncan, G. J., and S. D. Hoffman 1990 "Teenage Welfare Receipt and Subsequent Dependence Among Black Adolescent Mothers." *Family Planning Perspectives* 22:219–223.

Ellwood, D. T. 1988 *Poor Support.* New York: Basic Books.

Furstenberg, F. F., Jr. 1988 "Bringing Back the Shotgun Wedding." *Public Interest* 90:121–127.

———1989 "Supporting Fathers: Implications of the Family Support Act for Men." Paper presented at the forum on the Family Support Act sponsored by the Foundation for Child Development, Washington, D.C., November.

———1990 "Coming of Age in a Changing Family System." In S. Feldman and G. Elliott, eds., *At the Threshold: The Developing Adolescent.* Cambridge, Mass.: Harvard University Press.

——— 1991 "As the Pendulum Swings: Teenage Childbearing and Social Concern." *Family Relations.*

———, and A. Cherlin 1991 *Divided Families: What Happens to Children When Their Parents Part.* Cambridge, Mass.: Harvard University Press.

———, Jr., and C. W. Nord 1985 "Parenting Apart: Patterns of Childbearing After Divorce." *Journal of Marriage and the Family* 47:898–904.

Garfinkel, I., and S. McLanahan 1986 *Single Mothers and Their Children.* Washington, D.C.: Urban Institute Press.

———1990 "The Effects of the Child Support Provisions of the Family Support Act of 1988 on Child Well-Being." *Policy Review* 9:205–234.

Geronimus, A. T. 1987 "On Teenage Childbearing in the United States." *Population and Development Review* 13:245–279.

Gillis, J. R. 1985 *For Better, for Worse: British Marriages 1600 to the Present.* New York: Oxford University Press.

Glendon, M. A. 1989 *The Transformation of Family Law.* Chicago: University of Chicago Press.

Goode, W. J. 1960 "A Deviant Case: Illegitimacy in the Caribbean." *American Sociological Review* 25:21–30.

———1961 "Illegitimacy, Anomie, and Cultural Penetration." *American Sociological Review* 26:319–325.

———1971 "Family Disorganization." In R. K. Merton and R. Nisbet, eds., *Contemporary Social Problems,* 3rd ed. New York: Harcourt Brace Jovanovich.

Hayes, C. D. 1987 *Risking the Future,* Vol. 1. Washington, D.C.: National Academy Press.

Hoem, B., and J. M. Hoem 1988 "The Swedish Family: Aspects of Contemporary Developments." *Journal of Family Issues* 9:397–424.

Hofferth, S. L., and C. D. Hayes 1987 *Risking the Future,* Vol. 2. Washington, D.C.: National Academy Press.

Hogan, D. P., and E. Kitagawa 1985 "The Impact of Social Status, Family Structure, and Neighborhood on the Family Structure of Black Adolescents." *American Journal of Sociology* 90:825–855.

Laslett, P. 1972 "Introduction: The History of the Family." In P. Laslett and R. Wall, eds., *Household and Family in Past Time.* Oxford: Oxford University Press.

McLanahan, S., and K. Booth 1989 "Mother-Only Families: Problems, Prospects, and Politics." *Journal of Marriage and the Family* 51:557–580.

Malinowski, B. 1930 "Parenthood, the Basis of Social

Structure." In R. L. Coser, ed., *The Family: Its Structures and Functions.* New York: St. Martin's Press.

Miller, B. C., and K. A. Moore 1990 "Adolescent Sexual Behavior, Pregnancy, and Parenting." *Journal of Marriage and the Family* 52, no. 4:1025–1044.

Moore, K. A., M. C. Simms, and C. L. Betsey 1986 *Choice and Circumstance: Racial Differences in Adolescent Sexuality and Fertility.* New Brunswick, N.J.: Transaction Books.

Mott, F. 1990 "When Is Father Really Gone? Paternal–Child Contact in Father-Absent Homes." *Demography* 27:499–517.

National Center for Health Statistics 1990 *Advance Report of Final Natality Statistics, 1988.* Supp. to *Monthly Vital Statistics Report* 39, no. 4. Hyattsville, Md.: U.S. Public Health Service.

O'Connell, M., and M. J. Moore 1981 "The Legitimacy Status of First Births to U.S. Women Aged 15–24, 1939–1978." In F. F. Furstenberg, Jr., R. Lincoln, and J. Menken, eds., *Teenage Sexuality, Pregnancy, and Childbearing.* Philadelphia: University of Pennsylvania Press.

Popenoe, D. 1988 *Disturbing the Nest.* New York: Aldine De Gruyter.

Setzer, J. A., N. C. Schaeffer, and H. Charng 1989 "Family Ties After Divorce: The Relationship Between Visiting and Paying Child Support." *Journal of Marriage and the Family* 51:1013–1032.

Smith, D. S. 1978 "The Dating of the American Sexual Revolution: Evidence and Interpretation." In M. Gordon, ed., *The American Family in Social-Historical Perspective.* New York: St. Martin's Press.

Smollar, J., and T. Ooms 1987 *Young Unwed Fathers: Research Review, Policy Dilemmas, and Options.* Washington, D.C.: Maximus, Inc.

Teachman, J. D. 1990 "Still Fathers? The Reorganization of Parental Obligations Following Divorce." Paper presented at the Albany Conference on Demographic Perspectives on the American Family: Patterns and Prospects, April.

Thornton, A. 1989 "Changing Attitudes Towards Family Issues in the United States." *Journal of Marriage and the Family* 51:873–893.

Trussell, J. 1988 "Teenage Pregnancy in the United States." *Family Planning Perspectives* 20:262–272.

Vincent, C. E. 1961 *Unmarried Mothers.* New York: Free Press.

Vinovskis, M. 1988 *An "Epidemic" of Adolescent Pregnancy? Some Historical and Policy Considerations.* New York: Oxford University Press.

———, and P. L. Chase-Lansdale 1987 "Should We Discourage Teenage Marriage?" *Public Interest* 87:23–37.

Virginia Slims American Women's Public Opinion Poll 1985 A study conducted by The Roper Organization, Inc.

Wilson, W. J. 1987 *The Truly Disadvantaged.* Chicago: University of Chicago Press.

FRANK F. FURSTENBERG, JR.

IMPERIALISM AND COLONIALISM

Imperialism is among the most overused and contested terms in our political vocabulary, so much so that Hancock was led to brand it "a word for the illiterates of social science" (1950, p. 17). Viewed more hopefully, the study of imperialism seems dogged by two conceptual problems: the centrality of politics versus that of economics, and the awkward relationship between *imperialism* and *empire.*

Imperialism was first used in the 1830s to recall Napoleonic ambitions. It gained its classic meaning around the turn of the century as a description of the feverish colonial expansion of Britain, France, Germany, Russia, the United States, and Italy. But the term is seldom confined to formal colonial expansion; in particular, the continuing dependence of much of the third world on Western states and multinational corporations is often understood as neocolonialism or neoimperialism (Nkrumah 1966; Magdoff 1969).

Attempts to distill these diverse usages generally define imperialism as the construction and maintenance of relationships of domination between political communities. Such relations are often seen as explicitly political, either in the narrow sense of direct administrative control or more broadly as formal or informal control over state policy. Economic conceptions of imperialism sometimes develop an analogue to these notions, where relations of economic control or exploitation replace political domination.

This usage should be distinguished from the equation of imperialism with particular modes of production or types of economic systems. Lenin's statement that "imperialism is the monopoly stage of capitalism'' ([1917] 1939, p. 88) may be understood as such a definition. This usage fundamentally changes the terms of debate in ways that the extension from ''political'' to ''political and/or economic'' do not. Arrighi, among others, argues that Lenin is better understood as formulating a substantive proposition; he suggests the interpretation ''imperialism, or the tendency to war between capitalist countries, is a necessary consequence of the transformation of capitalism into monopoly or finance capital'' (1978, p. 14).

Even when imperialism is equated with the establishment and maintenance of political domination, an awkward relationship between *imperialism* and *empire* persists. Classically, empire refers to the great agrarian bureaucracies that dominated antiquity, from the Aztec to the Chinese, from ancient Sumer to Imperial Rome. It is not clear how much these structures have in common with the overseas colonial empires of Western states, much less with contemporary structures of dependence on foreign investment. For instance, while agrarian bureaucracies involved ethnic divisions, these separated classes (most importantly the ruling warrior class from others) rather than political communities or nations (Gellner 1983).

A second historical use of *empire* is the medieval image of a temporal parallel to the Roman church (Folz 1969; Guenee 1985). Rather than an alien and illegitimate structure, empire was seen as a political order unifying the Christian world. Revived by Charlemagne, the notion of a universal polity lived on, in an increasingly ghostly fashion, through the Holy Roman Empire. It receded into the background as a real political force with the construction of absolutist states and was lost as a compelling image with the rise of the nation-state.

In contrast to these historical understandings of empire, modern conceptions of imperialism rest on the notion that popular sovereignty forms the basis of political community. Only with the notion of popular sovereignty does domination refer to relationships between rather than within communities. If the criteria that the United Nations uses to identify colonialism today were applied before 1700, for example, all territories would be parts of empires and all peoples would be dependent subjects. It is thus no accident that the notion of imperialism arose with the nation-state; it connotes the expansionary drive of a community that is internally organized around (the myth of) popular sovereignty.

Some authors have used *colonialism* to refer to the construction and maintenance of colonies in a literal sense, groups of people who emigrate to form new societies in new lands. But today colonialism is generally synonymous with imperialism, though it has the specific connotation of Western domination over non-Western peoples.

WESTERN POLITICAL EXPANSION

While different theoretical analyses of imperialism often seek to understand different sets of events, they generally overlap in attending to the formation of Western colonial empires. This essay will thus briefly review the history of Western expansion and then consider some of the major arguments about the sources of imperialism.

Western overseas expansion can be described crudely as occurring in two stages, the colonial and the imperial. In the fifteenth and sixteenth centuries, sea-going powers constructed networks of colonial enclaves along the route to the East Indies. Less than half a century after the voyages of Columbus, Spanish conquistadores had laid waste to the Incan and Aztec empires and were sending gold and silver back to Spain. In the following two centuries, Spain, Portugal, Great Britain, France, and the Netherlands colonized virtually the whole of the Caribbean, Central and South America, and the North Atlantic seaboard. The colonial period per se came to a close with the decolonization of the Americas between 1776 and 1830, leaving Western states in control of vastly diminished overseas possessions.

The second period of expansion, one of imperial rather than colonial expansion, began after an interrugnum marked by British naval hegemony. In the three decades after 1880, a scramble for territory partitioned Africa, Southeast Asia, and the Pacific between Great Britain, France, Germany, Belgium, and Portugal, while the United States annexed the remains of the Spanish Empire. None of this expansion involved much metropolitan emigration; colonial officials, traders, planters, and missionaries formed a thin veneer on indigenous societies. These empires disintegrated as quickly as they were formed, as almost all Western dependencies became recognized sovereign states in the decades following World War II.

When examining the political structures of imperial rule, it is important to consider both metropolitan and indigenous traditions. Colonies tended to be formally organized along metropolitan lines (Fieldhouse 1966). Settler colonies mirrored domestic political structures quite directly (Lang 1975), while nonsettler colonies recall metropolitan structures in a more abstract fashion. For example, the British tried to fashion systems of local rule (Lugard [1922] 1965) while the French strove to create a unified, centralized administration. But the superficiality of most imperial rule led to great variation in actual administrative arrangements. Even empires whose guiding rationale was assimilation (the French and the Portuguese) depended heavily on indigenous authorities and traditions.

Overseas colonies also varied greatly in their economic relationship to the metropolis. Only a few colonies were the source of great riches for the metropolitan economy: most prominently, the American settler colonies, British India, and the Dutch East Indies (Indonesia). Others had a largely strategic value; much of the British empire, for instance, was acquired in the effort to maintain lines of communication to India. The great majority of colonies acquired after 1880 had rather little importance for the metropolis, either as markets for imperial products or as sources of raw materials (Fieldhouse 1973).

THEORIES OF IMPERIALISM

The starting point for modern theories of imperialism is John Hobson's *Imperialism: A Study* ([1902] 1965). A liberal critic of the Boer War, Hobson saw imperial expansion as a search for new outlets for investment. He found the roots of this search in the surplus capital amassed by increasingly monopolistic corporate trusts. Hobson viewed imperial expansion as costly for the nation as a whole and sought to expose the special interests promoting imperialism. He also contended that capital surpluses could be consumed domestically by equalizing the distribution of income.

Lenin's *Imperialism: The Highest Stage of Capitalism* ([1917] 1939) provides the most influential statement of an economic analysis of imperialism. Lenin agreed with Hobson that imperialism flowed from the need to invest outside the domestic economy, drawing explicitly on Hilferding's ([1910] 1981) analysis of finance capital as a stage of capitalism. He was concerned to show that imperialism was a necessary rather than an avoidable result of the dynamics of capitalism (in contrast to Hobson's anticipation of Keynes) and that the expansionary impulse could not be globally coordinated (versus Kautsky's notion of an ultra-imperialism). Lenin argued that the unevenness of development makes imperialist war inevitable, as "late starters" demand their own place in the sun.

More contemporary writers like Baran and Sweezy (1966), Frank (1967), and Wallerstein (1974) draw upon both the Marxist tradition and Latin American theories of *dependencia* to suggest an alternative economic analysis of imperialism. They argue that international economic relations involve a net transfer of capital from the "periphery" to the "core" of the economic system and point to the continuities in this process from early colonial expansion to contemporary neoimperialism. This is in sharp contrast with the Leninist tradition, which argues that imperialism develops the productive powers of noncapitalist societies and emphasizes the special affinity of imperialism and monopoly capital.

Others writers consider political ambitions or relationships to be the taproot of imperialism. Schumpeter (1951) turned the Marxist perspective on its head. He noted that the characteristic motif of the ancient empires is military expansion for its own sake. Schumpeter argued that imperialism appears as an atavistic trait in the landed aristocracy of modern societies, and stresses the mismatch between the social psychology of the warrior and the industrious, calculating spirit of capitalism.

Other analyses focusing on political processes emphasize the anarchical structure of the Western state system (Cohen 1973; Waltz 1979). In the absence of an enforceable legal order, states are forced to expand when they can or decline relative to more aggressive states. This perspective explains European imperialism in the nineteenth century as the product of increasing levels of international competition and conflict.

Whether economic or political, most analyses of imperialism find its sources in the logic of the West, ignoring indigenous peoples in the process. Some recent work, led by the historians John Gallagher and Ronald Robinson, has sought to redress this imbalance. Their seminal essay "The Imperialism of Free Trade" (1953) emphasizes the continuity in British policy between the informal imperialism of the mid-eighteenth century and the rush for colonies after 1880. In *Africa and the Victorians,* Robinson, Gallagher, and Denny (1961) argued that it was largely change in the periphery, particularly increasing resistance to Western influence, that led Western powers to replace informal domination with formal empire. In later work, Robinson (1972) has emphasized the other side of the coin—the extent to which Western imperialism was dependent on local collaboration.

The theoretical approaches reviewed above differ partly because they seek to explain somewhat different, though overlapping, events. Different theoretical aims make the study of imperialism a contested and messy business; they also point to the importance of the debate. Whether as the last stage of capitalism, the workings of an anarchical state system, or the evolving relationship between Europeans and the rest of the world, imperialism seems crucial to the violence and the dynamism of the twentieth century.

(SEE ALSO: *Decolonialization; Global Systems Analysis; Transnational Corporations*)

REFERENCES

Arrighi, Giovanni 1978 *The Geometry of Imperialism.* London: New Left Books.

Baran, Paul, and Paul Sweezy 1966 *Monopoly Capital.* New York: Monthly Review Press.

Cohen, Benjamin J. 1973 *The Question of Imperialism.* New York: Basic Books.

Fieldhouse, David K. 1966 *The Colonial Empires.* New York: Dell.

——— 1973 *Economics and Empire, 1830–1914.* Ithaca, N.Y.: Cornell University Press.

Folz, Robert 1969 *The Concept of Empire in Western Europe from the Fifth to the Fourteenth Century.* London: Arnold.

Frank, Andre Gunder 1967 *Capitalism and Underdevelopment in Latin America.* New York: Monthly Review Press.

Gallagher, John, and Ronald Robinson 1953 "The Imperialism of Free Trade." *Economic History Review* S5:1–15.

Gellner, Ernest 1983 *Nations and Nationalism.* Oxford: Basil Blackwell.

Guenee, Bernard 1985 *States and Rulers in Later Medieval Europe.* Oxford: Basil Blackwell.

Hancock, William K. 1950. *The Wealth of Colonies.* Cambridge: Cambridge University Press.

Hilferding, Rudolf (1910) 1981 *Finance Capital.* London: Routledge and Kegan Paul.

Hobson, John A. (1902) 1965 *Imperialism: A Study.* New York: Allen and Unwin.

Lang, James 1975 *Conquest and Commerce: Spain and England in the Americas.* New York: Academic Press.

Lenin, Vladimir Ilich (1917) 1939 *Imperialism: The Highest Stage of Capitalism.* London: International Publishers.

Lugard, Frederick J. D. (1922) 1965 *The Dual Mandate in British Tropical Africa.* 5th ed. London: Cass.

Magdoff, Harry 1969 *Age of Imperialism.* New York: Monthly Review Press.

Nkrumah, Kwame 1966 *Neo-Colonialism: The Last Stage of Imperialism.* London: International Publishers.

Robinson, Ronald 1972 "Non-European Foundations of European Imperialism: Sketch for a Theory of Collaboration." In Roger Owen and Bob Sutcliffe, eds., *Studies in the Theory of Imperialism.* Bristol: G. B. Longman.

———, John Gallagher, and Alice Denny 1961 *Africa and the Victorians: The Official Mind of Imperialism.* London: St. Martin's Press.

Schumpeter, Joseph 1951 "The Sociology of Imperialism." In Schumpeter, *Imperialism and Social Classes.* New York: Kelley.

Wallerstein, Immanuel 1974, 1980, 1989 *The Modern World-System.* 3 vols. Cambridge: Cambridge University Press.

Waltz, Kenneth 1979 *Theory of International Politics.* Reading, Mass.: Addison-Wesley.

Weber, Max 1958 *The Protestant Ethic and the Spirit of Capitalism.* New York: Scribners.

DAVID STRANG

IMPRESSION FORMATION *See* Affect Control Theory and Impression Formation.

INCEST Incest is illicit sex or marriage between persons socially or legally defined as related too closely to one another. All societies have rules regarding incest. Incest is conceptualized in four ways: as a proscribed or prescribed marriage form; as a taboo; as prohibited coitus; and as child abuse. The first three conceptualizations are most closely related to early scholars (mid-1800s to mid-1900s), who tended to overlap them. The last conceptualization has become prominent more recently.

Incest-as-marriage rules are usually proscriptive ("Thou shalt not"). Prescriptive ("Thou shalt") incestuous marriage rules have been documented for royalty in Old Iran and ancient Egypt and for Mormons in the United States (Lester 1972). That some groups proscribe while others prescribe incestuous marriages has caused some to be skeptical of many theories about incest, especially theories that assume that incest avoidance is natural, close inbreeding is genetically disadvantageous, or that there is an incest taboo.

John F. McLennan ([1865] 1876), a lawyer, coined the terms *endogamy* (within-the-group marriage) and *exogamy* (outside-the-group marriage). He defined incest as endogamy. Based on his analyses of marriage in Ireland, Australia, ancient Greece, and other societies, he concluded that rules proscribing endogamy evolved as a group survival mechanism. He reasoned that as members of one tribe or group married into others, "blood ties" emerged. These blood ties encouraged reciprocity between groups and cooperation and harmony within groups. Anthropologist Lewis Henry Morgan agreed with McLennan's definition of incest as endogamy and with McLennan's assumption that proscribing incest promoted both exogamy and group survival. Morgan assumed, however, that incest originally became prohibited due to the presumed deleterious effects of inbreeding. Tylor (1889) elaborated on McLennan's notion of exchange and reciprocity among exogamous groups. He noted that men made political alliances with men in other groups by exchanging women in marriage. The common thread among these theories is the focus upon incest rules as social organizational principles. A shared weakness is the reliance upon analyses of primitive or premodern groups. These inclinations are also found in varying degrees in writings by Sir James Frazer, Herbert Spencer, Brenda Seligman, Robert Briffault, Bronislaw Malinowski, George Murdock, and Claude Lévi-Strauss. Many of these and other writers also fail to differentiate between incest rules and exogamy rules. What one group calls incestuous marriage may not biologically be such. Likewise, some groups' exogamy rules permit biologically incestuous marriage. Recognizing that incest rules are socially defined, Sumner (in his famous tome *Folkways*) countered Morgan and presaged today's sociobiologists. He argued that incest rules should be modified as researchers gathered genetic evidence that dispelled fallacious beliefs that all incestuous matings are deleterious.

Sociologist Emile Durkheim's *Incest: The Nature and Origin of the Taboo* ([1898] 1963) is an infrequently cited magnum opus. Based on ethnographic research in Australia, this book emphasized and illustrated the social and moral origins of incest taboos. Durkheim noted the ways in which prohibitions against incest and penalties for rule violations organize social groups internally. Cooperation and alliances with other groups via exogamy are consequently prompted. Durkheim contends that the incest taboo has a religious origin. It is derived from the clan's sentiments surrounding blood, specifically menstrual blood. While blood is taboo in a general way, contact with the blood of the clan is taboo in specific ways. Durkheim reasoned that menstrual blood represents a flowing away of the clan's life blood. The taboo against blood is thus associated with women of the clan. This renders women taboo for and inferior to men of the same clan. The taboo relates to intercourse in general and to marriage in particular. Blood and incest are presumed to be related such that a man violating the taboo is seen as a murderer.

Durkheim contended that the origin of the taboo is lost to the consciousness of clans over time but that the taboo itself is replaced by a generalized repugnance of incest. This repugnance prompts men to exchange women with other groups, thus facilitating political alliances between men of different groups. In addition, in his *The Division of Labor in Society* (1893), Durkheim posited that when incest loses its religiously based criminal status, prohibitions against it are or will be codified into law. Prefiguring more recent research on incest as child abuse, Durkheim noted also that incest violations are most likely to occur in families in which members do not feel morally obligated to be dutiful to one another and to practice moral restraint ([1898] 1963, p. 102).

Sigmund Freud focused on the incest taboo ([1913] 1950) and infantile sexuality ([1905] 1962). Through his tale of the primal horde, Freud posited that in the original family there was a jealous and violent father who engaged his daughters in incest. The jealous brothers banded together, killed, and ate the father. Horrified by their deeds, the brothers made incest taboo. For Freud, this (the moment when humans made incest rules) was when humans became social. He assumed that very young (Oedipal) children sexually desire their opposite-sex parent. Little boys then suffer from castration anxiety, fearing that the father will become aware of their desires and punish them. While little girls see their mothers as inferior to men, they also know them to be more powerful than they. Thus, little girls resignedly align themselves with their mothers, repress their incestuous impulses, and experience penis envy.

Even though Freud's theories were based on conjecture and focused on the bourgeois nuclear family of his day, they have nonetheless influenced many social scientists, including French anthropologist Jean Claude Lévi-Strauss ([1949] 1969) and American sociologist Talcott Parsons (1954). Lévi-Strauss agreed with Freud that humans became social with the creation of incest rules. Borrowing from the emphasis on the exchange of women, found in the works of Durkheim and Marcel Mauss, and Durkheim's assumption that women of a clan become the symbol (totem) for the clan, Lévi-Strauss posited that exogamy represents a special form of alliance-creating reciprocity. Since incest involves sexuality, incest rules and the exchange of women represent a unique social connection between the biological and the cultural. Although frequently lauded by social scientists, the work of Lévi-Strauss adds little to previous theories about incest.

Parsons incorporated Freud's theory of infantile sexuality into his structural-functionalist view of the American nuclear family. Like functionalists before him, he assumed that incest rules exist to prevent role confusion within the nuclear family and to encourage alliances with other families. He contended that the mother was to exploit her son's Oedipal desires as if she had him on a rope. At earlier ages she was to pull him toward her, encouraging heterosexuality. At later ages she was to push him away, encouraging him to establish relationships with nonrelated females. Tugging and pulling on the rope were also designed to assist the son in internalizing society's incest rules and guide him in creating his own nuclear family.

Parsons assumed that little girls also experience an erotic attachment to their mothers. He argued that as the mother severed this attachment, it was her responsibility to instill in the daughter an aversion to father–daughter and brother–sister incest. Failure to do this would result in family disorganization and in the daughter's inability to become a normatively functioning adult. Parsons contended that incest aversion would be realized if the mother kept the erotic bond with her husband intact. Parsons's analysis has thus assisted in perpetuating what child abuse researchers have sought to eradicate: placing blame on mothers when fathers incestuously abuse their daughters (see Finkelhor 1984; Vander Mey and Neff 1986; Russell 1986).

Psychologist Edward Westermarck (1891) contended that family and clan members develop a sexual aversion to one another due to the dulling effects of daily interaction and the sharing of mundane tasks. This aversion prompts the development of laws and customs proscribing incest among persons with a shared ancestor and set of obligations based on clan membership. Westermarck noted that failure to develop this aversion and the propensity to violate incest laws were due to alcoholism, membership in the lower social classes, inability to control the sex drive, lack of alternative sexual outlets, social and geographic isolation, and failure to have developed normative, family-like feelings of duty. Variations on Westermarck's thesis appear in writings today. Some focus on a learned aversion that Oedipal children develop as their fantasies cannot be realized, due to their lack of full sexual maturation. Westermarck's thesis is weak because if there were a natural aversion to incest, then laws prohibiting it would be unnecessary. Furthermore, a growing body of literature suggests that persons who share mundane tasks and interact daily do not develop a sexual aversion to one another (see Vander Mey and Neff 1986).

Sociobiologists (e.g., Parker 1976; van den Berghe 1980) variously incorporate Freudian theses, Westermarck's thesis, and the assumption that human social behavior follows a fitness maxim such that a group establishes prescriptive or proscriptive incest rules that enhance a group's survival to its genetic advantage. Sociobiologists typically use the functionalist assumption that incest rules regulate the internal dynamics of the procreating group and encourage affiliation with other nuclear groups. Violations of incest rules are assumed to be caused by the factors identified by Westermarck. Many sociobiologists link intercourse directly to procreation. This is not always true of adult–adult intercourse. The assumption has no merit when one tries to explain why adult–child and child–child intercourse occurs. Equally problematic is the frequent reliance on the rules proscribing incest among royals. Dismissed is the role that ethnocentrism plays in such rules. Finally, serious questions arise when research on primates, birds, or other nonhumans is extrapolated to human social behavior and organization.

Of current concern is incest as a serious and severe type of child abuse. As child abuse, incest is any form of sexual touching, talking, or attempted or actual intercourse between an adult and a child or between two children when the perpetrator is significantly older than the victim or forces the victim to engage in actions against his or her will. The perpetrator and victim are related either by consanguinity or affinity. Incest is abuse because it harms the victim and violates the child's basic human rights. Its negative effects linger throughout victims' lives (Russell 1986). That the sexual victimization of children is nothing new, but rather ancient, is well documented (Rush 1980; deMause 1982). Public recognition of incest as child abuse, however, has its roots in research and public discourse of roughly the past fifteen years.

Had Freud not abandoned his first psychoanalytical paper, "The Aetiology of Hysteria" ([1896] 1946), he could have been heralded as the savior of children. In this paper he described incest and other sexual abuse experienced by eighteen patients when they were children. He linked his adult patients' problems to their experiences of childhood sexual trauma. However, when his paper was coldly received and then ignored by senior psychologists, and Freud faced professional ostracization, he dismissed these findings (see Jurjevich 1974; Masson 1984). He reasoned that his patients were incorrectly recalling masturbatory childhood fantasies of sexual encounters with adults (Freud [1905] 1962). Freud then associated adult neurosis and hysteria with unfulfilled childhood incest fantasies.

Freud's revamped theories quickly became popular. Several writers then recounted case studies of children who had experienced sex with an adult. The children were described as seductive and provocative. They were not seen as victims; rather, they were seen as sexual initiators (see Vander Mey and Neff 1986). Although Swedish sociologist Svend Riemer (1940) and American sociologist S. Kirson Weinberg (1955) tried to bring attention to incest as a form of family deviance that sometimes resulted in harm to victims, Freudian theory held fast until the late 1960s. The "discovery" of child abuse, in conjunction with the civil rights movement, the anti-Vietnam War movement, and the resurgence of the women's rights movement, refocused attention such that the physical abuse of children and rape of women became seen as serious wrongs inflicted on other humans and as special types of social problems. Since that time, theories and research have explored in great detail why and how incestuous abuse occurs and its lasting negative effects. Laws protecting children against such abuse have been improved. These laws mandate that treatment services be available for victims, perpetrators, and families (Fraser 1987). They also stipulate penalties (fines, imprisonment) for convicted abusers. These operate on a sliding scale, with harsher penalties applied to cases in which the victim is very young or has suffered serious physical or psychological trauma due to the abuse. Some cases are handled in family courts. Others, especially those involving serious harm to the child, are heard in criminal courts. Although variable in scope, laws in European nations prohibit and punish incestuous child abuse (Doek 1987). As with statutes in the United States, applicable penalties often depend on the victim–perpetrator relationship, the age of the victim, and the seriousness of harm to the victim. And, as in the United States, these laws are still inadequate. However, efforts to refine legal statutes and penalties continue. Refinement is needed, for instance, for statutes that designate only men as perpetrators and only females as victims. Laws are also needed that specifically define and punish child–child incestuous abuse.

Feminists focus on father–daughter incest. They refer to it as rape to emphasize the specific type of abuse that it is. The term *rape* also illustrates the point that if an adult male forced another person to engage in intercourse with him, he would be arrested for the very serious crime of rape. However, if he rapes his own child, it is called incest, which is often seen as a disgusting, private, family problem (Brownmiller 1975).

Feminists see incest as commonplace, originating in and perpetuated by patriarchy (Rush 1980). A general feminist approach to father–daughter incest incorporates a discussion of the sex-role socialization of males and the male-as-superior patriarchal ideology as causal factors in incest. The contention is that females ultimately are rendered second class citizens, the property of men, and sexual outlets for men (see Rush 1980). Problems with a general feminist perspective on incest include a focus limited to father–daughter incest, the monocausal linkage of patriarchy to incest, the portrayal of all incest perpetrators as male and all incest victims as female, and the oversimplified view of male sex-role socialization (Vander Mey, 1991).

American feminist sociologist Diana Russell (1986) extends and refines the general feminist approach to incest. She argues that males are socialized to sexualize the power given them by virtue of the fact that they are male. This includes sexualizing the power they have over their own children. Moreover, Russell recognizes that mothers and children can be incest perpetrators. She advocates androgynous socialization of children, more equality between men and women, and more public awareness of the harsh realities of incestuous abuse.

Welsh psychologist Neil Frude (1982) relied upon existing empirical and clinical research to articulate a five-factor explanatory model of father–daughter incest. These five factors are: sexual need (of the perpetrator); attractive partner; opportunity; disinhibition; and sexual behavior. A strength of Frude's model is the attention paid to the intertwisting of sex and power. Weaknesses include the fact that incest perpetrators are not usually sexually deprived, victim attractiveness is often irrelevant, and families are not usually closed systems today. American sociologist David Finkelhor (1984) offers a somewhat similar model, although it differs from Frude's model in that Finkelhor pays keen attention to the myriad ways in which larger social forces and cultural ideology are related to child sexual abuse. Finkelhor's model has the added strength of being applicable to several types of incest and other sexual abuse.

American sociologists Brenda Vander Mey and Ronald Neff (1986) have constructed a research-based ecological model of father–daughter incest. They begin with the assumption that there is no incest taboo. Rather, there are rules proscribing adult–child incest. They contend that characteristics of the society, the neighborhood, the family and the marital dyad, and the father–daughter dyad differentially affect the probability that a daughter will be sexually abused by her father. These levels of influence interact in complicated ways. Father–daughter incest is associated with male dominance in society and in the family, residence in a violent neighborhood, social isolation of the family, family disorganization, and a father's lack of empathy for his wife and children. Mitigating factors decreasing the likelihood of incest include a father's conformity to rules against incest, sex education of the daughter, and media announcements of adult–child incest as wrong and illegal. This model is strong in its reliance on research and theoretical principles. Although this model is limited to father–daughter incest, it does provide information that can assist in identifying children at risk for incestuous abuse. Vander Mey (1991) suggests, however, that a general systems model be constructed that taps factors correlated with a range of incestuous abuse.

Incestuous abuse is seen as an international social problem today. At least four journals frequently carry the latest research on this topic. These are: *Child Abuse and Neglect; Journal of Family Violence; The Journal of Interpersonal Violence;* and The *Journal of Child Sexual Abuse.*

(SEE ALSO: *Sexual Violence and Abuse*)

REFERENCES

Brownmiller, Susan 1975 *Against Our Will: Men, Women and Rape.* New York: Simon and Schuster.

deMause, Lloyd 1982 *Foundations of Psychohistory.* New York: Creative Roots.

Doek, Jack E. 1987 "Sexual Abuse of Children: An Examination of European Criminal Law." In P. B. Mrazek and C. H. Kempe, eds., *Sexually Abused Children and Their Families.* New York: Pergamon.

Durkheim, Emile (1893) 1963 *The Division of Labor in Society,* trans. G. Simpson. New York: Free Press.

———(1898) 1963 *Incest: The Nature and Origin of the Taboo.* A. Ellis, trans. New York: Lyle Stuart.

Finkelhor, David 1984 *Child Sexual Abuse: New Research and Theory.* New York: Free Press.

Fraser, Brian G. 1987 "Sexual Child Abuse: The Legislation and the Law in the United States." In P. B. Mrazek and C. H. Kempe, eds., *Sexually Abused Children and Their Families.* New York: Pergamon.

Freud, Sigmund (1896) 1946 "The Aetiology of Hysteria." In E. Jones, ed., and J. Riviere, trans. *Collected Papers.* New York: The International Psycho-Analytical Press.

———(1905) 1962 "My Views on the Part Played by Sexuality in the Aetiology of the Neurosis." In P. Reiff, ed., *Sexuality and the Psychology of Love.* New York: Collier Books.

———(1913) 1950 *Totem and Taboo.* J. Strachey, trans. New York: Norton.

Frude, Neil 1982 "The Sexual Nature of Sexual Abuse: A Review of the Literature." *Child Abuse and Neglect* 6:211–223.

Jurjevich, Ratibor-Ray M. 1974 *The Hoax of Freudism: A Study of Brainwashing the American Professionals and Laymen.* Philadelphia: Dorance.

Lester, David 1972 "Incest." *The Journal of Sex Research* 8:268–285.

Lévi-Strauss, Jean Claude (1949) 1969 *The Elementary Structure of Kinship.* J. H. Bell, J. R. von Sturmer, and R. Needham, trans. Boston: Beacon Press.

Masson, Jeffrey M. 1984 *The Assault on Truth: Freud's Suppression of the Seduction Theory.* New York: Farrar, Straus, and Giroux.

McLennan, John F. (1865) 1876 *Primitive Marriage: An Inquiry into the Origin of the Form of Capture in Marriage Ceremonies.* London: Bernard Quaritch.

Parker, Seymour 1976 "The Precultural Basis of the Incest Taboo: Toward a Biosocial Perspective." *American Anthropologist* 78:285–305.

Parsons, Talcott 1954 "The Incest Taboo in Relation to Social Structure and the Socialization of the Child." *British Journal of Sociology* 5:101–117.

Riemer, Svend 1940 "A Research Note on Incest." *American Journal of Sociology* 45:566–575.

Rush, Florence 1980 *The Best Kept Secret: Sexual Abuse of Children.* New York: McGraw-Hill.

Russell, Diana E. H. 1986 *The Secret Trauma: Incest in the Lives of Girls and Women.* New York: Basic Books.

Tylor, Edward B. 1889 "On the Method of Investigating the Development of Institutions; Applied to Laws of Marriage and Descent." *Journal of the Royal Anthropological Institute* 18:245–269.

van den Berghe, Pierre 1980 "Incest and Exogamy: A Sociobiological Reconsideration." *Ethology and Sociobiology.* 1:151–162.

Vander Mey, Brenda J. 1991 "Theories of Incest." In W. O'Donohue and J. Geer, eds., *The Sexual Abuse of Children: Research, Theory, and Therapy.* Hillsdale, N.J.: Erlbaum.

———, Brenda J., and Ronald L. Neff 1986 *Incest as Child Abuse: Research and Applications.* New York: Praeger.

Weinberg, S. Kirson 1955 *Incest Behavior.* New York: Citadel Press.

Westermarck, Edward (1891) 1922 *The History of Human Marriage.* New York: Allerton.

BRENDA J. VANDER MEY

INCOME DISTRIBUTION IN THE UNITED STATES The United States today is characterized by both an increasing concentration of wealth and widespread poverty. These trends, however, are somewhat obscured if one looks at only the information on yearly money income reported by American householders and families. This entry examines trends from 1960 to 1990 as well as the most recent Bureau of the Census data on all three topics: income distribution, wealth, and poverty.

INCOME DISTRIBUTION

Data on money income are published each year by the Bureau of the Census, based on information from approximately 55,000 households scientifically selected to represent the entire nation. Respondents are asked about all sources of money income for the preceding year, including wages, Social Security benefits, welfare payments, workers' compensation, returns on investments, and pensions. Although the reported amounts tend to be somewhat lower than the aggregate estimates derived from tax records, these data are considered to be as refined as can be expected for such a major undertaking.

Household Income. In 1988, when the median yearly money income of all American households was $27,225, 17 percent of households had incomes of under $9,999, in contrast to 3.2 percent reporting incomes of $100,000 or more. Compared with similar data from 1968, adjusted for inflation (so that the median in 1968 was only $900 lower than in 1988), these numbers indicate that the proportion of households at the top earnings level had more than doubled (up from 1.3 percent), while the percent in the lowest level had declined slightly (from 18.8 percent).

The largest percentage decline, however, occurred in the middle of the income distribution, among households reporting money incomes between $25,000 and $35,000: from 20.6 percent in 1968 to 16 percent in 1988. Overall, the proportion of households with incomes between $15,000 and $50,000 had declined from almost 60 percent in 1968 to 52 percent in 1988, leading many scholars to refer to the "disappearing middle" in the American income spectrum.

Because "households" can be composed of one person, often a young person beginning worklife or an older individual living on a limited income, household income is typically lower than that for "families," which consist of at least two persons related by blood, marriage, or adoption. Therefore, it is important to examine family income in order to test the disappearing middle thesis.

Family Income. As expected, the proportion of families at the bottom of the distribution in 1988 was smaller than for households—only 10.8 percent below $9,999—while the percentage at the top was somewhat higher—almost 4 percent. But in comparison with 1968, there was only a slight increase in the proportion at the bottom, while those with incomes of $75,000 and over had more than doubled. In addition, the percentage in the middle, between $25,000 and $50,000, declined from over 44 percent of all families in 1968 to almost 37 percent in 1988. In other words, there was a clear upward thrust in the distribution of family income in the United States from 1968 to 1988. In this sense, it can be claimed that, in terms of money income, American families are, on average, better off in 1990 than they were in the late 1960s. Such aggregate numbers, however, hide important differences by race and Hispanic origin among families and households.

Subgroup Differences. For example, while only 8.5 percent of white families had money incomes below $10,000 in 1988, 27.3 percent of black families and 20.3 percent of Hispanic-origin families fell into that category, reflecting the higher proportion of single-parent families within these two populations. Comparable percentages for households were 14.8 percent for white but fully one-third for black and close to one-fourth for households headed by a person of Hispanic origin.

In general, also, family and household incomes vary systematically by region of the country (highest in the Northeast and lowest in the South), by age of householder (highest for those ages forty-five to fifty-four, lowest for those fifteen to twenty-four), by number of wage earners, and by sex of householder. Incomes of female householders, in all regions, at all ages, and in all racial-ethnic categories, are typically less than half the income for married-couple units or even those occupied by a male householder, no wife present. For example, the 1988 median money income for all married-couple families was $36,389 in contrast to $17,672 for a family with a female householder, no husband present. Most of this income differential reflects variation in labor force participation rates, but even when women are employed full-time year-round, their median income in 1988 was $17,606, compared to $26,656 for a full-time, year-round male worker.

At the other end of the income distribution, households and families classified as white are three times more likely than those headed by blacks or Hispanics to report money incomes in excess of $100,000. Although the proportion of all units at the top income level has more than doubled over the past two decades, this does not mean that the wealth of the nation is more evenly distributed than in the past.

WEALTH

While measuring income is fraught with difficulties, including underreporting, it is relatively straightforward when compared to measuring net wealth: the total value of all assets owned by a family, household, or person, less what is owed. Such assets include investment portfolios, bank accounts, real estate, homes and their furnishings, insurance policies and annuities, pension equity, real estate, vehicles, and the contents of safe deposit boxes. Total assets, minus debts, equals net worth.

The first systematic study of American wealthholding was conducted by the Federal Reserve Board (FRB) in 1963–1964. At that time, researchers found that the top 0.5 percent of households (the "super rich") owned 25 percent of the total net assets of the nation. The next 0.5 percent ("very rich") accounted for an additional 7 percent, and the 9 percent of households composing the plain "rich" owned 33 percent, leaving approximately 35 percent of the total net assets of the United States to the remaining 90 percent of the population.

Although comparable data were not gathered for the next twenty years, there was scattered evidence from the Internal Revenue Service's estate tax records to suggest that the share of assets owned by the super rich had declined between 1965 and 1976 to a low of 14.4 percent. This drop was due in part to an extended stock market slump and in part to changes in tax policies as well as to the growth of social welfare programs, including Aid to Families with Dependent Children, liberalization of Social Security benefits, and the introduction of Medicare/Medicaid, all of which tended to shift income from the more affluent to the more needy.

When the Internal Revenue Service withdrew access to its estate tax records from researchers in 1976, reliable data on wealth were difficult to obtain. This situation changed in 1983 and 1984 when two separate surveys of wealthholding were conducted, one by the Bureau of the Census and one by the Federal Reserve Board, designed to be comparable to its 1963 study. The U.S. Bureau of the Census (1986) survey of 26,000 living units, selected for representativeness, asked about household wealth and asset ownership, including bank accounts, investments, pensions, real estate, vehicles, and business ownership.

Unfortunately, the Census Bureau's random sample contained very few living units at the top of the asset scale, so it is difficult to generalize about the very rich and super rich from these data. In contrast, the Federal Reserve Board study, while relatively small—a basic random sample of 3,800 living units—was augmented with an additional 435 high-asset households (Avery and Elliehausen 1986). The FRB also gathered information on a broader range of assets than did the Bureau of the Census. In addition, the FRB data have been reexamined by researchers from the University of Michigan in an analysis prepared for the Joint Economic Committee of the U.S. Congress (1986); this analysis also permits direct comparison with the 1963 study. For these reasons, we believe that the FRB data are the more accurate indicators of the distribution of wealth in the United States at the end of the 1980s.

The major finding is that between 1976 and 1983 the downward trend of asset ownership by the super rich was dramatically reversed. From owning less than 15 percent of the net wealth of the nation in 1976, the super rich accounted for a full 35 percent just six years later. In large part, this increase reflected changing stock market values, but it was also reinforced by Reagan administration policies on taxes and welfare that shifted wealth from the poor to the affluent.

The top 1 percent of American wealthholders—the super rich and the very rich—today own more than 40 percent of the net assets of the country, and the top 10 percent own 72 percent of the total wealth. When compared to the 1963 data, it is clear that wealth today is more concentrated than it was in the 1960s and that the steepest rise occurred in the 1980s. To the extent that we have comparable data, wealth in America today is more concentrated than at any time since 1927, before the stock market crash and the Great Depression, when the share of net assets owned by the super rich also exceeded 30 percent of the total.

Even in the depths of the Great Depression, the share of net assets owned by the super rich did not fall below 25 percent. This was also the time when one-third of the nation could be described as ill-fed, ill-housed, ill-clothed, and jobless in a society without an extensive public social welfare system.

POVERTY

The one-third of the nation deprived of adequate income, food, and housing in 1930 was not very different in size or background characteristics from those who were counted as poor in the late 1950s. Despite the introduction of Social Security for the retired, disabled, and dependents of deceased workers, and the other programs of the New Deal designed to minimize the effects of poverty, 22.4 percent of the American population was classified as poor in 1959. Their plight evoked images of the impoverished of the Great Depression: old people, rural Yankee families of Appalachia, unemployed white working men, grim-faced farmers, and possibly a dignified black couple. Faced with such daunting numbers, it became necessary to set standards of eligibility for the array of welfare programs that had gradually been introduced and expanded since the 1930s.

Defining Poverty. By 1964, the Social Security Administration had devised a method for defining poverty. Back in 1955, the Department of Agriculture had discovered that families of three or more persons spent one-third of their income on food. As the Department of Agriculture had also computed the price of the least expensive nutritionally adequate food plan, the Social Security Administration simply multiplied the cost of that food basket by three, and with a few corrections for family size, rural or urban residence, and age and sex of householder, arrived at a dollar figure that demarcated the poor from the nonpoor. Households with income over that line were officially not poor; those that fell below the threshold became officially poor.

The value of the economy food plan is adjusted

each year to the cost-of-living index, but the basic formula remains unchanged even though housing costs now outstrip the proportion of income spent on food. There have been changes in the index, such as no longer distinguishing rural from urban (the rural threshold was lower, presumably because country folk could grow some of their own food), or male from female heads of household (the latter were assumed to need less food than the former). Only size of household and age of householder have been retained in the calculations.

In 1990, the poverty threshold for a single person was approximately $5,500, slightly higher if under age sixty-five, and somewhat lower if over age sixty-five, on the assumption that older people eat less than younger ones. The poverty line for a two-person family was slightly over $7,000 and that for a family of four was about $11,500. These are the dollar values deemed adequate to house, feed, and clothe members of a household. Those with money income above the threshold are no longer eligible for additional benefits, including both income support (Aid to Families with Dependent Children, Supplemental Security Income) and in-kind programs (e.g., food stamps, Medicaid, housing subsidies). As low as these amounts may seem, there was a concerted effort during the Reagan administration to recalculate "income" to include the dollar value of in-kind benefits, which would have reduced the poverty rate by 25 to 30 percent, without any additional assistance to the poor. Although this new number continues to be included in Census Bureau publications (e.g., 1990c), the official poverty level remains calculated on the basis of income received or earned.

The poverty *rate,* then, represents the proportion of individuals, families, or households whose income falls below the threshold. Throughout the early 1960s, between 22 and 19 percent of all Americans were officially classified as poor. Programs introduced in the Johnson administration's War on Poverty helped to bring this figure down to slightly over 11 percent in the early 1970s. The poverty rate remained under 12 percent until the 1980s, when the recession of 1982–83, combined with Reagan administration cutbacks in social welfare programs, raised the poverty rate to 15.2 percent, before slowly declining to its current 13 percent.

Who Are the Poor? Poverty, however, is not evenly distributed among Americans. Although 65 percent of the poverty population in 1988 was white, this represents only 10 percent of all American whites. In contrast, 31.6 percent of blacks and 26.8 percent of persons of Hispanic origin had incomes below the poverty line in 1988, as did 20 percent of persons of "other races" (Asian, American Indian). Married couples fared much better than did unrelated individuals or persons in female-headed households, regardless of race or ethnicity, but, compared to whites, smaller proportions of American blacks and Hispanics live in married-couple families. At the extremes, while under 5 percent of white married couples fell below the poverty line, 56.3 percent of families headed by a black woman were so classified. Today, close to one-half of all black children and 40 percent of children of Hispanic origin will spend part of their lives in households below the poverty level, compared to 15 percent of children in white families.

In terms of age, one of every five American children is poor, in contrast to one in ten adults ages eighteen to sixty-four. Among the elderly (age sixty-five and over), 12 percent live in poverty, slightly below the national rate. This was not always so. Indeed, the high proportion of older people living in poverty was a major impetus for the social welfare reforms of the 1930s and the 1960s. Because the elderly could be perceived as "deserving" poor, it was possible to create a voting constituency favorable to such initiatives during both periods. Amendments to the Social Security Act in 1965 and 1972 broadened coverage, extended benefits, and initiated the Medicare program for reimbursing limited health care costs. As a consequence, poverty among the elderly declined from a post-Depression high of 35.2 percent in 1959 to its current 12 percent, but there are signs that housing and medical costs are once more outstripping the income resources of many elderly, especially for the very old, the frail, and the widowed—the vast majority of whom are women.

Indeed, it appears that poverty has increasingly become a problem for women of all ages, particularly those who are not married: teenage mothers, displaced homemakers, divorcees in general, and frail elderly widows. But the "feminization of poverty" (Pearce 1978) since 1970 is only partly due to an increase in female householders. Wives of the unemployed or of low earners also suffer. The basic causes of poverty in the United States today are low wages and limited employment opportunities for large numbers of men and women, especially racial-ethnic minorities; cutbacks in social welfare programs at all levels of government; and a decline in average earnings among young families in general, but most particularly for those headed by high school dropouts. People who work full-time, year-round at the minimum wage still fall below the poverty threshold for a family of three.

The Near Poor. In addition to those who fall below the official poverty level, millions of other individuals and families float precariously above that dollar threshold. The Bureau of the Census also counts individuals and families whose income is 125 percent of the poverty line—the "near poor." Including the near poor would have raised the 1988 poverty rate for families to over 14.5 percent and to almost 41 percent for female householders. In addition, the Bureau of the Census estimates that another 5 to 6 percent of Americans have been lifted above the poverty line by virtue of Social Security benefits to retired workers, survivors of deceased workers, and the disabled.

It appears, then, that poverty and near poverty are widespread, touching the lives of one in four Americans. The line between official poverty and nonpoverty is very thin, and individuals and families tend to slip under it and rise again with changes in employment, health, and marital status. That is, contrary to popular opinion, the poverty population is not characterized by long-term welfare dependency. Fewer than 10 percent remain on the welfare rolls for a decade or more, primarily women who entered the system as very young unwed mothers and who have been unable to develop job skills or find employment that pays enough to lift the family out of poverty. For most others, poverty and nonpoverty are temporary states. An extended illness, divorce, and job loss will plunge the unit below the threshold; remarriage, employment, and recovery from illness pulls the unit above the line (Duncan et al. 1984; Ruggles 1988; U.S. Bureau of the Census 1990a, 1990b).

Also contrary to public opinion, there is no evidence that poor women have children in order to increase their welfare benefits, or that variations in benefit levels affect the formation of single-parent families (Ellwood 1988). The prevalence of female householders among blacks is due primarily to a shortage of marriageable men. Young black males are disproportionately victims of homicide and accidental deaths; many are imprisoned; and large numbers are unemployed or underemployed.

Finally, living in poverty is a troubled existence. The poor are more likely than the nonpoor to be ill, to be without adequate health care, to feel emotional anguish, to be victims of crime, to fail in marriage, and to see their children suffer from malnutrition, crippling disease, and early death. In addition, as the stock of low-income rental or subsidized housing steadily diminished throughout the 1980s—due to the phasing out of federal programs combined with owners' decisions to convert much of this housing to condominiums—many of the poor and near poor entered the ranks of America's homeless. What remained of federal housing assistance under the Reagan administration was tainted by graft and political favoritism.

If there is a "culture of poverty" characterized by the intergenerational transmission of maladaptive attitudes toward work and marriage, as conservative critics of the welfare system claim (Lewis 1961; Murray 1984), sociologists tend to explain the persistence of such behaviors as normal responses to the unchanging structural conditions that create and maintain impoverishment—low wages, uncertain employment, inadequate housing and health care, failing schools, an indifferent public, and an often hostile government. Anyone living under these circumstances would most likely respond in similar ways. That is, rather than explaining social patterns by reference to the characteristics of individuals, sociologists examine the contexts in which that behavior takes place.

FUTURE TRENDS

Will the context for the distribution of income in the United States undergo change in the near future? There does not appear to be any major thrust toward revising the tax structure, to make the system more progressive, that is, to tax higher incomes at significantly higher rates. Indeed, quite the contrary appears to be the case at the state and local level, where the trend has been away from relatively progressive income taxes toward property and sales taxes that apply the same rate to all payers.

Nor does there appear to be much public sentiment toward raising welfare benefits in order to lift households over the poverty threshold. In general, eligibility rules and procedures tend to be more punitive than meliorative, so that large numbers of people eligible for in-kind benefits are not enrolled. The most recent attempts to reduce long-term welfare dependency involve state-sponsored "workfare" programs whereby single mothers are trained for entry into the labor force. During the training period and for some time afterward, the family continues to receive income assistance, Medicaid coverage, and child care. To date, workfare has not had a major impact on the poverty rate, in large part because the jobs for which the women are being trained do not raise their income sufficiently to compensate for the loss of health care coverage.

Behind the American public's resistance to changes in either the tax structure or the welfare system is a set of deeply ingrained attitudes about wealth and poverty. Based on the set of values often referred to as the "work ethic," these attitudes and beliefs have been central to the development of capitalism: work as a "calling" (sacred task); success as a sign of personal virtue; failure as a signal of moral flaw; and each person's responsibility for her or his conduct in this world. From this perspective, Americans tend to see success and failure as individually determined. Thus, poverty is thought to be due to laziness, lack of talent, or loose morals, rather than being linked to societal factors such as changes in the occupational structure, the flight of jobs and capital from central cities, and the subsequent deterioration of housing and schools (Feagin 1986). Conversely, the successful are thought to be endowed with special gifts of talent and virtue, including a willingness to work hard.

There are also indications that it will be harder than in the past to generate a collective commitment to alleviate poverty. America's poor today are different from the impoverished of the 1930s and even the late 1950s: less likely to be white, to be married, or to be male. The sympathy that is so readily evoked by the plight of an unemployed coal miner and his family is rarely extended to the dark-skinned inner city unwed mother who actually has fewer children on average than Appalachian whites.

Therefore, unless there is a major shift in values and political leadership, it is unlikely that there will be any marked reversal of current trends in the distribution of income, wealth, and poverty in the United States through the remainder of this century. Wealth will continue to become concentrated, even as the proportion of high wealthholders increases. The middle of the income distribution will continue to shrink, albeit slowly. And one in four Americans, and a higher proportion of children, will continue to live in or near poverty.

COMPARATIVE PERSPECTIVES

Any discussion of wealth, poverty, and the distribution of income within a population must take into account the vast differences between modern industrial societies and the less developed nations. Poor people in high-income societies are rarely as deprived of the basic necessities of survival as are most people in the third world, where income inequality is typically higher than in industrial societies (World Bank 1989). But Americans do not compare themselves to Sudanese; rather, they measure their circumstances against those of other Americans to whom they feel similar. It is a sense of relative rather than absolute deprivation that tends to fuel hostility, violence, indifference, or withdrawal into a world of drug-induced oblivion.

Yet, comparing only modern industrial societies, there is evidence that the extent of poverty and associated social problems—for example, single-parent families, teenage pregnancy, homicide, substance abuse, homelessness, infant mortality, violent crime—is greater in the United States than in other Western democracies. This is so largely because the United States has the least extensive social welfare system of any modern state. Alone among its industrialized peers, the United States is without a comprehensive family policy, lacks a national health insurance system, and emphasizes limitations rather than entitlements to benefit programs. As a consequence, there are few institutionalized mechanisms, other than Social Security, for the redistribution of income that narrow the gap between the very rich and very poor or that substantially reduce both the likelihood and impact of poverty. In the absence of a revitalization of a sense of collective responsibility, income inequality will continue to characterize the United States.

(SEE ALSO: *Homelessness; Poverty; Social Stratification*)

REFERENCES

Avery, Robert B., and Gregory E. Elliehausen 1986 "Financial Characteristics of High-Income Families." *Federal Reserve Bulletin* 72:163–176.

Duncan, Greg J., Richard D. Coe, Mary E. Corcoran, Martha S. Hill, Saul D. Hoffman, and James N. Morgan 1984 *Years of Poverty, Years of Plenty: The Changing Economic Fortunes of American Workers and Families.* Ann Arbor: Institute for Social Research, University of Michigan.

Ellwood, David T. 1988 *Poor Support: Poverty in the American Family.* New York: Basic Books.

Feagin, Joe R. 1986 *Social Problems: A Critical Power-Conflict Perspective,* 2nd ed. Englewood Cliffs, N.J.: Prentice-Hall.

Lewis, Oscar 1961 *Children of Sanchez.* New York: Random House.

Murray, Charles 1984 *Losing Ground.* New York: Basic Books.

Pearce, Diana 1978 "The Feminization of Poverty: Women, Work, and Welfare." *Urban and Social Change Review* February:1–17.

Ruggles, Patricia 1988 *Short Term Fluctuations in Income and Their Relationship to the Characteristics of the Low Income Population.* Survey of Income and Program Participation Working Paper No. 8802. Bureau of the Census. Washington, D.C.: U.S. Government Printing Office.

U.S. Bureau of the Census 1986 *Household Wealth and Asset Ownership: 1984.* Current Population Reports, Series P-70, No. 7. Washington, D.C.: U.S. Government Printing Office.

———1989 *Money Income and Poverty Status in the United States: 1988 (Advance Data from the March 1989 Current Population Survey).* Current Population Reports, Series P-60, No. 166. Washington, D.C.: U.S. Government Printing Office.

———1990a *Transitions in Income and Poverty Status: 1985-1986.* Current Population Reports, Series P-70, No. 18. Washington, D.C.: U.S. Government Printing Office.

———1990b *Trends in Income, by Selected Characteristics: 1947 to 1988.* Current Population Reports, Series P-60, No. 167. Washington, D.C.: U.S. Government Printing Office.

———1990c *Measuring the Effect of Benefits and Taxes on Income and Poverty: 1989.* Current Population Reports, Series P-60, No. 169-RD. Washington, D.C.: U.S. Government Printing Office.

U.S. Congress 1986 *The Concentration of Wealth in the United States: Trends in the Distribution of Wealth Among American Families.* Washington, D.C.: Joint Economic Committee.

World Bank 1989 *World Development Report 1989.* New York: Oxford University Press.

BETH B. HESS

INDIAN SOCIOLOGY Reviewers of Indian sociology generally trace its origin to the works of several British civil servants, missionaries, and Western scholars during the eighteenth and nineteenth centuries (Srinivas and Panini 1973; Rao 1978; Mukherjee 1979; Dhanagare 1985; Singh 1986). British administrators wanted to understand the customs, manners, and institutions of the people of India in order to run their administration smoothly. Christian missionaries were interested in learning local languages, folklore, and culture to carry out their activities. The origin, development, and functioning of the various customs and traditions, the Hindu systems of caste and joint family, and the village or tribal community and its economy and polity were some of the prominent themes of study. The first all-India census was conducted in 1871. Several ethnographic surveys, monographs, census documents, and gazetteers produced during this period constitute a wealth of information that is of interest to sociologists even today. Mukherjee (1979, p. 24) observes that the works of the civil servants, missionaries, and others during the colonial rule in India "provided the elements from which the British policy for ruling the subcontinent crystallized and also in turn helped to produce the pioneers in Indian sociology." Further, the available studies of Indian society and culture became an important source for testing various theories by scholars like Marx and Engels, Maine, and Weber.

The first universities in India were established in 1857 at Bombay, Calcutta, and Madras. Formal teaching of sociology started at the University of Bombay in 1914, at Calcutta University in 1917, and at Lucknow University in 1921. Prior to India's independence in 1947, only three other universities (Mysore, Osmania, and Poona) were teaching sociology. There was no separate department of sociology; it was joined with the department of economics (Bombay and Lucknow), economics and political science (Calcutta), anthropology (Poona), or philosophy (Mysore). Only a limited number of courses in sociology were taught, and they were fashioned by teachers according to their interests. Courses included such topics as social biology, social problems (such as crime, prostitution, and begging), social psychology, civilization, and prehistory. "In the case of teaching of Indian social institutions the orientation showed more Indological and philosophical emphasis on the one hand and a concern for the social pathological problems and ethnological description on the other. Strong scientific empirical traditions had not emerged before Independence" (Rao 1978, pp. 2–3).

Although many of the pioneers in sociology were educated at Calcutta, substantial impact on Indian sociology during the first half of the twentieth century was made at Bombay and Lucknow universities. Patrick Geddes, the first chairperson of the Department of Sociology and Civics at Bombay University, was a town planner and human geographer. His reports on the town planning of Calcutta, Indore, and the temple cities of south India contain much useful information and demonstrate his keen awareness of the problems of urban disorganization and renewal (Srinivas and Panini 1973, p. 187). G. S. Ghurye succeeded Geddes in 1924. He was trained as a social anthropologist at Cambridge University. There is a wide range of themes in his research work and writings: from castes, races, and tribes in India to cities and civilization, from Shakespeare on conscience and justice to Raiput architecture, and from Indian Sadhus to sex habits of a sample of middle class people of Bombay. He indicated several unexplored dimensions of Indian society, culture, and social institutions. During his teaching career of thirty-five years at Bombay University, he guided about eighty research students. Several of his students (for example, M. N. Srinivas, K. M. Kapadia, I. P. Desai, Y. B. Damle, A. R. Desai, and M. S. A. Rao) later on made a great impact on the development of sociology in India.

R. K. Mukherjee and D. P. Mukherji taught sociology at Lucknow University; both of them were trained in economics at Calcutta University. R. K. Mukherjee made a series of micro-level analyses of problems concerning the rural economy, land, population, and working class in India as well as the deteriorating agrarian relations and conditions of the peasantry, intercaste tensions, and urbanization. D. P. Mukherji's interests were diverse; they ranged from music and fine arts as peculiar creations of the Indian culture to the Indian tradition in relation to modernity. He was a professed Marxist and attempted a dialectical interpretation of the encounter between the Indian tradition and modernity; this encounter unleashed many forces of cultural contradiction during the colonial era (Dhanagare 1985, pp. 323–324).

B. N. Seal and B. K. Sarkar were two of the

leading sociologists of that time at Calcutta University. Seal was a philosopher and a comparative sociologist: He wrote on the origin of race, positive sciences and the physico-chemical theories of the ancient Hindus, and the differences and similarities between Vaishnavism and Christianity. He stressed the need for a statistical approach, inductive logic, and methodology to appraise the contextual reality comprehensively. Sarkar was a historian and economist by training. He opposed the persistent general belief that Hinduism is otherworldly. He was also one of the few who discussed Marx, Weber, and Pareto at a time when they were not fashionable with sociologists in India and abroad (Mukherjee 1979, pp. 33–35). S. V. Ketkar and B. N. Dutt, both of whom specialized in Indological studies in the United States, and K. P. Chattopadhyay, a social anthropologist trained in the United Kingdom, are some of the other noteworthy pioneers of Indian sociology.

Mukherjee (1979) points out that the goals set by the pioneers ranged from an idealized version of oriental culture to the materialist view of social development. They were involved in bibliographical research to establish the historical data base and strongly advocated empirical research. But in the days of the pioneers, the interaction between theoretical formulations and the data base remained at a preliminary stage.

Some of the outstanding features in the development of Indian sociology since India's independence are organization of professional bodies of sociologists, lack of a rigid distinction between sociology and social anthropology, debates regarding the need for indigenization of sociology and the relevance of Indian sociology, diversification and specialization into various subfields, and participation of sociologists in interdisciplinary research.

There has been a tremendous increase in the number of universities, colleges, and institutes teaching sociology. In most universities, teaching of sociology started first at the graduate level and then at the undergraduate level. Universities and institutions offering degrees in interdisciplinary areas such as management, rural development, planning, communication, and nursing include some sociology courses in their training program. Of late, some states have introduced sociology courses at the higher secondary level also.

There was no professional body of sociologists during the colonial period. Ghurye was instrumental in establishing the Indian Sociological Society in 1951, and R. N. Saksena was instrumental in organizing the first All-India Sociological Conference in 1956. These organizations merged in 1967 into a single all-India professional body of sociologists. The Indian Sociological Society has at present over 1,000 life members. Several regional associations of sociologists have also been formed during the last two decades.

The development of sociology in India, from the viewpoint of theory, methodology, and research interests, has been significantly influenced by that in the Western countries. Several Western scholars, a majority of them initially from the United Kingdom and Europe, and later on from the United States, have carried out studies in India. Similarly, many of the leading sociologists in India have been trained in the United Kingdom and the United States. There has been a steady increase in the participation of Indian sociologists in various international seminars, workshops, and conferences. The organization of the Eleventh World Congress of Sociology in New Delhi in 1986 indicates recognition of the development of Indian sociology and its contribution. However, with a rise in the cost of higher education and a fall in the availability of financial assistance at Western universities, there has been of late a decline in the number of Indian students going abroad for advance study in sociology.

Two journals of sociology, *The Indian Journal of Sociology,* started in 1921 by Alban G. Widgery (a British professor working in Baroda College), and *The Indian Sociological Review,* started in 1934 with R. K. Mukherjee as its editor, were short-lived. There are now only a few all-India journals of sociology: *Sociological Bulletin* (a biannual journal of the Indian Sociological Society since 1952), *Contributions to Indian Sociology* (edited by two French scholars, Louis Dumont and D. F. Pocock, from its inception in 1957 to 1963, when its editorship passed on to Indian sociologists), and

Social Change (published by the Council for Social Development since 1971). Occasionally, articles of sociological contents and relevance are published in other journals such as *Economic and Political Weekly* and the journals published by some universities and regional associations.

Initially, no rigid distinction was made between social anthropology and sociology, but they separated as teaching disciplines in the 1950s. In the field of research, however, the distinction between social anthropology and sociology continues to be blurred. Ghurye, Srinivas, S. C. Dube, and Andre Beteille, among others, have argued that a sociologist, in the Indian context, cannot afford to make any artificial distinction between the study of tribal and folk society and the advanced sections of the population; nor can sociological studies be confined to any single set of techniques. Yogesh Atal (1985) points out that this is true of several countries in Asia and the Pacific; social anthropologists have extended the scope of their investigation to microcommunities in rural as well as urban settings in their own country, and sociologists have found the anthropological method of field work and participant observation useful in their research. Even the Indian Council of Social Science Research (ICSSR) treats both these disciplines together in its two surveys of research, the first covering the period up to 1969 (Indian Council of Social Science Research 1972–1974) and the other from 1969 to 1979 (Indian Council of Social Science Research 1985–1986); the same approach continues for the third survey, now under way, for the period 1979 to 1987.

There have been continuous debates regarding the need for indigenization of sociology (or "sociology for India") and the relevance of Indian sociology (Unnithan, Singh, Singhi, and Deva 1967; Sharma 1985). One direction of the debate started with the suggestion of Dumont and Pocock (1957, p. 7) that "in principle . . . a sociology of India lies at the point of confluence of Sociology and Indology." Proponents of the Indological approach in sociology argue that the contextual specificity of Indian social realities could be grasped better from the scriptural writings. Gupta (1974) points out the need for separating normative and actual behavior. Oommen (1983, p. 130) pleads that "if sociology is to be relevant for India as a discipline it should endorse and its practitioners should internalize the value-package contained in the Indian Constitution," that is, socialism, secularism, and democracy rather than hierarchy, holism, pluralism, and so forth as pointed out by the Indologists. Another direction of the debate is identified with a paradigm of Indian sociology free from academic colonialism, which is manifested in concepts and methods borrowed from other cultures, particularly the West, that supposedly have no relevance to the Indian social, historical, and cultural situation (Singh 1986, p. 14). However, most sociologists are not hostile to using Western concepts, models, and analytical categories, but they want their adaptation to suit the Indian sociocultural setting. Singh (1986) analyzes the contents and salient orientations of the presidential addresses delivered by Srinivas, Saksena, Mukherjee, Dube, Desai, and Gore at the conferences of the Indian Sociological Society. He observes that these addresses profess a deep concern with the issue of relevance in the contexts of social policies, normative analysis of these policies, and the role of sociologists in understanding, appraising, or promoting these normative objectives of development and change in India.

In the 1950s and 1960s, several micro-level studies of caste, joint families, and village communities, mostly from the viewpoint of structural-functional aspects and change, were carried out. Srinivas introduced the concepts of dominant caste, Sanskritization, Westernization, and secularization to understand the realities of intercaste relations and their dynamics (Dhanagare 1985, p. 331). Change in the structural and functional aspects of family in different parts of India was the focal point of most studies in the area of marriage, family, and kinship. The village studies focused on stratification and mobility, factionalism and leadership, jajmani (patron–client) relationship, contrasting characteristics of rural and urban communities, and linkages with the outside world.

Indian sociology during the last two decades shows both continuity and change in research.

Caste and stratification, village communities, and social change have continued to be themes of research, but the approach has shifted from the functional to the conflict viewpoint. The descriptive studies of a single village community or other unit in a single social setting are replaced by analytical comparative studies of social structure across time and space. Interest in the area of marriage, family, and kinship has declined. Women's studies have gained tremendously in importance. Several studies have been conducted in the fields of education, urban sociology, social movements, voting behavior, communication, and industrial relations. Sociologies of medicine, law, science, and professions have also begun to develop. Now, the thrust is on studying various processes. For example, with a concern for equality and distributive justice, there is an increasing emphasis on examining the process of education as a vehicle of social change as it affects the existing system of stratification, women, and weaker sections.

India started its first Five-Year Plan in 1952. Since then social scientists, particularly economists and sociologists, have been involved in conducting diagnostic, monitoring, and evaluative studies concerning a variety of developmental programs at micro as well as macro levels. Policy and programs concerning urban and rural community development, Panchayati Raj, family planning, education, removal of untouchability, uplift of weaker sections (scheduled castes, scheduled tribes, and other disadvantaged castes), and rehabilitation of people affected by large-scale projects (construction of big dams, industrial estates, capital towns, etc.) have been some of the important areas of research by sociologists. At times, the various ministries of the central and the state governments, the ICSSR, and other funding agencies have sponsored all-India studies that have tended, albeit in a small way, to strengthen an interdisciplinary approach in social research. For example, the Indian Space Research Organization conducted in 1975 and 1976 a satellite instructional television experiment in 2,330 villages spread over twenty districts of six states in India for a period of one year (Agrawal et al. 1977); the ICSSR sponsored a nationwide study of the educational problems of scheduled-caste and -tribe students (Shah 1982). During the 1970s and the 1980s, several social research institutes have been established in different parts of India. Also, many universities have established interdisciplinary units for women's studies. The most prominent sociology departments and social research institutes are located in Delhi, Bombay, Ahmedabad, Jaipur, Chandigarh, Poona, Bangalore, Hyderabad, and Trivandrum.

Several universities have gradually switched over to the use of the regional language as a medium of instruction at the undergraduate level, and some at the graduate level also. Inadequate availability of textbooks in regional languages has been a major handicap in the teaching and learning process. Statistics has as yet not become an integral component of sociology curricula in a large number of colleges and universities. Although surveys are widely used in sociological research, most research publications hardly go beyond the use of descriptive statistics. There has been a strong plea for developing concepts and measurements that fit the Indian situation, but concerted efforts in this matter are still lacking.

(SEE ALSO: *Caste and Class*)

REFERENCES

Agrawal, Binod C., J. K. Doshi, Victor Jesudason, and K. K. Verma 1977 *Satellite Instructional Television Experiment: Social Evaluation—Impact on Adults.* Bangalore: Indian Space Research Organization.

Atal, Yogesh 1985 "Growth Points in Asian and Pacific Sociology and Social Anthropology." In *Sociology and Social Anthropology in Asia and the Pacific.* Paris and New Delhi: UNESCO and Wiley Eastern.

Dhanagare, D. N. 1985 "India." In *Sociology and Social Anthropology in Asia and the Pacific.* Paris and New Delhi: UNESCO and Wiley Eastern.

Dumont, Louis, and D. F. Pocock 1957 "For a Sociology of India." *Contributions to Indian Sociology* 1:7.

Gupta, Krishna Prakash 1974 "Sociology of Indian Tradition and Tradition of Indian Sociology." *Sociological Bulletin* 23:14–43.

Indian Council of Social Science Research 1972–1974 *A Survey of Research in Sociology and Social Anthropology.* 3 vols. Bombay: Popular Prakashan.

———1985–1986. *Survey of Research in Sociology and Social Anthropology, 1969–1979.* 3 vols. New Delhi: Satvahan Publications.

Mukherjee, Ramkrishna 1979 *Sociology of Indian Sociology.* New Delhi: Allied Publishers.

Oommen, T. K. 1983 "Sociology in India: A Plea for Contextualisation." *Sociological Bulletin* 32:111–136.

Rao, M. S. A. 1978 "Introduction." In *Report on the Status of Teaching of Sociology and Social Anthropology,* Part 1: "Recommendations." New Delhi: University Grants Commission.

Shah, Vimal P 1982 *The Educational Problems of Scheduled Caste and Scheduled Tribe School and College Students in India.* New Delhi: Allied Publishers.

Sharma, Surendra 1985 *Sociology in India: A Perspective from Sociology of Knowledge.* Jaipur: Rawat Publications.

Singh, Yogendra 1986 *Indian Sociology: Social Conditioning and Emerging Concerns.* New Delhi: Vistar Publications.

Srinivas, M. N. and M. N. Panini 1973 "The Development of Sociology and Social Anthropology in India." *Sociological Bulletin* 22:179–215.

Unnithan, T. K. N., Yogendra Singh, Narendra Singhi, and Indra Deva, eds. 1967 *Sociology for India.* New Delhi: Prentice-Hall.

VIMAL P. SHAH

INDIVIDUALISM Individualism is a doctrine concerning both the composition of human society and the constitution of sociocultural actors. The term was invented in the 1820s, apparently, in France (Swart 1962). Its first appearance in English dates from the 1835 translation of Alexis de Tocqueville's study of the United States (Tocqueville [1850] 1969). The basic notion conveyed by the newly coined word, that the individual is sovereign vis-à-vis society, was intensely controversial, for it symbolized the death of one established order and the rise of another. As an early French critic saw it, individualism "destroys the very idea of obedience and of duty, thereby destroying both power and law," leaving nothing "but a terrifying confusion of interests, passions and diverse opinions" (cited in Lukes 1973, p. 6).

Individualism should be distinguished from historically specific constitutions of the individuality of human beings. The word *individual,* used to discriminate a particular human being from collectivities *(family, state),* had been in circulation for centuries prior to Tocqueville, and individualizations had been practiced under one description or another long before that, at least as evidenced in the oldest surviving texts of human history. However, premodern constitutions of individuality did not become the focus of a distinctive doctrine called individualism. That development came in response to the profound changes of social structure and consciousness that had been slowly accumulating during the seventeenth and eighteenth centuries. In the transformation from a medieval to a modern world, new transparencies of meaning evolved, among the most important a particular conception of *the individual.* The enormous power of that conception is reflected in the fact that people of modern society have generally had no doubt as to what an individual *is.* The reference has been self-evident because the object referred to, an *individual,* has been self-evident, pregiven, natural.

But one must remember that *the individual* is a construct. Like all constructs, it is historically variable. The meaning of individualism's individual was formed under specific historical circumstances that, in practice as well as ideology, increasingly prized values of rational calculation, mastery, and experimentation; deliberate efforts toward betterment of the human condition; and a universalism anchored in the conviction that human nature is basically the same everywhere at all times and that rationality is singular in number. These commitments were manifested in the doctrine of individualism (as indeed in the formation of the modern social sciences). By the time of Tocqueville and the newly coined word, individualism's individual had become integral to much of the practical consciousness of modern society. Human beings were being objectified as instances of *the individual,* that is, as instances of a particular kind of individuality.

The forces created during that formative period wrought great changes in the fabric of society, many of which continue to reverberate. Of course, as historical circumstances have changed, both the individual of individualism and the constitution of individuality have changed. Nonetheless, a certain transparency of meaning remains today in our practical consciousness of the individual, and it is still informed by a doctrine of individualism. Thus, when a sociologist today says that "a natural unit of observation is the individual" (Coleman 1990, p. 1), he or she can safely assume that most readers will know exactly what is meant.

The remainder of this article offers cursory accounts of (1) the development of individualism during the seventeenth, eighteenth, and nineteenth centuries; (2) the recent shifts of emphasis in individualism's conception of the individual; and (3) some current issues and concerns. More extended treatments can be found in Macpherson (1962); Lukes (1973); Abercrombie, Hill, and Turner (1986); and Heller, Sosna, and Wellbery (1986), among others.

THE SELF-REPRESENTING INDIVIDUAL

Although elements of individualism can be seen in expressions of practical affairs as early as during the twelfth-century renaissance, (Macfarlane 1978; Ullmann 1966), the first more or less systematic statement of the doctrine came during the 1600s. Scholars such as René Descartes, Thomas Hobbes, and John Locke believed that, to understand a whole (e.g., society), one had first to understand the parts of which it was composed. In the case of society, those "parts," the building blocks of a society, were instances of the individual. Although disagreeing on various specific issues —for example, whether human agency is distinct from a natural world of causal necessity (Descartes) or a product of that causal necessity (Hobbes)—these seventeenth-century scholars displayed remarkable confidence in their understanding of the individual as a presocial atom. Their individual was a highly abstract being, squatting outside the world.

In the premodern order of European society, social relations had been organic, corporate, and mainly determined by family lineage and other group-based traits. Sovereignty was a complex relation of duty, responsibility, and charity, focused on a specific location in the hierarchical order of organic community. Certainly members of the community were individualized, but the distinction was constituted primarily by their positions in the hierarchical order. It is clear from surviving documents of the twelfth century, for example, that one individual knight was discriminable from any other in ways that we would describe as "personality." With rare exception, however, that discrimination was local. Otherwise, knights were discriminable mainly by pedigree, lines of fealty, and quality of chivalry. Individuals could rise (and fall) through gradations of rank, but vertical movement was first within the family or household group. A knight who aspired to still higher standing had first to be retained in another, more powerful, family.

In the new order, in contrast, social relations were conceived as contractual rather than organic, based on achieved traits (rather than on traits fixed at birth or by family lineage) of individuals free of the constraints of community. City life was once again the center of gravity in territorial organization, having displaced the manorial system. The new individual was conceived as a wholly separate entity of self-identical integrity, a "bare individual" who could freely consent to enter into concert with other equivalently constituted individuals, each propelled by self-interest. This was, as Macpherson (1962) describes it, the advent of "possessive individualism," and it correlated well with the developing motivations of capitalism.

By the end of the eighteenth century, individualism had attained mature statement in treatises by David Hume, Adam Smith, and Immanuel Kant, among others. This mature statement, worked out in the context of rapidly changing politico-economic institutions, emphasized the centrality of a *self-representing individual.* The chief claim—that "every individual appears as the autonomous subject of his [or her, but primarily his] decisions and actions" (Goldmann [1968] 1973, p. 20)—served as linchpin to formalized explanations of the political and economic rights of members of society, especially the propertied members. Expressions of the chief claim in moral and legal rights of the individual became enshrined in newly invented traditions, in legitimizing principles such as *popular sovereignty* and *inalienable rights,* and in documents of public culture such as the Declaration of the Rights of Man and the U.S. Constitution (Hobsbawm and Ranger 1983; Morgan 1988). The prayerful injunction "God bless the squire and his relations and keep us in our proper stations" had been replaced by the almost wholly secular "*I* pledge allegiance to the flag" (i.e., to an abstract sign). Although the claim of autonomy emphasized the universality of rights and the particularity of the *I,* the practical emphasis on a self-representing individual was formulated in politico-economic terms that "necessitated" elaborate definitions and procedures for the defense of "property rights" long before equivalent attention would be given to, say, "rights of the handicapped."

Much like the individual of organic community, the self-representing individual is a substantial presence, manifest as the embodiment of a uniform human nature and, as such, is the bearer of various traits, dispositions, and affirmations. However, the site of the self-representing individual's capacity for agency and potential for autonomy is neither the community nor the accumulated traits, dispositions, and affirmations. Rather, it is deeply interior to what became a new *inner nature* of being human. Beneath the faculty of reason, beneath all feeling and emotion and belief, there is *the will.* Emile Durkheim ([1914] 1973) described it as the egoistic will of the individual pole of *homo duplex;* for George Herbert Mead (1934) it was "the principle of action." But before either of those sociologists, the master theorizer of the self-representing individual, Kant, had formulated the basic principle as the pure functioning of the I through time. Only because I can unite a variety of given representations of objects in *one* consciousness, Kant ([1787] 1929, B133) argued, is it possible for me to "represent to myself the *identity of consciousness*" throughout those representations. In other words, the very possibility of knowledge of the external world is dependent on the temporal continuity of the I. The individual is absolute proprietor of this pure functionality, this willing of the I as basic principle of action; the individual owes absolutely nothing to society for it.

By conceiving the essential core of human individuality as a deeply interiorized, radically isolated, pure functionality, connections between the individual and the substantive traits that she or he bears become arbitrary. The individual is formally free to exercise a choice of which traits to bear, free to be mobile geographically, socially, culturally, personally. Ascriptive traits (e.g., sex, skin color) are devalued in favor of achieved traits, and one set of achieved traits can always be exchanged for yet another set. This principle of freely exchangeable traits, an aspiration directing progress toward *the good society,* depended on new means of socialization (or internalization of norms) to ensure sufficient regularity in the processes of exchange. Indeed, the self-representing individual was central to a distinctive regimen of behavior, a new practical meaning of *discipline* (Foucault [1975] 1977). As the doctrine of individualism expressed it, the contractual, associative forms of social relation, though looser fitting in their constraints than the old organic community, were complemented by the figure of *the self-made man* who had internalized all the norms of rectitude and propriety so nicely as to merit life in an unprecedentedly free society. When reality failed the image, there were courts and legal actions for deciding conflicts of interest and the clash of individuals' rights. Notably, not a single book on the law of torts had been published in English by the mid-1800s; the explosive growth of tort law and third-party rules was only beginning (Friedman 1985, pp. 53–54).

Because the doctrine of individualism provided a set of answers to questions that were foundational to sociology (as to the social sciences in general) —What is the individual? How is society possible? and others—virtually every topic subsequently addressed by sociology has in one way or another involved aspects of individualism. Given the composition of individualism's self-representing individual, the most prominent issues have often centered on questions of relationship between the rise of individualism and the development of new forms of politico-economic organization as manifested in capitalism, bureaucracy, and the modern state. Indeed, that relationship was the focus of one of the great controversies occupying many early sociologists (Abercrombie et al. 1986). Hardly anyone doubted the existence or importance of a relationship. Rather, the debates were about such issues as causal direction (which caused which?), periodizations (e.g., when did capitalism begin?), and whether ideas or material conditions (each category conceived as devoid of the other) were the primary motive force. In many respects the debates were a continuation of the struggles they were about.

Other, more specific topics addressed by sociologists have also involved aspects of the rise of individualism. Several have already been mentioned (e.g., a new regime of discipline). Additional examples are the development of sectarian (as opposed to churchly) religions, followed by an even more highly privatized mystical-religious consciousness of the isolated individual; changes in domestic architecture, such as greater emphasis on individualized spaces for privacy and functionally specialized rooms; changes in table manners, rules of courtesy, and other refinements of taste; emergence of a *confessional self* and practices of diary keeping; increased emphasis on romantic love (affective individualism) in mate selection; new forms of literary discourse such as the novel and the autobiography; and the rise of professionalism (see Abercrombie et al. 1986; Perrot [1987] 1990).

THE SELF-EXPRESSING INDIVIDUAL

The figure of the self-representing individual proved to be unstable, even as the meaning of representation gradually changed. This was mainly because the same factors that had produced this version of individualism's individual also led to dissolution of the transparent sign. For example, whereas clothing, manners, bodily comportment, and similar traits had been, in the old order, reliable signs (representations) of a person's rank or station in life, the sign became increasingly arbitrary in its relationship to ground. This loosening of the sign, together with a proliferation of signs in exchange, led to a new universalism of *the empty sign*. The prototype was money and the commodity form: Devoid of intrinsic value and capable of representing everything, it represents nothing in particular. As one scholar described the process, borrowing a clause from Karl Marx, "all that is solid melts into air" (Berman 1983).

At the same time, the rhetoric of transhistorical forms of value (e.g., the commodity, inalienable rights) allows for an enormous amount of individual variation in the sociocultural conditions under which that rhetoric can succeed. Individualism's emphasis on the bare individual was being increasingly generalized, further reducing the import of group-based relations and traits. In the mid-1800s, for instance, the distinction between public affairs and private matters was drawn at the door of home and family. Family life provided the chief "haven" of organic relations, nurturant domesticity, and refuge from the trials of work and politics. But soon the haven itself became a site of struggle toward still greater individuation. Of the many factors contributing to this rebellion against the traditional restraints of family, one of the most important was a new culture of sexuality, which manifested a more general and growing concern for the interior interests and needs of the individual.

Precedent for this concern can be seen in Kant's conception of the self-representing individual (because of the transcendental I, every individual has in common the potential for *self-actualization),* as well as in romanticist movements of the early 1800s. However, the creation of a new "inner discourse of the individual" has been mostly a twentieth-century phenomenon. The psychology of Sigmund Freud and his disciples formed part of that development, certainly; but another part was formed by the conception of a new "social citizenship" (Marshall 1964), which emphasized an individual's right to social welfare in addition to the earlier mandates of political and economic rights. A new figure of individualism's individual gradually emerged, the *self-expressing individual.*

The individualism of the self-representing individual promoted the idea that all interests are ultimately interests of the bare individual. The new version of individualism both extends and modifies that idea. Whereas the self-representing individual puts a premium on self-control and hard work, the self-expressing individual generalizes the value of *freedom of choice* from politico-economic exchange relations to matters of personal life-style and consumption preferences (Inglehart 1990). The central claim holds that "each person has a unique core of feeling and intuition that should unfold or be expressed if individuality is to be realized" (Bellah, Madsen, Sullivan, Swidler, and Tipton 1985, p. 336), and each person has the right to develop his or her unique capacities for self-expression. A recent change in divorce law partly illustrates the import of that claim. Prior to the 1960s one of the few organic relations still surviving in modern society was the marital bond; few conditions were deemed grave enough to have legal standing as grounds for breaking it. With the invention of *no fault divorce* (relatively noncontroversial legislation that spread rapidly from state to state; Jacob 1988), the marital relation became a civil contract much like any other, and a spouse's freedom to choose divorce in the interest of satisfying unfulfilled needs of self-expression gained recognition.

Not only does individualism's self-expressing individual remain a trait-bearing substantial entity, but also the variety of bearable traits is greatly expanded by the shift in emphasis from self-control to self-expression through life-style experimentation. Moreover, this shift in emphasis is accompanied by the stipulation that only those traits that an individual can freely choose to assume, and then jettison, should be relevant criteria by which to discriminate and evaluate individuals. Criteria falling outside the bounds of individual choice (*immutable* traits, whether biologic or sociocultural) are deemed to be both irrelevant and, increasingly, violations of an individual's rights. In conjunction with the *entitlements* logic of social citizenship, this stipulation of a radically individualistic freedom of reversible choice has been linked to the emergence of a generalized expectation of "total justice" (Friedman 1985).

By the same token, the doctrine of individualism has always contained a large fictive component. Long after the doctrine proclaimed the sovereignty of the bare individual, for example, the actual individuality of human beings continued to be heavily marked by ascriptive traits (e.g., gender, race) and by sociocultural inheritances from one's parents. The shift to an expressive individualism reflects efforts to situate the agency of a free individual outside the separately conceived domain of relations of domination. Rather than attempt to change those relations, the self-expressing individual would "transcend" them by concentrating on a logic of rights pertaining to the free expression of individual will in a domain of "personal culture" (Marcuse [1937] 1968).

Fictions can be productive in various ways, however. The fictions of individualism have often been made taskmasters, as women, African-Americans, the handicapped, and other human beings discriminated primarily by ascriptive or group-based criteria have struggled to make reality conform to doctrinal image.

SOME CURRENT ISSUES

Because individualism has been one of the professional ideologies of the social sciences *(methodological individualism),* a perennial issue concerns the proper structure of explanation, specifically whether explanation of any sociocultural phenomenon must ultimately refer to facts about individuals and, if so, what precisely that means (Lukes 1973, pp. 110–122). No one denies that collectivities are composed of individuals. But that truism does not settle how *composition* is to be understood or what constitutes the individual. In short, the allegedly methodological issue involves a number of conceptual issues, including several located at the intersection between individualism's individual and historical variations in the actual constitution of individuality (Heller et al. 1986). The doctrine of individualism has consistently conceptualized the individual as a distinct and self-contained agent who acts within, yet separate from, a constraining social structure. Rather than being an ensemble of social relations, individualism's individual is the substantial atom out of which any possible social relations are composed. This has certain implications for the empirical field.

Some sociologists contend, for example, that individualism's self-expressing individual is an accurate depiction of contemporary reconstitutions of individuality and that, in this new form of the individual, the substance of selfhood, an individual's self-identical integrity, is being evacuated. Bellah et al. indict the emergence of "a language of radical individual autonomy" in which people "cannot think about themselves or others except as arbitrary centers of volition" (1985, p. 81). Others argue that the emphasis on individual autonomy and separation is an expression of masculine, patriarchal values, as contrasted with feminine values of social attachment (Gilligan 1982, pp. 22–23). Still others see the development of an entirely new "order of simulacra" (Baudrillard [1976] 1983), in which simulation or the simulacrum (representation) substitutes for and then vanquishes the real (e.g., television images establish the parameters of reality). The alleged result is a collapse of "the social" into the indifference of "the masses," who no longer care to discriminate among "messages" (beyond their entertainment effects) because one simulation is as good as another.

Equally contentious issues surround the evident growth in people's sense of entitlement and in the array of legal rights claimed and often won on behalf of *individual choice.* Individualism's figure of the self-expressing individual is held by some to be the harbinger of a new age of democracy, by others the confirmation of a continuing trend toward greater atomization (Friedman 1985). Both assessments point to the emergence of a *rights industry* that promotes the invention of new categories of legal right pertaining to everything from the guaranteed freedom to experiment with unconventional life-styles without risk of discrimination or retribution, to the rights of animals both individually and as a species (Norton 1987), to the possibility of endowing genes with *subjectlike powers* and, thus, legal standing (Oyama 1985, p. 79). Some critics contend that the expansion of concern for increasingly particularized and "arbitrary" individual choices comes at the expense of diminished concern for social outcomes. "Unless people regain the sense that the practices of society represent some sort of natural order instead of a set of arbitrary choices, they cannot hope to escape from the dilemma of unjustified power" (Unger 1976, p. 240). The conviction recalls that of the early French critic quoted in the initial paragraph.

(SEE ALSO: *Capitalism; Democracy*)

REFERENCES

Abercrombie, Nicholas, Stephen Hill, and Bryan S. Turner 1986 *Sovereign Individuals of Capitalism.* London: Allen and Unwin.

Baudrillard, Jean (1976) 1983 *In the Shadow of the Silent Majorities.* New York: Semiotext(e).

Bellah, Robert N., Richard Madsen, William M. Sullivan, Ann Swidler, and Steven M. Tipton 1985 *Habits of the Heart.* Berkeley, Calif.: University of California Press.

Berman, Marshall 1983 *All That Is Solid Melts into Air.* London: Verso.

Coleman, James S. 1990 *Foundations of Social Theory.* Cambridge, Mass.: Harvard University Press.

Durkheim, Emile (1914) 1973 "The Dualism of Human Nature and Its Social Conditions." In Robert Bellah, ed., *Emile Durkheim on Morality and Society.* Chicago: University of Chicago Press.

Foucault, Michel (1975) 1977 *Discipline and Punish,* Alan Sheridan, trans. New York: Pantheon.

Friedman, Lawrence 1985 *Total Justice.* New York: Russell Sage Foundation.

Gilligan, Carol 1982 *In a Different Voice.* Cambridge, Mass.: Harvard University Press.

Goldmann, Lucien (1968) 1973 *Philosophy of the Enlightenment,* Henry Maas, trans. Cambridge, Mass.: MIT Press.

Heller, Thomas C., Morton Sosna, and David E. Wellbery 1986 *Reconstructing Individualism.* Stanford, Calif.: Stanford University Press.

Hobsbawm, Eric, and Terence Ranger (eds.) 1983 *The Invention of Tradition* Cambridge: Cambridge University Press.

Inglehart, Ronald 1990 *Cultural Shift in Advanced Industrial Society.* Princeton, N.J.: Princeton University Press.

Jacob, Herbert 1988 *Silent Revolution.* Chicago: University of Chicago Press.

Kant, Immanuel (1787) 1929 *The Critique of Pure Reason,* 2nd ed., trans. Norman Kemp Smith. London: Macmillan.

Lukes, Steven 1973 *Individualism.* Oxford: Basil Blackwell.

Macfarlane, Alan 1978 *The Origins of English Individualism.* Oxford: Basil Blackwell.

Macpherson, C. B. 1962 *The Political Theory of Possessive Individualism.* Oxford: Oxford University Press.

Marcuse, Herbert [1937] 1968 "The Affirmative Character of Culture." In *Negations,* Jeremy J. Shapiro, trans. Boston: Beacon.

Marshall, T. H. 1964 *Class, Citizenship, and Social Development.* New York: Doubleday.

Mead, George Herbert 1934 *Mind, Self, and Society,* ed. Charles W. Morris. Chicago: University of Chicago Press.

Morgan, Edmund S. 1988 *Inventing the People.* New York: Norton.

Norton, Bryan G. 1987 *Why Preserve Natural Variety?* Princeton, N.J.: Princeton University Press.

Oyama, Susan 1985 *The Ontogeny of Information.* Cambridge: Cambridge University Press.

Perrot, Michelle (ed.) (1987) 1990 *A History of Private Life,* vol. 4, Arthur Goldhammer, trans. Cambridge, Mass.: Harvard University Press.

Swart, Koenraad W. 1962 "'Individualism' in the Mid-Nineteenth Century (1826–1860)." *Journal of the History of Ideas* 23:77–90.

Tocqueville, Alexis de (1850) 1969. *Democracy in America,* 13th ed., J. P. Mayer, ed. George Lawrence, trans. New York: Doubleday.

Ullmann, Walter 1966 *The Individual and Society in the Middle Ages.* Baltimore: Johns Hopkins University Press.

Unger, Roberto Mangabeira 1976 *Law in Modern Society.* New York: Free Press.

LAWRENCE HAZELRIGG

INDUSTRIAL SOCIOLOGY The term *industrialization* connotes the development of social organizations, generally in a nation-state, in which large manufacturing enterprises loom large and in which supportive providers of public and private services grow with them in tandem. Industrial sociological studies accordingly focus on the "causes" or prerequisites for, the correlates of (in family, community, and other social settings), and the consequences of the industrialization process. The key consequences under examination have been the "rights, privileges, and immunities" of parties to labor contracts; the social and economic relationships among investors, producers, workers, consumers, and, in turn, the circumstances of dependents, communities, and regions; and finally, the resulting stabilities and changes in the social, economic, and political structures of the nations in which all these persons live. Those whose research and teaching agendas include several of these broad domains draw very heavily on specialists in economic development, social stratification, public policy, organizations, urban sociology, community studies, labor markets, and economic sociology.

Industrial sociology as a distinguishable if very broad field of study may truly be said to have been born in the late 1770s, so continuous with their forebears' interests have been many of the specific subjects of concern of investigators since that time. Systematic studies of social organizations in industrial societies date from the long-celebrated if not always carefully read analyses by Adam Smith, who joined philosophical issues having to do with economic activities and related "moral sentiments" earlier and then turned to his more widely known and enduring work on the social (macroscopic) and organizational (microscopic) roles in society of capitalists and, more famously, of labor. Smith regarded labor and its effective mobilization and utilization, not the fruits of mercantilism (i.e., the quantity of gold and silver imported from colonies and the exportation of finished goods), as the real sources of what he termed the wealth of nations.

His analyses and urgings about the benefits of free trade, of the constrained roles of government in economic affairs, of the critical roles of increasingly differentiated divisions of labor, and of the emergence of the "factory system" in late-seventeenth- and early-eighteenth-century England staked out most of the basic subjects of modern industrial sociologists' research studies: economic organizations; managers' and workers' ways; the correlates of technology and divisions of labor; economic exchange and trade; and questions about the roles of central governments in economies and about innumerable regulatory measures affecting workplaces.

Industrial sociologists can also trace their roots to Charles Dickens' very popular literary treatments of life in early-nineteenth-century England and to other early and more pointedly social, economic, and political reformers in Europe. Thus investigators now undertake studies with debts: to English and French critics, commentators, and philosophers captured in the term "the Enlightenment"; to Henri St. Simon's urgings about the application of scientific rationality to social organization; to Karl Marx's historicist treatments of capitalism's "maturer" states; to the pros and cons in arguments about nascent trade union movements; to debaters arguing over alternative welfare, trade, and other initiatives by governments; and to assessments of the philosophical legitimacy of the emerging stratification of societies, as variant forms of aristocracy gave way to variant forms of more representative governments. Dickens' characterization of an employers' association that resisted safety guards on moving machine parts as "The Association for the Mangling of Operatives" and his and his audiences' concerns about the improvement of working conditions presaged a great deal of the work of industrial sociologists in the twentieth century. Continuities since the nineteenth century, in all but methods of research, have been notable. The subjects pursued include the forces that virtually compel ever more differentiated divisions of labor; effect patterns of national income distribution; contribute to the rise, expansion, and characters of both "blue collar" labor forces and, overlapping with them, the expansion of middle classes in urban centers; contribute to the rise of trade unions and the resulting growth of new systems of law that have changed the nature of property and property claims to include more than physical capital and realty; cause the decline in small agricultural holdings, small towns, and rural areas; and, withal, the forces that generally make social life more secular, political life democratic, and working life more bureaucratic.

During the period 1900–1950 much of the macroscopic-level research that continued to add to present-day conceptions of the body of industrial sociological literature was actually performed by institutional economists—principally students of labor, management, and the "legal foundations of capitalism," in the tradition of the "Wisconsin" or (J. R.) "Commons" School (Commons and Associates 1926, 1935, 1936). These investigators also founded the field of industrial relations, whose practitioners' work has perennially overlapped with that of industrial sociologists. In recent times sociologists have essentially inherited what has come to be seen as the "institutional tradition" in economics, a tradition in that discipline that has given way to mathematical modeling and econometrics.

In the period after World War I, industrial sociologists gave increasing attention to the positive and negative social effects of business cycles: "Busts" undoubtedly helped to purge national economies of many types of waste and inefficiencies and thus contributed to subsequent "booms." At the same time, however, busts sparked unwelcome recessions and depressions, with their subversive effects on growth; employment levels; and thus on the living standards, attitudes, and behavior of most citizens. Researchers' attentions focused correlatively on the growth of large corporations; the pros and cons of aggressive competition; and the possibly leavening effects of unions and of interventions by the "positive state" against the centralization of economic and thus, potentially, of political power in private hands, such that some of the less salutary correlates of capitalist systems could be controlled. Generally the researchers sought not to traduce "big business" but to identify constraints on private economic power that would not reduce the benefits to societies of large corporations' productive capacities.

Systematic attention toward the middle of this period was also given to what is now termed the global economy, often in the form of studies of the effects of international trade barriers that contributed so significantly to the collapse of the Western industrial economies—the so-called Crash of '29 and the Great Depression. The political and economic interdependencies among nations—and those among classes of economic actors within them—became increasingly palpable to researchers, who began to see economies more clearly in terms of the structures of individual industries and industry groupings—new chapters in the all-important story of the causes and correlates of the division of labor (Brady 1943). Additionally, unions were gaining in their appeal, beyond skilled tradesmen, to industrial assembly workers. Among the questions pursued by sociologists were those having to do with the prospects that a coherent working *class* would emerge in the United States out of the ferment of the pre-World War II era. Incipient "class warfare" could be tamed, if not quashed, by reforms that are collectively referred to nowadays as revisions in (Jean-Jacques Rousseau's) "social contract" and as social "safety nets."

Finally, by the 1920s and into the 1940s, there were growing concerns about whether Benito Mussolini's "corporate state" and Adolph Hitler's Third Reich represented a kind of conspiracy of fascists with Italy's and Germany's financial and manufacturing leaders (Neumann 1942) against those, especially in the three Communist Internationals, who were perceived by conservatives to be urging workers to turn to the revolutionary political left. This subject earned much increased attention after World War II; joined by historians' work in the 1950s, the social scientific literature on the social sources of totalitarian systems has become extensive, one of the recurring questions in this literature being whether the seeds of "totalitarianism of the right" germinate especially well in "capitalist" soil (B. Moore 1973). The answers from sociologists' studies, however, have tended to focus on the fragility of support for democratic institutions in most societies. These studies have analyzed the vulnerabilities of democracies to losses of popular confidence of large numbers of citizens victimized by major and long-enduring economic collapses, rather than on the contradictions in capitalism per se, as a key reason for the appeal of social movements on the political right. Sufferings from traumatic social, political, and economic discontinuities, sociologists reported, could all too easily contribute to the delivery of loyalties of many, from Rome and Naples in Italy, Marienthal in Austria, Berlin in Germany, and Buenos Aires in Argentina, to demagogues and "scapegoaters." Indeed, these studies led social psychologists among sociologists to important and widely influential discoveries about scapegoating phenomena that, among others, could generate poisonous race and ethnic relations (Adorno et al, 1950).

At what we may call the "messoscopic"—middle levels—of analyses, industrial sociologists, in loose confederation with the more institutionally oriented scholars among labor economists, turned their attention in the pre-World War II period to the implications of the levels of aggregate demand (and deficiencies thereof) for the structures and experiences of communities before and during the Great Depression (as in Muncie, Indiana, in the United States); to the disinclinations of unemployed Americans to "blame the system" (rather than themselves) for their sad circumstances during the Great Depression; and to the pros and cons of government intervention in national economies and of the construction of the aforementioned "safety nets" for victims of economic downturns.

Not least among sociologists' interests were those in the stratification of societies, especially respecting the distribution of wealth and income among individuals and families; the behavior of economic elites in local communities; and the causes and correlates of social mobility. In the latter matter, evidence mounted that the economic successes and failures of individuals could not be attributed simply to their ambition, "drive," and hard work—or their lack of these oft-praised qualities. Indeed, many successes and failures are grounded in opportunity structures, not the least important of which are individuals' access to third-party "bonding" agents and access to formal education and training. While most economists have equated their educational achievement, or lack thereof, to earners' incomes without further ado, sociologists have urged that imperfections in markets enabled American employers to assume that better-educated workers were more productive and to pass on the costs of such an assumption to consumers (Berg 1970). For economists, better-educated workers are paid more because they are more productive, but their measure of productivity is income, not actual output.

The advent of World War II brought many industrial sociologists to focus, not without a degree of patriotic fervor, on organizational arrangements in relation to the need to heighten productivity gains in what President Franklin D. Roosevelt called the world's arsenal of democracy. Studies of workers' groups in industry in the late 1920s, many conducted by applied sociologists linked to academic business schools—at Harvard University especially—had already indicated that most workers were as responsive to work group "peer pressures" to fix production quotas at rates below those contemplated by managers and by their time-and-motion experts, as to economic incentives. These findings were replicated many times between 1929 and 1985. This view of workers' motives continues to inform many sociologists' urges that we go beyond conventional economic studies of wage administration in seeking to understand the ways of citizens in their workplaces. At issue are the respective roles of communitarian and individualistic predispositions of workers.

With few very notable exceptions, and for the majority's own good reasons, economists conceive of production organizations as essentially unproblematic "givens" into which resources are pumped and from which outputs flow. Sociologists' lessons about organizations as social systems, which balanced the valuable lessons taught by economists, were widely applied in electrical appliances, the airframes industry, and in automobile, steel, and other industrial settings. The lesson: Identify work groups and win over workers' groups and these groups' leaders to corporate aims and reap the benefits of the not-so-rugged individualists in workplaces who more often respond favorably to group norms than to group-disrupting industrial incentive-type pay plans. As it turned out, these lessons were perhaps applied somewhat more assiduously in Japan from 1960 to 1990 than in the United States, where worker participation in organizational decision making and work reforms have appealed to comparatively fewer employers despite the possible benefits of "humanized" personnel policies. Researchers have discovered that U.S. managers' interests in worker participation tend to wax when there are "tight" labor market conditions and wane when they are "loose." In Western managers' theory at least, human resources are factors of production—commodities—and the treatments of these factors are functions more of short-run market conditions than of long-term concern about the qualities of work life (O'Toole 1974). The latter concerns find more expression in collective bargaining relationships and in remedial legislation, with the endorsement and help of many sociologists who are skeptical of managers as patrons, than in initiatives by employers who are skeptical of the benefits of "codeterminative" relations with workers, like those requiring worker representations on boards of directors under laws in Germany and the Scandinavian countries.

THE CONTEMPORARY SCENE

In present-day industrial sociology the main subjects of study have been: (1) the increasingly important roles of education and training in shaping Americans' opportunities (Jencks et al. 1979); (2) in the relationships between the significant differences in circumstances between those who manage and work in "core" industries and managers and workers in "internal labor markets," and the lower-paid, appreciably less capitalized, smaller, more vulnerable establishments in the "peripheries" of economies (Kalleberg 1983); (3) in the correlates—income and otherwise—of discrimination against women and minorities; and (4) in the problems of those who simply are not well integrated into the labor force—the so-called underclass (Wilson 1987). These newer topics have taken their places with continuing studies of work groups; industrial conflict; mobility patterns; the evolving roles of public policies and the state; the politics of income distribution; and intramural studies of organizations, their decision-making arrangements, and, more recently, their "cultures."

Studies by industrial sociologists are increasingly comparative in character, as these researchers seek to identify cultural and political factors such as belief systems and constitutional arrangements, respectively, that play in upon the effectiveness of different nations' populations in efforts to mobilize human and other resources, motivate leaders and their human charges, design productive organizations, and make and provide goods and services (Lincoln and Kalleberg 1990; Cole 1989).

Overall, industrial sociologists have contributed to the delineation of options facing leaders in government, but less to enterprises, unions, and urban communities. During the period until 1970, industrial sociologists' investigations moved in increasingly specialized directions.

One thrust brought a large group of the fields' leaders to concentrate on organizations—especially large, complex organizations (Stinchcombe 1990; Coleman 1982; Thompson 1967). In rich elaborations and embellishments on Max Weber's pioneering work on bureaucracies, sociologists ventured into "the Japanese factory"; the Tennessee Valley Authority; banks; mental hospitals; British coal mines; gypsum mines; a state employment agency; schools, prisons, and equivalent "total institutions"; a foundry; the U.S. Military Academy; steel mills (in the United States and Europe), German, Soviet, and Czech manufactories; the military establishment; French family firms; social movements; labor unions; merchant ships; American soldiers' organized experiences in and out of World War II combat; and the YMCA, to mention just a few contexts and populations about which studies were completed (Perrow 1986; Hall 1987).

While the vast body of literature produced by the observers in this disparate array of organizations has received little acclaim in the media, it is an important sign of the importance of these investigators' findings, assessments, and consequent theories that their work is basic to the curricula of the very influential graduate schools of business and management, from Harvard to Berkeley, from Seattle to Miami, and from Maine to Los Angeles—and in Scandinavia; Germany; France; the United Kingdom; Japan; and, by 1990, in Moscow. The lessons learned: It is possible to design a great many optional variations on the specific structures of hierarchical organizations, their intramural arrangements, and the "production relations" therein, to meet the exigencies confronting managers and their charges in dealings with each other, with competitors, clients, customers, suppliers, subcontractors, regulators, third-party insurers, community forces, and with labor market developments.

Industrial sociologists, whether "majors" from colleges or holders of masters and doctoral degrees—some as consultants or as technicians or managers in corporate settings—offer prescriptions for improving employee morale and marketing programs (from demographic assessments to surveys of customer attitudes); for designing optimal "mixes" of wage and salary schedules with supplementary benefits; for reducing absenteeism and turnover; for productivity "enhancement"; for designing therapeutic (rather than custodial) environments in mental health care agencies; and for constructing occupational safety programs, grievance machinery, and quality control programs.

A second group moved away from these more microscopic studies of organizations to study the social, economic, and political development of whole societies, some in historical terms, during the post-World War II era, including India's, China's, Italy's, Japan's, and Germany's (actually "redevelopment" in the two last cases) and the USSR's systems. Among the lessons were important figures about the stabilities of some and the flexibilities of other social and cultural values that gave distinctive national shape to individual countries' brands of industrialization. It is clear that while the "common denominators" in the paths to both growth and development—the latter a matter of the degree of distributive justice in a society and the former a matter of increases in gross natural product—are numerous, there are instructive differences as well (Moore 1965; Inkeles and Smith 1974).

Indeed, a consortium of scholars, many of them sociologists, studying "industrialization and industrial man" in comparative-international terms, produced well over forty volumes and a great many shorter pieces on the convergences and divergences among industrial and industrializing nations over the period 1955–1975 (Dunlop et al. 1975). These works of scholarship have helped thousands of leaders in governments, large corporations, labor unions, and international agencies to make judgments about investments (both public and private); social, political, and economic policies; and the aptness of designs of organizations in what is now truly a global economy in which nations' planning efforts are turning, more and more, toward "market" and away from "command" economies. The conclusions by the end of 1990, in a continuing body of research following the preceding twenty-four months of changes in Eastern Europe and the USSR, are that the "marketizing" and democratization movements in previously planned economies will assuredly reduce divergences among industrial systems but will by no means eliminate entirely the influence of discrete national cultures in shaping the practices and institutions, from child rearing to legal structures, that help, in turn, to shape social relations in a given nation's enterprises, as some sociologists have long argued.

A third constituency moved "below" organizational levels to study the dynamics of work groups within organizations, picking up on the work of the aforementioned human relations school before, during, and after World War II. This group of scholars drew heavily on earlier sociologists' insights and theories—from Georg Simmel, Charles Cooley, and George Herbert Mead and especially from the massive post-World War II publications of data and analyses from one of the first very-large-sample and sophisticated social scientific surveys of wartime American soldiers (Inkeles 1964). These reports gave abundant corroboration to the findings in industry, by earlier human relations investigators, concerning the critical importance, in efforts to understand individual attitudes and behavior, of small groups and their norms (Homans 1950). The applications of these findings, in studies of satisfaction, leadership, morale, productivity, grievances, absenteeism, turnover, and incentive systems have become staples in training programs for supervisors and foremen in the United States, and in delineating jobs and designing work flows across American industries (Porter et al. 1975; Perrow 1986).

A fourth group has focused on industries and occupations as special and highly significant aspects of organizations' "external environments" and as subsets of America's systems of social stratification. Sociological studies of whole industries—their personnel and collective bargaining policies especially—have often informed public agencies' regulations, legislators' bills, and the decisions of judges. Analyses of differences among industries and occupations have helped leaders in government, business, and labor unions to understand better the dynamics of industrial conflict; the character and effectiveness of organizations; and the complexities in identifying the effects of physical technology—capital—in the spinning of "webs of rules" (Kerr et al. 1973) that, for all of their de facto and even informal character, function very much like governance systems in the workaday world (Kalleberg and Berg 1987). These systems, in their most formal states—arbitration procedures, for example—sometime mature into what the U.S. Supreme Court in 1960, in a "trilogy" of cases that defined the role of arbitration in industrial relations, called "systems of industrial common law" (i.e., as legal systems virtually unto themselves). Otherwise, more implicitly, as with work rules that establish "how fast is fast, how fair is fair, and how reasonable is reasonable," the webs of rules define relationships and codes applicable to both employers and employees that afford a kind of lubrication to the mechanics of human interactions in bureaucratic machines, with their close tolerances, involving millions of persons in hundreds of thousands of workplaces. Sociological studies of the costs and benefits to employees and employers (and ultimately to the public) of work rules, for example, have helped transform emotionally charged arguments about "featherbedding" into coherent and constructive debates about nonmonetary dimensions of working conditions. Studies of work rules suggest that "informal" organizations within parent organizations are really not as much informal as they are what French sociologist Durkheim long ago called "the noncontractual element of contracts"; sociologists have demonstrated that though these patterned, enduring, and bilaterally honored arrangements do not appear on organizations' wall charts, they are significant components of organizational life, not mere shadows of more palpable structures.

Meanwhile, the discovery in international comparisons of data on grievances and strikes—that there are numerous short strikes and many grievances in the United States and few but long strikes and virtually no grievances in Western Europe—has led researchers, employers, and union leaders to appreciate the value of expeditious "on-site" bargaining relationships, on a day-to-day basis, such that emotional affect in disagreements may be drawn off and tensions relaxed before out-and-out conflicts disrupt production and social relations.

At the same time, the costs as well as the benefits of federal laws requiring that unions be democratic have helped us to make more realistic estimates about democratic arrangements' capacities to function as panaceas; democracy, for example, offers no guarantees against corruption, nor does it assure harmonious relations between parties to collective bargaining agreements. Sociologists have also documented a kind of (perhaps understandable) hypocrisy about democracy: Many lay observers and most labor columnists are delighted by unionists who vote to ratify contracts or to "decertify" their bargaining agents, but are appalled by "strike votes."

Still another group of specialists has concentrated its attentions on worker satisfactions, dissatisfactions, and work experiences, by use of survey research designs that involve both periodic "snapshots" of different working Americans (and Japanese and West Europeans) and repeated observations of the same respondents over long time periods. These designs also make it possible to study "cohort effects," which is to say the effects of reaching a given age in different time periods, each with their different qualities regarding a variety of social realities (Quinn et al. 1974). Thus there are significant differences, for example, in the experiences (and their attitudes about them) of workers, depending on whether they entered the labor force in 1960, 1970, 1980, or 1990. Sociologists can accordingly raise thoughtful questions about the implications, for public and private policies, of changing *social* definitions of aging, for example, in juxtaposition and contrast with essentially arbitrary public *policies* that fix eligibilities for a number of services and benefits on the basis of the chronological ages of individuals; not all those now sixty-five years old think, act, or want to be thought of as a homogeneous class of "senior citizens," nor have they had the same "life histories" as those who reached that age in 1940, 1960, or 1980.

Finally, the advent and continuing engagements of the civil rights movement have sparked the expenditure of a great deal of research effort on the comparative socioeconomic opportunities of men and women, and of minority group members in these two groups (Jaynes and Williams 1989; Jacobs 1989). The findings by sociologists in these investigations have figured prominently in the drafting of legislation, legal suits, and employment policies, as well as in landmark civil rights decisions in courts at all levels.

In their work, as noted at the outset, industrial sociologists have drawn on work by sociologists in virtually every one of the profession's own major areas of interest with alacrity and have, in turn, seen much of their work inform the work of these other specialists. There has been similar intellectual commerce with social psychologists, industrial relations practitioners, and with full-time nonacademic social scientist practitioners in private enterprises, public agencies, universities, and in research and other organizations in foreign lands, especially in the United Kingdom; Yugoslavia; Germany; Japan; France; Scandinavia; Canada;

Italy; and what has, for so long, been called Eastern Europe.

(SEE ALSO: *Complex Organizations; Labor Movements and Unions; Organizational Effectiveness; Professions; Work and Occupations; Work Orientation*)

REFERENCES

Adorno, T. W., et al. 1950 *The Authoritarian Personality.* New York: Harper.

Berg, Ivar, 1970 *Education and Jobs: The Great Training Robbery.* New York: Praeger.

Brady, Robert A. 1943 *Business as a System of Power.* New York: Columbia University Press.

Cole, Robert E. 1989 *Strategies for Learning: Small Group Activities in American, Japanese, and Swedish Industry.* Berkeley, Calif.: University of California Press.

Coleman, James 1982 *The Asymmetric Society.* Syracuse, N.Y.: Syracuse University Press.

Commons, John R., and Associates 1926, 1935, 1936 *History of Labor in the United States.* New York: Macmillan.

Dunlop, John, et al. 1975 *Industrialism and Industrial Man Reconsidered.* Princeton, N.J.: Inter-University Study of Human Resources in National Development.

Glazer, Nathan 1975 *Affirmative Discrimination: Ethnic Inequality and Public Policy.* New York: Basic Books.

Hall, Richard 1987 *Organizations: Structures, Process and Outcomes.* Englewood Cliffs, N.J.: Prentice-Hall.

Homans, George 1950 *The Human Group.* New York: Harcourt, Brace.

Inkeles, Alex 1964 *What Is Sociology?* Englewood Cliffs, N.J.: Prentice-Hall.

———and David H. Smith 1974 *Becoming Modern: Industrial Change in Six Developing Countries.* Cambridge, Mass.: Harvard University Press.

Jacobs, Jerry 1989 *Revolving Doors: Sex Segregation and Women's Careers.* Stanford, Calif.: Stanford University Press.

Jaynes, Gerald David, and Robin M. Williams, Jr. (ed.) 1989 *A Common Destiny: Blacks and American Society.* Washington, DC: National Academy Press.

Jencks, Christopher, et al. 1979 *Who Gets Ahead? Determinants of Economic Success in America.* New York: Basic Books.

Kalleberg, Arne (ed.) 1983 "Capital, Labor and Work: Determinants of Work-Related Inequalities, a Special Issue." *International Sociology Journal* August.

———, and Ivar Berg 1987 *Work and Industry Structures, Markets and Processes.* New York: Plenum.

Kerr, Clark, John T. Dunlop, Fredrick Harbison, and Charles A. Meyers 1973 *Industrialization and Industrial Man* London: Penguin.

Lincoln, James R., and Arne L. Kalleberg 1990 *Culture, Control and Commitment: A Study of Work Organization and Work Attitude in the U.S. and Japan.* Cambridge: Cambridge University Press.

Miller, Delbert, and William Form 1980 *Industrial Sociology in Organizational Life.* New York: Harper and Row.

Moore, Barrington 1973 *Social Origins of Dictatorship and Democracy: Lord and Peasant in the Making of the Modern World.* Boston: Beacon Press.

Moore, Wilbert E. 1965 *The Impact of Industry.* Englewood Cliffs, NJ: Prentice-Hall.

Neumann, Franz 1942 *Behemoth: The Structure and Practice of National Socialism.* New York: Oxford University Press.

O'Toole, James (ed.) 1974 *Work and the Quality of Life: Resource Papers for Work in America.* Cambridge, Mass.: MIT Press.

Perrow, Charles 1986 *Complex Organizations: A Critical Essay.* New York: McGraw-Hill.

Porter, Lyman W., et al. 1975 *Behavior in Organizations.* New York: McGraw-Hill.

Quinn, Robert P., et al. 1974 *Job Satisfaction: Is There a Trend?* Monograph 30. Washington, DC: U.S. Government Printing Office.

Stinchcombe, Arthur L. 1990 *Information and Organization* Berkeley: University of California Press.

Thompson, James D. 1967 *Organizations in Action.* New York: McGraw-Hill.

Wilson, William J. 1987 *The Truly Disadvantaged: The Inner City, the Underclass and Public Policy.* Chicago: University of Chicago Press.

IVAR BERG

INDUSTRIALIZATION IN LESS DEVELOPED COUNTRIES In the two hundred years since the Industrial Revolution in England, the process of industrialization has had perhaps more impact on all the nations of the world than any other complex set of forces. This process has not been uniformly introduced in all countries, nor has it occurred at the same time or at the same rate. Despite the common features of industrialization, these differences in its introduction and adoption have produced inequities among nations and among people on a scale never before experienced.

In describing various countries and regions of the world, certain terms have been adopted, first by official agencies such as the United Nations and national governments, and then more generally by scholars, journalists, and those interested in making sense out of international relations. According to a now commonly used United Nations classification, *more developed countries* (MDCs) comprise all of Europe, North America (excluding Mexico), Japan, Australia, New Zealand, and the USSR; *less developed countries* (LDCs) constitute the remainder. This classification mirrors the famous "North–South divide" coined by former chancellor Willy Brandt (1980) in his commission's report to the World Bank. Also, MDCs may be equated with the capitalist Western nations (First World countries) and the communist Eastern-bloc countries (Second World), while the LDCs constitute the remaining nonaligned countries of the Third World (Crow and Thomas 1983, p. 8).

In some cases, the underlying variable upon which these distinctions are made is economic, in other cases it is political, and in still others it is unspecified. However, generally speaking, MDCs are "rich" and LDCs are "poor." In 1986, the per capita gross national product among all MDCs was US$10,700, while in the LDCs it was only US$640, or almost seventeen times less *(1988 World Population Data Sheet)*. The major explanation for this vast discrepancy is that MDCs are fully industrialized whereas LDCs are not. In 1985, the industrial market economies produced fully 82 percent of total world manufactures (World Bank 1987, p. 47). Considering that LDCs comprise 77 percent of the world's population *(1988 World Population Data Sheet)*, their industrial output, and therefore their standard of living, are dramatically lower than those of the MDCs.

INDUSTRIALIZATION DEFINED

Industrialization is a complex process comprised of a number of interrelated dimensions. Historically, it represents a transition from an economy based on agriculture to one in which manufacturing represents the principal means of subsistence. Consequently, two dimensions of industrialization are the work that people do for a living (economic activity) and the actual goods they produce (economic output). Other dimensions include the manner in which economic activity is organized (organization), the energy or power source used (mechanization), and the systematic methods and innovative practices employed to accomplish work (technology). Table 1 specifies these dimensions and also lists indicators commonly used to measure them.

According to these indicators, MDCs are fully industrialized. On average, close to one-third of the labor forces in these countries are employed in industry; manufacturing makes up approximately one-quarter of the gross domestic product; the overwhelming majority of workers are employees of organizations; commercial energy consumption is high (over 4,500 kilograms of oil equivalent per capita); and professional and technical workers comprise 15 percent of the work force (Hedley forthcoming). Furthermore, virtually all of the registered patents and industrial designs in force are held in the MDCs (Kurian 1984, pp. 217–219). Industrial activity and the services associated with it constitute the major driving force and source of income in these industrially developed countries.

In contrast, none of the LDCs is fully industrialized, as measured by these five dimensions of industrialization. Whereas manufacturing accounts for a significant proportion of many of these countries' total output, most do not achieve industrial status on any of the other dimensions. Manufacture in these countries is accomplished largely by traditional methods that have varied little over successive generations. Consequently, although manufacturing, or the transformation of raw materials into finished goods, is indeed an essential component of industrialization, there is considerably more to the process. Because industrialization is multidimensional, it therefore cannot be measured by only one indicator.

In general, LDCs may be classified into three major groups according to how industrialized they

Table 1
Dimensions and Measures of Industrialization

1. *Economic Activity*
   a. Percentage of labor force in manufacturing
   b. Percentage of labor force in industry

2. *Economic Output*
   a. Manufacturing as a percentage of gross domestic product
   b. Industry as a percentage of gross domestic product
   c. Gross output per employee in manufacturing
   d. Earnings per employee in manufacturing

3. *Organization*
   a. Wage and salary earners as a percentage of the labor force
   b. Number of manufacturing establishments employing fifty or more workers per capita

4. *Mechanization*
   a. Commercial energy consumption per capita
   b. Total cost of fuels and purchased electrical energy per employee in manufacturing

5. *Technology*
   a. Percentage of professional and technical workers in labor force
   b. Registered patents in force per capita
   c. Registered industrial designs in force per capita

are. The first and smallest group, referred to in the literature as *newly industrializing countries* (NICs), contains the most industrialized, in that they achieve industrial status on at least two of the dimensions listed in Table 1. According to Frederick Clairmonte and John Cavanagh (1984, p. 84), just four of these NICs, all situated in east Asia (Taiwan, South Korea, Hong Kong, and Singapore), accounted for over half of the total industrial exports of all developing countries in 1980. Other important NICs, most notably Brazil and Mexico, are located in Latin America. Although China and, to a lesser degree, India (because of their huge population bases) contribute significantly to the manufactured exports of LDCs (World Bank 1987, pp. 228–229), they have not developed their industrial infrastructures to the same extent as these NICs and, therefore, do not belong in the most industrialized group of LDCs.

A subgroup of NICs are the high-income, oil-exporting nations (e.g., United Arab Emirates, Kuwait, Saudi Arabia, and Libya). While they do not have large manufacturing bases, they do have significant proportions of their labor forces involved in industry (oil exploration and refining), a substantial component of professional and technical workers (many of them imported), and high per capita commercial energy consumption (World Bank 1987). Consequently, although they are concentrated in just one industry, they are more industrialized than most other LDCs, according to the criteria specified in Table 1. As a result of their petrodollars, they have acquired an industrial infrastructure that in other countries has taken decades upon decades to establish.

The second, very large, group of LDCs in terms of industrialization are those countries with a traditionally strong manufacturing base that also have a substantial agricultural component. Their economies straddle the agricultural and industrial modes of production. China and India are in this group, as are most of the non-European countries that form the Mediterranean basin. The goods that these LDCs predominantly manufacture (e.g., apparel, footware, textiles, and consumer electronics) are essential to their own domestic markets and, because they are labor intensive, also compete very well in the international marketplace. In addition, they export natural resources and agricultural products. Other countries included in this semi-industrial group of LDCs are most of the nations in South America, as well as many in south and east Asia.

The third and final group of LDCs are not industrialized on any of the five dimensions listed in Table 1. On average, fewer than 10 percent of their labor forces are employed in industry; anywhere from 60 to over 90 percent work in agriculture. Manufacturing contributes less than one-tenth to their national products; the bulk of income derives from natural resources, and cash crops grown exclusively for export. Per capita gross national product is very low, usually below US400 (World Bank 1987). Most of these nonindustrial LDCs are located in Africa and Asia.

Of these three groups of LDCs, the semi-industrial cluster of nations is by far the largest, constituting just over half the world's population. China and India alone make up two-thirds of this group. The second largest group, ranging between 10 and 15 percent of the world total, is the nonindustrial countries, and NICs, including high-income oil exporters, comprise less than 10 percent. Thus, approximately one-quarter of the world is fully industrialized, another 10 percent are industrializing, half are semi-industrial, and the remaining 15 percent are nonindustrial.

CORRELATES OF INDUSTRIALIZATION

Research has demonstrated that industrialization is directly related to national and individual income, urbanization, the development of an infrastructure (e.g., communication and transportation networks, education, and health and welfare programs), and the overall quality of life (Hedley forthcoming). For example, concerning income, in 1850 when the Industrial Revolution was well under way, per capita income in the industrialized MDCs was 70 percent higher than in the nonindustrialized LDCs (Murdoch 1980, p. 246). However, one hundred years later the difference had grown to over 2000 percent, and by 1980, just thirty years later, the average citizen in the MDCs was earning almost 4000 percent, or 40 times, more than her or his counterpart in the LDCs. Per capita income in the LDCs was US$245, while in the MDCs it was US$9,648 (Seligson 1984). For a variety of reasons, the direct relationship between industrialization and income is increasing.

In a comprehensive, worldwide study of 124 countries, Richard Estes (1988) examined the relationship between national economic development and the "capacity of nations to provide for the basic social and material needs of their populations." From 1970 to 1983, he measured the progress of these nations using thirty-six indicators grouped into ten dimensions of national well-being. Table 2 presents his detailed and exhaustive list of measures. To determine the effect of national development on these indicators of progress, Estes classified nations into four major groups: (1) twenty-four First World countries; (2) eight Second World countries; (3) sixty-seven Third World countries; and (4) twenty-five Fourth World countries (i.e., the least developed Third World countries officially "designated by the United Nations as LDCs . . . targeted for priority international development assistance"). Thus, the first two categories represent MDCs and the latter two are LDCs (the Fourth World countries correspond approximately to the nonindustrial nations described earlier).

From the scores on each of the ten dimensions, or subindexes, Estes constructed a cumulative Index of Social Progress for each country, which ranged between −8 (Ethiopia) and +208 (Denmark). Table 3 presents the values on this index for each of the group of countries mentioned, first in 1970 and then in 1983. The extreme differences in total scores between MDCs and LDCs are indicative of how poorly off people living in less developed countries are, relative to their fellow human beings in the more prosperous, developed nations. With the exception of the defense, geog-

Table 2
Index of Social Progress Indicators by Subindex

1. *Education Subindex*
   - School enrollment ratio, first level (+)*
   - Pupil–teacher ratio, first level (−)
   - Percent adult illiteracy (−)
   - Percent GNP in education (+)

2. *Health Status Subindex*
   - Male life expectancy at 1 year (+)
   - Rate of infant mortality (−)
   - Population in thousands per physician (−)
   - Per capita daily calorie supply (+)

3. *Women Status Subindex*
   - Percent eligible girls in first level schools (+)
   - Percent adult female illiteracy (−)
   - Length of time legislation in effect protecting legal rights of women (+)

4. *Defense Effort Subindex*
   - Military expenditures as percent of GNP (−)

5. *Economic Subindex*
   - Per capita gross national product (+)
   - GNP per capita annual growth rate (+)
   - Average annual rate of inflation (−)
   - Per capita food production index (+)
   - External public debt as percent of GNP (−)

6. *Demography Subindex*
   - Total population (−)
   - Crude birth rate (−)
   - Crude death rate (−)
   - Rate of population increase (−)
   - Percent of population under 15 years (−)

7. *Geography Subindex*
   - Percent arable land mass (+)
   - Natural disaster vulnerability index (−)
   - Average death rate from natural disasters (−)

8. *Political Participation Subindex*
   - Violations of political rights index (−)
   - Violations of civil liberties index (−)
   - Composite violations of human freedoms (−)

9. *Cultural Diversity Subindex*
   - Largest percent sharing same mother tongue (+)
   - Largest percent sharing same religious beliefs (+)
   - Largest percent with same racial/ethnic origin (+)

10. *Welfare Effort Subindex*
    - Years since first law:
      - Old age, invalidity, death (+)
      - Sickness and maternity (+)
      - Work injury (+)
      - Unemployment (+)
      - Family allowance (+)

* The sign specifies the direction of "progress."
SOURCE: Richard J. Estes, *Trends in World Social Development: The Social Progress of Nations, 1970 to 1987,* (New York: Praeger, 1988), pp. 2–3.

TABLE 3
Index of Social Progress by Developmental Status of Country, 1970 and 1983

Developmental Status of Country	*Number of Countries*	*Year* 1970	*Year* 1983	*Percentage Change 1970–1983*
First World	24	163	172	+ 5.5
Second World	8	158	142	−10.1
Third World	67	87	91	+ 4.6
Fourth World	25	45	43	− 4.4

SOURCE: Adapted from Richard J. Estes, *Trends in World Social Development: The Social Progress of Nations, 1970–1987.* (New York: Praeger, 1988), pp. 40–41.

raphy, and cultural diversity subindexes, LDCs at best score only half as well as MDCs in providing for the basic needs of their citizens, and in the most disadvantaged, Fourth World, countries, the differences are even greater.

With respect to changes in the Index of Social Progress over the fourteen-year period represented in Table 3, the developed market economies of the First World registered the greatest advance. Thus, even in this brief interval, the evidence indicates that the gap between MDCs and LDCs is increasing. The least developed Fourth World countries actually declined from what little "progress" they had initially achieved. As Estes (1988, p. 43) states, "Increased militarism and internal political oppression—coupled with *decreased* government expenditures for health, education, fertility control and related programs—are only suggestive of the high level of 'mal-development' that characterizes current social trends."

As indicated, there is a strong direct relationship between industrialization and economic development, and as Estes's research demonstrates, this relationship impinges directly upon the quality of life of people everywhere. Unfortunately for the vast majority of the world's citizens, their circumstances do not even approximate those structural features of society that most people in the more developed countries have largely come to take for granted (see Table 2).

PATHS OF DEVELOPMENT

Various schemes, proposals, and strategies have been suggested whereby LDCs can begin to share the same advantages as those presently enjoyed by MDCs. For example, two World Bank commissions under the direction of the former prime minister of Canada, Lester Pearson (1969), and the ex-chancellor of West Germany, Willy Brandt (1980), have made recommendations concerning such things as the institution of a modified and more equitable world financial structure, the liberalization of international trading policy, an increase in agricultural and energy production, and the establishment of a more workable international negotiating process. Similarly, the LDCs themselves have made proposals regarding what has come to be known as the New International Economic Order (see Tinbergen 1976). In a slightly different vein, the World Commission on Environment and Development (1987) has presented various options and strategies whereby economic development can occur in ecologically sound ways.

Generally, there are two dominant strategies of economic development: inwardly focused import substitution and outwardly oriented export promotion (see Balassa 1981, pp. 1–26). Countries employing import substitution attempt to industrialize by manufacturing for their own domestic markets the majority of those products they have normally been importing. According to this strategy, these countries become not only industrialized but also economically self-sufficient, thus diminishing their heavy reliance upon MDCs for expensive manufactured imports. India and many Latin American countries have established economies that are illustrative of this approach. On the other hand, countries emphasizing export promotion concentrate on those goods, both primary and manufactured, that have traditionally contributed to their economies and that, therefore, can earn export income. Successful pursuit of this strategy results in more profitable manufactured goods making up an increasing share of total exports, and consequently, there occurs both industrial and economic development. The four east Asian NICs mentioned exemplify this approach.

While the viability of either of these strategies obviously depends upon many factors (e.g., size of domestic market, natural resources, education and skills of the labor force, presence and type of foreign investment, and sociopolitical conditions), the evidence to date favors the outward orientation as the preferred path of development (see Syrquin and Chenery 1989). According to the World Bank (1987, pp. 92–94), "Outward orientation encourages efficient firms and discourages inefficient ones. And by creating a more competitive environment for both the private and public sectors, it also promotes higher productivity and hence faster economic growth."

Although there are monumental barriers to industrialization and economic development for the LDCs, they can be overcome (see Hedley 1985). To the extent that nothing is done, and the gap between the rich and the poor continues to widen, dire predictions have been made as to possible consequences. In fact, there is already an increase in world disorder. Manifestations of this deterioration include multiplying acts of terrorism and civil disobedience, illegal migration, increased crime, widespread famine, and internal disputes that escalate into international conflicts. Further instability may be introduced through large-scale default on debt repayment, expropriation and curtailment of the activities of transnational corporations, formation of cartels among LDCs to limit the supply of necessary goods to the developed nations, breakdown of international bodies and diplomatic communication, and finally, revolution and war.

To the extent that the now industrialized countries are not cognizant of the difficulties faced by the LDCs and do not act to ameliorate them, the rich nations along with the poor will suffer the calamitous consequences. As Lester Pearson prophesied, "Before long, in our affluent, industrial, computerized jet society, we shall feel the wrath of the wretched people of the world. There will be no peace" (cited in Tinbergen 1976, p. 59).

(SEE ALSO: *Modernization Theory; Transnational Corporations*)

REFERENCES

Balassa, Bela 1981 *The Newly Industrializing Countries in the World Economy.* New York: Pergamon.

Brandt Report 1980 *North–South: A Program for Survival. Report of the Independent Commission on International Development Issues.* Cambridge, Mass.: MIT Press.

Clairmonte, Frederick F., and John H. Cavanagh 1984 "Transnational Corporations and Global Markets: Changing Power Relations." In Pradip K. Ghosh, ed., *Multi-national Corporations and Third World Development,* pp. 47–91. Westport, Conn.: Greenwood.

Crow, Ben, and Alan Thomas 1983 *Third World Atlas.* Milton Keynes, U.K.: Open University Press.

Estes, Richard J. 1988 *Trends in World Social Development: The Social Progress of Nations, 1970–1987.* New York: Praeger.

Hedley, R. Alan 1985 "Narrowing the Gap between the Rich and the Poor Nations: A Modest Proposal." *Transnational Perspectives* 11(2–3):23–27.

——— Forthcoming *Making a Living: Technology, Industry, and Change.* New York: Harper Collins.

Kurian, George T. 1984 *The New Book of World Rankings.* New York: Facts on File.

Murdoch, William W. 1980 *The Poverty of Nations: The Political Economy of Hunger and Population.* Baltimore: Johns Hopkins University Press.

Pearson Report 1969 *Partners in Development: Report of the Commission on International Development.* New York: Praeger.

Seligson, Mitchell A. 1984 "The Dual Gaps: An Overview of Theory and Research." In Mitchell A. Seligson, ed., *The Gap between Rich and Poor: Contending Perspectives on the Political Economy of Development,* pp. 3–7. Boulder, Colo.: Westview.

Syrquin, Moshe, and Hollis Chenery 1989 "Three Decades of Industrialization." *World Bank Economic Review* 3(2):145–181.

Tinbergen, Jan 1976 *Reshaping the International Order.* New York: Dutton.

World Bank 1987 *World Development Report 1987.* New York: Oxford University Press.

World Commission on Environment and Development 1987 *Our Common Future.* Oxford: Oxford University Press.

1988 World Population Data Sheet 1988 Washington, D.C.: Population Reference Bureau.

R. ALAN HEDLEY

INFANT AND CHILD MORTALITY

The term *mortality* refers to the rate at which death occurs to members of a population. It is measured not by a count of deaths but by quotients that relate deaths to the size of the population in which those deaths occur. The most common measure of infant mortality is the infant mortality rate, the ratio of deaths that occur to children below age one in a particular year to births that occur in that year. This ratio is an excellent approximation to the probability that a newborn child will die before his or her first birthday.

The age referent for "child mortality" is less clear-cut. Among demographers, the term is used most frequently to refer to the probability that a newborn child will die before his or her fifth birthday. Obviously, such a measure of child mortality reflects infant mortality as well. The first five years of life are among the ages of highest mortality, matched in most populations only by the very old ages. In contrast, ages five to fifteen are usually the ages of lowest mortality.

Knowledge about levels of infant and child mortality is drawn from many sources. For prehistoric populations, the only evidence is derived from skeletal remains, which are not thought to provide a reliable account because of the fragility of infant skeletons and uncertainties about burial practices. After writing skills were developed, burial inscriptions and genealogies offered new sources of information. However, these records are also thought to be unreliable because infants and very young children would not have achieved the social significance that is typical of adults. Therefore, it is less likely that their deaths would be recorded.

It is only with the advent of modern vital statistics in eighteenth- and nineteenth-century Europe that a clear picture emerges about levels of infant and child mortality. For the earlier period, which covers the vast fraction of human evolution, the most that can be said is that infant and child mortality were undoubtedly very high by modern standards. It is likely that 20 percent to 30 percent of newborns died before their first birthday, and 30 percent to 60 percent before their fifth (Acsadi and Nemeskeri 1970).

There are reasons to believe that infant and child mortality rose when people settled in agricultural communities, and remained higher than had been typical in nomadic groups. Settlement in larger and denser communities allowed some bacterial and viral diseases, such as measles and smallpox, to be sustained from year to year by virtue of the larger number of new victims who could be attacked each year and who could pass the disease on to others who had not acquired immunities (Cockburn 1963). This speculation, which has a sound theoretical basis, has been supported by observations of contemporary nomadic groups (Howell 1979) and of low-density populations into which new diseases are introduced (McNeil 1976; Cockburn 1963).

When vital statistics on births and deaths first became available for European populations, they revealed very high levels of infant and child mortality. Sweden, the first country to have complete national data, had an infant mortality rate of 18 percent to 23 percent over the period 1778–1832 and a probability of dying before age five of about 30 percent (Keyfitz and Flieger 1968). Substantial annual fluctuations in these indexes were evident, reflecting both the natural cycle of diseases and epidemics and variations in the adequacy of annual harvests.

As other nations developed their systems of vital registration, Sweden was found to have one of the lowest infant and child mortality levels in Europe, probably owing to its rural character, low density, and mild summers. Southern and Eastern Europe had exceptionally high infant mortality, with European Russia having an infant mortality rate of 27.7 percent as late as 1896–1897. Some of the high infant mortality in Eastern Europe has been traced to its unusually short periods of breast-feeding, undoubtedly the most important health protection that could be offered an infant before the twentieth century.

High infant mortality was not confined to the poorer lands of Eastern and Southern Europe. England, the home of the industrial revolution and by 1900 one of the three richest countries in the world in terms of per capita income, had an infant mortality rate of 16 percent in 1901. Moreover, the rate had improved little since vital statistics became available in 1836. Data on infant mortality by area within England suggested that the most important source of variation was size and density of an area, rather than its economic circumstances (Woods 1985). It seems likely that the fall of infant mortality during the nineteenth century had been impeded by the rapid urbanization of the British population. Sweden, where urbanization was much less advanced, showed a slow and irregular improvement in infant mortality during the nineteenth century.

A new era in infant and child mortality was ushered in around 1880 in most of the now-industrialized world. Rates of improvement were much faster than they had been, and backsliding became infrequent. These countries have now achieved infant mortality rates on the order of 1 percent, with relatively little international variation. Most of the improvement occurred in the period 1880–1930. The most likely cause of the accelerated decline during this period was a revolution in bacteriology. The germ theory of disease was empirically validated in the 1870s and 1880s and led to a much clearer understanding of the nature of most of the diseases that were killing children. Previous theories of disease causation had stressed the maintenance of balance among bodily "humours" and the importance of foul-smelling atmospheric contaminants, derived from such sources as decaying vegetation, slaughterhouses, and sewers, as sources of disease. Before the germ theory, the role of contagious mechanisms was clearly recognized only for such spectacularly episodic diseases as cholera and typhus.

The ascendance of the germ theory was not instantaneous, and it met with resistance in many quarters, including physicians wedded to old practices. But by 1910 it had clearly become the dominant view among public health authorities who were responsible for making environmental improvements that reduced the incidence of disease. Bacterial counts rather than odor became the dominant criterion for water quality, and water supplies were improved in nearly all municipalities. Equally important for child survival were governmentally mandated improvements in the cleanliness of milk supplies, a process that began later and extended into the 1930s. An excellent review of these and other developments in the United States is provided in Ravenel (1921). The fact that infant and child mortality declined much faster in urban than in rural areas, which had much weaker public health programs, is additional evidence of the importance of public intervention in speeding health advances (Davis 1973).

Individual parents concerned with the survival of their children also had new and improved strategies for use in the home. The germ theory stimulated such practices as sterilization of bottles and milk, washing of hands, and isolation of sick family members. Information about the value of these practices was disseminated through many routes by public authorities. In the United States, the Children's Bureau, founded in 1912, was an especially effective agent of change. One of its publications, *Infant Care,* became the largest-selling publication in the history of the U.S. Government Printing Office (Ewbank and Preston 1990).

Physicians and drugs probably played a minor role in the modernization of infant and child mortality, a position supported most forcefully by Thomas McKeown (1976) with reference to England and Wales. Until the advent of sulfa drugs and antibiotics in the late 1930s and 1940s—by which time infant mortality rates had fallen by two-thirds—physicians had few drugs that could arrest the progress of disease. The main progress appears to have been made in the area of prevention rather than cure, and it was the combination of public authorities and parents that proved most effective in this arena. McKeown himself stresses the importance of improvements in the quantity of food available. But this explanation appears seriously inadequate both in England (Szreter 1988) and in the United States (Preston and Haines 1991).

That advances in lowering levels of infant and child mortality did not rely heavily on improved standards of living is also suggested by the experiences of the developing countries of Asia, Africa, and Latin America. The United Nations (1989) estimated that the average infant mortality rate for the developing world was 8.9 percent in 1980–1985, a rate that would have been the envy of England and Wales or the United States in 1900, even though they were already much richer countries than the typical developing country today.

Data on infant and child mortality in developing countries are much less adequate than in the industrialized world. A few nations in Latin America and East Asia have good systems of vital statistics, and India has useful vital data for a representative sample of its population. However, information for most countries is derived from questions asked of women on censuses or surveys about the number of children they have borne and the number of them who have survived.

The data that are available suggest that infant and child mortality during the twentieth century started from a substantially higher level and declined even faster than in developed countries. Data for rural China in the 1920s indicate a probability of dying before age five of about 38 percent, and Chilean data suggest a level of 40 percent in 1920 (Hill 1991). These countries had levels of about 3.9 percent and 2.3 percent, respectively, in the 1980s.

The sources of declining child mortality in developing countries are probably much the same as in developed countries. In particular, public health programs appear to have been successful in many areas. Their most spectacular successes probably pertain to antimalarial programs, where mosquito control could increase survival dramatically in a very short period. Many such programs were deployed in the 1945–1955 period, some under the instigation of international agencies and foundations (Preston 1980). Antibiotics and drug therapy probably played a larger role in the mortality decline in developing countries, in part because little improvement had occurred before their advent. Immunization has also been a potent weapon in the decline in child mortality in developing countries.

DIFFERENTIALS IN INFANT AND CHILD MORTALITY

Many studies have examined differences in infant and child mortality among social groups within the same population. These can be summarized by saying that geographic location was a decisive factor in child mortality during the period 1600–1900 and that social location has become the dominant factor during the twentieth century. Before there was a clear understanding of the nature of infectious diseases, they made very heavy inroads among all social groups, rich and poor alike. Richer groups were somewhat better protected than poorer ones, probably because of better nutrition and more spacious housing. But where one lived—especially the population density in one's area—seemed to be a more important factor. Larger cities suffered higher child mortality than small towns, which in turn had higher mortality than rural areas (Weber 1899). These residential differences are manifest in occupational differences as well. In the United States in the 1890s, children of farmers had 15 percent lower child mortality than children of professionals. Size of place was the single most important correlate of child mortality (Preston and Haines 1991).

In the course of the twentieth century, urban-rural differences narrowed to insignificance, while social class differences in child mortality tended to widen. The largest data series pertains to England and Wales, where the Registrar General defines social class in terms of father's occupational group. Pamuk (1988) has shown that social class differences in infant mortality widened in England and Wales between 1921 and 1971, despite the 1947 introduction of the British Health Service, which tended to equalize access to medical care. One may speculate that as environmental conditions improved, especially in cities, individual differences in resources and information acquired greater latitude in influencing child mortality.

In developing countries, existing data series fail to show that cities have had substantially worse child mortality conditions than rural areas. In fact, larger cities at present tend to have lower child mortality than rural areas. It is likely that this reversal of the patterns that were displayed earlier in the developed world is a reflection of the concentration of health services in cities. It also reflects the higher educational attainments of urban residents.

A large United Nations study investigated recent patterns of social and residential differences in child mortality in fifteen developing countries. The variable that emerged as most persistently and strongly related to child mortality was the mother's education (United Nations 1985). Each additional year of schooling for the mother reduced child mortality levels by about 6 percent on average. This influence was much stronger than that pertaining to the father's education or occupation, even though these variables would typically be more closely associated with a household's economic circumstances.

Caldwell (1990) argues that the strength of association between mother's education and child mortality in part reflects the fact that schooling elevates a woman's position in the home. It also exposes her to Western ideas and values and helps to break traditional, sometimes fatalistic, approaches to household management and interpersonal relations. Clelland and van Ginneken (1988) present evidence that in a number of countries better-educated mothers are more likely to use the preventative or curative services offered by modern medicine.

Since death is a biological event, social and economic influences on infant and child mortality must work through intervening biological mechanisms. Probably the most important of these mechanisms in the United States at present is birth weight (Institute of Medicine 1985). Very-low-birth-weight babies are at much higher risk of death, despite technological advances that have sharply improved their survival chances. Many of the other biomedical influences on infant mortality, such as the widely observed U-shaped relationships between infant mortality and age of mother or birth order of child, are primarily reflections of birth-weight differences.

The distribution of birth weights also helps to explain why the United States ranks only fifteenth to twentieth in the world in infant survival. Its set of infant mortality rates *at a particular birth weight* is about the lowest in the world. But it has a substantially higher fraction of births at very low weights. Why birth weights are lower in the United States is not clearly understood but may reflect poorer standards of prenatal care and weaker social support, including marital support, for mothers.

(SEE ALSO: *Birth and Death Rates; Health Promotion*)

REFERENCES

Acsadi, G., and J. Nemeskeri 1970 *History of Human Life Span and Mortality*. Budapest: Akad. Kiado.

Caldwell, J. 1990 "Cultural and Social Factors Influencing Mortality Levels in Developing Countries." *Annals of the American Academy of Political and Social Science* 510:44–59.

Clelland, J. G., and J. K. van Ginneken 1988 "Maternal Education and Child Survival in Developing Countries: The Search for Pathways of Influence." *Social Science and Medicine* 27:1357–1368.

Cockburn, A. 1963 *The Evolution and Eradication of Infectious Diseases*. Baltimore: Johns Hopkins University Press.

Davis, K. 1973 "Cities and Mortality." International Union for the Scientific Study of Population. *International Population Conference: Liège, 1973* 3:259–282. Liège: IUSSP.

Ewbank, D., and S. H. Preston 1990 "Personal Health Behavior and the Decline in Infant and Child Mortality: The United States, 1900–30." In J. Caldwell, ed., *What We Know About the Health Transition*. Canberra: Australia National University Press.

Hill, K. 1991 "The Decline of Childhood Mortality." Manuscript, Department of Population Dynamics, The Johns Hopkins University.

Howell, N. 1979 *The Demography of Dobe! Kung*. New York: Academic Press.

Institute of Medicine 1985 *Preventing Low Birthweight*. Washington, D.C.: National Academy of Sciences Press.

Keyfitz, N., and W. Flieger 1968 *World Population: An Analysis of Vital Data*. Chicago: University of Chicago Press.

McKeown, T. 1976 *The Modern Rise of Population*. New York: Academic Press.

McNeil, W. 1976 *Plagues and People*. Garden City, NY: Anchor Press.

Pamuk, E. 1988 "Social Class Inequality in Infant Mortality in England and Wales from 1921 to 1980." *European Journal of Population* 4:1–21.

Preston, S. H. 1980 "Causes and Consequences of Mortality Declines in Less Developed Countries During the Twentieth Century." In R. A. Easterlin, ed., *Population and Economic Change in Developing Countries*. Conference Report 30, Universities-National Bureau Committee for Economic Research. Chicago: University of Chicago Press.

———, and M. Haines 1991 *Fatal Years: Child Mortality in Late Nineteenth Century America*. Princeton, N.J.: Princeton University Press.

Ravenel, M. P. (ed.) 1921 *A Half Century of Public Health*. New York: American Public Health Association.

Szreter, S. 1988 "The Importance of Social Intervention in Britain's Mortality Decline c. 1850–1914: A Reinterpretation of the Role of Public Health." *Social History of Medicine* 1:1–37.

United Nations 1985 *Socioeconomic Differentials in Child Mortality in Developing Countries.* New York: United Nations.

———1989 *World Population Prospects, 1988.* New York: United Nations.

Weber, Adna F. 1899 *The Growth of Cities in the 19th Century: A Study in Statistics.* New York: Macmillan.

Woods, R. 1985 "The Effects of Population Redistribution on the Level of Mortality in Nineteenth-Century England and Wales." *Journal of Economic History* 45 (3):645–651.

SAMUEL H. PRESTON

INFORMATION SOCIETY The increased reliance on activities directly associated with the production, distribution, and utilization of information has led to the characterization of many of the advanced countries of the world as information societies. The term *information society* and similar concepts such as information age and knowledge economy describe a society in which there is great dependence on use of information technologies to produce all manners of goods and services. In contrast to the industrial society, which relied on internal combustion engines to augment the physical labor of humans, the information society relies on computer technologies to augment their mental labor.

Trends in labor force composition both define and measure the extent to which a nation can be described as an information society. Machlup (1962) was perhaps the first to describe U.S. society in these terms. He estimated in 1958 that nearly one-third of the labor force worked in information industries such as communications, computers, education, and information services, and accounted for 29 percent of the gross national product (GNP). Using a slightly different methodology, Porat (1977) estimated that information activities had risen to just under half of the U.S. GNP by 1967.

Advances in the capabilities of information technologies to process large quantities of information quickly have been a crucial factor in the development of the information society. These technologies are of two types, computing power and transmission capability (Mayo 1985). Development of inexpensive silicon integrated circuits containing as many as a million transistors on a single chip by the mid-1980s made it possible to pack tremendous information processing power into very little space. Desktop microcomputers now have processing power comparable to the largest mainframe computers of the previous decade. Corresponding breakthroughs have occurred in photonics as a result of the development of laser technology and ultrapure glass fiber. The result of these developments is the ability to transmit enormous quantities of information long distances on tiny optic fibers without amplification. For example, by the mid-1980s, AT&T Laboratories had transmitted 420 million bits per second of information over 125 miles without amplification. Efforts to connect much of the world with fiber optics are now proceeding at a very rapid pace. The practical effect of these and related advancements such as facsimile and satellite transmission technologies will be to make computers even more commonplace and easy to use, and to make communications among them equally commonplace and inexpensive. Thus, the information society must now be considered in the early stages of its existence.

James Beniger (1986) views the information society as long in its development as a result of a crisis of control evoked by the industrial revolution in the late 1800s. Industrialization speeded up material processing systems. However, innovations in information processing and communications lagged behind innovations in the use of energy to increase productivity of manufacturing and transportation systems. Development of the telegraph, telephone, radio, television, modern printing presses, and postal delivery systems all represented innovations important to the resolution of the control crisis, which required replacement of the traditional bureaucratic means of control that had been depended on for centuries before.

An entirely new stage in the development of the information society has been realized through recent advances in microprocessing technology, and the convergence of mass media telecommunications and computers into a single infrastructure of societal control (Beniger 1986). An important factor in this convergence is digitalization of all information so the distinctions between types of information such as words, numbers, and pictures become blurred and communications between persons and machines and between machines become impossible. Therefore, it is concluded by Beniger that digitalization allows the transformation of information into a generalized medium for processing and exchange by the social system, much as common currency and exchange rates, centuries ago, did the same for the economic systems of the world (1986).

An important attribute of the information society is the search for improvements in productivity primarily through the substitution of information for energy, labor, and physical materials. In practical terms, this means such things as supplying workers with computerized workstations that are networked to other workstations, utilizing computer software to retool equipment in distant locations, and sending facsimile or computer transmissions, which eliminates physical delivery of messages; these improvements make organizational production, distribution, and management decisions more efficient. One indicator of the extent to which industries in a developing information society seek productivity improvements through the use of information equipment is that in 1984 40 percent of all U.S. investment in durable equipment was spent on the purchase of computers and communication equipment, up from only 10 percent in 1960 (U.S. Congress 1988). The use and impact of these technologies are pervasive, influencing nearly all institutions, from those in education to those in the political realm (Weinberg 1990).

The implications of living in a fully developed information society are many (Dillman 1985). Chief among them is the breaking down of geographic barriers, whereby businesses are more connected to other businesses and consumers in other countries than they are to those in their own nation, thus providing a basis for the development of the global economy. Information technologies provide the potential for overcoming remoteness. They may also result in a dramatic modification of the relationship between worker and workplace, as technologies facilitate telecommuting from one's home as a means of dealing both with urban congestion and rural isolation. Such technologies also provide a basis for forming new groups and maintaining group identities that geographic separation heretofore made impossible. The emergence of global networks of information also puts pressure on all societies to conform to emergent international norms of openness and accountability (Weinberg 1990).

The information society differs significantly from the mass society with which it is sometimes contrasted (Dillman 1985). Whereas the latter emphasizes one-way communication, large-scale mass production of products and ideas, and the creation of uniformity, the information society emphasizes two-way communication, batch or even single-unit production, and development of a pluralism of interests. The information society can be considered an extension of the postindustrial society concept described by Daniel Bell (1973), with more recognition being given to the role of information technologies as the major driving force in transforming societal organization.

Quite different views exist about the possible effects of the development of a full-fledged information society. One view is that it will empower workers, providing direct access to opportunities unavailable to them in an industrial society except by high organizational position and proximity to centralized positions of power. For example, Harlan Cleveland (1985) describes information as being fundamentally different than the resources for which it is being substituted, for example, not being used up by one who consumes it and hence making its use possible by others. It is also easily transportable from one point to another. Cleveland projects that the information society will force dramatic changes in long-standing hierarchic forms of social organization, terminating many existing taken-for-granted hierarchies based on control, secrecy, ownership, early access, and geography. A similar view is provided by Masuda (1985), writing in a Japanese context, who envisions the development of participatory democracies, the eradication of educational gaps between urban and rural areas, and the elimination of a centralized class-based society.

A more pessimistic view of the consequences of knowledge becoming the key source of productivity is offered by Castells (1989). Fundamentally, the new information infrastructure that connects virtually all points of the globe to all others allows for great flexibility in all aspects of production consumption, distribution, and management. To take advantage of the efficiencies offered by full utilization of information technologies, organizations plan their operations around the dynamics of their information-generating units, and not around a limited geographic space. Individual nations lose the ability to control corporations. Information technologies, therefore, become instrumental in the implementation of fundamental processes of capitalist restructuring. Efforts are made to increase the rate of profits by substituting machines for workers, and the decentralization of production threatens the position of labor unions. In contrast to the view offered by Cleveland, the stateless nature of the corporation is seen as contributing to an international hierarchical functional structure in which the historic division between intellectual and manual labor is taken to an extreme. The consequences for social organization are to dissolve localities as functioning social systems and to supersede societies.

There is little doubt that the development of a full-fledged information society can produce dramatic changes in existing social structures and relationships. However, it remains to be seen whether the nature of those impacts will be primarily determined by the structural requirements of the new technologies as they seek to fulfill their development potential, or whether their impact will be primarily influenced by necessary adaptation to other forces of social change.

(SEE ALSO: *Mass Media Research*)

REFERENCES

Bell, Daniel 1973 *The Coming of Post-Industrial Society: A Venture in Social Forecasting.* New York: Basic Books.

Beniger, James R. 1986 *The Control Revolution: Technological and Economic Origins of the Information Society.* Cambridge, Mass.: Harvard University Press.

Castells, Manuel 1989 *The Informational City.* Cambridge: Basil Blackwell.

Cleveland, Harlan 1985 "The Twilight of Hierarchy: Speculations on the Global Information Society." *Public Administration Review* 45:185–196.

Dillman, Don A. 1985 "The Social Impacts of Information Technologies in Rural North America." *Rural Sociology* 50:1–26.

Machlup, Fritz 1962 *The Production and Distribution of Knowledge in the United States.* Princeton, N.J.: Princeton University Press.

Masuda, Yoneji 1981 *The Information Society as Post-Industrial Society.* Tokyo: Institute for the Information Society; Bethesda, Md.: World Future Society.

Mayo, John S. 1985 "The Evolution of Information Technologies." In Bruce R. Guile, ed., *Information Technologies and Social Transformation.* Washington, D.C.: National Academy of Engineering, National Academy Press.

Porat, M. U., et al. 1977 *The Information Economy.* OT Special Publication 77–12. Washington, D.C.: U.S. Department of Commerce.

U.S. Congress, Office of Technology Assessment 1988 *Technology and the American Transition: Choices for the Future.* OTA-TET-2A3. Washington, D.C.: U.S. Government Printing Office.

Weinberg, Nathan 1990 *Computers in the Information Society.* Boulder, Colo.: Westview Press.

DON A. DILLMAN

INHERITANCE Statutory and common laws governing inheritance have a profound effect on the formation or dissolution of household structures and the patterns of inheritance transfers over generations. A society, for any political or social reason, can initiate and promulgate a law or civil code controlling inheritance; inevitably, new laws or codes cause drastic change in the structure and functions of family systems.

In order to understand the subject of inheritance, it will be necessary to define many terms. To *inherit* is by law to receive property, resources, or, often, status from an ancestor at her or his decease or to take by intestate succession or by will. *Intestate succession* is a transfer of resources according to legal procedures that control distribution of the resources when there is no will. A person is *intestate* when he or she has not made a will. In a *will,* usually a written document, a person (or *testator*) makes a deposition of his or her property, and the deposition takes effect, at least in modern societies, upon the testator's death. A will is changeable and revocable during the lifetime of a testator.

Takers are successors or beneficiaries. *Impartible inheritance* is a situation, established by statute, in which the property and resources are indivisible and are given to one person *(devisee);* this type of inheritance is likely to occur within family households primarily in rural areas of most historic societies, especially in Eastern and Western Europe. *Partible inheritance,* dividing assets for conveyance to one's heirs, is linked to nuclear family households found in those locations where there is accelerated industrialization and urbanization.

Any system of inheritance promotes the continuity of family and societal structures over generations. The transfer of resources from the older to the younger generation helps maintain a family's position and power in the social order. Such transfers also provide stability to existing societal caste and class arrangements and ordinarily are ensconced deeply in tradition and myth. It is more likely that inheritance systems function to perpetuate existing social structures than to change society's organizations and institutions.

INHERITANCE, LAWS, AND CHANGE

Those most affected by changes in laws are persons with little power in society. This is evident in eighteenth- and nineteenth-century European societies, in which the promulgation of laws and decrees drastically affected the structure and practices of rural families. For example, Gaunt (1983) indicates that in nineteenth-century central Europe, in a section that is now part of Czechoslovakia, the decree to conscript unmarried men for military duty caused parents of serf families to encourage early marriage of their children. As a consequence, the incidence of complex family households increased, and there were changes in the patterns of inheritance succession. During a labor shortage in eighteenth-century Poland, fiefdom rulers encouraged endogamous marriage and attempted to restrict their chattels from leaving their villages. The economy was based on household unit sharecropping. The peasants encouraged complex family households consisting of two or more conjugal units, while the Polish lords favored neolocal household residence (Kochanowicz 1983). The inheritance outcomes of these efforts to circumvent political, economic, and social measures, often repressive in intent, affected existent family structures, their forms, and inheritance patterns.

The possession of equities, property, possessions, resources, and land (especially in the case of European peasants) determined whether these would compose an impartible or partible inheritance. For example, an impartible inheritance pattern is most likely when land is the primary family asset. In addition, the transfer of authority over these rights depended upon the timing of "stepping down," a process deeply embedded in the cultural traditions of the society (Gaunt 1983; Plakans 1989). Stepping down usually occurred through a retirement contract, which was essentially a will that indicated the conditions of the transfer from parents to children. This *inter vivos* phenomenon, a conveyance of property and other equities while the individual was alive and engaged in stepping down, was "one made of preserving intergenerationally the match between family and the property that provides its livelihood" (Sorensen 1989, p. 199). Stepping down, or disengaging, usually occurred when the oldest son married or when the parents were near or at retirement age. Stepping down was invoked by law or tradition, and it resulted in variations in inheritance patterns and in the organization of the life course of various family members.

Sorensen (1989) provides a detailed retirement contract of his great-grandfather on his mother's side, a prosperous farm family in the western part of Jutland, Denmark. The transfer of this medium-sized farm, substantially undervalued, when Laurids Poulsen was fifty-six, was apparently to make certain that the property remained in the family to buttress its position in the society.

It is not explicitly stated in the Poulsen retirement agreement that the heir, Alfred, would care for his parents in their declining years. The contract's provisions enabled Laurids and his wife, Maren, to be independent. Yet in this situation and, as Sorensen (1989) indicates, in Scandinavia since before the Middle Ages, transferring property to a son implied the promise of care in old age. Thus, there existed two motivations for conveying property to a son, but the stronger proved to be the hope of maintaining the property in the family over generations.

In former ages, conveying property and its accompanying position, status, and power was the intent of inheritance patterns. The preservation and maintenance of the family unit was the goal. Impartible inheritance expressed this intent of maintaining the family property and social position, but it created obvious winners and losers. The transfer of a family's property to a single heir meant that other family members could leave to seek opportunities elsewhere or remain with the family enterprise in a subservient position.

The possibilities for fuller expression of family members' abilities, where talent and skills and not family membership determined the individual's life course trajectory, would come at a later period. Partible inheritance reduced the requirement that family members subordinate their desires, interests, and expectations to those of the family unit. Changes in a society's demographics, such as fertility and mortality, and changes in the means of producing goods and services resulted in lessened need for impartible inheritance. Partible inheritance became identified with the modern period of Western civilization.

MODERN PERIOD

Rules for succession and rules for inheritance of property are related but distinct from one another. Inheritance of property usually follows lines of succession to social position. Codified systems of secular law governing inheritance and status succession emerge in complex societies and are sufficiently precise and uniform to meet the majority needs of the population (Radcliffe-Brown 1935).

For urbanites in complex societies such as those in Europe and the United States, the transfer of land, dwelling unit, tools, and equipment is less critical to the survival and maintenance of the family over generations than it is for the rural resident. Economic assets other than land and buildings—that is, personal mementos and possessions—become the content of such transfers.

Rural landholders of modest means were unable to effect a pattern of impartable inheritance. Increasing societal complexity nurtured corporate agriculture in preference to the family farm. The reduction in the number of family-owned farms, the increasing dependence of farm family members upon the larger, mostly urban society for jobs that are not located close to the farm dwelling, price supports, and payment for nonproduction have diminished the possibilities for maintaining the family farm over generations. Partible inheritance has become the norm.

This shift to partible inheritance under new rules of succession meant that for the first time the claims of the surviving spouse outweighed those of the surviving kin of one's lineage, a reversal of the pattern found in eighteenth- and nineteenth-century Europe and in primitive societies (Benedict 1936; Hoebel 1966). Under U.S. state statutes governing intestacy the surviving spouse and children share in the estate. The spouse receives at least one-third, depending on the number of surviving children and the specifics of the state law governing inheritance. If there is no surviving spouse the children share and share alike. Where there is no surviving spouse or children the estate passes to grandchildren. In the absence of grandchildren the next to receive are grandparents, then siblings, then more distant relatives.

Where testacy exists the estate usually passes to the surviving spouse. This horizontal transfer in the generational line of succession is uniquely modern and represents an evolution from the

Roman definition of inheritance as "succession to the entire legal position of a deceased man" (Maine 1963, p. 208). In Rome the heir functioned as a guardian or executor of the estate to perpetuate the honor and status of the deceased and family survivors and to keep intact and extend the estate's holdings. The stepwise shift from decedent to surviving spouse and subsequent vertical transfer of equities to children after the death of the surviving spouse resulted in a family system based more on individual relationships, feelings, perceptions, and interactions and less on tradition, primogeniture, and maintaining properties and estates.

The pattern of conveying all property to the spouse, to be discussed further in this article, is a practice seemingly not in consonance with the concept and exercise of testamentary freedom.

TESTAMENTARY FREEDOM

Testamentary freedom, the individual's right to will away property to persons outside the family or to distribute to a number of heirs and legatees related by blood, consanguinity, or adoption, is a fundamental Anglo-American concept of the U.S. inheritance system. The primogeniture system, which passed all property to a single heir and was most suited for the wealthy, was replaced in eighteenth-century England by a new law of the land—testamentary freedom. This occurred at the time England disposed its feudal land tenure system. The 1789 French Revolution, in keeping with its ideology of justice, freedom, equality, and fraternity, and for more concrete social and political reasons, enacted laws requiring equal distribution of a deceased person's assets among surviving children. Colonial settlers in the United States undoubtedly inspired by and enamored of the changes in English and French societies, brought with them this notion of testamentary freedom as part of their intellectual and cultural heritage.

At first blush the practice of testamentary freedom would seem at least to contradict if not destroy the major intent of an inheritance system. According to Edmund Burke, "the power of perpetuating our property in families is one of the most valuable and interesting circumstances belonging to it, and that which tends the most to the perpetuation of society itself" (1910, p. 121). The major question is whether testamentary freedom as it is practiced negates what Burke suggests is a most critical process for generational and societal continuity.

Testamentary freedom, like justice or liberty, is a relative and not an absolute condition. In practice it accommodates to family continuity over generations; a multilineal descent system; a highly differentiated society where the majority of assets owned by individuals are moveable; and values that espouse rationality, choice, freedom, and democracy. The right of an individual to dispose of property according to her or his wishes is recognized if the individual disposes property in a responsible fashion—when one takes care of one's kin, thus maximizing the possibilities of family continuity and orderly social relationships among family members. Testamentary freedom is not exercised absolutely. It accommodates to the norms of responsibility. Empirical data support the idea that compromise occurs among the interests of the individual's family and state in the exercise of testamentary freedom (Sussman, Cates, and Smith 1970).

Courts, social norms, and societal economic patterns limit the expression of testamentary freedom. Courts use the soundness of mind principle in determining if an individual acts in a responsible fashion. Knowing what one possesses, the nature of the business in which one is engaged, and the natural objects of one's bounty are the essential components of the legal definition of a sound mind. In practice, courts almost universally consider the well-being of the family in addition to considering whether an individual has knowledge of his or her assets and successors (Cates and Sussman 1982). Neglecting or abandoning the family is viewed as unnatural, and being unnatural is equated with being of unsound mind. The media abound with cases regarding will contests involving decedents' bequests to loved pets, charities, strangers, or acquaintances. Preventing a distant relative from taking from or receiving an adequate share of an estate may result in legal action. Sussman, Cates, and Smith (1970) report a case in which charities were the major beneficiaries. The sole surviving relative, a niece, contested the will and lost, but she received a large out-of-court settlement of $150,000. Courts, plaintiffs, and defendants normally favor out-of-court settlements because of lower economic and psychic costs. In 1965, when this case occurred, a settlement of $150,000 was judged to be ample compensation. The settlement was also an indication that the well-being of a distant family member had been considered.

Prevalent social norms foster concern for the well-being of surviving family members. Believing that families should take care of their own and that family members should not be pauperized, the state has more than a legal interest in seeing that testamentary freedom be exercised with regard for the well-being of the family.

PATTERNS OF GENERATIONAL DISTRIBUTIONS

Complex societies have developed systems of statewide resource transfers that have replaced in part some of the functions of the family inheritance system. These large-scale transfer systems, based on the principle of serial service, are society's way of taking care of those deemed dependent, those unable to contribute to the gross national product through gainful employment. Preponderant numbers of the very young and the elderly receive support from such transfers. The preeminent philosophical notion is that the young adult and middle age generations, individuals ages sixteen to sixty five, pay through their earnings for government-initiated entitlement and needs programs such as Social Security, Medicare, Medicaid, educational grants, welfare payments, and so forth, programs to maintain and enhance the lives of the less fortunate. These generations may participate in these programs somewhat grudgingly, but they do so with the knowledge that they were supported during their childhood and with the expectation of being supported by these same programs in their old age. This pattern of society-wide transfers is characteristic of serial service.

Such massive transfers have reduced the economic burden of families in caring for dependent members. In some instances these programs have diminished the need for family members to provide extensive and intensive social and emotional support (Kreps 1965). Social Security pensions and other vested retirement programs, in both the private and public sectors, provide sufficient income for an increasing number of retirees. Most of them will be able to live independently or with minimal support from their relatives during their later adult years. Being economically independent or quasi-independent in old age with little need to rely upon the family's financial resources is a radical shift from earlier periods, when older relatives depended on the determinations of the inheritance system.

The society-wide transfer system based on universal taxation has not completely replaced the family inheritance system. One can view the former as an impersonal, bureaucratized, and universal system enacted primarily by statute or charter and monitored by official regulations. Participants become part of a large formal system and once they qualify are treated in a uniform manner. The use of computers and identification numbers increases the impersonality of support systems.

The family inheritance system, on the other hand, is influenced but not controlled by large-scale economic transfers. It exists and functions within a set of norms that extoll interpersonal relationships, continuity of marriage and blood lines, symbolic meanings, feelings of filial piety, nurturance, support, care, distributive justice, and reciprocity.

These institutional systems and programs that mutually support families probably condition the bases upon which individual inheritance dispositions are made. Sussman, Cates, and Smith (1970) indicate that as a consequence of the growth of society-wide transfer programs,

> *Inheritance transfers may be less a consequence of acts of sexual reciprocity, based upon what specific individuals of one generation in a family do for others of another generation, but more a function of serial service. Serial service (a concept elaborated by William Moore, 1967) involves an expected gene-*

rational transfer that occurs in the normal course of events. It is expected that parents have to help their young children, and middle aged children may be called upon to give care or arrange for care of an aged and often ailing parent. This is within the cycle of life, and services of this kind are expected and are not based upon reciprocal acts. Whatever parents have in the way of worldly possessions will in due course be passed on to lineal descendants. (p. 10)

Since the 1970s there has been a strong movement to reduce, or at best not increase, taxation to support benefit systems that assure society-wide economic transfers across generational lines. Those who support a reduction in such transfers strongly believe that the society has reached its absorptive capacity to pay increasingly higher costs for retirement and a variety of services to dependent family members. The cutback in government programs coupled with the exhortation that the government "should get off the back of family members" and the reglorification of the myth that families in ancient times cared for their own have resulted in increasing burdens for families in the care of their elderly and dependent members. This shift away from society to family responsibility for family members suggests a new look at family economic transfers and the role such inheritance plays in intergenerational relationships and in the solution of long-term care of aged and other dependent members.

INHERITANCE ISSUES FOR THE 1990S

Believing they do not want to be a burden to their children, older adults with economic resources and few relatives for whom to function as primary caregivers when needed are spending their inheritance on travel and other leisure activities and for total medical and physical care as they move from independent to dependent living. A likely result is the diminishing of available funds to heirs and legatees and increased importance of family heirlooms. These gifts express the meaning and significance of the relationships between family members prior to the death of the testator.

The increasing unavailability of relatives, especially children, to care for aged family members will result in the assignment of heirs and legatees who are not related by blood or marriage. These are friends and service providers who supply social support, care, and nurturance and are "like family." Elders in the latter part of this century and well into the twenty-first, that is, members of the World War II baby boom generation, will be searching for a relative or someone to care for them in their declining years. Their drastically low reproduction rates and the consequences of the gender revolution begun in the 1960s will result in the availability of a severely limited number of immediate family members or distant relatives able or willing to provide care. Elderly people will turn to persons not related by blood or marriage—members of the individual's wider family (Marciano 1988). Wider family members are not a certain age, nor must they conform to traditional social norms; they are not related by blood or marriage. Bondings express deep friendship and voluntary informal contracted obligations and expectations. Wider family members today are on call and respond to requests for assistance immediately. They act and feel that they are at home in each other's household.

The consequence is an increasing incidence in the naming of such persons in wills and the probability that courts in the future will uphold their right to share the estate even in the case of intestacy. The courts may rule that traditional patterns of distribution to surviving family beneficiaries be modified to include those who provided care and nurturance to the deceased. The basis for such action is the notion of distributive justice, which invokes fairness. Those who have voluntarily provided services, intimacy, friendship, and care should be recognized and even rewarded. They have fulfilled the role of filial responsibility.

The dark side of this pattern is the exploitative friend, surrogate, or service provider who manipulates the care receiver and takes over the estate through an *inter vivos* transfer or by a rewriting of the will. This sorcerism, coupled with an increasing number of will contests, will keep attorneys in good financial stead and courts very busy for a long time.

Distributive justice, a just and fair distribution of resources as perceived by a testator or promulgated by the laws of intestacy, will be characteristic of transfers to family and kin as well as wider family members in the coming decades. A component of distributive justice is equality (Piaget 1932), a standard that is invoked by statutes governing intestacy. Equality is determined by the degree of relationship of the deceased to the survivor. Thus, upon the death of a parent intestate, equal shares are given to surviving children. If a spouse survives, she or he usually receives one-third of the estate, and the remaining two-thirds are distributed to surviving children.

Equity is another component of distributive justice. It implies a just and fair condition. It is not the same as equality. It is the "distribution of rewards and costs between persons" (Homans 1961, p. 74). Equity is the component most suited to arrangements for payment of rewards for incurred costs. Hence, both family and nonfamily members can expect rewards in property inheritance in relation to the costs incurred in caregiving and related activities. Such exchanges will become normative and generally accepted. Reciprocity is to be recognized and rewarded.

Portending the future, testators will increasingly enter into contracts with either family or nonfamily (wider) members, setting forth conditions and expectations of needed supports and caregiving (Hanks and Sussman 1990). Such contracts, seemingly as legal as any other contract, are likely to be challenged in the courts by those who stand to inherit under the laws of descent and succession. The rootedness of these contracts in distributive justice, with its fairness and equity principles, suggests that their validity will be sustained.

Contracts can involve *inter vivos* transfers or declarations in a will. For example, a middle-aged testator can give resources to a young relative or member of a wider family with a pay-back arrangement of care and service when needed by the benefactor. A will provision can readily be made. The exact instrument that will enhance its legality needs to be developed in consultation with attorneys. Such contracts, similar to prenuptial agreements, drawn with both parties of sound mind, should be legal. These contracts will have provisions for modification and cancelation, like any other contract. The major point is that such contracts can reduce the concerns of an aging population regarding their life-style in very old age and diminish their total dependence upon institutional forms of care. The "inheritance contract" fosters independence and utilization of one's resources in meeting health and social needs. Caretaking as a family enterprise can reduce potentially the outlay of public monies currently expended for health and social service programs. This reduction in the economic burden of government is not tantamount to the elimination of current universal support programs. At best the inheritance contract helps provide meaningful relationships, establishes a procedure for planning and expending one's resources, and encourages individuals to rely less upon governmental institutions.

Openness in discussing wills is a new departure from the past and leads to forthrightness in discussing other family matters. Hanks (1989) reports in her sample of 111 corporate family members that 88 percent discussed their wills and 60 percent their funeral arrangements. Such openness with relatives can reduce future will contests and result in conversations and negotiations regarding foreseeable generational transfers and caregiving arrangements. The symbolic meaning attached to the passing on of jewelry, paintings, furniture, books, and other household items has been given very little attention (Sussman, Cates, and Smith 1970). Allocations of these items demonstrated to the recipients the kind of emotional and affective relationship they had with the deceased. More individuals experienced pain and depression from not receiving a promised or expected heirloom than from receiving a lesser share of property or equities. Strong feelings are aroused because of the memories connected with these heirlooms, and the deceased cannot be asked regarding her or his feelings and emotions toward the heir. Openness in discussing wills and related matters can reduce misunderstandings and misinterpretations regarding the meaning attached to the transfer of heirlooms and the trauma of not knowing.

In the 1990s and future decades inheritance will continue its patterns of transfer and distribution of properties and equities over generations. It will be a different system from that found in rural areas in historic or current time. It will continue to be insignificant in the generational transfer of status and power except for the wealthy classes. Things that will distinguish inheritance in the future from that of the past is the emergence of the inheritance contract; openness in discussing will contents with potential beneficiaries; greater inclusion of distant family relatives in wills; increased number of will contests; and increased incidence in the number of older adults who spend money on leisure activities or on their own health care rather than contribute it to their children's inheritance.

(SEE ALSO: *Intergenerational Resource Transfers*)

REFERENCES

Benedict, Ruth 1936 "Marital Property Rights in Bilateral Society." *American Anthropologist* 38:368–373.

Burke, Edmund 1910 *Reflections on the French Revolution and Other Essays.* New York: DuHon.

Cates, Judith, and Marvin B. Sussman 1982 *Family Systems and Inheritance Patterns.* New York: Haworth Press.

Gaunt, David 1983 "The Property and Kin Relationships of Retired Farmers in Northern and Central Europe." In Richard Wall, Jean Robin, and Peter Laslett, eds., *Family Forms in Historic Europe.* Cambridge: Cambridge University Press.

Hanks, Roma 1990 "Inheritance and Caregiving: Perceptions in Veteran and Corporate Families." Unpublished paper, College of Human Resources, University of Delaware.

———, and Marvin B. Sussman 1990 "Inheritance Contracting: Policy Implications of Inheritance and Caregiving Patterns." Unpublished paper, College of Human Resources, University of Delaware.

Hoebel, Edgar A. 1966 *Anthropology.* New York: McGraw-Hill.

Homans, George C. 1961 *Social Behavior: Its Elementary Forms.* New York: Harcourt, Brace and World.

Hooyman, Nancy R. 1989 "Women as Caregivers of the Elderly: Implications for Social Welfare Policy and Practice." In David E. Bregel and Arthur Bloom, eds., *Aging and Caregiving.* Newbury Park, Calif.: Sage.

Kochanowicz, Jasalav 1983 "The Peasant Family as an Economic Unit in the Polish Feudal Economy of the Eighteenth Century." In Richard Wall, Jean Robin, and Peter Laslett, eds., *Family Forms in Historic Europe.* Cambridge: Cambridge University Press.

Kreps, Juanita 1965 "The Economics of Intergenerational Relationships." In Gordon F. Streib and Ethel Shanas, eds., *Social Structure and the Family.* Englewood Cliffs, N.J.: Prentice-Hall.

Maine, Henry S. 1963 *Ancient Law.* Boston: Beacon Press.

Marciano, Teresa D. 1988 "Families Wider Than Kin." *Family Science Review* 1:115–124.

Piaget, Jean 1932 "Retributive and Distributive Justice." In *Moral Judgement of the Child.* New York, Harcourt, Brace and World. Reprinted in Edgar Borgatta and Henry J. Meyer, eds., *Sociological Theory.* New York: Alfred A. Knopf, 1956.

Plakans, Andrejs 1989 "Stepping Down in Former Times: A Comparative Assessment of Retirement in Traditional Europe." In David I. Kertzer and K. Warner Schaie, eds., *Age Structuring in Comparative Perspective.* Hillsdale, N.J.: L. Erlbaum.

Radcliffe-Brown, Alfred R. 1935 "Patrilineal and Matrilineal Succession." *Iowa Law Review* 20:286–303.

Sorensen, Aage B. 1989 "Old Age, Retirement, and Inheritance." In David I. Kertzer and K. Warner Schaie, eds., *Age Structuring in Comparative Perspective.* Hillsdale, N.J.: L. Erlbaum.

Sussman, Marvin B., Judith N. Cates, and David T. Smith 1970 *The Family and Inheritance.* New York: Russell Sage Foundation.

MARVIN B. SUSSMAN

IN-LAW RELATIONSHIPS Within kinship systems, relationships with in-laws are a special category that has not been widely studied. In his seminal discussion of American kinship, Schneider (1968) argued that blood and marriage are the two basic principles defining kinship. Blood or consanguine relationships are bound together by genetic material, but relationships based on marriage are bound together by law and a code of conduct that accompanies them. In-law relationships are unique in that they are defined through a third party by both a marriage and a blood relationship. In many cultures, both historically and currently, anthropologists argue that in-law relationships were important to societies because they represented an alliance between two groups of blood relations (Wolfram 1987). In these cultures, in-law relationships are (or were) clearly defined and circumscribed by explicit institutional arrangements and prescribed and proscribed behaviors (Goetting 1990). In Western ideology, however, the husband-wife marital bond is the central family tie and supersedes claims of the extended family. Although general consensus exists as to the rules of membership, the codes of conduct associated with in-law relationships remain nebulous, and actual interactions and sentiments assigned to these relationships are subject to individuals' definitions (Goetting 1990). What patterns do exist and have been observed are restricted to relationships between parents-in-law and children-in-law. Other in-law relationships such as that between sisters- or brothers-in-law appear to be solely based on friendship or idiosyncratic relations (Finch 1989). In fact, Wolfram (1987) notes that such relationships are of so little importance that there are no recognized kinship terms for many of them.

The uncertainty associated with in-law relationships is underscored by the stereotyping of these relationships that exists in the popular culture, witnessed particularly in jokes about mothers-in-law. The problematic nature of the relationship is also underscored in the popular and clinical literatures, as well as studies of early years of marriage that focus on adjustment of in-laws and the influence of in-laws on the marital relationship.

The bulk of research on in-law relationships has focused on assistance and support patterns. These patterns reflect the distinctive feature of in-law relations, which is that they are generally conducted both through, and, in a sense, for the sake of a third party (Finch 1989). Children-in-law primarily receive support from parents-in-law as indirect beneficiaries of parental aid to married children. Hence, the primary patterns of contact and support between children-in-law and their parents-in-law reflect customary patterns of parent-child relationships.

Studies demonstrate that over the life cycle, aid between parents and children tends to be unidirectional from parents to children and that parental aid is most concentrated in the early year of children's marriages and decreases over time (Goetting 1990). Financial aid most often begins and is concentrated in early years of marriage, whereas aid in the form of services reaches a peak during the preschool years of the grandchildren. Both gender and class differences have been observed (Adams 1964). The wife's parents tend to be a source of greater aid in terms of service, while sons' parents tend to provide financial aid. More frequent financial help is given to middle-class than to working-class children and children-in-law. Working-class parents, when they live close by, give what they can in services. Consistent with this indirect pattern of support, in-laws usually are not primary or critical resources during times of personal crisis.

The presence of grandchildren also appears to influence in-law relationships. The birth of the first child has been reported to transform the mother-in-law/daughter-in-law relationship into one involving significant support patterns. In her study of mother-in-law and daughter-in-law relationships, Fischer (1983) notes that daughters with preschool children needed and received more help from both mothers and mothers-in-law. Mothers-in-law were more likely to give things, whereas mothers were more likely to do things. Daughters-in-law tended to seek help and advice more frequently from their mothers than from their mothers-in-law and were more likely to express ambivalence about help from their mothers-in-law. Parents-in-law have also been observed to benefit children-in-law by providing advice on child rearing and marriage and by serving as source of socialization into marriage roles (Goetting 1990).

Just as there is little evidence of direct support from parents-in-law to their children-in-law, research is consistent in demonstrating that children-in-law make a minimal direct contribution to the care of their elderly parents-in-law. The flow of support for in-laws from the child generation to the parent generation is also indirect and reflects patterns of gender differences associated with parent care. Parents are more likely to turn to daughters and, thereby, sons-in-law for help than to sons and daughters-in-law. However, most help to the elderly does not entail financial support but is more restricted to services and help with household tasks and personal care (Schorr 1980). This type of support is primarily performed by daughters, not sons nor sons-in-laws. There is some evidence, however, that sons-in-law who are spouses of daughters who serve as primary caregivers provide more help than do other persons with elderly parents-in-law (Brody and Schoonover 1988).

Although daughters are the preferred caregivers for elderly parents, when daughters are not available, parents turn to sons and daughters-in-law. In these situations, daughters-in-law often provide more direct service than their husbands, reflecting women's role as kin keepers (Finch 1989). In fact, in the hierarchy of sources of support for the elderly, daughters-in-law take precedence over sons (Schorr 1980). There is some evidence that caring for mothers-in-law is perceived as more stressful and requiring more tasks than does caring for a mother (Steinmetz 1988).

Support for parents-in-law can also take place in the form of co-residence. Again, the stronger kinship tie of women appears to dictate a greater number of mothers living with daughters and sons-in-law than with sons and daughters-in-law. Social class has also been observed to be associated with different patterns of support. There is a greater flow of financial aid from middle-class children to parents and parents-in-law than is true of working-class families, but a greater flow of service and co-residence among the working class.

The requirement of a third party as a defining factor for an in-law relationship makes these relationships uniquely vulnerable to dissolution when the marriage of the third party is dissolved owing to divorce or death. Recently, attention has been given to the in-law relationship under such conditions. Along with gender differences, the presence or absence of children from the dissolved marriage appears to influence the continuance of in-law relationships. Johnson (1989) argues that once a marriage has produced offspring, in-laws become affinal relatives who are defined not only by the order of law, but also by their recognition of a biological linkage to the child. Thus, when the legal basis of the relationship is dissolved, there remains a relationship based on common biological linkage. It is this tie, combined with the tendency in Western culture for mothers rather than fathers to retain custody of the children after a divorce, that appears to influence in-law relationships after divorce. Overall, research has established that divorce decreases in-law contact and support to various degrees, but the extent of these decreases differs by gender and the presence or absence of grandchildren. There is more interaction and support given between divorced women and their former in-laws than between divorced men and their ex-in-laws. (Goetting 1990; Johnson 1989). It has been suggested that this greater contact may be motivated by the desires of grandparents to maintain access to grandchildren. Not only do maternal grandparents have less contact with ex-sons-in-law than do paternal grandparents with ex-daughters-in-law, but the extent of contact between the paternal grandparents and ex-daughters-in-law tends to diminish over time as grandchildren grow and their needs diminish (Johnson 1989).

Conclusions are conflicting regarding the impact on in-law relationships of death of the third party who serves as the connector. In her pioneering study of widows, Lopata (1970) concluded that most widows received little help from their in-laws after the death of their spouse. In contrast, more recent studies (Anderson 1984; Townsend and Poulschock 1986) suggest that widowhood may lead to an expansion of an individual's support network to include in-laws as confidants and sources of help in times of personal crisis.

In summary, in-law relationships are perhaps the kin relationships most subject to voluntary definitions and individual interpretations. Most often, "in-laws serve as a reservoir of supplemental resources to be tapped as social norms dictate and practicalities allow" (Goetting 1990, p. 86). It must be stressed, however, that research focused on in-law relationships has been limited and the patterns reported here apply mainly to mainstream American culture. Although variation by social class has been observed and reported by some researchers, other demographic factors have been virtually ignored. Future research needs to address variations associated with ethnicity, regional residence, and urban and rural populations.

(SEE ALSO: *American Families; Intergenerational Relations; Kinship Systems and Family Types)*

REFERENCES

Adams, B. N. 1964 "Structural Factors Affecting Parental Aid to Married Children." *Journal of Marriage and the Family* 26 (3):327–331.

Anderson, T. B. 1984 "Widowhood as a Life Transition: Its Impact on Kinship Ties." *Journal of Marriage and the Family* 46 (1):105–114.

Brody, E. M., and C. B. Schoonover 1988 "Patterns of Parent-Care when Adult Daughters Work and When They Do Not." *Gerontologist* 5:372–381.

Finch, J. 1989 *Family Obligations and Social Change.* Cambridge: Polity Press.

Fischer, L. R. 1983 "Mothers and Mothers-in-law." *Journal of Marriage and the Family* 45 (1):187–192.

Goetting, A. 1990 "Patterns of Support among In-laws in the United States: A Review of Research." *Journal of Family Issues* 11 (1):67–90.

Johnson, C. L. 1989 "In-law Relationships in the American Kinship System: The Impact of Divorce and Remarriage." *American Ethnologist* 16 (1):87–99.

Lopata, H. Z. 1970 "The Social Involvement of Widows." *American Behavioral Scientist* 14:4–57.

Schneider, D. 1968 *American Kinship: A Cultural Account.* Englewood Cliffs, N.J.: Prentice-Hall.

Schorr, A. L. 1980 *Thy Father and Thy Mother . . . A Second Look at Filial Responsibility and Family.* Publication No. 13–1195. Washington, D.C.: U.S. Government Printing Office.

Spicer, J. A. C. Hempe 1975 "Kinship Interaction after Divorce." *Journal of Marriage and the Family* 37:113–119.

Steinmetz, S. K. 1988 *Duty Bound: Elder Abuse and Family Care.* Newbury Park, Calif.: Sage.

Townsend, A. L., and S. W. Poulshock 1986 "International Perspectives on Impaired Elder's Support Networks." *Journal of Gerontology* 41 (1):101–109.

Wolfram, S. 1987 *In-Laws and Out-Laws: Kinship and Marriage in England.* London: Croom Helm.

RHONDA J. V. MONTGOMERY

INSTITUTIONS *See* American Society.

INTEGRATION *See Segregation and Desegregation.*

INTELLECTUALS Modern societies face a growing dilemma posed by the fact that key institutions and their elites are increasingly dependent upon intellectuals, particularly those in universities, research institutes, and the cultural apparatus generally. Yet, the leaders in these same social units are among the major critics of the way in which the society operates, sometimes calling into question the legitimacy of the social order and its political structure. A ruling elite, even one that is conservative and anti-intellectual, cannot respond to such challenges by crushing the intellectuals, unless it is willing to incur the punitive costs which such suppression entails. As the Polish "revisionist" philosopher Leszek Kolakowski (1968, p. 179) wrote while still a member of the Communist party, "the spiritual domination of any ruling class over the people . . . depends on its bonds with the intelligentsia . . . ; for the less one is capable of ruling by intellectual means, the more one must resort to the instruments of force." Decades earlier, the classically liberal (laissez-faire) economist and sociologist Joseph Schumpeter (1962, p. 150) argued that under capitalism the dominant economic class must protect the intellectuals, "however strongly disapproving" they are of them, because they cannot suppress intellectual criticism without initiating a process of repression which will undermine their own freedom.

The word *intellectual* is fraught with ambiguities. The meanings attached to it are diverse (Lipset and Dobson 1972, pp. 137–140). In the loosest sense in which the word is used in common parlance today, intellectuals may be said to be all those who are considered proficient in and are actively engaged in the creation, distribution, and application of culture. Edward Shils (1968, p. 179) has suggested a comprehensive definition: "Intellectuals are the aggregate of persons in any society who employ in their communication and expression, with relative higher frequency than most other members of their society, symbols of general scope and abstract reference, concerning man, society, nature and the cosmos." For analytic purposes, however, it is desirable to distinguish between several types. It is particularly useful to emphasize the much smaller category of "creative intellectuals," whose principal focus is on innovation, the elaboration of knowledge, art, and symbolic formulations generally. Included in this group are scholars, scientists, philosophers, artists, authors, some editors, and some journalists, as distinguished from the more marginally intellectual groups who distribute culture, such as most teachers, clerics, journalists, engineers, free professionals, and performers in the arts, as well as those who apply knowledge in the course of their work, such as practicing physicians, lawyers, and engineers. To differentiate them from the intellectuals, they may be categorized as the *intelligentsia.*

The creative intellectuals are the most dynamic group within the broad stratum: Because they are innovative, they are at the forefront in the development of culture. The intelligentsia are dependent upon them for the ideational resources they use in their work. Much of the analytic literature dealing with intellectuals has emphasized their seemingly inherent tendency to criticize existing institutions from the vantage point of general conceptions of the desirable, ideal conceptions which are thought to be universally applicable. Thus, Joseph Schumpeter (1950, p. 147) stressed that "one of the touches that distinguish [intellectuals] . . . from other people . . . is the critical attitude." Raymond Aron (1962, p. 210) argued that "the tendency to criticize the established order is, so to speak, the occupational disease of the intellectuals." Richard Hofstadter (1963, p. 38) noted: "The modern idea of the intellectual as constituting a class, as a separate social force, even the term *intellectual* itself, is identified with the idea of political and moral protest." Lewis Coser (1970, p. viii) in defining the term stated: "Intellectuals are men who never seem satisfied with things as they are. . . . They question the truth of the moment in higher and wider truth."

These concerns are iterated by the fact that "intelligentsia" and "intellectuals," the two words most commonly used to describe those in occupations requiring trained or imaginative intelligence, were used first in the context of describing those engaged in oppositional activities. "Intelligentsia," first began to be used widely in Russia in the 1860s, referring to the opposition to the system by the educated strata. It was generally defined as "a 'class' held together by the bond of 'consciousness,' 'critical thought,' or 'moral passion'." (Malia 1961 p. 5) "Intellectual" as a noun first secured wide usage in France during the infamous Dreyfus case in 1898. A protest against Dreyfus's unjust imprisonment (after a biased court-martial), signed by a variety of writers and professors, was published as the "Manifesto of the Intellectuals." The anti-Dreyfusards then tried to satirize their opponents as the self-proclaimed "intellectuals" (Bodin 1962, pp. 6–9; Hofstadter 1963, pp. 38–39). The term was picked up in the United States in the context of characterizing opponents to World War I.

The American intellectual also has been seen as a source of unrest. Many have called attention to this phenomenon, seeing it as a continuing one in American history (May 1963; Hayek 1949, pp. 417–433). Richard Hofstadter (1965, pp. 111–112) described their stance of alienation as "historical and traditional," and pointed out that "even the genteel, established intellectuals of the mid-nineteenth century were in effect patrician rebels against the increasing industrialization and the philistinism of the country. So that it has been the tradition of American intellectuals of all kinds and stamps to find themselves at odds with American society: this, I think, to a degree that is unusual elsewhere." A century ago, Whitelaw Reid (1873, pp. 613–614), the editor of the *New York Tribune,* pointed to the role of the American "Scholar in Politics" as a foe of the "established," and a leader of the "radicals."

The reader should not get the impression that intellectual and student involvement in protest is confined to left-wing or progressive movements. This is not true, as witnessed, for example, by the intellectuals and students who constituted a core segment of activist support for the Fascist party of Mussolini, and of the National Socialist party of Hitler, before they took power, as well as among fascist and assorted anti-Semitic right-wing extreme groups in France and various countries in Eastern Europe up to World War II (Hamilton 1971; Röpke 1960, pp. 346–347). In Eastern Europe and the Soviet Union, intellectuals have been in the forefront of the struggles against Communist regimes, behavior that is perceived as left, i.e. opposition to statism, authoritarianism, and severe stratification.

In the United States, although scattered groups of right-wing intellectuals have emerged at times, the record seems to validate Richard Hofstadter's (1963, p. 39) generalization that for almost all of this century the political weight of American intellectuals has been on the progressive, liberal, and leftist side. Quantitative data derived from attitude surveys, the earliest dating back to before World War I, plus assorted other reports of the political orientations of the American professoriate, down to the present, strongly indicate that American intellectuals have consistently leaned in this direction (Lipset and Dobson 1972, pp. 211–289; Lipset 1991). This bias, to a considerable extent, reflects the absence or weakness of a legitimate national conservative tradition in America. National identity and national ideology are linked to a value system that emphasizes egalitarianism and populism, stemming from an elaboration of principles enunciated in the Declaration of Independence. Thus, when American intellectuals point up the gap between the real and the ideal, whether the latter is represented by what was in a bygone Jeffersonian laissez-faire era (a utopia of equal yeoman farmers) or what it should be (a classless participatory future), they challenge the system for not fulfilling the ideals implicit in the American Creed.

Still, the argument is frequently made that inherent in the structural changes since World War II, which have been described as leading to a "postindustrial society," has been a growing interdependence between political authority and intellectualdom, which should have reduced the critical stance. Modern developed socioeconomic systems are highly dependent on superior research and development resources, which mean better support for universities, and research centers, and the much larger component of persons who have passed through the higher education system—thus creating a mass, high-culture market that pays for the institutions and products of the artistic community (Bell 1973). Governments are increasingly a major source of financing for intellectualdom, ranging from artists to scientists. Recognition and financial rewards from the polity conceivably should help to reduce the historic tensions and the intellectual's sense of being an outsider. A further trend pressing in this direction is the fact that the complexities involved in "running" an advanced industrial or postindustrial society forces laymen, both political and economic leaders, to seek advice in depth from, to defer to, the scholarly-scientific community (Dahl 1989, pp. 334–335; Gagnon 1987). Many, therefore, have seen these trends as fostering the role of the intellectual as participant, as leading to the "interpenetration" of scholarship and policy (Shils 1968; Brint 1991).

These developments, however, have not led to the decline in the critical role of the intellectual in the United States, although patterns elsewhere appear somewhat different (Lerner, Nagai, and Rothman 1990, p. 26). A number of analyses of different American scholarly disciplines have emphasized the significant presence of political radicals among them and their greater alienation from the powers than in Western European societies

(Lipset 1991). In seeking to explain this trans-Atlantic difference, a Swedish scholar, Ron Eyerman (1990) notes that unlike the situation in America, Swedish (and I would add European) intellectuals are not an "alienated stratum" opposed to the state "because the avant-garde tradition was absorbed through a reformism [that] put intellectual labor to use in service of society," that is, largely through the labor and socialist movements. While the overwhelming majority of American intellectuals view themselves as outsiders, and have had little experience in directly influencing power that could moderate their sense of alienation, many European intellectuals have worked in a somewhat more integrated context. And most are, it should be noted, still on the left politically, though less radical relative to their national spectrums than their American counterparts.

The dilemma remains for intellectuals everywhere of how to obtain the resources necessary to pursue creative activity without "selling out," without tailoring creative and intellectual work to the demands of employer, patron, or consumer. In modern times in the West, the emphasis on originality, on innovation, and on following the logic of development in various creative fields—be they painting, music, literature, physics, or sociology—has been responsible for a recurrent conflict between intellectuals and those who pay for their works or exert control through the state, churches, businesses, the market, or other institutions. Intellectuals have often felt themselves to be dependent on philistines while wanting to do whatever they liked according to the norms of their field.

Much of the discussion has focused on the tensions created for unattached intellectuals. It has been asserted "that free-lance intellectuals are more receptive to political extremism than are other types of intellectuals . . . [since] the free-lance intellectual . . . has been dependent on an anonymous and unpredictable market. . . . Rewards are much less certain to be forthcoming for the free-lance intellectual, the form of reward less predictable, and the permanence of the recognition more tenuous. . . . [They] tend to be more dependent on their audience, over which they have relatively little control, and to feel greater social distance from it (Kornhauser 1959, pp. 186–187)."

To understand the continued anti-establishment emphasis of intellectuals, even when well rewarded, it is important to recognize the relationship of this emphasis to their concern for creativity or innovation. The capacity for criticism, for rejection of the status quo, is not simply a matter of preference by some intellectuals. Rather, it is built into the very nature of their occupational role. The distinction between integrative and innovative roles implies that those intelligentsia involved in the former, like teachers, engineers, and exponents of mass culture, use ideas—scholarly findings—to carry out their jobs; those in the latter activities, like scholars, poets, and scientists, are concerned with the creation of *new* knowledge, *new* ideas, *new* art. To a considerable extent, in such endeavors, one is much more rewarded for being original than for being correct—an important fact, a crucial aspect of the role insofar as we consider that such intellectuals tend to be socially critical.

(SEE ALSO: *Postindustrial Society*)

REFERENCES

Aron, Raymond 1962 *The Opium of the Intellectuals.* New York: Norton.

Bell, Daniel 1973 *The Coming of Post-Industrial Society.* New York: Basic Books.

Bodin, Louis 1962 *Les Intellectuels.* Paris: Presses Universitaires de France.

Brint, Stephen 1991 "The Powers of the Intellectuals." In William Julius Wilson, ed., *Sociology and the Public Agenda.*

Coser, Lewis 1970 *Men of Ideas.* New York: The Free Press.

Dahl, Robert A. 1989 *Democracy and Its Critics.* New Haven: Yale University Press.

Eyerman, Ron 1990 "Intellectuals and the State: A Framework for Analysis; with special reference for the United States and Sweden." Unpublished paper, Department of Sociology, University of Lund, Sweden.

Gagnon, Alain (ed.) 1987 *Intellectuals in Liberal Democ-*

racies: Political Influence and Social Involvement. Westport, Conn.: Greenwood Press.

Hamilton, Alastair 1971 *The Appeal of Fascism: A Study of Intellectuals and Fascism, 1919–1945.* London: Anthony Blond.

Hofstadter, Richard 1963 *Anti-Intellectualism in American Life.* New York: Alfred A. Knopf.

——— 1965 "Discussion." In A. Alvarez, ed., *Under Pressure.* Baltimore: Penguin Books.

Kolakowski, Leszek 1968 *Marxism and Beyond.* London: Pall Mall Press.

Kornhauser, William 1959 *The Politics of Mass Society.* New York: Free Press.

Lerner, Robert, Althea K. Nagai, and Stanley Rothman 1990 "Elite Dissensus and Its Origins," *Journal of Political and Military Sociology* 18 (Summer): 25–39.

Lipset, Seymour Martin 1991 "No Third Way: A Comparative Perspective on the Left." In Daniel Chirot, ed., *The End of Leninism and the Decline of the Left.* Seattle: University of Washington Press.

———, and Richard Dobson 1972 "The Intellectual as Critic and Rebel: With Special Reference to the United States and the Soviet Union." *Daedalus* 101 (Summer 1971):137–198.

Malia, Martin 1961 "What is the Intelligentsia?" In Richard Pipes, ed., *The Russian Intelligentsia.* New York: Columbia University Press.

May, Henry 1963 *The Discontent of the Intellectuals.* Chicago: Rand McNally.

Reid, Whitelaw 1873 "The Scholar in Politics." *Scribner's Monthly,* vol. 6.

Röpke, Wilhelm 1960, "National Socialism and the Intellectuals." In George B. de Huszar, ed., *The Intellectuals.* New York: Free Press.

Schumpeter, Joseph 1950 *Capitalism, Socialism and Democracy.* New York: Harper Torchbooks.

Shils, Edward 1968 "Intellectuals." In David L. Sills, ed. *International Encyclopedia of the Social Sciences,* vol. 7. New York: Macmillan and Free Press.

SEYMOUR MARTIN LIPSET

INTELLIGENCE Intelligence is a hypothetical concept, or latent variable, on which individuals differ or vary from each other. The concept of intelligence is not itself directly observable or measurable. Intelligence, an abstract continuum, is distinct from its nonabstract presumed indicators or measures; "intelligence" (concept) is distinct from "intelligence test" (indicator). The accuracy of the indicator—that is, its validity and reliability—is a matter of how accurately it measures observable phenomena presumed to reflect differing amounts of intelligence. The IQ or "intelligence quotient" is thus an operational, observable, presumed indicator of the concept, intelligence, and not the concept itself.

Various definitions of intelligence have appeared since the idea of a unitary coordinating "mental" faculty was used by the ancient Greek philosophers. The principal formulation of the modern notion of intelligence as some kind of mental capacity began in 1850 with Herbert Spencer and Sir Francis Galton. Since then, definitions of intelligence have varied but generally involve a notion of "potential," "ability," or "capacity" as distinct from actual achievement, attainment, or accomplishment. It is a cognitive disposition as distinct from an affect or emotion. Researchers have defined intelligence as "the ability to carry on abstract thinking" (Terman 1916, inventor in 1916 of the still popular Stanford–Binet IQ test); "innate general cognitive ability" (Burt 1972); and "the ability to adapt to the environment" (Thorndike 1905). Some have distinguished two kinds or "dimensions" of intelligence: certain given characteristics of the individual's nervous system (called "fluid" intelligence by R. B. Cattell) versus intelligence acquired through learning, experience, education, and social environment (called "crystallized" intelligence by Cattell).

The development of psychological testing for intelligence began in the early 1900s with A. Binet in France, who invented the notion of IQ as the ratio (quotient) of mental age to chronological age; J. M. Cattell in the United States; and C. Spearman and C. L. Burt in England. This inaugurated the continuing controversy of whether intelligence is reducible to some common set of highly correlated abilities or capacities (the unidimensional theory) or whether it is a matter of several, or many, relatively uncorrelated or independent (nonoverlapping) abilities or capacities (the multidimensional theory).

MEASUREMENT

Measurement accuracy—or, conversely, measurement error—is the degree to which presumed indicators of intelligence (intelligence tests such as the Stanford-Binet or the Wechsler Adult Intelligence Scales [WAIS], or the "ability" portion, as distinct from the achievement sections, of the popular Scholastic Aptitude Test [SAT]) accurately reflect or measure the extent to which an individual possesses intellectual ability. The degree of measurement accuracy is called the validity and reliability of the indicator(s). Validity is the degree to which the score on an indicator reflects the unknown, unobserved score on the concept "intelligence." Reliability refers to the stability or consistency of an indicator across, for example, different times (test–retest reliability), different forms or wordings of the same test (equivalent forms reliability), or different researchers. Hence, measurement accuracy (and its complement, measurement error) is the relationship or "epistemic" correlation between indicator and concept. Since the true score on the concept is not directly observable or measurable, validity is assessed indirectly, as by observing the relationships among several presumed indicators themselves.

A closely allied issue of measurement is whether the concept intelligence is unidimensional or multidimensional. In 1904 Spearman maintained that there was a statistical dimension or factor (called simply *g*) for "general intelligence," and that this factor accounted for, and correlated very highly with, specific separate abilities or performances on tests. This view—that intelligence is fundamentally reducible to one basic, though general, master capacity—is still somewhat popular today. This would mean that persons who score high on one type of ability (say, mathematics) would tend to score high on certain other abilities as well (such as reading comprehension, vocabulary, verbal analogies, and so on); and that persons who score low on one ability would also tend to score low on others. In fact, modern-day factor analysis, a set of techniques for assessing the extent to which many indicators may be parsimoniously accounted for by their relationship to (correlations with) a fewer number of variables called factors, began with Spearman's analyses.

This unidimensional formulation was challenged by L. L. Thurstone's multidimensional principle, which argued that intelligence consists of six or seven largely uncorrelated or nonoverlapping skills or capacities, called "primary abilities," such as spatial, quantitative, verbal, and inductive. Today, the multidimensional view of intelligence predominates over the strict unidimensional view, and it is argued that intelligence probably reflects both some unidimensionality as well as quite a bit of multidimensionality.

From 1960 to about 1975, important contributions to the multidimensional view were made by J. P. Guilford, who theorized that intelligence was so multidimensional that it could be broken down into as many as 120 specific abilities. A number of these abilities encompass what has come to be called creative intelligence. While the unidimensional view stressed individual abilities at inductive and also deductive reasoning, creative intelligence stresses "divergent" reasoning, or the ability to draw new and unanticipated conclusions or inferences. Debates in the professional literature now center on the question of whether creativity is a separate trait itself or whether it bears some relationship or overlap to unidimensional general intelligence. Some studies have shown significant correlation or overlap between general intelligence and creativity; others have shown little or no overlap and have concluded that the two are quite independent. It has been noted, however, that while measures of general intelligence correlate moderately to strongly with creativity for individuals in the low to normal ranges on both, the two types of abilities differ markedly and are virtually independent at the extreme upper ranges, namely among uniquely gifted individuals. Finally, a recent multidimensional formulation is that of H. Gardner, who posits seven independent abilities: logical–mathematical, linguistic, spatial, musical, interpersonal, intrapersonal, and body-kinesthetic.

Reliability of measures of intelligence have been assessed mainly by examining how stable one's intelligence scores for different types of abilities remain as a function of increasing age. Most studies show moderate to high correlations (of about 0.70) between IQ at age five and IQ during the late teenage years. The famous and long-term (forty-year) "studies of genius" by Terman, carried out on a large sample (1,528 persons initially) from the mid-1920s through the mid-1960s, demonstrated that high-IQ individuals consistently remain high in IQ from childhood right on through the retirement years. Other studies show only slightly less stability over such long periods of time for individuals who are in the normal (90–110) IQ range. Finally, studies of problem-solving ability show that it tends to decline relatively little before old age but that the speed of solving unfamiliar problems tends to decline with age.

Attempts to alter or increase IQ by means of specific coaching or environment-manipulation programs have met with some limited success. In general, such attempts to increase IQ are more successful for individuals in the normal ranges of IQ than for individuals who score either very high or very low in IQ. Programs geared to specific abilities (as increasing math skills) are more likely to result in an increase in that particular ability rather than in other abilities not addressed by the program. Recent evidence shows that such attempts to increase IQ among black and Hispanic youths can result in gains of up to 20 IQ points and that such gains do persist at least for several years. Finally, studies of the effect of coaching to increase SAT scores show that after removing the effect of test experience—that is, subtracting out the average difference between first and subsequent test scores for matched control, individuals who have not had an intervening coaching seminar—(most people score higher the second time they take the SAT than on their first attempt), some increase in SAT scores results, depending on the length and type of coaching program. There is no evidence that coaching has differing effects on males versus females, or upon white, black, or Asian groups.

Validity of measures of intelligence has been most often assessed through what is called predictive, or criterion, validation—finding the degree of relationship (size and direction of correlation and of slope) between some measure of intelligence, taken at one point in time, and some other "criterion" measure taken later, such as grades obtained later on in college or the type of occupation chosen after graduation. The higher the correlation or slope or both between test score and criterion, the higher the predictive validity of the test.

In general, studies show that predictive validity is better at the extremes (for those scoring either very high or very low on the test) than for individuals within the normal range. Oden's forty-year follow-up analysis of the Terman gifted group showed that individuals scoring 140 or higher on the Stanford-Binet IQ test when they were in their teens were 40 years later disproportionately more likely to have graduated from college (71 percent of the males and 67 percent of the females in the sample had graduated from college, with 40 percent and 24 percent respectively having gotten advanced graduate or professional degrees). Similarly, high proportions of both men (47 percent) and women (64 percent) became professionals. These predictions were not perfect, however. A small percentage of individuals dropped out of high school or college; some were unsuccessful at their chosen profession or remained unemployed; and a few committed suicide. These numbers were small. The entire sample was white, largely of middle class origins, and from urban California. Thus, no conclusions can be drawn regarding race, socioeconomic, or regional differences.

GROUP AND CULTURAL DIFFERENCES

Predictive validity has been assessed in many studies for different racial and ethnic groups (white, black, Hispanic, Asian). It is generally found that whites tend to score *on the average* about one standard deviation higher than blacks and Hispanics on IQ tests (about 15 IQ points higher) and on ability tests such as the SAT (about 50 to 100 SAT points higher, on a scale of 200 to 800). Since the 1980s, Asians have scored on the average slightly higher than or the same as whites on the quantitative portions of such tests, and either the same as or somewhat lower than whites on the verbal portions.

These average differences are regarded as being environmental in origin, reflecting group differences in education, socioeconomic status, childhood socialization, language, nutrition, and cultural advantages. There is no evidence whatever that such *between-group* differences are in any way genetic in origin. (*Within-group* differences in IQ that may be genetic in origin are discussed below under "Nature versus Nurture.")

Average differences in test scores reflect not only differences in social environment, but they may reflect lack of equivalence between groups in the predictive validities of the test. A test may be more predictively valid for one group than for another; namely, a test may have less measurement error for one group than for another. This is determined by assessing the relationship between the test score (*X*) at one point in time and some criterion measure (*Y*) such as college grades at a later point in time for the two groups being compared. Equivalent slopes and correlations for two groups would be interpreted as equal predictive validity for the two groups. Higher correlation or slope means higher predictive validity; lower correlation or slope means lower predictive validity. Different slopes or correlations for two groups would be evidence that the test (*X*) is not as valid for one group as for the other and that the test does not predict as well for one group as for the other.

A large number of studies show roughly equivalent test-to-grade predictions for whites and blacks. Such studies show that test scores and grades are moderately correlated for whites, correlating in some studies as low as 0.15 and in other studies up to about 0.60, with an average correlation of about 0.35, and with the correlations for blacks falling in the same range. This evidence suggests that one can, to a modest extent, predict later grades (such as first-year college grades) from ability test scores (SAT scores) and that these predictions are roughly the same for whites and blacks.

However, a significant number of studies (about one-fourth of those done) show some differences in either slope or correlation or both for whites compared to blacks and Hispanics, with the slopes and correlations being greater for whites, with blacks and Hispanics being roughly the same. This means that, at least for these studies, the test is less predictively valid for blacks and Hispanics than for whites. This is evidence for relatively more measurement error (thus measurement bias) in the case of blacks and Hispanics. Considerably less data are available on Asians; some studies show equal predictive validities, a few show less, and very few show slightly higher predictive validities for some Asian groups.

Apart from the question of validity, average differences in the test score itself exist on the basis of race and ethnicity, of socioeconomic status (social class and the linguistic and cultural differences associated with class differences), and of gender.

In almost every multiracial nation in the world, race differences are strongly confounded with social class differences. Thus, it is difficult to separate the effects of race on IQ from the effects of social class. In studies of race differences in intelligence in countries where white culture is the dominant culture, as in the United States, it has been consistently found that groups classified as Negro, black, or colored are disproportionately represented among the lower classes, and they also score lower on intelligence tests than those classified as white. These are *average* differences, as the distributions of scores for the two groups overlap considerably. In most cases, individuals were tested by white examiners, and there is evidence that one performs somewhat better on a test when examiner and examinee are of the same race.

In the United States, studies over the years have consistently found that Northern blacks, on average, score higher on IQ tests than Southern blacks. In some cases Northern blacks have scored higher, on average, than Southern whites. These differences reflect the differences in both socioeconomic status as well as region. Comparing whites and blacks of the same socioeconomic status and the same region lessens their average differences in IQ scores considerably. The differences between blacks and whites are further reduced when linguistic and cultural biases are removed from the tests. Similar findings are obtained in comparisons of whites and Hispanics. With regard to the relative effects of race versus class, in studies in which children of different races have been matched by socioeconomic status of their families (by parental occupation, education, income, and neighborhood), social class shows a stronger relative effect than race. Thus, average differences in IQ by class for individuals of the same race exceed average differences by race for individuals of the same social class.

Gender differences in intelligence, like race differences, are confounded by the differences in social status that men and women occupy in society. In all known societies, gender is correlated with social status; in the vast majority of societies and particularly the United States, women have been traditionally forced to occupy lower average social and economic status than men. Hence, like the minority-to-white comparison, the female-to-male comparison reveals some differences in IQ, with females scoring less on abilities defined as valuable (such as quantitative ability) by society. It used to be thought that the variability in IQ scores is greater among men than among women, with proportionately more men than women in both the gifted as well as the severely retarded range. More recent studies have shown this not to be the case and that with adequate sampling designs (absent in many past studies) the extremes of the distribution are equal for males and for females, as are the middle ranges. While recent studies show average IQ scores to be roughly equal for males and females, differences do arise on specific abilities: Men score higher, on average, in numerical reasoning, gross motor skills, spatial perception, and mechanical aptitude; women score higher, on average, in perception of detail, verbal facility, and memory. These average differences may reflect differences between the sexes in childhood socialization and differences in societal expectations or norms pertaining to men and women. Finally, there is some limited evidence that sex-typing (gender bias) in certain test questions, even in the quantitative sections, is present and thus may account for a portion of the gender difference.

NATURE VERSUS NURTURE

Since the mid-nineteenth century a controversy has raged in the social, behavioral, and natural sciences: Are human differences in intelligence influenced more by biological heredity (nature), by social environment (nurture), or primarily by combinations (interactions) of both? The contemporary approach to the issue has been to attempt to estimate empirically what is called the broad heritability coefficent (h^2), defined as the proportion of the total differences (total variance) in intelligence in a population that is causally attributable to genetic factors. Equivalently, it is the proportion of variance in intelligence that is accounted for by the genetic similarity between pairs of biological relatives. Consequently, if heritability in a population is 30 percent, then statistically speaking 30 percent of the differences in intelligence among individuals in that population are due to genetic factors, assuming that intelligence is validly and reliably measured. A 30 percent heritability would mean that 70 percent of the differences in intelligence in the population would be due to environment or to combinations or interactions, or to the covariance, of genes and environment.

The environment includes a large range of variables such as education, social class, cultural advantages or disadvantages, childhood socialization, nutrition, and many others. The heritability coefficient is not a characteristic of a single individual but of a specific population being studied at the time. Virtually all heritability estimates to date are based on white populations. The heritability estimate is not generalizable from one population to another; thus, for example, heritability estimates on whites cannot be generalized to blacks or any other racial or ethnic group. Nor can the heritability coefficient be used to draw conclusions about between-group average differences. Heritability has been variously estimated to be as low as 20 percent and as high as 80 percent, depending on the methodological accuracy of the study, the statistical assumptions used, types of biological relatives studied, and a host of other things. Some argue convincingly that heritability is impossible to estimate in any reliable way. The most recent reliable studies tend to center on a heritability of 40 to 50 percent.

How then is the heritability of intelligence actually calculated or estimated? One must first assume that IQ score validly measures intelligence, a conclusion that, as already noted, is subject to controversy. Assuming that IQ score measures at least some aspects of intelligence validly, then heritability is estimated by comparing pairs of individuals of varying degrees of biological relatedness: If any pair of individuals who are biologically related to each other are also similar in IQ, and if individuals who are more highly related biologically are also more similar in IQ, then, assuming equal environmental similarities for the different types of pairs, genes are hypothesized to be a cause of their IQ similarity.

Identical (monozygotic) twins are genetically identical to each other; they are genetic clones of one another. It is noted that identical twins raised together in the same family are very similar in IQ and in other traits suspected of high genetic causation, such as height. Their average IQ pair correlation is about 0.90, which is very high. This correlation reflects both their genetic similarity and their environmental similarity, since they were raised together. Pairs of fraternal (dizygotic) twins are less related biologically and, like ordinary brothers and sisters, share on the average half of their genes in common. Their similarity in IQ is about 0.60 in correlation. Ordinary siblings (brothers and sisters) correlate about 0.50 in their IQs, thus showing the effects of their lower environmental similarity in relation to the fraternal twin pairs. Pairs of first cousins are even less in biological overlap, and they correlate still less in IQ, at about 0.15. Finally, pairs of unrelated individuals picked at random do not correlate at all in IQ (the pair correlation is zero). In general, then, the closer the biological overlap of pairs of persons, the more similar they are in IQ, thus suggesting that genetic similarity is at least partly responsible for the similarity in IQ.

Such comparisons, however, do not rule out the effect of environment. Identical twin pairs raised together have very similar environments in addition to their identical genes; thus, environmental similarity could also be a cause of their similarity in IQ. By similar reasoning, fraternal twins are less similar to each other genetically, but also less similar environmentally, than are identical twin pairs. For example, it has been shown that fraternal twin pairs are less likely to play together, study together, and are treated less similarly by parents and teachers, than are identical twin pairs. Hence, the lower environmental similarity could be a cause of their lower similarity in IQ. Consequently, the effects of both genetic similarity and environmental similarity are confounded and entangled in such comparisons.

There have been four procedures used to attempt to disentangle the effects of environmental similarity from the effects of genetic similarity for pairs of relatives. The first of these is widely regarded as the best single–kinship procedure for estimating heritability: the study of identical twins who have been raised separately. In such instances, if the twins were separated virtually at birth (because of the death of a parent or other family problems) and raised in randomly differing environments and scattered over a wide range of environments, then any remaining similarity in their IQs would be caused genetically, since all they have in common would be their genes (and since the effects of prenatal environment are assumed to be slight). Also, with these givens, the magnitude of the resulting IQ correlation is a direct estimate of the magnitude of the heritability of IQ.

Given the extreme rarity of separated identical twins, there have been only four studies to date of pairs of separated identical twins (Newman, Freeman, and Holzinger 1937; Bouchard et al. 1990; Shields 1962; Juel-Nielsen 1965; a fifth study, Burt 1957, 1972 has been thoroughly discredited as having fabricated and falsified data on twins). These studies find the IQ similarity (correlation) of separated twins to be between 0.62 and 0.77. This would suggest strong genetic causation for the IQ similarity.

Methodological critics, however, discovered that quite a few of the twin pairs in three out of these four studies were not actually raised separately but were instead raised in different branches of the same family, or were separated not at birth but later during the teenage years, or were raised in social environments that were very similar in many respects. In quite a few cases the twins had actually attended the same schools for the same number of years before being tested for IQ. When the truly separated twins are singled out for analysis, their pair correlation, and thus the heritability estimate, falls to 0.30 or 0.40.

The second procedure for estimating IQ heritability, less methodologically pure than studying separated identical twins, is to compare the IQ correlation of identical twins raised together to that for fraternal twins raised together. When this is done, heritability estimates in the range of 0.50 to 0.60 are obtained. For this procedure to be valid, one must assume that identical twins raised together are no more similar in their environments than are fraternal twins raised together, a questionable assumption.

A third procedure is the converse of the first: the study of unrelated pairs of individuals adopted into the same family. Whereas identical twins raised separately provide pairs with perfect genetic similarity and dissimilar environments, the study of adopted unrelated pairs raised together provides us with the study of high similarity in family environment but zero genetic similarity. Hence, any IQ similarity for such pairs is entirely due to environment (and only family environment, not nonfamily environment). Such studies estimate environmental effects to be around 0.30, and thus heritability would be no more than 0.70.

A fourth procedure, the most up to date, called the multikin method, in effect averages the results for many kinships together. The procedure solves algebraically for the value of the heritability coefficient by utilizing an overidentified least-squares solution system for several simultaneous equations, where one equation is stated for each type of kinship (relative) such as identical twins raised together; identical twins apart; fraternal twins together; siblings together; parent-offspring pairs; cousins raised together; pairs of adopted children; and parent-adopted pairs. In such analyses, a number of (often implausible) assumptions must be made, such as zero measurement error, no sample bias, equal (or estimated) environmental similarity, no gene-by-environment interaction, and others. One such analysis found that the best-fitting set of equations yielded a heritability estimate of 0.51. Similar multikin analyses that include a direct estimate of environmental similarity for certain pairs of relatives yield somewhat lower heritability estimates, at about 0.40.

Considering all four methodologies, and granting for the moment all the necessary statistical assumptions (many of which are implausible), a tentative estimate of (broad) heritability of intelligence for Western white populations would be between 0.40 and 0.50, or 40 to 50 percent.

CONCLUSION

How is the study and measurement of intelligence important to sociology and the social sciences? What are the uses of intelligence measurement?

First, the study of intelligence involves a large number of disciplines and fields. For example, the relative effects of nature (genes) and nurture (social environment), and their interaction upon intelligence, is multidisciplinary and is analyzed and debated in the professional literature in biology (particularly population genetics), sociology, psychology, economics, and education.

Second, the history of the measurement of intelligence has been very closely tied to the development of empirical measurement in general in the social and behavioral sciences, and certainly in sociology. Developments in measurement theory, the distinction between concepts and indicators, and the development of techniques to assess validity and reliability of indicators—including recent work in multi-indicator models—has grown partly, though significantly, out of the study of the measurement of intelligence.

Third, among all the subspecialties in the discipline of sociology, the Sociology of Education has probably employed the concept and measurement of intelligence most productively. Intelligence has been used in at least three ways: (1) as an effect (as, when considering the relative effects of nature versus the effects of early home environment, schooling, and other environmental variables); (2) as a cause (a considerable amount of research in the sociology of education has evaluated the effects, or lack thereof, of measured intelligence upon performance in school, upon occupational achievement and earnings in later life, and also upon such phenomena as criminality; (3) as a control variable whose relative effects are analyzed in combination with other variables. For example, an important body of literature in status attainment has shown that when the effects of schooling, intelligence, and home environment upon later occupational achievement are analyzed, then the effects of schooling may be less than the combined effects of intelligence and home environment. Similarly, there are studies that show that the effects of teacher expectations upon student performance in the classroom are present in addition to (but not in place of) the effects of measured intelligence upon performance in the classroom.

(SEE ALSO: *Sex Differences; Socialization*)

REFERENCES

Bouchard, T. J., Jr., and M. McGue 1981 "Familial Studies of Intelligence: A Review." *Science* 212: 1055–1058.

———, et al 1990. "Sources of Human Psychological Differences: The Minnesota Study of Twins Reared Apart." *Science* 250: 223–228.

Burt, C. 1957 "The Relative Influence of Heredity and Environment on Assessments of Intelligence." *British Journal of Statistical Psychology* 10:99–104.

———1972 "Inheritance of General Intelligence." *American Psychologist* 27:175–190.

Chipmer, H. M., M. J. Rovine, and R. Plomin 1990 "LISREL Modeling: Genetic and Environmental Influences on IQ Revisited." *Intelligence* 14:11–29.

Dorfman, D. D. 1978 "The Cyril Burt Question: New Findings." *Science* 201:1177–1186.

Goldberger, A. S. 1978a "Heritability." Social Systems Research Institute, University of Wisconsin, Madison. Typescript. (Revised version of paper presented at Newmarch Lectures in Economic Statistics at University College London, June 6 and 7, 1978.)

———1978b "Pitfalls in the Resolution of IQ Inheritance." In N. E. Morton and C. S. Chung, eds., *Genetic Epidemiology.* New York: Academic Press.

Guilford, J. P. 1968 "The Structure of Intelligence." In D. K. Whitla, ed., *Handbook of Measurement and Assessment in the Behavioral Sciences.* Boston: Addison-Wesley.

Hearnshaw, L. S. 1979 *Cyril Burt, Psychologist.* Ithaca, N.Y.: Cornell University Press.

Jencks, C., et al. 1972 *Inequality: A Reassessment of the Effect of Family and Schooling in America.* New York: Basic Books.

Jensen, A. R. 1967 "Estimation of the Limits of Heritability Traits by Comparison of Monozygotic and Dizygotic Twins." *Proceedings of the National Academy of Sciences* 58:149–156.

———1969 "How Much Can We Boost IQ and Scholastic Achievement?" *Harvard Educational Review* 39:1–123.

———1980 *Bias in Mental Testing.* New York: Free Press.

Juel-Nielsen, N. 1965 "Individual and Environment: A Psychiatric-Psychological Investigation of Monozygous Twins Reared Apart." *Acta Psychiatrica et Neurologica Scandinavica,* Monograph supp. 183.

Kamin, L. J. 1974 *The Science and Politics of IQ.* Potomac, Md.: Lawrence Erlbaum Associates.

Morton, N. E., and C. S. Chung (eds.) 1978 *Genetic Epidemiology.* New York: Academic Press.

———, and D. C. Rao 1978 "Quantitative Inheritance in Man." *Yearbook of Physical Anthropology* 21:12–41.

Newman, H. H., F. N. Freeman, and K. J. Holzinger 1937 *Twins: A Study of Heredity and Environment.* Chicago: University of Chicago Press.

Oden, M. H. 1968 "The Fulfillment of Promise: 40-year Follow-up of the Terman Gifted Group." *Genetic Psychology Monographs* 77:3–93.

Plomin, R., J. C. DeFries, and J. C. Loehlin 1977 "Genotype–Environment Interaction and Correlation in the Analysis of Human Behavior." *Psychological Bulletin* 84:309–322.

Shields, J. 1962 *Monozygotic Twins Brought Up Apart and Brought Up Together.* London: Oxford University Press.

Taylor, H. F. 1980 *The IQ Game: A Methodological Inquiry into the Heredity–Environment Controversy.* New Brunswick, N.J.: Rutgers University Press.

——— 1981 "Biases in *Bias in Mental Testing.*" *Contemporary Sociology* 10:172–174.

——— 1992 "Group Differences and the Methodology of Standardized Testing." In J. H. Stanfield, ed., *Methods in Race and Ethnic Relations Research.* Beverly Hills, Calif.: Sage.

Terman, L. M. 1916 *The Measurement of Intelligence.* Boston: Houghton Mifflin.

Thorndike, E. L. 1905 "Measurement of Twins." *Journal of Philosophy, Psychology, and Scientific Method* 2:547–553.

HOWARD F. TAYLOR

INTERGENERATIONAL RELATIONS

Throughout recorded history, much concern has been expressed about relations among the generations. Historians have identified changing patterns of relationships between the old and the young, pointing out that in some epochs veneration of the aged was common, while in other eras, the aged were more likely to be held up to scorn and ridicule. In contemporary American society, these contrasts are more muted, and themes of both consensus and conflict are present.

Sociologists have explored intergenerational relations extensively, using both macrosociological and microsociological approaches. Scholars who have taken a macrosociological approach have examined the discontinuity caused by the succession of different groups of individuals who were born during the same time period and who therefore age together (Foner 1986). Sociologists refer to such groups as *cohorts.* Many important questions have been raised regarding relations among cohorts, including: How do people differ as a result of membership in a specific cohort? How and why do cohorts come into conflict with one another? Does a "generation gap" exist?

In contrast, sociologists who have taken a microsociological approach have focused on intergenerational relations within families. These scholars have examined the content and quality of relationships among family members in different generations, posing such questions as: How much contact do adult children have with their parents? What kinds of exchanges occur between older and younger generations? What is the role of grandparents in families? Under what circumstances does conflict among the generations in families occur? It is essential to study both levels and to draw connections between them.

MACROSOCIOLOGICAL PERSPECTIVES

Mannheim's View of Generations. Karl Mannheim provided one of the most enduring analyses of relations between cohorts (Mannheim, however, used the term *generation* instead of the contemporary sociological term *cohort,* used here). Mannheim argued that the individuals born into a given cohort experience the same set of sociopolitical events that occur while they are growing up; this sets them off as a special social group. Merely by their location in a given cohort, members will show certain similarities, as they are endowed with "a common location in the historical process" (Mannheim 1952, p. 290).

Thus, position within a cohort—like position within the socioeconomic structure—limits members to a narrow range of possible experiences and predisposes them to characteristic modes of thought. These differences can lead to conflict between the cohorts, as younger cohorts try to impose their views on society. The older cohort, on the other hand, has a major stake in preserving the existing social order. The interaction between these divergent cohort groups, according to Mannheim, is a critically important aspect of human social life.

To be sure, Mannheim did not compare belonging to a cohort with belonging to a more concrete group—such as a family—in that a cohort lacks a clear organizational framework. Further, he noted that there can be differences within cohorts. That is, within the same cohort, subgroups (in Mannheim's terms, *generational units*) can form, and these subgroups differ from each other and may even be antagonistic toward one another. Nevertheless, Mannheim viewed location in a cohort as a powerful influence on people's lives, analogous to class position. This concern with the continual succession of cohorts, and with its effects on social life, has found its clearest contemporary expression in age stratification theory.

Age Stratification Theory. Age stratification theory begins with the fundamental assumption that in order to understand intercohort relations, we need to see society as *stratified* according to age. Consistent with Mannheim, this view holds that society is divided into a hierarchy of socially recognized age strata. Each stratum consists of members who are similar in age and whose behavior is governed by the same set of norms for behavior appropriate for their age group. Further, members of various age strata differ in their abilities to obtain and control social resources. For example, young people in most societies have less power and fewer resources than do middle-aged adults.

The duties, obligations, and privileges associated with age strata vary according to individual attributes, but they are always influenced by the structural aspect of age. Thus, in a society various cohorts may have greatly divergent views on filial responsibility, expectations for independence of children, and other values.

Sociologists see such differences among cohorts as the basis for possible conflict of interest in society. In fact, conflict regarding continuity and discontinuity has been a major theme in macrosociological approaches to relations between age groups. As Bengtson (1989, p. 26) notes, members of the older cohort desire continuity: They want to transmit to younger cohorts "what is best in their own lives." Correspondingly, they fear discontinuity: that young people will choose to live by very different sets of values. What has come to be known as the "problem of generations" reflects "the tension between continuity and change, affirmation and innovation, in the human social order over time" (Bengtson 1989, p. 26).

As an example, an age stratification perspective on intergenerational relations can be applied to the political realm. When the age stratification system is viewed as analogous to other stratification systems (e.g., class or gender), it follows that group solidarity can develop within each age cohort and that conflict—both overt conflict and conflict of interests—may occur between two different cohorts.

On a basic level, members of older and younger cohorts find different political issues more salient; for example, the elderly are more likely to focus on old-age pensions and health benefits, while the young are concerned with issues such as educational loans or the military draft (Riley, Foner, and Waring 1988). Divergences in political ideology among older and younger cohorts have been examined, with the fairly consistent finding that the current aged cohort is generally more conservative than younger cohorts. (However, these cross-sectional differences do not highlight the fact that people change their political attitudes over time, in line with changes in the society as a whole.)

Do divergent interests and attitudes result in age-related collective political action? Sociologists have examined whether the aged constitute a self-defined political group that sets its agenda against those of other age strata. On the whole, it is not clear that a voting block can be organized around old-age interests, as political differences vary greatly within the cohort. Further, the elderly are a heterogeneous group. There are differences in socioeconomic status and racial and ethnic background within the aged cohort. In addition, the interests of the "young-old" (sixty-five to seventy-five) may differ from the "old-old" (over seventy-five), with the former more concerned with retirement issues, income maintenance, and leisure opportunities, and the latter interested more heavily in funding for medical services and long-term care. The overall evidence shows that the aged are willing to act together on some issues (like Social Security) but not on others.

A recent political development, however, may create more polarization among cohorts and thus lead to an upswing in age-based politics. This is the rising concern over "generational equity." Streib and Binstock (1988) have summarized the issue in the following way. The elderly in developed nations were seen as a disadvantaged group from the 1950s to the early 1970s. They were portrayed as having low economic and social status, compared with younger persons. By the late 1970s, however, some scholarly and popular literature began to assert that old people had in fact overbenefited, and the elderly came to be seen as potentially burdensome economically to younger generations.

The older generation has at times been viewed as a scapegoat for a number of problems (Binstock 1983). In particular, the elderly have come to be seen as demanding resources for themselves and thus depriving children of quality schooling, health care, and other services. Organizations have arisen whose goal is to advocate the interests of the young at the expense of the older cohort. These groups have the expressed goal of establishing "generational equity" by transferring resources back to the young.

In the face of such attacks, it is conceivable that the elderly will begin to coalesce into a more unified generational unit. In response to these claims, however, there has developed a countermovement that encourages cooperation among advocates for youth *and* the elderly. On the level of practice, this interest has led to the development of intergenerational programs that bring old and young together.

The macrosociological approach provides important insights into intergenerational relations and has obvious relevance for public policy on aging issues. It is equally critical, however, to examine intergenerational relations on the microsocial level.

MICROSOCIOLOGICAL APPROACHES: A FOCUS ON THE FAMILY

In recent years, many sociologists have focused on the smaller world of the family in an attempt to understand intergenerational relations. The family resembles the larger society in that it is the locus of both intergenerational consensus and conflict. There is considerable family solidarity, indicated by feelings of affection and attachment that result from a shared history and close contact (Bengtson, Rosenthal, and Burton 1988), as well as inequalities of power and social resources. The twin themes of solidarity and conflict are evident throughout sociological research on the topic.

The way in which these themes are worked out in families is affected by dramatic changes in the age structure of American society. In particular, average lifespan has increased, which means that family members will spend more time than ever before occupying intergenerational family roles. Further, increased life expectancy leads to a greater likelihood that families will spend longer periods of time caring for disabled elderly relatives.

Societal changes have also increased the complexity of intergenerational relations. For example, the high divorce rate found in contemporary American society raises the likelihood that adult children will return to their parents' homes, often bringing their own young children with them. Women's unprecedented participation in the labor force and their return to college in great numbers may also affect intergenerational relations. To be sure, the acquisition of these nonfamilial roles provides new and enriching opportunities for women; however, it may alter the time that has traditionally been devoted to "kinkeeping" between the generations.

It is possible to comment on only a few major themes in this review. The most widely studied area is that of parent–child relations in later life, including patterns of intergenerational contact and factors that affect the quality of adult child–elderly parent relationships. Two additional issues are relations with grandparents in the family and the importance of changing dependencies among the generations over the life course.

Contact between Parents and Children. A major concern of researchers has been to understand patterns of contact between adult children and older parents. Research on this issue has gone through two major phases. First, there was a period in which the nuclear family was held to be isolated. This view was based in part on Talcott Parson's analyses of family relations, which held that modernization had brought about the decline of the extended family (DeWit and Frankel 1988). During this period, it was widely believed that because of the geographic mobility of children, families abandoned their elderly relatives. This view also held that most elderly persons rarely saw their children and that family members no longer provided care for older relatives (Shanas 1979).

In the second phase, many prominent researchers devoted considerable effort to demonstrating that this view is inaccurate. Investigators such as Ethel Shanas, Marvin Sussman, and Eugene Litwak, as well as later researchers, clearly established that older persons have frequent contact with family members and that few are totally isolated from kin. Further, most aged family members are involved in a network of emotionally and instrumentally supportive relationships.

A major factor in determining the frequency of contact is physical proximity. Numerous studies have found that the frequency of intergenerational contact is greatly affected by geographical distance between households, with more distant children interacting less often with parents. However, it is clear that many geographically distant children nevertheless continue to interact to a significant degree with parents (DeWit and Frankel 1988). Further, several studies have found that some parents and children are able to maintain close ties despite being separated by great distances. Thus, it appears that distance is only one of several variables that are important in determining the quality of parent–child relationships.

Quality of Parent–Child Relationships. Researchers have moved beyond simply establishing patterns of contact to examining factors that affect the quality of parent–child relations in later life. A number of factors appear to have an impact on relationship quality.

Increased parental dependency is frequently cited as a factor that negatively affects the quality of aged parent–adult child relations. Studies have highlighted imbalanced exchanges and perceptions of inequity between the generations as major causes of family disharmony. For example, several investigations have suggested that an increase in parents' dependence upon their adult children may reduce positive feelings between the generations. Other studies have found that adult children's feelings of closeness and attachment are reduced when parents' health declines. As parents' health deteriorates, adult children are likely to need to increase their levels of support to previously independent parents, as well as to accept a lessening or termination of the parents' provision of support—thus disrupting the previously established flow of support between the generations.

A second factor affecting parent–child relations is *gender*. Studies of the effects of gender consistently demonstrate stronger affectional ties between mothers and daughters than between any other combination (Rossi and Rossi 1990). Mothers report more positive affect with adult daughters than with sons and are more likely to rely on daughters than on sons as confidants and comforters. Daughters in turn report greater feelings of closeness to mothers and are more likely to turn to them as confidants than to fathers.

Third, the *age of the child* affects relationships with parents. Theories of adult development and intergenerational relations lead to the expectation that a child's age will be negatively related to parent–child conflict and positively related to closeness. This literature suggests that maturational changes are likely to reduce differences between parents and adult children, thus minimizing the bases for conflict between them. For example, Bengtson (1979) suggests that, as children mature, their orientations become more similar to those of their parents. Similarly, Hagestad (1987) posits both that differences between parents and children become muted across time and that there is greater tolerance for differences that remain. A variety of empirical findings support these assertions.

Fourth, changes in the degree of *status similarity* between adult children and their parents may affect their relationship. In particular, many studies have found a consistent pattern of increased closeness in intergenerational relations when children begin to share a larger number of adult statuses with their parents (Adams 1968; Young and Willmott 1957). For example, the mother–daughter relationship appears to assume greater importance from the daughters' perspective when they themselves become mothers (Fischer 1986). Conversely, decreases in status similarity may negatively affect adult child–parent relations. For example, the status dissimilarity that develops when daughters surpass their mothers educationally may have particular potential for creating difficulties between the generations (Suitor 1987).

Grandparenthood. In recent years, sociologists have shown increasing interest in studying the role of grandparents in families. The demographic shifts noted above have brought about changes in the nature of grandparenthood in several ways. First, more people now survive to become grandparents than ever before. Second, the entry into grandparenthood is likely to occur in midlife, rather than in old age; thus, the duration of grandparenthood may extend to four decades or more. Third, the role of grandparent is not clearly defined in American society, and the normative expectations, privileges, and obligations are ambiguous (Hagestad 1985).

Studies have uncovered several consistent findings about grandparenthood. Contrary to popular stereotypes, most grandparents do not wish to take on a parental role toward their grandchildren. Rather, they generally prefer a more distant role in the grandchildren's lives. Nevertheless, grandparents are also a critical resource for families in times of trouble, as studies of divorce and teenage parenting make clear (Troll 1985).

Perhaps the most consistent finding in over twenty-five years of research is diversity in grandparenting styles. A number of typologies have been identified that array grandparents along a continuum from intense involvement and assumption of parental responsibilities, on the one hand, to relative alienation from grandchildren on the other (Neugarten and Weinstein 1964).

The most ambitious study to date used a representative survey to examine styles of grandparenting and to uncover factors that determine the adoption of a particular style (Cherlin and Furstenberg 1986). Andrew Cherlin and Frank Furstenberg were able to identify five basic grandparenting styles. *Detached* grandparents have little contact with their grandchildren. *Passive* grandparents visit somewhat more frequently but carefully maintain a distance from their grandchildren's lives. *Supportive* grandparents have more contact and focus on providing services to the grandchildren. *Authoritative* grandparents exert parent-like influence to a relatively great degree. Finally, *influential* grandparents combine involvement both in the provision of services and in adopting a parental role.

Cherlin and Furstenberg found that geographical distance was the most critical factor in determining which style of grandparenting developed. Detached grandparents were much more likely to live far away, while the most involved grandparents lived in close proximity to the grandchildren. Further, grandparents practiced "selective investment" in their grandchildren. They had more intense relationships with some grandchildren and more distant relationships with others. Other studies have affirmed this finding and have also pointed to the importance of gender: Grandmothers tend to have closer relationships with grandchildren than grandfathers do.

Research interest has also highlighted the effects of children's marital disruption on the relationship between grandparents and grandchildren. Despite suggestions in the popular media that relations between grandchildren and grandparents are damaged when adult children divorce, studies have shown that this is not necessarily the case. Cherlin and Furstenberg (1986) found that "custodial grandparents" (that is, those whose adult children were awarded custody of the grandchildren) tended to maintain very close ties with their grandchildren, while "noncustodial grandparents" were less likely to maintain such ties. Since custody of minor children continues to be awarded more frequently to mothers than to fathers, this means that ties with maternal grandparents are more likely to be maintained or strengthened following a divorce, while ties with paternal grandparents are more vulnerable—particularly in terms of frequency of interaction.

Changing Dependencies. Social scientists have convincingly demonstrated that children and parents continue to depend on one another for both emotional and instrumental support throughout the life course (Hill 1970). The literature on intergenerational relations, however, has focused more heavily on children's support to elderly parents than on the reverse. Thus, before turning to a brief discussion of the issue of caregiving to the elderly, it is important to emphasize the *reciprocal* nature of intergenerational assistance.

Sussman (1985) has provided a model of parent–child relations across the lifespan that emphasizes the cyclical shift in relations with parents. In the beginning, parents provide a substantial amount of assistance to their offspring, even into the children's early married life. Then, as children become more independent—and possibly move away—there is a decrease in intergenerational helping. Finally, as elderly parents begin to decline in health, they come to depend more heavily on their children. This cyclical view of support is important in that it stresses patterns of *mutual* aid between the generations (see also Rossi and Rossi 1990). Further, it should be noted that it is usually only very late in the life course that children's provision of support exceeds that of parents, and even then only when parents become frail and disabled.

In the past decade, several hundred articles have been published examining the experiences of families at this stage of the life course. Research has documented the strains experienced by middle-aged children when parents become dependent, including practical problems of managing competing demands on their time and energy, as well as emotional stress, increased social isolation, guilt, and feelings of inadequacy.

Besides establishing both the prevalence of support for aged parents and problems in providing care, researchers have attempted to determine who is most likely both to become a caregiver and to experience the greatest stress from caregiving. Two of the most consistent findings involve the issues of gender and the relationship to the elderly person. First, women are substantially more likely to become caregivers than are men, and they experience much greater stress and disruption in their daily lives from caregiving (Horowitz 1985). Second, when the elderly person is married, it is the spouse who almost always becomes the primary caregiver. Thus, adult children generally become caregivers only when the care recipient's spouse is not available to occupy this status. Further, spouses appear to experience greater physical and financial strain than do adult child caregivers (Cantor 1983).

Although research has focused on the detrimental consequences of caregiving, recent evidence suggests that most caregivers can also identify positive consequences of caregiving. These positive aspects usually involve feelings of gratification derived from helping someone they love, and fulfilling expectations of filial responsibility. Thus, the issue of changing dependencies in later life reflects the twin themes of consensus and conflict evident throughout theory and research on intergenerational relations.

(SEE ALSO: *Filial Responsibility; Inheritance; In-Law Relationships; Intergenerational Resource Transfers; Parental Roles; Social Mobility*)

REFERENCES

Adams, Bert N. 1968 *Kinship in an Urban Setting.* Chicago: Markham.

Bengtson, Vern L. 1979 "Research Perspectives on Intergenerational Interaction." In Pauline K. Ragan, ed., *Aging Parents.* Los Angeles: University of Southern California Press.

——— 1989 "The Problem of Generations: Age Group Contrasts, Continuities, and Social Change." In V. L. Bengtson and K. W. Schaie, eds., *The Course of Later Life: Research and Reflections.* New York: Springer.

———, Carolyn Rosenthal, and Linda Burton 1988 "Families and Aging: Diversity and Heterogeneity." In R. H. Binstock and L. K. George, eds., *Handbook of Aging and the Social Sciences,* 3d ed. San Diego: Academic Press.

Binstock, R. H. 1983 "The Aged as Scapegoat." *Gerontologist* 23:136–143.

Cantor, Majorie 1983 "Strain among Caregivers: A Study of Experience in the United States." *Gerontologist* 23:597–604.

Cherlin, Andrew J., and Frank F. Furstenberg, Jr. 1986 *The New American Grandparent: A Place in the Family, A Life Apart.* New York: Basic Books.

DeWit, David J., and B. Gail Frankel 1988 "Geographic Distance and Intergenerational Contact: A Critical

Assessment and Review of the Literature." *Journal of Aging Studies* 2:25–43.

Fischer, Lucy Rose 1986 *Linked Lives: Adult Daughters and Their Mothers.* New York: Harper and Row.

Foner, Anne 1986 *Aging and Old Age: New Perspectives.* Englewood Cliffs, N.J.: Prentice-Hall.

Hagestad, Gunhild O. 1985 "Continuity and Connectedness." In V. L. Bengtson and J. F. Robertson, eds., *Grandparenthood.* Newbury Park, Calif.: Sage.

——— 1987 "Dimensions of Time and the Family." *American Behavioral Scientist* 29:679–694.

Hill, Reuben 1970 *Family Development in Three Generations.* Cambridge, Mass.: Schenkman.

Horowitz, Amy 1985 "Family Caregiving to the Frail Elderly." In C. Eisdorfer et al., eds., *Annual Review of Gerontology and Geriatrics.* New York: Springer.

Johnson, Elizabeth S. "'Good' Relationships between Older Mothers and Their Daughters: A Causal Model." *Gerontologist* 18:301–306.

Mannheim, Karl 1952 *Essays on the Sociology of Knowledge,* Paul Kecskemeti, trans. London: Routledge and Kegan Paul.

Neugarten, Bernice L., and K. K. Weinstein 1964 "The Changing American Grandparent." *Journal of Marriage and the Family* 26:199–204.

Riley, Matilda White, Anne Foner, and Joan Waring 1988 "Sociology of Age." In *Handbook of Sociology.* Newbury Park, Calif.: Sage.

Rossi, Alice S., and Peter H. Rossi 1990 *Of Human Bonding: Parent–Child Relations across the Life Course.* New York: Aldine de Gruyter.

Shanas, Ethel 1979 "Social Myth as Hypothesis: The Case of the Family Relations of Old People." *Gerontologist* 19:3–9.

Streib, Gordon, and Robert H. Binstock 1988 "Aging and the Social Sciences: Changes in the Field." In R. H. Binstock and L. K. George, eds., *Handbook of Aging and the Social Sciences.* 3d ed. San Diego: Academic Press.

Suitor, J. Jill 1987 "Mother–Daughter Relations When Married Daughters Return to School: Effects of Status Similarity." *Journal of Marriage and the Family* 49:435–444.

Sussman, Marvin 1985 "The Family Life of Older People." In R. H. Binstock and E. Shanas, eds., *Handbook of Aging and the Social Sciences.* New York: Van Nostrand Reinhold.

Troll, Lillian E. 1985 "The Contingencies of Grandparenting." In V. L. Bengtson and J. F. Robertson, eds., *Grandparenthood.* Newbury Park, Calif.: Sage.

Young, Michael, and Peter Willmott 1957 *Family and Kinship in East London.* London: Routledge and Kegan Paul.

KARL PILLEMER
J. JILL SUITOR

INTERGENERATIONAL RESOURCE TRANSFERS The transfer of resources between individuals of different generations occurs on both the societal level, as the outcome of public policy or within the context of the private sector, and the family level, as in the exchange of emotional support and material goods. This discussion of the intergenerational exchange of resources will consider, first, the flow of resources within the context of the family; second, intergenerational transfers on the societal level; and last, the issue of equity in the transfer of resources intergenerationally. It is important to note at this point that the meaning of the word *generation* varies from setting to setting. In the family environment, the reference is primarily to lines of descent (grandparents, parents, children, etc.). However, each family member is also a member of a particular birth cohort, or group of individuals born during the same period of historical time, such as 1920–1924, and, at any given time, a member of a particular age group, such as sixty-five- to sixty-nine-year-olds. Each of these is also reflected in the intergenerational exchange within the context of the family and in the intergenerational exchange of a society's resources. Finally, the exchange process may also include the concept of generation that connotes a group of individuals, usually part of the same birth cohort, that shares a common set of political or social beliefs (e.g., the "Woodstock Generation").

RESOURCE TRANSFERS WITHIN THE CONTEXT OF THE FAMILY

Resources exchanged among family members vary greatly in size and type. Examples range from the ordinary, everyday exchange of care involved in child rearing or household chores to the bequest of substantial financial or material resources to descendants in a will. Over the last several decades a number of perspectives have developed regarding such familial exchanges. One such perspective views the resource-transfer process in terms of *reciprocity of exchanges among family members.* Analysts have examined reciprocity as a motivator of interdependence over time; at different points in the family structure (e.g., parent–child, sister–brother); and within the context of individual family members' perceptions of how much each member has given or received in the past (viz., Sussman 1965). *Exchange theory* specifically views all kinds of social interactions as the exchange of rewards between individuals where the group or individual with the greater amount of *social power* regulates the exchange process (Dowd 1975). Regarding resources to older family members, Horowitz and Shindelman view reciprocity in terms of the "credits earned" by the older individual for providing resources in the past to the family member currently on the giving end (Horowitz and Shindelman 1983).

In contrast, the *life cycle model* of family intergenerational transfers maintains that the distribution of resources among the generations in the family takes on a curvilinear shape: Individuals in the middle generations, and most likely middle-aged, transfer the bulk of family resources to those who are either younger or older. (For an illustration, see the works of Reuben Hill [1965, 1970] regarding his study of three-generational families in the Minneapolis-St. Paul area; also discussed in Sussman 1965.) In contrast, the *role continuity model of family intergenerational transfers* asserts that, except in families where the older generations are financially strained, older family members redistribute their wealth to successive generations in the family (see Riley and Foner 1971; Kalish 1975; Covey 1981 for further discussion). Finally, the giving and receiving of resources in the family can be viewed as *hierarchical/sequential* activities. From this perspective, individuals first seek aid from members of their nuclear family; failing that, from members of their extended family; and, only as a last resort, from institutional sources such as government programs, banks, and the educational system (viz., Morgan 1983).

A great variety of resources, both material and psychosocial in nature, are exchanged among members of nuclear and extended families. These include the giving and receiving of material gifts of all manner and size, the provision of help during emergencies (as when a family member is ill or in need of sudden and immediate shelter) and aid or financial resources, such as babysitting or nursing, offering advice, taking care of household maintenance, and inheriting assets of all kinds upon the death of family members.

In Western societies prior to industrialization, inheritance was a mechanism for passing on from father to son the means of family economic support, the farm or business (milling, smithing, etc.) that traditionally remained within the family for generations. With the arrival of industrialization and the movement of economic support to the factory or the office, the content and impact of inheritance grew more varied. While monetary and property assets are still very common, items with more symbolic significance, such as mementos or heirlooms, are often the most cherished (Sussman, Cates, and Smith 1970; Rosenfeld 1979; Schorr 1980).

The provision of care to family members is a resource transfer that occurs in every emotionally healthy family the world over. Family members frequently give or receive care for conditions that are quite taxing and of an indefinite duration, such as Down's Syndrome in a child or Alzheimer's disease in an older parent. However, most care-giving involves the many ordinary, everyday activities that are necessary to the survival and well-being of family members, for example, the typical care and feeding of infants and children, the performance of daily chores and house repairs, the giving of advice and emotional support, and the nursing of relatives during episodes of acute illness.

The intergenerational nature of this transfer is underscored in data from a national survey of Americans conducted by Louis Harris and Associates in conjunction with the National Council on the Aging, which found that between 70 percent and 81 percent of individuals in age groups between 18 to 64 years old helped either their parents or their grandparents through illnesses. Between 57 percent and 65 percent in these age groups helped parents or grandparents by fixing things around the house or keeping house for them (Winston 1976). Likewise, the same organization found that, of the 82 percent of the American public 65 years of age and older who had children or grandchildren, 78 percent of those 65 to 69, 65 percent of those 70 to 79, and *57 percent of those 80 and older* helped out younger family members when the latter were ill. Moreover, 65 percent of the 65- to 69-year-olds; 53 percent of the 70- to 79-year-olds; and *34 percent of those 80 and older* took care of grandchildren (Louis Harris and Assos. 1975). Medium-range parental expenditures for child-rearing during the age span from birth to age seventeen, with both spouses working full-time and year-round, was estimated by one analyst, in 1981 dollars, to be nearly $97,000 for the first child and over $91,000 for the second child (Espenshade 1984).

Noninheritance economic transfers within the family take a variety of forms: gifts, loans, payment of bills or down payments, and emergency financial help, for example. The directionality of this assistance, in both nuclear and extended families, is from parents of all ages to children of all ages and from adult children to older parents. For instance, the Louis Harris study determined that between 38 percent and 50 percent of the individuals in age groups 65 and older with children or grandchildren helped out younger family members with money, while between 24 percent and 46 percent of individuals 18 to 64 helped out older family members with economic transfers. United States Bureau of the Census national survey data found that over 900,000 parents were at least partially supported by sons or daughters (mean support from sons of $1,561 and from daughters of $1,347), while nearly half a million children 21 and over were at least partially supported by parents, receiving an average of $4,408 from fathers and $2,878 from mothers (U.S. Bureau of the Census 1989).

The transfer of goods and services among family members includes sharing the same household; making major purchases such as furniture, a car, or a large appliance; making smaller purchases such as clothing; and doing major repairs. Again, the Harris data show that substantial intergenerational transfers occur. For example, 90 percent of those Americans 65 years and older who had children or grandchildren gave those offspring gifts, while between 92 percent and 96 percent of adults 18 to 64 years old gave gifts to parents or grandparents (Louis Harris and Assos. 1975; Winston 1976).

INTERGENERATIONAL RESOURCE TRANSFERS ON THE SOCIETAL LEVEL: FROM ONE BIRTH COHORT/AGE GROUP TO ANOTHER

On the societal level, the concept of intergenerational transfers shifts from resource exchanges among specific individuals of the same lineage to transfers to and from large groups of people of one birth cohort or age group to large groups of people in the same or other birth cohorts or age groups. These exchanges take place in several arenas: (1) the public policy arena, where the transfer is usually in the form of resources defined in statutes and laws (examples in the United States include the Social Security system, Aid to Families with Dependent Children, school bonds); (2) the private sector, where transfers are in the form of wages or goods (examples include jobs that support workers and nonworkers, corporate profits that supply tax revenue); and (3) the creative arena (examples of these transfers include art, music, literature, and the fruits of social and physical science research).

Products of Public Policy. The outcomes of public policy are transfers that affect everyone in a society. Frequently, these resources are multifaceted, affecting a broad range of individuals. For instance, in the United States the term *Social Security* is commonly used to refer to Old-Age and Survivors Insurance retirement income and the death survivors' component of a larger piece of legislation that also includes a disability insurance program, an unemployment insurance component, and the public assistance Supplemental Security Income program. As a totality, then, these components of the social security legislation go to a wide range of individuals in a number of different circumstances. Moreover, it is important to note that, while resources stemming from public policy may be received by specific individuals at a particular point in time or over a particular span of time, in another sense each has a larger impact that far exceeds that exchange. For example, the issuance of a school bond in a community directly and immediately provides educational resources to a particular cohort of school-age residents. However, indirectly, those resources affect the lives of other members of the family, resulting in improved quality of life for them as well. Additionally, from a longitudinal perspective, the resources invested in educational infrastructure and materials benefit future generations of the community's students.

Outcomes of the Private Sector. Intergenerational resource transfers resulting from private-sector activity affect both the *active working population,* composed of individuals who are primarily in their young adult and middle years, and the so-called *dependent population,* composed of children and older people supported by the active working population. This transfer occurs through both the wages that workers earn and the tax revenue, funneling through the public sector, that workers provide. The precise age boundaries for these classifications vary from society to society according to culture and the primary means of economic support (agricultural or industrial). However, even within the age span of the active working population, one finds individuals who are part of the dependent population, such as those who are disabled or unemployed in their age groups. Moreover, within the age span of the dependent population one finds working school-age children and retirees working part-time or part-year.

In the United States, the *total dependency ratio* is generally considered to be the number of persons under 18 and those age 65 and over (together, the two dependent populations) for every 100 working-age individuals 18 to 64 years of age. The *youth dependency ratio* is generally the number of persons under 18 for every 100 individuals 18 to 64, while the *old-age dependency ratio* is the number of persons 65 and older for every 100 persons 18 to 64 years of age. In the United States, while the youth dependency ratio has declined from 51 in 1950 to a projected 41.9 by mid-1990, the old-age dependency ratio has climbed from 13.3 in 1950 to a projected 20.6 by mid-1990. Additionally, the old-age dependency ratio is expected to increase to 37 by 2030, at the height of the so-called Baby Boom retirement years, and to continue climbing to a projected 41.9 by 2080, due to the increasing numbers of the elderly projected to live into their 80s and 90s (U.S. Bureau of the Census 1984).

However, none of these ratios takes into consideration the possible impact of the following on intergenerational resource transfers: (a) the current and future contributions of elderly persons and youth who are employed; (b) the potential for increased labor force participation among those sixty-five and older; (c) the changes in the Social Security Act to gradually increase the age of eligibility for full Social Security retirement benefits to sixty-seven over a twenty-seven-year period, beginning in the year 2000; (d) the growing number of working women, who have different and, as yet, somewhat uncharted, labor force participation patterns; and (e) the growing economy (Crown 1985; Kingson, Hirshorn, and Cornman 1986).

Current Cohorts of Children and the Heterogeneity of the Elderly: Two Special Considerations of Intergenerational Transfers. In the United States, intergenerational resource transfers that are the products of public policy and private-sector activity support individuals of all ages. Of growing importance, however, is a consideration of the effect of the nature of such transfers upon two groups, current cohorts of children and the elderly, at any time when they are viewed as a heterogeneous group. Regarding the former, it is clear that, at present, many children live in poverty or near poverty and, thus, are not receiving from older generations (both older family members and older generations on the societal level) the resources they need to live satisfactory lives *as children.* For instance, in 1985, eleven million children 18 or younger were without health insurance, and over 23 percent of all live births in 1986 were to unmarried mothers, up from 10.7 percent of live births in 1970 (Chollet 1987; U.S. Department of Health and Human Services 1989). Also, in 1988, 19.4 percent of U.S. children eighteen and younger lived in households that were below the poverty level (U.S. Bureau of the Census, 1989). Moreover, limited access during childhood to such resources as health care and education, in particular, leads to reduced economic opportunities and productivity in adulthood. Thus, without the infusion of such resources, children are unable to prepare themselves for a productive adulthood in which they are capable of successfully joining the active working population to sustain themselves. Moreover, they are also not able to provide support for those individuals, young and old, who will then compose a large part of the dependent population of the future. (For instance, persons age seventeen and under in 1990 will be twenty to thirty-seven years of age in 2010, when the first wave of the Baby Boom cohort will begin to retire and forty to fifty-seven years of age in the year 2030, when the full weight of the Baby Boom retirement will be felt.)

Regarding the heterogeneity of the elderly, it is important to keep in mind that older people in Western societies vary greatly not only in chronological age (forty marks the onset of protection under the U.S. Age Discrimination in Employment Act; eighty-five is generally considered the onset of the "oldest old") but also in income, health, and activity status. In addition, the elderly vary, on these and other factors, according to race and gender. As a result, in old age *chronological age alone is not an adequate indicator of the need for a substantial infusion of public or private sector resources.* Indeed, some older people are still greater producers than consumers of society's resources. Likewise, for any particular individual, certain times *during* old age require a greater amount of societal resources than other times.

Outcomes of Creativity. The fruits of research, music, literature, systems of jurisprudence, and other cultural and scientific products represent very important types of societal-level intergenerational transfers. As long-term transfers that cross the generations of a society and frequently move from one society to another, these are resources that traverse both time and geography. (For instance, disease-resistant hybrid strains of rice developed in the United States and used in agricultural settings around the world benefited not only Americans alive during and after the mid-1950s but also people in other societies over succeeding decades.) Frequently, especially regarding the products of scientific research, those in the same birth cohort as the originator(s) or creator(s) do not feel the full impact, positive or negative, of the outcome themselves; this becomes part of the birthright, for better or worse, of the generations that follow. For example, those in the generation of the developers of the diphtheria/pertussis/tetanus vaccine, given routinely to infants, faced the risk of these diseases themselves during childhood. On the other hand, individuals in the same birth cohort as the developers of the atomic bomb have not lived the entire span of their lives, including childhood, coping with the implications of this scientific outcome

THE ISSUE OF EQUITY IN THE INTERGENERATIONAL TRANSFER OF RESOURCES

In recent years, the equity of intergenerational transfers has been a prominent topic of discussion in both the press and various academic settings. Consideration usually centers on the allocation process for resources resulting from public policy. However, it is important to keep in mind that much of the time these resources affect individuals within the context of the family. While there are many perspectives regarding the justification and procedure for transferring resources across generations, four particular factors appear to underlie each of these perspectives, each one subject, itself, to multiple meanings. When there is disagreement in the procedure for and direction of resource distribution across generations, it is frequently due to disagreement regarding the meaning of one or more of these factors (Hirshorn 1991). These are (1) the concept of the generation, discussed previously; (2) the issue of whether the resource transfer results in one party's experiencing an absolute or relative gain or loss in comparison with others; and (3) the perception of the resource "pie" to be allocated (e.g., Is it constant in size? Expandable?); and (4) the idea of *distributive justice,* or fairness in the rationale for deciding how to allocate resources (e.g., transfers can be based on level of need, on merit, or on equal shares for all, among other criteria).

Intergenerational Inequity Perspective. One of the most discussed perspectives in recent years argues that there is *intergenerational inequity* in the transfer of resources in the United States, particularly resources resulting from public policy. It focuses on the relative welfare of current cohorts of youth and current cohorts of the elderly. This perspective maintains, moreover, that, in the United States in recent decades, the welfare of the young, especially those under the age of eighteen, has diminished as a result of the enhanced status of the elderly, who have been accumulating sizable proportions of the nation's personal wealth and, at the same time, been on the receiving end of the bulk of the resources stemming from social policy (Medicare and Social Security retirement funds are singled out especially). Moreover, those adhering to this view maintain, the absolute size of public expenditures directed at the elderly is a major cause of the current budget deficit and other economic problems facing the United States at present. The assumption is that sufficient funds will not exist in the future to insure that those who are currently children and young adults will receive their fair share of these very resources, Social Security retirement and public sector health care support, in their own old age (Preston 1984a; 1984b; Lamm 1985; Kingson, Hirshorn, and Harootyan 1986). Among the problems with this perspective is that it assumes that the elderly, as a group, are all doing well in absolute terms; thus it does not take into consideration the variation within the older population that makes this group quite heterogeneous regarding health status, economic status, living arrangements, and other factors. Moreover, this perspective relies on the idea that the correct concept for use in assessing the equity of public resources transferred across generations—one that would result in social justice—is *numerical equality.* Yet, equal expenditures do *not* result in equal levels of return, no matter who receives the transfer. Finally, given the wide range of types of resources transferred within the context of the family and in the public and private sectors, it is meaningless even to try to arrive at an accurate measure of which generation/birth cohort/age group is faring better as a whole (Kingson, Hirshorn, and Cornman 1986).

Common Stake Perspective. An alternative view of intergenerational resource transfers notes the *common stake* that all generations/birth cohorts/age groups have in the wide variety of intergenerational exchanges. This perspective emphasizes the importance of using the concept of the *life course* in assessing the giving and receiving of resources at all levels and contexts, societal and familial. Thus, it emphasizes that, at some points along the life course, one generally takes more of certain kinds of resources than one gives, while at other points along the life course the opposite is true (e.g., hands-on care is very strong in infancy and sometimes in old age; tax revenues for education are very prominent during childhood). Moreover, generally we do not give the same resources to and take the same resources from the very same people, not within the context of the family or on the societal level. For instance, usually we do not provide the unstinting, continuous, and comprehensive care we received in infancy to our *parents* but we do to our own children.

This perspective also stresses the fact that the same intergenerational resource transfer affects some individuals directly and others indirectly. For example, the public sector program, Aid to Families with Dependent Children, provides *direct* support to children in families headed by parents who are unable to provide sufficient work-related income; thus, family funds are freed to purchase such items as needed medical supplies for, say, an ailing grandparent. *Indirectly* affected by another public transfer that flows intergenerationally is the schoolchild, living with a grandparent, whose lunch money comes from the latter's monthly Social Security check. Finally, the common stake viewpoint underscores the need for current and future generations of the elderly to concern themselves with the welfare of children and young people and vice versa—for the sake of all concerned (Kingson, Hirshorn, and Cornman 1986).

(SEE ALSO: *Filial Responsibility; Inheritance; Intergenerational Relations; Social Mobility)*

REFERENCES

Chollet, Deborah 1987 "A Profile of the Nonelderly Population without Health Insurance." Washington, D.C.: Employee Benefit Research Institute Education and Research Fund.

Covey, H. 1981 "A Reconceptualization of Continuity Theory." *Gerontologist* 21:628–633.

Crown, William H. 1985 "Some Thoughts on Reformulating the Dependency Ratio." *Gerontologist* 25:166–171.

Dowd, James J. 1975 "Aging as Exchange: A Preface to Theory." *Journal of Gerontology* 30:584–594.

Espenshade, Thomas J. 1984 "Investing in Children: New Estimates of Parental Expenditures." Washington, D.C.: Urban Institute Press.

Hill, Reuben 1965 "Decision Making and the Family Life cycle." In E. Shanas and G. Streib, eds., *Social Structure and the Family,* Englewood Cliffs, N.J.: Prentice-Hall.

———1970 *Family Development in Three Generations.* Cambridge, Mass.: Schenkman.

Hirshorn, Barbara 1991 "Multiple Views of the Intergenerational Flow of Society's Resources." *Marriage and Family Review,* special edition on intergenerational relations.

Horowitz, Amy, and L. Shindelman 1983 "Reciprocity and Affection: Past Influences on Current Caregiving." *Journal of Gerontological Social Work* 5 (3):5–20.

Kalish, Richard 1975 *Late Adulthood.* Monterey, Calif.: Brooks/Cole.

Kingson, Eric R., B. A. Hirshorn, and J. M. Cornman 1986 *Ties That Bind: The Interdependence of Generations* (report from the Gerontological Society of America). Washington, D.C.: Seven Locks Press.

Kingson, Eric R., B. A. Hirshorn, and L. K. Harootyan 1986 "The Common Stake: The Interdependence of Generations" (a policy framework for an aging society). Washington, D.C.: Gerontological Society of America.

Lamm, Richard D. 1985 *Mega-Traumas, America at the Year 2000,* Boston: Houghton Mifflin.

Louis Harris and Associates, Inc. 1975 "The Myth and Reality of Aging in America." Conducted for the National Council on the Aging, Inc., Washington, D.C.

Morgan, James N. 1983 "The Redistribution of Income by Families and Institutions and Emergency Help Patterns." In G. J. Duncan and J. N. Morgan, eds., *Five Thousand American Families: Patterns of Economic Progress.* Institute of Social Research 16. Ann Arbor: University of Michigan.

Preston, Samuel H. 1984a Children and the elderly: Divergent paths for America's dependents. *Demography,* 435–457.

———1984b Children and the Elderly: Scientific American. *Demography,* 251: 44–49.

Riley, Matilda W., and A. Foner 1971 "Social Gerontology and the Age Stratification of Society." *Gerontologist* 11, Part 1: 79–87.

Rosenfeld, J. P. 1979 *The Legacy of Aging: Inheritance and Disinheritance in Social Perspective.* Norwood, N.J.: Ablex.

Schorr, Alvin 1980 ". . . Thy Father and Thy Mother . . .: A Second Look at Filial Responsibility and Family Policy." Washington, D.C.: Social Security Administration.

Sussman, Marvin B. 1965 "Relations of Adult Children with Their Parents in the United States." In E. Shanas and G. Streib eds., *Social Structure and the Family: Generational Relationships.* Englewood Cliffs, N.J.: Prentice-Hall.

———, J. Cates, and D. Smith. 1970 *The Family and Inheritance,* New York: Russell Sage Foundation.

U.S. Bureau of the Census 1984 "Projections of the Population of the United States, by Age, Sex and Race: 1983–2080." Current Population Reports, Ser. P-25, No. 952. Washington, D.C.: U.S. Government Printing Office.

———1989 *Money Income and Poverty Status in the United States: 1988* (Advance Data from the March 1989 Current Population Survey). Washington, D.C.: U.S. Government Printing Office.

U.S. Department of Health and Human Services, National Center for Health Statistics 1989 *Health, United States, 1988.* DHHS Pub. NO. (PHS) 89-1232. Washington, D.C.: U.S. Government Printing Office.

Winston, Ellen 1976 "Aging in America," No. 6, Implications for Service Providers. Washington, D.C.: National Council on Aging.

BARBARA HIRSHORN

INTERGROUP AND INTERORGANIZATIONAL RELATIONS The focus here is first on the meaning of intergroup relations and next on interorganizational relations. The emphasis in both cases will be mainly on research and conceptualizations based in the United States.

INTERGROUP RELATIONS

A group is a collection of persons who have shared problems and act together in response to those problems, have shared expectations, and have a sense of common destiny. There are many kinds of groups, ranging from informal friendships to ethnic groups, to societies, and even to intersocietal groups. Intergroup relations refers to patterns of relationships that develop between groups. Extensive reviews of the literature in intergroup relations may be found in Seeman (1981) and Stephan (1985).

Although intergroup relations refers to all types of groups, it is not possible to avoid focusing on ethnic-racial group relations, because this has been the central concern in the United States since the social sciences and sociology, in particular, became established academic disciplines. Intergroup relations has been approached from the level of analysis of the group on the one hand, and from a social psychological perspective on the other.

This latter approach examines intergroup relations from the point of view of the individual and his or her relations with a group. In the latter part of the nineteenth century the United States experienced huge immigration from Southern, Central, and Eastern Europe. Since the new immigrants arrived from cultures that were markedly different from those Americans who were already established here, conflicts developed, a pattern in some ways not materially different from conflicts that now exist between U. S. citizens and recent immigrants from Central and Latin America and Asia. The history of research on intergroup relations in sociology shows a profound emphasis on problems created by these massive immigrations.

Lieberson (1980) has studied thoroughly the question of why those who migrated to the United States from South, Central, and Eastern Europe after 1880 in large numbers (such as Italians, Russians, Lithuanians, Poles, etc.) have been so much more successful than blacks. He found that blacks, in part because of their visibility, confronted much more serious social and competitive disadvantages than did these groups, even though the European groups did have many obstacles to overcome. Because of the slave period and the initial contacts with Africans, white society had and still has very unfavorable dispositions toward blacks, much more unfavorable than their dispositions toward white Europeans and even more unfavorable than their dispositions toward Asian immigrant groups. The competitive threat of Asian groups at the same time period was not nearly as great, since the Asian immigration was much smaller. Blacks also faced greater barriers than did Europeans from labor unions. Thus, Lieberson asserts that blacks and Europeans confronted intrinsically different situations that produced very different sets of opportunities for socioeconomic advancement.

Conflict and competition between groups is only one—albeit important—pattern that may develop, although it is the adaptation that is most likely to make headlines and be reported on the television news. William Graham Sumner (1906) applied the concept of ethnocentrism to explain intergroup conflict. Ethnocentrism is a ". . . view of things in which one's own group is the center of everything, and all others are scaled and rated with reference to it." Sumner believed that ethnocentrism served to highlight and even exaggerate differences between groups and hence contributed to in-group cohesion and strong hostility to the out-group.

One of the oldest social-psychological theories of intergroup relations stresses personality determinants. The leading exponent of this view is Gordon Allport (1954). Allport's definition of prejudice has two components: attitude and belief. Allport defines ethnic prejudice as "an antipathy based upon a faulty and inflexible generalization." In his book Allport refers to the generality of prejudice. A number of studies in this tradition report large intercorrelations of prejudices—that is, persons who are anti-Semitic are also anti-Catholic and antiblack (Epstein and Komorita 1965). The claim is that these views stem from a deep-seated personality syndrome, called by Allport "the prejudiced personality." The prejudiced person is highly moralistic and has a need for definiteness, among other features. As Seeman has noted (1981), the evidence on cross-group generality and its personality basis is easily challenged on both methodological and theoretical grounds. In general, the trait approach has slowly given way to a more situationalist view.

A note on discrimination and prejudice is in order, since much of the intergroup relations literature concerns these concepts. Discrimination is typically defined as treating people unequally due to their group membership, while prejudice is often seen as "a rigid, emotional attitude toward a human group" (Simpson and Yinger 1972). As Seeman (1981, p. 380) points out, in prejudice persons are categorized wrongly or prejudged, and this process is a complex rather than a simple one:

> *The error comes in misconceiving and misjudging such a group, and the individual members thereof, as a consequence of misreading the nature of the category involved. Often enough the misreading occurs because the cultural and historical sources of supposed category qualities are not taken into account or are attributed to irrelevant features of the category, that is, to blackness, Jewishness, and so on. What makes all this extremely tricky is that (a) it is difficult to demonstrate what, in fact, the appropriate characterizations are for the social categories we find it necessary to employ; and (b) given the powerful control that majorities exercise, pressures are generated that tend to socialize the members of a given category into the very features we discern: to make Jews "intellectual," blacks "hostile," Chicanos "indolent," and women "dependent." Thus, though demonstrable relevance (correctness) of the attributed qualities to the category is critical, there is typically a seeming relevance (a misread relevance) that beclouds the issue both for the participant and the analyst.*

Robert E. Park was one of the first leading sociologists of race relations and is identified with ecological theory (Park and Burgess 1921). Park viewed human beings as competing for territory much like plants and other animals. Ecological processes foster competition for limited resources. The distribution of the population is itself shaped by competition over scarce resources, and this competitive process structures the economic interdependence of groups and individuals. Competition also makes people aware of their status and induces them to view themselves as of superior or of inferior status depending on their social situation. Those who see themselves as superior express their consciousness of felt superiority and seek to maintain their privileged position through prejudice. Hence, the intergroup competitive process expresses itself through the development of moral and political order. This order is a product of such processes, in addition to competition, as conflict, accommodation, and assimilation. Racial consciousness is therefore seen as developing out of the competitive process, which is born in the competitive struggle for status. An "inferior" status group might not wish to compete and instead establish a niche within the division of labor, and this might lead to a stable equilibrium.

A dominant intergroup relations paradigm is derived from Marxist thought and is called conflict theory. By this view, race relations and their consequences emerge from the system of social stratification in the society. Societies are seen as constantly changing. Societies distinguish between and among their members and award some greater rewards, such as power, prestige, and money, than others. The result is social inequality, which becomes an essential part of the stratification system. Hence, the stratification system is simply the structured inequalities of groups or categories of individuals. The different groups in the society, such as classes, or ethnic-racial groups, compete for the limited resources available. Three conditions are necessary for intergroup conflict and inequalities to result (Cox 1948; Vander Zanden 1983).

First, there must be at least two identifiable groups. People must be aware of their group and another group on the basis of some characteristic or set of characteristics. These may be physical or not—that is, beliefs or values are sufficient.

Second, the two groups must compete with one another or feel they are competing for a limited pool of resources, such as money or land or jobs. Group members will protect their own interests by seeking to obtain resources for themselves, if necessary at the expense of members of the other group.

Third, the two groups cannot have exactly the same amount of power so that one group can claim an advantage in obtaining resources that another group also seeks. Under these conditions, one group becomes more dominant as the competition develops. The more powerful group defines the other group as inferior. As the group with less power seeks to protect and assert its interests, the dominant group may feel threatened and aggrandize to an even greater degree, and tension may mount. Most members of the dominant group soon find it easy and appropriate to view the other group in very negative terms.

Assimilation involves adapting another culture in place of one's native culture and usually is applied to the process that occurs when persons adjust to a new society and culture by adopting it. For example, many Asian groups have recently immigrated to the United States. Typically their children learn English, dress in American style, eat American food, and are seen as and regard themselves as Americans. However, many adult Asians, although completely or partially bilingual, will retain an affinity for their native culture and understandably are more comfortable conversing in their original tongue.

Accommodation refers to a decision by two or more groups to put aside a significant difference that exists between them in order to stress common interests. This leads to cultural pluralism—that is, a number of different cultural patterns coexisting in the same society. The United States is a pluralistic society in that it permits many distinctive religious, ethnic, and racial groups to exist side by side. The need of new Asian groups to retain their cultural identities is reflected in the existence in many large cities of Chinatowns, Koreatowns, and Japantowns. Some areas in large cities have signs only in Chinese or in both Chinese and English. This has produced some conflict with non-Chinese residents in these communities and has sparked "English-only" movements and resistance to bilingual instruction in public schools.

A great deal of research has been undertaken examining the impact of intergroup contact on intergroup hostility and prejudice (see reviews by Williams 1977 and Stephan 1985). Many of the early studies looked at naturally occurring intergroup contacts. A substantial number of laboratory and field investigations have been undertaken focusing on those characteristics of intergroup contacts that foster positive intergroup outcomes. Stephan (1985) summarizes the findings with regard to this problem in a list of thirteen propositions, such as: "Cooperation within groups should be maximized and competition between groups should be minimized" and "Members of the in-group and the out-group should be of equal status both within and outside the contact situation."

INTERORGANIZATIONAL RELATIONS

An organization is a group with three main features: a goal or set of goals, a boundary, and a technology (Aldrich 1979). Although we say organizations have goals, what is meant is that much of what organizations actually do seems as if it is directed to a shared objective or set of objectives. This may be for appearance sake, and/or the organization may really be goal-oriented. The boundary feature simply refers to the distinction that an organization makes between members and nonmembers. Finally, technology refers to the organization's division of labor or to the set of activities that the organization performs as part of its daily routines in processing new materials or people.

Each of these characteristics can be illustrated by the university. Its goals are often set forth, albeit in glowing and idealized terms, in its general catalog. These typically include teaching, research, and public service. One must apply to become a member of the university—student, faculty, or staff. And such statuses are frequently difficult to come by. The university's technology includes its classrooms and laboratories as well as the lecture and discussion methods of instruction.

Interorganizational relations refers to the relations between or among two or more organizations. There have been several recent overviews of the field of interorganizational relations (Pfeffer and Salancik 1978; Aldrich 1979; Van de Ven and Ferry 1980; Aldrich and Whetten 1981; Mulford 1984; Galaskiewicz 1985).

Every organization has relationships with other organizations. In the case of the university, if it is to function it must have students, and to recruit them it must have relationships with high schools, junior colleges, and other universities. These students (and faculty and staff) must eat, work, and play, so the university has relationships with food, housing, energy, and other suppliers of various kinds in the community. And, of course, the university needs other resources, especially funds, and therefore must relate to government agencies and alumni to obtain them (Clark 1983).

Organizations are ambivalent about establishing an interorganizational relationship to obtain resources (Yuchtman and Seashore 1967). On the one hand they want and need resources if they are to survive; but on the other hand organizations wish to maintain their autonomy, and insofar as they establish an interorganizational tie, they will be expected to reciprocate, and hence their freedom will be constrained. It is assumed that organizations want their autonomy from other organizations, but their survival needs induce them to relinquish some autonomy.

Galaskiewicz (1985) claims that interorganizational relations take place for three major reasons: to obtain and to allocate resources, to form coalitions to enhance power, and to achieve community acceptance or legitimacy.

Interorganizational relations research has been undertaken at three levels: the dyad (Hall et al. 1977), the action set (Hirsch 1972), and the network (Galaskiewicz 1979; Burt 1983). The simplest form of interorganizational relation is the dyad, which simply refers to the relationships of two organizations to one another. The action set concept developed from Merton's (1957) notion of role sets. Caplow (1964) and Evan (1966) took Merton's idea and applied it to the relationships between a focal organization, such as a university, and its pairwise relationship with other organizations with whom it interacts. One might examine the relationship between a university and the office of the mayor of the city within which it is located, and then study the effects of changes in this relationship as they influence other relationships in the set of organizations (Van de Ven and Ferry 1980). Aldrich (1979) has termed the group of organizations that constitute a temporary alliance for a particular or limited goal the "action set."

Networks of organizations contain the complete set of ties that connect all the organizations in a population of organizations (Aldrich 1979; Van de Ven and Ferry 1980; Hall 1987). Although the approaches of Aldrich and Van de Ven and Ferry are not identical conceptually, both orientations toward networks focus on identifying within a particular organizational population all connections of a specified kind that take place. Hence, the analysis of networks is far more complex than that of action sets or dyads.

The body of knowledge in the area of interorganizational relationships is not extensive, and what there is has focused on social services. There exists quite a bit of theoretical information but very few large data bases. With the exception of research on corporate board of directors' interlocks (Burt et al. 1980 and Burt 1983), there is very little work on the private sector.

An early area of interest to theorists has been the general state of the organizational and interorganizational environment. Aldrich (1979) has identified six dimensions of environments: capacity, homogeneity/heterogeneity, stability/instability, concentration/dispersion, domain consensus/dissensus, and turbulence. Capacity refers to the relative level of resources available in the organization's environment. A rich environment refers to one where resources are plentiful, while a lean environment is the opposite.

Homogeneity/heterogeneity refers to the extent to which organizations, individuals, or even social forces that influence resources are relatively similar or different. For example, does a focal organization deal with a relatively uniform and a highly heterogeneous population? If one contrasted the labor force that a Japanese and an American firm draws from to recruit, one would find that the Japanese firm confronts a more homogeneous environment than does its American counterpart. This is, of course, because American workers are much more heterogeneous than are Japanese workers in education, ethnic-racial background, and many other features (Cole 1979).

Stability/instability concerns the degree of turnover in various elements of the environment. Again, if Japanese and American firms are compared, we would anticipate greater turnover in the latter than in the former. The advantage of low turnover or a stable environment is that it permits the organization to develop fixed routines and structures.

Aldrich (1979) refers to the extent to which resources are distributed evenly in the environment or concentrated in a particular area as concentration/dispersion. The RTD is the major bus company in Los Angeles, and its potential ridership is dispersed over an area of more than 400 square miles. Such long transportation lanes present major problems, in contrast, for example, with the Santa Monica Bus Company, whose ridership is concentrated in a much smaller and geographically homogeneous area.

Organizations differ in the extent to which their claim to a specific domain is contested or acknowledged by other organizations. Domain consensus refers to a situation wherein an organization's claim to a domain is recognized, while domain dissensus refers to a situation where disagreement exists over the legitimacy of an organization's domain.

The final organizational dimension is turbulence. This term refers to the extent to which there are increasing environmental interconnections; the more interconnections, the greater the turbulence. Areas where many new organizations are emerging are generally areas of greater turbulence.

A great deal of the work on interorganizational relations has concerned delivery systems and stressed coordination (Rogers and Whetten 1982; Mulford 1984). This is because a central problem in service delivery involves overcoming the segmentation and fragmentation of services created by the large number of organizations with overlapping responsibilities and jurisdictions. Bachrach (1981) has identified a number of factors that discourage coordination among organizations serving the chronically mentally ill, including budget constraints, lack of a mandate to engage in interorganizational planning, and confusion due to separate funding streams for care. Other factors also discourage coordination, such as differences in organizational activities and resources; multiple network memberships and consequent conflicting obligations felt by constituent organizations; and a lack of complementary goals and role expectations (Baker and O'Brien 1971).

Each organization in a delivery system relies on the other organizations in the system, since no single unit can generate all the resources necessary for survival. Hence, the organizations in a system enter into exchanges with other organizations and consumers. It is assumed that each organization or system seeks to better its bargaining position. This perspective on delivery systems as interorganizational networks is generally labeled the resource dependence perspective (Pfeffer and Salancik 1978).

Contingency theory (Lawrence and Lorsch 1967) assumes that organizational functioning depends on the intertwining of technological and environmental constraints and the structures that emerge to deal with these constraints. The theory assumes, as does system theory more generally, that there is no single most effective way to organize (Katz and Kahn 1966), that the environment within which an organization functions influences the effectiveness of an organization, and that different organizational structures can produce different performance outcomes.

(SEE ALSO: *Organizational Structure; Social Network Theory; Systems Theory*)

REFERENCES

Aldrich, Howard 1979 *Organizations and Environments.* Englewood Cliffs, N.J.: Prentice-Hall.

———, and D. A. Whetten 1981 Organizational Sets, Action Sets, and Networks: Making the Most of Simplicity. In P. C. Nystrom and W. H. Starbuck, eds., *Handbook of Organization Design,* vol. I. New York: Oxford University Press.

Allport, Gordon W. 1954 *The Nature of Prejudice.* Reading, Mass.: Addison-Wesley.

Bachrach, Leona L. 1981 "Continuity of Care for Chronic Mental Patients: A Conceptual Analysis." *American Journal of Psychiatry* 138 (11):1449–1456.

Baker, Frank, and Gregory O'Brien 1971 "Intersystem Relations and Coordination of Human Service Organizations." *American Journal of Public Health* 61 (1):130–137.

Burt, Ronald S. 1983 *Corporate Profits and Cooptation: Networks of Market Constraints and Directorate Ties in the American Economy.* New York: Academic Press.

———, K. P. Christman, and H. C. Kilburn, Jr. 1980 "Testing a Structural Theory of Corporate Cooptation: Interorganizational Directorate Ties as a Strategy for Avoiding Market Constraints on Profits." *American Sociological Review* 45:821–841.

Caplow, Theodore 1964 *Principles of Organization.* New York: Harcourt, Brace Jovanovich.

Clark, Burton 1983 *The Higher Education System.* Berkeley: University of California Press.

Cole, Robert E. 1979 *Work, Mobility, and Participation.* Berkeley: University of California Press.

Cox, Oliver C. 1948 *Caste, Class and Race: A Study in Social Dynamics.* New York: Monthly Review Press.

Epstein, R., and S. S. Komorita 1965 "Parental Discipline, Stimulus Characteristics of Outgroups, and Social Distance in Children." *Journal of Personality and Social Psychology* 2:416–420.

Evan, William 1966 "The Organization Set: Toward a Theory of Interorganizational Relations." In J. Thompson, ed., *Approaches to Organizational Design.* Pittsburgh, Pa.: University of Pittsburgh Press.

Galaskiewicz, Joseph 1985 "Interorganizational Relations." *Annual Review of Sociology* 11:281–304.

Hall, Richard H. 1987 *Organizations: Structures, Processes, and Outcomes,* 4th ed. Englewood Cliffs, N.J.: Prentice-Hall.

———, J. Clark, P. Giordano, P. Johnson, and M. Van Roekel 1977 "Patterns of Interorganizational Relationships." *Administrative Science Quarterly* 22:457–474.

Hirsch, Paul M. 1972 "Processing Fads and Fashions: An Organization-Set Analysis of Cultural Industry Systems." *American Journal of Sociology* 77:639–659.

Katz, Daniel, and Robert L. Kahn 1966 *The Social Psychology of Organizations.* New York: Wiley.

Lawrence, Paul R., and J. W. Lorsch 1967 *Organization and Environment: Managing Differentiation and Integration.* Cambridge, Mass.: Graduate School of Business Administration, Harvard University.

Lieberson, Stanley 1980 *A Piece of the Pie: Black and White Immigrants Since 1880.* Berkeley: University of California Press.

Merton, Robert K. 1957 *Social Theory and Social Structure.* New York: Free Press.

Mulford, C. L. 1984 *Interorganizational Relations: Implications for Community Development.* New York: Human Sciences Press.

Park, Robert E., and E. W. Burgess 1921 *Introduction to the Science of Sociology.* Chicago: University of Chicago Press.

Pfeffer, Jeffrey, and G. Salancik 1978 *The External Control of Organizations: A Resource Dependence Perspective.* New York: Harper & Row.

Rogers, David L., and D. A. Whetten 1982 *Interorganizational Coordination: Theory, Research, Implementation.* Ames, IA: Iowa State University Press.

Seeman, Melvin 1981 "Intergroup Relations." In M. Rosenberg and R. H. Turner, eds., *Social Psychology: Sociological Perspectives.* New York: Basic Books.

Simpson, George E., and J. M. Yinger 1972 *Racial and Cultural Minorities,* 4th ed. New York: Harper and Row.

Stephan, Walter G. 1985 "Intergroup Relations." In Gardner Lindzey and Eliot Aronson, eds., *Handbook of Social Psychology,* vol. II. New York: Random House.

Sumner, William Graham 1906 *Folkways.* Boston: Ginn.

Van de Ven, Anderson H., and D. L. Ferry 1980 *Measuring and Assessing Organizations.* New York: Wiley.

Vander Zanden, J. W. 1983 *American Minority Relations,* 4th ed. New York: Alfred A. Knopf.

Williams, Robin M. 1977 *Mutual Accommodation: Ethnic Conflict and Cooperation.* Minneapolis: University of Minnesota Press.

Yuchtman, Ephraim, and S. Seashore 1967 "A Systems Resource Approach to Organizational Effectiveness." *American Sociological Review* 32:891–903.

OSCAR GRUSKY

INTERMARRIAGE Intermarriage among people of different races, religion, nationality, and ethnicity would be a subject of little concern in many societies (Degler 1971). That should be expected of a culturally diverse society such as the United States. Indeed, the United States is the most racially and culturally diverse nation in the Western, industrialized world. The heterogeneous composition of the United States should lend itself to a high degree of tolerance and acceptance of diversity in marriage patterns among its constituent groups (Spickard 1989). As of the 1990s, intermarriage rates among populations defined as ethnic minorities in the United States are practically normative (U.S. Bureau of the Census 1985). Only between blacks and whites has intermarriage remained such a rare practice as to continue to be regarded as socially deviant behavior. For that reason, our discussion of intermarriage will focus largely on those two groups.

Slavery had its greatest impact on interracial relations of the Africans brought to the United States. Most of the slaves who came in the beginning were males. The number of black females was not equal to that of males until 1840. As a result, the number of sexual relations between black slaves and indentured white women was fairly high. Some of these interracial relationships were more than casual contacts and ended in marriage. The intermarriage rate between male slaves and free white women increased to the extent that laws against them were passed as a prohibitive measure. Before the alarm over the rate of intermarriages, male slaves were encouraged to marry white women, thereby increasing the property of the slavemaster since the children from such unions were also slaves (Jordan 1968).

The end of slavery did not give the black woman any right to sexual integrity. What slavery began, racism and economic exploitation continued to impose on the sexual lives of black women. In the postbellum South, black women were still at the mercy of the carnal desires of white men. According to historians, black women were forced to give up their bodies like animals to white men at random. Many have noted that many Southern white men had their first sexual experience with black women. In some cases the use of black women as sexual objects served to maintain the double standard of sexual conduct in the white South. Many white men did not have sexual relations with white women until they married. Some Southern white men were known to joke that until they married they did not know that white women were capable of sexual intercourse (Cash 1960; Dollard 1957).

It was the protection of the sexual purity of the white women that partially justified the establishment of racially segregated institutions in the South. The Southern white man assumed that black men have a strong desire for intermarriage and that white women would be open to proposals from black men if they were not guarded from even meeting with them on an equal level. As Bernard (1966, p. 75) writes, "The white world's insistence on keeping Negro men walled up in the concentration camp (of the ghetto) was motivated in large part by its fear of black male sexuality."

The taboo on intermarriage is mostly centered on black men and white women. One reason for this is that white men and black women have engaged in coitus since the first black female slaves entered this country. Some black slave women were forced to engage in sexual relations with their white masters; others did so out of desire. Children resulting from these interracial sexual unions are always considered black, and the prevalent miscegenation of black women and white men has produced a much lighter-skinned American black than their African ancestor.

Traditionally, white fear of interracial relations has focused on the desire to avoid mongrelization of the races. Such a fear lacks any scientific basis since many authorities on the subject of racial types seriously question that a pure race ever existed on this planet. Most authorities note it is an actual fact that the whole population of the world is hybrid and becoming increasingly so. At any rate, the rate of miscegenation in the past almost certainly casts doubt on any pure race theory for the United States (Day 1972).

Since the interracial taboo is mostly centered on black men and white women, it is not strange that these two groups may have a certain curiosity about each other. Inflaming this curiosity are the sexual stereotypes mutually held by blacks and whites about each other as sexual partners. Just as these sexual stereotypes may stimulate the curiosity of white women, the black male may be equally attracted by the concept of sacred white womanhood applied to all white women. Especially in the South, the penalties for a black man having sex with a white female were extremely severe. Her status as forbidden fruit could only add to the natural attraction that most men feel toward the opposite sex. What is taken for granted by most white men became a forbidden pleasure to black males.

Regardless of the social taboos, intermarriage does take place between the races—most noticeably in the North. Despite the problems inherent in interracial marriages, such unions appear to be increasing. The U.S. Supreme Court ruling of 1967 that all laws prohibiting marriage between members of different races are unconstitutional, along with the status gains for blacks in the 1960s, influenced this increase. It has also been noted that most partners in this type of marriage are in the same educational brackets as their spouses. Despite this increase, black–white marriages are still less than 1 percent of all marriages in the United States (Spickard 1989). Little research is available on the success of interracial marriages. Authorities who have studied the subject generally have concluded these marriages have a fairly good chance of survival. The external pressures faced by interracial couples are often great but do not appear to be overwhelming (Cretser and Leon 1982).

CONTEMPORARY BLACK AND WHITE MARRIAGE

The 1970s and 1980s witnessed a significant increase in interracial dating and marriage. Among the reasons for this change in black–white dating and marriage was the desegregation of the public school system, the work force, and other social settings. In those integrated settings, blacks and whites met as equals. There were, of course, other factors such as the liberation of many white youth from parental control and the racist values parents conveyed to them (Staples 1981).

Although no studies have yet yielded any data on the subject, there appears to be a decline in black male–white female couples and an increase in black female–white male pairings (U.S. Bureau of the Census 1985). Several factors seem to account for this modification of the typical pattern. Many black women are gravitating toward white men because of the shortage of black males and their disenchantment with those they are able to meet. In a similar vein some white men are dissatisfied with white females and their increasing and vociferous demands for sex-role parity. At the same time there is a slight but noticeable decrease in black male–white female unions. A possible reason is that they are no longer as fashionable as they were in the 1960s and 1970s. Also, much of their attraction to each other was based on the historical lack of access to each other and the stereotype of black men as superstuds and white women as forbidden fruit (Staples 1981). Once they had extensive interaction, the myths were exploded and the attraction consequently diminished (Hernton 1965).

We should be fairly clear that there are relatively normal reasons for interracial attractions and matings. At the same time it would be naive to assume that special factors are not behind them in a society that is stratified by race. Given the persistence of racism as a pervasive force, many interracial marriages face rough going. In addition to the normal problems of working out a satisfactory marital relationship, interracial couples must cope with social ostracism and isolation. A recent phenomenon has been the increasing hostility toward such unions by the black community, which has forced some interracial couples into a marginal existence (Hare and Hare 1984). Such pressures cause the interracial marriage rate to remain very low. Fewer than 3 percent of all marriages involving a black person are interracial.

There are many factors and problems associated with interracial dating. Because of the unique and historical relationships between the races, such interracial dating practices often have a different motivation and character than the same behavior between members of the same race (Beigel 1966). Heer (1974) used an analysis of census data to interpret the changes in interracial marriages in the period between 1960 and 1970. Among his major findings was the shift of such marriages from the South to the North, an increase in black husband–white wife unions, and a fairly high rate of dissolution of such marriages.

No other issue provokes such an emotional response as that of interracial dating and marriage. If blacks are asked if they have ever dated a member of another race, two types of responses emerge. One group is so strongly opposed to it that they give a strident No. The other group has engaged in mixed dating and is quite defensive about it. Some of the latter group think it is a hostile, even stupid, question and assumes there is something strange about people who date across the color line. Whether strange or not, it is undeniable that interracial dating is a controversial activity (Staples 1981). Male–female relationships without the racial element are a controversial topic, and race has historically been a volatile and emotional issue. It is a fact that the scars of nearly 400 years of the worst human bondage known are not healed, and disapproval by many black and white people of interracial love affairs is one of the wounds.

Intermarriage is certainly nothing new in the United States. Its meaning and dynamics have, however, changed over the 400 years since blacks entered this country. In the era before slavery black male and white female indentured servants often mated with each other. During the period of black bondage, most mixed sexual unions took place between white men and female slaves, often involving coercion by the white partner. A similar pattern of miscegenation occurred after slavery, with a white man and a black woman as the typical duo. When blacks moved to larger cities outside the South, the black male–white female pairing became more common. As is commonly known, legal unions between the races was prohibited by law in many states until 1967. Legal prohibitions were not the only deterrent to such biracial unions. This country's history is replete with acts of terror and intimidation of interracial couples who violated the society's taboos on miscegenation. While blacks and whites came together in love and marriage over the years, it was generally at a high cost ranging from death to social ostracism (Stember 1976).

Around 1968 society witnessed the first significant increase in interracial dating. This was the year that blacks entered predominantly white college campuses in comparatively large numbers. Contemporaneous with this event was the sexual and psychological liberation of white women. While white society disapproved of all biracial dating, the strongest taboo was on the black male–white female bond. Hence, they became the dominant figures in the increments of biracial dating. The college campus became an ideal laboratory for experiments in interracial affairs. Young white women, who were not as racist as their parents, were liberated from parental and community control. Their student cohorts were more accepting or indifferent to their dating across racial lines. One study revealed that as many as 45 percent of the white female students had dated interracially (Willie and Levy 1972). There were, of course, regional differences: While 20 percent of all Americans had dated outside their race, the South had the lowest incidence of biracial dating (10 percent), while the West and young people had the highest rate (one out of three; Downs 1971).

Those changes in interracial dating practices coincided with the civil rights movement and a greater white acceptance of blacks as racial equals. Moreover, in the university setting the blacks and whites who dated were peers. They had similar educational backgrounds, interests, and values. Along with increments in racial unions came what appeared to be a change in public attitudes toward biracial couples. A 1985 poll indicated that only a minority of white Americans would not accept their child's marrying outside his or her race (Schuman, Steel, and Bobo 1985). This poll result could be misleading. Many people tend to give the liberal answer they think is proper or expected when asked about controversial issues such as interracial marriage. However, when confronted with the issue on a very personal level, their response is likely to be much different. Whether parents approve or not, it is clear that biracial matches have become part of the changing American scene. Mixed couples can be observed daily in the cities of the deep South and are commonplace in such liberal bastions as New York, Boston, and San Francisco; and parental approval is irrelevant to a number of black and white singles who have deviated from other norms related to sexual orientation, sex roles, sexual behaviors, marriage, and the like.

FACTORS IN INTERRACIAL MARRIAGES

The increase in interracial dating has resulted in an increase in interracial marriages. Using selective data, Heer (1974) found definite evidence of an upward trend in the percentage of blacks marrying whites. The interracial marriage rate was particularly high in those areas where residential segregation by race was low and where there are minimal status differences between the white and black population. However, Heer also discovered that marriages between black men and white women are much more common than those between white men and black women. In the western region, for example, the interracial marriage rate of black men is 12.3 percent and of black women 3.1 percent (Tucker and Mitchell-Kernan 1990).

Other factors may propel people into an interracial marriage. Some students of the subject assert that uneven sex ratios are a basic cause. Wherever a group in nearness to another group has an imbalance in sex ratio, there is a greater likelihood of intermarriage. If the groups have a relatively well-balanced distribution of the sexes, members will marry more within their own group (Guttentag and Secord 1983; Parkman and Sawyer 1967).

In interracial marriages, one always looks for ulterior motives. It is said that people marry interracially because of rebellion against their parents, sexual curiosity, and other psychological reasons. But many marriages that are homogeneous take place for the same reasons. There are all kinds of unconscious variances that attract individuals in many marriages. Thus, people may marry "their own kind" for the weirdest reasons, yet these reasons do not make each marriage suspect. Perhaps the imputation of ulterior motives to interracial couples says more about the individual making these interpretations and about the society we live in than about the couple who intermarry.

While the proportion of western black men dating interracially is much higher than black women, the difference is not so great when it comes to interracial marriages nationally. While black women are deprived of many dates by white women, the vast majority of black males are still available to them for marriage. Moreover, a great number of black women marry white men. The percentage of dating relationships between black women and white men that result in marriage may be even greater than the corresponding percentage for black men and white women.

In the past, many of the black men who married white women were of a higher social status than their wives. In fact, this marrying down was so common that sociologists formulated a theory about it. They hypothesized that the black groom was trading his class advantage for the racial caste advantage of the white bride (Davis 1941; Merton 1941). But contemporary interracial marriages are more likely to involve spouses from the same social class. Furthermore, when intermarriages involved members of different social classes, there was a pronounced tendency for black women to marry up rather than to marry down (Heer 1974; Monahan 1976).

Consequently, one reason that black women marry white men is to increase their station in life.

Of course, this is true of many marriages. One exception, however, is black female entertainers. Because they are closely associated with white males in the course of their jobs, many of them form interracial unions. Most of the celebrated cases in recent years have involved famous black women who married white men not equally famous or wealthy.

While the motivation for an interracial marriage may or may not differ from that of intraracial marriages, there are problems that are unique to interracial marriages. When researchers studied interracially married couples they discovered that courtship in most cases had been carried on clandestinely and, further, that many of them were isolated from their families following the marriage. The white families, in particular, frequently refused to have anything to do with children who entered into interracial marriages (Golden 1954; Porterfield 1982; Spickard 1989).

Other outstanding social problems encountered by the couples centered on such factors as housing, occupation, and relationships with family and peers. Several of the spouses lost their jobs because of intermarriage, while others felt it necessary to conceal their marriages from their employers. The children born of such marriages identified themselves with and were accepted by the black community. In sum, the couples had to rely upon themselves and their own power of determination to continue the marriage (Wilkinson 1975).

As for the sociocultural factors that promote or deter interracial marriages, several explanations have been put forth to explain the variation in intermarriage patterns in the United States. Tucker and Mitchell-Kernan (1990) hypothesized that certain environments are more racially tolerant of intermarriage than are others. Their hypothesis is based on the findings from U.S. census data showing interracial marriage rates highest in the West and lowest in the South (U.S. Bureau of the Census 1985). Similar to their explanation is the argument by Blau and Schwartz (1984) that the larger the group size as a proportion of the population, the less likely it is that members will marry outside their group. Second, they suggested that the more heterogeneous an area's population, the more likely it is that people will marry outside their group. Both the aforementioned propositions imply that intermarriage is a function of environmental forces, not individual motivations.

SUMMARY

Interracial mating is a subject fraught with controversy. Those who oppose it often combine a hostility toward racial equality with invidious assessments of the private thoughts and lives of interracial couples. Many men and women mate for no more complex reasons than meeting, liking each other as individuals, and choosing to transcend the societal barriers to their relationship. Only in societies similar to the one in the United States does a biracial union take on any greater significance. For centuries, Latin American nations have undergone such a fusion of the races that only nationality, language, and religion remain as sources of identity. But the painful history of race relations in North America militates against the natural mixing of individuals from different races. Instead of regarding interracial dating and marriage as a matter of personal choice, many minorities have taken up the call for racial purity so common to their white-supremacy adversaries of the past.

Despite the opposition to biracial unions, they will continue to increase, among both men and women, as long as the social forces that set intermarriage in motion are extant. There is, for example, the class factor. As long as middle-class blacks occupy token positions in the upper reaches of the job hierarchy, most of the people they meet in their occupational world will be white. Considering the fact that the job setting is the paramount place for meeting mates, it is only natural that many blacks will date and marry whites. Those whites will be the people they most often encounter and with whom they share common values, interests, and life-styles. Almost twenty-five years ago, E. Franklin Frazier (1957, p. 335) predicted:

The increasing mobility of both white and colored people will not only provide a first-hand knowledge of each for the other but will encourage a certain cosmopolitanism. That means there will be a growing number of marginal people who will break away from their cultural roots. These marginal people will help create not only an international community but an international society. In becoming free from their local attachments and provincial outlook, they will lose at the same time their racial prejudices, which were a product of their isolation. Many of these marginal people will form interracial marriages because they are more likely to find suitable marriage partners in the cosmopolitan circles than within their native countries.

Not all blacks who consort with nonblacks will do so for noble motives. Because blacks tend to stereotype each other in negative terms, many will cross the color line to find what they believe is "absent" in their own race. However, many of the alleged advantages of the white female actually result from her longer tenure and security in her class position. It is easier, for instance, to enact the traditional female role when the men in your class and race can fulfill the normative masculine role, and few black males have been allowed that opportunity in a racially stratified society.

The wave of the future, however, does not seem to be the black male–white female dyad. Increasingly, black women are dating and marrying white males. The attention of society in general and black women in particular has focused on black men and white women, and the fact that the most common interracial pairs in the 1960s were black women and white men has been overlooked. Some studies reveal that as many as 49 percent of black women have dated white men. As black women ascend in the middle class world, they, too, will mate on the basis of proximity and class interests. Previously, fewer black women engaged in interracial mating because white males were not interested in them, at least not for marriage. As racial barriers drop in the society in general, especially among the middle classes, the opportunity structure will increase for black women, and the outcome will be the same for them as for black men. Whether their biracial unions will be any more durable may depend primarily on the trajectory of social forces in the society at large.

(SEE ALSO: *Courtship; Discrimination; Ethnicity; Mate Selection Theories; Race)*

REFERENCES

Beigel, Hugo G. 1966 "Problems and Motives in Interracial Relationships." *Journal of Sex Research* 2:185–205.

Bernard, Jessie 1966 *Marriage and Family among Negroes.* Englewood Cliffs, N.J.: Prentice-Hall.

Blau, Peter, and Joseph E. Schwartz 1984 *Crosscutting Social Circles: Testing a Macrostructural Theory of Intergroup Relations.* Orlando, Fla.: Academic Press.

Cash, W.J. 1960 *The Mind of the South.* New York: Vintage.

Cretser, Gary, and Joseph Leon 1982 *Intermarriage in the United States.* New York: Haworth Press.

Davis, Kingsley 1941 "Intermarriage in Caste Societies." *American Anthropologist* 43:376–395.

Day, Beth 1972 *Sexual Life between Blacks and Whites: The Roots of Racism.* New York: World Publishing.

Degler, Carl N. 1971 *Neither Black nor White.* New York: Macmillan.

Dollard, John 1957 *Caste and Class in a Southern Town.* Garden City, N.Y.: Doubleday.

Downs, Joan 1971 "Black/White Dating." *Life,* 28 May, 56–61.

Frazier, E. Franklin 1957 *Race and Cultural Contacts in the Modern World.* New York: Alfred A. Knopf.

Golden, Joseph 1954 "Patterns of Negro–White Intermarriage." *American Sociological Review* 19:144–147.

Guttentag, Marcia, and Paul F. Secord 1983 *Too Many Women? The Sex Ratio Question.* Beverly Hills, Calif.: Sage.

Hare, Nathan, and Julia Hare 1984 *The Endangered Black Family.* San Francisco: Black Think Tank.

Heer, David 1974 "The Prevalence of Black-White Marriage in the United States, 1960 and 1970." *Journal of Marriage and the Family* 36:246–258.

Hernton, Calvin 1965 *Sex and Racism in America.* New York: Doubleday.

Jordan, Winthrop D. 1968 *White Over Black: American Attitudes toward the Negro 1550–1812.* Chapel Hill: University of North Carolina Press.

Merton, Robert 1941 "Intermarriage and Social Structure: Fact and Theory." *Psychiatry* 4:361–374.

Monahan, Thomas P. 1976 "The Occupational Class of Couples Entering Into Interracial Marriages." *Journal of Comparative Family Studies* 7:175–192.

Parkman, Margaret A., and Jack Sawyer 1967 "Dimensions of Ethnic Intermarriage in Hawaii." *American Sociological Review* 32:593–608.

Porterfield, Ernest 1982 "Black-American Intermarriage in the United States." In Gary A. Cretser and Joseph J. Leon, eds., *Intermarriage in the United States.* New York: Haworth Press.

Schuman, Howard, Charlotte Steel, and Lawrence Bobo 1985 *Racial Attitudes in America.* Cambridge, Mass.: Harvard University Press.

Spickard, Paul R. 1989 *Mixed Blood: Intermarriage and Ethnic Identity in Twentieth-Century America.* Madison: University of Wisconsin Press.

Staples, Robert 1981 *The World of Black Singles: Changing Patterns of Male/Female Relations.* Westport, Conn.: Greenwood Press.

Stember, Charles Herbert 1976 *Sexual Racism.* New York: Elsevier.

Tucker, M. Belinda, and Claudia Mitchell-Kernan 1990 "New Trends in Black American Interracial Marriage: The Social Structural Context." *Journal of Marriage and the Family* 52:209–218.

U.S. Bureau of the Census 1985 *Census of the Population, 1980.* Vol. 2, *Marital Characteristics.* Washington, D.C.: U.S. Government Printing Office.

Wilkinson, Doris Y. 1975 *Black Male/White Female: Perspectives on Interracial Marriage and Courtship.* Cambridge, Mass.: Schenkman.

Willie, Charles V., and Joan D. Levy 1972 "Black Is Lonely." *Psychology Today,* March, 76–86.

ROBERT STAPLES

INTERNAL MIGRATION Migration is the relatively permanent movement of individuals or groups over varying distances to change places of residence; permanence and distance are its major defining dimensions. Internal migration occurs within the boundaries of a given country. Migration is a type of geographic mobility status.

DEFINITIONS

The following definitions are standard in the field of social demography (Bogue 1985):

Mobility status. A classification of the population based on a comparison between the place of residence (destination) of each individual in a census enumeration or survey and the place of residence (origin) at some specified earlier date. Mobility status in terms of the distance of the move falls into four main categories: nonmovers, local movers, intrastate migrants, and interstate migrants. They may be looked at more specifically in the list below:

1. *Nonmovers* or nonmobile persons live in the same house at the time of the census as at the date of origin.
2. *Movers* or mobile persons live in a different house and are further classified as to where they were living at the earlier date.
   a. *Local movers* are mobile persons who live in the same county at census time as at the date of origin.
   b. *Migrants* are mobile persons who live in a different county at census time than at the date of origin. Migrants may be further subclassified:
      1. *Intrastate migrants* live in a different county but within the same state.
      2. *Interstate migrants* live in a different state.
      3. *Interregional migrants* live in a different geographic division or census geographic region; they are also interstate migrants.

Mobility interval. The lapsed time between the date specified for previous residence and the date of enumeration is usually either one year or five years. Recent census enumerations specify five years, and the Current Population Surveys have specified intervals of one, two, three, four, and five years.

Metropolitan mobility. A system of subdividing mobile persons into categories by place of residence at the beginning and the end of the mobility interval and according to standard metropolitan statistical areas (SMSAs) is as follows:

1. Within the same SMSA
2. Between SMSAs
3. From outside SMSAs to SMSAs
4. From SMSAs to outside SMSAs
5. Outside SMSAs at both dates

Mobility rates. The number of persons in a specified mobility status per one hundred or per one thousand population of the area in which they resided at the end of the mobility interval is a mobility rate. Such rates may refer to any of the categories of nonmobile or mobile persons specified above. Mobility rates may be specific for age, race, sex, or other traits. The denominator may also be the origin date or the midpoint of the migration interval.

Migration flows. The key distinction is that either the origin or the destination is unknown. There are two types of flows:

1. *In-migration* is comprised of migrants arriving at a particular place of destination, with no reference to the place of origin. In-flows could also arrive at a specified type of place, such as central cities or metropolitan areas.
2. *Out-migration* is comprised of migrants departing from a particular area, with no reference to the place of destination. Out-flows may also depart from specified types of places, such as places outside SMSAs or suburban metropolitan rings of SMSAs.

Migration streams. These connect an origin to a destination. There are three types of migration streams:

1. *Specific streams.* Streams that connect particular places within a category, such as streams between specific cities, counties, states, or regions. This is the major use of the term.
2. *Typological streams.* Streams that connect types of places, such as streams between all central cities and suburbs in a state or the nation.
3. *Counterstreams.* When a stream between two places endures, it usually generates a counterstream, a smaller stream in the opposite direction. The stream and counterstream are referred to as an exchange.

Net migration. This is the difference obtained when the number of out-migrants is subtracted from the number of in-migrants in a particular place or type of place. A location that experiences a loss of population through migration is said to have a negative net migration; one that gains population through migration has a positive net migration. Because of its birth and death rates, an area may have a negative net migration and continue to have a growing population. There is no such thing as a net migrant, however.

Return migration. The census contains an item that identifies the state of birth. Return migrants are those persons who return to their state of birth during the mobility interval.

MIGRATION RESEARCH

Net migration rates before 1940 were estimated using a survival-rate method, adding births and subtracting deaths and attributing most of the resulting decade population change to migration (Bogue and Beale 1961). The 1940 census was the first to include a mobility item. It asked where persons lived five years before. In 1950, after World War II, there was so much population movement that a one-year interval was substituted in the census. In 1960 the five-year mobility interval was restored and has been retained in subsequent decades. Because of these measurement changes, the 1960 and 1970 censuses were the first from which decade changes could be derived. Thus, several landmark studies appeared in the 1960s, breaking new ground and setting patterns for future migration research (Long 1988). Henry S. Shryock's (1964) work showed the importance of studying gross migration flows, in addition to the prevailing dependence on net migration. Ira S. Lowry (1966) introduced econometric modeling to migration research. Finally, Lansing and Mueller (1967) helped introduce survey approaches to analyzing internal migration.

U.S. MOBILITY

Americans are unusually mobile (Bogue 1985). Only Canada and Australia have populations as mobile as that of the United States. In a single year 17 percent of U.S. inhabitants move from one domicile to another, and about 6 percent change their county of residence. At current mobility rates average Americans live at fourteen different addresses during their lifetimes. Of these thirteen moves, three are as a dependent moving with parents and ten are on their own volition. People who have lived their entire lives at the same address account for no more than 2 percent or 3 percent of the adult population. Perhaps no more than 10 percent to 15 percent of people spend their entire lives in their county of birth.

When the five-year mobility interval is used, the mobility rates are not five times as large as those for a single year because persons who move several times within the interval are counted only once. Nearly one-half of the population is mobile over a five-year period, and more than one-fifth are migrants. Since 1980 there appears to have been no diminution in the tendency to migrate, but there has been an apparent reduction in local mobility.

One can discover contradictory findings in the mobility literature. These contradictions are often due to the data bases being analyzed (Long 1988). Some data bases use mortgage data, leaving out renters; others, such as the Annual Housing Survey, use households; and some, such as most census publications, use individuals as their units of analysis, each data base giving somewhat different results. In addition, some data sources offer little information on the characteristics of migrants. The individual master file of the Internal Revenue Service includes state and county migration data but includes no personal characteristics, and several large moving companies provide data on their customers, also without personal characteristics (Kahley 1990).

Reasons for Migration. Migration may occur in response to changing economic, social, or political conditions. *Push factors* are conditions in the sending population that impel or stimulate migration. Conditions that attract in-migrants are classified as *pull factors* (Ravenstein 1889; Lee 1966).

Declining economic opportunities, political instability, or the weakening of place ties may stimulate out-migration. Expanding economic opportunities, potential for advancement, the presence of family members and friends, or previous vacationing or residential experience tend to attract migrants. Not surprisingly, rural communities with high birthrates and regions with limited opportunities are areas of high outmigration, whereas urban, industrial regions and communities with expanding opportunities tend to have high in-migration (Prehn 1986).

Labor-force migration is viewed as an equilibrating mechanism that redistributes population as local economies rise and fall relative to one another. It contributes to economic expansion in the receiving population. Nonlabor-force migration responds more to amenity and social network factors, previous experience, and cost of living, but not to economic opportunities.

Wilbur Zelinski (1971) proposed a macro-level three-stage model of national internal migration. First, with the onset of modernization, the overall level of migration increases, primarily in the form of rural-to-urban moves. Second, as industrialization and modernization spread to more regions, migration may continue to increase because improved transportation and communication increase the availability of information and decrease the uncertainty of moving. Interurban moves become more important and eventually become the majority of all moves. Finally, at advanced stages, when level-of-living differences among areas have diminished, there may be more urban-to-rural movement and more "consumer-oriented" migration toward warm climates or locations with other amenities (Long 1988).

Differential Migration. What population characteristics predict migration? Characteristics that indicate less entanglement with social obligations, greater need for employment, and higher job skills are good predictors. Men are more mobile with respect to residence than women, although the difference is small. The single migrate at higher rates than the married. For several decades, blacks have been more mobile than whites. However, in 1980 whites migrated at higher rates than blacks, although blacks continued to be more mobile locally. Hispanics migrated internally at a rate between those of the black and the white populations. Persons with higher levels of education are more likely to migrate than those who are less well educated.

Age and Mobility. The shape of the age

profile of migrants in the United States has been consistent for decades, changing only gradually over time. The younger children are, the more likely they are to migrate. The migration rate of children bottoms out in the early teens and does not increase rapidly until the late teens. More than one-third of Americans in their young adult years, ages twenty to twenty-four, the peak migration years during the life course, moved at least once between 1982 and 1983, and nearly one-half of this mobility was migratory. Not surprisingly, this age corresponds with college graduation and marriage for many. The increasing age of children in the home, particularly once they begin their formal schooling, dampens the attractiveness of migration for their parents. The age-specific migration rate declines slowly at first, then more steeply until age thirty-five, after which it slowly declines throughout the middle years to a life-course low point just before the retirement years. The retirement migration hump between ages sixty and seventy is small by comparison to the early adulthood migration bulge. The final increase in age-specific migration rises at the end of life and is related largely to health issues. The elderly as a broad age category are only about one-half as mobile as the general population.

MIGRATION AND REGIONAL REDISTRIBUTION OF POPULATION

Three large interregional flows of internal migration have been occurring in the United States for many decades.

Westward Movement. For a long time, there has been a high-volume flow of persons into the Pacific region, principally California, as well as a high-volume flow into the mountainous southwestern states. The 1970–1980 decade had a higher volume of westward movement than any previous decade. Mountain states that previously had been suffering losses all made positive gains, and Colorado, Nevada, and Arizona continued the large gains of the previous decade.

Northward Movement from the South. The southern region lost population heavily between the close of the Civil War and 1950. A very large share of the migrating population was absorbed by industrial centers in the Northeast and East-North-Central regions. Both white and black migrants have flowed along these channels in great numbers. Some southern states, however, particularly Florida and Texas, were exceptions. Between 1970 and 1980 the net outflow from the South completely disappeared. Those who leave the South prefer the West rather than the North as a destination, and in-migrants to the South currently balance the out-migrants. Every state in the Northeast and North-Central regions suffered a net migration loss during the decade, resulting in a major regional migration turnaround (Bogue 1985).

The Southward Movement to the Gulf Coast and the Southern Atlantic Seaboard. The entire Gulf Coast, from the mouth of the Rio Grande in Texas across the coastal portions of lower Louisiana, Mississippi, and Alabama, and on to include all of Florida, has undergone a much more rapid and intensive economic development than the southern and southeastern parts of the United States lying away from the coast. Although this trend is a very old one, it accelerated rapidly in the 1970s.

As of 1980 there were only two regional migration streams instead of three: movement toward the South and Southwest, and movement toward the West. The Northeast and the North-Central region are the sources from which these migrants come (Bogue 1985).

One of the macro-level processes that affects geographic mobility in our time is metropolitan deconcentration. Many nonmetropolitan counties in the United States experienced a slowing of population decline in the 1960s, and in the 1970s their net migration rates climbed above the break-even point, signaling a genuine and widespread "rural-urban turnaround." Older people seem to have been in the vanguard of migration to nonmetropolitan counties; the turnaround for them happened in the 1960s rather than the 1970s. This reversal of a long-term trend of rural-to-urban migration has been of great interest to demographers. Mounting evidence now indicates that although deconcentration continues in nonmetropolitan America for the population as a whole, metropolitan counties by the late 1980s were outgrowing nonmetropolitan ones (Long and DeAre 1988).

RETIREMENT MIGRATION

Demography has tended traditionally to focus on youthful migration, and labor-force migration in particular. Increasing attention, however, is being given to nonlabor-force-motivated migration, particularly to the migration of persons of retirement age (Longino 1990). For the elderly, interstate flows are highly channelized—that is, half of the interstate migrants, regardless of their origin, flow into only seven of the fifty states. Florida dominates the scene, having received about one-quarter of all interstate migrants aged sixty or over in the five years preceding the 1960, 1970, and 1980 censuses. Although Florida, California, and Arizona have different major recruitment areas, they are the only states that attract several unusually large streams from outside their regions. Florida draws primarily from east of the Mississippi River, and Arizona and California draw from west of it. Among the elderly, the special characteristics of the destination tend to be more important than the distance. Warm climate, economic growth, and lower cost of living are still important causal factors.

Distance selectivity of elderly migration has been studied. Local movers are generally not as economically and socially well off as nonmovers, and migrants are more so. Interstate migrants tend to have the most positive characteristics.

Permanence is an important but difficult dimension of migration to study. The census assumes that one's "usual place of residence" is not temporary. In reality, however, much of the migration among older people may be temporary. Further study needs to develop a serious research literature on nonpermanent migration. So far, studies of elderly seasonal migrants have shown them to be relatively advantaged, attracted by nonlabor-force issues such as climate, cost of living, and the locations of family members and friends.

Metropolitan-to-metropolitan migration predominates among the elderly. Of the one-third who were changing environmental types, no increase occurred between the 1960 and 1980 censuses in the proportion moving out of metropolitan areas in each decade. The movement in the opposite direction, up the metropolitan hierarchy, however, declined, both among older intrastate and interstate migrants. The net difference made it appear as though the flow from cities increased. Metropolitan-to-nonmetropolitan migrants, especially those moving longer distances, tend to have more income, to be married, and to live in their own homes. A higher proportion of nonmetro-to-metro migrants is older, widowed, and living dependently, especially with their children.

The cycle of migration for a job when one is young, and returning to one's roots after retirement, has been an appealing notion to theorists. Andrei Rogers (1990), however, recently demonstrated that elderly persons are not any more likely to return home than are the nonelderly; the probabilities of return migration by the elderly are lower than those of the general population even after controlling for the different mobility levels of the two populations. There is wide state variability, however. The southeastern region is unusually attractive to older return migrants, and return migration is uncommonly high among older blacks moving into that region.

INTERNATIONAL COMPARISONS OF INTERNAL MIGRATION

There is little research comparing countries on internal migration because measures, data sources, and units of analysis differ widely among countries. Consequently, international organizations have not published compendiums of national comparative data on migration as they have on fertility and mortality. In addition, internal migration is conceived differently in certain types of cultures. In some small countries or where there is little new housing stock, residential movement is very limited. Further, in countries where, for historical reasons, transportation routes primarily connect the peripheral towns to a central national capital, migration is also limited. However, in countries such as the United States, with widely dispersed regional centers and major cities, internal migration is amplified and culturally expected.

Some tentative generalizations can be drawn from existing studies that compare internal migration in the United States with that of other countries (Long 1988). The U.S. national average for moves is higher than that of most other countries because (1) cities in the South and West are growing; (2) a relatively large minority of people who repeatedly move elevates the U.S. averages for lifetime moves above that for most other countries; and (3) during the past two decades the baby-boom generation in the United States has moved through the life-cycle stages that have the highest rates of geographic mobility.

Comparative studies have also given attention to older migrants, although their mobility rates are lower than for the young. Rogers (1989) argued that as the populations of industrialized nations age, the internal migration patterns of elderly persons will change. Elderly migration levels are low in countries in the first stage of this population transition. In the second stage of the transition, large, long-distance flows to particular principal destination regions appear. The third stage continues to exhibit large numbers of elderly migrants, but their moves now include a significant number of short-distance moves to more dispersed inland regions. Rogers and his colleagues (1990) argue from comparative data that England is in the third stage, the United States is transitioning between the second and the third, Italy is well into the second, and Japan is in the first stage.

Since 1970, for most developed countries, population aging has brought declining national rates of internal migration (Long 1988). For the United States, the decline appears to be greater for local moves than for long-distance movement. Urbanization was the dominant redistribution trend in the 1950s in fourteen European countries studied by Fielding (1989). The relationship between net migration and settlement size began to break down, however, in the 1960s—first in the countries of northwestern Europe in the mid-1960s, then in the countries and regions of the southern and Western European periphery through the 1960s, and in the case of Spain, into the 1970s. By the 1970s, most of the countries of Western Europe were recording counterurbanization, where the net flow was away from cities and toward smaller settlements. That counterurbanization became less dominant in the early 1980s but was not replaced by urbanization. Only in West Germany and Italy did the counterurbanization relationship persist. The United States experienced a similar pattern of long-term urbanization, reversed in the 1970s and then nearly reversed again in the 1980s (Frey 1990).

WHY IT IS DIFFICULT TO PREDICT FUTURE MIGRATION

There are several trends that could potentially reduce migration, some only in the short run. These demographic, economic, and social trends might have countervailing effects on recent and future levels of interstate migration (Long 1988). First, a generally slower economic growth in the late 1970s compared with the 1960s may have dampened interstate migration, particularly among the young. Second, the increased laborforce participation of women increased the number of dual-career households. Dual career households tend to have lower rates of long-distance migration. Third, housing conditions in the 1970s may have depressed interstate migration when a potential increase in salary was exceeded by the cost of a much more expensive mortgage at the new location. Fourth, migrants were more likely to move to smaller, cleaner cities with lower crime rates during the 1970s. These migrants may be less likely than others to make a second move.

In contrast, other trends could increase migration rates (Long 1988). First, the age composition has shifted. There were more persons in the twenty-to-thirty age range in the 1980s, the prime mobility age sector. The baby-boom generation is actually less likely to make long moves, on average. However, in the short run the incidence of migration increased anyway, because of their large numbers. In the long run, as baby boomers leave their prime mobility years, their aging will likely dampen the incidence of moving. Second, the rising level of education may increase migration: Each new cohort of adults has a higher level of education than their seniors. Third is household change: Married couples are increasingly likely to divorce, a situation favoring migration, but at the same time there are more dual-career couples in the population, which favors nonmobility.

As we have seen, many factors motivate migration. These factors need further study, which will certainly generate new research hypotheses to be tested by migration researchers in the 1990s.

(SEE ALSO: *Population; Retirement*)

REFERENCES

Bogue, Donald J. 1985 *The Population of the United States: Historical Trends and Future Projections.* New York: Free Press.

———, and Calvin L. Beale 1961 *Economic Areas of the United States.* New York: Free Press.

Fielding, A. J. 1989 "Migration and Urbanization in Western Europe since 1950." *The Geographical Journal* 155:60–69.

Frey, William H. 1990 "Metropolitan America: Beyond the Transition." *Population Bulletin* 45:1–51.

Kahley, William J. 1990 "Measuring Interstate Migration." *Economic Review* 75 (2):26–40.

Lansing, John B., and Eva Mueller 1967 *The Geographic Mobility of Labor.* Ann Arbor: Institute for Social Research, University of Michigan.

Lee, Everett S. 1966 "A Theory of Migration." *Demography* 3:47–57.

Long, Larry H. 1988 *Migration and Residential Mobility in the United States.* New York: Russell Sage Foundation.

———, and D. DeAre 1988 "U.S. Population Redistribution: A Perspective on the Nonmetropolitan Turnaround." *Population and Development Review* 14: 433–450.

Longino, Charles F., Jr. 1990 "Geographic Distribution and Migration." In R. H. Binstock and L. K. George, eds., *Handbook of Aging and the Social Sciences,* 3rd ed. San Diego, Calif.: Academic Press.

Lowry, Ira S. 1966 *Migration and Metropolitan Growth: Two Analytic Models.* San Francisco: Chandler.

Prehn, John W. 1986 "Migration." *The Encyclopedic Dictionary of Sociology,* 3rd ed. Guilford, Conn.: Dushkin.

Ravenstein, E. G. 1889 "The Laws of Migration." *Journal of the Royal Statistical Society* 52:245–301.

Rogers, Andrei 1989 "The Elderly Mobility Transition: Growth, Concentration and Tempo." *Research on Aging* 11:3–32.

———1990 "Return Migration to Region of Birth Among Retirement-Age Persons in the United States." *Journal of Gerontology: Social Sciences* 45:S128–S134.

———, John F. Watkins, and Jennifer A. Woodward 1990 "Interregional Elderly Migration and Population Redistribution in Four Industrialized Countries: A Comparative Analysis." *Research on Aging* 12: 251–293.

Shryock, Henry S. 1964 *Population Mobility within the United States.* Chicago: Community and Family Study Center, University of Chicago.

Zelinski, Wilbur 1971 "The Hypothesis of the Mobility Transition." *Geographical Review* 61:219–249.

CHARLES F. LONGINO, JR.

INTERNATIONAL LAW International law is the system of rules and principles governing relations at the interstate level. It originally developed in response to the needs of states but in recent times has grown to include international organizations and, to some extent, individuals.

International law as a systematic body of rules began in Europe in the seventeenth century. Before then, and from earliest history, rules existed governing the interrelations of various groups of people (Nussbaum 1958). But the rules were systematized in Europe only when the contacts among peoples became regular and frequent and the idea of a single ruler for all known society foundered. That occurred with the collapse of the Holy Roman Empire during the Thirty Years War (1618–1648). The state system developed in its place, characterized by a number of kingdoms and principalities, each equal to the others, sovereign within its own borders, and subject to no outside sovereign. Hugo Grotius, a Dutchman who lived during this time, wrote a seminal book, *De Jure Belli ac Pacis* (1620–1625), describing legal rules, derived from natural law, by which these states could achieve peaceful coexistence and, when they failed, how they could conduct their wars with some semblance of humanity. His book popularized international law, and he is generally considered the founder of international law.

The rules and principles Grotius described reflected the characteristics of states. The fundamental notion that states were sovereign and equal became a principle of international law. And because the rulers of states respected that principle as law, they were less likely to wage war or to annex their neighbors. International law helped create the success of the state system and in turn reflected the features of the system.

Grotius derived his rules from natural law, thus suggesting that nature was superior to states. By the nineteenth century, however, theorists abandoned natural law as a source of international law. Instead, they looked at the behavior of the states themselves as the source of international law. International lawyers became positivists, and the state became for international law the ultimate political entity. The rules of international law could guide and could set out regular procedures to ensure the smooth and peaceful conduct of international relations, but they permitted states wide prerogatives. Governments acquiesced in international legal rules because their states benefited from an orderly system of international relations in which they gave up few of the attributes of absolute sovereignty. For example, the rules did not speak to what states did internally, no matter how egregious. Individuals were not considered subjects of international law. Nor did the rules restrain states from the use of force. International law described permissible uses of force, but states could in effect use force whenever they chose.

By the twentieth century pressures for change began to develop. Technological advances in war and communications accounted for movements aimed at restraining states in their use of force and abuse of human beings. People such as Elihu Root, U.S. Secretary of State in Theodore Roosevelt's administration, wanted international law to provide the vehicle for restraint. Governments started experimenting with dispute settlement through arbitration and courts. They formed the League of Nations to help them control states' uses of force. International law and international institutions were being substituted for unbridled state sovereignty. The concept was a radical departure from the past and came about only over the course of half a century and two world wars.

After World War II, governments were willing in theory to contemplate real restraints on their ultimate sovereign prerogatives. The United Nations was created as an entity under international law. Its charter committed states to uphold human rights, to cooperate in solving world problems, to abandon the use of force, and to follow the commands of the organization itself. The idea was to lessen state sovereignty for the good of the whole world community. Thus, the state began to lose its place as the ultimate political entity almost exactly 300 years after its rise.

Certain international legal norms are now theoretically superior to the wills of the states. In other words, a certain amount of natural law now characterizes the system again. In addition, the state is making way for other types of political institutions such as regional arrangements, although if the state should ever become finally obsolete so will international law. The current form of international law and many of its rules and principles presuppose a system of coequal entities without a single sovereign.

While the state system remains intact, however, international law has taken on an increasingly important role in governing the relations of states in an interdependent, technologically linked world. It does this even though international law has never had the institutions typical of domestic law: a legislature for making law, an executive to enforce it, and a judiciary to adjudicate and interpret it. In some respects international law still functions as it did in the nineteenth century because the system benefits the state. Nevertheless, law does get made, enforced, and adjudicated, and social movements are at work putting demands on states to form and live by new norms of international law.

Because of the informal condition in which international law exists, however, some legal thinkers argue it is not law at all but rather moral precepts or mere guidelines. Most prominent of these thinkers was John Austin, who described law as a series of commands backed by sanctions. International law has no overarching authority to issue commands, and the sanctions are irregular. But Austin's criticism depends on his definition of law. If law is defined as behavior or behavioral restraint induced by a sense of obligation, international law, in its sphere, is law. Positivist international lawyers also point out that in the end the states acknowledge that international law is law, and that is the relevant indicator.

International legal rules have two basic sources: custom and treaty. Rules of customary international law are created through practices that states engage in because they believe they have a legal obligation to do so. Treaties are the explicit agreements states make with each other to be bound. As the need for international law has grown, states have relied on treaties as a law-making vehicle more and more. The general multilateral treaty has become a common form of law making for important international concerns. For almost ten years nearly every state of the world attended a conference to negotiate a comprehensive treaty on the law of the sea. Because so many states attended and the treaty was so long in the making, the treaty began to take on the characteristics of customary international law, irrespective of its status as a treaty. A similar conference will convene in 1992 to discuss climate, and suggestions have been made to convene such a conference for trade.

When no rule of custom can be found and no treaty exists, international courts have in some disputes turned to a third source of law—general principles of law. These are principles commonly found in domestic legal systems and can serve to fill any gaps in international law, which suffers from its ad hoc law-making process. Theorists consider general principles a subsidiary source of international law because general principles are not made in a positive sense by all the states of the system, and they may be applied to a state that did not wish to be bound by them. Custom and treaty, however, generally allow states to opt out of a rule, thus reflecting the traditional view that the states are superior to the system of law. In the last thirty years, however, states have accepted that certain principles cannot be derogated from because they are considered peremptory norms or *jus cogens*. Examples of such norms are the prohibitions on genocide, the slave trade, and the use of force to advance a state's political agenda. With the concept of *jus cogens*, international law has again taken on some elements of natural law.

Jus cogens also exemplifies the extent to which international law has overcome cultural relativity. As new states emerged in the 1960s, scholars from these states questioned whether international law should be binding on them since it was a European product that had aided in perpetuating colonialism. These criticisms have faded, however, because it became clear that international law also created the thing desired most by newly independent countries—statehood. Moreover, because international law is made by states, the new majority could begin to re-create international law. The process of international law has succeeded to the point of bringing states together in accepting that certain principles are overriding, despite the particular value systems of individual states.

Like the law-making system, the law-adjudicating system in international law depends on states volunteering to use it. The system does have courts, in particular, the International Court of Justice. But no state needs to subject itself to the court unless it wishes to do so. The court does have limited compulsory jurisdiction in the case of states that agree to submit cases to it in advance of disputes arising. Nicaragua brought a case against the United States under such an agreement in 1986. States can also agree on an ad hoc basis to submit disputes to arbitral tribunals. The vast majority of international law is adjudicated informally, however. If a state violates international law, such as when Iraq invaded Kuwait in 1990, most states in the system will pronounce their views regarding the legality of the action. Assessing these evaluations leads to conclusions regarding lawfulness. Thus, states make and adjudicate the law themselves.

States also enforce international law themselves. International law is notorious for being poorly enforced. In fact, however, most international law is in fact observed most of the time. Because the states must agree to the law, they tend to make only the laws they want and are willing to live by. Otherwise they opt out of the rules, as the United States has done for some of the new law of the sea. Law is not so well observed, however, in those areas that make headlines—war, human rights, terrorism—which perhaps accounts for international law's poor reputation for enforcement.

When a rule of international law is violated, the state that is harmed is allowed to take action against the perpetrator. For example, if a fishing treaty between state A and state B is violated because state A's fishermen overfish in state B's waters, state B might be entitled to terminate the treaty and prevent future fishing by state A. This system works to some extent, but states have tried to improve on it in recent decades by, first, giving the United Nations and, in particular, the Security Council authority to police some violations of international law and to expand the ability of domestic institutions in enforcing international law by expanding the concept of universal jurisdiction.

The Security Council has authority to maintain peace. In article 42 of the U.N. Charter, it is given the power to call on member states to contribute troops to fight at the direction of the council. The idea comes very close to having an international police force. It has only been used once, however—in Korea in the 1950s. Other attempts have been stymied by the cold war antagonism of the United States and the Soviet Union, each of which has a veto over invocation of article 42. As a sort of substitute, the Secretary General has regularly sent troops, contributed voluntarily by U.N. members, to serve a peacekeeping role. Peacekeeping troops are not supposed to take enforcement action. But enforcement action may be a possibility again with the end of the cold war. Following Iraq's invasion of Kuwait in 1990, the council ordered worldwide economic sanctions and permitted the use of force, both to enforce the sanctions and to push Iraqi troops out of Kuwait.

Another solution to enforcement has been the widening of universal jurisdiction. To prevent states from interfering in each other's affairs, international law contains principles of jurisdiction defining when and where a state may enforce rules of domestic or international law. In some instances any state may take action. This concept of universal jurisdiction is as old as international law. It was originally developed to handle the problem of piracy. Pirates are defined as persons who commit crimes for profit on the high seas. Generally they do not fly any state's flag, and they act outside the territorial jurisdiction of any state. Typically, the state where the act took place or the state of the pirate's nationality would have jurisdiction, but those categories often do not exist for pirates. The state of the victim might have jurisdiction, but the international system developed the rule that any state may board a vessel that fails to fly a flag and that any state may arrest, try, and punish pirates.

After World War II, universal jurisdiction was expanded to include the concept of crimes against humanity. The victorious allied powers tried German and Japanese individuals, holding them personally responsible for human rights abuses, characterized as crimes against humanity and thus crimes for which any state in the world could take jurisdiction. The Nuremburg and Japanese War Crimes Trials broke new ground in international law by holding that individuals had rights and responsibilities not only under their nation's law but under international law and by expanding the scope of a state's jurisdiction.

Individual responsibility and expanded state jurisdiction are being included today in a variety of treaties, especially related to human rights, narcotics, and terrorism. Customary international law now permits universal jurisdiction over persons who have committed genocide or war crimes. The International Court of Justice has also suggested that important human rights may be enforced by any state regardless of its connection with the violation because the obligation to respect human rights is an obligation owed to all people; it is a right *erga omnes*.

International law will need these improvements

in enforcement. The scope of questions now covered by international law grows annually with the increasing interdependence of the world and the technological advances that bring peoples into conflicting contact. The need to protect the global environment is the newest challenge for international law. States may soon decide they need an international organization to regulate the world trading system. The problems of development, health, communications, education, population, and use of space on earth and in outer space are all new problems in need of attention. Add to them the old problems of war, territorial disputes, governing international organizations, treaties, dispute resolution, refugees, human rights, diplomatic immunity, law of the sea, air space, recognition of new states, and so on, and the growing importance of international law becomes apparent. International law will continue to serve as a means of conducting smooth international relations, its traditional role, but it will also continue to assume new importance as a means of solving problems. In order to achieve this, however, international law must improve its institutions and be accepted by more states, whose own sovereignty will diminish as international law advances.

(SEE ALSO: *Genocide; Law and Legal Systems; Sociology of Law; War)*

REFERENCES

Brownlie, Ian 1990 *Principles of Public International Law.* Oxford: Clarendon Press.

Janis, Mark 1988 *An Introduction to International Law.* Boston: Little, Brown.

Max Planck Institute for Comparative Public Law and International Law 1981 *Encyclopedia of Public International Law.* New York: North-Holland.

Nussbaum, Arthur 1958 *A Concise History of the Law of Nations.* New York: Macmillan.

Parry, Clive, and John Grant 1988 *Encyclopedic Dictionary of International Law.* New York: Ocean Publications.

Stone, Julius 1983 "A Sociologial Perspective on International Law." In R. St. J. McDonald and D. M. Johnston, eds., *The Structure and Process of International Law: Essays in Legal Philosophy Doctrine and Theory.* The Hague: Martinus Nijhoff.

MARY ELLEN O'CONNELL

INTERNATIONAL MIGRATION

International migration is a term used to refer to change of usual residence between nations. The number of international migrants is always very much less than the total number of persons traveling across international frontiers, because the overwhelming majority of such travelers do not intend to change their usual residence. International migration is contrasted with *internal migration,* which refers to a change of usual residence within a nation. The term *immigration* is used to denote the flow of persons establishing a usual residence in a given nation whose last residence was in some other nation. The term *emigration* is used to denote the flow of persons relinquishing a usual residence in a given nation to establish residence in some other nation. Net international migration denotes the difference between the number of persons immigrating to a given nation in a given period and the number emigrating from that nation in the same period.

Immigratory and emigratory events constitute two of the four components of national population change; the other two components are births and deaths. For most nations, population change is determined predominantly by the balance of births and deaths (natural increase). However, for a few nations in certain periods, the net international immigration has also been an important component of the total population change.

In determining the number of persons who have changed residence among nations, national statistical agencies must specify the meaning of a change in usual residence. The United Nations suggests (1978, p. 57) that international movements with an intended stay of more than one year be classified as international migration. Unfortunately, there is considerable lack of uniformity among nations with respect to how international migration is defined. For example, according to data of the Mexican government, some 46,000 Mexicans emigrated to the United States in 1973; according to data of the United States government, the number of permanent legal immigrants from Mexico was about 72,000 (United Nations 1978, pp. 605–623). Also, many governments, including the United States, collect data on immigration but not on emigration. Finally, all data on immigration published by governments refer to legal immigration only. Data on illegal or undocumented immigration cannot be tabulated.

Certain terms useful for the study of either international or internal migration will now be explained. A *migration stream* is defined as the total number of migratory events from Place A to Place B during a given time. The *counterstream* is defined as the total number of migratory events from Place B to Place A. The sum of events in the stream and counterstream is termed the *gross interchange* between A and B. The *effectiveness of migration* is defined as the ratio of the net migration between A and B and the gross interchange between the two places. The effectiveness of migration can therefore vary from a low of 0 to a high of 1. For most pairs of geographic units the effectiveness of migration tends to be much closer to 0 than to 1.

Petersen (1975, pp. 321–324) makes very useful distinctions among the concepts of free, impelled, and forced migrations. In free migration the will of the migrant is the main factor. In impelled migration the will of the migrant is subordinated to the will of other persons. In forced migration the will of other persons is paramount, and the will of the migrant is of no weight at all. Another useful term is *return migration,* defined as migration back to a place in which one had formerly resided. *Chain migration* (MacDonald and MacDonald 1964) is also a frequently used concept. It refers to the common pattern whereby a given individual migrates to a particular destination in which he or she already has kin or friends who have previously migrated from his or her own area of origin.

MIGRATION DIFFERENTIALS

It is universally observed that the propensity for international migration is strongest among young adults. Other differentials in migration tend to be limited to particular cultures or locales. Because the highest propensity for international migration is among young adults, the contribution of international migration to population change is often considerably greater than the net international migration by itself. This is because the birth rate for migrants is higher than for the total population, and the death rate is lower.

DETERMINANTS OF THE VOLUME OF INTERNATIONAL MIGRATION

Demographers analyze the determinants of the volume of a migratory stream into two components. The first concerns the specific propensity to migrate for individuals of each given type. The second concerns the number of individuals of each given type. The volume of a migratory stream can be calculated as the sum of the products obtained by multiplying the specific propensity to migrate for individuals of each given type by the number of individuals of that type.

The determinants of the propensity to migrate may conveniently be analyzed in terms of a preference system, a price system, and the total amount of resources available for all goals (Heer 1975, pp. 94–96). The preference system describes the relative attractiveness of various places as goals for potential migrants, compared to other goals that their resources would allow them to pursue. An area's attractiveness is the balance between the positive and negative values that it offers.

Among the most important of the positive values is the prospect of a better-paying job. Other positive values achieved by migration include the chance to live in a more favorable climate, freedom from persecution, opportunity for marriage, and continuation of marital ties. In the case of forced migration, the positive value achieved is simply to save one's own life.

However, international migration also creates negative values. A major disincentive to migration is that it involves a disruption of interpersonal relationships with kin and old friends. Chain migration is so attractive precisely because it mitigates the disruption of such relationships (Massey, Alarcon, Durand, and Gonzalez 1987).

Other negative values created by international migration are the necessity to learn new customs and, often, a new language. Laws restraining legal entry or departure are also, of course, very important deterrents to international migration and will be discussed later in more detail.

The price system describes the costs in money, energy, and time, which cannot be used in the pursuit of other goals, imposed by a given migration decision. Since the cost of international migration generally varies in direct proportion to the distance traveled, the number of immigrants to a given place tends to vary inversely with the distance.

The total resources available for all goals also affects the decision to migrate. If the only drawback to migration is the expense of the move, an increase in monetary income should increase the probability of migration.

MAJOR STREAMS OF INTERNATIONAL MIGRATION

Certain major streams of international migration deserve mention, either because they have had important historical consequences or because they otherwise exemplify unusual patterns. One of the earliest streams of international migration with historical significance was the westward movement of nomadic tribes in Europe and Central Asia at the time of the fall of the Roman Empire. The many tribes that moved westward during this period included those speaking Celtic, Germanic, and Ural-Altaic languages. As the easternmost tribes moved westward, they pushed forward the tribes in front of them. One suggested explanation for this extensive migration is that the grasslands of Central Asia had become desiccated. A second possibility is that an expanding Chinese Empire disrupted the life of the nomadic tribes near its borders and, thus, provoked the movement of all the other tribes (Bury 1928; Huntington 1924; Teggart 1939).

The European and African migrations to North America, South America, and Oceania have probably had more important historical consequences than any other migratory stream. This flow began slowly after Columbus's voyage to America in 1492. It has been estimated that over sixty million Europeans left for overseas points in the centuries since then. However, net migration was lower, since many of those leaving Europe later returned (United Nations 1953, pp. 98–102). The migration from Africa to the New World was almost wholely a forced migration of slaves. The first slaves were brought to the colony of Virginia in 1619, and the slave trade in the United States was not legally ended until 1808. During the period of slave trade, about 400,000 Africans were brought to the United States (U.S. Bureau of the Census 1909, p. 36). The impact of the migration of slaves is revealed by the fact that, in 1790, 20 percent of the four million persons in the United States were black.

The emigration from Puerto Rico to the mainland United States, of major magnitude in the years following World War II, is of interest because it exemplifies an extremely high rate. According to the 1970 Census of the United States, the combined total of the population of Puerto Rico and of persons in the United States of Puerto Rican birth or parentage was about 4.1 million, of which around 1.4 million were in the United States. Thus 33.9 percent of all Puerto Ricans were on the mainland (U.S. Bureau of the Census 1971, p. 48; 1973, p. 1).

Immigration into Israel following World War II is likewise noteworthy because it exemplifies an extremely high rate. In 1948, when independence was established, the total population of Israel was 650,000; by 1961, after the influx of more than 1 million immigrants, it had risen to 2.2 million (Bouscaren 1963, pp. 89–90; United Nations 1966, p. 113).

Perhaps the world's largest gross interchange in a short time took place in India and Pakistan following the 1947 partition of British India and the establishment of these two areas as independent states. This migration is also of interest because it was impelled rather than free. In the face of violence, Hindus and Sikhs in Pakistan moved to India and Muslims in India moved to Pakistan. From 1947 through 1950, ten million persons migrated from Pakistan to India and 7.5

million from India to Pakistan (Spate 1957, p. 119).

The two most recent major streams of international migration exemplify what has been termed *labor migration.* The first stream was the large-scale migration of workers into the prosperous nations of northern and western Europe from poorer nations in the Mediterranean region such as Italy, Spain, Portugal, Yugoslavia, Greece, Turkey, Algeria, and Morocco. This stream began around 1960 and ended in 1973, following the sudden elevation of petroleum prices by the Organization of Petroleum Exporting Countries (OPEC). The proportion of the total population that was foreign increased substantially in all of the northwest European nations. For example, from 1960 to 1970, the foreign population of the German Federal Republic increased from 1 percent to 5 percent and that of Switzerland from 9 percent to 16 percent (Van de Kaa 1987, p. 42). The second major stream has been the large-scale migration of workers into the major oil-producing nations in the Persian Gulf region out of such nations as Jordan, Egypt, Yemen, Pakistan, and India. For example, from 1957 through 1975, 70 percent to 75 percent of the total labor force in Kuwait consisted of foreigners (Birks and Sinclair 1981, p. 459).

CONSEQUENCES OF INTERNATIONAL MIGRATION

One may examine the possible consequences of international migration for the individual, the area of net emigration, the area of net immigration, and the larger social system, which includes areas of net emigration and net immigration. The discussion must be in part speculative, since knowledge about these topics is incomplete.

Before a move, an immigrant will have anticipated a net balance of favorable consequences. Sometimes, however, reality will fall short of expectations, and dissatisfaction will provoke the immigrant to either return to her or his nation of origin or, on occasion, move on to some other nation.

Net emigration may have several important consequences for an area. By relieving population pressure, it may cause the average level of wage and salary income to rise. Remittances from emigrants may also be helpful. On the other hand, net emigration may cause the value of land and real estate to decline. Moreover, areas of net emigration suffer the loss of investments made to raise and educate children who spend their productive years elsewhere. This loss is particularly large when the individual receives a higher education prior to emigration. Such a loss is termed *brain drain.* Finally, since emigration rates are selective by age, nations with substantial net emigration may have relatively few young adults relative to the number of children and the aged.

Net immigration may also have important consequences. If the area is definitely underpopulated, the resultant population increase may help the nation to achieve economies of scale (reduction in the cost of goods obtainable by increasing the scale of production and marketing) and, thus, raise the general standard of living. Under other circumstances, net immigration may result in some decline in average wage and salary income. In either case, a net flow of immigrants tends to raise the price of land and real estate. Furthermore, in general, net immigration increases the proportion of young adults in the total population. Dependent on their composition, immigrants may receive either more or less in government benefits than the amount of their tax payments. Finally, net immigration may make the population more heterogeneous with respect to race, religion, or language.

For the system comprising the nations of both net inflow and net outflow, the direct effect of international migration is of course to promote a redistribution of population. If migrants have been responsive to differences in job opportunities, this redistribution may further the economic development of the total system. Moreover, a substantial amount of international migration responsive to job opportunities might also induce a decline in the degree to which there is economic inequality among nations. Unrestricted international migration might make the poor nations richer and the rich nations less prosperous. However, there is substantial disagreement among scholars as to what the effect of unrestricted immigration from the poor nations might be on the prosperity of the rich nations such as the United States. Julian Simon (1984) believes that net immigration to the United States will serve to increase its average income. Kingsley Davis, on the other hand, takes a much more pessimistic view (1981, pp. 428–429).

LEGISLATION AFFECTING IMMIGRATION AND EMIGRATION

National laws concerning immigration have varied from almost complete prohibition to positive encouragement. Laws restricting emigration are now relatively rare but have been of important consequence in modern times for at least one nation, the USSR.

In the seventeenth and eighteenth centuries a mercantilist ideology, which saw a large population as the key to national wealth and power, encouraged many of the governments of Europe to attempt to prohibit emigration and to encourage immigration. In the late seventeenth century, the French minister Colbert enacted legislation prescribing the death penalty for persons attempting to emigrate or helping others to emigrate, except to a French colony. In 1721, Prussia passed a similar law. Moreover, the Prussian emperor Frederick the Great invested state funds in subsidizing the settlement of immigrants. In Russia both Tsar Peter and Tsarina Catherine subsidized colonists from abroad, mostly from Germany (Glass 1940, pp. 94–96).

The nineteenth century, influenced by the economic doctrines of laissez faire, was the great period of unrestricted international migration. During this century the European governments freely permitted emigration, and the newly independent United States of America welcomed millions of immigrants.

After World War I, the United States government took a more active role in restricting international immigration. The major events in this connection were changes in immigration law in 1921 and 1924 that greatly restricted the number of immigrants to the United States, establishing a quota for each of the countries outside the Western Hemisphere. Furthermore, each of the nations of northwestern Europe was given a much larger quota relative to its population than those of southern or eastern Europe. This was done even though, in the immediately preceding years, rates of immigration from southern and eastern Europe had been much higher than those from northwestern Europe. The justification made at the time for the quota differentials was the presumed greater ease with which immigrants from northwestern Europe could assimilate themselves (Eckerson 1966, pp. 4–14).

By the 1960s, a changing climate of opinion with respect to the inferiority or superiority of different ethnic groups made it possible for President Kennedy to advocate the abolition of the discriminatory national-origins quota system, and a law accomplishing this was enacted in 1965 under the Johnson administration. The 1965 law called for the abolition of the national-origins quota system as of July 1, 1968, but, nevertheless, imposed an overall annual quota of 170,000 immigrants from outside the Western Hemisphere and 120,000 from within it (exclusive of immediate relatives of U.S. citizens). This legislation granted preference to persons with relatives already in the United States, to persons with needed occupational skills, and to refugees. Additional legislation passed in 1976 abandoned the separate quotas for the two hemispheres and imposed a 20,000 limit on quota immigrants from any nation in the Western Hemisphere (the 20,000 limit had previously been in existence only for Eastern Hemisphere nations). The major effect of the 1976 legislation was to make it more difficult for Mexicans legally to enter the United States.

Some nations, while placing severe restrictions on immigrants in general, have made use of positive inducements to encourage immigration from selected nations or groups. Currently the best example of such legislation is that of Israel, which has committed itself to encouraging the immigration of Jews from anywhere in the world. Formerly, Canada and Australia also exemplified such policies of selective encouragement. Each of these nations subsidized immigrants from European nations while placing severe restrictions on the immigration of nonwhites (Bouscaren 1963, pp. 105–108, 141–144; Petersen 1964, pp. 301–322).

The United States, Australia, Canada, and Israel have laws that allow immigrants permanent residence leading to citizenship. In recent decades, other nations, particularly in northwestern Europe and in the Persian Gulf, have had policies that encouraged only labor migration, that is, migration of workers, mostly male, who were supposed to return to their native countries following a fixed term. In the case of the European nations at least, these policies had unintended results. The contract workers were allowed to extend their stays beyond the times originally set for them to leave. Finally, they were allowed to bring their dependents to live with them. Hence, they became permanent immigrants even though this was not the result intended by original policy (United Nations 1982).

In many nations of the world, particularly in the United States, a major phenomenon is the existence of illegal, or undocumented, immigrants. A necessary condition for the existence of illegal immigration is a lack of congruence between the laws regulating the supply of legal immigrant opportunities and the demand for them. For example, the demand to immigrate to the United States from a particular nation should be a reflection of that nation's population size and the average propensity to immigrate to the United States if there were no legal restrictions. Accordingly, nations with large population size are likely to have more immigrant demand than nations with small populations; yet all nations, without regard to population size, have the same 20,000 person annual quota. Furthermore, national differences in individual propensity to immigrate to the United States should be a function of such variables as the difference in standard of living compared with that of the United States, proximity to the United States, degree of similarity with the language and culture of the United States, and prior existence of immigrants that allows for chain migration. Given Mexico's population size and presumed high average propensity for immigration to the United States, one can easily explain why a very large proportion of all undocumented persons in the United States are from that nation (Heer 1990).

Rising concern over the extent of undocumented immigration into the United States led the U.S. Congress to enact the Immigration Reform and Control Act of 1986. The intent of the legislation was to eliminate the presence of undocumented aliens in the United States either by legalizing their status or by forcing them to leave the country. This act had two key provisions. The first was the imposition of sanctions upon employers who knowingly employed illegal aliens. The second was the provision of a process whereby undocumented persons who had lived in the United States continuously since January 1, 1982, or had worked in U.S. agriculture for ninety days in the period from May 1985 to May 1986 were allowed to become temporary legal residents. After a short time, they would be allowed to become permanent legal residents. The success of employer sanctions is problematic because sanctions can be applied only if the employer knowingly hires illegal aliens and because it is relatively easy for an undocumented person to present to the potential employer either fake documents or the documents of some other legally resident person. On the other hand, over three million persons applied for legalization of status after the act was passed, among whom about 2.3 million were from Mexico (U.S. Immigration and Naturalization Service 1990).

In 1989 more than three-quarters of the world's 5.2 billion persons lived in one of the less developed nations. The annual rate of natural increase in these nations was around 2.1 percent; in the developed nations it was only 0.6 percent. In the developed nations per capita gross national product was $12,070; in the less developed nations, only $670 (Population Reference Bureau 1989). These facts imply a strongly increasing demand for immigration to the developed nations from the less developed. Given the current barriers to legal immigration imposed by the developed nations, undocumented immigration will be of increasing prevalence unless the governments of the developed nations take extraordinary measures to curb it.

(SEE ALSO: *Ethnicity; Population)*

REFERENCES

Birks, John, and Clive A. Sinclair 1981 "Demographic Settling amongst Migrant Workers." In *International Population Conference, Manila 1981,* vol. 2, pp. 449–469. Liège, Belgium: International Union for the Scientific Study of Population.

Bouscaren, Anthony T. 1963 *International Migration Since 1945.* New York: Praeger.

Bury, B. 1928 *The Invasion of Europe by the Barbarians.* London: Macmillan.

Davis, Kingsley 1981 "Emerging Issues in International Migration." In *International Population Conference, Manila 1981,* Vol. 2, pp. 419–429. Liège, Belgium: International Union for the Scientific Study of Population.

Eckerson, Helen F. 1966 "Immigration and National Origins." *Annals of the American Academy of Political and Social Science* 367:4–14.

Glass, David V. 1940 *Population Policies and Movements in Europe.* Oxford: Clarendon Press.

Heer, David M. 1975 *Society and Population,* 2nd ed. Englewood Cliffs, N.J.: Prentice-Hall.

———1990 *Undocumented Mexicans in the United States.* New York: Cambridge University Press.

Huntington, Ellsworth 1924 *Civilization and Climate.* New Haven, Conn.: Yale University Press.

MacDonald, John S., and Leatrice D. MacDonald 1964 "Chain Migration, Ethnic Neighborhood Formation, and Social Networks." *Milbank Memorial Fund Quarterly* 52:82–97.

Massey, Douglas, Rafael Alarcon, Jorge Durand, and Humberto Gonzalez 1987 *Return to Aztlan: The Social Process of International Migration from Western Mexico.* Berkeley, Calif.: University of California Press.

Petersen, William 1964 *The Politics of Population.* Garden City, N.Y.: Doubleday.

———1975 *Population,* 3rd ed. New York: Macmillan.

Population Reference Bureau 1989 *World Population Data Sheet.* Washington, D.C.: Population Reference Bureau.

Simon, Julian 1984 "Immigrants, Taxes, and Welfare in the United States." *Population and Development Review* 10:55–69.

Spate, O. H. K. 1957 *India and Pakistan: A General and Regional Geography.* New York: Dutton.

Teggart, Frederick J. 1939 *Rome and China: A Study of Correlations in Historical Events.* Berkeley, Calif.: University of California Press.

United Nations 1953 *The Determinants and Consequences of Population Trends.* New York: United Nations.

———1966 *United Nations Demographic Yearbook, 1965.* New York: United Nations.

———1978 *United Nations Demographic Yearbook, 1977.* New York: United Nations.

———1982 *International Migration Policies and Programmes: A World Survey.* New York: United Nations.

U.S. Bureau of the Census 1909 *A Century of Population Growth in the United States: 1790–1900.* Washington, D.C.: U.S. Government Printing Office.

———1971 *U.S. Census of Population: 1970.* Final Report PC(1)-A1. Washington, D.C. U.S. Government Printing Office.

———1973 *U.S. Census of Population: 1970.* Final Report PC(2)1E. Washington, D.C.: U.S. Government Printing Office.

U.S. Immigration and Naturalization Service 1990 *Provisional Legalization Application Statistics, January 9, 1990.* Washington, D.C.: U.S. Immigration and Naturalization Service.

Van de Kaa, Dirk J. 1987 "Europe's Second Demographic Transition." *Population Bulletin* 42:1–59.

DAVID M. HEER

INTERPERSONAL ATTRACTION

Everyone meets many people. With some there is a natural fit; with others there isn't. Liking a person is quite different from liking chocolate, or liking to ski. Liking someone implies feelings of warmth, intimacy, and consideration and a desire for time spent together. Interpersonal attraction plays a large part in the formation of all relationships except for those into which a person is born, that is, all nonascriptive relationships. Everyone uses tactics that are expected to recruit potential partners; the specific tactics used in presenting oneself, as well as the characteristics for which an individual looks in others, will vary depending upon whether what is sought is friendship or love or a good working partner (McCall 1974, p. 392). Even though liking someone is based on many factors that can't always be defined, a person does know upon meeting someone whether he or she is in fact liked. This perceived liking in turn draws us toward the other (Sprecher and Hatfield 1982, p. 79). Men and women operate differently in the area of choosing people as being attractive. For example, men are more inclined to reject a person who disagrees with them than are women, and more likely to choose the same type of person as a friend and as a marriage partner (Lindzay and Aronson 1969, p. 97).

First impressions don't necessarily last. Nisbett, reanalyzing Newcomb's data in 1989, found that people's liking of other people after sixteen weeks' acquaintance was not predicted very well by their initial liking of these others after one week's acquaintance (Nisbett and Smith 1989, p. 72).

THEORETICAL EXPLANATIONS OF INTERPERSONAL ATTRACTION

Homans, working from the perspective of exchange theory, states that people consider the rewards versus the costs of any potential relationship (Lindzay and Aronson 1969, p. 83) and are attracted to those people who provide the most reward at the least cost. From this perspective, the ideal relationship is one in which both participants have equal costs and rewards, so that neither feels cheated or exploited. Newcomb asserts that frequency of interaction is an important determinant of attraction, a view known as the *propinquity perspective.* The basic assumption is that the more frequently one interacts with others, the more attractive they become. It is expected that frequency of interaction will lead to increasing similarity of beliefs and values and that this *assumed similarity* will in turn lead to increased attraction. This perspective ignores the possibility that getting to know a person better may actually reveal many differences (Lindzay and Aronson 1969, pp. 94–95). Despite the idea's appeal to common sense, there is little evidence of increasing reciprocity of interpersonal attraction over time (Kenny and LaVoie 1982, p. 54).

People do prefer those who are similar in background, interests, and values. They want to talk about things that interest them and do things familiar to them. A person who can provide social support by having similar beliefs and values is a likely potential friend. Despite the folk wisdom that opposites attract, similarity is more powerful than complementarity. The exceptions are those with strong needs on either end of the dominance–submission continuum or the nurturance–succorance continuum (Argyle 1969, p. 213); when strong needs exist in these areas, complementarity is more powerful.

FORMING RELATIONSHIPS

First meetings proceed cautiously. In every cultural group there are conventions about how long the preliminaries must last. These conventions vary depending upon the age and gender of the participants, as well as where the meeting takes place.

In general, encounters that grow into close social relationships have the following characteristics: (1) a smooth pattern of interaction develops; (2) role relationships are clear, with participants agreeing on the definition of the situation and its rules and accepting the self-image presented by the other; (3) each comes to see the other and the link between them as special; (4) as trust grows, disclosure grows (Argyle 1969, pp. 207–208). The goals of the encounter determine the interpersonal attraction tactics used. For example, when characteristics of potential dating partners were varied along two dimensions, physical attractiveness and personality desirability, undergraduate males chose physical attractiveness as the deciding variable (Glick 1985, p. 561). Therefore, a female hoping for a date would find that increasing physical attractiveness would be more effective than showing what a nice personality she had.

In a culture that, like the United States, values openness, psychological awareness, and emotional vulnerability, self-disclosure increases likability.

Those who disclose little are less apt to be found attractive by others (Montgomery 1986, p. 143).

PLAYING AND WORKING TOGETHER

Competition has an interesting relationship with interpersonal attraction. Rees found that during intragroup competition, football players reported the most liking and respect for those who played their own position yet outperformed them (Rees and Segal 1984, p. 329). Riskin also found that males, when given background data indicating both the degree of competitiveness and the degree of work mastery in target males, rated the most competitive as most attractive, as long as they were also seen as having ability. In addition, these competitive males were assumed by the male subjects to be more attractive to women (Riskin and Wilson 1982, pp. 449–450). Numerous studies have shown that emergent leaders are given high interpersonal-attraction ratings by both sexes.

The workplace provides a setting where qualities of competitiveness, ability, and leadership are displayed. It might be assumed that this leads to the formation of romantic attachments. Though this does in fact occur, the work setting also provides for additional complexity in the handling of personal attraction. Attraction and intimacy must be seen in the context of outsiders' view of the relationship. Attempts must be made to balance the demands of the job and those of the relationship. Role relationships within the workplace are expected to contain a degree of distance that is at odds with the demands of "getting closer." Despite these problems, people do get romantically involved with co-workers. One study of 295 adults (average age: thirty-two) revealed that 84 had been involved in a romantic relationship with someone at work and 123 had been aware of a romance in their workplace. Such relationships are more likely to occur in less formal organizations, especially those that are very small or very large. The person most likely to enter into such a relationship is a female who is young, new, and of low rank (Dillard and Witteman 1985, p. 113).

FRIENDSHIP

Being perceived as friendly, pleasant, polite, and easy to talk to increases a person's ability to attract potential friends. If in addition similar values, interests, and backgrounds are present, the likelihood of friendship is even greater (Johnsons 1989, p. 387). In ongoing relationships friendship has nothing to do with the participants' rating of each other's physical appearance. Nevertheless, at the initial meeting stage a person judged as being too physically attractive will be avoided. In one study, sixty undergraduate males were shown a male target population (previously rated from 1 to 5 by a male and female sample) and were asked who among this group they would like to meet. The most attractive were chosen less frequently; they were judged to be more egocentric and less kind. It was the moderately attractive who were seen as being the type of person most of the subjects would like to meet. Explaining these findings in terms of exchange theory, one would say that most people rate themselves as bringing moderate attractiveness to a relationship and feel that extreme attractiveness throws off the equality (Gailucci 1984).

Though it is often assumed that young people do not see older people as potential friends, a review of forty research reports reveals that perceived agreement in attitudes tends to neutralize young adults' general perception of older adults as unattractive. Elders may perceive young people as attractive or unattractive, but they still prefer to associate with individuals who are middle-aged or older (Webb, Delaney, and Young 1989).

SEXUAL ATTRACTION AND ROMANTIC RELATIONSHIPS

While males and females alike differ in their ability to distinguish between friendly and sexually interested behavior, males are more likely to see sexual intent where females see only friendly behavior. When shown videotapes of five couples, each showing a male and a female behaving in either a friendly or a sexually interested way, males consistently saw more sexual intent (Shotland and Craig 1988, pp. 66–73).

Men and women also differ as to the relative importance of physical features and personal qualities in determining the choice of romantic partners. Even though both sexes rated personal qualities as being more important than physical features, males placed greater emphasis on the physical than did women (Nevid 1984). Despite this, there seems to be a point at which attempting to increase physical appeal by dressing to reveal the body has a negative effect on one's appeal as a marital partner. Hill reports that when male and female models wore very tight clothes that displayed a great deal of skin, they were rated as being very attractive as potential sex partners but their marital potential was lowered. High-status dressing had the opposite effect for both males and females: Ratings of physical, dating, sexual, and marital attractiveness all increased as the status of clothing increased (Hill, Nocks, and Gardner 1987, p. 144).

A shared sense of humor is another important component of loving and liking. When a humor test comprising cartoons, comic strips, and jokes was given to thirty college couples, along with a test that measured how much the partners loved and liked each other, a strong correlation between shared humor and a predisposition to marry was found (Murstein and Brust 1985). It can probably be assumed that the shared humor comes before the relationship, as well as serving as a factor that enhances it.

TRYING TO ATTRACT OTHERS

Though different factors come into play when one is evaluating someone as a potential friend or a potential work partner or a potential romantic partner, there seem to be inferred qualities that make a stranger appear to be likable or not likable. One study found that when videotapes of women were shown to males and females to judge, those most often chosen were apt to be described as sociable, cheerful, and positive emotionally; the underchosen were more apt to be described as negative and moody (Hewitt and Goldman 1982).

A modern form of presentation of self that tells quite a bit about what people feel makes them appear attractive is the personal ad. No longer are these dismissed as being for the desperate; rather, they are seen as just another way to introduce oneself. A study of the responses to different sets of physical characteristics referred to in ads showed that tall men and thin women received the greatest number of responses (Lynn and Shurgot 1984, p. 351). In these ads it can also be seen that people present themselves as happy, able, capable, and very successful. It is interesting to note that the richer a man claims to be, the younger, taller, and prettier a woman he wants. The younger and prettier a woman presents herself as being, the more successful a man she wishes to meet.

(SEE ALSO: *Courtship: Exchange Theory; Love; Mate Selection Theories; Personal Relationships; Social Psychology*)

REFERENCES

Argyle, Michael 1969 *Social Interaction.* Chicago: Aldine.

Dillard, James P., and Hal Witteman 1985 "Romantic Relationships at Work: Organizational and Personal Influences." *Human Communication Research* 12:99–116.

Gailucci, N. 1984 "Effects of Men's Physical Attractiveness on Interpersonal Attraction." *Psychological Reports* 55:935–938.

Glick, Peter 1985 "Orientations Toward Relationships: Choosing a Situation in Which to Begin a Relationship." *Journal of Experimental Social Psychology* 21:544–562.

Hewitt, J., and Morton Goldman 1982 "Traits Attributed to Over- and Under-Chosen Women." *Psychological Reports* 5:431–439.

Hill, Elizabeth, Elaine Nocks, and Lucinda Gardner 1987 "Physical Attractiveness: Manipulation by Physique and Status Displays." *Ethnology and Sociobiology* 8:143–154.

Johnsons, Martin R. 1989 "Variables Associated with Friendship in an Adult Population." *Journal of Social Psychology* 129:379–390.

Kenny, David A., and Lawrence LaVoie 1982 "Reciprocity of Interpersonal Attraction: A Confirmed Hypothesis." *Social Psychology Quarterly* 45:54–58.

Lindzay, Gardner, and Elliot Aronson 1969 *The Handbook of Social Psychology,* Vol. 3. Reading, Mass.: Addison Wesley.

Lynn, Michael, and Barbara A. Shurgot 1984 "Responses to Lonely Hearts Advertisements: Effects of Reported Physical Attractiveness, Physique, and Coloration." *Personality and Social Psychology Bulletin* 10:349–357.

McCall, George J. 1974 "A Symbolic Interactionist Approach to Attraction." In T. L. Huston, ed., *Foundations of Interpersonal Attraction.* New York: Academic Press.

Montgomery, Barbara 1986 "Interpersonal Attraction as a Function of Open Communication and Gender." *Communication Research Reports* 3:140–145.

Murstein, Bernard I., and Robert G. Brust 1985 "Humor and Interpersonal Attraction." *Journal of Personality Assessment* 49:637–640.

Nevid, Jeffrey F. 1984 "Sex Differences in Factors of Romantic Attraction." *Sex-Roles* 11:401–411.

Nisbett, Richard E., and Michael Smith 1989 "Predicting Interpersonal Attraction from Small Samples: A Re-analysis of Newcomb's Acquaintance Study." *Social Cognition* 7:67–73.

Rees, C. Roger, and Mady-Wechsler Segal 1984 "Intragroup Competition, Equity and Interpersonal Attraction." *Social Psychology Quarterly* 47:328–336.

Riskin, John, and David Wilson 1982 "Interpersonal Attraction for the Competitive Person: Unscrambling the Competition Paradox." *Journal of Applied Social Psychology* 12:444–452.

Shotland, R., and Jane Craig 1988 "Can Men and Women Differentiate Between Friendly and Sexually Interested Behavior?" *Social Psychology Quarterly* 51:66–73.

Sprecher, Susan, and Elaine Hatfield 1982 "Self-Esteem and Romantic Attraction: Four Experiments." *Recherches de Psychologie Sociale* 4:61–81.

Webb, Lynn, Judith Delaney, and Lorraine Young 1989 "Age, Interpersonal Attraction and Social Interaction: A Review and Assessment." *Research on Aging* 11:107–123.

ARDYTH STIMSON

INTERPERSONAL POWER In its broadest sense, interpersonal power refers to any cause of any change in the behavior of one actor, B, which can be attributed to the effect of another actor, A. It sometimes refers to the capacity to cause such change (Weber [1918] 1968), sometimes to actual use of that capacity (Simon 1953; Dahl 1957), but always to overcoming the "resistance" of B (Weber [1918] 1968), hence causing B to do something B would not otherwise do (Dahl 1957). Interpersonal power is therefore the power of one individual "over" another as opposed to an individual's power to do something, the capacity of an actor to attain some goal (as in Russell 1938). "Power over" always implies a relation between two actors rather than referring to an attribute of an actor. It is sometimes thought of as "micro" power and contrasts with "power to," which is attributed to collectives (Hawley 1963; Parsons 1963) and is thought of as "systemic" or "macro" power.

Adequate description of a power relation will typically refer to: (1) the *bases* of power (the bases of A's power over B are the resources that are possessed by A that are instrumental to the goals of B); (2) the *means* of power (the ways in which A uses these resources to change the behavior of B); (3) the *strength* of power (the costs to B if B does not comply with demands by A); (4) the *costs* of power (the costs of A of having to exercise power over B); (5) the *amount* of power (the extent to which A is able to get B to do something that B would not otherwise have done); (6) the *scope* of power (the acts with respect to which the amount of A's power over B is greater than zero); and (7) the *domain* of power (the persons over whom the amount of A's power is greater than zero). However, there is a great deal of disagreement over which of these constitute power and what kinds of bases, means, costs, and particularly compliance the word covers.

CONCEPTS OF POWER

In his work on power, Simon (1953) treats the effects rather than the causes of power and covers by the one word a whole family of concepts describing the effects of all the human causes of human conduct. Force, power, influence, authority, and manipulation all have a strong family resemblance to each other, and Dahl (1957), March (1955), and Simon (1953) have all treated them as one process. But French and Raven (1959) have pointed out important ways in which the dynamics of different kinds of power differ, and March (1966) has shown compellingly that treating them all as one unitary process leads only to a dead end.

The laws of *force,* for example, differ in a fundamental way from the laws governing power. In using force, A does not require B to choose between compliance or noncompliance. A kills B, imprisons B, drags B, wrestles B to the ground, but does not require choice by B. Threat of force requires a choice, but threat of force is a different process (Goode 1972). A threat may be futile if B has decided to die for a cause; the threat may not accomplish its purpose. Actual force will accomplish its purpose whether B chooses to comply or not. It simply removes B as a factor opposed to A's wishes.

Like force, *manipulation* does not require that B choose between complying or not complying with the wishes of A. A may control B by controlling the information at B's disposal, by preventing certain choices being open to B, or by activating motives of B known to lead B to do what A wants. In some sense, B may be said to make choices (hence the difference from force), but A does not require B to choose between compliance and noncompliance. A controls the conditions that govern how B analyzes the choice to be made.

Although there are more than one narrow senses of the term *power,* all are distinguished from force and manipulation by the fact that power involves a choice by B between compliance and noncompliance. But this is true also of influence and authority. What distinguishes power is that it involves external sanctions. In Blau (1964) B is coerced to do something, X, by threat of a penalty for noncompliance. In Festinger (1953), B is induced to do X by a promise of reward for compliance or coerced to do X by threat of a penalty for noncompliance. Both rewards and penalties are external to the actor. They make no internal change, no change in the actor's state of mind. B does not change views privately, even if B conforms publicly. *Influence,* on the other hand, persuades B that X is right according to B's own interests, hence B complies privately as well as publicly. Compliance is willing in the case of influence, "forced" (Festinger 1953) in the case of power. If compliance were not observable to A, B would still comply in the case of influence but would not in the case of power. Hence, power is highly dependent on observability, but influence is not (French and Raven 1959).

Authority differs from both: It refers to a claim by A, accepted by B, that A has a legitimate right to expect compliance by B, even if compliance runs counter to B's own preferences (Barnard 1938). It differs from influence because whether B likes or does not like X is irrelevant. It differs from power in that B is expected to comply (and, if B accepts A's authority, does comply) because it is right, not because it is expedient. If B accepts A's legitimate authority, then B complies with A's commands whether compliance is observable to A or not. Furthermore, the power that legitimate authority makes possible has different effects because it is legitimate. Power exercised outside the scope of legitimate authority creates "reactance" (Brehm 1966), but power exercised inside the scope of legitimate authority does not (French and Raven 1959).

French and Raven (1959) also distinguish reward from punishment power and hence inducement from coercion. Coercion causes reactance; inducement does not. But they are so indissolubly connected that it becomes difficult to treat them as distinct processes. A reward foregone is a cost, and a penalty foregone is a reward. Hence, withholding a reward is equivalent to imposing a penalty, and withholding a penalty is equivalent to giving a reward. In order to distinguish the two, one would have to be able to separate giving something from withholding something. This might be possible in principle, but not in the case of power. Power depends on the contingency of sanctions; that is, A must be able to give *or* withhold something, depending on whether B does not comply. It is difficult to have one without the other. Thus, probably the most satisfactory concept of interpersonal power is Festinger's forced compliance (1953), compliance that is public but not private, caused either by threat of penalty or promise of reward.

This still leaves the question of whether power is potential or actual. Weber ([1918]: 1968) emphasized the capacity of one actor to overcome the resistance of another whether or not the capacity is actually used. Simon (1953) and Dahl (1957) have objected to making inferences from a potential that might or might not actually be used. Research in fact consistently shows that not all potential power is used (see below), and Dahl in particular has argued that power has an effect only if used. On the other hand, Friedrich (1937) has argued that B might comply with the preferences of A because of anticipated reward or punishment, even if A says or does nothing that overtly demands compliance by B. Bachrach and Baratz (1962) go further and argue that certain kinds of acts that involve B doing nothing (nondecisions) occur without B even needing to know what A will do, simply because B knows what A *could* do. Both arguments imply that sheer existence of potential power has an effect whether used or not. The effect does not even have to be intended.

The issue of intentionality is another of the disputed questions in conceptualizing power, but not only can potential power have an effect without being used, there are even theories, such as Cartwright (1959) and Emerson (1962; 1972), in which "use" of power occurs without necessarily being intended by anyone.

The dispute over potential versus actual power refers more to causes, the dispute over broad versus narrow concepts of power more to effects. Thus, another ambiguity of power is whether one is referring to causes, effects, or the process relating the two.

THE CAUSAL APPROACH TO POWER

As process, power most typically refers to an exchange of "resources" (characteristics or objects instrumental to the attainment of goals). The only exception is the "causal" approach to power. Simon (1953) pointed out the similarity between the concept of "power over" and causality, leading to a long-standing tradition in which the former is defined in terms of the latter (as in Dahl 1957; Nagel 1975). But this led to so many difficulties that March (1966) concluded that the concept of power was superfluous. Although Nagel (1975) attempted to give the concept more explanatory power by narrowing it (to the effects of A's preferences on B), this led to little further advance, possibly because causal modeling gives one little insight into the process relating causes to effects.

But "process" theories themselves divide into four types: field theory; rational choice or decision, theories of exchange; behavioral exchange theory; and a neo-Weberian "resistance" theory of exchange.

THE FIELD THEORY OF POWER

In field theory, power is the ability to activate forces in the life space of another in the direction of X (Cartwright 1959). The capacity to activate such forces depends on the motive base of B, thought of as a tension system, which, when activated by A, produces a vectored force that reduces the tension. Thus, power depends on the needs of B as much as on the wishes of A. It was this approach that gave rise to the concept of a "resource": Transferable resources give rise to power. But use of power by A faces not only opposing forces leading B away from X but also resistance due to the exercise of power itself. (This resistance was later termed *reactance* by Brehm 1966 to distinguish it from resistance due to B's dislike of doing X itself.) A's "control" over B is the outcome of the opposing forces acting on B. Thus, the outcome of the reduction of tension in the force field is distinguished from A's power in a manner corresponding to the distinction between actual versus potential power. In field theory, therefore, success—that is, actual compliance by B—is not the measure of A's power since there are many forces other than A affecting B's behavior.

Field theory, like the causal approach to power, treats the whole family of power concepts as power, excluding only physical force. But research in this tradition was much concerned with differences between different types of power, including reward power, punishment power, expert power, legitimate power, and referent power (power arising from B's attraction to A, which causes a desire to be similar to A). It was found that both reward and punishment power depend on A's ability to observe B's behavior, while the other forms of power do not. Coercion increased but reward decreased reactance. Legitimacy normatively constrained power so that using it outside its legitimate scope reduced its effect. Use of coercion when it is legitimate decreased reactance, while use of rewards when they are not legitimate increased reactance (French and Raven 1959). Because of reactance, use of coercion depends on restraints that prevent B from leaving the field.

EXCHANGE THEORIES OF POWER

The most important difference between field theory and exchange theories is that in the latter alternatives become the most important factor in the analysis of power. The reason is that, assuming voluntary relations, an actor may do things which she or he would prefer not to do because they are nevertheless preferable to any available alternative. Thus, an abused wife may not leave her husband because separation or divorce are either even less desirable or even more costly. But exchange theories themselves come in three somewhat distinct forms: rational choice, or decision theory; behavioral exchange theory; and resistance theory.

Rational Choice Theories of Exchange and Power. Thibaut and Kelley (1959) offer perhaps the earliest rational choice model of the exchange process applied to power. They treat all interaction by analogy to the exchange of goods and services, each actor's participation in exchange being determined by choice among alternatives, the outcomes of which are characterized by their rewards and costs. Rewards are simply the positive values, costs the negative values, associated with the consequences of choosing an alternative. The value that results from the algebraic sum of rewards and costs is the payoff for a given act. Given interaction between two actors, A and B, payoffs are a joint function of the choices made by each. A matrix of joint payoffs for alternative actions by A and B formulates the conditions determining interaction between the two, in particular whether a relation forms and persists. Thibaut and Kelley treat payoffs in terms of their subjective value for the actors, hence in terms of their "utility" (although they do not use the term). In general, actors are assumed to maximize utility and continue in a relation only if for each actor a course of action is better than the best available alternative.

Thibaut and Kelley deal largely with stable relations rather than with particular acts. Power in a relation arises out of the "dependence" of the actors on each other. It can take either (or both) of two forms: A may be able to control the outcomes of B independently of any act by B, hence control B's fate, or A may be able to make rewards and costs contingent on B's behavior, hence control B's behavior. But an important principle of the theory is that control of an individual's fate can be converted into behavioral control.

There are many variants of the decision-theoretic approach to exchange, each differing with respect to how they treat the choice that underlies it. Value can be treated as objective (for example, in monetary terms) or subjective (for example, in terms of the meaning of money to the actor). The latter gives rise to a utility theory, such as in Thibaut and Kelley (1959) Blau (1964), and Bacharach and Lawler (1981). The relation between choice of an alternative and its outcome can be treated deterministically (as is true of all three of the utility theories just cited) or probabilistically. If value is treated objectively and outcomes probabilistically, one has an *expected utility* theory as in Harsanyi (1962). Among probabilistic theories, probability itself can be treated objectively or subjectively: In March (1955) the probabilities are objective, in Nagel (1968) and Tedeschi, Schlenker, and Bonoma (1975) they are subjective. In the latter case one has a *subjective expected utility* theory. In all these variants of decision theory, the central axiom is that the actor maximizes whatever the theory's criterion of choice.

Despite the variations among these theories, in general they predict that, given a conflict of interest, A is more likely to use power when more is at stake, when the cost of exercising power is less, when the likelihood of compliance is greater, and when there are fewer alternative means of obtaining compliance. The costs of exercising power include the relative depletion of A's stock of resources, the likelihood of retaliation, and the effect of reactance on subsequent relations with B. In general, the evidence supports these predictions, although "use" sometimes refers to whether or not A prefers to impose his or her will on B, sometimes to whether or not, if A does have such a preference, it is accomplished by manipulating rewards and punishments rather than by other means, and sometimes to whether or not A's behavior is overt and explicit, communicating threats or promises, or is covert. Rational choice theories also will in general predict that B is more likely to comply with A's preferences the larger the reward-attached to compliance, the larger the penalty attached to noncompliance, the greater the credibility is of A's promises of reward or threat of penalty, and the fewer the alternatives available to B. Again, the evidence largely supports these predictions. But it is well to keep in mind that with respect to both use and compliance, the evidence deals largely with voluntary relations.

Unlike other decision theories, subjective expected utility theory (especially Nagel 1968) makes use of Friedrich's (1937) "law of anticipated reactions," in which compliance occurs without directives, threats, or promises by A. In the case of punishment, not only is there no visible exercise of power by A, but compliance by B may appear to be willing because there is no visible resistance. In addition, if one takes into account that the law of anticipated reactions can be applied to A as well as to B, A may know in advance that B will comply and therefore know that it is unnecessary visibly to exercise power in order to achieve A's objective (Samuel and Zelditch 1989).

Bacharach and Lawler (1981) have pointed out that even though relative power in a relation is necessarily zero-sum, meaning that a gain by one actor implies loss by the other, relative power can be distinguished from absolute power, the sheer quantity of resources controlled by an actor. Hence, relative power can be distinguished from total power, the sum of the resources possessed by A and B. Total power, unlike relative power, is a variable that can increase for both actors at the same time. Bacharach and Lawler argue that total power has an effect independent of relative power, especially on the use of punitive power capabilities. Given a conflict of interest, if punitive power is an available tactic, the likelihood of its use by the more powerful actor increases as his or her relative power increases but decreases as total power increases.

Thibaut and Kelley note that all these ideas are more useful as the pattern of exchange becomes more stable, hence, the focus of exchange theory is often not only on the fact that power is relational, which is true even at the level of a unit act, but on the structure of relations arising from enduring patterns of repeated exchanges. The most influential theory of this kind has been Emerson's theory of power–dependence relations (1962; 1972). Though it originally grew out of Thibaut and Kelley, this theory has come to be associated more recently with behavioral exchange theory, a theory originating in the work of Homans.

Behavioral Exchange Theory. Homans (1961) behaviorized exchange theory by transforming rewards and costs into reinforcement contingencies and the process of exchange into mutual operant conditioning. Many fundamental concepts of decision theory, however, survive in behavioral exchange theory. Choices are determined by maximizing profit, which is the difference between rewards and costs. Costs in Homans take a form more like costs in economics than in Thibaut and Kelley, becoming opportunity costs, that is, profit foregone by choosing X over not-X. But, as in Thibaut and Kelley, exchange occurs at a point at which for both actors exchange is more profitable than each actor's best available alternative. Thus, A uses power in Homans—where "use" means attempts to direct the behavior of another—when it is more profitable than any alternative available to A, and B complies when compliance is more profitable than noncompliance. Homans, however, gives more emphasis than does Thibaut and Kelley to the effect of satiation on the value of a reward: Accumulation of rewards brings diminishing returns. Hence, poor actors are more responsive than are rich ones to offers of any given level of reward for doing an otherwise undesired act.

Emerson's power–dependence theory, perhaps the most influential theory of interpersonal power, was originally a utility theory of relations like Thibaut and Kelley's (Emerson 1962). But Emerson (1972) followed Homans in behaviorizing exchange theory, except that, unlike Homans, Emerson again dealt with relations rather than acts. Power–dependence theory is formulated in terms of two actors whose social relations entail ties of mutual dependence. "Power" is the amount of B's resistance that can be overcome by A: It is potential rather than actual power that is used to describe the relation. Power is a function of dependence, which arises from the control by one actor of resources on which another depends for achieving his or her goals. Dependence varies directly with an actor's motivational investment in goals but inversely with the availability of alternative sources of resources outside the relation. The "power advantage" of one actor over another is a function of the net balance of each one's dependence on the other. If net balance is zero, power is equal, or "balanced." A relatively unique feature of Emerson's theory is that balanced power is assumed to be stable, while imbalance creates pressures to change the power relation in the direction of balance. There are four kinds of balancing operations. B may (1) reduce motivational investment in the goals mediated by A, withdrawing from the relation; (2) increase the number of alternative sources of the resource (extend networks); (3) increase A's motivational investment in goals mediated by B (for example, by offering status to A); or (4) deny to A alternative sources of resources mediated by B (coalition formation). Attention to these operations leads one to distinguish use of power from change of power—increasing or decreasing dependence in the relation. These assumptions about balance have had a major impact on the study of organizations (beginning with Thompson 1967), but other exchange theories have tended to reject the balance assumption, especially Blau (1964), who instead treats the balance mechanisms as means by which A maintains or increases power over B.

"Use" in power–dependence theory comes to mean something quite different from what it means in decision or field-theoretic formulations: It refers now to asymmetries in the outcomes of exchange. It is assumed that use of power, in the more usual sense, increases until an equilibrium is reached, at which point the less powerful actor is receiving no more benefits than the best alternative source could provide. While power imbalance does in fact increase asymmetry of exchange, it has been consistently found that use is suboptimal. It is constrained in part by search costs (Molm 1987b) and in part by commitment to the other and concern for equity (Cook and Emerson 1978). Furthermore, use of punishment power depends not only on punishment capability but also on reward capability: Those weaker in reward power are, other things being equal, more likely to use punishment power (Molm 1987a).

The most significant development in the behavioral exchange theory of power has been its extension to networks of dyadic relations. Interpersonal power is not necessarily confined to a dyadic relation, as Coleman has shown (Coleman 1973). But except for Coleman, interpersonal power has usually been treated as dyadic. More complex structures are possible, however, by connecting dyads into networks (Emerson 1972). Study of such networks has rapidly developed as a central preoccupation of research on interpersonal power, especially preoccupation with the question of determinants of power at a position within a network. Most of this research has been concerned with negatively connected networks. A negative connection is one such that exchange in one relation decreases the value of exchange in another, while a positive connection increases its value. Thus, if A must choose which of two offers of exchange to accept from two others, B and C, AB is negatively connected to AC because choice of AB excludes exchange between A and C. Subsequent research has concentrated on the effects of varying structures of negatively connected networks. Centrality of a position turns out not to predict asymmetry of exchange very well, hence, much theory and research has been directed at discovering what alternative concept of power of a position does predict asymmetry of exchange. Cook and Emerson (1978) proposed "vulnerability" as an alternative and defined it as the effect that removing a position would have on the total quantity of resources available for exchange in a network. An intuitively appealing concept, this idea works well for many networks, though Markovsky, Miller, and Patton (1988) have objected that there are certain structures for which it does not accurately predict asymmetries. Their alternative conception derives from resistance theory.

Resistance Theory. Willer's (1981) resistance theory objects to the importance of satiation in behavioral exchange theory and as an alternative goes back to Weber's concept of power as overcoming resistance. Willer conceives of interaction as exchange of sanctions. The value of a sanction is a function of its objective value multiplied by its quantity, but value is not itself a function of quantity, hence, there is no satiation effect. Willer focuses instead on the "preference alteration state" of the actor (P_A), consequent on sanctions, and defines resistance as the ratio of two differences: the best possible outcome minus the value of P_A is divided by P_A minus the worst possible outcome B will accept, called P_A at confrontation. Exchange occurs at equiresistance.

The emphasis on resistance leads the theory to incorporate coercion and conflict more easily within the same framework as voluntary exchange. But in addition it leads to a different understanding of power at a position in a network. As in Cook and Emerson (1978), power at a position depends on alternatives, but Markovsky, Miller, and Patton (1988) propose a graph-theoretic index of power based on Willer's concept of exclusion. The difference between the two is that in Markovsky, Miller, and Patton exclusion is relative to the number of exchanges sought, while in Cook and Emerson actors seek to make a single exchange at a given point in time. It is "advantageous" in resistance theory to be connected to positions that have few alternatives relative to the number of exchanges sought and disadvantageous to be connected to positions that have many alternatives relative to the number sought. In negatively connected networks, an odd number of positions is advantageous, an even number disadvantageous. The ratio of advantageous to disadvantageous paths leading out from a point in a network (counting overlapping paths only once) gives the graph-theoretic index of power at that point in the network. The logic of the argument can be extended to inclusion as well as to exclusion. An inclusive connection is one such that exchange in one cannot occur until exchange in another also occurs. Inclusive relations, for example, increase the power of peripheral positions in a network.

(SEE ALSO: *Decision-Making Theory and Research; Exchange Theory*)

REFERENCES

Bacharach, Samuel B., and Edward J. Lawler 1981 *Bargaining: Power, Tactics, and Outcomes.* San Francisco: Jossey-Bass.

Bachrach, Peter, and Morton S. Baratz 1963 "Decisions and Nondecisions: An Analytical Framework." *American Political Science Review* 57:632–642.

Barnard, Chester I. 1938 *The Functions of the Executive.* Cambridge, Mass.: Harvard University Press.

Blau, Peter M. 1964 *Exchange and Power in Social Life.* New York: Wiley.

Brehm, Jack W. 1966 *A Theory of Psychological Reactance.* New York: Academic Press.

Cartwright, Dorwin 1959 "A Field Theoretical Conception of Power." In Dorwin Cartwright, ed., *Studies in Social Power.* Ann Arbor: University of Michigan Press.

Coleman, James S. 1973 *The Mathematics of Collective Action.* Chicago: Aldine.

Cook, Karen S., and Richard M. Emerson 1978 "Power, Equity, and Commitment in Exchange Networks." *American Sociological Review* 43:721–739.

Dahl, Robert A. 1957 "The Concept of Power." *Behavioral Science* 2:201–215.

Emerson, Richard M. 1962 "Power–Dependence Relations." *American Sociological Review* 27:31–41.

———1972 "Exchange Theory." In Joseph Berger, Morris Zelditch, and Bo Anderson, eds., *Sociological Theories in Progress,* vol. 2. Boston: Houghton Mifflin.

Festinger, Leon 1953 "An Analysis of Compliant Behavior." In Musafir Sherif and Milbourne O. Wilson, eds., *Group Relations at the Crossroads.* New York: Harper.

French, John R. P., and Bertram Raven 1959 "The Bases of Social Power." In Dorwin Cartwright, ed., *Studies in Social Power.* Ann Arbor: University of Michigan Press.

Friedrich, Carl J. 1937 *Constitutional Government and Politics: Nature and Development.* New York: Harper and Bros.

Goode, William J. 1972 "The Place of Force in Human Society." *American Sociological Review* 37:507–519.

Harsanyi, John C. 1962 "Measurement of Social Power, Opportunity Costs, and the Theory of Two-Person Bargaining Games." *Behavioral Science* 7:67–80.

Hawley, Amos 1963 "Community Power and Urban Renewal Success." *American Journal of Sociology* 68:422–431.

Homans, George C. 1961 *Social Behavior: Its Elementary Forms.* New York: Harcourt Brace Jovanovich.

March, James G. 1955 "An Introduction to the Theory and Measurement of Influence." *American Political Science Review* 49:431–451.

———1966 "The Power of Power." In David Easton, ed., *Varieties of Political Theory.* Englewood Cliffs, N. J.: Prentice-Hall.

Markovsky, Barry, David Willer, and Travis Patton 1988 "Power Relations in Exchange Networks." *American Sociological Review* 53:220–236.

Molm, Linda 1987a "Extending Power–Dependence Theory: Power Processes and Negative Outcomes." In Edward J. Lawler and Barry Markovsky, eds., *Advances in Group Processes: Theory and Research,* vol. 4. Greenwich, Conn.: JAI Press.

———1987b "Linking Power Structure and Power Use." In Karen S. Cook, ed., *Social Exchange Theory.* Newbury Park, Calif.: Sage.

Nagel, Jack H. 1968 "Some Questions about the Concept of Power." *Behavioral Science* 13:129–137.

———1975 *The Descriptive Analysis of Power.* New Haven, Conn.: Yale University Press.

Parsons, Talcott 1963 "On the Concept of Political Power." *Proceedings of the American Philosophical Society* 107, no. 3:232–262.

Russell, Bertrand R. 1938 *Power: A New Social Analysis.* London: Allen and Unwin.

Samuel, Yitzhak, and Morris Zelditch, Jr. 1989 "Expectations, Shared Awareness, and Power." In Joseph Berger, Morris Zelditch, Jr., and Bo Anderson, eds., *Sociological Theories in Progress: New Formulations.* Newbury Park, Calif.: Sage.

Simon, Herbert 1953 "Notes on the Observation and Measurement of Political Power." *Journal of Politics* 15:500–516.

Tedeschi, James T., Barry R. Schlenker, and Thomas V. Bonoma 1973 *Conflict, Power, and Games.* Chicago: Aldine.

Thibaut, John W., and Harold H. Kelley 1959 *The Social Psychology of Groups.* New York: Wiley.

Thompson, James D. 1967 *Organizations in Action.* New York: McGraw-Hill.

Weber, Max (1918) 1968 *Economy and Society.* Guenther Roth and Claus Wittich, eds.; trans. by Ephraim Fischoff et al. New York: Bedminster Press.

Willer, David 1981 "Quantity and Network Structure." In David Willer and Bo Anderson, eds., *Networks, Exchange, and Coercion.* New York: Elsevier/Greenwood.

MORRIS ZELDITCH, JR.

INTERVIEW PROCEDURES *See* Case Studies; Ethnomethodology; Field Research Methods; Survey Research.

INVENTIONS Sociologists have studied independent inventors, industrial research laboratories, the process of technological innovation, the effects of technology on society, and the influence of social factors on technological development, yet the sociology of invention largely remains to be synthesized, or invented, from the above elements and related themes. Indeed, one common notion of invention is that it is the putting together of elements of existing technology in a new format to solve a problem. The sociological perspective views invention as a series of incremental improvements to a technical process rather than as a single great innovation (Gilfillan 1970). For example, the diesel engine has been shown to be the result of such an extended process of invention by many persons rather than the sole accomplishment of the individual who was given eponymous recognition.

Even the notion of a succession of individual inventors working to improve a technology has been revised in light of the scale of cooperative effort required in many technical fields. Under contemporary conditions of technical complexity, invention has been professionalized and bureaucratized in R&D laboratories. In the late nineteenth century, United States corporations such as General Electric established laboratories, often headed by scientists drawn from universities, to improve existing products and develop areas of research likely to lead to new products. Under these conditions, development of new devices is a group effort or even a combination of a coordinated effort and a competitive race among several groups to achieve the desired goal. Kidder (1981) depicts the internal struggle between two branches of a computer corporation to invent its next product and the network of competitive and cooperative relationships within one of the groups.

Application of theory to making new devices has become a technique of organized invention. World War II successes in developing radar, the proximity fuse, and the atomic bomb exemplified the ability of large-scale, well-organized, and well-funded programs to invent toward a goal, combining theoretical understanding with trial-and-error approaches. These successes lent support to an even stronger version of the relationship between theory and invention: the notion of a unidirectional flow from basic to applied research to technological development as expressed by Vannevar Bush in his postwar manifesto for government support of science, *The Endless Frontier.* The premise was that scientists, well funded and allowed to follow their research instincts wherever they led them, would, as a by-product of their unfettered investigations, produce useful innovations. There are certainly significant examples of new technologies, such as lasers, emerging from the "meandering stream" of basic research. Nevertheless, the exigencies of international economic competition have led to a call for "directed basic research" in which exploration is targeted to specific economic and technological goals, such as the development of materials with novel properties.

While the sociology of invention is often presumed to be solely about the creation of physical artifacts to solve problems, it is also recognized that there are social inventions. Organizational and attitudinal innovations are deliberately sought to solve problems. For example, the "quality circle" bringing together workers and managers to solve industrial production problems across hierarchical lines and the "T" group for exploration and resolution of group process issues can be viewed as social inventions, as can "matrix organization" and bureaucracy itself.

Extending the sociology of invention to the realm of the social would seem to include all efforts at planned social change. However, even if the definition is limited to the creation of physical artifacts, the role of the social in facilitating or retarding technological innovation is a large one. Among the social elements identified in this process are the roles of:

Social movements in calling attention to a problem area and creating support for work on technical solutions, such as rocketry in early twentieth-century Germany (Bainbridge 1983) and birth control in the United States

Economic concentrations of power, such as oligopolistic and monopolistic corporations, in settling on an existing technology, such as the automobile industry and its commitment to the internal combustion engine to the virtual exclusion of electric or other alternatives, and electric lamp producers as manufacturers of incandescent bulbs who, for a time, ignored or deliberately blocked the introduction of fluorescent lighting until a new company eventually succeeded in bringing it to market (Bright 1947).

Governments also play an important role in shaping the development of technologies to achieve public policy goals. For example, the United States Army subsidized the development of the transistor through its procurement policy of purchasing large numbers of the devices during the 1950s in order to miniaturize battlefield communications equipment. The existence of a customer willing to pay high prices encouraged new firms to enter the industry (Etzkowitz 1984). Production in larger quantities led to improvements in the technology, and lower prices resulted in civilian uses, first in hearing aids and portable radios and then in an ever increasing number of consumer electronic devices. Indeed, a probabilistic relationship called "the learning curve" has been identified in which an increase in the scale of production of a device, with a concomitant lowering of its cost, brings with it a speeding of the process of invention (Nelson 1962). In the 1970s a proposal made in response to the energy crisis—to have the army purchase a large number of solar cells to meet its needs for electricity production and thereby induce a learning curve for that technology—failed through lack of sufficient political support. More recently, government environmental regulations have induced a wave of technological innovations in the steel and coal industries, relatively stagnant technical areas in the United States, that not only have reduced pollution but also have resulted in more efficient production processes.

The ability to attract a source of capital, whether public or private, is crucial to sustaining the process of invention. In 1869 Thomas Edison, a budding inventor of telegraphic devices, moved from Boston, then the technological center of the United States, to New York, its financial center. He also oriented his inventing skills to meeting the need of the financial industry for improved communication, thereby improving his chances of gaining financial support.

Availability of venture capital has been found to be a crucial determinant of technological innovation. Given that a new device or process has been invented outside of an existing firm, or even within a firm that does not perceive it as relevant to its business, what happens next? Often nothing, unless people and resources can be brought together to mount an effort to introduce the invention into use. Entrepreneurship and invention, and organizational and technical innovation, are inevitably intertwined. In the course of such ventures, inventors and scientists sometimes become businesspersons. The success of individual firms and the growth of groups of related technical firms in areas such as Silicon Valley in California and along Route 128 near Boston have become the basis of strategies for regional economic development elsewhere. Contemporary state government efforts to encourage technological innovation typically include a component to provide capital for new technical firms as part of their repetoire of initiatives (Etzkowitz 1990).

Time as well as money is a factor in the process of invention, and the two are often related. The ability to collapse the time frame necessary to make an invention allows increased access to funds under conditions of strict time limitations for return of capital on investment. In the late nineteenth century Edison noted that his backers expected a return within three years, a time frame that has not changed appreciably in the United States to this day. He successfully attempted to speed up the pace of invention to meet this requirement. Conversely, the availability of capital for long-term investment in Japan allows the support of longer-term programs of technological innovation. Similarly, when a Swiss firm with a longer time frame than United States stockholders typically allow purchased an interest in Genentech, a United States biotechnology company, the firm was able to continue research programs that it was about to eliminate. These instances illustrate the conditions of temporal and financial exigency under which invention often takes place.

Beyond the role of social factors in shaping the course of technological development is the question of the extent to which physical artifacts are an embodiment of social structures. Nuclear reactors have been found to require a bureaucratic form of organization to operate and control (Winner 1986). Other technologies, such as computers and solar cells, are variable in scale, and social impetuses can lead to a line of inventions emphasizing one characteristic or another, such as centralization of control in mainframe computers or decentralization in personal computers (Etzkowitz 1991). Nonetheless, some social structures have been viewed as a result of the invention and introduction of particular physical artifacts, such as the growth of dispersed suburbs following from the mass production of automobiles. The ubiquity of these connections between physical devices and social structures suggests that it is problematic to meaningfully view these two spheres in isolation from each other (Collins 1987).

Finally, there is the issue of the relationship of science to technology. One view is that although invention was formerly an untutored occupation, evolving independently of science, it has now been incorporated into science. A long-term relationship has been noted in which basic understanding of physical phenomena later results in practical devices that utilize earlier discoveries. For example, Marconi's patent application of 1896 for a long-range radio transmitter was "the technological embodiment of Maxwell's theory of the electromagnetic field, stated thirty years earlier (Aitken 1976, p. 209). A major scientific advance in the understanding of a physical phenomenon had been translated into a working device. Typically, each phase was conducted by different persons, with different professional outlooks and goals: discovery and theoretical advance versus commercial and military use.

More recently these processes have been collapsed into each other, sometimes with the same individuals involved in each phase. For example, the first successful insertion of foreign DNA into a host microorganism in 1973 was quickly followed, from 1976 on, by the founding of small entrepreneurial firms to make industrial applications of this new genetic technique in the production of new drugs and chemicals (Office of Technology Assessment 1984). Herbert Boyer, a university professor who was a leading figure in developing these gene-splicing techniques was also a cofounder of Genentech, a company organized to develop pharmaceutical and other products using those techniques. Other molecular biologists with university appointments soon participated in organizing their own companies. Subsequent academic research in this field has been carried out with the knowledge that commercial implications are an imminent possibility, and an increasing number of researchers and universities actively seek out the industrial potential of research (Etzkowitz 1990).

Another view is that technological innovation still largely proceeds on an alternative path to science and is also an independent sphere out of which scientific discoveries can flow. Invention is based on solving problems in industry, often by trial-and-error, "cut-and-try" methods. A theoretical understanding is worked out, if at all, after a working device is created. The invention of the transistor is often viewed as the classic example of the use of theory to aid in the invention of a device, but even in this instance the starting point was a commercial need to develop a more efficient alternative to existing mechanical switching devices for telephones. Solid-state physics was focused upon by researchers at Bell Laboratories as an area likely to produce a new type of switching device, and further pursuit of fundamental research on the solid state eventually led to the invention of the transistor.

On the other hand, the ovonic effect in polycrystalline silicon is an example of the development of theory following from the invention of a device. Stanford Ovshinsky, a self-taught expert on materials who formerly worked in the auto industry, found a way to line up molecules of silicon so that he could produce solar cells that generate electricity more simply and potentially more cheaply than do conventional methods. This new form of silicon, at first dismissed by professionally trained scientists, was later accepted when one of them developed a theoretical explanation for the property that Ovshinsky had obtained. Many contemporary inventors are not working on high-technology devices but on gadgets that will meet a need, will attract public attention, and will sell. Artifacts such as "Rubik's cube" shade into novelties like the "pet rock," and the notion of technical advance becomes separated from the concept of invention. Many contemporary professional, or at least self-identified, inventors work in these low-tech areas of innovation (Whalley 1986).

The relationship among science, applied research, and industrial problem solving are reconciled in a multidirectional model of technological innovation in which they are viewed as alternative, mutually influencing sources of invention. Projects often viewed as exemplifying the application of basic science to development of a device, such as the World War II United States effort to build an atomic bomb, also relied on "cut and try" techniques as well as on guidelines derived from theory. For example, in an effort to devise a fine-screen filter device to produce purified uranium, scientists accompanied by army officers went to a printing plant and attempted to adapt its sophisticated lithography equipment to solve the problem. Edison's collection and testing of a range of materials to produce an effective electric lamp filament is a classic example of the systematic use of this method. However, Edison, who is often viewed as the prototypical "trial-and-error" inventor, also had trained scientists on the staff of his "invention factory" and used a repertoire of electrical components with known properties to build devices to solve different problems.

Efforts to balance and integrate these apparently divergent approaches can be found in university research centers in the United States. They are often funded by a multiplicity of sources with different goals, from the most basic to the highly applied. To meet the needs of their sponsors and achieve their own intellectual goals, researchers attempt in the course of the same project to reconcile different goals by, for example, at one and the same time producing methods to analyze mortgage securities for the financial industry while advancing the theory of parallel processing in computer science (Etzkowitz 1991b). Thus, science and invention increasingly become organizationally and intellectually intertwined in government, industry, and university laboratories.

(SEE ALSO: *Diffusion Theories; Science; Technology and Society)*

REFERENCES

Aitken, Hugh 1976 *Syntony and Spark: The Origins of Radio.* New York: Wiley.

Bainbridge, William 1983 *The Spaceflight Revolution.* New York: Wiley.

Bijker, Wiebe, Thomas P. Hughes, and Trevor Pinch 1987 *The Social Construction of Technological Systems.* Cambridge, Mass.: MIT Press.

Bright, Arthur 1947 *The Electric Lamp Industry: Technological Change and Economic Development from 1800 to 1947.* New York: McGraw-Hill.

Collins, Randall 1987 "A Theory of Technology." In Collins, *Weberian Sociological Theory.* Cambridge: Cambridge University Press.

Etzkowitz, Henry 1984 "Solar Versus Nuclear Energy: Autonomous or Dependent Technology?" *Social Problems* (April):418–434.

———1990 "The Capitalization of Knowledge." *Theory and Society* 19:107–121.

———1991a "Technology and Social Change: Alternative Paths." In Henry Etzkowitz and Ronald Glassman, eds., *The Renascence of Sociological Theory.* Itasca, Ill.: Peacock.

———1991b "Regional Industrial and Science Policy in the United States." *Science and Technology Policy* (April).

Gilfillan, S. C. 1970 (1935) *The Sociology of Invention.* Cambridge, Mass.: MIT Press.

Kidder, Tracy 1981 *The Soul of a New Machine.* Boston: Little, Brown.

Nelson, Richard 1962 "The Link Between Science and Invention: The Case of the Transistor." In Nelson, *The Rate and Direction of Inventive Activity.* Princeton, N.J.: National Bureau of Economic Research.

Office of Technology Assessment 1984 *Commercial Biotechnology: An International Analysis.* Washington D.C.: Office of Science and Technology.

Whalley, Peter 1986 *The Social Production of Technical Work.* Albany, N.Y.: SUNY Press.

Winner, Langdon 1986 *The Whale and the Reactor: The Search for Limits in an Age of High Technology.* Chicago: University of Chicago Press.

HENRY ETZKOWITZ

ITALIAN SOCIOLOGY The birth of sociology in Italy is variously dated, depending on the causes that are adduced for it or on the perspectives from which it is viewed. Indeed, even the conceptualization of sociology changes; hence, it is in a certain sense more important to determine when each "sociology" was born. We can distinguish two types of sociology and two corresponding ways of generating cultural and professional training. The first type is positivist (or neopositivist) sociology, tied to quantitative empirical research, which aims to discover the laws and the causal relationships that can be drawn from the data and from experience; the second type is humanistic sociology, which interprets its role as a critical science, raises questions, is propaedeutic, and places social phenomena in their historical context. The two places for training professional sociologists are the research center and the university, respectively; each type of institution has an ambivalent and fluctuating relationship with the two sociologies.

Both types of sociology and both kinds of training, together with their origins, take on specific meanings according to the historical period, and hence depend on the process of complexification of Italian society and the parallel development of different Italys (at least the three indicated by Bagnasco 1977).

THE ORIGINS OF ITALIAN SOCIOLOGY

Many historians of sociology derive Italian sociology from the political thought of Niccolo Machiavelli (1469–1527), because of his interest in leadership and its connection with the structures within which the prince must exercise his will. The type of political sociology practiced by Vilfredo Pareto, Gaetano Mosca, Seipio Sighele, Roberto Michels and Camillo Pellizzi can also be related to this current of thought. This school, largely academic in origin, is based in political science, the philosophy of politics, and the philosophy of law. Associated with, and grafted onto it is a sociology of law, also rooted in the universities, as is shown by the great number of articles published in the first issues of *Quaderni di sociologia* (Notebooks of Sociology), a review founded in 1951. Philosophy (Roberto Ardigò), political science (Gaetano Mosca), and law (Carlo Francesco Gabba, Rodolfo Laschi, Enrico Ferri, Icilio Vanni) became "godfathers" to Italian sociology. This may be explained by the dominant themes: the legitimation, explanation, and order that accrue to leadership and political structures as they develop. There were also economists, often (though not always), with a socialist background and orientation—Ginseppe Toniolo, Achille Loria, and Pareto—always aiming to study society in macroscopic terms, in a way closely linked to political science.

Besides these currents linked to the sphere of public action, there was the study of the private sphere as it deviated from the established order—as examined from the perspectives of political science, philosophy, and economics. Cesare Lombroso, Enrico Morselli, Scipio Sighele, and Alfredo Niceforo, some of them with medical training, studied the criminal personality, constructed typologies of the "delinquent man," elaborated pseudobiological explanations of deviant behavior, and thus attempted to interpret the relationship between society and the deviant (the duty of society being to lock up and prevent the deviant from causing further harm).

The sociological bent of these Italian protosociologists, who were generally university professors, was taken from Auguste Comte and Herbert Spencer. Hence, in their work we find a search for the laws underlying the social phenomena studied, the confidence that one can understand these phenomena by means of an inductive method borrowed from the natural sciences, and the awareness that it is possible to describe and explain social reality with the positivist method. Italian sociological positivism (from 1865 to the rise of Fascism) worked out a paradigm of social analysis that was fairly homogeneous and characterized by naturalistic determinism in the form of evolutionistic organicism. It was carried out by means of a positivist inductive method, although the basis of determinism varied during the history of positivism. For Lombroso, Niceforo, and others the bases of such determinism were in biology and evolution (the theories of instinct and atavism), while for Pareto the structure of social activity took its model from economics. Another distinctive characteristic of this positivism was to consider society, social phenomena, and subjects in normative but exclusively objective terms. Roberto Ardigò worked along these lines as a theorist of human action, but after a certain point he became increasingly aware of the importance of "nonlogical" actions, of interiorization, and of socialization—the possibility of a voluntaristic theory. It is thus possible, in his case, to speak of a positivism of the subject, which foreshadows the work of Pareto.

The positivist approach was used by Socialist and Catholic scholars, as well as by liberals. This perspective was shared by the founders of *Rivista italiana di sociologia* (Italian Review of Sociology), which was published from 1897 to 1922.

Positivism—mainly a French and English current of thought—began to decline when its naturalistic-determinist presuppositions were left behind and other variables had been introduced, thus leading to interpretations of society in more complex terms (Mosca, Pareto, Michels, Gaetano Salvemini); also, it was questioned when a progressive and optimistic determinism was replaced by a pessimistic determinism (as in Michels, with his iron law of oligarchy). Positivism was reborn with the formation of the Chicago school of urban and ecological studies at the end of the 1930s.

In Italy positivism was replaced by the idealism of Benedetto Croce and Giovanni Gentile, who were strongly critical of positivism's main ideas and naturalistic research methods. The polemical debate in 1900–1901 between Pareto and Croce in the pages of *Il Giornale degli economisti (The Journal of Economists)* is emblematic.

The technologically hard core of positivism is the research method, particularly "the experimental method that has given such brilliant results in the natural sciences," as Pareto wrote in his "Discorso per il Giubileo" (1917; "Discourse for the Jubilee").

This explains why, among the positivist sociologists, there were many demographers and statisticians (including Angelo Messedaglia, Loria, Niceforo, and Livio Livi) during the years of Fascism (1920–1940) and why the preeminence of idealism—the point of reference for sociology—lay primarily in statisticians such as Corrado Gini, Vittorio Castellano, Marcello Boldrini, and Nora Federici.

Gini, in particular, was active in founding the Istituto Centrale di Statistica (Central Institute of Statistics) in 1926; this agency was set up to organize census taking in Italy. In 1928 he founded the Comitato Italiano per lo Studio dei Problemi della Popolazione (Italian Committee for the Study of Population Problems), the school of statistics at the University of Rome (1929), the Italian section of the Institut International de Sociologie (1932), the Società Italiana di Sociologia (Italian Society of Sociology) in 1937, and the Facoltà di Scienze Statistiche, Demografiche e Attuariali (Faculty of Statistical, Demographic, and Actuarial Sciences) at the University of Rome (1936). In this period Gini also founded, or was a founding member of, many journals, such as the *Bollettino bibliografico di scienze sociali e politiche* (1924; Bibliographical Bulletin of Social and Political Sciences), *La vita economica italiana* (1926; Italian Economic Life), and *Gems* (1934).

To sum up, Italian sociology was born through the importation of positivist ideas, paradigms, and methodological creeds, and it tried to solve the problems that society or the classes in power considered important in the second half of the nineteenth century and the first half of the twentieth—the existing forms of power and their legitimation, as well as the control of deviance. Its content therefore concerned the philosophy of law, political doctrines, socialism, the social thought of the Catholic church, criminality and alienation, and related matters. In the first half of the twentieth century, in particular during the Fascist period, the study of demographics and statistics remained alive, as did the charismatic components and fatal distortions of power (Michels). So, too, did the irrational and subjective element in society, in the form of residues and derivations (Pareto).

The themes and problems of concern were closely linked to the period in which Italian sociology developed. Socially, Italy was still traditional and sociology was developed within the universities, in the context of more-or-less formally recognized courses.

1945 TO THE 1960S

The postwar period witnessed a profound rupture in Italian society, in its culture, and hence in its sociology. That society became much more complex, and its emerging culture became part of sociological study. Thus problems such as those in the South of Italy—urbanization, migration, the large concentrations of workers—were brought to consciousness. Second, Italian sociologists were very receptive to foreign ideas and schools of thought. Thus, alongside the survival in academic circles of the influence of Comte, Spencer and Darwin, and in the work of Gini, Livi, and Castellano, the American influence became dominant and the German tradition regained importance, primarily through research institutes.

In other words, there was first an accumulation of theory and research that was incorporated into university sociology courses; later came the first chair of sociology, which was awarded to Franco Ferrarotti, at Rome in 1962. Scholars did not yet have sociological training, since no academic structures for that purpose existed; therefore they came from fields such as classical studies, political science (still very much oriented toward law), economics and commerce, medicine, law, and so forth.

One effect of this complexity was the subdivision of sociology into many branches: development and modernization; urban and rural sociology; the sociology of labor, of the economy, of migrations.

This period lasted from the end of World War II to the founding of the first faculty of sociology at Trento and the reform of the faculties of political sciences; it saw the incubation of a new direction in Italian sociology. Since that time there has been the development of the Faculty at the University of Rome, and many other universities have acquired significant faculty strength in sociology. Let us now examine these currents.

The Sociology of Development and the Mezzogiorno. One of the problems the new Italy had to face was the reduction of the developmental gap between North and South, in particular how to enable the society of the South and of the islands to overcome their state of underdevelopment. Even before World War II the "Southern question" had been posed and announced by the actions and writings of Guido Dorso and Salvemini, among others. But it was only after 1946 that the problem became a subject of study and institutional intervention. Some of the institutions that deal with intervention and training, as well as with sociological research on the problems of the Mezzogiorno, are the Associazione per lo Sviluppo dell'Industria nel Mezzogiorno (SVIMEZ; Association for the Development of Industry in the Mezzogiorno), the CENTRO per la Formazione e studi per il Mezzogiorno (Center for Professional Training and Studies of the Mezzogiorno), the Associazione Nazionale per gli Interessi del Mezzogiorno (ANANI; National Association for the Interests of the Mezzogiorno), the Movimento di Collaborazione Civica (Movement of Civic Collaboration), the Unione Nazionale per la Lotta contro il analfabetismo" (National Union for the Fight Against Illiteracy), and UNRRA-Casas (Instituto per lo Sviluppo dell'ediliza Sociale; the Institute for the Development of Public Housing).

Projects and plans were drawn up within and in cooperation with these agencies. They include the pilot project for the Abruzzi, the Sardinia project, the Center for Studies and Initiatives in western Sicily, the Center for Community Development at Palma di Montechiaro, and the Molise and Avigliano projects. It was in these institutions that sociological and anthropological studies on development, modernization, and the community were carried out. Tulio Tentori (1956), Guido Vincelli (1958), Danilo Dolci (1955, 1957, 1960), Gilberto Antonio Marselli (1963), Lidia de Rita (1964), Maria Ricciardi Ruocco (1967), Lucia Pinna (1971), Gualtiero Harrison and Maria Callari Galli (1971), and Giovanni Mottura and Enrico Pugliese (1974) are among those whose works reveal a social commitment together with testing of the theories of modernization. They show an awareness of their limits as well, as elaborated by the English-language sociological tradition; moreover, there was a strong element of utopianism in this mixture of social commitment and scientific rigor.

It was not just the ideas of American and northern European scholars that were studied and applied to the modernization of the South of Italy; scholars themselves were committed to the task. At the same time, some classic research was carried out, important both because it was cited by Italian scholars and because it was rejected by them (in particular by Alessandro Pizzorno and

Marselli). One of the books that became an object of controversy was Edward C. Banfield's *The Moral Basis of a Backward Society* (1958). Other often-cited foreign research works included Joseph Lopreato's *Social Stratification and Mobility in a South Italian Town* (1961), Felix Gross's *Value Structure and Social Change* (1979), and Johann Galtung's *Members of Two Worlds: A Development Study of Three Villages in Western Sicily* (1971).

Sociological study of modernization also entered the universities through sociology courses that took their place alongside rural economics. The most important center for these courses was the Faculty of Agriculture at Portici, and the most significant sociologists were Marselli, Pugliese, Mottura, and Emanuele Sgroi.

The Sociology of Work and Economics. The sociology of work and economics arose in the research agencies, in research centers of large industries, and in labor unions.

One very important research center for the training of Italian sociologists was Olive Hi's Ufficio Studi e Relazioni Sociali (Research and Social Relations Office) at Ivrea. Adriano Olivetti, building a company and a community, surrounded himself with sociologists, economists, communications experts, and planners. Ferrarotti, Pizzorno, Luciano Gallino Paolo Ceri, and Antonio Carbonaro worked and studied at the facility. They, and many more, devoted themselves to industrial relations and the rationalization of staff selection in large industries operated by enlightened and paternalistic entrepreneurs like Olivetti. Very often, however, the left-wing slant of their training and their impression of being manipulated led these sociologists to leave the research center after a short stay and to continue their sociological training at universities in the United States. In this cultural climate, which also was indebted to nineteenth-century models of integration of the company, the community, and territorial planning, the review *Comunità* published essays with a strong cultural and social commitment. The publishing house of the same name made available to the Italian public the classics of German and, especially, American sociology.

Another forum for the training of sociologists (especially in the sociology of labor) was the research offices of the labor unions (and, to a lesser extent, of the political parties). In particular, future sociologists such as Aris Accornero, Guido Baglioni, Gian Primo Cella, and Guido Romagnoli were directed toward studies on factory work. The factory and labor union conflicts were the main subjects of their research, with a consequent tendency to identify the "organization" with the factory (a pamphlet on the sociology of organizations by G. Bonazzi is, significantly, entitled "Dentro e fuori la fabbrica" (1982)—"Inside and Outside the Factory") and the labor union. These sociologists had few contacts with foreign scholars; when they did, such contacts were oriented toward France and particularly toward the Institut des Sciences Sociales du Travail, (the Institute of the Social Science of Labor) in Paris.

Urban Sociology and the Sociology of Planning. Other institutions in which sociologists (this time urban sociologists) were trained in the 1950s and 1960s were the planning offices set up by the territorial governments (large municipalities and provinces in northern Italy), particularly the Istituto Lombardo di Studi Economici e Sociali (ILSES; Lombard Institute of Economic and Social Studies) in Milan and the Centro Studi Sociali e Amministrativi (CSSA; Center for Social and Administrative Studies) in Bologna. The former trained the sociologists Pizzorno, Gianni Pellicciari, Massimo Paci, Alberto Martinelli, Guido Martinotti, Paolo Guidicini; the latter, Achille Ardigò, Guidicini, Giuliano Piazzi, and Pietro Bellasi. There was also the Ufficio Studi Sociali e del Lavoro (Office for Social and Labor Studies) in Genoa, where Luciano Cavalli carried out his *Inchiesta sugli abituri* (1957; Survey on Slums).

ILSES dealt with research on neighborhoods, on participation in neighborhoods, and, in general, on the structure of the city. The approaches were borrowed from the concepts and research of the Chicago school and the group that had formed around Paul Henry Chombart de Lauwe. Thus, among other things, Ernest W. Burgess's model of concentric areas was verified for Italian cities (in Rome and Milan), as was Hoyt's model of sectors. The results of these researches found expression in anthologies on the Chicago school: Guido Martinotti's *Città e analisi sociologica* (1968; The City and Sociological Analysis); manuals of urban sociology such as Franco Demarchi's *Società e spazio* (1969; Society and Space); and a manual of urban research based largely on that carried out by ILSES and CSSA, Paolo Guidicini's *Manuale della ricerca sociologica* (1968; Manual of Sociological Research).

The sociologists who worked at ILSES developed close contacts with the United States (particularly Martinotti, Paci, and Martinelli) and with the United Kingdom (Guidicini).

International Sociology. Sociology entered the universities and enabled them to train both theoretical and empirical sociologists, but no attention was given to international sociology. International sociology in Italy was developed by the Istituto di Sociologia Internazionale di Gorizia (ISIG) (Institute of International Sociology of Gorizia), founded by Demarchi in 1969. This branch of sociology seeks its identity in the synthesis of ideas from political sociology, the sociology of international relations, of ethnic relations, of borders, of towns, and of territories. Relations were developed with scholars from the United States, from Eastern Europe, and from the countries of the European Economic Community. From the United States, the Institute took the research methodology of multivariate analysis, under the direction of Edgar F. Borgatta; it was one of the first institutions in Italy to adopt these techniques. Its researchers later held important positions in various universities: Renzo Gubert, Alberto Gasparini, Raimondo Strassoldo, Bruno Tellia, Bernardo Cattarinussi, and Giovanni Delli Zotti.

Among the cited research organizations ISIG is one of the few that carries out an active program that is not encompassed by university activities. There are at least two reasons for this. First, Italian sociology has tended not to be interested in international relations. Second, there has been an acceleration of international interdependence; in recent years there has been great change in the relations between Western and Eastern Europe, and between Europe and the rest of the world. Under the recent direction of Alberto Gasperini, ISIG has responded to the need for such study, with emphasis on Eastern Europe and the USSR.

Academic Institutionalization of Italian Sociology. The most intense activity of the research agencies occurred in the 1950s and 1960s; it was scientific in the full sense of the word, since concrete problems were tackled empirically, starting from a theory (generally developed abroad) and ultimately returning to the theory. This way of doing research, and of training for research, is quite different from the method adopted in the universities, because it is tied to concrete problems and specific deadlines.

Moreover, in this period, together with the ideas and plans designed to establish sociology in the universities (the first chair in sociology was awarded to Ferrarotti in 1962), sociology was taking on an identity as an academic discipline. The first issue of *Quaderni di sociologia* (Notebooks of Sociology) was published in 1951, edited by Nicola Abbagnano and Ferrarotti, and in 1957 the Associazione Italiana di Scienze Sociali (AISS; Italian Association of Social Sciences) was founded. In 1959 the Centro Nazionale di Prevenzione e Difesa Sociale (National Center for Prevention and Social Defense) in Milan, together with AISS, organized the Fourth World Congress of Sociology at Stresa; and from then until 1974 Italian sociologists (Angelo Pagani and Guido Martinotti) held the post of secretary of the International Sociological Association. Italian sociology was now mature and ready to enter the universities with its own sociologists, their empirical experience, and their theoretical preparation; hence it was able to extend the discipline.

SINCE THE 1960S

Italian sociology, as a discipline and as scientific research, has developed strongly. The heart of this development lies more in the universities and university teachers than in the nonacademic instiutes that played such a large role until the 1960s. All this happened with the consolidation of socioltogy in the university system (which had the function of training young researchers and became the channel for legitimizing the scientific character of sociological research). Subsequent developments were the publication of dictionaries and encyclopedias of sociology, the foundation of the Associazione Italiana di Sociologia (Italian Association of Sociology), and the formation and coordination of sociological interests in specific areas.

Sociology in the Italian Universities. The complexity of Italian society requires a strong sociological reading of reality, and the nonacademic agencies have so far considered could not long meet this need. Moreover, a strong impulse to legitimize sociological analysis came from the student protest movement, which in the mid-1960s reached Europe from the United States.

Thus sociology entered the universities mainly with the establishment in Trento of the Istituto Universitario di Scienze Sociali (University Institute of Social Sciences, later the Faculty of Sociology) in 1962, and with the reform of political science faculties in 1968.

The Faculty of Sociology at Trento. The Istituto Universitario di Scienze Sociali was officially founded on September 12, 1962, on the initiative of the Provincia Autonoma di Trento (the Autonomous Province of Trento) and the Istituto Trentino di Cultura (the Trento Institute of Culture) and of Prof. Giorgio Braga, lecturer at the Università Cattolica in Milan. The governing body is composed of ten professors: three jurists, two economists, one statistician, one mathematician (the director, Mario Volpato), one moralist, and the sociologists Braga (vice director) and Franco Ferrarotti. The first sociologists to teach there were not from the Milan area. Later Milanese came to Trento: Francesco Alberoni and Guido Baglioni. The first teachers at Trento were from several regions: Giorgio Braga (from the Università Cattolica in Milan), Franco Ferrarotti (Rome), Filippo Barbano (Turin), Sabino Acquaviva (Padua), Franco Demarchi (Trento), and Achille Ardigò (Bologna). The students who enrolled in the first year (226), and even more in the immediately following years, were strongly motivated to study social problems and came increasingly from regions far from Trento.

The Faculty of Sociology, with its four-year program, grants two types of degrees in sociology: general and special. The general course trains teachers and researchers in the sociological disciplines who will work in universities, international institutions, and centers of research on economic and social problems. The special sociology course prepares students for management careers in public administration and in private firms (in particular, for research, public relations, and personnel), in social insurance offices, agencies for agricultural development, welfare agencies, labor unions and political parties, business consultancy agencies, marketing research offices, and town planning bodies.

As can be seen, this university planning aimed at the extension of the university; moreover, it set out to deal with a society that was both complex and predictable in its organization of problems and phenomena to be studied and, if possible, solved.

Things changed with the arrival of the student protest movement; at the University of Trento different models of teaching and organization were experimented with, leading it to occupy a unique position in the Italian university system. A "critical university," managed by a joint committee of teachers and students, was formed. The director of the institute and experimenter with this model was Francesco Alberoni, who attracted other teachers interested in this project, in particular from Milan. This situation lasted until 1970; meanwhile, it triggered experimentation at other Italian universities, and to some extent contributed to the reform of the faculties of political science. In subsequent years, while the Institute was transformed into the first Faculty of Sociology in the Italian university system, degree courses (corsi di laurea) in sociology emerged, often within existing *facoltà di magistero* (education faculties) at Rome, Naples, Salerno, and Urbino.

The Reform of the Faculties of Political Science. Sociology was offered in twenty-three Italian universities in 1964–1965, a total of thirty-eight courses taught by twenty-seven professors. It was episodically and marginally introduced into the faculties of law, letters, arts, economics, and political science, and often the same person was asked to teach several courses: for example, Alberoni taught four different courses in sociology at the same time at the Università Cattolica of Milan. The courses were scattered throughout Italy: four courses in Rome and Milan (Università Cattolica); three courses in Bari and Florence; two in Bologna, Cagliari, Milan (Università Statale), Naples, and Palermo; and one course each at the universities of Catania, Ferrara, Genoa, Messina, Milan (Polytechnic), Padua, Pavia, Pisa, Salerno, Siena, Turin, Trieste, Urbino, and Venice. For the most part the teachers were "masters": Achille Ardigò, Gianfranco Morra, Anna Anfossi, Franco Leonardi, Camillo Pellizzi, Giovanni Sartori, Luciano Cavalli, Renato Treves, Francesco Alberoni, Sabino Acquaviva, Eugenio Pennati, Agostino Palazzo, Franco Ferrarotti, Vittorio Castellano, Antonio Carbonaro, Filippo Barbano, Angelo Pagani, and Alessandro Pizzorno.

In 1990 the situation has completely changed, both in terms of the number of universities in which sociology is taught (now 42), obviously expanded by the establishment of new universities, and in terms of the number of courses and teachers (now 360). Moreover, some very substantial centers of sociology have been established, and sociology is taught in all the Italian universities. The universities with the greatest numbers of sociology courses are (in descending order): Rome (54), Bologna (32), Turin (31), Milan (23), and Trento (21). Those with fewer than twenty but at least ten courses are Padua (17), Naples (16), Calabria (14), Florence (13), Salerno (12), Catania (11), and Palermo (10).

One very important technical reason for these profound changes in the teaching of sociology was the reform of the faculties of political science. The first faculty of political science in Italy was established in 1875 at Florence (and called Cesare Alfieri). It was designed to train public officials and, in general, it prepared men for an active life and public debate. As time passed, while it kept these functions, this faculty tended to become transformed into a faculty of social science. After World War II the need was increasingly felt to reform the faculties of political science, detaching them from other faculties (particularly from the law faculties) and giving them an updated cultural core. Subsequently such faculties were divided into two biennia: The first is based on fundamental courses (including sociology), and the second is organized into five courses of study (indirizzi)—international, historical, economic, administrative, and social. In this last course (political-social) some true sociological curricula are offered; they are obviously more concentrated in the faculties of political science at Rome, Bologna, Turin, Padua, and Milan. At present the political-social course of studies is available in the following universities: Turin, Milan (Università Statale and Università Cattolica), Pavia, Trieste, Padua, Bologna, Florence, Pisa, Cambrino, Rome (LUISS), Naples, Bari, Messina, Catania, and Palermo.

The Future of Sociology in the Universities. At present, the teaching of sociology is concentrated in the Faculties of Sociology at Trento and Rome, the degree courses in sociology at the universities of Urbino, Naples, and Salerno; and in the several faculties of political science. Sociology courses are also offered by other faculties (such as economics and commerce, architecture, medicine, letters and philosophy, and arts), but the current tendency is to reduce this spread. There are at least two reasons for this: the "zero growth" of sociology (i.e., sociology departments have the right only to replace sociologists who leave the university or switch to other disciplines), and other disciplines' expansion of their number of chairs.

In the future, there will therefore be a tendency to strengthen sociology where it is already strong (in the faculties of political science) or through the creation of new degree courses in sociology; however, it is likely to disappear or to be excluded from the mainstream where it is peripheral (in the faculties of economics and commerce, architecture, and others). There are other ways in which the universities can train sociologists, such as Ph.D. programs; courses or schools of specialization for those who already have a degree; and special-purpose schools or diploma courses for those who plan to attend the university for only two years after their secondary schooling.

REFERENCES

Accornero, Aris, and Francesco Carmignani 1986 *I paradossi della disoccupazione.* Bologna: Il Mulino.

Acquaviva, Sabino, and Enzo Pace (eds.) 1984 *Dizionario di sociologia e antroplogia culturale.* Assisi: Cittadella.

Alberoni, Francesco (ed.) 1966 *Questioni di sociologia.* Brescia: La Scuola.

———1968 *Statu nascenti.* Bologna: Il Mulino

Amendola, Giandomenico, and Antonio Tosi (eds.) 1987 "La sociologia dell'abitazione." *Sociologia e ricerca sociale* 22:1–173.

Ammassari, Paolo 1970 *Worker Satisfaction and Occupational Life.* Rome: University of Rome.

Ardigò, Achille 1980 *Crisi di governabilità e mondi vitali.* Bologna: Cappelli.

———(ed.) 1984 "Per una rifondazione del welfare state." *La ricerca sociale* 32:1–155.

———1988 *Per una sociologia oltre il post-moderno.* Bari: Laterza.

Ardigò, Roberto 1910 *Opere filosofiche.* Padova: Draghi.

Associazione Italiana di Sociologia 1989 *L'Italia dei sociologi: Problemi, prospettive, indirizzi di ricerca.* Bologna: AIS.

———1990 *Annuario della sociologia italiana 1989/90.* Bologna: Barghigiani.

Bagnasco, Arnaldo 1977 *Tre Italie.* Bologna: Il Mulino.

Banfield, Edward C. 1958 *The Moral Basis of a Backward Society.* Glencoe, Ill.: Free Press.

Barbano, Filippo, and Giorgio Sola 1985 *Sociologia e scienze sociali in Italia, 1861–1890.* Milan: Angeli.

Barberis, Corrado 1988 *La classe politica municipale.* Milan: Angeli.

Boileau, Anna Maria, and Emidio Sussi 1981 *Dominanza e minoranze.* Udine: Grillo.

Bonazzi, Giuseppe 1982 *Dentro e fuori della fabbrica.* Milan: Angeli.

Burgalassi, Silvano, and Gustavo Guizzardi (eds.) 1983 *Il fattore religione nella società contemporanea.* Milan: Angeli.

Caizzi, Bruno (ed.) 1962 *Nuova antologia della questione meridionale.* Milan: Comunità.

Castellano, Vittorio 1968 *Introduzione alla sociologia e primi elementi de morfologia sociale.* Rome: Ilardi.

Cattarinussi, Bernardo, and Carlo Pelanda (eds.) 1981 *Disastro e azione umanà.* Milan: Angeli.

Cavalli, Luciano 1957 *Inchiesta sugli abituri.* Genoa: Office of Social and Labor Studies.

Cella, Gian Primo (ed.) 1979 *Il movimento degli scioperi nel XX secolo.* Bologna: Il Mulino.

Crespi, Franco (ed.) 1987 *Sociologia e cultura.* Milan: Angeli.

Delli Ziotti, Giovanni 1983 *Relazioni transnazionali e cooperazione transfrontaliera.* Milan: Angeli.

Demarchi, Franco 1969 *Società e spazio.* Trento: Istituto Superiore di Scienze Sociali.

———, Aldo Ellena, and Bernardo Cattarinussi (eds.) 1987 *Nuovo dizionario de sociologia.* Rome: Paoline.

De Rita, Lidia 1964 *I contadini e la televisione.* Bologna: Il Mulino.

Dolci, Danilo 1955 *Banditi a Partinico.* Bari: Laterza.

———1957 *Inchiesta a Palermo.* Turin: Einaudi.

———1960 *Spreco.* Turin: Einaudi.

Donati, Pierpaolo 1983 *Introduzione alla sociologia relazionale.* Milan: Angeli.

Ferrarotti, Franco 1972 *Trattato di sociologia.* Turin: Utet.

Gallino, Luciano 1978 *Dizionario di sociologia.* Turin: Utet.

———1980 *La società. Perché cambia, come funziona.* Turin: Paravia.

Galtung, Johan 1971 *Members of Two Worlds: A Development Study of Three Villages in Western Sicily.* Oslo: Universitetforlaget.

Gasparini, Alberto 1975 *La casa ideale.* Venice: Marsilio.

———1982 *Crisi della città e sua reimmaginazione.* Milan: Angeli.

———, and Paolo Guidicini (eds.) 1990 *Innovazione technologica e nuovo ordine urbano.* Milan: Angeli.

Gini, Corrado 1960 *Organismo e società.* Rome: Ilardi.

Giorio, Giuliano 1985 *Società e sistemi sociali.* Milan: Angeli.

Gross, Feliks 1970 "Value Structure and Social Change." *Revue Internationale de Sociologie* 1(3):85–120.

Gubert, Renzo 1972 *La situazione confinaria.* Trieste: Lint.

———1976 *L'identificazione etnica.* Udine: Del Bianco.

Guidicini, Paolo (ed.) 1968 *Manuale della ricera sociologica.* Milan: Angeli.

———1987 *Manuale per le ricerche sociali sul territorio.* Milan: Angeli.

Harrison, Gualtiero, and Maria Callari Galli 1971 *Né leggere, né scrivere.* Milan: Feltrinelli.

Izzo, Alberto 1977 *Storia del pensiero sociologico.* Bologna: Il Mulino.

La Rosa, Michele 1986 "La sociologia del lavoro in Italia." *In Sociologia del lavor.* 26–27:1–137.

Lentini, Orlando 1981 *La sociologia italiana nell'età del positivismo.* Bologna: Il Mulino.

Lopreato, Joseph 1961 "Social Stratification and Mobility in a South Italian Town." *American Sociological Review,* vol. 4.

Lotti, Luigi, and Gianfranco Pasquino 1980 *Guida alla facoltà di scienze politiche.* Bologna: Il Mulino.

Marselli, Gilberto Antonio 1963 "American Sociologists and Italian Peasant Society: With Reference to the Book of Banfield." *Sociologia Rurale* 3:15–32.

Martinotti, Guido (ed.) 1968 *Città e analisi sociologica.* Padua: Marsilio.

Melotti, Umberto (ed.) 1988 "Dal terzo mondo in Italia. Studi e ricerche sulle imigrazioni straniere." *Quaderni del terzo mondo* 31–32:1–18.

Minardi, Everardo, and Michele Colasanto (ed.) 1988 *Ricerca e formazione. I problemi della sociologia italiana.* Bologna: AIS.

Mosca, Gaetano 1962 *Storia delle dottrine politiche.* Bari: Laterza.

Mottura, Giovanni and Enrico Pugliese 1975 *Agricoltura, Mezzogiorno e mercato del lavoro.* Bologna: Il Mulino.

Negrotti, Massimo 1979 *Uomini e calcolatori.* Milan: Angeli.

Niceforo, Alfredo 1953 *Avventure e disavventure della personalità e della umana società.* Milan: Bocca.

Pagani, Angelo (ed.) 1960 *Antologia di scienze sociali.* Milan: Angeli.

Pareto, Vilfredo 1964 *Trattato di sociologia generale.* Milan: Comunità.

Pellizzi, Camillo 1964 *Rito e linguaggio.* Rome: Armando.

Pinna, Luca 1971 *La famiglia esclusiva: parentela e clientelismo in Sardegna.* Bari: Laterza.

Pinto, Diana (ed.) 1981 *Contemporary Italian Sociology.* Cambridge: Cambridge University Press.

Pizzorno, Alessandro 1960 *Comunità e razionalizzazione.* Turin: Einaudi.

Pollini, Gabriele 1987 *Appartenenza e identità.* Milan: Angeli.

Regini, Marino (ed.) 1988 *La sfida della flessibilitàa.* Milan: Angeli.

Ricciardi Ruocco, Maria 1967 *Inchiesta a Marsala.* Manduria: Lacaita.

Savelli, Asterio 1989 *Sociologia del turismo.* Milan: Angeli.

Scaglia, Antonio 1988 *Sociologia: Dalle scienze della natura alla scienza dell'agire umano.* Milan: Angeli.

Scivoletto, Angelo (ed.) 1983 *Sociologia del territorio.* Milan: Angeli.

Sgroi, Emanuele 1991 *La questione ambientale da allarme a progetto: Le nuove professionalità.* Naples: CUEN.

Strassoldo, Raimondo 1976 *Ambiente e società.* Milan: Angeli.

———1979 *Temi de sociologia delle relazioni internazionali.* Gorizia: ISIG.

Sturzo, Luigi 1960 *La società, sua natura e leggi.* Bologna: Zaniechelli.

Sussi, Emidio, and Danilo Sedmak 1984 *L'assimilazione silenziosa.* Trieste: Editoriale Stampa Triestina.

Tentori, Tullio 1956 *Il sistema di vita nella comunità materana.* Rome: UNRA-Casas.

Vincelli, Guido 1958 *Una comunità meridionale. Montorio dei Frentani.* Turin: Taylor.

Visentini, Luciano 1984 *Tra mestiere e vocazione: La sociologia del lavoro in Italia.* Milan: Angeli.

ALBERTO GASPARINI

J

JAPANESE SOCIOLOGY Japanese sociology divides roughly into three stages of development: Pre–World War II, with emphasis on theoretical and philosophical orientations, influenced primarily by European sources (especially German); Post–World War II, with emphasis on empirical orientations, influenced primarily by the United States; and the present, with emphasis on both theoretical and empirical orientations (see, e.g., Odaka 1950; Halmos 1966, and Koyano 1976, on the history of Japanese sociology). In a general sense, the development of Japanese sociology reflects that country's social and cultural change, as well as national policies. The significant Western influence exhibits some time lag in terms of its expression in Japanese sociology.

PRE–WORLD WAR II STAGE (1893–1945)

Japanese sociology began as a European import and reflected a conservative stance. This occurred shortly after the Meiji Restoration of 1868. E. F. Fenollosa (1853–1908), an American professor, first taught sociology at the University of Tokyo in 1878. Three years later, Shoichi Toyama (1848–1900) began teaching at the same university; in 1893, he became the first professor of sociology in Japan and is regarded as the founder of Japanese sociology. Toyama, and later Nagao Ariga (1860–1921), a student of Fenollosa and the first sociologist in Japan to publish, both introduced aspects of Herbert Spencer's organic analogy for society. The works of Spencer and John Stuart Mill were particularly significant during these early years and were translated frequently.

Tongo Takebe (1871–1945), successor to Toyama in 1898, introduced Comte to Japan. Takebe combined Comte's positivism with Confucian philosophy and social thought to fit Japanese society. Takebe also founded the Japan Institute of Sociology in 1913, an organization replaced by the Japan Sociological Society in 1924. A new approach began to take hold in the 1910s, the psychological approach initiated by Ryukichi Endo (1874–1946) at Waseda University. Endo drew on Franklin Giddings's theory of *consciousness of kind* to explain social phenomena.

During the 1910s other Western sociological theories were brought to Japan, largely through the work of Shotaro Yoneda (1873–1945) at Kyoto University. Yoneda looked at society and culture from a sociopsychological perspective and was an important teacher, who introduced many Western sociologists' ideas to Japan, including those of Gabriel Tarde, Emile Durkheim, Georg Simmel, and Franklin Giddings. Yoneda laid the groundwork for the subsequent strong influence of the German school of sociology.

From this point forward, until the end of World War II, the German school was the dominant influence in Japanese sociology. There were two major divisions that grew out of the German school: *formale Soziologie* (formal sociology) and, later, *Kultursoziologie* (cultural sociology). The major proponent of the former was Yasuma Takata (1883–1972), a student of Yoneda. Takata (1989) successfully changed the view of sociology from that of a synthesis of the social sciences to one in which sociology stood by itself as separate and independent, drawing in particular on the work and influence of Max Weber, Georg Simmel, Ferdinand Toennies, and Robert MacIver.

New influences, however, were seen in the 1920s. Formal sociology was seen as abstract and out of touch with the real world. As a consequence, cultural sociology gained a stronger foothold in both Germany and Japan. Pioneering the work in cultural sociology in Japan was Eikichi Seki (1900–1939). No doubt a reaction to the Depression of 1929, cultural sociology gained popularity for its closer ties with the social realities of the day. Although a theory of cultural sociology fitting the Japanese society seemed imminent, it never really unfolded. While there were also French and American influences on Japanese sociology during the prewar period, they were minor compared with those of Germany. Jyun'ichiro Matsumoto (1893–1947), of Hosei University, saw a need to synthesize formal and cultural sociology into what he would call "general sociology." At the same time, Masamichi Shimmei (1898–1988), of Tohoku University, sought to take Matsumoto's thoughts and combine them with Simmel's general sociology and the thinking of Karl Mannheim.

Because Western theory and thought dominated Japanese sociology in the prewar period, little of the work analyzed Japanese society. There were, however, a handful of notable empirical studies, especially in family and rural sociology, a tradition begun at the University of Tokyo by Teizo Toda (1887–1955). Toda had studied at the University of Chicago, where he learned about survey methodologies being used in the United States. Toda analyzed statistics on the Japanese family structure, using census and other current and historical data. Kizaemon Aruga (1897–1979) worked in the area of rural sociology, linking his findings with previous folklore studies and working toward clarifying the condition of social strata in prewar Japan. Lack of financial support, however, hindered the development of empirical research during this time.

Two phenomena in particular worked against the development of Japanese sociology prior to World War II. First, Japanese sociology focused on European sociology rather than on studies of its own society. The second phenomenon, bolstered by government officials and scholars inclined toward nationalistic militarism, involved a distorted public image: that sociology and sociologists were associated with socialism because of the two words' similarity in the Japanese language (sociology *shakaigaku* and socialism *shakaishugi*). Many thought that sociology was the study of socialism or social revolution and that sociologists were socialists and, therefore, a sinister threat to national security. As World War II grew closer, and during the war, increasingly publications were censored, academic freedom was severely curtailed, and meetings and conventions could not be held.

POSTWAR STAGE (1946–1960)

Defeat and U.S. occupation brought drastic social changes to Japan. The traditional family system collapsed; land reform was the order of the day. Indeed, the traditional Japanese value system was pulled out from under the nation. "Democratization" was the new buzzword. The term *sociology* was released from taboo. Educational reforms in the 1950s now required sociology courses for a general university education. More and more departments of sociology were formed, particularly at private colleges and universities. Suddenly, many sociologists were needed. American influences were rampant in all areas of Japanese society, and sociology was no exception. Many American sociological theories came to influence Japanese sociology, the strongest of which was that of Talcott Parsons.

As the importance of empirical study was growing in the United States, Japanese sociologists also began to develop a strong interest in empirical work. They studied American research methods, ultimately leading to a rapid increase in surveys and in research based on the results of these surveys. To many, the empirical studies of Japanese sociology moved the entire discipline from one of art and humanity to one of social science. However, many surveys were carried out for fact-finding purposes rather than hypothesis testing for theory construction.

Along with the vast changes in Japanese society in the postwar period came a virtually unlimited number of topics for sociological study and investigation, particularly from an empirical standpoint. This marked a time of diversification for Japanese sociology and signaled the establishment of a number of subdisciplines in the field.

The Japan Sociological Society joined the International Sociological Association in 1950. Two years later, a survey on social stratification and mobility was conducted under the auspices of the Japan Sociological Society, in cooperation with the International Sociological Association. This survey was repeated three years later on a nationwide scale and, subsequently, every ten years. In 1954, the Institute of Statistical Mathematics in Tokyo began a nationwide time-trend survey of the Japanese national character, a survey conducted every five years since, with the objective of analyzing changes (or lack thereof) in general social attitudes among the Japanese since World War II.

Although the postwar period saw great social change in Japan, within academic circles, senior sociologists, most of whom belonged to the prewar generation, prevailed. A generational change among leading Japanese sociologists took place in the 1960s, marking the end of the postwar period (Koyano 1976).

THE PRESENT STAGE (1960 ONWARD)

Since the 1960s, American sociology has gained an ever-dominating influence over Japanese sociology. With the exception of Talcott Parsons and his structural-functionalism, however, no major American sociologists have had significant influence over the theoretical aspects of Japanese sociology. Marxist sociology has tended to influence many of the younger Japanese sociologists from a theoretical perspective. Since the 1960s, the number of sociologists in Japan has grown markedly, to the point where there are more sociologists in Japan than in any other country except the United States. While there were about 300 sociologists teaching at colleges and universities in Japan in the 1970s, their number grew to about 1,000 by the late 1980s, and the Japan Sociological Association boasted over 2,200 members.

As a result of American influences, economic development, and a host of other factors, Japanese sociology has continuously diversified since the early 1960s. These circumstances have brought forth a wide variety of challenging research topics for sociologists and have created a situation in which there are no especially influential figures in Japanese sociology, although each subdiscipline does have its major proponents.

Currently there are about thirty subdisciplines, the most prominent of which are: (a) social thought and the history of sociology (representing 10.5 percent of the 1,945 members of the Japan Sociological Society who selected first-choice subdisciplines in 1988); (b) sociology of the family (9.0 percent); (c) general sociological theories (8.4 percent); (d) rural sociology and community studies (7.9 percent); (e) industrial sociology and management (7.2 percent); (f) social welfare, social security, and medical sociology (7.1 percent); (g) sociology of education (5.8 percent); and (h) urban sociology (5.1 percent). While family and rural sociology held greatest significance in the prewar era, their dominance has since waned.

Sociologists who study industrial sociology,

management, urban sociology, social welfare, social security, and medical sociology have increased in number continuously since World War II. Publication of articles originating from the various subdisciplines breaks down as follows: (a) sociology of the family (7.4 percent); (b) social thought and the history of sociology (7.2 percent); (c) general social theories (6.5 percent); (d) sociology of education (6.5 percent); (e) urban sociology (6.2 percent); (f) rural sociology and community studies (5.8 percent); (g) industrial sociology and management (5.2 percent); (h) social problems (5.1 percent); and (i) social welfare, social security, and medical sociology (5.1 percent). These figures were derived from lists of publications in the *Japanese Sociological Review* from 1984 through 1988. The total figure was 7,426 articles (and 927 books) for the five-year period, most of which appeared in Japanese.

Unlike the United States, in Japan there is no rigid screening or referee system for publications, with the exception of a few well-known journals such as the *Japanese Sociological Review (Shakaigaku Hyoron), The Study of Sociology (Shakaigaku Kenkyu),* and *Sociology (Soshiorogi).* With regard to presentations at meetings of the Japan Sociological Society, the five regional associations, and the associations of various subdisciplines, there are, in many cases, no rigid referee systems. Heated debate is rare and, thus, academic stimulation from published or presented controversies is quite limited.

By the late 1980s, 33 of Japan's 501 colleges and universities had doctoral programs in sociology. The major institutions with such programs included the public universities of Hokkaido, Tohoku, Tokyo, Hitotsubashi, Tokyo Metropolitan, Nagoya, Kyoto, Osaka, Kobe, and Kyushu and the private universities of Waseda, Keio, and Hosei. Also, there were about 700 graduate students studying sociology, 490 of whom were doctoral candidates (see Committee on the Education of Sociology 1988). In general, two years are required to obtain a master's degree and an additional three years to finish course work for the doctoral programs. More than 80 percent of those who finish the master's program go on to the doctoral program. Most who obtain master's degrees do not complete their doctoral theses within three years. Rather, after finishing their doctoral course work, they obtain teaching or research positions and often finish their doctorates at a later stage in their careers. Forty-one persons obtained doctoral degrees in sociology during the period 1977 to 1986, ten from public graduate schools and thirty-one from private graduate schools. There has been a surplus of recently graduated sociologists vis-à-vis the number of teaching positions available. In the late 1980s there were about forty sociology professors who held doctoral degrees in literature and about thirty who held doctoral degrees in sociology, with several others having their doctoral degrees in related fields.

Compared to other social sciences such as economics, the number of professors who obtained their doctoral degrees in sociology from foreign educational institutions has been limited. For instance, only about twenty Ph.D. holders teaching at Japanese colleges and universities in the late 1980s obtained their degrees in the United States, although their numbers have been increasing.

In Japan, there are no major university research centers such as the Institute for Social Research at the University of Michigan or the National Opinion Research Center at the University of Chicago. However, there are some research institutions that have carried out major surveys since the 1950s, some on a continuing basis, including surveys targeting trends in social attitudes. These include the Japanese Prime Minister's Office, the Institute of Statistical Mathematics, Mainichi Press, Jiji Press, and Nippon Hoso Kyokai, a Japanese broadcasting organization (see Sasaki and Suzuki 1991). Each one of these endeavors is independent and generally does not provide its data to outside researchers, making secondary analysis of such data a difficult task in Japan. On occasion, surveys, including cross-national studies, are funded by agencies such as the Japanese Ministry of Education, the Japan Society for the Promotion of Science, and the Toyota Foundation. On a regional or local basis, funds are sometimes provided by prefectural or municipal governments.

With the exception of a few research groups doing cross-national studies, in general Japan's sociologists have limited contact with researchers in other nations. This can be attributed primarily to the language barrier and lack of experience in exchanging ideas. However, there are now about two hundred Japanese sociologists who have done, or are presently doing, internationally comparative sociological research, although many of these are not actually collaborating with other nations' researchers. In this regard, the most popular subdisciplines are rural sociology, community studies, urban sociology, culture, religion, industrial sociology and management, and sociology of the family. The most popular locations for study are Asia, followed by the United States and Western Europe.

The language barrier also hinders foreign scholars from coming to Japan to study. Again, this is changing, and more and more activity is being seen in industrial sociology including Japanese management, the sociology of education, and medical sociology, all of which are viewed from abroad as particularly successful elements of Japan's economic and social development. On a less pragmatic plane, the sociology of religion has gained popularity as a topic for study in Japan.

Japanese sociology does not enjoy a wide-ranging reputation in the rest of the world. This has been attributed to lack of integration and coordination. Indeed, Japanese sociology has relied substantially upon foreign influence and has not excelled with regard to the development of original theoretical or empirical ideas. Sociology is comparatively popular in Japan, where there is a strong demand for books on the subject. As a consequence, Japanese scholars often feel little need to publish in foreign languages. Publication in English in particular would be essential to the mutual exchange of ideas and research results now and in the future. At the same time, Japanese sociologists will need to invite their foreign colleagues to meetings and conventions, as occurred in 1991 when the International Congress of the International Institute of Sociology (the oldest sociological association in the world) met in Japan for the first time in the history of Japanese sociology.

Japanese sociologists make little effort to integrate their empirical research findings with sociological theory, preferring to limit their studies to specific features of society, without investigating the overall social structure and process. Foreign influences will no doubt encourage Japanese sociology to integrate empirical research results and to construct theories accordingly. This suggests the need for greater theoretical and methodological training in graduate programs. Of course, major funding is likely to continue to center around empirical study both within Japan and comparatively with other nations.

While Japanese sociology enjoys a significant amount of useful data, it is disparate. The establishment of a central data archive will be imperative for secondary analysis, graduate training, and empirical study in general. As data gathering becomes increasingly expensive, the usefulness and need for such archives will become even more essential.

In terms of the disciplines within Japanese sociology that will take on greater and greater importance, cross-national studies will certainly become more popular. Along these same lines, time-trend studies will increase in popularity, in an effort to discover what changes and what does not change in society. Finally, whereas Japanese sociologists traditionally have not been consulted in the industrial, business, and governmental environments, this will change as Japanese sociologists acquire greater methodological skills and theoretical knowledge, as well as empirical research experience. Indeed, some graduate students will have to seek nonacademic employment in view of the lack of teaching positions at present. Japanese sociology will therefore become more pervasive and useful in Japanese society.

REFERENCES

Committee on the Education of Sociology, Japan Sociological Society 1988 "Research Report on a Survey of the Problem of Post-Graduate Students." *Japanese Sociological Review* 39:314–334. (In Japanese)

Halmos, P. (ed.) 1966 "Japanese Sociological Studies." *Sociological Review Monograph,* no. 10. Keele, United Kingdom: University of Keele.

Koyano, Shogo 1976 "Sociological Studies in Japan: Prewar, Postwar and Contemporary Stages." *Current Sociology* 24:1–196.

Odaka, Kunio 1950 "Japanese Sociology: Past and Present." *Social Forces* 28:400–409.

Sasaki, Masamichi, and Tatsuzo Suzuki. 1991 "Trend and Cross-National Study of General Social Attitudes." *International Journal of Comparative Sociology* 31:193–205.

Takata, Yasuma 1989 *Principles of Sociology.* Tokyo: University of Tokyo Press/New York: Columbia University Press.

MASAMICHI SASAKI

JUVENILE DELINQUENCY AND JUVENILE CRIME The year 1990 apparently witnessed the growth and spread of street crime in America with a parallel growth in the fear of youth gangs. Youth violence seemed to grow in many cities in 1990: Boston, Philadelphia, Washington, Richmond, Los Angeles, Phoenix, New York, and others. The year ended with a public shootout by warring gangs at a theater showing *Godfather III.* The parks are places where muggings, as well as "wildings" (gang rapes and violent attacks on women, especially) can take place. No wonder the year ended on a dismal note.

In a comment made in 1959, but which is still relevant to those who are intrigued, frightened, or perplexed by the "heedlessness" of today's youth, Teeters and Matza stated: "It has always been popular for each generation to believe its children were the worst, the most lawless and the most unruly" (p. 200). We are also reminded by them that "Sir Walter Scott in 1812 deplored the insecurity of Edinburgh where groups of boys between 12 and 20 years scoured streets and knocked down and robbed all who came in their way" (p. 200). Apropos of delinquency, such remarks underscore the relativity of opinions and the brevity of trends. They also remind us that while juvenile delinquency is a relatively new legal category that subjects children to court authority, it is also a timeless and ubiquitous part of life. As such, I shall consider here some of the varieties of modern data on juvenile misconduct.

The term "modern" underscores the fact (emphasized by writers such as Gibbons and Krohn [1991], Empey [1982], and Short [1990]) that "juvenile delinquency" is a relatively recent social construction. It grew out of legal and humanitarian concern for the well-being of children and was designed to allow children to be handled outside the criminal law. The first juvenile court, established in Cook County, Illinois, in 1899, was designed to meet the special needs of children at a time of great industrialization in the United States. The data of delinquency, however, are not limited to the legal status of "juvenile delinquent," because sociologists are just as interested in unofficial as in official acts of delinquency. More specifically, it is well known that much of the behavior defined by law as delinquent is not detected, not reported, or not acted on by legal agents of control.

Moreover, different jurisdictions have different legal definitions of delinquency. Within the United States, for example, while the statistics defining delinquency are similar in the fifty states and District of Columbia with respect to age and type of offense requiring juvenile court control, there are more differences than similarities. First, the laws vary in terms of the age limits of juvenile court jurisdiction; thirty-one states and the District of Columbia set seventeen years of age as the upper age limit, twelve states set sixteen years, six set fifteen years, and one sets eighteen years. Moreover, in many states the delinquency laws empower the juvenile court to remand youths under the maximum juvenile court age to criminal courts. In such cases, the offenses are often those for which adults may be arrested: index crimes (see below). In addition, some states have passed legislation that requires certain cases, such as homicides, or youths charged with serious offenses, to be dealt with by the criminal court. In these cases, the juvenile acquires the legal status of criminal. Finally, it should be noted that all American state jurisdictions contain an omnibus clause or provision, referred to as status offenses, that awards the court jurisdiction over youths who have behaved in ways not forbidden by criminal law. While these provisions differ from state to state, it is of interest to note a few examples of these conditions. They include engaging in indecent behavior, knowingly associating with vicious or immoral persons, growing up in idleness or crime, being incorrigible, and wandering in the streets at night. Critics note that these behavior categories are so vaguely defined that nearly all youngsters could be subjected to them.

Such different procedures and practices caution us against making easy generalizations both within and between countries when examining official data. Indeed, other shortcomings likewise warn against drawing firm conclusions when unofficial data are examined. Although methodological shortcomings may exist in the study of delinquency, there may be advantages in utilizing all the data of delinquency (official and unofficial) in pursuit of its understanding. Thus, the study of official delinquency data places much of the focus on the actions of official agents of control (the police, the courts), while the study of unofficial—including hidden—delinquency often allows students to examine the processes leading to the behavior. Moreover, as Vold and Bernard (1986) and others have noted, unofficial data, especially self-reports, frequently focus on trivial offenses, while the more serious offenses often do not appear in self-reports but in reports of official agencies.

In sum, our concern here will be to discuss those topics of delinquency which are of the greatest concern: the frequency, the severity, and the duration of delinquency, from both individual and aggregate perspectives. These will devote some attention to trends. In the following section, the focus is on the extent of delinquent behavior.

EXTENT OF AND TRENDS IN DELINQUENCY

In addressing the matter of the extent of delinquency, it is important to note the admonitions of Empey and Erickson (1966), Hirschi (1969), Matza (1964), and others that delinquency is not only transient but also widespread. Many juveniles engage in delinquency only occasionally, and some engage in it more frequently. Gibbons and Krohn (1991) call delinquency "a sometime thing," while Matza describes the process of drifting into and out of delinquency. Moreover, it should be kept in mind that some acts of delinquency are serious acts of criminality and others are petty, trivial acts. As we consider both official and unofficial data on juvenile delinquency and juvenile crime, we will encounter these various clarifying factors.

Official Delinquency. The most serious crimes committed by youth and adults in the United States are referred to as index crimes and are compiled by the FBI, based on reports of approximately sixteen thousand law enforcement agencies throughout the country. These index crimes, reported in Uniform Crime Reports, are divided into two major types: violent (homicide, rape, robbery, and aggravated assault) and property (burglary, larceny-theft, motor vehicle theft, and arson). Nonindex offenses are those considered to be relatively petty, such as liquor law violations, disorderly conduct, and sex offenses (except forcible rape, prostitution, and commercialized vice).

Index crimes are reported annually by the FBI and sometimes as estimates for the United States as a whole from a sample of reporting agencies. In 1988, the FBI's Uniform Crime Reports indicated that of all arrests in the United States in 1987, approximately 16.5 percent were of youths under eighteen years of age; 15 percent of the arrests for violent crime in 1987 (murder and manslaughter, forcible rape, robbery, and aggravated assault) were of persons under eighteen years of age.

One of the most striking facts about officially recorded delinquency is that, contrary to public fears, it has declined in recent years in the United States. For the period between 1978 and 1987, there was an 8 percent reduction in the total number of arrests of persons under eighteen. Consistent with and extending the latter data, the subsequent Uniform Crime Report presents data showing that while total arrests increased by over 20 percent between 1979 and 1988, arrests of persons under eighteen years of age declined by about 12 percent. This decline in arrests of youths under eighteen must be interpreted with caution. During the period 1980–1989, the percent change in number of persons under eighteen who were arrested continued to show a decline, but a smaller one of 7 percent.

Underscoring this caution is the fact that while the Uniform Crime Report shows a decline in index arrests for urban, suburban, and rural youth alike for the period 1979–1988, the number of index arrests increased substantially across these residential categories between 1965 and 1977. Peter and Lucille Kratcoski, in viewing this dramatic change, suggest that it could be due to "movement of the 'baby-boom' segment of the population through the high offense years during the mid-70s followed by a reduction in the under-18 population since 1978" (1990, p. 15). Gibbons and Krohn (1991) also suggest that such trends may be due to shifts within the delinquency-eligible youth group. Further, the latter authors suggest that such trends may reflect increased or decreased concern about youthful misconduct.

Consistent with the decreasing trend in juvenile arrests is the fact that the numbers of youngsters who have been sent to juvenile courts (that is, officially processed) have decreased since 1975. Index and nonindex delinquency cases referred to courts in 1985 numbered 534,000, while court status offense cases in the same year numbered some 88,000, about one-sixth of the delinquency cases, according to the U.S. Department of Justice. Status offenses in 1985 were fairly equally apportioned among the four categories of runaway, ungovernability, liquor law, and truancy violations. Among the delinquency cases referred to juvenile courts in 1985, 9.1 percent involved index crimes of violence, 42.6 percent involved index property crimes, and over 48 percent involved nonindex delinquency. Considering delinquent cases (violations of criminal statutes) and status cases together for 1984, Gibbons and Krohn (1991) indicate that less than 5 percent of the youth population appeared in juvenile courts in 1984. This figure includes both petitioned (officially processed) and nonpetitioned cases.

A notable exception to the decline in arrests and court referrals of persons under eighteen years of age is the increase in murder and nonnegligent manslaughter. More specifically, the Uniform Crime Report shows that between 1980 and 1989 there was an increase from 1,189 to 1,733 cases of murder and nonnegligent manslaughter by the under-eighteen group, an increase of over 45 percent. Indeed, there was a general increase in index crimes of violence for the under-eighteen group of 5.7 percent for that period. Forcible rape showed an increase of 22.8 percent, and aggravated assault increased by 33.7 percent. Only robbery showed a decline, of 21.1 percent. The data for 1990 will, no doubt, exaggerate these trends, given the substance of preliminary reports in the media.

Cohort Study. One of the first longitudinal studies of delinquency was conducted by Wolfgang, Figlio, and Sellin (1972) in Philadelphia. They traced the police contacts of all boys born in 1945 who lived in the city between their tenth and eighteenth birthdays. One of their aims was to trace the volume and frequency of delinquent careers up to age eighteen in a cohort of 9,945. They found that 35 percent of these boys (3,475) were involved with the police at least once during the time between their tenth and eighteenth birthdays. Of these 3,475 boys with police contacts, 54 percent were repeaters. The total number of delinquent events (offenses) for the 3,475 delinquent boys amounted to 10,214 through age seventeen. Thus, it is clear that the number of offenses far outnumbers the number of offenders found in the cohort. One must note, then, that longitudinal study of delinquents yields data with important differences from those obtained when cross-sectional studies of persons arrested are conducted. Examples of other longitudinal studies include the Provo Study, the Cambridge-Somerville Study, the Vocational High Study, and, in Britain, the National Survey of Health and Development.

Self-Reports: Offender Reports and Victim Reports. Official reports of crime and juvenile delinquency have been criticized for years because they are widely believed to underreport the volume of offenses. Moreover, there was considerable belief, especially among those with a conflict perspective, that official reports underreported middle-class crime and delinquency. In an effort to detect "hidden" delinquency, sociologists developed a technique designed to produce a more accurate picture. The technique used by Short and Nye (1958), in a number of studies of hidden delinquency, consisted of having juveniles in a school or other population complete questionnaires and reveal the extent to which they engaged in law-violating behavior. They found that delinquency was widespread throughout the juvenile population. Subsequently, Williams and Gold (1972) and Empey and Erickson (1966) embarked on studies employing self-reports. These writers found that 88 percent and 92 percent of their study groups, respectively, had engaged in violations. Hindelang, Hirschi, and Weis (1981) present a similar volume of law-violating behavior in their Seattle study. Criticisms of the self-report method followed many of these studies, centering on issues of respondent misrepresentation, respondent recall, and weaknesses of study groups. A major criticism (by Nettler [1984], for example) was that self-reports elicited minor or petty infractions for the most part. Because of its obvious utility, the self-report technique has been greatly improved in recent years, becoming an important, if not the dominant, method of measurement in studies focusing on the extent and cause of delinquency.

A number of students of delinquency agree that many of the improvements in self-report studies have been contributed by Delbert Elliott and his colleagues (Regoli and Hewitt [1991]; Gibbons and Krohn [1991]; Bartol and Bartol [1989]). Elliott and his colleagues have initiated a panel design that employs periodic interviews instead of questionnaires. The study, called the National Youth Survey (NYS), utilizes a national probability sample of 1,726 adolescents aged eleven to seventeen in 1976 and covers over one hundred cities and towns in the United States. In contrast with earlier self-report studies, Elliott asks his respondents about a full range of activities designed to get at serious as well as minor infractions. In addition, his respondents are asked whether they were caught when engaging in delinquent and criminal activities.

Another attempt to ascertain the volume of delinquency in the United States is represented by the National Crime Survey (NCS). This survey, an effort to ascertain the extent of victimization in the population of the United States, was begun in 1973 after an initial study sponsored by the President's Commission on Law Enforcement and Administration of Justice in 1967. Interviews are conducted semiannually by the Bureau of the Census in a large national sample of sixty thousand households (Bartol and Bartol 1989). The survey was intended to supplement the Uniform Crime Report (UCR) data and measures the extent to which persons and households are victims of rape, robbery, assault, burglary, motor vehicle theft, and larceny. Binder, Geis, and Bruce note that one of the major findings of the 1967 study of victims by the President's Commission was the revelation that "actual crime was several times that indicated in the UCR" (1988, p. 34). In the current victim interviews, if the respondent has been victimized, he or she will be asked questions about characteristics of both victim and offender, including victim perceptions of the offender. Binder and his colleagues warn about the difficulty of age discrimination by the victim under stress and suggest that this method cannot be relied on too heavily in measuring delinquency.

Nevertheless, Laub (1983) has found NCS data useful in addressing the issue of the extent and change in delinquency volume. In an analysis of NCS data obtained between 1973 and 1980, he found no increase in juvenile crime over those years. He further noted that data from the National Center for Juvenile Justice supported this conclusion. It would seem, then, that NCS data, UCR data, and juvenile court data are in some agreement that delinquency has not increased recently, contrary to much public opinion. While self-report data indicate that violations are consistently widespread in American society, it is important to note that these reports involve primarily minor violations. Indeed, to the extent that almost everyone engages in minor violations, it may make sense to focus primarily on serious violations. Nettler (1984), noting that self-report studies find a large number of minor infractions, suggested that such violators are best described as lying on a continuum rather than as "delinquent" or "nondelinquent." The cohort studies by Wolfgang and his colleagues (1972) showed that serious violations involved only a small proportion of the study groups.

FACTORS RELATED TO DELINQUENCY

Age and Gender. In the United States, in Britain, and in other countries of Europe where delinquency is recognized and studied, there is general agreement that it peaks in adolescence (ages fifteen to eighteen) rather than in childhood. (This is not to say, however, that delinquency is not on the increase among younger children. A study by the FBI in 1990 found that the arrest rate for rape among males twelve years and under has more than tripled since 1970. [Boston Globe, January 14, 1991, p. 25]). The UCR shows that 15.5 percent of all arrests in 1989 involved persons under eighteen years of age. This age group produced 27.3 percent of arrests for index crimes, however. Male arrests peaked at age seventeen (4.1 percent of all male arrests), followed by age sixteen (3.3 percent of arrests). Considering arrests of females under eighteen, the peak age was sixteen (4.0 percent of all female arrests), followed by age seventeen (3.9 percent). Earlier studies and analyses by Empey and Erickson (1966), by Wolfgang (1983), and by Braithwaite (1981) are consistent with this picture, with sixteen years being the peak year for juvenile misconduct.

It has consistently been found that males outnumber females in UCR arrest data. Thus, in both 1988 and 1989, males were arrested four times more frequently than females, among those under eighteen. For those under eighteen in both 1988 and 1989, males outnumbered females eight to one in arrests for violent offenses. However, James Short (1990) points out that lately the gender ratio has declined substantially. Recent UCR trends suggest that Short may be correct when considering serious violations among those under eighteen. Thus, between 1980 and 1989 violent crime increased by 4.5 percent for males under eighteen and by 16.5 percent for comparable females. Considering all arrests for males and females under eighteen, males showed a *decline* of 8.5 percent between 1980 and 1989, while females showed an *increase* of 1.1 percent for the same period. This could be indicative of major changes to come.

Perhaps Hagan's power-control theory is relevant here. Hagan et al. (1987) suggest that childrearing styles in the home (the power structure) are determined in part by the nature of the parents' occupations. The two main types of childrearing styles are patriarchal and egalitarian. In occupations the two types are command (managerial) and obey (subject to others' authority). In the egalitarian family where both parents work in authority positions, the mother's authority means she has a substantial amount of power in the home, and this leads to the daughters' having increased freedom relative to sons. This situation is reversed in patriarchal families, controlled by fathers and sons. In the egalitarian family, the adolescent daughter has an increased willingness to take risks. Hagan assumes that willingness to take risks is a fundamental requirement for delinquency. He also predicts that female delinquency will be high in mother-only homes. The absence of a father leaves a void in male power, allowing the adolescent girl more freedom, greater risk taking, and an increased tendency to deviate. The theory needs to be tested more fully.

With respect to self-reports, the reports of the NYS suggest that age was not related to involvement in delinquent acts. Although males admitted to more infractions than did females, the differences are much less pronounced than those seen in the UCRs. Again, it should be emphasized that efforts are being made to enhance the ability of self-report studies to elicit information on more serious infractions.

Race and Class. UCRs for 1985 and 1989 present data on arrests by race in the United States. Among persons arrested and under eighteen years of age, blacks showed an increase from 23 percent in 1985 to 28 percent in 1989, while whites showed a decrease from 75 percent to 70 percent. The remainder of the arrests by race were attributed to Native Americans, Asians, Pacific Islanders, and Alaskan Natives. The proportion of index violent crime for blacks under eighteen increased from 52 percent in 1985 to 53 percent in 1989, while the comparable proportions for whites were 46 percent and 45 percent. Meriting considerable concern are the figures for murder and nonnegligent homicide. Here, blacks under eighteen accounted for 51 and 61 percent, respectively, of these crimes in 1985 and 1989; whites accounted for 48 and 37 percent during the same two years. This increase in the proportion of murder and nonnegligent manslaughter accounted for by blacks under eighteen is accompanied by the fact that the number of such crimes doubled for blacks and increased by 30 percent for whites during the five-year period. Aggravated assaults also increased substantially during this period for both whites and blacks under eighteen. Some consolation, perhaps, may be taken from the fact that among those under eighteen, the number of forcible rapes declined among blacks and showed a 1 percent increase for whites between 1985 and 1989. Among this age group property crimes showed a fair decline for whites and remained almost the same for blacks.

The dramatic overall increase in crimes of violence in recent years brings to mind Jackson Toby's (1967) classic work on delinquency in affluent society, as well as Durkheim's (1951) discussion of rising expectations in his theory of anomie. In Toby's case, he was trying to account for the rise in theft crimes in a variety of countries. He took special note of adolescent crime in industrial countries like Japan, Sweden, and Great Britain, but also included developing countries such as Nigeria and India in his analysis. Toby suggested that the resentment of poverty is likely to be greater among the relatively poor in an affluent society than among the poor in a poor society. He suggests, however, that envy is at work not only in the more affluent societies like Japan but also in countries with rising standards of living, such as India and Nigeria. Moreover, Toby suggests that not only adults but also the young are subject to rising expectations. It may be that relative deprivation can account for at least some of the rise in youth violence in the United States. Toby's work also suggests that the presence of such envy could be heightened where the inhibiting effect of schools or families is missing in either affluent or developing societies. Here Toby's thesis greatly resembles control theory. The increase in single-parent families among blacks, persisting educational inequalities for blacks, and chronic employment problems for black youth may tend to lessen social controls and could be factors in the greater increase in violence among them.

Social class has been, by far, the most controversial of all the factors studied in connection with juvenile delinquency. The argument seems to revolve around both method and theory. Some argue about the impact of social class, others debate the measurement of social class, and a few argue about both. In recent years, several writers have attempted to review the research on class and delinquency or crime. Tittle and his associates (1978), noting that nearly every sociological theory of crime or delinquency had class as a key factor, reviewed thirty-five such studies. Their findings suggested to Tittle and his colleagues that the class and crime-delinquency connection might be a "myth" because the relationship could not be confirmed empirically.

Subsequently, John Braithwaite (1981) criticized Tittle's study not only as incomplete but also as having come to the wrong conclusions. He reviewed fifty-three studies that used official data and forty-seven studies that used self-reports in the study of delinquency. Braithwaite forcefully argues that the class-crime relationship is no myth. Of the studies using official records, Braithwaite found that the vast majority (forty-four) showed lower-class juveniles to have substantially higher offense rates than middle-class juveniles. Of the forty-seven self-report studies, he concluded that eighteen found lower-class juveniles reported higher levels of delinquent behavior, seven reported qualified support for the relationship, and twenty-two found no relationship. Braithwaite is critical of self-report studies when (1) they do not closely examine the lowest group on the social class continuum (the lumpenproletariat) and (2) they do not include serious offenses and chronicity in their data gathering. While the argument may continue, Braithwaite and others seem to be less critical of self-report studies when they correct these apparent shortcomings.

Apparently the work of Elliott and Ageton (1980) has done much to defuse this issue. They found, for example, that the relationship between class and self-reported delinquency is totally a consequence of the difference between the lowest class group and the rest of the sample, with no difference between the working and middle classes. Recent writers like Messner and Krohn (1990), Hagan and Palloni (1990), and Colvin and Pauly (1983) have apparently profited from these debates; their work shows an inclination to refine the "objective" measure of class, using insights from conflict theory as they formulate explanations of delinquency. Indeed, it is safe to say that social class is alive and well, but it is more broadly conceptualized now; many of the new theories include patterns of child rearing, job experiences, and family structure that are incorporated into the framework of a more radical neo-Marxist perspective. The effort by sociologists in the United States and in other countries to better understand juvenile delinquency appears to be entering a new and more urgent phase.

(SEE ALSO: *Crime, Theories of; Criminal and Delinquent Subcultures; Criminology; Juvenile Delinquency, Theories of; Socialization*)

REFERENCES

Ageton, Suzanne, and Delbert Elliott 1978 *The Incidence of Delinquent Behavior in a National Probability Sample of Adolescents.* Boulder, Colo.: Behavioral Research Institute.

Bartol, Curt, and Anne Bartol 1989 *Juvenile Delinquency: A System Approach.* Englewood Cliffs, N.J.: Prentice-Hall.

Binder, Arnold, Gilbert Geis, and Dickson Bruce 1988 *Juvenile Delinquency: Historical, Cultural, Legal Perspectives.* New York: Macmillan.

Braithwaite, John 1981 "The Myth of Social Class and Criminality Reconsidered." *American Sociological Review* 46:36–57.

——— 1989 *Crime, Shame, and Reintegration* Cambridge: Cambridge University Press.

Colvin, Mark, and John Pauly 1983 "A Critique of Criminology: Toward an Integrated Structural-Marxist Theory of Delinquency Production." *American Journal of Sociology* 89:513–551.

Durkheim, Emile 1951 *Suicide,* J. A. Spaulding and George Simpson, trans. New York: Free Press.

Elliott, Delbert, and Suzanne Ageton 1980 "Reconciling Race and Class Differences in Self-Reported and Official Estimates of Delinquency." *American Sociological Review* 45:95–110.

Empey, Lamar T. 1982 *American Delinquency,* rev. ed. Homewood, Ill.: Dorsey.

———, and Maynard Erickson 1966 "Hidden Delinquency and Social Status." *Social Forces* 44:546–554.

Gibbons, Don, and Marvin Krohn 1991 *Delinquent Behavior,* 5th ed. Englewood Cliffs, N.J.: Prentice-Hall.

Hagan, John, and Alberto Palloni 1990 "The Social Reproduction of a Criminal Class in Working-Class London, Circa 1950–1980." *American Journal of Sociology* 96:265–299.

———, J. Simpson, and A. R. Gillis 1987 "Class in the Household: A Power-Control Theory of Gender and Delinquency." *American Journal of Sociology* 92:788–816.

Hindelang, M. J., Travis Hirschi, and Joseph Weis 1981 *Measuring Delinquency.* Beverly Hills, Calif.: Sage.

Hirschi, T. 1969 *Causes of Delinquency.* Berkeley: University of California Press.

Kratcoski, Peter, and Lucille Dunn Kratcoski 1990 *Juvenile Delinquency,* 3rd ed. Englewood Cliffs, N.J.: Prentice-Hall.

Laub, John 1983 "Trends in Serious Juvenile Crime." *Criminal Justice and Behavior* 10:485–506.

Matza, David 1964 *Delinquency and Drift.* New York: Wiley.

McCord, William, Joan McCord, and Irving Zola 1959 *Origins of Crime: A New Evaluation of the Cambridge-Somerville Study.* New York: Columbia University Press.

Messner, Steven, and Marvin Krohn 1990 "Class, Compliance Structures, and Delinquency: Assessing Integrated Structural-Marxist Theory." *American Journal of Sociology* 96:300–328.

Nettler, Gwynn 1984 *Explaining Crime,* 3rd ed. New York: McGraw-Hill.

Regoli, Robert, and John Hewitt 1991 *Delinquency in Society.* New York: McGraw-Hill.

Short, James 1990 *Delinquency in Society.* Englewood Cliffs, N.J.: Prentice-Hall.

———, and F. Ivan Nye 1958 "Extent of Unrecorded Juvenile Delinquency: Tentative Conclusions." *Journal of Criminal Law, Criminology and Police Science* 49:296–302.

Teele, James E. (ed.) 1970 *Juvenile Delinquency: A Reader.* Itasca, Ill.: Peacock.

Teeters, Negley, and David Matza 1959 "The Extent of Delinquency in the United States." *Journal of Negro Education* 28:200–213.

Tittle, Charles R., Wayne Villemez, and Douglas Smith 1978 "The Myth of Social Class and Criminality: An Empirical Assessment of the Empirical Evidence." *American Sociological Review* 43:643–656.

Toby, Jackson 1967 "Affluence and Adolescent Crime." In *1967 President's Commission on Law Enforcement and Administration of Justice: Task-Force Report on Juvenile Delinquency and Youth Crime.* Washington, D.C.: U.S. Government Printing Office. Reprinted in James E. Teele, ed., *Juvenile Delinquency: A Reader.* Itasca, Ill.: Peacock, 1970.

U.S. Department of Justice 1984 *Juvenile Court Statistics.* Washington, D.C.: U.S. Department of Justice.

———1988 *Crime in the United States.* Washington, D.C.: U.S. Department of Justice.

———1989 *Crime in the United States.* Washington, D.C.: U.S. Department of Justice.

Vold, George, and Thomas Bernard 1986 *Theoretical Criminology.* New York: Oxford University Press.

Williams, Jay, and Martin Gold 1972 "From Delinquent Behavior to Official Delinquency." *Social Problems* 20:209–229.

Wilmott, Peter 1966 *Adolescent Boys in East London.* London: Routledge and Kegan Paul.

Wolfgang, Marvin 1983 "Delinquency in Two Birth Cohorts." *American Behavioral Scientist* 27:75–86.

———, Robert Figlio, and Thorsten Sellin 1972 *Delinquency in a Birth Cohort.* Chicago: University of Chicago Press.

JAMES E. TEELE

JUVENILE DELINQUENCY, THEORIES OF The topic of juvenile delinquency is a fertile area for construction of sociological theory. Three major sociological traditions, including structural functionalism, symbolic interactionism, and conflict theory, contribute to the explanation of delinquency. Much of the work in this area seeks to explain why officially recorded delinquency is concentrated in the lower class, or in what is today more often called the underclass. This entry considers the most prominent theories of delinquency under the theoretical rubrics noted above.

STRUCTURAL FUNCTIONALISM AND DELINQUENCY

Structural-functional theories regard delinquent behavior as the consequence of strains or breakdowns in the social processes that produce conformity. These theories focus on institutions, such as the family and school, that socialize individuals to conform their behavior to values of the surrounding society and on the ways in which these institutions can fail in this task. Wide agreement or consensus is assumed about which behaviors are valued and disvalued in society. The question structural-functional theories try to answer is, why do many individuals during their adolescence behave in ways that challenge this consensus? That is, why do many adolescents violate behavioral norms that nearly all of us are assumed to hold in common?

Anomie Theory. The roots of functional theory are found in Durkheim's notion of *anomie* ([1897] 1951). To Durkheim, this term meant an absence of social regulation, or normlessness. Merton (1938, 1957) revived the concept to describe the consequences of a faulty relationship between goals and the legitimate means of attaining them. Merton emphasized two features of social and cultural structure: culturally defined goals (such as monetary success) and the acceptable means (such as education) to their achievement. Merton argued that in our society success goals are widely shared, while the means of or opportunities for attaining them are not.

Merton's theory is used to explain not only why individual adolescents become delinquents but also why some classes are characterized by more delinquency than others. Since members of the lower- or underclass are assumed to be most affected by the disparity between the goals and the means of attaining success, this class is expected to have a higher rate of delinquent behavior. Merton outlined a number of ways individuals adapt when faced with inadequate means of attaining their goals. Among these, *innovation* involves substituting illegitimate for legitimate means to goal attainment; it is the resort to this adaptation that is thought to account for much theft among adolescents from the underclass.

Subcultural Theory. Group-based adaptations to the failure to attain success goals involve the *delinquent subculture.* Cohen (1955) suggests that children of the underclass, and potential members of a delinquent subculture, first experience a failure to achieve when they enter school. When assessed against a "middle class measuring rod," these children are often found lacking. A result is a growing sense of "status frustration." Underclass children are simply not prepared by their earliest experiences to satisfy middle class expectations. The delinquent subculture therefore emerges as an alternative set of criteria or values that underclass adolescents can meet.

Cohen argues that these subcultural values represent a complete repudiation of middle class standards; the delinquent subculture expresses contempt for a middle class life-style by making its opposite a criterion of prestige. The result, according to Cohen, is a delinquent subculture that is "nonutilitarian, malicious, and negativistic"—an inversion of middle class values. Yet this is only one possible type of subcultural reaction to the frustration of failure. As we see next, many subcultural responses are elaborated in the theoretical tradition of structural functionalism.

Differential Opportunity Theory. Cloward and Ohlin (1960) argue that to understand the different forms that delinquent and ultimately criminal behavior can take, we must consider the different types of illegitimate opportunities available to those who seek a way out of the underclass and where these opportunities lead. Different types of community settings produce different subcultural responses. Cloward and Ohlin suggest that three types of responses predominate, each one leading to its own respective subculture: a stable criminal subculture, a conflict subculture, and a retreatist subculture.

The *stable criminal subculture* offers, as its name suggests, the most promising (albeit still illegitimate) prospects for upward economic mobility. According to Cloward and Ohlin, this subculture can emerge only when there is some coordination between those in legitimate and in illegitimate roles—for example, between politicians or police and the underworld. One pictures the old-style political machine, with protection provided for preferred types of illegal enterprise. Only in such circumstances can stable patterns be established, allowing opportunities for advancement from adolescent to adult levels of the criminal underworld. When legitimate and illegitimate opportunity structures are linked in this way, the streets become safe for crime, and reliable upward mobility routes can emerge for aspiring criminals.

Violence and conflict, on the other hand, disrupt both legitimate and illegitimate enterprise. When both types of enterprises coexist, violence is restrained. However, in the "disorganized slum," where these spheres of activity are not linked, violence can reign uncontrolled. Cloward and Ohlin see these types of communities as producing a *conflict subculture.* A result of this disorganization is the prevalence of adolescent street gangs and their violent activities, making the streets unsafe for more profitable crime.

The *retreatist subculture* includes adolescents who fail in their efforts in both the legitimate and illegitimate opportunity structures. These "double failures" are destined for drug abuse and other forms of escape.

Cloward and Ohlin's theory played a role in encouraging the Kennedy and Johnson administrations of the 1960s to organize the American War on Poverty, which attempted to open up legitimate opportunities for youth and minorities in the underclass (see Moynihan 1969). However, another important variant of structural-functional theory argued that the most important cause of delinquency was not a strain between goals and means but rather a relative absence of goals, values, commitments, and other sources of social control.

Social Disorganization Theory. The earliest North American efforts to explain crime and delinquency in terms of social control focused on the absence of social bonds at the community level. Entire neighborhoods were seen as being socially disorganized, as lacking the cohesion and constraint that could prevent crime and delinquency. This work began in the late 1920s, when Clifford Shaw and Henry McKay (1931, 1942) sought to identify areas of Chicago that were experiencing social disorganization. They explored the process that characterized these communities. What they found were indications of what they assumed to be social disorganization—truancy, tuberculosis, infant mortality, mental disorder, economic dependency, adult crime, and juvenile delinquency. In Chicago, the rates of these conditions were highest in the slums near the city center; they diminished in areas farther away from the center. Since these problems were assumed to be contrary to the shared values of area inhabitants, they were taken as indications that these areas were unable to realize the goals of their residents. In other words, they were taken as indicators of social disorganization.

Shaw and McKay also attempted to determine the sorts of community characteristics that were correlated with delinquency so that they could infer from these characteristics what the central components of social disorganization were and how they caused delinquency. Three types of correlates were identified: the economic status of the community, the mobility of community residents, and community heterogeneity. The implication was that poverty, high residential mobility, and ethnic heterogeneity led to a weakening of social bonds or controls and, in turn, to high rates of delinquency. All of this was being said of the neighborhoods Shaw and McKay studied; it was left to later theories to spell out the meaning of weakened neighborhood bonds or controls for individuals.

Control Theory. At the level of individuals, to have neither goals nor means is to be uncommitted and thus uncontrolled. Hirschi (1969) has argued that the absence of control is all that really is required to explain much delinquent behavior. There are other types of controls (besides *commitment* to conformity) that may also operate: *involvement* in school and other activities; *attachments* to friends, school, and family; and belief in various types of values and principles. Hirschi argues that delinquent behavior is inversely related to the presence of these controls. Alternatively, as these controls accumulate, so too does conformity. According to control theory, the more committed, attached, involved, and believing individuals are, the greater is their bond to society. Again, Hirschi's point is that no special strain between goals and means is necessarily required to produce delinquent behavior; all that is required is the elimination of the constraining elements of the social bond.

In each of the theories that we have considered thus far, values or beliefs play some role in causing delinquency. It is argued that the presence of success goals or values without the means to obtain them can produce deviant behavior, as can the absence of these goals or values in the first place. It is an emphasis on these values, and the role of the school and family in transmitting them, that ties the structural-functional theories together.

SYMBOLIC INTERACTIONISM AND DELINQUENCY

Symbolic-interactionist theories of delinquency are concerned less with values than with the way in which social meanings and definitions can help produce delinquent behavior. The assumption, of course, is that these meanings and definitions, these symbolic variations, affect behavior. Early versions of symbolic-interactionist theories focused on how adolescents acquired these meanings and definitions from others, especially peers; more recently, theorists have focused on the role of official control agencies, especially the police and courts, in imposing these meanings and definitions on adolescents. The significance of this difference in focus will become apparent as we consider the development of the symbolic-interactionist tradition.

Differential Association Theory. Edwin Sutherland (1939; 1949) anticipated an emphasis of the symbolic-interactionist perspective with his early use of the concept of *differential association.*

This concept referred not only to associations among people but also, and perhaps even more importantly, to associations among ideas. Sutherland's purpose was to develop a general theory that explained delinquency as well as adult criminality. He argued that people violate laws only when they define such behavior as acceptable and that there is an explicit connection between people and their ideas (that is, definitions). So, for example, delinquent behavior is "learned in association with those who define such behavior favorably and in isolation from those who define it unfavorably," and this behavior occurs when "the weight of the favorable definitions exceeds the weight of the unfavorable definitions."

Although Sutherland intended his theory to be general and explicitly to include the explanation of delinquency, his best-known applications of the theory were in his famous studies of professional theft and white-collar crime. Nonetheless, Sutherland's emphasis on white-collar illegality was important for the study of delinquency because it stressed the ubiquity of criminality, and, as we see next, it helped to mitigate delinquency theory's preoccupation with underclass delinquency.

Neutralization Theory. While most of the theories we have considered to this point portray the delinquent, especially the underclass delinquent, as markedly different from "the rest of us," Sykes and Matza (1957, 1961) follow Sutherland's lead in suggesting that the similarities actually outnumber the differences. Their argument is based in part on the observation that underclass delinquents, like white-collar criminals, usually exhibit guilt or shame when detected violating the law.

Sutherland had argued that individuals become white-collar criminals because they are immersed with their colleagues in a business ideology that defines illegal business practices as acceptable. Sykes and Matza (1957) argue that the delinquent, much like the white-collar criminal, drifts into a deviant life-style through a subtle process of justification. "We call these justifications of deviant behavior techniques of neutralization," they write, "and we believe these techniques make up a crucial component of Sutherland's definitions favorable to the violation of law" (p. 667).

Sykes and Matza list four of these *neutralization techniques:* denial of responsibility (e.g., blaming a bad upbringing), denial of injury (e.g., claiming that the victim deserved it), condemnation of the condemners (e.g., calling their condemnation discriminatory), and an appeal to higher loyalties (e.g., citing loyalty to friends or family as the cause of the behavior). Sykes and Matza's point is that delinquency in the underclass, as elsewhere, is facilitated by this kind of thinking. A question lingered, however: Why are these delinquencies of the underclass more frequently made the subjects of official condemnation?

Labeling Theory. Franklin Tannenbaum (1938) anticipated a theoretical answer to this question. He pointed out that some aspects of juvenile delinquency—the play, adventure, and excitement—are a normal part of teenage street life and that, later in their lives, many nostalgically identify these activities as an important part of their adolescence. But others see such activities as a nuisance or as threatening, so they summon the police.

Tannenbaum's concern is that police intervention begins a process of change in the way the individuals and their activities are perceived. He suggests that there is a gradual shift from defining specific acts as evil to defining the individual as evil. Tannenbaum sees the individual's first contact with the law as the most consequential, referring to this event as a "dramatization of evil" that separates the child from his or her peers for specialized treatment. Tannenbaum goes on to argue that this dramatization may play a greater role in creating the criminal than any other experience. The problem is that individuals thus singled out may begin to think of themselves as the type of people who do such things—that is, as delinquents. From this viewpoint, efforts to reform or deter delinquent behavior create more problems than they solve. "The way out," Tannenbaum argues, "is through a refusal to dramatize the evil." He implies that the less said or done about delinquency the better.

Sociologists have expanded Tannenbaum's perspective into what is often called a labeling, or societal reactions, theory of delinquency and other kinds of deviance. For example, Lemert (1967) suggests the terms *primary deviance* and *secondary deviance* to distinguish between acts that occur before and after the societal response. Acts of primary deviance are those that precede a social or legal response. They may be incidental or even random aspects of an individual's general behavior. The important point is that these initial acts have little impact on the individual's self-concept. Acts of secondary deviance, on the other hand, follow the societal response and involve a transformation of the individual's self-concept, "altering the psychic structure, producing specialized organization of social roles and self-regarding attitudes." From this point on, the individual takes on more and more of the "deviant" aspects of his or her new role (Becker 1963, 1964). The societal response has, from this viewpoint, succeeded only in confirming the individual in a deviant role: for example, by potentially making adolescent delinquents into adult criminals through the punitive reactions of the police, courts, and others.

In the end, symbolic interactionists do not insist that all or even most delinquent behavior is caused by officially imposed labels. Being labeled delinquent is thought, rather, to create special problems for the adolescents involved, often increasing the likelihood that this and related kinds of delinquent behavior will be repeated. The point is that not only the actor but also reactors participate in creating the meanings and definitions that generate delinquency. The symbolic interactionists note that the poor are more likely than the rich to get caught up in this process. This point is further emphasized in conflict theories.

CONFLICT THEORY AND DELINQUENCY

The most distinctive features of conflict theories include attention to the role of power relations and economic contradictions in generating delinquency and reactions to it. For example, conflict theories have focused on the role of dominant societal groups in imposing legal labels on members of subordinate societal groups (Turk 1969). The fact that subcultural groups typically are also subordinate groups ties this work to earlier theoretical traditions discussed above.

An Early Group-Conflict Theory. George Vold (1958) was the first North American sociologist to write explicitly about a group-conflict theory of delinquency. He began with the assumption that criminality involves both human behavior (acts) and the judgments or definitions (laws, customs, or mores) of others as to whether specific behaviors are appropriate and acceptable or inappropriate and disreputable. Of the two components, Vold regarded judgments and definitions as more significant. His salient interest was in how groups impose their value judgments by defining the behaviors of others as illegal.

Vold regarded delinquency as a "minority group" behavior. For example, he argues that "the juvenile gang . . . is nearly always a 'minority group', out of sympathy with and in more or less direct opposition to the rules and regulations of the dominant majority, that is, the established world of adult values and powers" (p. 211). In this struggle, the police are seen as representing and defending the values of the adult world, while the gang seeks the symbolic and material advantages not permitted it under the adult code. At root, Vold argues, the problem is one of intergenerational value conflict, with adults prevailing through their control of the legal process.

A Theory of Legal Bureaucracy. According to this viewpoint, determining which groups in society will experience more delinquency than others may be largely a matter of deciding which laws will be enforced. Chambliss and Seidman (1971) observe that in modern, complex, stratified societies such as our own, we assign the task of resolving such issues to bureaucratically structured agencies such as the police. The result is to mobilize what might be called the primary principle of legal bureaucracy. According to this principle, laws will be enforced when enforcement serves the interests of social control agencies and their officials; and laws will not be enforced when enforcement is likely to cause organizational strain. In other words, the primary principle of legal bureaucracy involves maximizing organizational gains while minimizing organizational strains.

Chambliss and Seidman conclude that a consequence of this principle is to bring into operation a "rule of law," whereby "discretion at every level . . . will be so exercised as to bring mainly those who are politically powerless (e.g., the poor) into the purview of the law" (p. 268). Theoretical work of this kind coincided with important research on the policing of juveniles (e.g., Reiss 1971). According to the conflict theorists, poor minority youth appear disproportionately in our delinquency statistics more because of class bias and police and court prejudice than because of actual behavioral differences.

Recent Structural Theories. Some recent theories of delinquency have combined conflict theory's structural focus on power relations with etiological questions about sources of delinquent behavior as well as reactions to it. Thus Spitzer (1975) begins the formulation of a Marxian theory of delinquency (and deviance more generally) with the observation, "We must not only ask why specific members of the underclass are selected for official processing, but also why they behave as they do" (p. 640).

A recent effort to answer behavioral questions with insights from conflict theory is an "integrated structural-Marxist theory" proposed by Colvin and Pauly (1983). This theory integrates elements of control theory and Marxian theory. The theory is comprehensive, and only some of its most striking features can be outlined here. These features include a Marxian focus on working class parents' experiences of coerciveness in the workplace, which Colvin and Pauly suggest lead to coerciveness in parenting, including parental violence toward children. In turn, Colvin and Pauly argue that such children are more likely to be placed in coercive control structures at school and to enter into alliances with alienated peers. All of these experiences make delinquent behavior more likely, including the violent and instrumental kinds of delinquent behavior that may be precursors of adult criminality.

Power-control theory is another recent structural formulation (Hagan 1989) that attempts to explain large and persistent gender differences in delinquency by taking power relations into account. Power relations in the family are the starting point of this theory. The cornerstone of the theory is the observation that, especially in more patriarchal families, mothers more than fathers are involved in controlling daughters more than sons. A result of this intensified mother–daughter relationship is that daughters become less inclined to take what they perceive as greater risks of involvement in delinquency. Police and other processing agencies act on stereotypes that extend these gender differences in officially recorded delinquency. Power-control theory generally predicts that in more patriarchal families, sons will be subjected to less maternal control, develop stronger preferences for risk taking, be more delinquent, and more often be officially labeled for being so.

These structural approaches illustrate a trend toward theoretical integration in this tradition and elsewhere in the study of delinquency (Messner, Krohn, and Liska 1989). These integrations involve theories that are often thought to be in apposition if not opposition to one another. One of the distinctive features of sociological theories of delinquency is the richness of their diversity, and it is not yet clear whether diversity or integration will provide the greater source of theoretical and empirical advancement in years to come.

(SEE ALSO: *Crime, Theories of; Criminology; Juvenile Delinquency and Juvenile Crime*)

REFERENCES

Becker, Howard 1963 *Outsiders: Studies in the Sociology of Deviance.* New York: Free Press.

——— 1964 *The Other Side: Perspectives on Deviance.* New York: Free Press.

Chambliss, William, and Robert Seidman 1971 *Law, Order and Power.* Reading, Mass.: Addison-Wesley.

Cloward, Richard, and Lloyd Ohlin 1960 *Delinquency and Opportunity: A Theory of Delinquent Gangs.* New York: Free Press.

Cohen, Albert 1955 *Delinquent Boys.* New York: Free Press.

Colvin, Mark, and John Pauly 1983 "A Critique of Criminology: Toward an Integrated Structural-Marxist Theory of Delinquency Production." *American Journal of Sociology* 89 (3):512–552.

Durkheim, Emile 1951 (1897) *Suicide,* trans. John Spaulding and George Simpson. New York: Free Press.

Hagan, John 1989 *Structural Criminology.* New Brunswick, N.J.: Rutgers University Press.

Hirschi, Travis 1969 *Causes of Delinquency.* Berkeley: University of California Press.

Lemert, Edwin 1967 *Human Deviance, Social Problems and Social Control.* Englewood Cliffs, N.J.: Prentice-Hall.

Merton, Robert 1938 "Social Structure and Anomie." *American Sociological Review* 3:672–682.

———1957 *Social Theory and Social Structure.* New York: Free Press.

Messner, Steven, Marvin Krohn, and Allen Liska 1989 *Theoretical Integration in the Study of Deviance and Crime: Problems and Prospects.* Albany: State University of New York Press.

Moynihan, Daniel P. 1969 *Maximum Feasible Misunderstanding.* New York: Free Press.

Reiss, Albert 1971 *The Police and the Public.* New Haven, Conn.: Yale University Press.

Shaw, Clifford, and Henry McKay 1931 *Social Factors in Juvenile Delinquency.* Washington, D.C.: National Commission of Law Observance and Enforcement.

———1942 *Juvenile Delinquency and Urban Areas.* Chicago: University of Chicago Press.

Spitzer, Steven 1975 "Toward a Marxian Theory of Deviance." *Social Problems* 22:638–651.

Sutherland, Edwin 1939 *Principles of Criminology.* Philadelphia: Lippincott.

———1949 *White Collar Crime.* New York: Dryden.

Sykes, Gresham, and David Matza 1957 "Techniques of Neutralization: A Theory of Delinquency." *American Sociological Review.* 26:664–670.

———1961 "Juvenile Delinquency and Subterranean Values." *American Sociological Review* 26:712–719.

Tannenbaum, Frank 1938 *Crime and the Community.* Boston: Ginn.

Turk, Austin 1969 *Criminality and the Legal Order.* Chicago: Rand McNally.

Vold, George 1958 *Theoretical Criminology.* New York: Oxford University Press.

JOHN HAGAN

K

KINSHIP SYSTEMS AND FAMILY TYPES Kinship systems are mechanisms that link conjugal families (and individuals not living in families) in ways that affect the integration of the general social structure and enhance the ability of the society to reproduce itself in an orderly fashion. Kinship performs these social functions in two ways. First, through relationships defined by blood ties and marriage, kinship systems make possible ready-made *contemporaneous networks* of social ties sustained during the lifetimes of related persons and, second, they enable the *temporal continuity* of identifiable family connections over generations, despite the limited lifespan of a family's members. Variations in norms governing the structure of contemporaneous networks and the modes of temporal continuity compose the basis for the typologies of kinship systems described in this article.

In conceptualizing connections between kinship systems and family types, social scientists have applied either of two approaches. Some have developed typologies from historical analyses (and evolutionary schemes) that depict the transition of Western societies from ancient or medieval origins to modern civilizations. Other social scientists construct typologies that cut across diverse historical periods. Each historical era then constitutes a unique medium in which the structural typologies are expressed.

MODERNITY, FAMILY PATTERNS, AND KINSHIP SYSTEMS

There are at least three ways to develop historical typologies related to kinship and family. One way is to hypothesize a linear historical progression, which includes a family type existing at the beginning point in time, a particular historical process that will act upon the family and kinship structures (e.g., urbanization or industrialization), and a logical outcome at the end of the process. A second approach builds upon the above approach by positing a transitional family type that emerges during the historical process and gives way in the final stages of the process to another family type. A third approach is to devise a family type based upon a configuration of attributes peculiar to a particular historical era (e.g., the Victorian family, the American colonial family) and implies that any historical era represents a unique convergence of diverse factors.

Bipolar Typologies. By and large, sociologists have drawn a connection between kinship and family on the basis of a distinction between traditionalism and modernity. Generally, this distinction draws upon Henry Maine's (1885) depiction of the transformation of social relations in early societies. Maine argued that social relations changed from those based on ascriptive status (deriving from birth) to relations created and sustained through voluntary contractual arrangements. Maine's theory has evoked a series of typologies that, in large measure, refine the status–contract distinction. For instance, an ideal type developed by Ferdinand Tönnies ([1887] 1957) has provided a backdrop for later typologies. The Tönnies typology itself refers to a shift from *Gemeinschaft* (community) as a form of social organization based upon an existential will (*Wesserwille*)), which is suited to feudalism and peasant society, to *Gesellschaft* (society) as a social form based upon rational will (*Kurwille*), which fits an urban environment under modern capitalism. Contemporary family typologies, in building upon Tönnies's conceptual scheme, portray a weakening of kinship obligations and constraints.

One position, rooted in George P. Murdock's (1949) analysis of cross-cultural archives, has resulted in the main sequence theory of social change in kinship structure (Naroll, 1970). Main sequence theory pertains to the way differential gender contributions to production of material resources affects the use of kindred as human resources/property. This theory holds that basic changes in kinship are initiated by a shift in the relative importance of men and women to the economic life of the society. First, there is a modification in the economic division of labor by gender. (For example, in hoe cultures, women tend to do the farming; when plows are introduced, men become the farmers.) Second, the shift in sexual division of labor generates a change in married couples' choices of residence, the major alternatives being near the husband's relatives (patrilocal), the wife's (matrilocal), or anywhere the couple desires. (Plow cultures tend toward patrilocal residence.) Third, the change in choice of residential site affects the line of descent and inheritance favored in the kinship system: the husband's side (patrilineal), the wife's (matrilineal), or both sides (bilateral). (Plow cultures show a greater inclination toward patrilineality than do hoe cultures.) Fourth, the transfer to lineage affiliation generates a change in kinship terminology, particularly in ways that show tribal or clan membership, or, in modern societies, the dissolution of larger kinship structures. As applied to the emergence of modernity, main sequence theory predicts a continual emancipation from kinship constraints. An increase in the proportion of women in the labor force will produce a trend toward neolocal residence, which in turn will lead to increased emphasis upon bilaterality, weakening sibling ties and obligations to both sides of the extended family, and in the long run to changes in kin terminology and identity (e.g., voluntarism in choice of surnames).

In a variation of main sequence theory, urban sociologists such as Wirth (1956) and Burgess, Locke, and Thomas (1963) wrote on the effects of transferring the economic base of societies from the land to urban centers. The theme of their work is to be found in the German proverb "Stadt Luft macht frei" ("city air makes one free"). For example, Burgess, Locke, and Thomas described a progression from what they named the institutional family to the companionship family. In this conceptualization, the institutional family, embedded in a larger kinship group, is characterized by patriarchy, clearly defined division of household labor by sex, and high fertility. Its unity is derived mainly from external constraints—social mores, religious authority, fixity in location, position in the social structure, and the value of familism (i.e., values giving priority to the collective welfare of the family over that of individual members). Burgess, Locke, and Thomas regarded the institutional family as an adaptation to relatively immobile, rural, agricultural societies and believed its way of life was fixed over time. By way of contrast, urban society, which is characterized by mobility, anonymity, and change, makes inoperative the social control mechanisms developed to maintain stable, rural societies. With the withering of these external controls on rural family life, Burgess, Locke, and Thomas proposed that the companionship family is bound together by internal forces—mutual affection, egalitarianism, a sense of belonging, common interests—and affords freedom from the demands of traditional family and kinship ties.

Unlike the urban sociologists, structural functionalists such as Talcott Parsons (1954) place considerable emphasis on the interaction of subsystems in the larger social system. In part, structural functionalists are concerned with economic and kinship factors in structuring nuclear family relationships. Parsons describes American kinship as "a 'conjugal' system in that it is made up *exclusively* of interlocking conjugal families" (1954, p. 180) and is multilineal (i.e., bilateral) in descent. Parsons associates kinship solidarity with unilineal descent, that is, with a "structural bias in favor of solidarity with the ascendant and descendant families in any one line of descent" (1954, p. 184). The absence of such bias in the American descent system, Parsons suggests, is in large measure responsible for "the structural isolation of the individual conjugal family." The importance Parsons attributes to unilineality as a factor in facilitating strong dependence upon kin ties is exemplified by his highlighting two exceptions to the structural isolation of the conjugal family in America—the upper class elements, whose status depends on the continuity of their patrilineages' solidarity, and the lower class elements, in which there is "a strong tendency to instability of marriage and a 'mother-centered' type of family structure" (Parsons 1954, p. 185). However, Parsons regards the urban middle classes as characterizing "the focal American type of kinship." Since in the middle classes the residence of the conjugal family typically is neolocal, and the conjugal family is economically independent of "the family of orientation of either spouse," the role of the conjugal family in U.S. society can be, for theoretical purposes, understood as master of its own destiny, rid of the impediments of extended-family ties.

In reaction to those sociologists who see modernity as inimical to bonds of kinship, other social scientists (e.g., Adams [1968]; Firth, Hubert, and Forge [1969]; Litwak [1985]; Mogey [1976]; Shanas et al. [1968]; and Sussman [1959]) turn their attention to the attenuated functions of kinship in contemporary society. Just as Goode (1963) notes a "fit" between the needs of modern capitalist society for a socially and geographically highly mobile population and the flexibility of the isolated conjugal family system, the revisionists indicate a similar fit between the existence of a highly mobile population and the presence of kin who give emergency aid and social support to relatives. The revisionists shift our attention away from constraints imposed by kinship loyalties and obligations and direct it instead to sources of services, goods, and emotional support that cannot readily be supplied by bureaucracies, markets, or other agencies. In his typology, Litwak (1960a and 1960b) distinguishes the isolated nuclear family (without kinship resources) from the traditional extended family (implying a hierarchy of authority), on the one hand, and from the modified extended family (which consists of a network of related but autonomous nuclear families), on the other. Although the revisionists have not destroyed the foundation of the bipolar family typologies, they do focus on a previously neglected area of analysis.

Three-Stage Typologies. Some modernization typologies introduce a third, transitional stage between traditional and modern kinship and family structures. These typologies accept the position that initially there is an emancipation from traditional kinship constraints and obligations, but they also propose that at some point new values of modernity emerge to fill the vacuum left by the dissipation of the old kinship constraints. For example, building on the work of LePlay, Zimmerman and Frampton (1966) offer a scheme of transformation in which families change from a patriarchal form to a stem-family structure and thence to an unstable type. Zimmerman and Frampton begin with the premise that each social organization derives its "essential character" from a triad of "imperishable institutions"—family, religion, and property. However, in their view, "familism is necessary in all complete social organization to a degree more imperative than the need for property" (1966, p. 14). Zimmerman and Frampton regard the patriarchal family as the most familistic form. The patriarchal type is rooted in idealistic religion and is characterized by a common household of a patriarch and his married sons and their families, wherein the property is held in the name of the "house," with the father as trustee. They identify the patriarchal form as having been prevalent among agriculturists in the Orient, in rural Russia, and among Slavonic peasants.

With urbanization and industrialization, however, the unstable family becomes predominant. Zimmerman and Frampton associate the unstable family with materialism and individualism and the resulting atomization of social life. Individuals are "freed from all obligations toward their parents and relatives" (1966, p. 15), and the identity of each conjugal family as a social unit ends with the death of the parents and the dispersal of the children.

The stem family represents a transitional state between the patriarchal and unstable forms. The stem family extends branches into urban centers while retaining its roots in the ancestral lands. As a result, the stem family provides a balance between the security of the traditional influences and resources of the "house" and the freedom and resources of the cities. (However, historical researchers yield less idyllic descriptions of the stem family than the Zimmerman and Frampton portrait. See Berkner 1972.)

A less romantic depiction of a transitional family type is drawn by Lawrence Stone (1975) in his typology of the English family's movement from feudalism to modernity. Stone posits the existence of a dual historical process. He places the decline of the importance of kin ties in the context of the emergence of a powerful, centralized state, and he then regards the rise of the modern family as an ideological emergence accompanying the development of capitalism.

According to Stone's typology, feudal England emphasized (1) kin-group responsibility for crimes and treasonable acts of members and (2) the institution of cousinship with its broad obligations. As political and economic power moved away from the traditional, landed elite to the state and the entrepreneurial class, the common law of the courts no longer recognized criminal and civil deviance as a kin-group responsibility, and cousinship lost its effectiveness. To fill the vacuum left by the decline of kinship as a factor in one's destiny, the relatively denuded conjugal family had to take over the task of guiding the destiny for its members. Consequently, by the sixteenth century, as an intermediate step toward the modern family, there was a trend toward authoritarianism in husband–wife interaction, and family governance took the form of patriarchy.

Stone (1975, p. 15) suggests that it was not until the eighteenth century that the spread of individualism and utilitarianism gave rise to a more companionate and egalitarian family structure. This last family form has been designated by Alan Macfarlane (1986) as the Malthusian marriage system, in which (1) marriage is seen as ultimately the bride's and groom's concern rather than that of the kin group; (2) marital interaction is supposed to be primarily companionate; and (3) love is supposed to be a precursor of marriage. Functionally, the Malthusian system yields relatively fewer children—by choice—than earlier family forms.

The Problem of Structure in Modernity Typologies. Typologies depicting historical transformations in family and kinship place much emphasis on the "fit" between the needs of modern industrial society and the presence of the conjugal family type (Parsons 1954; Litwak 1960a; 1960b). Despite this conjecture, Parsons (1954, p. 184) suggests that in Western society an "essentially open system" of kinship, with its "primary stress upon the conjugal family" and its lack of larger kin structures, has existed for centuries, long before the modern period. Like Macfarlane (1986), Parsons dates its establishment in late medieval times "when the kinship terminology of the European languages took shape." Moreover, Goode's (1963) analysis of family trends in eleven societies indicates that acceptance of modern, conjugal family ideology may precede economic and industrial development rather than come as a subsequent adaptation. Such findings cast doubt on the validity of the dichotomy between traditional societies and modernity as providing a theoretical basis for the typologies discussed above.

Parsons argues that (1) there is an incompatibility between corporate kinship and multilineal systems, and (2) in large measure, this incompatibility accounts for the prevalence of highly adaptable, structurally independent conjugal households in modern societies. However, findings by Davenport (1959), Mitchell (1963), Pehrson (1957), Peranio (1961), and others that corporate structures of kinship (such as clans) do exist in some multilineal kinship systems undercut Parsons's argument that such structures are to be found only in unilineal systems. Nevertheless, if multilateral kinship systems can accommodate corporate structures, then they can also include other kinship elements that sustain loyalties to descent groups and facilitate segmentation of the society.

The Problem of Connecting Kinship and Family in Modernity Typologies. Revisionists of the isolated conjugal family position have presented considerable evidence of residual elements of kinship ties in contemporary society. However, they do not adequately explain the connections between types of kinship systems and variation in performance of family functions in different parts of the social structure. Their main concern is with changes in kinship and family, changes that are consistent with the general loosening of tradition in modern society. But their focus on emancipation from tradition diverts their attention (1) from the influence of emerging ethnic, religious, or class interests upon patterns of integration of family networks in the larger social structure, and (2) from the temporal dimensions of kinship, which go beyond living kin to departed ancestors and generations yet to come.

Additionally, given the fact that the family-kinship typologies described above have their roots in the distinction between tradition and modernity, they overlook those nonindustrial, primarily nonurban societies in which families approach the companionship model as well as those ethnic and religious segments of industrial, primarily urban societies where strong familistic tendencies persist. Except for Stone (1975) and Zimmerman and Frampton (1966), these typologies are based on the concept of emancipation from tradition, and they do not deal explicitly with the emergence of new family values (other than flexibility and freedom). Most of all, their emphasis on emancipation from the constraints of tradition precludes their explaining why cohesive forces of family and kinship may remain strong (or increase in strength) in the face of an economic and social environment that is hostile to stable family life. (Exceptions are Sennett [1970] and Harris and Rosser [1983].)

A TRANSHISTORICAL TYPOLOGY OF KINSHIP AND FAMILY SYSTEMS

For well over a millennium, church intellectuals have been aware of variations in marital selection and their implications for family structure and kinship ties as well as for social structure. Early in the fifth century, in his *De Civitate Dei (City of God),* Saint Augustine of Hippo (1966, vol. 4, pp. 503–505) noted that in early biblical times demographic insufficiencies made it necessary for Jews to practice kinship endogamy. However, he proposed that marrying close relatives, and thereby creating multiple family ties with the same people, restricted the potential expanse of social circles that could be tied into a coherent community. Kinship endogamy tends to divide societies into segments. On the other hand, marrying persons from previously unrelated families would "serve to weld social life securely" by binding diverse peoples into an extensive web of relationships. Later, in the twelfth century, Gratian suggested that God commanded the Hebrews to select relatives as mates "because the salvation of man was realized in the pure Jewish race" but that the Christian faith, which could be readily spread through teaching, made kinship endogamy obsolete (Chodorow 1972, p. 74).

Gratian's argument suggests that the differences between Judaic and Christian marriage systems have broad implications for contemporaneous functions of kinship as well as for temporal functions, connecting past and future generations. The discussion that follows presents a kinship and family typology derived ultimately from Augustine's and Gratian's depictions of marriage systems as well as from issues pertaining to descent.

This typology involves theoretical concerns drawn from sociology and anthropology.

Contemporaneous and Temporal Functions of Kinship Systems. Both marriage systems and descent rules affect the character of links between contemporaneous networks of families. A major controversy that at one time occupied many social anthropologists was whether marriage systems (i.e., marital alliances between groups) are more fundamental in generating forms of social organization than are descent rules or vice versa. At stake in the controversy was the issue of whether the social solidarity undergirding descent rules is more fundamental than the ideas of reciprocity and exchange involved in marriage systems. In the end, Africanists favored descent rules, while Asianists leaned toward marital alliances. In their assessment of the controversy, Buchler and Selby (1968) found evidence for the validity of both views.

However, despite the chicken-and-egg character of the controversy, the alliance–descent issue highlights the contradictory nature of kinship structure. This contradiction is depicted in the opposing views of structuralists such as Claude Lévi-Strauss (1969), who supports the alliance position, and functionalists such as Meyer Fortes (1969), who argues for the descent position.

Alliance theories of kinship systems identify the primary function of kinship as the integration of networks of related families into the contemporaneous social fabric. Alliance adherents begin with marriage as the central element in structuring the way kinship operates. To alliance theorists, the significance of marriage lies in the idea that marriage is essentially a mode of exchange whose primary reason for existence is to inhibit conflict in society. In their view, kin groups exist as organized entities to effect marital exchanges. According to Lévi-Strauss, the leading figure in alliance theory, "exchange in human society is a universal means of ensuring the interlocking of its constituent parts" (1963, p. 2). In unilineal systems, women are exchanged for equivalent valuable property, services, or both; in bilateral systems (which by their nature become multilateral in the long run), commitments to each other's relatives are exchanged. In bilateral kinship, bride and groom are of presumably equivalent value. Thus, in general, alliance theorists regard descent groupings primarily as a necessary ingredient for sustaining the marriage exchange system over the generations.

The descent theory of kinship systems rests on the assumption that the continued welfare of kindred over the generations is the primary function of kinship. In particular, Fortes regards "filiation"—being ascribed the status of a child of one's parents, with all the lifetime rights and obligations attached to that status (1969, p. 108)—as the "crucial relationships of intergenerational continuity and social reproduction" (pp. 255–256). He proposes that, as a concomitant of filiation, "the model relationship of kinship amity is fraternity, that is sibling unity, equality, and solidarity" (p. 241), and he provides a biblical example of the tie between David and Jonathan. But he also notes that "the Euro-American kinship institutions and values of Anglo-Saxon origin are imbued with the same notion of binding force of kinship amity" (p. 242), and he cites the mother–daughter relationship in England (in research findings by Young and Willmott [1957]) as exemplifying that same moral code of diffuse but demanding reciprocal obligations.

On the one hand, alliance theory postulates that the basic drive in kinship organization is derived externally, from the kind of alliances appropriate to the structure of power in the community. Collectively, marital alliances create between families a network of links that integrate them in reference to overarching religious, economic, and political institutions. On the other hand, descent theory ascribes the bases of organization to internal demands, structural factors in the persistence of the kindred: rules governing residential location, division of labor and authority among members, and the various economic and political functions to be performed by the kinship system (Buchler and Selby 1968, p. 129).

Given the contradiction in the impulse for kinship organization, there is an apparent "impasse between the alliance and filiation point of view" (Buchler and Selby 1968, p. 141). What appears to be at issue is the depiction of the kinds of reciprocity norms that define the character of kinship. Descent theory presumes that an axiom of amity (i.e., prescriptive altruism or general reciprocity) is basic to the coherence of kin groups; alliance theory holds that balanced reciprocity (i.e., the rightness of exchanges for overt self-interest, opportunistic individualism, or noumenal norms) is in the final analysis the glue that integrates families and kin groups into a coherent whole.

The contradiction is apparent in many ways. For example, in biblical references and religious writings, the Ten Commandments enjoin one to honor parents and, conversely, to "cleave" to one's spouse and maintain peace in the household. In terms of kinds of reciprocity, one commandment involves unconditional giving or honoring, while the other concerns maintaining domestic peace (implying fair give-and-take).

Similarly, contemporary writers on marriage generally find the concept of balanced reciprocity appropriate in describing the quality of husband–wife ties. For example, Walster and Walster (1978) report that marriages work best when both husband and wife (as well as lovers) believe that each is receiving a fair exchange for what he or she offers in the relationship. Moreover, in their review of research on the quality of marriage, Lewis and Spanier (1982) note the importance of the symmetry of exchange in establishing and maintaining strong marital ties. However, in the socialization of children and in the allocation of resources, the rule of amity (or prescriptive altruism) is supposed to prevail. For example, parents are ordinarily expected to make "sacrifices" for their children when necessary; to do otherwise is to be a "bad" parent. In the American court system, the general rule for the disposition of children in cases of divorce, child neglect or abuse, or adoption is that the court should base its decision on the welfare of the child rather than on the interests of the parents or other parties.

To some extent, the descent–marriage contradiction can be obscured by compartmentalizing marital, parental, and filial conduct and by dividing responsibilities of husband and wife. However, conflicts in norms for dealing with family members and kindred may occur for several reasons, but they occur principally because of scarcities of time and resources required to carry out duties and obligations in the face of a wide range of simultaneous and conflicting demands. Since the resulting dilemmas are widespread in the society, there is a need for a general rule. Because contradictory alliance and descent impulses are operative, each group is pushed to establish a coherent kinship scheme that gives priority to one impulse over the other or at least establishes some form of compromise between them.

There is evidence that rules governing marital functions conflict with those pertaining to descent functions, paralleling the alliance–descent controversy in kinship systems. Where descent functions are given precedence in family organization, marital functions are subordinated (and vice versa). Examples of this inverse relationship are (1) if husband–wife unity is central, then the unity between siblings is peripheral (and the reverse), and (2) if marriage between close affines is forbidden, first-cousin marriage is permitted (and vice versa). These examples are discussed in the sections that follow.

Marital Unity versus Unity of the Sibling Group. Comparisons between societies indicate that ties between siblings have an inverse relationship to husband–wife ties. Where descent is valued over alliance or marriage in kinship relations, brother–sister bonds are particularly close (Parsons 1954), while the husband–wife relationship is relatively distant. In such family systems (whether or not its therapeutic implications are true), parents are expected to remain together for the sake of the children, and this expectation expresses the priority of descent over marital ties. Conversely, in family systems where the marriage function is more valued, the husband–wife relationship is intense (e.g., the importance of the give-and-take of love and of companionship for marriage) and the brother–sister relationship is competitive, distant, or both and the incest taboo justifies their apartness (see Lopata [1973] on widows and their brothers). In societies where priority is given to marital bonds over descent ties, the presence of children is of less importance in dissolving an unhappy marriage, and there is greater ambiguity about what is best for the children. The mere fact that the strength of brother–sister ties and that of marital ties vary inversely in different societies lends support to the proposition that there is a contradiction in the family system between its marital functions and its descent functions.

Affines and Cousins in American Marriage Law. The opposition between marital and descent functions in the family is also illustrated by the inverse relationship in American law of marriages considered to be incestuous: As a general tendency, states that *forbid* second marriages between a person and certain affines (such as that person's parents-in-law and sons- or daughters-in-law) *allow* first cousins to marry, while those that *permit* marriage between close affines *forbid* first-cousin marriage (Farber 1968, pp. 27–28). If the preferred function of marriage is to reinforce close consanguineous kinship ties, then this pattern of marital prohibitions signals a subordination of affinal bonds to those of consanguinity. Marrying into the family of the former spouse will not reinforce any of the other existing bonds of consanguinity. Consequently, although first-cousin marriage is to be permitted in order to reinforce intimate kinship ties, marriage with close affines should be avoided. However, if marriage is considered to be primarily a mechanism for creating new bonds between previously unrelated families, then a second marriage into the same family merely serves to maintain the affinal bonds initiated in the first marriage.

Social Structure and Kinship Systems. The presence of contradictory impulses in organizing kinship ties produces a predicament in establishing priorities between them. This contradiction evokes a question: Which circumstances lead some societies (and ethnic and religious subgroups) to give priority to descent and others to favor alliance assumptions in their kinship and family organization (Farber 1975)? In their analyses of the relationship between kinship organization and social structure, both Paige (1974) and Swanson (1969) distinguish between societies that feature the legitimacy of special interests—factionalism—in organizing social life and those that feature the importance of common interests—communalism—as an organizing theme.

Factions are a means for gathering forces and mobilizing members for conflict or competition with other factions. They emerge as a reaction to perceived danger to their well-being from other groups (cf. Douglas 1966). Factions emerge where either (1) special interest groups vie for superiority over other groups for access to power, wealth, or some other property, or (2) groups sense a danger to their continued autonomous existence as an ethnic or religious entity.

In kinship organization, the mobilization of property and of members in factionalism involves generating norms to facilitate the pulling inward of human, symbolic, and material resources. (Consequently, this type of kinship organization, associated with factionalist social structure, can be called *centripetal.)* This centripetal tendency permits each kin group to separate itself from competing groups. As a result, kin groups favor norms strengthening *descent* relationships over norms facilitating new alliances with other groups through marriage. Insofar as descent group norms are rooted in the axiom of amity, one would expect centripetal kinship organization to feature the norm of prescriptive altruism over balanced reciprocities in kinship and family relations (see Farber 1975).

Jewish family norms provide some insight into the relationship between centripetal kinship systems and the application of the axiom of amity. In its basic ideology and in the code of laws supporting that ideology, Judaism assigns a major significance to the concept of nurturance (Farber 1984). Since nurturance is a central feature of maternal giving, it can be regarded as a metaphor for the axiom of amity. The *Code of Jewish Law (Shulkhan Arukh)* offers numerous instances that signify the place of nurturance in Judaism (Ganzfried 1963). For example, the code sublimates feeding and eating into sacred, ritualistic acts. The act of eating is invested with holiness, to be enjoyed in abundance, particularly on feast days and the Sabbath. A connection is made in the code between providing food and giving gifts and charity. It proposes that festive occasions are also times for charity to the needy and for sending gifts. In addition to drawing a connection between food and charity, the code applies the metaphor of the parent–child relationship to charity giving and assigns a priority to family in its general concept of nurturance: First parents, then offspring, and "other kinsmen take precedence over strangers" (Ganzfried 1963, chap. 34). The injunction to nurture children involves an emphasis not only on food but on other aspects as well (for example, an exaggerated emphasis on elaborated linguistic codes for use in childrearing). Zena Smith Blau (1974, p. 175) writes that "whatever Jewish mothers did for their children—and they did a great deal—was accompanied by a flow of language, consisting of rich, colorful expressive words and phrases." The aim of socialization is presumably to turn the child into a *Mensch*—to transform the child from a receiver of nurture to a giver of nurture (Zborowski and Herzog 1952, p. 335). Hence, in traditional Judaism, the concept of nurturance seems to tie together the kinship emphasis on descent and the axiom of amity in organizing family relationships.

As opposed to factionalism, communalism implies a situation in which special interests are subordinated to common concerns of diverse groups. In stateless societies, these common concerns may well emerge from economic interdependence or the presence of a common enemy. In societies with a centralized government, the state presumably symbolizes a concern for the common welfare of the populace. Other unifying concerns may exist as well, for example, the presence of a universal church (as opposed to competing sects and denominations), nationalism (as opposed to ethnic self-determination), a centralized bureaucracy or market (as opposed to regional competition for dominance), and so on. The common concerns would best be served if members of kin groups were to be dispersed by marriage to previously unrelated people living throughout the society. This dispersal would maximize the number of diverse kin groups with which any family is connected, and it would thereby scatter kinship loyalties, obligations, and property as widely as possible. (Consequently, this kind of kinship system, associated with communalism, can be called *centrifugal.)*

In contrast to the centripetal system, the centrifugal system subordinates kinship ties to conjugal family ties and extends marital prohibitions widely in order to inhibit marriages that would merely reinforce existing consanguineous ties. According to the theory outlined above, in centrifugal kinship systems, in which marriage functions are given priority over descent functions, the appropriate norm for defining family interaction is balanced reciprocity—exchange rather than the axiom of amity.

In the United States, although the centrifugal kinship system appears in a wide range of socioeconomic, religious, and ethnic groups, it is found disproportionately at lower socioeconomic levels, where families seek improved integration into the larger society (Farber 1981).

The application of balanced exchange as a norm in family and kinship is exemplified in a study of poor families by Carol Stack (1974). She describes the prevalence of "swapping" as a named, bartering norm governing both ties between kin and between family members in their struggle for survival. Stack notes that "reciprocal obligations last as long as both participants are mutually satisfied" and that they continue such exchange relationships as long as they can "draw upon the credit they accumulate with others through swapping" (p. 41). Indeed, according to Stack, "those actively involved in domestic networks swap goods and services on a daily, practically an hourly, basis" (p. 35). But this exchange does not constitute a playing out of the axiom of amity since "the obligation to repay carries kin and community sanctions" (p. 34) and it extends beyond family and kin to friends. Although swapping may involve some element of trust, it exists to ensure exchanges in the lean times that predictably recur in domestic networks that are too marginal in resources to be magnanimous. It pays to create numerous bartering arrangements rather than to accumulate obligations within a very small network of intimate kin. Thus, in its own way, swapping mimics the proliferation of networks of previously unrelated families characteristic of centrifugal kinship systems.

Related Transhistorical Typologies. Variations on issues pertinent to the structural contradiction typology have been developed in other transhistorical schemes associated with the role of marriage and descent systems in organizing family and kinship systems. For instance, Guichard (1977) distinguishes between Eastern/Islamic and Western/Christian kinship systems. According to his typology, in the Eastern system, (1) descent is patrilineal; (2) marital ties are weak and polygyny and easy divorce are permitted; (3) close ties exist between kin related through male lineage groups; (4) strong preference is given to endogamy within patrilineages; and (5) the sexes are segregated and women are relatively secluded within the home. In contrast, in the Western system, (1) kinship is bilineal or bilateral/multilateral, with ties to the maternal family considered important and with an emphasis on affinal connections as well; (2) marital bonds are the dominant unifying feature in family and kinship, with monogamy as prescribed and with extended kin ties as weak; (3) kin ties are defined according to individual connections rather than by lineage groups, with an emphasis upon the ascending line rather than the descending line and with little importance attached to lineal continuity or solidarity; (4) kinship exogamy is prescribed, with endogamy permitted primarily for economic reasons; and (5) interaction between the sexes occurs in a wide range of circumstances.

In his reaction to Guichard, Goody (1983) revives the anthropological controversy between alliance theory and descent theory. Goody criticizes Guichard for basing his typology upon marital norms (i.e., the endogamy–exogamy distinction) and suggests that by not starting with descent factors (i.e., inheritance practices), Guichard has overlooked a more fundamental distinction—that between kinship systems in which property is passed from one generation to the next through both sexes (by means of inheritance and dowry) and those systems in which property is transmitted unisexually (usually through males). Goody contends that passing property down unisexually encourages the development of corporate kinship groups (e.g., African systems). However, the use of bilateral devolution discourages such corporate structures, and Goody places both Eastern and Western systems in Guichard's dichotomy in the bilateral category. He faults Guichard for overstating the existence of corporate structures in Eastern kinship and proposes that Guichard's Western type represents merely a later historical development away from its roots in the Eastern system. Goody sees the primary problem of explaining the character of family and kinship in Western society as one of discerning how European societies shifted from preferred kinship endogamy (e.g., first-cousin marriage) to prescribed exogamy.

In his analysis of European kinship, Goody considers the changes introduced by the Christian (i.e., Roman Catholic) church from its beginnings to the late medieval period. He interprets the shift from kinship endogamy to exogamy mainly as a strategic move by the church to gain control over the lives of its members. As part of this effort, it had to wrest access to resources (especially productive land) from enduring control by family and kin. As a result, church laws evolved favoring those norms that might enhance allegiance to the church and weaken competition from the family and the state. In consequence, the church favored: (1) the use of testation permitting bequests to the church; (2) the prescription of kinship exogamy as a means for inhibiting both the reinforcement of close kin ties and the passing down of resources exclusively within lineages; (3) the requirement of the consent of both bride and groom in marriage; (4) late marriage as a means for weakening family control over mate selection; (5) prohibition of divorce even for childless couples; and so on.

Goody seems to overstate his case in trying to interpret the shifts in kinship in ways that are consistent with his basic typology. For example, in giving primacy to inheritance patterns, Goody asserts that the ban on divorce in Roman Catholicism was devised primarily to encourage bequeathing estates to the church in case of childlessness. But, in fact, when there were no children, bequests usually were made "to brothers and sisters and to nieces and nephews" (Sheehan 1963, p. 75). Moreover, Goody's explanation of the ban ignores the widespread practice of bequeathing a portion of one's estate to the church even when one left a widow, children, or both. Michael Sheehan (1963, p. 298) reports that these bequests were made for the good of the soul. "Among the Anglo-Saxons, bequests to the parish church became so general that they were eventually required by law." This practice was not restricted to England. According to Sheehan, "Christians in the Mediterranean basin had developed the practice of bequeathing part of their estate in alms" (p. 303). Thus, church heirship in medieval Christian Europe was tied to repentance regardless of the existence of familial beneficiaries. Since church acquisition did not have to depend on bequests from childless couples, it is unlikely that the ban on divorce derives primarily from the desire of the church for additional benefices.

In addition, Goody dismisses the intermittent presence of kinship endogamy in medieval Europe as opportunistic deviations from the moral injunctions of the church. Yet, as Duby (1977) indicates, in medieval Europe the ebb and flow in kinship endogamy was tied to the amount of emphasis given to strengthening lines of descent. For example, Duby notes that in northern France, from before the tenth century to about the middle of the eleventh century, there was little utilization of the concept of lineage and only vague awareness of genealogy and knowledge about ancestors. Prior to that time, even members of the aristocracy considered their family to consist of "a horizontal grouping" of neighbors and kin "whose bonds were as much the result of marriage alliances as of blood" (Duby 1977, p. 147). Then, beginning with the tenth century, there was a change in ideas and norms regarding kinship—a conscious strengthening of lineage by controlling marriage, which frequently took place between close relatives (despite impediments in canon law [Canon Law Society 1983]). To summarize, Goody's argument is that medieval deviation from canon law consisted of opportunistic economic decisions and did not derive from a different set of norms. But Duby describes the coordination of kinship endogamy with the emerging notion of the legitimacy of lineage—a complex of ideas that requires a consensus among the kin in order to be effective. Hence, it appears that the change in marriage rules and in the significance of lineage signaled more than ad hoc departures from church law.

There is still another reason for questioning Goody's conclusions: Goody makes the point that through bequests the Catholic church became the largest landowner in Europe. In his focus upon the growth of exogamy as a consequence of devolution of estates to both sexes, he has overlooked the church's own involvement as a major heir in the inheritance system. Particularly in the light of the church's view that ties through faith are equivalent to blood ties, the church is identified with spiritual kinship (Goody 1983, pp. 194ff). However, if it is legitimate to consider the church as an heir on par with familial heirs, then the system becomes one of *trilateral* devolution—sons, daughters, *and* the church. In that case, the European system differs markedly from the Eastern kinship system described by Guichard. Indeed, in contrast to Judaism and Islam, Christianity, at least until the end of the medieval period, saw family and kinship ties as *competitive* with church interests and the strategies the church applied to weaken these ties altered both the marriage and the inheritance systems. The data imply that, despite their contradictory implications, both the marriage or alliance component and the descent component should be addressed as equal factors in organizing family life.

A task that remains is to integrate typologies of the emergence of modern kinship systems with transhistorical, structural typologies.

(SEE ALSO: *Alternative Life-Styles; American Families; Family and Household Structure; Family Roles*)

REFERENCES

Adams, Bert N. 1968 *Kinship in an Urban Setting.* Chicago: Markham.

Augustine, Saint 1966 *The City of God against the Pagans.* Cambridge, Mass.: Harvard University Press.

Berkner, Lutz 1972 "The Stem Family and the Developmental Cycle of a Peasant Household: An Eighteenth-Century Example." *American Historical Review* 77:398–418.

Blau, Zena Smith 1974 "The Strategy of the Jewish Mother." In Marshall Sklare, ed., *The Jew in American Society.* New York: Behrman House.

Bott, Elizabeth 1972 *Family and Social Network.* New York: Free Press.

Buchler, Ira R., and Henry A. Selby 1968 *Kinship and Social Organization.* New York: Macmillan.

Burgess, Ernest W., Harvey J. Locke, and Mary Margaret Thomes 1963 *The Family: From Institution to Companionship.* New York: American Book Company.

Canon Law Society of Great Britain and Ireland 1983 *The Code of Canon Law.* London: Collins Liturgical Publications.

Chodorow, Stanley 1972 *Christian Political Theory and Church Politics in the Mid-Twelfth Century.* Berkeley: University of California Press.

Davenport, W. 1959 "Nonunilinear Descent and Descent Groups." *American Anthropologist* 61:557–572.

Douglas, Mary 1966 *Purity and Danger.* London: Routledge and Kegan Paul.

Duby, Georges 1977 *The Chivalrous Society.* London: Edward Arnold.

Farber, Bernard 1968 *Comparative Kinship Systems.* New York: Wiley.

———1975 "Bilateral Kinship: Centripetal and Centrifugal Types of Organization." *Journal of Marriage and the Family* 37:871–888.

———1981. *Conceptions of Kinship.* New York: Elsevier.

———1984. "Anatomy of Nurturance: A Structural Analysis of the Contemporary Jewish Family." Paper presented at Workshop on Theory Construction and Research Methodology, National Council on Family Relations, San Francisco, October.

Firth, Raymond, Jane Hubert, and Anthony Forge 1969 *Families and Their Relatives.* New York: Humanities Press.

Fortes, Meyer 1969 *Kinship and Social Order.* Chicago: Aldine.

Ganzfried, Solomon 1963 *Code of Jewish Law (Kitzur Shulkhan Arukh),* rev., annot. ed. New York: Hebrew Publishing Company.

Goode, William J. 1963 *World Revolution and Family Patterns.* New York: Free Press.

Goody, Jack 1983 *The Development of the Family and Marriage in Europe.* New York: Cambridge University Press.

Guichard, P. 1977 *Structures sociales 'orientales' et 'occidentales' dans l'Espagne musulmane.* Paris: Mouton.

Harris, C. C., and Colin Rosser 1983 *The Family and Social Change.* Boston: Routledge and Kegan Paul.

Lévi-Strauss, Claude 1963 *Structural Anthropology.* New York: Basic Books.

———1969 *The Elementary Structures of Kinship.* Boston: Beacon Press.

Lewis, Robert A., and Graham B. Spanier 1982 "Marital Quality, Marital Stability and Social Exchange." In F. Ivan Nye, ed., *Family Relationships: Rewards and Costs.* Beverly Hills, Calif.: Sage.

Litwak, Eugene 1960a "Occupational Mobility and Extended Family Cohesion." *American Sociological Review* 25:9–21.

———1960b "Geographical Mobility and Extended Family Cohesion." *American Sociological Review* 25:385–394.

———1985 *Helping the Elderly: The Complementary Roles of Informal Networks and Formal Systems.* New York: Guilford Press.

Lopata, Helena Znaniecki 1973 *Widowhood in an American City.* Cambridge, Mass.: General Learning Press.

Macfarlane, Alan 1986 *Marriage and Love in England: Modes of Reproduction 1300–1840.* New York: Basil Blackwell.

Maine, Henry S. 1885 *Ancient Law.* New York: Henry Holt.

Mitchell, William E. 1963 "Theoretical Problems in the Concept of the Kindred." *American Anthropologist* 65:343–354.

Mogey, John 1976 "Content of Relations with Relatives." In J. Caisenier, ed., *The Family Life Cycle in European Societies.* Paris: Mouton.

Murdock, George Peter 1949 *Social Structure.* New York: Macmillan.

Naroll, Rauol 1970 "What Have We Learned from Cross-Cultural Surveys?" *American Anthropologist* 75:1227–1288.

Paige, Jeffery M. 1974 "Kinship and Polity in Stateless Societies." *American Journal of Sociology* 80:301–320.

Parsons, Talcott 1954 "The Kinship System of the Contemporary United States." In Talcott Parsons, ed., *Essays in Sociological Theory.* New York: Free Press.

Pehrson, R. N. 1957 *The Bilateral Network of Social Relations in Konkama Lapp District.* Bloomington: Indiana University Research Center in Anthropology, Folklore, and Linguistics.

Peranio, R. 1961 "Descent, Descent Line, and Descent

Group in Cognatic Social Systems." In V. E. Garfield, ed., *Proceedings of the Annual Meeting of the American Ethnological Association.* Seattle: University of Washington Press.

Sennett, Richard 1970 *Families Against the City: Middle Class Homes of Industrial Chicago, 1872–1890.* Cambridge, Mass.: Harvard University Press.

Shanas, Ethel, Peter Townsend, Dorothy Wedderburn, Henning Friis, Paul Milhøj, and Jan Stehouwer 1968 *Old People in Three Industrial Countries.* New York: Atherton Press.

Sheehan, Michael M. 1963 *The Will in Medieval England: From the Conversion of the Anglo-Saxons to the End of the Thirteenth Century.* Toronto: Pontifical Institute of Medieval Studies.

Stack, Carol B. 1974 *All Our Kin.* New York: Harper Colophon Books.

Stone, Lawrence 1975 "Rise of the Nuclear Family in Early Modern England: The Patriarchal Stage." In Charles E. Rosenberg, ed., *The Family in History.* Philadelphia: University of Pennsylvania Press.

Sussman, Marvin 1959 "The Isolated Nuclear Family: Fact or Fiction?" *Social Problems* 6:333–340.

Swanson, Guy E. 1969 *Rules of Descent: Studies in the Sociology of Parentage.* Anthropological Papers, no. 39. Ann Arbor: Museum of Anthropology, University of Michigan.

Tönnies, Ferdinand [1887] 1957. *Community and Society.* East Lansing: Michigan State University Press.

Walster, Elaine, and G. William Walster 1978 *A New Look at Love.* Reading, Mass.: Addison-Wesley.

Wirth, Louis 1956 *Community Life and Social Policy.* Chicago: University of Chicago Press.

Young, Michael, and Peter Willmott 1957 *Family and Kinship in East London.* London: Routledge and Kegan Paul.

Zborowski, Mark, and Elizabeth Herzog 1952 *Life Is with People: The Culture of the Stetl.* New York: Schocken Books.

Zimmerman, Carle C., and Merle E. Frampton 1966 "Theories of Frederic LePlay." In Bernard Farber, ed., *Kinship and Family Organization.* New York: Wiley.

BERNARD FARBER